THE MODERN CONTRACT
OF GUARANTEE

AUSTRALIA
Law Book Co.—Sydney

CANADA and **USA**
Carswell—Toronto

HONG KONG
Sweet & Maxwell Asia

NEW ZEALAND
Brookers—Wellington

SINGAPORE and **MALAYSIA**
Sweet & Maxwell Asia
Singapore and Kuala Lumpur

THE MODERN CONTRACT OF GUARANTEE

English Edition

Dr James O'Donovan

Professor of Law
University of Western Australia
Barrister and Solicitor of the
Supreme Court of Western Australia

and

Dr John Phillips

Professor of English Law
King's College, London
Barrister of the Middle Temple

London
Sweet and Maxwell
2003

Published in 2003 by
Sweet & Maxwell Limited of
100 Avenue Road, London NW3 3PF
www.sweetandmaxwell.co.uk
Typeset by MFK Mendip, Frome, Somerset
Printed in Great Britain by MPG Books

No natural forests were destroyed to make this product;
only farmed timber was used and replanted

ISBN 0421 641 401

A CIP catalogue record for this book is available from the British Library

PREFACE

The Modern Contract of Guarantee is a practical treatise on the law of suretyship in modern commercial practice. The work is intended as a detailed reference text for those in the legal profession who practise in this area of law (either as litigators or as those drafting commercial contracts) and also as a scholarly analysis and evaluation of the law of suretyship. In our view a reference guide to this complex area of law should also identify uncertainties in law and indicate how those uncertainties should be resolved, as well as question existing dogma and provide suggestions for reform. To most readers this statement of the book's purposes will be uncontroversial, but it requires emphasis because a view appears to have developed in some sections of legal academe that a treatise written for the benefit of the wider legal community is *ipso facto* lacking in intellectual rigour. Our modest hope is that the work is both scholarly and useful.

The sub-title to the book—*English Edition*—may appear puzzling, but it reflects the fact that the work was first published (in 1985) as an analysis of the Australian law of guarantees. It is now in its third Australian edition. The *English Edition* has, of course, necessitated very substantial re-writing, but we have deliberately not ignored our Australian heritage and the product of 20 years research. We have included Australian (and other Commonwealth) case examples when they provide the reader with a clearer understanding of English law, or when they address issues not yet considered by English courts. We consider that it is an important feature of a text upon which lawyers rely for guidance that predictions are made (with the assistance of case law from other common law jurisdictions) as to the likely outcome of future litigation.

The law governing contracts of guarantee is complex and is not governed solely by orthodox contractual principles. The tri-partite relationship between guarantor, creditor and principal debtor, and the financial vulnerability of the guarantor's position, means that the legal regime is an amalgam of contract, equitable principles, and statute law (the latter being especially important in respect of the position upon insolvency and in respect of consumer transactions). In terms of the contract law the book does not simply seek to reiterate fundamental contractual jurisprudence, but rather applies it specifically to contracts of guarantee. Additionally, as there is not often a clear distinction between guarantees and other forms of contractual security, the book analyses the law governing other types of contract, in particular, performance bonds and indemnities.

The book is divided into four parts. Part I analyses the law governing *Formation and Validity* (Chapters 1 to 4). As the majority of guarantees are written instruments in standard form, it might be reasonably supposed (vitiating factors such as non-disclosure and undue influence apart) that the legal issues governing formation would be relatively settled. Yet many problems continue to arise, most notably in respect of whether or not there is sufficient consideration for the guarantee; the validity of execution by partners, trustees, company directors as well as unincorporated associations, and local councils with limited statutory powers; and the effect of a failure of a co-surety to execute the guarantee. We also address the different ways in which the requirements of the Statute of Frauds can be satisfied (with a practical focus on matters which must be included in the written evidence) and, in the light of the recent House of Lord's decision in *Actionstrength Ltd v International Glass Engineering In.Gl.En. SpA*, the impact of estoppel on the formation of guarantees.

It is, however, in relation to vitiating factors such as non-disclosure and undue influence that there has been the most voluminous case law over recent years. This case law is examined and re-assessed in Chapter 4, especially in the light of *Royal Bank of Scotland v Etridge*. This leads to a critical analysis of the extent to which the creditor can protect its position by relying on a certificate of advice given by a solicitor and a discussion of the duty imposed upon a solicitor when giving advice to a prospective guarantor. Chapter 4 also considers the impact of the Unfair Contract Terms Act 1977 and the Unfair Terms in Consumer Contracts Regulations 1999, and, where that legislation applies, which categories of clauses in guarantees may be invalid. The impact of illegality is also addressed and, in particular, whether guarantees can constitute preferences and the effect of the provisions of the Companies Act 1985 dealing with guarantees of loans to directors and guarantees as prohibited financial assistance in the purchase of shares.

Part II of the book, *Liability and Discharge* (Chapters 5 to 9), investigates, first, (in Chapter 5) the scope of the guarantor's liability. The general principles of construction applicable to contracts of guarantee are reasonably well settled, but numerous specific problems of construction continue to arise in respect, for example, of the failure to identify the correct creditor or principal debtor, or to properly describe the principal transaction. The effect of specific provisions, such as "all account" clauses and conclusive evidence certificates as to amount of the indebtedness, are analysed, and importantly, the potential impact of estoppel by convention on the extent of the guarantor's liability.

Chapters 6 to 9 investigate the bases for discharging the guarantor. Historically the onerous burden of suretyship is well chronicled. In Elizabethan times one commentator, echoing the scriptures, warned of the dangers of acting as a surety:

"If any desire thee to be his surety, give him a part of what thou has to spare; if he press thee further, he is not thy friend at all, for friendship rather chooses harm to itself than offereth it. If thou be bound for a stranger, thou art a fool; if for a merchant, thou puttest thy estate to learn to swim; if for a churchman, he hath no inheritance; if for a lawyer, he will find an evasion by a syllable or word to abuse thee; if for a poor man, thou mayest pay it thyself; if for a rich man, he needs not; therefore, from suretyship, as from manslayer or enchanter, bless thyself."

Over time, and no doubt as a judicial response to the need to provide safeguards for the guarantor, the courts developed particular rules whereby the guarantor was discharged in circumstances which were perceived as prejudicing his position. These principles are detailed in Chapters 6 to 9, and include discharge by release of the principal debtor; by a variation of the principal contract; and by the creditor improperly dealing with collateral securities. Despite the inclusion of provisions designed to exclude these rules, there has been much modern case law which has revisited and refined these principles. This has occurred, in part, because such clauses have not been appropriately drafted for their intended purpose. In these chapters, therefore, there is also particular emphasis on assessing the strengths and also weaknesses of such exclusion clauses. In our view it is only when the clauses are placed in their appropriate legal context that their function can be properly understood by the commercial lawyer. This is a general theme which is followed elsewhere in the work in situations where it is usual for the creditor to attempt to exclude the guarantor's rights.

Part III is a detailed analysis of the right of the parties. In Chapter 10 there is focus upon the creditor's enforcement of the guarantee both by extra-curial methods and by court action. Thus there is an examination of the creditor's rights of proof in the bankruptcy or liquidation of the principal debtor; the nature (both substantively and procedurally) of the action to enforce the guarantee; the rights of third parties and other assignees to enforce the guarantee, including the impact of the Contracts (Rights of Third Parties) Act 1999; and potential restraints upon enforcement as a result of statutory limitation periods (especially in the light of the Civil Liability (Contribution) Act 1978 and *Hampton v Minns*), estoppel and *res iudicata*.

The rights of the guarantor both before and after payment are dealt with in Chapters 11 and 12 respectively. As regards the former there is emphasis on the guarantor's (strangely under-utilised) right to *quia timet* relief and his rights of set-off, where the law remains complex and uncertain. Chapter 12 explores in detail the guarantor's rights of indemnity, contribution and subrogation. Some current issues include whether or not co-guarantors who have received no benefit from the guarantor should be liable to contribute equally to the common debt; the application of subrogation to cross guarantees within corporate group structures; and the effectiveness of clauses designed to exclude the right of subrogation (in the light of *Liberty Mutual Insurance (UK) Ltd v HSBC Bank Plc*).

The last part of the book—Part IV, *Guarantees in Particular Contexts*—has two Chapters. Chapter 13 analyses the nature of conditional and unconditional performance bonds and Chapter 14 assesses the application of conflict of law principles to guarantees. We have changed the structure of the work from previous Australian editions in that the law applicable to bills of exchange and consumer credit discussed in separate Chapters in this part has been re-located within the relevant sections of the substantive Chapters in Parts I to III. A similar approach has been adopted to leases. We have made this change because we believe that the future law of guarantees as applied in those contexts is likely to be better understood in the light of the general law of guarantees and, indeed, it is the general law that is likely to influence how the law develops in those areas.

The law is stated as at March 31, 2003.

James O'Donovan and John Phillips
October 2003

CONTENTS

Refer also to the detailed contents list at the beginning of each chapter.

TABLE OF CASES

All references are to paragraph numbers

Australia

Canada

European Union

Hong Kong

Ireland

New Zealand

Nigeria

South Africa

United Kingdom

United States of America

TABLE OF STATUTES

All references are to paragraph numbers

TABLE OF RULES AND STATUTORY INSTRUMENTS

All references are to paragraph numbers

TABLE OF EC LEGISLATION

All references are to paragraph numbers

Part I

FORMATION AND VALIDITY

CHAPTER 1

DEFINITION AND DISTINCTIONS

1. HISTORICAL BACKGROUND

Suretyship is as ancient as the pyramids and nearly as distinctive. More **1–01** than 2,500 years before the dawn of Christianity, a contract of suretyship was recorded on a tablet found in the Library of Sargon I, King of Accad and Sumer.[1] The earliest known code of suretyship law was that of Hammurabi enacted about 2250 BC, some 500 years after the reign of Sargon I.[2] This code, which provided for a system of state fidelity insurance, anticipated the concept of a corporate surety by more than 4,000 years.[3]

1–02   The *Old Testament* records an instance of suretyship between Joseph, Governor of Egypt and his perfidious brothers,[4] and the *Book of Proverbs* testifies that such contracts were used extensively by the ancient Hebrews during the reign of King Solomon.[5] The practice of taking hostages for the performance of a promise or an obligation was the most elementary form of suretyship in this period,[6] but it appears that contracts of suretyship were also used to secure repayment of debts. The Hebrews gave such undertakings orally in the presence of witnesses[7] and there is no evidence of written contracts of suretyship executed prior to 670 BC.[8]

1–03   By the time Gauis wrote his *Commentaries* circa AD 150, the Romans had developed a highly complex law of suretyship.[9] The modern doctrines of contribution, reimbursement and subrogation had their counterparts in Roman law, though in a different form. By the time of Justinian, the *fidejussor*, which bears a striking resemblance to a modern guarantee, was the dominant, if not exclusive, form of suretyship.[10] Certain peculiar features of the Roman law of suretyship died with the Empire but its core has shown a remarkable durability, surviving even today in modern continental codes.[11] English law, on the other hand, developed in an insular and distinctive manner owing little to Roman jurisprudence.[12] What is surprising, therefore, about the English law of suretyship is not its divergence from Roman law but the areas of similarity.

1–04   In Anglo-Saxon England, the surety was a means of enforcing the criminal law and maintaining peace and good order. In this sense the surety was directly connected with the administration of justice.[13] Every person was required to have a *borh* or surety who was responsible for the

---

[1] W. D. Morgan, "The History and Economics of Suretyship" (1927) 12 Corn. L.Q. 153.
[2] T. Hewitson, *Suretyship: Its Origin and History in Outline* (1927), p.11.
[3] Morgan, *op. cit.*, at 154.
[4] *Genesis* 37, 39, 41, 42. See also Hewitson, *op. cit.*, p.4. The familar story of Damon and Pythias is a similar example of ancient suretyship. Richard Edwards wrote a play by that name in 1550. See H Gerwig, *University Handbook for Readers and Writers* (1965), p.177; J. W. Mason, *Radio Talks*, Season 1923–1924, p.6; J. W. Mason, *Origin and History of Suretyship*, pp.4–5, cited in Morgan, *op. cit.*, at 157, n.11.
[5] 970–928 B.C. See, *e.g. Proverbs* 11:15: "He that is surety for a stranger shall smart for it; and he that hateth suretyship is sure"; *Proverbs* 17:18: "A man void of understanding striketh hands, *and* becometh surety in the presence of his friend"; and *Proverbs* 22:26: "Be not thou one of them that strike hands, *or* of them that are sureties for debts."
[6] Hewitson, *op. cit.*, p.4.
[7] *Proverbs* 17:18; *Job* 17:3.
[8] Morgan, *op. cit.*, at 156.
[9] Morgan, *op. cit.*, at 158. See also W. H. Loyd, "The Surety" (1917) 66 Uni of Penn L. Rev. 40 at 43–47; Hewitson, *op. cit.*, pp.27–33.
[10] Morgan, *op. cit.*, at 160.
[11] See generally P. K. Jones Jr, "Roman Law Bases of Suretyship in Some Modern Civil Codes" (1977) 52 Tul L. Rev. 129.
[12] Hewitson, *op. cit.*, pp.62–63.
[13] Morgan, *op. cit.*, at 160–161; Hewitson, *op. cit.*, pp.76–82.

criminal acts of the principal.[14] This concept can probably be traced to the earlier collective liability of the family which later gave rise to a duty of members of the family to act as surety for each other.[15] In the Middle Ages, too, the vassal was expected by some customs to act as pledge for the lord. Thus Anglo-Saxon law demanded: "that every lord have his household in his own borh".[16] To fail to protect the surety against liability was a gross breach of faith for which the law ultimately granted redress.[17]

The frankpledge which first appeared around AD 1150 was simply the Anglo-Saxon frithborh systematised and applied communally.[18] The simplest description of the operation of the frankpledge is: **1–05**

"that all men in every ville of the whole realm were by custom under obligation to be in the suretyship of ten, so that if one of the ten commit an offence, the nine have him to justice".[19]

Thus it was used to secure the punishment of the offending members **1–06** who disturbed the peace and good order of the community. In this way it served a similar purpose to the *communitas* of the 7th and 8th centuries.[20]

Sureties were also used to secure repayment of debts. In this capacity the **1–07** surety was little more than a hostage whose position was described by Brissaud, writing in the early Middle Ages, as follows:

"The creditor kept him near himself, sometimes sequestrated, or even in irons; he was authorised to take vengeance upon him if the debtor did not pay his debt at maturity; just as he would have taken vengeance upon the person of the debtor (it was death, mutilation, slavery for debts). Such a prospect as this must have led the hostage to neglect no means of getting the debtor to free himself of the obligation. Also, thenceforth one can account for two of the most remarkable characteristics of the primitive suretyship: First, in giving surety, the debtor frees himself; secondly, the death of the surety destroys the right of the creditor; the fact of being in his hands like a pledge could not be transmitted to the heirs of the hostage. Of course, moreover, the creditor had to feed his hostage, which gave rise to the gibe, '*The banquet of a hostage is a costly banquet*'. In order to avoid these expenses, the creditor gave up the person of his hostage, or, rather, did not demand that the hostage should be handed over to him as soon as the contract was made. He contented himself with the promise that the hostage would present himself at the first summons at the place which was appointed beforehand, or which should be designated afterwards,—a town, a castle, or an inn,—and from which place he was forbidden to

---

[14] Thorpe, *Ancient Laws and Institutes of England*, Ethelred I, 1; Athelstan V, 4, cited in Morgan, *op. cit.*, p.160, n.35.
[15] See Loyd, *op. cit.*, at 42.
[16] Ethelred I, 1, cited in Hewitson, *op. cit.*, p.69, n.4.
[17] Loyd, *op. cit.*, at 42.
[18] Hewitson, *op. cit.*, p.70; Morgan, *op. cit.*, at 161.
[19] W. A. Morris, *The Frankpledge System* (Harvard Historical Series), Vol. 14, p.15.
[20] See Hewitson, *op. cit.*, p.71.

depart until the debt should be paid. The laws seldom had to see the carrying out of this promise, because it was made a point of honour to keep it; and, if necessary, excommunication would have had satisfaction from the recalcitrant hostage (perjury or quasi-perjury) or else he would have been taken by force (intervention of the magistrates). Shutting up in prison was the natural penalty for the infraction of this order; Beaumanoir recommended that one give the hostage who had suffered this punishment better nourishment than is furnished to prisoners for some crime. At the same time, the hostage, and, as a consequence, the debtor, was charged with the expenses occasioned by the sojourn of the former in prison."[21]

1–08   In Anglo-Saxon times, the surety was an indispensable feature of every business transaction. A law of King Ethelred declared: "No man could either buy or exchange unless he have *borh* and witnesses."[22] No further formality was required at this time, nor was consideration necessary until later when suretyship was seen as a contractual relationship.

1–09   The growth of trade and commerce accelerated the development of the guarantee as a means of securing payment of debts owed to merchants. The merchant guild guaranteed the trading debts of each of its members by a form of suretyship analogous to frankpledge. The guarantee was by the members individually, jointly and collectively.[23] Unlike the frankpledge, which also relied upon the association of certain persons into a group, it served a purely commercial purpose. This mercantile arrangement was later challenged by legislation which declared that a merchant stranger could not be pressed for a debt in a city, borough, town, market or fair unless he was either debtor, pledgor or main pernor.[24]

1–10   In 1283, the Statute of Acton Burnell codified the remedies of a merchant against a debtor's surety, rendering the surety's moveables liable to execution.[25] Two years later, the merchant's remedies were extended to the debtor's land.[26] Yet even apart from actions based upon the statutes De Mercatoribus, proceedings to enforce undertakings similar to guarantees were not uncommon in the 13th century. Examples could be found in the King's Court[27] and in the local courts.[28]

1–11   Juristically, the surety's relationship with the creditor was that of the body-pledge down to the end of the 13th century, although that relation was obscured by the fact that, upon default, the creditor had recourse to

[21] *Brissaud's History of French Private Law* (Continental Legal History Series, 1969), Vol. 3, p.574. See also F. Pollock & F. W. Maitland, *The History of English Law* (2nd ed., 1923), Vol. 2, p.211.
[22] Ethelred I, 3, cited in Morgan, *op. cit.*, at 162 and in Hewitson, *op. cit.*, p.66. Ethelred reigned from 866–871 A.D. Guarantees were one of the earliest contractual obligations recognised by English law: Holdsworth, *History of English Law*, Vol. 2 (2nd ed.) at 185.
[23] Hewitson, *op. cit.*, pp.74–75.
[24] See 3 Ed I c. XXIII and 27 Ed III c. XVII. See also Hewitson, *op. cit.*, p.75.
[25] 11 Ed I, De Mercatoribus (1283).
[26] 13 Ed I, Stat 3.
[27] *Case of M de B* (1221), cited in F. W. Maitland (ed.), *Note Book* (1887), pl 1543, 1574, 1641 and 1649.
[28] *Selden Society*, Vol. 23, p.26. See also Hewitson, *op. cit.*, pp.47 and 117.

the surety's property, rather than the surety's person.[29] Instances of this form of body-pledge are recorded as late as the 13th and 14th centuries.[30]

The 14th century saw a gradual transition from the hostage relationship to a contractual relationship between the parties.[31] Notionally at least the medieval form of suretyship involved the surrender of the surety's body as a pledge and a submission by the surety to the power of the creditor. In primitive German law, the token of this submission was provided by offering one's hand. In time English law, too, came to regard the surety's surrender to the creditor as purely symbolic. The essence of the relationship was inexorably changing from power to consent. Once this concept of consent crept into suretyship, the transition from plegiatio, or body-pledge, to contract began.[32] Eventually, English law acknowledged that the surety's duty to answer for the debt of another stemmed from the surety's promise which was either under seal or supported by consideration.[33] Suretyship was no longer seen as the substitution of the surety's person for that of the debtor. It came to be regarded as a contractual obligation which arose by way of accession to the debtor's liability.[34]

1–12

By the time of Queen Elizabeth I, therefore, suretyship was not simply the concomitant of administrative justice, it was also an adjunct of good faith and credit, playing a vital role in trade and commerce.[35] But even then the onerous burden of suretyship was becoming clear. Sir Walter Raleigh, echoing scriptural warnings[36] against acting as a surety, wrote:

1–13

"If any desire thee to be his surety, give him a part of what thou has to spare; if he press thee further, he is not thy friend at all, for friendship rather chooses harm to itself than offereth it. If thou be bound for a stranger, thou art a fool; if for a merchant, thou puttest thy estate to learn to swim; if for a churchman, he hath no inheritance; if for a lawyer, he will find an evasion by a syllable or word to abuse thee; if for a poor man, thou mayest pay it thyself; if for a rich man, he needs not; therefore, from suretyship, as from manslayer or enchanter, bless thyself."[37]

One clue to the widespread use of the contract of suretyship in Elizabethan England is the fact that the plot of Shakespeare's *Merchant of Venice* revolves around such a contract. The arrangement between

1–14

---

[29] Hewitson, *op. cit.*, p.118.
[30] Hewitson, *op. cit.*, p.67.
[31] Hewitson, *op. cit.*, p.118. Suretyship was a contractual relationship when Glanvill wrote: Loyd, *op. cit.*, p.48. See W. Holdsworth, *A History of English Law* (7th ed., 1922), Vol. 3, pp.414–416.
[32] See W. W. Story, *The Law of Contracts* (5th ed., 1865), Vol. (11), p.319, n.1 and Hewitson, *op. cit.*, p.118.
[33] After some judicial vacillation, the need for consideration was ultimately recognised in the 16th century: see *Year Book*, 12 Hen VIII, Mich pl 3. However, in the 14th century, local courts were busily enforcing unwritten agreements: Hewitson, *op. cit.*, p.120.
[34] See Loyd, *op. cit.*, at 42–43.
[35] Hewitson, *op. cit.*, pp.8–9. See also W. Holdsworth, *A History of English Law* (7th ed., 1922), Vol. 2, pp.83–84. Elizabeth I reigned from 1558–1603 A.D.
[36] See above, n.5.
[37] Quoted in Morgan, *op. cit.*, at 162.

Antonio and Shylock, under which Shylock could take his pound of flesh if Antonio's friend, Bassanio, failed to pay his debt to Shylock on the due date, is a crude form of guarantee. The master playwright would not have chosen this subject unless he was confident that it was familiar to his audience.

1–15 Although suretyship came to be accepted as an accessory contract, the distinctive features of this contract were not overlooked. In particular, it was recognised that most contracts of guarantee are entered into for the benefit of another. Mindful of this, equity developed ways of alleviating the surety's burden on grounds of natural justice.[38] Hence, the equitable doctrines of contribution, subrogation and reimbursement play a significant part in the law of suretyship.[39]

1–16 In modern legal parlance, the term "contract of suretyship" has largely fallen into disuse and been replaced by the term "contract of guarantee". Such contracts, which are further regulated by statutory provisions affecting their form and enforceability,[40] are the central theme of this book. The term "suretyship", in the modern context, is usually reserved for suretyship which serves as an adjunct of administrative or judicial justice. This form of suretyship falls outside the scope of this book which focuses upon the contemporary contract of guarantee.

1–17 It is now appropriate to define the term "guarantee" and to describe the relationship between the parties to such a contract.

2. DEFINITIONS

1–18 In essence, a guarantee is a binding promise of one person to be answerable for a present or future debt or obligation of another if that other defaults.[41] In *Moschi v Lep Air Services Ltd*,[42] Lord Diplock expressed the view that the nature of the guarantor's obligation was "to see to it that the debtor performed his own obligations to the creditor".[43] But this view, as a matter of general principle,[44] was rejected by Mason

---

[38] Hewitson, *op. cit.*, p.126.
[39] See below, Chapters 11 and 12.
[40] See below, Ch.3.
[41] *Yeoman Credit Ltd v Latter* [1961] 1 W.L.R. 828; *Sunbird Plaza Pty Ltd v Maloney* (1988) 166 CLR 245; *Direct Acceptance Finance Ltd v Cumberland Furnishing Pty Ltd* [1965] N.S.W.R. 1504; *Total Oil Products (Aust) Pty Ltd v Robinson* [1970] 1 N.S.W.R. 701; *General Surety Co Ltd v Francis Parker Ltd* (1977) 6 B.L.R. 18; *Re Richards Ex p. Lloyd, Official Receiver* (1935) 8 A.B.C. 37; *W. C. Angliss Co (Aust) Pty Ltd* (1935) 8 A.B.C. 37; *Browning v Stallard* (1814) 5 Taunt 450; 128 E.R. 764; *Commercial Banking Co of Sydney Ltd v Patrick Intermarine Acceptances Ltd (in liq)* (1978) 52 A.L.J.R. 404 at 406; *Western Dominion Investment Co v MacMillan* [1925] 2 D.L.R. 442, affirmed in [1925] 4 D.L.R. 562, CA. Sir Wilfred Greene M.R. collected different legal definitions of the term "guarantee" in his judgment in *Re Conley* [1938] 2 All E.R. 127 at 130–131. See also at 135–138 *per* Luxmore J.
[42] [1973] A.C. 331 at 348.
[43] *ibid*. See also *General Produce Co v United Bank Ltd* [1979] 2 Lloyd's Rep. 255 at 258 *per* Lloyd J.
[44] But the question will be dependent on the precise form of guarantee: see Lord Reid in *Moschi v Lep Air Services Ltd* [1973] A.C. 331 at 344–345, whose comments were approved by Mason C.J. in *Sunbird Plaza Pty Ltd v Maloney* (1988) 166 C.L.R. 245 at 256.

C.J. in *Sunbird Plaza Pty Ltd v Maloney*,[45] who regarded it as "fictitious and quite unrealistic to suggest that this version of the guarantor's undertaking, rather than a promise to 'answer for' the debt or default, of another, is the true nature of the guarantor's obligation".[46] The distinction, as discussed later in the text, may be important when the principal contract is determined,[47] and it is also relevant in identifying the creditor's correct form of action when commencing proceedings against the guarantor.[48]

The person who makes the promise to be answerable for the debt or obligation of another is called the guarantor or the surety; the person to whom the promise is made is called the creditor[49]; and the person on whose behalf the promise is made is called the "principal debtor", or simply, "the principal". In most English common law jurisdictions, the terms "surety" and "guarantor" are used interchangeably and this practice is followed in this book. However, in some jurisdictions, particularly in the United States of America, the terms "surety" and "guarantor" are distinguished.[50] Technically, a guarantee is the undertaking that the debt shall be paid.[51] Generally in a contract of guarantee there are at least two obligations, one primary and the other secondary.[52]   1–19

(i) The principal obligation

A contract of guarantee is predicated upon the existence of a valid principal obligation owed by the principal debtor.[53] If there is no such principal obligation, generally the guarantee fails. Consequently, a valid guarantee depends upon the existence of a promise made to a person to whom a debtor is already answerable or is to become answerable.[54] The   1–20

---

[45] (1988) 166 C.L.R. 245.
[46] *ibid.* at 256.
[47] See below, paras 6–121 to 6–144.
[48] See below, paras 10–201 to 10–214.
[49] The term "creditor" will be used throughout this book even though the principal obligation may be a lease or a building contract, as distinct from a debt.
[50] See L. P. Simpson, *Handbook of the Law of Suretyship* (Minn., West Publishing 1950), pp.16–23.
[51] *Campbell v McIsaac* (1873) 9 N.S.R. 287, Can CA. A relation of suretyship can exist between two parties who are both primarily liable to a creditor but who *as between themselves* have assumed the positions of principal and surety. In the absence of notice of the true relationship between the parties, the creditor's rights against them are unaffected: *Forster v Ivey* (1901) 2 O.L.R. 480, affirming (1900) 32 O.R. 175, CA. See also *Overend, Guerney & Co (Liquidators) v Oriental Financial Corp (Liquidators)* (1874) L.R. 7 H.L. 348.
[52] *Western Dominion Investment Co v MacMillan* [1925] 2 D.L.R. 442, affirmed in [1925] 4 D.L.R. 562, CA. See also *Stephen's Commentaries on the Laws of England* (18th ed., 1925), Vol. III, p.265.
[53] *Lakeman v Mountstephen* (1874) L.R. 7 H.L. 17 at 24 *per* Lord Selborne; *Swan v Bank of Scotland* (1835) 10 Bli N.S. 627; 6 E.R. 231, HL; *Lougher v Molyneux* [1916] 1 K.B. 718; *Morin v Hammond Lumber Co* [1923] 1 D.L.R. 519, reversing *Morin v Hammond Lumber Co* (1922) 68 D.L.R. 519. It is on this basis that a guarantee should be distinguished from a novation of the principal contract where one obligor is substituted for another.
[54] *Harburg India Rubber Comb Co v Martin* [1902] 1 K.B. 778 at 784, *per* Vaughan Williams L.J.; *Re Conley, Ex p. Trustee v Barclays Bank Ltd* [1938] 2 All E.R. 127 at 130–131; *Yeoman Credit Ltd v Latter* [1961] 1 W.L.R. 828 at 830–831; *Total Oil Products (Aust) Pty Ltd v Robinson* [1970] 1 N.S.W.R. 701 at 703. *Cf. Kimball Lumber Co v Anderson* (1916) 27 D.L.R. 555, Sask CA.

principal obligation need not, however, be contractual. The guarantor's
undertaking to answer for the debt, default or miscarriage of another
within the terms of the *Statute of Frauds* can be applied to non-contractual
liabilities of the principal debtor.[55]

1–21   In terms of general principle, not only must the principal obligation
exist, but it must also remain unchanged throughout the life of the
guarantee.[56] Even slight unauthorised changes in the primary obligation
may discharge the guarantor.[57] Moreover, if the principal obligation
determines, so does the guarantee.[58]

(ii) The secondary obligation

1–22   The distinctive feature of a contract of guarantee is the secondary
obligation which is assumed by the surety or guarantor.[59] A guarantee is
not a representation that the principal debtor is credit-worthy.[60] The main
and immediate object of the transaction must be that the guarantors, or
their property, will be answerable to the creditor.[61] The liability of the
guarantor is secondary or auxiliary in the sense that it is in addition to
the primary liability of the principal debtor, but this does not prevent the
creditor from enforcing the guarantee before instituting proceedings
against the principal debtor.[62] It is not necessary for a guarantor to assume
personal liability for the debt of another since the person who provides a
pledge of property without incurring liability beyond the pledge is
nevertheless properly classified as a guarantor.[63] But where a guarantor
merely assumes a personal liability, the guarantee is not, strictly speaking,

---

[55] See *Re Young and Harston's Contract* (1885) 31 Ch. D. 168, CA; *Kirkham v Marter* (1819) 2
B. & Ald. 613 at 617; 106 E.R. 490 at 491 *per* Holroyd J.
[56] *Coady v J Lewis & Sons Ltd* [1951] 3 D.L.R. 845.
[57] *Western Dominion Investment Co v MacMillan* [1925] 2 D.L.R. 442, affirmed in [1925] 4
D.L.R. 562, CA: see below, paras 7–01 to 7–058.
[58] *Stacey v Hill* [1901] 1 K.B. 660, CA. But the guarantee may contain clauses preserving the
guarantor's liability in the circumstances referred to in this paragraph and may nevertheless
properly be classified as a guarantee: see below, paras 1–98 to 1–107.
[59] *Turner Manufacturing Co Pty Ltd v Senes* [1964] N.S.W.R. 692; *Coady v J Lewis & Sons
Ltd* [1951] 3 D.L.R. 845.
[60] *R v Gurofsky* (1919) 16 O.W.N. 19.
[61] The mere fact that an agreement may create a liability for the debt of another does not in
itself make the agreement a contract of guarantee: *McPherson v Forlong* [1928] 3 W.W.R. 45
(Can). Further, where a company director agrees with a bank to provide security in the future
in respect of the director's contingent and future obligations to the bank, including "successive
transactions", this agreement extends to the director's obligations as a guarantor of a
subsequent loan made by the bank to the director's company: *Fountain v Bank of America
National Trust & Savings Association* (1992) 5 B.P.R. 97 at 410.
[62] *Mallett v Bateman* (1865) 16 CB(NS) 530 at 543; 143 E.R. 1235 at 1240 (the principal debtor
is not exonerated); *Fahey v MSD Spiers Ltd* (1973) 2 N.Z.L.R. 655 at 659.
[63] *Edwards v Lennon* (1866) 6 S.C.R. (NSW) Eq 18; *Perry v National Provincial Bank of
England* [1910] 1 Ch. 464, HL; *Re Conley Ex p. Trustee v Barclays Bank Ltd* [1938] 2 All E.R.
127 (CA); *Bank of New Zealand v Baker* [1926] N.Z.L.R. 462; *Smith v Wood* [1929] 1 Ch. 14;
Bolton v Salmon [1891] 2 Ch. 48 at 53. Accordingly, where a husband mortgages his interest in
the matrimonial home as security for a debt, and his wife joins in that mortgage including a
covenant to pay, she becomes a surety in equity for the payment of the debt: *Standard Realty
Co v Nicholson* (1911) 24 O.L.R. 46 at 52 *per* Riddell J. As she has charged her own property
as security for her husband's debt, she it entitled to have her property exonerated out of her
husband's estate: *Rowlatt on Principal and Surety* (5th ed., 1999) by G. Moss Q.C. and D.

a security since it does not provide the creditor with recourse to specific property to secure performance of the principal debtor's obligation.[64] By the same token, any implication that a mortgage imposes a personal obligation on the mortgagor to repay the mortgage debt is readily rebutted where the mortgage is granted as security for the debt of another. In this situation s.28(1) of the Land Registration Act 1925 does not apply so the mortgagor will not be subjected to an implied personal covenant to repay.[65]

Jordan C.J. aptly described the general nature of a contract of guarantee **1–23** in *Jowitt v Callaghan*:[66]

"The contract of guarantee or suretyship is a contract between two persons which is intended by them to secure the performance of the obligation of a third person to one of them. The existence, present or future, of the obligation of a third person, and an intention in the parties to the contract to secure the performance of that obligation, are essential features of a contract of guarantee. If these elements are present, the contract is one of guarantee whether the promise be collateral to the promise of a principal obligor and in the nature of a distinct and separate promise to perform the principal obligation if it does not: *Inland Revenue Commissioners v Holder* [1931] 2 K.B. 81 at 101–102; *Elder v Northcott* [1930] 2 Ch. 422 at 430; or whether it be a joint promise with the principal obligor by virtue of which an immediate obligation is assumed to the obligee which is joint with that of the principal obligor: *Permanent Trustee Co of New South Wales Ltd v Hinks* (1934) 34 S.R. (NSW) 130 (in which case, there is suretyship in equity though not at common law: *Wauthier v Wilson* (1912) 28 TLR 239); and whether the promise be a promise to be personally liable if the principal obligor does not perform the obligation, or a promise merely that certain property of the promisor shall be a security for the performance of the principal obligation: *Re Conley Ex p. Trustee v Barclay's Bank Ltd* [1938] 2 All E.R. 127."[67]

The guarantor's liability is secondary or accessory in the sense that it is **1–24** contingent upon the principal debtor's continuing liability and, ultimately, the debtor's default.[68] The fact that the guarantor's liability is secondary does not, however, prevent the creditor from proceeding first against the

---

Marks, at 7. See also *Re Pittortou* [1985] 1 W.L.R. 58 (where the wife's security was given for the joint benefit of the couple's business and family affairs).

[64] For this reason a creditor need not value a guarantee when it submits a proof of debt in the bankruptcy or liquidation of an insolvent principal debtor: *Re Smeltzer* (1987) 67 C.B.R. (NS) 270, Ont. SC.

[65] *Fairmile Portfolio Management Ltd v Davies Arnold Cooper (A Firm)* [1998] E.G.C.S. 149.

[66] (1938) 38 S.R. (NSW) 512.

[67] *ibid.*, at 516.

[68] *Guild & Co v Conrad* [1894] 2 Q.B. 885 at 896; *Coady v J Lewis & Sons Ltd* [1951] 3 D.L.R. 845; *Western Dominion Investment Co v MacMillan* [1925] 2 D.L.R. 442, affirmed in [1925] 4 D.L.R. 562, CA. See also *Commercial Banking Co of Sydney Ltd v Patrick Intermarine Acceptances Ltd (in liq)* (1978) 52 A.L.J.R. 404 at 406. It is common practice, however, to insert a clause in guarantees making the "surety" a principal debtor so far as the creditor is concerned: see below, paras 1–101 and 7–28. The fact that the guarantee is an accessory

guarantor before it sues the principal debtor.[69] It appears, therefore, that the principal debtor's primary liability merely connotes that he will *ultimately* be liable to indemnify the guarantor in respect of amounts paid by the guarantor in reduction of the principal debt.[70] The guarantor's collateral obligation is dependent upon the primary obligation as it existed when the secondary liability arose.[71] Thus if the principal debtor is excused or the principal's liability terminates, the guarantor is generally discharged from his secondary obligation.[72]

1–25   The surety's liability must not be different in kind or greater in extent than that of the principal debtor,[73] and generally, there must be no liability imposed upon the surety apart from the promise to answer for the debt.[74] In this sense the liability of the guarantor and the principal debtor must generally be co-extensive. For this reason, there is no suretyship in a recourse agreement under which a dealer agrees, upon default of the customer, to pay not just the amount then due by the customer under the purchase agreement but all amounts which would be paid if that agreement had run its full course.[75]

1–26   Many of the cases which have explored the nature of the guarantor's secondary obligation are more concerned with the question of whether the guarantor's promise falls within the Statute of Frauds.[76] Observations from those cases about the nature of a guarantor's undertaking must be viewed in that light. Hence, statements to the effect that guarantors must have no interest in the debt other than their promise, and that the guarantor must

---

contract prevents it from merging with the principal debt or obligation: *White v Cuyler* (1795) 6 Term R. 176; 101 E.R. 497; *Clarke v Henty* (1838) 3 Y. & C. 187 at 189; 160 E.R. 667 at 668.
[69] See below, paras 11–11 to 11–28.
[70] See below, Ch. 12 as to the right of indemnity.
[71] *Western Dominion Investment Co v MacMillan* [1925] 2 D.L.R. 442, affirmed in [1925] 4 D.L.R. 562, CA. As to the difference between a guarantee and collateral security, see *Thackwell v Gardiner* (1851) 5 De G. & Sm. 58; 64 E.R. 1017. See also *W. Thomas & Co Ltd v Welk* [1935] S.A.S.R. 165, where it was held that a letter from a creditor in which he agreed that on dissolution of a partnership a continuing partner should take over the liabilities and receive the assets of the partnership, did not amount to a novation of his principal obligations so as to release the outgoing partners. Cf. *Australian Joint Stock Bank v Hogan* (1902) 2 S.R. (NSW) 7.
[72] *Stacey v Hill* [1901] 1 K.B. 660, CA (which involved a guarantee of a lease disclaimed by the lessee's trustee in bankruptcy under s.55(2) of the Bankruptcy Act 1883). See below, para. 6–149. In certain cases, however, the guarantor may yet be liable under a specific provision in the guarantee on the basis of an indemnity or an estoppel: *Alliance Acceptance Co Ltd v Hinton* (1964) 1 D.C.R. (NSW) 5. See below, para.1–100.
[73] *Direct Acceptance Finance Ltd v Cumberland Furnishings Pty Ltd* [1965] N.S.W.R. 1504 at 1510.
[74] *Coady v J Lewis & Sons Ltd* [1951] 3 D.L.R. 845 at 847; *Duncan, Fox & Co v North and South Wales Bank* (1880) 6 App. Cas. 1 at 13, in which Lord Selborne emphasised that the surety and principal debtor are liable for the "same debt".
[75] *Yeoman Credit Ltd v Latter* [1961] 1 W.L.R. 828; *Direct Acceptance Finance Ltd v Cumberland Furnishings Pty Ltd* [1965] N.S.W.R. 1504; *Cameo Motors Ltd v Portland Holdings Ltd* [1965] N.Z.L.R. 109 at 113. *Cf. Unity Finance Ltd v Woodcock* [1963] 2 All E.R. 270; [1963] 1 W.L.R. 455. However, in certain cases, the fact that the creditor may be able to sue the guarantors as joint primary obligors with the principal debtor, for example, under a covenant to pay interest, does not prevent the transaction from being a guarantee: this primary liability does not exclude the guarantors' secondary liability as sureties: *Permanent Trustee Co of New South Wales Ltd v Hinks* (1934) 34 S.R. (NSW) 130 at 140, *per* Jordan C.J.
[76] See below, paras 3–06 to 3–22.

enter the transaction simply to undertake the secondary obligation,[77] should be confined to the question of whether or not a particular undertaking by guarantors is within the statute. Similarly, the principle that if the promisors derive any direct benefit such as a payment or a transfer of property from the transaction their promise is not a guarantee should be restricted to the context of the Statute of Frauds.[78] These principles are of no assistance in determining the more general question of whether an undertaking is a guarantee. Thus an undertaking can be properly classified as a guarantee even if promisors derive a direct benefit from their promise and even if the undertaking is, for that reason, unenforceable under the Statute of Frauds.

An arrangement is not a guarantee if the promisor undertakes an independent obligation which extinguishes the principal debtor's liability.[79] But a person does not assume the principal debtor's primary obligation simply by directly promising to repay the principal debtor's debt. As long as the debtor's principal obligation to pay remains intact, such a promise may constitute a guarantee.[80]   **1–27**

3. THE MODERN SCOPE OF SURETYSHIP

In *Duncan, Fox & Co v North and South Wales Bank*,[81] Lord Selborne identified three classic situations in which suretyship arises. In the first, there is an agreement to constitute the relationship of principal and surety for a particular purpose, and the creditor thereby secured is a party to this arrangement in the sense that the creditor and the principal debtor agree from the outset that the surety's liability is merely secondary, and that the primary liability rests with the principal debtor.[82] There may be one agreement, for example a mortgage, to which the creditor, the principal debtor and the surety are all parties. Under such an agreement, the liability of the principal debtor and the surety may be joint or joint and several. Alternatively, the creditor's acceptance of the surety's secondary liability   **1–28**

---

[77] *Permanent Trustee Co of New South Wales Ltd v Hinks* (1934) 34 S.R. (NSW) 130 at 138; *Doyle v McKinnon* [1925] 3 D.L.R. 334.

[78] *Sutton & Co v Grey* [1894] 1 Q.B. 285; *Healy v Cornish* (1863) 3 S.C.R. (NSW) Eq. 28. As we shall see, a promise can be classified as a guarantee within the Statute where the promisors receive merely an indirect benefit as a result of their promise, for example, where the promisors are released from obligations under another guarantee: *Healy v Cornish*, above.

[79] *Guild & Co v Conrad* [1894] 2 Q.B. 885 at 896; *Permanent Trustee Co of New South Wales Ltd v Hinks* (1934) 34 S.R. (NSW) 130; *Coady v Lewis & Sons* [1951] 3 D.L.R. 845 at 847. If the transaction effects a novation of the original agreement between the creditor and the principal debtor whereby a third party assumes the debtor's liability, it is not a guarantee: *Browning v Stallard* (1814) 5 Taunt 450; 128 E.R. 764; *Re International Life Assurance Society & Hercules Insurance Co. Ex p. Blood* (1870) L.R. 9 Eq. 316; *Nat'l Pole & Treating Co v Blue River Pole & Tie Co* [1929] 3 D.L.R. 638, reversed on the facts in [1930] 3 D.L.R. 996.

[80] *Permanent Trustee Co of New South Wales Ltd v Hinks* (1934) 34 S.R. (NSW) 130 at 137–138.

[81] (1880) 6 App. Cas. 1, approved in *A. M. Spicer & Son Pty Ltd (in liq) v Spicer* (1931) 47 CLR 151; *Re Hodgetts Ex p. Official Receiver* (1949) 16 A.B.C. 201. See also *Forster v Ivey* (1901) 2 O.L.R. 480.

[82] (1880) 6 App. Cas. 1 at 11.

may be signified in a separate instrument to which the principal debtor is not a party. This is by far the most common form of suretyship.

1–29   In the second situation, there is an agreement between two co-debtors that one will assume the primary liability as principal debtor and the other will undertake the secondary liability as guarantor. To this contract of suretyship, the creditor is a stranger.[83] In the absence of notice of this arrangement, the creditor is entitled to treat both co-debtors as principal debtors since there is no contract of suretyship between the creditor and the guarantor.[84] But as between the co-debtors, one is guarantor for the other and, under this contract of suretyship, the guarantor acquires certain rights and incurs certain liabilities vis-à-vis the principal debtor.[85] A similar type of suretyship can be implied from an agreement by continuing partners to indemnify a retiring partner against any past or future debts or liabilities incurred in the business.[86]

1–30   Where a creditor is later given notice or becomes aware[87] of this contract of suretyship between the creditor's co-debtors, the arrangement attracts some of the incidents of suretyship so far as the creditor is concerned; but it does not make the creditor's contract with the co-debtors one of guarantee.[88] Nor does it make the co-debtor who has agreed to act as guarantor a surety for all purposes as between himself and the creditor.[89] But once the creditor receives notice of the suretyship it is expected to respect the rights of the co-debtor who has assumed the position of surety, despite the fact that the creditor has never specifically agreed to the co-debtor assuming such a position.[90] Thus the creditor's

---

[83] *ibid.* See also *Israel v Foreshore Properties Pty Ltd* (1980) 30 A.L.R. 631.

[84] See *Duncan, Fox & Co v North and South Wales Bank* (1880) 6 App. Cas. 1 at 11–12, *per* Lord Selborne L.C. and *Nicholas v Ridley* [1904] 1 Ch. 192. *Cf. York City & County Banking Co v Bainbridge* (1880) 43 L.T. 732 (which suggests that the creditor is entitled to treat both co-debtors as principal debtors unless *the creditor agrees* that one is merely a surety for the other).

[85] *Duncan, Fox & Co v North and South Wales Bank* (1880) 6 App. Cas. 1 at 11–12. In particular, if the guarantor is required to pay the debt he or she is entitled to an indemnity from the principal debtor: *ibid.* at 11 *per* Lord Selborne.

[86] *Australian Joint Stock Bank v Hogan* (1902) 2 S.R. (NSW) 7. *Cf. W Thomas & Co Ltd v Welk* [1935] S.A.S.R. 165, where the outgoing partners became guarantors on dissolution of the firm and continuation of the business by one of the partners. As to the liability of retiring and continuing partners, see *Stevens v Britten* [1954] 1 W.L.R. 1340.

[87] The initial liability of two principal debtors may be changed by a subsequent express or implied agreement that one of those debtors shall be surety only. Thus the course of dealings between a newly-constituted firm and a creditor subsequent to the retirement of a partner may relieve that partner of primary liability and render that partner liable merely as a surety. Indeed, in such a case it is not necessary to give the creditor an express notice of the usual agreement between continuing partners in order to indemnify a retiring partner against any past or future debts incurred in the business: *Oakeley v Pasheller* (1836) 10 Bli N.S. 548; 6 E.R. 202; *Overend, Gurney & Co (Liquidators) v Oriental Financial Corp (Liquidators)* (1874) L.R. 7 H.L. 348; *Rouse v Bradford Banking Co* [1894] A.C. 586.

[88] *Permanent Trustee Co of New South Wales Ltd v Hinks* (1934) 34 S.R. (NSW) 130 at 140. See also *Harris v Ferguson* (1922) 63 DLR 672, CA; *Maytag Co Ltd v Kolb* (1915) 32 D.L.R. 221, Sask SC.

[89] *Oakeley v Pasheller* (1836) 10 Bli. N.S. 548; 6 E.R. 202; *Overend, Gurney & Co (Liquidators) v Oriental Financial Corp (Liquidators)* (1874) L.R. 7 H.L. 348; *Rouse v Bradford Banking Co* [1894] AC 586; *Permanent Trustee Co of New South Wales Ltd v Hinks* (1934) 34 S.R. (NSW) 130 at 140.

[90] *Rouse v Bradford Banking Co* [1894] A.C. 586; *Hollier v Eyre* (1842) 9 Cl. & Fin. 1; 8 E.R. 313; *Overend, Gurney & Co (Liquidators) v Oriental Financial Corp (Liquidators)* (1874) L.R.

rights and obligations vis-à-vis this party turn on circumstances and arrangements unknown to the creditor at the date of the contract with the co-debtors.[91] While this appears to offend contractual principles, it must be remembered that the guarantor's rights in this context are not founded on contract[92] but on equity.[93]

Just as it is possible for a contract of suretyship to exist between two co-debtors without the concurrence of the creditor, it is equally possible for a surety to guarantee the liability of a third person in such a way as to create a contract of suretyship against the creditor, but not as against the principal debtor. Thus a recourse agreement in the form of a guarantee[94] entered into by a dealer at the request of a finance company, whereby the dealer guarantees the due performance of a hire-purchase agreement, may create a contract of suretyship as against the finance company (the creditor) but not against the hirer (the principal debtor). In a similar vein, when a surety guarantees a loan made to a subsidiary company at the request of its parent, there may be no contract of suretyship between the surety and the subsidiary.[95] While the principal debtor is not a party to these contracts of suretyship, it may nevertheless be liable, as a result of equitable principles, to indemnify the surety against any liability the surety incurs as a result of the suretyship.[96]

1–31

The third situation described by Lord Selborne in *Duncan, Fox & Co v North and South Wales Bank*[97] is not dependent upon a contract of suretyship. It arises when there is a primary and secondary liability of two persons, say A and B, for the same debt but the debt is, as between the two, the debt of A only.[98] Lord Selborne identified this third class of cases in this way:

1–32

"Cases in which there is, strictly speaking, no contract of suretyship, but in which there is a primary and secondary liability of two persons for one

---

7 H.L. 348; *Goldfarb v Bartlett* [1920] 1 K.B. 639; *AGC (Advances) Ltd v West* (1984) 5 N.S.W.L.R. 590; *Jenkins v Wyatt* (1900) 21 L.R. (NSW) 322. Parol evidence is admissible to show that the creditor knew that one of the co-debtors was principal and the other was surety: *Mutual Loan Fund Association v Sudlow* (1858) 5 C.B. (NS) 449; 141 E.R. 183. The onus is on the party seeking relief as a surety to show that the creditor was aware of the true relationship between the parties when the instrument was executed or when the creditor subsequently dealt with the real principal debtor: *Burnard v Lysnar* [1927] N.Z.L.R. 757 at 764.

[91] See *Chitty on Contracts* (28th ed., 1999), Vol. 2, p.1298, para.44–004.

[92] See *Permanent Trustee Co of New South Wales Ltd v Hinks* (1934) 34 S.R. (NSW) 130 at 140.

[93] *ibid.* See also *Wythes v Labouchere* (1859) 3 De & G 593; 44 E.R. 1397; *Oriental Financial Corp v Overend Gurney & Co* (1871) L.R. 7 Ch. App. 142, affirmed 7 H.L. 348 at 361 *per* Lord Cairns. Indeed, this principle applies even where the contract between the creditor and the co-debtors is under seal: *Rees v Berrington* (1795) 2 Ves. Jun. 540; 2 W. & T.L.C. Eq. (8th ed.), p.571 *per* Lord Loughborough.

[94] Normally "recourse agreements" take the form of indemnities but they can be drafted as guarantees.

[95] See, *e.g. Brown, Shipley & Co Ltd v Amalgamated Investment (Europe) BV* [1979] 1 Lloyd's Rep. 488.

[96] This right of indemnity will be founded on a restitutionary claim or the doctrine of subrogation: see below, Ch. 12.

[97] (1880) 6 App. Cas. 1 at 11–12.

[98] *Sherwin v McWilliams* (1921) 17 Tas. L.R. 94: such an agreement between the two debtors does not *in itself* affect the rights of the creditor.

and the same debt, by virtue of which, if it is paid by the person who is not primarily liable, he has a right of reimbursement or indemnity from the other."[99]

1–33   Indeed, in this form of constructive suretyship, equity ensures that B's rights are not materially different from those of a surety by express agreement at law. This appears to be true whether B attended to the payment of the debt out of personal responsibility or by realisation of a security which B had given in support of the principal debt.[1]

1–34   The classic illustration of this principle is the relationship of an indorser to an acceptor of a bill of exchange, the liability of the indorser being secondary to the primary liability of the acceptor.[2]

1–35   *A M Spicer & Son Pty Ltd (in liq) v Spicer*[3] provides another illustration of this principle. At Spicer's request, Howie paid a company £10,000 in return for an allotment of 10,000 preference shares in the company to Spicer. Spicer covenanted with Howie to repay this sum with interest and deposited the shares, a transfer thereof and the title deed to certain property with Howie as security. The preference shares were, therefore, encumbered with Spicer's debt to Howie who was thus in a position to make claims against the company.

1–36   When the company went into liquidation, a new company was formed to acquire the assets of the old company and to discharge its liabilities. The share capital in the new company was allotted to members of the old company in the proportion of one share for every two shares held in the capital of the old company. Accordingly 5,000 preference shares in the new company were allotted to Spicer. Initially Howie refused to assent to this arrangement but the liquidators ultimately obtained his agreement on the following terms: (1) that he advance a further £3,000 to the new company and (2) that the new company issue him with a debenture conferring a floating charge over its assets to secure the £3,000 together with the earlier payment of £10,000 and the interest thereon. Howie subsequently appointed a receiver under the debenture and obtained payment of more than £12,000 through a realisation of the secured assets of the new company.

1–37   The High Court of Australia held unanimously that a relation analogous to that of principal and surety existed between Spicer and the new company. Since payment of Spicer's debt to Howie would discharge the liability secured by the preference shares, Spicer's liability was clearly

---

[99] *Duncan, Fox & Co v North and South Wales Bank* (1880) 6 App. Cas. 1 at 13. Parol evidence is admissible to show, as between the two co-obligors in a bond, that one is surety for the other: *Bolton v Cooke* (1825) 3 L.J.O.S. 87.
[1] *Re Hodgetts Ex p. Official Receiver* (1949) 16 A.B.C. 201 at 206–207. See also *Smith v Wood* [1929] 1 Ch. 14.
[2] As in *Duncan, Fox & Co v North and South Wales Bank* (1880) 6 App. Cas. 1. A similar principle applies where one person gives another a promissory note securing an advance to a third party. See *Pooley v Harradine* (1857) 7 El. & Bl. 431; 119 E.R. 1307; *Greenough v McLelland* (1860) 2 E. & E. 424; 119 R.R. 778 (creditor knew of the suretyship arrangement at the time he took the note); *Leicestershire Banking Co Ltd v Hawkins* (1900) 16 T.L.R. 317 (where the priority of the securities held for the surety was in issue).
[3] (1931) 47 C.L.R. 151.

primary. It was equally clear that Howie's claims against the company through the preference shares given as security were merely secondary. Hence, as soon as the debt was paid by the new company or by a realisation of its assets, the company was entitled to recoup the payment from Spicer and resort to the securities which Spicer had given Howie.[4]

Lord Selborne's third situation,[5] as illustrated by *A. M. Spicer & Son Pty Ltd (in liq) v Spicer*,[6] might not be the only context in which suretyship arises in the absence of a contract of suretyship. Recent developments in relation to estoppel suggest that suretyship may also arise where there is no binding contract of guarantee but merely a gratuitous promise to answer for the debt or liability of another. This suggestion first stemmed from an obiter dictum of Goff J. at first instance in *Amalgamated Investment & Property Co Ltd (in liq) v Texas Commerce International Bank Ltd.*[7] Subsequent developments[8] in respect of estoppel in Australia indicate that it is probable that a party who acts unconscionably in inducing an assumption by the creditor that a contract of guarantee exists (or will exist) will be estopped from denying this state of affairs provided that the creditor acts on the assumption.[9] Although no contract of suretyship exists, the party estopped would, in the words of Lord Selborne, incur "a secondary liability ... for one and the same debt, by virtue of which ... he has a right of reimbursement or indemnity from the [principal debtor]."[10]   **1–38**

Suretyship will not always arise where there is a primary and secondary liability of two persons for the same debt. For example, a mortgagor of property which is sold subject to the mortgage does not become a surety for the purchaser.[11] Nor is the assignor of a lease a surety of the assignee even if the assignee covenants to indemnify the assignor against liability for breaches of covenants in the lease.[12] Similarly, a transferor of shares does not become the surety of the transferee even if the transferor is liable by statute to pay calls on the shares if the transferee defaults.[13] In all these cases the secondary liability which remains with the transferor or assignor is "a vestige of the original primary liability".[14] A guarantee, on the other hand, creates a liability which is almost invariably intended to be of a secondary nature.   **1–39**

---

[4] *A M Spicer & Son Pty Ltd (in liq) v Spicer* (1931) 47 C.L.R. 151 at 185–186 *per* Dixon J.
[5] See *Duncan, Fox & Co v North and South Wales Bank* (1880) 6 App. Cas. 1 at 11–12.
[6] (1931) 47 C.L.R. 151.
[7] [1981] 2 W.L.R. 554 at 574.
[8] *Waltons Stores (Interstate) Pty Ltd v Maher* (1988) 164 C.L.R. 387; *Commonwealth v Verwayen* (1990) 64 A.L.J.R. 540.
[9] *e.g.* by making advances to the principal.
[10] *Duncan, Fox & Co v North and South Wales Bank* (1880) 6 App. Cas. 1 at 12. See also below, para.2–90.
[11] *Re Errington, Ex p. Mason* [1894] 1 Q.B. 11 at 14. Indeed, the mortgagor has an implied right of indemnity against the purchaser: *Waring v Ward* (1802) 7 Ves. Jun. 332 at 337; *Bridgman v Daw* (1891) 40 W.R. 253.
[12] *Baynton v Morgan* (1888) 22 Q.B.D. 74; *Selous Street Properties Ltd v Oronel Fabrics Ltd* (1984) 269 E.G. 643 and 743; *Allied London Investments v Hambro Life Assurance Ltd* (1984) 269 E.G. 41; *Re Russell; Russell v Shoolbred* (1885) 29 Ch. D. 254; *Johns v Pink* [1900] 1 Ch. 296.
[13] Companies Act 1985, s.502(2)(c); *Re Contract Corporation; Hudson's Case* (1871) L.R. 12 Eq. 1 at 6; *Helbert v Banner* (1871) LR 5 HL 28; *Roberts v Crowe* (1872) LR 7 CP 629.
[14] K.P. McGuinness, *The Law Of Guarantee* (2nd ed., 1996), p.34.

1–40   Suretyship covers a broad spectrum.[15] It arises when one spouse
guarantees the debt of the other[16] and when the debts of a company are
guaranteed by its directors.[17] It can also appear in transactions involving
unincorporated associations[18] and partnerships.[19] As a means of securing
contractual obligations, guarantees are used in a wide variety of contexts:
banker and customer,[20] mortgagor and mortgagee,[21] landlord and tenant,[22]
vendor and purchaser,[23] sale of goods[24] and hire purchase[25] (particularly
where the purchaser or hirer is an infant),[26] building contracts,[27]
performance[28] and fidelity bonds.[29] Guarantees may also be given by
governments to promote sporting bodies, to foster the growth of small
businesses or to assist industrial development or export trade.[30] An
ordinary promissory note or bill of exchange can create a relationship
analogous to suretyship,[31] and the maker or acceptor of an accommodation
note or bill is properly classified as a guarantor because he undertakes to

[15] For a full account of the roles that guarantees play in business transactions, see K.P.
McGuinness, *The Law of Guarantee* (1986), pp.5–19.
[16] *Bank of A/asia v Levy* (1895) 6 Q.L.J. 208; *Union Bank v Crate* (1911) 19 O.W.R. 299,
affirmed in (1913) 3 D.L.R. 686, CA.
[17] As examples of a guarantee of a company's debts, see *Shaw v Royce Ltd* [1911] 1 Ch. 138
and, as to guarantees of dividends on shares, see *Taylor v Reid* (1929) 42 C.L.R. 371. As to
guarantees of schemes of arrangement, see *Re Hickinbotham* (1879) 5 V.L.R. (L) 101.
[18] See *Dalgety v Harris* [1977] 1 N.S.W.L.R. 324, CA; *Re Marantha Ski Club Co-op Ltd* [1977]
A.C.L.C. 29,256.
[19] See *Australian Joint Stock Bank v Hogan* (1902) 2 S.R. (NSW) 7; *Colonial Bank of New
Zealand v Smith* (1888) 6 N.Z.L.R. 659.
[20] See *Campbell v Russell* (1938) Q.W.N. 10. As to guarantees of overdrafts, see *Queensland
National Bank Ltd v Queensland Trustees Ltd* (1899) 9 Q.L.J. 282; *Commercial Bank v
Moylan* (1870) 1 A.J.R. 123; *Bank of A/asia v Crotchett* (1878) 4 V.L.R. (L) 226.
[21] *Re Law Guarantee Trust & Accident Society Ltd* [1914] 2 Ch. 617; *Re Mercantile Finance
Trustees & Agency Co of Australia Ltd*; (1896) 22 V.L.R. 381; *Hancock v Williams* (1942) 42
S.R. (NSW) 252.
[22] See *Stone v Geraldton Brewery Co* (1898) 1 W.A.L.R. 23; *Sacher Investments Pty Ltd v
Forma Stereo Consultants Pty Ltd* [1976] 1 N.S.W.L.R. 5; *International Leasing Corp (Vic) Ltd
v Aiken* [1967] 2 N.S.W.R. 427.
[23] *Western Dominion Investment Co v MacMillan* [1925] 2 DLR 442, affirmed in [1925] 4
D.L.R. 562, CA.
[24] See *Schureck v McFarlane* (1923) 41 W.N. (NSW) 3; *Turner Manufacturing Co Pty Ltd v
Senes* [1964] N.S.W.R. 692.
[25] *Payton v S. G. Brookes & Sons Pty Ltd* [1977] W.A.R. 91. See also *Guthrie v Motor Credits
Ltd* (1963) 37 A.L.J.R. 167 (a guarantee of a car dealer's obligations to a finance company).
[26] See below, paras 5–15 to 5–17. See also *Yeoman Credit Ltd v Latter* [1961] 1 W.L.R. 828;
Alliance Acceptance Co Ltd v Hinton (1964) 1 D.C.R. (NSW) 5.
[27] See *A/asian Conference Association Ltd v Mainline Constructions Pty Ltd (in liq)* (1978) 53
A.L.J.R. 66; *Purcell v Raphael* (1867) 7 S.C.R. (NSW) 138.
[28] As to performance bonds, see generally *Edward Owen Engineering Ltd v Barclay's Bank
International Ltd* [1977] 3 W.L.R. 764, CA: see below, Ch. 13. See also *Re Patrick Corp Ltd
and the Companies Act* [1981] 2 N.S.W.L.R. 328.
[29] As to fidelity guarantees, see *Kennaway v Treleavan* (1839) 5 M. & W. 498; 151 E.R. 211;
Newbury v Armstrong (1829) 6 Bing. 201; 130 E.R. 1257; *London Chartered Bank v
Sutherland* (1871) 2 A.J.R. 17; *Dougharty v London Guarantee & Accident Co* (1880) 6 V.L.R.
(L) 376; *National Mortgage & Agency Co of New Zealand Ltd v Stalker* [1933] N.Z.L.R. 1182.
[30] See below, Ch. 13. See, *e.g.* Exports and Investment Guarantees Act 1991, discussed in G.
Andrews and R. Millett, *Law of Guarantees* (3rd ed., 2000), Ch. 15.
[31] See below, paras 1–44 to 1–54; *Duncan, Fox & Co v North and South Wales Bank* (1880) 6
App. Cas. 1; *Ex p. Yonge* (1814) 3 V. & B. 31 at 40; 35 E.R. 391 at 394; *Hartland v Jukes* (1863)
1 H. & C. 667; 158 E.R. 1052; *Pioneer Bank v Canadian Bank of Commerce* (1916) 31 D.L.R.
507.

be answerable for the debt of the party accommodated.[32] Even certain letters of credit can amount to guarantees.[33] It may be necessary for trustees, executors or administrators to give or take guarantees in the performance of their duties.[34] In international trade, guarantees appear in several different guises: tender bonds, performance guarantees and repayment guarantees.[35] Indeed, it is difficult to imagine a more versatile arrangement than a contract of guarantee.

Guarantees can be limited to a specific principal transaction, such as a contract of sale, a lease or a building contract, or they can apply to all transactions and dealings between the creditor and the principal debtor. The former are called specific guarantees; the latter "all accounts" or "all moneys" guarantees. Moreover guarantees can be limited in duration or can extend for an indefinite period as continuing guarantees. **1–41**

Sureties are often required to ensure that a party attends the court or complies with its orders. Equitable principles of the general law of suretyship are generally not applicable in this context.[36] Technically, such sureties are not guarantors and, for this reason, a discussion of those forms of suretyship lies beyond the scope of a book on the modern contract of guarantee.[37] **1–42**

4. THE APPLICATION OF PRINCIPLES OF SURETYSHIP TO NEGOTIABLE INSTRUMENTS

The application of the principles of suretyship depends, to a degree, upon whether or not the negotiable instrument was accepted for value. **1–43**

(i) Where a negotiable instrument is accepted for value

Strictly, in the case of a bill accepted and indorsed for value, the relationship between the acceptor, on the one hand, and the drawer and indorsers, on the other, is not that of principal debtor and surety, though it **1–44**

---

[32] See *Re Acraman; Ex p. Webster* (1847) De G 414; *Bailey v Edwards* (1864) 4 B. & S. 761; 122 E.R. 645; *Ex p. Yonge* (1814) 3 V. & B. 31 at 40; 35 E.R. 391 at 394 *per* Lord Eldon L.C. See below, para.1–59.

[33] See *Commercial Banking Co of Sydney Ltd v Patrick Intermarine Acceptances Ltd* (1978) 52 A.L.J.R. 404. Generally, however, letters of credit involve direct, independent undertakings which are not guarantees. A standby letter of credit is merely an instrument of payment under which the issuing bank's obligation is independent of the primary obligation of the borrower and the bank's liability is not dependent upon the borrower's default: *Commercial Banking Co of Sydney Ltd v Patrick Intermarine Acceptances Ltd*, above.

[34] As to guarantees given to trustees by beneficiaries, see *Union Bank of Australia Ltd v Whitelaw* [1906] V.L.R. 711. As to guarantees by trustees, executors and administrators, see *Jenkins v Wyatt* (1900) 21 L.R. (NSW) 322 and *Estate of Gracey* (1917) 17 S.R. (NSW) 239.

[35] ICC (International Chamber of Commerce) *Uniform Rules for Demand Guarantees* (1992) ICC Publication No.458 and *Uniform Customs and Practice for Documentary Credits* (1993 Revision) ICC Publication No.500.

[36] *Rastall v A-G* (1871) 18 Gr. 138; 17 Gr. 1 (Can); *Thomakakis v Sheriff of NSW* (1993) 33 N.S.W.L.R. 36.

[37] See, C. Chatterton, *Bail: Law and Practice* (1986) and F. Paterson, *Understanding Bail in Britain* (1996).

is analogous thereto.[38] Prima facie the acceptor's position is merely similar to that of a principal debtor since the acceptor is primarily and absolutely liable to pay the bill according to its tenor.[39] The drawer and indorsers are *treated* as sureties for the acceptor and are only liable if the acceptor defaults.[40] They are in a sense only quasi-sureties since they do not enjoy all the rights which a surety enjoys under a normal guarantee.[41] But while they are treated as sureties in respect of the acceptor, they are not co-sureties as between themselves. Thus, where a bill is accepted by the drawee and later indorsed by the drawer and then by subsequent indorsers to the holder, as between the holder and the acceptor, the latter is principal debtor and the drawer and the indorsers are the sureties; but as between the holder and drawer, the drawer is prima facie a principal debtor and the subsequent indorsers are the principal's sureties. Equally, as between the holder and the first indorser, prima facie the first indorser is the principal and the second and subsequent indorsers are the sureties, and so on.[42] On a bill payable to the order of a third person, the payee is a subsequent party and is consequently a surety for the drawer.[43] This chain of liability is particularly important when considering the question of discharge since a discharge of prior parties to the bill releases subsequent parties, although the converse is not true.[44] The holder of the bill, of course, assumes the position occupied by a creditor in an ordinary guarantee. Similar principles govern the respective liabilities of the parties who draw or indorse a cheque.[45]

---

[38] *Duncan, Fox & Co v North and South Wales Bank* (1880) 6 App. Cas. 1 at 11 *per* Lord Selborne, 14 *per* Lord Blackburn. See also *Scholefield Goodman & Sons Ltd v Zyngier* [1984] VR 445; on appeal: [1986] A.C. 562; *Re Conley* [1938] 2 All E.R. 127 at 131 *per* Lord Greene M.R. *Cf. Rouquette v Overmann* (1875) L.R. 10 Q.B. 525 at 536–537; *Cook v Lister* (1863) 32 L.J.C.P. 121 at 127.

[39] See *Rowe v Young* (1820) 2 Bligh P.C. 391 at 467; 4 E.R. 372 at 407; *Jones v Broadhurst* (1850) 9 C.B. 173 at 181; 137 E.R. 858 at 861 per Cresswell J. See also Bills of Exchange Act 1882, s.54. A drawee who accepts the bill becomes primarily liable thereon: *Philpot v Briant* (1828) 4 Bing 717 at 720; 130 E.R. 945 at 946. As to the relations inter se of joint acceptors who are not partners, see *Harmer v Steele* (1849) 4 Exch. 1 at 13; 154 E.R. 1100 at 1105.

[40] *Rowe v Young* (1820) 2 Bligh P.C. 391 at 467; 4 E.R. 372 at 407; *Jones v Broadhurst* (1850) 9 C.B. 173 at 181; 137 E.R. 858 at 861 *per* Cresswell J; *Maxal Nominees Pty Ltd v Dalgety Ltd* [1985] 1 Qd R 51; *Bills of Exchange Act* 1882, s.55(1) and (2). *Cf. Scholefield Goodman & Sons Ltd v Zyngier* [1986] A.C. 562.

[41] In particular, it appears that they cannot claim the equities of a surety while the bill is current and before it is dishonoured: *Duncan, Fox & Co v North and South Wales Bank* (1880) 6 App. Cas. 1 at 22–33 *per* Lord Watson. See also *Ex p. Yonge* (1814) 3 Ves. & B. 31; 35 E.R. 391.

[42] See *Horne v Rouquette* (1878) 3 Q.B.D. 514 at 518, where Brett L.J. cited with approval a passage which now appears in N. Elliott, J. Odger and J.M. Phillips, *Byles on Bills of Exchange and Cheques* (27th ed., 2002), pp.464–465. See also *Ewin v Lancaster* (1865) 5 B. & S. 571 at 577; 122 E.R. 1306 at 1308.

[43] The payee occupies the same position as the first indorsee and the second indorser of a bill drawn payable to the indorser's order: see *Claridge v Dalton* (1815) 4 M. & S. 226; 105 E.R. 818; *Byles on Bills of Exchange and Cheques* (27th ed., 2002), p.465.

[44] On the general question of discharge, see below, Chs 6–9.

[45] See *Byles on Bills of Exchange and Cheques* (27th ed., 2002), para.21–95 and A. L. Tyree, *Australian Law of Cheques and Payment Orders* (1988), paras 12.22–12.24.

(a) Stranger signing bill

Under continental legal systems, a stranger can assume a liability as a **1–45** guarantor just by signing a bill of exchange.[46] Under this principle, called an "aval", the stranger assumes the same liability as the party for whom he intervened.[47] Thus, where an aval is given on behalf of an acceptor, the stranger incurs the liability of an acceptor; if nothing is said, the aval is deemed to have been provided for the drawer, who is the "surety" on the face of the bill.

English law does not recognise an aval for the honour of the acceptor **1–46** even if this aval is constituted by a stranger's signature on the bill.[48] But it does allow a stranger's indorsement on a bill to operate as an aval where the stranger indorses the bill to a person who is about to take the bill. Such an indorsement creates no obligation to those who were previously parties to the bill, but it does enure for the benefit of subsequent parties.[49]

A bank guarantee or an aval on a bill of exchange is governed by the law **1–47** of the country where it is delivered.[50] But if the courts of the country where it was signed refused to recognise that law and summarily rejected a claim under that guarantee, a local court may be prepared to hear the claim to prevent the guarantee being subverted. It would be necessary to establish that the local court would fully explore the merits of the case and that the transaction had a solid connection with the local jurisdiction, for example, through the incorporation of the defendant company in that jurisdiction.[51]

In *Steele v M'Kinlay*,[52] a stranger, James M'Kinlay, signed the back of a **1–48** bill drawn by Walker on, and accepted by, M'Kinlay's two sons. The bill was later indorsed by the drawer. At the time of the action both Walker and James M'Kinlay were dead and there was no evidence why or in what capacity M'Kinlay had signed. Walker's representatives sued M'Kinlay's representatives on the bill. Under the law merchant, a person who wrote an indorsement on a bill with intent to become a party to it would, in a dispute with subsequent holders, incur all the liabilities of a proper indorser.[53] Consistent with these principles, the court held that although

[46] See the Geneva Convention, Ch IV, Arts 30, 31 and 32. It appears that the aval can be traced directly to the civil law doctrine of negotiorum gestio: L. Aitken, "Negotiorum Gestio and the Common Law—A Jurisdictional Approach" (1988) 11 Syd. L.R. 566 at 577–580.

[47] For a discussion of the use of avals in trade financing, see R. Lombardi, "Avals and Quasi-Indorsements of Negotiable Instruments" (1988) 14 Mon. L.R. 264. For a discussion of the operation and effect of the aval and the impact of the UNCITRAL Convention, s.G, Arts 47–49, see E. Wong, "The UNCITRAL Convention on International Bills of Exchange" (1988) 4 B.L.B. 70.

[48] See *Jackson v Hudson* (1810) 2 Camp. 447 at 448; 170 E.R. 1213 at 1214, approved in *Steele v M'Kinlay* (1880) 5 App. Cas. 754 at 772. Moreover, in *Ferrier v Stewart* (1912) 15 C.L.R. 32 at 41, Isaacs J. appeared to pay lip service to the doctrine of aval.

[49] See *Hill v Lewis* (1709) 1 Salk 132 at 133; 91 E.R. 124 at 125; *Penny v Innes* (1834) 1 C.M. & R 439; 149 E.R. 1152.

[50] *Banco Atlantico SA v British Bank of the Middle East, Financial Times*, June 5, 1990, CA.

[51] *ibid.*

[52] (1880) 5 App. Cas. 754.

[53] *ibid.*, at 782. See also *McDonald & Co v Nash & Co* [1924] A.C. 625 at 650 per Lord Sumner; *Grunzweig und Hartmann Montage GmBH v Irvani* [1988] 1 Lloyd's L.R. 460, where the defendant was held liable for the value of dishonoured bills because he had signed them as

M'Kinlay was, in effect, an indorser he could not, in the absence of a special contract, be regarded as an acceptor since this would make him liable to the drawer, a prior holder of the bill. A memorandum in writing was necessary to prove the special contract, and in its absence M'Kinlay was not liable to the drawer. It is interesting to note that the bill in *Steele v M'Kinlay* was drawn by Walker payable to "me or my order" and that he indorsed it. On this basis, M'Kinlay's prior indorsement could have rendered him liable to Walker, not as drawer but as payee or holder.[54]

1–49   The Bills of Exchange Act 1882 does not recognise an aval. However, s.56 provides: "Where a person signs a bill otherwise than as drawer or acceptor, he thereby incurs the liabilities of an indorser to a holder in due course." By this section, the signatory is liable not as guarantor but as an indorser, and the liabilities incurred by such a stranger are those of an indorser to a holder in due course.[55] These liabilities do not extend to prior holders as such so the stranger will not be liable to a drawer qua drawer or a payee qua payee, although a drawer or payee may of course become a holder subsequent to the stranger's indorsement.[56] Since the stranger's liabilities are limited to subsequent holders of the bill, the section produces a result similar to that achieved in *Steele v M'Kinlay* and thereby gives statutory force and recognition to Lord Watson's interpretation of the law merchant in that case.[57] But it is perhaps going too far to assert that the section has adopted the principle of aval[58] since it does not render the stranger liable to prior holders *as such*.

(b) Signature as a backer

1–50   A person who signs a bill of exchange other than as drawer or acceptor must do so as an indorser or as a stranger.[59] Either way such a person will, by virtue of s.56 of the Bills of Exchange Act 1882, incur the liabilities of an indorser to a holder in due course.[60] Where a person not liable on a bill signs it with intent to guarantee payment by the acceptor to the drawer, that person is said to "back" the bill. Under s.56, such a person attracts all the liabilities of an indorser to a holder in due course, although he may be liable to parties other than such a holder.[61] That person's liabilities may

---

backer before the words "bon pour aval pour les tires" (meaning literally "good as a guarantee for the drawers") were added above his signature on legal advice.
[54] See *Byles on Bills of Exchange and Cheques* (27th ed., 2002), para.17–15.
[55] This appears to be the plain meaning of the words of the section, although its general interpretation appears to assume that the signatory is liable only to a holder in due course and no one else: see *Byles on Bills of Exchange and Cheques* (27th ed., 2002), para.17–13.
[56] See *Ferrier v Stewart* (1912) 15 C.L.R. 32 at 37 *per* Griffith C.J.
[57] (1880) 5 App. Cas. 754 at 782.
[58] *Cf. Robinson v Mann* (1901) 31 S.C.R. 484 at 486 *per* Sir Henry Strong C.J. (Can). See also *Grant v Scott* (1919) 59 S.C.R. 227.
[59] See *Byles on Bills of Exchange and Cheques* (27th ed., 2002), para.17–13.
[60] See *Grunzweig und Hartmann Montage GmBH v Irvani* [1988] 1 Lloyd's L.R. 460 at 466; L. Aitken, "Backing Bills and the Aval" (1990) 6 B.L.B. 6.
[61] See above, paras 1–45 to 1–49. *Grunzweig und Hartmann Montage GmBH v Irvani* [1988] 1 Lloyd's Rep. 460 at 466; *Rowe & Co Pty Ltd v Pitts* [1973] 2 N.S.W.L.R. 159 (where the defendant was held liable as an indorser even though the plaintiff was not a holder in due course because he took the bill after notice of dishonour).

extend to any subsequent holders of the bill but not to prior holders as such.[62] A person who backs a bill can be liable under the section even if a holder inserts the word "guarantor" after the person's signature on the bill.[63] This statutory liability does not depend upon the law of suretyship.[64]

Oral evidence is admissible to establish the intention behind the backer's indorsement.[65] This intention can be gleaned from the circumstances surrounding the indorsement[66] and it is a question of fact whether or not the backer signed the instrument as a principal or as a surety.[67] It is not necessary to show that the stranger signing the bill was a party to an agreement between the parties that the stranger was to sign as guarantor as long as the stranger had notice of the agreement before he indorsed the bill.[68] Nor is it conclusive that the word "directors" was inserted after the signatures of the strangers on the bill, since it may be merely descriptive and does not necessarily exclude their personal liability on the bill.[69] It is not necessary to produce a written memorandum satisfying the *Statute of Frauds* in order to render a signatory liable as an indorser under s.56.[70] Moreover, a signatory can be liable under the section even if he signed the bill before it was delivered to the payee and indorsed by the payee[71] and even though the bill has not been indorsed to the signatory.[72]

1–51

A signatory cannot, however, be liable as an indorser under s.56 of the Bills of Exchange Act 1882 unless the instrument is a bill of exchange or a

1–52

---

[62] See *Ferrier v Stewart* (1912) 15 C.L.R. 32 at 37 *per* Griffith C.J. See also *McCall Bros v Hargreaves* [1932] 2 K.B. 423.
[63] *Trimper v Frahn* [1925] S.A.S.R. 347. Similarly in *Walker v O'Reilly* (1861) 7 U.C.L.J. 300, the following indorsement on the back of a promissory note did not prevent the signatory being liable as an indorser, rather than a guarantor: "I guarantee payment of the within."
[64] See *Robinson v Mann* (1901) 31 S.C.R. 484 at 486 *per* Sir Henry Strong C.J. See also *McCall Bros v Hargreaves* [1932] 2 K.B. 423 at 429. If the holder of the cheque is not a holder in due course, there is a rebuttable presumption that the stranger signed the cheque with the intention to become liable thereon. s. 75(2)(b). As to evidence in rebuttal, see *Bondina Ltd v Rollaway Shower Blinds* [1986] 1 All E.R. 564.
[65] *McDonald & Co v Nash & Co* [1924] A.C. 625.
[66] *ibid.* See also *Macdonald v Whitfield* (1883) 8 App. Cas. 733.
[67] *Noonan v White* (1879) 1 A.L.T. 2. See also *Wilders v Stevens* (1846) 15 M. & W. 208: 153 ER 824. This proposition is not limited to bills of exchange as a person can sign a promissory note as surety: *MacKenzie v West* (1890) 16 V.L.R. 588; *Markwell Bros v Bennett* [1904] Q.W.N. 13; *Hartland v Jukes* (1863) 1 H & C 667. A party to a promissory note can join therein as a surety even if that party's purpose is to enable the principal debtor to raise money to apply towards the discharge of certain obligations to that party: *Shepley v Hurd* (1879) 3 O.A.R. 549.
[68] See *Douglas v Hutton* (1856) 1 V.L.T. 37.
[69] *Elliott v Bax-Ironside* [1925] 2 K.B. 301. Cf. *Bondina Ltd v Rollaway Shower Blinds* [1986] 1 All E.R. 564 (where the form of the cheque makes it clear that the signatory was signing merely in a representative capacity, the presumption will be rebutted).
[70] *McCall Bros v Hargreaves* [1932] 2 K.B. 423 at 429.
[71] See *Durack v West Australian Trustee, Executor & Agency Co Ltd* (1945) 72 C.L.R. 189; *Laidley v McMillan* (1870) 9 S.C.R. (NSW) 118. Where there is extrinsic evidence that the parties intended the defendant to be liable in the event of the principal's default, the order and position of the parties' signatures is immaterial. Nor does it matter that the plaintiff's indorsement was restrictive: *Yeoman Credit Ltd v Gregory* [1963] 1 WLR 343. See also *Grant v Scott* (1919) 59 S.C.R. 227 at 231.
[72] Normally, the indorser of a bill of exchange cannot be sued as such unless the bill has been indorsed to him: *Wood v M'Mahon* (1877) 3 V.L.R. (L) 282; *Singer v Elliott* (1888) 4 T.L.R. 524. The person who signs a bill either as an indorser or as a stranger is precluded from setting up the defence that the person suing on the bill was himself a previous indorser: *Glenie v Bruce Smith* [1907] 2 K.B. 507, affirmed in [1908] 1 K.B. 263.

promissory note.[73] It also appears that a person cannot be liable as an indorser if that person signs a promissory note after it matures, at least where the payee to whose order the note was made has never indorsed it.[74] Even if a person signs the instrument while it is current, that person's liability as an indorser can be excluded if the words "sans recours" are added to his signature.[75] Where the bill is incomplete at the time the person backs the bill with his signature, it appears that the person cannot be held liable as an indorser under the section if the omission is material and cannot be cured by invoking s.20.[76] In such a case, the person could still be held liable as a guarantor but only if there is a written memorandum satisfying the Statute of Frauds.[77]

(c) Guarantees embodied in the negotiable instrument

1–53   If a bill of exchange bears an indorsement to the effect that in case of non-payment of the bill by the acceptor the bill is to be presented to the defendant, and the defendant then signs this indorsement, this constitutes a valid guarantee and no other evidence apart from the bill is necessary to satisfy the Statute of Frauds.[78] But the defendant's indorsement must make it clear that he intended to undertake the liability of a surety. It is not sufficient for the defendant to write on the bill: "I know this to be a genuine firm."[79]

(d) Guarantees outside the negotiable instrument

1–54   Where a person does not sign a negotiable instrument but guarantees the obligations of one of the parties thereto by a separate document, that person can be held liable as a guarantor provided the document satisfies

---

[73] To be a promissory note, the instrument must contain an unconditional promise to pay a certain sum of money: *Lamb v Somerville* (1909) 29 N.Z.L.R. 138. See also Bills of Exchange Act 1882, s.83.

[74] *Robertson v Lonsdale* (1892) 21 O.R. 600 CA.

[75] See N. Elliott, J. Odgers and J.M. Phillips, *Byles on Bills of Exchange and Cheques* (27th ed., 2002), p.198.

[76] See also *McCall Bros Ltd v Hargreaves* [1932] 2 K.B. 423; *Ferrier v Stewart* (1912) 15 C.L.R. 32. Cf. *Erikssen v Bunting* (1901) 20 N.Z.L.R. 388.

[77] *McCall Bros Ltd v Hargreaves* [1932] 2 K.B. 423. *Singer v Elliott* (1888) 4 T.L.R. 524 suggests that such a memorandum will also be necessary where the bill is not negotiated, but that case was not officially reported and the judgments of the Court of Appeal do not expressly refer to the Bills of Exchange Act. Moreover, it appears that *Wilkinson v Unwin* (1881) 7 Q.B.D. 636 was not cited to the court, nor was the court's attention drawn to the equivalent of s.20 of the Bills of Exchange Act: 1882. Consequently, Goddard J. in *McCall Bros Ltd v Hargreaves* at 428 doubted whether *Singer v Elliott* could now be regarded as an authority.

[78] *J. W. Holmes & Co v Durkee* (1883) Cab. & El. 23; *Stagg, Mantle & Co v Brodrick* (1895) 12 T.L.R. 12 CA. Although under general law such a signatory would not have been liable as an indorser because his indorsement was not part of the bill of exchange, that signatory might be liable as an indorser under s.56 of the Bills of Exchange Act 1882.

[79] *Ulster Banking Co v Mahaffy* (1881) 15 I.L.T. 94.

the Statute of Frauds.[80] It must be clear, however, that the person has given an unequivocal promise to pay on the default of the principal: a letter stating "we are honest enough to pay you" does not constitute a guarantee on behalf of the maker of a promissory note.[81] These principles operate independently of the law merchant and the Bills of Exchange Act 1882.

(e) Liability on a bill of exchange or a cheque

The Statute of Frauds need not be satisfied where an action is brought **1–55** on the bill or cheque itself seeking to hold a party liable under the Bills of Exchange Act 1882.[82] In such a case, the order of the signatures of the parties is immaterial.[83] Any bona fide holder of a bill or cheque can fill in the material particulars which are missing from the bill or cheque.[84] Even a bill of exchange or cheque indorsed in blank can be enforced in this way without reference to the Statute of Frauds or indeed the law of suretyship.[85]

(f) Variation of the parties' prima facie liabilities

The positions and liabilities which parties assume on a negotiable **1–56** instrument can be varied or even reversed by agreement between them.[86] Thus, the acceptor of a bill of exchange or the maker of a promissory note can agree to exchange positions with the party who was originally liable upon that party's default.[87] Similarly, where A and B are primarily liable on the face of a negotiable instrument and A alone is sued, it is competent for her to show that she was merely a surety for B.[88] Similar principles apply to cheques. The form of the instrument, therefore, is not the sole factor determining the rights and liabilities of the parties.

---

[80] *Macdonald v Whitfield* (1883) 8 App Cas 733; *Morris v Stacey* (1816) Holt N.P. 153; 171 E.R. 196; *Steele v M'Kinlay* (1880) 5 App Cas 754; *Reihe v Heller* (1929) 35 O.W.N. 272, CA; *Wambold v Foote* (1878) 2 O.A.R. 579. See also *Yeoman Credit Ltd v Gregory* [1963] 1 WLR 343 at 345, where Megaw J. found that there was no general contract of guarantee on the evidence. See also *Overend Gurney & Co Ltd v Oriental Financial Corp Ltd* (1874) L.R. 7 H.L. 348 at 358. Thus an action cannot be brought on a mere oral promise to indorse the commercial paper of the plaintiff's debtor: *Leiser & Co v Canadian Pacific Timber Co* [1920] 1 W.W.R. 735, BC.
[81] *Reihe v Heller* (1929) 35 O.W.N. 272, CA. A similar principle applies, mutatis mutandis, to cheques.
[82] *Wilkinson v Unwin* (1881) 7 Q.B.D. 636; *Standard Bank v Alta Enrg Co* (1917) 33 D.L.R. 542.
[83] *McDonald & Co v Nash & Co* [1924] A.C. 625; *McCall Bros Ltd v Hargreaves* [1932] 2 K.B. 423; *National Sales Corp Ltd v Bernardi* [1931] 2 KB 188.
[84] *ibid.* See also *Erikssen v Bunting* (1901) 20 N.Z.L.R. 388; *Carter v White* (1883) 25 Ch. D. 666; *Re Duffy's Estate* (1880) 5 L.R. Ir. 92.
[85] *Glenie v Bruce Smith* [1908] 1 K.B. 263.
[86] See *Overend Gurney & Co Ltd v Oriental Financial Corp Ltd* (1874) L.R. 7 H.L. 348; *Greenough v M'Clelland* (1860) 30 L.J.Q.B. 15; *Rouse v Bradford Banking Co* [1894] AC 586.
[87] *ibid.*
[88] *Ewin v Lancaster* (1865) 6 B. & S. 571; 122 E.R. 1306; *Rouse v Bradford Banking Co* [1894] A.C. 586 at 591; *Pooley v Harradine* (1857) 7 E. & B. 431; 119 E.R. 1307.

1–57   Once the holder or other party seeking to enforce the instrument is notified of a change in the relationship of the parties, that party is bound by it whether he consents or not.[89] It is immaterial whether the party knew of the real relationship between the parties when he took the bill of exchange or promissory note[90] as long as he had notice of the true position at the time of his dealings with the principal.[91] If a defendant can establish that he is merely a surety to the knowledge of the claimant, the defendant can invoke any defences available to a guarantor under the law of suretyship.[92]

1–58   Originally neither the common law nor equity would allow parol evidence to vary the terms of a written instrument.[93] But now such evidence is admissible to establish the true relationship of the parties, whether a question of an indemnity arises between the principal debtor and the guarantor, or a question of contribution between co-sureties.[94]

(ii) Where a negotiable instrument is accepted or indorsed otherwise than for value

1–59   There is a prima facie presumption that every party to a bill or cheque is deemed to have become a party thereto for value.[95] This presumption can be rebutted by evidence that the instrument was signed by one party for the accommodation of another. Where a person lends his name to another for the other's accommodation, the party accommodated undertakes to pay the bill or cheque at maturity and also to indemnify the first person if that person is compelled to pay the bill or honour the cheque for

---

[89] See *Pooley v Harradine* (1857) 7 E. & B. 431; 119 E.R. 1307; *Overend Gurney & Co Ltd v Oriental Financial Corp Ltd* (1874) L.R. 7 H.L. 348 at 360; *Greenough v M'Clelland* (1860) 30 L.J.Q.B. 15; *Neill & Co Ltd v Esther* (1894) 13 N.Z.L.R. 220. Cf. *Strong v Foster* (1855) 17 C.B. 201; 139 E.R. 1047; *York City & County Banking Co v Bainbridge* (1880) 43 L.T. 732; *Ball v Gilson* (1858) 7 C.P. 531 (Can), which suggest that it is necessary for the holder or payee to consent to the change.

[90] Cf. *Ball v Gilson* (1858) 7 C.P. 531 (Can); *Manley v Boycot* (1853) 2 E. & B. 46; 118 E.R. 636; *Pooley v Harradine* (1857) 7 E. & B. 431; 119 E.R. 1307.

[91] *Overend Gurney & Co Ltd v Oriental Financial Corp Ltd* (1874) L.R. 7 H.L. 348; *Pooley v Harradine* (1857) 7 E. & B. 431; 119 E.R. 1307; *Oakeley v Pasheller* (1836) 10 Bli. (NS) 548.

[92] See S. D. Phipson, *Evidence* (15th ed., 2000), para.42–32. See also *Hollier v Eyre* (1842) 9 Cl. & F. 1 at 45; 8 ER 313 at 332; *Davies v Stainbank* (1855) 6 De G.M. & G. 679; 43 E.R. 1397; *Greenough v M'Clelland* (1860) 30 L.J.Q.B. 15; *Overend Gurney & Co Ltd v Oriental Financial Corp Ltd* (1874) L.R. 7 H.L. 348; *Neill & Co Ltd v Esther* (1894) 13 N.Z.L.R. 220. See further *Bechervaise v Lewis* (1872) L.R. 7 C.P. 372.

[93] See *Pooley v Harradine* (1857) 7 E. & B. 431; 119 E.R. 1307. At law, it was thought that such evidence was inadmissible because it contradicted the terms of a written instrument: *Fentum v Pocock* (1813) 5 Taunt 192; 128 ER 660. See also *Bailey v Edwards* (1864) 4 B. & S. 761; 122 E.R. 645. The same resistance was seen in the context of promissory notes: *Price v Edmunds* (1829) 10 B. & C. 578; 109 E.R. 566; *Nafis v Soules* (1853) 2 C.P. 412 (Can). This approach was later revised where it could be shown that there was a contemporaneous agreement that the principal should be treated as a surety: *Manley v Boycot* (1853) 2 E. & B. 46; 118 E.R. 686.

[94] *Reynolds v Wheeler* (1861) 30 L.J.C.P. 350; *Godsell v Lloyd* (1911) 27 TLR 383. See also *Hunters v Evans* (1830) 9 Sh. (Ct of Sess) 76, where the acceptor of a bill of exchange was allowed to prove by the oath of the holder that he was known to be the mere surety of another party who was primarily liable for the debt.

[95] Bills of Exchange Act 1882, s.30.

him.[96] Indeed, as a consequence of this liability, the drawer of the bill as the party accommodated is obliged to provide funds to the accommodation party in advance of the maturity date, usually by discounting replacement bills.[97] For this reason, the High Court of Australia in *Coles Myer Finance Ltd v Federal Commissioner of Taxation*[98] specifically rejected the view that the drawer of an accommodation bill does not come under a liability to the acceptor until the acceptor makes payment under the bill. Consequently, the indorsement of a negotiable instrument for the accommodation of another does in fact create the relationship of principal and surety between the parties,[99] and the accommodation party is entitled to all the rights and benefits of a surety.[1] In a similar vein, the maker of an accommodation note assumes the position of surety in relation to the party accommodated.[2] The relationship of principal and surety can also arise between the joint and several makers of a promissory note[3] and in such a case the order of signatures thereon is immaterial.[4]

The Bills of Exchange Act 1882 recognises accommodation facilities. **1–60** Section 28(1) defines an accommodation party to a bill as "a person who has signed a bill as a drawer, acceptor, or indorser, without receiving value therefor, and for the purpose of lending his name to some other person".[5] Moreover, s.28(2) provides: "An accommodation party is liable *on the bill* to a holder for value, and it is immaterial whether, when such holder took the bill, he knew such party to be an accommodation party or not" (emphasis added).[6]

These subsections interface with, but do not encroach upon, the general **1–61** law of suretyship. In the first place, they render the accommodation party liable, not as surety, but on the bill itself. Moreover, the accommodation party is liable only to a holder for value. A holder is defined in s.2 as "the payee or indorsee of a bill or note who is in possession of it, or the bearer thereof". The definition of a holder in due course in s.29 connotes the addition of "value" in the sense of consideration sufficient to support a

---

[96] A similar proposition, which now appears in *Byles on Bills of Exchange and Cheques* (27th ed., 2002), p.262, was quoted with approval in *Sleigh v Sleigh* (1850) 5 Ex. 514; 155 E.R. 224. See also *Yates v Hoppe* (1850) 9 C.B. 541; 137 E.R. 1003; *Reynolds v Doyle* (1840) 1 Man & G 753; 133 E.R. 536; *K. D. Morris & Sons Pty Ltd (in liq) v Bank of Queensland Ltd* (1980) 146 C.L.R. 165 at 202 per Aickin J.
[97] See *K. D. Morris & Sons Pty Ltd (in liq) v Bank of Queensland Ltd* (1980) 146 C.L.R. 165 at 202.
[98] (1993) 176 C.L.R. 640.
[99] *Harris v Lerner* [1924] 2 D.L.R. 518. See also *Oriental Financial Corp v Overend Gurney & Co* (1871) L.R. 7 Ch. App. 142 at 150; *Davies v Stainbank* (1855) 6 De G.M. & G. 679 at 696; 43 E.R. 1397 at 1404; *Coles Myer Finance Ltd v FCT* (1993) 176 C.L.R. 640 at 657.
[1] *Lysnar v Burnar* [1927] N.Z.L.R. 757 at 771 *per* Reed J. (a case involving a promissory note). An IOU can also be given as a guarantee: *R. v Chambers* (1871) L.R. 1 C.C.R. 341. As to the definition of an accommodation party, see s.28(1) of the Bills of Exchange Act 1882.
[2] *Bechervaise v Lewis* (1872) L.R. 7 C.P. 372.
[3] *Lysnar v Burnar* [1927] N.Z.L.R. 757.
[4] *Cullen v Bryson* (1892) Q.R. 2 S.C. 36 (Can); *Rutherford v Taylor* (1915) 24 D.L.R. 822.
[5] "Value" in this context refers to the discount or part of it and does not include bank fees for services in providing financial accommodation: *Oriental Financial Corp v Overend, Gurney & Co* (1871) L.R. 7 Ch. App. 142 at 151.
[6] *Cf. Smith v Knox* (1799) 3 Esp. 46; 170 E.R. 533; *Fentum v Pocock* (1813) 5 Taunt 192 at 196; 128 E.R. 660 at 662; *Harrison v Courtauld* (1832) 3 B. & Ad. 36; 110 E.R. 14.

simple contract or even an antecedent debt or liability.[7] Thus, a mere donee, recipient, thief or finder is not a holder for value. By contrast, under the general law of suretyship, it appears that an accommodation party can be liable as surety to any holder or payee.[8] Secondly, an accommodation party can be liable on the bill to a holder for value even though the holder was not aware when it took the bill that the party was merely an accommodation party.[9] By contrast, under the general law of suretyship, an accommodation party can enjoy the rights of a surety as against a holder of the bill only if the holder knew that a relationship of principal and surety existed between the parties to the bill before it dealt with the real principal.[10]

5. PRINCIPLES OF CLASSIFICATION

1–62   A consistent thread of principle linking the threefold classification of Lord Selborne in *Duncan, Fox & Co v North and South Wales Bank*,[11] and other authorities[12] defining the nature of a guarantee is that suretyship exists where there is a primary and secondary liability for the same debt, with the party who is secondarily liable having a right of reimbursement from the primary obligor. One of the perennial problems in the law of guarantees, however, is how to identify these features in a particular transaction and thereby establish that the contract is one of guarantee. The courts have established certain principles to assist in this inquiry and have highlighted the cardinal features of contracts of guarantee by comparing and contrasting them with other similar contracts.

1–63   In order to determine whether a contract is one of guarantee the court looks at the natural meaning[13] and the substantial character of the document itself,[14] and the nature of the transaction between the parties.[15] No precise formula is required in order to create a guarantee[16] but the words used must not be equivocal.[17] It is a question of fact in each case

---

[7] See Bills of Exchange Act 1882, s.28. Consideration may be given at any time: s.28(2); *Diamond v Graham* [1968] 1 WLR 1061.

[8] See above, para.1–59.

[9] Bills of Exchange Act 1882, s.28(2).

[10] *Overend Gurney & Co Ltd v Oriental Financial Corp Ltd* (1874) L.R. 7 H.L. 352 (surety discharged because creditor gave time to the principal even though the creditor was not aware of the real relationship between the parties until after a cause of action accrued against both of them).

[11] (1880) 6 App. Cas. 1. See above, paras 1–28 to 1–32.

[12] See above, paras 1–18 to 1–27.

[13] *Pearson v Goldsbrough Mort & Co Ltd* [1931] S.A.S.R. 320 at 327; *Edwards v Lennon* (1866) 6 S.C.R. (NSW) Eq. 18; *A A Davison Pty Ltd v Seabrook* (1931) 37 A.L.R. 156.

[14] *Seaton v Heath* [1899] 1 Q.B. 782.

[15] *Re Sudell Ex p. Simpson* (1834) 3 Deac. & Ch. 792.

[16] *Welford v Beazely* (1747) 3 Atk. 503; 26 E.R. 1090. See also *Bradley Bros Ltd v Scott* [1923] N.Z.L.R. 1050; *Colwell v Hatfield* (1832) 1 N.B.R. 282, CA ("You can tell C or any one that will supply him with hay, that I will accept C's order payable in the Spring") and *Rains v Storry* (1827) 3 C. & P. 130 (NP).

[17] *Ulster Banking Co v Mahaffy* (1881) 15 I.L.T. 94; *Bancroft v Milligan* (1913) 16 D.L.R. 648, CA.

whether the contract is a guarantee.[18] The court examines the substance, not the form, of the transaction;[19] it goes beyond the words used by the parties in an effort to ascertain the true nature of the arrangement.[20] The label which the parties place on the contract is not conclusive, for some terms are not words of substance:[21] in many cases, courts have held contracts described by the parties as "guarantees" to be indemnities[22] or even warranties,[23] and the converse is also true.[24]

The words used must not be merely an overture. To support a guarantee **1–64** they must amount to a firm undertaking to pay if the principal debtor defaults. Consequently, the words "I am prepared to back him for one month's credit to 30 pounds" constitute a guarantee,[25] but more equivocal words such as "I have no objection to your supplying goods or extending credit to the debtor" are not sufficient.[26]

The words used by the parties are not considered in isolation. They must **1–65** be construed in the light of the surrounding circumstances present at the time the instrument was executed.[27] The court attempts to ascertain the true intention of the parties at the time when the arrangement was made.[28]

---

[18] *Doyle v McKinnon* [1925] 3 D.L.R. 334.
[19] *Harburg India Rubber Comb Co v Martin* [1902] 1 K.B. 778 at 784; *Clipper Maritime Ltd v Shirlstar Container Transport Ltd* [1987] 1 Lloyd's Rep 546 at 555; *Re Australian & Overseas Insurance Co Ltd* [1966] 1 N.S.W.R. 558 at 565; *Re International Life Assurance Society and Hercules Insurance Co; Ex parte Blood* (1870) L.R. 9 Eq. 316; *Bancroft v Milligan* (1913) 16 D.L.R. 648, CA; *Guild & Co v Canrad* [1894] 2 Q.B. at 892 *per* Lindley L.J. It is the immediate and main object and not the nature of the contract which determines whether it is a guarantee or an indemnity: *McPherson v Forlong* [1928] 3 W.W.R. 45. Cf. *Western Dominion Investment Co v MacMillan* [1925] 1 W.W.R. 852, affirmed [1925] 4 D.L.R. 562, CA.
[20] *Burnard v Lysnar* [1927] N.Z.L.R. 757. The court will examine closely the nature of the obligations imposed on the parties to see if they are consistent with a contract of guarantee: *Yeoman Credit Ltd v Latter* [1961] 1 W.L.R. 828.
[21] *Re Denton's Estate; Licences Insurance Corp & Guarantee Fund Ltd v Denton* [1904] 2 Ch. 178; *Re Australian & Overseas Insurance Co Ltd* [1966] 1 N.S.W.R. 558 at 565; *Guild & Co v Conrad* [1894] 2 Q.B. 885 at 892 *per* Lindley L.J. The fact that the contract provides that the surety is to be liable "as principal debtor" does not necessarily convert a guarantee into an indemnity, although it may well displace some technical principles of the law of suretyship, for example, the discharge of a guarantor as a result of the creditor giving time to the principal debtor or releasing the principal debtor. See *Heald v O'Connor* [1971] 1 W.L.R. 497 at 503 *per* Fisher J.; *General Produce Co v United Bank* [1979] 2 Lloyd's Rep. 255 at 259 *per* Lloyd J.
[22] *Re Sudell, Ex p. Simpson* (1834) 3 Deac. & Ch. 792. In *Phoenix Assurance Co Ltd v Wren* [1950] S.A.S.R. 89, the contract was held to be one of insurance, even though it was expressed to be a bond for the payment of entertainment tax.
[23] *Waterson v Barclay* (1863) 3 S.C.R. (NSW) 14.
[24] *Re Australian & Overseas Insurance Co Ltd* [1966] 1 N.S.W.R. 558; *Western Dominion Investment Co v MacMillan* [1925] 2 D.L.R. 442; *Bell v Welch* (1850) 9 C.B. 154; *Crown Lumber Co Ltd v Engel* (1961) 28 D.L.R. (2d) 762. See also *Re Denton's Estate; Licences Insurance Corp & Guarantee Fund Ltd v Denton* [1904] 2 Ch. 178; *Trade Indemnity Co v Workington Dock & Harbour Board* [1937] A.C. 1 at 16–17 (a contract of guarantee, not a contract of insurance).
[25] *A. A. Davison Pty Ltd v Seabrook* (1931) 37 A.L.R. 156.
[26] *M'Iver v Richardson* (1813) 1 M. & S. 557; 105 E.R. 208; *Mozley v Tinkler* (1835) 1 Cr. M. & R. 692; 149 E.R. 1258.
[27] *Bristol & West Building Society v Freeman & Pollard (A Firm)* (unreported, Queen's Bench Division, Judge Raymond Jack Q.C., February 20, 1996); *Edwards v Lennon* (1866) 6 S.C.R (NSW) Eq. 18 at 30; *Gorman v Norton* (1887) 8 L.R. (NSW) 479 at 487; *Doyle v McKinnon* (1925) 56 O.L.R. 298, affirmed 57 O.L.R. 104, CA. Thus in *Yeoman Credit Ltd v Latter* [1961] 1 W.L.R. 828, the Court of Appeal thought it was significant that all parties knew the principal debtor was an infant.
[28] *Gorman v Norton* (1887) 8 L.R. (NSW). 479 at 487.

It may take note of the fact that the contract is between business persons.[29] In this exercise, it considers the effect which the document has on the person to whom it is addressed.[30] If the creditor as a reasonable person acted upon the document as if it were a guarantee the court may hold the promisors to their undertaking, regardless of the promisors' private intentions at the time.[31]

1–66   Extrinsic evidence has been held admissible to determine whether as between two obligors one is principal and the other is surety, when the creditor is not a party to any such agreement.[32] In respect of ascertaining the relationship between the creditor and the obligor, however, it has been stated that such evidence is inadmissible and that the status of the obligor must be determined by the instrument itself.[33] However, in *AGC (Advances) Ltd v West*,[34] Hodgson J. in the Supreme Court of New South Wales admitted extrinsic evidence to show that a party named as the principal borrower in the relevant instrument was in fact a guarantor only and the party named as guarantor was the principal debtor. This represents a modern, more flexible approach to the admissibility of extrinsic evidence.

1–67   In applying these principles of classification the courts often divide transactions into different categories. Perhaps the most fundamental distinction to be drawn is between a contract of guarantee and a primary liability.

6. DISTINCTION BETWEEN GUARANTEE AND PRIMARY LIABILITY

1–68   The difference between these two undertakings is easy to state but often difficult to discern. As we have seen, a guarantee is a collateral undertaking to answer for the debt or to perform the obligation of another on his default. It is distinct from a transaction in which one party assumes a direct, absolute liability on a given date[35] or as soon as money is lent or goods are delivered to a third party.[36] Here the liability is not

---

[29] *A. A. Davison Pty Ltd v Seabrook* (1931) 37 A.L.R. 156.

[30] *ibid.; Gorman v Norton* (1887) 8 L.R. (NSW) 479 at 486; *Heislter v Anglo-Dal Ltd* [1954] 1 W.L.R. 1273 at 1280 *per* Romer L.J., CA. In *Westminster Trust Co v Brymner* (1920) 54 D.L.R. 244, the court considered how the transaction was treated by the parties.

[31] *Gorman v Norton* (1887) 8 L.R. (NSW) 479 at 486.

[32] In such a case the creditor will be precluded from treating the party who is in fact a surety as a principal debtor, when the creditor has notice of the arrangement between the two obligors: see *AGC (Advances) Ltd v West* (1984) 5 N.S.W.L.R. 590.

[33] *Hollier v Eyre* (1842) 9 Cl. & Fin. 1; 8 E.R. 313; *Edwards v Lennon* (1866) 6 S.C.R. (NSW) Eq. 18 at 29–30.

[34] (1984) 5 N.S.W.L.R. 590 at 603. Hodgson J. acknowledged that "the circumstances in this case go, perhaps, a little further" than previous authority (but not discussed on appeal: (1986) 5 N.S.W.L.R. 610). See also *Manzo v 555/255 Pitt Street Pty Ltd* (1990) 21 N.S.W.L.R. 1 at 814; *Custom Credit Corp Ltd v Heard* (1983) 33 S.A.S.R. 45.

[35] *Evans v Jones* (1864) 3 H. & C. 423; 159 E.R. 595. It usually involves a new and original promise for distinct consideration of benefit to the defendant: *Tumblay v Meyers* (1858) 16 U.C.R. 143.

[36] *Turner Manufacturing Co Pty Ltd v Senes* [1964] N.S.W.R. 692. See also *Stadium Finance Co Ltd v Helm* (1965) 109 Sol. Jo. 471, CA.

contingent upon another's default.[37] Nor is it founded upon the other's primary obligation to pay. Indeed the essence of the arrangement is that the third party assumes no liability to pay.[38]

There are some well-established examples of primary liability. An **1-69** absolute undertaking to pay a certain sum on a given day is a classic illustration.[39] Moreover, the acceptor of a bill of exchange and the maker of a promissory note are primarily liable thereon.[40]

But often the determination of whether a primary or secondary liability **1-70** is being undertaken is an issue of some difficulty. As indicated,[41] the wording of the agreement must be construed in the light of the surrounding circumstances to ascertain the true nature of the agreement. Yet the wording of the instrument may be far from precise.

Statements such as: "Let him have the goods, I will be your **1-71** paymaster"[42] or even in certain contexts "I will see you paid"[43] can impose a primary liability. But statements such as: "You need not worry— remember I am in charge down there now. I'll see you paid"[44] or simply "Don't trouble about the payment; I'll see you paid"[45] usually suggest that the promise is a guarantee rather than an agreement by the promisor to assume primary liability.

The words of the instrument may, however, not be decisive. It has been **1-72** seen that in *AGC (Advances) Ltd v West*[46] Hodgson J. held that the position of the party who was the principal borrower according to the instrument was in reality the guarantor, whilst the party designated as the guarantor was in fact the principal borrower. His Honour reached this conclusion because it was clear from the extrinsic evidence and the surrounding circumstances that the party referred to as the "guarantor" had undertaken to assume the initial liability for all the obligations of the "borrower" pursuant to the deed.

A further complicating factor is that the status of a party can change as a **1-73** result of a subsequent variation or a change of circumstances. Thus in *Reade v Lowndes*,[47] the creditor entered into a new arrangement with the surety (after having obtained judgment against him) whereby a primary liability was undertaken. Conversely, a person may ostensibly contract as a

---

[37] *Andrews v Smith* (1835) 2 Cr M. & R. 627; 150 E.R. 267; *Re Thomson* [1927] 2 D.L.R. 254. See also *Susan v Jans* [1923] G.L.R. 593; *Dixon v Hatfield* (1825) 2 Bing 439; 130 E.R. 375.
[38] *Gordon v Martin* (1731) Fitz G. 302; 94 E.R. 766; *Birkmyr v Darnell* (1704) 1 Salk. 27; 91 E.R. 27; *Permanent Trustee Co of New South Wales Ltd v Hinks* (1934) 34 S.R. (NSW) 130.
[39] *Evans v Jones* (1839) 5 M. & W. 295; 151 E.R. 126.
[40] See *Colonial Bank of A/asia v Ettershank* (1875) 4 A.J.R. 185; affirmed by the Privy Council in (1875) 4 V.L.R. (L) 239. See above, para.1–44.
[41] See above, paras 1–62 to 1–67.
[42] See *Birkmyr v Darnell* (1704) 1 Salk 27; 91 E.R. 27.
[43] *ibid.* See also *Lakeman v Mountstephen* (1874) LR 7 HL 17; *Gorman v Norton* (1887) 8 L.R. (NSW) 479.
[44] *Bradley Bros Ltd v Scott* [1923] N.Z.L.R. 1050 (guarantee unenforceable because it did not comply with the Statute of Frauds).
[45] *Kinnear v New Zealand Loan & Mercantile Agency Co* (1905) 25 N.Z.L.R. 784. See also *John C. Love Lumber Co Ltd v Moore* [1963] 1 O.R. 245; *Nichols v King and Garside* (1849) 5 U.C.Q.B. 324, CA.
[46] (1984) 5 N.S.W.L.R. 590, referred to above, para.1–66. See also *Manzo v 555/255 Pitt St Pty Ltd* (1990) 21 N.S.W.L.R. 1.
[47] (1857) 23 Beav. 361; 53 E.R. 142.

primary obligor and yet subsequently assume liability as a surety only. For example, a partner who retires from a partnership after securing an indemnity from the remaining partners may no longer be primarily liable, but acquire the status of a guarantor of the partnership debts.[48] If the creditor becomes aware of this arrangement, the creditor's actions may release the surety in accordance with the usual grounds for discharge.[49] A clause in the agreement with the original partners providing that all the partners shall remain principal obligors despite a change in the composition of the partnership or the resignation of one of the partners will not preclude the retiring partner from acquiring the status of a surety because, as indicated, the wording is not determinative.

1–74   The issue of whether a primary or secondary liability has been undertaken has arisen in respect of some common commercial transactions.

(i) The supply of goods upon credit

1–75   There is a rebuttable presumption that the persons to whom goods are delivered are primarily liable.[50] But the key question is to whom was the credit given[51] or, more expansively, did the defendant's actions lead the claimant to believe the supply in question was on the defendant's credit?[52] If the goods were actually sold to the defendant on his credit, it is immaterial that they were delivered to a third party.[53] Thus if A supplies goods to B on B's credit, B will be primarily liable even if they were, by arrangement, delivered to C, a third party. To establish a primary liability, the defendant's undertaking to pay should precede the delivery of the goods to the third party.[54] But entries in the vendor's books of account[55] and applications for, or promises of, payment[56] are cogent factors

---

[48] *Rouse v Bradford Banking Co* [1894] A.C. 586. As another example, see *Reid v Royal Trust Corp of Canada* (1985) 20 D.L.R. (4th) 223.

[49] See below, Chs 6–9. See also *Rouse v Bradford Banking Co* [1894] A.C. 586 (the giving of time to the remaining partners, although held on the facts not to amount to the giving of time).

[50] See *Pearson v Goldsbrough Mort & Co Ltd* [1931] S.A.S.R. 320 at 326; *Edwards v Lennon* (1866) 6 S.C.R. (NSW) Eq. 18.

[51] *Forth v Stanton* (1668) 1 Wms. Saund. 210 at 211; 85 E.R.217 at 222. If the credit was extended solely to the debtor, the transaction is one of primary liability: *Pearson v Goldsbrough Mort & Co Ltd* [1931] S.A.S.R. 320.

[52] *Smith v Rudhall* (1862) 3 F. & F. 143 at 144; 176 E.R. 64 at 65.

[53] *Pearson v Goldsbrough Mort & Co Ltd* [1931] S.A.S.R. 320. See also *Henderson v O'Dowd* (1867) 7 S.C.R. (NSW) 48.

[54] *Pearson v Goldsbrough Mort & Co Ltd* [1931] S.A.S.R. 320 at 326.

[55] *Storr v Scott* (1833) 6 C. & P. 241, N.P.; 172 E.R. 1224.

[56] See *Darnell v Tratt* (1825) 2 C & P 82; 172 E.R. 37. *Cf. Anderson v Hayman* (1789) 1 Hy. Bl. 120; 126 E.R. 73.

suggesting that the defendant has undertaken a direct, primary liability to pay; indeed, sometimes, they are the only clues to the parties' intentions.[57]

(ii) Letters of comfort

A letter of comfort is a document which contains various statements of fact and intention addressed to a lender by, for example, a parent company in respect of one of its subsidiaries or by the government in respect of a public entity.[58] In the context of the law of guarantees, what is significant is that the letter will invariably contain a statement that the subsidiary or public utility, as the case may be, will be maintained in a financial position to meet its loan commitments to the intending lender.[59] Thus in *Banque Brussels Lambert SA v Australian National Industries Ltd*,[60] the relevant part of the letter stated:

1–76

"We [ANI Ltd] take this opportunity to confirm that it is our practice to ensure our affiliate Spedley Securities Ltd, will at all times be in a position to meet its financial obligations as they fall due. These financial obligations include repayment of all loans made by your bank under the arrangements mentioned in this letter."

Rogers C.J. of the Supreme Court of New South Wales held that this undertaking was promissory and intended to be legally binding,[61] but rejected the argument that the undertaking was in the nature of a guarantee:

1–77

"the letter makes clear that the defendant is not assuming secondary liability for the debts of the principal debtor. It is not suggested that the letter makes the defendant liable for the debt of Spedley conditioned merely on non-payment by Spedley. The statements made in the letter are more remote from the liability of Spedley to repay the facility. By reason of this, a failure to adhere to the statements made will, at best,

---

[57] *Simpson v Penton* (1834) 2 Cr. & M. 430 at 433, *per* Bayley B.; 149 E.R. 828 at 829–830.
[58] As to whether a parent company can be held liable for fraudulent trading under s.213 of the Insolvency Act 1986 as a result of issuing a letter of comfort, see *Re Angustus Barnett & Son Ltd* [1986] B.C.L.C. 170 (parent company was not a party to the carrying on of its subsidiary's business for an allegedly fraudulent purpose). Compare *Re Gerald Cooper Chemicals Ltd* [1978] Ch. 262.
[59] Other elements will include a statement that the parent is aware of the proposed borrowing by the subsidiary and that the parent will not reduce its shareholding in the subsidiary without the lender's consent: see generally G. Walker, "Letters of Cold Comfort" *Banking Law Bulletin* (1989), Vol. 5, p.120.
[60] [1989] 21 N.S.W.L.R. 502. See also *BNZ v Ginivan* [1991] 1 NZLR 178; *Chemco Leasing v Rediffusion* [1987] 1 F.T.L.R. 201; *Commonwealth Bank of Australia v TLI Management Pty Ltd* [1990] V.L.R. 510 (letter of comfort embodied merely statements of the defendant's intentions).
[61] *Cf. Kleinwort Benson Ltd v Malaysia Mining Corp Bhd* [1989] 1 W.L.R. 379 (discussed below, para.2–10), where the Court of Appeal held that a letter of comfort in similar terms was merely a statement of present fact and not a promise as to future conduct; hence, it had no contractual effect: see Note (1989) 63 A.L.J. 370. See, similarly, *Re Atlantic Computers plc (in administration)* [1995] B.C.C. 696.

give rise merely to a claim for damages and throw up considerable questions of causation."[62]

1–78   Rogers C.J. is clearly correct in concluding that the author of the letter did not expressly assume a secondary liability for the debts of the principal.[63] But it is at least arguable that the second sentence of the relevant part of the letter, which makes specific reference to the fact that "[t]hese financial obligations include the repayment of all loans", is an implied promise to pay the loans if the subsidiary does not and thus falls within the definition of a guarantee. Certainly somewhat different wording with, for example, some reference to default by the borrower might well result in a letter of comfort being held to be a guarantee.

1–79   Even on the analysis of Rogers C.J. it is also arguable that a letter of comfort imposes a liability which is at least somewhat analogous to that imposed on a guarantor. One consequence is that the beneficiary of the letter should be under similar obligations to those imposed upon a creditor who has the benefit of a contract of guarantee, for example, in respect of the duty of the creditor to preserve securities for the enforcement of the principal contract. But there is no indication in the cases that the courts view letters of comfort in this light.

1–80   The view that a letter of comfort does not constitute a guarantee often coincides with the intentions of the company, or other party providing the letter, who does not wish to give a guarantee because a guarantee would exceed its borrowing limits, or because it would result in a contingent liability appearing on its balance sheet.[64]

(iii) Letters of credit

1–81   A letter of credit is an instrument of payment whereby an issuing bank (the issuer) assumes an independent obligation, distinct from the principal obligation of the borrower, to make payment upon the production of specified documents, for example, a demand or a certificate, or when certain events occur.[65] A letter of credit is not qualified by reference to the contract between the borrower and the beneficiary of the letter so there is no need for the issuer to inquire whether the borrower is in default before paying the beneficiary. Unlike a guarantee, a letter of credit does not create an accessory obligation which is contingent upon the borrower's

---

[62] [1989] 21 N.S.W.L.R. 502 at 522.

[63] With respect, however, the reliance that Rogers C.J. places upon the fact that the breach of the undertaking contained in the letter of comfort gives rise to an action for damages is misplaced. Many guarantees are so drafted that the appropriate action may be in damages as well as in debt: see below, paras 6–123 to 6–125.

[64] P. Wood, *Law and Practice of International Finance* (1980), para.13.5.

[65] *Commercial Banking Co of Sydney Ltd v Patrick Intermarine Acceptances Ltd* (1978) 52 A.L.J.R. 404.

default and dependent upon the continued existence of the borrower's principal obligation.[66]

(iv) Put options

A put option is an agreement by which one party agrees to assume a particular obligation or to do a particular act or to purchase particular property if certain events happen or if required to do so by the grantee.   **1–82**

For example, the put option may entitle the creditor at a future date to **1–83** require the grantor of the option to purchase shares at a price stipulated in the option when the creditor has taken these shares as security from the borrower in respect of the granting of a loan facility.[67] The agreement ensures that the creditor is protected in the event of a fall in value of the shares. It has been argued that a put option is in the nature of a guarantee because the essential purpose of the agreement is to secure the obligations of the borrower.[68] But in *Standard Chartered Bank Australia Ltd v Greater Pacific Investments Ltd*,[69] this argument was rejected because the put option was not expressly made conditional upon a breach of the terms of the loan facility and the grantor of option had no right of recourse against the borrower in the event of being called upon to purchase the shares. Furthermore, in the usual case, the liabilities of the grantor of the option will be entirely different from those of the borrower because the share price will bear no correlation to the money owed by the borrower pursuant to the loan facility. A primary liability is imposed because, in the words of Lord Selborne in *Duncan, Fox & Co v North and South Wales Bank*,[70] it cannot be said that "there is a primary liability of two persons for *one and the same debt*".[71]

The fact that a put option may be granted as security for the due **1–84** payments of a debt is not in itself sufficient to attract the incidents of suretyship as between the grantor and the grantee of the option. However, in an exceptional case, a put option may constitute a guarantee or at least place the grantor of the option in the position of a surety if the following conditions are satisfied:

> (a) if the exercise of the put option by the lender is expressly conditioned on the default of the borrower;[72]

[66] An excellent discussion of the law relating to standby letters of credit is found in K.P. McGuiness, *The Law of Guarantee* (1986), Ch. 12. For a similar unconditional obligation, see the discussion of performance bonds, below, Ch. 13.
[67] As in *Standard Chartered Bank Australia Ltd v Greater Pacific Investments Ltd* (1989) 5 W.A.R. 541.
[68] See *Mallet v Bateman* (1865) L.R. 1 C.P. 163 at 171 *per* Pollock C.B. and K.P. McGuiness, *The Law of Guarantee* (2nd ed., 1996), p.44.
[69] (1989) 5 WAR 541. As to the nature of a put option and the need for the offeree to accept within a reasonable time, see also *Chemco Leasing Spa v Rediffusion Ltd* [1987] 1 F.T.L.R. 201.
[70] (1880) 6 App. Cas. 1.
[71] *ibid.* at 13 (emphasis added).
[72] *Standard Chartered Bank Australia Ltd v Greater Pacific Investments Ltd* (1991) 5 W.A.R. 541. See also *Mallett v Bateman* (1865) L.R. 1 C.P. 163.

(b) if the amount payable by the grantor upon the exercise of the put option is conditioned on the state of accounts between the borrower and the lender, so that the purchase price is equivalent to the amount of the debt owing by the borrower[73] or a specified part of it;[74]

(c) if the grantor of the option retains his right of recourse against the borrower,[75] who remains primarily liable to the lender;[76] and

(d) if the amount paid by the grantor to the lender upon the exercise of the put option is paid in discharge of the whole or part of the borrower's debt.[77]

A modern put option would rarely satisfy these conditions.

(v) Subordination agreements

1-85   A subordination agreement is an agreement under which one creditor, whose debt ranks in priority to or equal with the debts of other creditors of the same debtor, agrees to postpone or defer payment of his debt until the other creditors have been paid. Such an agreement is valid even though it varies the *pari passu* principle inherent in insolvency legislation.[78]

1-86   A subordination agreement bears some similarity to a guarantee in that it provides creditors with some extra assurance that they will be paid because they are not competing with the subordinated creditor. But a subordination agreement is not a guarantee because it is not a binding promise to be responsible for the debt, default or miscarriage of another party.

1-87   The courts perform their most difficult exercise in differentiating between a primary and a secondary liability when they draw the distinction between a guarantee and an indemnity. The difficulties inherent in this exercise, which merits separate discussion,[79] are accentuated because an

---

[73] See *Standard Chartered Bank Australia Ltd v Greater Pacific Investments Ltd* (1989) 5 W.A.R. 541.
[74] Unless this condition is satisfied, the grantor of the put option is not answerable for the debt of another. It should not be necessary, however, for the option price to be the full amount of the borrower's debt because a guarantor can limit his liability to a specified portion of the principal debt or even to a specific amount. But a put option cannot amount to a guarantee if the grantor is liable to purchase the property for an amount in excess of the debt owing by the borrower.
[75] *Standard Chartered Bank Australia Ltd v Greater Pacific Investments Ltd* (1991) 5 W.A.R. 541 suggests that this is a necessary element of a guarantee or suretyship, but the guarantor's right of indemnity can be expressly or impliedly excluded by agreement.
[76] See *Mallett v Bateman* (1865) L.R. 1 C.P. 163 at 171 *per* Pollock C.B.
[77] This is implicit in obiter dicta in *Standard Chartered Bank Australia Ltd v Greater Pacific Investments Ltd* (1991) 5 W.A.R. 541.
[78] *Re Maxwell Communications Corp plc (No. 2)* [1994] 1 All E.R. 737 at 753–755; *Horne v Chester & Fein Property Developments Pty Ltd* [1987] V.R. 913; *United States Trust Co of New York v Australia & New Zealand Banking Group Ltd* (1995) 13 A.C.L.C. 1225.
[79] See below, paras 1–88 to 1–107.

indemnity is often used to secure the due performance of another's obligations.

7. DISTINCTION BETWEEN GUARANTEE AND INDEMNITY

The performance of an obligation or the payment of a debt of another **1–88** may be secured not by a guarantee, but by a contract of indemnity. The distinction between a contract of guarantee and a contract of indemnity[80] is that in a contract of indemnity a primary liability is assumed whether or not a third party makes default[81] whilst, as has been seen, in a contract of guarantee the surety assumes a secondary liability to the creditor for the default of another who remains primarily liable to the creditor.[82] The contract of indemnity, therefore, is "a contract by one party to keep the other harmless against loss"[83] and is not dependent on the continuing liability of the principal debtor. The obligation has no reference in law to the debt of another.[84] In other words, an indemnity imposes a primary obligation which is independent of the continuing obligation of another.[85]

The distinction between the two types of contract is important for **1–89** several reasons. First, the statutory provision which requires certain types of contracts to be evidenced in writing in general applies to guarantees and not to indemnities.[86] Secondly, as the guarantor's liability is usually treated as being co-extensive with that of the principal, the guarantor's liability will be affected by the discharge of the principal or by the fact that the principal contract is void or unenforceable, but an indemnifier's liability is less likely to be affected by these matters.[87] Thirdly, a guarantor has been

---

[80] "Indemnity" in this section is referred to in this narrow sense. In a wider sense, the term "indemnity" may embrace recompense for any loss or liability which one person has incurred, which may arise by contract (*e.g.* a contract of insurance) or by operation of law (*e.g.* an employer has a right of indemnity against an employee when held vicariously liable to a third party as a result of the employee's negligence: *Lister v Romford Ice & Cold Storage Co Ltd* [1957] A.C. 555). An example of a right of indemnity which may arise as a result of operation of the law in the context of the law of guarantees is the guarantor's right of indemnity from the principal: see below, Ch. 12.

[81] See, *e.g. Guild & Co v Conrad* [1894] 2 Q.B. 885 at 882.

[82] *Yeoman Credit Ltd v Latter* [1961] 1 W.L.R. 828 at 831; *Total Oil Products (Aust) Pty Ltd v Robinson* [1970] 1 N.S.W.R. 701; *Goulston Discount Co Ltd v Clark* [1967] 2 Q.B. 493 at 496–497; *Argo Caribbean Group Ltd v Lewis* [1976] 2 Lloyd's Rep. 289 at 296.

[83] *Yeoman Credit Ltd v Latter* [1961] 1 W.L.R. 828 at 830–831; *Total Oil Products (Aust) Pty Ltd v Robinson* [1970] 1 N.S.W.R. 701 at 703; *Davys v Buswell* [1913] 2 K.B. 47 at 53–55. An indemnity is an independent obligation to make good a loss: *Sutton & Co v Grey* [1894] Q.B. 285 at 288–289 *per* Lord Esher M.R.

[84] *Clipper Maritime Ltd v Shirlstar Container Transport Ltd* [1987] 1 Lloyd's Rep. 546 at 555; *Harburg India Rubber Comb Co v Martin* [1902] 1 K.B. 778 at 784.

[85] *Clement v Clement* (1996) 71 P. & C.R.D. 19.

[86] Guarantees are *prima facie* unenforceable if they do not satisfy the requirements of s.4 of the Statute of Frauds 1677. See below, paras 3–149 to 3–153. Not surprisingly, the need to distinguish guarantees from indemnities for the purposes of the Statute of Frauds "has raised many hair-splitting distinctions of exactly that kind which brings the law into hatred, ridicule and contempt by the public": *Yeoman Credit Ltd v Latter* [1961] 1 W.L.R. 829 at 835 *per* Harman L.J.

[87] See, *e.g. Yeoman Credit Ltd v Latter* [1961] 1 W.L.R. 828; *Goulston Discount Co Ltd v Clark* [1967] 2 Q.B. 493. *Cf. Bentworth Finance Ltd v Lubert* [1968] 1 Q.B. 680 (where there

held to be discharged from liability by certain types of conduct of the creditor. Such conduct will discharge an indemnifier in some, but not all, cases in which a guarantor is discharged.[88]

1–90   Although it is a question of construction in each case,[89] it may be relatively easy to determine whether a contract is one of indemnity rather than of guarantee. For example, in the context of an undertaking to a finance company entering into a hire-purchase contract, an undertaking in these terms will be construed as an indemnity:

> "I agree to indemnify you against any loss you may suffer by reason of the fact that the hirer under the said agreement for any cause whatsoever does not pay the amounts which he would have paid if he completed his agreement by exercising the option to purchase. The loss is recoverable whether or not the hirer is in breach of the provisions of the agreement. Loss shall mean the difference between the total amount the hirer would have had to pay to acquire title to the goods under the hire-purchase agreement, plus your expenses, less payments received by you."[90]

1–91   An example of a guarantee in a similar context would be a promise to "guarantee the obligations of the hirer under the agreement".

1–92   Another example is *ANZ Banking Group Ltd v Beneficial Finance Corp Ltd*[91] where the Judicial Committee of the Privy Council decided that a "take-out" letter in the following terms was an indemnity, rather than a guarantee:

> "It is hereby agreed as follows:
>
> 1. In the event of the bank's liability in respect of the loan not being satisfied on or before the expiration of two (2) years (the expiration date) from the date hereof Beneficial undertakes upon receipt of ninety (90) days notice in writing from the bank to pay or otherwise make such arrangements (the take-out) as are satisfactory to the bank to discharge the liability to the bank under the said loan."

1–93   In doubtful cases, the courts will decide whether the contract is one of indemnity rather than a contract of guarantee by a careful perusal of all the provisions of the agreement to ascertain if the rights of the creditor against

---

was no hire-purchase contract because there was an implied condition of the agreement that a log-book would be provided). See below, paras 5–131 and 6–97. But note *Citicorp Australia Ltd v Hendry* (1985) 4 N.S.W.L.R. 1.
[88] *e.g.* see below, paras 6–67 to 6–71, 6–90 to 6–93 and 7–65 to 7–74.
[89] *Moschi v Lep Air Services Ltd* [1973] A.C. 331 at 349; *Alfred McAlpine Construction Ltd v Unex Corp Ltd* (1994) 38 Com. L.R. 38.
[90] See a similar example in *Goulston Discount Co Ltd v Clark* [1967] 2 Q.B. 493. See also *Yeoman Credit Ltd v Latter* [1961] 1 W.L.R. 828, CA (an indemnity). *Cf. Western Credit Ltd v Alberry* [1964] 2 All E.R. 938, CA (a guarantee). Note that the position has been modified by the Minors' Contracts Act 1987.
[91] [1983] 1 N.S.W.L.R. 199. For further examples, see *Anglomar Shipping Co Ltd v Swan Hunter Shipbuilders Ltd* [1980] 2 Lloyd's Rep. 456; *Alfred McAlpine Construction Ltd v Unex Corp Ltd* (1994) 38 Con LR 63.

the party entering into the contract are different in extent from those available against the debtor.[92] Thus, the agreement will be construed as an indemnity if the contract, according to some of its clauses, operates to render the promisor liable in circumstances in which the principal is not in default,[93] or renders the promisor liable for a greater amount than the principal.[94] By reference to these criteria, a contract by which a dealer agrees to indemnify a finance company against losses arising from a consumer credit contract has been held to be an indemnity.[95]

Other factors may also indicate whether the contract is one of indemnity or guarantee. The fact that the words "guarantee" or "indemnity" appear in the instrument are indications of the intentions of the parties, especially if the expressions are repeated a number of times[96] or appear in the heading to the instrument,[97] but they are not decisive[98] and the essential nature of the agreement must always be considered.[99]   **1–94**

If the agreement contains a provision preserving the liability of the guarantor in the event of the creditor giving time to the principal to perform the principal obligation, this will suggest that the contract is one of guarantee because, if the contract were one of indemnity, there would be no need for such a provision since an indemnifier is not discharged by such conduct of the creditor.[1] Conversely, the contract may well be one of indemnity if the parties know that the principal contract is void (for example as a result of the principal's infancy), because if it were construed as a guarantee the transaction would be ineffective since there would be no   **1–95**

---

[92] This is the approach taken in *Yeoman Credit Ltd v Latter* [1961] 1 W.L.R. 828 at 830–833; *Argo Caribbean Group Ltd v Lewis* [1976] 2 Lloyd's Rep. 289 at 296; *Direct Acceptance Finance Ltd v Cumberland Furnishing Pty Ltd* [1965] N.S.W.R. 1504; *Total Oil Products (Aust) Pty Ltd v Robinson* [1970] 1 N.S.W.R. 701; *Cameo Motors Ltd v Portland Holdings Ltd* [1965] NZLR 109.

[93] *Yeoman Credit Ltd v Latter* [1961] 1 W.L.R. 828 at 832–833. *Direct Acceptance Finance Ltd v Cumberland Furnishing Pty Ltd* [1965] N.S.W.R. 1504 at 1509.

[94] *Direct Acceptance Finance Ltd v Cumberland Furnishing Pty Ltd* [1965] N.S.W.R. 1504 at 1509; *Argo Caribbean Group Ltd v Lewis* [1976] 2 Lloyd's Rep. 289 at 296.

[95] *Direct Acceptance Finance Ltd v Cumberland Furnishing Pty Ltd* [1965] N.S.W.R. 1504; *Goulston Discount Co Ltd v Clark* [1967] 2 Q.B. 493; *United Dominions Trust (Commercial) Ltd v Eagle Aircraft Services Ltd* [1968] 1 All E.R. 104, CA. *Cf. Unity Finance Ltd v Woodcock* [1963] 1 WLR 455, where it was held that, on similar wording, a recourse agreement was a guarantee. The case can probably be explained on the narrower ground that the creditors had repossessed the goods illegally and were seeking an indemnity from the consequences of their own illegal act: see this explanation in *Goulston Discount Co Ltd v Clark* [1967] 2 Q.B. 493. In *Direct Acceptance Finance Ltd v Cumberland Furnishing Pty Ltd* [1965] N.S.W.R. 1504, the N.S.W. Court of Appeal doubted *Unity Finance Ltd v Woodcock* [1963] 1 W.L.R. 455.

[96] *Heald v O'Connor* [1971] 1 W.L.R. 497 at 503.

[97] *Goulston Discount Ltd v Clark* [1967] 2 Q.B. 493 at 498 *per* Danckwerts L.J. *Western Credit Ltd v Alberry* [1964] 2 All E.R. 938 at 940 *per* Davies L.J.; *Crown Lumber Co Ltd v Engel* (1961) 28 D.L.R. (2d) 762.

[98] *Total Oil Products (Aust) Pty Ltd v Robinson* [1970] 1 N.S.W.R. 701; *Western Credit Ltd v Alberry* [1964] 2 All ER 938 at 940 *per* Davies L.J.

[99] *Yeoman Credit Ltd v Latter* [1961] 1 W.L.R. 828 at 833.

[1] *Western Credit Ltd v Alberry* [1964] 2 All E.R. 938 at 940 *per* Davies L.J. *Western Dominion Investment Co v MacMillan* [1925] 2 DLR 442, affirmed in [1925] 4 D.L.R. 562, CA. But the fact that the agreement makes no provision for a demand being made on the principal debtor does not convert what would otherwise be a guarantee into an indemnity: *Chiswell Shipping Ltd v State Bank of India* [1987] 1 Lloyd's Rep. 165.

valid principal obligation, and the parties could not have intended this result.[2]

1–96   The difficulty of determining whether the contract is one of guarantee or indemnity is reflected in modern forms of contract used to secure the obligation of another, some of which cannot easily be classified into these two separate categories. The most commonly found forms are as follows:

1–97   *(a) A simple guarantee*: Some guarantees merely contain one simple undertaking to guarantee the obligations of a named principal. The agreement contains no special clauses and is clearly a contract of guarantee according to traditional definitions. Surprisingly, this form is still used by some finance companies.

1–98   *(b) A guarantee containing clauses preserving the guarantor's liability in certain circumstances*: The form of this guarantee is the same as in para.(a) above, but it also contains clauses which preserve the liability of the guarantors in circumstances in which they would otherwise be discharged (for example, by the creditor varying the principal contract or impairing securities held for the enforcement of the principal obligation).[3] Even if the agreement contains a clause to the effect that the creditor may treat the guarantor "as a principal debtor" it will probably still be viewed as a contract of guarantee,[4] but this may not be the case if certain clauses specifically preserve the guarantor's liability in circumstances where the principal is no longer liable: see below, para.(c).

1–99   *(c) A guarantee which contains clauses preserving the liability of the guarantor in specified circumstances where the principal is no longer liable*: The form of this guarantee is the same as in para.(b) above, but it also contains clauses which, in specified and limited situations, preserve the liability of the guarantor in circumstances in which the principal will no longer be liable to the creditor. Examples are the preservation of the guarantor's liability where the principal is released by the creditor, and where the principal contract is void because of the principal's infancy. In the first of these examples, an assumption has been made that the contract remains properly classified as a guarantee,[5] whilst in the second it has been suggested that the contract is in fact one of indemnity.[6] In such situations, therefore, the question of categorisation is an open one.

1–100   Where the terms of the instrument confine the preservation of the guarantor's liability to one or at least a small number of situations in which the principal is no longer liable, it is difficult to conclude that the contract renders the creditor "harmless against loss" within the definition of an indemnity. Yet it cannot be said the contract is strictly a guarantee because liability may be incurred in these specific situations without the default of

---

[2] *Yeoman Credit Ltd v Latter* [1961] 1 W.L.R. 828 (but see this factor criticised in a note in (1961) 24 M.L.R. 644 at 647–648.)
[3] See below, Chs 7 and 8.
[4] *Heald v O'Connor* [1971] 1 W.L.R. 497 at 503; *General Produce Co v United Bank Ltd* [1979] 2 Lloyd's Rep. 255 at 259. See also below, para.1–101.
[5] e.g. *Bank of Adelaide v Lorden* (1970) 45 A.L.J.R. 49, where the terminology of guarantee is used.
[6] *Alliance Acceptance Co Ltd v Hinton* (1964) 1 D.C.R. (NSW) 5. Note, however, that an alternative basis of this decision was that the clause operated as an estoppel against the guarantor.

the principal. It may be that this type of contract should be regarded as a hybrid, generally being in the nature of a guarantee but containing elements of an indemnity. At least one authority has recognised this possibility.[7]

(d) A guarantee containing a "principal debtor" clause: A guarantee **1–101** which contains clauses preserving the liability of the guarantor in certain circumstances when the principal is no longer liable (as in para. (c) above) will invariably also contain a "principal debtor" clause, whereby the creditor is "given liberty to act as though the guarantor were a principal debtor".[8] It is clear that the effect of such a clause, even standing alone, may be to preserve the guarantor's liability in circumstances in which he would otherwise be discharged, for example, where the creditor improperly releases a security[9] or grants the principal an extension of time to repay the debt.[10] Depending on its precise construction, the clause may also obviate the necessity for a demand to be made upon the guarantor before issuing proceedings.[11]

The dominant view, however, is that the incorporation of a "principal **1–102** debtor" clause does not convert what would otherwise be interpreted as a contract of guarantee into a contract of indemnity.[12] The effect of a "principal debtor" clause in particular contexts is considered elsewhere in the text.[13]

(e) Simple indemnity: Some forms of contract securing the obligation or **1–103** the payment of a debt of another are clearly indemnities. An example is given earlier in this section.

(f) A combined "guarantee and indemnity": The contract securing the **1–104** obligation or payment of another may be drafted in such a way that it expressly contains a promise to guarantee and a promise to indemnify. An example is an agreement in these terms:

"(1) I will upon demand pay to you such sum or sums of money as at any time or from time to time have become payable by the customer but be unpaid by her/him. (2) I will indemnify and keep indemnified you, your

---

[7] *General Surety & Guarantee Co Ltd v Francis Parker Ltd* (1977) 6 Build. L.R. 18 at 21.
[8] An example taken from *Fletcher Organisation Pty Ltd v Crocus Investments Pty Ltd* [1988] 2 Qd. R. 517.
[9] *ibid.*
[10] *Heald v O'Connor* [1971] 1 W.L.R. 497. See also *Brown Bros Motor Lease Canada Ltd v Ganapathi* (1983) 139 D.L.R. (3d) 227.
[11] *Esso Petroleum Co Ltd v Alstonbridge Properties Ltd* [1975] 1 W.L.R. 1474 at 1478. *Cf. Re Taylor; Ex p. Century 21 Real Estate Corp* (1995) 130 A.L.R. 723, where Burchett J. emphasised that the issue was one of construction of the particular guarantee, and added "[N]o generalisation is possible."
[12] *Citicorp Australia Ltd v Hendry* (1985) 4 N.S.W.L.R. 1 at 20 *per* Clarke J. (at first instance); *Heald v O'Connor* [1971] 1 W.L.R. 497. See also *Clipper Maritime Ltd v Shirlstar Container Transport Ltd* [1987] 1 Lloyd's Rep. 546 at 555; *Brown Bros Motor Lease Canada Ltd v Ganapathi* (1983) 139 D.L.R. (3d) 227. *Cf. Fletcher Organisation Pty Ltd v Crocus Investments Pty Ltd* [1988] 2 Qd. R. 517 at 526–527, 536, where the effect of a principal debtor clause is equated with a specific variation of the contractual arrangements whereby the guarantor clearly assumes a primary liability. See also K.P. McGuinness, *The Law of Guarantee* (1986), p.26, who suggests that the effect of a principal debtor clause is "to render the obligation of the surety absolute and unconditional".
[13] See below, paras 5–127, 6–68 to 6–69, 7–28, 7–84, 8–30, n.71, 8–98 to 8–99 and 10–118 to 10–121.

successors and assigns from all loss or damage suffered and all claims costs and expenses made against or incurred by you in any way arising out of or consequent upon your having entered into such agreement, whether arising out of a breach by the customer of any of the terms and conditions thereof or otherwise including any such loss or damage, etc. as aforesaid as may arise from the said agreement being (for whatever reason) unenforceable against the customer. (3) No relaxation or indulgence which you may from time to time or at any time extend to the customer shall in any way prejudice or act as a waiver of your strict rights against me hereunder."

1–105 In this situation the agreement has sometimes been construed simply as a guarantee, despite the inclusion of an indemnity provision. Thus in *Stadium Finance Co Ltd v Helm*,[14] the Court of Appeal held that an agreement containing the above clauses and headed "indemnity form" was in fact a guarantee, with the result that the contract was unenforceable against the guarantor when the principal contract was void due to the principal's infancy. Russell L.J. was of the view that, as most people were not prepared to subject themselves to the nuisance of primary liability, a clearer form must be adopted before the instrument could be construed as an indemnity.[15] The construction of a contract in this form as a guarantee is more likely if the obligation is only to attach in the event of the failure of the principal to discharge his obligations,[16] since this in indicative of a secondary liability.

1–106 Another possibility is to construe the agreement as two separate obligations of guarantee and indemnity and, indeed, this appears to be the usual approach.[17] However, even if the instrument is treated as embodying separate obligations, the interrelationship of the guarantee and the indemnity may well have a significant impact on the effectiveness of the provisions.[18] In particular, the fact that the substantial part of the document (apart from the indemnity clause) is drafted as a guarantee can, at least on one view, result in the indemnity provision being much less effective from the creditor's point of view.[19] An illustration is *Citicorp Australia Ltd v Hendry*,[20] where it was held that an indemnity provision did not preserve the obligor's liability when the sums payable pursuant to

---

[14] (1965) 109 S.J. 471. *Cf.* however *Total Oil Products (Aust) Pty Ltd v Robinson* [1970] 1 N.S.W.R. 701 at 703–704, where it was held that a particular clause in a contract which was phrased in terms of a guarantee was a promise of indemnity.

[15] See also *Re Taylor, Ex p. Century 21 Real Estate Corp* (1995) 130 A.L.R. 723.

[16] *Re Taylor, Ex p. Century 21 Real Estate Corp* (unreported, Fed Ct of Australia, Burchett J. June 27, 1995) at 9–10.

[17] *Citicorp Australia Ltd v Hendry* (1985) 4 N.S.W.L.R. 1 at 20 *per* Clarke J. (at first instance). The matter was treated similarly on appeal (1985) 4 N.S.W.L.R. 1 at 36, where the instrument was referred to as a "guarantee/indemnity document". See also *James Hardie & Co Pty Ltd v Burrows* (unreported, Vic Sup Ct, July 5, 1991).

[18] *The "Barenbels"* [1985] 1 Lloyd's Rep. 528 at 532, although here the obligations were embodied in the same clause.

[19] In *Citicorp Australia Ltd v Hendry* (1985) 4 N.S.W.L.R. 1 at 20, Clarke J. in fact regarded "the agreement as a whole as an agreement of guarantee" and the indemnity as an "additional" liability.

[20] (1985) 4 N.S.W.L.R. 1.

the principal contract were irrecoverable as being in the nature of a penalty. The indemnity clause (as well as the guarantee) had been drafted on the basis that there was an existing obligation of the principal to pay, which was not the case because the sums as a matter of law were at no stage recoverable from the principal.[21]

As the above analysis of common forms indicates, the distinction **1–107** between a contract of guarantee and one of indemnity is often blurred, and it is always essential to give effect to the particular wording in each case, rather than attempt a rigid categorisation.[22] The authors in this work have, therefore, on many occasions looked at the law in regard to both types of contract. Indeed, as the modern forms of guarantee often contain elements of an indemnity this is why the authors have entitled the work *The Modern Contract of Guarantee*. Instances of the treatment of a contract of indemnity, or a guarantee which contains elements of indemnity, are found in Chapter 5 (where the principles of construction applicable to a contract of indemnity are analysed), Chapters 6–8 (where the effect of circumstances discharging the guarantor are considered also in relation to the indemnifier) and Chapters 10–12 (where the rights of an indemnifier are discussed).

8. DISTINCTION BETWEEN GUARANTEE AND WARRANTY

In common parlance, the terms "guarantee" and "warranty" are used **1–108** interchangeably. There is some historical basis for this usage for it appears that the words were once the same, the letter "g" of the Norman-French being convertible with the "w" of the German and English, as in the names William and Guillaume.[23] In general, however, the term "guarantee" should be used to describe a collateral contract "by which one person is bound to another for the due fulfilment of a promise or engagement of a third party",[24] while the term "warranty" should be reserved for "a contract as to the title, quality or quantity of a thing sold"[25] or an undertaking that the title, quality or quantity of the subject matter of a contract is as it appears to be or as it has been represented. Unlike a guarantee, a warranty does not necessarily relate to the obligations of a

---

[21] See below, para.5–129 and note, in particular, a different interpretation in *Gulf Bank KSC v Mitsubishi Heavy Industries Ltd* [1994] 2 Lloyd's Rep. 145 at 151.

[22] *Alfred McAlpine Construction Ltd v Unex Corp Ltd* (1994) 38 Con. L.R. 63.

[23] H.A. de Colyar, *A Treatise on the Law of Guarantees* (3rd ed., 1897), pp.1–2. The Old French noun "garantie" and verb "garantie" were derived from the Frankish word "garant", itself a derivation of an earlier form "warrant", meaning a warrant or supporter: K.P. McGuinness, *The Law of Guarantee* (2nd ed., 1996), p.23.

[24] *Parson's Law of Contracts* (5th ed.), Vol. ii, p.3, quoted in H.A. de Colyar, *op. cit.*, p.2.

[25] *ibid.* A retailer's obligation to effect repairs to goods sold is a warranty, not a guarantee: See, *e.g. Adams v Richardson & Starling Ltd* [1969] 1 W.L.R. 1645. Technically, a "warranty" is a subsidiary term of a contract which gives rise to a right to damages if the term is breached, but which does not give the injured party a right to treat the contract as at an end: *Oscar Chess Ltd v Williams* [1957] 1 All E.R. 325 at 328 *per* Denning L.J., CA.

third party. In *Nicholls v Nordheimer*,[26] a promise that a piano would be free from defects at the time of sale and for five years thereafter was held to constitute an oral contract of guarantee and was, therefore, unenforceable under the Statute of Frauds. The above definition of "warranty" suggests that this decision is erroneous. Generally, oral or written assurances as to the quality or performance of consumer goods are warranties, not guarantees.

1–109 *Waterson v Barclay*[27] is a clear example of such a warranty in relation to realty. William White agreed to sell to the plaintiff land on which the defendant had a claim. The defendant gave the plaintiff a signed memorandum containing the following promise:

> "I ... do hereby guarantee a genuine title to the farm purchased by ... [the plaintiff] from William White ... in consideration of his causing to be placed to my account, or in the Commercial Bank, Sydney, at once, the amount of the balance of purchase money."

1–110 The Supreme Court of New South Wales held that this document constituted a warranty that the vendor held, and should be in a position to convey, a valid title to the land.

This work is not concerned with warranties as to the title, quality or quantity of property sold.

9. DISTINCTION BETWEEN GUARANTEE AND INSURANCE

1–111 Like an indemnity, a contract of insurance is a direct, positive and independent contract: the insurer agrees to pay money upon the happening of a specified event.[28] Where the event is a default by a debtor, the contract bears a striking resemblance to a guarantee.[29] But a contract of insurance does not depend on the existence of a principal debtor or his default. It creates a form of primary liability usually to pay money on the occurrence of the specific event; it is not a collateral obligation to answer for the debt or default of another person.

1–112 The difference between a contract of insurance and a contract of guarantee depends on three distinct but related factors: the nature of the contract, the obligations it creates, and the way it is effected.

---

[26] (1871) 22 U.C.C.P. 48, Can CA.
[27] (1863) 3 S.C.R. (NSW) 14.
[28] *Yeoman Credit Ltd v Latter* [1961] 1 W.L.R. 828; *Dane v Mortgage Insurance Corp* [1894] 1 Q.B. 54 at 61 *per* Lord Esher M.R.; *Prudential Insurance Co v IRC* [1904] 2 K.B. 658 at 663 *per* Channell J. A contract of insurance secures some benefit, usually but not necessarily the payment of a sum of money: *ibid.*
[29] *Dane v Mortgage Insurance Corp Ltd* [1894] 1 Q.B. 54 at 61 *per* Lord Esher M.R.; *Finlay v Mexican Investment Corporation* [1897] 1 Q.B. 517 See also M.C. Blair, "The Conversion of Guarantee Contracts" (1966) 29 Mod. L. Rev. 522 on the distinction between contracts of guarantee and contracts of insurance.

A contract of insurance is a matter of speculation.[30] The insurer bears **1–113** the risk of the loss. The insured party has the means of knowledge as to the risk[31] and must make full disclosure of all material facts to the insurer.[32] The insured generally puts the risk before the insurer as a business transaction, and the insurer fixes the premium on the risk stated. This is why a contract of insurance requires the parties to exercise a high standard of good faith; this is why it is a contract uberrimae fides.[33] In a contract of guarantee the creditor does not generally explain or represent to the surety the risk the surety is undertaking; in general, the surety knows the risk or at least he is expected to ascertain it exactly. The creditor has no general duty to disclose to the guarantor all material facts within the creditor's knowledge.[34] Usually, the surety assumes the secondary obligation from motives of friendship to the debtor or because of some business association, not as a result from any direct bargaining between the creditor and the surety. Often the surety derives no premium or any other pecuniary benefit from the transaction.[35]

A contract of insurance is not a promise to pay if a third party defaults[36] **1–114** or a promise to pay what the principal debtor should have paid.[37] Nor is it necessary for an insurance contract to relate to the conduct or performance of another person.[38] In *Dane v Mortgage Insurance Corp Ltd*,[39] Lord Esher M.R. illustrated this central point by reference to marine insurance:

"A policy on a ship, for instance, is not an undertaking to pay the amount insured, if somebody else, for example, the owner of another ship that has caused the loss, does not, but to pay such amount on the loss of the ship."[40]

---

[30] *Cf. Re Australian & Overseas Insurance Co Ltd* [1966] 1 NSWR 558 (a contract of guarantee) with *Dane v Mortgage Insurance Corp Ltd* [1894] 1 Q.B. 54 (a contract of insurance). In both cases, an insurance company undertook to repay on default of a financial institution a customer's deposit.

[31] *Seaton v Heath* [1899] 1 Q.B. 782 at 793 *per* Romer L.J.

[32] Or at least the insurer does not have the same means of knowledge as to the risk: *ibid.*

[33] See, *e.g. Royal Bank v Fleming* [1933] O.R. 601, CA.

[34] *Lindsay v L. Stevenson & Sons Ltd* (1891) 17 VLR 112; *London General Omnibus Co Ltd v Holloway* [1912] 2 K.B. 72 at 81 *per* Farwell L.J. Nevertheless, creditors have a limited duty of disclosure to prospective guarantors. See below, paras 4–02 to 4–21.

[35] *Seaton v Heath* [1899] 1 Q.B. 782. For this reason, "Sureties have for very many years been favoured in equity": *London General Omnibus Co Ltd v Holloway* [1912] 2 K.B. 72 at 81 *per* Farwell L.J.

[36] *ibid.* at 793 (the insurer undertakes to pay the loss incurred by the insured in the event of certain specified contingencies occurring.)

[37] *Bristol & West Building Society v Freeman and Pollard (a firm)* (unreported, Queen's Bench Division, Judge Raymond Jack Q.C., February 20, 1996).

[38] *Re Law Guarantee Trust and Accident Society Ltd; Liverpool Mortgage Insurance Co's Case* [1914] 2 Ch. 617 at 629–630 *per* Buckley L.J.

[39] [1894] 1 Q.B. 54 at 60.

[40] *ibid.* A contract under which a party undertakes to provide a customer with consideration in kind by supplying replacement services rather than money to compensate for the loss suffered in an uncertain event (namely the financial failure of a supplier) is a contract of insurance: *Re Sentinel Securities Plc* [1996] 1 W.L.R. 316 at 326–327. See also *Department of Trade and Industry v St Christopher Motorists' Association Ltd* [1974] 1 W.L.R. 99.

1–115   Although the insurer promises to pay on a certain event or by reference to a formula,[41] the insurance contract is treated as one of indemnity so that if the insured party saves anything on the loss, the amount salvaged must be credited to the insurer.[42]

1–116   A contract of guarantee also differs from a contract of insurance in the way it is effected.[43] The former is a contract between persons who occupy, or ultimately assume, the positions of creditor, debtor and surety;[44] the method of achieving this result matters little in the present context. A contract of insurance, on the other hand, is usually formed and accepted by the issue of a policy in response to a proposal signed by the insured party.[45] This procedure is vitally important as the proposal generally forms the basis of the contract

1–117   The form of the policy may suggest that the contract is one of insurance rather than of guarantee.[46] Insurance policies are usually issued on printed forms designed for the particular kind of insurance involved. Although a contract of guarantee is generally unenforceable unless it is evidenced in writing,[47] no other formalities are required; the contract can be formed merely by a letter of guarantee with no special phrases or terms of art.[48] If the document contains provisions which attempt to preserve the liability of the promisor despite a failure or release of the debtor's liability, it may persuade the court to construe it as a guarantee as such provisions are redundant in a contract of insurance.[49]

1–118   Finally, a contract of insurance is void unless the party to be insured has an insurable interest in the subject matter.[50] A similar statutory requirement is not necessary for contracts of guarantee where the interests of the creditor and the debtor are so manifest.

Again, this book is not concerned with contracts of insurance.

10. CONCLUSION

1–119   The elements of suretyship in its modern forms are well established. Yet it is still difficult in many cases to determine whether a particular arrangement is a contract of guarantee or some other similar undertaking. Parties often assume the position of sureties without understanding the risk they have undertaken and the obligations they have assumed. It is expected that they know the risk or can, at least, find out the necessary

---

[41] See, *e.g. Bristol & West Building Society v Freeman & Pollard (a firm)* (unreported, Queen's Bench Division, Judge Raymond Jack Q.C., February 20, 1996).
[42] [1894] 1 Q.B. 54 at 61.
[43] *ibid.*
[44] *Seaton v Heath* [1899] 1 Q.B. 782; *Re Australian & Overseas Insurance Co Ltd* [1966] 1 N.S.W.R. 558.
[45] *Re Albert Life Assurance Co, Ex p. Western Life Assurance Society* (1870) L.R. 11 Eq. 164.
[46] *Phoenix Assurance Co Ltd v Wren* [1950] S.A.S.R. 89.
[47] On the other hand, see *Re Australian & Overseas Insurance Co Ltd* [1966] 1 N.S.W.R. 558.
[48] See below, paras 2–03 to 2–06.
[49] *Trade Indemnity Co Ltd v Workington Harbour & Dock Board* [1937] A.C. 1.
[50] M.A. Clarke, *The Law of Insurance Contracts* (4th ed., 2002), Chs 3 and 4; A. McGee, *The Modern Law of Insurance*, Ch. 4.

information. Often this is a misconception. Sureties often accept their secondary obligation from motives of friendship or family ties. They themselves receive no benefit yet they assume a potentially onerous burden.

The technicalities of modern suretyship can also affect creditors **1–120** adversely. The creditor may assume that a contract of indemnity or insurance has been formed in such a way as to protect its advance or investment. If the court finds that the contract is one of guarantee, the creditor may in certain circumstances forfeit rights it would otherwise enjoy. Indeed, the creditor's rights may be unwittingly jeopardised by its own actions in granting the a concession as to time or amount.

The role of the law in this area should be to dispel any doubts about the **1–121** true nature of a transaction by clarifying the circumstances in which suretyship arises. Unfortunately authorities in this area form a thicket which lawyers often find difficult to penetrate. The parties to the contract learn of its consequences when it is too late to disengage themselves from a bargain they made largely in ignorance.

CHAPTER 2

FORMATION OF THE CONTRACT OF GUARANTEE

1. INTRODUCTION

In this chapter the general principles relating to the formation of a **2–01** contract of guarantee will be considered. No attempt will be made to provide a comprehensive treatment of this area of the law of contract. Rather the chapter will be directed at the particular problems which guarantees raise in relation to offer and acceptance, privity, capacity, consideration, uncertainty and conditions precedent.

2. MUTUAL ASSENT OF THE PARTIES IS REQUIRED

No special words are necessary to create a contract of guarantee. The **2–02** relation of suretyship will arise from the agreement of the parties if they manifest their intention clearly.[1] As we have seen, most contracts of guarantee are concluded by means of offer and acceptance between the creditor and the guarantor, and the principal debtor may be a party to this agreement.[2] Whatever the genesis of the guarantee, the parties must concur in the subject of the contract.[3] While general contractual principles require the parties to the guarantee to be ad idem as to the terms of their agreement, they do not usually protect a party against a unilateral mistake, a secret reservation or an erroneous construction of the contract.[4]

3. THE OFFER OF GUARANTEE AND CONTRACTUAL INTENTION

(i) General principles

The offer to guarantee will usually be made by the guarantor or his **2–03** lawfully authorised agent.[5] The guarantor's offer must be clear and definite such as:

---

[1] *Dane v Mortgage Insurance Corp Ltd* [1894] 1 Q.B. 54, CA. A person may not guarantee his own debt or obligation: *Miles v Zuckerman* [1931] O.R. 368, CA. *Cf. Heisler v Anglo-Dal Ltd* [1954] 1 W.L.R. 1273, where the word "guarantee" was not used in its technical legal sense. For this reason it is unlikely that a partner can guarantee a debt of a partnership. But a person may guarantee the obligation of a spouse or a corporation of which he is the sole or principal shareholder: *Standard Realty Co v Nicholson* (1911) 24 O.L.R. 46; *Cooperative Trust v Lobstick Village* (1991) 1 B.L.R. (2d) 147 at 157.
[2] See *Duncan, Fox & Co v North and South Wales Bank* (1880) 6 App. Cas. 1 at 11, discussed above, paras 1–28 to 1–33.
[3] *Preston v Luck* (1884) 27 Ch. D. 497. See also *Bank of Nova Scotia v MacDonald* (1968) 69 D.L.R. (2d) 504 (NS).
[4] *Preston v Luck* (1884) 27 Ch. D. 497. See, however, below, Ch.4.
[5] As to the actual or ostensible authority of agents to bind their principals to a guarantee, see *Freeman & Lockyer v Buckhurst Part Properties (Mangal) Ltd* [1964] 2 Q.B. 480 and *John Davidson (Pipes) Ltd v First Engineering Ltd* (2001) S.C.L.R. 73.

"I hereby hold myself responsible for and guarantee the payment of the [principal debt] to you."[6]

2–04   Vague or equivocal statements will not suffice;[7] they must be promissory and show an intention to be legally bound.[8] Nor will a mere overture to provide a guarantee constitute an offer capable of acceptance.[9] The central question is whether or not it is sufficiently clear from the documentation and the surrounding circumstances that there is an intention to enter a legally binding obligation.[10] Indeed, much may depend on the surrounding circumstances. In *Sorby v Gordon*,[11] the statement: "I am quite willing to guarantee the first shipment" was sufficient in the light of the dealings between the parties. Similarly, in *A. A. Davison Pty Ltd v Seabrook*,[12] the defendant was held liable as guarantor on a document addressed to a manufacturer in the following terms: "I am prepared to back him, the buyer, for 1 month credit to £30." A contract of guarantee was established when the manufacturer supplied the buyer with goods on the faith of this statement. But it should not be assumed that an officer of a corporation is offering a personal guarantee when he is merely stating his intention as a director or officer that his corporation will be liable as a guarantor.[13] Additionally an offer of guarantee, even if specific in nature, which is contained in a document headed "subject to contract" will not constitute a legally binding offer capable of acceptance, unless the condition "subject to contract" is subsequently waived or otherwise replaced.[14]

2–05   Conduct is also significant. The deposit of title deeds by a property owner with a bank as security for a customer's overdraft may constitute a guarantee.[15]

---

[6] *Van Wart v Carpenter* (1861) 21 U.C.Q.B. 320, CA. A promise to furnish a guarantee can be satisfied by the provision of a personal guarantee of the promisor: *Heisler v Anglo-Dal Ltd* [1954] 2 All E.R. 770.

[7] *Westhead v Sproson* (1861) 6 H. & N. 728; 158 E.R. 301 (a conditional guarantee); *Morrell v Cowan* (1877) 6 Ch. D. 166 at 170. See *Ulster Banking Co v Mahaffy* (1881) 15 I.L.T. 94 (IR); *Helliwell v Dickson* (1862) 9 Gr 414, Ch. R., CA.

[8] *Motemtronic Ltd v Autocar Equipment Ltd* (unreported, Court of Appeal, Civil Division, June 20, 1996). The same principle applies to contracts of indemnity. Hence a bank will not be liable as an indemnifier merely because it signs letters of indemnity provided by its customer to a carrier: *Pacific Carriers Ltd v Banque Nationale de Paris* (unreported, NSW Sup Ct, Hunter J., October 16, 2001).

[9] *M'Iver v Richardson* (1813) 1 M. & S. 557; 105 E.R. 208. See also *Symmons v Want* (1818) 2 Stark 371; 171 E.R. 676; *Mozley v Tinkler* (1835) 1 C.M. & R. 692; 149 E.R. 1258; *Nash v Spencer* (1896) 13 T.L.R. 78; *Newport v Spivey* (1862) 1 New Rep. 30; 7 L.T. 328.

[10] *Bradley West Solicitors Nominee Co Ltd v Keeman* [1994] 2 N.Z.L.R. 111 at 117.

[11] (1874) 30 L.T. 528.

[12] (1931) 37 A.L.R. 156. See also *Kosky v Outstanding Outdoors Ltd* (unreported, NZ High Ct, June 6, 1995), where a brochure issued by the New Zealand Spa and Pool Association to a customer of one of its members stated that "your customer is registered with us and insured with us", and then "for a modest premium you will receive a guarantee covering your pool shell". This was held to constitute an enforceable guarantee by the Association.

[13] *The Technology Partnership v Afro-Asian Satellite Communications (UK) Ltd* (unreported, Court of Appeal (Civil Division), October 12, 1998) at p.11 of Lexis transcript, *per* Peter Gibson L.J.

[14] *Carlton Communications plc v Football League* (unreported, August 1, 2002), paras 49–61.

[15] *Deutsche Bank AG v Ibrahim* (unreported, HC, Ch Div, January 13, 1992).

The terms of the offer must be addressed to the creditor, rather than the **2–06** principal debtor,[16] and the offer must be accepted within a reasonable time or it will lapse in accordance with normal contractual principles.[17] The offer may be revoked at any time before acceptance.[18] Moreover, it cannot be accepted after the offeree has notice of the death of the offeror.[19]

The ambit of the offer will determine the scope and extent of the **2–07** guarantor's obligation and will prescribe the exact conditions upon which the guarantee is to be given. This means that the guarantor will be discharged if there is a breach of such a condition.[20] Similarly, if the offer is in respect of a named principal, a change in the identity of the principal or in the principal's condition may discharge the guarantor.[21]

Where a mortgage is granted to secure another's debt, the mortgagor **2–08** does not necessarily assume a personal obligation to repay the debt. The mortgagor's liability may be restricted to the value of the secured property. This is so even though s.28(1) of the Land Registration Act 1925 provides, in effect, that a personal covenant to pay is implied in a registered mortgage unless there is an entry on the register negating such an implication.[22]

(ii) Letters of comfort

The difficulty of ascertaining whether the relevant statement is **2–09** promissory and evinces an intention to be legally bound is illustrated in the context of letters of comfort. It has been seen[23] that, although letters of comfort are not usually construed as contracts of guarantee, in the authors' view the beneficiary of the letter should be under similar obligations to those imposed upon a creditor who has taken a guarantee as security.

[16] *A A Davison Pty Ltd v Seabrook* (1931) 37 A.L.R. 156; *Helliwell v Dickson* (1862) 9 Gr 414, Ch. R. CA; *Nash v Spencer* (1896) 13 T.L.R. 78; *Castling v Aubert* (1802) 2 East 325; 102 E.R. 393; *Brueckner v Carroll* (unreported, NSW Sup Ct, Santow J, December 14, 1994). A guarantee involves a promise to the creditor, not merely a promise to provide the principal debtor with additional funds: *Phillips v Bateman* (1812) 16 East 356; 104 E.R. 1124.
[17] *Cf. Pope v Andrews* (1840) 9 Car. & P. 564 at 568; 173 E.R. 957 at 959 (which suggests that the offeree is bound expressly to dissent within a reasonable time). A lapsed offer may be revived if the offeror re-opens the offer to the offeree, or if the original offeree offers to accept the offer and both parties concur; *O'Young and Lum v Reid & Co Ltd* [1932] A.L.R. 278; 6 A.L.J. 76.
[18] *Offord v Davies* (1862) 12 C.B.N.S. 748; 142 E.R. 1336. See also *Bristol, Cardiff & Swansea Aerated Bread Co v Maggs* (1890) 44 Ch. D. 616.
[19] *Coulthart v Clementson* (1879) 5 Q.B.D. 42. See also *Re Silvester Midland Railway Co v Silvester* [1895] 1 Ch. 573 and *Dickinson v Dodds* (1876) 2 Ch. D. 463, CA. An agreement by the executors of a deceased guarantor to continue the liability in return for an extension of time by the creditor will be invalid if it is beyond their powers: *Union Bank v Clark* (1908) 12 O.W.R. 532, affirmed in (1910) 14 O.W.R. 298.
[20] *Blest v Brown* (1862) 4 De G.F. & J. 367; 45 E.R. 1225; *Lumberman's Bank & Trust Co v Sevier* (1928) 149 Wash 118, 270: see below, pp. 8–01 to 8–93.
[21] Unless, of course, the guarantee clearly indicates that it is intended to survive such changes: see below, paras 9–53, *et. seq.*
[22] *Fairmile Portfolio Management Ltd v Davies Arnold Cooper (a firm)* [1988] E.G.C.S. 149. It appears that the principle also applies to unregistered land. See s.117(2) of the Law of Property Act 1925.
[23] See above, paras 1–76 to 1–80.

2–10   Whether a letter of comfort is legally binding and promissory will be dependent on the precise wording and the surrounding circumstances.[24] Thus in *Kleinwort Benson Ltd v Malaysia Mining Corp Bhd*,[25] the English Court of Appeal held that a letter of comfort imposed no contractual obligation when the wording of the relevant part of the letter ("it is our policy to ensure that the business of [our subsidiary] is at all times in a position to meet its liabilities to you") was consistent with a statement amounting only to a representation of fact. Furthermore, the surrounding circumstances showed, inter alia, that the letter of comfort was only entered into after the parent company had refused to assume joint and several liability with the borrower or to give a guarantee.

2–11   Rogers C.J. of the Supreme Court of New South Wales took a different view of a letter of comfort in *Banque Brussels Lambert SA v Australian National Industries Ltd*,[26] where the wording of the letter was, of course, not identical and the circumstances showed that the creditor had made it clear that a binding obligation was required. The letter was held to be legally binding. But what is significant is not that the interpretation of the letter was different from the construction of the document in *Kleinwort Benson Ltd v Malaysia Mining Corp Bhd*,[27] but that Rogers C.J. criticised the approach of the Court of Appeal in the latter case in subjecting the letters to "minute textual analysis". Rogers C.J. clearly favoured a more robust approach to construction which would not allow "statements made by businessmen, after hard bargaining and made to induce another business person to enter into a business transaction" to "reside in a twilight zone of merely honourable agreement".[28]

2–12   Sometimes, a letter of comfort will contain a clause expressly stating that "this document is not intended to be a guarantee and . . . is an expression of present intention by way of comfort only".[29] Even adopting the broader approach of Rogers C.J. in *Banque Brussells Lambert SA v Australian National Industries Ltd*,[30] this will provide a strong indication that the letter is not contractually binding.[31]

---

[24] *Motemtronic Ltd v Autocar Equipment Ltd* (unreported, Court of Appeal, Civil Division, June 20, 1996), where the court held that an assurance given by a company director to induce another party to enter into a contract was merely a statement of comfort, not intended to be legally binding.

[25] [1989] 1 All E.R. 785; [1989] 1 W.L.R. 379.

[26] (1989) 21 N.S.W.L.R. 502. See also *BNZ v Ginivan* [1991] 1 N.Z.L.R. 178 at 180.

[27] [1989] 1 All E.R. 785; [1989] 1 W.L.R. 379.

[28] Of course, as the question is simply one of interpretation it could not be said that the law of New South Wales is different from that in England: *Esanda Finance Corp Ltd v Wordplex Information Systems Ltd* (1990) 19 N.S.W.L.R. 146. Cf. also, in Victoria, the interpretation of the letter in *Commonwealth Bank of Australia v TLI Management Pty Ltd* [1990] V.R. 510.

[29] See *Re Atlantic Computers plc (in administration)* [1995] B.C.C. 696.

[30] (1989) 21 N.S.W.L.R. 502.

[31] Although, as indicated, it will be a question of construction in each case: see generally *Re Atlantic Computers plc (in administration)* [1995] B.C.C. 696.

4. ACCEPTANCE OF THE OFFER

In accordance with normal contractual principles the method of **2–13**
acceptance will depend upon the terms of the offer.[32] But often the
promisor's offer to provide a guarantee may be accepted by conduct.[33]
Thus, in an offer to furnish a guarantee when goods are supplied to the
principal, the acceptance of the offer will take place when the goods are
supplied.[34] In many such cases there will be no need for an express
communication of acceptance because the terms of the offer of guarantee
will be taken to have impliedly waived this normal requirement.[35] Where
the creditor acts in reliance upon the offer of guarantee, the guarantor will
only be bound if the creditor's actions in response to the offer correspond
exactly with its terms.[36] For example, an offer to act as guarantor of a loan
repayable on demand will not bind the offeror as surety for a loan on
different terms.[37] An acceptance by conduct, therefore, comprises two
elements: the offeree must know of the offer, and the offeree must act in
reliance upon its terms.[38]

Even where communication of acceptance would prima facie be **2–14**
unnecessary, for example, because of the operation of the postal rule,
the offer of guarantee may expressly or impliedly stipulate that written
notification of acceptance is required. For example, in *Mozley v Tinkler*,[39]
Baron Parke considered that on its true construction an offer of guarantee

---

[32] As a general rule, communication of acceptance is required before the contract is
complete: *Tallerman & Co Pty Ltd v Nathan's Merchandise (Vic) Pty Ltd* (1957) 98 C.L.R. 93
at 111. See also *M'Iver v Richardson* (1813) 1 M & S. 557; 105 E.R. 208 and *Newport v Spivey*
(1862) 1 New Rep. 30; 7 L.T. 328. An offer of guarantee (not under seal) can be revoked at
any time before it is accepted or acted on in such a way as to raise a promissory estoppel. See
Dickinson v Dodds (1876) 2 Ch. D. 463; *Daulia Ltd v Four Millbank Nominees Ltd* [1978] 1
Ch. 231 at 239 *per* Goff L.J. (as he then was). Where the terms of the offer do not limit the
time for acceptance, the offeree's response must be communicated to the offeror within a
reasonable time: *Marsden & Son v Capital & Counties Newspaper Co Ltd* (1901) 46 Sol. J. 11,
CA; *Payne v Ives* (1823) 3 Dow & Ry K.B. 664 at 668. See also *Pope v Andrews* (1840) 9 Car.
& P. 564; 173 E.R. 957 (creditors' retention of guarantee for three weeks constituted
acceptance in the circumstances).
[33] See, *e.g. Sorby v Gordon* (1874) 30 L.T. 528 and *Jays Ltd v Sala* (1898) 14 T.L.R. 461 While
it is true that acceptance can be inferred from the creditor's words and conduct, inferences
that might be drawn in dealings between two parties might not be as readily drawn in the
tripartite arrangement involved in a guarantee: *Dalgety Australia Ltd v Harris* [1977] 1
N.S.W.L.R. 324 at 328.
[34] *Jays Ltd v Sala* (1898) 14 T.L.R. 461; *Oldershaw v King* (1857) 2 H. & N. 517; 157 E.R. 213;
Westhead v Sproson (1861) 6 H. & N. 728; 158 E.R. 301; *Morrell v Cowan* (1877) 6 Ch. D. 166
at 170; *Smith v Passmore* (1883) 4 L.R. (NSW) 274; *S. H. Lock Discounts & Credits Pty Ltd v
Miles* [1963] V.R. 656; *Bank of Montreal v Sperling Hotel Co Ltd* (1973) 36 D.L.R. (3d) 130.
See also *Raikes v Todd* (1838) 8 Ad & El 846 at 857; 112 E.R. 1058 at 1062 *per* Patterson J;
Robertson v Healy (1866) 5 S.C.R. (NSW) 290; *Chapman v Sutton* (1846) 2 C.B. 634; 135 E.R.
1095; *Bank of Montreal v Germain* [1976] WWD 75 (Alberta) (as to further advances to the
principal debtor).
[35] See, *e.g. Sorby v Gordon* (1874) 30 L.T. 528.
[36] *Luck v Ilka* [1951] Q.S.R. 281. See also *Royal Bank of Canada v Kiska* [1967] 2 O.R. 379;
Glyn v Hertel (1818) 8 Taunt 208; 129 E.R. 363.
[37] *Luck v Ilka* (1951) Q.S.R. 281.
[38] *Dalgety Australia Ltd v Harris* [1977] 1 N.S.W.L.R. 324. See also *Reuss v Picksley* (1866)
L.R. 1 Exch 342 at 352. *Cf. Jays Ltd v Sala* (1898) 14 T.L.R. 461.
[39] (1835) 1 Cr. M. & R. 692; 149 E.R. 1258 (original emphasis). See also *Gaunt v Hill* (1815) 1
Stark 10; 171 E.R. 386; *Newport v Spivey* (1862) 7 L.T. 328.

in the following terms required the actual communication of a notice of acceptance:

> "Mr France informs me, that you are about publishing an arithmetic for him and another person, and I have no objection to being answerable as far as £50. *For my reference*, apply to Messrs Brooke and Co of this place."

2–15   A general guarantee, which is not in its terms restricted to any particular person or persons, can be accepted by anyone who knows of the offer and acts in reliance upon it.[40] By contrast, a special guarantee can be accepted only by the person or persons with whom the offeror has expressed an intention to contract. For example, an offer to a partnership cannot be accepted by the firm after a change of partners.[41] Nor can an offer to an individual be accepted by the firm in which that individual later becomes a partner.[42]

2–16   Where a guarantee is addressed to a group of companies and it is not clear which company in the group is the offeree, extrinsic evidence and the consideration clause may be used to establish that the guarantee is in fact addressed to the particular company with whom the principal debtor was trading at the date of the execution of the guarantee.[43] In some circumstances, where the guarantee is addressed to the wrong company in the group, the court may order rectification of the guarantee to accord with the final intention of the parties at the time of execution of the guarantee.[44] But rectification requires convincing proof that the guarantee does not embody the common intention of the parties and a strong case for substituting the name of another company as offeree.[45]

2–17   If the offer of guarantee is made to two persons in the alternative it must be accepted by one or the other of the offerees since the defendant guarantors are entitled to know to whom they are responsible. Thus in *Lott v Collins*,[46] the defendant escaped liability on his guarantee of rent payable by a sublessee of a certain farm because his promise was made to the plaintiff lessee or the lessor in the alternative. In the absence of an acceptance by the lessee or the lessor, the guarantor could not be liable.

2–18   The court rejected a submission that the plaintiff had accepted the defendant's offer by granting the sublease in reliance on the guarantee. It is arguable that this submission should have been accepted since this

---

[40] *Cf. Harris v Stevens* (1902) 1 O.W.R. 109 (Can).
[41] See below, paras 9–63 to 9–64.
[42] *ibid.*
[43] *Boral Resources (Qld) Pty Ltd v Donnelly* [1988] 1 Qd. R. 506. See also *Re Rogers Ex p. CMV Parts Distributors Pty Ltd* (1989) 20 F.C.R. 561, where it was clear that the reference in the guarantee to the "Group" was to be read distributively and not as a description of obligations owed jointly to all companies in the group.
[44] *Elders Lensworth Finance Ltd v Australian Central Pacific Ltd* [1986] 2 Qd. R. 364. See also below, para. 5–98.
[45] *Pukallus v Cameron* (1982) 56 A.L.J.R. 907 at 909; *Australian Gypsum Ltd & Australian Plaster Co Ltd v Hume Steel Ltd* (1930) 45 C.L.R. 54 at 64; *Slee v Warke* (1949) 86 C.L.R. 271 at 281.
[46] (1869) 8 S.C.R. (NSW) 104. *Cf. Bradford Old Bank Ltd v Sutcliffe* [1918] 2 KB 833.

conduct on the part of the plaintiff should have amounted to a sufficient acceptance to render the guarantee enforceable.[47]

An offer (not under seal) can be revoked at any time prior to **2–19** acceptance.[48] Moreover, an undertaking to provide security in respect of a *proposed* agreement or transaction regulated by the Consumer Credit Act 1974 can be, in effect, revoked where the surety gives the creditor a notice under s.106 of the Act. Upon receipt of such notice, the creditor is required to return any property or money it has received in respect of the suretyship and cancel any entry relating to the security which appears in any register.

5. PRIVITY OF CONTRACT

Offer and acceptance are not the only essential elements of a valid **2–20** contract of guarantee. A court will not entertain an action for breach of contract unless there is privity of contract between the claimant and the defendant. This is equally true of actions to enforce a guarantee. While privity of contract between the guarantor and the principal debtor is not necessary,[49] privity of contract between the surety and the person seeking to recover on the guarantee is essential.[50] Thus a landlord could not enforce a third party's written undertaking addressed to the landlord's tenant to be responsible for the rent.[51] As a general rule, the claimant may not enforce a guarantee at law unless the claimant was a party to the contract.[52]

The Contracts (Rights of Third Parties) Act 1999 makes inroads into the **2–21** doctrine of privity of contract[53] but it is wrong to assert that it abolishes the doctrine.[54] The Contracts (Rights of Third Parties) Act 1999 does not have retrospective effect. Moreover, it does not apply to contracts made before the end of the period of six months beginning with November 11, 1999, the

---

[47] See generally *Brogden v Metropolitan Railway Co* (1877) 2 App. Cas. 666 and *Robophone Facilities Ltd v Blank* [1966] 3 All E.R. 128. It may be, however, that the creditor's positive act in granting the sublease was not done in response to the defendant's offer of guarantee.
[48] *Dickinson v Dodds* [1876] 2 Ch. D. 463; *Daulia Ltd v Four Millbank Nominees Ltd* [1978] 1 Ch. 231 at 239.
[49] *Western Dominion Investment Co v MacMillan* [1925] 2 D.L.R. 442, affirmed in [1925] 4 D.L.R. 562, CA.
[50] *Re Bodner Road Construction Ltd* (1963) 43 W.W.R. 641 (Man). See also *Tobin Tractor (1957) Ltd v Western Surety Co* (1963) 40 DLR (2d) 231 (Sask). *Cf. Rattenbury v Fenton* (1834) 3 My. & K. 505; 40 E.R. 192. Note that the Law Commission recommended changes to the privity of contract rule: Consultation Paper No. 121 "Privity of Contract: Contracts for the Benefit of Third Parties" (1991). See Contracts (Rights of Third Parties) Act 1999 which allows third parties in their own right to enforce a term of a contract for their benefit. See generally M. Dean, "Removing a Blot on the Landscape–The Reform of the Doctrine of Privity" [2000] J.B.L. 143. The Act received Royal Assent on November 11, 1999. Compare s.11 of the Property Law Act 1974 (Qld) and s.55 of the Property Law Act 1969 (WA).
[51] *Nash v Spencer* (1896) 13 T.L.R. 78.
[52] But if the principal debtor executed the guarantee as trustee of the creditor, he may be able to hold the guarantor liable in equity: *Gregory and Parker v Williams* (1817) 3 Mer. 582; 36 E.R. 224. See also *Fletcher v Fletcher* (1844) 4 Hare 67; 67 E.R. 564; *Vandepitte v Preferred Accident Insurance Corp of New York* [1933] AC 70. See also below, paras 10–160 to 10–199.
[53] *Alfred McAlpine Ltd v Panatown Ltd* [2001] 1 A.C. 518 at 535 *per* Lord Clyde.
[54] See *Alfred McAlphine Ltd v Panatown Ltd* [2001] 1 A.C. 518 at 544 *per* Lord Goff and *Johnson v Gone Wood & Co* [2001] 1 All E.R. 481 at 507.

day on which the Act came into force, except where a contract made within that period expressly states that the Act is to apply to it.[55]

2–22   The general rule[56] does not, however, prevent the creation of a trust of a promise to guarantee the debt of another. Nor does it preclude possible arguments as to the creation of an estoppel by conduct based on the decision in *Waltons Stores (Interstate) Ltd v Maher*.[57]

2–23   The circumstances in which a creditor who is not an original party to the guarantee may enforce it are dealt with in Chapter 10.[58]

6. CAPACITY OF THE PARTIES

(i) Mental incapacity and drunkenness

2–24   A contract of guarantee will not be binding on the guarantor if the guarantor lacked the mental capacity to contract when he gave the guarantee. Where the guarantor lacks this faculty, the agreement will be voidable at his option if the creditor knows of the guarantor's insanity or intellectual handicap.[59] A similar principle should apply where the guarantor is incapable of contracting by reason of senility.[60] In all these cases the court will refuse to hold the guarantor to the bargain if he did not have the ability to understand the nature and effect of his act, and the creditor was aware of this condition.[61] Indeed, earlier dicta suggest that a lunatic's contract of guarantee can be set aside, at the lunatic's option, if the contract is not "fair and bona fide", even if the creditor was oblivious of the guarantor's incapacity.[62] But these dicta are contrary to the weight

---

[55] s.10(3).
[56] See also below, Ch. 10.
[57] (1988) 164 C.L.R. 387 at 452.
[58] See below, paras 10–173 to 10–200.
[59] See *Molton v Camroux* (1848) 2 Exch. 487, affirmed in (1849) 4 Exch. 17; *York Glass Co Ltd v Jubb* (1925) 42 T.L.R. 1, CA; *Imperial Loan Co v Stone* [1892] 1 Q.B. 599 at 601; *Bradford Old Bank Ltd v Sutcliffe* [1918] 2 K.B. 833 CA. But since a contract of guarantee is not usually beneficial to a guarantor who lacks the requisite mental capacity, it should not be necessary to enquire whether the creditor knew of the guarantor's incapacity: *Van Patton v Beals* (1877) 46 Iowa 62. Cf. *Wadsworth v Sharpsteen* (1853) 8 N.Y. 388 and *Crawford v Scovell* (1880) 94 Pa 48.
[60] See *Earl of Aylesford v Morris* (1873) 8 Ch. App. 484 at 490–491; *Fry v Lane* (1888) 40 Ch. D. 312; *Dark v Boock* [1991] 1 N.Z.L.R. 496, HC; *Gibbons v Wright* (1954) 91 C.I.R. 423; *Jenkins v Morris* (1880) 14 Ch. D. 674 CA (the fact that a guarantor suffers from delusions does not make the guarantee voidable), and the cases cited above, n.59.
[61] *Imperial Loan Co v Stone* [1892] 1 Q.B. 599 at 601. See generally G.H. Treitel, *The Law of Contracts* (11th ed., 2003), p.557; *Chitty on Contracts* (28th ed., 1999), Vol. I, paras 8.067 and 8.077. See also *Doty v Mumma* (1924) 305 Mo. 188. The onus is on the guarantor to show that the creditor was aware of his condition: *Scott v Wise* [1986] 2 N.Z.L.R. 484 at 492 *per* Somers J.; *Hart v O'Connor* [1985] A.C. 1000, PC.
[62] *Molton v Camroux* (1849) 4 Exch. 17. A similar rule applies in equity: see *Niell v Morely* (1804) 9 Ves. Jun. 478 at 481–482; 32 E.R. 687, at 688–689 per Sir William Grant M.R. and *Price v Berrington* (1849) 7 Hare 394; 68 E.R. 163. See also R. Goff and G. Jones, *The Law of Restitution* (5th ed., 1998), pp.636–637.

of authority. However, relief may be granted in equity[63] where the creditor took advantage of the guarantor's mental frailty.[64]

Extreme drunkenness is a defence to an action to enforce a guarantee,[65] but unless the guarantor proceeds with reasonable promptness to repudiate the contract, the guarantor may be held to his undertaking.[66] Generally, however, a guarantee given by a drunkard will be voidable because the extent of inebriety will be apparent to the creditor.   **2–25**

(ii) Infancy

In accordance with general principles, an infant will not have the legal capacity to enter into a contract of guarantee because it is difficult to envisage circumstances in which the contract could be regarded as being for the infant's benefit.[67] Even if an infant's guarantee is in some way connected with a beneficial contract of service entered into by the infant, he would probably not be bound. Thus an infant who guaranteed repayment of a loan to his employer or master under an apprenticeship would not be liable on the guarantee. Where the guarantee is void, it cannot be ratified by the minor on attaining majority.[68]   **2–26**

Where the creditor enters into the principal contract with a minor, the contract will not be binding on the minor because of his incapacity. It does not automatically follow that a guarantee in respect of the principal contract will be unenforceable. Section 2 of the Minors' Contracts Act 1987 provides, in effect, that such a guarantee will not be unenforceable by reason only of the fact that it relates to a principal contract with a minor.[69]

---

[63] See *Wiltshire v Marshall* (1866) 14 L.T. 396; *Selby v Jackson* (1844) 13 L.J. Ch. 249; *Blomley v Ryan* (1956) 99 C.L.R. 362. See also below, paras 4–155 to 4–159.

[64] See below, paras 4–155 *et. seq.*, as to the general principles of unconscionability.

[65] See *Gore v Gibson* (1845) 13 M. & W. 623; 153 ER 260; *Molton v Camroux* (1849) 4 Exch. 17 at 19 *per* Patterson J.; *Matthews v Baxter* (1873) L.R. 8 Exch. 132; *Blomley v Ryan* (1956) 99 C.L.R. 362; *Pitt v Smith* (1811) 3 Camp. 33; 170 E.R. 1296.

[66] *Howard v Currie* (1879) 5 V.L.R. (Eq.) 87. See also *Scates v King* (1870) 1 V.R. (Eq.) 100.

[67] See generally, as to infants' contracts, *Chitty on Contracts* (28th ed., 1999), para.8–002; G.H. Treitel, *The Law of Contract* (11th ed., 2003), pp.539–557.

[68] *Beam v Beatty* (1902) 4 O.L.R. 554 at 559 *per* Garrow J.A. (Can). See also *Pearson v Calder* (1916) 35 O.L.R. 524 at 530, CA (guarantee in respect of a debt of a minor). As to guarantees of the debts of a minor, see the Minors' Contracts Act 1987.

[69] It is no longer necessary, therefore, to draw a distinction between an indemnity relating to a minor's principal contract, which was enforceable under the common law, and a guarantee of minor's principal contract, which was not enforceable under the common law. See *Coutts & Co v Browne–Lecky* [1947] K.B. 104; *Stadium Finance Co Ltd v Helm* (1965) 102 S.J. 471. Compare *Wauthier v Wilson* (1912) 28 T.L.R. 239; *Yeoman Credit Ltd v Latter* [1961] 1 W.L.R. 828.

(iii) Companies

2–27   Under the common law, a guarantee granted by a company beyond its legal capacity was void.[70] This doctrine of *ultra vires* created problems for third parties who took a company guarantee in good faith.

2–28   The doctrine of *ultra vires* in its application to ordinary limited companies was fundamentally changed by s.35 of the Companies Act 1985. This provision was enacted to bring English law on *ultra vires* into conformity with European Community law as contained in the First Company Law Directive (68/151/EEC) (as amended).

2–29   Sections 108 to 112 of the Companies Act 1989, which came into force in 1991,[71] have further modified the effect of the *ultra vires* doctrine. Section 108 replaces s.35 of the Companies Act 1985 with a cluster of new provisions, ss.35–35B. Under s.35 in its present form, the validity of an act done by a company shall not be called into question on the ground of lack of capacity by reason of anything in the company's memorandum.[72] Thus, a guarantee granted by a company *ultra vires* is no longer void.[73] Section 35 does not, however, prevent a guarantee being challenged on the grounds that it involved an *abuse of power* by *the directors* of the guarantor company.[74]

2–30   Sections 35A and 35B provide protection for third parties in their dealings with companies. So far as persons dealing with a company in good faith are concerned, the power of the board of directors to bind the company, or authorise others to do so, is deemed to be free of any limitation under the company's constitution.[75] And a person shall not be regarded as acting in bad faith by reason only of knowledge that an act is beyond the powers of the directors under the company's constitution.[76] Indeed, a third party is not even bound to inquire whether the transaction is permitted by the company's memorandum or whether there is any limitation on the powers of the board of directors to bind the company or authorise others to do so.[77]

---

[70] *Macgregor v Dover and Deal Rly Co* (1852) 18 Q.B. 618; 28 L.J. Q.B. 69; 118 E.R. 233; *Ashbury Rly Carriage Co v Riche* (1875) L.R. 7 H.L. 653 at 693–694; *Re Cleveland Trust* [1991] B.C.C. 33.

[71] See Companies Act 1989 (Commencement No.8 and Transitional and Saving Provisions) Order 1990 SI 1990/2569, art.4. The Commencement Order preserves the operation of s.35 of the Companies Act 1985 in its original form in respect of "any act done by a company prior to February 4, 1991": SI 1990/2569, art.7(i).

[72] Sections 35 and 35A of the Companies Act 1985 do not apply to the acts of a company which is a charity except in favour of a person who (a) gives full consideration in relation to the act in question; and (b) does not know that the act in question is not permitted by the company's memorandum or is beyond the powers of the directors, or who does not at the time know that the company is a charity.

[73] The better view is that the section prevents both the company and the third party raising the company's lack of capacity as a defence.

[74] See *Rolled Steel Products (Holdings) Ltd v British Steel Corporation* [1986] Ch. 246 at 302–304

[75] Companies Act 1985, s.35A(1), inserted by s.108 of the Companies Act 1989. This section is intended to enable people to deal with the company in good faith without being adversely affected by any limitations on the company's capacity or its rules of internal management: *TCB Ltd v Gray* (1986) 2 B.C.C. 99,044.

[76] Companies Act 1985, s.35A(2), inserted by s.108 of the Companies Act 1989.

[77] Companies Act 1985, s.35B, inserted by s.108 of the Companies Act 1989.

However, the *ultra vires* doctrine will still operate *within* the company **2–31** for the purpose of defining the directors' duties to their shareholders because the directors are still required to observe any limitations on their powers flowing from the company's memorandum.[78] The company may, by special resolution, ratify any action by the directors beyond the company's capacity but this will not absolve the directors or any other person of any liability incurred as a result of an *ultra vires* transaction.[79]

Moreover, a member of the company may bring proceedings to restrain **2–32** the granting of a guarantee which would be beyond the company's capacity or beyond the powers of the directors.[80] However, these proceedings will not be available in relation to a guarantee which has already been granted or executed.

Where the principal contract is *ultra vires* the principal debtor company, **2–33** the guarantors may be liable if they have assumed the risk of non-payment for any reason but not if they have only assumed liability on the grounds of financial inability of the principal debtor.[81] In any event, a party may be liable as an indemnifier, as distinct from a guarantor, even if the loss arises under a principal contract that is *ultra vires*.[82]

(iv) Incorporated associations

In the United Kingdom there is no general incorporation legislation for **2–34** voluntary associations. Consequently, the legal capacity of an incorporated association to grant a guarantee will, in the absence of any specific legislation governing its operations,[83] be governed by the common law doctrine of *ultra vires*.[84]

In *Rosemary Simmons Memorial Housing Association Ltd v United* **2–35** *Dominions Trust*,[85] a charitable corporation's capacity to enter into a guarantee depended upon a construction of the objects clause in its constitution. Mervyn Davies J. was prepared to imply a power to provide guarantees as to transactions in which the corporation itself was involved. But his Lordship did not imply a power gratuitously to guarantee the liabilities of a third party with whom the corporation had no legal nexus, namely, a new, incorporated and non-charitable association which the

---

[78] Companies Act 1985, s.35(3), inserted by s.108 of the Companies Act 1989.
[79] *ibid.*
[80] Companies Act 1985, s.35(2) and s.35A(4), inserted by s.108 of the Companies Act 1989. Nor does s.35 prevent a guarantee being challenged on the grounds that it involved an *abuse of power* by the directors of the guarantor company. See *Rolled Steel Products (Holdings) Ltd v British Steel Corporation* [1986] Ch. 246 at 302–304.
[81] See *Gerrard v James* [1925] Ch. 616. See also *Heald v O'Connor* [1971] 1 W.L.R. 497 at 506. The *ultra vires* doctrine has been largely abrogated by ss.35–35B of the Companies Act 1985. See *TCB Ltd v Gray* [1985] Ch. 621; aff'd [1987] Ch. 458.
[82] See *Yeoman Credit Ltd v Latter* [1961] 1 W.L.R. 828.
[83] See, *e.g. Den Norske Creditbank v Sarawak Economic Development Corp* [1988] 2 Lloyd's Rep. 616.
[84] *Rosemary Simmons Memorial Housing Association Ltd v United Dominions Ltd* (1987) 3 B.C.C. 65, (guarantee and mortgage granted by charitable housing association in respect of the liabilities of a third party declared void).
[85] (1987) 3 B.C.C. 65.

corporation decided to use to undertake a building project. Hence, the guarantee in question was void.

2-36   On the other hand, in *Den Norske Creditbank v Sarawak Economic Development Corp*[86] the legal capacity of a statutory corporation was governed by the Act under which the corporation was constituted. That Act provided that the corporation had power:

> "to do all things expedient or reasonably necessary or incidental to the discharge of its duties, and in particular, but without prejudice to the generality of the foregoing ... (d) to guarantee, within such limits as shall be fixed by the Minister, any loans made by any bank ... for any purpose for which the corporation might itself have granted such loan."

2-37   It was argued that the corporation could only guarantee loans made by a bank, as defined in the Act, and it could only give a guarantee within a limit fixed by the relevant Minister. It was common ground that the loan was not made by a bank within the statutory definition. Nevertheless, Phillips J. gave judgment against the corporation under the guarantee since it came within the general wording of the Act granting the corporation power to do "all things expedient or reasonably necessary or incidental to the discharge of its duties".

(v) Voluntary associations

2-38   Since an unincorporated association has no legal personality it cannot give a binding guarantee unless it is authorised by statute or by rules of court. But the person or persons who actually provide the guarantee, ostensibly on behalf of the unincorporated association, may be taken to have contracted personally and they may be held personally liable on the guarantee.[87] Moreover, under the laws of agency, they may be held to have contracted on behalf of the members of the association.[88] This may render one or more of the members of the association, including the trustees of its funds, liable to be sued in a representative action to enforce the guarantee.[89]

---

[86] [1988] 2 Lloyd's Rep. 616. See also *Credit Suisse v Borough Council of Allerdale* [1995] 1 Lloyd's Rep. 315.
[87] *Bradley Egg Farm Ltd v Clifford* [1943] 2 All E.R. 378, CA. See also *Carlton Cricket & Football Social Club v Joseph* [1970] V.R. 487 and *Smith v Yarnold* [1969] 2 N.S.W.R. 410.
[88] *Ideal Films Ltd v Richards* [1927] 1 K.B. 374. See also J.F. Keeler, "Contractual Actions for Damages Against Unincorporated Associations" (1971) 34 Mod L.R. 615.
[89] See, *e.g.* CPR, r.19.6(1) and (5). As to *ultra vires* guarantees given by charitable housing associations, see *Rosemary Simmonds Memorial Housing Assocation Ltd v United Dominion Trust Ltd* [1987]1 All E.R. 281.

(vi) Government guarantees and guarantees by public authorities

Guarantees given by the government in respect of funds raised by, or financial accommodation afforded to, public authorities or other bodies take one of three forms.[90] The first type depends upon the provision of the Act constituting the public authority. The second type depends upon the terms of legislation establishing central borrowing authorities to co-ordinate and control the raising of capital by public authorities. These central borrowing authorities may be empowered to raise funds or obtain financial accommodation as agents of their respective public authorities or to advance the funds they raise directly to the public authorities.[91] The relevant legislation usually provides an express statutory guarantee of specified obligations of the borrowing authority, or expressly empowers a government official, usually the Chancellor, to execute a formal guarantee for and on behalf of the government.[92]

2–39

The capacity of the government to provide guarantees of the first two types depends upon the construction of the relevant enabling legislation in each case. As the guarantees are intended to support the public authority in achieving its public purposes, there is no doubt that this legislation is within the constitutional competency of Parliament.[93] But if the statutory power is limited to guaranteeing the raising of money by direct borrowings, or the issue of prescribed securities, it will not extend to guarantees of more sophisticated fundraising techniques such as the discounting of negotiable instruments.[94] Moreover, the statutory authority to support the fundraising of public authorities and other bodies may be limited to the provision of a simple guarantee, as distinct from a guarantee which contains an indemnity clause.[95] The powers of public authorities created by, or pursuant to, legislation are limited to those that are directly conferred on them by the relevant legislation and those that are fairly incidental to the express powers.[96] As Phillips J. observed in *Den*

2–40

---

[90] See generally the excellent article by M. Breheny and J. Beaven, "Australian Federal and State Government Guarantees.—A Legal Overview" (1986) 4 J.I.B.L. 231, on which this section draws heavily. See also M. Breheny, "Government Guarantees—An Overview" (1986) 1 (No. 5) Banking Law Bulletin 76; R.I. Milliner, "Government Guarantees" (Law Society of Western Australia, Continuing Legal Education: General Services 1989); E. Nosworthy, "Contracts with Governments—Some Problems Relating to Crown Capacity in Australia" in Papers Presented at the 22nd Australian Legal Convention, Brisbane 1983 (Law Council of Australia, 1984), p.97.

[91] See M. Breheny and J. Beaven, "Australian Federal and State Government Guarantees—A Legal Overview" (1986) 4 JIBL 231 at 232. For a discussion of the third type of government guarantee see para.2–46.

[92] M. Breheny and J. Beaven, "Australian Federal and State Government Guarantees—A Legal Overview" (1986) 4 J.I.B.L. 231 at 232.

[93] See R.I. Milliner, "Government Guarantees", above n.90.

[94] See *Chow Yoong Hong v Choong Fah Rubber Manufactory* [1962] A.C. 209; *Re Securitibank Ltd (No. 2)* [1978] 2 N.Z.L.R. 136 and *Brick & Pipe Industries Ltd v Occidental Life Nominees Pty Ltd* (1991) 9 A.C.L.C. 324.

[95] See above, para.1–106. See also M. Breheny and J. Beaven, "Australian Federal and State Government Guarantees—A Legal Overview" (1986) 4 JIBL 231 at 233.

[96] *New South Wales v Bardolph* (1934) 52 C.L.R. 455 at 496 *per* Rich J.; *A-G v Great Eastern Railway Co* (1880) 5 App. Cas. 473 at 478; *A-G v Crayford UDC* [1962] Ch. 575. See also

Norske Creditbank v Sarawak Economic Development Corp,[97] "if a statute is to prevent a statutory company from exercising powers which are naturally expedient for the pursuit of its objects clear wording is required".[98]

2–41 Moreover, the mere fact that there is a statutory requirement that a minister of the Crown satisfies or approves any contract in which a Crown corporation is a party is not sufficient to render any contract entered into without such approval *ultra vires*.[99]

2–42 However, in *Sutton LBC v Morgan Grenfell & Co Ltd*[1] the Court of Appeal held that the Housing Associations Act 1985 only enabled a local authority to guarantee loans taken out by housing associations registered under s.4 of the Act. These express restrictions on how local authorities were to discharge their function of providing accommodation for the homeless were not overridden by the power of local authorities under s.111 of the Local Government Act 1972 to incur financial obligations to facilitate the discharge of their functions.

2–43 A local authority cannot circumvent restrictions on its borrowing or investment powers by guaranteeing the debts of a limited liability company formed specifically to carry out unauthorised activities.[2] Even a broad power "to do anything (whether or not involving the ... borrowing ... of money ...) which is calculated to facilitate, or is conducive or incidental to" the discharge of the local authority's functions must be construed in the light of the relevant statutory provisions, particularly the restrictions placed on the authority's borrowing and investment powers.[3] Accordingly, a local authority has no implied power to discharge its statutory functions by forming a limited liability company and guaranteeing the company's debts. Any such guarantee is *ultra vires* and void,[4] and an estoppel will not cure this invalidity.[5]

2–44 The system of Parliamentary control of supply expenditure through approval of Estimates does not prevent the government from entering into

---

Hazell v Hammersmith & Fulham London Borough Council [1992] 2 A.C. 1. In that case, the House of Lords held that a local council, which had in good faith exceeded its powers, was not empowered to take such steps as were necessary to mitigate the loss caused by its *ultra vires* actions. It would be difficult to apply this proposition to an *ultra vires* guarantee. See also M. Pearce, "Hammersmith and Fulham" (1991) 6 B.L.B. 61.

[97] [1988] 2 Lloyd's Rep. 616.
[98] *ibid.* at 620.
[99] *Australian Broadcasting Corp v Redmere Pty Ltd* (1988) 166 C.L.R. 454.
[1] [1997] 6 Bank L.R. 156. See also *Crédit Suisse v Waltham Forest LBC* [1997] Q.B. 362.
[2] *Crédit Suisse v Waltham Forest London Borough Council* [1996] 4 All E.R. 176; *Crédit Suisse v Allerdale Borough Council* [1997] Q.B. 306 at 332; *Wandsworth London Borough Council v Winder* [1985] A.C. 461; *Hazell v Hammersmith and Fulham London Borough Council* [1992] 2 A.C. 1; *R. v Richmond upon Thames London Borough Council, Ex p. McCarthy & Stone (Developments) Ltd* [1992] A.C. 48. See also P. Cane, "Do Banks Dare Lend to Local Authorities?" (1994) 110 L.Q.R. 514. See also Local Government Act 1972, s.111 and Local Government (Miscellaneous Provisions) Act 1976, s.19. *Cf. Den Norske Creditbank v Sarawak Economic Development Corporation* [1989] 2 Lloyd's Rep. 35.
[3] *ibid.*
[4] *Crédit Suisse v Waltham Forest London Borough Council* [1996] 4 All E.R. 176. See also *Sutton London Borough Council v Morgan Grenfell Co Ltd, The Times*, November 7, 1996.
[5] *Moss Steamship Co Ltd v Whinney* [1912] A.C. 254 at 266; *British Mutual Banking Co v Charnwood Forest Ry Co* (1887) 18 Q.B.D. 714.

a guarantee before an Estimate has been approved.[6] When Parliament approves the Estimates and passes an Appropriation Act in a particular financial year, it is authorising *expenditure* in that year, not financial *commitments* to be undertaken in that year.[7] Consequently, appropriation is not necessary for the validity of a government guarantee, and the government can enter into a guarantee years before it is necessary for it to obtain approval of the Estimates, including the actual liability under the guarantee.[8]

Another basis on which it is sometimes alleged that governments lack the capacity to provide an effective guarantee is the doctrine of executive necessity.[9] The rationale of this doctrine is that it is not competent for the government to fetter its future executive action. It cannot by contract hamper its freedom to respond to the needs of the community and the welfare of the State.[10] But the doctrine of executive necessity should not apply to a commercial contract like a guarantee because this would offend the public policy that the parties should be held to their bargain and it might jeopardise the government's commercial reputation.[11] A guarantee should not be seen as an impedient to executive action or a fetter on the government's discretion[12] but rather as a legitimate exercise of freedom of executive action.[13] It appears, therefore, that the doctrine of executive necessity should not be invoked to deny the Crown or the government the power to provide a guarantee.

2–45

The third type of government guarantee is an executive guarantee furnished without any express statutory authorisation by a government[14] or a statutory authority apparently representing the Crown.[15] The Government has power to enter into contracts without any specific statutory authorisation or any prior appropriation of funds in the ordinary

2–46

---

[6] C. Turpin, *Government Contracts*, p.25.

[7] *ibid.*

[8] *Commercial Cable Co v Government of Newfoundland* [1916] 2 A.C. 610 at 617; *Kidman v Commonwealth of Australia* (1925) 32 A.L.R. 1 at 2–3; Mitchell, *The Contracts of Public Authorities* (1954), pp.70–73; Street, *Governmental Liability: A Comparative Study* (1953), pp.87–89. Cf. *Churchward v The Queen* (1865) L.R. 1 Q.B. 173 at 209.

[9] See generally C. Turpin, *Government Contracts*, pp.19–25 and N. Seddon, *Government Contracts: Federal, State and Local* (2nd ed., 1999), pp.169–172; P. W. Hogg, "The Doctrine of Executive Necessity in the Law of Contract" (1970) 44 A.L.J. 154.

[10] *Rederiaktiebolaget Amphitrite v The King* [1921] 3 K.B. 500 at 503 *per* Rowlatt J.

[11] *ibid.*

[12] This principle against contracts fettering the exercise of discretions by public authorities is closely related to the doctrine of executive necessity: *Ayr Harbour Trustees v Oswald* (1883) 8 App. Cas. 623 at 634 and C. Turpin, *Government Contracts*, p.22.

[13] C. Turpin, *Government Contracts*, p.25.

[14] M. Breheny and J. Beaven, "Australian Federal and State Government Guarantees—A Legal Overview" (1986) 4 J.I.B.L. 231.

[15] The general test for determining whether or not a statutory authority is an agent or representative of the Crown focuses upon the degree of control which the Crown is entitled to assert over the authority's statutory activities: M. Breheny and J. Beaven, "Australian Federal and State Government Guarantees—A Legal Overview" (1986) 4 J.I.B.L. 231; P.W. Hogg, *Liability of the Crown* (1971), pp.213–214. See also *Re Kearney Ex p. Japanangka* (1984) 58 A.L.J.R. 231; *Sharkey v Fisher* (1980) 33 A.L.R. 173; *Townsville Hospitals Board v Council of the City of Townsville* (1982) 56 A.L.J.R. 789; *Bradken Consolidated Ltd v Broken Hill Pty Co Ltd* (1979) 145 C.L.R. 107; *Superannuation Fund Investment Trust v Commissioner of Stamps (SA)* (1979) 26 A.L.R. 99.

course of government administration.[16] This falls within its unwritten constitutional power to attend to peace, order and good government of its constituency.

(vii) Express clauses in the guarantees relating to incapacity

2–47   To avoid problems of incapacity, modern guarantees often contain a clause along the following lines:

> "This guarantee shall be deemed to be fully effectual between the principal debtor, the creditor and the guarantor/s irrespective of whether it may in fact be of no effect (or be unenforceable) for any reason whatsoever including the infancy or other incapacity of the principal debtor or the guarantor/s or either or any of them to enter into the principal transaction hereby secured or this guarantee or any collateral security."

2–48   Where the principal contract is defective due to the principal's incapacity, such a clause may estop any person who signs the guarantee from arguing that it is invalid on that basis.[17] But the clause is not likely to avail the creditor where the guarantee is invalid due to the guarantor's incapacity because the clause, being part of the guarantee, will itself be of no effect.

7. CONSIDERATION

2–49   Unless the contract of guarantee is under seal,[18] it must be supported by consideration.[19] The onus of proof is on the claimant to establish that there is sufficient consideration.[20] The consideration for the guarantee must

---

[16] *New South Wales v Bardolph* (1934) 52 C.L.R. 455. The absence of an appropriation may, however, prevent the government from satisfying a debt owing under a contract: *Kidman v Commonwealth* (1925) 37 C.L.R. 233; *New South Wales v Bardolph* (1934) 52 C.L.R. 455 and N. Seddon, *Government Contracts* (The Federation Press, Sydney, 1999), para.206.

[17] See *Alliance Acceptance Co Ltd v Hinton* (1964) 1 D.C.R. (NSW) 5.

[18] Deeds executed by individuals need not be executed under seal: Law of Property (Miscellaneous Provisions) Act 1989, s.1(1)(b), which came into force on July 31, 1990. Moreover, on the same date the requirement of a company to have a common seal was abolished. However, deeds are still commonly referred to as "documents executed under seal": G. Andrews and R. Millett, *Law of Guarantees* (3rd ed., 2000), para.2.08.

[19] *Barrell v Trussell* (1811) 4 Taunt 117; 128 E.R. 273; *French v French* (1841) 2 Man. & G. 644; 133 E.R. 903; *Sheffield v Castleton (Lord)* (1700) 2 Vern. 393; 23 ER 853; *Saunders v Wakefield* (1821) 4 B. & Ald. 595; 106 E.R. 1054. Note, however, the possibility of establishing the existence of a guarantee by means of the doctrine of estoppel by convention; that is, if the parties assume the guarantee is valid and binding, whilst it is in fact not supported by consideration, the guarantee may still be effective in some circumstances: See Goff J. in *Amalgamated Investment & Property Co Ltd (in liq) v Texas Commerce International Bank Ltd* [1982] Q.B. 84 at 108 and see above, para.1–38 and *Performance Systems Inc v Pezim* [1971] 5 W.W.R. 433.

[20] *Lau v Leff* (1968) 87 W.N. (Pt. 2) NSW 305; [1968] 2 N.S.W.R. 367 (this case, in fact, concerned a contract of indemnity).

move from the person to whom the guarantee is given;[21] although indeed the whole consideration need not move from that person.[22] In the context of a guarantee, the consideration will be in the form of the creditor incurring some detriment in reliance on the promise to guarantee,[23] rather than conferring a benefit upon the guarantor.[24] Indeed, the notion that the guarantor obtains a direct advantage from the arrangement has been held to be inconsistent with the concept of a guarantee enforceable under the Statute of Frauds.[25]

If there is a total failure of the consideration for a guarantee, it cannot be enforced.[26]   **2–50**

In recent times, the doctrine of consideration has been considerably eroded by the decision in *Williams v Roffey Bros & Nicholls (Contractors) Ltd*[27] where the Court of Appeal held that the "practical benefit" to the promisor from the promisee's performance of an existing contractual   **2–51**

---

[21] *Dutchman v Tooth* (1839) 5 Bing N.C. 577; 132 E.R. 1222 (CP); *Fleming v Bank of New Zealand* [1900] A.C. 577 (PC) (consideration moving from creditor's agent sufficient); *Rattenbury v Fenton* (1834) 3 My. & K. 505; 40 E.R. 192 (where there was no consideration passing from the creditor to the promisor or to any other party because the creditor was unaware of the promise); *Bank of Montreal v Sperling Hotel Co* (1973) 36 D.L.R. (3d) 130 (Man). Consideration moving from the principal debtor to the guarantor will not suffice: *Dutchman v Tooth* (1839) 5 Bing N.C. 577; 132 E.R. 1222; *Fleming v Bank of New Zealand* [1900] A.C. 577 at 587, PC; *French v French* (1841) 2 Man. & G. 644; 133 ER 903; *Astley Industrial Trust Ltd v Grimston Electric Tools Ltd* (1965) 109 S.J. 149; *Power v Ahern* [1935] Q.W.N. 22 (Aust).
[22] *Hodson v Lee* (1847) 9 L.T.O.S. 312 at 313, *per* Patterson J.
[23] Any damage to another or suspension or forbearance of another's right is a sufficient foundation for an undertaking: *Pillans and Rose v Van Mierop and Hopkins* (1765) 3 Burr 1663; 97 E.R. 1035. See also *Jones v Ashburnham* (1804) 4 East 455; 102 E.R. 905; *Bailey v Croft* (1812) 4 Taunt 611; 128 E.R. 470. Even the delivery up of a guarantee which does not comply with the Statute of Frauds may be good consideration for a fresh guarantee: *Haigh v Brooks* (1839) 10 Ad. & E. 309 at 334; 113 E.R. 119 at 128.
[24] *Pillans and Rose v Van Mierop and Hopkins* (1765) 3 Burr 1663; 97 E.R. 1035; *Erskine-Smith Co v Bordeleau* [1929] 2 D.L.R. 877. See also *Fitzgerald v Dressler* (1859) 7 C.B. (NS) 374; 141 E.R. 861; *Davys v Buswell* [1913] 2 KB 47. It is not necessary for either party to a contract to derive any direct or personal benefit from the transaction: *Fred T. Brooks Ltd v Claude Neon Gen Advertising Ltd* [1932] 2 D.L.R. 45, Ont CA. See also *Seaton v Heath* [1899] 1 Q.B. 782 at 793 *per* Romer L.J. (reversed on other grounds in *Seaton v Burnand* [1900] AC 135 (HL)); *Royal Bank v Kiska* [1967] 2 O.R. 379 (CA). It is not necessary for individual guarantors to derive any benefit from their guarantees, although some sureties are compensated for assuming their liabilities as guarantors. See L. Aitken, "The Compensated Surety" [1992] L.M.C.L.Q. 177; *Tricontinental Corp Ltd v HDFI Ltd* (1990) 21 N.S.W.L.R. 689, CA; *Corumo Holdings Pty Ltd v C. Itoh* (1991) 24 N.S.W.L.R. 370.
[25] See below, Ch. 3.
[26] *Cooper v Joel* (1859) 1 De G.F. & J. 240; 45 E.R. 350; *Cornell v Bradford* [1929] Q.W.N. 45; *Walton v Cook* (1888) 40 Ch. D. 325; *Rolt v Cozens* (1856) 18 C.B. 673; 139 E.R. 1534. *Cf. Re Barber & Co, Ex p. Agra Bank* (1870) L.R. 9 Eq. 725 at 734; *Chan v Cresdon Pty Ltd* (1989) 168 C.L.R. 242; *Latter v White* (1870) L.R. 8 Q.B. 622; 5 H.L. 572. *Cf. Glegg v Gilbey* (1876) 2 Q.B.D. 6 and 209 (where the guarantor remained liable because the creditor was not paid the amount promised under a deed of composition). See also *Ex p. Gilbey* (1878) 8 Ch. D. 248; Where a debtor defaults in paying an instalment due under a composition or scheme governed by the Bankruptcy Act 1914, the court can cancel the scheme and declare the debtor bankrupt, thereby discharging the guarantors of their liabilities under the composition or scheme: *Walton v Cook* (1888) 40 Ch. D. 325. *Cf. Cole v Lynn* [1942] 1 K.B. 142, where creditors covenanted under a deed of arrangement not to sue the principal debtor but expressly preserved their rights against the surety. The surety was held to be entitled to an indemnity from the principal debtor in respect of any payments made to the creditors under the deed.
[27] [1990] 1 All E.R. 512, CA.

obligation can provide consideration for the promisor's promise to pay the promisee more than the original contract price.[28] Interestingly, the Court of Appeal in *Re Selectmove Ltd*[29] was not prepared to extend this principle by allowing a promise to accept part payment of a debt to extinguish the original obligation to pay the whole debt. Any such extension would be inconsistent with *Foakes v Beer*,[30] where the House of Lords held that the payment of a smaller sum than the amount due does not discharge the debt because the debtor provides no consideration for the creditor's promise to accept less than the original debt. The reconciliation of these seemingly inconsistent decisions may lie in the field of promissory estoppel.[31] If they cannot be reconciled, there is more to be said for retaining the rule in *Foakes v Beer* than extending *Williams v Roffey Bros & Nicholls (Contractors) Ltd* to cover an agreement to accept less as well as an agreement to pay more.[32]

2–52   For the present, it is sufficient to note that neither strand of authority creates problems in the tripartite arrangement which is inherent in a guarantee. The performance of an existing contractual obligation by the principal debtor to repay a loan, to complete a building contract or to comply with its covenants under a lease will not provide consideration for a guarantee of the principal debt or obligation. As we have seen, the consideration for a guarantee must move from the promisee,[33] *i.e.* the creditor, although it need not move in favour of the guarantor. The consideration for a guarantee is not provided by the principal debtor performing an existing contractual obligation to the creditor. Equally, the performance of an existing contractual obligation by the creditor to provide further advances to the principal debtor does not provide consideration for a new guarantee of the principal debt.[34] But an agreement to provide further advances beyond the agreed amount of an existing loan facility or to extend the time for payment under an existing loan facility could clearly provide consideration for a guarantee of the principal debtor's new obligation.[35]

2–53   Similarly, an agreement to perform an existing legal duty, for example, to comply with a subpoena, could constitute good consideration for a guarantee of payment for compliance if the agreement imposes a more onerous obligation or an obligation to perform the duty in a particular way, for example, an obligation not merely to produce documents but to

[28] See generally N. J. Hird and A. Blair, "Minding Your Own Business–Williams v Roffey Re-visited: Consideration Reconsidered" [1996] J.B.L. 254 and J. W. Carter, A. Phang and J. Poole, "Reactions to Williams v Roffey" (1995) 8 J.C.L. 248.

[29] [1995] 1 W.L.R. 474. See also *Re C (A Debtor)* (unreported Court of Appeal, May 11, 1994) to similar effect.

[30] (1884) 9 App. Cas. 605.

[31] See J. O'Sullivan, "In Defence of Foakes v Beer" (1996) C.L.J. 219 at 226–227; N. J. Hird and A. Blair, "Minding Your Own Business–Williams v Roffey Re-visited: Consideration Reconsidered" [1996] J.B.L. 254.

[32] J. O'Sullivan, "In Defence of Foakes v Beer" (1996) C.L.J. 219.

[33] See above, para.2–49.

[34] This does not constitute any detriment to the creditor. See *Pillans and Rose v Van Mierop and Hopkins* (1765) 3 Burr 1663; 97 E.R. 1035; *Jones v Ashburnham* (1804) 4 East 455; 102 E.R. 905.

[35] See K.P. McGuinness; *The Law of Guarantee* (2nd ed., 1996), para.4.184.

explain them.[36] Moreover, where a person contracts with a third party to perform an existing legal duty, this can constitute consideration for a guarantee of payment for the service because it exposes the creditor to a private action by the third party to enforce the duty.[37] Conversely, an agreement by a creditor to accept a promise to pay part of the existing principal debt may be good consideration for a new guarantee of that part of the debt because the creditor is agreeing to accept less in return for the right to recover the lesser amount from the principal debtor *and* the guarantor.

(i) Evidence of consideration

The Statute of Frauds 1677 was intended to deal with the mischief   2–54
of frauds and perjuries and to avoid actions to enforce promises based on illegal consideration.[38] Judicial interpretation of s.4 of that Act required the consideration for the promise of a guarantor to appear in the guarantee itself.[39] This interpretation allowed sureties to escape liability through many unjust and technical defences.[40] Accordingly, in 1856, s.3 of the *Mercantile Law Amendment Act* was passed. It provided, in effect, that no promise to answer for the debt, default or miscarriage of another was to be deemed unenforceable by action because of the fact that the consideration for the promise did not appear in writing.

While it is no longer necessary under this legislation for the   2–55
consideration to appear on the face of the instrument of guarantee,[41] (which can then be proved by parol evidence)[42] the parties may specify the consideration in the document itself. If they do so, they may be bound by their clear statement of the consideration and may not be allowed to dispute it if, for instance, it is challenged on grounds of illegality or because the expressed consideration is past consideration.[43]

---

[36] *Glasbrook Brothers Ltd v Glamorgan County Council* [1925] A.C. 270. *Cf. Collins v Godefroy* (1831) 1 B. & Ad. 950; 109 E.R. 1040 (where the plaintiff had done no more than perform an existing legal duty).
[37] K.P. McGuinness, *The Law of Guarantee* (2nd ed., 1996), para.4.190.
[38] *Wain v Warlters* (1804) 5 East 10 at 17–18; 102 E.R. 972 at 975.
[39] See, *e.g. Morley v Boothby* (1825) 3 Bing 108; 130 E.R. 455; *Saunders v Wakefield* (1821) 4 B & Ald 595; 106 E.R. 1054. It was necessary for the agreement or memorandum to show the consideration expressly or by necessary inference: *Raikes v Todd* (1838) 3 Ad. & E. 846; 112 E.R. 1058.
[40] See *Halsbury's Laws of England* (4th ed., 1978), Vol. 20, para.122, n.1.
[41] *ibid*; *Vetro Glass Pty Ltd v Fitzpatrick* [1963] S.R. (NSW) 697; *Elanco Pty Ltd v Wyman* (unreported, Qld Sup Ct, Connolly J. No.1985 of 1978). This is so even in those jurisdictions where contracts which cannot be performed within one year must be in writing: *Barron v Geddes* (1897) 19 A.L.T. 27; 3 A.L.R. 159. But where one guarantee is substituted for another, the consideration supporting the original may be relied upon to support its substitute: *Northern Crown Bank v Elford* (1917) 34 D.L.R. 280.
[42] *Lilley v Midland Brick Co Pty Ltd* (1993) 9 W.A.R. 339. Extrinsic evidence is admissible to prove the consideration for a guarantee. See *Pao On v Lau Yiu Long* [1980] A.C. 614 at 631–632 *per* Lord Scarman.
[43] *Elanco Pty Ltd v Wyman* (unreported, Qld Sup Ct, Connolly J., No. 1985 of 1978); *Oldershaw v King* (1857) 2 H. & N. 517; 157 E.R. 213.

2–56   The consideration supporting the guarantee should not be a matter of conjecture.[44] The court will examine the guarantee itself in the light of the surrounding circumstances, for example, the state of the accounts between the parties.[45] In construing the consideration in the guarantee, the court will attempt to give business sense and efficacy to the agreement,[46] and parol evidence is admissible to explain and interpret the consideration where it is ambiguously expressed.[47]

(ii) Common forms of consideration

(a) *Entering into the principal transaction or transactions, or agreeing to do so*

2–57   The usual form of consideration provided by the creditor is the creditor's action in entering into the principal transaction (for example, by the supply of particular goods;[48] the making of advances to the principal;[49] the entering into a lease;[50] or, in a fidelity guarantee, by the creditor entering

---

[44] See *Raikes v Todd* (1838) 8 Ad. & E. 846; 112 E.R. 1058.

[45] *Bell v Welch* (1850) 9 C.B. 154; 137 E.R. 851. See also *Lisala Pty Ltd v Britannia Ave Pty Ltd* (unreported, SA Sup Ct, Full Ct, May 20, 1992). The word "guarantee" does not of itself import a consideration: *Johnson v Fitzgerald* (1897) 29 N.S.R. 339, CA; *Guthrie v O'Connor* (1875) 36 U.C.Q.B. 372, CA.

[46] *S. H. Lock Discounts & Credits Pty Ltd v Miles* [1963] V.R. 656 at 658 *per* O'Bryan J. See also *Lisala Pty Ltd v Britania Ave Pty Ltd* (unreported, SA Sup Ct, Full Ct, May 20, 1992), where a particularly inelegant statement of consideration was construed as the creditor's promise to deliver the balance of the goods to the principal. The construction placed on the words of the guarantee will not necessarily reflect grammatical strictness; rather it will explain the intention of the parties: *Goldshede v Swan* (1847) 1 Exch. 154; 154 E.R. 65.

[47] E.g. *Broom v Batchelor* (1856) 1 H. & N. 255; 156 ER 1199. See also *Wynne v Hughes* (1873) 21 W.R. 628 (Ex); *Crears v Hunter* (1887) 19 Q.B.D. 341, CA. Extrinsic evidence is admissible to prove the consideration for a guarantee. See *Pao On v Lau Yiu Long* [1980] A.C. 614 at 631–632 *per* Lord Scarman. However, the general rule is that extrinsic evidence of the parties' intentions and negotiations is not admissible. See *Prenn v Simmonds* [1971] 1 W.L.R. 1381 at 1385 *per* Lord Wilberforce; *Lep Air Services Ltd v Rolloswin Ltd* [1973] A.C. 331 at 354. See below, paras 5–05 to 5–07.

[48] *Mockett v Ames* (1871) 23 L.J. 729; *Morrell v Cowan* (1877) 7 Ch. D. 151; *Wood v Benson* (1831) 2 C. & J. 94; 149 E.R. 40; *Johnston v Nicholls* (1845) 1 C.B. 251; 135 E.R. 535; *Raikes v Todd* (1838) 8 Ad. & E. 846 at 857; 112 E.R. 1058 at 1062 *per* Patterson J.; *Robertson v Healy* (1866) 5 SCR (NSW) 290; *Chapman v Sutton* (1846) 2 C.B. 634; 135 E.R. 1095; *Bank of Montreal v Germain* [1976] W.W.D. 75 (Alta).

[49] *Hartland v Jukes* (1863) 1 H. & C. 667; 158 E.R. 1052; *Grahame v Grahame* (1887) 19 L.R. Ir. 249; *Edwards v Jeavons* (1848) 8 C.B. 436; 137 E.R. 579; *Broom v Batchelor* (1856) 1 H. & N. 255; 156 E.R. 1199; *Smith v Passmore* (1883) 4 L.R. (NSW) 274; *S. H. Lock Discounts & Credits Pty Ltd v Miles* [1963] V.R. 656; *Westhead v Sproson* (1861) 6 H & N 728; 158 E.R. 301. See also *Mockett v Ames* (1871) 23 L.T. 729. It may be different where the creditor has reason to believe that the guarantor expects further advances to be made but does not make any further advances, see *Bank of Montreal v Sperling Hotel Co Ltd* (1973) 36 D.L.R. (3d) 130. A guarantee granted in consideration of further advances or supplies by the creditor to the principal debtor can extend to existing debts and liabilities, even if there is no obligation to provide the further advances or supplies: *Russell v Moseley* (1822) 3 Brod & B. 211; 129 E.R. 1264; *Kennaway v Treleavan* (1839) 5 M. & W. 498; 151 E.R. 211; *Johnston v Nicholls* (1845) 1 C.B. 251; 135 E.R. 535; *White v Woodward* (1848) 5 C.B. 810; 136 E.R. 1097; *Oldershaw v King* (1857) 2 H. & N. 399, 517; 157 E.R. 165 and 213; *Harris v Venables* (1872) L.R. 7 Ex. 235.

[50] *Chan v Cresdon Pty Ltd* (1989) 168 C.L.R. 242.

into a contract of employment with the principal).[51] This is often stated to be the consideration in the guarantee. In cases in which the consideration is the actual act of entering into the principal transaction, the guarantee will only become binding when that act occurs, that is, by the actual supply of goods, the actual making of advances or entering into the lease.[52] If the stipulated act does not take place, the consideration for the guarantee will totally fail.[53]

In each case, a precise construction of the statement of consideration is necessary in order to determine if the relevant act has occurred. In *Gobblers Inc Pty Ltd v Stevens*,[54] for example, where the consideration was stated in the guarantee to be "granting this lease to the lessee", it was held that there was no consideration when no lease was executed at all and the lessee was simply allowed into occupation, despite the fact that a statutory tenancy was thereby created. On the other hand, in *Chan v Cresdon Pty Ltd*,[55] where the consideration was similarly expressed to be "entering into this lease", the execution of an instrument equivalent to an equitable lease was held to satisfy this description, even though other wording in the guarantee indicated the guarantor would only be liable for obligations arising pursuant to a registered lease.[56]

2–58

Instead of the act of entering into the principal transaction, the consideration may be the promise of the creditor to enter into the principal transaction in the future, and the contract of guarantee will then become binding when the creditor so agrees rather than at the later date of entering into the transaction.[57]

2–59

---

[51] See *Newbury v Armstrong* (1829) 6 Bing 201; 130 E.R. 1257; *Kennaway v Treleavan* (1839) 5 M. & W. 498; 151 E.R. 211. Consideration may also be found in the actions of a creditor company in ensuring that goods be supplied by one of its subsidiary companies to the principal: *Bunnings Ltd v Ravi* (unreported, WA Sup Ct, January 27, 1994).

[52] *Greenham Ready Mixed Concrete Ltd v CAS (Industrial Development) Ltd* (1965) 109 S.J. 209 (the consideration was "recommencing to supply" the principal); *National Australia Bank Ltd v McKay* (1995) A.T.P.R. 41–409 (consideration constituted by provision of "banking accommodation"); *Hill Equipment & Refrigeration Co Pty Ltd v Nuco Pty Ltd* (1992) 110 F.L.R. 25; *Chan v Cresdon Pty Ltd* (1989) 168 C.L.R. 242; *Bank of Montreal v Sperling Hotel Co Ltd* (1973) 36 D.L.R. (3d) 130 (Man); *Westhead v Sproson* (1861) 6 H. & N. 728; 158 E.R. 301; *Morrell v Cowan* (1877) 6 Ch. D. 166 at 170. See also *Greenham Ready Mixed Concrete v CAS (Industrial Developments) Ltd* (1965) 109 S.J. 209.

[53] *Cornell v Bradford* [1929] Q.W.N. 45; *Cooper v Joel* (1859) 1 De G.F. & J. 240; 45 E.R. 350. Note also that a creditor who does not comply strictly with the requirement of consideration may be in breach of a condition upon which the guarantee is based: see, *e.g. Australian Joint Stock Bank v Costello* (1989) 6 W.N. (NSW) 94. See also below, para.2–89.

[54] (1994) A.N.Z. Conv R. 110. See also *Mayes v Concrete Properties Ltd* (1994) A.N.Z. Conv. R. 113; *AGC Ltd v Benson* (unreported, NSW CA, December 12, 1991).

[55] (1989) 168 C.L.R. 242. See also *National Australia Bank v McKay* (unreported, Vic Sup Ct, May 5, 1995).

[56] On the facts, there was no liability as the lease had not been registered: see below, paras 5–44 to 5–49.

[57] *Mercantile Bank of Australia Ltd v Weigall* (1895) 16 A.L.T. 192; *Farrow Mortgage Services Pty Ltd (in liquidation) v Collins* (1995) A.N.Z. Conv. R. 431 at 432. The cases cited in n.52 are properly explained on the basis that the stipulated consideration was the act of entering into the principal transaction, rather than the agreement to do so. Where the guarantee is given "in consideration of your agreeing to supply" the principal debtor but the amount to be supplied is left to the discretion of the creditor, the guarantee will only be enforceable if and when the creditor provides the supplies: *Westhead v Sproson* (1861) 6 H. & N. 728; *Morrell v Cowan* (1877) 6 Ch. D. 166 at 171. Cf. *White v Woodward* (1848) 5 C.B. 810; 136 E.R. 1097 (where the goods had already been supplied).

2–60   It has been held that the creditor's "promise to consider a request" to
enter into the principal transaction is not good consideration.[58] But if the
clause imposes an express or implied requirement that the creditor must
act bona fide or reasonably in considering a request, it is not clear why this
should be so as the argument that the consideration is illusory is then
rebutted.[59]

(b) Forbearance to sue for a past debt

2–61   If the creditor agrees to forbear from suing the principal for a past debt
or actually does so at the guarantor's express or implied request, this will
constitute good consideration[60] for a guarantee of that past debt or future
transactions, or both. The same applies if the creditor promises to give
time to the principal at the guarantor's request.[61] The mere fact of
forbearance will not be sufficient consideration; it must be at the express or
implied request of the guarantor,[62] which cannot be inferred simply from
proof of an act of forbearance.[63] The forbearance must also relate to a
serious claim honestly held, not a vexatious or frivolous matter.[64]

2–62   A promise to suspend or abandon curial proceedings against a debtor for
seizure and sale of his goods or to suspend or abandon proceedings out of
court for the appointment of a receiver to enforce a security can also

---

[58] *Coghlan v S. H. Lock (Aust) Ltd* (1987) 61 A.L.J.R. 289 at 292, disagreeing with McHugh
J.A. in the New South Wales Court of Appeal: (1985) 4 N.S.W.L.R. 158. *Cf.* G. Moss and D.
Marks, *Rowlatt on Principal and Surety* (5th ed. 1999), p.11. However, the actual advance of
money in response to the guarantors' promise does provide consideration for their liability:
Coghlan v S.H. Lock (Australia) Ltd (1986) 61 A.L.J.R. 289 at 292, PC.

[59] In another context, see *Godecke v Kirwan* (1973) 129 C.L.R. 629.

[60] *Murphy v Timms* [1987] 2 Qd. R. 550; *Miles v New Zealand Alford Estate Co* (1886) 32 Ch.
D. 266; *Colonial Bank of A/asia v Kerr* (1889) 15 V.L.R. 314; *Harris v Venables* (1872) L.R. 7
Exch. 235; *Oldershaw v King* (1857) 2 H. & N. 517; 157 E.R. 213; *Payne v Wilson* (1827) 7 B.
& C. 423; 108 ER 781; *Paulger v Butland Industries Ltd* [1989] 3 N.Z.L.R. 549; *Pacific Projects
Ltd (in liq.)* [1990] 2 Qd. R. 541. See also *Crears v Hunter* (1887) 19 Q.B.D. 341 (forbearance
to sue the principal debtor at the request of the guarantor was good consideration); *Oldershaw
v King* (1857) 2 H. & N. 517; 157 E.R. 213 (an agreement to forbear for a reasonable time was
good consideration); *Miles v New Zealand Alford Estate Co* (1886) 32 Ch. D. 266 (agreement
to abandon proceedings).

[61] *Isbell Dean (Bean) Co v Avery* [1923] 1 D.L.R. 708, CA.

[62] *Crears v Hunter* (1887) 19 Q.B.D. 341 at 346, *per* Lopes J.; *Provincial Bank of Ireland v
Donnell* [1934] N.I. 33; *Miles v New Zealand Alford Estate Co* (1886) 32 Ch. D. 266. For this
reason, the mere act of maintaining a customer's overdrawn account does not constitute
sufficient consideration for a guarantee: *Royal Bank of Canada v Salvatori* [1928] 3 W.W.R.
501 at 508, PC ("continuing to deal" with the principal debtor involves a bona fide fresh
transaction between the creditor and the principal debtor).

[63] *Murphy v Timms* [1987] 2 Qd. R. 550. See also *NZI Bank Ltd v Philpott* [1990] 2 N.Z.L.R.
403. *Cf. Glegg v Bromley* [1912] 3 K.B. 474 at 491 *per* Parker J. (where the creditor forbore to
act upon the faith of a mortgage) and *Fullerton v Provincial Bank of Ireland* [1903] A.C. 309 at
313–316.

[64] *Miles v New Zealand Alford Estate Co* (1886) 32 Ch. D. 266 applying *Callisher v
Bischoffsheim* (1870) L.R. 5 Q.B. 449; *Tempson v Knowles* (1849) 7 C.B. 651; 137 E.R. 258 (on
compromises). The guarantor carries the onus of proving that the creditor's claim was
frivolous or vexatious by way of defence: *Miles v New Zealand Alford Estate Co* (1886) 32 Ch.
D. 266 at 299 *per* Fry L.J.

sustain a guarantee.[65] The same applies to a composition with creditors,[66] and even a promise to request the sheriff to discontinue execution proceedings against the debtor will suffice.[67] A forbearance to take proceedings against a debtor company will not, however, prevent the creditor from serving a statutory demand upon it pursuant to s.268 of the Insolvency Act 1986.[68]

The forbearance or the giving of time must be on the part of the person **2–63** to whom the debt is owed or the person charged with the collection of the debt. A receiver appointed by the court has a duty to collect the debts of the estate. If that receiver gives one of the estate's debtors time to pay, this is good consideration for a guarantee of the debt.[69]

There can be no forbearance if there is no person capable of being **2–64** sued.[70] For this reason, it is not sufficient to rely upon a consideration to forbear generally. Unless there is a debtor, the claimant's forbearance to sue is no detriment to the claimant and, therefore, no consideration for a guarantee.[71] Likewise, the giving of time to the principal will not support the guarantee when the principal is not indebted to the creditor.[72] Similarly, where the consideration for the guarantee is the withdrawal of legal process it is not necessary to prove that the claim would have succeeded; it is sufficient that the abandoned suit was a "serious claim honestly made".[73]

---

[65] *Clarke & Walker Pty Ltd v Thew* (1967) 116 C.L.R. 465 (an undertaking not to sue or take any proceedings against a company does not include service of a statutory demand under s.268 of the Insolvency Act 1986 nor, similarly, extra-curial action for the recovery of a secured debt, for example, exercising a power of sale or appointing a receiver). See also *Harris v Venables* (1872) L.R. 7 Exch. 235 (where the creditor agreed to withdraw a winding up petition against the debtor company in return for the guarantee). An agreement to suspend or abandon proceedings against a debtor can support a guarantee even though the creditor may be free at a later time to revive the proceedings or bring a fresh suit against the debtor: see *Harris v Venables*, above.

[66] *Tempson v Knowles* (1849) 7 C.B. 651; 137 E.R. 258.

[67] *Pullin v Stokes* (1794) 2 Hy. Bl. 312; 126 E.R. 568.

[68] *Clarke & Walker Pty Ltd v Thew* (1967) 116 C.L.R. 465; 41 A.L.J.R. 139.

[69] *Willatts v Kennedy* (1831) 8 Bing. 5; 131 E.R. 301.

[70] *Jones v Ashburnham* (1804) 4 East 455; 102 E.R. 905. See also *Papworth v Johnson* (1614) 2 Bulst 91; 80 E.R. 984; *White v Bluett* (1853) 23 L.J. Ex. 36; *Pyers v Turner* (1592) Cro. Eliz. 283; 78 E.R. 537. Cf. *Dunton v Dunton* (1892) 18 V.L.R. 114; *Ward v Byham* [1956] 1 W.L.R. 496, CA (a promise to perform an existing duty can be good consideration). Moreover, if there is no one who can sue for the principal debt, a promise to forbear from suing is not consideration: *White v Bluett* (1853) 23 L.J. Ex. 36.

[71] *ibid.*

[72] *Pyers v Turner* (1592) Cro. Eliz. 283; 78 E.R. 537.

[73] *Miles v New Zealand Alford Estate Co* (1886) 32 Ch. D. 266 at 283 *per* Cotton L.J. and at 291 *per* Bowen L.J.; *Callisher v Bischoffscheim* (1870) L.R. 5 Q.B. 449 (forbearance to sue in respect of a disputed claim is good consideration even it turns out that the claim was completely unfounded).

2-65   The older cases suggest that a promise to forbear for a short time is too indefinite to constitute consideration for a contract of guarantee.[74] But more recent decisions indicate that the parties need not define the time given to the debtor. On this basis, agreements to forbear for a reasonable time or for a convenient time have been held sufficient to sustain a guarantee.[75]

2-66   A creditor who breaks its promise to forbear to sue for the principal debt will be unable to enforce a guarantee given in consideration of this promise.[76]

(c) Nominal consideration

2-67   The creditor may merely give a nominal consideration for the guarantee (for example, one pound), which can be stipulated in the guarantee as the consideration.[77] As Wilmot J. observed in *Pillans and Rose v Van Mierop and Hopkins*,[78] "the least spark of a consideration will be sufficient".[79] This procedure has the advantage that the guarantee becomes immediately binding and cannot be withdrawn before the creditor actually enters into the principal transaction.[80]

---

[74] See *Lutwitch v Hussey* (1583) Cro. Eliz. 19; 78 E.R. 286; *Beven v Cowling* (1626) Poph 183; 79 E.R. 1277; *Philips v Sackford* (1595) Cro. Eliz. 455; 78 E.R. 694; *Semple v Pink* (1847) 1 Exch. 74; 154 E.R. 31. *Cf. Emmott v Kearns* (1839) 5 Bing (NC) 559; 132 E.R. 1214 (agreement to forbear for two months). In *Wynne v Hughes* (1873) 21 W.R. 628 at 629, Baron Pollack opined that the effect of *Semple v Pink* had been overridden by *Oldershaw v King* (1857) 2 H. & N. 517; 157 E.R. 213. See also *Harris v Venables* (1872) L.R. 7 Exch. 235. It was argued in *Semple v Pink* that the cases in which the law implies a reasonable time are those in which the particular act requires some time to be performed. This proposition, which was apparently accepted by the court, must now be open to question. Moreover, the main question before the court in *Semple v Pink* was whether there was a variance between the guarantee proved and that set out in the declaration. If the guarantors stipulate a date on or before which they will pay and the creditor forbears until that date, the guarantee is enforceable even though it did not specify the time of forbearance: *Rolt v Cozens* (1856) 18 C.B. 673; 139 E.R. 1534. *Cf. Harris v Venables* (1872) L.R. 7 Exch. 235 (where the consideration was the withdrawal of a winding up petition, not forbearance to proceed with another petition for 18 months).

[75] *Oldershaw v King* (1857) 2 H. & N. 517; 157 E.R. 213 (where it was unnecessary to decide this point as the contract itself disclosed a sufficient consideration for the guarantee); *Mapes v Sidney* (1624) Cro. Jac. 683; 79 E.R. 592; *Barber v Mackrell* (1892) 40 W.R. 618; 41 W.R. 341. See also *Emmott v Kearns* (1839) 5 Bing (NC) 559; 132 E.R. 1214 (agreement to forbear for two months); *Johnson v Whitchcott* (1639) 1 All Abr. 24 at 33; *Beven v Cowling* (1626) Poph 183; 79 E.R. 1277; *Barber v Mackrell* (1892) 68 L.T. 29; 41 W.R. 341. See also *Wynne v Hughes* (1873) 21 WR 628; *Nikaldi Sportswear Inc v Mear* (1977) 5 B.C.L.R. 79 (Can). But note that in *Baryo Investments v Smith* (unreported, WA Sup Ct, Owen J. January 20, 1992), Owen J. indicated that "[t]here may well be circumstances in which failure to specify a minimum period during which forbearance is to operate may be fatal to the enforcement of the guarantee". However, it may be possible to construe the agreement in such a way as to imply a specific period of forbearance: See *Payne v Wilson* (1827) 7 B. & C. 423; 108 E.R. 781.

[76] *Cooper v Joel* (1859) 1 De G.F. & J. 240; 45 E.R. 350 (surety was entitled to have the guarantee delivered up to be cancelled); *Rolt v Cozens* (1856) 18 C.B. 673; 139 E.R. 1534.

[77] e.g. *Johnston v Nicholls* (1845) 1 C.B. 251; 135 E.R. 535 (small credit advances to principal debtor); *Dutchman v Tooth* (1839) 5 Bing N.C. 577; 132 E.R. 1222 (creditor advanced 2s 6d to the guarantor).

[78] (1765) 3 Burr 1663; 97 E.R. 1035.

[79] *ibid.* at 1666; 197 E.R. 1035 at 1036.

[80] See below, para.9–26, for a fuller discussion of this difficulty.

(d) Consideration in relation to negotiable instruments

In the context of negotiable instruments, some of the contractual **2–68** principles dealing with consideration remain the same, while some are modified. Section 30(1) of the Bills of Exchange Act 1882 provides that every party whose signature appears on a bill is prima facie deemed to have become a party to the bill for value. Moreover, the Act provides that valuable consideration for the bill may be constituted by any consideration sufficient to support a simple contract or by an antecedent debt or liability.[81] One general principle which remains intact is that the consideration for a promissory note given by way of guarantee must move from the promisee but it need not move in favour of the promisor.[82] In *Standard Bank v Alberta Engineering Co*,[83] two directors of a company, on being released from certain existing guarantees, executed a promissory note intended as security for the company's indebtedness to a bank. In an action by the bank on the note, the court held that the release from the existing guarantees was sufficient consideration to support the promissory note as a guarantee: the consideration for the promissory note, namely the release from the existing guarantees, moved from the promisee, that is, the creditor under those guarantees; it was not necessary for this consideration to move in favour of the promisor, namely the parties responsible under the promissory note.

Consideration in the context of negotiable instruments often takes a **2–69** simple form. Since the mere acceptance of a bill of exchange is an obligation to pay it,[84] an acceptance will bind the acceptor even if the acceptor has no funds of the drawer and even though he receives no consideration,[85] as in the case of an accommodation bill.[86] The currency and whole purpose of bills of exchange as legal institutions demand this result.[87] By the law merchant, bills of exchange are treated as special contracts even though they are merely simple contracts.[88]

The delivery of a promissory note, by which a stranger promises to pay **2–70** money to the deliverer, is good consideration for a promise and it is not necessary to prove upon what consideration the note was made.[89] Hence in *Meredith v Chute*,[90] the plaintiff was able to show that he had provided consideration for the defendant's promise simply by delivering to the defendant at his request a promissory note by one Hurst: he did not have to prove that Hurst's note was given for consideration since the defendant himself had, in effect, admitted this by giving his promise to the plaintiff.

Where a creditor undertakes to forbear to sue the principal debtor or **2–71** actually forbears to sue the debtor at the surety's express or implied

[81] See Bills of Exchange Act 1882, s27(1).
[82] See *Chitty on Contracts* (28th ed., 1999) Vol. 1, paras 3–035 and 3–037.
[83] (1917) 33 D.L.R. 542.
[84] See *Pillans v Van Mierop* (1765) 3 Burr 1663; 97 E.R. 1035.
[85] See *Simmonds v Parminter* (1747) 1 Wils K.B. 185; 95 E.R. 564.
[86] See above, para.1–59.
[87] *Pillans v Van Mierop* (1765) 3 Burr 1663; 97 E.R. 1035.
[88] *ibid.*
[89] *Meredith v Chute* (1702) 2 Ld Raym 759; 92 E.R. 7.
[90] *ibid.*

request, this constitutes a sufficient consideration for the surety's guarantee.[91] Even an agreement to forbear for an unspecified period constitutes consideration, at least where a reasonable time can be inferred or where the guarantor has benefited from the forbearance.[92] Similarly, in *Barber v Mackrell*,[93] a guarantee of the payment of some old bills was supported by a promise to draw new bills for the same amounts, even though the duration of the new bills was not specified.

2–72   Future dealings between the parties can furnish the necessary consideration.[94] In *Bank of Montreal v Germain*,[95] a consideration of future dealings was sufficient to support a promissory note. Similarly, the granting of credit or an agreement to enter into relations is sufficient consideration.[96] So too, the obtaining of bill stamps and the drawing of bills thereon at the plaintiff's own expense was sufficient consideration to sustain a guarantee of bills, which were to be drawn by the plaintiff and for which the defendant had agreed to arrange acceptances.[97]

(iii) Past consideration

2–73   A guarantee given simply for past or executed consideration will fail.[98] One initial problem is that the statement of consideration in the guarantee may itself give the appearance of being past consideration. Thus, the guarantee may be given "in consideration of an account having been opened"[99] or an "advance having been made". Although 19th-century

---

[91] G. Moss and D. Marks, *Rowlatt on Law of Principal and Surety* (5th ed., 1999), para.2–06, p.12; *Oldershaw v King* (1853) 2 H. & N. 517; *Miles v New Zealand Alford Estate Co* (1886) 32 Ch. D. 266.

[92] G. Moss and D. Marks, *Rowlatt on Law of Principal and Surety* (6th ed, 1994), para.2–06, p.13.

[93] (1892) 40 W.R. 618; 41 W.R. 341.

[94] See above, paras 2–57 to 2–60. As to promissory notes given for existing debts and further advances, see *Mayhew v Crickett* (1818) 2 Swanst 185; 36 E.R. 585; *Re Boys; Ex p. Hop Planters Co* (1870) L.R. 10 Eq. 467.

[95] [1976] W.W.D. 75 (Alta).

[96] *Lloyd's v Harper* (1880) 16 Ch. D. 290 at 319; *Bluck v Gompertz* (1852) 7 Exch. 862; 155 E.R. 85 and 1199.

[97] *Bluck v Gompertz* (1852) 7 Exch. 862; 155 E.R. 1199.

[98] *French v French* (1841) 2 Man. & G. 644; 133 E.R. 903; *Forth v Stanton* (1669) 1 Wms Saund 210; 85 E.R. 217; *Jones v Ashburnham* (1804) 4 East 455 at 463; 102 E.R. 905 at 908; *Wigan v English and Scottish Law Life Assurance Association* [1909] 1 Ch. 291 at 297; *Currie v Misa* (1875) L.R. 10 Ex. 153, affirmed on other grounds: *Misa v Currie* (1876) 1 App. Cas. 554; *Astley Industrial Trust Ltd v Grimston Electric Tools* (1965) 109 S.J. 149; *Power v Ahern* [1935] Q.W.N. 22.

   Simmons v Keating (1818) 2 Stark 426; 171 E.R. 694, which appears to be an exception to this principle, can be explained on the ground that the creditor agreed, at the guarantor's request, to supply goods to the principal debtor before the guarantee was given and the delivery of the goods did not take place until after the guarantee was given. See *Pao On v Lau Yiu Long* [1980] A.C. 614 at 628–631, PC. A promise to perform a pre-existing contractual obligation to a third party can be valid consideration: *New Zealand Shipping Co Ltd v A. M. Satterthwaite & Co Spraggon (Australia) Pty Ltd* [1975] A.C. 154 at 168, PC. *Port Jackson Stevedoring Pty Ltd v Salmond & Spraggon (Australia) Pty Ltd* (1978) 139 C.L.R. 231 at 273–274; *Pao On v Lau Yiu Long* [1980] A.C. 614 at 632, PC: *Scotson v Pegg* (1861) 6 H. & N. 295; *New Zealand Shipping Co Ltd v A. M. Satterthwaite & Co Ltd (The Eurymedon)* [1975] A.C. 154 at 168.

[99] See a similar example in *White v Bank of Victoria* (1882) 8 V.L.R. (M) 8.

authority indicates that in such a case the guarantee will fail because the parties will be bound by the statement of consideration contained in the guarantee,[1] McHugh J.A. in *Breusch v Watts Development Division Pty Ltd*[2] specifically left open the question as to whether the courts could look beyond the document to ascertain whether good consideration in fact existed.

Even on the traditional view, however, the guarantee will not always fail. First, consideration expressed in terms of the future supply of goods or the making of advances to the principal may support a guarantee of past indebtedness, as well as those future obligations.[3] This will not be the case, however, in the rare case where the guarantee is construed by consideration, and one relating to past indebtedness, which will accordingly fail for want of consideration.[4]

2–74

Secondly, it is open to the creditor to show that the guarantee has been orally agreed upon before the consideration is executed and has only later been reduced to writing.[5] The statement of the consideration in the written document is then only a written memorandum of the prior binding agreement.[6]

2–75

In a similar vein, a guarantee given after the creditor has supplied the principal debtor with goods may be supported by consideration if the supply was done at the guarantor's request and on the understanding that a guarantee would be provided.[7]

2–76

Thirdly, the courts have been ready to avoid a literal interpretation of the expressed statement of consideration in the guarantee where it might appear on the face of it to be past consideration.[8] In *Breusch v Watts Development Division Pty Ltd*,[9] McHugh J.A. stated:

2–77

"Acting upon the principle, ut res magis valeat quam pereat, the courts, where possible, have invariably held that the words of a guarantee imported an executory or future consideration rather than a past or

---

[1] *Oldershaw v King* (1857) 2 H. & N. 517; 157 E.R. 213.
[2] (1987) 10 N.S.W.L.R. 311 at 317, with Hope J.A. and Glass J.A. concurring. In the court below, Yeldham J. held that it was permissible to look beyond the document to see if there was good consideration for the guarantee.
[3] *Johnston v Nicholls* (1845) 1 C.B. 251; 135 E.R. 535; *White v Woodward* (1848) 5 C.B. 810; 136 E.R. 1097.
[4] *Wood v Benson* (1831) 2 Cr. & J. 94; 149 E.R. 40. See also *Smith v Passmore* (1883) 4 L.R. (NSW) 274.
[5] See *Mumford v Gething* (1859) 7 C.B.N.S. 305; 141 E.R. 834; *Dodge v Pringle* (1860) 29 L.J. Ex. 115. This argument was raised in *Ahern v Power* [1935] QWN 22 but rejected because there was no evidence that the defendant had the necessary animus contrahendi at the time he gave his promise. For this reason a creditor who takes a guarantee in these circumstances would be well advised to ensure that the guarantee is executed as a deed under seal or is supported by nominal consideration flowing to the guarantor.
[6] *ibid.*
[7] See *Simmons v Keating* (1818) 2 Stark 426; 171 E.R. 694; *Pao On v Lau Yin Long* [1980] A.C. 614; *Re Casey's Patents* [1982] 1 Ch 104 at 115–116; *Bradford v Roulston* (1858) 8 I.C.L.R. 468.
[8] See, *e.g. Broom v Batchelor* (1856) 1 H. & N. 255; 156 E.R. 1199; *Butcher v Steuart* (1843) 11 M. & W. 857 at 874; 152 E.R. 1052 at 1059; *Goldschede v Swan* (1847) 1 Exch. 154; 154 E.R. 65 (instrument was sufficiently ambiguous to allow parol evidence to be admitted to show that the advance was made simultaneously with the execution of the guarantee).
[9] (1987) 10 N.S.W.L.R. 311.

executed consideration. The decided cases proceed upon the principle that the words of a guarantee document, referring to the supply of goods or credit, are to be construed, if possible, as including the future supply of those goods or that credit. The cases also establish that, in determining whether the words of the guarantee were intended to have a future operation, it is permissible to ascertain what were the prior dealings between the parties and what was contemplated as to the future course of their dealings."[10]

2-78   As an example of these principles, in *S H Lock Discounts & Credits Pty Ltd v Miles*,[11] the creditor's consideration was expressed to be "your having, at my request agreed to make loans to C". Despite the use of the past tense, the statement of consideration was interpreted to mean the making of future loans to the principal debtor, C, from time to time on the faith of the guarantee. Similarly in *National Australia Bank Ltd v McKay*,[12] Hansen J. held that the term "banking accommodation" did not connote past consideration since the reality of the arrangement between the parties was that it was broad enough to include a *continuation* of the customer's account in debit.

2-79   As McHugh J.A. indicates in *Breusch v Watts Development Division Pty Ltd*,[13] parol or other extrinsic evidence can also be readily admitted to interpret the consideration as relating to future events and thus save the guarantee, on the basis that the statement of consideration is ambiguous so that the normal exception to the parol evidence rule in the case of ambiguous agreements is applicable.[14] Indeed, the admission of oral evidence has apparently been allowed where the statement of the consideration refers reasonably clearly to past events. Thus, in *Broom v Batchelor*,[15] the promise of guarantee was made "in consideration of the credit given by [the creditor] to [the principal]", but oral evidence was admitted to show that the consideration actually intended by the parties was future credit.[16]

---

[10] *ibid.* at 314. See also *S. H. Lock Discounts & Credits Pty Ltd v Miles* [1963] V.R. 656 and *Steele v Hoe* (1849) 14 Q.B. 431; 117 E.R. 168; *Broom v Batchelor* (1856) 1 H. & N. 255; 156 E.R. 1199; *Hoad v Grace* (1861) 7 H. & N. 494; 158 E.R. 567; *Wood v Priestner* (1866) L.R. 2 Ex. 66 and 282.
[11] [1963] V.R. 656. See also *King v Cole* (1848) 2 Exch. 628; 154 E.R. 642 ("having released"); *Tanner v Moore* (1846) 9 Q.B. 1; 115 E.R. 1176 ("having agreed"); *Johnston v Nicholls* (1845) 1 C.B. 251; 135 E.R. 535 (where the wording of the guarantee was equivocal); *Morrell v Cowan* (1877) 6 Ch. D. 166 ("having at my request agreed to supply"); *NEC Information Systems Australia Pty Ltd v Linton* (unreported, NSW Sup Ct, Wood J., April 17, 1985).
[12] (1995) A.T.P.R. 41-409.
[13] (1987) 10 N.S.W.L.R. 311.
[14] See also *Broom v Batchelor* (1856) 1 H. & N. 255; 156 E.R. 1199; *State Bank of Victoria v Voss* (unreported, Vic Sup Ct, May 17, 1991); *Steele v Hoe* (1849) 14 Q.B. 431; 117 E.R. 168; *Goldshede v Swan* (1847) 1 Exch. 154; 154 E.R. 65; *Butcher v Steuart* (1843) 11 M. & W. 857; 152 E.R. 1052; *Hamilton v Watson* (1845) 12 Cl. & Fin. 109; 8 E.R. 1339; *Colbourn v Dawson* (1851) 10 CB 765; 138 ER 302; *Bainbridge v Wade* (1850) 16 Q.B. 89; 117 E.R. 808; *Haigh v Brooks* (1839) 10 Ad. & El. 309; 113 E.R. 119; *Lilley v Midland Brick Co Pty Ltd* (1993) 9 W.A.R. 339.
[15] (1856) 1 H. & N. 255; 156 E.R. 1199.
[16] See *Butcher v Steuart* (1843) 11 M. & W. 857 at 874; 157 E.R. 1052 at 1060; *Goldshede v Swan* (1847) 1 Exch. 154; 154 E.R. 65 and *King v Cole* (1848) 2 Exch. 628; 154 E.R. 642.

Even though the consideration as expressed in the guarantee is drafted **2–80** so as to refer to future events, the consideration may still be past. Thus, if the consideration as expressed in the guarantee is the act of the creditor in concluding the principal transaction, the guarantee will be of no effect if the creditor enters into the principal transaction prior to the execution of the guarantee.[17] For example, in *Astley Industrial Trust Ltd v Grimston Electric Tools Ltd*,[18] the guarantee was expressed to be "In consideration of your hiring to the hirer etc", but the guarantee was executed four days after the hiring agreement was concluded. The consideration was, therefore, past and the guarantee of no effect. If, however, the principal transaction is executed simultaneously with the guarantee, this will be sufficient consideration,[19] and it has been held that if the two transactions are executed at the same meeting it does not matter which instrument was signed first: the court will treat them as if they were signed concurrently.[20] Furthermore, the result in the *Astley Industrial Trust* case may be avoided if the consideration is construed as the performance, rather than the execution of the principal contract, provided that the guarantee is entered into prior to such performance.[21]

The possibility that the principal contract may be executed before the **2–81** date of the execution of the guarantee has led to the inclusion of a type of clause in the guarantee which contemplates that evidence of other consideration may be introduced if this happens. The clause might state that the guarantee is given in consideration of the creditor entering into the principal transaction "or (if the transaction has already been entered into) you [the creditor] extending other valuable consideration to the principal debtor". Evidence of such consideration may be adduced because it is no longer necessary for the consideration to appear on the face of the document.[22]

While there is a statutory presumption under s.27 of the Bills of Exchange Act 1982 that an antecedent debt or liability is sufficient consideration for a promissory note or bill of exchange, this is not sufficient to support a guarantee given in the form of a promissory note or bill of exchange. Even where the guarantee is given in the form of a promissory note or bill of exchange for the payment of a debt it appears that it is necessary for the creditor to prove some consideration, apart from an antecedent debt or liability, for the giving of the bill or note. This

---

Extrinsic evidence will not, however, in all cases clarify the nature and character of the consideration and save the guarantee. *e.g.* in *Bell v Welch* (1850) 9 C.B. 154; 137 E.R. 851 the consideration was expressed to be money "advanced or to be advanced" to the principal debtor up to a certain limit. The surrounding circumstances revealed that the limit had already been exceeded. Since this consideration was past, the guarantee failed.

[17] *Astley Industrial Trust Ltd v Grimston Electric Tools Ltd* (1965) 109 S.J. 149; *French v French* (1841) 2 Man. & G. 644; 133 E.R. 903. There may be difficult factual issues as to when the respective contracts have been executed: *Natcomp Holdings Pty Ltd v Peters* (unreported, Vic Sup Ct, August 24, 1993).

[18] (1965) 109 S.J. 149.

[19] *Goldshede v Swan* (1847) 1 Exch. 154; 154 E.R. 65. See also *Butcher v Steuart* (1843) 11 M. & W. 857; 152 E.R. 1052; *Broomfield v Walker* (1870) 9 S.C.R. (NSW) 189.

[20] *M'Ewan v Newman* (1874) 5 A.J.R. 167.

[21] *Hill Equipment & Refrigeration Co Pty Ltd v Nuco Pty Ltd* (1992) 110 F.L.R. 25.

[22] See above, para.2–54 and below, para.3–06.

consideration could take the form of forbearance to sue the principal debtor on the antecedent debt or liability.[23] Consequently, in relation to a guarantee in the form of a promissory note or bill of exchange there must still be some relationship between the giving of the bill or the making of the note, on the other hand, and the antecedent debt or liability on the other.[24]

(iv) Illusory consideration

2–82   The guarantee will not be binding if the consideration expressed in the instrument is illusory or a sham.[25] Thus in *Reid Murray Holdings Pty Ltd (in liq) v David Murray Holdings Pty Ltd*,[26] the expressed consideration was the creditor "having at the request of the guarantor advanced or agreed to advance" sums of money to certain debtors. Mitchell J. in the Supreme Court of South Australia held that there was no consideration for the guarantee as the evidence established that no such request had in fact been made and that there was no intention that the stated consideration should exist.[27]

(v) Illegal consideration

2–83   Illegal consideration will not sustain a contract of guarantee.[28] Thus a guarantee to assist one of the parties to break the law is void.[29] A

---

[23] See *Oliver v Davis* [1949] 2 K.B. 727 (where it was held that if the antecedent debt or liability was that of a third party, there had to be some relationship between the giving of the bill or note and that debt or liability). See also G. Andrews & R. Millett, *Law of Guarantees* (3rd ed., 2000), para. 2.09 and *Crofts v Beale* (1851) 11 C.B. 1722; 138 E.R. 436.
[24] *Oliver v Davis* [1949] 2 K.B. 727 at 737, *per* Evershed M.R. *Cf.* K.P. McGuinness, *The Law of Guarantee* (1986), para.4.192.
[25] *Reid Murray Holdings Ltd (in liq) v David Murray Holdings Pty Ltd* (1972) 5 S.A.S.R. 386; *Hodson v Lee* (1847) 9 L.T.O.S. 312 at 313 (Lord Denman C.J.); *White v Woodward* (1848) 5 C.B. 810; 136 E.R. 1097.
[26] (1972) 5 S.A.S.R. 386.
[27] *ibid.* at 396. The guarantee was saved, however, because it was in the form of a deed: see below, paras 2–84 to 2–86. The courts will lean against a construction that renders the consideration illusory: *Castlemaine Tooheys Ltd v Axming Pty Ltd* (unreported, Qld Sup Ct, July 3, 1987).
[28] *Wood v Barker* (1865) L.R. 1 Eq. 139; *Coles v Strick* (1850) 15 Q.B. 2; *Herman v Jeuchner* (1885) 15 Q.B.D. 561; *Coleman v Waller* (1829) 31 Y. & J. 212; 148 E.R. 1156; *McKewan v Sanderson* (1875) L.R. 20 Eq. 65. Hence, a guarantee given in order to stifle a criminal prosecution is void: *Cannon v Rands* (1870) 23 L.T. 817; *Jones v Merionethshire Permanent Benefit Building Society* [1891] 2 Ch. 587, affirmed in [1892] 1 Ch. 173, CA. *Cf. Coutts & Co v Browne-Lecky* [1947] K.B. 104 at 111; *Heald v O'Connor* [1971] 2 All E.R. 1105. The unenforceable guarantee can be ordered to be delivered up or cancelled: *Jackman v Mitchell* (1807) 13 Ves. Jun. 581; 33 E.R. 412. A contract of indemnity given in respect of a principal debt or obligation which is void is not necessarily itself void and unenforceable: *Yeoman Credit Ltd v Latter* [1961] 1 W.L.R. 828. But see *Haseldine v Hosken* [1933] 1 K.B. 822 (solicitor was not entitled to claim under an indemnity insurance policy for the loss he suffered as a result of entering into a champertous agreement) and *Smith v White* (1866) L.R. 1 Eq. 626 (immoral contract).
[29] *Cannon v Rands* (1870) 23 L.T. 817. See also *Jones v Merionethshire Permanent Benefit Building Society* [1892] 1 Ch. 173; *Ritchie v Smith* (1848) 6 C.B. 462; 136 E.R. 1329. Compare *Lougher v Molyneux* [1916] 1 K.B. 718 (a guarantee of a loan prohibited by statute was held to

guarantee which is contrary to the policy of the bankruptcy laws is also void.[30] For example, in *Nerot v Wallace*,[31] a promise, made by a friend of the bankrupt to pay such sums as the bankrupt had received and had not accounted for, in consideration that the assignees and the commissioners of bankruptcy would forbear to examine him in relation to those sums was held to be void on this basis. Similarly, as it is the right of all unsecured creditors involved in bankruptcy proceedings to share assets rateably, a guarantee which has the effect of granting one unsecured creditor a preference, priority or advantage over other unsecured creditors in such proceedings is void.[32]

8. DEEDS

A guarantee executed as a deed need not be supported by consideration. It is no longer necessary for a deed executed by an individual to bear a seal.[33] It appears to be sufficient that the individual signed a document bearing an indication of a seal with the intention of executing it as a deed.[34] Even where the document was not executed with this intention, the guarantor may be held liable on the basis on an estoppel if the document specifically states that it was "signed, sealed and delivered" and the creditor relied on this representation of fact by making advances in reliance on the document.[35]   **2–84**

It is no longer necessary for companies in England and Wales to have a common seal.[36] Accordingly these companies can execute a guarantee as a deed without affixing a common seal. All that appears to be necessary is for the companies to intend to execute the document as a deed.   **2–85**

If the guarantee is to be effective as a deed it must comply with the relevant statutory requirements in respect of its execution.[37] The modern

---

be unenforceable). A guarantee given in consideration of an agreement to abort a criminal prosecution is not enforceable: *Jones v Merionethshire Permanent Benefit Building Society* [1891] 2 Ch. 587, affirmed [1892] 1 Ch. 173; *Cannon v Rands* (1870) 23 L.T. 817; *Seear v Cohen* (1881) 45 L.T. 589 (a general threat of criminal proceedings). As to whether a bank guarantee given to persuade the creditor to discontinue criminal or quasi-criminal. G. Andrews & R. Millett, *Law of Guarantees* (3rd ed., 2000), para.2.18.

[30] *Nerot v Wallace* (1789) 3 Term Rep. 17; 100 E.R. 432.

[31] (1789) 3 Term Rep. 17; 100 E.R. 432. *Cf. Kaye v Bolton* (1795) 6 Term Rep. 134; 101 E.R. 474.

[32] *McKewan v Sanderson* (1875) 44 L.J. Ch. 447. See also *Jackman v Mitchell* (1807) 13 Ves. J. 581; 33 E.R. 412; *Coleman v Waller* (1829) 3 Y. & J. 212; 148 E.R. 1156; *Wood v Barker* (1865) L.R. 1 Eq. 139; *Coles v Strick* (1850) 15 Q.B. 2; 117 E.R. 358.

[33] Law of Property (Miscellaneous Provisions) Act 1989, s.1(1)(b), which came into force on July 31, 1990.

[34] *Stromdale & Ball Ltd v Burden* [1952] 1 Ch. 223 at 230 *per* Danckwerts J.; *Procopia v D'Abbondanzo* (1975) 35 D.L.R. (3d) 641 at 646 affirmed in (1976) 58 D.L.R. (3d) 368; *Re Sandilands* (1871) L.R. 6 C.P. 411; *National Provincial Bank of England v Jackson* (1886) 33 Ch. D. 1 at 14.

[35] See *TCB Ltd v Gray* (1986) 2 B.C.C. 99,044; *Stromdale & Ball Ltd v Burden* [1952] 1 Ch. 223. See also *Partnership Pacific Ltd v Smith* (unreported, NSW Sup Ct, April 5, 1991), p.8.

[36] G. Moss and D. Marks, *Rowlatt on Principal and Surety* (5th ed., 1999), p.9 states that the requirement that companies in England and Wales have a common seal was abolished on July 31, 1990. See also G. Andrews and R. Millett, *Law of Guarantees* (3rd ed., 2000), para.2.08.

[37] See Law of Property (Miscellaneous Provisions) Act 1989, s.1(2).

approach to the formal requirements for the execution of a deed is that if a person signs a document bearing wax or wafer or other indication of a seal, with the intention of executing the document as a deed, that is sufficient adoption or recognition of the seal to constitute due execution as a deed.[38] In a case in which the formalities are not met, however, the guarantor may nevertheless be estopped from denying that the document was executed.[39]

2–86   A guarantee in the form of a properly executed deed will probably not be invalidated because of a statement that it is entered into for a consideration which does not exist and which is known by both guarantor and creditor not to exist,[40] unless the consideration is illegal so that the whole transaction is void for illegality.[41]

9. UNCERTAINTY

2–87   A guarantee, like any other contract, may be void because the terms of the guarantee are uncertain.[42] The tendency, however, has been for the courts to interpret the guarantee with regard for the fact that it is a commercial document,[43] and there are few cases where a guarantee has been held void on this basis. Thus, if the guarantee is given in consideration of further advances being made to the principal, there is no necessity to specify the details of the amount of the advances or the time at which they will be made.[44] As we have seen, the guarantee will be enforceable as soon as a bona fide advance is made.[45] It has been

---

[38] *Stromdale & Ball Ltd v Burden* [1952] 1 Ch. 223 at 230 *per* Danckwerts J.; *Procopia v D'Abbondanzo* (1975) 35 DLR (3d) 641, affirmed in (1976) 58 D.L.R. (3d) 368.
[39] *TCB Ltd v Gray* (1986) 2 B.C.C. 99,044. See also *Partnership Pacific Ltd v Smith* (unreported, N.S.W. Sup Ct, April 5, 1991) at 8.
[40] *Reid Murray Holdings Ltd (in liq) v David Murray Holdings Pty Ltd (in liq)* (1972) 5 S.A.S.R. 386 at 396. See also *Rose v Poulton* (1831) 2 B. & Ad. 822 at 826–831; 109 E.R. 1348 at 1350–1351 (where the issue was not decided); *Bunn v Guy* (1803) 4 East 190 at 200; 102 E.R. 803 at 806. These cases are analysed in *Reid Murray Holdings Ltd (in liq) v David Murray Holdings Pty Ltd* (1972) 5 S.A.S.R. 386 at 395–396. *Cf. British American Oil Co Ltd v Ferguson* [1951] 2 D.L.R. 37 at 45 and *H.A. de Colyar's Law of Guarantees and of Principal and Surety* (3rd ed., 1897), p.21.
[41] *Reid Murray Holdings Ltd (in liq) v David Murray Holdings Pty Ltd* (1972) 5 S.A.S.R. 386 at 396.
[42] *Oldershaw v King* (1857) 2 H. & N. 517; 157 E.R. 213; *G. Scammell v Nephew Ltd v Ouston* [1941] A.C. 251 at 268–269 *per* Lord Wright; *Relwood Pty Ltd v Manning Homes Pty Ltd* [1990] 1 Qd. R. 481 (FC) (guarantee not enforceable because the requisite credit limit had not been agreed). *Cf. Caltex Oil (Australia) Pty Ltd v Alderton* (1964) 81 W.N. (Pt. 1) (NSW) 297 at 298. This principle applies equally to indemnities: *State Bank of India v Kaur* [1996] 5 Bank L.R. 158; [1995] N.P.C. 43.
[43] See the general principles of construction set out below in Ch. 5, and, in this context, *Caltex Oil (Aust) Pty Ltd v Alderton* (1964) 81 W.N. (Pt 1) (NSW) 297; *Broadlands Finance Ltd v Williamson* (unreported, NZ High Ct, February 7, 1984); *Hillas & Co v Arcos Ltd* [1932] All E.R. Rep. 494 at 503; *per* Lord Wright; *Nicolene Ltd v Simmonds* [1953] 1 Q.B. 543 at 551 *per* Denning L.J., CA.
[44] *White v Woodward* (1848) 5 C.B. 810; 136 E.R. 1097. See also *Simpson v Manley* (1831) 2 Cr. & J. 12; 149 E.R. 5, where the consideration was the "giving of credit", and this was interpreted to mean a fair and reasonable credit. See also below, para.3–69 and especially *Vetro Glass Pty Ltd v Fitzpatrick* [1963] 63 S.R. (NSW) 697.
[45] *ibid.*

suggested[46] that, where the expressed consideration is a promise to supply goods or make advances, rather than the actual supply or making of the advances, the agreement will be too indefinite in the absence of details being specified in the guarantee as to the type or amount of the goods or advances. However, it is thought unlikely that a court would today strike down a guarantee for this reason.[47]

Apart from the statement of consideration, the terms of the guarantee must be sufficiently certain, although extrinsic evidence is admissible to resolve any ambiguity in those terms.[48] The relevant parties must be properly identified[49] as well as the principal transactions to which the guarantee relates[50] and the amount of the guarantor's liability.[51]

Where there is an inconsistency in the terms of the guarantee and it **2–88** cannot be resolved by reading the document as a whole, the court may as a last resort adopt the principle of interpretation that an earlier clause prevails over a later clause.[52]

10. CONDITIONS PRECEDENT TO THE OPERATION OF THE GUARANTEE

A contract of guarantee will not come into effect unless all express or **2–89** implied conditions precedent to the operation of the guarantee are satisfied. A condition precedent may relate, for example, to the necessity for the creditor to obtain a co-guarantor,[53] or an additional security,[54] or to the fact that the principal transaction must be entered into upon certain terms.[55] It may also be a condition precedent that the goods which constitute the subject matter of the principal transaction are in existence.[56] Such terms are considered in detail elsewhere in the text,[57] but one general point which may be made here is that, in accordance with normal contractual principles, extrinsic evidence of the condition precedent may be admitted to establish that the contract has not yet come into operation.[58] If the condition is not satisfied, the consequence is that a

---

[46] Fry J. in *Morrell v Cowan* (1877) 6 Ch. D. 166 at 171 (reversed on other grounds in (1877) 7 Ch. D. 151).
[47] See in support of this view *Lindsay v L Stevenson & Sons Ltd* (1891) 17 V.L.R. 112 at 115 (where a guarantee given "in consideration of your promise to do a considerable portion of your business" with the principal was held to be sufficiently certain).
[48] See below, para.5–05.
[49] See below, paras 5–13 to 5–21 and 10–160 *et. seq.* and *Re A & K Holdings Pty Ltd* [1964] V.R. 257; *Triaca v Summaries Pty Ltd* [1971] V.R. 347.
[50] See below, para.5–44; *Westhead v Sproson* (1861) 6 H. & N. 726; 158 E.R. 301; *Helliwell v Dickson* (1862) 9 Gr. 414, and *Mercantile Credits Ltd v Harry* [1969] 2 N.S.W.R. 248.
[51] See below, para.5–30 and *Caltex Oil (Aust) Pty Ltd v Alderton* (1964) 81 W.N. (Pt 1) (NSW) 297; *Relwood Pty Ltd v Manning Homes Pty Ltd* [1990] 1 Qd. R. 481.
[52] *Kench v Forsyth* [2002] T.A.S.S.C. 1 (unreported, Supreme Court of Tasmania, January 14, 2002.
[53] See below, paras 3–87 to 3–99.
[54] See below, paras 8–57 to 8–61.
[55] See below, paras 5–44 to 5–49.
[56] See below, para.8–69.
[57] See above, nn.53–56.
[58] *Pym v Campbell* (1856) 6 E. & B. 370; 119 E.R. 903.

clause in the guarantee itself which purports to protect the creditor from a failure, for example, to obtain the signature of a co-guarantor will be ineffective for that purpose; the clause is itself part of the guarantee, and the guarantee has no legal effect as a result of the failure of the condition precedent.[59]

11. CONDUCT FALLING SHORT OF AN EXPRESS CONTRACTUAL COMMITMENT

2–90   This chapter has focused upon the elements required for the formation of a guarantee according to normal contractual principles. Even if there is no concluded contract of guarantee, however, a person negotiating as a prospective guarantor may potentially incur personal liability on the basis of an estoppel. In *Brueckner v Carroll*,[60] a solicitor, who acted for the borrower and who had been asked by the borrower to provide a guarantee, sent a draft (and unexecuted) document embodying the principal transaction to the creditor. A clause in the document stated that, in the event of default, the obligations of the borrower would be guaranteed by the (named) solicitor. Santow J. held that the clause did not constitute a firm offer of guarantee, but was meant simply to indicate to the creditor the "kind of thing that might be entered into in a more formal fashion".[61]

2–91   Nevertheless, the creditor sought to argue that the solicitor was estopped from denying that he had guaranteed the principal obligation. The court rejected this claim as there was no evidence to support a finding that the solicitor had encouraged or acquiesced in any assumption made by the creditor that a binding guarantee had come into existence.[62] Despite this finding, *Brueckner v Carroll*[63] does illustrate a possible liability for persons who in prior negotiations indicate a willingness to assume the position of guarantor.[64]

---

[59] *Molsons' Bank v Cranston* (1918) 45 D.L.R. 316.
[60] (1995) A.T.P.R. 41–379.
[61] *ibid.*, at 40,238.
[62] It is unlikely, however, that a claim based on estoppel (if proved) would be defeated by an absence of writing: see below, paras 3–161 to 3–170.
[63] (1995) A.T.P.R. 41–379. See also *CSR Ltd v Price* (unreported, NSW Sup Ct, April 29, 1993).
[64] Estoppel may also be relevant in determining the scope of the guarantor's liability: see below, paras 5–94 to 5–96.

CHAPTER 3

FORMAL REQUIREMENTS

1. INTRODUCTION

3–01   In the eyes of the law a contract of guarantee has always been a solemn undertaking. Guarantors seldom derive any benefit, yet they can incur substantial liabilities through their suretyship. Whilst the common law was generally sympathetic to guarantors, it did not demand that the contract of guarantee be in writing.[1] This requirement was introduced by the Statute of Frauds 1677, which stated that no action could be brought upon a special promise to answer for the debt, default or miscarriage of another unless it, or some memorandum or note thereof, was in writing and signed by the party to be charged or that party's lawfully authorised agent.[2] The principal object of the statute was to prevent fraud and perjury by withdrawing the right to sue on certain agreements if they could only be established by oral evidence.[3] By requiring a guarantee to be proved by objective written evidence, the statute reduced the risk that false claims would be accepted. The statute reflected the legislature's concern that certain contracts might be established by "false evidence, or by evidence of loose talk, when it never was really meant to make such a contract".[4] Guarantees are usually continuing contracts and evidence of their formation may be difficult to find after the lapse of time.[5] The statute also served a subsidiary purpose of ensuring that guarantors did not lightly assume the mantle of suretyship. As the Albert Institute of Law Research

---

[1] See *Wood Bros v Gardner* (1886) 5 E.D.C. 189 (SAf).
[2] Statute of Frauds 1677, 29 Car II, c.III, s.4.
[3] *Re Hoyle; Hoyle v Hoyle* [1893] 1 Ch. 84 at 98; *Saunders v Wakefield* (1821) 4 B. & Ald. 595; 106 E.R. 1054; *Barkworth v Young* (1856) 4 Drew 1; 62 E.R. 1; *Welford v Beazely* (1747) 3 Atk. 503; 26 E.R. 1090. In *Motemtronic Ltd v Autocar Equipment Ltd* (unreported, Court of Appeal, Civil Division, June 20, 1996) Henry L.J. expressed the view that the mischief aimed at by s.4 of the Statute of Frauds 1677 remains as valid as it ever did.
[4] *Steele v M'Kinlay* (1880) 5 App. Cas. 754 at 768, quoted with approval by the Court of Appeal in *Actionstrength Ltd v International Glass Engineering IN.GL.EN SpA* [2002] 1 WLR 566 (see, on appeal to the House of Lords [2003] 2 W.L.R. 1060).
[5] Law Reform Commission of Tasmania, Report No. 50: *Suretyship and Guarantee* (1987), p.11.

and Reform noted in 1985, a secondary purpose of the writing requirement is to caution people, particularly inexperienced or unsophisticated people, against entering into contracts without proper thought.[6]

There are two main reasons why a detailed analysis of these formal requirements is warranted. First, not all guarantees are caught by the Statute of Frauds. It is, therefore, necessary to determine what promises fall within the statute and what promises are enforceable without writing. Secondly, since the statute extends to most guarantees, it is vital to ensure that the statutory requirements are satisfied, otherwise the guarantee in question may be unenforceable. While most modern commercial guarantees comply with the formal requirements, guarantees given in less sophisticated contexts may run foul of the statute.[7] **3–02**

For these reasons, this chapter is concerned with the formal requirements of a contract of guarantee, whether they derive from the Statute of Frauds or some other source. The execution of such a contract fits neatly within this compass. **3–03**

2. ELECTRONIC COMMERCE

Under s.8(1) of the Electronic Communications Act 2000, "the appropriate Minister *may* by order made by statutory instrument modify the provisions of (a) any enactment or subordinate legislation ... in such manner as he may think fit for the purpose of authorising or facilitating the use of electronic communications" (emphasis added) for the purposes of the making of contracts. **3–04**

This provision will soon be suspended by the United Kingdom's implementation of EC Directive 2000/31 of June 8, 2000 [2000] O.J. L178/1 on electronic commerce in the Internal Market (Directive on Electronic Commerce). Article 9 (1) of this directive provides that "Member States shall ensure that their legal system allows contracts to be concluded by electronic means" and it requires Member States to ensure that contracts are not deprived of legal effectiveness on the ground that they are made by electronic means. Member States can provide for exceptions to this rule, notably in relation to "contracts of suretyship granted and on collateral securities furnished by persons acting outside their trade, business or profession". This suggests that it will be necessary for UK law to draw a distinction between business sureties and non-business sureties. The formal requirements for guarantees granted by non-business sureties may continue to be governed by s.4 of the Statute of Frauds. **3–05**

---

[6] Report No. 44: "The Statute of Frauds and Related Legislation" (June 1985).
[7] For an example of an equitable mortgage by deposit which was held to be unenforceable because it was, in effect, a guarantee which did not comply with the statute, see *Deutsche Bank v Ibrahim, The Financial Times* December 13, 1991.

3. THE MODERN STATUTORY PROVISIONS

(i) No longer restricted to "special promises"

3–06   The Statute of Frauds applied to "any *special* promise to answer for the debt, default or miscarriage of another person",[8] and a promise was not special in this sense unless it was supported by consideration.[9] The term "special" in this context means "collateral" or "secondary."[10] It is not intended to be restricted to contracts under seal or contracts of record.[11] This led the courts to deny the plaintiff recovery on a promise unless the promise was reduced to writing which contained some specialty. A written agreement did not create a specialty unless it contained the consideration for the promise.[12] However, as a result of s.3 of the Mercantile Law Amendment Act 1856 a contract of guarantee shall not be invalid by reason only of the fact that the consideration does not appear on the face of the instrument.

(ii) What promises are caught by the statute?

(a) Promise must be made to the creditor

3–07   The statute is directed at promises "to answer for the debt, default, or miscarriage of another person". The term "debt" refers to an existing contractual liability;[13] the term "default" refers to a future liability in contract or otherwise;[14] the term "miscarriage" is broad enough to cover

---

[8] Statute of Frauds 1677, 29 Car. II, c. III, s.4 (emphasis added). A special promise does not include an implied promise arising by operation of law: *Gray v Hill* (1826) Ry. & M. 420; 171 E.R. 1070. The words "debt, default or miscarriage" appear to be wide enough to cover any form of civil liability in contract, in tort or under statute. See *Castling v Aubert* (1802) 2 East 325 at 330–331 *per* Lord Ellenborough C.J.; *Kirkham v Marter* (1819) 2 B. & Ald. 613 at 616. The Statute applies equally to guarantees and binding agreements to provide a guarantee: *Mallet v Bateman* (1865) L.R. 1 C.P. 163 at 170; *Compagnie Générale d'Industrie et de Participations v Myson Group Ltd* (1984) 134 N.L.J. 788. Consequently, a promise by a third party to pay compensation to a victim of a tort in consideration of the victim's not suing the tortfeasor is within the statute: *Kirkham v Marter* (1819) 2 B & Ald 613; 106 E.R. 490. The statute also applies to an agreement to give a guarantee: *Compagnie Générale d'Industrie et de Participations v Myson Group Ltd* (1984) 134 NLJ 788; *Mallett v Bateman* (1865) L.R. 1 C.P. 163. For a more detailed analysis of the meaning of the words "debt, default or miscarriage", see H.A. de Colyar's *Law of Guarantees* (3rd ed., 1897), pp.50–53.
[9] *Saunders v Wakefield* (1821) 4 B. & Ald. 595 at 600; 106 E.R. 1054 at 1056. In Canada, the word "special" has been interpreted to mean "collateral", so that a direct undertaking to pay the debt of another is not caught by the statute: *Sarbit v Hanson & Booth Fisheries (Can) Co Ltd* [1950] 4 D.L.R. 34 CA.
[10] *Sarbit v Booth Fisheries Ltd* (1951) 58 Man. R. 377 at 386, *per* Coyne J.A., CA.
[11] *Holmes v Mitchell* (1859) 7 C.B.N.S. 361 at 370; 141 E.R. 856 at 859. The term "special promises" does not extend to implied promises that arise by operation of law such as an implied promise to pay for repairs: *Gray v Hill* (1826) Ry. & M. 420 (NP); 171 E.R. 1070.
[12] *Saunders v Wakefield* (1821) 4 B. & Ald. 595 at 600; 106 E.R. 1054 at 1056.
[13] *Castling v Aubert* (1802) 2 East 325; at 330–331; 102 E.R. 393 at 395 *per* Lord Ellenborough C.J.
[14] *Re Young & Harston Contract* (1885) 31 Ch. D. 168; *Kirkham v Marter* (1819) 2 B. & Ald. 613, 106 E.R. 490 at 491 *per* Holroyd J.: "both the words miscarriage and default apply to a promise to answer for another with respect to the non-performance of a duty, though not

any other form of civil liability.[15] To attract the statute, the promise must be made to a person to whom another is answerable.[16] It follows that the modern formal requirements only apply to promises made to a creditor,[17] since the promise must be made to a person capable of bringing an action for the debt.[18] They have no application to promises made to the debtor alone,[19] unless the debtor has constituted himself a trustee of the promise for the creditor.[20] Hence, where only one person is liable to the creditor, and another person trading with that person agrees to reimburse him for any debts incurred in the course of the business, the statute does not apply.[21]

(b) The promisor must undertake a personal liability

To fall within the statute, the promise must impose on the promisor and the promisor's assets a personal liability for the debt.[22] A promise to pay the debt of a third party if that party furnishes the promisor with the means to liquidate the debt need not be in writing.[23] There is no guarantee within the statute unless the promisor's own funds or assets are put in jeopardy.[24] Equally, an agreement that property already pledged for one debt shall remain pledged for another is merely an agreement to appropriate the fund in a different manner and it is not within the statute.[25]

3–08

---

founded upon a contract". In this context "default" means not doing what is reasonable in the circumstances: *ibid.*

[15] *Kirkham v Marter* (1819) 2 B. & Ald. 613 at 616; 106 E.R. 490 at 491 (the word "miscarriage" covers wrongful acts which attract civil liability).

[16] But a guarantee is not invalidated simply because there is a mistake in the name of the creditor: *W.R. Brock Co v Young* (1910) 8 E.L.R. 244, NS. Where one person promises to indemnify another to induce him to provide a guarantee of a third party's debt, the promise is not within the statute: *Eastwood v Kenyon* (1840) 11 Ad. & El. 438; 113 E.R. 482, Q.B.; *Wildes v Dudlow* (1874) L.R. 19 Eq. 198 at 200; *Reader v Kingham* (1862) 13 C.B. (NS) 344. A promise made by one co-debtor to another is not within the statute: *Thomas v Cook* (1828) 8 B. & C. 728; 108 E.R. 1213; *Rae v Rae* (1857) 61 Ch.R. 490; *Wildes v Dudlow* (1874) L.R. 19 Eq. 198. *Eastwood v Kenyon* (1840) 11 Ad. & El. 438; 113 E.R. 482. However, it is not necessary for the guarantee to be addressed to the creditor. See below, para.10–168.

[17] *Eastwood v Kenyon* (1840) 11 Ad. & EL. 438; 113 E.R. 482. Accordingly, an oral promise made to a person who is not a party to the contract between the creditor and the principal debtor, that the debtor will perform the contract, is enforceable: *Hargreaves v Parsons* (1844) 13 M. & W. 561; 153 E.R. 235; see also *Reader v Kingham* (1862) 13 C.B.N.S. 344; *Love's case* (1706) 1 Salk 28; 91 E.R. 28; *Cripps v Hartnoll* (1863) 4 B. & S. 414; 122 E.R. 514.

[18] *Re Hoyle; Hoyle v Hoyle* [1893] 1 Ch. 84 at 99. For this reason, a guarantee by one partner to indemnify his co-partners against any loss in respect of his son's debt to the firm was not within the statute.

[19] *Eastwood v Kenyon* (1840) 11 Ad. & El. 438; 113 E.R. 482.; *Castling v Aubert* (1802) 2 East 325; 102 E.R. 393; *Gregory & Parker v Williams* (1817) 3 Mer. 582; 36 E.R. 224; *Adams v Dansey* (1830) 6 Bing 506; 130 E.R. 1376; *Wildes v Dudlow* (1874) L.R. 19 Eq. 198; *Re Bolton* (1892) 8 T.L.R. 668; *Guild & Co v Conrad* [1894] 2 Q.B. 885.

[20] See *Gregory v Williams* (1817) 3 Mer. 582; 36 E.R. 224.

[21] *Adams v Dansey* (1830) 6 Bing. 506; 130 E.R. 1376.

[22] *Harvey v Edwards Dunlop & Co Ltd* (1927) 39 C.L.R. 302 at 311 *per* Higgins J.

[23] *Castling v Aubert* (1802) 2 East. 325; 102 E.R. 393. See also *Andrews v Smith* (1835) 2 Cr. M. & R. 627; 150 E.R. 267 (In both cases it was held that the promisor's undertaking was direct and original, not collateral. Thus, it was not within the statute.

[24] See the Court of Appeal *Actionstrength Ltd v International Glass Engineering IN.GL.EN SpA* [2002] 1 W.L.R. 566 at 575 *per* Simon Brown L.J.

[25] *Macrory v Scott* (1880) 5 Exch. 907; 155 E.R. 396.

3–09   In *Harvey v Edwards Dunlop and Co Limited*[26] the respondent entered
into an oral contract with the appellant and a company in which the
appellant was interested. In consideration of the respondent refraining
from signing judgment in an action against the company, the appellant
agreed to arrange for an attorney to sell certain property belonging to the
appellant and pay a portion of the proceeds of sale to the respondent to
meet the amount of the judgment. Knox C.J. and Gavan Duffy and Starke
JJ. held that the contract fell within the Statute of Frauds as a special
promise to answer for the debt of another and that there was a sufficient
memorandum in the correspondence and the power of attorney to satisfy
the statute. Higgins J. dissented, holding that the agreement was not a
special promise to answer for the debt of another because the contract did
not impose on the promisor and his assets generally a liability for the
judgment debt: the liability was imposed on the proceeds of sale of some of
the appellant's property.[27]

3–10   On the other hand, a promise to pay the debt of another out of money
due to the promisor himself when he receives the funds falls within the
statute.[28] In *Actionstrength Ltd v International Glass Engineering
IN.GL.EN SpA*[29] the claimant (a subcontractor) agreed to supply labour
to the first defendant (the main contractor), who had contracted to build a
factory for the second defendant (the building owner). The main
contractor failed to pay the subcontractor amounts due under the supply
contract. On the assumed facts, the subcontractor complained to the
building owner who orally agreed that it would attempt to persuade the
main contractor to pay the outstanding amounts and failing that, it would
withhold moneys due from the building owner to the main contractor and
pay the subcontractor out of these funds. In consideration of the building
owner's promise, the subcontractor continued to supply labour for the
contract works. The issue was whether the building owner's promise to the
subcontractor was a promise to answer for the default of the main
contractor.

3–11   The Court of Appeal held that the building owner's promise fell within
the statute and it was unenforceable because of the absence of written
evidence. The fact that the substance of the building owner's promise was
to redirect to the subcontractor funds owed by the building owner to the
main contractor did not take the promise outside the statute. There was no
justification for reading into s.4 of the Statute of Frauds words to the effect
that the promise must be a promise to answer for the debt of another "out
of the general assets of the promisor". A promise falls within the statute

---

[26] (1927) 39 C.L.R. 302.
[27] This reasoning did not find favour with the Court of Appeal in *Actionstrength Ltd v
International Glass Engineering IN.GL.EN SpA* [2002] 1 W.L.R. 566. See also *Bolton v
Darling Downs Building Society* (1935) St. R. Qd. 237, where a member of a building society
that advanced money to a mortgagor was held to have guaranteed repayment of the loan
because he lodged shares with the society as collateral security. In this case there was no
suggestion that the arrangement was not a guarantee simply because only some of the
promisor's assets were provided as security.
[28] *Morley v Boothby* (1825) 3 Bing. 107 and *Halsbury's Laws of England* 4th ed., reissue,
Vol 20 (1993), para.152.
[29] [2002] 1 W.L.R. 566, appeal dismissed on other grounds [2003] 2 W.L.R. 1060.

even if the promisor undertakes to be liable for the debt of another only in respect of *specific funds* within his control.[30] It is not necessary for the promisor to assume a general liability out of all his assets for the debt of another.

The building owner's promise fell within the statute because its payment   **3–12** under the oral agreement with the subcontractor would not have extinguished the building owner's liability to pay the main contractor in the absence of its direction or consent. As the main contractor would still be entitled to be paid by the building owner, any payment to the subcontractor out of the funds retained by the building owner would be treated as a payment out of the building owner's funds. Its promise to the subcontractor was, therefore, a promise to answer for the main contractor's debt out of the building owner's funds and it was within the statute.[31]

A promise to answer for the debt of another may fall within the statute   **3–13** even if the assumption of personal liability by the guarantor is not immediate, as where the guarantor promises to give a guarantee upon the happening of a certain event such as the delivery of goods or the provision of services.[32] Equally, a personal promise by a company director to find the money to meet the first instalment of a debt owing by one of the company's subsidiaries could fall within the statute.[33] But an undertaking to procure *another party* to sign a guarantee is not within the statute, since the only person liable on this promise is the promisor himself, and the proposed guarantor has not yet undertaken to be answerable for the debt, default or miscarriage of another.[34] Thus an oral contract to procure a guarantee is enforceable.[35]

If a contract contains a promise which answers the statutory description,   **3–14** that is enough to attract the operation of the formal requirements; it is immaterial that the contract contains another promise or an alternative promise. Thus in *Marginson v Ian Potter & Co*,[36] Gibbs and Mason JJ. expressed the view that a promise by a third party to pay a company's debt

---

[30] Cf. *Harvey v Edwards Dunlop & Co Ltd* (1927) 39 C.L.R. 302 at 311, where only one of the five justices of the High Court of Australia, namely Higgins J., suggested the statute does not apply if the liability attaches to a particular asset belonging to the promisor, rather than to the promisor's assets generally. In *Actionstrength Ltd v International Glass IN.GL.EN SpA* [2002] 1 W.L.R. 566, the Court of Appeal specifically rejected this suggestion because it could not be justified in principle or on the terms of the statute.
[31] On the other hand, if payment to the subcontractor under its oral agreement with the building owner extinguishes the owner's liability to pay the main contractor, then the payment is treated as a payment out of the funds of the main contractor and the statute does not apply.
[32] *Mallet v Bateman* (1865) L.R. 1 C.P. 163. See also *Leiser & Co v Canadian Pacific Timber & Logging Co. Ltd* [1920] 1 W.W.R. 735 (BC).
[33] See *Motemtronic Ltd v Autocar Equipment Ltd* (unreported, Court of Appeal, Civil Division, June 20, 1996), where the Court found that there was no intention to create legal relations.
[34] *Bushell v Beavan* (1834) 1 Bing N.C. 103; 131 E.R. 1056.
[35] *Leiser & Co v CP Timber etc Co* [1920] 1 W.W.R. 735 (BC). But only nominal damages will be awarded for breach of such a contract if the proposed guarantee would be unenforceable under the statute: *Bushell v Beavan* (1834) 1 Bing. N.C. 103; 131 E.R. 1056. Where one party induces another to provide a guarantee of a third party's debt by a promise that the first party will indemnify that other against such a liability, he will be held to the indemnity even if it is not in writing: *Wildes v Dudlow* (1874) L.R. 19 Eq. 198.
[36] (1976) 136 C.L.R. 161 at 168–169.

to its creditor, or to put the company in funds so as to enable it to pay the debt, could fall within the statute. It was necessary for the first option contained in such a promise to be evidenced in writing even if the promisor elected to perform the alternative promise which did not fall within the statute. However, the enforceability of any part of the contract, other than the guarantee, may depend on whether the guarantee is severable.[37]

(c) The promise must be collateral

3–15   The statute applies only where the promise secures the debt, default or miscarriage of *another person*.[38] There must be a principal debtor,[39] though he need not exist at the time the guarantee is given,[40] and this principal debtor must be a legal person.[41] A guarantee of the debt of an unincorporated association is not caught by the statute because such bodies have no legal personality.[42] By contrast, an oral promise by a

---

[37] See *Chater v Beckett* (1797) 7 Term Rep. 201; 101 E.R. 931 (severance not possible); *Lord Lexington v Clarke* (1689) 2 Vent. 223; 86 E.R. 406 (entire agreement; severance not possible); *Thomas v Williams* (1830) 10 B. & C. 664; 109 E.R. 597 (entire agreement; severance not possible); *Wood v Benson* (1831) 2 Cr. & J. 94; 149 E.R. 40 (severance possible).

[38] Thus the statute does not apply to a promise to pay an amount unless it is the debt of another. A promise by an employee to repay his own debt to his employer out of moneys deducted from his wages at his request or with his consent is not within the statute: *Steggall & Co v Lymburner* (1912) 14 W.A.L.R. 201. Moreover, in *Barrell v Trussell* (1811) 4 Taunt. 117; 128 E.R. 273, for example, it was held that a promise given in consideration of forbearance to sell under an apparently absolute bill of sale was not within the statute as the bill did not appear to be security for any debt. Moreover, a promise by one guarantor to indemnify another is not within the statute: *Thomas v Cook* (1828) 8 B. & C. 728; 108 E.R. 1213. For the promise to fall within the statute, the principal debtor must remain liable: *Browning v Stallard* (1814) 5 Taunt 480; 128 E.R. 764 (a novation); *Commercial Bank of Tasmania v Jones* [1893] A.C. 313, PC. See also *Taylor v Hilary* (1835) 1 C.M. & R. 741; 149 E.R. 1279; *Goodman v Chase* (1818) 1 B. & Ald. 297; 106 E.R. 110; *Butcher v Stewart* (1843) 11 M. & W. 857; 152 E.R. 1052; *Emmett v Dewhurst* (1851) 3 Mac & G. 587; 42 E.R. 386.

[39] *Houlditch v Milne* (1800) 3 Esp. 86, N.P.; 170 E.R. 547; *Tomlinson v Gill* (1756) Amb. 330; 27 E.R. 221. See also *Birkmyr v Darnell* (1805) 1 Salk 27; 91 E.R. 27; *Lakeman v Mountstephen* (1874) L.R. 7 H.L. 17; *Harburg India Rubber Comb Co v Martin* [1902] 1 K.B. 778 at 784.

[40] *Lakeman v Mountstephen* (1874) LR 7 HL 17. It was decided in *Lexington (Lord) v Clarke* (1689) 2 Vent 223; 86 E.R. 406 that a promise to pay the debt of a deceased person falls within the statute even if no legal personal representative has been appointed. But see *Tomlinson v Gill* (1756) Amb. 330; 27 E.R. 221, where it was held that a promise by a person that he would make good any deficiency of assets to pay the debts of an intestate, provided that the widow of the intestate would permit him to be joined by her in the letters of administration, was outside the statute. This case could be explained on the ground that the promise was made to the intestate's widow who was not a creditor and that this alone was sufficient to take the case outside the statute. However, Lord Hardwicke apparently based his decision on the fact that there was not a promise on a new consideration. *Tomlinson v Gill* would appear to represent the better view.

[41] *Houlditch v Milne* (1800) 3 Esp. 86; 170 E.R. 547; *Tomlinson v Gill* (1756) Amb. 330; 27 E.R. 221. A guarantee of a promise to supply goods to an infant is not within the statute, unless both parties assume that the supplies are necessaries: *Harris v Huntbach* (1757) 1 Burr. 373; 97 E.R. 355. Compare *Fane v Bancroft* (1897) 30 N.S.R. 33.

[42] *Wedley v Green* (1958) 13 D.L.R. (2d) 174. Nor is the liability of a retired partner within the statute: *Rouse v Bradford Banking Co* [1894] A.C. 586. As to guarantees of partnership debts generally, see *Lacy v M'Neile* (1824) 4 Dow & Ry. K.B. 7 (where it was held that a promise by a partner to guarantee a partnership debt which had been assigned to a new creditor was not within the statute) and *Fane v Bancroft* (1897) 30 N.S.R. 33 (Can). *Cf. Devaux v Steinkeller* (1839) 6 Bing N.C. 84; 133 E.R. 33. A new partner in a firm can be made

substantial shareholder to guarantee repayment of a debt owed by his company to a supplier was unenforceable under the statute because the company, as a separate legal entity, was the principal debtor.[43]

A promise to pay one's own debt is not within the statute.[44] Consequently, the statute does not apply to:

3–16

(a) an agreement to pay a sum to compromise a claim against the promisor and third parties, even if the promisor may have a good defence to the claim against him;[45]

(b) a promise to pay money owed by the promisor to the promisee in discharge of a debt owed by the promisee to a third party;[46] and

(c) a promise by a judgment debtor to allow the judgment creditor to treat the judgment as security for the creditor's debt to a third party.[47]

Even a direct, independent or original undertaking to pay another's debt need not be reduced to writing since the promisor has assumed a personal liability for the debt.[48] The promise to pay the debt of another will only be

---

liable to an existing creditor without writing under the statute, as the original debtor's liability is replaced by the joint liability of the partners: *Re Lendon and Lendon Ex p. Lane* (1846) De. G. 300.

[43] *Shea v George Lindsay Ltd* (1910) 15 W.L.R. 362; 20 Man. R. 208 (Can). See also *Harburg India Rubber Comb Co v Martin* [1902] 1 K.B. 778.

[44] *Eastwood v Kenyon* (1840) 11 Ad. & El. 438; 113 E.R. 482; *Guild & Co v Conrad* [1894] 2 Q.B. 885; *Marginson v Ian Potter & Co* (1976) 136 C.L.R. 161 (where the promisor guaranteed repayment of his own debt incurred on his behalf as an undisclosed principal); *Hodgson v Anderson* (1825) 3 B. & C. 842; 107 E.R. 945 (where the debtor promised to pay his own debt *Ardern v Rowney* (1805) 5 Esp. 254; N.P.; 170 E.R. 803 (a promise to be answerable for a debt only to the extent of the promisor's own indebtedness to the creditor is not within the statute); *Commercial Bank of Tasmania v Jones* [1893] A.C. 313 (the *Statute of Frauds* has no application to an action against a debtor by the assignee of an equitable assignment of the debt); *Gillies v Brown* (1916) 31 D.L.R. 101 (promise by president of company: held not to be a guarantee of the company's debt). A promise by a person to answer for her or his spouse's debt is, however, unenforceable unless in writing: *Beard v Hardy* (1901) 17 T.L.R. 633, CA; *Jeffrey v Alyea* (1916) 30 D.L.R. 341, CA.

[45] *Orrell v Coppock* (1856) 2 Jur. N.S. 1244; 26 L.J. Ch. 269; *Stephens v Squire* (1696) 5 Mod. Rep. 205; 87 E.R. 610. See G. Andrews and R. Millett, *Law of Guarantees* (3rd ed., 2000), para.3.05.

[46] *Andrews v Smith* (1835) 2 Cr. M. & R. 627; 150 E.R. 267; *Hodgson v Anderson* (1825) 5 Dow & Ry. K.B. 735; 107 E.R. 945; *Re Lendon and Lendon, Ex p. Lane* (1846) De G. 300; 10 Jur. 382. See G. Andrews and R. Millett, *Law of Guarantees* (3rd ed., 2000), para.3.11.

[47] *Macrory v Scott* (1850) 5 Exch. 907; 155 E.R. 390 (an agreement stating that property already pledged for one debt shall remain pledged for another is not within the statute). See G. Andrews and R. Millett, *Law of Guarantees* (3rd ed., 2000), para.3.05.

[48] *Andrews v Smith* (1835) C.M. & R. 627; 150 E.R. 267; *Dixon v Halfield* (1825) 2 Bing 439; 130 E.R. 375; *Walker v Taylor* (1834) 6 C. & P. 752, N.P.; 172 E.R. 1448; *Bampton v Paulin* (1827) 4 Bing 264; 130 E.R. 769; *Croft v Smallwood* (1793) 1 Esp. 121; 170 E.R. 299; *Bayne v Hare* (1859) 1 L.T. 40; *Lane v Burghart* (1841) 1 Q.B. 933; 113 E.R. 1389; *Harris v Huntbach* (1757) 1 Burr 373; 97 E.R. 355 (where it was held that the defendant's undertaking was original because the principal debtor was known to be an infant); *Wambolt v Arenburg* [1963] 4 D.L.R. 399; *Doyle v McKinnon* [1925] 3 D.L.R. 334; *McDonald v Glass* (1851) 8 U.C.Q.B. 245 (CA); *Bateman and Matthews v Spencer* [1923] 4 D.L.R. 170; *McPherson v Forlong* [1928] 3 W.W.R. 45; *Howes v Martin* (1764) 1 Esp. 162 (an indemnity against the demand of another is not within the statute). There is no promise to answer for the debt, default or miscarriage of another person where one party, at the request of another, enters into a recognisance for the appearance of a third party to answer a criminal charge: *Cripps v Hartnoll* (1863) 4 B. & S.

caught if it is collateral to, co-extensive with, and dependent upon, the principal debtor's obligation.[49] Where the liability assumed by the promisor is of a different nature and extent from the liability assumed by the principal debtor, the statute does not apply since the promisor's liability is original, not secondary.[50] Nor does the statute apply where a person agrees with the creditor to become jointly liable with the principal debtor because this is a principal liability, not a collateral obligation.[51] Even a promise by one partner to indemnify his co-partners against any individual loss if a debtor of the firm fails to pay his debt is not within the statute because it is not a promise to pay the debt to all the partners who could sue for the debt.[52]

3-17   Whether a promise creates a collateral liability or guarantee within the statute or an original or primary liability outside the statute is a matter of construction having regard to the words used and the surrounding circumstances.[53] In particular, it depends on whether there would be any liability upon the promisor apart from his promise and, if not, whether the liability of the principal debtor would subsist.[54] Hence, if there is an original liability having no reference to the debt another, so that the promisor is liable whether or not another party is liable and whether or not that other party defaults, the statute does not apply because the promisor's

---

414; 122 E.R. 514. Moreover, where one party to a contract transfers the benefit of the contract to a third party and guarantees the performance of the contractor, the guarantee is not within the statute as it operates merely as an undertaking to procure the contractor to perform its obligations: *Hargreaves v Parsons* (1844) 13 M. & W. 561; 153 E.R. 235. However, in *Green v Cresswell* (1837) 10 A. & E. 453; 113 E.R. 172 Lord Denman C.J. held that an indemnity against becoming bail in civil proceedings was within the statute, because the indemnifier was promising to answer for the default of another. However, this decision may be of dubious authority. See *Wildes v Dudlow* (1874) L.R. 19 Eq. 198; *Re Bolton* (1892) 8 T.L.R. 668 and *Guild v Conrad* [1894] 2 Q.B. 885.

[49] *Birkmyr v Darnell* (1704) 2 Ld Raym 1085; 91 E.R. 27; *Read v Nash* (1751) 1 Wils. 305; 95 E.R. 632; *Hargreaves v Parsons* (1844) 13 M & W 561; 153 E.R. 235; *Fish v Hutchinson* (1759) 2 Wils 94; 95 E.R. 704; *Huey v Doody* (1921) 49 N.B.R. 424; 63 D.L.R. 115 (CA); *Hoener v Merner* (1884) 7 O.R. 629.

[50] See, *e.g. Goulston Discount Co Ltd v Clark* [1967] 2 Q.B. 493; *Guild & Co v Conrad* [1894] 2 Q.B. 885. For this reason, recourse agreements taken by hire purchase companies from car dealers to the effect that the car dealer will pay the hire purchase company for all losses arising from the hirer's default are indemnities which do not fall within the statute: *Yeoman Credit Ltd v Latter* [1961] 1 W.L.R. 828; *Goulston Discount Co Ltd v Clark* [1967] 2 Q.B. 493, CA. *Cf. Western Credit Ltd v Alberry* [1964] 2 All E.R. 938. See also Consumer Credit Act 1974, s.113(7), as amended by the Minors' Contracts Act 1987, s.4(1).

[51] *Thomas v Cook* (1828) 8 B. & C. 728; 108 E.R. 1213; *Wildes v Dudlow* (1874) L.R. 19 Eq. 198. This is so even if the promisor and the principal debtor agree that, as between themselves, the principal debtor shall remain primarily liable.

[52] *Re Hoyle, Hoyle v Hoyle* [1893] 1 Ch. 84.

[53] Where the substance of the promise is an undertaking to be answerable for the debt of another, the statute applies even if the promise involves redirecting to the creditor moneys owed by the guarantor to the principal debtor: *Actionstrength Ltd v International Gas Engineering IN.GL.EN SpA* [2002] 1 W.L.R. 566. There is no magic in the words: "I'll see you paid." In certain circumstances, they can support an original undertaking; in others, a collateral undertaking within the statute: *Birkmyr v Darnell* (1704) 2 Ld. Raym. 1085; 91 E.R. 27 and *Matson v Wharam* (1787) 2 T.R. 80; 100 E.R. 44. Nor is a reference to the imposition of a primary liability decisive: *Clipper Maritime Ltd v Shirlstar Container Transport Ltd* [1987] 1 Lloyd's Rep. 546 at 555.

[54] *Doyle v McKinnon* [1925] 3 D.L.R. 334; *Coady v J Lewis & Sons Ltd* [1951] 3 D.L.R. 845; *Davys v Buswell* [1913] 2 K.B. 47 at 53–54.

undertaking is original or primary, not collateral.[55] Such promises are in the nature of an indemnity. Even a promise to indemnify someone who is himself a surety or guarantor for another falls outside the statute.[56]

As an illustration of these principles, let us consider whether a promise **3–18** to pay for goods supplied to another constitutes a guarantee within the statute. The cardinal question is: to whom did the supplier give the credit?[57] This is a question of fact having regard to the whole transaction.[58] However, if a tradesman makes out an account for goods in the name of a particular person, it must be taken that they were supplied on the credit of that person, unless it can be established by unequivocal evidence that the credit was, in fact, given to another.[59] And a tradesman may be required to produce his books in order to show on whose credit the goods were delivered.[60] If it appears that the goods were supplied on the credit of the promisor, that person's promise need not be in writing since the promisor is primarily liable for his own debt.[61] This is so where the promisor has undertaken to pay for the goods whether or not the other party fails to pay

---

[55] *Harburg India Rubber Comb Co v Martin* [1902] 1 K.B. 778 at 784; *Clipper Maritime Ltd v Shirlstar Transport Ltd* [1987] 1 Lloyd's Rep. 546 at 555; *Guild & Co v Conrad* [1894] 2 Q.B. 885. *Mountstephen v Lakeman* (1871) L.R. 7 Q.B. 196; 7 H.L. 17. If the promise was given for the express purpose of protecting the creditor against the possibility that the principal debtor might not be liable for the debt, the promise is a principal obligation and not within the statute: *Lakeman v Mountstephen* (1874) L.R. 7 H.L. 17 at 23 (there must be a principal debtor existing at the time of the promise or constituted by subsequent events). As to the distinction between a guarantee, on the one hand, and a primary liability on the other, see above, para.1–68.
[56] *McPherson v Forlong* [1928] 3 W.W.R. 45; *Cripps v Hartnoll* (1863) 4 B. & S. 414; 122 E.R. 514; *Wildes v Dodlow* (1874) L.R. 19 Eq. 198; *Keens v Baldwin* (1922) 22 O.W.N. 395. *Cf. Green v Cresswell* (1839) 10 Ad. & E. 453; 113 E.R. 172.
[57] *Austen v Baker* (1698) 12 Mod. Rep. 250; 88 E.R. 1299; *Storr v Scott* (1833) 6 C. & P. 241, N.P.; 172 E.R. 1224.; *Keate v Temple* (1797) 1 Bos. & P. 158; 126 E.R. 834; *Croft v Smallwood* (1793) 1 Esp. 121; *Beard v Hardy* (1901) 17 T.L.R. 663, CA and *Guild & Co v Conrad* [1894] 2 Q.B. 885 at 895 *per* Lopes L.J.
[58] *Lakeman v Mountstephen* (1874) L.R. 7 H.L. 17; *Darnell v Tratt* (1825) 2 C. & P. 82; 172 E.R. 37; *Simpson v Penton* (1834) 2 Cr. & M 430; 149 E.R. 828. The language used by the parties will not necessarily be decisive in determining whether the transaction creates a primary or collateral liability: *Simpson v Penton* (1834) 2 Cr. & M. 430; 149 E.R. 828.
[59] *Storr v Scott* (1833) 6 C. & P. 241, N.P.; 172 E.R. 1224. See also *Austen v Baker* (1698) 12 Mod. Rep. 250; 88 E.R. 1299.
[60] *Austen v Baker* (1698) 12 Mod. Rep. 250; 88 E.R. 1299. But even if credit is given to the promisor, the promise may yet be within the statute if the original debtor is not discharged: *Barber v Fox* (1866) 1 Stark 270; 171 E.R. 470. If one of several defendants promises to pay a sum by way of compromise of the whole claim, the statute does not apply even if the other defendants remain liable: *Orrell v Coppock* (1856) 26 C.J. Ch. 269; 2 Jur. N.S. 1244.
[61] This is so even if the consideration is exclusively for the use of another and even if there is further consideration for the promise: see *Edge v Frost* (1824) 4 D. & C. 243. See also *Fitzgerald v Dressler* (1859) 7 CB NS 374 at 379 and 392; *Sutton & Co v Grey* [1894] 1 Q.B. 285 at 288. And the promise would not, it appears, be retrospectively brought within the statute if the person who enjoys the consideration later ratifies the transaction and assumes liability for it: see *Lakeman v Mountstephen* (1874) L.R. 7 H.L. 17 and Rowlatt, *The Law of Principal and Surety* (5th ed., 1999), para.15–01. It appears that, where goods or services are supplied on the joint credit of two persons, the statute does not apply even though the seller knows that they are intended for the use of only one of the parties and that the other party joined in the undertaking simply to procure the supply on credit for this purpose: *Hampson v Merriott*, Lancaster Spring Assizes 1806 per Chambre J. reported in *Fell on Mercantile Guarantees* (2nd ed., 1820), pp.27, 28. Where it is not clear on whose credit the goods are supplied, see *Storr v Scott* (1833) 6 C. & P. 241; 172 E.R. 1224.

for them.[62] But if the goods were supplied on the credit of the person to whom they were delivered, the promisor's promise to pay for the goods can amount to a guarantee within the statute since it creates only a secondary liability.[63]

(d) The promise can relate to either an existing liability or an inchoate liability of another

3–19   The statute applies where the promise to answer for the debt, default or miscarriage is in relation to an *existing liability* of another person.[64] Thus, a promise to answer for the existing liability of a third party under a contract[65] or a tenancy agreement[66] requires written evidence. Equally, the statute can apply where the liability of the debtor has not yet crystallised, for example, where there is a promise to see that the creditor is paid for goods to be delivered to the debtor or work to be done for the debtor under an existing contract.[67] No action can, therefore, be brought on an oral promise to guarantee payment for goods not yet delivered to the principal debtor.[68] The statute also catches a guarantee that a promissory note made by another will be paid at maturity,[69] but not a promise purporting to guarantee that certain stock will pay a dividend because in this situation the principal does not even assume a contingent liability.[70]

---

[62] *Lakeman v Mountstephen* (1874) L.R. 7 H.L. 17 at 23; *Edge v Frost* (1824) 4 D. & R. 243. *Simpson v Penton* (1834) 2 Cr. & M. 430; 149 E.R. 828. Indeed, G. Andrews and R. Millett in *Law of Guarantees* (3rd ed., 2000), para.3.06 rightly contend that a simple test of whether a promisor's liability is original or collateral is to ask whether the promisor would be liable irrespective of whether the principal is liable or in default.

[63] See *Anderson v Hayman* (1789) 1 Hy. Bl. 120; 126 E.R. 73.

[64] *Sarbit v Hanson & Booth Fisheries (Canadian) Co Ltd* [1950] 4 D.L.R. 34. The term "debt" in s.4 of the statute covers existing or contemplated liabilities. The term "default" catches debts payable in future and, with the term "miscarriage", covers tortious liability.

[65] *Barber v Fox* (1866) 1 Stark 270, N.P.; *Edwards v Kelly* (1817) 6 M. & S. 204; 105 E.R. 1219; *Castling v Aubert* (1802) 2 East 325; 102 E.R. 393; *Clipper Maritime Ltd v Shirlstar Container Transport Ltd* [1987] 1 Lloyd's Rep. 546 (guarantee of obligations under a charter of a ship); *Fish v Hutchinson* (1759) 2 Wils 94; 95 E.R. 704 (promise to pay subsisting debt of another). See also *Tomlinson v Gell* (1837) 6 Ad. & El. 564; 112 E.R. 216 (a promise to pay the plaintiff's legal costs already incurred in return for his promise to discontinue the suit).

[66] *Rounce v Woodyard* (1846) 8 L.T.O.S. 186.

[67] *Watkins v Perkins* (1697) 1 Ld. Raym. 224; 91 E.R. 1046; *Peckham v Faria* (1781) 3 Doug K.B. 13; 99 E.R. 514; *Matson v Wharam* (1787) 2 Term Rep. 80; 100 E.R. 44. A promise covering a contemplated liability which arises subsequently in the course of a transaction between the creditor and the debtor is within the statute: *Lakeman v Mountstephen* (1874) L.R. 7 H.L. 17. There is no longer any doubt that the statute applies to promises to answer for another's future debts. See *Peckham v Faria* (1781) 3 Doug K.B. 13; 99 E.R. 514.

[68] *Jones v Cooper* (1774) 1 Cowp. 227; 98 E.R. 1058; *Anderson v Hayman* (1789) 1 Hy. Bl. 120; 126 E.R. 73.

[69] *Wambold v Foote* (1878) 2 O.A.R. 579 (Can).

[70] *Quance v Brown* [1926] 2 D.L.R. 824, CA.

(e) The principal debtor must remain liable

The statute will not apply unless the principal debtor whose debt or **3–20**
obligation is guaranteed remains primarily liable.[71] If the effect of the
arrangement between the parties is to extinguish the principal debtor's
liability or to release the principal, then the promisor's undertaking need
not be in writing.[72] Where the creditor agrees to release the principal
debtor in return for a new agreement under which the guarantor alone or
the guarantor and the principal debtor jointly or severally are to be liable,
the contract is not within the statute.[73] Indeed, any novation of the
agreement between the creditor and the principal debtor which extinguishes the debtor's liability is beyond the statute.[74] But the creditor's
release of the principal debtor will not take the promisor's undertaking
outside the statute unless it is absolute in the sense that, after the release,
the principal debt no longer subsists. Hence, it is not sufficient that the
creditor promises the surety alone that the creditor will not sue the debtor
for some time, since such undertakings by the creditor do not relieve the
principal debtor of liability.[75]

A different result may occur where a third party's promise induces the **3–21**
debtor's creditors to enter into a general scheme of arrangement. Creditors
who become parties to an arrangement whereby a third party takes over
the principal debtor's property and undertakes to pay the debtor's debts
are prevented from bringing an action against the debtor. However, such a
scheme of arrangement does not itself formally release the debtor, and
thus the debtor remains liable to the individual creditors until they agree to
accept the composition and release the debtor. At the relevant time,
namely the date of the arrangement between the promisor and the
creditors,[76] the principal debtor is still liable. Hence, the promise falls
within the statute as a promise to answer for the debt of another who

---

[71] *Fish v Hutchinson* (1759) 2 Wils 94; 95 E.R. 704; *Mawbrey v Cunningham* (1773), cited in 2
Term Rep. at 81; 100 E.R. at 44; *Rounce v Woodyard* (1846) 8 LTOS 186; *Gull v Lindsay*
(1849) 4 Exch. 45; 154 E.R. 1118.
[72] *Goodman v Chase* (1818) 1 B. & Ald. 297; 106 E.R. 110; *Re Lendon and Lendon, Ex p.
Lane* (1846) De G. 300; *Commercial Bank of Tasmania v Jones* [1893] A.C. 313. An
agreement to purchase another's debt need not be in writing: *Anstey v Marden* (1804) Bos. &
P.N.R. 124; 127 E.R. 406. Cf. *Emmett v Dewhurst* (1851) 3 Mac. & G. 587; 42 E.R. 386.
Similarly, the novation of an existing contract falls outside the statute: *Browning v Stallard*
(1814) 5 Taunt 450; 128 E.R. 764, CA; *Scarf v Jardine* (1882) 7 App. Cas. 345 at 351, HL;
Commercial Bank of Tasmania v Jones [1893] A.C. 313, PC.
[73] See *Goodman v Chase* (1818) 1 B. & Ald. 297; 106 E.R. 110; *Butcher v Steuart* (1843) 11 M.
& W. 857; 152 E.R. 1052.; *Browning v Stallard* (1814) 5 Taunt 450; 128 E.R. 764; '*Re Lendon
and Lendon, Ex p. Lane* (1846) De G. 300; 10 Jur. 382.
[74] *Re Lendon and Lendon, Ex p. Lane* (1846) De G. 300; *Commercial Bank of Tasmania v
Jones* [1893] A.C. 313; *Lacy v M'Neile* (1824) 4 Dow & Ry. K.B. 7; *Hodgson v Anderson*
(1825) 3 B. & C. 842; 107 E.R. 945; *Butcher v Steuart* (1843) 11 M. & W. 857; 152 E.R. 1052; *Re
Errington, Ex p. Mason* [1894] 1 Q.B. 11; *Re Guthrie & Co Ex p. Bank of A/asia* (1884) 2
N.Z.L.R. 425; *Gull v Lindsay* (1849) 4 Exch. 45; 154 E.R. 1118. Nor does the statute apply
where the parties strike a new agreement: *Walker v Taylor* (1834) 6 C. & P. 752; 172 E.R.
1448; *Browning v Stallard* (1814) 5 Taunt 450; 128 E.R. 764.
[75] *Rothery v Curry* (1748) Tr. 21 Geo. II, cited in Buller's N.P. 281; *Lee v Bashpole* (1685)
Comber bach 163; 90 E.R. 406; *King v Wilson* (1731) 2 Strange 873; 93 E.R. 908; *Fish v
Hutchinson* (175) 2 Wils 94; 95 E.R. 704.
[76] See Low Kee Yang, *The Law of Guarantees in Singapore and Malaysia* (Butterworths,
1992), p.75.

remains liable. The subsequent discharge of the principal debtor upon the
creditors' acceptance of the composition would arguably not be sufficient
to take the promise outside the statute.[77]

3–22   On the other hand, where the creditors agree to *accept the promise of
payment* by a third party *as satisfaction* of their debts, the principal debt is
discharged at the date of the agreement and the third party's promise does
not fall within the statute.[78] Similarly, the promise will be outside the
statute where it amounts to a purchase of debts which, in effect, preserves
the debts as distinct from discharging them.[79] In this situation, therefore,
the third party's undertaking falls outside the statute only where it is given
in return for an immediate release of the debtor by his creditors.[80] If the
release of the debtor does not occur until the creditors receive the full
amounts payable to them under the scheme of arrangement, the debtor
remains liable to them at the date of the scheme of arrangement and the
third party is, therefore, promising to answer for the debts of another
within the statute.[81]

(f) Formal Requirements in Relation to Bills of Exchange

3–23   A person who draws or indorses a bill of exchange may assume one of
two liabilities: either a liability on a guarantee constituted by the bill or a
liability on the bill itself under the law merchant or ss.54 and 55 of the Bills
of Exchange Act 1882.[82] The Statute of Frauds may not be invoked as a
defence in an action on the bill of exchange itself,[83] but it may be relied
upon in an action on the guarantee whether embodied in the bill or
contained in correspondence.[84] It is this latter action which warrants
attention.

---

[77] *Chater v Beckett* (1797) 7 Term Rep. 201. Note, however, that in this case the court did not
consider whether the principal debtor remained liable notwithstanding the defendant's
promise. See also *Bird v Gammon* (1837) 3 Bing N.C. 883; 132 E.R. 650. Cf. *Anstey v Marden*
(1804) 1 Bos & P.N.R. 124; 127 E.R. 406 (an original contract to purchase the debts of the
debtor was not within the statute).
[78] *Morris v Baron* [1918] A.C. 1 at 35; *Elton Cop Dyeing Co v Broadbent* (1920) 122 L.T. 142;
British Russian Gazette v Associated Newspapers [1933] 2 K.B. 616.
[79] *Anstey v Marden* (1804) 1 Bos. P. N.R. 124; 127 E.R. 406.
[80] *Bird v Gammon* (1837) 3 Bing N.C. 883 at 889; 132 E.R. 650 at 653. See also *Emmet v
Dewhurst* (1851) 3 Mac. & G. 587 at 596; 42 E.R. 386 at 390. Cf. *Anstey v Marden* (1804) 1 Bos
P.N.R. 124; 127 E.R. 406 (where there was an agreement to purchase the debt of another;
held: not within the statute).
[81] See *Case v Barber* (1681) T. Raym. 450; *Chater v Beckett* (1797) 7 Term Rep. 201; *Emmett v
Dewhurst* (1851) 3 Mac. & G. 587.
[82] *Stagg, Mantle & Co v Brodrick* (1895) 12 T.L.R. 12, CA; *Shaw & Co v Holland* [1913] 2
K.B. 15; *Glenie v Bruce Smith* [1908] 1 K.B. 263; *Wilkinson v Unwin* (1881) 7 Q.B.D. 636. See
also *Jenkins & Sons v Coomber* [1898] 2 Q.B. 168.
[83] For cases in which an indorser was sued on the bill of exchange, see *Jenkins & Sons v
Coomber* [1898] 2 Q.B. 168; *Shaw & Co v Holland* [1913] 2 K.B. 15; *Glenie v Bruce Smith*
[1908] 1 KB 263; *National Sales Corp Ltd v Bernardi* [1931] 2 K.B. 188; *McCall Bros Ltd v
Hargreaves* [1932] 2 K.B. 423; *Re Gooch Ex p. Judd* [1921] 2 K.B. 593. The fact that the third
party's indorsement appears below the word "guarantor" does not prevent that third party
from being held liable as an indorser: *Trimper v Frahn* [1925] S.A.S.R. 347. See also s.56 of the
Bills of Exchange Act 1882.
[84] A surety may be held to the guarantee even though he did not sign the bill as guarantor:
Morris v Stacey (1816) Holt N.P. 153; 171 E.R. 196.

Where the contract between the creditor, the debtor and the surety is **3–24** contained in the negotiable instrument, no further evidence apart from the instrument is required to answer the statute if the obligation appearing on the face of the instrument is the precise obligation assumed by the surety.[85] Thus a person can simply be sued as a guarantor on the basis of his indorsement of a bill of exchange,[86] provided that the indorsement clearly constitutes an undertaking to be liable as guarantor in case of default by the acceptor of the bill.[87] If there are any doubts about the capacity in which a person signs a bill of exchange or cheque, they can be resolved, for example, by a subsequent letter signed by the defendant confirming that he indorsed the bill or cheque as guarantor: the bill or cheque and the letter will be read together thereby satisfying the need for a written memorandum.[88]

The defendant may be liable as guarantor even though he did not **3–25** indorse the bill of exchange or cheque.[89] It is enough for the defendant to write a letter to the creditor enclosing the bill or undertaking to see the creditor paid if the bill is not honoured when it is due.[90]

Not all promises to pay the debt of another are within the Statute of **3–26** Frauds. For example, a promise to pay the debt of another if that other defaults is not within the statute unless the principal debtor remains under the primary liability to pay the debt or honour the principal obligation.[91] But a release of the principal debtor from existing liability will not always take the case outside the statute. Where a creditor agrees to forgo its present claim against the debtor and take from the debtor a bill or note in its place in return for a third party's undertaking to meet the debtor's new liability, this undertaking will be unenforceable unless the statute is satisfied.[92]

If a vendor agrees to supply goods to another and draw bills upon the **3–27** purchaser for the price in exchange for a promise by a third party to take over the bills from the vendor, indorsed without recourse to the vendor, or indorsed with a collateral indemnity to the indorser against his liability as indorser, this promise is within the statute: in substance this is a guarantee of the intended debt.[93] But not all such promises to purchase debts require writing. Thus, where the intention of the parties is that the purchaser of the debt should collect the debt for himself and this is reflected in the price which the vendor is paid for relinquishing the right to recover the debt, the statute will not apply.[94]

---

[85] *J.W. Holmes & Co v Durkee* (1883) Cab. & El. 23.
[86] *Stagg, Mantle & Co v Brodrick* (1895) 12 T.L.R. 12, CA; *G & H Montage v Irvani* [1989] Fin. L.R. 390, CA.
[87] *ibid.* See also *Ulster Banking Co v Mahaffy* (1881) 15 I.L.T. 94.
[88] *Singer v Elliott* (1888) 4 T.L.R. 524 CA.
[89] See *National Sales Corp Ltd v Bernardi* [1931] 2 K.B. 188; *Jenkins & Sons v Coomber* [1898] 2 Q.B. 168.
[90] *ibid.*
[91] See above, paras 3–20 to 3–22.
[92] *Maggs v Ames* (1828) 4 Bing 470; 7 L.J. (O.S.) C.P. 75; 130 E.R. 849; *Emmett v Dewhurst* (1851) 3 Mac. & G. 587; 21 L.J. Ch. 497.
[93] *Mallett v Bateman* (1865) 16 C.B. (N.S.) 530; 35 L.J.C.P. 40.
[94] G. Moss and D. Marks, *Rowlatt on Principal and Surety* (5th ed., 1999), para.3–12.

3–28   Nor is the Statute of Frauds applicable where the promisor undertakes to pay the creditor upon the debtor's default, not from the promisor's own funds, but from assets of the debtor which the promisor has, or expects to have, in his hands.[95] When the drawee of a cheque promises the payee to pay the amount of the cheque out of a balance which the drawee holds to the credit of the drawer, the promise is enforceable without writing.[96] In such a case the promisor is, in effect, surrendering a lien over the debtor's property. The promisor is not promising to answer personally for the principal debt and the promise is not, therefore, within the statute.[97]

3–29   A promise to indemnify a person against any loss that person might incur by becoming a surety on the face of a bill of exchange, a promissory note or a cheque does not require writing whether the promise comes from a stranger or a party who is a principal in the transaction.[98] Thus, in *Guild & Co v Conrad*,[99] where the plaintiffs accepted bills drawn on them by an overseas firm upon the defendant's oral undertaking to find money to enable the plaintiffs to answer their acceptances, the statute did not apply, it being clear that the drawers were not expected to be able to pay the bills.

(iii) Guarantees outside the statute

(a) The general principle

3–30   In some cases, the promisor undertakes to be answerable for the debt, default, or miscarriage of another, in substance and in fact, yet the statute does not apply.[1] In *Harburg India Rubber Comb Co v Martin*[2] Vaughan Williams L.J. explained this phenomenon in the following terms:

> "In each of these cases there was in truth a main contract—a larger contract and the obligation to pay the debt of another was merely an incident of the larger contract. As I understand those cases, it is not a question of motive—it is a question of object. You must find what it was that the parties were in fact dealing about. What was the subject matter of the contract? If the subject matter of the contract was the purchase of property—the relief of property from a liability, the getting rid of encumbrances, the securing greater diligence in the performance of the duty of a factor, or the introduction of business into a stockbroker's office—in all those cases there was a larger matter which was the object of the contract. That being the object of the contract, the mere fact that

---

[95] *Pillans v Van Mierop* (1765) 3 Burr 1663 at 1666–7; 97 E.R. 1035 at 1036–7.
[96] *Ardern v Rowney* (1805) 5 Esp. 254; 170 E.R. 803.
[97] *Harvey v Edwards Dunlop & Co Ltd* (1927) 39 C.L.R. 302.
[98] *Batson v King* (1859) 4 H. & N. 739; 28 L.J. Ex. 327; *Wildes v Dudlow* (1874) L.R. 19 Eq. 198; 44 L.J. Ch. 341; *Re Bolton* (1892) 8 T.L.R. 668; 36 S.J. 608. *Cf. Green v Cresswell* (1837) 10 Ad. & E. 453; 4 Jur. 169.
[99] [1894] 2 Q.B. 885.
[1] A promise which is not within the statute may, nevertheless, constitute a guarantee for other purposes: *Heald v O'Connor* [1971] 1 W.L.R. 497.
[2] [1902] 1 K.B. 778.

as an incident to it—not as the immediate object, but indirectly—the debt of another to a third person will be paid, does not bring the case within the section."[3]

On this analysis, if the principal object of the contract is other than to secure the debt of a third person, the guarantee will fall outside the statute.[4] The courts have accepted that the rule embraces several categories of cases.

3–31

(b) "Relief of property cases"

The statute will not apply if the object of the contract is not simply to be answerable for the debt of another, but to protect property in which the promisor has a legal or equitable interest.[5] Thus a guarantee given to remove an encumbrance from the property,[6] to gain a security,[7] or to avoid the exercise of a power to sell[8] or distrain[9] such property does not require written evidence.[10] It appears to be

3–32

---

[3] ibid., at 786. See also Huggard v Representative Church Body [1916] 1 I.R. 1; Sutton & Co v Grey [1894] 1 Q.B. 285; Ideal Plumbing & Heating Ltd v Pearce (1957) 24 W.W.R. 320, (Can); Macrory v Scott (1850) 5 Exch. 907 at 914; 155 E.R. 396 at 399–400; Gilles v Brown (1916) 53 S.C.R. 557 (a promise to a debtor to pay his debt is not within the statute).

[4] As Low Kee Yang has pointed out, it is often difficult to discern "what the parties are about". He notes that the American rule focuses on the object of the promisor, not the object of both parties: see L. P. Simpson, Handbook of the Law of Suretyship (1950), p.138; Low Kee Yang, The Law of Guarantees in Singapore and Malaysia (1992), p.85.

[5] Fitzgerald v Dressler (1859) 7 C.B.N.S. 374; 141 E.R. 861; Marginson v Ian Potter & Co (1976) 136 C.L.R. 161. See also generally J. Williams, The Statute of Frauds Section IV (1932), pp.18–20, which contains a detailed analysis of the cases. Low Kee Yang suggests that this principle is not really one category of the main object rule but rather a complementary rule with an independent operation: see Low Kee Yang, The Law of Guarantees in Singapore and Malaysia (1992), p.87.

[6] Harburg India Rubber Comb Co v Martin [1902] 1 K.B. 778 at 793 per Cozens-Hardy L.J. (where his Lordship introduced a new category of "the document cases" to explain this principle); Castling v Aubert (1802) 2 East 325; 102 E.R. 393 ; Thomas v Williams (1830) 10 B. & C. 664; 109 E.R. 597; Wood v Benson (1831) 2 Cr. & J. 94; 149 E.R. 40; Fitzgerald v Dressler (1859) 7 C.B.N.S. 374; 141 E.R. 861. Compare Huggard v Representative Church Body [1916] 1 I.R. 1. Moreover, if a creditor gives up property on which he has a lien for a debt to a third person, other than a purchaser, in consideration of a promise by the third person to pay the debt, the promise is not within the statute: Williams v Leper (1766) 3 Burr 1886; 97 E.R. 1152; Castling v Aubert (1802) 2 East 325; 102 E.R. 393; Houlditch v Milne (1800) 3 Esp. 86; Edwards v Kelly (1817) 6 M. & S. 204; 105 E.R. 1219; Thomas v Williams (1830) 10 B. & C. 604; 109 E.R. 597; Bampton v Paulin (1827) 4 Bing 264; 130 E.R. 769. Consequently, a promise by sub-purchaser to pay the vendor direct to secure the release of the vendor's lien does not fall within the statute: Fitzgerald v Dressler (1859) 7 C.B.N.S. 374; 141 E.R. 861. See also Marginson v Potter & Co (1976) 11 A.L.R. 64 (Aus). But the statute does apply where the promise to guarantee payment of a debt of another is given in consideration of a lien not being asserted. See Gull v Lindsay (1849) 4 Exch. 45 at 52; 154 E.R. 1118 at 1121.

[7] Marginson v Ian Potter & Co (1976) 136 C.L.R. 161 at 171; Fitzgerald v Dressler (1859) 7 C.B.N.S. 374; 141 E.R. 861; Williams v Leper (1766) 3 Burr 1886, 1890; 97 E.R. 1152, 1153.

[8] Barrell v Trussell (1811) 4 Taunt 117; 128 E.R. 273; Marginson v Ian Potter & Co (1976) 136 C.L.R. 161.

[9] See, e.g. Williams v Leper (1766) 3 Burr 1886; Bampton v Paulin (1827) 4 Bing 264; Thomas v Williams (1830) 10 B. & C. 664.

[10] Cf. Davys v Buswell [1913] 2 K.B. 47, where the promise was given merely in response to a threat to stop supplies of goods to the company. There was no question of the promise being given to prevent seizure of the goods.

necessary in these cases for the property to be surrendered to the guarantor or his order.[11]

3–33 A modern example is *Marginson v Ian Potter & Co*,[12] where the appellant guaranteed the debts of a company (incurred through trading losses) to a firm of stockbrokers. The company had in fact contracted as agent for a syndicate of which the appellant was a member and which was an undisclosed principal. Gibbs and Mason J.J., at least on the narrow basis of their reasoning, held that the object of the appellant's promise was to free shares held by the company on behalf of the appellant and the other co-syndicators from an exercise of a power of sale which the firm of stockbrokers was entitled to exercise pursuant to its brokerage contract.[13]

3–34 Although the cases are not entirely consistent, if the promise relates to property in which the promisor has a commercial interest only, as a shareholder or director (rather than a legal or equitable interest), the statute will apply.[14] Thus in *Davys v Buswell*[15] the Court of Appeal held that the statute applies even if the promisor is a debenture-holder with a floating charge over the assets and undertaking of the debtor company. Although it might be in the interests of a debenture-holder to assist the debtor to carry on its business and obtain further deliveries of goods which might ultimately be realised by a receiver and manager appointed by the debenture-holder, this is not a sufficient interest to excuse the debenture-holder from complying with the statute.

3–35 The statute does not apply to a promise by a third party to pay a debt out of the proceeds of realisation of property given to the third party by a creditor who has a lien on the property[16] or a promise to pay the debt out of funds of the debtor coming into the hands of the promisor.[17] The rationale is that the object of the transaction is not merely to pay the debt of another but rather to give the promisor an independent interest in the

---

[11] See *Clancy v Piggott* (1835) 2 Ad. & El. 473; 111 E.R. 183; *Rounce v Woodyard* (1846) 8 L.T.O.S. 186; *Bull v Collier* (1842) 4 I.L.R. 107 at 113; *Fennell v Mulcahy* (1845) 8 I.L.R. 434. *Cf. Houlditch v Milne* (1800) 3 Esp. 86.

[12] (1976) 136 C.L.R. 161.

[13] *ibid.*, at 171. For a broader basis, see below, para.3–37.

[14] *Marginson v Ian Potter & Co* (1976) 136 C.L.R. 161 at 171, *per* Gibbs J. (as he then was) and Mason J. (as he then was). See also *Harburg India Rubber Comb Co v Martin* [1902] 1 K.B. 778 at 791; *Davys v Buswell* [1913] 2 K.B. 47 at 58. *Cf.* however, *John C. Love Lumber Co Ltd v Moore* (1962) 36 D.L.R. (2d) 609, CA, in which an owner's promise to pay the subcontractors of his builder if the builder did not, was held not to require writing because the owner had a "financial and property interest" in the work being completed on time: see also *Active Customs Brokers Ltd v Sack* (1987) 37 B.L.R. 229; 25 OAC 305, Ont Div Ct (guarantor was acting president of debtor company).

[15] [1913] 2 K.B. 47. The decision is cited by Gibbs J. and Mason J. in *Marginson v Ian Potter & Co* (1976) 136 C.L.R. 161 at 171 as authority for the proposition stated in the text. But Jacobs J. (at 173) takes the view that there the debenture-holder did have an equitable interest in the assets of the company, and the proper explanation of the case is that the object of the contract was to protect a property right.

[16] *Williams v Leper* (1766) 3 Burr 1886; 97 E.R. 1152; *Castling v Aubert* (1802) East 325; *Houlditch v Milne* (1800) 3 Esp. 86; *Edwards v Kelly* (1817) 6 M. & S. 204; 105 E.R. 1219; *Thomas v Williams* (1830) 10 B. & C. 664; 109 E.R. 597; *Bampton v Paulin* (1827) 4 Bing 264; 130 E.R. 769; *Walker v Taylor* (1834) 6 C. & P. 725.

[17] See *Dixon v Hatfield* (1825) 2 Bing 439; 130 E.R. 375; *Andrews v Smith* (1835) 3 Cr. M. & R. 627; 150 E.R. 267; *Sweeting v Asplin* (1840) 7 M. & W. 165 at 170–171; 151 E.R. 723 at 725–726; *Walker v Rostron* (1842) 9 M. & W. 411; 152 E.R. 174; *Cf. Morley v Boothby* (1825) 3 Bing 107; 130 E.R. 455. See also *Parkins v Moravia* (1824) 1 C. & P. 376.

transaction. The promisor is not a stranger who guarantees a debt but an interested party who is seeking to remove an encumbrance or charge on his own interest. For this reason, the principle is subject to two restrictions. First, an oral promise to pay more than the amount charged on the goods is unenforceable.[18] Secondly, the goods must be surrendered to the promisor, not the debtor.[19]

(c) "The purchase cases"

If the substance of the transaction is to purchase the debt held by the promisee, the statute will not apply, even though an incidental result of such a contract is to secure to the vendor payment of part of the sum owing.[20] It is not entirely clear why the principle of Vaughan Williams L.J. in *Harburg India Rubber Comb Co v Martin*[21] needs to be invoked at all in this context or because the transaction is not one of guarantee but simply constitutes an assignment of the debt.[22]   **3–36**

(d) "The antecedent liability cases"

In *Marginson v Ian Potter & Co*,[23] Jacobs J. indicated that a separate category of cases existed in which the promise related to a debt for which the promisor was antecedently liable.[24] His Honour held on the facts (which are stated earlier in the text) that the appellant's antecedent liability stemmed from the principle that the debtor company, as agent or trustee for the appellant, was entitled to be indemnified by him against debts which it incurred in acting on his behalf in the same transactions. The   **3–37**

---

[18] *Thomas v Williams* (1830) 10 B. & C. 664; 109 E.R. 597 (under duress tenant's goods were surrendered to a broker for sale on his undertaking to pay not merely the arrears of rent but also future rent: held: the statute applied).

[19] *Fennell v Mulcahy* (1845) 8 I.L.R. 434; *Rounce v Woodyard* (1846) 8 L.T.O.S. 186. *Cf. Houlditch v Milne* (1800) 3 Esp. 86.

[20] See this category in J. Williams, *The Statute of Frauds Section IV* (1932), p.21; and see, for example, *Anstey v Marden* (1804) 1 B. & P. (N.R.) 124, 133; 127 E.R. 406, 409. *Cf. Mallett v Bateman* (1865) 16 C.B. (N.S.) 530; 143 E.R. 1235, where Blackburn J. and Pollock C.B. appear to suggest that a promise to purchase a debt is always within the statute. However, these dicta should be confined to cases where the principal object of the transaction was to ensure that the creditor's debt be paid from one source or another. They should not apply to the situation where a third party purchases the creditor's debt and collects it for itself: G. Moss and D. Marks, *Rowlatt on Principal and Surety* (5th ed., 1999), para.3–12.

[21] [1902] 1 K.B. 778. See also *Castling v Aubert* (1802) 2 East 325.

[22] An assignment, of course, may require other formalities to be complied with before it is effective.

[23] (1976) 136 C.L.R. 161 at 174. See also *Orrell v Coppock* (1856) 2 Jur. N.S. 1244; 26 L.J. Ch. 269.

[24] See above, para.3–33. Consequently, a promise to pay a sum to compromise the liability of another is not within the statute if the promisor is alleged, rightly or wrongly, to be liable for the same debt: *Orrell v Coppock* (1856) L.J. Ch 269. See also *Pillans v Van Mierop* (1765) 3 Burr 1664 at 1666–1667; 97 E.R. 1035 at 1036 (a promise to honour a bill to be drawn on the promisor for the account of a third party).

stockbrokers, to whom the debt was incurred, were entitled to claim this right of indemnity through subrogation.[25] The result was that the appellant's promise was not solely to answer for the debt, default or miscarriage of another, but had the wider objective of discharging an antecedent liability to a third party (that is, the company).[26]

3–38   It has been seen[27] that Gibbs and Mason J.J. apparently based their decision on the ground that the appellant's promise had the object of relieving the property from an exercise of the power of sale. But their Honours also refer to the fact that "the [appellant's] promise related to a debt for which he was antecedently liable",[28] indicating that this was an alternative basis for their decision. Gibbs and Mason J.J., however, regarded the antecedent liability as founded on a different ground from that suggested by Jacobs J., namely, that the appellant was liable not to the company but to *the firm of the stockbrokers* as an undisclosed principal on whose behalf the company acted. By the date of the action against the appellant, however, the appellant and the other syndicators were no longer liable because the firm of stockbrokers had obtained a judgment against the company.[29] But again, on this analysis it would appear that there is no need to invoke the special principle in *Harburg India Rubber Comb Co v Martin*[30] because the effect of the appellant's promise to the stockbrokers was simply to revive a primary liability. The promise was not a guarantee at all because the promise did not secure a secondary liability.

(e) Del credere agents

3–39   A del credere agent is one who is engaged to negotiate sales on a higher scale of commission than ordinary agents. This higher reward is paid in consideration of the agent's taking greater care in sales to customers and in assuming responsibility for their solvency and their performance of the contracts[31] The agent's promise is not the only factor which connects him to the transaction: the agent's involvement is required by the customary terms of his employment.[32] Ultimately, this arrangement may result in the liability of a del credere agent for the debt of one or more of the purchasers, but that is not its immediate object. Consequently, a contract for the employment of a del credere agent need

---

[25] (1976) 136 C.L.R. 161 at 175.
[26] *ibid.*
[27] See above, para.3–33.
[28] (1976) 136 C.L.R. 161 at 171.
[29] (1976) 136 C.L.R. 161 at 169. The general rule is that the liability of an undisclosed principal merges in the judgment obtained against the agent by a third party: see *Petersen v Moloney* (1951) 84 C.L.R. 91 at 102–104.
[30] [1902] 1 K.B. 778.
[31] For a concise statement of the nature of a del credere agent's liability, see *Morris v Cleasby* (1816) 4 M. & S. 566; 105 E.R. 943. See also *Wolff v Koppel* (1843) 5 Hill, New York Rep. 458.
[32] *Fleet v Murton* (1871) L.R. 7 Q.B. 126 at 133; *Sutton & Co v Grey* [1894] 1 Q.B. 285 (where the promisor agreed to introduce clients to stockbrokers upon terms which were similar to those which apply to a del credere agent).

not satisfy the statute.[33] The responsibility of a del credere agent is not a collateral undertaking but rather an incident of the agency.[34]

Although these four categories of cases (b) to (e) have been identified as situations in which the guarantee is only "an incident" to a contract having a wider objective, they are probably not exclusive categories.[35] Thus if the creditor can show that the guarantee is given as a subsidiary part of a major transaction, involving quite different rights and obligations, it is arguable the statute will not apply.

3–40

By the same token, the mere fact that the promisor derives some benefit, such as a fee or commission, in return for his undertaking to be answerable for the debt, default or miscarriage of another is not, in itself, sufficient to take the promise outside the statute.[36] It is not the promisor's motive but rather the main object of the contract that determines whether the promise must comply with the statute.[37]

3–41

4. FALSE REPRESENTATIONS AS TO CREDIT

Section 4 of the Statute of Frauds did not apply to false and fraudulent representations as to the credit of a third person.[38] At common law an action for deceit lay upon such a representation even in the absence of writing.[39] As oral guarantees were unenforceable under the statute, plaintiffs sought damages in such actions at common law.[40] This gap in s.4 was so exploited that it was necessary to introduce s.6 of the Statute of Frauds Amendment Act 1828.[41] (Lord Tenterden's Act), which provided that no action could be brought upon a false representation as to the credit

3–42

---

[33] *Couturier v Hastie* (1852) 8 Ex. 40, reversed on other grounds in (1856) 5 H.L.C. 673; *Harburg India Rubber Comb Co v Martin* [1902] 1 K.B. 778 at 793. Some commentators argue that the main object in a del credere agent situation is ultimately to provide a guarantee and that the del credere agent's promise should not fall outside the statute: see, *e.g.* Low Kee Yang, *The Law of Guarantees in Singapore and Malaysia* (1992), p.86. But this ignores the other important elements of the del credere agent's position, namely the higher reward and the extra care involved in selecting customers. The guarantee of the customers' solvency is merely one aspect of the arrangement. See generally Bowsted and Reynolds, *Agency* (17th ed., 2001), para.1–038.

[34] G. Moss and D. Marks, *Rowlatt on Principal and Surety* (5th ed., 1999), para.3–21.

[35] A possible further category is where the guarantor does not incur personal liability but charges his property by way of security for another's debt: see G.H. Treitel (11th ed., 2003), pp.182–183 and the cases there cited. But in *Bank of Scotland v Wright* [1990] BCC 663 at 680, Brooke J. doubted the existence of this category. In any event, in this situation the charge will invariably be in writing. Note also that an oral agreement varying the mode of performance of a guarantee obligation can probably be relied upon by way of defence: *Re a Debtor* (unreported, HC, Ch. D., November 25, 1991).

[36] Compare *Sutton & Co v Grey* [1894] Q.B. 285.

[37] *Harburg Indian Rubber Comb Co v Martin* [1902] 1 K.B. 778 at 786 *per* Vaughan Williams L.J.

[38] *Ex p. Carr* (1814) 3 Ves. & B. 108; 35 E.R. 420, LC.

[39] *Paisley v Freeman* (1789) 3 Term Rep. 51; 100 E.R. 450.

[40] Sometimes, however, the court would deny relief on the ground that there was nothing more than a guarantee unenforceable under the Statute of Frauds: see, *e.g. Smith v Harris* (1817) 2 Stark. 47, N.P.; 171 E.R. 568.

[41] 9 Geo IV, c.14.

of another unless it was in writing[42] and signed by the party making the representation.[43] Given the historical background to this section, a slight digression to consider its present scope may be excused.

3–43   Early in the life of Lord Tenterden's Act, it was established that s.6 only applied to fraudulent misrepresentations as to another's credit.[44] It was not enough for the representation to be false[45] or merely careless.[46] It was necessary to show that the defendant knew the statement was untrue and that the defendant made it with the intention of inducing the plaintiff to act upon it. Furthermore, the plaintiffs were required to prove that they acted on the misrepresentation to their detriment.[47] It did not matter that the plaintiffs were partly influenced by oral statements, provided their actions were substantially induced by the written representation.[48] These principles have survived.

3–44   The section applies to false representations as to the credit of *"any other person"*.[49] In this context "person" includes a company.[50] Moreover, a representation by a partner as to the credit of the partner's firm is caught by the section,[51] but the firm itself is not liable for the representation even if the other partners knew and approved of it.[52] Only the party signing the representation can be charged with it.[53]

3–45   Unlike s.4 of the Statute of Frauds, s.6 of the Statute of Frauds Amendment Act 1828 applies whether or not the party to be charged obtains a benefit from the credit, money or goods supplied to the other person on the faith of that party's representation.[54] As s.6 is limited in its application to fraudulent misrepresentations as to credit, it will not protect those in the finance industry from an action in tort for negligent misstatement. Indeed, the repeal of the section has been recommended because it is illogical that a fraudulent misrepresentation, in addition to a promise, should be in writing: "a promise is a promise, a fraud is a fraud, and the difference is significant."[55]

---

[42] No representation, no matter how false or fraudulent, was of any legal effect if it was made for the purpose stated in the section: *Clydesdale Bank Ltd v Paton* [1896] A.C. 381. See also *Haslock v Fergusson* (1837) 7 Ad. & El. 86; 112 E.R. 403 and *Swann v Phillips* (1838) 8 Ad. & El. 457; 112 E.R. 912.

[43] See *UBAF Ltd v European American Banking Corp* [1984] 2 All E.R. 226, where the Court of Appeal held that, for the purposes of s.6 of Lord Tenterden's Act, a representation signed on behalf of a company by its duly-authorised agent acting within the scope of his authority, or by an officer or employee acting in the course of his duties in the business of the company, constituted a representation made by the company and signed by it.

[44] *Banbury v Bank of Montreal* [1918] A.C. 626; *Behn v Kemble* (1859) 7 C.B.N.S. 260; 141 E.R. 816; *Paisley v Freeman* (1789) 3 Term Rep. 51; 100 E.R. 450.

[45] *Behn v Kemble* (1859) 7 C.B.N.S. 260; 141 E.R. 816.

[46] *Bishop v Balkis Consolidated Co* (1890) 25 Q.B.D. 512.

[47] *Behn v Kemble* (1859) 7 C.B.N.S. 260; 141 E.R. 816.

[48] *Tatton v Wade* (1856) 18 C.B. 371; 139 E.R. 1413.

[49] Emphasis added.

[50] *Banbury v Bank of Montreal* [1918] A.C. 626; *Hirst v West Riding Union Banking Co* [1901] 2 K.B. 560.

[51] *Devaux v Steinkeller* (1839) 6 Bing N.C. 84; 133 E.R. 33; *Turnbull & Co v Mackay* [1932] N.Z.L.R. 1300. See also *Fortune v Young* [1918] S.C. 1.

[52] *Turnbull & Co v Mackay* [1932] N.Z.L.R 1300.

[53] *Williams v Mason* (1873) 28 L.T. 232. This is because s.6 is directed at the mental fraud of the person making the representation. See also *Swift v Jewsbury* (1874) L.R. 9 Q.B. 301.

[54] *Pearson v Seligman* (1883) 48 L.T. 842, CA.

5. THE FORM OF WRITTEN EVIDENCE REQUIRED BY THE STATUTE OF FRAUDS

(i) The general principles

Leaving aside guarantees outside the statute and false representations as to credit, let us now consider what written evidence is needed for guarantees within the statute.[56] Section 4 requires that the guarantee itself or some memorandum or note thereof shall be in writing.[57]

3–46

It provides two separate ways in which a contract of guarantee may be made enforceable. The first way is by having a written agreement signed by the parties to be charged or their agent; the second way is by having a note or memorandum of the agreement signed in a similar manner. In the latter case the agreement itself may be oral as long as there is written evidence of the agreement to satisfy the statute.

3–47

Elpis Mairtime Co Ltd v Marti Chartering Co Inc[58] illustrates the application of both these methods of complying with the statute. In that case, negotiations for a charterparty were conducted partly by telephone and partly by telex between the owners' brokers, Tramp Maritime Co Ltd ("Tramp"), and the charterers' brokers, "Marti". During these negotiations Tramp insisted that Marti should itself provide a guarantee, initially only in respect of the charterers' liability for demurrage but ultimately the guarantee was extended to include the charterers' liability for freight. Marti orally agreed to provide such a guarantee in its own right.[59] The guarantee was incorporated in a written charterparty which consisted of several pages. The front sheet was stamped and signed for the owners as principals. It was also stamped and signed for Marti with the following words typed above the stamp and signature: "For and on behalf of charterers as brokers only". On all the succeeding pages except the last three there appeared a stamp and signature for Marti but without the qualification that they were inserted only as brokers for the charterers. At the end of the last page of the charterparty, there was a stamp and signature for Marti with the word "charterers" typed above them. Clause 24 of the charterparty, which was on the second page of the additional typed pages, stated that Marti guaranteed "outstanding demurrage, if any and for balance freight".

3–48

After the voyage was completed the owners claimed a sum due to them in respect of demurrage and freight. The charterers paid nothing, and an

3–49

---

[55] See the Law Reform Commission of Tasmania Report No. 50, "Suretyship and Guarantee" (1987), pp.13–14.

[56] As a result of the Mercantile Law Amendment Act 1856, it is no longer necessary for the consideration for the promise to appear in the written evidence of the guarantee. Some of the earlier cases which decided that the writing was insufficient simply because the consideration was not apparent on its face should, therefore, be treated with caution as they might be decided differently today: see above, para.3–06.

[57] Writing includes typing, printing, lithography, photography and other ways of representing or reproducing words in a visible form: Interpretation Act 1978, s.5 and Sch.1.

[58] [1992] 1 A.C. 21.

[59] It was this fact which enabled their Lordships to distinguish *Young v Schuler* (1883) 11 Q.B.D. 651. See below, para.3–51.

arbitration award for the full amount of the claim, with interest and costs, was ultimately entered against them. No amount of the award was paid by the charterers.

3–50   In the present proceedings, the owners sought to enforce the guarantee against Marti. Marti contended, *inter alia*, that the guarantee was unenforceable because it did not comply with s.4 of the Statute of Frauds 1677.

3–51   In determining whether the guarantee was enforceable against Marti, the House of Lords considered two alternative assumptions. On the first assumption, Marti affixed its signature to the page of the charterparty containing the guarantee as a contracting party. On that assumption, the prior oral agreement by Marti to provide a guarantee was subsumed in the written agreement contained in clause 24 of the charterparty. This written agreement was signed by Marti on its own account. Accordingly, on this assumption the guarantee was signed by the party to be charged and the requirements of s.4 of the statute were satisfied.[60]

3–52   The alternative assumption was that all Marti's signatures on the charterparty, including the signature on the page containing the guarantee in clause 24, were affixed by Marti solely as agents for the charterers. On this assumption, Marti was never a party to the document in its own right and the prior oral agreement of guarantee between Marti and the owners was not subsumed in clause 24 of the charterparty.[61] The original oral agreement of guarantee remained intact and the only remaining question was whether clause 24 of the charterparty constituted a sufficient memorandum or note of the prior oral guarantee to satisfy the statute. Their Lordships decided that Marti's intention or capacity to sign was "wholly irrelevant"[62] to the question whether Marti signed in its own right or as agents for the charterers as well. They concluded that clause 24 of the charterparty contained all the terms of the prior oral guarantee and it was, therefore, a sufficient note or memorandum of this guarantee to comply with the statute. Consequently, it made no difference whether Marti signed as a contracting party in its own right or as agent for the charterers. Either way, Marti's guarantee satisfied s.4 of the Statute of Frauds 1677 and the owners were entitled to summary judgment for the full amount of their claim.

3–53   Since the object of the statute is to exclude parol evidence,[63] any writing embodying the terms of the agreement and signed by the person to be charged or that person's lawfully authorised agent, is sufficient.[64] The memorandum need not be addressed to the creditor as long as the creditor can be identified from the memorandum evidencing the guarantee[65] or from a written answer accepting the guarantee offered.[66]

---

[60] [1992] 1 A.C. 21 at 32.
[61] [1992] 1 A.C. 21 at 33.
[62] *ibid.*
[63] Under the modern law of evidence it is doubtful whether there is a danger of contracts of guarantee being established by false evidence or evidence of loose talk so there is less justification for rendering oral guarantees unenforceable: *The Technology Partnership v Afro-Asian Satellite Communications (UK) Ltd* (unreported, Court of Appeal (Civil Division), October 12, 1998) at p.10 of the Lexis transcript, *per* Peter Gibson L.J.

The intention of the person who signs the document or memorandum is immaterial.[67] All that is required is evidence under the hand of the alleged guarantor or that person's lawfully authorised agent that he has given a promise which falls within the terms of the statute. This written evidence must contain a sufficient admission that a contract of guarantee was entered into and a statement of the terms of the contract.[68] A letter to an agent or friend of the person sought to be charged may be sufficient;[69] so too may an affidavit in a different matter;[70] even a signed entry in a personal diary will suffice.[71] Moreover, the requirements of the statute can be satisfied by a recital in a will which confirms that the testator has guaranteed certain debts.[72] It is no objection in all these cases that the document signed by the party to be charged was not intended to serve as a guarantee,[73] although the signature must convey approval of the contents of the memorandum.[74] A note or memorandum which denies the existence of a contract to guarantee will obviously not satisfy the statute[75] but written evidence that unambiguously recognises the existence of the contract yet purports to repudiate it may be sufficient.[76] Indeed, the idea of

---

[64] *Re Hoyle; Hoyle v Hoyle* [1893]1 Ch. 84 at 99. No special form is necessary: *Jones v Williams* (1841) 7 M. & W. 493; 10 L.J. Ex. 120; 151 E.R. 860; *Gibson v Holland* (1865) L.R. 1 C.P. 1 at 5–6; *Bailey v Sweeting* (1861) 9 C.B. (N.S.) 843; 142 E.R. 332. But the memorandum or note must indicate the existence of the alleged guarantee and state its terms: *The Technology Partnership v Afro-Asian Satellite Communications (UK) Ltd* (unreported, Court of Appeal (Civil Division), October 12, 1998).

[65] *Williams v Lake* (1863) 2 E. & E. 349; 121 E.R. 132; *Williams v Byrnes* (1863) 1 Moo P.C.C.N.S. 154; 15 E.R. 660, PC. *Cf. Glover v Halkett* (1857) 2 H. & N. 487; 157 E.R. 201; *Brettel v Williams* (1849) 4 Exch. 623; 154 E.R. 1363; *Vandenbergh v Spooner* (1866) L.R. 1 Exch. 316; *Gibson v Holland* (1865) L.R. 1 C.P. 1 (contract for purchase of goods). But see *Walton v Dodson* (1827) 3 C. & P. 162.

[66] *Williams v Byrnes* (1863) 1 Moo P.C.C.N.S. 154 at 198; 15 E.R. 660 at 675; *Re Agra and Masterman's Bank* (1867) L.R. 2 Ch. App. 391. If the evidence shows that the party to whom the guarantee was addressed is merely an agent, the principal can enforce the guarantee: *Bateman v Phillips* (1812) 15 East 272; 104 E.R. 847; *Gibson v Holland* (1865) L.R. 1 C.P. 1. *Cf. Walton v Dodson* (1827) 3 C. & P. 162; *Garrett v Handley* (1825) 4 B. & C. 664; 107 E.R. 1208 (a guarantee given to one partner for the benefit of all the partners can be enforced by the several partners of the firm).

[67] *Re Hoyle; Hoyle v Hoyle* [1893] 1 Ch. 84; *Elpis Maritime Co Ltd v Marti Chartering Co Inc* [1991] 3 All E.R. 758. See also *Jones v Victoria Graving Dock Co* (1877) 2 Q.B.D. 314 (an entry in a company minute book signed by the company chairman was a sufficient memorandum). See also below, para.3–56.

[68] *Tiverton Ltd v Wearwell Ltd* [1975] 1 Ch. 146; *Motemtronic Ltd v Autocar Equipment Ltd* (unreported, Court of Appeal, Civil Division, June 20, 1996).

[69] See *Bailey v Sweeting* (1861) 9 C.B. N.S. 843; 142 E.R. 332; *Re Hoyle; Hoyle v Hoyle* [1893] 1 Ch. 84 at 99; *Bateman v Phillips* (1812) 15 East 272; 104 E.R. 847. *Cf. Allaway v Duncan* (1867) 16 L.T. 264 (letter by attorney not sufficient in the circumstances).

[70] *Re Hoyle; Hoyle v Hoyle* [1893] 1 Ch. 84 at 100.

[71] *ibid.*, cited with approval by the House of Lords in *Elpis Maritime Co Ltd v Marti Chartering Co Inc, The Maria D* [1992] 1 A.C. 21 at 32–33.

[72] *Re Hoyle; Hoyle v Hoyle* [1893] 1 Ch. 84. Even an admission in pleadings that there is an enforceable guarantee will suffice: *Lucas v Dixon* (1889) 22 Q.B.D. 357 at 361 *per* Bowen L.J. It would, however, appear to be necessary for the plaintiff to discontinue the proceedings and commence another action because otherwise the memorandum or note of the guarantee would not be in existence before the commencement of the action. See *Lucas v Dixon* (1889) 22 Q.B.D. 357 at 363 *per* Fry L.J.

[73] What matters is the substance, not the form, of the contract: *Seaton v Heath* [1899] 1 Q.B. 782 at 792 *per* Romer L.J.; *Re Denton's Estate* [1904] 2 Ch. 178.

such an undertaking need not be present in the mind of the person signing the memorandum.[77] Nor is it necessary for the agreement between the parties to be finalised before the memorandum is given. Thus a memorandum may be sufficient to satisfy the statute although it is signed by the party to be charged before the agreement is concluded by verbal acceptance.[78]

3–54   The memorandum must be in existence when the action on the guarantee is commenced. For this reason, an admission in an affidavit in the cause that there is an enforceable guarantee will not suffice.[79]

3–55   With the advent of electronic communications it became necessary to modify legislation dealing with formal requirements in relation to documents and instruments. Under s.8 of the Electronic Communications Act 2000 the appropriate Minister may by order made by statutory instrument modify the provisions of any enactment, including s.4 of the Statute of Frauds 1677. To authorise or facilitate the use of electronic communications or electronic storage, the appropriate Minister may make orders determining how written evidence of a guarantee may be provided in electronic communications. The only qualification on this power is that the method authorised by the Minister must be "no less satisfactory" than the current requirements under s.4 of the Statute of Frauds 1677.

---

[74] *Clipper Maritime Ltd v Shirlstar Container Transport Ltd* [1987] 1 Lloyd's Rep. 546 at 554, in which Staughton J. was of the view that an answer back of the receiver of a telex (as opposed to the sender) would not constitute a valid signature since it only authenticates the document and does not convey approval of the contents.

[75] *Thirkell v Cambi* [1919] 2 K.B. 590; *Tiverton Estates v Wearwell* [1975] Ch. 146; (the words "subject to contract" showed that the signatory did not acknowledge the contract) *Daulia Ltd v Four Millbank Nominees Ltd* [1978] Ch. 231. Cf. *Law v Jones* [1974] Ch. 112, CA.

[76] *Thirkell v Cambi* [1919] 2 K.B. 590 at 595; *Dewar v Mintoft* [1912] 2 K.B. 373. See also *Bailey v Sweeting* (1861) 9 C.B.N.S. 843; 142 E.R. 332; *Wilkinson v Evans* (1866) L.R. 1 C.P. 407; *Buxton v Rust* (1872) L.R. 7 Exch. 279; and G. Andrews and R. Millett, *Law of Guarantees* (3rd ed., 2000), para.3.22.

[77] *Re Hoyle; Hoyle v Hoyle* [1893] 1 Ch. 84 at 98.

[78] *Stewart v Eddowes* (1874) L.R. 9 C.P. 311; *O'Young and Lum v Reid & Co Ltd* [1932] A.L.R. 278. See below, paras 3–81 to 3–86. See also *Parker v Clark* [1960] 1 W.L.R. 286 at 295–296 per Devlin J.; *Reuss v Picksley* (1866) L.R. 1 Ex. 342.

[79] *Middleton v Brewer* (1790) 1 Peake 20; *Spurrier v Fitzgerald* (1801) 6 Ves. Jun. 548; 31 E.R. 1189. As to whether this problem can be overcome by discontinuing the action and commencing another, see *Lucas v Dixon* (1889) 22 Q.B.D. 357 at 363 per Fry L.J.; *Farr, Smith & Co Ltd v Messers Ltd* [1928] 1 K.B. 397 (a reconstituted action may be treated as a new action for this purpose) and *Grindell v Bass* [1920] 2 Ch. 487 at 493.

(ii) Connected documents

The need for written evidence of a guarantee under the statute can be   **3–56**
satisfied by several documents if they are connected together.[80] Before
documents can be read together for this purpose, the document signed by
the party to be charged must contain an express or implied reference to
some other document which provides the necessary terms.[81] It is
sufficient if the documents are connected by necessary inference and
natural intendment.[82] No such inference can be drawn where the
documents sought to be linked are inconsistent as to the terms of the
guarantee.[83] Nor is it sufficient that the documents refer to one another:
there must be a clear agreement to provide a guarantee.[84] Furthermore, a
document will not be incorporated by reference in another simply
because the subject matter and one of the parties are the same.[85] But if
the requisite nexus exists, it does not matter that the guarantor has never
seen the other document which is to be read together with the one he or
she has signed.[86]

In *Thomson v McInnes*,[87] Griffith L.J. was of the view[88] that there must   **3–57**
generally be a definite reference to another document, not just to a
transaction in the course of which another document may or may not have
been written. But this test probably no longer represents the law, and it is
now sufficient that another transaction is referred to, with the transaction

---

[80] *Coe v Duffield* (1822) 7 Moore C.P. 252; *Macrory v Scott* (1850) 5 Exch. 907; 155 E.R. 396; *Brettel v Williams* (1849) 4 Exch. 623; 154 E.R. 1363; *Williams v Byrnes* (1863) 1 Moo P.C.C.N.S. 154 at 198; 15 E.R. 660 at 675, PC; *Sheers v Thimbleby* (1897) 76 L.T. 709; 13 T.L.R. 451; *Cf. Timmins v Moreland Street Property Co* [1958] 1 Ch. 110 (it was impossible to find any such reference in the cheque in this case).

[81] *Long v Millar* (1879) 4 C.P.D. 450; *Timmins v Moreland Street Property Co Ltd* [1958] 1 Ch. 110 at 130 *per* Jenkin L.J. Cheques which do not refer to the specific transaction cannot be used to satisfy the statute: *Harvie v Gibbons* (1980) 109 D.L.R. (3d) 559, Alta, CA (where an incomplete reference on a cheque, endorsed by the vendor, was supplemented by a map drawn by the purchaser in the vendor's presence at the time of the agreement, and by an unsigned note of a conversation with the vendor's executrix after the vendor's death). See also *Harvey v Edwards Dunlop & Co Ltd* (1927) 39 C.L.R. 302; *De Leuil v Jeremy* (1964) 65 S.R. (NSW) 137; *Glass v Pioneer Rubber Works of Australia Ltd* [1906] V.L.R. 754; *Tooth & Co Ltd v Bryen (No.2)* (1922) 22 S.R. (NSW) 541. If the reference to the other document is unclear, oral evidence may be adduced to identify it: *Timmins v Moreland Street Property Co Ltd* [1958] Ch. 110; *Long v Millar* (1879) 4 C.P.D. 450. Parol evidence is admissible to establish the requisite nexus: *Long v Millar* (1879) 4 C.P.D. 450; *Ridgway v Wharton* (1857) 6 H.L. Cas. 238; 10 E.R. 1287.

[82] *Ballantine v Harold* (1893) 19 V.L.R. 465. But the connection cannot be established solely by parol evidence: *Boydell v Drummond* (1809) 11 East 142; 103 E.R. 958; *Timmins v Moreland Street Property Co Ltd* [1958] Ch. 110 at 130 *per* Jenkins L.J.; *Smith v Dixon* (1839) 3 Jur. 770; *Peirce v Corf* (1874) L.R. 9 Q.B. 210; *Long v Millar* (1879) 4 C.P.D. 450. See also *Jay v Gainsford* (unreported, Court of Appeal, October 4, 1977).

[83] See *Corcoran v O'Rourke* (1888) 14 V.L.R. 889.

[84] *Motemtronic Ltd v Autocar Equipment Ltd* (unreported, Court of Appeal, Civil Division, June 20, 1996).

[85] *Nicholls v Davis* (1889) 15 V.L.R. 184.

[86] *Macrory v Scott* (1850) 5 Exch. 907; 155 E.R. 396.

[87] (1912) 12 C.L.R. 562.

[88] *ibid.*, at 569.

being explained and the appropriate document being identified by parol evidence.[89]

3–58   Where the relevant documents are physically connected, the cross-reference from one to another may be implied simply from the connection.[90] Thus in *M'Ewan v Dynon*[91] a guarantee was attached to an account by folding the corners of both documents several times. This annexure satisfied the Statute of Frauds because it constituted an implicit reference in the guarantee to the attached account.

3–59   If an agreement which creates a debt refers to an attached guarantee of the debt the terms of the agreement may be incorporated in the guarantee annexed.[92] A guarantee described in an instrument as an attached document may be incorporated by reference even though it is annexed later with the assent of both parties.[93] Moreover, a deed which refers to a guarantee as an attached document may be read together with the guarantee even if the latter is detached and then signed by a defendant who has not seen the deed.[94]

3–60   The authorities give some examples of documents which can be read together to provide a sufficient memorandum of a guarantee. An indorsement on an envelope can be taken to refer to a piece of letter paper contained therein for the purpose of ascertaining whether there is a sufficient memorandum within the statute.[95] Correspondence between the parties,[96] even subsequent correspondence signed by the guarantor's agent,[97] can be incorporated by reference in a guarantee. A power of attorney and a course of correspondence between solicitors were so connected in one case as to constitute a memorandum in writing.[98] Similarly, where a deed of variation extending the term of a lease was signed by the guarantor of the lease, the deed and guarantee in the lease were read together so as to render the guarantor liable for the rent during the extended term.[99] Even a reference in a signed document to an unsigned document which contained full particulars of the transaction and which

---

[89] *Woden Squash Courts Pty Ltd v Zero Builders Pty Ltd* [1976] 2 N.S.W.L.R. 212 at 218; *Stokes v Whicher* [1920] 1 Ch. 411 at 418; *Elias v George Sahely & Co (Barbados) Ltd* [1983] 1 A.C. 646 at 655.

[90] *M'Ewan v Dynon* (1877) 3 V.L.R. (L) 271; *Pearce v Gardner* [1897] 1 Q.B. 688.

[91] (1877) 3 V.L.R. (L) 271. Cf., however, the harsh decision in *Corcoran v O'Rourke* (1888) 14 VLR 889 that separate memoranda on different sides of the same piece of paper did not satisfy the Statute of Frauds.

[92] *Chambers v Rankine* [1910] S.A.L.R. 73.

[93] *Lawrence v Fordham* [1922] V.L.R. 705. In this context, the term "attached" may be interpreted liberally to include "accompanying".

[94] *Macrory v Scott* (1850) 5 Exch. 907; 155 E.R. 396.

[95] *Freeman v Freeman* (1891) 7 T.L.R. 431. But words written on an envelope containing no reference to the letter enclosed inside may not be read together to provide a sufficient memorandum: *Tomlinson Bros & Co v Daniels* (1930) 33 W.A.L.R. 101. Cf. *Richard v Stillwell* (1883) 8 O.R. 511.

[96] *Bristol, Cardiff and Swansea Aerated Bread Co v Maggs* (1890) 44 Ch. D. 616 at 625; *Hussey v Horne Payne* (1879) 4 App. Cas. 311; *Redhead v Cator* (1815), as reported in 1 Stark 14, NP; 171 E.R. 387; *Coe v Duffield* (1822) 7 Moore C.P. 252; *Sheers v Thimbleby & Son* (1897) 76 L.T. 709 (defendant's letter dated September 15 together with the plaintiff's letter dated September 16).

[97] *Brettel v Williams* (1849) 4 Exch. 623; 154 E.R. 1363.

[98] *Harvey v Edwards Dunlop & Co Ltd* (1927) 39 C.L.R. 302.

[99] *Goodaston v F.H. Burgess Plc* [1998] L. & T.R. 46.

was sent to a solicitor to be reduced to form was enough to allow the documents to be read together.[1]

Where the parties to a lease, including the guarantors, purport to extend **3–61** the term of the lease by deed, the original lease is surrendered and a new lease is granted by operation of law.[2] Moreover, the combination of the original lease and the extension deed is a sufficient note or memorandum of the guarantee to satisfy the Statute of Frauds. Consequently, the guarantors cannot escape liability on the ground that there was no express written guarantee of the new lease.[3]

Where the guarantors terminate a continuing guarantee at the same time **3–62** as the principal debtor terminates the principal contract, the liability of the guarantors will not be revived when a new main contract is executed.[4] There is no implication that the revoked guarantee will apply to the new contract, and the written evidence supporting the original guarantee cannot support an implied guarantee in relation to the new contract.[5] But the written evidence supporting the original guarantee might satisfy the statute in relation to the revived guarantee if there is an express agreement to that effect.[6]

(iii) Contents of the memorandum

(a) Names of the parties

The parties to a contract of guarantee must be specified expressly in the **3–63** contract or be identifiable by a reasonable construction of the contract or by a reference to a linked document.[7] It is not necessary that they be named in the guarantee itself.[8]

Extrinsic oral evidence is admissible to enable the parties to a contract **3–64** to be specifically identified when they have been described in the

---

[1] *Ridgway v Wharton* (1857) 6 H.L. Cas 238; 10 E.R. 1287.
[2] *Jenkin R. Lewis & Son Ltd v Kenman* [1971] 1 Ch. 477.
[3] *Goodaston Ltd v F.H. Burgess Plc* [1998] L. & T.R. 46.
[4] *Silverburn Finance UK Ltd v Salt* [2001] Lloyd's Rep. Bank 119.
[5] *ibid.*
[6] *ibid.*, at 124, *per* Rix L.J.
[7] All the parties must be identified or identifiable: *Riley v Melrose Advertisers* (1915) 17 W.A.L.R. 127; *Williams v Byrnes* (1863) 1 Moo P.C.C. (NS) 154; 15 ER 660; *Williams v Lake* (1859) 2 E & E 349; 121 E.R. 132; *Imperial Bank of Canada v Nixon* [1926] 4 D.L.R. 1052, CA. See also *AGS Electronics Ltd v Sherman* (1979) 19 B.C.L.R. 22, SC and *Sims v Robertson* (1921) 21 S.R. (NSW) 246, where there was a sufficient description of the parties in the light of the surrounding circumstances; *A Macdonald & Co v Fletcher* (1915) 22 B.C.R. 298 (Can) (parol evidence was not admissible to show that the ledger on which the guarantee was written belonged to the plaintiffs); *Freeman v Freeman* (1891) 7 T.L.R. 431 (parol evidence was admissible to connect an envelope which mentioned the plaintiff's name with a guarantee enclosed in the envelope). But where a guarantee is given in return for a cash consideration it is not necessary for the memorandum to state the name of the person who provided the consideration: *Dutchman v Tooth* (1839) 5 Bing N.C. 577; 132 E.R. 1222. Note the possibility of rectification of the guarantee where the names of the parties are not specified: see below, paras 3–79 to 3–80.
[8] *Rossiter v Miller* (1878) 3 App. Cas. 1124 at 1153.

memorandum in general terms.[9] Thus a written guarantee in favour of "each and every member of The Wholesale Spirit Merchants' Association of Victoria [and the] Wine and Producers' Association of Victoria"[10] or "all those who are unsecured creditors of the debtor at a certain date"[11] is a sufficient memorandum.[12] The function of the evidence in this context is simply explanatory, enabling the parties possessing the characteristics described to be identified. Similarly, oral evidence is admissible to show the composition of the members of a firm when an abbreviated description of the firm appears in the memorandum[13] or to show the precise identity of the company when the company name is abbreviated.[14]

3–65   Even if there may be a conflict of fact for the judge to decide as to those persons coming within the general description in the memorandum, the evidence is admissible.[15] However, it is not possible to adduce extrinsic evidence when the memorandum contains little or no guidance as to the characteristics of a person alleged to be a party.[16] To admit such evidence in these circumstances would be to prove the intention of the maker of the

[9] *Rosser v Austral Wine & Spirit Co Pty Ltd* [1980] V.R. 313; *Re A & K Holdings Pty Ltd* [1964] V.R. 257; *Sims v Robertson* (1921) 21 S.R. (NSW) 246; *Expotech Pty Ltd v Kwiatkowski* (unreported, Qld Sup Ct, April 7, 1995) (where the phrase "your offer of guarantee" was construed as relating to a particular offeror by reference to a prior conversation); *Bateman v Phillips* (1812) 15 East 272; 104 E.R. 847. The parol evidence rule does not bar such evidence. But it is not sufficient for the document to refer incidentally to the parties without making it clear that they are parties to the contract: *Vandenbergh v Spooner* (1866) L.R. 1 Exch. 316 (where the vendor's name as vendor was not mentioned in the document even though it occurred as part of the description of the goods); *Newell v Radford* (1867) L.R. 3 C.P. 52 and G. Andrews and R. Millett, *Law of Guarantees* (3rd ed., 2000), para.3.23. As to parol evidence of vitiating factors affecting a written guarantee, see K.P. McGuiness *The Law of Guarantee* (2nd ed., 1996), para.5.42.
[10] *Rosser v Austral Wine & Spirit Co Pty Ltd* [1980] V.R. 313.
[11] *Re A & K Holdings Pty Ltd* [1964] V.R. 257.
[12] *Jones v Williams* (1841) 7 M. & W. 493; 151 E.R. 860; *Marsden & Son v Capital & Counties Newspaper Co Ltd* (1901) 46 Sol. Jo. 11. The name of the principal debtor can be proved in a similar way: *Kelly, Douglas & Co v Locklin* (1912) 8 D.L.R. 1039; *Re Agra and Masterman's Bank* (1867) L.R. 2 Ch. App. 391. *Cf. Wiliams v Lake* (1863) 2 E. & E. 349; 121 E.R. 132; *Williams v Byrnes* (1863) 1 Moo P.C.C.N.S. 154; 15 E.R. 660, PC. *Cf. Glover v Halkett* (1857) 2 H. & N. 487; 157 E.R. 201; *Brettel v Williams* (1849) 4 Exch. 623; 154 E.R. 1363; *Vanderbergh v Spooner* (1866) L.R. 1 Exch. 316 (where the vendor's name appeared in the document merely as part of the description of the goods purchased); *Gibsonv Holland* (1865) L.R. 1 C.P. 1 (the note or memorandum was sufficient even though it passed between one of the parties to the contract and his agent rather than between the contracting parties themselves). But see *Walton v Dodson* (1827) 3 C. & P. 162; 172 E.R. 369 (a guarantee which is not addressed to anyone may be enforced by the party to whom it is given or for whose use it was delivered; a guarantee addressed to one of the two parties may be enforced by both if it is shown that the parties to whom it was addressed did not carry on a separate business).
[13] *Rosser v Austral Wine & Spirit Co Pty Ltd* [1980] V.R. 313 at 316, 318, overruling *King v Grimwood* (1891) 17 V.L.R. 253.
[14] *Rodrick v City Mutual Life Assurance Society* (1897) 18 N.S.W.L.R. (Eq) 128. See also *Tower Paint v Laboratories Ltd v 126 019 Enterprises Ltd* (1983) 27 Alta L.R. (2d) 154, Q.B. (principal debtor identified by its business name; true identity of debtor not in question: guarantee enforceable).
[15] *Rosser v Austral Wine & Spirit Co Pty Ltd* [1980] V.R. 313 at 315–316, referring to *Di Biase v Rezek* [1971] 1 N.S.W.L.R. 735.
[16] *ibid.* See also *Williams v Lake* (1859) 2 E. & E. 349; 121 E.R. 132 (a document was not a sufficient note or memorandum because it did not in any way identify the party for whom it was intended); *A Macdonald & Co v Fletcher* (1915) 22 B.C.R. 298 (Can) (a guarantee endorsed on a ledger was not enforceable because there was nothing to show that the ledger belonged to the plaintiff).

document as to the parties to the contract, which is not permissible. As Asprey J.A. explained in *Di Biase v Rezek*:[17]

"For example, if an agent purported to contract (without binding himself personally) on behalf of his 'client' or 'clients', evidence as to who were the party or parties on whose behalf he intended to contract would be inadmissible because such evidence, if admitted, would only go to show which of his clients he intended to be the contracting party. The evidence would be proof only of the agent's intention. But if, on the other hand, he purported so to contract on behalf of the 'proprietor' of a given property the fact of the proprietorship can be determined independently of any intention entertained by the agent (see *Rossiter v Miller* (1878) 3 App. Cas. 1124 at 1140–1)."[18]

The distinction between admitting oral evidence when there is simply a conflict of fact to decide and excluding it when it is relevant to show the intention of the author is easier to state than apply in particular cases. It is fair to say, however, that the modern tendency is for the courts to err on the side of generosity in the admitting of extrinsic evidence in order to determine the identity of the parties to the memorandum.[19] **3–66**

The identity of the principal debtor must be stated in the memorandum[20] or it must be ascertainable from a reasonable construction of the memorandum or by reference to a linked document.[21] Otherwise, the memorandum will not satisfy the Statute of Frauds. Extrinsic evidence is not admissible to establish the identity of the principal debtor.[22] **3–67**

Where a company which has provided a guarantee changes its name and a related company assumes the name of the original guarantor, the creditor will still be entitled to enforce the guarantee if the related company is estopped by deed from denying that it is the guarantor referred to in the original guarantee.[23] Moreover, a corporate guarantor will not be able to escape liability under its guarantee simply by changing its name.[24] **3–68**

---

[17] [1971] 1 N.S.W.L.R. 735.
[18] *ibid.* at 742. The passage was approved in *Rosser v Austral Wine & Spirit Co Pty Ltd* [1980] V.R. 313 at 315–316. See also *Bateman v Phillips* (1812) 15 East 272; 104 E.R. 847; *Gibson v Holland* (1865) L.R. 1 C.P. 1 (a letter signed by the party to be charged and addressed to his agent can be a sufficient note or memorandum). *Cf. Walton v Dodson* (1827) 3 Car. & P. 162; 172 E.R. 369 (a guarantee given to one of two partners may be enforced by both if it is shown that the partner to whom it was addressed was not carrying on a separate business); *Garrett v Handley* (1825) 4 B. & C. 664; 107 E.R. 1208 (the partners of a firm can enforce a guarantee given to one of them if there is evidence that it was given for the benefit of them all).
[19] As illustrated by *Rosser v Austral Wine & Spirit Co Pty Ltd* [1980] V.R. 313; *Di Biase v Rezek* [1971] 1 N.S.W.L.R. 735; *Re A & K Holdings Pty Ltd* [1964] V.R. 257.
[20] *State Bank of India v Kaur* [1995] 5 Bank L.R. 158; [1995] N.P.C. 43, CA.
[21] See above, para.3–56.
[22] *State Bank of India v Kaur* [1995] 5 Bank L.R. 158; [1995] N.P.C. 43, CA.
[23] *Re Patrick Corp Ltd* (1981) 5 A.C.L.R. 646.
[24] Companies Act 1985, s.28(7).

(b) Terms of the contract

3–69   The general rule is that all the material terms of the contract sued upon, except the consideration,[25] must be evidenced in writing.[26] Thus in *Holmes v Mitchell*,[27] the words "I will take any responsibility myself respecting it, should there be any" in a letter written by the defendant to the plaintiff relating to a proposed mortgage was held not to constitute a sufficient memorandum. Williams J. stated:

> "It will be observed, that, at the time the letter was written, *no mortgage existed*. The letter is silent as to the sum to be advanced, as to the rate of interest, as to the nature of the security, whether a mortgage in fee or for years, and as to the land to be charged. The letter, if read by itself without reference to any previous conversations, would be a promise to be responsible for any sum of money, however large, at any rate of interest, secured by any kind of mortgage, on any land, with any title. That, however, would be an unreasonable construction, and is not its true meaning; it evidently refers to previous conversations in which these particulars were supplied. The whole promise, therefore, is not in writing, as the statute requires that it should be."[28]

3–70   Furthermore, the statute will not be satisfied by a memorandum which contains terms materially different from those of the alleged oral agreement between the parties.[29]

3–71   Despite this apparently inflexible approach, there are several qualifications which make the creditor's task in seeking to establish that the memorandum contains the material terms much easier.

3–72   First, extrinsic evidence can be admitted to explain the meaning of ambiguous expressions in the document,[30] although it cannot be used to

---

[25] If there is good consideration for the guarantee, oral evidence is admissible to prove what it is. Parol evidence, however, will not be admitted to explain the guarantor's promise in the sense of identifying the principal debt. See below, para.5–05.

[26] *State Bank of India v Kaur* (1996) 5 Bank L.R. 158; [1995] N.P.C. 43 (limit of guarantor's liability omitted); *Holmes v Mitchell* (1859) 7 C.B.N.S. 361; 141 E.R. 856; *Birmingham Joinery Ltd v Phillips* [1999] E.W.C.A. 787 (February 26, 1999); *Luck v Ilka* [1951] Q.S.R. 281; *Albert Building Society v Pratt* (1893) 19 V.L.R. 195; *Sinclair Scott & Co Ltd v Naughton* (1929) 43 C.L.R. 310 at 318, 328–329. It is sufficient for the note or memorandum to refer to the principal debt "together with interest thereon" as this will be interpreted as interest at the contractual rate payable by the principal debtor: *MP Services Ltd v Lawyer* (1996) P. & C.R. D 49. But there is no need for the statement of consideration to appear in the memorandum: see also *Forbes v Clarton* (1878) 4 V.L.R. 22.

[27] (1859) 7 C.B.N.S. 361; 141 E.R. 856.

[28] *ibid.*, at 370; 859. *Cf. Birmingham Joinery Ltd v Phillips* [1999] E.W.C.A. (February 26, 1999), where the liability to be guaranteed was agreed at a meeting and accurately set out in a letter relied on as a memorandum or note of the guarantee.

[29] *Smith v Lush* (1952) 52 S.R. (NSW) 207. But a memorandum which provides written evidence of an offer which has lapsed can meet the statutory requirements if the parties revive the promise by verbally confirming that the memorandum reflects their agreement: *O'Young v Walter Reid & Co Ltd* (1932) 47 C.L.R. 497.

[30] *Perrylease Ltd v Imecar AG* [1987] 2 All E.R. 373 at 380; *Sheers v Thimbleby & Son* (1897) 76 L.T. 709 at 711–712; *Expotech Pty Ltd v Kwiatkowski* (unreported, Qld Sup Ct. April 7, 1995).

establish the terms themselves, that is, "to explain the promise".[31] For example, in *Perrylease Ltd v Imecar AG*,[32] a guarantee "in respect of the proposed leasing by the lessee from Perrylease Limited of motor vehicles" was interpreted in accordance with extrinsic evidence to embrace any leasing agreement subsequently entered into between the creditor and the principal debtor. *Holmes v Mitchell*[33] was distinguished on the basis that the letter in that case contained "no details whatever of the contract between surety and creditor"[34] and that the decision "was not a case of a written contract at all".[35] But *Perrylease Ltd v Imecar AG* is also probably illustrative of a more liberal trend to the admissibility of extrinsic evidence as an aid to interpretation, at least where the guarantee is embodied in a formal agreement.[36] This trend reached its high-water mark in *Houlahan v Australian & New Zealand Banking Group Ltd*[37] where Higgins J. held that the "identification of the indebtedness to be guaranteed might well be regarded as implied".[38] In his Honour's judgment, it did not matter that the guarantee contained no reference to the proposed overdraft facility to be guaranteed. With respect, the guarantee should contain some reference to the principal transaction to which the guarantee relates. This is a material term of the contract of guarantee and it should be evidenced in writing. If there is no express or implied indication as to what principal transaction is guaranteed, then the note or memorandum of the guarantee does not satisfy the Statute of Frauds.[39]

Secondly, the creditor may waive the benefit of a term which is omitted from the memorandum if that term is exclusively for its benefit.[40] Such relief is not available, however, when the memorandum contains terms beyond those included in the oral agreement.[41]   **3–73**

Thirdly, the creditor may rely on the fact that a term is implied.[42] For example, if the instrument does not specify the date from which it is to operate, a term may be implied in the written guarantee that it is to commence immediately unless otherwise expressly agreed.[43]   **3–74**

Finally, and importantly, there is authority that a guarantee in general terms of "advances" is a sufficient memorandum, even without the use of   **3–75**

---

[31] *Perrylease Ltd v Imecar AG* [1987] 2 All E.R. 373 at 380.
[32] [1987] 2 All E.R. 373. *Cf. Houlahan v Australia & New Zealand Banking Group Ltd* (1993) 110 F.L.R. 259.
[33] (1859) 7 C.B.N.S. 361; 141 E.R. 856.
[34] [1987] 2 All E.R. 373 at 380.
[35] *ibid.*
[36] There is also evidence of this approach in much earlier cases, *e.g. Sheers v Thimbleby & Son* (1897) 76 L.T. 709 at 712, in which Chitty J. interpreted a guarantee of "the safety of the above investments" in the light of the surrounding circumstances. Williams J. in *Holmes v Mitchell* (1859) 7 C.B.N.S. 361; 141 E.R. 856 adopted a much more restrictive attitude to the use of the extrinsic evidence in the context of a guarantee contained in a letter.
[37] (1993) 110 F.L.R. 259.
[38] *ibid.*, at 265.
[39] See also above, para.3–06.
[40] *Johnson v Humphrey* [1946] 1 All E.R. 460; *Hawkins v Price* [1947] Ch. 645. It will be necessary for the plaintiff to give the defendant notice that the plaintiff has waived terms in his favour before he enforces the guarantee: *Morten v Marshall* (1863) 2 H. & C. 305; 159 E.R. 127.
[41] *Smith v Lush* (1952) 52 S.R. (NSW) 207 at 211.
[42] *Ward v National Bank of New Zealand* (1886) 4 N.Z.L.R. 35.
[43] *ibid..*

extrinsic evidence to interpret the expression. In *Vetro Glass Pty Ltd v Fitzpatrick*,[44] the view was taken that the word "advances" sufficiently set out the promise and identified the debt. It was to be construed as "a promise to pay anything and everything comprehended in an advance to a named debtor".[45] The promise did not have to set out the amount owing, even if this was not known to the promisor.[46]

3–76   Where the terms of a written guarantee complying with the statute are varied, the new terms also must be evidenced by a document which satisfies section 4.[47] Otherwise, the guarantee, as varied will be unenforceable.[48] In theory, the original guarantee would still be enforceable[49] but in practice the defendant guarantor would be able to raise the variation as a defence to an action based on the original guarantee because s.4 does not bar such a defence.[50]

(c) Recognition of a legal obligation

3–77   The dominant view is that the memorandum must contain not only the terms of the contract, but also an express or implied recognition that the contract was entered into.[51] This requirement, however, is likely to be satisfied in respect of a memorandum containing clear words of guarantee, unless some part of the memorandum contains a denial of liability or the document is stated to be "subject to contract".[52]

3–78   Where the termination of the principal contract results in the revocation of a related guarantee, there can be no implied renewal of the guarantee

---

[44] (1963) 63 S.R. (NSW) 697.

[45] *ibid.*, at 700. Reliance was placed on *Parkinson v Booth* (1934) 34 S.R. (NSW) 185. In that case, however, there was an express term limiting the liability of the guarantor to a fixed amount and the court distinguished *Holmes v Mitchell* (1859) 7 C.B.N.S. 361; 141 E.R. 856 on that basis.

[46] *ibid.*

[47] See *Goss v Lord Nugent* (1833) 5 B. & Ad. 58; 110 E.R. 713; *Anglophoto Ltd v Stutz* (1968) 12 C.B.R. (NS) 186; *Hawrish v Bank of Montreal* [1969] S.C.R. 515; *Bank of Montreal v Barraclough* (1929) 36 O.W.N. 42, CA.

[48] *ibid.*

[49] See *Morris v Baron & Co* [1918] A.C. 1 at 16; *Price v Dyer*, 17 Ves. 356 at 365; 34 E.R. 137 at 140; *Robinson v Page* (1826) 3 Russ 114 at 121; 38 E.R. 519 at 521. If the guarantor consents to the material alteration or is estopped from complaining about it, there is no need to satisfy the statute because the creditor will be suing on the original guarantee: *Crédit Suisse v Borough Council of Allerdale* [1995] 1 Lloyd's Rep. 315 at 370–371. *Bank of Scotland v Wright* [1991] B.C.L.C. 244 at 263–266.

[50] See *Re A Debtor* (unreported, Ferris J.) *The Times*, November 25, 1991. The court will not admit oral evidence of a collateral contract which is inconsistent with the terms of a written guarantee. See *Hawrish v Bank of Montreal* [1969] S.C.R. 515, where the Supreme Court of Canada held that evidence of oral assurances limiting the guarantor's liability under a written guarantee was inadmissible because the guarantee was a continuing guarantee which contained an entire agreement clause and a clause stating that no representations were made by the creditor to the guarantor. See also *Hoyt's Proprietary Ltd v Spencer* (1919) 27 C.L.R. 133 at 130 *per* Knox C.J. See also G. Andrews and R. Millett, *Law of Guarantees* (3rd ed., 2000), para.3.18.

[51] *Tiverton Estates Ltd v Wearwell Ltd* [1975] Ch. 146 at 156–157; *Martyn v Glennan* [1979] 2 N.S.W.L.R. 234; *Coogee Esplanade Surf Motel Pty Ltd v Commonwealth* (1976) 50 A.L.R. 363.

[52] See these difficulties in other contexts in *Thirkell v Cambi* [1919] 2 K. B. 590; *Griffiths v Young* [1970] Ch. 675; *Law v Jones* [1974] Ch. 112.

on the renewal of the principal contract because such an implication would not satisfy the formal requirements of the Statute of Frauds.[53]

(d) Rectification

Although the guarantee, or note or memorandum, must contain the names of the parties and the material terms, this does not preclude rectification of the agreement so as to make it conform with the real intention of the parties. The contract so rectified is capable of constituting a written memorandum.[54] Thus in *Whiting v Diver Plumbing & Heating Ltd*,[55] the guarantee was rectified to include the name of the principal debtor. On one view, rectification in these circumstances might be seen "as driving a horse and cart"[56] through the statutory provisions; on another, "it is simply another example of equity relieving against the rigours of the statute".[57] Certainly, it is difficult to see how a rectification of the guarantee to reflect the parties' true intentions defeats the purposes of the statute.[58] In any event, when the written instrument is rectified there may well be a sufficient note or memorandum to satisfy the statute.[59]

3–79

However, the better view appears to be that the court should not grant a rectification order where the guarantee omits the name of the principal debtor.[60]

3–80

---

[53] *Silverburn Finance (UK) Ltd v Salt* [2001] 2 All E.R. (Comm) 438; [2001] Lloyd's Rep. Bank 119.

[54] *United States of America v Motor Trucks Ltd* [1924] A.C. 196 at 201; *Whiting v Diver Plumbing & Heating Ltd* [1992] 1 N.Z.L.R. 560. As to the relatively strict burden of proof in an action for rectification, see *Joscelyne v Nissen* [1970] 2 Q.B. 86; *Crane v Hegeman-Harris Co Inc* [1939] 1 All E.R. 662 at 664. See also *Craddock Bros v Hunt* [1923] 2 Ch. 136 and R.P. Meagher, D. Heydon and M. Leeming, *Equity Doctrines & Remedies* (4th ed., 2002), para.26–050 and S.M. Waddams, *The Law of Contracts* (3rd ed., 1993), p.243. As to the scope of the remedy of rectification, see *Frederick E. Rose (London) Ltd v William H. Pim Jnr & Co Ltd* [1953] 2 Q.B. 450; *Vaudeville Electric Cinema Ltd v Muriset* [1923] 2 Ch. 74; *United States of America v Motor Trucks Ltd* [1924] A.C. 196; *H.F. Clarke Ltd v Thermidaire Corp* (1973) 33 D.L.R. (3d) 13 at 20–21, reversed on other grounds, but approved on this point: 54 D.L.R. (3d) 385 at 387.

[55] [1992] 1 N.Z.L.R. 560.

[56] *ibid.*, at 569.

[57] *ibid.*, at 569.

[58] See *United States of America v Motor Trucks Ltd* [1924] A.C. 196 at 200–201 *per* Earl of Birkenhead.

[59] *United States of America v Motor Trucks Ltd* [1924] A.C. 196 at 201.

[60] *Imperial Bank v Nixon* [1926] 4 D.L.R. 1052 at 1059. (Can). See also *A. Macdonald & Co v Fletcher* (1915) 22 B.C.R. 298, CA (not clear who was the creditor); *Vandenbergh v Spooner* (1866) L.R. 1 Exch. 316. But *cf. Newell v Radford* (1867) L.R. 3 C.P. 52.

6. EXECUTION OF GUARANTEES

(i) Introduction

3–81　　There are special formal requirements for guarantees executed as deeds. A deed of guarantee must be executed in the presence of an attesting witness.[61] But it appears that a party could be prevented by an estoppel by convention or an estoppel by representation from relying on a lack of proper attestation.[62] The question depends in each case on the purpose of the statute and its underlying policy.[63]

3–82　　Section 4 of the Statute of Frauds requires the guarantee or some memorandum or note thereof to be in writing "and signed by the party to be charged therewith or some other person thereunto by him lawfully authorised".[64]

3–83　　The party to be charged with the guarantee is the guarantor or surety. That person's signature or the signature of his agent is essential if the guarantee is to be enforced. Signatories are liable for their own undertakings, even though they are acting for another, unless they can show that on agency principles they should be held to have expressly or impliedly negatived their personal liability.[65] Generally the intention or capacity of the party signing the memorandum is immaterial.[66] Thus a note or memorandum evidencing the guarantee may be signed by the alleged guarantor in another capacity (for example as agent for the principal debtor).[67] Intention may be important, however, where one party signs the guarantee once in two different capacities. For example, a guarantee so executed by a person as an officer of that person's company and also in his private capacity binds both that person and the company as long as there is nothing to indicate that he signed the guarantee solely for and on behalf of the company.[68]

---

[61] Law of Property (Miscellaneous Provisions) Act 1989, s.1.
[62] See *Shah v Shah* [2001] 4 All E.R. 138.
[63] See *Godden v Merthyr Tydfil Housing Association* (1997) P. & C.R. D 1.
[64] See above, paras 3–06 *et. seq.* Under Scottish law the guarantor's signature must be witnessed by two witnesses: *Governor and Company of the Bank of Scotland of the Mound v Butcher* (unreported, Court of Appeal, Civil Division, July 28, 1998).
[65] See *Stanley Yeung Kai Yung v Hong Kong & Shanghai Banking Corp* [1981] A.C. 787 at 794–795 *per* Lord Scarman. Consequently, the signature of a guarantor as a witness or as an agent may be sufficient to satisfy the Statute if there was other evidence that he orally agreed to provide a guarantee: *Elpis Maritime Co Ltd v Marti Chartering Co Inc The Maria D* [1992] 1 A.C. 21; *Welford v Beezely* (1747) 1 Ves. Sen. 6; 27 E.R. 855; *Wallace v Roe* [1903] 1 I.R. 32. As to agency principles, see below, paras 3–100 to 3–108.
[66] *Re Hoyle; Hoyle v Hoyle* [1893] 1 Ch. 84; *Elpis Maritime Co Ltd v Marti Chartering Co Inc* [1991] 3 All E.R. 758. In *Godwin v Francis* (1870) L.R. 5 C.P. 295 it was held that the statute was satisfied by the signature of the party to be charged on instructions for a telegraphic message accepting the plaintiff's written offer. The capacity in which the signatory signs the document is only relevant if the guarantee is the written document itself. It will then be relevant to consider whether the signatory intended to assume a personal liability: See *Elpis Maritime Co Ltd v Marti Chartering Co Inc, The Maria D* [1992] 1 A.C. 21 and *Re Hoyle; Hoyle v Hoyle* [1893] 1 Ch. 84 at 99.
[67] *Elpis Maritime Co Ltd v Marti Chartering Co Inc* [1991] 3 All E.R. 758.
[68] *Ontario Marble Co Ltd v Creative Memorials Ltd* (1963) 39 D.L.R. (2d) 149.

The memorandum may be signed in a variety of ways:[69] by a printing of **3–84** the guarantor's name[70] if done with the guarantor's authority;[71] by initials;[72] or even by a mark, where the signatory is illiterate.[73] The signature need not be at the foot or end of the guarantee or on each page of it. It is enough that the signature, wherever it appears, authenticates the whole document.[74] It is not even necessary for the signature to be witnessed.[75] But the casual insertion of the promisor's name in a guarantee does not amount to a sufficient signature.[76]

While the party to be charged must sign the guarantee or the **3–85** memorandum or note thereof, it is not necessary to obtain the creditor's signature.[77] Once the creditor has acted upon the guarantee, the guarantor will be bound thereby.[78] Even where a document purporting to guarantee the payment of moneys was expressed as an inter partes deed, it was not necessary for the person to whom the moneys were payable to execute the deed, either because it was sufficient for him to be named in the deed or because the document could be enforced as a deed poll.[79]

The circumstances surrounding the execution of a guarantee can affect **3–86** its validity and enforceability.[80] If there is evidence of fraud or undue influence, misrepresentation or a lack of the necessary understanding on the part of the guarantor, this can vitiate the guarantee.[81] In the absence of such factors, a deaf and blind person was held to a guarantee where he clearly understood its contents and made a rational decision to sign it.[82] A defendant incurred no liability, however, where she signed a blank form

---

[69] The signature may be printed or pencilled: *Geary v Physic* (1826) 5 B. & C. 234; 108 E.R. 87.
[70] *Saunderson v Jackson* (1800) 2 Bos. & Pul. 238; 126 E.R. 1257; *Casey v Irish International Bank* [1979] I.R. 364, SC.
[71] *Schneider v Norris* (1814) 2 M. & S. 286; 105 E.R. 388. See also *Leeman v Stocks* [1951] Ch. 941.
[72] *Goods of Blewitt* (1880) L.R. 5 P.D. 116; *Chichester v Cobb* (1866) 14 L.T. 433; *Jacob v Kirk* (1839) 2 Mood & R. 221 (NP); 174 E.R. 269; *Chichester v Cobb* (1866) 14 L.T. 433; *Decouvreur v Jordan The Times*, May 25, 1987.
[73] *Baker v Dening* (1838) 8 Ad. & E. 94; 112 E.R. 771; *Selby v Selby* (1817) 3 Mer. 2; 36 E.R. 1. It appears that the guarantee can even be executed by signed instructions for a telephonic or telegraphic message: *Godwin v Francis* (1870) L.R. 5 C.P. 295.
[74] *Gladstone v Ball* (1862) 1 W. & W. (Eq) 277; *Caton v Caton* (1867) L.R. 2 H.L. 127; *Durrell v Evans* (1862) 1 H. & C. 174; 158 E.R. 848; *Hill v Hill* [1947] Ch. 231 at 240 *per* Morton L.J.; *Bluck v Gompertz* (1852) 7 Exch. 862; 155 E.R. 1199. Where a company director signed a contract on behalf of the company but neglected to sign a guarantee in the same document, his signature as a director bound him as a guarantor because this was his intention: *VSH Ltd v BKS Air Transport and Stevens* [1964] 1 Lloyd's Rep. 460.
[75] *Canadian Imperial Bank v Hardy Bay Inn Ltd* [1985] 1 W.W.R. 405 at 408.
[76] *Stokes v Moore* (1786) 1 Cox Eq. Cas. 219; 29 E.R. 1137. Similarly, a memorandum signed "your affectionate mother" will not satisfy the statute: *Selby v Selby* (1817) 3 Mer. 2; 36 E.R. 1.
[77] *Liverpool Borough Bank v Eccles* (1859) 4 H. & N. 139; 157 E.R. 789. However, where the guarantee is couched in such a way that it requires the signature of the creditor to accept the surety's offer of guarantee, then it will be necessary for the creditor to sign the document.
[78] *Liverpool Borough Bank v Eccles* (1859) 4 H. & N. 139; 157 E.R. 789; *Laythoarp v Bryant* (1836) 2 Bing N.C. 735; 132 E.R. 283.
[79] *Lincoln Contractors Pty Ltd v Searle* [1982] Qd. R. 71.
[80] See *Union Bank of Australia Ltd v Whitelaw* [1906] V.L.R. 711.
[81] See below, Ch. 4.
[82] *Vickers v Bell; Bell v Vickers* (1864) 9 L.T. 600; on appeal: (1864) 4 De G.J. & Sm. 274; 46 E.R. 924.

which was later filled in by her husband as a guarantee.[83] And a guarantor does not necessarily sign a note or memorandum in such a way as to signify assent if he merely fills in his name, or allows another to fill in his name, as well as other details on a standard guarantee form.[84]

(ii) Conditions precedent to execution

(a) Execution of the guarantee by co-guarantors

3–87   It may be contemplated that more than one guarantor will execute the guarantee. There is rarely an express term in the guarantee to this effect, but a term may be implied from the form of the guarantee,[85] and accompanying documents.[86] Thus in *Stramit Industries Ltd v Reinhardt*,[87] this result was inferred from a statement on the credit application (which embodied the instrument of guarantee on the back of the document) stating "personal guarantees will be signed by all directors in the case of proprietary limited companies".

3–88   Less obviously, a clause in the guarantee providing that the liability of the guarantors shall be "joint and several" invariably carries with it the implication that the guarantee shall not be binding unless all those named in the guarantee execute it,[88] even if one of the guarantors is insolvent.[89] This presumption,[90] arising from the form of the documentation, is not a rule of law[91] and can be rebutted by other evidence indicating that one guarantor agreed to remain liable despite the failure of one guarantor to

---

[83] *Hall v Merrick* (1877) 40 U.C.Q.B. 566.
[84] See *Morton v Copeland* (1855) 16 C.B. 517; 139 E.R. 861. Cf. *VSH Ltd v BKS Air Transport Ltd* [1964] 1 Lloyd's Rep. 460; *Young v Schuler* (1883) 11 Q.B.D. 651 and *Decouvreur v Jordan The Times*, May 25, 1987, CA (where a person orally agreed to guarantee the obligations of a party under a court order and printed and partly wrote his name on a draft minute of guarantee drawn up by counsel but failed to add his usual signature: held liable.) See G. Andrews and R. Millett, *Law of Guarantees* (3rd ed., 2000), para.3.24.
[85] *Marston v Charles H. Griffith & Co Pty Ltd* (1985) 3 N.S.W.L.R. 294 at 300–301; *Evans v Bremridge* (1855) 25 L.J. Ch. 102, affirmed in (1856) 25 L.J. Ch. 334; *National Provincial Bank of England v Brackenbury* (1906) 22 T.L.R. 797; *Hansard v Lethbridge* (1892) 8 T.L.R. 346.
[86] *Stramit Industries Ltd v Reinhardt* [1985] 1 Qd. R. 562; *Bleyer v Neville Jeffress Advertising Pty Ltd* (unreported, NSW CA, December 15, 1987); *City Bank v Reynolds* (1888) 9 L.R. (NSW) 472.
[87] [1985] 1 Qd. R. 562. There was also reliance on oral evidence.
[88] *Marston v Charles H Griffith & Co Pty Ltd* (1985) 3 N.S.W.L.R. 294 at 300–301; *Keith Murphy Pty Ltd v Custom Credit Corp Ltd* (1992) 6 W.A.R. 332; *Evans v Bremridge* (1855) 25 L.J. Ch. 102, affirmed in 1856 25 L.J. Ch. 334; *National Provincial Bank of England v Brackenbury* (1906) 22 T.L.R. 797; *Fitzgerald v M'Cowan* (1898) 2 I.R. 1. Cf. *Cumberlege v Lawson* (1857) 1 C.B.N.S. 709; 140 E.R. 292, where these words apparently did not have this effect. This case is contrary to the weight of authority.
[89] *Fitzgerald v M'Cowan* (1898) 2 I.R. 1. However, it is not sufficient that the guarantee simply makes provision for several unnamed guarantors: *Tasman Finance Pty Ltd v Edwards* (unreported, NSW Sup Ct, December 8, 1992); *Shaftesbury Nominees Pty Ltd v Brixmond* (unreported, Qld Sup Ct, March 2, 1994). See also *Dallas v Walls* (1873) 29 L.T. 599.
[90] As described in *Keith Murphy Pty Ltd v Custom Credit Corp Ltd* (1992) 6 W.A.R. 332 at 344; *Marston v Charles H Griffith & Co Pty Ltd* (1985) 3 N.S.W.L.R. 294 at 300–301.
[91] *Taubmans Pty Ltd v Loakes* [1991] 2 Qd. R. 109; *Shaftesbury Nominees Pty Ltd v Brixmond Pty Ltd* (unreported, Qld Sup Ct, March 2, 1994).

execute the guarantee.[92] For example, the Supreme Court of South Australia in *Walter & Morris Ltd v Lymberis*[93] held that a guarantee signed by an individual guarantor was binding, even though it was in a form appropriate to a joint and several guarantee. This conclusion was reached primarily on the basis of a clear finding of fact that the guarantor, when he signed the guarantee, contemplated that no other person was intended to be a guarantor jointly with him; and the case is illustrative of the recent trend to interpret guarantees in the light of surrounding circumstances and commercial reality.

If a term is imposed that additional guarantors be obtained, each **3–89** guarantor must also execute the guarantee according to any condition attaching to his liability.[94] Thus, where a guarantee stated that a guarantor's liability (expressed to be "joint and several" with other guarantors) was limited to £50 and he eventually executed the guarantee without the agreement of the other guarantors on the basis that his liability was to be limited to £25, the other guarantors were not bound.[95]

The obligation on the creditor to obtain other guarantors may also be **3–90** established by oral evidence outside the terms of the guarantee.[96] The burden of proof is on the guarantor to show that it is clearly contemplated that additional guarantors *must* be obtained, rather than that there is a mere contemplation that such guarantors *might* be obtained.[97] This burden of proof has proved difficult to satisfy. For example, no agreement was found where the creditor proposed that an additional guarantor be obtained, but there was no further evidence to suggest that the guarantee was dependent upon obtaining a further guarantor.[98] Similarly, where there was a promise by the principal borrower prior to the execution of the guarantee that the principal contract would be secured by the "personal obligation of this firm and the individual partners", this was not interpreted as a condition that all the partners should execute the

---

[92] *Walter & Morris Ltd v Lymberis* (1965) S.A.S.R. 204; *Marston v Charles H Griffith & Co Pty Ltd* (1985) 3 N.S.W.L.R. 294 at 300–301; *Taubmans Pty Ltd v Loakes* [1991] 2 Qd. R. 109; *Midland Brick Co Pty Ltd v Lilley* [1991] 2 Qd. R. 109.

[93] [1965] S.A.S.R. 204. See also *BP Australia Ltd v Anderson* (unreported, SA Sup Ct, November 9, 1994); *Citibank Savings Ltd v Vago* (unreported, NSW Sup Ct, May 1, 1992); *Tasman Finance Pty Ltd v Edwards* (unreported, NSW Sup Ct, December 8, 1992).

[94] *Ellesmere Brewery Co v Cooper* [1896] 1 Q.B. 75.

[95] *ibid.* Lord Russell also emphasised the fact (at 79–82) that the remaining guarantors' rights of contribution would be prejudicially affected by the alteration, but if it is a condition of the contract that each guarantor execute the agreement it is unnecessary to show such prejudice. This was the case in this instance because the guarantors' liability was expressed to be "joint and several". It should also be noted that the guarantor who made the alteration was held not bound by the guarantee because he undertook liability only on the basis that the other guarantors remained liable (at 82–83). But it is thought that the guarantor who made the alteration would be liable if he clearly gave consent to a change in the contractual arrangements, in terms that he consented to remain liable despite the release of the other guarantors.

[96] *Leaf v Gibbs* (1830) 4 C. & P. 466 (NP); 172 E.R. 785; *Traill v Gibbons* (1861) 2 F. & F. 358 (NP); 175 E.R. 1095; *Ward v National Bank of New Zealand* (1883) 8 App. Cas. 755 also contemplates the admission of oral evidence.

[97] *Horne v Ramsdale* (1842) 9 M. & W. 329; 152 E.R. 140; *Re Smith, Fleming & Co Ex p. Harding* (1879) 12 Ch. D. 557 at 564; *Coyte v Elphick* (1874) 22 W.R. 541 (statement in recital of deed of guarantee contemplating that loan be secured by several sureties was not sufficient); *Dallas v Walls* (1873) 29 L.T. 599.

[98] *Traill v Gibbons* (1861) 2 F. & F. 358 (NP); 175 E.R. 1095.

guarantee before those who did so became legally bound.[99] What is required before the burden is satisfied is a clear understanding that the contract of guarantee is to be executed by particular guarantors.[1]

3–91   Where it is contemplated (by implication from the words "joint and several" or otherwise) that the guarantee shall not be binding until all co-guarantors execute it, an implication also arises that a *valid execution* is necessary.[2] Thus where the guarantee is void as against one of the parties, for example, because of forgery[3] or because of a failure to comply with statutory requirements,[4] the other guarantors will be discharged. Such situations have been treated as analogous to those in which the co-guarantor does not sign at all.[5] This analogy is, of course, less readily drawn where the guarantee is only voidable as against the intended surety because, for example, of unilateral mistake or unconscionability.[6] But it would be somewhat odd if the other guarantors remained liable when a co-guarantor was discharged, for example, on the grounds of common mistake at law (which renders the contract void) but not when he was discharged on the basis of unilateral mistake as to the terms of the guarantee (which renders the contract voidable).

3–92   In those cases referred to in this section where the guarantor was discharged because of the failure of an intended co-guarantor to execute the agreement, the proper legal basis was that there had been a breach of an express or implied condition or a failure of a condition precedent to that effect.[7] But some of the 19th century decisions[8] make some reference to the guarantor being discharged in equity, which led the Court of Appeal of the Supreme Court of New South Wales in *Bleyer v Neville Jeffress Advertising Pty Ltd*[9] to conclude that equity provided an additional basis of discharge. Hope J.A. stated:[10]

---

[99] *Re Smith, Fleming & Co Ex p. Harding* (1879) 12 Ch. D. 557.
[1] As in *City Bank v Reynolds* (1888) 9 L.R. (NSW) 472; *Stramit Industries Ltd v Reinhardt* [1985] 1 Qd. R. 562. See also *Elliott v Davis* (1800) 2 Bos. & P. 338; 126 E.R. 1314, where a guarantor not only signed for himself but also on behalf of a co-guarantor without having any authority to do so. The court drew the inference that the guarantor had agreed only to be bound if the co-guarantor also became a party to the agreement. This is another rare example of a decision where a guarantor has succeeded in showing that he intended to be bound only if a co-guarantor was obtained.
[2] *James Graham & Co (Timber) Ltd v Southgate-Sands* [1985] 2 All E.R. 344; *McNamara v Commonwealth Trading Bank of Australia* (1984) 37 S.A.S.R. 232.
[3] *James Graham & Co (Timber) Ltd v Southgate-Sands* [1985] 2 All E.R. 344.
[4] *McNamara v Commonwealth Trading Bank of Australia* (1984) 37 S.A.S.R. 232 (failure to comply with s.44 of the Consumer Transactions Act 1972 (SA)).
[5] *ibid.*, at 239.
[6] See below, paras 4–54 and 4–155.
[7] As cogently explained by O'Connor L.J. in *James Graham & Co (Timber) Ltd v Southgate-Sands* [1985] 2 All E.R. 344.
[8] *Evans v Bremridge* (1855) 25 L.J. Ch. 102, affirmed in (1856) 25 L.J. Ch. 334; *Hansard v Lethbridge* (1892) 8 T.L.R. 346. But in *James Graham & Co. (Timber) Ltd v Southgate-Sands* [1985] 2 All E.R. 344 at 350–351 O'Connor L.J. was of the view that, questions of pleadings apart, the guarantors would have been discharged at law.
[9] (Unreported NSW CA, December 15, 1987). See also *Keith Murphy Pty Ltd v Custom Credit Corp Ltd* (1992) 6 W.A.R. 332 at 344, where it was said to be irrelevant that the guarantors did not know what they were signing.
[10] Kirby P. agreed with the reasoning of Hope J.A. The rule appears to extend beyond liability for misrepresentation in equity.

"A guarantor, even though liable at law, may be relieved of his obligation in equity in a number of circumstances, of which those relevant to the present proceedings are if he enters into the guarantee on the basis of a belief or understanding, induced in whole or in part by some statement or other act by or on behalf of the creditor, including the terms of any document provided by the creditor ... that another person or other persons will also guarantee the debt."

The possibility of discharge in equity in the manner described will be important when the evidence is not sufficiently cogent to establish a condition or condition precedent that all intended guarantors will execute the agreement before it becomes legally binding.[11] This may occur, for example, where liability is not expressed to be "joint and several", which normally implies that such a condition exists.[12]   **3–93**

In contradistinction to discharge in law for breach of condition or a failure of a condition precedent, however, relief in equity will be discretionary.[13] In this context it is said that equity operates "on the conscience"[14] of the creditor, so that the guarantor may not be discharged in equity when one of the co-guarantors' signatures is a forgery and the creditor has neither actual nor constructive knowledge of the relevant circumstances.[15]   **3–94**

Clauses are often found in the modern contract of guarantee purporting to render an individual guarantor liable despite the failure of other guarantors to execute the guarantee. An example is: **3–95**

"This guarantee shall bind each of the signatories hereof notwithstanding that one or more of the persons named herein as a guarantor may never execute the same."

If there are other indications in the guarantee itself that it is a condition that co-guarantors must execute the agreement (for example, by the use of the words "joint and several"), the conflict between the two provisions may be resolved by any available extrinsic evidence.[16] In its absence, it is thought that the specificity of this clause will override any such indications and that the guarantors who do execute the agreement will be bound.   **3–96**

Many guarantees also embody a clause stating that the release of a guarantor by the creditor will not discharge a co-guarantor. Such a   **3–97**

---

[11] *Stramit Industries Ltd v Reinhardt* [1985] 1 Qd. R. 562 is an example of discharge of a guarantor on this basis. In *Marston v Charles H. Griffith & Co Pty Ltd* (1985) 3 N.S.W.L.R. 294 at 301, Powell J. was of the view that where the guarantee is embodied in a deed which imposes "joint and several" liability, the guarantor will be bound at law if the intended co-guarantors do not sign, although equitable relief will be available. But this special rule applying to deeds is inconsistent with the reasoning of O'Connor L.J. in *James Graham & Co (Timber) Ltd v Southgate-Sands* [1985] 2 All E.R. 344, and is thought to be incorrect.
[12] See the cases cited above, n.88.
[13] *James Graham & Co (Timber) Ltd v Southgate-Sands* [1985] 2 All E.R. 344, especially at 354.
[14] *ibid.*
[15] *ibid.* Cf., however, *Keith Murphy Pty Ltd v Custom Credit Corp Ltd* (1992) 6 W.A.R. 332 at 345.
[16] As in *Westpac Banking Corp v Smith* (unreported, Vic Sup Ct, September 4, 1991).

provision is unlikely to displace the presumption arising from the words "joint and several", since it merely preserves the liability of the co-guarantor in the light of the creditor's subsequent conduct. It does not negate the implication that all the guarantors must execute the instrument in the first place.[17]

3–98   Sometimes, however, oral evidence may establish that it is a condition precedent to the operation of the guarantee that other guarantors must sign. Thus, in *Molsons Bank v Cranston*,[18] parol evidence established that the guarantee, which was under seal, was not to be binding until all the directors had signed it. Some directors did not sign. A clause in the guarantee itself in similar wording to that set out above was held to be ineffective to preserve the liability of a guarantor who did execute the agreement. As the condition precedent to the operation of the guarantee had not been fulfilled, the clause, which was itself part of the guarantee, was also of no legal effect. Oral evidence in these circumstances is admissible as a result of the established exception to the parol evidence rule allowing the admissibility of extrinsic evidence to show that the contract is not yet operative.[19] A clause of this type in the guarantee is probably also sufficient to exclude the guarantor's discharge on equitable grounds unless the guarantor's belief that other guarantors will sign is induced not by the form of the document but by a statement by or on behalf of the creditor.[20]

(b) Execution of the guarantee by the principal debtor

3–99   Sometimes the guarantor will undertake a liability on condition that the principal debtor becomes a party to the same instrument.[21] Thus, if the guarantor agrees to assume liability in a "joint and several" bond with the principal, prima facie, it will be a condition of the guarantor's liability that the principal executes the deed.[22] This inference may no doubt be negated by extrinsic evidence showing that when the guarantor signed the guarantee it was not intended that the principal should sign.[23] It appears to be sufficient compliance with the condition if the principal executes a separate instrument under seal by which the guarantor will acquire by

---

[17] *Keith Murphy Pty Ltd v Custom Credit Corp Ltd* (1992) 6 W.A.R. 332 at 345–346.
[18] (1918) 45 D.L.R. 316.
[19] See generally G. H. Treitel, *The Law of Contract* (11th ed., 2003), pp.195–196; *Pym v Campbell* (1856) 6 El. & Bl. 370; 119 E.R. 903; *Molsons Bank v Cranston* (1918) 45 D.L.R. 316. On the other hand, it could be argued that an express clause stating that the guarantee is not subject to any condition precedent excludes parol evidence of such a condition. See *Royal Bank v 634 535 Ontario Inc* (1992) 7 B.L.R. (2d) 91 at 97 *per* Hockin J. (Ont Gen Div). But if there is in fact such a condition precedent, the contract will not be binding unless the condition precedent is satisfied.
[20] In such a case the guarantor may be able to rely on rescission in equity, as a result of a misrepresentation, see below, paras 4–36 to 4–50.
[21] *Bonser v Cox* (1841) 4 Beav 379; 49 ER 385; *Ward v National Bank of New Zealand* (1883) 8 App. Cas. 755.
[22] Ibid.
[23] See *Walter & Morris Ltd v Lymberis* [1965] S.A.S.R. 204, where a similar conclusion was reached when the liability of the co-guarantor was expressed as "joint and several".

subrogation the equivalent rights of specialty against the principal upon paying the creditor.[24] Generally, however, it is not necessary for the principal debtor to sign the guarantee.

(iii) Execution by directors and other agents

The Statute of Frauds contemplates that the guarantee can be signed by **3–100** the surety's lawfully authorised agent.[25] The authority conferred upon the agent need not be in writing[26] and may even be founded upon a course of dealings between the parties.[27] The onus is on the party seeking to enforce the guarantee to prove that the agent was authorised to sign the document as a record of agreement on behalf of the defendant.[28] An agent acting within the scope of his authority can bind the principal even if the agent has acted in his own interests, at least where the other party acts bona fide in ignorance of the terms of the agent's written authority.[29] There is a sufficient memorandum for the purposes of the statute if the document signed by the agent can be read with another document which is not so executed.[30] It appears however that one of the contracting parties may not

[24] *Cooper v Evans* (1867) L.R. 4 Eq. 45.
[25] The agent's mandate can be conferred by verbal authority or verbal ratification: *Emmerson v Heelis* (1809) 2 Taunt. 38 at 48; 127 E.R. 989 at 993; *Maclean v Dunn* (1828) 4 Bing. 722 at 727; 130 E.R. 947 at 949. The agent of one party can be authorised by another party to sign the document on the latter's behalf: see *Durrell v Evans* (1862) 1 H. & C. 174 at 187, 191; 158 E.R. 848 at 853, 855; *Caton v Caton* (1867) L.R. 2 H.L. 127. *Cf. Dixon v Broomfield* (1814) 2 Chit 205, where a mere note written by the clerk of the promisee in the presence of the guarantor to record the terms of the promise was not done with the requisite authority to bind the guarantor. Where one guarantor purports to sign a guarantee on behalf of another guarantor without his authority, the signature is a forgery: *CSR Ltd v Price* (unreported, NSW Sup Ct. Cole J, 29 April 1993). As to the authority of brokers and auctioneers to sign guarantees on behalf of their principals, see H.A. de Colyar, *Law of Guarantees* (3rd ed, 1897), pp.161–162. As to the admissibility of oral evidence to establish that an agent signed on behalf of an undisclosed principal, see *Higgins v Senior* (1841) 8 M. & W. 834; 151 E.R. 1278; *Basma v Weekes* [1950] A.C. 441; *Young v Schuler* (1883) 11 Q.B.D. 651, CA; *Canadian Welsh Anthracite Coal Co v Pember* (1927) 32 O.W.N. 75, Div Ct.
[26] *Pain v Flynn* (1884) 10 V.L.R.(E) 131; *Rhodes Pty Ltd v Galati* [1961] W.A.R. 180; *Waller v Hendon & Co* (1723) 2 Eq. Cas. Abr. 50; 22 E.R. 44; *Cave v MacKenzie* (1877) 46 L.J. Ch. 564; *James v Smith* [1891] 1 Ch. 384, affirmed on other grounds in (1891) 65 L.T. 544 (CA; *Emmerson v Heelis* (1809) 2 Taunt 38; 127 E.R. 989; *Coles v Trecothick* (1804) 9 Ves. 234; 32 E.R. 592. *Cf. Cooke v Jackson* (1850) 15 L.T.O.S. 523.
[27] See *Watkins v Vince* (1818) 2 Stark 368 (NP); 171 E.R. 675. *Cf. Hasleham v Young* (1844) 5 Q.B. 833; 114 E.R. 1463.
[28] *Banbury v Bank of Montreal* [1918] A.C. 626 (a case involving negligent advice); *Yonge v Toynbee* [1910] 1 K.B. 215, CA; *John Griffiths Cycle Corpn Ltd v Humber & Co Ltd* [1899] 2 Q.B. 414 at 418 (reversed on a different point *sub nom. Humber v Griffiths* (1901) 85 L.T. 141). A solicitor who is to draft a contract does not have implied authority to sign it on behalf of his client: *Smith v Webster* [1876] 3 Ch. 49; *Bowen v Duc D'Orléans* (1900) 16 T.L.R. 226, CA. Hence, it is a question of fact in each case whether the solicitor was authorised to sign the note or memorandum as evidence of a guarantee: See, *e.g. Forster v Rowland* (1861) 7 H. & N. 103; 158 E.R. 410; *Earl of Glengal v Barnard* (1836) 1 Keen 769 at 787, on appeal (1848) 2 H.L. Cas. 131; 49 E.R. 571; *Smith v Webster* (1876) 3 Ch. 49 at 57, CA; *Bowen v Duc D'Orléans* (1900) 16 T.L.R. 226, CA.
[29] *Hambro v Burnard* [1904] 2 K.B. 10. It does not matter that the guarantor signed the memorandum in his capacity as agent of the principal debtor rather than in his own right as guarantor because the intention of the signatory is irrelevant: *Elpis Maritime Co Ltd v Marti Chartering Co Inc, The Maria D* [1992] 1 A.C. 21.
[30] *Ridgway v Wharton* (1857) 6 H.L. Cas. 238; 10 E.R. 1287.

act as authorised agent of the other and bind that other by his signature, even if his actions are authorised or later ratified.[31]

3–101   General principles of the law of agency determine whether an agent has express, implied or ostensible authority to bind the principal.[32] A person can sign as agent of a surety even if he is not *sui juris*.[33] A guarantee signed without authority by an agent will not bind the principal; but if such a guarantee is adopted by the principal orally, it will be enforceable under the statute.[34]

3–102   If the signatory does not sign "as agent" of the surety, parol evidence is admissible to prove the capacity in which he signed the document. In this way an undisclosed principal can become liable on a guarantee.[35]

3–103   Where a party executes a guarantee or third party mortgage under a power of attorney, the supervening mental incapacity of the principal terminates the attorney's actual authority.[36] However, the Enduring Powers of Attorney Act 1985 enables a person to execute an enduring power of attorney which ensures that the attorney's authority continues notwithstanding the guarantor's supervening mental incapacity.[37] But what capacity must the grantor possess at the time the enduring power of attorney is granted?

3–104   According to Hoffmann J. (as he then was) in *Re K, Re F*[38] it is sufficient that the grantor of the enduring power of attorney understands the nature and effect of the power; it is not necessary that the grantor is able to perform all the acts which the power of attorney authorises. However, the better view appears to be that a higher level of capacity is required to grant an enduring power of attorney. In *Gibbons v Wright*,[39] the High Court of Australia unanimously held that the law "requires, in relation to each

---

[31] *Wright v Dannah* (1809) 2 Camp. 203; 170 E.R. 1129; *Farebrother v Simmons* (1822) 5 B. & Ald. 333; 106 E.R. 1213; *Sharman v Brandt* (1871) L.R. 6 Q.B. 720. *Cf. Burnard v Lysnar* (1929) N.Z.P.C.C. 538, and see above, n.25.

[32] See generally *Bowstead and Reynolds on Agency* (17th ed. 2001), Ch. 3. As to execution of guarantees by directors on behalf of their companies, see *Re Eva Life Assurance Society* [1866] W.N. 309; *Colman v Eastern Counties Rly Co* (1846) 10 Beav. 1; 50 E.R. 481; *In re Cunningham & Co; Simpson's Claim* (1887) 36 Ch. D. 532. As to the issues of directors lacking authority and constructive notice,see Gower's *Principles of Modern Company Law* (6th ed. by P. Davies) (Sweet & Maxwell, London,1997), pp. 213–217. For illustrations of the application of the indoor management rule, see *Pacific Coast Coal Mines Ltd v Arbuthnot* [1917] A.C. 607 at 611; *Re Athenaeum Life Assurance Society Ex p. Eagle Insurance Co* (1858) 4 K. & J. 549; 70 E.R. 229. See also *John Davidson (Pipes) Ltd v First Engineering Ltd* 2001 S.C.L.R. 73.

[33] *Watkins v Vince* (1818) 2 Stark 368; 171 E.R. 675 (signature by infant son binding on father).

[34] *Ronald v Lalor* (1872) 3 V.R. (Eq.) 98. See also *Maclean v Dunn* (1828) 4 Bing 722; 130 E.R. 947; *Marsh v Joseph* [1897] 1 Ch. 213. The surety can ratify the signature of his agent either orally or in writing because it is not necessary for the agent to be authorised in writing: *Maclean v Dunn* (1828) 4 Bing 722 at 727; 130 E.R. 947 at 949. As to ratification generally, see *Marsh v Joseph* [1897] 1 Ch. 213, CA.

[35] See *Young v Schuler* (1883) 11 Q.B.D. 651.

[36] *Drew v Nunn* (1897) 4 Q.B.D. 661; *Harrington v Bailey* (1961) 351 S.W. 2d 946; *Kuder v United National Bank* (1985) 497 A. 2d 1105 (DC App); *Kelly v Ramplin* (No.1) (unreported, NSW Sup Ct. Holland J., September 15, 1976).

[37] See R. Mundar, "The Capacity to Execute an Enduring Power of Attorney in New Zealand and England: A Case of Parliamentary Oversight?" (1989) 13 N.Z.U.L.R. 253.

[38] [1988] 1 All E.R. 358.

[39] (1954) 91 C.L.R. 423. See also R. Mundar, "The Capacity to Execute an Enduring Power of Attorney in New Zealand and England: A Case of Parliamentary Oversight?" (1989) 13 N.Z.U.L.R. 253.

particular matter or piece of business transacted, that each party shall have such soundness of mind as to be capable of understanding the general nature of what he is doing by his participation".[40] Their Honours expected a higher level of capacity for the execution of a power of attorney than for the creation of other agencies. They suggested that the grantor must be capable of understanding the nature of the acts or transactions which the particular power of attorney purports to authorise. The more general the power of attorney, the higher the level of capacity required of the grantor. It is not sufficient for the grantor merely to understand what he is doing in general terms and to intend its consequences.

Where the guarantee takes the form of a third party mortgage, **3–105** registration of the mortgage in the Land Register cures any invalidity caused by a failure to register the power of attorney used to execute the mortgage under the general property law statutes.[41] The mortgagee acquires an indefeasible interest in the property upon registration of the mortgage, subject only to the well-recognised exceptions to the indefeasibility principle.[42-43]

A person does not become liable on a guarantee just by signing the **3–106** document if it was never intended that that person would become a guarantor and if he was not named as a party in the guarantee. Hence, a person who signs a guarantee merely as an agent for another named party does not become liable as a guarantor.[44] But it appears that personal liability will not necessarily be excluded simply by adding the words "as agent" or "director" to the signature on a guarantee.[45] Similarly, the fact that the signatories executed the document near the printed words "authorised signatory" does not necessarily establish that they were simply signing for and on behalf of their company if there was no provision for any other type of signature.[46] The court will look at the whole of the document and the surrounding circumstances known to the parties to ascertain whether there is any objective evidence of an intention by the signatory to assume a personal liability as a guarantor.[47] If possible, evidence of the circumstances in which the guarantee was

---

[40] (1954) 91 C.L.R. 423 at 437.
[41] See *Broadlands International Finance Ltd v Sly* (1987) 4 B.P.R. 97,280, a case decided upon s.163 of the Conveyancing Act 1919 (NSW).
[42-43] See *Broadlands International Finance Ltd v Sly* (1987) 4 B.P.R. 97,280 at 9,423. See Land Registration Act 2002, R. Megarry, *A Manual of the Law of Real Property* (1993) and K. Gray, *Elements of Land Law* (2nd ed., 1993).
[44] *General Credits Ltd v Ebsworth* [1986] 2 Qd. R. 162. See also above, para.3–101.
[45] *Re Fletcher Ex p. Hanimex Pty Ltd* (1984) 9 A.C.L.R. 30. *Cf. Ariadne Steamship Co Ltd v James McKelvie & Co* [1922] 1 K.B. 518 at 535, *per* Atkin J; *National Commercial Banking Corp of Australia Ltd v Cheung* (1983) 1 A.C.L.C. 1326.
[46] *Deeks v Little Moreton Pty Ltd, t/a HR Products* (unreported, WA Sup Ct (FC), March 10, 1995).
[47] See *Universal Steam Navigation Co Ltd v James McKelvie & Co* [1923] A.C. 492; *NEC Information Systems Pty Ltd v Linton* (unreported, NSW Sup Ct, Wood J. April 17, 1985); *Scottish Amicable Life Assurance Society v Reg Austin Insurances Pty Ltd* (1985) 9 A.C.L.R. 909 (an indemnity case); *Re Fletcher Ex p. Hanimex Pty Ltd* (1984) 9 A.C.L.R. 30; *Clark Equipment Credit of Australia Ltd v Kiyose Holdings Pty Ltd* (1989) 21 N.S.W.L.R. 160 at 174 *per* Giles J; *Miles v Zuckerman* [1931] O.R. 368, CA; *Cook v Smith* (1932) 41 O.W.N. 155, CA. See also D. Curtis, "Signer Beware—The Liability of the Signatory to a Contract" (1987) 3 Aust Bar Rev. 65. See also *Johnson Co v Imperial Fisheries Ltd* (1911) 19 W.L.R. 285 (Can). *Cf. Welsh Anthracite Coal Co v Pember* (1927) 32 O.W.N. 75.

signed should be adduced to assist the court in determining whether the
agent or officer signed in his personal capacity or on behalf of his principal
or company.[48]

3–107   Even if the directors of the principal debtor did not intend to assume a
personal liability by signing the guarantee, they may be liable to make a
contribution to the assets of the debtor company if they were guilty of
fraudulent or wrongful trading under s.213 or s.214 of the Insolvency Act
1986. They can incur this form of liability under s.213 if, in the course of
the winding up of the debtor company, it appears that any business of the
company has been carried on with intent to defraud creditors of the
company or for any fraudulent purpose.

3–108   A similar liability can be imposed on the directors under s.214 if, at some
time before the commencement of an insolvent liquidation of the debtor
company, they knew or ought to have concluded that there was no
reasonable prospect that the company would avoid going into insolvent
liquidation.[49] However, the directors' personal liability under these
provisions is not as easy to establish as the liability of directors under
the insolvent trading provisions of the Australian Corporations Act 2001.
In that context the New South Wales Court of Appeal in *Hawkins v Bank
of China*[50] held that directors could incur a personal liability for insolvent
trading if they signed a company guarantee at a time when there were
reasonable grounds to suspect that the company was insolvent.[51]

(iv) Execution by partners

3–109   Agency principles permeate many areas of partnership law and, together
with the partnership deed, govern the ability of an individual partner to
bind the partner's firm by signing a guarantee. A partner can commit the
current members of her or his firm to a guarantee by signing the firm name
thereon.[52] But this liability will arise only where it is clear that the
guarantee was necessary for carrying the partnership contract into effect[53]

---

[48] *Deeks v Little Moreton Pty Ltd t/a HR Products* (unreported, WA Sup Ct (FC), March 10,
1995).
[49] Note the defences available to the directors under s.214(3) and (4).
[50] (1992) 26 N.S.W.L.R. 562.
[51] See A.D. Brown, "Does Section 592 Apply to Guarantees? The Risks Increase After the
Hawkins Case" (1993) C.S.L.J. 34 at 41–42. Section 592 of the Corporations Act 2001 (Cth)
was the Australian insolvent trading provision. See now s.588G of the Corporations Act 2001
(Cth).
[52] *Re Smith, Fleming & Co Ex p. Harding* (1879) 12 Ch. D. 557. See *Hope v Cust*. Sittings at
Guildhall after Michaelmas Term, 1774, cited by Lawrence J. in *Shirreff v Wilks* (1800) 1 East
48 at 53; 102 E.R. 19 at 21.
[53] *Duncan v Lowndes* (1813) 3 Camp. 478; 170 E.R. 1452; *Brettel v Williams* (1849) 4 Exch.
623; 154 E.R. 1363. Cf. *Ex p. Gardom* (1808) 15 Ves. Jun. 286; 33 E.R. 762. In determining
whether an act is in the ordinary course of a partnership's business, the court will examine the
nature and scope of the business by reference to the agreement between the partners: *Walker
v European Electronics Pty Ltd* (1990) 23 N.S.W.L.R. 1. It is not sufficient that the guarantee
was given incidentally to advance objects within the scope of the partnership: *Duncan v
Lowndes* (1813) 3 Camp 478; 170 E.R. 1452 (it is not incidental to the general power of a
partner to bind his co-partners to a guarantee of the debts of another); *Brettel v Williams*
(1849) 4 Exch. 623; 154 E.R. 1363 (guarantee did not bind the firm because there was no
evidence that it was necessary for carrying into effect the partnership contract); *Hasleham v
Young* (1844) 5 Q.B. 833; 114 E.R. 1463; (a guarantee by a solicitor for a client was not

or that the other partners have adopted the guarantee.[54] The firm will not be bound by the guarantee simply because it was given to advance the business of the partnership.[55] For these reasons, it will be difficult to enforce a guarantee in a firm's name executed by one of the partners. If the signing partner, however, has the necessary express or implied authority, or if the other partners give their consent to the giving of the guarantee, or subsequently ratify it, the firm will be bound by the signature.[56]

Thus in *Bank of Scotland v Henry Butcher*,[57] a firm of surveyors **3–110** guaranteed the overdraft of the bank's customer, with which it had a consultancy arrangement. The guarantee was signed by four of the firms' thirteen partners "as partners [in the firm] and as individuals". By the terms of the partnership deed a partner could enter into a guarantee with the consent of the other partners. Although the other partners did not pass a resolution giving the partners who signed the guarantee authority to execute the guarantee, it was held that they had either consented or acquiesced in the giving of the guarantee[58] because of the following circumstances:[59]

(a) The practice of the partnership was not to deal with any matters by formal resolution. Each partner reported its activities to the executive committee and the rest of the firm was kept informed by the circulation of the executive committee minutes. If any partner wished to object he had five days to do so, and in the absence of any objection from the other partners the matter would be taken as agreed.

(b) All the partners were aware of the consultancy agreement (which was accepted as being binding as the partnership) and that the guarantee was an integral part of that agreement.

(c) The partnership as a whole knew that the overdraft guaranteed was continuing to rise and that steps were being taken to extricate the partnership from the guarantee, thus indicating

---

[54] *Brettel v Williams* (1849) 4 Exch. 623; 154 E.R. 1363. See also *Duncan v Lowndes* (1813) 3 Camp 478; 170 E.R. 1452; *Sandilands v Marsh* (1819) 2 B. & Ald. 673; 106 E.R. 511. *Cf. Bank of Scotland v Henry Butcher & Co* [2001] 2 All E.R. (Comm) 691, where a guarantee bearing the signature of four of the partners bound the partnership because the signing of the guarantee was an act relating to the partnership business and the partnership affirmed the transaction.

[55] *ibid.* But see *Ex p. Gardom* (1808) 15 Ves. 286; 33 E.R. 762 and *Hope v Cust* (1774), cited in (1800) 1 East 48 at 53; 102 E.R. 19 at 21. See also *Duncan v Lowndes* (1813) 3 Camp 478; 170 E.R. 1452; *Crawford v Stirling* (1802) 4 Esp. 207; 170 E.R. 693 and *Hasleham v Young* (1844) 5 Q.B. 833; 114 E.R. 1463.

[56] *Bank of Scotland v Henry Butcher* [2001] 2 All ER (Comm) 691; *Duncan v Lowndes* (1813) 3 Camp 478; 170 E.R. 1452; *Sandilands v Marsh* (1819) 2 B & Ald 673; 106 E.R. 511. See *Re Crowder Ex p. Nolte* (1826) 2 Gl. & J. 295, LC. *Cf. Ex p. Harding; In re Smith, Fleming & Co* (1879) 12 Ch. D. 557.

[57] [2001] 2 All ER (Comm) 691.

[58] It was held in the alternative that the partnership had ratified the guarantee.

[59] See especially para.53.

(that the partnership considered that it was bound by the guarantee.[60]

3–111   Nevertheless, in general, a creditor who wishes to take a guarantee from a firm should ensure that all the partners sign the memorandum because the giving of such a security would not usually be necessary to implement the partnership contract.[61]

(v) Execution by trustees

3–112   A guarantee executed by trustees in favour of a creditor will be binding upon the trustees personally[62] unless it is expressly stipulated that the trustees sign only in their capacity as trustees and disclaim any personal liability.[63] It is not sufficient for the trustees merely to contract "as trustees"; they must stipulate expressly that the creditor may look only to the trust assets for payment.[64]

3–113   In deciding whether the intention of the parties to the contract of guarantee was to exclude the personal liability of the trustee, the court takes into account the following factors: the nature, purpose and subject matter of the contract; the capacity and duties of the parties to make the contract in one form rather than another; the precise words used in the guarantee; and the circumstances of the case,[65] including the background facts and the negotiations and correspondence between the parties. There is no difficulty in admitting extrinsic evidence to establish the capacity in which a party executed a guarantee because such evidence is not concerned with the parties' actual intentions as to the meaning of the terms of the guarantee.[66] The question of the capacity in which a trustee executed a guarantee is a matter to be determined objectively in the light of this evidence and not on the basis of the subjective intentions of the parties.[67]

---

[60] Note that it was also held that the partners who signed the guarantee were also bound as individuals (see paras 55–66).

[61] See *Hawtayne v Bourne* (1841) 7 M. & W. 595; 151 E.R. 905. See also, generally, *Lindley & Banks on Partnership* (18th ed. 2002), Ch. 12.

[62] See *Vacuum Oil Co Ltd v Wiltshire* (1945) 72 C.L.R. 319; *Lumsden v Buchanan* (1865) 4 Macq 950; *Muir v City of Glasgow Bank* (1879) 4 App. Cas. 337; *Re Anderson Ex p. Alexander* (1927) 27 S.R. (NSW) 296.

[63] In which case the guarantee will bind the trust assets: *Helvetic Investment Corp Pty Ltd v Knight* (1982) 7 A.C.L.R. 225, reversed on appeal but not on this point: *Helvetic Investment Corp Pty Ltd v Knight* (1984) 9 A.C.L.R. 773 (liability not limited to the assets of the trust). See also *Re Anderson Ex p. Alexander* (1927) 27 S.R. (NSW) 296 at 300 *per* Long Innes J.; *Lumsden v Buchanan* (1865) 13 L.T. 174; *Muir v City of Glasgow Bank* (1879) 4 App. Cas. 337 at 355, 388.

[64] *Watling v Lewis* [1911] 1 Ch. 414 at 424.

[65] *Muir v City of Glasgow Bank* (1879) 4 App. Cas. 337 at 345–346; *Helvetic Investment Corp Pty Ltd v Knight* (1982) 7 A.C.L.R. 225, reversed on appeal but not on this point: (1984) 9 A.C.L.R. 723.

[66] *Re Interwest Hotels Pty Ltd* (in liq) (1993) 12 A.C.S.R. 78; *Codelfa Construction Pty Ltd v Rail Authority* (1982) 149 C.L.R. 337.

[67] *Re Interwest Hotels Pty Ltd* (in liq) (1993) 12 A.C.S.R. 78 at 120.

In *Helvetic Investment Corp Pty Ltd v Knight*,[68] a trustee was held **3–114** personally liable under a guarantee and this liability was not limited to the trust assets. The defendant was the sole trustee of "The John Knight Family Trust" as well as the managing director of J F Knight Fabrics Pty Ltd ("the company"). All but one of the shares in the company were apparently owned by the John Knight Family Trust. The company borrowed money from the plaintiff who stipulated that a guarantee "signed by all the shareholders of the company" be given to support the loan. The company sent a printed form of guarantee to the defendant to be completed. On the guarantee, in the space provided for the description and particulars of the guarantor, the defendant wrote "The John Knight Family Trust". The following indorsement appeared in the execution clause:

"THE JOHN KNIGHT FAMILY TRUST

J. Knight Trustee"

It appeared that Mr Knight also signed each page of the guarantee.

The Court of Appeal of New South Wales found that the writing on the **3–115** guarantee construed in its proper context indicated that the defendant was personally liable on the guarantee and his liability was not limited to the assets of the trust. The indorsement in the execution clause merely described the legal person to whom the trusts and the trust property pertained; it was not intended to limit liability to the trust assets. As Glass J.A. observed, "[l]anguage which asserts that Mr Knight executed the instrument because he was the trustee of the trust falls short of stipulating that he contracted only in that capacity".[69] It is apparent, therefore, that if a trustee wishes to exclude personal liability and confine the liability to the trust assets, the trustee must do so by clear language in the guarantee. The trustee cannot simply rely upon the fact that the guarantor is described as the trust itself, or the fact that he signs the guarantee "as trustee". The trustee should insert the words "as trustee only" or "as trustee and not otherwise" and insert a further clause expressly disclaiming any personal liability.

The result in *Helvetic Investment Corp Pty Ltd v Knight* is consistent **3–116** with the general principle that trustees as legal owners of the trust assets are personally liable for the consequences of their own actions.[70]

In *Re Interwest Hotels Pty Ltd* (in liq),[71] it was even clearer that the **3–117** guarantee was given by the trustee company in its personal capacity. In that case, Interwest was the trustee of the J & K Avram Unit Trust and one of a number of guarantors of a loan. Interwest had no assets in its own right

---

[68] (1984) 9 A.C.L.R. 773.
[69] *ibid.*, at 774.
[70] See also *Elders Trustee & Executor Co Ltd v E G Reeves Pty Ltd* (1987) 78 A.L.R. 193 at 253–256.
[71] (1993) 12 A.C.S.R. 78.

and was a trading trust company with a paid up capital of $2. Some of the other guarantors were trustees and the deed of guarantee noted that they acted solely in that capacity. Neither the sealing clause nor the terms of the guarantee gave any indication of the capacity in which Interwest was acting, and it executed the deed of guarantee in its own name.

3–118   Eames J. found that there is no rule that a company is, without more, presumed to be acting in capacities other than its personal capacity when it executes a document.[72] The guarantee itself and the extrinsic evidence in this case indicated that Interwest had signed the deed of guarantee solely in its personal capacity. It was not necessary for the trustee to add the words "in its personal capacity" when it executed the guarantee as this was the effect of the general law in any event.[73] The fact that Interwest was known to have acted in the past only in a trustee capacity did not prevent it from asserting that on this occasion it acted in its own right, but it carried a heavy evidentiary burden to establish that the other party accepted the contract on a basis that defied commercial logic.[74]

3–119   His Honour's finding that the guarantee bound Interwest only in its own right did not destroy the efficacy of the deed, but it did mean that the lender's recourse against Interwest would be limited to its negligible assets.[75]

3–120   *Re Interwest Hotels Pty Ltd* (in liq) is a salutary reminder to lenders to be careful, in taking guarantees from trustees, to ensure that the guarantee binds both the trustee and the trust assets. While it is true that lenders may be able to invoke the trustee's right of indemnity from the trust assets by subrogation,[76] this remedy will not be available unless the trustee's liability under the guarantee was properly incurred in the administration of the trust.[77] If the liability was incurred by the trustee in the trustee's own right and not in the proper performance of the trustee's duties as trustee, then no right of subrogation will be available and the lender's recovery will be restricted to the trustee's own assets.

3–121   As Eames J. himself observed, "This case demonstrates the potential for fraud and unfairness which might accompany the activities of a trading trust company, and also the potential for loss, even where there is no intended unfairness, which the unwary creditor will suffer if the creditor does not sufficiently take care for his own protection."[78]

3–122   Where a trustee executes a guarantee without power or authority to do so, the trustee will be denied his normal right of indemnity from the trust

---

[72] *ibid.*, at 85.
[73] *ibid.*, at 85.
[74] *ibid.*, at 86.
[75] *ibid.*, at 120.
[76] See *Re Johnson; Shearman v Robinson* (1880) 15 Ch. D. 549 at 552.
[77] *Re Interwest Hotels Pty Ltd* (in liq) (1993) 12 A.C.S.R. 78 at 85.
[78] *ibid.*, at 116.

assets[79] and the creditor will have no right of recourse to the trust assets[80] or to the beneficiaries.[81]

Modern contracts of guarantee sometimes contain clauses along the following lines:

3–123

> "In the event that the guarantor enters into this guarantee as trustee of any trust or is giving this guarantee for the purpose of or in order to benefit any trust of which the guarantor is a trustee ... the guarantor has full complete and valid authority pursuant to the trust to enter into this guarantee and to grant security over any trust property."

Such clauses assist the creditor in establishing that it took the guarantee from the trustee without notice of any breach of trust, and they may create an estoppel by representation against the trustee.[82]

3–124

(vi) Execution by or on behalf of companies

At common law, there was an ancient and technical rule,[83] that a company could not manifest its intention by any personal act or oral discourse and that it spoke and acted only by its common seal.[84] It was later recognised that it was not necessary for a company entering into contracts in the ordinary course of business to affix its seal. Certainly it is now clear that contracts of guarantee need not be executed by companies under seal.[85] As regards execution in the form of a deed the present position is that a company may execute a guarantee by deed by affixing its common seal to the document (pursuant to s.36A(2) of the Companies Act 1985).[86] It is no longer necessary, however, for a

3–125

---

[79] Trustee Act 2000, s.31(2) and *Lewin on Trusts* (17th ed., 2000), paras 21.03A and 21.03B. As to issues of execution without power, see *AGC (Advances) Ltd v Feakle Nominees Pty Ltd* (unreported, Vic Sup Ct. May 2, 1991).

[80] See generally *Octavo Investments Pty Ltd v Knight* (1979) 144 C.L.R. 360 and *Re Suco Gold Pty Ltd* (in liq) (1983) 33 S.A.S.R. 99. See also *Kemtron Industries Pty Ltd v Commissioner of Stamp Duties* Q.L.R. 18/5/84; H.A.J. Ford, "Trading Trusts and Creditors' Rights" (1981) 13 M.U.L.R. 2.

[81] See generally *Hardoon v Belilios* [1901] A.C. 118; *Balsh v Hyham* (1728) 2 P. Wms. 453; 24 E.R. 810; *Re German Mining Co Ex p. Chippendale* (1853) 4 De G.M. & G. 19; 43 E.R. 415.

[82] *Alliance Acceptance Co Ltd v Hinton* (1964) 1 DCR (NSW) 5.

[83] See Chancellor Kent, *Commentaries on American Law* (1827), Vol. 2, p.232, cited in *Australian Capital Television Pty Ltd v Minister for Transport and Communications* (1989) 7 A.C.L.C. 525 at 533 *per* Gummow J.

[84] *Australian Capital Television Pty Ltd v Minister for Transport and Communications for the Commonwealth* (1989) 7 A.C.L.C. 525 at 533 *per* Gummow J.

[85] *Re Fireproof Doors Ltd* [1916] 2 Ch. 142; *Reuter v Electric Telegraph Co* (1856) 6 El. & Bl. 341; 119 E.R. 892; (a company incorporated by Royal Charter); *South of Ireland Colliery Co v Waddle* (1868) 3 L.R.C.P. 463 (a company can contract without affixing its seal if the contract is for a purpose connected with its objects).

[86] Companies Act 1985, s.36A(3). Section 350 of the Companies Act 1985 provides that a company which has a common seal shall have its name engraved in legible characters on the seal. Nevertheless, if the company obtaining the bond has used a seal engraved with its trading name rather than its registered name, this will not in itself render the bond a nullity or unenforceable by a third party beneficiary against a surety which has validly sealed the bond. See *OTV Birwelco v Technical and General Guarantee Co Ltd* [2002] 4 All E.R. 668.

company in England or Wales to have a common seal.[87] Under s.36A(4) of the Companies Act 1985[88] a document signed by a director and the company secretary or by two directors and expressed to be executed by the company will have the same effect as if it were executed under the common seal of the company.[89] Nothing in s.36A requires a company to use its registered name rather than its trading name in the body of the deed or bond.[90]

3–126   Guarantees given by companies under hand may be executed in accordance with s.36 of the Companies Act 1985. That section provides that any contract which, if made between private persons, would by law be required to be in writing, signed by the parties to be charged therewith, may be made on behalf of a company in writing and signed by any person acting under its express or implied authority.[91] Written contracts made by companies can be varied or discharged in the same manner. The persons who are normally authorised to sign documents on behalf of companies are one or more of the directors. Whether they are authorised to bind their company to a guarantee will depend upon whether they have the necessary express, implied or ostensible authority.[92] Clearly, a managing director would have the usual authority to sign a guarantee on behalf of a company,[93] but an individual director does not have the usual authority to bind the company to a guarantee.[94] However, the general power of management which is usually vested in the board of directors may give it sufficient authority to enter into a

[87] The requirement that companies in England and Wales have a company seal was abolished on July 31, 1990.
[88] Section 36A of the Companies Act 1985 was brought in effect by s.130 of the Companies Act 1989.
[89] See also s.36A(5) which provides that "a document executed by a company which makes it clear on its face that it is intended by the person or persons making it to be a deed has effect, upon delivery, as a deed; and it shall be presumed, unless a contrary intention is proved, to be delivered upon its being so executed".
[90] According to Judge Thornton Q.C. in *OTV Birwelco v Technical and General Guarantee Co Ltd* [2002] 4 All E.R. 668.
[91] See generally G. Andrews and R. Millett, *Law of Guarantees* (3rd ed., 2000), para.3.26.
[92] See generally *Hely-Hutchinson v Brayhead Ltd* [1968] 1 Q.B. 549; *Freeman and Lockyer v Buckhurst Park Properties (Mangal) Ltd* [1964] 1 Q.B. 48 at 504–505 *per* Diplock L.J.; *Colman v Eastern Counties Rly Co* (1846) 10 Beav. 1; 50 E.R. 481; *Re Cunningham & Co Ltd*; *Simpson's Claim* (1887) 36 Ch. D. 532. A managing director has usual or customary authority to bind the company to a guarantee of loans to a subsidiary, and to indemnities given to persons, who have guaranteed such loans, see *Hely-Hutchinson v Brayhead Ltd* [1968] 1 Q.B. 549. A managing director may even have the implied authority to bind his company to a guarantee of debts owed by other persons in certain circumstances. See, *e.g. British Thomson-Houston Co Ltd v Federated European Banks Ltd* [1932] 2 K.B. 176. *Cf. Re Cunningham & Co Ltd*; *Simpson's Claim* (1887) 36 Ch. D. 532 at 540, where it was held that the giving of a promissory note in the name of the company as a guarantor was not, in the circumstances, within the power of the overseas manager of the company. Where a contract does not fall within the authority of a director because he is abusing his authority, "no contract comes into existence": *Jyske Bank (Gibraltar) Ltd v Spgeldnaes* (unreported, Court of Appeal July 29, 1999).
[93] *Hely-Hutchinson v Brayhead Ltd* [1968] 1 Q.B. 549.
[94] *Re Haycraft Gold Reduction & Mining Co* [1900] 2 Ch. 230; *Brick & Pipe Industries Ltd v Occidental Life Nominees Pty Ltd* (1991) 9 A.L.C.C. 324. Neither the chair of the board of directors nor the company secretary has the implied usual authority to give guarantees on behalf of their companies: *Hely-Hutchinson v Brayhead Ltd* [1968] 1 Q.B. 549 at 584; *Panorama Developments (Guildford) Ltd v Fidelis Furnishing Fabrics Ltd* [1971] 2 Q.B. 711; *Donato v Legion Cabs (Trading) Co-op Society Ltd* [1966] 2 N.S.W.R. 583.

guarantee on behalf of the company if the guarantee is within the scope of the company's business.[95]

An individual director who purports to sign a guarantee on behalf of his **3–127** company may be held personally liable as a guarantor,[96] either because the document which he signed was a sufficient note or memorandum of his earlier oral contract of guarantee or because he has undertaken a personal liability as a surety on the terms of the document.[97] It is imperative, therefore, that directors ensure that the terms of corporate guarantees clearly exclude any personal liability and confirm that they are signing the guarantee only on behalf of the company and not in their personal capacity.[98] But these disclaimers of personal liability will count for little if the guarantee which is expressed to be executed for and on behalf of a particular company is intended to secure the debts or liabilities of that company.[99] In this situation, the court may be inclined to interpret the guarantee as a personal guarantee by the director of the company's debts and liabilities.

(vii) Guarantees by governments and public authorities[1]

The ordinary principles of agency determine whether or not a Crown **3–128** servant has authority to bind the Crown to a guarantee. Thus a guarantee

[95] Compare *Re West of England Bank Ex p. Booker* (1880) 14 Ch. D. 317 and *Re Cunningham & Co Ltd*; *Simpson's Claim* (1887) 36 Ch. D. 532. See also *Richardson v Landecker* (1950) 50 SR (NSW) 250; *Black v Smallwood* (1966) 117 C.L.R. 52 at 60. In *Re West of England Bank*; *Ex p. Booker* (1880) 14 Ch. D. 317 the court held that the directors of a joint stock bank had authority to guarantee interest payable on debentures issued for the purpose of forming another company which was important to the business of the bank.

[96] See *Johnson v Imperial Fisheries Ltd* (1911) 19 W.L.R. 285; 16 B.C.R. 445 (Can). However, the company itself will not be bound in this situation: see *White v Bank of Victoria* (1882) 8 V.L.R. (M) 8 (where the directors did not purport to execute the guarantee on behalf of their company) and *Brick & Pipe Industries Ltd v Occidental Life Nominees Pty Ltd* (1991) 9 A.CL.C. 324. However, the other directors could adopt the guarantee on behalf of the company, thereby rendering it liable as a surety: *Re Dover and Deal Railway, Cinque Ports Thanet & Coast Junction Co*; *Londesborough's (Lord) Case* (1854) 4 De G.M. & G. 411 at 421; 43 E.R. 567 at 571. The directors could also have incurred liability for a breach of warranty of authority where the guarantee was ultra vires: See *Chapleo v Brunswick Permanent Building Society* [1881] 6 Q.B.D. 696 (a case involving an unincorporated building society). But *ultra vires* is no longer an issue in relation to incorporated companies: See ss.108 and 109 of the Companies Act 1989.

[97] See *Sun Alliance Pensions Life and Investments Services Ltd v RJL and Anthony Webster* [1991] 2 Lloyd's Rep. 410 and *VSH Ltd v BKS Air Transport* [1964] 1 Lloyd's Rep. 460.

[98] See also *W. & T. Avery Ltd v Charlesworth* (1914) 31 T.L.R. 52 (an agreement on behalf of the company to pay a sum of money); *Chapman v Smethurst* [1909] 1 K.B. 927 (company liable on a promissory note signed on its behalf by its managing director); *Re Dover & Deal Railway Etc Co, Lord Londesborough's Case* (1854) De G.M. & G. 411 at 421; 43 E.R. 567 at 571; *Dutton v Marsh* (1871) LR 6 Q.B. 361 (directors did not exclude personal liability on a promissory note). Cf. *Alexander v Sizer* (1869) L.R. 4 Exch. 102.

[99] See *Minorities Finance Ltd v Attam* (unreported, CAT No.1094 of 1989, November 13, 1989, cited in G. Andrews and R. Millett, *Law of Guarantees* (3rd ed., 2000), para.3.26.

[1] As to the general issues which must be addressed in relation to guarantees by governments and public authorities, see K.P. McGuinness, *The Law of Guarantees* (2nd ed., 1996), para.5.56. See generally M. Breheny and J. Beaven, "Australian Federal and State Government Guarantees—A Legal Overview" (1986) 4 JIBL 231; R. I. Milliner, "Government Guarantees" (The Law Society of Western Australia, Continuing Legal Education: General Series, 1989); M. Breheny, "Government Guarantees—An Overview"

executed by the servant within the scope of the servant's actual authority or, subject to certain limitations, within the ambit of the servant's usual or ostensible authority will bind the Crown.[2] Usually the servant with actual authority to commit the Crown to a guarantee is the Minister responsible for the administration of the particular activity or venture covered by the guarantee. This actual authority will be confirmed by administrative arrangements published from time to time[3] or by specific statutory provisions authorising the Minister or other appropriate official to execute the guarantee. Any procedural requirements relating to the form or execution of these guarantees must be observed, otherwise the guarantee will be invalid and unenforceable.[4] It is, of course, possible for Crown servants below the rank of Minister to be given actual authority to provide a guarantee binding on the Crown but it may be more difficult to establish that this authority has been conferred in such cases. Similarly, it is often difficult to establish that a Crown servant has usual authority to bind the Crown to a guarantee.[5]

3–129   In a case of ostensible authority, the principal holds out the agent as having authority to contract on the principal's behalf. In the context of government contracts, this presents a problem because:

"No public officer, unless he possesses some special power, can hold out on behalf of the Crown that he or some other public officer has the right to enter into a contract in respect of the property of the Crown when in fact no such right exists."[6]

Generally, therefore, the only official with the requisite actual authority to hold out a Crown servant will be the Minister responsible for the particular area of government to which the guarantee relates. In the absence of specific statutory power, a holding out by any other Crown servant will not support the estoppel by representation necessary to bind the Crown on the basis of the ostensible authority of the servant who provided the guarantee.

3–130   The doctrine of constructive notice, which once loomed large in any discussion of corporate contracting, has its counterpart in the area of

(1986) 1 (No. 5) *Banking Law Bulletin* 76; E. Campbell, "Commonwealth Contracts" (1970) 44 A.L.J. 14; E. Campbell "Federal Contract Law" (1970) 44 A.L.J. 580; E. Nosworthy, "Contracts with Governments: Some Problems Relating to Crown Capacity in Australia" in *Papers presented at the 22nd Australian Legal Convention Brisbane 1983* (Law Council of Australia, 1984), pp.97–105 and M. I. Aronson and H. Whitmore, *Public Torts and Contracts* (1982).
[2] P. W. Hogg, *Liability of the Crown* (1971), p.126. See also N. Seddon, *Government Contracts* (2nd ed., 1999, The Federation Press, Sydney), pp.89–97.
[3] See E. Nosworthy, "Contracts with Governments", *op. cit.*, at 100.
[4] See *Commercial Cable Co v Government of Newfoundland* [1916] 2 A.C. 610; *Commonwealth v Colonial Ammunition Co Ltd* (1924) 34 C.L.R. 198; *Nicholas v Western Australia* [1972] W.A.R. 168; *Cudgen Rutile (No. 2) Ltd v Chalk* [1975] A.C. 520; *ABE Copiers Pty Ltd v Secretary Department of Administrative Services* (1985) 7 F.C.R. 94.
[5] See G.H. Treitel, "Crown Proceedings: Some Recent Developments" (1957) *Public Law* 321, where *Robertson v Minister of Pensions* [1949] 1 K.B. 227, a controversial example of such authority, is discussed. See also E. Nosworthy, "Contracts with Governments", *op. cit.*, at 101.
[6] *A-G (Ceylon) v A. D. Silva* [1953] A.C. 461 at 479, PC.

government contracts. A third party dealing with a Crown servant is deemed to have notice of any statutory restriction or limitation placed on the servant's authority to provide a guarantee binding on the Crown.[7] Thus, a statutory provision limiting a government guarantee given by the Minister for Trade, for example, to the sum advanced to the principal debtor and interest thereon at the rate of 10 per cent would be binding on the creditor. Equally, an express statutory provision limiting a Crown servant's authority will prevent a third party from holding the Crown liable to a guarantee given in excess of that authority. Conversely, a creditor taking a guarantee executed by a Crown servant cannot invoke an express statutory provision to establish a holding out by the Crown unless the creditor had actual knowledge of the provisions and relied on it.[8]

(viii) Alterations after signature

Where a guarantee is materially altered after signature[9] the guarantor will not be bound by the amended document unless he indorses it. It is not necessary for the guarantor to sign the indorsement containing the alteration, but he should do something which authenticates his original signature;[10] he must confirm in some way that the signature extends to the altered guarantee. If the guarantor orally assents to the alteration and later concludes an agreement, it appears that the document may still be a sufficient memorandum even though it was not reproduced to the guarantor at the time of his verbal assent to the alteration.[11] In effect, the defendant in such a case agrees that his original signature should operate as a signature to what has become a complete agreement between the parties.[12]

3–131

It is hardly necessary to state that the persons who attest the affixing of a company's seal to a guarantee given by a company will not be personally liable if the imprint of the seal is later crossed out without their consent or authority.[13]

3–132

---

[7] *R. v Woodburn* (1898) 29 S.C.R. 112 at 123 (Can).
[8] See *Freeman and Lockyer v Buckhurst Park Properties (Mangal) Ltd* [1964] 2 Q.B. 480 at 504–505.
[9] The insertion of the name and address of a purported service agent, without the knowledge and consent of the guarantor, did not constitute a material alteration of the guarantee as it did not alter or accelerate the guarantor's liability: *Raiffeisen Zentralbank Osterreich AG v Crossseas Shipping Ltd* [2000] 1 All E.R. (Comm) 76 (discussed in detail, below paras 8–36 to 8–45).
[10] *Bluck v Gompertz* (1852) 7 Exch. 862; 155 E.R. 1199. *Cf. Stewart v Eddowes* (1874) L.R. 9 C.P. 311 (where parol evidence was admitted to show what was the condition of a document when it became a contract between the parties).
[11] *Stewart v Eddowes* (1874) L.R. 9 C.P. 311; *Koenigsblatt v Sweet* [1923] 2 Ch. 314. See also *O'Young and Lum v Reid & Co Ltd* [1932] A.L.R. 278 at 284. In general terms, contracts which themselves must be made in writing can only be varied by writing: *Rattrays Wholesale Ltd v Meredyth-Young & A'Court Ltd* [1997] 2 N.Z.L.R. 363. But s.4 of the Statute of Frauds 1677 does not require guarantees to be in writing; it is sufficient that there is some written note or memorandum of the guarantee signed by the guarantor or his lawfully authorised agent.
[12] *ibid.* Parol evidence of such an agreement is admissible: *Stewart v Eddowes* (1874) L.R. 9 C.P. 311.
[13] *National Commercial Banking Corp of Australia Ltd v Cheung* (1983) 1 A.C.L.C. 1326.

3–133   A guarantee which contains a mistake in the written statement of an existing contract can be corrected by an unsigned indorsement by the defendant on the guarantee itself. Such an indorsement will be regarded as an authentication of the defendant's signature on the original guarantee, and that document, with the indorsement, will be accepted as a sufficient memorandum under the statute.[14] But a signature made before an alteration will not authenticate the amendment if the change effects a variation of the contract already concluded and binding on the parties.[15]

(ix) Forgeries

3–134   The general rule is that a contract is avoided insofar as it applies to a person whose signature as guarantor was forged.[16] It is not sufficient for a defendant simply to swear that what appears to be his signature is irregular or forged where there is independent evidence of disinterested parties confirming that the defendant signed the guarantee.[17] Forgery must be proved.[18] By the same token, if the claimant fails to prove that the defendant signed the guarantee it will not be enforceable.[19]

3–135   The general rule does not apply to a third party mortgage of registered land without any fraud on the part of the mortgagee.[20] In *Grgic v Australian & New Zealand Banking Group Ltd.*[21] the mortgagor's signature on a third party mortgage was forged by an imposter and the signature was attested and certified by bank officers without any knowledge of the forgery. The New South Wales Court of Appeal held that the bank acquired an indefeasible title as mortgagee because the registered proprietor of the land had no personal equity in the form of a legal or equitable cause of action against the bank.

3–136   The bank officers had certified that the mortgagor was "personally known" to them, but this did not constitute "fraud" in the relevant sense of actual fraud. As Powell J.A. pointed out:

---

[14] See *Bluck v Gompertz* (1852) 7 Exch. 862; 155 E.R. 1199 (an undertaking to get two drafts upon a third party accepted by him and to see that the drafts were duly paid was altered by an indorsement by the defendant charging the amount of one of the drafts).

[15] *New Hart Builders Ltd v Brindley* [1975] Ch. 342 at 352 *per* Goulding J; *Stewart v Eddowes* (1874) LR 9 CP 311; *Koenigsblatt v Sweet* [1923] 2 Ch. 314.

[16] *J. R. Watkins Medical Co v Lee* (1920) 52 D.L.R. 593 at 595 (obiter dicta); *CSR Ltd v Price* (unreported, NSW Sup Ct. Cole J. April 29, 1993). Inferential support for this proposition can be drawn from Lord Loreburn's judgment in *Ruben and Ladenburg v Great Fingall Consolidated* [1906] A.C. 439 at 443. Not every forgery invalidates a guarantee. A forged alteration to a document does not render the document void unless the alteration goes to the essence of the agreement: *Lombard Finance Ltd v Brookplain Trading Ltd* [1991] 1 W.L.R. 271 (deletion of word "Company" from name of the principal debtor in the guarantee). But where the alteration is material, the whole of the document is corrupted and rendered void: *Pigot's Case* (1614) 11 Co. Rep. 261; 77 E.R. 1177.

[17] *R v Chesley* (1889) 16 S.C.R. 306 (Can).

[18] *Farrow Mortgage Services Pty Ltd v Trewhitt* (unreported, Vic Sup Ct, Hedigan J., November 29, 1994).

[19] *Equuscorp Pty Ltd v Wright* [2002] U.S.C. 109 (unreported, Vic Sup Ct, Byrne J., April 12, 2002).

[20] *Small v Tomassetti* [2001] N.S.W.S.C. 1112 (unreported, NSW Sup Ct, Campbell J., November 26, 2001).

[21] (1994) 33 N.S.W.L.R. 202.

"In the circumstances, it being well-established that a person who presents for registration a document which is forged, or has been fraudulently or improperly obtained, is not guilty of 'fraud' if he honestly believes it to be a genuine document which can be properly acted upon (*Assets Co Ltd v Mere Roihi* [1905] AC 176 at 210; *Mayer v Coe* (1968) 88 WN (Pt 1) (NSW) 549) and that a less than meticulous practice as to the identification of persons purporting to deal with land registered under the provisions of the [Real Property] Act does not constitute a course of conduct so reckless as to be tantamount to fraud (*Ratcliffe v Watters* (1969) 89 WN (Pt 1) NSW 496 at 500) ..."[22]

As common law forgery involves the false making of a document or a false alteration of a document going to its substance and altering its nature and effect,[23] it is not a forgery to make or alter a document so that it merely tells a lie.[24] Accordingly, a guarantee will not be a forgery simply because it contains a false representation that a solicitor witnessed the guarantor's signature and certified that he explained the document to the guarantor.[25] **3–137**

It has been seen[26] that there may exist a condition of the guarantee that a number of persons shall execute the instrument as guarantors, for example, by implication from the words "joint and several". If such a term exists, and one of the signatures is forged, then the co-guarantors will be discharged because there has not been a *valid* execution of the guarantee by all guarantors in compliance with the term.[27] Alternatively, the other guarantors may be discharged in equity.[28] **3–138**

7. WHEN MUST THE MEMORANDUM BE IN EXISTENCE?

It is not necessary for the note or memorandum evidencing an oral guarantee to be made contemporaneously with it.[29] Usually the written evidence comes into existence after the oral agreement to provide a guarantee and this is sufficient to satisfy the Statute of Frauds.[30] **3–139**

---

[22] *ibid.*, at 222. See also *Small v Tomassetti* [2001] N.S.W.S.C. 1112 (NSW Sup Ct, Campbell J., November 26, 2001).
[23] *Brott v The Queen* (1992) 173 C.L.R. 426.
[24] *ibid.*
[25] *Farrow Mortgage Services Pty Ltd v Trewhitt* (unreported, Vic Sup Ct, Hedigan J. November 29, 1994).
[26] See above, paras 3–87 to 3–98.
[27] *James Graham & Co (Timber) Ltd v Southgate-Sands* [1985] 2 All E.R. 344. *Cf. CSR Ltd v Price* (unreported NSW Sup Ct, Cole J., April 29, 1993). It was not clear from the judgment in this case whether the guarantee was expressed to be joint and several. See also above, para.3–92.
[28] See above, paras 3–92 to 3–94. Note also clauses which may preclude discharge on this basis: see above, paras 3–95 to 3–97.
[29] *Longfellow v Williams* (1804) Peake, Add. Cas. 225; *Re Hoyle; Hoyle v Hoyle* [1893] 1 Ch. 84.
[30] In *Barkworth v Young* (1856) 4 Drewry 1 at 12; 62 E.R. 1 at 5 a written memorandum made approximately 14 years after the contract was acceptable.

3–140   The memorandum can be made at any time after the contract but it must be in existence before an action on the guarantee is commenced.[31] As the Statute of Frauds was merely intended to prescribe evidentiary requirements for certain promises,[32] this principle appears to be anomalous. It is, however, supported by the terms of s.4 itself.[33] Thus the section will not be satisfied by an incomplete memorandum coupled with further material in the pleadings[34] or in an affidavit filed in the proceedings.[35] However, if a written admission is made in the course of proceedings, the requirements of the statute can be accommodated by discontinuing the action and instituting another at a later time relying on that admission.[36]

3–141   A written offer to guarantee the debt, default or miscarriage of another can be evidenced by a note or memorandum brought into existence before the contract of guarantee was concluded by the creditor's acceptance of the written offer of a guarantee.[37] While the terms of s.4 of the Statute of Frauds 1677 appear to be based on the premise that the requisite note or memorandum relates to an existing agreement, it is now established that a note or memorandum containing an offer of guarantee and signed by the guarantor can satisfy the statute even if it is only later unconditionally accepted by the creditor.[38] However, in *New Eberhardt Co Ex p. Menzies*[39] Bowen L.J. sounded a note of caution when he observed that the written offer cases "pushed the literal construction of the Statute of Frauds to a limit beyond which it would perhaps be not easy to go."[40] Consequently the court may impose a heavy burden of proof on a creditor who alleges that the guarantor's written offer to guarantee was later accepted orally.[41]

3–142   While it is important for the memorandum to be in existence before the action on the guarantee is commenced, it should not be in existence too early. A memorandum made more than six years before the action is commenced will not support the guarantee unless the guarantor revives it by a verbal promise within the limitation period.[42] A lapsed memorandum

---

[31] *Longfellow v Williams* (1804) Peake Add. Cas. 225 NP; 170 E.R. 252; *Sievewright v Archibald* (1851) 17 Q.B. 103; *Re Hoyle; Hoyle v Hoyle* [1893] 1 Ch. 84; *Lucas v Dixon* (1889) 22 Q.B.D. 357. In *Farr, Smith & Co v Messers Ltd* [1928] 1 K.B. 397 the memorandum was a pleading drafted in an earlier action; and in *Re Hoyle; Hoyle v Hoyle* [1893] 1 Ch. 84 it was a recital of the promise in the will of one of the guarantors. But where a defendant pays money into court on a plea of tender, this in effect admits the promise to guarantee payment and the plaintiff need not prove that there was written evidence of the guarantee: *Middleton v Brewer* (1790) Peake 20; 170 E.R. 64, (NP). *Semble*, the tender has to be made before the plaintiff's action is commenced.
[32] *Re Hoyle; Hoyle v Hoyle* [1893] 1 Ch. 84; *Thomson v Eede* (1895) 22 O.A.R. 105.
[33] *Re Hoyle; Hoyle v Hoyle* [1893] 1 Ch. 84.
[34] *Southern Suburban Land & Finance Co Ltd v Hughes* (1889) 15 V.L.R. 751.
[35] *Popiw v Popiw* [1959] V.R. 197. This is true even if those proceedings do not directly raise the Statute of Frauds: *Dudgeon v Chie* (1953) 55 S.R. (NSW) 450.
[36] *Lucas v Dixon* (1889) 22 Q.B.D. 357 at 363; *Farr, Smith & Co v Messers* [1928] 1 K.B. 397.
[37] See generally G. Andrews and R. Millett, *Law of Guarantees* (3rd ed., 2000), para.3.21.
[38] *Parker v Clark* [1960] 1 W.L.R. 286 at 295–296; *Powers v Fowler* (1855) 4 El. & Bl. 511; 119 E.R. 187; *Reuss v Picksley* (1866) L.R. 1 Ex. 342; *Smith v Neale* (1857) 2 C.B.N.S. 67; 140 E.R. 337; *Tiverton Estates Ltd v Wearwell* [1975] Ch. 146. *Cf. Munday v Asprey* (1878) 13 Ch. 855 at 857 per Fry J.
[39] (1889) 43 Ch. D. 118.
[40] *ibid.*, at 129.
[41] See *Watson v Davies* [1931] 1 Ch. 455 at 468 *per* Maugham J., and G. Andrews and R. Millett, *Law of Guarantees* (3rd ed., 2000), para.3.21.
[42] *Gibbons v McCasland* (1818) 1 B. & Ald. 690; 106 E.R. 253.

can be resuscitated in a similar manner. Where a lost memorandum is found, it can be reactivated by the parties if they verbally acknowledge that they signed the memorandum and that they are bound by the guarantee.[43]

The Statute of Frauds does not require the guarantee to be in writing: **3–143** written evidence of the guarantee is sufficient to satisfy the statute.[44] Accordingly, it is not necessary for the guarantee to remain in existence until the creditor sues the guarantor. If the note or memorandum evidencing the guarantee is lost or destroyed, oral evidence is admissible to prove that a note or memorandum satisfying the statute did exist before the creditor commenced its action against the guarantor.[45]

8. WHO MUST SUPPLY THE MEMORANDUM?

The memorandum must be supplied by the guarantor in the guarantor's **3–144** own right or on his behalf. A defendant will not be personally liable on a memorandum made clearly in the capacity of agent or attorney of another.[46] It is sometimes difficult to ascertain whether a guarantee is executed by a party as a principal or as an agent. In *Allaway v Duncan*,[47] the defendant, an attorney, wrote to the plaintiff in the following terms:

> "[The debtor] has handed me your letter of the 3rd respecting the non-payment of the bill for 91 pounds due on Saturday. I am now making arrangements for an advance to [the debtor], to enable him to pay this and other claims upon him, and if you will have the goodness to hold the bill for a few days, I shall be prepared on his behalf to take it up."

The plaintiff had no further communication with the defendant. It was **3–145** held that the defendant's letter did not render him personally liable as surety for the amount of the bill of exchange. One reason why the defendant was excused was because he had written to the plaintiff in the character of an agent. With respect, there was no clear indication in the defendant's letter that he was an attorney and this fact was not known to the plaintiff when he received the letter. The decision might be more soundly based on the ground that the letter was not sufficiently clear to create a contract of suretyship.[48]

---

[43] *O'Young and Lum v Reid & Co Ltd* [1932] A.L.R. 278.
[44] *Re Hoyle; Hoyle v Hoyle* [1893] 1 Ch. 84 at 97 *per* Lindley L.J. and at 100 *per* A.L. Smith L.J.; *Laythorp v Bryant* (1836) 2 Bing N.C. 735; 132 E.R. 283.
[45] *Barrass v Reed*, *The Times* March 28, 1898; *Crays Gas Co v Bromley Gas Consumers Co The Times* March 23, 1901, CA, cited in G. Andrews and R. Millett, *Law of Guarantees* (3rd ed., 2000), para.3.21 and K.P. McGuinness, *The Law of Guarantee* (2nd ed., 1996), para.5.19. In general, see *Cole v Gibson* (1750) 1 Ves. Sen. 503 at 505; 27 E.R. 1169 at 1170.
[46] But see *Redhead v Cator* (1815), as reported in 1 Stark 14 NP; 171 E.R. 387, where an agent for foreign vendors was held liable on a guarantee that shipments of goods imported for sale would be in conformity with the revenue laws of Great Britain. See also *National Commercial Banking Corp of Australia Ltd v Cheung* (1983) 1 A.C.L.C. 1326.
[47] (1867) 16 L.T. 264.
[48] *ibid.*, at 265, *per* Byles and Keating JJ.

3–146   It is not enough merely for the defendant to be present when the memorandum is completed; the defendant must actually authorise the agent to execute the memorandum on his behalf. Hence, in *Dixon v Broomfield*,[49] a memorandum written by the plaintiff's clerk in the presence of the defendant did not satisfy the statute.

9. HOW MUST THE MEMORANDUM BE ADDRESSED?

3–147   To satisfy the Statute of Frauds, it is not necessary for the memorandum to be addressed to the other contracting party.[50] But a memorandum which is not addressed to any particular person, or which is addressed to the whole world is defective.[51] In general, it should be given or addressed to the person for whom the guarantee is intended, namely, the creditor.[52] However, it is sufficient for the memorandum to be addressed to the creditor's attorney provided the attorney receives it in that capacity.[53] In some cases, it is not even necessary for the creditor to be named in the memorandum as long as it contains references by which the creditor can be identified,[54] for it is sufficient that there be evidence of the guarantee under the hand of the guarantor or the guarantor's agent. Thus a memorandum addressed to a debtor's "unsecured creditors" or "trade creditors" may suffice. *Jones v Williams*[55] represents the high-water mark of this more lenient approach. The defendant wrote to a person inviting that person's brothers to join in a security for the repayment of money to be advanced to him to sustain a legal action. The plaintiff, who was merely the administrator of the estate of one of the brothers, and to whom the invitation was not specifically addressed, executed the bond in question and was allowed to recover on the guarantee.

3–148   If the memorandum is addressed to one of two parties with whom the principal debtor has contracted, only that party can enforce the

---

[49] (1814) 2 Chit. 205.
[50] *Gibson v Holland* (1865) L.R. 1 C.P. 1.
[51] *Brettel v Williams* (1849) 4 Exch. 623; 154 E.R. 1363; *Harris v Stevens* (1902) 1 O.W.R. 109 (Can). *Cf. Fortune v Young* [1918] S.C. 1 (Scot). Such a defect may not afterwards be rectified by the defendant's ratification of a delivery to a particular person who was not originally contemplated as a creditor: *Williams v Lake* (1859) 2 E. & E. 349; 121 E.R. 132. But a guarantee, not addressed to any particular person, will enure for the benefit of those to whom or for whose use it was delivered: *Walton v Dodson* (1827) 3 C. & P. 162 NP; 172 E.R. 369. *Cf. Williams v Lake* (above).
[52] *Williams v Lake* (1859) 2 E. & E. 349; 121 E.R. 132; *Huron County v Kerr* (1868) 15 Gr. 265 (Can); *A McDonald & Co v Fletcher* (1915) 22 B.C.R. 298, CA. It is not enough that the guarantor knows who the creditor is: *Williams v Byrnes* (1863) 1 Moo P.C.C. (NS) 154; 15 E.R. 660, PC. *Cf. Macrory v Scott* (1850) 5 Exch. 907; 155 E.R. 396.
[53] *Bateman v Phillips* (1812) 15 East 272; 104 E.R. 847; *Gibson v Holland* (1812) 15 East 272; 104 E.R. 847.
[54] *Sims v Robertson* (1921) 21 S.R. (NSW) 246. See also *Arvier v Watson* (1888) 14 V.L.R. 771. See also above, paras 3–63 to 3–68.
[55] (1841) 7 M. & W. 493; 151 E.R. 860.

guarantee.[56] But a memorandum of a guarantee directed to two parties in the alternative cannot support an action by either party.[57]

10. CONSEQUENCES OF FAILURE TO COMPLY WITH THE STATUTE

The words "no action shall be brought" in s.4 of the Statute of Frauds are taken to mean that an oral guarantee unsupported by written evidence cannot be enforced.[58] Even if the promisor's verbal undertaking falls partly within the statute and partly outside it, the promisor's undertaking cannot be enforced if it is one entire agreement which is not severable.[59]   **3–149**

The statute bars an action on an oral guarantee but it is not available as a defence in a suit relating to a matter quite independent of the contract of guarantee.[60] Thus, it will not prevent a plaintiff suing on a bill of exchange even if that instrument constitutes an incomplete memorandum of a guarantee. Such a suit is not an action to enforce a promise to answer for the debt of another.[61] Nor does the statute prevent the court from exercising its summary jurisdiction to compel its officers, including solicitors and attorneys, to perform their verbal guarantees to pay claims made against their clients.[62]   **3–150**

---

[56] *Stevenson v McLean* (1861) 10 U.C.C.P. 414, CA.
[57] *Lott v Collins* (1869) 8 S.C.R. (NSW) 104.
[58] *Barrell v Trussel* (1811) 4 Taunt 117; 128 E.R. 273; *Rann v Hughes* (1778) 4 Bro. P.C. 27; 2 E.R. 18. The statute renders the guarantee unenforceable but not void: *Maddison v Alderson* (1883) 8 App. Cas. 467; *Re Hoyle; Hoyle v Hoyle* [1893] 1 Ch. 84 at 97. A failure to satisfy the formal requirements of the statute is also a defence to a proof of debt in a bankruptcy or liquidation: *Re Solmon* (1974) 19 C.B.R. (NS) 165, Ont, SC. Even an oral guarantee given in a foreign country cannot be enforced in England because s.4 of the Statute of Frauds 1677 is regarded as part of English procedural law, which is governed by the *lex fori*: *Leroux v Brown* (1852) 12 C.B. 801; 138 E.R. 1119. Compare *Compagnie Generale d' Industrie v Myson Group Ltd* (1984) 134 N.L.J. 788, where Hirst J. held that a defence based on s.4 of the Statute of Frauds 1677 was not made out in an action to enforce a guarantee given by an English company under French law. See generally Ch. 14.
[59] *Lexington v Clarke* (1689) 2 Vent 223; 86 E.R. 406; *Chater v Beckett* (1797) 7 Term Rep 201; 101 E.R. 931; *Thomas v Williams* (1830) 10 B. & C. 664; 109 E.R. 597. In *Lyde v Higgins* (1804) 1 Smith K.B. 305, that part of the promise falling outside the statute was severed and enforced. See also *Wood v Benson* (1831) 2 Cr. & J. 94; 149 E.R. 40. As to severance generally, see *Bromley v Smith* [1909] 2 K.B. 235.
[60] *Coady v J Lewis & Sons Ltd* [1951] 3 D.L.R. 845 NS. But an oral guarantee may not be raised as a counterclaim to an unrelated claim: *Coady v J Lewis & Sons Ltd* [1951] 3 D.L.R. 845 at 848 (an oral guarantee may only be raised as a defence when the plaintiff is seeking to recover money or property which has passed in pursuance of the principal contract). See also *Lavery v Turley* (1860) 6 H. & N. 239; 158 E.A. 98, (Ex.) (where there was an accord and satisfaction so it was immaterial that the contract was not supported by written evidence).
[61] See *Glenie v Smith* [1908] 1 K.B. 263; *Wilkinson v Unwin* (1881) 7 QBD 636; *McCall Bros Ltd v Hargreaves* [1932] 2 K.B. 423; *G & H Montage GmbH v Irvani* [1988] 1 W.L.R. 1285, affirmed [1990] 1 W.L.R. 667 at 683–684, 686 and 691, CA.
[62] *Evans v Duncombe* (1831) 1 Cr. & J. 372; 148 E.R. 1465; *Re Greaves* (1827) 1 Cr. & J. 374; 148 E.R. 1466 (note). This is because the prefatory words of the section are "No action shall be brought whereby to *charge* the defendant" (emphasis added). The court will not allow the solicitor as an officer of the court to take advantage of his presumed knowledge that oral guarantees are generally unenforceable: *Re Greaves* (1827) 1 Cr. & J. 374; 148 E.R. 1466 (CP); *Re Patterson* (1832) 1 Dowl. 468. See also *Re A Solicitor* (1900) 45 S.J. 104. But s.4 of the Statute of Frauds 1677 should prevent oral guarantees given by solicitors in their private

3–151   In effect, the Statute of Frauds prevents an action being brought to enforce an oral guarantee. But can the statute be pleaded as a bar to a defence, counterclaim or set-off based on an oral guarantee? There are dicta in the judgment of North J. in *Miles v New Zealand Alford Estate Co Ltd*[63] which suggest that a plaintiff cannot plead the statute in reply to the defendant's defence or counterclaim.[64] But the contract which the defendant company sought to enforce in that case was not a guarantee but rather a contract in the articles of association granting the company a first charge on the shares of its members in respect of their liabilities to the company. Mr Justice North's remarks were not endorsed by the English Court of Appeal in *Sidebotham v Holland*[65] or the High Court of Australia in *Perpetual Executors and Trustees Association of Australia Ltd v Russell*.[66] Indeed, the better view appears to be that an oral guarantee may not be invoked as a defence or counterclaim to an action by the guarantor to recover a debt.[67] However, an oral guarantee may support an exercise of a liquidator's statutory right of set-off against the guarantor because this does not involve the bringing of an action, but rather a bookkeeping exercise.[68]

3–152   Even when the statute does apply it does not nullify an oral contract of guarantee; it merely renders it unenforceable.[69] Consequently, money paid by a guarantor to a creditor in the performance of such a contract cannot be recovered unless the consideration for the payment has failed.[70] It also appears that an oral guarantee may be raised by way of equitable set-off as a defence if it is so intimately connected with the plaintiff's claim that it "impeaches his title".[71] On the other hand, an oral guarantee will probably not support a counter-

---

capacity from being enforced: See G. Andrews and R. Millett, *Law of Guarantees* (3rd ed., 2000), para.3.29.

[63] (1886) 32 Ch. D. 266.

[64] *ibid.*, at 279.

[65] [1895] 1 Q.B. 378.

[66] (1931) 45 C.L.R. 146.

[67] *Coady v J. Lewis & Sons Ltd* [1951] 3 D.L.R. 845 at 847–848 *per* Doull J.; *Perpetual Executors and Trustees Association of Australia Ltd v Russell* (1931) 45 C.L.R. 146 at 153 *per* Gavan Duffy C.J. and Starke and McTeirnan JJ. See also at 155–157 *per* Evatt J.

[68] See *Hiley v People's Prudential Assurance Co Ltd* (1938) 60 C.L.R. 468 at 497. Compare *Re Solmon* (1974) 19 C.B.R. (NS) 165 (a failure to satisfy the requirements of the statute is a ground for rejecting the creditor's proof of debt in the bankruptcy or liquidation of the guarantor).

[69] The guarantee is unenforceable, but not void: *Maddison v Alderson* (1883) 8 App. Cas. 467. See also *Leroux v Brown* (1852) 12 C.B. 801; 138 E.R. 1119 and *Laythoarp v Bryant* (1836) 2 Bing N.C. 735; 132 E.R. 283. Such an unenforceable guarantee may be revived by an express promise: *Wilson v Marshall* (1864) 15 Ir. C.L.R. (NS) 466.

[70] *Noske Bros Pty Ltd v Leys* [1930] S.A.S.R. 43; *Coady v J. Lewis & Sons Ltd* [1951] 3 D.L.R. 845 (NS); *Sweet v Lee* (1841) 3 Man. & Gr. 452; 133 E.R. 1220. See also *Shaw v Woodcock* (1827) 7 B. & C. 73; 108 E.R. 652. Executors and administrators should not use the funds of the estate to pay a creditor a debt guaranteed by the deceased if the Statute of Frauds prevents the creditor from enforcing the guarantee. Indeed, they may not retain funds out of the estate where the deceased's guarantee was given to them in their own right: *Re Rownson* (1885) 29 Ch. D. 358. See also *Re Midgley* [1893] 3 Ch. 282 (it is a breach of duty for an executor to pay a statute-barred debt).

[71] Moreover, a liquidator should be able to exercise a statutory right of set-off in respect of an oral guarantee because this involves merely a bookkeeping exercise: *Hiley v People's Prudential Assurance Co Ltd* (1938) 60 C.L.R. 468.

claim as this effectively involves bringing an action against the plaintiff on the basis of the guarantee.[72] Moreover, since the statute does not affect the validity of a contract of guarantee but merely prescribes evidentiary requirements, oral evidence is admissible to prove that the necessary memorandum or note of the contract was lost.[73]

There are certain exceptions to the general rule that a verbal **3–153** guarantee is unenforceable. If the guarantee is not supported by written evidence because of fraud on the part of the principal debtor or the guarantor, the statute does not bar recovery.[74] Again, a promise to pay the debt of another needs no written evidence where the defendant admits in the pleadings that there is an enforceable contract, or where the defendant pleads a tender to the count on such promise and payment into court.[75] The defendant can, however, admit the existence of an oral guarantee and yet successfully plead the statute as a defence.[76]

11. PLEADINGS

A failure to comply with the statute must be expressly pleaded as a **3–154** defence;[77] otherwise it will not be necessary for the claimant to prove that the guarantee was in writing[78] and the court will assume that the guarantee is enforceable[79]

It is implicit in *Marsden & Sons v Capital & Counties Newspaper Co* **3–155** *Ltd*[80] that the Statute of Frauds should be pleaded by the defendant in the defence to an action to enforce an oral guarantee because if the point is not taken the guarantee can be enforced. For this reason, a statement of claim which pleads an oral contract of guarantee will not be struck out on the ground that it discloses no cause of action.[81] However, the defendant may be able to have the plaintiff's claims struck out under the other limbs of

---

[72] *Lavery v Turley* (1860) 6 H. & N. 239; 158 E.R. 98; *Coady v J. Lewis & Sons Ltd* [1951] 3 D.L.R. 845 at 848; *Re A Debtor (No.517 of 1991) The Times* November 25, 1991.
[73] *Barrass v Reed, The Times*, March 28, 1898; *Crays Gas Co v Bromley Gas Consumers Co, The Times*, March 23, 1901, CA; *Read v Price* [1909] 2 K.B. at 730 *per* Cozens-Hardy M.R. (parol evidence is admissible to prove the contents of written evidence which has been lost); *Barber v Rowe* [1948] 2 All E.R. 1050, CA (secondary evidence of a lost lease was admissible).
[74] *Whitchurch v Bevis* (1789) 2 Bro. C.C. 559; 29 E.R. 306, LC. See also *Maddison v Alderson* (1883) 8 App. Cas. 467 at 490.
[75] *Middleton v Brewer* (1790) Peake 20, NP; 170 E.R. 64; *Spurrier v Fitzgerald* (1801) 6 Ves. Jun. 548; 31 E.R. 1189.
[76] *Lucas v Dixon* (1889) 22 Q.B.D. 357 at 363 *per* Fry L.J. See also *Lavery v Turley* (1860) 30 L.J. Ex. 49; 158 ER 98; *Macrory v Scott* (1850) 20 L.J. Ex. 90; 155 E.R. 396. It is for the defendant to plead and prove non-compliance with the statute: *Marginson v Ian Potter & Co* (1976) 136 C.L.R. 161 at 168. See also *Spurrier v Fitzgerald* (1801) 6 Ves. Jun. 548; 31 E.R. 1189.
[77] *Clarke v Callow* (1876) 46 L.J.Q.B. 53 at 54 *per* Kelly C.B.; *Steadman v Steadman* [1976] A.C. 536 at 558.
[78] *Lucas v Dixon* (1889) 22 Q.B. 357, CA.
[79] *Steadman v Steadman* [1976] A.C. 530, at 557 and 558.
[80] (1901) 46 Sol. Jo. 11, CA.
[81] *Fraser v Pape* [1904] 91 L.T. 340; (the defendant has the option of relying on a failure to satisfy the requirements of the statute); *Linkmel Construction Ltd v New Spiral Housing Association* (unreported, CAT 205 of 1988, March 8, 1988), cited in G. Andrews and R. Millett, *Law of Guarantees* (3rd ed., 2000), para.3.27.

CPR, r.3.4(2) if he asserts that he is going to plead s.4 of the Statute of Frauds 1677 and there is no reasonable basis for arguing that the oral guarantee is evidenced by a sufficient note or memorandum.[82]

3–156   Where the defendant admits in his pleading or in an affidavit filed in the proceedings that there was a contract of guarantee, he will probably be unable to rely on s.4 of the Statute of Frauds 1677 unless he raises this defence simultaneously.[83] Certainly, the claimant will be entitled to enforce the guarantee where the defendant pleads tender after paying the money into court as this is consistent with an admission of liability.[84]

12. IMPACT OF EUROPEAN COMMUNITY LAW

3–157   Under European Community law, a creditor wishing to sue a guarantor domiciled in England should prima facie bring proceedings in England.[85] This may present problems if the guarantee is unenforceable in England because it does not comply with s.4 of the Statute of Frauds 1677.[86] Would the English court bar the plaintiff's action simply because the evidentiary requirements of the statute are not satisfied? Or would the English court take the view that this result would undermine the objectives of the Convention on Jurisdiction and the Enforcement of Judgments or the basic tenets of European Community Law.[87] These are difficult questions which have not yet been addressed in the courts. In the absence of judicial authority, it may be advisable for the plaintiff to explore the possibility of instituting proceedings against the English surety in another jurisdiction which does not have formal evidentiary requirements like the Statute of Frauds. If this were possible the plaintiff might be able in England to enforce a foreign judgment obtained against the English surety under the recognition of foreign judgments regime.[88]

---

[82] G. Andrews and R. Millett, *Law of Guarantees* (3rd ed., 2000), para.3.27. See generally S. Sime, *A Practical Approach to Civil Procedure* (5th ed., 2002), pp.233–234.

[83] See G. Andrews and R. Millett, *Law of Guarantees* (3rd ed., 2000), para.3.27 and *Lucas v Dixon* (1889) 22 Q.B.D. 357 at 361 *per* Bowen L.J.; *Cooth v Jackson* (1801) 6 Ves. Jun. 12; 31 E.R. 913; *Ridgeway v Wharton* (1854) 3 De G.M. & G. 677; 43 ER 266; *Heys v Astley* (1863) 4 De G.J. & S. 34; 46 E.R. 827. See also *Humphries v Humphries* [1910] 2 K.B. 531.

[84] *Middleton v Brewer* (1790) 1 Peake 20; 170 E.R. 64.

[85] See below, Ch. 14.

[86] See above, para.3–149, n.58.

[87] See below, Ch. 14.

[88] See generally P. Kaye, *Civil Jurisdiction and Enforcement of Foreign Judgments* (Abingdon, Oxon. Professional Books 1987); P. Kaye, *Law of the European Judgments Convention* (Chichester, Barry Rose, 1999); R. Galli, "The World and EC Draft Conventions on Jurisdiction, Recognition and Enforcement of Foreign Judgments in Civil Matters" (2000) 119 *Patent World 26*; M.M. Ernst, "Recognition and Enforcement of Foreign Money Judgments in the United States and the United Kingdom in the Light of Currency Conversion Problems" (1988) 3 *Emory Journal of International Dispute Resolution* 59; J. Harris, Recognition of Foreign Judgments at Common Law" (1997) 17 *Oxford Journal of Legal Studies* 477" and *Israel Discount Bank of New York v Hadjipateras* [1983] 3 All E.R. 129 (a defendant will not be able to rely on public policy to assert that a foreign judgment on a guarantee should not be recognized on the grounds that the guarantee was invalid because of coercion duress or undue influence if the defendant failed to raise the public policy defence available to him in the foreign court). See below Ch. 14.

13. THE EQUITABLE DOCTRINE OF PART PERFORMANCE

There is some doubt as to whether the equitable doctrine of part **3–158** performance applies to guarantees. On one view, the doctrine excludes guarantees from its ambit because it only applies to contracts relating to the disposition of an interest in land.[89] On another, part performance is limited to cases in which equity would entertain a decree of specific performance.[90] This latter interpretation would not as a matter of law preclude the operation of the doctrine because specific performance is today regarded as being potentially applicable to most types of contract.[91]

As a matter of proof, however, part performance is unlikely to be **3–159** successfully pleaded in respect of a guarantee. The doctrine of part performance requires conduct by the creditor which makes it inequitable for the guarantor to rely on the statute.[92] The general test is whether the acts relied upon as part performance are unequivocally and in their own nature referable to some such agreement as that alleged.[93] It is not sufficient simply that the creditor provides consideration for the guarantee, which has been fully executed.[94]

Since a guarantee is usually given to secure the repayment of the **3–160** principal debt or the performance of the principal obligation, it will be difficult for the claimant to satisfy this requirement. Thus, any action by the creditor in purported reliance on the guarantee might simply have been induced by the creditor's relationship with the principal debtor. For example, where a person acts on the faith of a guarantee by entering into a contract of sale with a purchaser and allowing the purchaser into possession, the action might well have been induced by the obligations imposed by the contract of sale.[95] Nor is it likely that the creditor can rely on acts such as the making of a demand upon the guarantor who the creditor alleges is bound, because this is evidence simply of the creditor's attempts to enforce the guarantee and not of part performance of the creditor's obligations.[96] For these reasons, the equitable doctrine of part performance cannot be relied upon by a creditor who wishes to enforce an oral guarantee.[97]

---

[89] *Britain v Rossiter* (1879) 11 Q.B.D. 123 at 129, 131; *Sarbit v Hanson & Booth Fisheries (Can) Co* [1950] 2 W.W.R. 545, reversed on other grounds in [1951] 2 D.L.R. 108, CA; *Rink v March* [1921] 1 W.W.R. 919.
[90] *McManus v Cooke* (1887) 35 Ch. D. 681 at 687. Cf. *Sinclair v Schildt* (1914) 16 W.A.L.R. 100. These issues were specifically left open by Staughton J. in *Clipper Maritime Ltd v Shirlstar Container Transport Ltd* [1987] 1 Lloyd's Rep. 546 at 556.
[91] But not all, see G.H. Treitel, *The Law of Contract* (11th ed., 2003), pp.1029 to 1037. *Chitty on Contracts* (28th ed., 1999), paras 28–017–28–026.
[92] *Clipper Maritime Ltd v Shirlstar Container Transport Ltd* [1987] 1 Lloyd's Rep. 546 at 556.
[93] *Maddison v Alderson* (1883) 8 App. Cas. 467 at 479.
[94] *ibid.* at 490.
[95] *Rink v March* [1921] 1 W.W.R. 919. See also the same difficulty in *Clipper Maritime Ltd v Shirlstar Container Transport Ltd* [1987] 1 Lloyd's Rep. 546 at 556.
[96] *Clipper Maritime Ltd v Shirlstar Container Transport Ltd* [1987] 1 Lloyd's Rep. 546 at 556.
[97] Any other result would negate the effect of the statute in relation to guarantees: *Maddison v Alderson* (1883) 8 App. Cas. 467; *Rink v March and Donawel* [1921] 1 W.W.R. 919 (Can). Cf. *Huron County v Kerr* (1868) 15 Gr. 265 (Can). However, it is possible for the equitable

14. THE EFFECT OF ESTOPPEL

3–161   There is a general principle that a party cannot set up an estoppel in the face of a statute.[98] This principle depends on the nature of the enactment, the purpose of the provision and its underlying social policy.[99] Certainly, it is true that an estoppel cannot be invoked to validate a transaction that is void on the ground of public policy. Hence, in *Godden v Merthyr Tydfil Housing Association*[1] a claim for damages for breach of contract was void because the contract was not in writing as required by s.2(1) of the Law of Property (Miscellaneous Provisions) Act 1989. But, as Viscount Radcliffe pointed out in *Kok Hoong v Leong Cheong Kweng Mines* Ltd,[2] not all statutes which declare offending transactions to be unenforceable or void are essentially prohibitory so as to preclude estoppels. Indeed, the Statute of Frauds 1677 merely regulates procedure by rendering an oral guarantee unenforceable; it does not strike at the essential validity of the guarantee. Nor are the terms of the Statute of Frauds so essentially prohibitory as to preclude an estoppel.[3]

3–162   In *Humphries v Humphries*[4] a tenant did not raise any defence under s.4 of the Statute of Frauds 1677 in a first action for arrears of rent. The landlord proved the lease to the satisfaction of the court and obtained judgment. In a subsequent action against the tenant for further arrears of rent under the same lease, the Court of Appeal held that the tenant was estopped by the earlier judgment from raising a defence under s.4.

3–163   Farwell L.J., delivering the judgment of the Court of Appeal, said:

> "It is argued that the decision of the Divisional Court is in contravention of the Statute of Frauds; but estoppel is merely a rule of evidence, and if the plaintiff can object to the reception of evidence on a particular fact because it is an issue which was properly raised by him and was or could have been traversed by the defendant in a former action, and has been determined in the plaintiff's favour in such action, there is no reason for disallowing the objection; but if there was no such definite issue, then the objection will fail. The application of the ordinary rules of evidence to cases arising under the Statute of Frauds is not of any greater interference with the statute than the application of Order XIX, r.15; nor is such application otherwise than in accordance with the true meaning of the Act, which is to prevent fraud and perjury".[5]

---

doctrine of past performance to co-exist with the formal requirements for a contract for the sale of land: *Actionstrength Ltd v International Glass Engineering IN.GL.EN Spa* [2003] 2 W.L.R. 1060 at 1067, *per* Lord Hoffmann.

[98] See *Kok Hoong v Leong Cheong Kweng Mines Ltd* [1964] A.C. 993 at 1015.
[99] *Yaxley v Gotts* [2000] Ch. 162 at 191, *per* Beldam L.J.
[1] [1997] N.P.C. 1; (1997) 74 P. & C.R.D. 1.
[2] [1964] A.C. 993 at 1015–1016.
[3] *ibid.* On the other hand, the requirement of a signature on a deed is regarded as fundamental to the public interest. See s.1 of the *Law of Property (Miscellaneous Provisions) Act* 1989 and *Shah v Shah* [2002] Q.B. 35 at 46.
[4] [1910] 2 K.B. 531, C.A.
[5] *ibid.*, at 536–537.

While *Humphries v Humphries*[6] turned primarily on a narrow issue of **3–164** estoppel, the Court of Appeal appeared to be receptive to the argument that the tenant was precluded by an estoppel *in pais* from raising s.4 of the Statute of Frauds 1677.[7] If such an estoppel could be raised against a guarantor it might enable the creditor to enforce an oral guarantee indirectly through the medium of estoppel. However, it would be necessary for the creditor to establish that it acted to its detriment in reliance on the guarantor's conduct. The mere advance of funds or supply of goods or services to the principal debtor might not have been induced by the guarantor's conduct. But it might be different where the creditor released one guarantor on receiving an oral assurance from another that a new written guarantee would be provided, or where the evidence clearly showed that the creditor was not prepared to make the advances or supply the goods or services to the principal debtor without the promised guarantee. It would not be as difficult to establish this type of estoppel against a guarantor as it would be to invoke the equitable doctrine of part performance[8]because it would not be necessary to establish that the creditor's actions were unequivocally referable to the provision of the guarantee[9] but the evidentiary difficulties should not be underestimated.[10]

There is the further problem that English courts generally take the view **3–165** that an estoppel can only act as a shield, not as a sword.[11] But, while it is true that estoppel is not, in itself, a cause of action, it can enable a party to enforce a cause of action which would otherwise be unavailable in the absence of the estoppel.[12]Consequently, where a guarantor induces a creditor to act to its detriment on the assumption that a written guarantee has been executed, the Statute of Frauds should not afford the guarantor any defence.[13] Any other result would allow the Statute of Frauds to cloak a fraud.[14] The underlying social policy reflected in that statute is to protect guarantors by requiring written evidence of their undertakings.[15] This

---

[6] [1910] 2 K.B. 531.

[7] G. Andrews and R. Millett, *Law of Guarantees* (3rd ed., 2000), para.3, 31.

[8] See above, para.3–158.

[9] *Maddison v Alderson* (1883) 8 App. Cas. 467 at 479.

[10] See generally *Decouvrer v Jordan*, CA CAT No. 525 of May 18, 1987 (*The Times*, May 24, 1987).

[11] See *Amalgamated Investment & Property Co Ltd v Texas Commerce International Bank Ltd* [1982] Q.B. 84 at 105 *per* Goff J. (as he then was) and at 131–132 *per* Brandon L.J. But see *Crabb v Arun District Council* [1976] Ch. 179 at 187 where Lord Denning M.R. pointed out that proprietary estoppel does give rise to a cause of action.

[12] *Crabb v Arun District Council* [1976] Ch. 179 at 187 *per* Denning M.R. approved in *Amalgamated Investment & Property Co Ltd v Texas Commerce International Bank Ltd* [1982] Q.B. 84 at 105. See also R. Halson, "The Offensive Limits of Promissory Estoppel" (1999) L.M.C.L.Q. 256.

[13] *Kok Hoong v Leong Cheong Kweng Mines Ltd* [1964] A.C. 993 at 1019 *per* Viscount Radcliffe (obiter dicta).

[14] Compare *Davies v Otty* (1865) 34 Beav. 208; 55 E.R. 875, where it was not honest for the defendant to retain land conveyed to him subject to an oral arrangement that the land would be transferred back to the original owner upon the happening of a certain event. It has been suggested that fraud (short of a change of possession) is not sufficient to justify nullifying the Statute of Frauds: *Maddison v Alderson* (1883) 8 App. Cas. 467 at 490.

[15] *Kok Hoong v Leong Cheong Kweng Mines Ltd* [1964] A.C. 993 at 1016 and *Re Hoyle; Hoyle v Hoyle* [1893] 1 Ch. 84 at 98. See also *Goodaston Ltd v FH Burgess Plc* [1998] L. & T.R. 46.

policy would not be served by allowing guarantors to hide behind the statute to avoid an estoppel raised against them on grounds of unconscionability.[16]

3–166 An oral promise to guarantee repayment of a debt will not be sufficient in itself to raise an estoppel by representation to overcome the lack of written evidence required by the Statute of Frauds 1677. In *Actionstrength Ltd v International Glass Engineering IN.GL.EN SpA*[17] the assumed facts for the purposes of the proceedings were that the first defendant ("Inglen") agreed to construct a factory for the second defendant ("St-Gobain"). The claimant ("Actionstrength") was a recruitment agency which agreed to provide construction workers at the factory site in return for payment by Inglen on monthly invoices. Inglen allegedly fell behind in payments and Actionstrength threatened to withdraw all labour from the site unless all Inglen's arrears were paid. After tripartite negotiations, St-Gobain's representative allegedly reached an oral agreement with Actionstrength that it would ensure that Actionstrength would receive any amount due from Inglen (if necessary by redirecting payments due by St-Gobain to Inglen) provided that Actionstrength agreed not to withdraw the workforce from the factory site. Actionstrength continued to supply labour for another month but the arrears of payments continued to spiral. After further negotiations between the parties broke down, Actionstrength withdrew the workforce and issued proceedings against both Inglen and St-Gobain. The claim against St-Gobain was based on the alleged oral guarantee. In its defence, St-Gobain pleaded s.4 of the Statute of Frauds 1677. The trial judge dismissed St-Gobain's application that the claim against it be struck out under CPR r.24.2 as having no real prospect of success because it was arguable that St-Gobain's promise was not "to answer for the debt ... of another person" within the statute. The Court of Appeal allowed an appeal against this order on the ground that it was clearly arguable that St-Gobain's oral guarantee was a promise to answer for Inglen's debt to Actionstrength. Simon Brown L.J. described Actionstrength's case on estoppel as "quite hopeless".[18] By the same token, his Lordship suggested that where a guarantor assures a creditor that his promise will be binding whether or not it is put in writing, the guarantor may not be able to hide behind the statute as a defence. But there would be no estoppel simply because the creditor acted to its detriment in reliance upon the guarantor's oral promise to answer for the debt or default of another.

---

[16] *Kok Hoong v Leong Cheong Kweng Mines Ltd* [1964] A.C. 993 at 1019 (obiter dicta). But the giving of general instructions for the preparation of a written guarantee is not sufficient to amount to fraud justifying the enforcement of an oral guarantee. See *Whitchurch v Bevis* (1789) 2 Bro C.C. 559 at 569; 29 E.R. 306 at 311. Nor is there fraud merely because the principal debtor obtained credit and cannot make restitution: *Maddison v Alderson* (1883) 8 App. Cas. 467 at 490.

[17] [2003] 2 W.L.R. 1060.

[18] [2002] 1 W.L.R. 566 at 576–577. Peter Gibson L.J. and Tuckey L.J. agreed with Simon Brown L.J. but did not examine the estoppel issue in their judgments.

A further appeal to the House of Lords was dismissed because any **3–167** estoppel based on the extension of credit on the faith of an oral promise of guarantee would be inconsistent with the statute and would render the statutory requirements nugatory. While Actionstrength assumed that it had an enforceable guarantee, there was nothing to show that St-Gobain induced or encouraged it to believe that assumption because section 4 rendered St-Gobain's oral guarantee unenforceable. Indeed, as Lord Bingham pointed out, "[i]f St-Gobain were held to be estopped in this case it is hard to see why any oral guarantor, where credit was extended to a debtor on the strength of a guarantee would not be similarly estopped".[19] In a similar vein Lord Hoffmann succinctly declared: "To admit an estoppel on these grounds would be to repeal the statute."[20]

An estoppel might arise, however, where a guarantor gives the creditor **3–168** an explicit assurance that he will not plead the statute as a defence[21] or represents that he has validly executed a guarantee,[22] when he knows that his signature was forged. It would still be necessary, of course, for the creditor to prove that it relied to its detriment on the assumption induced or encouraged by the guarantor.[23] Only then would an estoppel by representation arise; only then would it be unconscionable to allow the guarantor to plead the statute as a defence. Such a finding "would depend very much on the court's views, on the facts of any particular case, of the personalities and attributes of the two parties between whom the alleged estoppel was alleged to have arisen.[24] Interestingly, in *Bank of Scotland v Wright*[25] Brooke J. was not prepared to find an estoppel against the guarantor because "he was not an acute, experienced, commercially-minded businessman" and he could find nothing in his conduct to constitute active encouragement or influence of the creditor in its mistaken belief that there was an enforceable guarantee.[26]

The Statute of Frauds 1677 does not exclude the operation of an **3–169** estoppel by convention.[27] In *Coghlan v S H Lock*[28] the New South Wales Court of Appeal held that an estoppel by convention precluded a guarantor from relying on the statute as a defence. Moreover, in *Bank of Scotland v Wright*[29] Brooke J. suggested that an estoppel by convention

---

[19] *Actionstrength Ltd v International Glass Engineering IN.GL.EN SpA* [2003] 2 W.L.R. 1060 at 1064.
[20] [2003] 2 W.L.R. 1060 at 1068.
[21] [2003] 2 W.L.R. 1060 at 1074. See also *Commonwealth v Verwayen* (1990) 170 C.L.R. 394.
[22] [2003] 2 W.L.R. 1060 at 1064, *per* Lord Bingham, at 1064–1065, *per* Lord Woolf at 1069, *per* Lord Clyde and at 1073–1074, *per* Lord Walker. Lord Hoffmann (at 1068) declined to consider this issue. See also *Scotland v Wright* [1991] B.C.L.C. 244 at 266, *per* Brooke J.
[23] In *Actionstrength Ltd v International Glass Engineering IN. GL. EN SpA* [2003] 2 W.L.R. 1060 at 1070 Lord Clyde found another reason for rejecting the estoppel argument: "the acts of Actionstrength in keeping the labour force on site and continuing to work do not demonstrate a reliance on some assumption of the enforceability of the guarantee".
[24] *Bank of Scotland v Wright* [1991] B.C.L.C. 244 at 266 *per* Brooke J.
[25] [1991] B.C.L.C. 244.
[26] [1991] B.C.L.C. 244 at 266.
[27] See *Amalgamated Investment & Property Co Ltd v Texas Commerce International Bank Ltd* [1982] Q.B. 84.
[28] (1985) 4 N.S.W.L.R. 158. On appeal, this decision was reversed on other grounds: (1987) 8 N.S.W.L.R. 88, PC.
[29] [1991] B.C.L.C. 244 at 266.

might overcome the lack of written evidence of a guarantee. And in *Actionstrength Ltd v International Glass Engineering IN.GL.EN SpA*[30] Lord Bingham accepted that an estoppel by convention could apply in the context of a guarantee.

3–170   In summary, therefore, guarantors can be estopped from denying that their oral guarantees are enforceable where they have acted unconscionably in their dealings with the creditor. In an appropriate case the essentially evidentiary requirements of the Statute of Frauds can be displaced by estoppel by representation, estoppel in pais or estoppel by convention.[31]

15. FORMAL REQUIREMENTS FOR CONSUMER CREDIT TRANSACTIONS

3–171   Consumer credit legislation imposes additional formal requirements.[32]

3–172   Section 105 of the The Consumer Credit Act 1974, and accompanying regulations, prescribe formalities for the execution of guarantees and indemnities in respect of transactions to which the Act applies, that is, transactions involving the supply of credit not exceeding £25,000 to individuals, (including partnerships and sole traders) under consumer credit agreements, consumer hire agreements, or any linked transaction.[33]

3–173   There is a broad definition of surety and security in s.189(1) of the Act, which states:

> "Surety" means — the person by whom any security is provided, or the person to whom his rights and duties in relation to the security have passed by assignment or operation of law;

> "Security" means — a mortgage, charge, pledge, bond, debenture guarantee, bill, note or other right provided by the debtor or hirer, or at his request (express or implied) to secure the carrying out of the obligations of the debtor or hirer under the agreement;

The requirement that the debtor or hirer must have expressly or impliedly requested the security means that a recourse agreement[34] between a trader and a financial institution (entered into without the

---

[30] [2003] 2 W.L.R. 1060 at 1064.

[31] See also below, para.5–94 for the effect of estoppel on the scope of the guarantor's liability.

[32] There are also formal execution requirements for guarantees given by government bodies and statutory corporations. These depend on the terms of the relevant governing statute. See generally C. Turpin, *Government Contracts* (Harmondsworth, Penguin, 1972); M.I. Aronson and H. Whitmore, *Public Torts and Contracts* (Sydney, LBC, 1982); S. Perloff and H. Perloff, "Latent Defects in Government Contracts" (1997) 27 *Public Contract Law Journal* 87.

[33] There is much fuller discussion of these formalities in other texts. See A.G. Guest and M.G. Lloyd *Encyclopaedia of Consumer Credit Law*; paras 2–106 to 2–114; G. Andrews and R. Millett, *Law of Guarantees* (3rd ed., 2000) Ch 12, R. Goode, *Consumer Credit Act 1974*, paras 13.1–13.15, Ch. 14.

[34] Under such an agreement the dealer guarantees the indebtedness of its customers under hire purchase agreements between those customers and the finance house, *e.g. Unity Finance Ltd v Woodcock* [1963] 1 W.L.R. 455.

knowledge of the customer) is outside the scope of the statutory provisions. Even if the debtor or hirer has knowledge of the agreement, but has done nothing to facilitate it, this probably does not amount to an implied request.[35] Although the definition of surety is (oddly) wide enough to include a security provided by the debtor or hirer himself, s.105 specifically denies its application to such circumstances.[36]

Section 105(1) provides that any security provided in relation to a **3–174** regulated agreement shall be expressed in writing. It is insufficient (in contrast to the general statutory provisions governing the form of guarantees[37]) that the agreement is made orally and subsequently evidenced in writing.

Regulations have also been made[38] (as envisaged in s.105(2)) setting out **3–175** requirements as to the form of the security instrument and the information to be contained in it, but these regulations only apply to guarantees and indemnities, excluding a mortgage charge or pledge. As to the form of the security instrument, it must designate the type of contract, that is, either a "Guarantee subject to the Consumer Credit Act 1974", or an "Indemnity subject to the Consumer Credit Act 1974" or a "Guarantee and Indemnity subject to the Consumer Credit Act 1974,"[39] as the case may require. There must be a signature box in the appropriate form,[40] although the guarantee may be signed by someone on behalf of the guarantor.[41] There are various provisions regarding the use of particular words[42] and the size and legibility of lettering.[43]

Certain information must also be included in the guarantee/indemnity, **3–176** namely, the name and a postal address of the creditor or owner as well as that of the debtor or hirer and the surety.[44] Additionally there must be a "description of the subject matter to which the security to be provided by the surety relates".[45] This appears to contemplate the guarantee and/or indemnity being given in respect of a particular transaction or transactions, so it is unlikely that an "all monies" guarantee[46] can be utilised in respect of a regulated agreement.[47] The guarantee and/or indemnity must also set out a statement of the surety's rights in the form specified in Part III of the Schedule.

Pursuant to s.105 the guarantee/indemnity will not be properly executed **3–177** unless it conforms to the regulations and embodies all the terms of the

---

[35] See A.G. Guest and M.G. Lloyd, *Encyclopaedia of Consumer Credit Law* at para.2–106 on the basis that "the word 'request' presupposes on the part of the person making the request, some initiative, some action evidencing a desire for the thing requested".
[36] s.105(6).
[37] See above, para.3–06 *et. seq.*
[38] Consumer Credit (Guarantees and Indemnities) Regulations 1983 (SI 1983/1556).
[39] Reg. 3(1)(a), Sch., Pt I.
[40] Reg. 3(1)(d), Sch., Pt IV.
[41] S.105(4)(c) and Reg. 4(2).
[42] Reg. 3(2)(a)–(c).
[43] Reg. 3(5), 4(1) See also s.105(4)(c).
[44] Reg. 3(1) (b), Sch., Pt II.
[45] Sch. Pt II(c).
[46] See below Ch. 5.
[47] See A.G. Guest and M.G. Lloyd, *Encyclopaedia of Consumer Credit Law* para.3–234 for a fuller discussion.

security, other than implied terms.[48] The same result follows if the surety is not provided with a copy of the document when it is presented or sent to him for execution,[49] or if he is not given a copy of the executed agreement.[50] If the security is improperly executed in that it fails to comply with these provisions (or is not in writing) the security, so far as provided in relation to a regulated agreement, is enforceable against the surety only on the order of the court.[51] If an application for an order of enforcement is dismissed, other than on technical grounds,[52] the security will be treated as if it never had effect,[53] with the consequence that any property lodged with the creditor solely for the purpose of the security shall be returned by him forthwith, and any amount received by the creditor on realisation of the security shall, so far as it is referable to the agreement, must be repaid to the surety.[54] The creditor must also take any necessary action to ensure that entries in any register relating to the security are removed or cancelled.[55]

3–178   Some debate has arisen as to the consequences if the creditor proceeds to enforce a security without the necessary court order. There is no specific sanction provided, as s.106 is not activated in such circumstances.[56] It has been suggested that the debtor or surety should seek an injunction against a creditor who has enforced or threatens to enforce a security,[57] or alternatively, a declaration of unenforceability.[58] But a simpler course of action would be for the surety (if sued) to plead as a defence that no cause of action has arisen since an order of the court has not been obtained pursuant to s.105(7).

3–179   In the case of non-commercial agreements, (that is, those not made by a creditor or owner in the course of a business carried on by him) the surety may on payment of a fee request a copy of the underlying regulated agreement or security instrument (and a statement signed by the creditor showing the state of accounts between the creditor and debtor or hirer).[59] This is in addition to the creditor's obligations arising under s.105.[60] If the creditor fails to provide the necessary information he is not entitled, whilst the default continues, to enforce the security, so far as it is provided in relation to the agreement.[61] Additionally, the creditor commits an offence if the default continues for one month.[62]

---

[48] s.105(4)(a).
[49] s.105(4)(d).
[50] s.105(5)(a). Where the security is provided before the regulated agreement is made, a copy of that executed agreement must be given to the surety within seven days after it is made (s.105(5)(b)). Until the regulated agreement is made the surety has the right to treat the security as never having effect (See s.113(6) and s.106).
[51] s.105(7).
[52] See s.105(8). See for fuller discussion of the meaning of this term R. Goode, *Consumer Credit Act 1974*, para.13.12.
[53] s.106(a).
[54] s.106(b)(d).
[55] s.106(c).
[56] Note that this is not one of the events specified in s.113(3) which activates s.106.
[57] G. Andrews and R. Millett, *Law of Guarantees* (3rd ed., 2000), p.527.
[58] *ibid.*
[59] s.107.
[60] See above, para.3–177.
[61] s.107(4)(a).
[62] s.107(4)(b).

CHAPTER 4

FACTORS AFFECTING VALIDITY

1. INTRODUCTION

4–01   A contract of guarantee, like any other contract, can be nullified on a variety of grounds ranging from incapacity to duress and undue influence, from misrepresentation to illegality. Some of these grounds have already been discussed in Chapter 2. In this chapter, the remaining factors which may vitiate a contract of guarantee will be considered under several broad headings.

2. DUTY OF DISCLOSURE

(i) No general duty of disclosure

4–02   Unlike contracts of insurance, guarantees are not contracts of the utmost good faith[1] requiring full disclosure of all material facts by both parties. There is no universal obligation, therefore, upon the creditor to disclose all facts relating to its dealings with the principal debtor, or affecting the

---

[1] See generally the formulation of the rule in *Royal Bank of Scotland v Etridge* [2002] A.C. 773 at 812, para.81, *per* Lord Nicholls, at 848, para.187 *per* Lord Scott; *Hamilton v Watson* (1845) 12 Cl. & Fin. 109 at 118–119; 8 E.R. 1139 at 1343–1344; *Bank of Scotland v Henry Butcher* [2001] 2 All E.R. (Comm) 691, paras 74–80; *Crédit Lyonnais Bank v Export Credit Guarantee Dept* [1996] 1 Lloyd's Rep. 200 at 225–227; *Davies v London & Provincial Marine Insurance Co* (1878) 8 Ch. D. 469 at 475; *Lee v Jones* (1864) 17 C.B. (NS) 482 at 495; 144 E.R. 194 at 199; *Behan v Obelon Pty Ltd* [1984] 2 N.S.W.L.R. 637 at 639; *Seaton v Heath* [1899] 1 Q.B. 782 at 792; *Yerkey v Jones* (1939) 63 C.L.R. 649; *Goodwin v National Bank of Asia Ltd* (1968) 117 C.L.R. 173 at 175. Also see generally D. Murdoch, "Creditor's duty of disclosure in Contracts of Guarantee" (1995) 8(3) *Journal of Contract Law* 283.

debtor's credit.[2] Nor is the creditor expected to advise the proposed surety of every circumstance within the creditor's knowledge which it is material for the surety to know before he executes the guarantee.[3]

Sometimes the duty has been regarded as arising from the presumed basis of the guarantee,[4] but the most usual rationale is that the failure to make disclosure in such circumstances amounts to an implied representation that the undisclosed facts do not exist.[5]   **4–03**

Several reasons have been advanced to justify this general rule. Sometimes there is an appeal to practicalities and business efficacy.[6] Thus it is supported on the ground that otherwise no creditor could rely on a contract of guarantee unless the creditor communicated to the proposed sureties everything relating to its dealings with the principal debtor.[7] In *Hamilton v Watson*,[8] Lord Campbell went so far as to suggest that bankers would never obtain sureties if full disclosure of all material facts were required. In *London General Omnibus Co Ltd v Holloway*,[9] Farwell L.J. also stressed the difficulties which full disclosure would entail for bankers taking a guarantee: it would be necessary for them to state how the principal debtor's account had been kept, whether the principal debtor was in the habit of overdrawing, whether the principal debtor was punctual in his dealings, and whether the principal debtor performed her or his promises in an honourable manner. In some cases such a disclosure by the bank might constitute a breach of its duty of confidence.[10]   **4–04**

The general rule obviates these difficulties by allowing the creditor to assume that the proposed surety is acquainted with the principal debtor's position. The surety is presumed to know that the guarantee is intended to secure repayment of the principal's debts and that dissatisfaction with the principal debtor's account is the probable reason for the creditor's insistence that a guarantee be given.[11] It is left to the principal debtor to explain his financial position to the intending surety. At any rate, it is expected that the proposed sureties will have ready access to the principal debtor and his financial statements so that they can assess the risk for themselves.[12]   **4–05**

[2] *Isman v Widen* [1926] 1 D.L.R. 247 (Sask CA); *National Mortgage & Agency Co of New Zealand Ltd v Stalker* [1933] N.Z.L.R. 1182; *A.D. & J.A. Wright Pty Ltd v Custom Credit Corp Ltd* (1992) 108 F.L.R. 45.
[3] *Hamilton v Watson* (1845) 12 Cl. & Fin. 109; 8 E.R. 1339; *Davies v London & Provincial Marine Insurance Co* (1878) 8 Ch. D. 469.
[4] *Westpac Securities v Dickie* [1991] 1 N.Z.L.R. 657 at 662–663; *Behan v Obelon Pty Ltd* [1984] 2 N.S.W.L.R. 637 at 639.
[5] *Geest plc v Fyffes* [1999] 1 All E.R. (Comm) 672 at 682–683; *London General Omnibus Co Ltd v Holloway* [1912] 2 K.B. 72 at 78. See also below, paras 4–22 to 4–26.
[6] See *Levett v Barclays Bank Plc* [1995] 2 All E.R. 615 at 627.
[7] *Lee v Jones* (1864) 17 C.B. (NS) 482 at 503; 144 E.R. 194 at 202 *per* Blackburn J.
[8] (1845) 12 Cl. & Fin. 109; 8 E.R. 1339.
[9] [1912] 2 K.B. 72.
[10] *Tournier v National Provincial & Union Bank of England* [1924] 1 K.B. 461.
[11] *Fitzgerald v Jacomb* (1873) 4 A.J.R. 189 at 190.
[12] *Seaton v Heath* [1899] 1 Q.B. 782 at 792; *Behan v Obelon Pty Ltd* [1984] 2 N.S.W.L.R. 637; *Pooraka Holdings Pty Ltd v Participation Nominees Pty Ltd* (1991) 58 SASR 184 at 195; *A.D. & J.A. Wright Pty Ltd v Custom Credit Corp Ltd* (1992) 108 F.L.R. 45.

(ii) Unusual features must be disclosed

4-06   A duty is, however, imposed on the creditor to disclose facts in certain circumstances. On the present state of the authorities its precise formulation is unclear, but a useful starting point is the recent formulations of the rule by Lord Nicholls and Lord Scott in *Royal Bank of Scotland v Etridge*.[13] Lord Nicholls stated the principle in this way:[14]

> "..., stated shortly, a creditor is obliged to disclose to a guarantor any unusual feature of the contract between the creditor and the debtor which makes it materially different in a potentially disadvantageous respect from what the guarantor might naturally expect"[15]

The emphasis here is upon any "unusual feature of *the contract*" between creditor and debtor, which is in accordance with earlier authority to the effect that the unusual feature must amount to a "contractual condition or obligation"[16] of the principal obligation. In the mid nineteenth century in *Hamilton v Watson*[17] Lord Campbell had emphasised that the issue was "whether there be *a contract* between the debtor and the creditor to the effect that the position shall be different from that which the surety might naturally expect".[18] Subsequently, in *National Provincial Bank of England Ltd v Glanusk*,[19] it was held that the bank had no duty to disclose that it was suspicious that its customer was using the guarantor's own money to defraud him because there was "*no contract* between [the bank and the customer] altering the position".[20] Again in *Cooper v National Provincial Bank Ltd*[21] the bank's failure to disclose that the customer's bankrupt husband was allowed to operate the account did not discharge the guarantor in the absence of a "*contract*"[22] between the customer and the bank permitting him to do so, there being merely an informal authority given by the customer to her husband.

4-07   In *Royal Bank of Scotland v Etridge*[23] Lord Scott, however, defined the general obligation of disclosure as extending to unusual features of the "contractual *relationship*",[24] with the use of this word suggesting that even an informal (unusual) arrangement between creditor and debtor (not

---

[13] [2002] 2 A.C. 773.
[14] *ibid.*, at 812, para.81.
[15] See also the cases cited above n.1. Note that exceptionally the obligation to disclose may arise from a term of the offer of guarantee *Walkins Products Inc v Thomas* (1965) 54 D.L.R. (2d) 252 at 258.
[16] See this expression used in *Levett v Barclays Bank plc* [1995] 2 All E.R. 615 at 632(j), although elsewhere in the judgment there is a reference to "contractual arrangements" (at 630).
[17] (1845) 12 Cl. & Fin. 109; 8 E.R. 1139.
[18] *ibid.*, at 118–119; 1343–1344.
[19] [1913] 3 K.B. 335.
[20] *ibid.*, at 338.
[21] [1946] 1 K.B. 1.
[22] *ibid.*, at 7.
[23] [2002] 2 A.C. 773.
[24] *ibid.*, at 848, para.187.

amounting to a contractual term) should be disclosed.[25] Commonwealth authority also suggests that any "special arrangement"[26] between creditor and debtor should require disclosure. Thus in *Commercial Bank of Australia v Amadio*[27] it was held that, *inter alia*, the bank should have disclosed its practice of selectively dishonouring the cheques of its customer to create a façade of solvency and prosperity, which was clearly not an arrangement arising from a contractual condition. It is considered that the duty of disclosure should not be limited to unusual matters arising only as a result of a contractual condition since the guarantor may be equally prejudiced by an informal understanding between creditor and principal.

Nevertheless, most circumstances where the duty of disclosure have been imposed have arisen in the context of an unusual feature arising from a term of the contract between creditor and principal. Thus it has been held that an agreement that part of the advance secured by the guarantee should be applied to a pre-existing debt should have been disclosed.[28]   **4–08**

In *Levett v Barclays Bank plc*,[29] the bank failed to disclose the terms of   **4–09** the borrower's facility letter which were materially different from the terms of the guarantor's memorandum of deposit of Treasury stock, in that the facility letter contained no requirement of a demand upon default and gave the bank an automatic right to apply the proceeds of sale of the Treasury stock on the date of its maturity in paying out its loan. These unusual differences should have been disclosed since they significantly affected the guarantor's risk; it meant that the guarantor had no opportunity to discharge the loan and save the stock and the borrower had no incentive to pay it off.

---

[25] This is especially so since Lord Scott quotes (with apparent approval, at 848, paras 187–188) the much wider principle of Vaughan Williams L.J. in *London Omnibus Co Ltd v Holloway* [1912] 2 K.B. 72 at 78 whilst at the same time (as discussed below) disapproving of the extension of this formulation in the Australian case, *Pooraka Holdings Pty Ltd v Participation Nominees Pty Ltd* (1991) 58 S.A.S.R. 184.

[26] *Commercial Bank of Australia Ltd v Amadio* (1983) 151 C.L.R. 447 at 456.

[27] (1983) 151 C.L.R. 447. This decision was specifically referred to with approval in *Crédit Lyonnais Bank Nederland v Export Credit Guarantee Dept* [1996] 1 Lloyd's Rep. 200 and in *Geest plc v Fyffes plc* [1999] 1 All E.R. (Comm) 672 at 681–682. See also *Scales Trading Ltd v Far Eastern Shipping Co. Public Ltd* [2001] Lloyd's Rep. (Bank) 29, where there were fraudulent collusive arrangements between creditor and principal to avoid foreign exchange contracts, which could not be regarded as being a term of the contract between them. Even in *Cooper v National Provincial Bank* [1946] 1 K.B. 1 (discussed above) it was acknowledged that if the account guaranteed had "in truth" been the account of the undischarged bankrupt, the guarantor would have been discharged, even though this would merely have been a special arrangement between creditor and principal, rather than a condition of their contract (at 7).

[28] *Stone v Compton* (1838) 5 Bing N.C. 142; 132 E.R. 1059 (where the guarantee in fact recited that the debt was paid); *Pidcock v Bishop* (1825) 3 B. & C. 605; 107 E.R. 857 (where the creditor and principal agreed that the purchase price of goods, which was guaranteed, should be inflated so that the additional amount could be used to pay off the pre-existing debt). See also *Lee v Jones* (1864) 17 C.B. (NS) 482; 144 E.R. 194 (described below); *Vivian v Eynon* [1927] G.L.R. 447; *Hamilton v Watson* (1845) 12 Cl. & Fin. 109 at 119; 8 ER 1339 at 1343–1344 (where it was suggested that a contractual arrangement to use the money advanced to pay the creditor's bank should be disclosed). If the principal debtor and the creditor have entered into a secret agreement or arrangement giving the creditor an unfair preference, both the agreement and the guarantee can be set aside: *Pendlebury v Walker* (1841) 4 Y. & C. Ex. 424; 160 E.R. 1072. See also *Lewis v Jones* (1825) 4 B. & C. 506; 107 E.R. 1148.

[29] [1995] 2 All E.R. 615.

4–10   Another, more recent, example is *Royal Bank of Scotland v Bennett*.[30]
There the Royal Bank of Scotland increased the borrowing company's
overdraft facility, taking as security a guarantee from the wife of the major
shareholder of the company as well as a fixed and floating charge over the
company's new factory and business. An additional loan was made by
another lender, supported also by a fixed charge over the factory, and the
Royal Bank of Scotland agreed that this charge was to rank ahead of its
own fixed and floating charge. It was held that this "unusual feature" of
the overdraft facility should have been disclosed. The guarantor was
disadvantaged in a material respect because the ranking agreement
reduced the amount of company assets that would be available for
payment of the company's debt to the Royal Bank of Scotland, thereby
increasing the likelihood that the bank would have recourse to the
guarantee. It also diminished the value of the securities to which the
guarantor would be entitled to be subrogated on payment of the debt to
the bank.

4–11   There is support for the view that the duty of disclosure extends beyond
the requirement to disclose "a special arrangement" between creditor and
principal, of which the creditor is aware. Commonwealth authority
suggests that it requires disclosure of facts of which the creditor *ought to
have been aware*. In *Pooraka Holdings Pty Ltd v Participation Nominees
Pty Ltd*,[31] King C.J. in the Supreme Court of South Australia stated that
the duty of disclosure extended to any unusual feature surrounding the
transaction between the creditor and the surety (a) of which the creditor is
or ought to be aware, (b) of which the surety is unaware, and (c) which the
creditor appreciates, or in the circumstances ought to appreciate, might be
unknown to the surety and might affect the surety's decision to become a
surety.[32] But in *Royal Bank of Scotland v Etridge*[33] Lord Scott, expressly
referring to that decision, considered that "this statement of the extent of
the duty of disclosure may well be too wide".[34]

4–12   Similarly, in other jurisdictions there is also support for the view that the
duty of disclosure arises even where there is no special arrangement at all
between creditor and principal. It has been held in Australia that in certain
circumstances the fraud[35] of the principal should be disclosed and, in
Canada, the fact that the directors of the principal had started a new

---

[30] One of the appeals decided in *Royal Bank of Scotland v Etridge* [2002] 2 A.C. 773 at 871–878, paras 310–351.
[31] [1991] 58 S.A.S.R. 184.
[32] *ibid.*, at 193.
[33] [2002] 2 A.C. 773.
[34] *ibid.*, at 848, para.188.
[35] *Westpac Banking Corp v Robinson* (1990) A.S.C. 56–002 at 59,037–59,038, where there was a "virtual certainty of fraud" in respect of the principal debtor's own internal operations. *Cf.
National Provincial Bank of England Ltd v Glanusk* [1913] 3 KB 335, where there was "a suspicion" that the creditor was defrauding the principal; *Fitzgerald v Jacomb* (1873) 4 A.J.R. 189, where there was a belief that the principal was defrauding the creditor by forgery. In *Westpac Banking Corp v Robinson* (1990) A.S.C. 56–002 at 59,035, Brownie J. distinguished *National Provincial Bank of England Ltd v Glanusk* on the basis that in the latter case knowledge of the fraud was only gained by the creditor after the execution of the guarantee. An appeal from Brownie J.'s judgment was upheld: [1993] 30 N.S.W.L.R. 668, principally on the ground that the allegations of fraud against one of the vendors of the business related to the business itself which, by the time the guarantee was signed, was under the control of the

company in competition with the trading activities of the principal.[36] It has also been suggested that a duty of disclosure might be imposed in respect of a guarantee of the performance of the obligations of a contractor pursuant to a building contract, where the contractor had mistakenly omitted significant costs from the tender and had unsuccessfully sought a release from the contract on that basis.[37]

This does not, as yet, appear to be the law of England and Wales. As regards fraud, in *National Provincial Bank of England Ltd v Glanusk*[38] it was held that the bank's suspicions of fraud of the principal debtor need not be disclosed. Nevertheless there are some judicial suggestions that the duty of disclosure may extend to dishonest conduct. In *Bank of Scotland v Henry Butcher*[39] Michael Kallipetis sitting as a Deputy Judge of the High Court appeared to acknowledge that matters amounting to "equitable impropriety"[40] should be disclosed, and in *Crédit Lyonnais Bank Nederland v Export Credit Guarantee Department*[41] a distinction was drawn between mere suspicion of fraud (where there was no duty of disclosure) and actual knowledge of it. The Privy Council in *Scales Trading Ltd v Far Eastern Shipping Co. Public Ltd*[42] also rescinded a guarantee for non-disclosure because of fraudulent collusion between creditor and principal debtor, which related to false and inflated invoices designed to circumvent Russian foreign exchange restrictions. Indeed, it would be somewhat odd if the creditor was obliged to disclose an unusual contractual term of the principal agreement, but not the fraudulent practices of the principal. As will be seen,[43] there are also some general suggestions that the duty of disclosure should be somewhat broader in scope.

4–13

In *Royal Bank of Scotland v Etridge*[44] Lord Scott did in fact extend the duty of disclosure to unusual features of the contractual relationship "between the creditor and *other creditors of the principal debtor*".[45] Similarly, in *Behan v Obelon Pty Ltd*[46] the High Court of Australia specifically left open the question[47] of whether the duty as a matter of law

4–14

---

purchasers. Hence, the bank was under no duty to disclose the fraud allegations to the guarantors of the bank's loan to the purchasers.

[36] *Toronto Dominion Bank v Rooke* (1983) 3 D.L.R. (4th) 715.

[37] *Doe v Canadian Surety Co* [1937] S.C.R. 1, although the matter was not finally decided. See also *Stiff v Eastbourne Local Board* (1869) 20 L.T. 339, where a surety for a contractor was held entitled to be informed that the employer had entered into a separate arrangement with another party for completion of the same project.

[38] [1913] 3 K.B. 335.

[39] [2001] 2 All E.R. (Comm) 691.

[40] *ibid.*, at 715 para.80(7). On the facts it was alleged (but not proved) that the creditor was aware that the borrower had used the account for purposes other than his business.

[41] [1966] 1 Lloyd's Rep. 200 at 227.

[42] [2001] Lloyd's Rep. (Bank) 29. But the decision can be viewed as being based on the narrower ground that these were "unusual" contractual arrangements between creditor and debtor.

[43] See below, para.4–22.

[44] [2002] 2 A.C. 773.

[45] *ibid.*, at 848, para.188.

[46] (1985) 157 C.L.R. 326 at 330.

[47] *Cf.*, however, the view of the Court of Appeal of the Supreme Court of New South Wales: *Behan v Obelon Pty Ltd* [1984] 2 N.S.W.L.R. 637.

could extend to disclosure to one co-surety of information acquired by the creditor concerning the financial credit-worthiness of another co-surety.[48]

4–15   Another uncertainty is whether the duty to disclose unusual facts is a continuing duty. In *Toronto Dominion Bank v Rooke*,[49] the Court of Appeal of British Columbia held that the duty could apply to events occurring subsequent to the execution of the guarantee, in relation to a request by the creditor for the guarantor's consent to a variation of the principal contract. But there is no decisive English authority to support this view and such a duty would impose an unduly onerous burden on the creditor.[50] If *Toronto Dominion Bank v Rooke* were correct, it would mean that the creditor could not rely on a clause in the guarantee precluding the guarantor's discharge on the ground of variation of the principal contract, unless the creditor had disclosed all unusual facts at the date of a variation. Furthermore, if the continuing duty extends beyond cases of variation of the principal contract, the creditor would need to assess whether particular facts were unusual at all stages after the execution of the guarantee, for example, when granting further advances pursuant to a loan facility agreement.

4–16   American courts have, however, recognised a continuing duty of disclosure. In *Georgia Pacific Corp v Levitz*[51] the Arizona Court of Appeal held that a surety had a defence to an action to enforce a continuing guarantee where the creditor failed to disclose to the surety that the principal debtor was nearly insolvent before it extended further credit to the debtor. It is unlikely that a similar principle will be accepted in this jurisdiction because there is no clearly established doctrine of good faith and fair dealing in relation to contractual negotiations.

4–17   Whatever the precise ambit of the obligation to disclose unusual facts, one thing is clear: whether a feature is unusual will be dependent upon the particular transaction between creditor and principal and the surrounding circumstances. In *Lee v Jones*,[52] where a guarantee was given in respect of the obligations of a del credere agent, it was held that the creditor should have disclosed that the agent had not settled prior accounts because the terms of the guarantee and the annexed principal transaction indicated that the prior indebtedness should be disclosed.[53] But the existence of past

---

[48] In any event, the High Court held that there was no duty arising on the facts because the co-guarantors were co-venturers and the creditor was entitled to assume that each guarantor would make inquiries as to the solvency of the other.

[49] (1983) 3 D.L.R. (4th) 715.

[50] But note that in *National Provincial Bank of England Ltd v Glanusk* [1913] 3 K.B. 335, it was assumed the duty applied to facts arising after the date of execution, although it was held that no duty arose in the circumstances. *Toronto Dominion Bank v Rooke* (1983) 3 D.L.R. (4th) 715 was also referred to with apparent approval by Colman J. in *Geest plc v Fyffes plc* [1999] 1 All E.R. (Comm) 672 at 682.

[51] 716 P 2d 1057 (1986), applying *Sumitomo Bank of California v Iwasaki* 447 P 2d 956 (1968). See also *Restatement of Security*, s.124(1).

[52] (1864) 17 C.B. (NS) 482; 144 E.R. 194. See also *National Mortgage & Agency Co of New Zealand Ltd v Stalker* [1933] N.Z.L.R. 1182 at 1186.

[53] This decision could in fact be regarded as being based on fraudulent misrepresentation rather than non-disclosure. Shee J. states that "[it] is difficult to conceive language more obscure and better calculated to mislead, or dissimulation more insidious, than in this agreement" ((1864) 17 CB (NS) 482 at 496–497; 144 E.R. 194 at 200): see *Behan v Obelon Pty Ltd* [1984] 2 N.S.W.L.R. 637 at 638–639 for this explanation.

indebtedness will not normally be regarded as an unusual feature, for example, in respect of a guarantee of cash advances.[54]

If the fact is an unusual one prima facie requiring disclosure, what is the **4–18** position if the matter is also one in respect of which a duty of confidentiality arises from a banker-customer relationship? In the Australian case *Westpac Banking Corp v Robinson*[55] Brownie J. was of the view (without finally deciding) that there was a duty to disclose the fraud of the principal debtor and that such duty should prevail over the usual obligation of confidence, although the matter was not considered upon appeal[56] since it was there held that no duty of disclosure arose on the facts. The issue presents a dilemma for the creditor and the law provides no clear guidance. In each case the creditor has to assess whether the particular fact is an unusual one and then determine whether it should disclose the fact, and in doing so, risk breaching its duty of confidentiality to the customer. In the case of a guarantee given by a wife in respect of her husband's debts (and possibly guarantees given by other non-commercial guarantors) the decision in *Royal Bank of Scotland v Etridge*[57] imposes an obligation on banks to disclose the circumstances of the borrower's financial position to the guarantor's solicitors. If the borrower does not give consent to the disclosure of the information the transaction will not be allowed to proceed. This does not provide a direct answer to the issue under consideration here, but it does point to the fact that the safest course of action is for the creditor to obtain the written consent of the principal debtor before disclosing the essential facts to the guarantor.

Clauses in a guarantee may exclude the right to rescind the contract for **4–19** non-disclosure, even theoretically, on one view, for fraudulent non-disclosure.[58] But such clauses will be read narrowly,[59] and will be subject to the fairness tests in the Unfair Terms in Consumer Contracts Regulations 1999 (where those Regulations apply).[60]

(iii) What need not be disclosed

The extent of the creditor's duty to inform the guarantor of any unusual **4–20** features of the account to be guaranteed or matters which are not naturally

---

[54] *Hamilton v Watson* (1845) 12 Cl. & Fin. 109; 8 E.R. 1339; *National Mortgage & Agency Co of New Zealand v Stalker* [1933] N.Z.L.R. 1182 at 1187.
[55] (1990) A.S.C. 56–002 at 59,038.
[56] (1993) 30 N.S.W.L.R. 668. *Cf. Kabwand Pty Ltd v National Australia Bank Ltd* (1989) A.T.P.R. 40–950, where the court held that the bank was under no duty to the purchasers to disclose the true state of the vendor's business because of the bank's overriding duty of confidentiality towards the vendor, which was the bank's customer. In this case, however, the bank owed no duty to the purchasers who were also customers of the bank.
[57] [2002] 2 A.C. 773; see below, para.4–210.
[58] *HIH Casualty & General Insurance Ltd v Chase Manhattan Bank* [2001] 1 Lloyd's Rep. 30 at 44–45 (but this case dealt with the exclusion of liability for the fraudulent misrepresentations of an agent and could be so confined.) *Cf.*, however, *S. Pearson & Son Ltd v Dublin Corporation* [1907] A.C. 351 at 362, 365, although it is not clear whether the decision is based upon a legal rule or, more narrowly, upon the construction of the relevant clause.
[59] *ibid.* See also *Toomey v Eagle Star Insurance Co Ltd* [1995] 2 Lloyd's Rep. 88 at 91–92.
[60] See below, para.4–163.

to be expected in the principal transaction is most starkly revealed by an account of what need not be disclosed. Although, as indicated, whether or not a particular fact needs to be disclosed will be dependent on the precise circumstances, in general terms, it can be said that there is no obligation to volunteer information about the following matters, many of which affect the credit of the principal:[61]

(a) the principal debtor's existing indebtedness to the creditor,[62] previous defaults[63] or credit rating;[64]

(b) the fact that the creditor has previously refused to grant a home loan to the guarantor's child, who was a director of the principal debtor company;[65]

(c) the fact that the principal debtor whose account is guaranteed had overdrawn his account or consistently exceeded the overdraft limit,[66] that the principal debtor's cheques were being dishonoured,[67] or that the account was being closely monitored;[68]

(d) the likely future indebtedness or liability of the principal debtor to the creditor;[69]

(e) that notices of demand had been served by the creditor upon the principal;[70]

---

[61] *Commercial Bank of Australia Ltd v Amadio* (1983) 151 C.L.R. 447 at 455, 463; *Wythes v Labouchere* (1859) 3 De G. & J. 593; 44 E.R. 1397.
[62] *National Provincial Bank of England Ltd v Glanusk* [1913] 3 K.B. 335; *Midland Bank v Kidwai, Independent,* June 5, 1995, CA; *Union Bank of Australia Ltd v Puddy* [1949] V.L.R. 242 at 247; *Royal Bank of Scotland v Greenshields* [1914] S.C. 259; *London General Omnibus Co Ltd v Holloway* [1912] 2 K.B. 72; *Hamilton v Watson* (1845) 12 Cl. & Fin. 109; 8 E.R. 1339; *O'Brien v Australia & New Zealand Bank* (1971) 5 S.A.S.R. 347; *Boral Resources NSW Pty Ltd v Craig* (unreported, NSW Sup Ct, September 13, 1984) (not necessary to disclose an additional liability assumed by principal prior to execution of guarantee); *Commercial Bank of Australia Ltd v Amadio* (1983) 151 C.L.R. 447 at 455, 463 (no obligation to disclose that account to be guaranteed is overdrawn).
[63] See *Roper v Cox* (1882) 10 L.R. Ir. 200 (default under previous tenancy need not be disclosed); *Hamilton v Watson* (1845) 12 Cl. & Fin. 109; 8 ER 1339. Cf. *Britannia Steamship Insurance Association Ltd v Duff* (1909) 2 S.L.T. 193 at 195.
[64] *Hamilton v Watson* (1845) 12 Cl. & Fin. 109; 8 ER 1339.
[65] *Marzouk v Westpac Banking Corp* (unreported, NSW CA, October 14, 1992).
[66] *Commercial Bank of Australia Ltd v Amadio* (1983) 151 C.L.R. 447 at 456. See also *Kelly v Australian & New Zealand Banking Group Ltd* (unreported, Qld Sup Ct, Demack J, May 31, 1993) (co-guarantor exceeded overdraft limit); *Westpac Banking Corp v Robinson* (1990) A.S.C. 56–002 at 59,035, reversed on appeal (but not on this point) (1993) 30 N.S.W.L.R. 668.
[67] *ibid.*
[68] *Westpac Banking Corp v Robinson* (1990) A.S.C. 56–002 at 59,035, reversed on appeal (but not on this point) (1993) 30 N.S.W.L.R. 668.
[69] *Goodwin v National Bank of A/asia Ltd* (1968) 117 C.L.R. 173. It was not even necessary to disclose that the interest rate charged on the principal debt was over 30 per cent: *Seaton v Heath* [1900] A.C. 135.
[70] *Westpac Banking Corp v Robinson* (1990) A.S.C. 56–002 at 59,035, reversed on appeal (but not on this point) (1993) 30 N.S.W.L.R. 668.

(f) the fact that the principal debtor had personally guaranteed to the creditor the account of another party, thereby exposing himself and the surety to an additional contingent liability;[71]

(g) the fact that the creditor intends to enter into a new agreement with the principal debtor, leaving the surety's liability intact but extending credit to the principal debtor;[72]

(h) the principal debtor's conduct and behaviour, including the principal's irresponsibility in operating the business;[73]

(i) The fact that the customer's bankrupt spouse was able to draw on the customer's account, and that cheques had been drawn on the account but orders had been given by the drawer not to pay them;[74]

(j) the credit-worthiness of a co-guarantor, as the creditor can reasonably expect each co-guarantor to make his own inquiries regarding the financial worth of the others;[75] this is especially so if the co-guarantors are co-venturers;[76]

(k) the object or expected use of the advance secured by the guarantee[77] or the purpose of the guarantee itself;[78]

---

[71] *Goodwin v National Bank of A/asia Ltd* (1968) 117 C.L.R. 173; *Shotter v Westpac Banking Corp* [1988] 2 N.Z.L.R. 316 at 334; *Wythes v Labouchere* (1859) 3 De G. & J. 593; 44 E.R. 1397.

[72] *Bank of Nova Scotia v Neil* (1968) 69 D.L.R. (2d) 357, BC CA.

[73] See *Bank of Scotland v Henry Butcher & Co* [2001] 2 All E.R. (Comm) 691 where the court held that in the absence of proof of "equitable impropriety" it was not necessary for the creditor to inform the guarantors that the borrower was using the guaranteed account for the payment of restaurant and hotel expenses because the payments were not "so exceptional as to support the argument that the bank was aware that [the borrower] was using the account for purposes other than his business" (at para.80). *National Australia Bank Ltd v Le Maistre* (unreported, NSW Sup Ct, July 28, 1987) where the principal went "berserk with the urge for more stock"; *Union Bank of Australia Ltd v Whitelaw* [1906] V.L.R. 711. In *Westpac Banking Corp Ltd v Robinson* (1993) 30 N.S.W.L.R. 668, the bank's failure to disclose fraud allegations on the part of one of the vendors of a business did not amount to misrepresentation because the alleged defalcations concerned the business which, by the time the guarantee was signed, was already under the control of the purchasers: reversing *Westpac Banking Corp Ltd v Robinson* (1990) A.S.C. 56–001. See also *Kelly v ANZ Banking Group Ltd* (unreported, Qld Sup Ct, Demack J., May 31, 1993); *National Provincial Bank of England Ltd v Glanusk* [1913] 3 K.B. 335; *Bank of Scotland v Morrison* [1911] S.C. 593. The position in relation to fidelity guarantees is different: *Railton v Matthews* (1844) 10 Cl. & F. 934; 8.

[74] *Cooper v National Provincial Bank Ltd* [1946] K.B. 1, which may be restricted to its particular facts: To quote Lawrence L.J. at 7: "The fact that her husband to whom she gave this authority to draw on her account was an undischarged bankrupt does not make the authority so unusual that it ought to have been communicated by the bank to the intended surety". See also *Goad v Canadian Imperial Bank of Commerce* (1968) 67 D.L.R. (2d) 189 (Ont H Ct).

[75] *Behan v Obelon Pty Ltd* (1985) 157 C.L.R. 326 at 330; *Royal Bank of Canada v Hislop* (1989) 62 D.L.R. (4th) 228; *Kelly v Australian & New Zealand Banking Group Ltd* (unreported, Qld Sup Ct, Demack J., May 31, 1993).

[76] *Behan v Obelon Pty Ltd* (1985) 157 C.L.R. 326 at 330.

[77] *Lloyd's Bank Ltd v Harrison* (1925) 4 Legal Decisions Affecting Bankers 12; *Midland Bank v Kidwai, Independent*, June 5 1995, CA; *Sorrell v National Australia Bank* (unreported, Sup Ct WA, Full Ct, April 1, 1998).

[78] *North British Insurance Co v Lloyd* (1854) 10 Exch. 523; 156 E.R. 545 (creditor not bound to disclose that the guarantee was required because another surety wished to retire); *Westminster Bank Ltd v Cond* (1940) 46 Com. Cas. 60.

(l)   any anticipated logistical or technical difficulties which the principal debtor may have in discharging the principal obligation;[79]

(m)   the fact that the principal debtor whose account is guaranteed had entered into an arrangement with a company associated with the creditor on terms that the principal debtor would complete certain building work for no profit;[80]

(n)   the fact that the purchase price payable under the contract guaranteed greatly exceeds the true value of the property purchased;[81]

(o)   any difficulties which the principal debtor may have in performing the principal obligation as a result of the actions of a third party;[82] or

(p)   any other factor unconnected with the guarantee which may render the undertaking it contains more hazardous.[83]

4-21   Even a belief or suspicion by the creditor or one of its officers that the principal debtor did not have power as a trustee to enter into the principal transaction is not necessarily an unusual feature which must be disclosed to a prospective guarantor. This is certainly true where the guarantor's undertaking is in the form of a guarantee and indemnity because the guarantor can be liable in his capacity as an indemnifier even if the principal contract is void as an *ultra vires* transaction.[84]

If the undertaking is simply a guarantee, it is dependent upon the continuing existence and validity of the principal transaction, so if the principal transaction is *ultra vires*, the guarantee will be discharged in any event.[85]

(iv) A wider duty of disclosure?

4-22   It has been seen that there are some suggestions that the duty of disclosure extends beyond a requirement to disclose "a special arrange-

---

[79] *Trade Indemnity Co Ltd v Workington Harbour & Dock Board* [1937] A.C. 1 (the employer under a building contract is not usually obliged to inform the contractor and the surety of the difficulty of the site where the contract itself states that this is a matter for the expertise and experience of the contractor); *Lloyd's Bank Ltd v Harrison* (1925) 4 Legal Decisions Affecting Bankers 12.

[80] *Commercial Bank of Australia Ltd v Amadio* (1983) 151 C.L.R. 447 at 456 per Gibbs C.J. But see *Westpac Banking Corporation v Robinson* (1993) 30 N.S.W.L.R. 668 at 688 *per* Clarke J.A.

[81] *Pooraka Holdings Pty Ltd v Participation Nominees Pty Ltd* (1991) 58 S.A.S.R. 184 at 195 *per* King C.J.

[82] *Cooper v National Provincial Bank Ltd* [1946] K.B. 1.

[83] *Lindsay v L. Stevenson & Sons Ltd* (1891) 17 V.L.R. 112; *Wythes v Labouchere* (1859) 3 De G. & J. 593 at 609; 44 ER 1397 at 1404.

[84] *Seventy-sixth Emotion Pty Ltd v Australia & New Zealand Banking Group Ltd* (unreported, Vic Sup Ct, May 25, 1992).

[85] See, however, below, paras 5–113 to 5–114 regarding companies.

ment" between creditor and debtor, and that there is also an obligation to disclose arrangements between other parties, and perhaps also the creditor's knowledge of fraudulent activities of the principal debtor.[86] At a more general level, the rule of disclosure has sometimes been expressed in broader terms in accordance with its perceived rationale that it is based on an implied representation that the undisclosed facts do not exist. Thus in *London General Omnibus Co v Holloway*[87] Vaughan Williams L.J. (in interpreting an earlier formulation of the rule by Lord Campbell in *Hamilton v Watson*) said this[88]:

> "Lord Campbell, it is true, takes as his example of what might not be naturally expected an unusual contract between creditor and debtor whose debt the surety guarantees, but I take it this is only an example of the general proposition that a creditor must reveal to the surety every fact which under the circumstances the surety would expect not to exist, for the omission to mention that such a fact does exist is an implied representation that it does not."

London General Omnibus Co v Holloway[89] was concerned with a **4–23** guarantee of good behaviour of an employee (where special principles apply[90]), but it was nevertheless quoted without apparent disapproval by Lord Scott in *Royal Bank of Scotland v Etridge*.[91] Similarly in *Geest plc v Fyffes*[92] Colman J., adopting the same theoretical basis of the doctrine, held that in determining whether there had been an implied representation the court had to consider not only any express representations, and the nature of the contract between beneficiary of the guarantee and the debtor, but also the conduct of the beneficiary.[93] Indeed, it was described as a "helpful test" to determine "whether, having regard to the beneficiary's conduct in such circumstances, a reasonable potential surety would naturally assume that the true state of facts did not exist and that, had it existed, he would in all the circumstances necessarily have been informed of it".[94]

Arguably these formulations do no more than express the underlying **4–24** rationale for the duty of disclosure and should be read subject to the normal rule that only unusual facts need be disclosed. Yet, phrased in

---

[86] See above, paras 4–12 to 4–13.
[87] [1912] 2 K.B. 72.
[88] *ibid.*, at 78.
[89] [1912] 2 K.B. 72.
[90] See below, para.4–30.
[91] [2002] 2 A.C. 773 at 848, para.188, (in the context of disapproving the even wider proposition in *Pooraka Holdings Pty Ltd v Participation Nominees Pty Ltd* (1991) 58 S.A.S.R. 184). But note that the formulation by Vaughan Williams L.J. was disapproved by *Crédit Lyonnais Bank Nederland v Export Credit Guarantee Dept* [1996] 1 Lloyd's Rep. 200 at 226.
[92] [1999] 1 All E.R. (Comm) 672.
[93] *ibid.*, at 683.
[94] See also in support of a wider notion of the duty of disclosure based upon an implied representation *Union Bank of Australia v Puddy* [1949] V.L.R. 242 at 247 where Fullagar J. stated that "if a creditor knows or would reasonably believe the surety to be acting upon a particular assumption of fact and knows the assumption is unfounded, his conduct in not disclosing the truth may often be held to amount to a representation that the assumption is well founded".

terms of the law relating to misrepresentation, they provide a legal basis
for extending the duty of disclosure to embrace material as well as unusual
facts.[95] There is also the parallel development[96] in respect of guarantees
given by a wife in respect of her husband's debts (and possibly those given
by other non-commercial guarantors), where a much greater degree of
disclosure is required to be made to the potential guarantor's solicitor. This
may in the future influence a broadening of the scope of the general law
described in this section.

4–25   The parties can extend the creditor's duty of disclosure by an express
provision in the contract of guarantee. In *Formica Ltd v Secretary of State
Acting by the Export Credits Guarantee Department*,[97] the guarantee
provided, *inter alia*:

> "Without prejudice to any rule of law, it is declared that this guarantee
> is given on a condition that (a) the INSURED has at the date of this
> guarantee disclosed and will at all times during the operation of this
> guarantee promptly disclose all facts in any way affecting the risks
> guaranteed; and (b) in order to prevent or minimise any loss
> recoverable under this guarantee the INSURED shall (i) use all
> reasonable and usual care skill and forethought ... (ii) take all
> practical measures. . . ."

4–26   Colman J. held that the insured's contractual duty of disclosure in
accordance with this provision was sufficient to rebut the insured's claim
that certain documents were subject to legal advice privilege or litigation
privilege. However, any privileged documents provided to the defendants
under clause 4 would be privileged in their hands.

(v) A duty to answer questions

4–27   If the guarantor asks the creditor a direct question about a material
point, the creditor must give the information honestly and to the best of its
ability.[98] Sureties are entitled to true, honest and accurate answers to their
questions about any matters germane to the guarantee.[99] However, if the
creditor's replies are misleading they will only release the sureties if they

---

[95] Note that in *Westpac Securities v Dickie* [1991] 1 N.Z.L.R. 657 at 662–663 Hardie Boys J.
suggested that a creditor's failure to disclose a material fact will vitiate the guarantee if the
fact is inconsistent with the presumed basis of the contract: "in each case it will be a question
of the materiality of the fact concealed". See also a view that the guarantor can rescind for
even minor misrepresentations: *Davies v London & Provincial Marine Insurance Co.* (1878) 8
Ch. D. 469 at 475, discussed below, para.4–37.
[96] See *Royal Bank of Scotland v Etridge* [2002] A.C. 773 and below, paras 4–207 to 4–216.
[97] [1995] 1 Lloyd's Rep. 692.
[98] *Hamilton v Watson* (1845) 12 Cl. & Fin. 109; 8 E.R. 1339; *Goodwin v National Bank of A/
asia Ltd* (1968) 117 CLR 173; *Westminster Bank Ltd v Cond* (1940) 46 Com. Cas. 60; *O'Brien v
Australia & New Zealand Bank* (1971) 5 S.A.S.R. 347; *Fitzgerald v Jacomb* (1873) 4 A.J.R.
189; *Canadian Imperial Bank of Commerce v Larsen* [1983] 5 W.W.R. 179 (rescission granted
because of innocent misrepresentation about the financial status of the principal debtor).
[99] *Westminster Bank Ltd v Cond* (1940) 46 Com. Cas. 60; *O'Brien v Australia & New Zealand
Bank* (1971) 5 S.A.S.R. 347; *Fitzgerald v Jacomb* (1873) 4 A.J.R. 189.

amount to a misrepresentation.[1] In a sense, the creditor's obligation is a positive duty to abstain from misrepresenting the material facts. The creditor is not obliged to make inquiries elsewhere as to the financial position of the principal debtor.[2] It is merely required to answer truthfully from information within its own resources.[3]

On this basis a surety has a right to inquire periodically from the bank the amount for which the surety is liable under the guarantee. The bank should then disclose the amount of the surety's existing and contingent liabilities. If the amount of the debt secured is more than the limit of the guarantee, the surety should simply be advised that he is liable for the full amount stated in the guarantee,[4] but generally the surety is not entitled to know of the particulars of the customer's account or be given a copy of it.[5] The surety can also demand information as to the interest rate charged on the principal debt and the amount, if any, realised by the bank under its collateral securities.[6] On all these matters, the surety is entitled to a truthful answer.[7]

4–28

Paget's Law of Banking, citing *Hamilton v Watson*,[8] suggests that if a bank is questioned by an intending surety on a *material* matter the bank may disclose the information without breaching its duty of confidence, "the occasion justifying disclosure or the customer's authority for such disclosure being implied in the introduction of the surety".[9] But this is not thought to be correct. Although Lord Campbell in *Hamilton v Watson*[10] suggested (obiter) that the bank must answer questions relating to the principal's account and business dealings,[11] the issue of whether the duty of confidence imposes a qualification on such obligations is not specifically addressed.

4–29

(vi) Fidelity guarantees

The courts have devised special rules for fidelity guarantees. This form of suretyship is, in effect, a guarantee of the good behaviour of an employee or agent. An employer or principal would not normally be expected to retain in employment an employee or agent who has been guilty of dishonesty or misconduct. Thus a surety will not be held liable on a fidelity guarantee where the employer or principal fails to disclose any such defaults of which it is aware during the agent's or employee's service

4–30

---

[1] *Canterbury Farmers' Co-op Association (Ltd) v Lindsay* (1910) 29 N.Z.L.R. 793; *Parsons v Barclay & Co Ltd* (1910) 103 L.T. 196.
[2] *Parsons v Barclay & Co Ltd* (1910) 103 L.T. 196.
[3] *ibid.*
[4] A. Holden, *The Law and Practice of Banking* (8th ed., 1993), Vol. 2, pp.198–199.
[5] *Ross v Bank of New South Wales* (1928) 28 S.R. (NSW) 539. See, however, below paras 4–210 to 4–216, in respect of guarantees given by a wife in respect of her husband's borrowings.
[6] *ibid.*
[7] See *Ross v Bank of New South Wales* (1928) 28 S.R. (NSW) 539.
[8] (1845) 12 Cl. & Fin. 109; 8 ER 1339.
[9] *Paget's Law of Banking* (11th ed., 1994), p.592.
[10] (1895) 12 Cl. & Fin. 109; 8 E.R. 1339.
[11] (1845) 12 Cl. & Fin. 109 at 119; 8 E.R. 1339 at 1343.

even if the failure is not wilful, intentional or fraudulent.[12] The surety will also be discharged if the employer does not divulge facts which give it reason to believe that there has been misconduct.[13] In a continuing guarantee the employer remains under a duty to disclose to the surety any future dishonesty or misconduct of the employee. If the employer fails to do so, it will forfeit the benefit of the fidelity bond in respect of this conduct.[14]

4–31 Similarly, non-disclosure by an employer of the fact that to the employer's knowledge the employee has been guilty of defalcations in his service before the fidelity bond was executed amounts to a representation that the employee has not been guilty of such dishonesty.[15] It appears, however, that the employer is under no obligation to advise the surety of any misconduct of the employee in previous positions even if the employer is aware of it.[16] This principle is particularly harsh since fidelity guarantees are usually given on the understanding that, so far as the employer is aware, the employee is not dishonest.[17]

4–32 The disclosure required from the employer must be sufficiently complete to enable the proposed surety to decide whether or not he is prepared to allow the employee to be retained on the basis of the fidelity bond.[18] Where the employee has been guilty of falsifying books of account and fabricating entries, it is not sufficient to give the intending surety notice of defaults "to a large amount".[19]

4–33 There must be no fraudulent concealment from the surety.[20] But if the surety already knows the facts which he alleges were fraudulently withheld, he cannot avoid the guarantee.[21] On the other hand, an innocent failure to disclose details of the employee's misconduct will discharge the surety.[22] Mere delay in advising the surety of an employee's defalcation does not, however, nullify the fidelity bond in respect of that defalcation provided that the employer does not actively conceal it from the surety and

---

[12] *Smith v Bank of Scotland* (1813) 1 Dow 272; 3 E.R. 697, HL; *Phillips v Foxall* (1872) L.R. 7 Q.B. 666; *London General Omnibus Co Ltd v Holloway* [1912] 2 K.B. 72; *Sanderson v Aston* (1873) L.R. 8 Exch. 73; *Railton v Mathews* (1844) 10 Cl. & Fin. 934; 8 ER 993, HL; *Thomas v Watkins Products Inc* (1965) 54 D.L.R. (2d) 252, NB CA.
[13] *London General Omnibus Co Ltd v Holloway* [1912] 2 K.B. 72 at 80 *per* Vaughan Williams L.J.
[14] *Smith v Bank of Scotland* (1813) 1 Dow 272; 3 E.R. 697, HL. Quaere whether this rule applies if the employer is unable to dismiss the employee. See *Caxton & Arrington Union v Dew* (1899) 68 L.J.Q.B. 380 (where the obligees in respect of a bond for the due performance of a collector of rates had no power to dismiss the collector).
[15] *Phillips v Foxall* (1872) L.R. 7 Q.B. 666; *Sanderson v Aston* (1873) L.R. 8 Exch. 73; *Enright v Falvey* (1879) 4 L.R. Ir. 397.
[16] But see *Wythes v Labouchere* (1859) 3 De G. & J. 593 at 609; 44 E.R. 1397 at 1404.
[17] See *London General Omnibus Co Ltd v Holloway* [1912] 2 K.B. 72.
[18] *Enright v Falvey* (1879) 4 L.R. Ir. 397.
[19] *ibid.*
[20] *Peers v Oxford* (1870) 17 Gr. 472. See also *Ruthenian Farmers' Elevator Co Ltd v Hrycak* [1924] 3 D.L.R. 402.
[21] *Peers v Oxford* (1870) 17 Gr. 472. See also *Peel v Tatlock* (1799) 1 Box & Pul 419; 126 E.R. 986; *Goring v Edmonds* (1829) 3 Moo & P. 259; 6 Bing 94; 130 E.R. 1215; *Caxton & Arrington Union v Dew* (1899) 68 L.J.Q.B. 380.
[22] "The injury to the surety is the same, whether the non-disclosure was due to fraud or forgetfulness": *London General Omnibus Co Ltd v Holloway* [1912] 2 K.B. 72 at 82 *per* Farwell L.J.

the rights of the parties have not altered.[23] Generally, the employer's right to dismiss employees for misconduct is a right which the surety is entitled in equity to have exercised for his protection to minimise liability under the fidelity bond. If the employer waives the right to dismiss, the surety will normally be released.[24] But a surety will not be discharged where the employer treats the employee's defalcation as a loan in the books to conceal it from other employees, as long as this step does not amount to a waiver or a novation or a concealment from the surety.[25]

Sometimes a fidelity guarantee is given to an employer in return for an undertaking that periodical checks will be made on the employees to ensure that their accounts are accurate. Such an undertaking is usually found to be merely a representation of intention, not a warranty or a wilful misrepresentation. Consequently, a failure to conduct the checks will not excuse the surety.[26]

4–34

(vii) Effect of non-disclosure

Non-disclosure amounting to undue concealment constitutes a misrepresentation which can vitiate a contract of guarantee.[27] But the guarantee will not be automatically rescinded simply because of a non-disclosure amounting to a misrepresentation. General equitable principles will determine whether the guarantee should be rescinded in the circumstances of the case.[28]

4–35

3. MISREPRESENTATION

A misrepresentation of fact[29] by the creditor which induces the guarantor to enter into the guarantee will entitle the guarantor, in accordance with normal principles, to rescind the contract.[30] The

4–36

---

[23] *Peel v Tatlock* (1799) 1 Bos. & P. 419; 126 E.R. 986.
[24] *Phillips v Foxall* (1872) L.R. 7 Q.B. 666.
[25] *Peel v Tatlock* (1799) 1 Bos & P 419; 126 E.R. 986. See also *Mountague v Tidcombe* (1705) 2 Vern. 518; 23 E.R. 933.
[26] *A-G v Adelaide Life & Assurance Guarantee Co Ltd* (1888) 22 S.A.L.R. 5; *R. v National Insurance Co* (1887) 13 V.L.R. 301; *Benham v United Guarantee & Life Assurance Co* (1852) 7 Exch. 744; 21 L.J. (Ex.) 317; 155 E.R. 1149.
[27] See above, para.4–01; *Bank of India v Patel* [1982] 1 Lloyd's Rep. 506 at 515 *per* Bingham J., approved on appeal [1983] 2 Lloyd's Rep. 298 at 301–302 *per* Goff L.J.; *Westpac Banking Corp v Robinson* (1993) 30 N.S.W.L.R. 668 at 688, *per* Clarke J.A.
[28] *Mackenzie v Royal Bank of Canada* [1934] A.C. 468; *Westpac Banking Corp v Robinson* (1993) 30 N.S.W.L.R. 668. See also *Westpac Securities Ltd v Dickie* [1991] 1 N.Z.L.R. 657.
[29] A statement will be treated as true if it is substantially correct and the difference between the statement and the truth would not have induced a reasonable person to enter into the contract: *Avon Insurance v Swire* [2000] 1 All E.R. (Comm) 573.
[30] As to misrepresentation generally see J. Beatson, *Anson's Law of Contract* (28th ed., 2002), Ch. 6. G.H. Treitel, *The Law of Contract* (11th ed., 2003), Ch. 9. See also, in relation to guarantees, *Mackenzie v Royal Bank of Canada* [1934] A.C. 468. The misrepresentation may take the form of a false statement or undue concealment: *Willis v Willis* (1850) 17 Sim. 218; *Blest v Brown* (1862) 4 De G.F. & J. 367; 45 E.R. 1225.

misrepresentation, which must be of fact rather than opinion,[31] (but can be express or implied)[32] may relate to the financial position or state of accounts of the principal,[33] the creditor's policy and intentions as to terms of the principal contract,[34] or the need and purpose of the guarantee.[35] Common misrepresentations will also concern the extent of the guarantor's liability under the guarantee, for example, a false assertion that the guarantor's liability is limited in amount[36] or relates only to future indebtedness[37] or is not of a personal nature.[38] Although these statements involve a representation as to the contents of a legal document, they will probably still be viewed as representations of fact rather than law.[39]

4–37   While it is clear from this analysis that the general rules as to misrepresentation apply to guarantees, there is some suggestion that the courts will be inclined to allow a guarantor to rescind the contract even for the most minor misrepresentations. Thus, in *Davies v London & Provincial Marine Insurance Co*[40] Fry J. said:

"there is no consideration in this case, as in many cases of suretyship, for the contract so entered into; and therefore I think ... it is a contract in respect of which very little is sufficient. Very little said which ought not to have been said, and very little not said which ought to have been said, would be sufficient to prevent the contract being valid."[41]

4–38   This approach, which might be regarded as being contrary to the general contractual rule that the misrepresentation must be material, reflects the fact that a guarantee, although not a contract *uberrimae fidei*,[42] does

---

[31] See *National Bank of New Zealand v Macintosh* (1881) 3 N.Z.L.R. 217, where a misrepresentation honestly made that the principal was "all right and would be able to meet the liabilities" was held to be a statement of opinion.
[32] See *Geest plc v Fyffes plc* [1999] 1 All E.R. (Comm) 672, discussed above, para.4–23.
[33] *Ward v The National Bank of New Zealand* (1886) 4 N.Z.L.R. 35, CA; *Stone v Compton* (1838) 5 Bing (NC) 142; 132 E.R. 1059; *O'Brien v Australia & New Zealand Bank Ltd* (1971) 5 S.A.S.R. 347 at 353; *McKewan v Thornton* (1861) 2 F. & F. 594; 175 E.R. 1201; *Blest v Brown* (1862) 3 Giff 450; 66 E.R. 486. But a statement by the creditor that it had advice that the assets of the principal debtor were worth in excess of a certain amount does not amount to a representation that the assets are worth more than this amount: *Commonwealth Bank of Australia v Prentice* (unreported, Sup Ct, NSW, Barr A.J., December 14, 1995) (BC 9506814 at 13).
[34] *O'Brien v Australia & New Zealand Bank Ltd* (1971) 5 S.A.S.R. 347 at 353.
[35] *Canterbury Farmers' Co-op Association (Ltd) v Lindsay* (1910) 29 N.Z.L.R. 793; *O'Brien v Australia & New Zealand Bank Ltd* (1971) 5 S.A.S.R. 347. A mere expression of opinion by the creditor or the creditor's agent that reliance upon the guarantee was unlikely does not amount to a promise that the guarantee would never be enforced: *Morris v Wardley Australia Property Management Ltd* (1994) ASC 56–268.
[36] *Bank of New South Wales v Flack* [1984] A.C.L.D. 249.
[37] *O'Brien v Australia & New Zealand Bank* (1971) 5 S.A.S.R. 347 (misrepresentation that guarantee applied only to future indebtedness when in fact it covered past indebtedness); *Bank of Nova Scotia v Zackheim* (1983) 3 D.L.R. (4th) 760.
[38] *Bank of A/asia v Adams* (1889) 8 N.Z.L.R. 119.
[39] See, in other contexts, *Hirshfeld v L.B. & S.C. Ry* (1876) 2 Q.B.D. 1; *Horry v Tate & Lyle Refineries Ltd* [1982] 2 Lloyd's Rep. 416. See generally as to this distinction J. Beatson, *Anson's Law of Contract* (28th ed. 2002), pp.240–241.
[40] (1878) 8 Ch. D. 469.
[41] ibid., at 475. See also *Bank of New South Wales v Rogers* (1941) 65 C.L.R. 42 at 59–60.
[42] ibid.

impose a duty on the creditor to make disclosure in certain circumstances. However, the creditor's duty of disclosure is, as we have seen,[43] limited to the unusual features of the *principal transaction* which the guarantor would not naturally expect to exist. It does not warrant the suggestion that the contract of guarantee will be voidable where there is undue concealment of matters which are not unusual features of the principal transaction,[44] or where there is a non-material misrepresentation.

Although generally a misrepresentation must be made by the creditor (so that a misrepresentation by a co-guarantor or the principal debtor will not suffice), the creditor will be bound by a representation by such a third party in the rare case where he appoints him as agent to procure the guarantor's signature.[45] Alternatively, and more commonly, where a wife guarantees her husband's debts and is induced to execute the guarantee because of the husband's misrepresentations, the guarantee will be set aside if the creditor has constructive notice of her husband's conduct.[46] The same principle may apply to other "non-commercial" guarantors.[47]

4–39

The remedy that the guarantor will usually seek as a result of misrepresentations made to him is rescission of the guarantee. The usual factors precluding rescission will apply such as affirmation and lapse of time, and an inability to provide restitution.[48] The latter requirement means that in the (somewhat unusual) case where the guarantor has derived a benefit from the transaction, this must be restored.[49]

4–40

In the context of guarantees, a somewhat controversial issue that arises is whether or not the court has jurisdiction to give partial rescission. This possibility was denied in *TSB plc v Camfield*,[50] where a wife gave a charge (securing her husband's business debts) over a house, having been induced to do so on the basis of a misrepresentation by her husband that the charge was limited to £15,000, when it was in fact unlimited. The creditor was fixed with constructive notice of such misrepresentation. The court rejected the bank's argument that the guarantor was only entitled to have the guarantee set aside on the basis that it remained a valid security for £15,000.[51]

4–41

---

[43] See above, paras 4–02 to 4–21.
[44] *Cf.* G. Andrews and R. Millett, *Law of Guarantees* (3rd ed, 2000), para.5.15. The approach is also contrary to the general approach to misrepresentation. See *Avon Insurance v Swire* [2000] 1 All E.R. (Comm) 573 (see above n.29).
[45] *Barclays Bank plc v O'Brien* [1994] 1 A.C. 180 at 194A, 195 F–G. See below, para.4–178.
[46] *Barclays Bank plc v O'Brien* (*ibid.*); *Royal Bank of Scotland v Etridge* [2002] 2 A.C. 773. See below, paras 4–179 to 4–187.
[47] See below, paras 4–184 to 4–187.
[48] See generally, J. Beatson, *Anson's Law of Contract* (28th ed., 2002) pp.253–256.
[49] As in *Dunbar Bank v Nadeem* [1997] 2 All E.R. 253, discussed below, para.4–151, in the context of undue influence, where the same principle applies.
[50] [1995] 1 W.L.R. 430. See also *Castle Phillips Finance Co v Piddington* [1994] N.P.C. 155; *Molestina v Ponton* [2002] 1 Lloyd's Rep. 271; *Allied Irish Bank plc v Byrne* [1995] 2 F.L.R. 325 and, generally, an excellent analysis of the issue by J. O'Sullivan, "Undue Influence and Misrepresentation after *O'Brien*: Making Security Secure" (in *Restitution and Banking Law* 1998, ed. F. Rose), p.42. See also D.J. Meikle, "Partial Rescission–Removing the Restitution from a Contractual Doctrine" (2003) Vol. 19(3) J. of Contract Law 40.
[51] The court's reasoning was that it was too late to impose terms once the matter had reached court, as rescission had already occurred by the act of the representee. As pointed out by J. O'Sullivan, "Undue Influence and Misrepresentation after *O'Brien*: Making Security Secure" (in *Restitution and Banking Law*, 1998, ed. F. Rose), p.42 at pp.66–67, this reasoning is

4–42   Whilst this approach is clearly correct where the guarantor would not
have entered into a guarantee at all as a result of the misrepresentation, it
does seem an inflexible approach when it is proved clearly on the facts that
the guarantor would in any event have entered into a guarantee on certain
terms knowing the true facts (that is, in *TSB Bank plc v Camfield*,[52] if it
was shown that Mrs Camfield would have been prepared to enter into a
guarantee with an upper limit of £15,000).

4–43   The approach is also at variance with the flexible approach equity
adopts to issues of rescission, in particular, the approach of equity to
restitution as a condition of rescission. Restitution never required
complete restitution of the position which existed before the contract. It
allowed its remedies, particularly the power to order an account to be
taken, or to direct inquiries as to allowances to be made for deterioration,
to be employed to achieve practical restitution and justice.[53] In this way
equity was able to restore the parties substantially to the status quo.

4–44   A modern example is *O'Sullivan v Management Agency and Music Ltd*[54]
where an exclusive management agreement made by a composer was set
aside because of undue influence arising out of a fiduciary relationship
between the parties. The Court of Appeal granted rescission even though
the parties could not be restored to their original positions. Their
Lordships declared that a contract may be set aside in equity as long as
"the court can achieve practical justice between the parties"[55] and that
"the court will do what is practically just in the individual case,[56] by
granting rescission and restitution together with orders for accounts".[57]
This jurisdiction to do "what is practically just" echoes Lord Blackburn's
remarks in *Erlanger v New Sombrero Phosphate*[58] over a century earlier.

4–45   A different approach to the granting of partial rescission has been taken
in other jurisdictions. In Australia in *Vadasz v Pioneer Concrete (SA) Pty
Ltd*[59] the appellant was a director of Vadipile Drilling Pty Ltd
("Vadipile"), which carried on business as a foundation piling contractor.
The respondent supplied Vadipile with ready-mixed concrete on credit and
it sought a guarantee from the appellant. The respondent represented that
the guarantee would apply to Vadipile's future indebtedness but it was
expressed to cover both past and future indebtedness. In reliance upon the
appellant's guarantee, the respondent supplied Vadipile with large
quantities of concrete which had been used and could not be returned.
Moreover, Vadipile was insolvent.

---

fallacious since "it has never been suggested that the restitutionary consequences which flow
from rescission are achieved without intervention by the court".
[52] [1995] 1 W.L.R. 430.
[53] See generally *Erlanger v New Sombrero Phosphate Co.* (1878) 3 App. Cas. 1218; *Alati v
Kruger* (1955) 94 C.L.R. 216. A similar flexible approach has been adapted in relation to
mortgages and undue influence. See, generally, J. Beatson, *Anson's Law of Contract* (28th ed.,
2002), pp.256–257 and *O'Sullivan v Management Agency and Music Ltd* [1985] 1 Q.B. 428,
discussed below, para.4–44.
[54] [1985] 1 Q.B. 428.
[55] *ibid.*, at 458 *per* Dunn L.J.
[56] *ibid.*, at 466 *per* Fox L.J.
[57] *ibid.*, at 471 *per* Waller L.J.
[58] (1878) 3 App. Cas. 1218 at 1278–1279.
[59] (1995) 130 A.L.R. 570.

The High Court of Australia dealt with the appeal on the assumption **4–46** that the respondent's misrepresentation was fraudulent, although there was no positive finding of fraud. The only question for the court was whether equity required complete restitution of the position which existed before the contract as a condition of a rescission order. The evidence indicated that the appellant would have been prepared to enter into the guarantee if it had been confined to the future indebtedness of Vadipile because this was the only way that Vadipile could obtain future supplies of concrete. As a director of Vadipile, the appellant was fully aware of its financial position and stood to benefit personally from its operations. Against this background, the High Court applied the maxim that "he who seeks equity must do equity"[60] and ordered rescission of the appellant's guarantee but only in so far as it related to Vadipile's prior indebtedness.[61]

At the end of the day the court is faced with a choice. Either it follows **4–47** the clean and neat approach in *TSB Bank plc v Camfield*[62] and orders restitution in toto in all cases or it confines this approach to cases where the guarantor would not have provided the guarantee at all but for the misrepresentation and it grants rescission on terms where the evidence indicates that the guarantor would have been prepared to provide a more limited guarantee in the terms represented to him. The latter approach is more consistent with the historical genesis of equity's jurisdiction in this area and it enables the court to dispense practical justice.[63] In *Scales Trading Ltd v Far Eastern Shipping Co. Public Ltd*[64] the Privy Council left open the question of whether restitution can be ordered on terms and it may be that *TSB Bank plc v Camfield*[65] will not be regarded as a general rule applicable in all cases of misrepresentation.

If the courts do permit partial rescission such relief is likely to be more **4–48** appropriate where there has been a specific and precise misrepresentation as to the ambit of the guarantee, for example, as to the upper limit of liability (as in *TSB Bank plc v Camfield*)[66] or the duration of the guarantee, or the fact that it is confined to future indebtedness. In these cases there is more likelihood of proving that the guarantor would have been prepared to provide a more limited guarantee in the terms represented to him. But there is much less possibility of satisfying this burden of proof when the misrepresentation relates to the principal

---

[60] *Cheese v Thomas* [1994] 1 W.L.R. 129 at 136; *Vadasz v Pioneer Concrete (SA) Pty Ltd* (1995) 130 A.L.R. 570 at 579.
[61] Similarly it has been held that where a misrepresentation as to the customer's solvency induced the guarantor to provide a fresh guarantee to replace an existing guarantee of the customer's indebtedness, the guarantor is entitled to rescission of the new guarantee on terms that the bank is restored to its position under the original guarantee: see *Ward v National Bank of New Zealand* (1886) 4 N.Z.L.R. 35. See also *Brueckner v The Satellite Group (Ultimo) Pty* (unreported, NSW Sup Ct. May 23, 2003) where a rescission order was not granted because the guarantors would have entered into the guarantee even if there had been no undue concealment.
[62] [1995] 1 W.L.R. 430.
[63] *Erlanger v New Sombrero Phosphate Co* (1878) 3 App. Cas. 1218 at 1278–1279, *per* Lord Blackburn.
[64] [2001] 1 All E.R. (Comm) 319.
[65] [1995] 1 W.L.R. 430.
[66] *ibid.*

debtor's financial position or the creditor makes general statements that the guarantor's property will not be put in jeopardy.[67] Certainly partial relief would be inappropriate where (as is often the case) there is a combination of undue influence and misrepresentation (even of a specific nature) because it could not be said with certainty that the guarantor would have proceeded with the transaction but on different terms.[68]

4–49   Assuming *TSB Bank plc v Camfield*[69] remains the law, and that there is no power to order partial rescission in equity, it is unlikely that the creditor can utilise s.2(2) of the Misrepresentation Act 1967 to achieve the same result. This provides that "where a person has entered into a contract after a misrepresentation has been made to him otherwise than fraudulently and he would be entitled, by reason of the misrepresentation, to rescind the contract" the court has a power to award damages in lieu of rescission if it considers it equitable to do so "having regard to the nature of the representation and the loss that would be caused by it if the contract were upheld, as well as to the loss that rescission would cause to the other party".[70] But the measure of damages under the sub-section is the loss caused by the misrepresentation as a result of the refusal to allow rescission of the contract.[71] On the assumption that the law does not permit partial rescission, the loss would be the guarantor's total liability under the guarantee not (as the creditor would claim) the additional amount in excess of the more limited liability that the creditor misrepresented that the guarantor would have. Another reason for not utilising s.2(2) in the context of misrepresentation by third parties of which the creditor has constructive notice was given in *TSB Bank plc v Camfield*.[72] There the bank had constructive notice of a misrepresentation by the husband to the guarantor wife, and it was held that an award of damages against the husband would have been "an empty remedy".[73] No court could have formed the view that it was equitable to exercise its discretion to award damages in lieu of rescission since "the loss to the wife by upholding the legal charge in exchange for an award of damages against her husband would have far outweighed the loss that rescission would cause to [her husband]".[74]

---

[67] See *Garcia v National Australia Bank* (1998) 194 C.L.R. 395, where the court would not enforce the guarantee as a personal unsecured undertaking. Such assurances may in fact not amount to misrepresentations of fact at all but statements as to the future which would only be binding as contractual terms or by the application of the principles of estoppel (see below, para.5–94).

[68] See J. O'Sullivan, "Undue Influence and Misrepresentation after *O'Brien*: Making Security Secure" (in *Restitution and Banking Law* 1998, ed. F. Rose), p.42 at 67, and also for a fuller discussion of this issue.

[69] [1995] 1 W.L.R. 430.

[70] See generally J. Beatson, *Anson's Law of Contract* (28th ed., 2002), pp.257–259.

[71] *William Sindall plc v Cambridgeshire County Council* [1994] 1 W.L.R. 1016. See also J. Beatson, *Anson's Law of Contract"* (28th ed., 2002), pp.258–259.

[72] [1995] 1 W.L.R. 430.

[73] *ibid.*, at 439.

[74] *ibid.* Arguably, however, the analysis of the effectiveness of the wife's claim against the husband is misguided. All that s.2(2) requires is that the court determine whether it is equitable to award damages in lieu of rescission of the contract which (unlike s.2(1), discussed below) may be construed as being a contract–in this case the guarantee–other than one entered into directly with the misrepresentor.

Aside from seeking rescission, if the guarantor can prove that a **4–50** misrepresentation is fraudulent,[75] the creditor may be liable in the tort of deceit. This will be the case for example if the creditor insists that the signing of the guarantee is a formality and its enforcement may never be required even though he knows that the principal is hopelessly insolvent.[76] Even in the absence of fraud damages may be obtained against the creditor pursuant to the Misrepresentation Act 1967, s.2(1), in respect of a misrepresentation made by him, unless the creditor proves "that he had reasonable grounds to believe and did believe up to the time the contract was made that the facts represented were true". Section 2(1) does not apply, however, where the misrepresentation is made by a third party[77] (for example, a husband where the prospective guarantor is his wife) even though the creditor has constructive notice of the misrepresentation.[78] This results from the wording of s.2(1) which is limited in its terms to "where a person has entered into a contract after a misrepresentation has been made to him by another *party thereto*". Here the misrepresentation is not made by the other party to the contract (the creditor) but by a third party (the husband).

Many forms of guarantee contain clauses stating that the guarantor **4–51** acknowledges that the guarantor has not executed the guarantee as a result of any representation or promise by or on behalf of the creditor or stating that no servant or employee of the creditor has authority to make representations. At common law it was held that the guarantor was bound by such clauses,[79] although they were unlikely to be interpreted as embracing fraudulent representations.[80] Now, pursuant to s.3 of the Misrepresentation Act 1967, such clauses will be subject to the requirement of reasonableness in s.11(1) of the Unfair Contract Terms Act 1977.[81] Additionally such clauses are likely to be regarded as "unfair" within the meaning of the Unfair Terms in Consumer Contracts Regulations 1999, in circumstances where the Regulations apply.[82]

Sometimes a particular statement by the creditor does not amount to a **4–52** misrepresentation of existing fact (for example, a statement as to its policy regarding future enforcement of the guarantee) so that the equitable and statutory remedies for misrepresentation are unavailable. Nevertheless,

---

[75] *Derry v Peek* (1889) 14 App. Cas. 337. A fraudulent misrepresentation involves a false statement made knowingly or recklessly, with the intention that the person to whom it was addressed should act on it: *Standard Chartered Bank v Pakistan National Shipping Corp (No.2)* [2000] 1 Lloyd's Rep. 218 at 224. As to exemplary damages in cases of deceit, see *Kuddus v Chief Constable of Leicestershire Constabulary* [2001] 3 All E.R. 193 at 209. It may, however, be possible to award compound interest on damages for fraud: *Clef Aquitaine SARL v Laporte Materials (Barrow) Ltd* [2001] Q.B. 488.
[76] *Canterbury Farmers Co-op Assoc Ltd v Lindsay* (1910) 29 N.Z.L.R. 793.
[77] Unless the third party is the creditor's agent.
[78] See below, paras 4–179 to 4–187, as to when the creditor has constructive notice. As to s.2(1) of the Misrepresentation Act 1967 generally see J. Beatson, *Anson's Law of Contract* (28th ed., 2002), pp.248–250, and on this issue p.249, para.2.
[79] *Trade Indemnity Co Ltd v Workington Harbour & Dock Board* [1937] A.C. 1 at 18.
[80] See also above, para.4–19.
[81] See below, para.4–160. As to a fuller discussion, see J. Beatson, *Anson's Law of Contract* (28th ed., 2002), pp.260–262.
[82] See below, para.4–163.

the guarantor may have a defence based upon estoppel[83] or a claim on the basis of a collateral contract if the statement is sufficiently promissory.[84]

4. MISTAKE

4-53   Contracts of guarantee can also be set aside under the doctrine of mistake, which applies to contracts generally. Different kinds of mistake may be relevant.

(i) Unilateral mistake as to the terms of the guarantee

4-54   Sometimes the guarantor will allege that he has been mistaken about a fundamental term of the guarantee. For example, the guarantor may think that liability is limited to a specific amount or to debts arising from particular transactions,[85] whereas it is unlimited. If this mistake as to a fundamental term of the contract is known to the creditor, or (on one view) ought to have been known to the creditor,[86] no contract will arise at law.[87] Alternatively there is a parallel jurisdiction in equity to set aside the transaction, where it is "unconscientious"[88] for the creditor "to avail himself of the legal advantage which he has obtained".[89] The relationship between the different lines of authority in law and equity is unclear, but it is considered that setting aside the transaction in equity affords greater flexibility, allowing rectification,[90] or, possibly partial rescission.[91] On

---

[83] See, *e.g. Bank of Baroda v Shah* (unreported, Court of Appeal, July 30, 1999; 1999 W.L. 851947) where a bank was estopped from enforcing a guarantee against a company director because it reneged on an assurance that he would be released from his guarantee when he resigned as a director.

[84] See J. Beatson, *Anson's Law of Contract* (28th ed., 2002), pp.130–132.

[85] See, *e.g. Royal Bank of Canada v Hale* (1961) 30 D.L.R. (2d) 138; *Royal Bank of Canada v Oram* [1978] 1 W.W.R. 564; *ANZ Banking Group Ltd v Letore Pty Ltd* (unreported, Vic Sup Ct, Hansen J., December 22, 1994) (where the unilateral mistake arose from the bank officer's unilateral intention to apply the document according to its terms as an unlimited guarantee contrary to the agreement of the parties that it be held for a limited purpose).

[86] Probably constructive knowledge will only be sufficient to invoke the doctrine, however, where the creditor's conduct is unconscionable, for example, where the creditor seeks to prevent the guarantor discovering the mistake. See J. Beatson, *Anson's Law of Contract* (28th ed., 2002), pp.323–324 and the cases there cited (n.95).

[87] *Smith v Hughes* (1871) L.R. 6 Q.B. 597; *Hartog v Colin & Shields* [1939] 3 All E.R. 566. And see generally, J. Beatson, *Anson's Law of Contract* (28th ed, 2002), pp.323–326.

[88] *Torrance v Bolton* (1872) L.R. Ch. App. 118 at 124.

[89] *ibid.* As to unilateral mistake in equity see J. Beatson, *Anson's Law of Contract* (28th ed, 2002), pp.345–347. See also *Riverplate Properties Ltd v Paul* [1975] Ch. 133; *Taylor v Johnson* (1983) 151 C.L.R. 422; *Royal Bank of Canada v Oram* [1978] 1 W.W.R. 564; *West Sussex Properties Ltd v Chichester DC* [2000] N.P.C. 74.

[90] As to rectification, see *Riverplate Properties Ltd v Paul* [1975] 1 Ch. 133; *A. Roberts & Co Ltd v Leicestershire County Council* [1901] Ch. 555; *ANZ Banking Group Ltd v Letore Pty Ltd* (unreported Vict S. Court, Australia, December 22, 1994).

[91] On one view rescission is not available at all unless the creditor actually knows of the mistake (see J. Beatson, *Anson's Law of Contract* (28th ed., 2002), pp.346–347). There is also authority against the availability of partial rescission in the case of misrepresentation. See above, paras 4–41 to 4–48.

either basis the mistake must be in relation to a term of the contract; a mistake as to the commercial consequences of the contract is insufficient.[92]

There are some cases where the guarantor has been discharged on the grounds of unilateral mistake. Thus, the Supreme Court of British Columbia in *Royal Bank of Canada v Oram*[93] held that the defendant was released from his guarantee because the evidence established that the officer of the creditor bank with whom he dealt must have known he was labouring under a misapprehension. The guarantor believed that the guarantee related only to future indebtedness whereas it was also a guarantee of the past indebtedness of the principal. On the facts of *Royal Bank of Canada v Oram*, the defendant's misapprehension was in part induced by a misrepresentation by the bank's employee, but there is no need for a specific misrepresentation of fact since this would in any event give the usual right of rescission.

4–55

Despite the possible application of the principles of unilateral mistake to guarantees, the burden of proof imposed upon the guarantor to establish the requisite requirements for equitable intervention will be difficult to satisfy. It is not sufficient for the guarantor simply to show that he has made a mistake. The guarantor must also prove from express words, conduct, or previous dealings[94] that the creditor knew or had reason to know of that mistake.[95] Additionally where the equitable jurisdiction is invoked, the contract will not be set aside where the rights of strangers have already crystallised,[96] or, possibly, where the creditor has materially altered his position.[97]

4–56

(ii) Common mistake and mutual mistake

If the parties enter into a contract under a common mistaken assumption of "an essential and integral element of the subject matter"[98] of the contract, the contract will be void at law.[99]

4–57

[92] *Clarion Ltd v National Provident Institution* [2000] 1 W.L.R. 1888.
[93] [1978] 1 W.W.R. 564. See also *Royal Bank of Canada v Hale* (1961) 30 D.L.R. (2d) 138 (where the guarantor thought that he was guaranteeing a specific loan whereas in fact he was guaranteeing all direct and indirect debts of the principal).
[94] All this evidence will be relevant. See *McMaster University v Wilchar Const Ltd* (1971) 22 D.L.R. (3d) 9.
[95] *General Credits Ltd v Ebsworth* [1986] 2 Qd. R. 162 at 165, in which there was no proof of knowledge or complicity by the creditor.
[96] *Taylor v Johnson* (1983) 151 C.L.R. 422 at 433.
[97] *ibid.* But it is not thought that the specific bars which preclude rescission for misrepresentation (such as affirmation) are strictly applicable in this context.
[98] *Bell v Lever Bros Ltd* [1932] A.C. 161 at 235–236.
[99] See generally J. Beatson, *Anson's Law of Contract* (28th ed., 2002), pp.317–321; *Chitty on Contracts* (28th ed., 1999), Vol. 1 paras 5–024–5–028. It does not matter whether the cause of the mistake is an innocent act or omission of the creditor or an innocent or fraudulent act or omission of a third party. See *Chitty on Contracts* (28th ed., 1999), Vol. 2, para.44–024. The relevance of a fraud by a third party lies in the fact that it provides a reasonable ground for the guarantor's mistaken belief which is a condition of relief: *Associated Japanese Bank (International) Ltd v Crédit du Nord SA* [1989] 1 W.L.R. 255. According to the Court of Appeal in *Great Peace Shipping Ltd v Tsavliris Salvage (International) Ltd* [2002] 3 W.L.R. 1617, there is now no alternative equitable jurisdiction to set a contract aside on the basis of common mistake (*Cf. Solle v Butcher* [1950] 1 K.B. 671).

4–58   In the first Australian edition of this work, the authors boldly stated that principles of common mistake will be of "little practical application" in relation to guarantees.[1] In *Associated Japanese Bank (International) Ltd v Crédit du Nord SA*[2] it was held, however, that a guarantee of the performance of a lease was void for common mistake when the creditor and guarantors both erroneously believed that the goods which were leased existed at the date of the execution of the guarantee. Mr Justice Steyn was of the view that the "subject matter of the guarantee ... was *essentially* different from what it was reasonably believed to be"[3] since the creditor and the guarantors (because they had an interest in the goods through their contingent right of subrogation) regarded the existence of the goods as of fundamental importance as a security. After the authors' false prediction in the first edition, it would perhaps be churlish to cast doubt on the correctness of the decision, but other writers have done so on the basis that, in terms of the existing authorities, the mistake was not sufficiently fundamental.[4] Certainly, it is thought a mistake would not be sufficiently fundamental simply because the guarantor and creditor have made a mistake not as to the existence but merely as to the value of the security.

4–59   Exceptionally, a guarantee may be vitiated on the ground of mutual mistake, that is, where there is an insoluble ambiguity (in an objective sense) and the evidence shows the parties meant different things.[5] For example, the terms of the guarantee may reasonably be interpreted by the guarantor as imposing a limit upon the amount of liability, but conversely, the creditor may reasonably interpret the guarantee as being unlimited in amount.[6] The mistake destroys the apparent agreement of the parties.[7]

4–60   But there will be no operative mistake if the guarantor (as is often the case) has simply contracted upon an erroneous understanding of the meaning of the contract, as objectively construed by the court.[8] In this situation, only one party (the guarantor) is mistaken and the guarantee can only be vitiated on the ground of unilateral mistake, which will require proof that the creditor knew or had good reason to suspect that the guarantor was mistaken.[9]

4–61   A guarantor may be discharged from liability where he is mistaken as to the identity of the principal debtor. For example, in *De Brettes v*

---

[1] J. O'Donovan and J.C. Phillips, *The Modern Contract of Guarantee* (1985), p.129.
[2] [1989] 1 W.L.R. 255.
[3] *ibid*, at 269 (emphasis added).
[4] J.W. Carter, "An Uncommon Mistake" (1991) 3(3) J.C.L. 237.
[5] *Raffles v Wichelhaus* (1864) 2 H. & C. 906; 159 E.R. 373; *Lloyd's Bank plc v Waterhouse* (1991) 10 Tr. L.R. 161. See generally J. Beatson, *Anson's Law of Contract* (28th ed., 2002), pp.322–323; *Chitty on Contracts* (28th ed., 1999), Vol. 1, paras 5.032–5.033.
[6] See similarly *Houlahan v Australian & New Zealand Banking Group Ltd* (1992) 10 F.L.R. 259.
[7] *ibid.* But note that in *Houlahan v Australian & New Zealand Banking Group Ltd* (1992) 10 F.L.R. 259, the guarantee was enforced in respect of the limited amount, which does not accord with the accepted view that there is no concluded arguement.
[8] See generally J. Beatson, *Anson's Law of Contract* (28th ed., 2002), pp.322–323; *Chitty on Contracts* (28th ed., 1999), Vol. 1, para.5–033.
[9] See, in more detail, above, para.4–54.

Goodman[10] the vendor and the guarantor both believed that certain property was being sold to two co-purchasers. The agent, who purported to act on behalf of the "purchasers", only had authority to act for one of them. In these circumstances, the guarantor was relieved of liability under his guarantee of payment of one of the instalments of the purchase price.

(iii) Non est factum

Occasionally a person who signs a guarantee believing that it is a different transaction may successfully invoke the plea of non est factum.[11] The modern boundaries of this defence were redefined by the House of Lords in *Saunders v Anglia Building Society*,[12] Expressed in general terms, the criteria for a successful plea are the following:

4–62

1. The person relying on the plea usually must belong to a class of persons who, through no fault of their own, are unable to have any understanding of the purport of a particular document, because of blindness, illiteracy[13] or some other disability;[14] it will be only in exceptional cases that a person of "full age and understanding"[15] can take advantage of the defence.

2. The signatory must have made a fundamental mistake as to the nature or contents of the document being signed, having regard to the intended practical effect of that document; the document signed must be radically different from the one the signatory intended to sign.[16]

---

[10] (1855) 9 Moo P.C.C. 466; 14 E.R. 375. See also *Provident Accident & White Cross Insurance Co v Dahne and White* [1937] 2 All E.R. 255, where the court held that a surety was not liable under an agreement to indemnify a party providing a bond because the bond had been given to the wrong council. The undertaking was to indemnity the road authority against failure of a contractor to carry out his contract. The evidence showed that the guarantors would not have entered into such a document in respect of the Glamorgan County Council (in place of the Gower Rural District Council).

[11] The defence should be specifically pleaded: *Yerkey v Jones* (1939) 63 C.L.R. 649 at 663.

[12] [1971] A.C. 1004. See also, in Canada, *Royal Bank of Canada v Interior Sign Service Ltd* [1973] 2 W.W.R. 272, BC, and in Australia, *Petelin v Cullen* (1975) 132 C.L.R. 355.

[13] See, *e.g. Lloyds Bank v Waterhouse* (1991) 10 Tr. L.R. 161, CA. Illiteracy is not, in itself, however, a defence in an action to enforce a guarantee as it cannot be equated with mental incapacity or drunkenness: *Barclays Bank Plc v Schwartz* 1995 W.L. 1082384 (unreported, Court of Appeal, June 21, 1995).

[14] *PT Ltd v Maradona Pty Ltd* (1992) 127 A.N.Z. Conv. R. 513 (guarantor suffering from a stroke: plea of non est factum upheld).

[15] [1971] A.C. 1004 at 1016 *per* Lord Reid. Even though a person may be in a position of serious disadvantage from the point of view of the general rules applying to unconscionable transactions (see below, para.4–155) this will probably not by itself be sufficient to bring the signatory within this class of persons: *Broadlands International Finance Ltd v Sly* (1987) A.N.Z. Conv. Rep. 329.

[16] *Saunders v Anglia Building Society* [1971] A.C. 1004 at 1020, 1034. For the plea of non est factum, it is immaterial whether the signatory's fundamental mistake is induced by the creditor or a third party: *Lloyd's Bank v Waterhouse* (1991) 10 Tr. L.R. 161, CA; [1991] Fam. L.R. 23. But the plea is not available where the mistaken belief arises from the guarantor's solicitor, although of course the solicitor may be liable in negligence: *Bradley West Solicitor's Nominees Co Ltd v Keeman* [1994] N.Z.L.R. 111.

>   3. The signatory must show that he took all reasonable precautions
>   in the circumstances to ascertain the nature of the document.[17]

4–63   As a successful plea of non est factum renders a contract void,[18] these
stringent criteria have been formulated with a desire to protect the
interests of third parties. A guarantor will have some difficulty in satisfying
them. In many cases the guarantor will fail to prove an absence of
negligence[19] (see above, No.3) because the guarantor entered into the
guarantee without reading it and with an indifference as to what he was
signing.[20] Prior to the decision in *Saunders v Anglia Building Society*[21]
there were cases[22] where the defence succeeded, but those decisions are
not consistent with the requirement that the signatory must take
reasonable precautions to ascertain what he was signing.[23] Indeed, it was
at one time held[24] that the requirement was not essential to a successful
plea where the signature was induced by fraud, but this view was
specifically rejected in *Saunders v Anglia Building Society*.[25] Even illiterate
guarantors will be unable to rely on the plea of non est factum if they do
not ask for the documents to be read to them and their nature explained.
Consequently the plea will only be available to them where the guarantee
was read to them and they were misled into believing that the document
was fundamentally different from the one they believed they were
signing.[26]

---

[17] The onus is on the signatory to prove that he took care to inform himself of the purport and
effect of the document: *Saunders v Anglia Building Society* [1971] A.C. 1004 at 1027 *per* Lord
Wilberforce.

[18] For this reason, equitable considerations such as delay will not bar relief where the plea of
non est factum is successful: *George As Executor of the Estate of Kate Habsie George v Paul
George Pty Ltd* (unreported, Sup Ct, NSW Equity Division, Santow J., February 29, 1996)
(BC 9600347 at 28).

[19] Note that where the other party knows or has reason to suspect that the document was
executed under a misapprehension, on one view there is no need for the signatory to prove an
absence of negligence, unless a third party has taken an interest under the contract: *Petelin v
Cullen* (1975) 132 CLR 355 at 360. But in these circumstances the signatory will be able to rely
on the principles of unilateral mistake: see above, para.4–54.

[20] e.g. *Avon Finance Co Ltd v Bridger* [1985] 2 All E.R. 281; *NZI Ltd v Cane* (unreported, HC
(NZ), February 14, 1985); *Beneficial Finance Co of Canada v Telkes* [1977] 6 W.W.R. 22; *First
Independent Bank v Proby* [1966] 57 W.W.R. 360. In *Lloyd's Bank Plc v Waterhouse* (1991) 10
Tr.L.R. 161, Woolf L.J. held that the defendant had been careless by failing to disclose his
disability (illiteracy), but the majority (Purchas L.J. and Sir Edward Eveleigh) thought that
the defendant was not careless because he had energetically investigated the ambit of the
guarantee.

[21] [1971] A.C. 1004.

[22] *Muskham Finance Ltd v Howard* [1963] 1 Q.B. 904; *Carlisle & Cumberland Banking Co v
Bragg* [1911] 1 K.B. 489; *Carlton & United Breweries Ltd v Elliott* [1960] V.R. 320 (which
specifically stated that the signatory's negligence was immaterial); *J.R. Watkins Co v Hannah*
[1926] 4 DLR 93; *Rural Bank of New South Wales v Hobby* [1967] 1 N.S.W.R. 210.

[23] Negligence or carelessness in the context of a plea of non est factum is not the same as in
the tort of negligence: *Petelin v Cullen* (1975) 132 C.L.R. 355 at 360.

[24] *Carlisle & Cumberland Banking Co v Bragg* [1911] 1 K.B. 489.

[25] [1971] A.C. 1004 at 1019, 1038.

[26] *Hambros Bank Ltd v British Historic Buildings Trust* [1995] N.P.C. 179; *Barclays Bank v
Schwartz* [1995] 1 C.L.Y. 2492.

The guarantor will also have difficulty establishing that the mistake is   **4-64**
sufficiently fundamental.[27] The mistake does not have to be as to the legal
character of the document but may be as to the contents.[28] But it is unclear
if the guarantor is discharged where he believes that his liability is limited
to a specific amount, or extends only to particular transactions, if it is in
fact a more extensive liability. Some decisions[29] indicate that such mistakes
are not fundamental, but in *Lloyd's Bank Plc v Waterhouse*.[30] Purchas L.J.
was of the view that a guarantor's liability under an all-moneys guarantee
was fundamentally different from liability under a loan account for the
purchase of a farm, even though the all-moneys guarantee imposed an
upper limit on the guarantor's liability to the extent of the amount of the
loan. This was because the all-moneys guarantee would render the
guarantor liable for debts incurred in activities other than farming.[31]

It appears that a false belief that the principal transaction is secured is   **4-65**
not fundamental[32] or even that the signatory enters into a transaction
believing it to be one of guarantee whereas it is in fact one of indemnity,
imposing a liability on the signatory regardless of the principal's default.[33]

5. ILLEGALITY

(i) Overview

Guarantees which are unenforceable on grounds of illegality may   **4-66**
conveniently be grouped into four main categories:[34]

    (a) where the very making of the guarantee itself is expressly or
        impliedly prohibited by statute;

---

[27] But for a clear case of a mistake being fundamental, see *Westpac Banking Corp v McDougall* [1988] B.C.L. 865 (mistaken belief that the document gave authority to open a bank account).

[28] In *Saunders v Anglia Building Society* [1971] A.C. 1004, the House of Lords specifically stated this to be the case and overruled the earlier test based upon a distinction between the legal character and contents of a document. Earlier decisions had held that the defence was only available where the mistake was one as to the legal character of the document.

[29] *Bank of A/asia v Reynell* (1891) 10 N.Z.L.R. 257 (a difference between £500 and £5,000 was held not to be substantial, although the case was decided before the abolition of the rule that a mistake as to the contents of the document was sufficient to establish the plea, as indicated in n.29); *Canadian Imperial Bank of Commerce v Dura Wood Preservers Ltd* (1979) 102 D.L.R. (3d) 78; *Stewart and McDonald v Young* (1894) 38 Sol. J. 385.

[30] (1991) 10 Tr.L.R. 161.

[31] *Cf.*, however, the view of Woolf L.J. (with Sir Edward Eveleigh not discussing this issue).

[32] *Canadian Imperial Bank of Commerce v Dura Wood Preservers Ltd* (1979) 102 D.L.R. (3d) 78, SC. *Cf. Chiswick Investments v Pevats* [1990] 1 N.Z.L.R. 169 (mistake as to capacity).

[33] Zelling J. in *O'Brien v Australia & New Zealand Bank Ltd* [1971] 5 S.A.S.R. 347 at 357.

[34] See generally G.H. Treitel, *The Law of Contract* (11th ed., 2003), Ch. 12. *Chitty on Contracts* (28th ed., 1999), Vol. 1, paras 17–001–17–197; J. Beatson, *Anson's Law of Contract* (28th ed., 2002), Ch. 9. See also The Honourable Mr Justice P.D. Connolly, "Illegal Contracts—A Case for Surgery?" (Papers presented at the 22nd Australian Legal Convention, Brisbane, 1983), pp.58–67. See a similar classification by Gibbs A.C.J. in *Yango Pastoral Co Pty Ltd v First Chicago Australia Ltd* (1978) 139 C.L.R. 410 at 413 in the context of statutory illegality.

(b) guarantees to do something which infringe public policy or which are forbidden by statute;

(c) guarantees ex facie lawful which are made to effect a purpose which is rendered unlawful by statute or by public policy; and

(d) guarantees ex facie lawful but *performed* in a manner which contravenes a statute.

4–67 As we shall see, the effect of illegality upon guarantees depends upon a number of factors which are sometimes uncertain in their application.

(ii) Guarantees expressly or impliedly prohibited by statute

(a) The general principles

4–68 Guarantees which are expressly or impliedly prohibited by statute are unenforceable.[35] It is immaterial that the parties did not intend to break the law, and generally even an innocent party may not enforce such a guarantee.[36]

4–69 The defence of illegality in such cases is not merely a right of the defendant; it is an impediment to the plaintiff's cause of action so that the court can refuse to enforce the guarantee on grounds of public policy.[37]

4–70 An express prohibition can be inferred even if the prohibition is not explicit.[38] The court will acknowledge an express prohibition if the substance of the prohibition is sufficiently clear.[39]

4–71 In some cases, it is not clear whether the statute in question is intended to prohibit the guarantee or merely to exact a penalty for a contravention. In determining whether a guarantee is impliedly prohibited and therefore unenforceable, several factors are important. Perhaps the paramount consideration in these cases is the object of the statute.[40] Is the statute intended to protect the general public from possible fraud or injury or merely to impose a penalty for the benefit of revenue?[41] If the statute is

---

[35] *St John Shipping Corp v Joseph Rank Ltd* [1957] 1 Q.B. 267 at 283; *Levy v Yates* (1838) 8 A. & E. 129; 112 E.R. 785. See also *Archbolds (Freightage) Ltd v S. Spanglett Ltd* [1961] 1 Q.B. 374 at 384, *per* Pearce L.J.; at 388 *per* Devlin L.J. As to the effect of illegality on a contract, see *Standard Chartered Bank v Pakistan National Shipping Corporation (No.2)* [2000] 1 Lloyd's Rep. 218 at 227–228 and 231–232. As to pleading illegality, see *Birkett v Acorn Business Machines* [1992] 2 All E.R. (Comm) 429.

[36] *St John Shipping Corp v Joseph Rank Ltd* [1957] 1 Q.B. 267 at 283; *Anderson Ltd v Daniel* [1924] 1 K.B. 138; *Holman v Johnson* (1775) 1 Cowp. 341 at 343; 98 E.R. 1120 at 1121.

[37] *Bird v British Celanese Ltd* [1945] 1 K.B. 336; *Montague v Pooley* [1951] St. R. Qd. 291; *Clarke v Ritchey* (1865) 11 Gr. 499; *Jackman v Mitchell* (1807) 13 Ves. Jun. 581; 33 E.R. 412.

[38] *Re Mahmoud and Ispahani* [1921] 2 K.B. 716.

[39] *ibid.*

[40] *Meliss v Shirley and Fremantle Local Board of Health* (1885) 16 Q.B.D. 446 at 451–452; *Shaw v Groom* [1970] 2 Q.B. 504; *Bradshaw v Gilbert's A/asian Agency (Vic) Pty Ltd* (1952) 86 C.L.R. 209; *Pretorius Pty Ltd v Muir and Neil Pty Ltd* [1976] 1 N.S.W.L.R. 213.

[41] *Victorian Daylesford Syndicate Ltd v Dott* [1905] 2 Ch. 624; *Cope v Rowlands* (1836) 2 M. & W. 149; 150 E.R. 707; *Taylor v Crowland Gas & Coke Co* (1854) 10 Exch. 293; *Little v Poole* (1829) 9 B. & C. 192; 109 E.R. 71.

designed to protect the public[42] the courts will generally treat a guarantee given in breach of the statute as impliedly prohibited and unenforceable, whereas if the object of the statute would be adequately served by the sanction of a penalty for offenders the guarantee will not be impliedly prohibited and may be enforceable.[43] While the imposition of a penalty is sometimes said to raise a presumption of an implied prohibition,[44] this presumption can easily be rebutted.[45] In *Yango Pastoral Co Pty Ltd v First Chicago Australia Ltd*[46] it was assumed that the plaintiffs had carried on banking business without the authority required by s.8 of the Banking Act 1959 (Cth). Did this breach prevent the plaintiffs from recovering \$132,600 advanced to the defendants on the security of a mortgage, which was supported by a guarantee? The High Court of Australia considered that the central question was whether the mortgage and the guarantee were impliedly prohibited by the Act. It found that there was no implied prohibition because, *inter alia*, the penalty imposed by the Act was quite independent of the number of banking transactions conducted on any day of contravention; the penalty was not imposed in respect of each transaction. In other words, the penalty was directed at the carrying on of banking business, as distinct from the transactions involved in banking business. Moreover, s.8 of the Banking Act 1959 (Cth) did not prohibit any manner of performance for transactions involving mortgages (or guarantees), so that the contravention of the Act in carrying on banking business without the necessary authority did not render the mortgage (or guarantee) invalid or unenforceable on the grounds of an implied prohibition.[47]

Another relevant factor in determining whether a statute impliedly prohibits a guarantee is the reasonableness of the result.[48] If a finding of an implied prohibition would produce an absurd, inconvenient or unreasonable result, then the court may conclude that the guarantee is not impliedly prohibited.[49] In *Yango Pastoral Co Ltd v First Chicago Australia Ltd*[50] Mason J. observed that it might have been very inconvenient or unreasonable to treat all banking transactions as impliedly prohibited by the Banking Act 1959 (Cth) because depositors might, therefore, be prevented from recovering their money from a corporation carrying on banking business in breach of the Act.

4–72

---

[42] This factor is influential but not necessarily decisive: see, *e.g. Shaw v Groom* [1970] 2 Q.B. 504; *Yango Pastoral Co Pty Ltd v First Chicago Australia Ltd* (1978) 139 C.L.R. 410 at 414.
[43] See *Victorian Daylesford Syndicate Ltd v Dott* [1905] 2 Ch. 624 at 629–630; *Marks v Jolly* (1938) 38 S.R. (NSW) 351 at 357; *Chai Sau Yin v Liew Kwee Sam* [1962] A.C. 304; *Yango Pastoral Co Pty Ltd v First Chicago Australia Ltd* (1978) 139 C.L.R. 410 at 414.
[44] See *Dalgety & New Zealand Loan Ltd v C. Imeson Pty Ltd* [1964] N.S.W.R. 638.
[45] *ibid.*
[46] (1978) 139 C.L.R. 410. Cf. *Ambassador Refrigeration Pty Ltd v Trocadero Building & Investment Co Pty Ltd* [1968] 1 N.S.W.R. 75.
[47] See also *Kelly v Australian & New Zealand Banking Group Ltd* (unreported, Qld Sup Ct, Demack J., May 31, 1993) (where the guarantee served a purpose far removed from the allegedly illegal activity of carrying on the business of a real estate agent without a licence).
[48] See *Chitty on Contracts* (28th ed., 1999), vol. 1, para.17–145.
[49] See *St John Shipping Corp v Joseph Rank Ltd* [1957] 1 Q.B. 267; *Shaw v Groom* [1970] 2 Q.B. 504.
[50] (1978) 139 C.L.R. 410.

4–73   Examples of guarantees expressly or impliedly prohibited by statute include guarantees given to evade licensing laws[51] or the Money Lenders Acts,[52] or to circumvent a prohibition in the companies legislation on a company purchasing its own shares.[53]

(b) Can a guarantee constitute a preference?

4–74   A preference is not expressly prohibited by ss.239 and 340 of the Insolvency Act 1986, but it can be set aside as against the liquidator or the trustee in bankruptcy of the debtor who granted the preference.[54] For present purposes it will be sufficient to address the fundamental question whether a guarantee confers a preference on the creditor. The hallmark of a preference is that it puts the creditor in a better position in the liquidation or bankruptcy than it would have been in if the transactions or dealing had not occurred. Essentially, the effect of a preference is to give a creditor a priority or advantage over other unsecured creditors or priority creditors in respect of past indebtedness of the bankrupt debtor or insolvent company.[55]

4–75   But even where guarantee is given to a creditor in respect of the guarantor's past indebtedness, it is not a preference because it does not constitute a transaction or act involving a dealing with, or relating to, property of the guarantor.[56] A guarantee is essentially a personal obligation to answer for the debt or default of another if that other person defaults.[57] Consequently, a guarantee has no effect upon the statutory order of application of assets in the ultimate liquidation of the guarantor[58] since it usually creates merely an unsecured, personal liability. It does not improve the creditor's position in the bankruptcy or liquidation of the guarantor vis-à-vis other unsecured creditors of the guarantor. It appears, therefore, that the giving of a personal guarantee does not constitute a preference.

4–76   It is different where the "guarantee" takes the form of a third party mortgage under which the mortgagor pledges his assets to secure payment of the principal debt or performance of the principal obligation of the

---

[51] *Ritchie v Smith* (1848) 6 C.B. 462; 136 E.R. 1329. See also *Brown v Moore* (1902) 32 S.C.R. 93 (a guarantee of payment for the price of intoxicating liquor sold contrary to a statutory prohibition was held to be invalid).
[52] See *Scholefield Goodman & Sons Ltd v Gange* [1980] A.C.L.D. 33. The Moneylenders Acts have been replaced by the Consumer Credit Act 1974. Under s.40(2) of that act a regulated agreement with a person who carries on a consumer credit business without a licence is not illegal but merely unenforceable against the debtor unless the Director General of Fair Trading otherwise orders; *Chitty on Contracts* (28th ed., 1999) Vol. 1, para.17–149.
[53] See below, para.4–85.
[54] See generally S. Rajani, *Tolley's Corporate Insolvency* (1994) paras B9.4 and C10.4 and I.F. Fletcher, *The Law of Insolvency* (2nd ed., 1996), pp.642–643.
[55] *Re a Company No. 005009 of 1987 Ex p. Coop* (1988) 4 B.C.C. 424. *Cf. Robertson v Grigg* (1932) 47 C.L.R. 257; *Burns v Stapleton* (1959) 102 C.L.R. 97.
[56] *Re Jaques McAskell Advertising Freeth Division Pty Ltd (in liq)* [1984] 1 N.S.W.L.R. 249.
[57] See above, paras 1–18 to 1–27.
[58] *Burns v Stapleton* (1959) 102 C.L.R. 97 at 104.

borrower or principal obligor.[59] Such a guarantee clearly affects the assets of the guarantor/third party mortgagor. But does it relate to the past indebtedness of the third party mortgagor to the mortgagee? The answer would appear to be "no", unless the third party mortgage is expressed to cover some existing indebtedness or liability of the third party mortgagor to the mortgagee, in addition to the liability of the principal debtor. In general, therefore, a third party mortgage will not constitute a preference.

A guarantee might, however, be avoided where it is given to one   **4–77** creditor in a secret arrangement to obtain the creditor's support for a composition agreement. But here the guarantee is invalidated on the grounds that it offends public policy; not because it is a preference.[60]

While it is generally true that the *giving* of a guarantee or a third party   **4–78** mortgage does not constitute a preference, a preference may arise *in favour of a guarantor*. A contingent creditor such as a guarantor may be regarded as a creditor for the purposes of the preference provisions if that person was *already* a guarantor at the time of the transaction in question. It is not sufficient that he *becomes* a creditor as a result of that transaction.[61]

Consider the following example: a guarantor provides an all-accounts   **4–79** guarantee in respect of the liability of a company; the guarantor becomes concerned about his potential liability under the guarantee and advises the company that he will revoke his guarantee in respect of future advances by the lender to the company unless he receives some security from the company by way of counter-indemnity; the company gives the guarantor a mortgage over its shares in a listed public company. In this situation, the company has conferred a preference upon the guarantor as an unsecured contingent creditor of the company. If the lender enforced the guarantee and the guarantor paid some or all the principal debt, he would be entitled to an indemnity from the company in respect of any amounts he paid off the principal debt. In this sense he is a contingent creditor of the company, and the share mortgage gives him an advantage over unsecured creditors of the company in respect of debts due and owing to them in that it purports to exclude the shares from a pari passu distribution. The advantage is conferred in respect of an already existing contingent liability, so it is a preference.[62]

Four conclusions can be drawn from this analysis: **4–80**

(i) the giving of a guarantee does not of itself confer a preference upon the lender;

(ii) nor does the grant of a third party mortgage constitute a preference unless it secures past indebtedness of the mortgagor as well as the principal borrower;

[59] *Re Conley Ex p. The Trustee v Barclay's Bank* [1938] 2 All E.R. 127; *Jowitt v Callaghan* (1938) 38 S.R. (NSW) 512.
[60] *Lewis v Jones* (1825) 4 B. & C. 506 at 511; 107 E.R. 1148 at 1150; *Pendlebury v Walker* (1841) 4 Y. & C. Ex. 424; 160 E.R. 1072.
[61] *Re Jaques McAskell Advertising Freeth Division Pty Ltd (in liq)* [1984] 1 N.S.W.L.R. 249.
[62] It is no longer necessary to establish a dominant intention to prefer the creditor: *Re Mc Bacon Ltd* [1990] B.C.C. 78.

(iii) a preference can be conferred by the borrower on a guarantor in respect of an already existing contingent liability;

(iv) but where the guarantor is given a security by way of counter-indemnity as a condition precedent to the operation of his guarantee and to protect the guarantor against any liability he might later incur under the guarantee, a preference may arise.

(c) Guarantees of loans to directors and associates

4–81   Another situation where it may be possible to enforce a guarantee despite the existence of illegality is where the relevant statute itself states that the guarantee can be enforced in certain circumstances. A guarantee given contrary to s.330 of the Companies Act 1985 is an illustration. Section 330(2) prohibits a company from providing a guarantee in connection with a loan made to a director of the company, or of its holding company. Moreover, s.330(4) prohibits the company from providing a guarantee or any security in connection with a credit transaction made by any other person for a director of the company or his associates. A transaction or arrangement prohibited by s.330 is voidable at the option of the company unless:

(a) restitution is impossible;

(b) the director has indemnified the company for the loss and damage it has suffered; or

(c) "any rights acquired bona fide for value and without actual notice of the contravention by a person other than the person for whom the transaction or arrangement was made would be affected by its avoidance".

4–82   There is a general prohibition in s.330 of the Companies Act 1985 on a company entering into any guarantee or providing any security in connection with a loan made by any person to a director of the company or of its holding company.[63] Moreover, a "relevant company"[64] is prohibited from entering into a guarantee[65] or providing any security in

---

[63] Companies Act 1985, s.330(2).

[64] This term is defined in s.331(6) of the Companies Act 1985 to mean
"a company which—
   (a) is a public company, or
   (b) is a subsidiary of a public company, or
   (c) is a subsidiary of a company which has as another subsidiary a public company, or
   (d) has a subsidiary which is a public company."

[65] The term "guarantees" is defined in s.331(2) to include an indemnity and cognate expressions must be construed accordingly.

connection with a loan, a quasi loan[66] or a credit transaction[67] made by any other person for directors of the company or directors of its holding company or for persons connected with them.[68] A breach of these prohibitions can attract civil remedies[69] and criminal penalties.[70]

There are, however, exceptions to these statutory prohibitions. First, in the case of a relevant company which is a member of a group of companies, the company is not prohibited from entering into a guarantee or providing any security in connection with a loan or quasi-loan made by any person to another member of the group by reason only that a director of one member of the group is associated with another.[71] Consequently, guarantees provided in respect of inter-company loans in the same group are exempt. Secondly, there are specific exceptions relating to guarantees of minor business transactions relating to relevant companies[72] and guarantees in connection with a credit transaction made by any other person for its holding company.[73] Finally, there is an exception for a money-lending company entering into a guarantee in connection with any other loan or quasi loan.[74]

4–83

Where a company makes a loan contrary to the general prohibition in s.300 of the Insolvency Act 1986, it is not clear whether it can enforce a guarantee given by a third party to secure the loan. In *Corumo Holding Ltd v C Itoh Ltd*[75] Rogers C.J. of the Commercial Division of the Supreme Court of New South Wales held that such a guarantee was not affected by the illegality of the loan under similar legislation. On appeal, this issue did not require determination, but at least Meagher J.A. appeared to take a contrary view.[76] The question remains an open one, but as Rogers C.J. pointed out, if the company cannot enforce the guarantee, it may defeat

4–84

---

[66] A "quasi loan" is a transaction under which the creditor agrees to pay, or pays otherwise than in pursuance of an agreement, a sum for a borrower or agrees to reimburse, or reimburses otherwise than in pursuance of an agreement, expenditure incurred by another party for the borrower where the terms are that the borrowers will reimburse the creditor or where the borrower is under a liability to reimburse the creditor: s.331(3) of the Companies Act 1985.

[67] A "credit transaction" is defined as a transaction under which the creditor:
   (a) supplies any goods or sells any land under a hire-purchase agreement or a conditional sale agreement;
   (b) leases or hires any land or goods in return for periodical payments;
   (c) otherwise disposes of land or supplies goods or services on the understanding that payment is to be deferred: s.331(7).

[68] The range of connected persons is defined in s.364 of the Companies Act 1985.

[69] Generally, the offending guarantee or security is voidable at the insistence of the company unless restitution is no longer possible or unless the rights of innocent third parties have intervened: s.341 of the Companies Act 1985. The directors who authorised the offending transaction must account for any gain they made from the transaction and indemnify the company for any loss it suffers as a result of the transaction: s.341(2).

[70] Companies Act 1985, s.342.

[71] Companies Act 1985, s.333.

[72] Companies Act 1985, s.335.

[73] Companies Act 1985, s.336.

[74] Companies Act 1985, s.338. The term "money-lending company" is defined in s.338(2). The term "quasi-loan" is defined in s.331(3). See above, n.66.

[75] (1990) 3 A.C.S.R. 438.

[76] (1991) 5 A.C.S.R. 720 at 749–750. Samuels J.A. (at 738) "generally" agreeing; Kirby P. (at 723) expressing no opinion. See also *The Wan Development Sdn Bhd v Co-op Central Bank Bhd* (1989) 2 A.C.S.R. 61.

the objective of the legislation in protecting the company from having its assets misused.[77]

(d) Guarantees as illegal financial assistance to companies acquiring their own shares

4-85   Under s.151 of the Companies Act 1985, there is a general prohibition on a company or any of its subsidiaries giving financial assistance directly or indirectly to a person for the purpose of acquiring shares in the company.[78] It is immaterial whether the financial assistance is provided before or at the same time as the acquisition of the shares.[79] There is a further prohibition on a company or any of its subsidiaries giving financial assistance directly or indirectly to reduce or discharge any liability incurred by a person who has acquired shares in the company.[80]

4-86   In the present context the significance of these prohibitions is that "financial assistance" is defined to include financial assistance given by way of guarantee, security or indemnity, other than an indemnity in respect of the indemnifier's own neglect or default, or by way of release or waiver.[81]

4-87   Where the effect of the guarantee or indemnity is contrary to the prohibition in s.151 of the Companies Act 1985, the guarantee or indemnity is unlawful.[82] Any director who is a party to a breach of this section is guilty of misfeasance and is liable to indemnify the company against any loss caused by the default.[83] Criminal penalties may also be imposed on officers of the company who are guilty of a default under the section.[84]

4-88   The general prohibition on the giving of financial assistance for the purpose of acquiring shares in the company is relaxed in relation to private companies. The prohibition does not apply to a private company where the acquisition of the shares in question is or was an acquisition of shares in the company or, if it is a subsidiary of another private company, in that other company, provided that the provisions of ss.156 to 158 are compiled with in relation to the giving of the financial assistance.[85]

4-89   There are numerous exceptions from the general prohibition on the giving of financial assistance for the purpose of acquiring shares in the company.[86] For example, the prohibition does not apply if:

---

[77] (1990) 3 A.C.S.R. 438 at 451. But there are contrary arguments: see (1991) 5 A.C.S.R. 720 at 749, 750 *per* Meagher J.A.
[78] Companies Act 1985, s.151(1).
[79] *ibid.*
[80] Companies Act 1985, s.151(2).
[81] Companies Act 1985, s.152(1)(a)(ii).
[82] *Belmont Finance Corpn v Williams Furniture Ltd* [1979] Ch. 250; [1979] 1 All E.R. 118, CA. See also *Brady v Brady* [1988] 2 All E.R. 617.
[83] *Steen v Law* [1964] A.C. 287, PC; *Wallersteiner v Moir, Moir v Wallersteiner* [1974] 3 All E.R. 217.
[84] Companies Act 1985, s.151(3).
[85] Companies Act 1985, s.155.
[86] See generally Companies Act 1985, s.153.

(a) the company's principal purpose in giving that assistance is but an incidental part of some larger purpose of the company; and

(b) the assistance is given in good faith in the interests of the company.[87]

However, in the case of a public company, the exceptions relating to the lending of money in the ordinary course of its business and employee shareholding schemes do not apply unless the company has net assets which are not thereby reduced or, to the extent that these assets are thereby reduced, the assistance is provided out of distributable profits.[88]

(iii) Guarantees which infringe public policy

The second main category of guarantees which are illegal are guarantees which infringe public policy in the sense of "some definite and governing principle which the community, as a whole has already adopted either formally by law or tacitly by its general course of corporate life".[89] It is only where there is a substantial degree of impropriety that the guarantee is properly classified as "illegal".[90] Such guarantees are probably unenforceable whether or not the parties know of the illegality.[91] Hence, a guarantee given for the purpose of stifling a prosecution against the principal debtor may be attacked on grounds of public policy,[92] whether or not the alleged offender was in fact guilty and whether or not the prosecution was in fact stifled.[93] Moreover, a guarantee of legal costs incurred in champertous proceedings would be unenforceable as it offends the public policy against contracts prejudicial to the administration of justice.[94]

4–90

---

[87] Companies Act 1985, s.153(1).

[88] Companies Act 1985, s.154.

[89] *Wilkinson v Osborne* (1915) 21 C.L.R. 89 at 97. See also *A. v Hayden* (No 2) (1984) 56 ALR 82 at 109. G. Andrews and R. Millett, *Law of Guarantees* (3rd ed., 2000), para.5.59, cite guarantees of a contract to sell or supply prohibited drugs or hard-core pornographic material as guarantees which offend against public policy.

[90] G.H. Treitel, *The Law of Contract* (11th ed., 2003), Ch. 11; *Chitty on Contracts* (28th ed., 1999), Vol. 1, paras 17–003–17—005.

[91] *Thackwell v Barclays Bank Plc* [1986] 1 All E.R. 676; *Sydney Newspaper Publishing Co v Muir* (1888) 9 L.R. (NSW) 375.

[92] *Cannon v Rands* (1870) 23 L.T. 817; *Major v McCraney* (1898) 29 S.C.R. 182; *Jones v Merionethshire Permanent Benefit Building Society* [1892] 1 Ch. 173; *Williams v Bayley* (1866) L.R. 1 H.L. 200; *Osborn v Robbins* 36 NY 365 (1867); *People's Bank of Halifax v Johnson* (1892) 20 S.C.R. 541.

[93] *Cannon v Rands* (1870) 23 L.T. 817; *Seear v Cohen* (1881) 45 L.T. 589. But where there is additional consideration, *e.g.* a forbearance to sue in a civil suit, the mere promise not to institute a prosecution does not by itself make the guarantee void for illegality: *Jones v Merionethshire Permanent Benefit Building Society* [1892] 1 Ch. 173 at 184 *per* Bowen L.J. See *Rowlatt on the Law Relating to Principal and Surety* (4th ed., 1982), p.128. See also *Kerridge v Simmonds* (1907) 4 C.L.R. 253 and *Public Service Employees' Credit Union Co-op Ltd v Campion* (1984) 75 F.L.R. 131.

[94] *Cf. Re Trepca Mines Ltd* (No.2) [1962] Ch. 511. Note that G. Andrews and R. Millett, *Law of Guarantees* (3rd ed., 2000), para.5.59 suggest that it is unlikely that the court would refuse to enforce a guarantee provided as security for the costs of the plaintiff in proceedings which

(iv) Where the purpose of the guarantee is illegal

4–91   In the third category of illegal guarantees fall guarantees which on their face are lawful but which have as their purpose something which is forbidden by statute or which infringes some public policy identified by the courts.[95] In some circumstances the creditor may enforce such a guarantee if he was not implicated in the illegality.[96] An example of a guarantee in this category is a guarantee designed to evade a statutory prohibition such as a guarantee given as part of a sham transaction to avoid legislation limiting the amount of commission payable.[97]

(v) Where the performance of the guarantee is illegal

4–92   The final category of illegal guarantees is guarantees which are ex facie lawful but which are performed in a manner which infringes a statute.[98] Here, the guarantee *as formed* is not illegal but the performance of the guarantee constitutes a breach of an Act.[99] Once again, factors such as inconvenience, disproportionate penalties, unwitting breaches and injury to trade and commerce are relevant considerations in determining whether such a guarantee is illegal.[1] Guarantees in this category are enforceable by the creditor only if the creditor is innocent of the guarantor's illegal performance, and even then the codes are entirely consistent.[2] However, the creditor will not be regarded as innocent if he or she has been culpably negligent concerning the possible illegality.[3]

4–93   It should be emphasised that the effect of illegality on guarantees described in this section can only be stated in general terms. In determining the effect of illegality, the court considers a wide range of

are later successfully challenged by the defendant as champertous because this result would be unfair to the defendant.

[95] See The Honourable Mr Justice P.D. Connolly, "Illegal Contracts—A Case for Surgery?" (Papers Presented at the 22nd Australian Legal Convention, Brisbane, 1983), p.59.

[96] *Mason v Clarke* [1955] A.C. 778; See G.H. Treitel, *The Law of Contract* (11th ed., 2003) pp.486–490. For this reason the innocent bank in *Crédit Suisse v Borough Council of Allerdale* [1995] 1 Lloyd's Rep. 315 would have been able to counter the local authority's defence of illegality, but it could not refute the defence of *ultra vires*.

[97] *Williams v Fleetwood Holdings Ltd* (1973) 41 D.L.R. (3d) 636.

[98] Connolly, *op.cit.*, p.60. An example of where the performance of an obligation under a guarantee might be illegal is where payment by the means stipulated in the guarantee would infringe exchange control legislation: G. Andrews and R. Millett, *Law of Guarantees* (3rd ed., 2000), para.5.60. See also *Lloyds TSB Bank Plc v Rasheed Bank, The Times* January 19, 2000 where EU legislation passed in the aftermath of Iraq's invasion of Kuwait made it unlawful to pay claims arising out of guarantees given to any Iraqi person. See G. Andrews and R. Millett, *Law of Guarantees* (3rd ed., 2000), para.5.60.

[99] *St John Shipping Corp v Joseph Rank Ltd* [1957] 1 Q.B. 267 at 284. See, *e.g. B. and B. Viennese Fashions v Losane* [1952] 1 All E.R. 909 (where the plaintiff was not entitled to recover the price of goods supplied without an invoice because this supply breached art.10(1) of the Utility Mark and Apparel and Textiles (General Provisions) Order 1947 (SR & O 1947/2642), which was revoked by the Utility Goods (Revocation) Order 1952 (SI 1952/489)).

[1] See *Yango Pastoral Co Pty Ltd v First Chicago Australia Ltd* (1978) 139 C.L.R. 410 at 417 *per* Gibbs A.C.J.

[2] *Archbolds (Freightage) Ltd v S. Spanglett Ltd* [1961] 1 Q.B. 374 discussed by G.H. Treitel, *The Law of Contract* (11th ed., 2003), pp.486–489.

[3] See *Askey v Golden Wine Co Ltd* [1948] 2 All E.R. 35 and Connolly, *op.cit.*, p.60.

factors: the source of the illegality; innocence or knowledge of the illegality; the extent to which the illegal purpose of the guarantee has been achieved; whether the creditor is relying on the illegal guarantee or an independent cause of action; public policy considerations and severability of the illegal portion of the contract.[4] Moreover, the courts have adopted a wide spectrum of techniques to avoid any unfair results which might arise from an application of the strict rule that an illegal contract is enforceable.[5] The standard textbooks on contract law contain a comprehensive analysis of these techniques.[6]

(vi) Severance

A guarantee which contains an illegal provision is not necessarily invalid. The general test for determining whether the offending provisions are severable from the rest of the agreement was declared by Jordan C.J. in *McFarland v Daniell*:[7]   **4–94**

"When valid promises supported by legal consideration are associated with, but separate in form from, invalid promises, the test of whether they are severable is whether they are in substance so connected with the others as to form an indivisible whole which cannot be taken to pieces without altering its nature ... If the elimination of the invalid promises changes the extent only but not the kind of contract, the valid promises are severable."[8]

While this statement has been approved by the High Court of Australia[9] and the Privy Council,[10] it is not an exclusive test because there are no rules which will decide all cases.[11]   **4–95**

6. IMPROPER EXERCISE OF POWER

Under the general law, the directors of a company have a duty to exercise their powers bona fide in the best interests of the company and for a proper purpose.[12] This duty is particularly relevant to corporate guarantees. Where the directors breach these duties in granting a   **4–96**

---

[4] See *Chitty on Contracts* (28th ed., 1999), Vol. 1, paras 17–003–17–005.
[5] See Connolly, *op. cit.*, pp.62–65.
[6] See *Chitty on Contracts* (28th ed., 1999), Vol. 1, para.17–007.
[7] (1938) 38 S.R. (NSW) 337.
[8] *ibid.* at 345.
[9] *Thomas Brown & Sons Ltd v Fazal Deen* (1962) 108 C.L.R. 391 at 411.
[10] *Carney v Herbert* [1985] A.C. 301 at 310–311.
[11] *ibid.*, at 309.
[12] See generally *Piercy v S. Mills & Co* [1920] Ch. 77; *Hogg v Cramphorn Ltd* [1967] Ch. 254; *Bamford v Bamford* [1970] Ch. 212; *Charterbridge Corpn Ltd v Lloyd's Bank Ltd* [1970] Ch. 62; *Whitehouse v Carlton Hotels* (1987) 70 A.L.R. 251; *Colarc Pty Ltd v Donarc Pty Ltd* (1991) 4 A.C.S.R. 155; *Howard Smith Ltd v Ampol Petroleum Ltd* [1974] A.C. 821. See also L.C.B. Gower, *Principles of Modern Company Law* (5th ed., 1992), pp.553–558 and R.R. Pennington, *Company Law* (7th ed., 1995), pp.780–782. In relation to corporate guarantees, see *Re Efron's*

guarantee to a creditor in the name of the company the guarantee will be voidable at the option of the company if the creditor knew of the breach of duty or was put on inquiry.[13]

4–97   In *Northside Developments Pty Ltd v Registrar-General*[14] Brennan J. observed:

> "A creditor will ordinarily be put on inquiry when his debtor offers as security a guarantee given by a third party company whose business is not ordinarily the giving of guarantees, for the execution of guarantees and supporting securities for another's liabilities, not being for the purposes of a company's business nor otherwise for its benefit, is not ordinarily within the authority of the officers or agents of the company."[15]

His Honour continued:

> "Of course, the circumstances may show that the giving of such a guarantee ... is for the company's benefit. For example, it may be for the benefit of solvent companies within a group to guarantee the liabilities of a holding company in order to benefit the guarantor companies as well as other members of the group."[16]

4–98   Yet even where the guarantor companies are associated with the borrowing corporation and have legitimate interests in its survival, the guarantees will not be enforceable if the borrowing corporation was clearly insolvent and it was clear that the creditor would call upon the guarantees immediately.[17] It is not for the corporate benefit of the guarantor companies to provide a guarantee of the borrower's debts in these circumstances even though the guarantors would be entitled to an indemnity and rights of set off in respect of any amounts paid to the creditor under the guarantees.[18] If the creditor knew of this breach of duty by the directors of the guarantor companies or had been put on inquiry, the guarantees would not be enforceable. Nor would it be possible to obtain an order for specific performance of a covenant by the borrowing corporation to procure guarantees from its subsidiaries in this

---

Tie & Knitting Mills Pty Ltd (in liq) [1932] V.L.R. 8; *Re Hapytoz Pty Ltd (in liq)* [1937] V.L.R. 40.

[13] *Re David Payne & Co Ltd* [1904] 2 Ch. 608 at 613, 617–618 and 619–620. As to the extent of the inquiry required, see *Northside Developments Pty Ltd v Registrar-General* (1990) 8 A.C.L.C. 611.

[14] (1990) 8 A.C.L.C. 611.

[15] *ibid.*, at 632.

[16] *ibid.*, at 632. See also *Pyramid Building Society v Scorpion Hotels Pty Ltd* (1996) 4 A.C.L.C. 679 at 690.

[17] *ANZ Executors & Trustees Co Ltd v Qintex Australia Ltd* (1990) 8 A.C.L.C. 980.

[18] *ibid.* Cf. G.A. Nation III, "Some Thoughts About Intercorporate Guarantees, Fair Consideration, and Reasonably Equivalent Value" (1987–1988) 37 Drake L. Rev. 569, where it is suggested that such guarantees are supported by consideration because the guarantor corporation acquires an interest in the principal debtor's assets through its rights of exoneration, reimbursement and subrogation.

situation.[19] These principles were confirmed by the decision of the New South Wales Court of Appeal in *Bank of New South Wales v Fiberi Pty Ltd*.[20] In that case, the bank was held to have been put on inquiry by four factors:

(a) there appeared to be no commercial benefit for Fiberi Pty Ltd in entering into the guarantee and third party mortgage;

(b) the bank had not made a search to ascertain who were the proper officers of Fiberi Pty Ltd to execute the documents;

(c) the bank had not inquired whether one of the directors was the managing director of Fiberi Pty Ltd with authority to commit it to the guarantee and third party mortgage; and

(d) the land over which the mortgage was granted was a residential property and was unlikely to form part of Fiberi Pty Ltd's commercial property portfolio.[21]

A much more potent weapon for attacking guarantees which lack corporate benefit is s.238 of the Insolvency Act 1986. Where a company in liquidation[22] or subject to an administration order[23] entered into a transaction[24] with any person at an undervalue at a "relevant time", as defined in s.240, the liquidator or administrator can apply to the court under s.238 for an order restoring the position to what it would have been if the company had not entered into the transaction.[25]   **4–99**

A company enters into a transaction with a person at an undervalue if the terms of the transaction provide for the company to receive no consideration or consideration which is significantly less than the value of the consideration provided by the company.[26]   **4–100**

The "relevant time" for the purposes of s.238 is the period of two years ending with the onset of insolvency, where the undervalue transaction was with a person connected with the company, and six months ending with the onset of insolvency, where the undervalue transaction was with a person who is not connected with the company.[27] But these purviews apply to s.238 only if the company was unable to pay its debts at the time of the transaction or became unable to pay its debs in consequence of the transaction at an undervalue.[28] Undervalue transactions during the so-   **4–101**

---

[19] *ANZ Executors & Trustees Co Ltd v Qintex Australia Ltd* (1990) 8 A.C.L.C. 980.
[20] (1994) 12 A.C.L.C. 48.
[21] For a detailed analysis of this case, see O'Donovan, "Corporate Benefit in Relation to Guarantees and Third Party Mortgages" (1996) 24 A.B.L.R. 126.
[22] s.238 applies to a company that "goes into liquidation". This phrase is defined in s.247(2) of the Insolvency Act 1986.
[23] As to administration orders, see ss.8–27 of the Insolvency Act 1986.
[24] The term "transaction" is defined in s.436 of the Insolvency Act 1986.
[25] Insolvency Act 1986, s.238(1)–(3). There is a similar regime in relation to transactions at an undervalue by a debtor who becomes bankrupt. See s.339 of the Insolvency Act 1986.
[26] Insolvency Act 1986, s.238(4).
[27] Insolvency Act 1986, s.240(1)(a) and (b).
[28] Insolvency Act 1986, s.240(2). As to the meaning of the phrase "unable to pay its debts" see s.123 of the Insolvency Act 1986.

called "interim period" between the presentation of a petition for an administration order and the actual making of the administration order are also caught by s.238.[29]

4–102 Even if the undervalue transaction occurred at a relevant time, the court must not make an order under s.238 if it is satisfied:

(a) that the company entered into the transaction in good faith and for the purpose of carrying on its business; and

(b) that at the time of the transaction there were reasonable grounds for believing that the transaction would benefit the company.[30]

4–103 A guarantee or third party mortgage may well be a transaction at an undervalue if the benefits which will accrue to the company are outweighed by the detriment it will incur by entering into the transaction. If the guarantee or third party mortgage relates to past indebtedness of an insolvent company and it is likely that it will be enforced immediately, the transaction would clearly be a transaction at an undervalue.[31]

4–104 Section 238 of the Insolvency Act 1986 gives the court a broad power to make a remedial order. This could include an order releasing or discharging, wholly or partly, a security or guarantee given by the company under, or in connection with, the transaction and an order requiring the third party to repay to the company some or all the money it has received under the transaction.

4–105 Section 238 represents a time bomb so far as cross guarantees within corporate groups are concerned. It poses a serious threat to guarantees and third party mortgages which lack corporate benefit and it is only a matter of time before liquidators and administrators realise the potential of this provision.[32]

7. FETTERING DISCRETION AND EXECUTIVE NECESSITY

4–106 The directors of a company have a fiduciary duty not to fetter their discretion.[33] In *Coronation Syndicate Ltd v Lilienfield*,[34] Solomon J. explained this principle in the following terms:

[29] Insolvency Act 1986, s.240.
[30] Insolvency Act 1986, s.238(5).
[31] *ANZ Executors & Trustee Ltd v Qintex Australia Ltd (rec & man apptd)* [1991] 2 Qd. R. 360. See also *Pacific Projects Pty Ltd (in liq)* [1990] 2 Qd. R. 541 (where a guarantee and third party mortgage was successfully challenged under s.120 of the Bankruptcy Act 1966 (Cth), which was a predecessor of s.588 FB of the Corporations Act 2001 (Cth).
[32] For an example of a court order under s.242 of the Insolvency Act 1986 reducing a guarantee as a gratuitous alienation, see *Jackson v Royal Bank of Scotland* 2002 S.L.T. 1123.
[33] See *Clark v Workman* [1920] 1 Ir. R. 107; *Dawson International Plc v Coats Paton Plc* 1989 S.L.T. 655 (1st Div); *Thorby v Goldberg* (1964) 112 C.L.R. 597.
[34] 1903 T.S. 489.

"But the directors are in a fiduciary position, and it is their duty to do what they consider will best serve the interests of the shareholders. If, therefore, they have bound themselves by contract to do a certain thing, and therefore have bona fide come to the conclusion that it is not in the interests of the shareholders that they should carry out their undertaking, I do not think that the court would be justified in interfering with their discretion and compelling them to do what they honestly believe would be detrimental to the interests of the shareholders. ... For this breach of contract they may be personally liable in damages, but if that is their honest conviction I do not see how we can compel them to perform their contract."[35]

However, it is quite different where the directors resolve to provide a **4–107** guarantee for and on behalf of their company. While this guarantee creates merely a contingent liability, the directors may not later renege on the guarantee on the ground that it fetters their discretion as to future action and compels them to perform a contract which might not be in the best interests of the shareholders when the guarantee is enforced. The proper time for the exercise of the directors' discretion is at the time of the negotiation of the guarantee, not at the date when the contract is to be performed.[36] If, at the time the guarantee is executed, the directors were bona fide of the opinion that it was in the best interests of the company, then they are able to bind their company to do whatever is required under that contract.[37] Their fiduciary duty to retain their discretions presents no obstacle to enforcement of the guarantee.[38]

In the public arena, the rough equivalent of the duty not to fetter **4–108** discretion is the doctrine of executive necessity.[39] This doctrine prevents the executive arm of a government from restricting its future actions where a contract obliges the executive to exercise its statutory duties in a particular way.[40] In effect, the executive is not bound by a contract which inhibits it in carrying out its specific statutory duties or exercising its statutory discretions. Devlin L.J. captured the essence of the doctrine in *Commissioners of Crown Lands v Page*:[41]

"When the Crown, or any other person, is entrusted, whether by virtue of the prerogative or by statute, with discretionary powers to be exercised for the public good, it does not, when making a private contract in general terms, undertake (and it may be that it could not

---

[35] *ibid.*, at 497.
[36] *Thorby v Goldberg* (1964) 112 C.L.R. 597 at 605 *per* Kitto J.
[37] *ibid.*
[38] See also, LCB Gower, *Principles of Modern Company Law* (5th ed., 1992), pp.558–559.
[39] See M. Aronson and H. Whitmore, *Public Torts and Contracts* (1982), p.194, N. Seddon, *Government Contracts* (2nd ed., 1999), paras 5.2–5.9, and S.D. Hotop, "State Instrumentalities" (Law Society of Western Australia, Continuing Legal Education: General Services, 1989), pp.7–11.
[40] M. Breheny and J. Beaven, "Australian Federal and State Government Guarantees—A Legal Overview" (1986) 4 J.I.B.L. 231 at 235.
[41] [1960] 2 Q.B. 274.

even with the use of specific language validly undertake) to fetter itself in the use of those powers, and in the exercise of its discretion."[42]

4–109   His Lordship added that the doctrine did not necessarily mean "that the Crown can escape from any contract which it finds disadvantageous by saying that it never promised to act otherwise than for the public good".[43] The courts will draw a distinction between "an act done for a general executive purpose" and "an act done for the purpose of achieving a particular result under the contract in question".[44] Only the former type of act falls within the doctrine of executive necessity.

4–110   An analogous doctrine applies to statutory authorities so that where such an authority gives a contractual undertaking which is incompatible with the due exercise or performance of its statutory powers or duties, the undertaking is *ultra vires*.[45] The test of the validity of the contract or undertaking is whether it is consistent and compatible with the objects of the statutory authority's powers and duties.[46]

4–111   In *Ansett Transport Industries (Operations) Pty Ltd v Commonwealth*,[47] Mason J. (as he then was) considered this principle and the kindred doctrine of executive necessity in detail. His Honour noted the competing policy interests at stake:

> "Public confidence in government dealings and contracts would be greatly disturbed if all contracts which affect public welfare or fetter future executive action were held not to be binding on the government or on public authorities. And it would be detrimental to the public interest to deny to the government or a public authority power to enter a valid contract merely because the contract affects public welfare. Yet on the other hand the public interest requires that neither the government nor a public authority can by a contract disable itself or its officer from performing a statutory duty or from exercising a discretionary power conferred by or under a statute by binding itself or its officer not to perform the duty or to exercise the discretion in a particular way in the future."[48]

---

[42] *ibid.*, at 291. See also *Ayr Harbour Trustees v Oswald* (1883) 8 App. Cas. 623; *Rederiaktiebolaget Amphitrite v The King* [1921] 3 K.B. 500; *Ansett Transport Industries (Operations) Pty Ltd v Commonwealth* (1977) 139 C.L.R. 54.
[43] [1960] 2 Q.B. 274 at 293.
[44] *ibid.*
[45] *Ayr Harbour Trustees v Oswald* (1883) 8 App. Cas. 623; *Birkdale District Electric Supply Co Ltd v Southport Corp* [1926] A.C. 355; *Ransom & Luck Ltd v Surbiton BC* [1949] Ch. 180; *William Cory & Son Ltd v London Corp* [1951] 2 K.B. 476; *British Transport Commission v Westmorland County Council* [1958] A.C. 126; *R. v Liverpool Corp Ex p. Liverpool Taxi Fleet Operators' Association* [1972] 2 Q.B. 299; *Suttling v Director-General of Education* (1985) 3 N.S.W.L.R. 427; affirmed on appeal, but on different grounds in (1987) 162 C.L.R. 427. See S.D. Hotop, "State Instrumentalities" (Law Society of Western Australia, Continuing Legal Education: General Series, 1989), p.9.
[46] *Birkdale District Electric Supply Co Ltd v Southport Corp* [1926] A.C. 355 at 364.
[47] (1977) 139 C.L.R. 54.
[48] *ibid.*, at 74.

In his Honour's judgment, where a public authority *in which the* **4–112**
relevant power or discretion resides is itself a party to the contract in
question, the authority will have purported to place an anticipatory,
contractual fetter on its own future exercise of the statutory power or
discretion. This purported fettering will be ultra vires the public
authority.[49] On the other hand, where the public authority makes a
contract relating to the exercise of a statutory discretion *by an officer*
who is not a party to the contract, the making of the contract should not
necessarily be *ultra vires*. By the same token, the contract should not be
able to fetter the future exercise of the statutory discretion by the officer.
In this situation the contract would be valid and enforceable against the
public authority which is a party to it, but only by way of damages and
not through specific performance or injunctive relief. This result "would
work a reasonable compromise between the desirability of recognising
the binding nature of contracts and the need to preserve the free and
unfettered exercise of the discretion."[50]

In the case of a contract expressly authorised by statute, Mason J said **4–113**
that there could be "no room for the notion that the undertaking is invalid
on the ground that it is an anticipatory fetter on the exercise of a statutory
discretion".[51] Such a contract would be valid and enforceable, at least by
an action for damages.

The doctrine of executive necessity will seldom allow the Crown to **4–114**
escape liability on a commercial guarantee given on its behalf by a servant
or agent or provided by the express terms of a statute.[52] A guarantee
merely creates a specific, contingent obligation to pay money or perform
the principal obligation. It does not generally restrict the performance of
executive duties or the exercise of executive discretions.[53] In any event, the
party taking the guarantee can protect herself or himself against the
consequences of it being declared invalid by reason of the doctrine of
executive necessity by obtaining legislative approval or ratification of the
contract.[54]

8. TAKING ADVANTAGE OF ANOTHER

This section considers a variety of doctrines, mostly equitable, which **4–115**
may lead to a guarantee being set aside, in essence because the creditor has
in some way or other taken advantage of the guarantor. Although each has

---

[49] This was the result in *Ayr Harbour Trustees v Oswald* (1883) 8 App. Cas. 623; *Ransom &
Luck Ltd v Surbiton BC* [1949] Ch. 180; *British Transport Commission v Westmorland County
Council* [1958] A.C. 126; *Cudgen Rutile (No.2) Pty Ltd v Chalk* [1975] A.C. 520.
[50] *Ansett Transport Industries (Operations) Pty Ltd v Commonwealth* (1977) 139 C.L.R. 54 at
76.
[51] *ibid.*, at 77.
[52] See *Ansett Transport Industries (Operations) Pty Ltd v Commonwealth* (1977) 139 C.L.R.
54 at 74 *per* Mason J., 113 *per* Aickin J., 62 *per* Gibbs J.
[53] M. Breheny and J. Beaven, "Australian Federal and State Government Guarantees—A
Legal Overview" (1986) 4 J.I.B.L. 231 at 234.
[54] *Ansett Transport Industries (Operations) Pty Ltd v Commonwealth* (1977) 139 C.L.R. 54.

a different theoretical basis, more than one of these doctrines may well be applicable in a particular factual situation.

(i) Duress

4–116   On normal contractual principles a guarantee will be voidable on the basis of duress to the person, that is, if it is induced by actual or threatened violence to the guarantor or actual or threatened deprivation of the guarantor's liberty.[55] The same applies if the conduct is directed not to the guarantor himself but to the guarantor's family. Thus a threat to prosecute, or instigate a prosecution of, a person's son in order to induce that person to enter into a guarantee will vitiate the contract,[56] and a company guarantee will be set aside if the directors of the company have been induced to provide a guarantee by a threat to prosecute a family member.[57] Duress of goods, whereby a person enters into a guarantee by reason of an actual or threatened seizure or destruction of that person's goods is also capable of being a ground for setting aside the guarantee.[58]

4–117   The application of the principles of duress, however, is not confined to duress to the person and duress of goods. Duress is now based on a broad general principle, encompassing what is sometimes called the doctrine of economic duress. The basis of duress was originally considered to be founded on the fact that the will of the victim was overborne so as to vitiate any contractual consent.[59] The modern view however, is not the lack of consent but "the victim's intentional submission arising from the realisation that there is no other practical choice open to him".[60] Illegitimate pressure is applied to the victim, so he has no reasonable alternative but to submit to the demand.[61]

4–118   In determining whether or not a guarantee will be set aside on the ground of economic duress, a crucial question is when does the pressure extend beyond normal commercial hard bargaining and become "illegitimate". There are no English cases directly addressing this issue in the context of guarantees, but the matter was addressed in the Australian case of *Wardley (Australia) Ltd v McPharlin*.[62] The creditor informed an existing guarantor of moneys lent by way of mortgage that unless further

---

[55] See generally J. Beatson, *Anson's Law of Contract* (28th ed., 2002), pp.276–284; *Barton v Armstrong* [1976] A.C. 104; *Williams v Bayley* (1866) L.R. 1 H.L. 200.
[56] *Public Service Employees Credit Union Co-op Ltd v Campion* (1984) 75 F.L.R. 131, although the decision is (oddly) based on undue influence, despite being a classic illustration of duress to the person. See also *Seear v Cohen* (1881) 45 L.T. 589.
[57] *Mutual Finance Ltd v John Wetton & Sons Ltd* [1937] 2 K.B. 389.
[58] *Vantage Navigation Cpn v Suhail & Saud Bahwan Building Materials (The Alev)* [1989] 1 Lloyd's Rep. 138. There were earlier doubts whether an agreement entered into on this basis could be impugned. See generally J. Beatson, *Anson's Law of Contract* (28th ed., 2002), p.279.
[59] *Occidental Worldwide Investment Cpn v Skibs A/S Avanti* [1976] 1 Lloyd's Rep. 293 at 336; *North Ocean Shipping Co. Ltd v Hyundai Construction Co. Ltd* [1979] Q.B. 705 at 717, 719; *Pao On v Lau Yiu Long* [1980] A.C. 614 at 635.
[60] *Universe Tankships Inc of Monrovia v International Transport Workers Federation* [1983] 1 A.C. 366 at 400.
[61] See, generally, J. Beatson, *Anson's Law of Contract* (28th ed., 2002), p.278.
[62] (1984) 3 B.P.R. 9500.

guarantees were given to cover subsequent advances it would proceed to enforce its securities. It was legally entitled to do this because the principal debtor was in default. The guarantor, after protest, eventually agreed to sign a further guarantee "under duress", which (with some perspicacity) he noted on the guarantee. Rogers J. held that the guarantee could not be avoided on the basis of economic duress because the creditor, although "driving a hard bargain",[63] was simply threatening to exercise its legal rights in appropriate exercise of its powers.[64] Another example might be where the creditor states that he will exercise his rights to issue a winding up petition against a company unless the directors of the company give personal guarantees.

But in the context of a renegotiation of an existing agreement the pressure may well be illegitimate if the creditor threatens to exercise his powers in a way *not* authorised by the existing contractual arrangements or the general law, and the circumstances are such that the guarantor has been left with no viable alternative but to submit to the pressure,[65] perhaps without the opportunity of obtaining legal advice.[66] This is especially so if the creditor is not acting bona fide in the honest belief that this conduct is lawful.[67] A possible illustration is where the creditor induces the execution of a guarantee by a company director by threatening to terminate a loan facility agreement made with the company where there was no breach justifying termination and at a stage when the business of the company was crucially dependent on the continued availability of the loan facility. **4–119**

A defence of duress, although much less likely, is not precluded because the creditor's threat involves no breach of contract or other legal wrong,[68] at least provided that the threat is "immoral or unconscionable".[69] In some circumstances it is at least possible that a guarantee could be set aside on the basis of economic duress if it has been induced by the creditor's threat to exercise his proper legal rights, for example, if the creditor demands that a wife executes a personal guarantee (supported by charges over her **4–120**

---

[63] *ibid.*, at 9502. *Cf.*, however, *NZI Capital Corp Ltd v Ianthe Pty Ltd* (unreported, NSW Sup Ct, July 31, 1991), where pressure was applied to execute personal guarantees when a representation had been previously made that no such guarantees were required before the loan facility would be made available, reliance had been placed on that representation, and the facility was urgently required.

[64] See also *Shivas v Bank of New Zealand* [1990] 2 N.Z.L.R. 327.

[65] In other contexts, this factor has been regarded as highly relevant as indicating the existence of economic duress: *North Ocean Shipping Co Ltd v Hyundai Construction Co Ltd* [1979] 1 Q.B. 705; *Atlas Express Ltd v Kafco (Importers & Distributors) Ltd* [1989] Q.B. 833; *B & S Contracts & Design Ltd v Victor Green Publications Ltd* [1984] I.C.R. 419. *Cf.* the absence of this factor in *Pao On v Lau Yiu Long* [1980] A.C. 614. Indeed on one view the existence of a viable alternative precludes a finding of economic duress: *Vantage Navigation Cpn v Suhail & Saud Bahwan Building Materials (The Alev)* [1989] 1 Lloyd's Rep. 138; *Hennessy v Craigmyle & Co Ltd* [1986] ICR 461. See J. Beatson, *Anson's Law of Contract* (28th ed., 2002), pp.280–281.

[66] *Atlas Express Ltd v Kafco (Importers & Distributors) Ltd* [1989] Q.B. 833. *Cf. Pao On v Lau Yiu Long* [1980] A.C. 614, where advice was taken and there was no protest.

[67] But good faith in itself does not preclude a finding of economic duress: *Huyton SA v Peter Cremer Gmbh & Co* [1999] 1 Lloyd's Rep. 620 at 627.

[68] See *Universe Tankships of Monrovia v International Transport Workers Federation* [1983] 1 A.C. 366 at 401. And generally J. Beatson, *Anson's Law of Contract* (28th ed., 2002), pp.283–284.

[69] See this view expressed in *Alf Vaughan v Royscot Trust Ltd* [1999] 1 All E.R. (Comm) 856.

property) when there has been merely a technical breach of a loan made to her husband's company and when such a guarantee had never been contemplated pursuant to the original arrangements.

(ii) Undue influence

4–121   If a guarantor is induced to enter into a guarantee by the undue influence of the creditor (or of a third party for which the creditor is held accountable),[70] the guarantee can be set aside. A distinction is made between actual and presumed undue influence.

(a) Actual undue influence

Actual undue influence is constituted by "overt acts of improper pressure or coercion such as unlawful threats".[71] As an example in *Bank of Credit & Commerce International SA v Aboody*[72] an incident occurred in respect of one of the guarantees in that case, which was described as "redolent of undue influence":[73]

> "while [the solicitor] was still attempting to give his advice to Mrs Aboody, her husband had burst into the room uninvited and in a high state of excitement. He interrupted [the solicitor] with the words, 'Why the hell don't you get on with what you are paid to do and witness her signature?' There followed a scene which so distressed Mrs Aboody that she was reduced to tears. Both men were shouting. [The solicitor] was considerably shaken by the scene and finally said 'All right. Let her sign'"[74]

Less dramatically, wounding and insulting language by a husband towards his wife, including references to the wife's disloyalty (in refusing to sign the guarantee) in comparison to the support and loyalty of his other relatives can amount to undue influence.[75]

4–122   Sometimes, however, actual undue influence has been established on much less compelling evidence. In *UCB Corporate Services Ltd v Williams*,[76] (significantly decided after *Etridge*) the Court of Appeal accepted findings of the trial judge that actual undue influence had arisen,

---

[70] See below, paras 4–177 to 4–216, for the basis of this accountability.
[71] *Royal Bank of Scotland plc v Etridge (No.2)* [2002] 2 A.C. 773 (hereafter referred to as *Etridge*) at 795 para.8.
[72] [1990] 1 Q.B. 923.
[73] *ibid.*, at 974.
[74] *ibid.*, at 951–952.
[75] See the factual analysis at first instance in *Bank of Scotland v Bennett* [1997] 3 F.C.R. 193 at 822–827; as discussed in *Etridge op. cit.*, above, para.4–121, n.71 at 871–872, paras 310–316. See also *Steeples v Lea* [1998] 1 F.L.R. 138 at 147 where actual undue influence was established when an employee who "was of a trusting disposition and trusted her employer" entered into a guarantee after a "whispered" conversation with her employer in the presence of her solicitor which persuaded her to proceed.
[76] [2002] EWCA Civ 555.

primarily because of the husband's capacity to influence his wife allied with a failure to disclose facts which meant that the wife's potential liability was more extensive than she supposed. The trial judge had concluded in this way:

"I am satisfied that Mr Williams not only had the ability to influence Mrs Williams, but did influence her, by failing to disclose matters without knowledge of which Mrs Williams could not make an informed decision as to whether to sign the charge or not. Mrs Williams has satisfied me that her husband influenced her to such an extent that her independence of decision was substantially undermined. She executed it in ignorance of important matters relating to the transaction, and not because, in full knowledge of all such matters, she was persuaded that it was the right thing to do. I am satisfied that, in this case, actual undue influence was exerted by Mr Williams on his wife."[77]

This is clearly a broad view of the requirement of "improper pressure" to which *Etridge* refers and it is arguable that such facts should at the most only have established a presumption of undue influence.[78] Indeed, if the concept of actual undue influence is to be expanded in this way it is significant because, in contrast to presumed influence, actual undue influence does not require proof that the transaction is manifestly disadvantageous.[79] This means that in the case of an "ordinary" guarantee given by a wife to secure her husband's overdraft, (which as, will be seen, is not regarded in the usual case as manifestly disadvantageous)[80] the wife may succeed in having it set aside on the basis of actual undue influence, although a case pleaded on the basis of presumed undue influence would fail.

Invariably many factual situations, in which actual undue influence can form a basis of a guarantor's defence, will probably also provide the evidence necessary for a successful claim on the ground of duress.[81] This is especially so in commercial renegotiations, when it is argued that the execution of the guarantee has been induced by threats, for example, that no further credit will be given or that materials, which are urgently needed, will not be supplied.[82] Indeed, since the doctrines of actual undue influence and duress have such a similar application, there is good reason for a reassessment of whether they should exist as separate doctrines.[83]

4–123

---

[77] *ibid.*, at para.27.
[78] See below, para.4–124.
[79] *CIBC Mortgages v Pitt* [1994] 1 A.C. 200. As to blurring of the distinction between actual and presumed undue influence after *Etridge* see, however, A. Phang and H. Tjio, "The Uncertain Boundaries of Undue Influence" [2002] L.M.C.L.Q. 231 at 232–234.
[80] See below, paras 4–140 to 4–143.
[81] See above, para.4–116.
[82] See, *e.g. Thermo-Flo Corp Ltd v Kuryluk* (1978) 84 D.L.R. (3rd) 529, where the claim was unsuccessful.
[83] In *Etridge, op. cit.*, above, para.4–121, n.71. Lord Nicholls at 795 para.8, specifically stated that "today there is much overlap with the principle of duress as this principle has subsequently developed.

(b) Presumed undue influence

4–124   As the nomenclature suggests this form of undue influence arises out of a relationship between two persons where one has acquired over another a measure of influence or ascendancy, of which the ascendant person then takes advantage without (necessarily) any specific overt acts of persuasion.[84] In *Royal Bank of Scotland v Etridge*,[85] Lord Nicholls expanded upon this concept in wide terms:

> "(9) Typically this occurs when one person places trust in another to look after his affairs and interests, and the latter betrays this trust by preferring his own interests. He abuses the influence he has acquired…
>
> (11) Even this test is not comprehensive. The principle is not confined to cases of abuse of trust and confidence. It also includes, for instance, cases where a vulnerable person has been exploited. Indeed, there is no single touchstone for determining whether the principle is applicable. Several expressions have been used in an endeavour to encapsulate the essence: trust and confidence, reliance, dependence or vulnerability on the one hand and ascendancy, domination or control on the other. None of these descriptions is perfect. None is all embracing. Each has its proper place."

4–125   Lord Nicholls, supported by other members of the House of Lords, also clearly identified some form of blameworthy conduct on the part of the defendant as being an element of undue influence: "undue influence means that influence has been misused".[86] There is "a connotation of impropriety".[87] This is in sharp contrast to other jurisprudence (both academic[88] and judicial)[89] which had distinguished undue influence from unconscionable conduct on the basis that undue influence is concerned with the quality of consent, which has been vitiated because of the claimant's dependence upon the defendant, not necessarily because of any improper conduct by the defendant. As one court has put it:

---

[84] *Etridge, op. cit.*, above, para.4–121, n.71 at 795 paras 8 and 9.

[85] *Etridge, op. cit.*, above, para.4–121, n.71 at 795–796, paras 9 and 11.

[86] *Etridge, op. cit.*, above, para.4–121, n.71 at 800, para.32. Indeed the relevant paragraph is headed "a cautionary note".

[87] *ibid.* See also Lord Clyde at 816, para.93 who is of the view that undue influence includes "cases of coercion, domination, victimisation and all the insidious techniques of persuasion". Lord Hobhouse and Lord Scott do not appear to adopt a firm view on this issue, although Lord Scott at 838–839 paras 146–147 brackets together misrepresentation and undue influence by the husband as instances of the "husband's impropriety".

[88] Birks and Chin, "On the Nature of Undue Influence" in *Good Faith and Fault in Contract Law* (1995) p.57. See also on the relationship between unconscionability and undue influence: Thompson [1994] Conv. 233; Phang, "Undue Influence, Methodology, Sources and Linkages" [1995] J.B.L. 552; Capper "Undue Influence and Unconscionability: A Rationalisation" (1998) 114 L.Q.R. 479. As to the relationship between undue influence and equitable compensation see Ho, "Undue Influence and Equitable Compensation" in *Restitution and Equity* (2000 ed., Birks & Rose), p.193.

[89] *Commercial Bank of Australia Ltd v Amadio* (1983) 151 C.L.R. 447 at 461 (*per* Mason J.) and at 474 (*per* Deane J.), *Morrison v Coast Finance Ltd* (1965) 55 D.L.R. (3d) 710 at 713. See also the analysis of cases in Birks and Chin, *op. cit.*.

"Although unconscionable conduct ... bears some resemblance to the doctrine of undue influence, there is a difference between the two. In the latter the will of the innocent party is not independent and voluntary because it is overborne. In the former the will of the innocent party, even if independent and voluntary, is the result of the disadvantageous position in which he is placed and of the other party unconscientiously taking advantage of that position."[90]

The impact of this requirement of a "connotation of impropriety" is **4–126**
unclear. In the context of guarantees given by wives, Lord Nicholls indicated that this "cautionary note" was meant merely to emphasise that a "degree of hyperbole" may be only "natural when a husband is forecasting the future of his business" and, on that basis alone, the guarantee should not be regarded as being procured by the husband's undue influence. Indeed, the requirement may not have an unduly limiting effect upon the application of the doctrine. In one of the appeals decided in *Royal Bank of Scotland v Etridge*, (*Barclays Bank plc v Coleman*)[91] a presumption of undue influence was found to exist, even though the husband could not be regarded as "blameworthy" in any real sense. In that case the husband (as borrower) and the wife (as guarantor) were both Hasidic Jews and the wife's upbringing had "prepared her to expect and accept a position of subservience and obedience to the wishes of her husband".[92]

The presumption of undue influence was held to arise out of the **4–127**
relationship between them "in which Mrs Coleman was not merely disinclined to second guess her husband on matters of business, but appears to have regarded herself as obliged to do so".[93] There were no misrepresentations by the husband and the borrowings were made to support a business venture "which was no more disadvantageous to her than any transaction in which a wife agrees to become surety in order to support her husband's commercial activities".[94] The husband (and wife) were in reality simply following the cultural traditions of the community in making decisions about the family's business activities.[95]

The burden of proving an allegation of undue influence rests upon the **4–128**
party claiming to have been wronged (the guarantor),[96] and the court will draw appropriate inferences of fact from a balanced consideration of the totality of the evidence,[97] including the personality of the parties, their

---

[90] *Commercial Bank of Australia Ltd v Amadio* (1983) 151 C.L.R. 447 at 461.
[91] *Etridge, op. cit.*, above, para.4–121, n.71 at 865 paras 282–292. A number of separate appeals, including this one, were decided by the House of Lords in *Royal Bank of Scotland v Etridge*.
[92] *Etridge, op. cit.*, above, para.4–121, n.71 at 866 para.283.
[93] *Etridge, op. cit.*, above, para.4–121, n.71 at 868, para.291.
[94] *ibid.*
[95] It should also be said that the Court of Appeal in *Hammond v Osborn* [2002] EWCA Civ 885, which was decided subsequently to *Etridge*, specifically stated (when setting aside a gift on the basis of undue influence) that "the court does not interfere on the ground that *any wrongful act* has in fact been committed by the donee but on the ground of public policy" (para.32, *per* Sir Martin Nourse, Keene L.J. agreeing) (authors' italics).
[96] *Etridge, op. cit.*, above, para.4–121, n.71 at 796 para.13.
[97] *Etridge, op. cit.*, above, para.4–121, n.71 at 797 para.16.

relationship, and the extent to which the transaction cannot readily be accounted for by the ordinary motives of ordinary persons in that relationship.[98]

4-129   The task of a guarantor seeking to set aside a guarantee on the basis of undue influence is assisted, however, by two presumptions. The first[99] is where it is presumed that duties of trust and confidence arises as a matter of law by virtue of the status of the parties to the transaction. The second arises because, having regard to the particular circumstances, the claimant is shown to have placed trust and confidence in the other party and the transaction is one calling for an explanation.[1] This does not constitute a true legal presumption but simply a shift in the evidentiary onus. As described by Lord Nicholls in *Etridge* it constitutes "a rebuttable evidential presumption of undue influence",[2] with the legal and persuasive burden of proof remaining on the claimant throughout.

(c) Presumption of undue influence arising from a particular class of relationships

4-130   There is an irrebutable presumption in certain classes of relationships that one party has influence over the other.[3] The claimant need not prove he actually reposed trust and confidence in the other.[4] It is sufficient simply to show the existence of the relevant type of relationship[5] which include parent and child[6] and even a person in loco parentis and that person's charge; guardian and ward;[7] doctor and patient;[8] solicitor and client;[9] spiritual adviser and a member of his congregation;[10] a man and his fiancée (in certain circumstances);[11] and trustee and beneficiary.[12] The presumption is applied to these relationships because they are viewed as

---

[98] *Etridge, op. cit.*, above, para.4–121, n.71 at 796 para.13.

[99] This was referred to as the "2A" presumption by Slade L.J. *BCCI v Aboody* [1990] 1 Q.B. 923 at 953, approved by the House of Lords in *Barclays Bank plc v O'Brien* [1994] 1 A.C. 18 at 189–190.

[1] *Etridge, op. cit.*, above, para.4–121, n.71 at 796–797 paras 14–16.

[2] *Etridge, op. cit.*, above, para.4–121, n.71 at 797 para.16. See A. Phang and H. Tjio, "The Uncertain Boundaries of Undue Influence" [2002] L.M.C.L.Q. 231 at 232–234. The second "presumption" was referred by Slade LJ in *BCCI v Aboody (ibid.)* as the class 2B presumption, but this nomenclature was rejected by the House of Lords in *Etridge*. See especially Lord Hobhouse at 822 para.107, Lord Clyde at 816 para.92, Lord Scott at 842 para.161. See also K.N. Scott, "The evolving equity of undue influence" (2002) 18 Journal of Contract Law 236.

[3] *Etridge, op. cit.*, above, para.4–121, n.71 at 797 para.18.

[4] *ibid.*

[5] *ibid.*

[6] *Bullock v Lloyd's Bank* [1955] Ch. 317; *Bainbridge v Browne* (1881) 18 Ch. D. 188; *Powell v Powell* [1900] 1 Ch. 243.

[7] *Hylton v Hylton* (1754) 2 Ves. Sen. 547; 28 E.R. 349; *Hatch v Hatch* (1804) 9 Ves. 292; 34 E.R. 1043.

[8] *Mitchell v Humfray* (1881) 8 Q.B.D. 587; *Dent v Bennett* (1839) 4 My. & Cr. 269; 41 E.R. 105; *Radcliffe v Price* (1902) 18 T.L.R. 466.

[9] *Wright v Carter* [1903] 1 Ch. 27.

[10] *Allcard v Skinner* (1887) 36 Ch. D. 145.

[11] *Re Lloyd's Bank Ltd* [1931] 1 Ch. 289 *Cf. Zamet v Hyman* [1961] 1 W.L.R. 1442.

[12] *Beningfield v Baxter* (1886) 12 App. Cas. 167.

being likely to give one party authority or influence over the other, but there is no presumption that the confidence has been abused. This is a matter of evidence.[13]

Although it has been said that the categories of relationship are not **4–131** closed,[14] the presumption has been held not to apply to the following relationships: employer and employee;[15] principal and agent;[16] landlord and tenant;[17] but the most notable omission from the list of relationships to which the presumption applies is husband and wife.[18] There is no rational explanation for applying the presumption between a man and his fiancée and excluding it between a husband and wife but this distinction is drawn on the basis of policy, which some might regard as anachronistic. The courts take the view that there is nothing unusual in a wife showing her affection for her husband in a tangible way, for example, by guaranteeing repayment of his debts. The affection and confidence inherent in the marital state does not of itself amount to undue influence.[19]

(d) Evidentiary presumption of undue influence

The presumption of undue influence arising from a special relationship, **4–132** which shifts the evidentiary burden of proof from the complainant to the other party, is established by showing two matters:

(i) That the complainant reposed trust and confidence in the other party.

(ii) That the transaction is not readily explicable by the relationship between the parties and calls for an explanation.[20]

(i) The first element: reposing trust and confidence in the other party

As to the first requirement, proof of its existence may often be found to **4–133** exist in the relationship of husband and wife. Although (as we have seen) no legal presumption arises from the particular status of the parties "the court will nevertheless note, as a matter of fact, the opportunities of abuse which flow from a wife's confidence in her husband".[21] Thus in *Bank of Credit & Commerce International SA v Aboody*[22] a special relationship

---

[13] *Etridge, op. cit.*, above, para.4–121, n.71 at 482 para.104, *per* Lord Hobhouse.

[14] *Lloyds Bank Ltd v Bundy* [1975] Q.B. 326 at 341; *Allcard v Skinner* (1887) 36 Ch. D. 145.

[15] *Mathew v Bobbins* (1980) 124 S.J. 479.

[16] *Re Coomber; Coomber v Coomber* [1911] 1 Ch. 723 at 728.

[17] *Mathew v Bobbins*, (1980) 124 S.J. 479.

[18] *Yerkey v Jones* (1939) 63 C.L.R. 649; *Bank of Montreal v Stuart* [1911] A.C. 120; *Howes v Bishop* [1909] 2 K.B. 390.

[19] *Etridge, op. cit.*, above, para.4–121, n.71 at 797 para.19; *Yerkey v Jones* (1939) 63 C.L.R. 649 at 657 *per* Dixon J.

[20] *Etridge, op. cit.*, n.71 at 798 para.21, *per* Lord Nicholls.

[21] *Etridge, op. cit.*, n.71 at 797 para.19.

[22] [1990] 1 Q.B. 923. See also *Barclays Bank plc v Coleman* (above, n.91); *Dunbar Bank plc v Nadeem* [1997] 2 All E.R. 253, where Mrs Nadeem "was entirely happy to leave anything of a financial nature to her husband" and "if formal documents needed to be signed Mr Nadeem simply told her where to sign and she did so without question". In *Barclays Bank plc v Caplan* [1998] 1 F.L.R. 532 at 542 the presumption appears to have been established on the much less

probably existed between husband and wife because the wife, although intelligent and capable of independence, trusted her husband to such an extent that she "blindly and without a care"[23] signed company documents prepared for her signature.

The presumption of undue influence will not arise, however, simply because the wife would have "liked more time to consider whether or not to sign"[24] or where the guarantor has a "relative naiveté" in financial affairs[25] or where the wife is capable of, and does, exercise an independent judgment as to whether to execute the guarantee. As an example, in *Turner v Barclays Bank plc*[26] the wife was a "reasonably intelligent and careful person"[27] and "not by any means naive in financial matters and quite capable of making up her own mind".[28] She was responsible for the family finances and previously worked as a clerical assistant for the Inland Revenue.[29] Given this background Neuberger J. concluded, taking into account other evidence, that:

> "Mrs Turner was in no doubt influenced by the fact that the business had run profitably in the past and that Mr Turner had therefore showed himself as a competent businessman, albeit not in a very large way. She was influenced by the view which he took and communicated, as I have already mentioned, namely that the difficulties of the business would be temporary and sorted out in the next few months. In that sense, it can be said that she reposed trust and confidence in him. However, I do not consider that this was a blind trust and confidence: she applied her own judgment to his assessment of the prospects of the problem being a temporary one, and decided that she would accept his assessment as accurate."[30]

4–134   The establishment of the presumption will be much more difficult in commercial dealings, but in *Lloyds Bank Ltd v Bundy*[31] it was shown to exist in the context of a banker-customer relationship. The defendant, an elderly farmer, who was not conversant with business affairs, charged his only asset, a farmhouse, and provided guarantees to secure an overdraft granted by the bank to a plant-hire company operated by his son. Later, when the company's business deteriorated, the assistant manager of the bank interviewed the defendant in his son's presence. He told the defendant that the bank would continue to support his son's company only if the defendant increased his

---

cogent (and probably insufficient) evidence that "Mrs Caplan left her husband to conduct their joint financial affairs".

[23] [1989] 2 W.L.R. 759 at 766. But note that the wife's plea for relief was in fact based on actual undue influence.

[24] See *National Westminster Bank v Gill* which was one of the appeals decided in *Etridge op. cit.*, above, para.4–121, n.71 at 865 para.281.

[25] *Greene King plc v Stanley* [2001] EWCA Civ 1966.

[26] [1998] 1 F.L.R. 276.

[27] *ibid.* at 286.

[28] *ibid.*

[29] *ibid.*

[30] [1998] 1 F.L.R. 276 at 289.

[31] [1975] Q.B. 326.

guarantee and charge up to a figure of £11,000. The assistant manager also sketched the company's position but did not fully explain its accounts to the defendant. The defendant's son had explained to his father that the company's parlous condition was attributable to a number of bad debts, although the assistant manager was not satisfied that this was true. At the time of this interview the assistant manager realised that the defendant relied on him implicitly, in his capacity as bank manager, to advise him about the transaction. A guarantee and a charge covering the required amount had been prepared in advance ready for signature, and the defendant signed these documents at the interview. Some five months later, a receiving order was made against the defendant's son and the bank terminated the company's overdraft facilities.

Sir Eric Sachs and Cairns L.J. found that there existed a special **4–135** relationship between the bank and the defendant which gave rise to a duty of fiduciary care. While disclaiming any intention of cataloguing the elements of such a special relationship, Sir Eric Sachs provided some insights into its nature. His Lordship thought that a special relationship would arise in a commercial context:

"[w]here someone relies on the guidance or advice of another, where, the other is aware of that reliance, and where the person on whom reliance is placed obtains, or may well obtain, a benefit from the transactions or has some other interest in it being concluded."[32]

He then added:

"In addition, there must, of course, be shown to exist a vital element which in this judgment will for convenience be referred to as confidentiality. It is this element which is so impossible to define and which is a matter for the judgment of the court on the facts of any particular case."[33]

In *Lloyds Bank Ltd v Bundy*[34] the existence of the relationship of **4–136** dependency was supported by clear evidence of a longstanding relationship between the defendant and the bank, whereby the defendant placed trust and confidence in the bank officers. But a bank will not be held to have "crossed the line which divides a normal business relationship from one of undue influence"[35] merely by giving advice about the relevant transaction,[36] especially if the customer has experience in business affairs.[37]

In some cases proof of the first element required to establish the **4–137** presumption, that is, that the complainant reposed trust and confidence in

---

[32] *ibid.*, at 341. The "reliance factor" was again emphasised in *Re Brocklehurst* [1978] Ch. 14.
[33] [1975] Q.B. 326 at 341.
[34] [1975] Q.B. 326.
[35] *National Westminster Bank plc v Morgan* [1985] 1 A.C. 686 at 701.
[36] *ibid.* See also *Cornish v Midland Bank Plc* [1985] 3 All E.R. 513.
[37] *Shotter v Westpac Banking Corp* [1988] 2 N.Z.L.R. 316 at 333.

the other party, has seemingly been too easily inferred. In *Crédit Lyonnais Bank Nederland NV v Burch*[38] the defendant mortgaged her flat, valued at £100,000, with an equity of £70,000, as security for her employer's overdraft, which was in the region of £250,000–£270,000. It was held that the relationship of employer and employee had "ripened into"[39] a relationship of trust and confidence because of "the excessively onerous nature of the transaction into which she was persuaded to enter, coupled with the fact she did so, at the request of, and after discussion with, [her employer]".[40] In the absence of facts showing an antecedent relationship of trust and dependency, it is hard to discern that this first element which is necessary to establish the presumption is satisfied. The "onerous nature of the transaction" is pertinent not to the first, but the second requirement, namely, that the transaction is not readily explicable by the relationship between the parties. *Crédit Lyonnais Bank Nederland NV v Burch*[41] might be better regarded as coming within the wider definition of undue influence set out by Lord Nicholls in *Etridge* which includes "cases where a vulnerable person has been exploited."[42] Additionally, the facts would appear to justify setting aside the guarantee on the basis that it constituted an unconscionable bargain.[43]

(ii) The second element: the transaction is not readily explicable between the parties and calls for an explanation

4–138   The stated reason for the second element required to establish the presumption, is to prevent it being applicable to obviously "innocuous" transactions between those in a relationship of trust and confidence, such as a moderate Christmas, or birthday present by a child to a parent, or to an agreement whereby a client or patient agrees to be responsible for the reasonable fees of his medical or legal advisor.[44] The element encapsulates the requirement of "manifest disadvantage" which Lord Nicholls (rejecting previous judicial criticism)[45] reiterates in substance, although not in nomenclature. Lord Nicholls, who gave the leading judgment in *Etridge*,[46] saw the proper formulation of the principle as that set out by Lord Scarman in *National Westminster Bank plc v Morgan*:[47]

[38] [1997] 1 All E.R. 144. *Cf. Banco Exterior Internacional SA v Thomas* [1997] 1 All E.R. 46.
[39] *ibid.*, at 154.
[40] *ibid.* See similarly, *Steeples v Lea* [1998] 1 F.L.R. 138 where a junior employee also gave a guarantee, but there was also evidence of actual undue influence in this case as a result of a conversation with her employee in the presence of her solicitor (at 147).
[41] [1997] 1 All E.R. 144.
[42] See *Etridge, op. cit.*, above, para.4–121, n.71 at 795, para.11.
[43] This was not relied on in the case: see [1997] 1 All E.R. 144 at 152–153. As to unconscionability see below, para.4–155.
[44] *Etridge, op. cit.*, above, para.4–121, n.71 at 798, para.24; at 841, para.156.
[45] *Barclays Bank plc v Coleman* [2000] Q.B. 20 at 30–32. See also academic criticism: D. Tipaldy, "The Limits of Undue Influence" (1985) 48 M.L.R. 579; A. Phang and H. Tjio, "The Boundaries of Undue Influence" [2002] L.M.C.L.Q. 231 at 234–236.
[46] Lord Bingham in *Etridge, op. cit.*, above, para.4–121, n.71 at 794, para.3 states that Lord Nicholls' judgment "commands the unqualified support of all members of the House.
[47] [1985] A.C. 686 at 704.

"The Court of Appeal erred in law in holding that the presumption of undue influence can arise from the evidence of the relationship of the parties without also evidence that the transaction itself was wrongful in that it *constituted an advantage taken of the person subjected to the influence which, failing proof to the contrary, was explicable only on the basis that undue influence had been exercised to procure it.*"

This test, it will be observed, appears to do more than raise an evidentiary burden—if a transaction is explicable only on the basis that undue influence has been exercised, then it is more in the nature of an irrebuttable presumption.[48]

It is reasonably clear, however, (as held prior to *Etridge*) that the transactional disadvantage must be "obvious"[49] and not simply emerging only after "a fine and close evaluation of its various beneficial and detrimental features".[50] There will be some very clear cases, such as *Crédit Lyonnais Bank Nederland NV v Burch*, (already discussed)[51] where the employee had no financial interest in the business (other than keeping her job) and faced losing her home if the business failed.

4–139

In *Etridge* the House of Lords addressed the question of whether or not a wife's guarantee of her husband's bank overdraft, together with a charge on her share of the matrimonial home was a transaction manifestly to her disadvantage. Lord Nicholls considered that "in the ordinary case" a guarantee of this nature is not to be regarded as a transaction which, failing proof to the contrary, is explicable only on the basis that it has been procured by the exercise of the undue influence of her husband.[52] His Lordship said that[53]:

4–140

"[28] In a narrow sense, such a transaction plainly ('manifestly') is disadvantageous to the wife. She undertakes a serious financial obligation, and in return she personally receives nothing. But that would be to take an unrealistically blinkered view of such a transaction. Unlike the relationship of solicitor and client or medical advisor and patient, in the case of husband and wife there are inherent reasons why such a transaction may well be for her benefit. Ordinarily, the fortunes of husband and wife are bound up together. If the husband's business is the source of the family income, the wife has a lively interest in doing what she can to support the business.[54] A wife's affection and self-interest run hand-in-hand in inclining her to join with her husband in charging the matrimonial home, usually a jointly-owned asset, to obtain

[48] Lord Scott in fact points out the circularity of the reasoning (*Etridge, op. cit.*, above, para.4–121, n.71 at 840, para.155).
[49] *Bank of Credit & Commerce International SA v Aboody* [1990] 1 Q.B. 923 at 965.
[50] *ibid.* But inevitably there will be some evaluation of the facts. See, generally, J. O'Sullivan, "Undue Influence and Misrepresentation after O'Brien: Making Security Secure" in *Restitution and Banking Law* (1998, ed. F. Rose), p.42 at pp.48–56.
[51] See above, para.4–137.
[52] *Etridge, op. cit.*, above, para.4–121, n.71 at 800 para.30. See generally G. Andrews, "*Undue Influence—Where's the Disadvantage*" [2002] 66 Conv. 456, especially at 461–463.
[53] *Etridge, op. cit.*, above, para.4–121, n.71 at 799 para.28.
[54] *Cf.* earlier suggestions to the contrary in *Barclays Bank v Kennedy* [1989] 1 F.L.R. 36.

the financial facilities needed by the business. The finance may be needed to start a new business, or expand a promising business, or rescue an ailing business."

Earlier suggestions[55] that a guarantee given by a wife was manifestly disadvantageous simply because it put the matrimonial home at risk are therefore no longer correct, although it may be different where others (such as parents) execute a charge over their only significant asset in respect of borrowings for a business venture in which they have no financial interest.[56]

4-141   This is perhaps an uncontroversial analysis, but more difficulty arises in identifying the extraordinary guarantee to which Lord Nicholls alludes. In respect of the events surrounding the transaction itself, latitude is to be given to the "reasonable husband", who, when forecasting his business prospects, might naturally be expected to indulge in "a degree of hyperbole" which courts should not too readily treat as "exaggerations" or "misstatements".[57] Even though most guarantees have broadly similar standard terms, Lord Hobhouse in *Etridge* considered that no lender who had proper regard to the wife's interest would ask her to sign an unlimited guarantee,[58] so this may indicate the guarantee is manifestly disadvantageous. And in *Dunbar plc v Nadeem*[59] a decisive factor in arriving at the same view was that the guarantee was an "all monies" guarantee securing her husband's business debts.

4-142   One circumstance where a wife's guarantee may not be "ordinary" and may constitute a manifestly disadvantageous transaction is when the husband's borrowings are made for a speculative purpose, perhaps especially if it is for a commercial enterprise beyond the scope of the normal family business. An example is *Bank of Scotland v Bennett*[60] in which the husband had a total lack of experience in a speculative venture (a frozen fish business) and the loan had been rejected by a number of other financial institutions. Furthermore, the wife received no salary or dividends and took no part in the management of the company. By comparison, in *Bank of Credit & Commerce International SA v Aboody*,[61] the wife's guarantee did not constitute a manifestly disadvantageous transaction because there was a reasonable prospect that the funds provided by the bank would have enabled the company to survive, preserving the wife's income.[62] Additionally, the wife also held a 35 per cent shareholding in the company.

---

[55] *e.g. Midland Bank v Phillips* (unreported March 14, 1986).
[56] See, *e.g.* the circumstances set out in *Greene King plc v Stanley* [2001] EWCA Civ 1966 para.106, in holding that it was a transaction which called for an explanation.
[57] *Etridge, op. cit.*, above, para.4–121, n.71 at 800 para.32.
[58] *Etridge, op. cit.*, above, para.4–121, n.71 at 824 para.112.
[59] [1997] 2 All E.R. 253 at 265.
[60] See the analysis of the facts by the trial judge [1997] 3 F.C.R. 193. The case was eventually decided on different grounds by the House of Lords. See *Etridge op. cit.*, above, para.4–121, n.71 at 871–878, paras 310–351.
[61] [1990] 1 Q.B. 923.
[62] Note, however, that this was an actual undue influence case, and in *CIBC Mortgages v Pitt* [1994] 1 A.C. 200 it was subsequently held that in the case of actual undue influence it is unnecessary to prove that the transaction was manifestly disadvantageous to the party seeking

Normally a loan made to the husband and wife jointly[63] will not be **4–143** regarded as manifestly disadvantageous, but it may be otherwise if the facts reveal the loan has been made in some significant degree for the purposes of the husband's business. In *Dunbar Bank v Nadeem*,[64] for example, the loan was structured in terms of a joint purchase of a new leasehold interest in the matrimonial home, but to the bank's knowledge, it was in reality proposed and intended as short term security for the husband's business debts. Although the wife was able to acquire a joint interest in a leasehold property worth £400,000 (with a net equity of £44,000) for a loan of £260,000, the charge expressly made the wife liable for all her husband's borrowings, which were repayable on demand and when the husband was having difficulty servicing his interest obligations.[65]

One particular difficulty arising from the identification of this separate **4–144** element (required to raise the presumption) that the transaction is not readily explicable by the relationship between the parties is that it appears to exclude the creation of a presumption where there is a past history of excessive trust and dependence, but there is no evidence of any misrepresentation or overbearing behaviour in respect of the transaction in question and there are no other facts taking the transaction outside the category of an "ordinary guarantee". In such a case it can be shown that the complainant reposed trust and confidence in her husband, yet there are no special circumstances which would appear to make "the transaction itself" explicable only on the basis of undue influence. So the second prerequisite is not satisfied, and the complainant cannot establish what might justifiably be regarded as a classic case of presumed undue influence.

The presumption of undue influence should be determined on the basis **4–145** of an overall assessment of the evidence and not by evaluation of the evidence relating to the prior relationship, and then, as a separate further element, a determination of whether the transaction itself is explicable only on the basis of undue influence. Indeed, leaving aside Lord Nicholl's adoption of Lord Scarman's principle in *National Westminster Bank plc v Morgan*,[66] their Lordships' views in *Etridge*[67] are not inconsistent with this position.

Additionally, (as we have seen) in *Barclays Bank plc v Coleman*[68] (one **4–146** of the cases decided in *Etridge*) the presumption was held to arise because of an excessive relationship of trust and dependency, despite the fact that the guarantee "was no more disadvantageous to her than any transaction

---

to set it aside. But the analysis is still valid in respect of cases based on presumed undue influence.

[63] *CIBC Mortgages v Pitt* [1994] 1 A.C. 200.

[64] [1997] 2 All E.R. 253.

[65] *ibid.*, at 265.

[66] [1985] A.C. 686.

[67] *Etridge, op. cit.*, above, para.4–121, n.71 at 816 para.93, *per* Lord Clyde; at 842 para.158 where Lord Scott states that it is "the combination of the relationship and the nature of the transaction" that gives rise to the presumption.

[68] One of the appeals decided in *Etridge, op. cit.*, above, para.4–121, n.91. This result will be reinforced if there is proven "bullying" or "excessive" pressure at the time of entering the transaction. See *Barclays Bank plc v Harris*, another of the appeals decided in *Etridge* (*op. cit.*, above, para.4–121, n.71 at 858 para.244).

in which a wife agrees to become surety in order to support her husband's commercial activities".[69]

4–147   In *Etridge* Lord Nicholls makes it clear that the claimant may succeed in claim of undue influence even when the presumption is not available to him "for instance, where the impugned transaction was not one which called for an explanation".[70] Thus the claimant may still seek to set aside an "ordinary" guarantee (which is not "manifestly disadvantageous") on the basis of actual undue influence,[71] and without reliance on the presumption, provided that the facts justify such a claim.

(e) Rebutting the presumption

4–148   The presumption of undue influence is rebutted if the party benefiting from the transaction shows that it was entered into as a result of "the free exercise of an independent will".[72] The most usual way of doing this is to show that the complainant had independent advice before entering the transaction,[73] so as to "bring home to a complainant a proper understanding of what he or she is about to do".[74] The receipt of outside advice does not, however, necessarily show that the subsequent completion of the transaction was free from the exercise of undue influence because "a person may understand fully the implications of the proposed transaction ... and yet still be acting under the influence of another".[75] All the circumstances must be taken into account in determining whether or not the independent advice had an "emancipating effect".[76] Where the guarantor has been under the influence of the borrower (most commonly where a wife is under the undue influence of her husband) in the usual case the guarantee will not be set aside as against the bank if the bank receives confirmation from a solicitor acting for the wife that he has advised the wife appropriately.[77] The matter is more fully discussed later in this chapter,[78] and (as we will be seen) the decision of the House of Lords in *Etridge* has set out some new procedures in respect of future transactions.

---

[69] *Etridge, op. cit.*, above, para.4–121, n.71. *ibid.* at 867–868 para.291.
[70] *Etridge, op. cit.*, above, para.4–121, n.71 at 797 para.17.
[71] *Royal Bank of Scotland plc v Etridge (No.2)* [2002] 2 A.C. 773, and see above, paras 4–121 to 4–123. As to criticism of this result see A. Phang and H. Tijo, "The Uncertain Boundaries of Undue Influence" [2002] L.M.C.L.Q. 231 at 234–236.
[72] *Inche Noriah v Shaik Allie Bin Omar* [1929] A.C. 127 at 136; *Etridge, op. cit.*, above, para.4–121, n.71 at 798 para.20.
[73] *Etridge, op. cit.*, above, para.4–121, n.71 at 798 para.20; *Allcard v Skinner* (1887) 36 Ch. D. 145 at 190; *Bullock v Lloyd's Bank* [1955] Ch. 317; *Horry v Tate & Lyle Refineries Ltd* [1982] 2 Lloyd's Rep. 417 at 421.
[74] *Etridge, op. cit.*, above, para.4–121, n.71 at 798 para.20.
[75] *ibid.*
[76] *ibid.*
[77] *Etridge, op. cit.*, above, para.4–121, n.71 at 806 para.56.
[78] See below, paras 4–188 to 4–206.

(f) Consequences of undue influence

Proof of undue influence gives rise to a right of the guarantor to rescind **4–149** the guarantee not only when it is exercised by the creditor as against the guarantor,[79] but also where the creditor has actual or constructive notice of undue influence exercised by the third party (such as the principal borrower).[80] In *Bank of Credit & Commerce International SA v Aboody*[81] it was said that "at least in ordinary circumstances" it would not be appropriate to set aside a transaction which has been procured by the undue influence of the other party if it is established that the complainant would have entered into the transaction in any event. This view, however, was rejected by the Court of Appeal in *UCB Corporate Services Ltd v Williams*[82] in the case of actual undue influence since "actual undue influence is a species of fraud:"[83] Jonathan Parker L.J. (Kay, Peter Gibson L.J.J.) agreeing said:

> "That being so, I cannot see any reason in principle why (for example) a husband who has fraudulently procured the consent of his wife to participate in a transaction should be able, in effect, to escape the consequences of his wrongdoing by establishing that had he not acted fraudulently, and had his wife had the opportunity to make a free and informed choice, she would have acted in the same way. The fact is that the husband's fraud deprived the wife of the opportunity to make such a choice, and, as I see it, it is that fact which founds the wife's equity (as against her husband) to set aside the transaction."[84]

Thus in the case of actual undue influence the victim is entitled to have **4–150** the transaction set aside "as of right",[85] but it has been argued[86] that in the case of presumed undue influence there is merely an equity to have the transaction set aside. Given, however, the blurring of the distinction in *Etridge*[87] between actual and presumed undue influence[88] (with the latter being seen simply as constituting a shift in the evidentiary onus of proof rather than as a legal presumption), and the fact that undue influence is now seen as having "a connotation of impropriety"[89] (with a moral culpability akin to fraud) it is considered that the same principle should apply to presumed undue influence.

---

[79] *e.g. Lloyd's Bank Ltd v Bundy* [1975] B. 326.
[80] See below, paras 4–179 to 4–187.
[81] [1990] 1 Q.B. 923.
[82] [2002] EWCA Civ 555.
[83] Following this analogy in *CIBC Mortgages v Pitt* [1994] A.C. 200 at 209.
[84] *UCB Corporate Services Ltd v Williams* [2002] EWCA Civ 555 paras 85–91.
[85] *ibid.*
[86] *UCB Corporate Services Ltd v Williams* [2002] EWCA Civ 555, para.53.
[87] *op. cit.*, n.71.
[88] See generally A. Phang and H. Tjio, "The Uncertain Boundaries of Undue Influence" [2002] L.M.C.L.Q. 231.
[89] *Etridge, op. cit.*, above, para.4–121, n.71 at 800 para.32. See also below, para.4–125.

4–151   If the guarantee is to be rescinded, the parties must be restored to their original position, that is, there is a requirement of restitution.[90] In the usual case the guarantor receives no benefit from the guarantee itself, so it will be simply set aside without the court making any order of restitution. Sometimes, however, such an order will be appropriate. Thus, in *Dunbar Bank v Nadeem*[91] the charge executed by both the wife and husband was given not only as security for the husband's borrowings, but also for the purchase of the couple's joint interest in the leasehold property charged. The charge was set aside, but only on condition that the wife repaid to the bank the amount used to acquire her half share in the lease.

4–152   As a finding of undue influence vitiates consent the guarantee will usually be set aside in toto, but sometimes a number of separate undertakings may be executed by the guarantor (usually to facilitate further borrowings), only one of which is tainted by undue influence. In such a case this latter obligation may be severed from the agreement, leaving the other undertakings enforceable. Thus in *Barclays Bank plc v Caplan*[92] guarantees and charges signed by the wife were followed by the execution by her over a year later of a "side letter" which substantially increased her liability (and burdened her interest in the matrimonial home) in respect of her husband's business debts. Only the side letter was tainted with undue influence and J. Sumption Q.C. (sitting as deputy judge of the Chancery Division) held that the side-letter, as a separate and distinct instrument extending the obligations under the earlier guarantees and charges, could be severed from the transaction. The test for severance was met since there was no necessity to add to, or modify, the wording of the earlier guarantees, or alter the balance of rights and obligations therein contained.[93]

4–153   The right to rescind the contract may be lost by affirmation, which may be inferred from the action or inaction of the guarantor after the cessation of the undue influence which induced the guarantee.[94] There must however be a knowledge of the relevant facts and an "absolute release from the undue influence"[95] which had brought about the contract. Thus in *Moxon v Payne*[96] it was said that there must be "full knowledge of all the facts, full knowledge of the equitable rights arising from those facts, and an

---

[90] See J. Beatson, *Anson's Law of Contract* (28th ed., 2002), p.283.
[91] [1997] 2 All E.R. 253. See also *Midland Bank plc v Greene* [1994] 2 F.L.R. 827 and J. O'Sullivan, "Undue Influence and Misrepresentation after O'Brien: Making Security Secure" in *Restitution and Banking Law* (1998, ed. F. Rose), p.42 at 64–69.
[92] [1998] 1 F.L.R. 532.
[93] See the test for severance set out at [1998] 1 F.L.R. 532 at 546. See also *Chemidus Wavin Ltd v Société pour la Transformation et l'Exploitation des Resines Industrielles SA* [1978] 3 C.M.L.R. 514; *Lobb (Alec) Garages Ltd v Total Oil (Great Britain) Ltd* [1985] 1 W.L.R. 173; *Sadler v Imperial Life Assurance Co of Canada Ltd* [1988] I.R.L.R. 388 at 392. Cf. the position in respect of misrepresentation: *TSB Bank Ltd plc v Camfield* [1995] 1 W.L.R. 430; *Allied Irish Bank plc v Byrne* [1995] 2 F.L.R. 325 and above, paras 4–41 to 4–48.
[94] See generally J. Beatson, *Anson's Law of Contract* (28th ed., 2002), p.294 and the cases there cited.
[95] *ibid.*
[96] (1873) L.R. 8 Ch. App. 881 at 885.

absolute release from the undue influence by means of which the frauds were practised".

In the context of guarantees, therefore, the guarantor's right to rescind **4–154** will be barred by affirmation where the guarantor takes no steps to set aside the guarantee after taking legal advice, at a point in time when the facts indicate clearly that the guarantor is no longer under the influence of another (for example, where a wife has separated from her husband and blind devotion has been replaced, as is often the case, by bitter animosity).

(iii) Unconscionable bargains

The requirements for the application of the doctrine of unconscion- **4–155** ability were precisely set out by Mr Peter Millet Q.C. (as he then was), sitting as a High Court Judge, in *Alex Lobb (Garages) Ltd v Total Oil (Great Britain) Ltd*:[97]

"First, one party has been at a serious disadvantage to the other, whether through poverty, or ignorance, or lack of advice, or otherwise, so that circumstances existed of which unfair advantage could be taken: see, for example, *Blomley v. Ryan* (1956) 99 CLR 362,[98] where, to the knowledge of one party, the other was by reason of his intoxication in no condition to negotiate intelligently. Second, this weakness of the one party has been exploited by the other in some morally culpable manner: see, for example, *Clark v Malpas* (1862) 4 De G. F. & J. 401, where a poor and illiterate man was induced to enter into a transaction of an unusual nature, without proper independent advice, and in great haste. And third, the resulting transaction has been, not merely hard or improvident, but overreaching and oppressive. Where there has been a sale at an undervalue, the undervalue has almost always been substantial, so that it calls for an explanation, and is in itself indicative of the presence of some fraud, undue influence, or other such feature. In short, there must, in my judgment, be some impropriety, both in the conduct of the stronger party and in the terms of the transaction itself (though the former may often be inferred from the latter in the absence of an innocent explanation) which in the traditional phrase 'shocks the conscience of the court', and makes it against equity and good conscience for the stronger party to retain the benefit of a transaction he has unfairly obtained."

Few claimants in English courts have utilised these principles to argue that a guarantee should be set aside, preferring instead to base their claim on undue influence. This is so, even though the particular facts might

---

[97] [1983] 1 W.L.R. 87 at 94–95.
[98] The full list of examples provided by Fullagar J. in *Blomley v Ryan* were "poverty or need of any kind, sickness, age, sex, infirmity of body or mind, drunkenness, illiteracy or lack of education, lack of assistance or explanation where assistance or explanation is necessary".

appear to justify an application of the doctrine. As a striking example in *Crédit Lyonnais Bank Nederland NV v Burch*[99] Miss Burch as a junior employee was clearly at a special disadvantage vis-à-vis her employer, especially since she was not told of the indebtedness of the company's liabilities, which it was proposed that she should guarantee, or the extent of its overdraft facility. There was a lack of advice where "assistance or explanation [was] necessary". Then as to the second and third elements identified by Mr Millett (in the passage set out in the previous paragraph), there was an exploitation of this weakness by the employer and the guarantee (exposing Miss Burch to excessive financial risk with no potential benefit) could justifiably be regarded as "overreaching and oppressive". Nevertheless (as previously discussed) the guarantee was set aside on the basis of undue influence rather than unconscionability, even though it is arguable the facts did not justify the application of that doctrine.[1]

4–156 By contrast, in other common law jurisdictions, the principles of unconscionability have been widely applied as a basis for setting aside guarantees.[2] This has occurred partly as a result of an extended interpretation of the term "special disadvantage" which has been held to include emotional dependence,[3] lack of business acumen[4] and, most significantly, general matters not directly related to these personal characteristics of the guarantor. A survey of the decided cases indicates the following will be important, depending on the particular context: the circumstances of the negotiations and how the guarantee came to be signed;[5] the length and complexity of the documentation;[6] the relative bargaining positions of the parties;[7] the existence of a special relationship between the guarantor and creditor, giving rise to a relationship of trust;[8] any misrepresentations made or pressure applied;[9] a lack of knowledge of

---

[99] [1997] 1 All E.R. 144.
[1] See above, para.4–137.
[2] See, generally, J. O'Donovan and J. Phillips, *The Modern Contract of Guarantee* (3rd Australia ed., 1996), pp.176–185.
[3] *Louth v Diprose* (1992) 175 C.L.R. 621.
[4] *National Australia Bank Ltd v Nobile* (1988) A.T.P.R. 40–856 at 49,240, *per* Davies J.; *Household Financial Services Ltd v Price* (unreported, SA Sup Ct, Burley J., November 14, 1994)); *National Australia Bank Ltd v Le Maistre* (unreported, NSW Sup Ct, March 25, 1988); *Nolan v Westpac Corp* (1989) A.S.C. 55–930 at 58,515. See also *Beneficial Finance Corp Ltd v Karavas* [1991] 23 N.S.W.L.R. 256, where guarantors were relieved of liability because they lacked the "education, experience or intellectual capacity" to understand the magnitude and nature of the risks they had undertaken. This was a case decided under the Contracts Review Act 1980 (NSW).
[5] *Commercial Bank of Australia Ltd v Amadio* (1983) 151 C.L.R. 447 at 476–477 *per* Deane J.
[6] *ibid.*, at 476 *per* Deane J. See also *Re Ferdinando; Ex p. Australia & New Zealand Banking Group Ltd v Official Trustee in Bankruptcy* (1993) 42 F.C.R. 243.
[7] *Commercial Bank of Australia v Amadio* (1983) 151 C.L.R. 447 at 476 where Deane J. emphasises that "the bank, for its part, was a major national financial institution". See also *National Australia Bank Ltd v Nobile* (1988) A.T.P.R. 40–856.
[8] *Lloyds Bank Ltd v Bundy* [1975] 1 Q.B. 326; *National Australia Bank Ltd v Nobile* (1988) A.T.P.R. 40–856 at 49–243 *per* Davies J.
[9] *Commercial Bank of Australia Ltd v Amadio* (1983) 151 C.L.R. 447; *Bawn v Trade Credits Ltd* (1986) N.S.W. Conv. R. 55–290; *Nolan v Westpac Banking Corp* (1989) A.S.C. 55–930 at 58–515.

the financial position of the principal debtor;[10] the purpose of the loan[11] or the risk of default;[12] the existence of a relationship between the guarantor and a third party (such as the principal debtor), upon whose advice the guarantor relies;[13] a special and undisclosed arrangement between a bank and the principal debtor amounting to "more than an ordinary business relationship", especially if it inhibits the proper conduct of banking business.[14]

Commercial Bank of Australia Ltd v Amadio[15] itself provides an **4–157** illustration of the operation and interaction of some of the factors which may place the guarantor in a position of special disadvantage. Mr and Mrs Amadio as guarantors were held to be under a special disadvantage because of a variety of circumstances: their age and limited grasp of English; they were approached to sign a lengthy and complicated guarantee "in their kitchen when Mr Amadio was reading the newspaper after lunch and Mrs Amadio was washing the dishes"; they had placed trust in their son, the managing director of the principal debtor, who had misled them as to extent and duration of the guarantee; and it was not insignificant that the relationship between the bank and the principal debtor was more than a normal business arrangement, arising out of the bank's desire to protect its own position and that of its wholly owned subsidiary, which had financed many of the principal debtor's projects.

As has been seen, the expanded concept of undue influence in *Etridge* **4–158** and, in particular, the reference to "cases where a vulnerable person has been exploited"[16] may mean that similar factual circumstances to those occurring in *Crédit Lyonnais Bank Nederland NV v Burch*[17] can now more properly be brought within the concept of undue influence, despite (as we have seen[18]) the somewhat dubious basis for establishing a relationship of trust and confidence in that case. Indeed, if all the claimant is required to show is that "a vulnerable person has been exploited", rather than the elements of unconscionability set out in *Alex Lobb (Garages) Ltd v Total Oil (Great Britain) Ltd,*[19] its proof would appear somewhat easier.

---

[10] *Melverton v Commonwealth Development Bank of Australia* (1989) A.S.C. 55–921 at 58–459, where Hodgson J. thought a significant factor was the extent to which the guarantor did not appreciate the facts relevant to the risk that was being undertaken.
[11] *Burke v State Bank of New South Wales Ltd* (1995) 37 N.S.W.L.R. 53.
[12] *ibid.*
[13] *Commercial Bank of Australia Ltd v Amadio* (1983) 151 C.L.R. 447; *Nolan v Westpac Banking Corp* (1989) A.S.C. 55–930 at 58–514.
[14] *Commercial Bank of Australia Ltd v Amadio* (1983) 151 C.L.R. 447 at 468 *per* Wilson J., 473 *per* Deane J.
[15] (1983) 151 C.L.R. 447.
[16] See above, para.4–124.
[17] [1997] 1 All E.R. 144.
[18] See above, para.4–137.
[19] [1983] 1 W.L.R. 87. See above, para.4–155.

(iv) Inequality of bargaining power

4–159   In *Lloyds Bank Ltd v Bundy*[20] Lord Denning MR stated that the guarantee and charge in that case could be set aside not only on the basis of undue influence,[21] but, alternatively, on broader ground of "inequality of bargaining power",[22] which could be regarded as embracing the intervention of equity in all cases of coercion, undue influence, and unconscionable bargains. Lord Denning defined the concept in this way:[23]

"There are cases in our books in which the courts will set aside a contract, or a transfer of property, where the parties have not met on equal terms – when the one is so strong in bargaining power and the other so weak that, as a matter of common fairness, it is not right that the strong should be allowed to push the weak to the wall".

This general principle was, however, rejected in *National Westminster Bank plc v Morgan*,[24] so that inequality of bargaining power cannot now be regarded as a basis for setting aside guarantees. Indeed, the doctrine of undue influence (especially since its expanded scope in *Etridge*[25] to encompass "cases where a vulnerable person has been exploited")[26] and the potential application of the principles of unconscionability bargains,[27] are likely to encompass all cases necessitating the intervention of equity.

(v) Unreasonable or unfair terms

(a) Unfair Contract Terms Act 1977

4–160   As guarantees are (in the usual case) entered into "in the course of a business",[28] the Unfair Contract Terms Act 1977 has potential application in respect of the validity of clauses within the standard form guarantee. There are a number of relevant provisions. Section (2)(2) states that a person (the creditor in the context of guarantees) cannot "exclude or restrict his liability for negligence except in so far as the term or notice satisfies the requirement of reasonableness". Thus, in principle, the creditor cannot exclude any liability for the tort of negligence arising from his failure to explain the guarantee but this result is of little practical

---

[20] [1975] Q.B. 326.
[21] See the discussion above, paras 4–134 to 4–136.
[22] [1975] Q.B. 326 at 339.
[23] *ibid.*, at 336–337. See also *Clifford Davis Management Ltd. v WEA Records Ltd* [1975] 1 W.L.R. 61; *Arrale v Costain Civil Engineering Ltd* [1976] 1 Lloyd's Rep. 98; *Cresswell v Potter* [1978] 1 W.L.R. 255n; *Backhouse v Backhouse* [1978] 1 W.L.R. 243, at 252; *A. Schroeder Music Publishing Ltd v Macaulay* [1974] 1 W.L.R. 1308.
[24] [1985] A.C. 686.
[25] *op. cit.*, above, para.4–121, n.71.
[26] See above, para.4–124.
[27] See above, para.4–155.
[28] s.3.

import since it is now clear that the creditor owes no such general duty of care.[29] More significantly s.2(2), however, will not apply to a clause in a guarantee excluding the creditor's duty to act with reasonable care in preserving or realizing securities since that duty is founded in equity rather than upon the tort of negligence.[30] Section 3 of the Act governs various exclusions from liability. It states:

(3)(1) This section applies as between contracting parties where one of them deals as consumer or on the other's written standard terms of business.
(2) As against that party, the other cannot by reference to any contract term—
    (a) when himself in breach of contract, exclude or restrict any liability of his in respect of the breach; or
    (b) claim to be entitled—
        (i) to render a contractual performance substantially different from that which was reasonably expected of him or
        (ii) in respect of the whole or any part of his contractual obligation, to render no performance at all,

except in so far as (in any of the cases mentioned above in this subsection) the contract term satisfies the requirement of reasonableness."[31]

In the context of guarantees, the guarantor will either be dealing as a **4–161** consumer or, more commonly, on the other's (that is, the creditor's) written standard terms of business. Yet do provisions which are commonly termed exclusion clauses and which appear in standard form guarantees come within the terms of s.3? Section 3(2)(a), translated into the language of guarantor and creditor, means that as against "that party" (the guarantor) dealing on the other's (the creditor's) written standard terms of business the other (the creditor) cannot when *himself in breach of contract exclude or restrict any liability of his in respect of the breach*. Thus, to come within the ambit of s.3(2)(a) and be subject to the test of reasonableness, the relevant clause must restrict the *creditor's* liability in respect of the *creditor's* breach of contract. Many of the clauses in standard form guarantees, however, do not have this effect. They simply preserve the guarantor's liability in circumstances when otherwise under the general law the guarantor would be discharged, so there is no exclusion of any liability of the creditor in respect of his breach of contract.[32] Examples of such clauses are clauses preventing the guarantor being discharged in the event of a variation of the principal contract,[33] or if the creditor fails to

---

[29] See below, para.8–115.
[30] *China & South Seas Bank v Tan* [1990] 1 A.C. 536 at 543–544, disapproving *Standard Chartered Bank v Walker* [1982] 1 W.L.R. 1410.
[31] Note also that s.13 of the Act extends the operation of s.3(2).
[32] See *Chitty on Contracts* (28th ed. 1999), para.44–118.

[33] See below, para.7–27.

maintain securities for the benefit of the guarantor[34] or releases the principal debtor.[35] Nor, pursuant to s.3(2)(b)(i) is the creditor claiming to be entitled by such clauses, "to render a *contractual performance* substantially different from that which was reasonably expected of him", unless "contractual performance" is interpreted in a (probably unrealistically)[36] broad sense to include ancillary equitable duties, for example, to preserve and maintain securities for the benefit of the guarantor.[37]

4–162   Some clauses in standard form guarantees, however, may come within the ambit of s.3(2)(a). Thus if the guarantee, (possibly from wording in the recital or statement of consideration)[38] imposes a contractual obligation on the creditor to obtain or maintain a security, another clause in the guarantee purporting to preserve the guarantor's liability if the creditor fails to do so will "exclude or restrict" the liability of the creditor in respect of the breach of this contractual undertaking. It has also been said that a clause excluding the guarantor's right of set off will come within s.3(2)(a) (as extended by s.13) since it excludes or restricts the creditor's liability when himself in breach of contract in respect of his breach.[39] But it is not entirely clear that this is so since, in the context of guarantees, the most usual set off is where the creditor is not in direct breach of his obligations *to the guarantor* under the guarantee but of the terms of the principal transaction, and the guarantor seeks to rely on a set off[40] arising from the latter transaction. Indeed, in the case of a legal set off the creditor may not even be in breach of the guaranteed principal transaction at all, but of an entirely separate contract with the principal.[41]

(b) Unfair Terms in Consumer Contracts Regulations 1999

4–163   These Regulations,[42] implementing EC Directive 93/13/EEC, exercise control over contract terms. In one respect the Regulations are narrower in their application than the Unfair Contract Terms Act 1977 since their impact is limited to terms contained in contracts made between a seller or supplier acting in the course of his business and another not so acting ("the consumer").[43] Yet, in another respect the Regulations have a more extended impact since they control not only exemption clauses, but any contractual term which has not been individually negotiated, which is then

---

[34] See below, para.8–92.

[35] See below, para.6–74.

[36] At least, however, in such a case an obligation is imposed upon the creditor (*Cf. Paragon Finance plc v Nash* [2002] 1 W.L.R. 685 especially at paras 72–76).

[37] But even so it might be argued that the guarantor could not reasonably expect that the creditor would render a performance other than that as qualified by the clause. See *Chitty on Contracts* (28th ed. 1999), para.14–070.

[38] See below, paras 8–57 to 8–61.

[39] *Chitty on Contracts* (28th ed., 1999), para.44–118.

[40] See below, paras 11–46 to 11–88.

[41] See below, paras 11–75 to 11–94.

[42] SI 1999/283. See, generally, *Chitty on Contracts* (28th ed., 1999) paras 44–119–44–123, J. Beatson, *Anson's Law of Contract* (28th ed., 2002), pp.200–203.

[43] Reg. 4(1).

subject to a test of "unfairness".[44] An unfair term is one which, contrary to the requirements of good faith, causes a significant imbalance in the parties' rights and obligations to the detriment of the consumer.[45] Schedule 2 also provides a non-exhaustive list of terms which may be regarded as unfair. A determination that a term is unfair means that it is not binding upon the consumer, although the contract will continue to bind the parties if it is capable of doing so in the absence of that term.[46]

In terms of the application of the Regulations to guarantees, a guarantor may perhaps be regarded as "supplying a service"[47] to a creditor since a "supplier of services" has been interpreted widely to include other commercial contracts, such as contracts of insurance[48] and contracts for the supply of financial services.[49] But, even assuming this to be the case, there are differing views as to the which types of guarantee come within the ambit of the Regulations. On one view the Regulations apply only in the unlikely case where the guarantor is acting in the course of a business, but the creditor is not. This interpretation arises because the Regulations define "supplier" (that is, in this context, the guarantor) as one, who, "is acting for purposes relating to his trade, business or profession"[50] and "a consumer" (that is, the creditor) as "any natural person who ... is acting for purposes which are outside his trade, business or profession".[51] Examples in the context of guarantees will be rare since it follows from these definitions that the creditor must be a natural person making an advance to a third party, which is then guaranteed by a bank or other commercial enterprise. As in most cases the reverse is the position and the creditor is acting in the course of a business and the guarantor is not, on this view the impact of the Regulations would be minimal, but it does accord with the literal meaning of the statutory instrument. **4–164**

A second view[52] is that guarantees by individuals are governed by the Regulations but only where the guarantee relates to a contract for the supply of goods or services *to a consumer*. This derives some (albeit oblique) support from the decision of the European Court in *Bayerische Hypotheken- und Wechselbank AG v Dietzinger*[53] and its interpretation of EC Directive 85/577, designed to protect the consumer in respect of contracts negotiated away from business premises. The European Court held that the phrase "contracts under which a trader supplied goods or services to a consumer" in Art.(1)(1) included contracts of guarantee, but only where the principal contract itself consisted of a contract under which a trader supplies goods or services to a consumer. It has therefore been **4–165**

---

[44] Reg. 5(1).
[45] *ibid.*
[46] Reg. 8.
[47] Although this is not clear from the Regulations themselves.
[48] See Preamble to the Directive L23
[49] See also *Chitty on Contracts* (28th ed., 1999) Vol. 1 para.15–011.
[50] Reg. 3(1).
[51] *ibid.*
[52] See *Chitty on Contracts* (28th ed., 1999) Supplement para.44–120 (addition to n.84 on p.1360).
[53] [1998] E.C.R. I–1199.

suggested that a "similar distinction"[54] could be adopted for the purpose of Directive 93/13 on unfair terms in consumer contracts, and the United Kingdom enacting Regulations. Indeed, this is the authors' preferred position, since the Regulations would then dovetail neatly with the general consumer protection in respect of consumer loans.

4–166   Finally, it has been argued that all guarantees made by consumers might be governed by the Regulations. Although (as has been seen)[55] this interpretation is contrary to the definition of supplier in the Regulations, it is said[56] to be based on the fact that:

> "the European Court of Justice could possibly take the view that contracts of guarantee were so inextricably linked with the provision of financial services by financial institutions that to refuse to apply the Directive's harmonizing controls to them would perpetuate unnecessarily existing distortions in competition in that area of the supply of services."

This is a somewhat general ground for extending the scope of the Directive to all guarantees made by consumers. Indeed, on this view, the Regulations would have a far ranging impact since guarantees by wives and persons not involved in the business of the borrowing company would be the subject of control.[57]

4–167   Assuming a broad application of the Regulations, there are clearly some clauses in standard form guarantees which may be regarded as "unfair" in that they cause "a significant imbalance in the parties' rights and obligations to the detriment of the consumer". The requirement of "significant imbalance" is met if, looking at the contract as a whole, "the term is so weighted in favour of the supplier as to tilt the parties' rights and obligations under the contract significantly in his favour"[58] (such as imposing on the consumer a disadvantageous burden, risk or duty).[59] Additionally, the requirement of good faith is one of "fair and open dealing" and means that the terms should be expressed "fully, clearly and legibly, containing no concealed pitfalls or traps",[60] with "appropriate prominence being given to terms which might operate disadvantageously to the consumer".[61] Fair dealing also requires that "a supplier should not, whether deliberately or unconsciously, take advantage of the consumer's necessity, indigence, lack of experience, unfamiliarity with the subject matter of the contract [or] weak bargaining position".[62] In the context of guarantees the terms most likely to contravene the Regulations are these:

---

[54] See above, n.52.
[55] See above, para.4–164.
[56] *Chitty on Contracts* (28th ed., 1999) para.44–120, p.1360.
[57] Although not directors' guarantees.
[58] *Director of Fair Trading v First National Bank plc* [2002] 1 A.C. 481 at 494, para.17, *per* Lord Bingham.
[59] *ibid.*
[60] *ibid.*
[61] *ibid.*
[62] *ibid.* See also other considerations referred to by Lord Steyn at 499–500, para.36–37; Lord Millett at 505, para.54.

(a) Clauses which preserve the guarantor's liability if the creditor fails to **4–168** maintain or preserve a security given by the principal debtor to secure the principal debt.[63] Such clauses can be seen as creating a "significant imbalance" in the rights of the parties since they expose the guarantor to the unreasonable risk of the creditor improperly dealing with the security. If this happens the effect of such clauses is that the guarantor loses the benefit of the security to which he would otherwise be entitled by subrogation.[64]

(b) Clauses which exclude the guarantor's right of subrogation, even **4–169** after payment of the debt[65] (for the same reasons as outlined in the previous paragraph above (a)).

(c) Clauses excluding the guarantor's right of set off or counterclaim.[66] **4–170** Here an imbalance in the parties' rights and obligations is created because the effect of the clause is that the guarantor cannot avail himself of a legitimate claim that he (or the principal) would otherwise possess against the creditor. Moreover Schedule 2 states (in clause 1(b)) that a clause may be regarded as being unfair if it has the object and effect of "inappropriately excluding or limiting the legal rights of the consumer ... *including the option of offsetting a debt owed to the seller or supplier against any claim which the consumer may have against him*" (authors' italics).[67]

(d) Clauses preserving the liability of the guarantor even if the principal **4–171** debtor is released,[68] especially if the contract as a whole is drafted as one of guarantee rather than as one of indemnity. Arguably these clauses create a "significant imbalance" in the rights of the parties since an agreement which the guarantor legitimately assumes is one of guarantee (co-extensive with the principal's obligations under the principal contract) has been converted into one of indemnity without definite and clear wording to that effect. If the contract is, however, clearly designated as an indemnity such clauses might be regarded as simply reinforcing the nature and subject matter of the contract.[69] Indeed Regulation 6(2) states specifically that the assessment of the fairness of the term should not relate to "the definition of the main subject of the contract".

(e) Clauses preserving the liability of the guarantor if the creditor agrees **4–172** with the principal to vary the principal contract.[70] A "significant imbalance" results because the obligation originally guaranteed may become much more onerous. Although not directly relevant, clause 1(j) of Sch.2 give some support for this view because it refers to a term which may be regarded as unfair when it has the object or effect "of enabling the seller or supplier to alter the terms of the contract unilaterally without a

---

[63] See below, para.8–92.
[64] See below, para.12–254.
[65] See below, para.12–260.
[66] See below, paras 11–88 and 11–94.
[67] See also generally on the exclusion of rights of set-off (and the effect of the Unfair Contract Terms Act 1977): *Stewart Gill Ltd v Horatio Myer & Co Ltd* [1992] 1 Q.B. 600 at 606. See also, below, para.11–50.
[68] See below, para.6–74.
[69] See *Chitty on Contracts* (28th ed., 1999) para.44–121.
[70] See below, para.7–27.

valid reason which is specified in the contract". In the context of guarantees an agreement between the parties to the principal contract to vary its terms in essence amounts to a "unilateral" alteration from the guarantor's standpoint.

4–173   (f) Terms which provide that the guarantee is continuing without any specified upper limit upon liability.[71] In *Etridge*[72] Lord Hobhouse specifically stated[73] in the context of a wife's guarantee of her husband's borrowings that no bank "who had a proper regard to the wife's interest" could reasonably ask her to sign an unlimited guarantee. A similar argument could be made in respect of "all monies" clauses, which (as will be seen)[74] may impose quite unexpected liabilities upon the guarantor.

4–174   (g) So-called "conclusive evidence" clauses[75] may provide that a certificate signed by an officer of the relevant financial institution shall be regarded as conclusive evidence of the amount of the indebtedness. Clearly in terms of the burden of proof this results in a "significant imbalance" in the rights of the parties. Schedule 2 clause 1(q) specifically states that a clause may be regarded as being unfair if it excludes or hinders "the consumer's right to take legal action or exercise any other legal remedy, particularly by . . . unduly restricting the evidence available to him which, according to the applicable law, should lie with another party to the contract".

4–175   (h) Principal debtor clauses,[76] by which the guarantor is deemed to be a principal debtor in all respects. Although such clauses probably do not convert what is otherwise a contract of guarantee into a contract of indemnity,[77] they do have the effect of preserving the liability of the guarantor in the event of a variation of the principal contract,[78] so (for the reasons given above)[79] are arguably unfair. An additional reason for regarding them as unfair is that their meaning is uncertain, so that the guarantor is less able to understand the nature of his obligations.[80]

4–176   (i) Clauses preserving the liability of the guarantor in the event of a release of a co-guarantor.[81] A "significant imbalance" in the parties' rights and obligations may be created here because the guarantor's consent to such a release means that he will lose his right of contribution against co-guarantor, so (potentially) the whole burden of the liability will fall on him.

---

[71] See below, para.5–22.
[72] *op. cit.*, above, para.4–121, n.71.
[73] *ibid.*, at 824 para.112.
[74] See below, para.5–79.
[75] See below, para.5–102.
[76] See above, para.1–101.
[77] See above, para.1–101.
[78] See below, para.7–28.
[79] See above, para.4–172.
[80] Note that Sch.2, clause 1(i) expressly refers to terms which have the object and effect of irrevocably binding the consumer to terms with which he had no real opportunity of becoming acquainted before the conclusion of the contract.
[81] See below, para.8–29.

9. THE CREDITOR'S LIABILITY FOR THE CONDUCT OF THE PRINCIPAL DEBTOR OR OTHER THIRD PARTIES

Even if the creditor has not been directly responsible for acts which **4-177** vitiate the guarantee, the creditor may in some circumstances be held responsible for the conduct of the principal debtor or a third party. Most of the authorities concern the exercise of undue influence by the principal debtor towards the guarantor, but this issue is dealt with separately as the principles have potential application to other vitiating factors (such as misrepresentation). Two separate rules are relevant, although the second is the much more important.

(i) Agency

If the creditor appoints an agent to obtain the guarantor's signature the **4-178** creditor will be liable for any misrepresentations made, or undue influence exercised, by the agent.[82] Thus the creditor may appoint the principal borrower as agent to obtain the execution of the guarantee on its behalf. This is unlikely in any practical sense, and in *Barclays Bank plc v O'Brien*,[83] the House of Lords specifically rejected a previous view expressed by the Court of Appeal in *Shephard v Midland Bank plc*[84] (and other cases)[85] that the guarantor may set aside the guarantee if the creditor has "entrusted" the task of obtaining the guarantor's signature to someone (such as the borrower) who was, to the knowledge of the creditor, in a position to influence the guarantor and who then procured the signature of the guarantee by undue influence or misrepresentation. Nor will the bank's action in giving the guarantee to the husband or other third party to obtain the wife's signature clothe the husband with apparent authority to act on its behalf.[86]

(ii) Notice

The guarantee will be set aside if the creditor has actual knowledge of **4-179** any fraud, undue influence exercised or misrepresentations made by the borrower.[87] In *Woodchester Equipment Leasing Co v Capital Belts*[88] a

---

[82] *Barclays Bank plc v O'Brien* [1994] 1 A.C. 180 at 194A, 195 F-G. See also *Nightingale Finance Ltd v Scott* (unreported, November 18, 1997), where the agent's knowledge that the transaction was manifestly disadvantageous to the guarantor was imputed to the creditor.
[83] *Barclays Bank plc v O'Brien* [1994] 1 A.C. 180 at 194.
[84] [1987] 2 F.L.R. 175.
[85] See also *Barclays Bank plc v Kennedy* [1989] 1 F.L.R. 356 at 364; *Avon Finance Co Ltd v Bridger* [1985] 2 All E.R. 281; *Kings North Trust Ltd v Bell* [1986] 1 W.L.R. 119 at 124; *Challenge Bank Ltd v Pandya* (1993) 60 S.A.S.R. 330.
[86] *Barclays Bank v O'Brien* [1994] 1 A.C. 180 at 194-195.
[87] *ibid.*, at 195.
[88] Unreported (April 12, 1995, CAT No.335).

finance company was held to have actual knowledge of facts giving rise to a
fraud by the supplier of photocopying machines when it was sent a receipt
stating that the cost of equipment to be paid by the lessee of the equipment
under a rental plan was three times that indicated by an earlier statement.
Given that, additionally, it was known that the relevant salesmen were "a
pretty dodgy bunch" and that it was the practice of the finance company to
deliberately avoid making a check upon prices (despite the ready
availability of a book for this purpose) it was held that "it must have
been obvious that something was seriously wrong". The finance company
had deliberately turned "a blind eye" to the obvious,[89] and the guarantor
of payments under the rental plan was accordingly discharged.

4–180   In the (very likely) absence of any actual knowledge the creditor will also
be rendered liable for the conduct of borrower on the basis of the principles
of constructive notice as set out by the House of Lords in *Barclays Bank plc
v O'Brien*,[90] and as subsequently re-defined and extended by the same
court in *Etridge*.[91] In *Barclays Bank plc v O'Brien*[92] the principle was
formulated by Lord Browne-Wilkinson (in respect of circumstances where
a wife is guarantor for her husband's borrowings) in this way:

> "A creditor is put on inquiry when a wife offers to stand surety for her
> husband's debts by the combination of two factors: (a) the transaction is
> on its face not to the financial advantage of the wife; and (b) there is a
> substantial risk in transactions of that kind that, in procuring the wife to
> act as surety, the husband has committed a legal or equitable wrong that
> entitles the wife to set aside the transaction."[93]

This is, of course, not constructive notice as understood in property law,
when a purchaser is treated as having constructive notice of all that a
reasonably careful purchaser would have discovered. Here there is no duty
upon the lender to make inquiries; the doctrine is simply a mechanism for
fixing the lender with responsibility for wrongful conduct by the husband.[94]
There has been some rather sterile academic debate[95] in respect of the
inappropriate use of the terminology of constructive notice in this context,
but it is a debate about nomenclature rather than substance.

4–181   In terms of that substantive principle the House of Lords in *Etridge*
interpreted Lord Browne-Wilkinson's criteria in a manner that is less
favourable to creditors – and in two respects. First, it rejected the view
(accepted by the Court of Appeal) that the question of whether or not the
lender is "put on inquiry" should be judged in the light of the facts known
to the lender. This view had been set out by the Court of Appeal in

---

[89] See this test in *Feuer Leather Corpn v Frank Johnstone & Sons* [1981] Com. L.R. 251. See
also Lindley L.J. in *Manchester Trust v Furness* [1895] 2 Q.B. 539 at 545.
[90] [1994] 1 A.C. 180.
[91] *op. cit.*, above, para.4–121, n.71.
[92] [1994] 1 A.C. 180.
[93] *ibid.*, at 196.
[94] See Lord Nicholls in *Etridge*, *op. cit.*, above, para.4–121, n.71 at 802, para.39.
[95] As described by J. O'Sullivan, "Undue Influence and Misrepresentation after O'Brien:
Making Security Secure" *Restitution and Banking Law* (1998, ed. F. Rose), p.42 at pp.44–45.

Barclays Bank plc v Bennett[96] which stated that the court should "look at the transaction through the eyes of the lender and ask whether in the light of all the facts which the lender does know, it is put on inquiry that there is a real and substantial risk that the wife's apparent consent to the transaction may have been obtained by some improper conduct". This approach meant that when a lender, for example, knows that the wife is a shareholder, but is at the same time ignorant of the fact that the shareholding is a limited one and that the wife takes no active part in the management of the company, the lender is not caught by condition (a) of Lord Browne-Wilkinson's test, that is, the guarantor cannot show that the transaction is "not to the financial advantage of the wife". Even where condition (a) is satisfied the lender is put on inquiry within the meaning of condition (b) only if the lender "is aware that the parties are cohabiting or that the particular surety places implicit trust and confidence in the principal debtor in relation to her financial affairs".[97]

In *Etridge*, however, Lord Nicholls read Lord Browne-Wilkinson's text   **4–182**
restrictively to mean "quite simply, that a bank is put on inquiry whenever a wife offers to stand surety for her husband's debts".[98] Clearly this is a sensible approach. Not only does it accord with Lord Browne-Wilkinson's objective formulation (encapsulated in the phrase "in transactions of *that kind*") but it also avoids lengthy inquiries (and expensive litigation) as to the degree knowledge possessed by the lender. Additionally, even if the wife is a director or the secretary of the company, whose shares are held by her and her husband, and even if she has an equal shareholding with her husband, the creditor is nevertheless put on inquiry.[99] This prevents the structure of the company being manipulated to create a façade of active participation by the wife.

The principle in *Barclays Bank plc v O'Brien*[1] also applies where the   **4–183**
husband stands surety for his wife's debts and in the case of unmarried couples (whether heterosexual or homosexual), but in the latter case only where the creditor is aware of the relationship. Cohabitation is not essential.[2]

The second respect in which *Etridge*[3] interpreted the principles in   **4–184**
Barclays Bank plc v O'Brien[4] in a manner less sympathetic to creditors was more far reaching. Lord Nicholls, supported by the majority of the House, espoused a "wider principle" that the doctrine of notice should be extended to "every case where the relationship between the surety and debtor is non-commercial".[5] This extended category has the merit of removing the artificial distinction between different classes of relationships

---

[96] [1999] Lloyd's Rep. Bank 145. It was an approach also followed by the Court of Appeal in *Etridge* itself: [1998] 4 All E.R. 705. See also *Barclays Bank v Sumner* [1996] E.G.C.S. 65; *Bank of Cyprus (London) Ltd v Markou* [1999] 2 F.L.R. 17.
[97] *Etridge, op. cit.*, above, para.4–121, n.71 at 803, para.45.
[98] *Etridge, op. cit.*, above, para.4–121, n.71 at 803, para.44.
[99] *Etridge, op. cit.*, above, para.4–121, n.71 at 804, para.49.
[1] [1994] 1 A.C. 180 at 198; *Etridge, op. cit.*, above, para.4–121, n.71 at 804 para.47.
[2] *Etridge, op. cit.*, above, para.4–121, n.71 at 804 para.47; *Massey v Midland Bank plc* [1995] 1 All E.R. 929 at 933.
[3] *op. cit.*, above, para.4–121, n.71.
[4] [1994] 1 A.C. 180.
[5] *Etridge, op. cit.*, above, para.4–121, n.71 at 814 para.87.

since, as Lord Nicholls points out, "the reality of life is that relationships in which undue influence can be exercised are infinitely various".[6]

4–185   The danger, however, is that if the category is not sufficiently defined the lender will be unable to determine which transactions will be subject to the relevant procedures, creating uncertainty for lenders. Indeed, if the category is not precisely delineated lenders are likely to adopt special procedures in respect of all guarantees, illegitimately increasing the burden upon lenders and the costs of borrowing.

4–186   So what is meant by a "non-commercial guarantee"? Lord Nicholls himself excludes some unarguably obvious examples where the guarantor is paid a fee (as in an insurance bond) or there is a inter-company guarantee.[7] More generally, we are told, that "those engaged in business can be regarded as capable of looking after themselves".[8] So presumably a guarantee by a director will generally be viewed as a commercial guarantee. But there are some difficult cases. Is a guarantee given by a non-executive director, having no financial interest in the commercial activities of the borrower "engaged in business" in the relevant sense?

4–187   One circumstance where the creditor will not be put on inquiry is where a joint loan is made to husband and wife which is, so far as the creditor is aware, for their joint purposes. Thus in *CIBC Mortgages v Pitt*[9] the transaction consisted of a joint loan to husband and wife which the bank understood (from their joint application) to be for the purpose of discharging an existing mortgage on their matrimonial home and then using the balance of the funds to buy a holiday home. In fact the husband used the surplus funds to purchase shares, but "there was nothing to indicate to the [creditor] that this was anything other than a normal advance to husband and wife for their joint benefit".[10] But the bank will be put on inquiry if it knows that the funds, or part of the funds, are to be applied for the substantial benefit of the husband.[11]

(iii) How can the creditor protect its position?

4–188   Assuming, prima facie, the creditor has constructive notice of the guarantor's rights, the question inevitably arises as to the necessary procedures the creditor needs to take to preclude a subsequent claim that it had constructive notice of any undue influence or misrepresentations. A distinction needs to be made between those transactions which had been

[6] *Etridge, op. cit.*, above, para.4–121, n.71 at 813–814 para.86.
[7] *Etridge, op. cit.*, above, para.4–121, n.71 at 814, para.88.
[8] *ibid.*
[9] [1994] 1 A.C. 200.
[10] *ibid.*, at 204. See also *Hedworth v Scotlife Home Loans (No.2) Ltd* [1995] N.P.C. 91, where there was a joint loan made to husband and wife for the joint purpose of discharging an existing mortgage, although the application had erroneously stated the purpose of the loan to be "for business purposes". It was held that the wife was not entitled to take advantage of the information given to the bank so as to put the bank on inquiry, when there would have been no such duty imposed on the bank had the correct purpose of the loan been stated.
[11] *Dunbar Bank plc v Nadeem* [1997] 2 All E.R. 253. See also above, para.4–151.

executed prior to the decision in *Etridge*[12] and those which subsequently take place, and in respect of which additional procedures are now imposed.

(a) Transactions prior to Etridge

In *Barclays Bank plc v O'Brien*[13] Lord Browne-Wilkinson considered, in **4–189** the context of the approach in that case, that the lender should insist that the wife attend a private meeting (in the absence of her husband) at which she must be told of the extent of her liability as guarantor, warned of the risk she was running and urged to take independent advice. Exceptionally, however, where the lender knew of facts that would render the presence of undue influence "not only possible but probable", the lender must insist that the wife is independently advised.[14]

This procedure, however, not only failed to anticipate the growth in **4–190** telephone and internet banking, but the identification of the "exceptional" case meant that lenders inevitably adopted the practice of referring the wife to a solicitor for advice in nearly all cases. Such a referral avoided the possibility of failing to comply with the somewhat general guidelines as to the information to be provided. It was unclear whether advice as to the extent of liability and the risk involved the necessity to provide, for example, information as to the borrower's financial circumstances or a detailed analysis of the terms of the guarantee. Advice from an independent solicitor also precluded the guarantor from relying on assurances alleged to have been given orally at any private meeting with bank officials. In *Etridge* the House of Lords recognised this commercial reality[15] and considered it reasonable for lenders as "a suitable alternative"[16] to prefer advice to be given by an "independent legal adviser" and then rely on written confirmation from the solicitor that appropriate advice had been given.

As regards the effect of the confirmation, Lord Nicholls stated[17] the **4–191** position in this way:

"In respect of past transactions, the bank will ordinarily be regarded as having discharged its obligations if a solicitor who was acting for the wife in the transaction gave the bank confirmation to the effect that he had brought home to the wife the risks she was running by standing as surety."

At the same time the House of Lords specifically rejected[18] the view expressed by Millett L.J. in the Court of Appeal in *Crédit Lyonnais Bank*

---

[12] *op. cit.*, above, para.4–121, n.71.
[13] [1994] 1 A.C. 180 at 196–197. Prior to *Barclays Bank plc v O'Brien* a telephone call to the wife explaining the necessary facts and giving her time to consider the matter, might well have sufficed: *Turner v Barclays Bank plc* [1998] 1 F.L.R. 276 at 294.
[14] *ibid.*
[15] *Etridge, op. cit.*, above, para.4–121, n.71 at 805, para.55.
[16] *Etridge, op. cit.*, above, para.4–121, n.71 at 805–806 para.55.
[17] *Etridge, op. cit.*, above, para.4–121, n.71 at 812 para.80. See also at 806 para.56.
[18] *Etridge, op. cit.*, above, para.4–121, n.71 at 807 para.63.

Nederland NV v Burch[19] (and accepted by the Court of Appeal in *Etridge* itself)[20] that if the transaction is "one into which no competent solicitor could properly advise the wife to enter"[21] confirmation that legal advice has been given by a solicitor will be insufficient to avoid the creditor being fixed with constructive notice.

4–192   A general certification by the solicitor, without any detail as to information provided to the guarantor, will suffice, for example, a certification by a solicitor that "I hereby confirm that prior to the execution of this document I explained the contents and effect thereof to [the guarantor] who informed me that he/she understood the same".[22] In the usual case a statement by the solicitor that he has "explained" the terms and conditions (without any reference to the guarantor's *under-standing*) will suffice because "in ordinary cases" that understanding, once the explanation had been given, could be assumed.[23] The certification may also be given by a legal executive since the creditor is entitled to assume that a solicitor's firm will "not entrust such a task to a legal executive with insufficient experience to carry out the task properly".[24]

4–193   In *Etridge*[25] the House of Lords concluded, confirming previous Court of Appeal authority,[26] that a solicitor can give appropriate legal advice to the wife and give the relevant certification, even if the solicitor also acts for the lender or the husband, or both. This is so whether or not the lender deals directly with the husband and wife and has to take the initiative in requiring the wife to take legal advice, or, alternatively, deals throughout with the solicitor acting for the husband and wife.[27]

4–194   Additionally, even where (as is commonly the case) the bank requests the solicitor acting for the husband to undertake the conveyancing formalities on behalf of the bank as well as to advise the wife, in performing the latter task the solicitor is acting as agent for the wife and not the bank.[28] Thus the solicitor's failure to give adequate advice will not be imputed to the bank either generally or pursuant to s.199(1)(ii)(b) of the Law of Property Act 1925, which states:

---

[19] [1997] 1 All E.R. 144 at 157.
[20] [1998] 4 All E.R. 705 at 722 para.49.
[21] *ibid.*
[22] See *Etridge, op. cit.,* above, para.4–121, n.71 at 852 para.203. See also *Banco Exterior Internacional v Mann* [1995] 1 All E.R. 929.
[23] *National Westminster Bank plc v Amin* [2002] U.K.H.L. 9 para.24. But see below, para.4–205 for the extraordinary case.
[24] *Barclays Bank plc v Coleman,* one of the appeals decided in *Etridge, op. cit.,* n.71 at 868 para.292.
[25] *Etridge, op. cit.,* above, para.4–121, n.71 at 809–810 paras 73–74 *per* Lord Nicholls; at 817, para.96, *per* Lord Clyde.
[26] See generally, *Banco Exterior Internacional v Mann* [1995] 1 All E.R. 936; *Midland Bank Plc v Serter* [1995] 1 F.L.R. 1034; *Barclays Bank Plc v Thomson* [1997] 1 F.L.R. 156; *Bank of Baroda v Shah* [1988] 3 All E.R. 24; *Halifax Mortgage Services Ltd v Stepsky* [1996] 2 All E.R. 277.
[27] *Etridge, op. cit.,* above, para.4–121, n.71 at 809 para.71.
[28] *Etridge, op. cit.,* above, para.4–121, n.71 at 846 paras 176–179, *per* Lord Scott; at 810–811 paras 77–78, *per* Lord Nicholls. See also *Barclays Bank plc v Thomson* [1997] 1 F.L.R. 156; *Halifax Mortgage Services Ltd v Stepsky* [1996] 2 All E.R. 277.

(1) A purchaser shall not be prejudicially affected by notice of ... (ii) any ... matter or any fact or thing unless ... (b) in the same transaction with respect to which a question of notice to the purchaser arises, it has come to the knowledge of his counsel, as such, or of his solicitor or other agent, as such..."

As the solicitor is *not* the bank's solicitor in giving advice to the wife, s.199 (1)(ii)(b) does not apply unless (as will be seen)[29] the solicitor in question never does in fact become the wife's solicitor.

The House of Lords, therefore, unequivocally rejected the argument **4–195** that the solicitor advising the wife must act for the wife alone. Several reasons are given for this[30] but, with respect, none are persuasive. It is said that a solicitor acting for a wife alone will add significantly to the legal costs for the wife.[31] But the lender could be made responsible for re-imbursement of the wife's costs, which would then be an additional cost of borrowing. Where the husband has extensive business interests these costs will be absorbed by the borrowing companies themselves. It is true that in other cases the costs will be borne by the husband directly (and probably indirectly by the family as a whole), but even here it is doubtful that this concern should take precedence over the wife's entitlement to truly independent advice. In any event, it is probable that the additional costs involved will not be excessive.

Another argument is that the wife will be "happier" if advised by a **4–196** family solicitor, who may be better placed to advise because of his knowledge of the respective backgrounds of husband and wife.[32] Yet this emotional contentment during the course of the meeting seems less important than the potential disadvantage (which Lord Nicholl's acknowl-edges) "that [the wife's] interests may rank lower in the solicitor's scale of priorities, perhaps unconsciously, than the interests of her husband".[33] Do we willingly choose a medical practitioner who has a comforting "bedside manner" even though there is a possibility that he is not the best person to make a correct diagnosis? Indeed, the solicitor's knowledge of the husband's "history", especially if it is littered with ill-considered business decisions, may make him the least suitable person to advise.

Lord Nicholls does accept that "in every case the solicitor must consider **4–197** carefully whether there is any conflict of duty or interest and, more widely, whether it would be in the best interests of the wife for him to accept instructions from her",[34] but in truth there is always a conflict of interest. It is simply unrealistic to expect that a solicitor acting for a number of parties with differing interests, can give truly independent advice to all those parties. This is acknowledged by the solicitor's professional conduct rules themselves, which prevent solicitors acting for more than one party where

---

[29] See below, para.4–203.
[30] *Etridge, op. cit.*, above, para.4–121, n.71 at 809–810, paras.73–74.
[31] *ibid.*
[32] *Etridge, op. cit.*, above, para.4–121, n.71 at 809, para.73.
[33] *Etridge, op. cit.*, above, para.4–121, n.71 at 809, para.72.
[34] *Etridge, op. cit.*, above, para.4–121, n.71 at 810, para.74.

there is a risk of a conflict of interest[35] and also by the judicial rejection of the device of "Chinese Walls", which purport to divide a solicitor's firm into separate sections when the firm is acting for clients with conflicting interests.[36] It is not insignificant that in other Commonwealth countries the courts have insisted that the solicitor must act and be understood to act solely for the guarantor.[37] Indeed, this was the view of some earlier English authority.[38]

4–198   Whatever the merit of this criticism, however, it is clear from the decision in *Etridge* that the bank will ordinarily not have constructive notice of undue influence exercised, or misrepresentations made, by the husband if a solicitor acting for the wife (albeit also for the husband or bank) gives the bank confirmation to the effect that he has advised the wife of the risks involved in becoming a surety. Given this approach, however, are there any circumstances in which the lender *cannot* rely on the fact that the wife has been advised, with confirmation to that effect, or any circumstances whereby knowledge of any inadequate advice will be imputed to the bank? There are a number of possibilities:

(i) Knowledge of inadequate advice

4–199   In *Etridge* Lord Nicholls clearly stated[39] that confirmation from a solicitor acting for the wife will not suffice:

> "if the bank knows that the solicitor has not duly advised the wife or, I would add, if the bank knows facts from which it ought to have realized that the wife has not received the appropriate advice. In such circumstances the bank will proceed at its own risk."

Given that a certificate drafted by the solicitor in general terms will suffice to protect the position of the creditor,[40] there will be few circumstances in which the creditor should realise that the advice is inadequate. Lord Nicholls does set out the "core minimum" elements of the legal advice which the solicitor should provide,[41] although it is arguable that these requirements apply only to future transactions. In any event it is unlikely that the House of Lords in *Etridge* intended the "core minimum"

---

[35] See generally J. O'Sullivan, "Undue Influence and Misrepresentation after O'Brien: Making Security Secure" in *Restitution and Banking Law*, p.42 at pp.60–61.
[36] *ibid.*
[37] Notably Australia. See, *e.g. McNamara v Commonwealth Trading Bank* (1984) 37 S.A.S.R. 232. See generally, J. O'Donovan and J. Phillips, *The Modern Contract of Guarantee* (3rd Australian ed., 1996) at pp.192–195; Sneddon, "Unfair Conduct in Taking Guarantees and the Role of Independent Advice" (1990) Vol.13(2) U.N.S.W. L.J. 302; Sneddon, "Lenders and Independent Solicitor's Certificates for Guarantors and Borrowers: Risk Minimisation or Loss Sharing" (1966) Vol.24 A.B.L.R. 5.
[38] *Powell v Powell* [1900] 1 Ch. 243; *Re Coomber* [1911] 1 Ch. 723.
[39] *Etridge, op. cit.*, above, para.4–121, n.71 at 806 para.57. See also at 817 para.95, *per* Lord Clyde.
[40] See above, paras 4–191 to 4–195.
[41] See below, paras 4–217 to 4–221.

matters to be set out in the certificate so as to put the creditor on inquiry if they are not set out therein.[42]

One circumstance where the creditor should realise from the facts **4–200** known to it that the advice may not be adequate is where the transaction is structured in such a way that the documentation does not reveal that one party to the transaction is a surety. Thus in *Northern Rock Building Society v Archer*,[43] Mrs Archer mortgaged her property as surety for an advance which was made to enable her brother to set up in practice as a solicitor. Although Mrs Archer was in no position to meet the repayments (and it was intended throughout that the responsibility for the repayments should be that of her brother) Mrs Archer was named in the documentation as the borrower with her brother named as the guarantor. This was therefore the reverse of the true position so that the lender was not entitled to assume that the solicitor would know that Mrs Archer should receive advice appropriate to her actual status as guarantor.

It is unclear the extent to which the creditor must disclose other **4–201** information to the solicitor. As regards future transactions (after the handing down of the decision in *Etridge*)[44] the House of Lords specifically sets out the information which needs to be disclosed, but in respect of prior transactions it is thought it would not extend beyond the limited common law duty to disclose unusual facts.[45]

(ii) Inadequate confirmation

In *Bank Melli Iran v Samadi-Rad*[46] the creditor did not oblige the **4–202** solicitor to provide a certificate that appropriate advice had been given before the loan was made, but simply relied upon a letter forwarded seven days after completion, stating that the advice had been given. Morritt L.J. concluded that this procedure was insufficient:

" ... I should be most reluctant to conclude that a lender might rely alone on the undertaking of a solicitor that the surety would be separately advised by an unidentified solicitor, when there is no apparent difficulty in requiring and being given at the time of completion a specific assurance or warranty that she has been advised by a named solicitor, for it is a commonplace experience that "there's many a slip twixt cup and lip!"...[47]

---

[42] Although Lord Nicholls does state that "the bank should in every case obtain from the wife's solicitor a written confirmation *to the effect mentioned above*", but this is in a section said to apply only to future transactions (*Etridge, op. cit.*, above, para.4–121, n.71 at 812 para.79(4), (80).

[43] [1999] Lloyd's Rep Bank 32.

[44] *op. cit.*, above, para.4–121, n.71.

[45] See above, para.4–02.

[46] [1995] 2 F.L.R. 367.

[47] *ibid.*, at 375. Note that on the facts the creditor's solicitor did in fact require assurances that the undertaking had been performed, although the Court of Appeal said it would need to be determined at trial whether or not the assurances were sufficient (at 375).

Conversely, a more liberal approach was adopted in *Scottish Equitable Life plc v Virdee*[48] where it was held to be an adequate confirmation when the creditor was informed by the husband's solicitor that another solicitor had advised the wife, without any confirmation being received directly from the wife's solicitor.[49] And in *Bank of Baroda v Reyarel*[50] Hoffmann L.J. said that the bank could assume appropriate advice had been given when it knew the wife was being advised by a solicitor even if no certificate at all was provided. But it is difficult to see how these cases comply with the requirement set out in *Etridge* that "the bank will ordinarily be regarded as having discharged its obligations if a *solicitor acting for the wife* in the transaction gave the bank confirmation to the effect that he had brought home to the wife the risk she was running by standing as surety". Additionally, as Lord Scott points out in *Etridge*, "knowledge that a solicitor is acting for a surety wife does not, without more, justify the bank in assuming the solicitor's instructions extend to advising her about the nature and effect of the transaction".[51]

(iii) Knowledge imputed to the bank when the solicitor is in fact not acting as the wife's solicitor

4–203   It has been seen[52] that, although a solicitor may be acting for the creditor (on its instructions) in the matter of the conveyancing, when he gives advice to the wife he will be acting solely as the wife's solicitor. The responsibility for any inadequate advice will not be imputed to the creditor. If, however, it transpires that the solicitor never acted for the wife at all in giving her advice, then the solicitor's failure to give any advice will be the bank's failure, pursuant to s.199(1)(ii)(b) of the Law of Property Act 1925 since the solicitor is then acting for the bank alone. This is so despite any erroneous confirmation by the solicitor that he has given the wife a sufficient explanation of the transaction. Thus in *Midland Bank plc v Wallace*[53] the bank requested a solicitor "to attend to the necessary formalities for us in the signing of the enclosed legal charge by Mr and Mrs Wallace". The solicitor wrote to the bank confirming that Mr and Mrs Wallace had "executed the documents" and that he had "attested them stating the documents have been explained". Mrs Wallace never gave the solicitor instructions to give her advice and none was given. As Lord Nicholls explained,[54] Mrs Wallace could not be bound by the acts of "a stranger", when there was no relationship of principal and agent between

---

[48] [1999] 1 F.L.R. 863.
[49] But the mere witnessing of a signature by a solicitor would not relieve the lender from having constructive notice of the husband's undue influence (see *Scottish Equitable Life plc v Virdee* [1999] 1 F.L.R. 863 at 867).
[50] [1995] 2 F.L.R. 376.
[51] *Etridge, op. cit.*, above, para.4–121, n.71 at 844–845 para.168. See also at 825 para.115, *per* Lord Hobhouse and *UCB Corporate Services v Williams* [2002] EWCA Civ 555 paras 95–97.
[52] See below, para.4–194.
[53] One of the appeals decided in *Etridge, op. cit.*, above, para.4–121, n.71 at 859–862, para.248–266. See also *National Westminster Bank plc v Amin* [2002] UKHL 9.
[54] *op. cit.*, above, para.4–121, n.71 at 815 para.90(1). See also Lord Scott at 859–861 paras 248–521 where the facts are fully set out.

her and her solicitor, and the remedy of the bank lay against the solicitor for breach of warranty of authority:

"The bank was put on inquiry, because this was a case of a wife standing as surety for her husband's debts. As the evidence stands at present, Mr Samson's participation in the transaction does not assist the bank. He was not Mrs Wallace's solicitor. Deficiencies in the advice given by a solicitor do not normally concern the bank. That is the position where the solicitor is acting for the wife, or where the solicitor has been held out by the wife to the bank as her solicitor. But where the solicitor was not acting for the wife, the bank is in the same position as any person who deals with another in the belief that the latter is acting on behalf of a third party principal when in truth he is not. Leaving aside questions of ostensible authority or the like, the alleged principal is not bound or affected by the acts of such a stranger.[55] The remedy of the bank lies against the (unauthorized) 'agent'. If the bank has suffered provable loss, it has a claim for damages for breach of implied warranty of authority."

In *Midland Bank plc v Wallace*,[56] the bank had not requested the solicitor to give any advice about the legal charge and at least Lord Scott emphasized this fact.[57] But even if the bank had done so, it is difficult to see this would have altered the position that the solicitor never became *the wife's* solicitor.[58] This will be a question of evidence in each case, although if the solicitor does give advice and explanation regarding the transaction, (even if it is inadequate) this would probably constitute an implied retainer, especially if the wife is to be directly responsible for the fees.

Lord Nicholls in this passage,[59] contemplates that the wife may "hold out" the solicitor "as her solicitor". But any such representation by the wife must give the bank reason to assume that the solicitor's instructions extend to giving advice about the nature and effect of the legal charge. Thus, in *UCB Home Loans Corp Ltd v Moore*[60] the more insertion of a solicitor's name (purporting to represent husband and wife as a joint retainer) on the mortgage application form was not sufficient to create this assumption, because such instructions extended to no more than authorising retention of the solicitor to agree "the form of the security documents and make arrangements for them to be executed".[61] It was held that there was an arguable case that the lender should have checked the position with the wife and sought confirmation that she was separately

4–204

---

[55] *Cf.* earlier authority *Bank of Baroda v Shah* [1988] 3 All E.R. 24.
[56] *op. cit.*, above, para.4–121, n.71.
[57] *Etridge, op. cit.*, above, para.4–121, n.71 at 861 para.261.
[58] This was not the case in *Midland Bank plc v Wallace* (*op. cit.*, above, para.4–203, n.53) as the solicitor submitted his fee note directly to the bank. (see *Etridge op. cit.*, above, para.4–121, n.71 at 860 para.255).
[59] See above, para.4–203.
[60] One of the cases decided in *Etridge, op. cit.*, above, para.4–121, n.71 at 868–871, paras 294–309, especially at 871 para.307, *per* Lord Scott. See also Lord Hobhouse at 831–832, para.127.
[61] *Etridge, op. cit.*, above, para.4–121, n.71 at 871 para.307, *per* Lord Scott.

advised.[62] It is true that a special feature of this case was that the wife argued that the husband did not have authority to fill in the mortgage application form, so it is arguable she never instructed the solicitor at all.[63] But subsequently in *Lloyd's TSB Bank v Holdgate*[64] the Court of Appeal did not limit *UCB Home Loans Corp v Moore*[65] to this narrower ground, so on this view the lender will not be protected simply because the wife has gone to a solicitor in connection with a transaction unless the lender has "reason to assume that [the] instructions extended to giving [the wife] advice about the nature and effect of the legal charge".[66] It is considered, however, that an unambiguous statement by the wife that a particular solicitor represents her will convey a reasonable implication that the solicitor's instructions extend to giving an explanation of the transaction. But, in all cases, as a matter of caution the lender should confirm that the solicitor's instructions do so extend.

(iv) The "extraordinary" case: specially vulnerable groups

4–205   In *National Westminster Bank plc v Amin*,[67] decided by the House of Lords after *Etridge*, it was held that there was an arguable case that a solicitor who (erroneously) confirmed that independent advice had been given to the guarantor wife had not been retained by her as her solicitor.[68] But, alternatively, the House of Lords noted that Lord Nicholls in *Etridge*[69] had emphasised that *"ordinarily"* the bank could preclude a successful claim that it had constructive notice of the wife's right to have the guarantee set aside on the basis of undue influence or misrepresentation by seeking confirmation from the wife's solicitor that the transaction had been explained to her.[70] *National Westminster Bank plc v Amin*,[71] was, however, in the view of the House of Lords not an "ordinary" case. The bank was aware that Mr and Mrs Amin came from an ethnic minority group and could not speak English and "knew, therefore, that they might be specially vulnerable to exploitation in relation to transactions such as that which were being proposed".[72] In such circumstances the House of Lords suggested:

> (1) The bank's letter to the solicitor should have stated that "special care"[73] might be needed in advising Mr and Mrs Amin. It was totally inappropriate simply to ask the solicitor to attend to the

---

[62] See at 831–832, para.127 *per* Lord Hobhouse.
[63] This feature of the case is stressed by Lord Hobhouse in *Etridge, op. cit.,* above, para.4–121, n.71 at 832, para.127, with Lord Nicholls agreeing (at 815 para.90(3). The exact basis of the decision is not clear, because Lord Bingham (at 794 para.4) agrees with Lord Scott. Lord Clyde simply allows the appeal (at 818 para.97), but generally agreeing with Lord Hobhouse. See an analysis of the decision in *Lloyds TSB Bank v Holdgate* (unreported CA October 14, 2002).
[64] Unreported CA October 14, 2002, at paras 24, 40–43.
[65] *Etridge, op. cit.,* above, para.4–121, n.71 at 868–871, paras 294–309.
[66] See the language of Lord Scott in *Etridge, op. cit.,* above, para.4–121, n.71 at 871 para.307.
[67] [2002] UKHL 9.
[68] See above, para.4–203.
[69] *op. cit.,* above, para.4–121, n.71.
[70] See above, para.4–191.
[71] [2002] UKHL 9.
[72] *ibid.,* at para.24.
[73] [2002] UKHL. 9 at para.24(ii).

"necessary formalities" as the bank had done on the facts of the case.

(2) The bank should have sought "confirmation of Mr and Mrs Amin's apparent understanding of the transaction",[74] rather than being content with a statement from the solicitor that he had "explained" the terms and conditions of the transaction. Although "in ordinary cases ... that understanding, once the explanation had been given, could be assumed"[75] such an assumption would not be safe given Mr and Mrs Amin's cultural background and their inability to speak and understand English.

Thus, where the creditor knows the guarantor is "specially vulnerable to exploitation in respect of the proposed transaction" it appears that the creditor must draw the attention of the solicitor acting for the wife to the need for "special care" in giving advice, at least where the solicitor is also acting for the bank in respect of the conveyance. It should also seek an assurance that the guarantor has understood the nature of the transaction. The difficulty for the lender, of course, is to identify those potential guarantors coming within this category. Is it limited to those from an ethnic minority background, or does it include others who may be specially vulnerable for other reasons, for example, because of their educational background?

In *Etridge*[76] Lord Nicholls stated in respect of all wife guarantors **4–206** (whether in a vulnerable group or not) that where the bank believes or suspects that the wife has been mislead by her husband or is not entering the transaction of her own free will, the bank must inform the wife's solicitors of the facts giving rise to the belief or suspicion. This obligation, however, is limited in its application to future transactions.[77] This latter limitation is somewhat odd given the special treatment of "specially vulnerable" guarantors in *National Westminster plc v Amin*,[78] which is applicable to past transactions. If a bank in respect of past transactions needs to inform the solicitor that "special care" is needed in respect of giving advice to a "specially vulnerable" guarantor, surely it should also be under a general obligation in respect of those transactions to disclose its belief or suspicion of misrepresentation or undue influence.

(b) Additional procedures in respect of future transactions

In *Etridge*,[79] additional obligations were imposed upon lenders as **4–207** regards subsequent transactions (presumably the relevant date being the handing down of the decision). A failure to comply with these obligations

---

[74] *ibid.*, para.24(iv).
[75] *ibid.*
[76] *op. cit.*, above, para.4–121, n.71 at 812, para.79(3). See also below, para.4–214.
[77] *Etridge, op. cit.*, above, para.4–121, n.71 at 812 para.80.
[78] [2002] UKHL 9.
[79] *Op. cit.*, above, para.4–121, n.71.

will constitute an additional circumstance (together with those outlined in the previous section) where the lender will not be able to rely on a confirming certificate from the solicitor. These obligations, which appear only to apply to wives and not other "non-commercial" guarantors, may be conveniently classified in the following way:

(i) Direct communication with wife as to choice of solicitor

4–208   One of the faults in the procedures for ensuring the wife received appropriate advice prior to *Etridge* was that the wife, when becoming involved in the transaction at a late stage, often had no opportunity to exercise a choice as to the identity of her solicitor (which invariably was the husband's solicitor). Nor did the wife usually realise that the purpose of the advice was to protect the bank's position. Thus *Etridge*[80] requires, in respect of future transactions, that the lender should take steps to *check directly with the wife* the name of the solicitor she wishes to act for her and to inform her (by this direct communication) that, for the lender's own protection, it will require written communication from a solicitor acting for her, "to the effect that the solicitor has fully explained to her the nature of the documents and the practical implications they will have for her".[81] The bank should not proceed with the transaction until it has received an appropriate response from the wife.[82] This direct communication with the wife must contain the following information and requests:[83]

> (1) She should be told that the purpose of this requirement is that once she has signed the documents thereafter she should not be able to dispute that she is legally bound by them.

> (2) She should be asked to nominate a solicitor whom she is willing to instruct to advise her, separately from her husband, and act for her in giving the necessary confirmation to the bank.

> (3) She should be told that, if she wishes, the solicitor may be the same solicitor as is acting for her husband in the transaction. If a solicitor is already acting for the husband and the wife, she should be asked whether she would prefer that a different solicitor should act for her regarding the bank's requirement for confirmation from a solicitor.

4–209   One criticism of this well-intentioned procedure is that it is hardly likely to induce the wife to instruct an independent solicitor. It is almost inevitable that this direct communication becomes a matter of family discussion (or husband's persuasion). Indeed the explicit statement informing the wife that "if she wishes" her solicitor may be the same as the solicitor acting for her husband will invariably point the wife decisively in that direction. No specific guidance is given by the House of

---

[80] *op. cit.*, above, para.4–121, n.71.
[81] At 811 para.79(1).
[82] *ibid.*
[83] *ibid.*

Lords as to the result if the wife responds to this communication by stating that she does not wish to take legal advice at all. One previous judicial view[84] was that the lender was not under an obligation to ensure that the guarantor receives independent advice, but simply to advise the guarantor to seek advice and give her an opportunity to do so. But *Etridge* now appears to deny this possibility, by specifically stating that the bank should "in every case"[85] obtain confirmation from the wife's solicitor that advice has been given. This mandatory requirement also means that under the new procedures the bank will not be able to rely upon the fact that the wife had falsely represented to the bank that she is being advised by a particular solicitor.[86]

(ii) Provision of Financial Information

In *Etridge*[87] the House of Lords considered that a solicitor can only properly give advice to a wife if provided with information about her husband's affairs, which is in the peculiar knowledge of the lender. Thus the lender must now provide the solicitor with certain financial information that he requires for this purpose, as described by Lord Nicholls: **4–210**

"What is required must depend on the facts of the case. Ordinarily this will include information on the purpose for which the proposed new facility has been requested, the current amount of the husband's indebtedness, the amount of his current overdraft facility, and the amount and terms of any new facility. If the bank's request for security arose from a written application by the husband for a facility, a copy of the application should be sent to the solicitor."[88]

The confidential relationship between banker and customer will mean that the consent of the borrower to the release of this information will be needed, but, if no consent is given, the transaction will not be allowed to proceed.[89] And, if the bank does not provide the information, the solicitor must not confirm to the bank that the required advice has been given.[90] Nothing is said as to the obligation of the bank or solicitor if the prospective guarantor asks a specific question about a particular material matter, but there is existing authority[91] that such a matter must be disclosed.

There are a number of difficulties with the imposition of these obligations upon the lender, which is no doubt a well meaning attempt to improve the quality of legal advice. The bank's obligation to provide information, although easy to state in general terms, may not be so easily **4–211**

---

[84] *Coldunell v Gallon* [1986] Q.B. 1184 at 1201.
[85] *Etridge, op. cit.*, above, para.4–121, n.71 at 812, para.79(4).
[86] See above, para.4–204.
[87] *op. cit.*, above, para.4–121, n.71.
[88] *Etridge, op. cit.*, above, para.4–121, n.71 at 811–812, para.79(2).
[89] *ibid.*
[90] *Etridge, op. cit.*, above, para.4–121, n.71 at 808, para.67.
[91] *Hamilton v Watson* (1848) 12 Cl. & Fin. 109; 8 E.R. 1339. See also above, paras 4–27 to 4–29.

implemented in particular cases. Where the husband's business affairs are extensive, perhaps carried on through a number of related companies, even giving a realistic picture of his current indebtedness may prove troublesome. Similarly the borrower may have loan facilities at financial institutions other than the lender who is taking the guarantee as security, so that the disclosure of the particular overdraft granted by the latter may give a distorted picture of the husband's exposure. Indeed, historically these difficulties, now brushed aside in *Etridge*, have not escaped the notice of the judiciary. One of the primary reasons advanced for previously limiting the general rule of disclosure in respect of guarantees only to "unusual features of the contract between the creditor and debtor which makes it materially different in a potentially disadvantageous way from what the guarantor might expect"[92] (thus excluding facts relating to the general creditworthiness or financial position of the borrower) was the immense burden placed on banks in providing full and accurate information.[93] In *Hamilton v Watson*[94] Lord Campbell went so far as to suggest that lenders would never obtain sureties if full disclosure of material facts were required.

4–212   Indeed, the relationship between the procedure of disclosure set out in *Etridge* and this general rule of disclosure requires clarification. Lord Nicholls in *Etridge* saw no need "to re-visit"[95] the scope of the general disclosure principle. There are, indeed, few examples of its application since it is so narrowly based, on one view being limited to unusual facts arising from *a term of the contractual relationship between lender and borrower*.[96]

4–213   Despite Lord Nicholl's assertion that this general law of disclosure[97] applicable to contracts of guarantee does not require re-examination, the very scheme which his Lordship adopts does in fact modify the rule. The bank must now disclose the current amount of the husband's indebtedness and the amount of his current overdraft facility to the wife's agent (her solicitor). Such an obligation will also presumably extend to other "non-commercial" guarantors[98] (in Lord Nicholl's terminology). Furthermore the information which the lender must disclose depends "on the particular facts of the case". An additional matter that one might well suppose that the lender should disclose pursuant to this procedure is the lender's reasonable suspicion that the borrower has been fraudulent (despite, on one view, there being no obligation to disclose this under the general

---

[92] *Etridge, op. cit.,* above, para.4–121, n.71 at 812, para.81, *per* Lord Nicholls. See also, the principle stated in similar terms at 848 paras 185–188, *per* Lord Scott, who, however, also encompasses within the rule unusual features of the contractual relationship arising between "the creditor and other creditors of the principal debtor". See above, para.4–14.

[93] *e.g. London General Omnibus Co Ltd v Holloway* [1912] 2 K.B. 72; *Lee v Jones* (1864) 17 C.B. (NS) 482 at 503; 144 E.R. 194 at 202; *Levett v Barclays Bank plc* [1995] 2 All E.R. 615 at 627; *Hamilton v Watson* (1845) 12 Cl. & Fin. 109; 8 E.R. 1339. See above, para.4–04.

[94] (1845) 12 Cl. & Fin. 109; 8 E.R. 1339.

[95] *Etridge, op. cit.,* above, para.4–121, n.71 at 812, para.81.

[96] See above, para.4–06.

[97] See above, paras 4–02 to 4–35.

[98] This seems to follow from Lord Nicholl's assertion that there is "no rational cut-off point" between certain types of relationship (see *Etridge, op. cit.,* above, para.4–121, n.71 at 814 para.87), although the specific obligations are referred to in terms of husband and wife (at 811–812, para.79).

law).[99] Indeed, it would be somewhat odd if the lender is obliged to disclose the extent of the borrower's indebtedness or amount of his current overdraft facility but not suspicions of fraud.

(iii) Disclosure of facts indicating suspicion of misrepresentation or undue influence

In *Etridge*[1] Lord Nicholls set out this additional obligation.   **4–214**

"Exceptionally there may be a case where the bank believes or suspects that the wife has been misled by her husband or is not entering into the transaction of her own free will. If such a case occurs the bank must inform the wife's solicitors of the facts giving rise to its belief or suspicion."[2]

A failure to provide this information will presumably mean that the validity of the guarantee can be subsequently impugned on the basis of undue influence.

In the case of actual knowledge by the lender of a misrepresentation by   **4–215** the husband or, a specific threat amounting to duress, or of facts clearly indicating the existence of undue influence, this exception may be justifiable. But Lord Nicholls exception is wider than that, referring to a suspicion that the wife is not entering the transaction of her own free will. A bank official, who legitimately seeks clear and precise rules, may be justifiably perplexed. Is suspicion aroused because at a meeting at the bank the husband appears to have a somewhat overbearing manner or the wife appears to come from a cultural background where wives are generally subservient to the wishes of their husbands in financial matters? Presumably not, since these facts would not be sufficient by themselves to raise the presumption of undue influence, but one suspects the bank official will not be sure. There is an echo here of the "exceptional" case identified by Lord Browne-Wilkinson in *Barclays Bank plc v O'Brien*,[3] (detailing circumstances when advice was required to be given by a solicitor rather than by the bank) which very much influenced bank procedures and distorted the general scheme that his Lordship proposed in that case.

There is always a judicial reluctance to create fixed rules. Often   **4–216** generally worded exceptions (as here) are borne out of an understandable wish to achieve the desired result in every future case, not yet contemplated. But in the commercial world such exceptions create uncertainty and derogate from the legitimate expectation that the lender should be able to have confidence in its securities.

---

[99] See above, paras 4–12 to 4–13.
[1] *Etridge, op. cit.*, above, para.4–121, n.71.
[2] *ibid.*, at 812, para.79(3).
[3] [1994] 1 A.C. 180.

(iv) Solicitor's obligations: the nature and content of advice

4–217   As has been seen, the scheme envisaged by *Etridge*[4] is that in every case the bank must obtain a written confirmation from the wife's solicitor that the solicitor has given the requisite advice. The wife cannot then impugn the validity of the guarantee as against the lender, although the wife may have an action against her solicitor in negligence if the advice is inadequate. On the face of it the scheme provides certainty, giving the lender confidence in its security, but to achieve a balanced approach and to ensure the interests of the guarantor are protected there need to be safeguards that the advice given to the guarantor by the solicitor is satisfactory. In *Etridge*[5] the House of Lords does set out in some detail (as regards future transactions) the particular matters that need to be addressed in giving that advice.

4–218   At a doctrinal level *Etridge* rejected the view (which had been accepted by the Court of Appeal in the same case,[6] following *Crédit Lyonnais Bank Nederland NV v Burch*)[7] that the solicitor's duty is to satisfy himself that his client is free from influence. According to the House of Lords the solicitor's obligation is simply to explain the transaction and the risks involved in it.[8] There is also a rejection of the general proposition (again emanating from *Credit Lyonnais Bank Nederland NV v Burch*)[9] that the solicitor is under an obligation to veto the transaction if in his view the transaction is one which the guarantor could not sensibly enter and refuse to act if the guarantor insists on proceeding with it.[10] It is acknowledged, however, that "[t]here may, of course, be exceptional circumstances where it is glaringly obvious that the wife is being grievously wronged" and in "such a case the solicitor should decline to act further".[11] One instance given is that of a poor man divesting himself of all his property in favour of his solicitor.[12] In the context of guarantees it is difficult to contemplate such an "extreme example",[13] but a solicitor may perhaps be justifiably concerned at continuing to act when a wife without any independent means of support is asked to charge her sole capital asset (the matrimonial home) as security for borrowings for a venture which is unreasonably and obviously speculative.

4–219   On a more specific level, *Etridge* (whilst acknowledging that the content of legal advice will depend on the particular circumstances) set out a "core minimum"[14] of matters that should be covered by the solicitor in a face to face meeting with the wife in the absence of her husband, using non-

[4] *op. cit.*, above, para.4–121, n.71.
[5] *ibid.*
[6] *Royal Bank of Scotland plc v Etridge* [1998] 4 All E.R. 705 at 715.
[7] [1997] 1 All E.R. 144.
[8] *Etridge, op. cit.*, above, para.4–121, n.71 at 806–807 paras 58–59.
[9] [1997] 1 All E.R. 144.
[10] *Etridge, op. cit.*, above, para.4–121, n.71 at 807, para.61.
[11] *Etridge, op. cit.*, above, para.4–121, n.71 at 807 para.62.
[12] *ibid.*
[13] *ibid.*
[14] *Etridge, op. cit.*, above, para.4–121, n.71 at 808 para.65.

technical language.[15] It is instructive to set out the relevant part[16] of the judgment detailing these matters in full:

"*(1)* He will need to explain the nature of the documents and the practical consequences these will have for the wife if she signs them. She could lose her home if her husband's business does not prosper. Her home may be her only substantial asset, as well as the family's home. She could be made bankrupt.

(2) He will need to point out the seriousness of the risks involved. The wife should be told the purpose of the proposed new facility, the amount and principal terms of the new facility, and that the bank might increase the amount of the facility, or change its terms, or grant a new facility, without reference to her. She should be told the amount of her liability under her guarantee. The solicitor should discuss the wife's financial means including her understanding of the value of the property being charged. The solicitor should discuss whether the wife or her husband has any other assets out of which repayment could be made if the husband's business should fail. These matters are relevant to the seriousness of the risks involved.

(3) The solicitor will need to state clearly that the wife has a choice. The decision is hers and hers alone. Explanation of the choice facing the wife will call for some discussion of the present financial position, including the amount of the husband's present indebtedness, and the amount of his current overdraft facility.

(4) The solicitor should check whether the wife wishes to proceed. She should be asked whether she is content that the solicitor should write to the bank confirming he has explained to her the nature of the documents and the practical implications they may have for her, or whether, for instance, she would prefer him to negotiate with the bank on the terms of the transaction. Matters for negotiation could include the sequence in which the various securities will be called upon or a specific or lower limit to her liabilities. The solicitor should not give any confirmation to the bank without the wife's authority."

Additionally, the solicitor should obtain from the wife any information he needs, and "if the bank *fails for any reason* to provide the information requested by the solicitor, the solicitor should decline to provide the confirmation sought by the bank".[17] There is some potential here for commercial transactions to be delayed or aborted if a cautious solicitor requests unnecessary information, which the bank cannot easily locate and, because of lack of knowledge, is unable to supply.

4–220

---

[15] *Etridge, op. cit.*, above, para.4–121, n.71 808 para.66.
[16] *Etridge, op. cit.*, above, para.4–121, n.71 808 para.65.
[17] *Etridge, op. cit.*, above, para.4–121, n.71 at 808 para.67.

4–221   The professional burden placed upon the solicitor, who has a potential liability to the guarantor[18] arising from a breach of his professional duty of care, is high, perhaps excessively so. The omission of one of the mandatory core matters will mean that the advice is inadequate. Even if all those matters are covered the courts may find (with the prudence of hindsight) that particular circumstances warranted supplementary advice or the disclosure of additional facts. And the solicitor must also remember that he cannot accept instructions "in exceptional circumstances where it is glaringly obvious that the wife is being grievously wronged".[19]

10. LIABILITY OF CO-GUARANTORS WHEN VITIATING CIRCUMSTANCES ARE PROVED AGAINST ONE GUARANTOR

4–222   As a matter of principle, the fact that the contract is avoided against one co-guarantor will not discharge the other guarantors. But if (as is usual) the liability of the guarantors is joint and several this carries with it the implication that all the guarantors must execute the agreement before it becomes legally binding.[20] On this basis it has been held that, if the signature of one of the joint and several guarantors is forged, so that as regards that guarantor the guarantee is void and of no effect, all guarantors are discharged, even if they did not know of the forgery.[21] The same conclusion has been reached in Australia where the guarantee is void as against one guarantor because of a failure to comply with statutory requirements regarding execution.[22]

4–223   Arguably, therefore, the same result follows if the guarantee is void vis-à-vis one of the guarantors for other reasons, such as common mistake or illegality. But what is the position if the guarantee is not void but voidable? This is a crucial question since most of the common vitiating factors such as undue influence, unconscionability or duress render the contract voidable. In these cases it cannot be said that the guarantee is of no effect; it is simply liable to be set aside in equity. But it would be odd indeed if the co-guarantors were to be discharged, for example, where the relevant vitiating factor is common mistake but not where it is undue influence, unconscionability or duress.

4–224   The most sensible approach would be to preserve the liability of the co-guarantors in all situations in which the guarantee is void or is voidable and

---

[18] See, *e.g. McGregor v Michael Taylor & Co* [2002] 2 Lloyd's Rep. 468. Note also that the lender's solicitor may be liable to the lender for breach of its contract of retainer, if the contract stipulates certain requirements, *e.g.* the lender's solicitor must confirm that the borrower's solicitor also acts for the guarantor. See *Mercantile Credit Ltd v Fenwick* [1999] 2 F.L.R. 110, although it was held on the facts that the "Notes for Solicitors" did not impose this requirement as a term of the contract.

[19] See above, para.4–218.

[20] See above, para.3–87.

[21] *James Graham & Co (Timber) Ltd v Southgate-Sands* [1986] Q.B. 80.

[22] *McNamara v Commonwealth Trading Bank of Australia* (1984) 37 S.A.S.R. 232 (failure to comply with s.44 of the Consumer Transactions Act 1972, SA).

has been set aside, except in respect of forgeries when in reality there is no execution at all. Otherwise the result operates unfairly upon the creditor, who loses all its rights against the co-guarantors, despite there being no evidence that they had entered into the contract otherwise than as a result of their free and voluntary acts.

Part II

LIABILITY AND DISCHARGE

CHAPTER 5

THE SCOPE OF THE GUARANTOR'S LIABILITY

This chapter analyses the extent and scope of the guarantor's liability. This is a matter of construction in each case so the chapter begins with an analysis of the general principles of construction applicable to contracts of guarantee. The second section analyses particular problems of construction which may arise in determining the extent of the guarantor's liability and, in this context, the types of clauses which are commonly found in modern contracts of guarantee. Finally, the special difficulty of the extent of the guarantor's liability where the principal contract is defective in some way (that is, because it is void, voidable or unenforceable) is dealt with in section 3.

1. GENERAL PRINCIPLES OF CONSTRUCTION AFFECTING THE SCOPE OF THE GUARANTOR'S LIABILITY

(i) The general rule

Historically, the judicial approach to the construction of contracts of guarantee has been characterised by inconsistency. A number of different methods of construction have been suggested, but principally the cases have vacillated between two views.[1]   **5–01**

First, the courts have often stated that in cases of ambiguity the guarantee should be construed *in favour* of the guarantor.[2] For example, in *Eastern Counties Building Society v Russell*,[3] Hilbery J. said: **5–02**

> "Rather will the court in case of doubt lean in [the surety's] favour. Neither equity nor law will put a construction on the document which results in imposing on the surety any more than, on the strictest construction of the instrument, he must be said expressly to have undertaken, or so as to detract from the right given to the surety by the proviso defining the circumstances in which the surety is to be held discharged."[4]

Sometimes this rule of construction is expressed in more liberal terms than that laid down by Hilbery J., with an emphasis on a "fair but strict reading of the language of the guarantee"[5] rather than restricting the guarantor's obligation to that which "on the strictest construction of the instrument, he must be said to have expressly undertaken".

The second approach treats a guarantee like any other mercantile document or commercial contract.[6] Thus the guarantee should be given a   **5–03**

---

[1] At one time, a third view was that the guarantee should be construed against the guarantor: *Mayer v Isaac* (1840 6 M. 151 E.R. 554 at 557 ("the party who receives the instrument, and parts with his goods on the faith of it should rather have a construction put upon it in his favour"); *Jones v Mason* (1892) 13 L.R. (NSW) 157 at 162; *A.A. Davison Pty Ltd v Seabrook* (1931) 37 A.L.R. 156.

[2] *Eastern Counties Building Society v Russell* [1947] 1 All E.R. 500 at 503 (and the cases therein cited); *General Surety & Guarantee Co Ltd v Francis Parker Ltd* (1977) 6 Build. L.R. 18 at 21; *Glyn v Hertel* (1818) 8 Taunt. 208; 129 E.R. 363; *Ankar Pty Ltd v National Westminster Finance (Aust) Ltd* (1987) 162 C.L.R. 549; *Parker v Bayly* [1927] G.L.R. 265 at 267; *Mercantile Credits Ltd v Harry* [1969] 2 N.S.W.R. 248 at 249; *Duncombe v Australia & New Zealand Bank Ltd* [1970] Qd. R. 202 at 207; *Mercantile Credits Ltd v Buckeridge* [1980] W.A.R. 1 at 7; *Triaca v Summaries Pty Ltd* [1971] V.R. 347 at 351.

[3] [1947] 1 All E.R. 500.

[4] *ibid.*, at 503.

[5] *First National Finance Corp Ltd v Goodman* [1983] B.C.L.C. 203 at 213. See also *Ankar Pty Ltd v National Westminster Finance (Aust) Ltd* (1987) 162 C.L.R. 549 at 561 and *Tam Wing Chuen v Bank of Credit & Commerce Hong Kong Ltd* [1996] 2 B.C.L.C. 69, emphasising that the contra proferentem rule only applied in ambiguous cases.

[6] *Bacon v Chesney* (1816) 1 Stark. 192; 17 E.R. 443; *Stamford Spalding & Boston Banking Co v Ball* (1862) 4 De G. F. 310; *Straton v Rastall* (1788) 2 T.R. 366 at 370; 100 E.R. 197 at 199; *Hargreave v Smee* (1829) 6 Bing. 244 at 248; 130 E.R. 1274 at 1276; *Morten v Marshall* (1863) 3 H. & C. 310; *S.H. Lock Discounts & Credits Pty Ltd v Miles* [1963] V.R. 656 at 658; *Reid Murray Holdings Ltd (in liq) v David Murray Holdings*; (1972) 5 S.A.S.R. 386 at 406; *Craig v Finance Consultants Pty Ltd* [1964] N.S.W.R. 1012.

reasonable, business meaning and should not be construed so as to render the guarantee ineffective or illusory.[7]

5–04   These two approaches are, of course, not alternatives (since the former only applies in cases of ambiguity) and recent statements of principle articulate both views, but with an emphasis on treating the guaranteed as a commercial document. Thus in *Estates Gazette Ltd v Benjamin Restaurants Ltd*[8] the Court of Appeal put it this way:

> "Lastly it was submitted on behalf of the defendants that if there is an ambiguity or doubt upon the meaning of the suretyship covenant I should construe it in favour of the defendants and against the plaintiffs. Certainly it is true that neither equity nor law will put a construction on a contract of guarantee which results in imposing on the surety any greater obligation than that which on the strictest construction of the instrument he must be said expressly to have undertaken: see *Eastern Counties Building Society v Russell* [1947] 1 All E.R. 500. On the other hand, the words have to be fairly construed in their context and in accordance with their proper meaning without in any way favouring the guarantor, who is not placed in any more favourable position in this regard than any other contracting party. The so-called rule of construction is very much a matter of last resort."

It is not clear, however, why the strict "so-called rule of construction" should be described "as a last resort". A preferable formulation would be to state simply (as in *Melvin International SA v Poseidon Schiffahrt GmbH M.-V. Kalma*)[9] that guarantees are to be construed according to usual contractual principles, but cases of doubt and ambiguity are to be resolved in favour of the guarantor.

5–05   The principles applicable to the construction of commercial contracts, as formulated by Lord Hoffmann in *Investors Compensation Scheme Ltd v West Bromwich Building Society*,[10] permit a broad-ranging inquiry, construing the contract in its factual matrix. It is useful to re-state them here:

> "(1) Interpretation is the ascertainment of the meaning which the document would convey to a reasonable person having all the background knowledge which would reasonably have been available to the parties in the situation in which they were at the time of the contract.

[7] *ibid.*
[8] [1994] 1 W.L.R. 1528 at 1533, adopting the view of Millett J. in *Johnsey Estates Ltd v Webb* [1990] 19 E.G.L.R. 80 at 82. See similarly *Waydale Ltd v DHL Holdings (UK) Ltd (No.2)* 2001 S.L.T. 224 at 228 (strict rule of construction to be applied only where "ordinary rules of interpretation had been applied and failed to provide a solution"); *Tam Wing Chuen v Bank of Credit & Commerce Hong Kong Ltd* [1996] 2 B.C..C. 69; *De Vere Hotels Ltd v Aegon Insurance Co (UK) Ltd* (unreported October 15, 1997)
[9] [1999] 2 Lloyd's Rep. 374.
[10] [1998] 1 All E.R. 98 at 114–115. See also *Bank of Credit & Commerce International SA v Ali* [2002] 1 A.C. 251 (approving these principles). See also *Mannai v Eagle Star Assurance Co Ltd* [1997] A.C. 749; *Liberty Mutual Insurance Co (UK) Ltd v HSBC Bank plc, The Times*, May 4, 2001. See also J. Beatson, *Anson's Law of Contract* (28th ed., 2002), pp.160–163.

(2) The background was famously referred to by Lord Wilberforce as the 'matrix of fact', but this phrase is, if anything, an understated description of what the background may include. Subject to the requirement that it should have been reasonably available to the parties and to the exception to be mentioned next, it includes absolutely anything which would have affected the way in which the language of the document would have been understood by a reasonable man.

(3) The law excludes from the admissible background the previous negotiations of the parties and their declarations of subjective intent. They are admissible only in an action for rectification. The law makes this distinction for reasons of practical policy and, in this respect only, legal interpretation differs from the way we would interpret utterances in ordinary life. The boundaries of this exception are in some respects unclear. But this is not the occasion on which to explore them.

(4) The meaning which a document (or any other utterance) would convey to a reasonable man is not the same thing as the meaning of its words. The meaning of words is a matter of dictionaries and grammars; the meaning of the document is what the parties using those words against the relevant background would reasonably have been understood to mean. The background may not merely enable the reasonable man to choose between the possible meanings of words which are ambiguous but even (as occasionally happens in ordinary life) to conclude that the parties must, for whatever reason, have used the wrong words or syntax: see *Mannai Investments Co Ltd v Eagle Star Life Assurance Co. Ltd* [1997] A.C. 749.

(5) The 'rule' that words should be given their 'natural and ordinary meaning' reflects the common sense proposition that we do not easily accept that people have made linguistic mistakes, particularly in formal documents. On the other hand, if one would nevertheless conclude from the background that something must have gone wrong with the language, the law does not require judges to attribute to the parties an intention which they plainly could not have had. Lord Diplock made this point more vigorously when he said in *Antaios Cia Naviera SA v Salen Rederierna AB* [1985] A.C. 191 at 201 'if detailed semantic and syntactical analysis of words in a commercial contract is going to lead to a conclusion that flouts business commonsense, it must be made to yield to business commonsense'."

As regards evidence of the "matrix of fact", such surrounding circumstances will include the genesis, background, context and commercial purposes of the transaction, and knowledge of the market in which the parties are operating.[11] And, as the meaning of the guarantee is to be ascertained objectively, it is not essential that the surrounding circumstances be actually known by both creditor and guarantor before the evidence is admissible.[12]

[11] *Reardon Smith Line Ltd v Yngvar Hansen-Tangen* [1976] 1 W.L.R. 989 at 995–996.
[12] *ibid.*

5–06   The principles so far discussed have been enunciated in the (usual) context of the construction of guarantees drafted by the creditor. It has been suggested[13] that where the guarantor draws up the terms of the guarantee (as in the case of a conditional performance bond), any ambiguity should be resolved in favour of the creditor.[14] This leads to the more general question as to whether guarantees in different contexts should be construed differently. Are consumer guarantees to be construed differently from directors' guarantees and, in turn, is another approach to be adopted towards a company guarantee when the company is not paid fees for undertaking the obligation? There is no judicial support for any such approach and in the authors' view it is unnecessary. In any event the courts are entitled to take into account the commercial context in which the guarantee is executed in interpreting the instrument[15] and, indeed, the application of this tenet of construction may also achieve the objective of preventing corporate guarantors escaping liability on technical grounds.

5–07   Although the terms of the guarantee and the identity of the parties are required to be in writing pursuant to the Statute of Frauds[16] this does not preclude the admissibility of extrinsic evidence to explain the meaning of these terms[17] or precisely identify the parties to the guarantee.[18]

(ii) The recital as an aid to interpretation

5–08   As the recital is part of the guarantee, it is clearly admissible as an aid to interpreting the scope of the guarantor's liability.[19] Indeed, it will be seen later in the text that the words of the recital may even contain a condition upon which the guarantee is based (for example, that the creditor must obtain a particular security from the principal).[20] If, however, the meaning of the substantive part of the guarantee is clear as to the scope of the guarantee, the courts will not alter that interpretation as a result of some indication as to a contrary interpretation which may appear in the recital.[21] The main difficulty arises where the words of the recital are also clear and

---

[13] *Mercers of City of London v New Hampshire Insurance Co* [1992] 2 Lloyd's Rep. 365 at 368, *per* Parker L.J. See also the comments of Kirby P. in *Tricontinental Corp Ltd v HDFI Ltd* (1990) 21 N.S.W.L.R. 689 at 694–695 in respect of a compensated surety.
[14] *ibid.*
[15] *ibid.*
[16] 1677, 29 Car. II, c.3, s.4: see above, generally, Ch. 3.
[17] *Perrylease Ltd v Imecar AG* [1987] 2 All E.R. 373: see above, para.3–72. It will, of course, sometimes be a matter of difficulty as to whether the extrinsic evidence is being used to explain the terms of the guarantee or to introduce additional terms.
[18] *Rosser v Austral Wine & Spirit Co Pty Ltd* [1980] V.R. 313: see above, paras 3–63 to 3–68.
[19] *Bank of British North America v Cuvillier* (1861) 4 L.T. 159; *Australian Joint Stock Bank Ltd v Bailey* [1899] A.C. 396.
[20] *Greer v Kettle* [1938] A.C. 156. And see below, paras 8–57 to 8–61.
[21] *Australian Joint Stock Bank v Bailey* [1899] A.C. 396. As examples, see *Sansom v Bell* (1809) 2 Camp. 39; 170 E.R. 1074 (a reference to past indebtedness in the recital was held not to confine the guarantee to past transactions when the substantive part of the guarantee indicated it was to have both a retrospective and prospective effect); *Bank of British North America v Cuvillier* (1861) 4 L.T. 159.

are in direct conflict with the operative parts of the guarantee.[22] In this situation there are several cases[23] where the words of the recital have been construed to prevail over the substantive words of the guarantee. For example, in *Pearsall v Summersett*,[24] the substantive part of the guarantee related to "all such sum or sums as the plaintiff should or might thereafter become liable to pay", but the guarantor's liability was confined to debts incurred prior to the execution of the guarantee because of the wording of the recital which stated that the guarantee was given to secure such pre-existing debts.[25] There is one statement by the Privy Council[26] that in these cases of direct inconsistency the recital *must* be interpreted as qualifying the wording in the body of the guarantee, but it is doubtful if this is a firm rule of construction. Indeed, it is considered that the correct approach is to construe the guarantee as a whole[27] giving effect, where appropriate, to the operative part of the guarantee.[28]

(iii) The consideration clause as an aid to interpretation

If the guarantee is expressed to be given for a specified consideration, the consideration clause will be an integral part of the instrument and will be taken into account in the construction of the guarantee as a whole.[29] Thus, as will be seen, a condition upon which the guarantee is based may be found in the expressed consideration.[30] The consideration may also define the extent of the guarantor's liability[31] or identify the proper claimant.[32] Again, however, as in the case of the recital there is no rule that the expressed consideration must be construed as qualifying the general wording of the guarantee. Thus in *Bank of India v Trans Continental Commodity Merchants Ltd and Patel*,[33] where "in consideration of the Bank of India ... affording banking facilities" the guarantor promised "to

5–09

[22] Although the courts will strive to avoid any inconsistency: see *Dan v Barclays Australia Ltd* (1983) 57 A.L.J.R. 442 at 444–445.
[23] *Pearsall v Summersett* (1812) 4 Taunt. 593; 128 E.R. 463; *Kitson v Julian* (1855) 4 E. & B. 854; 119 E.R. 317; *Liverpool Water Works Co v Atkinson* (1805) 6 East 507; 102 E.R. 1382; *Peppin v Cooper* (1819) 2 B. & Ald. 431; 106 E.R. 423.
[24] (1812) 4 Taunt 593; 128 E.R. 463.
[25] *Cf.*, however, *Sansom v Bell* (1809) 2 Camp 39; 170 E.R. 1074, where there was a similar recital.
[26] *Australian Joint Stock Bank v Bailey* [1899] A.C. 396 at 400.
[27] An approach adopted by the New South Wales Court of Appeal in *Tucker v Broadlands International Finance Ltd* (unreported, NSW CA, September 12, 1986) at 9.
[28] See *Bank of India v Trans Continental Commodity Merchants Ltd and Patel* [1982] 1 Lloyd's Rep. 506 at 512, where Bingham J. held that the substantive part of the guarantee was so clear as to obviate reference to the consideration for the guarantee which appeared in the introductory recital; *Evans v Earle* (1854) 10 Exch. 1; 156 E.R. 330 (condition in guarantee not modified by recital).
[29] *National Bank of Nigeria Ltd v Awolesi* [1964] 1 W.L.R. 1311; *Bank of India v Trans Continental Commodity Merchants Ltd and Patel* [1982] 1 Lloyd's Rep. 506 at 512; *Geelong Building Society (in liq) v Encel* [1996] 1 V.R. 594; *National Bank of New Zealand v West* [1978] 2 N.Z.L.R. 451 at 458.
[30] As in *National Bank of Nigeria Ltd v Awolesi* [1964] 1 W.L.R. 1311. See below, paras 6–43 to 6–47.
[31] As in *National Bank of New Zealand Ltd v West* [1978] 2 N.Z.L.R. 451 at 458.
[32] *Boral Resources (Qld) Pty Ltd v Donnelly* [1988] 1 Qd. R. 506.
[33] [1982] 1 Lloyd's Rep. 506; on appeal: [1983] 2 Lloyd's Rep. 298 at 300.

pay on demand all and every sum and sums of money which are now or shall at any time be owing to the bank anywhere on any account whatsoever". Bingham J. held that the reference in the expressed consideration to "banking facilities" could not limit the scope of liability to sums incurred from "banking" transactions in view of the broad terms in the body of the guarantee.[34] As in the case of the recital to the guarantee, there is probably no firm rule of construction and the court is left to decide which part of the guarantee best reflects the parties' intentions in the light of the surrounding circumstances.[35]

(iv) Construction of contracts of indemnity

5–10   Contracts of indemnity are to be construed strictly in favour of the indemnifier[36] (as in the case of exclusion clauses), which is a clear difference in approach from that currently applicable to guarantees.[37] Given the blurred distinction in this context between guarantees and indemnities, there is a strong argument for applying the same principles of construction to both types of contract. On that basis indemnities would be interpreted according to normal contractual principles,[38] but with cases of ambiguity or doubt being resolved in favour of the indemnifier. Additionally, it has been said that a contract of indemnity should not be restricted by its recitals,[39] thus suggesting that in the case of an indemnity a recital is not relevant as an aid to construction (whereas, as we have seen,[40] in the case of a guarantee, it is permissible to refer to it). Again, there is no justification for adopting this separate approach.

5–11   In any event, as the law now stands it is clear that a contract of indemnity will not be construed as entitling the person in whose favour it was made to an indemnity against the consequence of that person's own negligence unless there is a clear provision to that effect.[41] It also follows that the indemnity will not readily be construed as extending to liabilities incurred through deliberate breaches of contract by the person in whose favour it was given. For example, if the indemnifier undertakes to keep the

---

[34] *ibid.*

[35] See generally, above, para.5–08.

[36] *Smith v South Wales Switchgear Ltd* [1978] 1 All E.R. 18; *General Surety & Guarantee Co Ltd v Francis Parker Ltd* (1977) 6 Build. L.R. 16 at 21.

[37] See above, para.5–04.

[38] There is some support for this approach because in a commercial context indemnities have been construed with the aim of "achieving 'a reasonable commercial' purpose". See *Rank Enterprises v Gerard* [1999] 2 Lloyd's Rep. 666 at 670 which led the court to construe the words "should any claims which have been incurred prior to the time of delivery" in an indemnity as meaning "should any claims *in respect of liabilities* which had been incurred prior to the time of delivery" be made.

[39] *Re Baker, Collins & Rhodes* (1881) 20 Ch. D. 230.

[40] See above, para.5–08.

[41] *Smith v South Wales Switchgear Ltd* [1978] 1 All ER 18; *Gertsen v Municipality of Metropolitan Toronto* (No. 2) (1973) 43 D.L.R. (3d) 504; *Albert Shire Council v Vanderloos* (1992) 77 L.G.R.A. 309; *EE Caledonia Ltd v Orbit Valve plc* [1995] 1 All E.R. 174; *Greenwell v Matthew Hall Pty Ltd* (No. 2) (1982) 31 S.A.S.R. 548; *Davis v Commissioner for Main Roads.* (1968) 41 A.L.J.R. 322 at 324. For a recent example of the construction of an indemnity see *Campbell v Conoco (UK) Ltd* [2003] 1 All E.R. (Comm.) 35.

other party "indemnified against ... any liability, loss, claim or proceedings whatsoever in respect of or arising out of the execution of a leasing contract", the indemnifier will probably not be liable for losses in respect of the leasing agreement which arise from the other party's negligence or deliberate breach of contract.[42]

2. PARTICULAR PROBLEMS OF CONSTRUCTION AFFECTING THE SCOPE OF THE GUARANTOR'S LIABILITY

The construction of particular guarantees will, of course, simply be a question of the interpretation of the relevant clauses in each case. Many of the older cases, especially those relating to fidelity guarantees,[43] examine wording that is unlikely to be repeated, but there are some common clauses and some general questions of construction determining the extent of the guarantor's liability which merit individual treatment. These matters will be dealt with in turn.   **5–12**

(i) Limitations upon liability in respect of the principal transactions embraced by the guarantee

(a) Is the guarantee prospective or retrospective?

Most modern guarantees clearly indicate that the guarantee applies to debts that have already been incurred by the principal as well as those which will arise as a result of future transactions. A common form of wording is a guarantee to pay "on demand ... all moneys which are now or may from time to time hereafter be owing or remain unpaid".[44] Provided that this substantive provision of the guarantee is clear, it is immaterial that there are other contrary indications in the recital to the guarantee or in the expressed consideration for the guarantee. Thus, where the consideration for the guarantee is forbearance to sue for past indebtedness[45] or where the recital in a deed refers to past indebtedness,[46] the guarantee will still be   **5–13**

---

[42] See a similar clause in *Smith v South Wales Switchgear Ltd* [1978] 1 All ER 18 at 22. *Cf.*, however, constructions in *Wright v Tyne Improvements Commissioners* [1968] 1 All E.R. 807; *Blake v Richards & Wallington Industries Ltd* (1974) 16 K.I.R. 151; *Great Western Railway Co v Port Talbot Dry Dock Co Ltd* [1944] 2 All E.R. 328; *Furness Shipbuilding Co v London & North Eastern Railway* [1934] All E.R. Rep. 54; *Warrellow v Chandler and Braddick* [1956] 3 All E.R. 305; *Smith v Vange Scaffolding & Engineering Co Ltd* [1970] 1 All E.R. 249.

[43] *e.g. Dougharty v London Guarantee & Accident Co* (1880) 6 VLR (L) 376.

[44] See a similar guarantee in *National Bank of A/asia v Mason* (1976) 50 A.L.J.R. 362. Other clear examples occur in *Saunders v Taylor* (1829) 9 B. & C. 35; 109 E.R. 14; *Burgess v Eve* (1872) L.R. 13 Eq. 450.

[45] *Coles v Pack* (1869) L.R. 5 C.P. 65.

[46] *Sansom v Bell* (1809) 2 Camp. 39; 170 E.R. 1074. Note, however, *Pearsall v Summersett* (1812) 4 Taunt 593; 128 E.R. 463, where the recitation of past obligations was held to confine the guarantee to retrospective obligations, despite the fact that the substantive part of the guarantee encompassed "sums as the plaintiff should or might thereafter become liable to pay". It is thought that this decision placed undue reliance on the recital where the substantive

both prospective and retrospective in nature if future dealings are clearly included in the main body of the guarantee. Similarly, oral evidence will not be admitted to confine the guarantee to past indebtedness, when it is clearly worded so as to have both a retrospective and a prospective operation.[47]

5–14   Sometimes, however, the substantive part of the guarantee may indicate with reasonable clarity that it is to be only prospective in nature or, alternatively, only retrospective in nature. Thus, in *Fahey v MSD Speirs Ltd*,[48] the guarantor was "to pay for any materials *which are purchased from* MSD Speirs Ltd by Fahey Construction Co Ltd" (emphasis added), and the Privy Council held that the guarantee related to future purchases of materials after the date of the guarantee and not past indebtedness. Conversely, the guarantee may be clearly retrospective in nature, being limited to the "existing indebtedness" of the principal.[49]

5–15   The main difficulties of construction arise when the substantive provision in the guarantee is ambiguous in that it does not indicate clearly whether the guarantee is retrospective or prospective in nature. Although the cases are not easily reconcilable,[50] they reveal some guidelines as to how this question of construction is to be resolved. In particular, if the consideration for the guarantee is the making of future advances by the creditor to the principal, this indicates that the guarantee is to be only prospective in nature.[51] Thus in *Morrell v Cowan*[52] the guarantee stated that "in consideration of you ... having at my request agreed *to supply and furnish goods to C*, I hereby guarantee to you ... the sum of 500 pounds" (emphasis added), and it was held that the guarantee was limited to goods actually supplied after the guarantee was executed. There has also been a tendency to interpret the expressed consideration in ambiguous cases as relating to future indebtedness[53] so as to avoid the conclusion that the consideration is past and therefore that the guarantee is ineffective because it is not supported by consideration.[54] Where the consideration is future advances, some judicial comments indicate that if the guarantee is to embrace past debts the agreement to cover such debts must be expressed

---

provision in the guarantee was clear. For a discussion of the effect of a recital and of this case, see above, para.5–08.

[47] *Hawrish v Bank of Montreal* (1969) 2 D.L.R. (3d) 600.

[48] [1975] 1 N.Z.L.R. 240. See also *Rank Xerox (Finance) Pty Ltd v Peddlesden* (1987) 5 S.R. (WA) 14 (agreements entered into "now and hereafter" not embracing agreements concluded prior to the date of the guarantee).

[49] Where the guarantee is only retrospective in nature, problems may arise as to the consideration for the guarantee: see above, para.2–73.

[50] See the discussion of *Pearsall v Summersett* (1812) 4 Taunt 593; 128 E.R. 463 above at n.46.

[51] *Morrell v Cowan* (1877) 7 Ch. D. 151 at 153–154 *per* James C.J.; *Glyn v Hertel* (1818) 2 Moo 134; 129 E.R. 363. *Cf.*, however, *Wilson v Craven* (1841) 8 M. & W. 584; 151 E.R. 1171, in which a guarantee under seal which recited the creditor's obligation to open a new account was held to be both retrospective and prospective in operation.

[52] (1877) 7 Ch. D. 151.

[53] See above, Chapter 2, paras 2–75 to 2–79, and especially *Chalmers v Victors* (1868) 18 L.T. 481; *Hoad v Grace* (1861) 5 L.T. 359; 158 E.R. 567; *Broom v Batchelor* (1856) 1 H. & N. 255; 156 E.R. 1199; *Goldshede v Swan* (1847) 1 Exch. 154; *Steele v Hoe* (1849) 14 Q.B. 431; 117 ER 168; *S.H. Lock Discounts & Credits Pty Ltd v Miles* [1963] V.R. 656.

[54] *ibid.*

in the clearest terms.[55] Yet more recent statements have referred to the commercial likelihood that the creditor would require the guarantee to be both prospective and retrospective,[56] and it is probable that the burden of showing that the guarantee is also retrospective in such circumstances is now less difficult to satisfy.

Other surrounding circumstances which have been held to indicate that   **5–16**
the guarantee is to have a prospective effect are that the guarantee has been given for an amount which is more than the amount of the existing indebtedness,[57] that the creditor refused to deliver further goods until the guarantee was executed,[58] and that transactions subsequent to the execution of the guarantee were concluded between principal and creditor.[59]

In cases of ambiguity in the substantive part of the instrument there may   **5–17**
also be indications in the recital or the surrounding circumstances showing that the guarantee is to have a retrospective effect. In particular, if the recital to the guarantee simply recites past indebtedness, this will tend to show that the guarantee is to be only retrospective in effect.[60] Thus in *Re Medewe's Trust*,[61] the deed recited that there was a balance due on three banking accounts. The guarantee, which was limited to a sum of £3,000 for whatever balance "which shall or may be found due on the balance of the said several accounts", was interpreted in reliance on the recital to refer to the existing indebtedness and not future advances. Although the word "shall" might be thought clearly to cover future indebtedness, it was interpreted as conveying an uncertainty as to the exact amount already owing by the principal to the creditor, which was to be settled by negotiations between them.

The determination of the question as to whether the guarantee is   **5–18**
prospective or retrospective or both affects the extent of liability under the guarantee, not merely because in the one case future debts are within the scope of the guarantee and in the other they are not. The distinction is also important because of the effect of the rule in *Devaynes v Noble, Clayton's Case*;[62] that is, the first sum paid into a current account is deemed to be the first paid out, and the first debit in the account is extinguished by the first deposit.

The problem arises when there are further dealings between principal   **5–19**
and creditor after the guarantee is given. Let us suppose that a retrospective guarantee is taken for a past debt of £1,000. The creditor then lends another £1,000 to the principal, who subsequently pays the creditor £800. Although the principal is still indebted to the creditor to the extent of £1,200, the money paid in is appropriated to the principal's earliest debts by reason of the rule in *Clayton's Case*. Thus the principal

---

[55] *Morrell v Cowan* (1877) 7 Ch. D. 151 at 154 *per* James C.J.
[56] *Fahey v MSD Speirs Ltd* [1975] 1 N.Z.L.R. 240 at 244; *Re Fletcher Ex p. Hanimex Pty Ltd* (1984) 9 A.C.L.R. 30 at 33 *per* Fox J.
[57] *Chalmers v Victors* (1868) 18 L.T. 481.
[58] *Smith v Passmore* (1883) 4 L.R. (NSW) 274 at 278.
[59] See *Wood v Priestner* (1866) L.R. 2 Exch. 66 at 69.
[60] *Re Medewe's Trust* (1859) 26 Beav. 588; 53 ER 1025.
[61] *ibid.*
[62] (1816) 1 Mer. 572; 35 E.R. 767.

debt to the creditor *before* the guarantee is given is reduced to £200, and, as the guarantee is retrospective (covering only those debts incurred prior to the execution of the guarantee), the guarantor's liability is reduced to £200.[63] If the payment to the creditor by the principal had been £1,000, the guarantor's liability would have been extinguished. In this example, a different result would be reached if the guarantee had been prospective, covering a specific debt of £1,000 incurred after the date of the guarantee. The guarantor would remain fully liable to the extent of his liability because the payment of £800 by the principal would be applied first of all to the existing indebtedness.[64]

5–20   Even in the case of a prospective guarantee, subsequent payments in will, however, eventually reduce and then extinguish the guarantor's liability unless the guarantee is made a continuing one.[65] For instance, in the above example, if the payments by the principal in reduction of the indebtedness amounted to £2,000, the guarantor's liability would be extinguished despite subsequent loans being made to the principal. The payment of £2,000 would be sufficient to extinguish both the existing indebtedness of £1,000 at the time the guarantee was taken *and* the subsequent loan of £1,000 which was within the ambit of the prospective guarantee.

5–21   One final consequential problem arising from the differentiation of retrospective and prospective guarantees is whether the transaction which is guaranteed occurs before or after the date of the guarantee. For example, a prospective guarantee of goods to be supplied to the principal will embrace goods delivered after the date of the guarantee, even though the supply contract was entered into before its execution.[66] Similarly, a prospective guarantee of "advances to be made" to a principal will probably embrace loans contracted for before the date of the guarantee but not received by the principal until after the date of the guarantee.

(b) Is the guarantee continuing or specific?

5–22   A guarantee may be specific in that the guarantor promises to guarantee a particular transaction. Examples include guarantees of hire-purchase or mortgage transactions where the principal's liability is fixed. A continuing guarantee, on the other hand, is one that guarantees a series of future transactions entered into between principal and creditor. Such a guarantee will be entered into where the principal buys goods from the creditor over a period of time or where the principal borrows money periodically from a bank. In this context, the distinction between a specific and continuing

---

[63] For a similar situation, see *Re Medewe's Trust* (1859) 26 Beav. 588; 53 E.R. 1025.
[64] For similar situations, see *Kirby v Duke of Marlborough* (1813) 2 M. & S. 18; 105 E.R. 289; *National Bank of New Zealand Ltd v Macintosh* (1881) 3 N.Z.L.R. 217.
[65] The effect of this is to exclude the rule in *Devaynes v Noble, Clayton's Case* (1816) 1 Mer. 572; 35 E.R. 767. The distinction between a specific and continuing guarantee is discussed below, para.5–22.
[66] *Simmons v Keating* (1818) 2 Stark 426; 171 E.R. 694. As another example, see *Tullamore UDC v Robins* (1913) 48 I.L.T. 180.

guarantee may be of the utmost importance in determining the extent of the guarantor's liability. For example, if the principal borrows £1,000 through an overdrawn account and the guarantee is for a specific sum of £1,000 rather than a continuing guarantee, the rule in *Devaynes v Noble, Clayton's Case*[67] will mean that the sums paid into the account are appropriated first of all to that sum. Thus if the principal repays £300, the guarantor's liability will be reduced by that amount to £700. If the principal eventually pays £1,000 to that account, the guarantor's liability will be extinguished, despite the fact that the principal has borrowed further sums from the creditor and is, therefore, still indebted to the creditor. Similarly, if the creditor periodically supplies goods to the principal but the guarantee secures a specific transaction, the guarantor's liability will be extinguished if the principal pays the creditor an amount to satisfy the principal's debt in relation to that transaction, even though the principal has failed to pay for goods subsequently purchased.[68]

Today, the guarantee in these situations is usually drafted so that it is clearly a continuing guarantee. The guarantee will relate to "all moneys which are now or may from time to time be owing or remain unpaid" by the principal to the creditor, and there may also be a specific reference to the guarantee being "a continuing security".[69] In less obvious cases, the court will construe the guarantee as continuing if there are phrases of a general character which convey the idea that the guarantee is to apply to a continued course of dealing between principal and creditor rather than a specific transaction or loan. The type of analysis which the courts have embarked upon is well illustrated by the judgment of Alderson B. in *Mayer v Isaac*,[70] in distinguishing the guarantee in the earlier case of *Nicholson v Paget*:[71]

5–23

"the words of guarantee [in *Nicholson v Paget*] were: 'I hereby agree to be answerable for the payment of £50 for T Lerigo, in case T Lerigo does not pay for the gin, Taking that according to its plain meaning, it refers to some particular amount of gin which the party was to receive from the plaintiff: but here the words are more general; the defendant says, 'In consideration of your supplying my nephew Vogel with china and earthenware, I hereby guarantee the payment of any bills you may draw on him on account therefore, to the amount of £200;' that is, according to the plain and natural meaning of the words, 'In consideration of your supplying my nephew generally with china and earthenware,—not any particular goods, but any china and earthenware,—I hereby guarantee you the payment of any bills you may draw on him on account of that

[67] (1816) 1 Mer. 572; 35 E.R. 767.
[68] As an example, see *Heffield v Meadows* (1869) L.R. 4 C.P. 595.
[69] It may be dangerous, however, for the creditor to rely upon the phrase "continuing security", standing alone: see *Bailey v Manos* (unreported, Fed Ct, SA, May 6, 1992).
[70] (1840) 6 M. & W. 605; 151 E.R. 554. See also *See v Farey* (1889) 10 L.R. (NSW) 72 at 75.
[71] (1832) 1 C. & M. 48; 149 E.R. 309. As other illustrations of a guarantee being confined to a specific sum of money, see *Kirby v Duke of Marlborough* (1813) 2 M. & S. 18; 105 E.R. 289; *City Discount Co v McLean* (1874) L.R. 9 C.P. 692; *Bovill v Turner* (1815) 2 Chit. 205; *Kay v Groves* (1829) 6 Bing. 276; 130 E.R. 1287; *J. Wiseman & Sons Ltd (in liq) v Harris* [1932] N.Z.L.R. 663.

general supply to be made to him.' If that be so, it cannot be doubted that this is a continuing guarantee; it contemplates the continuance of a supply on the one side, and on the other a liability for any default during that supply; and then it defines the extent to which the defendant will be bound upon this continuing or running guarantee, viz £200."[72]

5–24 The intention that the guarantee is to apply to a future series of transactions may be found in an express reference to such a continued course of dealing, for example, where the guarantee states that it is given "as an inducement to continue your dealings with [the principal]"[73] or is given "according to the custom of their trading with you".[74] The intention may also be inferred where the guarantee refers to "*any* goods" or "*any* debt" or "*any* sums of money" supplied or advanced to the principal.[75] In some cases, a reference in the guarantee simply to payment for the supply of "goods" (in the plural) or the payment of "an account" may lead to an interpretation that the guarantee is continuing,[76] but in these cases there is also the possibility that the guarantee may be confined to payment for a specific delivery of goods or to payment of the existing account.[77]

5–25 In cases in which the wording of the guarantee is neutral, (for example, "I hereby engage to be responsible for liabilities incurred by [the principal] to the extent of £50 to [the creditor]")[78] the courts may have regard to the surrounding circumstances to ascertain if the guarantee is continuing. For example, the fact that the principal's business is such that it requires periodic supplies or advances,[79] the nature of the past dealings between creditor and principal,[80] evidence that the object of the guarantee was to encourage or preserve the business,[81] and the fact that the guarantee would otherwise lack commercial utility may lead to an interpretation that the guarantee is continuing.[82] The courts have also had regard to the subsequent conduct of the parties (for example, an inquiry by the guarantor as to extent of the outstanding balance of the principal's account)[83] in arriving at the conclusion that the guarantee is continuing,

---

[72] (1840) 6 M. & W. 605 at 612–613; 151 E.R. 554 at 557.
[73] *Allan v Kenning* (1833) 9 Bing. 618; 131 E.R. 746.
[74] *Hargreave v Smee* (1829) 6 Bing. 244; 130 E.R. 1274.
[75] *Bastow v Bennett* (1812) 3 Camp. 220; 170 E.R. 1360; *Mason v Pritchard* (1810) 2 Camp. 436; 170 E.R. 1210; *Ross v Burton* (1848) 4 U.C.Q.B. 357 (Can); *Merle v Wells* (1810) 2 Camp. 413; 170 E.R. 1201; *Nottingham Hide, Skin & Fat Market Co Ltd v Bottrill* (1873) L.R. 8 C.P. 694 at 701.
[76] *Hitchcock v Humfrey* (1843) 5 Man. & G. 559; 134 E.R. 683; *Saddington v Byrne* (1864) 4 S.C.R. (NSW) 27.
[77] *Allnutt v Ashenden* (1843) 5 Man. & G. 392; 134 E.R. 616. See also the discussion of the words "any accounts" in *Wood v Priestner* (1866) L.R. 2 Exch 66 at 69 *per* Kelly C.B.
[78] This example is taken from *Chalmers v Victors* (1868) 18 L.T. 481.
[79] *See v Farey* (1889) 10 L.R. (NSW) 72 at 75, where Stephen J. emphasises the fact that the principals were "produce merchants".
[80] *Johnston v Nicholls* (1845) 1 C.B. 251 at 270–272; 135 E.R. 535 at 543; *L. Petrie Ltd v Frizzle* [1926] 2 D.L.R. 420 at 421.
[81] *Heffield v Meadows* (1869) L.R. 4 C.P. 595 at 599, in which Willes J. emphasised the fact that the guarantee was given because the creditor might otherwise refuse to deal with the principal; *Rainey v Dickson* (1860) 8 Gr. 450 (Can).
[82] *Guinness v Box* (1879) 5 V.L.R. 381 at 387 *per* Stephen J. See also *Fahey v MSD Speirs Ltd* [1975] 1 N.Z.L.R. 240 at 244.
[83] *Burgess v Eve* (1872) 26 L.T. 540 at 541; *Henniker v Wigg* (1843) 4 Q.B. 792; 114 E.R. 1095.

although the general contractual rule is that such evidence is inadmissible as an aid to the interpretation of a contract.[84]

Where the guarantor's liability is limited, it should not be inferred that the guarantee is for a specific sum if there are other indications that the guarantee is to be continuing.[85] For example, a guarantee of "all moneys which are now or may from time to time be owing or remain unpaid to the extent of £2,000" or "not exceeding £2,000" will generally be interpreted as designating the upper limit of the guarantor's liability rather than as being a guarantee of a specific sum of £2,000.[86] A different conclusion may be reached, however, where at the time the guarantee is given it is shown that a particular advance is to be made and the amount of that advance is exactly the same as the expressed limit of the guarantor's liability.[87]

5-26

Sometimes the effect of a clause providing that the guarantee is a continuing security may be negated by evidence that the parties had agreed that it was to be limited to a specific transaction. Thus, in the *Governor & the Company of the Bank of Ireland v McCabe*[88] there was clear oral evidence (including that given by bank officials) that a guarantee described in the written document as "a continuing security" was referable to a specific loan and would be discharged when the loan was repaid. One commentator[89] has asserted that the decision illustrates "the fallibility of the 'continuing security' provisions in standard form guarantees", but the circumstances of the case were unusual in that its intended effect was only negated by admissions by the creditors' officers that it was not to apply to subsequent transactions.

5-27

One special principle of construction arises in the context of a guarantee embodied in a promissory note, given for a fixed sum payable on a fixed day. The presumption is that the promissory note is intended to secure an advance made at the date of the note,[90] and the presumption is reinforced if the advance made is equivalent to the amount of the promissory note.[91] The presumption may be rebutted by evidence to the contrary (for example, in an attached memorandum)[92] showing that it is intended to cover future advances. If the promissory note is payable on demand, rather

5-28

---

[84] *Schuler AG v Wickman Machine Tools Ltd* [1974] A.C. 235 at 261, 263; *Whitworth Street Estates (Manchester) Ltd v James Miller & Partners Ltd* [1970] A.C. 583 at 603. See generally J. Beatson, *Anson's Law of Contract* (28th ed., 2002), pp.160–161.

[85] *Laurie v Scholefield* (1869) L.R. 4 C.P. 622; *Batson v Spearman* (1838) 9 Ad. & El. 298; 112 E.R. 1225; *Seller v Jones* (1846) 16 M. & W. 112; 153 E.R. 1121; *Browning v Baldwin* (1879) 40 L.T. 248 ("to the extent of 1,000 pounds further") *Saddington v Byrne* (1864) 4 S.C.R. (NSW) 27; *Mercantile Bank of Australia Ltd v Weigall* (1895) 16 A.L.T. 192; *See v Farey* (1889) 10 L.R. (NSW) 72.

[86] *ibid.*

[87] See *Plastic Decoration & Papier-Mache Co Ltd v Massey-Mainwaring* (1895) 11 T.L.R. 205, where the guarantee for the price of building works was limited to £1,300 and the amount due under the contract was at that time £1,300.

[88] Unreported, September 19, 1994.

[89] G. Andrews & R. Millett, *Law of Guarantees* (3rd ed., 2000), p.199. See also *Bailey v Manos*, unreported, Fed Ct, S.A., May 6, 1992.

[90] *Re Boys; Ex p. Hop Planters Co* (1870) L.R. 10 Eq 467; *Walker v Hardman* (1837) 4 Cl. & Fin. 258; 7 E.R. 99.

[91] *Re Boys Ex p. Hop Planters Co* (1870) L.R. 10 Eq. 467 at 470.

[92] *Hartland v Jukes* (1863) 1 H. & C. 667; 158 E.R. 1052; *Henniker v Wigg* (1843) 4 Q.B. 792; 114 E.R. 1095.

than on a fixed date, so that there is no clear indication that a definite advance is intended, the promissory note may be interpreted as a continuing security.[93]

5–29   The foregoing discussion has centred upon finding indications in the wording of the guarantee that it is continuing. But what is on the face of it a guarantee of a specific principal obligation may involve the guarantor in liability for additional amounts if the principal contract itself contemplates that the principal may be rendered liable for these amounts. Thus if there is a promise to guarantee the performance of *all* the obligations of a contractor under a building contract, and the building contract itself clearly contemplates subsequent loans being made to the contractor by the creditor to enable the work to be completed, the guarantor will be liable if the contractor defaults in repayment of the loans.[94]

(c) Is the guarantee limited in respect of the amount of the principal transaction guaranteed?

5–30   If the guarantee is a continuing guarantee covering future transactions, it will usually be construed as being unlimited in amount in the absence of any specific provision providing for a limit on liability.[95] Where a standard form guarantee is used and the form contains a clause providing for an upper limit on the guarantor's liability but the amount is left blank, the guarantee generally may be construed as being unlimited[96] and sufficiently certain.[97] Even if the parties fail to adopt the precise procedure set out in the guarantee for the creation of an unlimited guarantee, it may still be construed as being unlimited. In *Bank of Baroda v Patel*[98] a provision providing for a limit on the guarantor's liability was accompanied by a note in the margin of the document stating "delete if the guarantee to be unlimited". Despite the fact that there was no deletion, the guarantee was held to be unlimited when all the guarantors had placed their initials in the margin beside the note. A different result is reached, however, if the guarantee clearly indicates that there is to be an upper limit to the guarantor's liability, but the parties never reach an agreement as to this limit.[99]

5–31   Many guarantees do in fact provide for a restriction of the guarantor's liability to a certain fixed amount. A common wording is where the guarantor promises that he will guarantee the account of the principal in

[93] *Pease v Hirst* (1829) 10 B. & C. 122; 109 E.R. 396.
[94] This possibility is contemplated by *Trade Indemnity Co Ltd v Workington Harbour & Dock Board* [1937] A.C. 1. But note that on the facts the subsequent loans were not contemplated by the principal contract.
[95] *Coles v Pack* (1869) L.R. 5 C.P. 65.
[96] *Caltex Oil (Aust) Pty Ltd v Alderton* (1964) 81 W.N. (Pt. 1) (NSW) 297; *New Zealand Loan & Mercantile Agency Co Ltd v Paterson* (1882) N.Z.L.R. 1, 325, CA.
[97] *ibid.*
[98] [1996] 1 Lloyd's Rep. 391. *Cf.* however, *State Bank of India v Gurmit* [1996] 5 Bank L.R. when the guarantee was held not to be certain and not to comply with the Statute of Frauds, but additionally in this case there was no proper identification of the principal debtor (which was probably decisive).
[99] *Relwood Pty Ltd v Manning Homes Pty Ltd* [1990] 1 Q.d. R. 481.

respect of advances "up to a limit not exceeding £30,000" or "to the extent of £30,000". This provision will be effective to restrict the guarantor's liability to the amount expressed as the limit,[1] but the clause will not be interpreted as making the guarantee conditional upon the principal debtor's liability to the creditor being limited to that sum.[2] The creditor may, therefore, still grant advances in excess of the stipulated amount and the guarantor will remain liable up to the expressed limit of liability.[3]

A different result may be reached, however, if the limitation more obviously applies to the amount advanced than the amount guaranteed. An example might be "in consideration of advancing a sum not exceeding £3,000 to the principal, I guarantee the payment of that amount". The probability here is that, if the creditor lends an amount in excess of £3,000, the creditor will be in breach of a condition that the amount lent should not exceed that figure and the guarantee will be totally ineffective.[4]

5–32

In particular cases it will also be necessary to define the limit of the guarantor's liability with some clarity. If there is a number of co-guarantors, it must be made clear whether the limit applies to the total liability of all the guarantors or the liability of each individual guarantor.[5] Similarly, if the guarantee is given to a number of creditors (for example, members of an unincorporated association), it should be specified whether the instrument imposes a limit on the guarantor's liability to each creditor or the guarantor's liability to all the creditors. Thus in *Triaca v Summaries Pty Ltd*[6] a guarantee was given "to each and every member" of an

5–33

---

[1] Where a guarantor who had provided a limited guarantee repays the full amount of the principal debt as the result of a mutual mistake by both parties as to the extent of the guarantor's liability, it may be possible to recover the overpayment through a claim against the creditor for unjust enrichment. But no such claim will succeed where the guarantor's payment was attributable to other considerations and was not influenced by the guarantor's belief that he was liable for the whole of the principal debt: see *Killham v Banque National de Paris* (unreported, Vic Sup Ct, June 28, 1994).

[2] *Laurie v Scholefield* (1869) L.R. 4 C.P. 622; *Total Oil Products (Aust) Pty Ltd v Robinson* [1970] 1 N.S.W.R. 701 at 704; *Matthews Thompson & Co Ltd v Everson* (1934) 34 S.R. (NSW) 114 at 124; Sometimes a clearer form of expression is used, *e.g.* "the plaintiff shall not be entitled to recover from the guarantors a larger sum than 300 pounds": *Parkinson v Booth* (1934) 34 S.R. (NSW) 185.

[3] See criticism of this construction by the South Australian Law Reform Committee in its *Report Relating to the Reform of the Law of Suretyship* (39th Rep. 1977), p.5. The Committee recommends that "the law should be amended to provide that where an upper limit is specifically placed on a surety's liability in relation to a particular creditor, and that creditor advances moneys to the debtor beyond the limit of liability so imposed and accepted by the creditor without first obtaining the consent of the surety, the surety's liability should be diminished to the extent of those further advances".

[4] *Philips v Astling* (1809) 2 Taunt. 206; 127 E.R. 1056 is a similar example. Under a contract of guarantee of a bill of exchange of a specified amount, the guarantor was held not liable when a bill was given for a larger sum. But the courts have tended to avoid constructions which are unfavourable to the creditor in this way. See *Parker v Wise* (1817) 6 M. & S. 239; 105 E.R. 1232; *Gordan v Rae* (1858) 8 E. & B. 1065; 120 E.R. 396. See also *Queensland National Bank Ltd v Queensland Trustees Ltd* (1899) 9 Q.L.J. 282, where a clause in the guarantee stating that "the limit of the overdraft ... shall be £50,000" was interpreted as merely specifying the amount up to which the principal could draw *without further* communication to the bank.

[5] See *Imperial Bank v Kidd* (1922) 23 O.W.N. 19. See also a similar problem in *National Bank of New Zealand Ltd v Murland* [1991] 3 N.Z.L.R. 86, where it was held that, in the particular context, the word "several" meant that the guarantors would be liable proportionately to their shareholding in the principal debtor company.

[6] [1971] V.R. 347.

association of wine merchants and producers. A clause stated that "my liability to you under this guarantee shall not amount to more than three thousand dollars ($3,000) at any one time". It was argued by the defendant guarantor that this imposed a total limit upon his liability to all the creditors. The court rejected this argument concluding that it merely imposed a limit on the guarantor's liability to each creditor, but the facts do illustrate the need for unambiguous wording in this situation. One general factor, which influenced the court's decision and might be relevant in similar situations was that, if the guarantor's interpretation was correct, it would mean that no creditor would be aware at the time of supplying goods to the principal debtor whether or not the guarantee was security for the credit that was being provided without checking the position of all the other creditors.

5–34   A final situation necessitating clarity in specifying the extent of the guarantor's liability is where the principal transaction is secured. The limit of the guarantor's liability should not be expressed so as to indicate that the guarantor's liability is to cease upon the creditor recovering the stipulated sum by realisation of the security.[7]

(d) Is the guarantee a security for the whole debt or a part of the debt?

5–35   In situations where the guarantee is drafted with a limitation on the guarantor's liability, an issue of construction arises as to whether it is a guarantee of the whole of the outstanding indebtedness, but with a specified restriction on the extent of the guarantor's liability, or merely a guarantee of a part of the whole debt. The distinction has been described as "over-subtle",[8] but it is clearly established by authority[9] and several consequences flow from it. First, if the guarantee is construed as a guarantee of part of the debt rather than the whole of the outstanding indebtedness, the guarantor will be entitled upon payment of that part of the debt to share in the benefit of the securities given to the creditor to secure the principal transaction in the same proportion that the debt satisfied by the guarantor bore towards the full amount of the debt.[10] If the guarantee makes it clear that it is a guarantee of the whole of the indebtedness, the guarantor will not be entitled to the benefit of the securities until the whole debt has been satisfied.[11] This conclusion is often reinforced by a provision specifically stating that the guarantor is not entitled to share in any security until the creditor has been paid in full.

---

[7] See the guarantor's argument in *Naughton v Glasson* (1975) 49 A.L.J.R. 104.
[8] *Barclays Bank Trust Fund Ltd v TOSG Trust Fund Ltd* [1984] 1 All E.R. 628 at 641.
[9] *ibid.* See also *Ellis v Emmanuel* (1876) 1 Ex. D. 157.
[10] This arises from the general principal of subrogation that once the guarantor has paid in full he is entitled to be subrogated to securities held by the creditor: *Re Howe Ex p. Brett* (1871) 6 Ch. App. 838 at 841; *Dixon v Steel* [1901] 2 Ch. 602; *Re Butlers Wharf Ltd* [1995] 2 B.C.C. 717. For a more detailed discussion, see below, Ch. 12.
[11] *Gedye v Matson* (1858) 25 Beav. 310; 53 E.R. 655.

Secondly, if the guarantee is only for part of the debt, the guarantor will   **5–36**
be entitled on payment of that part of the debt to prove in the principal's
bankruptcy, and will be entitled to such proportion of the dividends on the
total principal debt as the payment bears to that debt.[12] The guarantor will
have no such right of proof if the guarantee covers the whole debt, but has
a limitation on the amount of the guarantor's liability.[13] Similarly, in the
case of a guarantee of the whole debt, payments by the guarantor prior to
the date of bankruptcy will not disentitle the creditor from proving in the
principal's bankruptcy for the full amount of the debt.[14]

Thirdly, where co-guarantors guarantee separate parts of the principal   **5–37**
debt rather than the whole of the outstanding indebtedness, no right of
contribution will arise between them.[15]

Given such serious consequences, it is important as a matter of   **5–38**
construction to differentiate a guarantee of the whole indebtedness from
a guarantee of part of a debt. In the case of a continuing guarantee of a
fluctuating balance (such as in the case of a guarantee of a debtor's current
account with a bank) with a limit on the liability of the guarantor, the
prima facie inference is that the guarantee is security for part only of the
debt.[16] An example would be a guarantee "of any debt which the principal
may contract from time to time as a running balance of account to any
amount not exceeding £400".[17] In these cases, therefore, it is important to
displace the prima facie inference by including a clause in the guarantee
that "the guarantee is to be a continuing guarantee *for the whole of* the
moneys hereby secured".[18] Other forms of expression may also lead to the
inference that the instrument is a guarantee of the whole indebtedness. For
example, in *Ulster Bank Ltd v Lambe*[19] reliance was placed on a provision

---

[12] *Barclays Bank Ltd v TOSG Trust Fund Ltd* [1984] 1 All E.R. 628 at 641; *Re Butlers Wharf Ltd* [1995] 2 B.C.C. 717 at 722; *Gray v Seckham* (1872) 7 LR Ch. App. 680; *Ex p. Rushforth* (1805) 10 Ves. 409; 32 E.R. 903; *Re Sass; Ex p. National Provincial Bank of England Ltd* [1896] 2 Q.B. 12 *Westpac Banking Corp v Gollin & Co Ltd* [1988] V.R. 397 at 405; *Seabird Corp Ltd (in liq) v Sherlock* (1990) 2 A.C.S.R. 111 at 116. See below, paras 10–28 to 10–53 for a more detailed discussion of this question.

[13] *Barclays Bank Ltd v TOSG Trust Fund Ltd* [1984] 1 All E.R. 628 at 641; *Ellis v Emmanuel* (1876) 1 Ex. D. 157 *Westpac Banking Corp v Gollin & Co Ltd* [1988] V.R. 397 at 405; *Seabird Corp Ltd (in liq) v Sherlock* (1990) 2 A.C.S.R. 111 at 115–116; *Re Sass Ex p. National Provincial Bank of England Ltd* [1896] 2 Q.B. 12 *Martin v McMullen* (1891) 18 O.A.R. 559. A specific provision in the guarantee often makes it clear that the guarantor is not entitled to receive any dividends until the creditor has been paid in full, *e.g. Re Rees Ex p. National Provincial Bank of England Ltd* (1881) 17 Ch. D. 98.

[14] *Ulster Bank Ltd v Lambe* [1966] N.I. 166: see below, paras 10–40 to 10–43.

[15] See below, para.12–42. The distinction between a guarantee of part of the debt and a guarantee of the whole debt also has consequences in respect of the rules of appropriation: see below, paras 6–23 to 6–35.

[16] *Barclays Bank Ltd v TOSG Trust Fund Ltd* [1984] 1 All E.R. 628 at 642; *Ellis v Emmanuel* (1876) 1 Ex. D. 157 (the conclusion is reached by Blackburn J. after an exhaustive review of earlier authorities); *Re D (a lunatic patient) (No.2)* [1926] V.L.R. 467 at 486; *Challenge Bank Ltd v Mailman* (unreported, NSW CA, May 14, 1993).

[17] *Bardwell v Lydall* (1831) 7 Bing. 489; 131 E.R. 189. See also the numerous other older examples cited in *Ellis v Emmanuel* (1876) 1 Ex. D. 157.

[18] Similarly, in *Re Sass Ex p. National Provincial Bank of England Ltd* [1896] 2 Q.B. 12 ("This guarantee is to security for the whole amount now due or owing").

[19] [1966] N.I. 161.

stating that "the guarantee shall be available as an *ultimate security for any balance*" which may be due to the bank.[20]

5-39   Despite the importance of the distinction between the two forms of guarantee, there are modern examples of infelicitous drafting. In the Australian case of *Challenge Bank Ltd v Mailman*,[21] the relevant clauses (which defined both "debt" and "guarantor") were drafted in such a way as to limit the liability of each guarantor to a specific part of the debt. There was no reference to each guarantor being liable for the whole indebtedness, albeit with a restriction on the extent of liability. Furthermore, another clause indicated that each guarantor could seek the transfer of any security, or part thereof, once each guarantor had paid "*its*" proportion of the debt.[22]

5-40   In situations where there is a specific guarantee of a fixed and ascertained sum (for example, a guarantee of a mortgage debt), but with a limitation on the guarantor's liability, there is no prima facie presumption that the guarantee is security for only part of the debt.[23] Indeed, it appears that the courts readily infer that such guarantees are guarantees of the whole indebtedness.[24]

(e) Is the guarantee limited in time?

5-41   The fact that the guarantee is limited in time may affect the extent of the principal transactions embraced by the guarantee. Most of the authorities relating to the question of whether the guarantee is of limited duration involve guarantees of the faithful discharge of an employee's duties. Such guarantees have usually been construed as being limited to the current term of the employee's appointment.[25] If the recital stipulates a particular period of employment, the guarantee may be confined to that period, despite clear wording in the substantive part of the guarantee purporting to extend the guarantee to the total period during which the employee continues in that employment.[26]

---

[20] *ibid.*, at 165. Lowry J. also laid emphasis on the fact that the guarantee was described as a "continuing guarantee", but this is inconsistent with the general principle of *Ellis v Emmanuel* (1876) 1 Ex. D. 157 which applied the presumption stated in the text specifically in respect of continuing guarantees.

[21] Unreported, NSW CA, May 14, 1993.

[22] In the case of a guarantee of part of a debt, a provision stating the guarantee is a "continuing security" and is to be in addition to, and without prejudice to, any other security held from, or on account of, the debtor will probably not negate the guarantor's rights in respect of proof and subrogation: see *Re Butlers Wharf Ltd* [1995] 2 B.C.C. 717 at 724–727 and the analysis of *Re Sass Ex p. National Provincial Bank of England* [1986] 2 Q.B. 12. *Cf.* suggestions to the contrary by Oliver L.J. in *Barclays Bank Ltd v TOSG Trust Fund* [1984] 1 All E.R. 626 at 641–642.

[23] *Ellis v Emmanuel* (1876) 1 Ex. D. 157 at 168–169.

[24] This appears to be the approach taken in *Ellis v Emmanuel* (1876) 1 Ex. D. 157.

[25] *Hassel v Long* (1814) 2 M. & S. 363; 105 E.R. 416; *Wardens of St Saviour's, Southwark v Bostock* (1806) 2 Bos. & Pul. N.R. 175; 127 E.R. 590. Note, however, that the guarantee may expressly apply to a subsequent re-appointment: *Augero v Keen* (1836) 1 M. & W. 390; 150 E.R. 485. The term of office may also not be limited in duration: *Birmingham Corp v Wright* (1851) 16 Q.B. 623; 117 E.R. 1019.

[26] *Liverpool Waterworks Co v Atkinson* (1805) 6 East 507; 102 E.R. 1382; *Peppin v Cooper* (1819) 2 B. & Ald. 431; 106 E.R. 423; *Kitson v Julian* (1855) 4 E. & B. 854; 119 E.R. 317; *Lord*

Such problems are less likely to occur today with the demise of this type **5–42**
of fidelity guarantee,[27] but the issue of construction may still be relevant in
other situations. For example, if there is a guarantee of a lease of a fixed
duration, the guarantee will expire at the date on which the lease expires,
unless it clearly extends to subsequent leases.[28]

A continuing guarantee of future advances, which does not state a time **5–43**
limit for the duration of the guarantee, will generally be construed as being
unlimited in duration.[29] Sometimes the terms of the guarantee may permit
the guarantor to determine the guarantee by giving a period of notice or a
specific time limit may be stipulated (for example, "this guarantee shall
expire three years from the date hereof"[30] or "this guarantee shall
continue in force for one year from the date hereof)."[31] The main difficulty
in this context is whether the guarantor's liability can be said to have arisen
during the period before the date of expiration. This issue is discussed
elsewhere.[32]

(f) Is the guarantee limited in respect of the type of principal transaction to be guaranteed?

The guarantee may be limited in respect of the type of principal **5–44**
transaction guaranteed. Such a limitation may often appear in the recital to
the guarantee or the expressed consideration for the guarantee. Thus in
United Dominion's Trust Ltd v Beech,[33] the guarantee stated that "*in
consideration of your extending certain banking facilities to [D Ltd] ... we
hereby jointly and severally guarantee the prompt payment of all or any
sums of money for which [the principal] may become liable to you and we
hereby jointly and severally guarantee to hold you harmless of any loss or
damage which you may sustain by reason of your having extended the
above-mentioned banking facilities*". The court held that the guarantee was
limited to sums of money owed by the principal in respect of *banking
transactions or facilities*. On the facts, this was not the case because the
relevant transaction was the utilisation of customers' money to purchase
debts and goods (rather than to make loans), which was not a banking
activity.[34]

Arlington v Merricke (1672) 2 Wms. Saund. 403; 85 E.R. 1215. These are examples of the
recital taking precedence over the substantive part of the guarantee, but in the authors' view
there is no rule of law that the recital should predominate: see above, para.5–08.
[27] But as a modern example of a fidelity guarantee involving a time limitation, see *QBE
Insurance (International) Ltd v Commercial Union Assurance Co of Australia* (1987) 5 ANZ
Insurance Cases 75,249.
[28] *Tayleur v Wildin* (1868) L.R. 3 Exch. 303; *A Plesser & Co Ltd v Davis* (1983) 267 E.G. 1039
(Q.B.) (a guarantee of lease not extending to a statutory continuation of the tenancy);
Junction Estates v Cope (1974) 27 P. & C.R. 482. See also, below, para.5–48.
[29] *Coles v Pack* (1869) L.R. 5 C.P. 65.
[30] *e.g. National House-Building Council v Fraser* [1983] 1 All E.R. 1090.
[31] *e.g. Hollond v Teed* (1848) 7 Hare 50; 68 E.R. 20.
[32] See below, paras 9–21 to 9–25, 9–32 to 9–35.
[33] [1972] 1 Lloyd's Rep. 546.
[34] *ibid.*, at 551.

5-45   Sometimes the recital or the statement of consideration may indicate that the guarantee is to be limited to a particular type of transaction, but the substantive part of the guarantee indicates a wider liability. In such a case the width of the guarantee may not be constrained by the recital or expressed consideration. This is illustrated by *Bank of India v Trans Continental Commodity Merchants and Patel*,[35] where the guarantee was similarly expressed to be in consideration of the bank "affording banking facilities" to the principal, but the guarantor then promised to pay all sums of money which should be owing to the bank "on any account whatsoever". Bingham J. took the view that the expression of consideration should not limit the guarantee to debts arising from banking facilities in view of the wide language which followed it.[36] Similarly, in *Phillips Petroleum Co v Quentin*[37] where a guarantee was given in consideration of the creditor "entering into certain agreements and/or leases and extending credit" to the principal borrower, the Privy Council held that the guarantee was not limited by this wording to agreements that had already been entered into or were in contemplation. Other provisions of the guarantee, most notably a clause providing for termination, contemplated that the guarantee was intended to embrace further, presently unidentified agreements.[38]

5-46   In determining the transactions to which the guarantee is to apply, the court may have regard to extrinsic evidence and the surrounding circumstances.[39] Extrinsic evidence has been admitted to show that the term "bills of exchange" in the guarantee was to be given a broad commercial meaning and was not to be interpreted according to the technical definition in the Bills of Exchange Act.[40]

5-47   If the guarantee relates only to a single principal transaction, that transaction must be properly identified.[41] If, therefore, a guarantee of the performance by a lessee of the terms of a lease could reasonably refer to

---

[35] [1982] 1 Lloyd's Rep. 506 on appeal: [1983] 2 Lloyd's Rep. 298 at 300. Note, however, that there are some authorities which have held that the words of the recital are to prevail over the wide language of the substantive part of the guarantee: see above, para.5–08.

[36] [1982] 1 Lloyd's Rep. 506 at 512; on appeal: [1983] 2 Lloyd's Rep. 298 at 300. Some guarantees are sufficiently widely expressed to cover any transaction negotiated between principal and creditor: see, *e.g. Traders Finance Corp Ltd v Brewster* (1967) 64 D.L.R. (2d) 554. Notice also the phrase "all accounts" guarantee, discussed below, para.5–79. For another example of this issue of construction, see *Lloyd's v Harper* (1880) 16 Ch. D. 290.

[37] Unreported, February 16, 1998.

[38] The guarantee was expressed to be a continuing guarantee and a notice of termination was required to notify the creditor that it should not "enter into ... further agreements [or] extend further credit on the security of the guarantee". According to the Privy Council this plainly contemplated that agreements concluded and credit extended after the date of execution could fall within the terms of the guarantee.

[39] See this principle discussed above, paras 5–01 to 5–07 and, in this context, *Davey v Phelps* (1841) 2 Man. & G. 300 at 305; 133 E.R. 760 at 762.

[40] *Dalgety Ltd v John J. Hilton Pty Ltd* [1981] 2 N.S.W.L.R. 169 at 173 (an affidavit by the plaintiff creditor was admitted as evidence to show this). Similarly, the expressions "renewal" of a bill of exchange (*Barber v Mackrell* (1892) 68 L.T. 29) and "to discount" a bill of exchange (*Utica City National Bank v Gunn* (1918) 118 N.Z. 607) have been given non-technical meanings.

[41] *Mercantile Credits Ltd v Harry* [1969] 2 N.S.W.R. 248. It is possible that oral evidence may be admitted to show to which transaction the guarantee relates: *Brunton v Dullens* (1859) 1 F. & F. 450; 175 E.R. 804.

either of two particular leases, and there is no evidence to indicate to which the guarantee is to apply, the guarantee will be void for uncertainty.[42] Similarly, the guarantor will not incur liability if the guaranteed transaction is never concluded.[43]

In the case of a guarantee referring to a particular transaction or arrangement, the guarantor will not be liable for the principal debtor's default in respect of a different transaction. In this context, in accordance with general principles,[44] any ambiguity will be resolved in favour of the surety. Guarantees of a lessee's obligation pursuant to a lease provide illustrations. Thus in *Jaskel v Sophie Nursery Products Ltd*[45] such a guarantee was construed as not extending to a separate transaction entered into as a result of a supplemental deed providing for a cash deposit to be maintained by the tenant at a certain level. And in *Junction Estates Ltd v Cope*[46] a guarantee that a tenant will perform all the tenant's covenants "herein before contained" was interpreted as applying to the initial term of the lease and not a statutory extension of the term. A similar approach to construction would mean that a guarantee of obligations "under the lease" will not extend to obligations arising pursuant to a renewal[47] of the lease upon the exercise of an option for renewal.[48]

5-48

Other examples of the guarantee not embracing the relevant transaction occur where the guarantor promises to guarantee only a transaction of a given amount, but the creditor enters into a transaction with the principal

5-49

---

[42] *Mercantile Credits Ltd v Harry* [1969] 2 N.S.W.R. 248.
[43] *Australian Guarantee Corp Ltd v Benson* (unreported, NSW Sup. Ct., December 12, 1991).
[44] See above, paras 5–01 to 5–09.
[45] [1993] E.G.C.S. 42. See also *West Horndon Industrial Park Ltd v Phoenix Timber Group* [1995] 20 E.G. 137 (guarantee of lease not encompassing licence imposing additional burdens on the tenant).
[46] (1974) 27 P. & C.R. 482. *Associated Dairies Ltd v Pierce* (1983) 265 E.G. 127. The same result may be reached in respect of the liability of the original tenant for his assignee's obligations, when the assignee's tenancy continues by virtue of statute after expiry of the term: *City of London Corp v Fell* [1993] Q.B. 589.
[47] As held in the Australian case *Yulin Pty Ltd v Japan Building Projects (Aust) Pty Ltd* [1991] ANZ Conv. R. 390. As another Australian example, where the construction arguably unfairly prejudiced the landlord see *Chan v Cresdon Pty Ltd* (1989) 168 L.L.R. 242 where the guarantee, which was embodied in the lease itself, related to the "due and punctual performance by [the lessee] of the obligations to be performed under this lease". The lease for a term of five years was executed in registrable form (in the required form E), but was in fact not registered pursuant to the Real Property Act 1861 (Qld). Although the majority of the High Court of Australia was of the view that a common law tenancy at will terminable on one month's notice was created and was also prepared to assume that an equitable lease (enforceable by a decree of specific performance) was also brought into existence, the court nevertheless held that the guarantor was not liable. Applying the strict rule of construction, the words "under this lease" contemplated, according to the High Court, only liability pursuant to a registered lease at law for a fixed term.
[48] But the issue of construction will depend upon the precise clause and somewhat different wording may lead to the guarantor remaining liable. See *Tessari v Bais Pty Ltd* (1993) 60 S.A.S.R. 59 at 75, where the guarantee did not use the words "under" this lease, but referred to obligations of the lessee contained in the lease, which were expressed to continue throughout any renewed term; *Abigroup v Sandtara Pty Ltd* (1993) A.N.Z. Conv. R. 358, where the guarantee contained the wording "in accordance with or by the virtue of or in consequence of this instrument"; *Collin Estates Ltd v Buckley* [1992] 40 E.G. 151, where a guarantee "to make good ... all losses, costs, damages and expenses" occasioned by the lessee's breach was held to embrace money payable pursuant to a court settlement between lessor and lessee.

for a larger amount,[49] or the guarantor promises to guarantee a particular borrowing facility but the creditor and principal enter into a different facility.[50]

(g) Is the guarantor liable for interest accruing on the principal transaction?

5–50   Most guarantees expressly make the guarantor liable for both the principal debt and the arrears of interest accruing on that debt.[51] In other cases it is a question of construction of the scope of the guarantee whether the guarantor is liable for interest.[52] Thus a guarantee which simply refers only to "advances" made to the principal probably does not cover amounts owing in respect of unpaid interest.[53] The courts may, however, have regard to the surrounding circumstances to ascertain whether the guarantee is intended to cover interest. For example, in *Fahey v MSD Speirs Pty Ltd*,[54] a guarantee to "pay for any materials which are purchased from [the creditor]" was held to embrace those parts of the amount claimed which consisted of an interest element on the overdue accounts because the guarantor was aware of the terms upon which the supplies were purchased.[55] Is it essential, therefore, that the guarantor be shown to possess actual knowledge of the fact that interest is payable according to the terms of the principal transaction before he can be rendered liable for such interest payments? It is thought that there is no such general rule. In *Fahey v MSD Speirs Pty Ltd*, the guarantee related in its terms to a specific, single obligation, that is, to pay for materials, so that the guarantee could reasonably be interpreted as not embracing a liability for interest. But many guarantees are general in nature whereby the guarantor's promise extends to all the obligations of the principal debtor under the principal obligation. In this case, if the principal contract imposes a liability to pay interest, the guarantor will also probably be liable for outstanding interest simply because it is one of the obligations guaranteed. It should be irrelevant that the guarantee itself does not specifically refer to the guarantor's liability for interest or that the guarantor does not know of the terms of the principal obligation.[56]

---

[49] *Philips v Astling* (1809) 2 Taunt. 206; 127 E.R. 1056
[50] *Clarke v Green* (1849) 3 Exch. 619; 154 E.R. 992 (a guarantee of a loan payable by instalments, but the principal loan agreement provided for the total amount owing to be payable upon default); *Luck v Ilka* [1951] Q.S.R. 281 (a guarantee of a loan repayable on demand, but the creditor entered a fixed term loan). See also *Dan v Barclays Australia Ltd* (1983) 57 A.L.J.R. 442.
[51]   e.g. *Bank of Adelaide v Lorden* (1970) 45 A.L.J.R. 49.
[52]   See generally *Fahey v MSD Speirs Pty Ltd* [1975] 1 N.Z.L.R. 240 at 243. Sometimes the question of construction is as to the amount of interest payable or the period for which it should be paid: *King v Greenhill* (1843) 6 Man. & G. 59; 134 E.R. 808.
[53]   *Reid Murray Holdings Ltd (in liq) v David Murray Holdings Pty Ltd* (1972) 5 S.A.S.R. 386 at 409.
[54]   [1975] 1 N.Z.L.R. 240.
[55]   *ibid.*, at 243.
[56]   In *Ackermann v Ehrensperger* (1846) 16 M. & W. 99; 153 E.R. 1115, Pollock C.B. appeared to take this view in holding that a surety for a bill of exchange was liable for interest from the date it became due. See also *Dawson v Raynes* (1826) 2 Russ. 466 at 471–472; 38 E.R. 411 at

Assuming that the guarantor is to be liable for interest, a problem of **5–51** construction may arise as to the extent of interest payable by the guarantor. If the guarantor's liability is limited, the limit will usually be expressed to apply to the capital sum,[57] and the guarantor will be liable additionally for all amounts of interest accruing on that sum, but occasionally the guarantee may make it clear that the upper limit of the guarantor's liability is inclusive of both capital and interest.[58] But, even in the former case, the guarantee will usually be interpreted as embracing interest accruing on the principal sums payable by the guarantor and not for interest payable on principal sums advanced by the creditor to the principal beyond the limit of the guarantor's liability.[59]

In the case of "top-slice" guarantees, when the guarantor is made liable **5–52** for the principal debt in excess of a certain amount, it is a matter of construction whether or not the guarantor incurs liability for interest upon only that amount or upon the total principal debt. In *Huewind Ltd v Clydesdale Bank plc*[60] the guarantors undertook to be responsible for a principal sum "in excess of the sum of Eight hundred thousand pounds sterling and of all interest due or to become due by the Principals". There was a further provision that the guarantor's "liability under this guarantee shall not exceed the sum of One million pounds sterling and interest thereon". It was held by the Outer House in Scotland that the guarantors' liability for interest was limited to interest on the principal sum in excess of the initial £800,000 but that their overall liability for interest was not to exceed the interest due on the maximum guaranteed sum of one million sterling.

Sometimes the guarantor will not be liable by the terms of the guarantee **5–53** for the principal sum at all, but will only be liable for interest. In this case the guarantee will probably not be interpreted, in the absence of clear wording to the contrary, as referring to interest accruing on the principal sum whilst it remains in arrears after the due date for payment.[61] This construction is influenced by the fact that the result would otherwise be that the guarantor would remain liable for interest in perpetuity and could only put an end to that liability by paying the principal sum itself.[62]

The creditor's right to recover interest under the guarantee may be **5–54** affected by other factors.

If the principal's liability for the debt ceases, the liability of the **5–55** guarantor for any future interest subsequently accruing will also cease. A specific example of the cessation of the guarantor's liability for interest by

---

412–413; *Canadian Imperial Bank of Commerce v Avenue Shoppers Plaza Ltd* (1967) 59 W.W.R. 369.

[57] *e.g. Bank of Adelaide v Lorden* (1970) 45 A.L.J.R. 49 (guarantor's liability not to exceed "the sum of $4,000 and interest on the said sum"). See also *Huewind Ltd v Clydesdale Bank plc* [1995] S.L.T. 392.

[58] *e.g. Dow Banking Corp v Mahnakh Spinning & Weaving Corp and Bank Mellat* [1983] 2 Lloyd's Rep. 561 (guarantor's liability not to "exceed a total of 6,000,000 pounds . . . including interest and charges").

[59] *Meek v Wallis* (1872) 27 L.T. 650.

[60] [1995] S.L.T. 392.

[61] *Ruddenklau and Gardner v Charlesworth* [1925] N.Z.L.R. 161. But a guarantee may cover interest over an indefinite period: *Cook v Fowler* (1874) L.R. 7 H.L. 27.

[62] *Ruddenklau and Gardner v Charlesworth* [1925] N.Z.L.R. 161 at 168.

determination of the principal's liability arose in *Bank of Adelaide v Lorden*.[63] The guarantor promised to pay on demand advances made to the principal debtor by the bank and any interest accruing on the sums advanced. The guarantee contained a clause preserving the liability of the guarantor in the event of a release of the principal so as to avoid the normal consequence of the guarantor being absolutely discharged by the release. The demand upon the guarantor was not made until after the date of the composition agreement which, on its proper construction, released the debtor and put an end to the debtor's future liability, including his liability to pay interest on the debt. Thus the debtor and, therefore, the guarantor could not be liable for any interest which would otherwise have accrued between the date of the composition agreement and the date of demand. However, interest would, of course, be payable after the date of demand by virtue of the statutory provisions regarding the payment of interest between the date the cause of action arises and the date of judgment.[64]

5–56   The creditor's right to recover interest is also affected by the obtaining of a judgment against the principal debtor as well as the principal debtor's bankruptcy or winding up. When a judgment is obtained, the accepted position is that the cause of action against the principal is merged in the judgment so that interest does not thereafter accrue pursuant to the contractual obligation but under the rules of court.[65] The effect of the debtor's bankruptcy or winding up is that no interest is thereafter recoverable[66] by the creditor as a provable debt.[67] The guarantor's obligation in respect of interest accruing on the principal debt is thus fixed at that point of time, although no doubt the guarantee can expressly make the guarantor liable for such interest. Where the principal obligation is secured and the creditor does not prove in the principal debtor's bankruptcy or winding up, the creditor should be entitled to interest until the date of payment.[68]

5–57   It is not only the principal debtor's insolvency or a judgment given against the principal debtor that affects the recovery of interest. No interest is recoverable as a provable debt accruing after the *guarantor's* bankruptcy or winding up.[69] But, again, this principle should not affect the creditor's right to recover interest up to the date of payment if the creditor has taken a further security from the guarantor and does not prove.[70] In respect of a judgment obtained against the guarantor, the doctrine of merger is similarly applicable, thus precluding the recovery of interest

---

[63] (1970) 45 A.L.J.R. 49.
[64] See below, Ch. 10.
[65] *Director of Fair Trading v First National Bank* [2001] 3 W.L.R. 1297 at 1301; *In re Sneyd Ex p. Fewings* (1883) 25 Ch. D. 338; *Faber v Earl of Lathom* (1897) 77 L.T. 1.
[66] *Re Moss Ex p. Hallet* [1905] 2 K.B. 307. See also Insolvency Act, 1986, s.183; Insolvency Rules 1986 r.4.93.
[67] *ibid.*, where the wording of bond was regarded as decisive.
[68] Pennington, *Corporate Insolvency* (2nd ed., 1997), p.330. See *also Re London, Windsor & Greenwich Hotels (Quartermaine's case)* [1892] 1 Ch. 639; *Re Securitibank* [1980] 2 N.Z.L.R. 714.
[69] *Re Amalgamated Investment & Property Co Ltd* [1984] 3 All E.R. 272; *Re Standard Insurance Co Ltd (in liq) and Companies Act 1936* [1970] 1 N.S.W.R. 599.
[70] *Re Securitibank Ltd* [1980] 2 N.Z.L.R. 714.

pursuant to the terms of the guarantee after the date of judgment[71] unless the guarantee specifically includes a liability to pay such interest on the amounts owing under the judgment.[72] It is for this reason that drafters often include a clause in the guarantee excluding the doctrine of merger by judgment.

Finally, it has been suggested that the guarantor may be relieved in equity of the payment of future interest if the creditor simply allows arrears of interest to accumulate without taking steps to minimise the guarantor's liability.[73] But this view would seem to conflict with the well-established rule that the creditor need not take steps to press for payment against the principal debtor.[74]

5–58

(h) Is the guarantor liable for costs incurred by the creditor as a result of enforcing the principal transaction?

Whether the guarantor is liable for costs incurred in enforcing the principal transaction will be dependent on the wording of the guarantee and the principal transaction. Sometimes the fact that the principal transaction does not refer to a liability for costs may be decisive. In *Hoole Urban District Council v Fidelity & Deposit Co of Maryland*,[75] a guarantor undertook to be responsible for the contractor's obligations under a building contract. The guarantor was held not to be liable for costs incurred by the plaintiff arising from arbitration proceedings with the contractor because the contractor's liability for costs did not arise by virtue of a breach of the provisions of the principal contract, which contained no undertaking as to costs, but under the arbitration award itself. If the principal contract is similarly drafted, the result will be the same where the creditor proceeds by court action against the principal debtor and receives an order for costs in the creditor's favour.[76] The creditor will be able to recover costs, however, if the principal contract specifically imposes a contractual obligation upon the principal to pay costs which might be awarded against him, because this is then one of the contractual obligations guaranteed.[77]

5–59

---

[71] See above, n.65.

[72] *ibid.* Note especially the clause in *McDonald v Scobie* [1980] Qd. R. 477.

[73] *Dawson v Raynes* (1826) 2 Russ. 466; 38 E.R. 411 (sureties of a bankrupt receiver held not to be liable for arrears of interest in circumstances in which no steps had been taken to compel the passing of his accounts).

[74] See below, paras 11–11 to 11–37.

[75] [1916] 1 K.B. 25.

[76] Note that in *Baker v Garratt* (1825) 3 Bing. 56 at 60; 130 E.R. 434 at 436, Best C.J. was of the view that the guarantor would not be liable for the costs of a fruitless action by the creditor against the principal debtor if the creditor had not given the guarantor notice of his intention to sue the principal.

[77] *Hoole Urban District Council v Fidelity & Deposit Co of Maryland* [1916] 1 K.B. 25 at 29–30. On the same principle, if there is a guarantee of an arbitration award, the guarantor will be liable for all the component parts of the award including costs: *Compania Sudamericana De Fletes SA v African Continental Bank Ltd* [1973] 1 Lloyd's Rep. 21. As another analogous example, see *Re Lockey* (1845) 1 Ph. 509; 41 E.R. 726 (principal's contractual obligation which was guaranteed was to obey orders of the Lord Chancellor, and the Lord Chancellor made an order as to costs).

5-60   A differently worded guarantee will also produce a different result. Most modern guarantees impose a specific liability upon the guarantor for the costs of enforcing the principal transaction within the definition of the moneys secured by the guarantee. Similarly, if the guarantor is liable for all moneys owing by the principal "on any account whatsoever", this may be interpreted as embracing the principal's liability for costs incurred by the creditor in taking proceedings against the principal. A guarantor may also be liable for the creditor's costs of suing the principal where the guarantee imposes an obligation on the creditor to sue the principal before proceeding against the guarantor.[78]

5-61   If the creditor has to take steps to enforce a security upon the principal's default (for example, by the appointment of a receiver), it is thought that a general guarantee of the principal's obligations under the principal contract will cover the expenses incurred in doing so,[79] at least if the steps taken are necessary in the circumstances.[80] This is because the expenses will be incurred as a necessary consequence of a breach of the contractual obligations of the principal and will arise as a result of a breach of those obligations. As a matter of precaution, however, if the creditor wishes to recover these costs, there should be a specific clause in the guarantee to that effect.

5-62   It is established that where there is a contract of indemnity the costs of legal proceedings properly incurred by the person indemnified are recoverable[81] unless it is clear that the person indemnified has no sustainable defence.[82] This liability for costs arises because in the usual case the indemnity on its proper construction embraces a liability for costs,[83] but it is possible that a contract of indemnity may, upon different wording, not cover such liability.[84] Solicitor and client costs may be recoverable by the holder of the indemnity, although this will be dependent on the precise terms of the indemnity in question.[85]

---

[78] *Guenard v Coe* (1914) 17 D.L.R. 47 at 51.
[79] *Maunsell v Egan* (1846) 9 Ir. Eq. R. 283 (surety for performance of receiver's duties liable for costs involved in the appointment of a new receiver and the obtaining of an order that tenants pay their rents to the new receiver); *Keily v Murphy* (1837) Sau. & Sc. 479 (costs of attachment against a tenant for non-payment of rent held to be chargeable against the surety).
[80] See this limitation referred to in *Hatch, Mansfield & Co Ltd v Weingott* (1906) 22 T.L.R. 366 (costs of recovering property in criminal proceedings against employee held to be recoverable from the guarantor of the obligations of the employee as this was a reasonable course to adopt in the circumstances). See also Best C.J. in *Baker v Garratt* (1825) 3 Bing. 56 at 60; 130 E.R. 434 at 436 (surety not liable for costs of frivolous action against principal).
[81] *Duffield v Scott* (1789) 3 T.R. 374; 100 E.R. 628; *Jones v Williams* (1841) 7 M. & W. 493; 151 ER 860; *The Millwall* [1905] P. 155; *Mee v DWD Hotels Ltd* (No.2) [1974] 2 N.Z.L.R. 272; *Howard v Lovegrove* (1870) L.R. 6 Exch. 43.
[82] *Howard v Lovegrove* (1870) L.R. 6 Exch. 43; *Smith v Compton* (1832) 3 B. & Ad. 407; 110 E.R. 146.
[83] An indemnity in relation to loss from "any claims or actions" is probably sufficient, *e.g.* *Schleimer v Brisbane Stevedoring Pty Ltd* [1969] Qd. R. 46.
[84] *Potter v LCC* (1905) 70 J.P. 35.
[85] *Mee v DWD Hotels Ltd (No.2)* [1974] 2 N.Z.L.R. 272 at 277. See also *Great Western Railway Co v Fisher* [1905] 1 Ch. 316 at 324; *Barnett v Eccles Corp* [1900] 2 Q.B. 423 at 428; *Born v Turner* [1900] 2 Ch. 211; *Wiffen v Bailey and Romford Urban Council* [1915] 1 K.B. 600 at 607; *Howard v Lovegrove* (1870) LR 6 Exch. 43. *Cf. Maxwell v British Thompson-Houston Co Ltd* [1904] 2 K.B. 342, which also held that the costs of an appeal were not recoverable.

(ii) Limitations upon liability arising from the designation of the parties in the guarantee

(a) Is the guarantee limited in respect of a particular principal debtor with whom the creditor must contract?

The guarantee may specify that it applies where the creditor advances   **5–63**
sums of money to, or enters into a transaction with, a named principal. If
advances are made to a person other than the named principal, such
advances will not be within the scope of the guarantee. This issue is
illustrated by *Reid Murray Holdings Ltd (in liq) v David Murray Holdings
Pty Ltd*,[86] where a guarantee was given to secure advances made by the
creditor to Reid Murray Electrics Pty Ltd and all its subsidiary companies.
It was held that the guarantee did not cover advances made to a firm in
which one of the subsidiary companies was merely a partner. The
guarantee did not specifically cover such advances and there was nothing
in the surrounding circumstances to indicate that advances made to the
partnership came within the scope of the guarantee.[87] The problem of
advances being made to a principal who is outside the ambit of the
guarantee is likely to be accentuated in circumstances where there is a
change in the constitution of the principal debtor (for example, by merger
and takeover).[88]

Where there is a reference to a number of principal debtors, care must   **5–64**
be taken to ensure that the guarantee embraces loans to each individual
company and not merely loans made to the companies jointly.[89]

Problems as to whether a particular principal comes within the ambit of   **5–65**
the guarantee may also arise in respect of a "mutual guarantee", whereby
each company in a particular group guarantees the debts of the others. If a
new company comes into the group and signs the relevant instrument of
guarantee, the companies which are already existing signatories to the
instrument will not thereby become guarantors of the new company unless
they specifically agree to do so, or unless the original guarantee is so
drafted as to encompass any company which signs it in the future.[89a] Clear
wording will be required before the guarantee will be construed as
referring to any principal other than the existing signatories.

---

[86] (1972) 5 S.A.S.R. 386.
[87] *ibid.*, at 408. Note that in *National Bank of New Zealand Ltd v West* [1978] 2 N.Z.L.R. 451
at 461, Richmond J. suggests that by reference to extrinsic evidence it may be shown that a
loan to an apparently independent party is in substance a loan to the named principal. But if
the principal is not named in the guarantee at all, parol evidence will probably not be admitted
to identify the principal: *Imperial Bank v Nixon* [1926] 4 D.L.R. 1052.
[88] See the issue discussed in this context below, paras 9–53 to 9–69, especially 9–67 and 9–68,
and see in particular *National Bank of New Zealand Ltd v West* [1978] 2 N.Z.L.R. 451.
[89] See *Wates Building Group Ltd v Jones* (1996) 59 Construction L.R. 97 where there was a
guarantee of the repayment of loans to "both of you", although it was in the event held by
reference to the broad, general terms of the substantive body of the guarantee that the
guarantee embraced loans made to each company individually.
[89a] *Ford & Carter Ltd v Midland Bank Ltd* (1979) 129 N.L.J. 543.

(b) Is the creditor correctly identified?

5–66   Subject to the general rules regarding enforcement,[90] a guarantee may only be enforced by the creditor named in the guarantee. Thus, upon an assignment of a lease, a guarantee given specifically to the assignor of the lessee's obligations to secure against the failure of the assignee to pay the rent will not enure for the benefit of the lessor.[91]

5–67   One difficulty is that, although a named creditor may be specified in the guarantee, the moneys payable pursuant to that guarantee may not be owing to that creditor.

5–68   In particular, problems may occur in the construction of the guarantee when the creditor does not lend moneys directly to the principal but does so through the intermediary of a subsidiary because of exchange control or tax considerations. The problem was raised in *Amalgamated Investment & Property Co Ltd (in liq) v Texas Commerce International Bank Ltd.*[92] The plaintiffs were the guarantors of a loan made by the defendant bank to a company (called "ANPP") which was closely associated with the plaintiffs. The money was advanced by the bank through a subsidiary company of the bank (called "Portsoken") so as to avoid exchange control restrictions. When the plaintiffs went into liquidation, the bank realised properties which were security for other loans made by the bank to the plaintiffs as principals and sought to apply the amount of the loans which remained outstanding to the plaintiffs' liability under the guarantee. The plaintiffs, acting through their liquidator, sought to restrain the bank from this course of action on the basis that they were under no liability to the bank as guarantors of the loan made by the bank to ANPP. The plaintiffs promised by the guarantee to pay "on demand all moneys which ... shall ... be due or owing or payable to you [that is, the bank] on any account whatsoever by the principal". It was argued that the plaintiffs were not liable under the guarantee because the loan was not owing by the principal (ANPP) to the bank but only by the principal to the bank's subsidiary (Portsoken). At first instance, Goff J. accepted this argument:

> "The words of the guarantee are clear, and under them the guarantee was applicable only to moneys due or owing or payable to the bank. It is plain, on the evidence before me, that the ... loan was advanced [to ANPP] not by the bank, but by Portsoken; no part of the loan was ever due or owing or payable to the bank—the creditor was always Portsoken. I can see no reason for departing from the natural and ordinary meaning of the words of the guarantee."[93]

5–69   On appeal, Goff J.'s decision on this issue was overruled on the ground that, having regard to the surrounding circumstances and the general setting of the transactions, the guarantee was wide enough to embrace not only moneys payable by ANPP to the bank itself but also moneys payable

---

[90] See, generally, below, Ch. 10.
[91] *Malyon v New Zealand Methodist Trust Assoc* [1993] 1 N.Z.L.R. 137.
[92] [1982] Q.B. 84. See note (1982) 56 A.L.J. 141.
[93] *ibid.*, at 94.

by ANPP to Portsoken, which Portsoken was then required to pass on to the bank.[94] The Court of Appeal had regard to previous correspondence between the parties which clearly indicated that the plaintiffs would be responsible for seeing that the bank was repaid,[95] the conduct of the parties at the time of the transaction[96] and the fact that Portsoken was merely the alter ego of the parent bank.[97] The approach taken by the Court of Appeal is really at variance with the express wording of the guarantee and thus arguably in conflict with the general rule that extrinsic evidence is only admissible as an aid to interpretation where the words of the guarantee are unclear.[98]

Problems may also occur in identifying the correct plaintiff when the guarantee names a number of parties as creditors, often companies in the same group. Prima facie, the obligations of the guarantors will be owed jointly to all the parties named in the guarantee.[99] The interpretation of the agreement as a whole, however, may show that the guarantee has not been addressed to all of those parties named. For example, in *Boral Resources (Qld) Pty Ltd v Donnelly*,[1] the guarantee, which was addressed to eleven companies, was given in consideration of "your having ... agreed to supply to [the principal debtor]" certain building materials. This clause, together with the surrounding circumstances, was held to indicate that the guarantee was addressed only to the company which had agreed to supply goods, that is, the company with which the principal debtor was trading when the guarantee was given. The contract of guarantee was with that company, and the other named parties could not enforce the guarantee.[2]

5–70

---

[94] *ibid.*, at 118–119 *per* Denning M.R., 124–125 *per* Eveleigh L.J., 129 *per* Brandon L.J.
[95] *ibid.*, at 124 *per* Eveleigh L.J.
[96] *ibid.*, at 118–119 *per* Denning M.R., 129 *per* Brandon L.J.
[97] *ibid.*, at 119.
[98] See the general principles above, paras 5–01 to 5–09. The guarantee is also unlikely to be affected if the creditor's name is simply misdescribed and this does not affect the guarantor's willingness to contract: *J.A. Johnstone Co Ltd v E.R. Taylor Const Ltd* (1965) 52 D.L.R. (2d) 20 at 28–29. Note, however, that both Goff J. and the Court of Appeal both agreed on the alternative basis of the decision, namely, estoppel: discussed in detail below, paras 5–94 to 5–96.
[99] *Re Rogers Ex p. CMV Parts Distributors Pty Ltd* (1989) 20 F.C.R. 561 at 565, where von Doussa J. was of the view that such a guarantee would "ordinarily be understood" in this way.
[1] [1988] 1 Qd. R. 506.
[2] See also *Re Rogers Ex p. CMV Parts Distributors Pty Ltd* (1989) 20 F.C.R. 561, where the guarantee was interpreted as being addressed to three companies which had agreed to supply goods to the principal debtor. The identification of a number of companies in this way will not render the guarantee uncertain: (1989) 20 F.C.R. 561 at 566. *Cf. Ramsay v Aira Pty Ltd* (unreported, SA Sup Ct, October 7, 1992) where it was held that all the companies in the same group were proper plaintiffs, even though the document was addressed only to the managing director of one of those companies. The evidence showed that, in their business dealings, documentation had been prepared without any real concern for the name of the particular company within the group.

(c) Is the guarantee limited by the capacity in which the guarantor executes the guarantee?

5–71 The guarantor may argue that he has not executed the guarantee in a personal capacity, but in another capacity, for example, as trustee on behalf of a family trust or on behalf of a company. The proper approach[3] in these circumstances is to ascertain the guarantor's intention from a construction of the document as a whole, including (but not limited to) the qualification attached to the signature, and in the light of the surrounding circumstances.

5–72 On this basis, if the guarantor clearly indicates in signing the guarantee that he is contracting *in a capacity as trustee of a family trust and is not undertaking personal liability*, the guarantor may only be liable in the capacity as trustee and only to the extent of the assets for the time being of the family trust.[4] Sometimes it is unclear if the guarantor is signing on behalf of a company or, alternatively, assuming personal liability. In *Nelson Gardner v Cowburn*[5] the director of a number of companies agreed to a repayment schedule for debts owing by one company and additionally agreed the following undertaking (set out in a letter written and sent to him by the creditor):

> "with immediate effect, personally and/or from your other companies guarantee that amount outstanding at any time over normal trading terms…"

It was argued that the guarantee was void for uncertainty as the identity of the guarantor was unclear because the letter could be interpreted as referring to either the director personally or one of his unnamed companies, but the Court of Appeal held that it constituted a personal undertaking by the guarantor, although the arrangements for payment could be made through any of the companies. The courts may also construe the document as imposing personal liability, even if there is some qualification to the guarantor's signature which might appear to negate such liability. In *Scottish Amicable Life Assurance Society v Reg Austin Insurances Pty Ltd*,[6] the signatures of two directors on an indemnity agreement were expressed to be made *on behalf of* the company. Nevertheless, it was held that the directors were personally liable. The

---

[3] This follows from the general principles of construction applicable to guarantees (see above, paras 5–01 to 5–09). See also *Clark Equipment Credit of Australia Ltd v Kiyose Holdings Pty Ltd* (1989) 21 N.S.W.L.R. 160.

[4] *Muir v City of Glasgow Bank and Liquidators* (1879) 4 App. Cas. 337; *Helvetic Investment Corp Pty Ltd v Knight* (1984) 9 A.C.L.R. 773 at 774, 778. Note that in *Helvetic Investment Corp v Knight* personal liability was not negated.

[5] Unreported, March 7, 1989.

[6] (1985) 9 A.C.L.R. 909 at 923–924. See also *Helvetic Investment Corp v Knight* (1984) 9 A.C.L.R. 773; *Re Fletcher; Ex p. Hanimex* (1984) 9 A.C.L.R. 30 (reference to the instrument being a "director's" guarantee did not negate personal liability); *NEC Information Systems (Aust) Pty Ltd v Linton* (unreported, NSW Sup Ct, April 17, 1985). *Cf. Clark Equipment Credit of Australia Ltd v Kiyose Holdings Pty Ltd* (1989) 21 N.S.W.L.R. 160, where (unlike the instant case) there was a "sensible explanation" of the signatures, namely, the execution of a factoring agreement by the company: see (1989) 21 N.S.W.L.R. 160 at 176.

contents of the indemnity agreement, which appeared to impose personal liability, and the surrounding circumstances, including a previous letter from the creditor to the directors stating that a "personal guarantee" was required, overcame the prima facie inference to be drawn from the qualification to the signature.

In the case of an execution of a guarantee by a company holding no assets in its own right, *the creditor* may strive to show that the company has executed the guarantee in its capacity as trustee, so that a claim can be made against the assets of the trust.[7] Again, the issue is determined objectively as a matter of construction, with reference to all the circumstances.[8]

5–73

(iii) The effect of particular phrases used in the guarantee upon liability

(a) The meaning of amounts "contingently owing"

Many guarantees are specifically drafted so as to cover not only moneys owing to the creditor but also moneys which are "owing contingently" to the creditor. In the context of guarantees there is a dearth of English authority, but the the effect of such clauses was discussed in the Australian High Court case *National Bank of A/asia Ltd v Mason*.[9] The guarantors in that case agreed to pay to the creditor "on demand ... all moneys which may from time to time hereafter be owing to the bank or remain unpaid from the customer on any account whatsoever ... *whether contingently or otherwise* including all moneys which the bank ... may hereafter ... become liable to pay for or on account of the customer". The guarantee was given in consideration of the bank making credit available to the principal debtor. The question arose as to whether this guarantee brought within its scope a possible future liability of the principal debtor company to the bank. On the facts, this possible liability could have arisen because of a pending action by payees of certain cheques which one of the guarantors had indorsed to the principal company and which were then credited to the principal company's account and collected by the bank. The payees disputed the authority of the guarantor to make these endorsements and brought an action against the guarantor who had indorsed the cheques, and also the bank. The bank argued that, since the action against it for damages might be successful, and the bank could then seek reimbursement from the principal company, this was a contingent liability of the company to the bank within the meaning of the guarantee. The issue was important because if the moneys came within the scope of the

5–74

---

[7] *Re Interwest Hotels Pty Ltd (in liq)* (1993) 12 A.C.S.R. 78.
[8] *ibid.*, where it was held that the company had executed the guarantee personally, rather than as trustee. A relevant fact was that the creditor had been put on notice that the company would not readily agree to the trust assets being exposed to liability: (1993) 12 A.C.S.R. 78 at 121.
[9] (1976) 50 A.L.J.R. 362.

guarantee they would also come within the terms of the mortgage,[10] which the guarantors had also given as security, and the guarantors would not be entitled to have the mortgage discharged. Such a discharge would otherwise have been possible because there were no other outstanding liabilities of the principal to the creditor, the overdraft having been paid.

5-75   The High Court unanimously rejected the bank's argument, holding that the guarantees did not extend to this possible liability of the principal company to the bank, and, in doing so, Barwick C.J. and Stephen J. gave indications of the possible scope of the phrase "owing ... whether contingently or otherwise" appearing in a guarantee.[11] Stephen J. construed the reference to contingent liabilities in this particular guarantee as merely referring to a description of the occasion (that is, the contingency) when it has occurred and has given rise to the actual indebtedness:

> "the phrase must, I think, be taken to refer not to contingent events upon the happening of which moneys will, for the first time, become 'now owing', but rather as descriptive of one instance of money being now owing, that is to say, where, in some transaction productive of liability only if some contingent event occurs, that event does occur. Thus the contingency which the clause refers to is not descriptive of the nature of the indebtedness of the bank but instead describes the contingent nature of the occasion which, the contingency having happened, has given rise to actual indebtedness."[12]

5-76   Thus confined, the words "whether contingently or otherwise" add nothing to the word "owing". Contingent liabilities would only fall within the ambit of the guarantee once the contingency had occurred and in that case the liabilities would be "owing" in any event. Although this conclusion was primarily reached by reference to other parts of the guarantee,[13] Stephen J. was also influenced by broader policy considerations. He referred to the inherent contradiction between a guarantee which refers to "moneys now owing" and at the same time seeks to include moneys only owing on a contingency.[14] Further, if the reference to moneys

---

[10] See the terms of the mortgage discussed by Barwick C.J.: (1976) 50 A.L.J.R. 362 at 365.
[11] The judgment of Murphy J., (1976) 50 A.L.J.R. 362 at 369, is short and he does not elaborate on a possible meaning of "contingently". Murphy J. held that the possible liability of the principal to the bank did not mean that there was "money owing" by the guarantor to the bank.
[12] (1976) 50 A.L.J.R. 362 at 368.
[13] In particular, Stephen J. emphasised the inclusion of a provision in the guarantee (cl. 4) whereby, if the guarantor determined the guarantee by notice in accordance with its terms, the guarantor must make provision up to the limit of the guarantee for any contingent liabilities arising from specified transactions. Stephen J. was of the view that the inclusion of this provision indicated that the guarantee did not extend to contingent liabilities as soon as they arose and whether or not the contingency occurred. If such contingent liabilities were included in the guarantee as soon as they arose, there would be no need for cl.4 governing contingent liabilities arising after determination. Arguably, however, this reasoning is defective because the purpose of cl.4 might not be to bring contingent liabilities which might arise after determination of the guarantee within its ambit, but merely to ensure that upon determination the guarantor pays the creditor an amount to cover the principal's liability in respect of those liabilities when other securities given by the guarantor may be released by the creditor.
[14] (1976) 50 A.L.J.R. 362 at 368.

payable on a contingency were read in a wide sense as being an event which might or might not occur, it would seem that the bank could demand payment from the guarantor of sums which might never become due to the bank from the principal, so that the liability of the guarantor would exceed rather than be co-extensive with that of the principal.[15]

Although reaching the same conclusion on the facts, Barwick C.J.   **5–77**
appears to have taken a broader view of the phrase "whether contingently or otherwise". The Chief Justice held that before the moneys will be "owing contingently" there must be some presently existing obligation out of which the ultimate liability will grow.[16] This definition was not satisfied on the facts because the principal company was at no stage under an existing obligation to pay damages to the bank; it was simply a liability which might subsequently arise out of the facts and from the past relationship of the parties.[17] However, Barwick C.J., unlike Stephen J., appeared to contemplate that, if the guarantee referred to "liabilities which are owed contingently", liabilities of the principal to the creditor being subject to an event which might never occur may be brought immediately within the scope of the guarantee, provided that an existing obligation has arisen. An illustration would be payments owing to the creditor under a contract where the payments need to be approved by a third party (for example, by the certificate of an architect) before they are payable.

It is considered that the approach taken by Barwick C.J. is more in   **5–78**
accordance with the existing (albeit limited) English authority. In *Banner Lane Realisations Ltd (in liq) v Berisford Plc*[18] the Court of Appeal held, in the context of the interpretation of a debenture charge, that the term "present and future indebtedness" would not by itself exclude cases where there is no present obligation at all but where that obligation arises in the future. As Morritt L.J. stated:

> "So the obligation of the principal debtor at the time the debenture was executed to indemnify the surety in the future *if* and to the extent that he the surety is called on to pay and does pay the sums due under the guarantee, in my view, falls within the expression 'present or future indebtedness' as used in the debenture" [authors' emphasis]

(b) An "all accounts" or "all moneys" guarantee

Many guarantees are widely drafted to include within their ambit "all   **5–79**
and every sum and sums of money which are owing or unpaid on any account whatsoever" There is no classic judicial definition of the phrase "all accounts", but it has been said not to be limited to an account

---

[15] *ibid.*, at 367.
[16] *ibid.*, at 366.
[17] *ibid.*
[18] [1997] 1 B.C.L.C. 380 at 388. See also *Re Rudd & Son Ltd* (1986) 2 B.C.C. 98, 955, below, para.5–80.

normally portraying the relation of banker and customer, for example, a current or loan account.[19] This conclusion is reinforced if the guarantee also refers to the contingent liability of the principal.[20]

5–80   Generally "all monies" clauses in guarantees have been broadly interpreted, and their potentially wide ambit have often not been restrained by the statement of consideration or recital which might indicate the guarantee is to be limited to a particular type of transaction.[21] Indeed, in *Re Rudd & Son Ltd*[22] a clause in a mortgage imposing an obligation to "pay to the bank all and every the sum of and sums of money which shall for the time being be owing to the bank ... on the current account of the firm or any other account" was construed as including contingent indebtedness (including, on the facts, the potential liability of the principal borrower to indemnify the bank in respect of suretyship bonds, even though no call had been made on those bonds).

5–81   One particular problem which has arisen, especially in respect of cross guarantees in a group structure, is whether an "all accounts" guarantee will embrace the liabilities of the principal debtor when those liabilities have been incurred in the debtor's capacity as a guarantor of a loan made by the creditor to a third party. Although the precise wording of the guarantee and the particular circumstances will be decisive, the general trend has been to interpret an "all accounts" guarantee to include such obligations.[23] Thus in *Bank of Scotland v Wright*,[24] the guarantee related to "sums ... due and to become due to you by your customer ... in any manner or way whatsoever". It was held to embrace the principal debtor's contingent liability to another company in the same group pursuant to a guarantee, once that liability had crystallised. A significant factor was that the guarantor at the date of the execution of the guarantee knew that it was to be part of an "interlinked mesh of securities" involving a cross guarantee given by the company whose debt he had guaranteed.[25]

---

[19] *National Bank of New Zealand Ltd v West* [1978] 2 N.Z.L.R. 451 at 457.

[20] *ibid.* In the case of an all-embracing guarantee of this type, there is no general duty owed by the principal debtor or its directors (if a company) to the guarantor not to increase the guarantor's liabilities. Exceptionally, however, in *Elliot v Wheeldon* [1993] B.C.L.C. 53, it was held to be "at least ... arguable" that "where A and B enter into a joint venture for the carrying on of a business through the medium of company C, with A as the continuing guarantor of C's liabilities, B owes a duty to A to conduct himself as a director of C in such a way as not, except in good faith, to increase A's liabilities under his guarantee" (at 57).

[21] See *Bank of India v TransContinental Commodity Merchants & Patel* [1982] 1 Lloyd's Rep. 506; *Phillips Petroleum Co v Quentin* (unreported February 16, 1998). See above, para.5–09.

[22] (1986) 2 B.C.C. 98, 955. See, similarly, *Banner Lane Realisations Ltd (in liq) v Berisford plc* [1997] 1 B.C.L.C. 380 in respect of the phrase "future indebtedness", discussed above, para. 5–78. See also *Catley Farms Ltd v ANZ Banking Group (NZ) Ltd* [1982] 1 N.Z.L.R. 430.

[23] But the creditor as a matter of caution should include a clause specifically referring to liabilities in respect of "any guarantee which has been given by the customer to a third party" (as in *Catley Farms Ltd v ANZ Banking Group (NZ) Ltd* [1982] 1 N.Z.L.R. 430).

[24] [1990] B.C.C. 663. See also *Coghlan v SH Lock (Aust) Ltd* (1987) 61 A.L.J.R. 289; *Cambridge Credit Corp Ltd v Lombard Australia Ltd* (1977) 136 C.L.R. 608, where a clause in a mortgage was given this meaning. *Cf.* McHugh J.A. in *Coghlan v SH Lock (Aust) Ltd* (1985) 4 N.S.W.L.R. 158 at 181, CA; *Re Clark's Refrigerated Transport Pty Ltd (in liq)* [1982] V.R. 989.

[25] In *Bank of Scotland v Wright* [1990] B.C.C. 663 at 675, Brooke J. regarded the surrounding circumstances as important and was of the view that the guarantee was not to be interpreted purely in reliance on "internal linguistic considerations".

There have, however, been some limitations imposed by judicial   **5–82**
interpretation on the scope of an "all moneys" guarantee. For example,
an "all monies" guarantee will not readily be interpreted as increasing the
scope of the guarantor's liability upon assignment and, in particular, as
covering debts owed by the principal debtor to third parties and assigned
to the creditor who enjoys the benefit of a guarantee, supported by a legal
charge. In *Kova Establishment v Sasco Investments Ltd*[26] John Martin
Q.C., sitting as a Deputy Judge of the High Court, referred with approval
to the comments of Brooking J. in the Australian case, *Re Clark's
Refrigerated Transport Pty Ltd (in liq)*,[27] where His Honour stated:

"In the first place, considering the matter generally and without regard
to the detailed provisions of the particular instruments here in question,
I cannot help thinking that when a person gives an 'all obligations'
mortgage or debenture he does not ordinarily contemplate that the
property the subject of the security will secure not only his present and
future obligations to the mortgagee or debenture holder but also any
debt or liability of his which may be assigned by a third person to the
secured creditor. It does seem strange that a man may lock up his
counting-house and go home for the night, in the comfortable knowledge that his only secured creditor is his banker, to whom he owes a
trifling sum secured by the usual boundless bank instrument, and unlock
the door in the morning to find that, by virtue of assignments of the large
but unsecured debts owed by him to his fellow merchants, and indeed to
the butcher, the baker and the candlestick maker, all his unsecured debts
have gone to feed his banker's insatiable security so that everyone of his
debts is now secured."

The precise construction will be dependent, of course, on the particular
wording of the guarantee. In *Kova Establishment v Sasco Investments Ltd*[28]
one provision that supported an interpretation that assigned debts were
not included within the guarantee was a clause providing for the payment
of interest payable upon the total debt at a defined rate after demand had
been made. As this rate might (and on the facts was) higher than the rate
payable on the principal debt, this meant that, when the assigned debts
become subject to the guarantee and legal charge, the effect would be to
alter the amount which the creditor was entitled to receive and which the
guarantor (but not necessarily the debtor) was obliged to pay.

Conversely, there may be an assignment of the benefit of the   **5–83**
"guarantee" (supported by a legal charge) securing certain indebtedness
of the borrower to another unsecured creditor of that borrower. Again all
"monies" clause will not, without clear wording, be construed as
converting the pre-existing unsecured loans of the creditor into secured
loans. As Hart J. put it in *Sandhurst Holdings Ltd v Grosvenor Assets
Ltd*:[29]

---

[26] [1998] 2 B.C.L.C. 83.
[27] *ibid.*, at 87. See also [1982] V.R. 989 at 995–996.
[28] [1998] 2 B.C.L.C. 83.
[29] Unreported July 17, 2001.

"it is contrary to one's expectations that a borrower who has voluntarily given security in respect of liabilities incurred to a particular person may find that the security comes to be applied to liabilities which he has incurred in a deliberately unsecured way to another person."[30]

Aside from issues of interpretation arising upon assignment, it does not appear that an all monies clause can be utilised to prejudice the position of the guarantor, for example, by prejudicing the exercise of the right of subrogation. This proposition derives from *Lloyds Bank Plc v Shorney*.[31] There Mr and Mrs Shorney gave a mortgage over their matrimonial home as part of a wider transaction in respect of which Mr Shorney had given a separate guarantee to secure a loan of £150,000 made by the bank to a company (in which Mr Shorney no longer had any interest). The mortgage limited Mr and Mrs Shorney's liability to £150,000 but also contained an "all monies" clause and a provision governing the right of subrogation. The mortgage secured:

"A (a) all money and liabilities (including further advances made hereafter by the Bank and secured directly or indirectly by this mortgage) whether certain or contingent which now are or at any time hereafter may be due owing or incurred from or by the Customer to the Bank anywhere on any current or other account or in any manner whatsoever whether as principal or surety and whether alone or jointly with any other person firm or corporation and in whatever style name or form including:"

The right of subrogation was addressed in clause 21:

"21. Until all money and liabilities and other sums due owing or incurred by the Customer to the Bank shall have been paid or discharged in full notwithstanding payment in whole or in part of any sum recoverable from the mortgagor hereunder or any purported release or cancellation hereof the Mortgagor shall not by virtue of any such payment or by any other means or any other ground (save as hereinafter provided):

(d) to be entitled to claim or have the benefit of any security or guarantee now or hereafter held by the Bank for any money or liabilities or other sums due or incurred by the Customer to the Bank or to have any share therein."

5–84   Subsequently (and unknown to Mrs Shorney) Mr Shorney gave further guarantees in respect of additional loans made to the borrowing company. When Mrs Shorney paid the debt of £150,000 which arose under the mortgage, it was held that the bank could not rely on clause 21 to deprive her of the right to the mortgage by way of subrogation on the basis of the

---

[30] See also *Katsikalis v Deutsche Bank (Asia) AG* [1988] 2 Qd.R. 641, where it was held that a mortgage which referred to sums "due owing or payable . . . on any account whatsoever" did not embrace a pre-existing debt owed by the principal debtor to an assignee of the mortgage, the assignor being another creditor who, subsequent to the creation of that debt, had made further advances (secured by the mortgage) to the same principal debtor.
[31] [2001] N.P.C. 121.

argument that Mr Shorney's liabilities (now increased by the further guarantees) had not "been paid or discharged in full". According to the Court of Appeal the increase in Mr Shorney's liabilities above £150,000 could not have been reasonably contemplated by Mrs Shorney since her liability under the mortgage (limited to that amount) reflected a guarantee precisely for that sum given by Mr Shorney in respect of the original borrowings of a company in which he was no longer interested. As a result the material increase in Mr Shorney's liabilities above £150,000 would prejudice her position if the bank relied on clause 21 since its application would deprive Mrs Shorney of the right of subrogation. The "all monies" clause A(a) (set out above) did not assist the bank since, according to Walker L.J. (Latham L.J. and Astill J. agreeing): "it seems to me that it is not permissible to look at the general wording of an "all monies charge" in order to suggest that Mrs Shorney should have contemplated further guarantees being entered into."[32] The circumstances of this case are somewhat unusual, but it does raise the possibility of the width of an "all monies" clause being restricted in respect of liabilities which the guarantor could not have reasonably contemplated.[33]

The creditor needs to give careful consideration to bringing proceedings   5–85
when separate securities containing "all monies" clauses are given to that creditor. In particular, if the defendant gives an "all monies" charge to the creditor and subsequently an "all monies" guarantee, the creditor cannot obtain a money judgment "in respect of the total amount outstanding under the [legal charge] and subsequently bring proceedings under the guarantee (having failed to include all the relevant amounts in the first claim)".[34]

(c) The meaning of "advances"

A common form of guarantee is a guarantee of "advances" to be made   5–86
to the principal.[35] Normally, "advances" means a furnishing of money for some specified purpose, although the furnishing need not necessarily be by way of loan.[36] The definition will exclude a situation in which a principal

---

[32] Another clause (16) provided that "The Bank may without any consent from the Mortgagor and without affecting this mortgage renew vary increase or determine any advances accommodation or facilities given or to be given by the customer". But the clause did not cover "what the Bank did in the instant case because the underlying transaction was a liability of Mr Shorney for the debts of the company".

[33] There are statements of a more general nature in the Court of Appeal's decision. Relying on the non-disclosure decision, *Levett v Barclays Bank* [1995] 1 W.L.R. 1260, it is asserted that "the case recognises that without consent, including consent by virtue of the terms of the guarantee itself, the Bank cannot act in a way that materially affects the surety's position". But there is little other support for a general "prejudice" principle of this nature (see below, paras 8–106 to 8–114) and *Levett v Barclays Bank* is clearly based on the much more limited basis of a breach of the creditor's duty of disclosure.

[34] *Lloyds Bank plc v Hawkins* [1998] Lloyd's Rep. Bank 379 at 385.

[35] In complicated transactions, the amount of the advance secured may sometimes be difficult to determine: *Euro-Pacific Finance Corp Ltd v Hielacher* (1980) 30 A.L.R. 1.

[36] *Burnes v Trade Credits Ltd* (1981) 34 A.L.R. 459 at 461. *Cf.*, in special circumstances, *Quainoo v NZ Breweries Ltd* [1991] 1 N.Z.L.R. 161 at 165–166, where it was held the expression embraced an existing, accumulated debt. On the facts, any other construction

sum has already been advanced by the creditor and all that occurs is that the term of repayment of the original principal sum is extended. This transaction will not be a "further advance" within the meaning of the guarantee.[37] On this basis, the roll-over of a commercial bill or facility will not constitute an "advance" since the transaction does not involve the provision of an additional sum of principal. The term "advance" will also exclude mere book-keeping transactions.[38] Thus if a bank allows the principal to pay off the overdraft on one account by drawing a cheque on a newly opened account, which is then debited with the amount of the cheque, the transaction will not amount to "an advance".[39]

5–87   If the guarantee in this form is intended to relate both to past and future indebtedness, this should be expressly stated ("sums of money already advanced or to be advanced"). Similarly, there should be an express reference to the inclusion in the guarantee of unpaid interest if (as is usual) it is intended that the guarantee should cover such liability, because the term "advance" has been construed as not including amounts payable by way of interest.[40]

(d) Scope of liability when the guarantee relates to "moneys secured by the mortgage"

5–88   It will be seen that this expression may have important effects on the liability of the guarantor upon a discharge or release of a mortgage,[41] but, even apart from that situation, if the guarantee makes it clear that the only obligation which is guaranteed is the money secured by a mortgage rather than all sums which are owed by the principal debtor to the creditor, the guarantor will not be liable for debts incurred which were never secured by the mortgage at all. Thus in *Buckeridge v Mercantile Credits Ltd*,[42] the defendant guarantor argued that he could not be liable for moneys owed independently by virtue of a debenture which the creditor held as security together with a mortgage. His argument was that the wording in the guarantee, which referred to "all moneys owing ... by the mortgagors" should be interpreted as "all moneys owing ... by the mortgagors *under the mortgage*".[43] This construction was rejected, but the case does illustrate the need to avoid wording which may be interpreted to mean that the guarantor is only liable for sums secured by the mortgage.

---

would have been "unreasonable and unrealistic" because it was clear that no additional cash sums were made or intended to be made.
[37] *Burnes v Trade Credits Ltd* (1981) 34 A.L.R. 459.
[38] *AJS Bank v Costello* (1890) 6 W.N. (NSW) 94.
[39] *ibid.*
[40] *Reid Murray Holdings Ltd (in liq) v David Murray Holdings Pty Ltd* (1972) 5 S.A.S.R. 386 at 409.
[41] See below, para.6–54.
[42] (1982) 56 A.L.J.R. 28.
[43] *ibid.*, at 31 (emphasis added).

(iv) The effect of the terms of the principal transaction upon liability

The terms of the principal transaction will naturally determine the extent of the guarantor's liability because the guarantor's liability will be co-extensive with that of the principal debtor. But there are two particular issues of liability affected by the terms of the principal transaction which merit individual consideration.   **5–89**

(a) Scope of liability where there is a discrepancy between the guarantee and the principal transaction

Sometimes the guarantee and the principal transaction may be so drafted that it is apparent that the liability of the guarantor as defined in the contract of guarantee does not exactly correspond with the obligation of the principal as defined in the principal transaction. There is no English authority, but guidance as to how this discrepancy can be resolved can be obtained from the New Zealand case of *Perrott v Newton King Ltd*.[44] There the mortgagor's liability was to pay interest on the principal sum so long as the principal sum should "remain unpaid", but the guarantor of the mortgage promised by the terms of the guarantee to pay arrears of interest while any money remained "owing" on the mortgage. The guarantor was held to be released by the principal's bankruptcy from a liability to pay interest, because after the mortgagor's bankruptcy, the principal sum could no longer be regarded as being "owing".[45] A different result would have been reached if the guarantee, like the mortgage, had contained the words "remain unpaid".[46] But Kennedy J. said that in such cases the words in the guarantee and not the words in the principal transaction must define the guarantor's liability: **5–90**

"The plaintiffs, claiming as they do under the agreement of guarantee, must take their rights to be defined by the agreement of guarantee itself, although that agreement creates a liability which does not exactly correspond with the obligation the performance of which is secured by the memorandum of mortgage ... I know of no principle which would permit the assumption that the liability guaranteed was co-extensive with that undertaken by the mortgagor in the mortgage so that the court may by interpretation hold that words of the guarantee have the same meaning as different words in the memorandum of mortgage."[47]

This was, of course, a case in which the liability of the guarantor was reduced in accordance with the provisions of the guarantee and any   **5–91**

---

[44] [1933] N.Z.L.R. 1131.
[45] See on this issue, below, paras 6–91 to 6–93.
[46] *ibid.* See especially *Re Fitzgeorge Ex p. Robson* [1905] 1 K.B. 462.
[47] [1933] N.Z.L.R. 1131 at 1157. The other members of the New Zealand Court of Appeal (Myers C.J., Herdman J.) did not directly discuss the point raised by Kennedy J. but clearly agreed that the words in the guarantee should predominate.

reference to the provisions of the principal transaction would have enlarged the guarantor's liability. Kennedy J., however, was of the view that the same principle applies where the wording of the guarantee indicates a more extensive liability than that which the principal will incur under the principal transaction[48] (for example, where the guarantee of a lessee's obligations under a lease recites that a particular rent is payable, but the lease itself indicates that a lower rent is payable by the lessee).[49] It is thought, however, that in such cases the general principle of co-extensiveness would lead the courts to strive for an interpretation which would make the liabilities of principal and guarantor the same,[50] except where the instrument clearly indicated that the "guarantor" had assumed a wider independent liability. This view is supported by the fact that, as has been seen, the courts may construe a contract as a guarantee, even though it contains an indemnity clause.[51]

(b) Scope of liability where the principal transaction provides for the whole sum to be payable on the principal's default

5–92   The question arises as to whether a guarantor will be liable for the total sum which is owed by the debtor, when that sum has become payable by the debtor as a result of a clause in the principal transaction providing that the whole of the principal sum is payable upon any default by the debtor. If the guarantee itself can be construed simply as a guarantee of each sum arising under the principal transaction as it would *normally* fall due, the guarantor will not be liable for the whole of the principal sum. Again the relevant authority is from New Zealand. Thus in *Parker v Bayly*,[52] where the guarantee of a mortgagor's obligation related to the payment of moneys "whenever the same may under or by virtue of the said memoranda of mortgage ... be due and payable", it was held that these words were intended to apply to the periodic payments of interest and capital provided for in the mortgage, and not to render the guarantor liable to pay the whole sum which was immediately due under the mortgage upon a default by the principal.[53] It was considered that liability for the total sum did not strictly arise "under or by virtue of" the mortgage within the meaning of the guarantee (except in a secondary sense), but by virtue of a default under the mortgage on the part of the mortgagors.[54] The inclusion of a principal debtor clause, whereby the guarantor is deemed to be a principal debtor in respect of his relationship with the creditor, did not alter this construction because the effect of such a clause was not to

---

[48] [1933] N.Z.L.R. 1131 at 1157–1158.
[49] See a similar example quoted by Kennedy J. *ibid.*, at 1158. See also *Lainson v Tremere* (1834) 1 Ad. & E. 792; 110 E.R. 1410.
[50] This is especially likely to be the case where the guarantee is contained in the principal transaction: *Joint Stock Bank v Mortimer* (1867) 6 S.C.R. (NSW) 248 at 252.
[51] See above, paras 1–104 to 1–106 and especially *Stadium Finance Co Ltd v Helm* (1965) 109 S.J. 471.
[52] [1927] G.L.R. 265.
[53] *ibid.*, at 267–268.
[54] *ibid.*

enlarge the ambit of the guarantor's obligations, but merely to deprive the guarantor of his equitable rights to be discharged in certain circumstances (for example, by a variation of the principal contract).[55]

It will, however, probably be unusual for a modern contract of guarantee to be construed (as in *Parker v Bayly*) in a restricted way. For example, if the guarantor has guaranteed the due and punctual performance of all the principal's obligations, the guarantee will be interpreted as embracing the principal obligation in the mortgage whereby the principal is obliged to pay the whole amount owing upon the principal's default. The guarantor will then become immediately liable for the whole mortgage debt upon any default by the principal.[56]

5–93

(v) The effect of the doctrine of estoppel upon the scope of liability

The possibility of widening the extent of the guarantor's liability by reference to the doctrine of estoppel is illustrated by the decision of the Court of Appeal in *Amalgamated Investment & Property Co Ltd (in liq) v Texas Commerce International Bank Ltd*.[57] The facts of the case have been previously set out.[58] The Court of Appeal held, first, that a guarantee of "all moneys which ... shall ... be due and owing to [the bank] on any account whatsoever by the principal" included, as a matter of construction, moneys which were payable not to the bank directly but to the bank's subsidiary. This aspect of the decision is considered in detail elsewhere.[59] Secondly, the court was of the view that, even assuming that this construction of the guarantee was erroneous, the guarantors were estopped by convention from denying that the loan came within the guarantee. The estoppel arose because the evidence, including negotiations subsequent to the execution of the guarantee,[60] indicated that the parties assumed the truth of a certain state of affairs, namely, that the guarantee effectively bound the guarantors to discharge the indebtedness of the principal to the bank's subsidiary. The bank in pursuance of this belief had acted in a way which it would not otherwise have done (for example, by rearranging its securities).[61] The facts, therefore, came within the principle of estoppel by convention, which was described by the court in these terms:

5–94

---

[55] *ibid.* Note, however, that in *Gilmer and Gilmer v Ross* [1932] N.Z.L.R. 507 the principal debtor clause was regarded as enlarging the liability of the guarantor in this context, but reliance on the principal debtor clause was probably unnecessary in view of the wording of the substantive part of the guarantee.

[56] *e.g.* see the terms of the guarantee in *Gilmer and Gilmer v Ross* [1932] N.Z.L.R. 507. This conclusion assumes that the relevant clause in the principal contract does not amount to a penalty provision. As to the consequences of this: see below, para.5–110.

[57] [1982] Q.B. 84, CA.

[58] See above, para.5–68.

[59] *ibid.*

[60] See especially [1982] Q.B. 84, CA at 119–120.

[61] *ibid.*, at 120 *per* Denning M.R., 131 *per* Brandon L.J.

"This form of estoppel is founded, not on a representation of fact made by a representor and believed by a representee, but on an agreed statement of facts the truth of which has been assumed, by the convention of the parties, as the basis of a transaction into which they are about to enter."[62]

5–95   It is clear from this definition that a definite and specific representation of fact is not necessary to found the estoppel,[63] and this removes one obstacle which has sometimes prevented an argument based on estoppel succeeding in this context.[64] The estoppel can probably also rest on a foundation of assumed law, for example, as to the effect of the instrument of guarantee.[65] But what is required (and what is not explicitly stated in the definition in the previous paragraph) is that the party estopped must induce by action or inaction the assumption in the mind of the other party so that it would be unfair or unjust to allow a departure from the assumption.[66]

5–96   The doctrine of estoppel by convention has been applied by courts in other jurisdictions where there was an agreed assumption that the guarantee was addressed to all companies within a group structure, although the guarantee only expressly referred to one of the companies as the creditor.[67] It has also been applied where the guarantee itself indicates it will apply to loans made to a particular company, but there is an agreed assumption that the guarantee will embrace loans made to a number of companies within the group.[68] Potentially, estoppel may also enable the creditor to recover in respect of the indirect liability of the principal debtor (for example, the latter's obligations as guarantor of a third person's debts) when the wording of the guarantee may not include such liability.[69] It may also be utilised to reduce the scope of the guarantor's liability,[70] but is unlikely to be applied to extend the guarantor's liability beyond that imposed upon the principal debtor[71] (that is, to convert a contract of guarantee into a contract of indemnity).

---

[62] *ibid.*, at 126 *per* Eveleigh L.J., 130–131 *per* Brandon L.J.
[63] *Coghlan v SH Lock (Aust) Ltd* (1985) 4 N.S.W.L.R. 158 at 166.
[64] See, *e.g. United Dominion's Trust Ltd v Beech* [1972] 1 Lloyd's Rep. 546 at 552.
[65] *Eslea Holdings Ltd v Butts* (1986) 6 N.S.W.L.R. 175. *Cf.*, however, *Con-Stan Industries of Australia Pty Ltd v Norwich Winterthur Insurance (Aust) Ltd* (1986) 60 A.L.J.R. 294 at 300, which was analysed by Samuels J.A. in *Eslea Holdings Ltd v Butts* (1986) 6 N.S.W.L.R. 175 at 185–189.
[66] *Coghlan v SH Lock (Aust) Ltd* [1985] 4 N.S.W.L.R. 158, at 167–168; *Bank of Scotland v Wright* [1990] B.C.C. 663 at 677, 679.
[67] *Eslea Holdings Ltd v Butts* (1986) 6 N.S.W.L.R. 175.
[68] *Coghlan v SH Lock (Aust) Ltd* (1985) 4 N.S.W.L.R. 158. But note that, on appeal, the Privy Council approached the matter simply on the basis of the construction of the terms of the guarantee: (1987) 3 B.C.C. 183.
[69] As argued in *Bank of Scotland v Wright* [1990] B.C.C. 663, where the wording of the guarantee was in any event sufficiently wide to cover such indirect liabilities.
[70] *e.g. National Westminster Finance NZ Ltd v National Bank of NZ Ltd* [1996] 1 N.Z.L.R. 548, where the guarantor was held liable to pay a net amount after allowing for credit balances in other accounts.
[71] *Securum Finance Ltd v Ashton* [2002] 2 All E.R. (D) 380, where Peter Smith J. said that this would lead to a "bizarre result" (at para.58) and that *Amalgamated Investment & Property Co Ltd (in liq) v Texas Commerce International Bank Ltd* should not be extended to where the principal's liability did not "actually exist".

Amalgamated Investment & Property Co Ltd (in liq) v Texas Commerce International Bank Ltd[72] in fact concerned an action by the guarantors to restrain the bank from applying moneys, received from the realisation of properties securing other loans made to the guarantors as principals, in diminution of their liability as guarantors. Some doubt was expressed in that case as to whether the principle of estoppel by convention would enable the creditor to succeed in an action to enforce the guarantee itself. In particular, Eveleigh L.J. considered that if estoppel was utilised in this way it would be treating the estoppel "as having the effect of an assumpsit".[73] It is true that this accords with the present English law[74] in respect of promissory estoppel, but it does mean that the outcome will be dependent upon the precise way the litigation unfolds. Indeed, in Australia it is now clear that estoppel can found a cause of action[75] and in the context of proprietory estoppel even English courts have created rights based upon estoppel.[76] Given that there is also an emerging view that different forms of estoppel should be unified in a wider doctrine based upon unconscionability,[77] it may be that English courts will soon recognise that estoppel can be a cause of action. Certainly there seems no reason even under existing authority why estoppel cannot *assist* the creditor in an action to enforce the guarantee. The cause of action is still a claim for debt or damages (as the case may be)[78] pursuant to the guarantee; the estoppel simply prevents the creditor relying on the strict wording of the guarantee. In *Amalgamated Investment & Property Co Ltd (in liq) v Texas Commerce International Bank Ltd*[79] Brandon L.J. in fact appeared to recognise this in stating that whilst a person "cannot in terms found a cause of action upon estoppel, he may, as a result of being able to rely on an estoppel, succeed on a cause of action on which, without being able to rely on that estoppel, he would necessarily have failed".[80]

(vi) Where a restriction on the scope of liability arises from a mistake

Occasionally there may be a mistake in the final written guarantee **5–97** which, if not corrected, will have the effect of restricting the scope of the guarantor's liability. For example, the wrong principal or creditor may be designated in the guarantee so that loans made to the intended principal are not embraced by the guarantee, or the moneys are owed to the incorrect creditor. One possibility in this situation is that the guarantee can

---

[72] [1982] Q.B. 84.
[73] *ibid.*, at 126.
[74] *Combe v Combe* [1951] 2 K.B. 215 at 224. See generally J. Beatson *Anson's Law of Contract* (28th ed., 2002) pp.118–20.
[75] *Waltons Stones (Interstate) Pty Ltd v Maher* (1988) 164 C.L.R. 387.
[76] *Crabb v Arun DC* [1976] Ch. 179 and generally J. Beatson *Anson's Law of Contract* (28th ed., 2002) pp.120–121.
[77] See generally J. Beatson *Anson's Law of Contract* (28th ed., 2002) pp.122–124.
[78] See below, Ch. 10.
[79] [1982] Q.B. 84.
[80] *ibid.*, at 131–132.

be rectified to correct the mistake. The necessary conditions are, however, not easy to satisfy. There must be convincing evidence that the guarantee at the date of its execution does not accurately reflect the common intention and common outward accord of the guarantor and creditor.[81] This cannot be shown where there has been confusion as what has been agreed, or where the parties simply fail to address the question at all.[82]

5–98   Additionally there must be a literal mistake in the wording of the guarantee rather than a mistake by the parties as to the intended effect of a term.[83] As a result cases where guarantees have been rectified are rare. There appear to be no English decisions, although in Australia a claim for rectification of a guarantee was allowed by substituting the name of another creditor when another company in the same group had clearly been erroneously inserted in that capacity in the final written instrument.[84]

(vii) Proof of the guarantor's liability

(a) Judgment or award obtained by the creditor against the principal

5–99   If the guarantee in general terms secures the due performance of the obligations of the principal debtor, the guarantor will not be bound by a judgment or arbitration award obtained by the creditor against the principal. The award will not be evidence against the guarantor and the extent of the guarantor's liability must be strictly proved.[85] The reason for this is that the guarantor might otherwise be bound by an admission of the principal debtor in the course of an arbitration without the authority of the guarantor, or by the principal failing to contest properly the arbitration proceedings.[86] The rule applies even where the arbitration award arises out of an arbitration clause contained in the principal contract.[87] This was the case in *Bruns v Colocotronis*,[88] where the guarantee was also expressed in these general terms: "The guarantor guarantees and undertakes to procure

---

[81] See generally J. Beatson, *Anson's Law of Contract* (28th ed., 2002), p.339 and the cases there cited.
[82] *ibid.*
[83] *Frederick E Rose (London) Ltd v William H Pim Jnr Co Ltd* [1953] 2 Q.B. 450 and see J. Beatson *Anson's Law of Contract* (28th ed., 2002), p.340.
[84] *Elders Lensworth Finance Ltd v Australian Central Pacific Ltd* [1986] 2 Qd R.364. See also *Houlahan v ANZ Banking Group* (1992) 110 F.L.R. 259, where the guarantor argued that the written document should be rectified because it did not represent the parties' common intention that the guarantor's liability be limited. Although the court discussed the issue in terms of mutual mistake, it was in essence a claim for rectification.
[85] *Re Kitchin Ex p. Young* (1881) 17 Ch. D. 668; *Bruns v Colocotronis* [1979] 2 Lloyd's Rep. 412; *Alfred McAlpine Construction v Unex Corp* [1994] N.P.C. 16; *Begley v A-G (NSW)* (1910) 11 C.L.R. 432; *Guenard v Coe* (1914) 6 W.W.R. 922. The same rule should apply to a contract of indemnity: *Peterborough Real Estate Invt Co v Ireton* (1884) 5 O.R. 47. An exception is where statute provides otherwise: *Re Scottish Loan & Finance Co Ltd* (1944) 44 S.R. (NSW) 461.
[86] *Bruns v Colocotronis* [1979] 2 Lloyd's Rep. 412 at 418–419.
[87] *ibid.*
[88] *ibid.*

the due performance and payment of *all* liabilities and obligations of the Owners arising under or out of the agreements".

A different result is reached, however, if the guarantee contains clear **5–100** wording making the guarantor liable to pay sums awarded against the principal debtor, for example, a guarantee of the amounts payable under "any arbitration award rendered ... according to [the terms of the principal contract]"[89] when the guarantor will be liable for *all* the component parts of the award, including interest and costs awarded by the arbitrator.[90] Even if there is no specific guarantee of the amounts payable under the award, the courts may sometimes infer from more general language that the guarantor intended to guarantee the payments under the award. Thus in *Compania Sudamerica De Fletes SA v African Continental Bank Ltd*,[91] the defendant guarantors issued a letter of guarantee which provided that "we guarantee ... the due fulfilment of *any* obligation and the full and total payment without discount up to an amount not exceeding £13,200 sterling". It was held that this clause standing alone was sufficient to render the guarantor liable for the total amount of the award in circumstances where the principal contract contained an arbitration clause.[92] It is arguable, however, that the wording of the guarantee was little different from that in *Bruns v Colocotronis* (quoted above), where the creditor's claim, arising in very similar circumstances, was denied. A clearer reference in the guarantee to the guarantor's liability for the amounts payable under an award should be necessary to displace the normal rule regarding the non-binding nature of arbitration awards.

(b) Architect or surveyor's certificate

A guarantor of the performance of a contractor's obligations under a **5–101** building contract will not be bound by the certificate of an architect as to the cost of completing the work, even though the architect is empowered to determine that matter as between the contractor and the owner.[93] The guarantor is entitled to have liability proved against him,[94] unless the guarantor agrees in the guarantee that the architect's certificate is to be conclusive evidence of the extent of liability as against the guarantor,[95] or

---

[89] See the second sentence of the guarantee in *Compania Sudamericana De Fletes SA v African Continental Bank Ltd* [1973] 1 Lloyd's Rep. 21. As another example, see *Guardians of the Poor of the Belford Union v Pattison* (1856) 11 Exch. 623; 156 E.R. 980. *Cf.* the insufficient wording in *Alfred McAlpine Construction Ltd v Unex Corp Ltd* [1994] N.P.C. 16.

[90] *Compania Sudamericana De Fletes SA v African Continental Bank Ltd* [1973] 1 Lloyd's Rep. 21. But it is still open to the guarantor to show that the award was collusively and fraudulently entered up: *Hutchison v Hooker* (1883) N.Z.L.R. 2 (SC) 134.

[91] [1973] 1 Lloyd's Rep. 21. See also *Sabemo Pty Ltd v De Groot* (1991) 8 B.C.L. 132.

[92] [1973] 1 Lloyd's Rep. 21 at 26.

[93] *Powell River Paper Co Ltd v Wells Construction Co & American Surety Co of New York* [1912] 2 D.L.R. 340; *Sabemo Pty Ltd v De Groot* (1991) 8 B.C.L. 132, in respect of an architect's progress certificate. This proposition also follows from *Re Kitchin Ex p. Young* (1881) 17 Ch. D. 668.

[94] *British America Assurance Co v Redekopp* (1973) 38 D.L.R. (3d) 631.

[95] As to conclusive evidence certificates, see below, para.5–102.

agrees in some other way to the determination of the extent of that liability by the architect.[96]

(c) Prima facie or conclusive evidence certificate

5–102   Sometimes a guarantee contains a clause stating that a certificate signed by a bank officer shall be either prima facie or conclusive evidence of the extent of the guarantor's liability. In the case of a provision stating that the statement by the creditor shall be prima facie evidence of the amount owed, it appears that a presumption is raised of the veracity of the statement which the guarantor must then displace.[97] The guarantor may make an application seeking a direction that the creditor justify the calculation.[98]

5–103   The effect of a conclusive evidence clause was considered in *Bache & Co (London) Ltd v Banque Vernes et Commerciale de Paris*[99] where the clause read:

"Notice of default shall from time to time, be given by the [claimant] to [the defendants] and on receipt of any such notice [the defendants] will forthwith pay ... the amount stated therein as due, such notice of default being as between [the claimants and the defendants] conclusive evidence that [the defendants'] liability hereunder has accrued in respect of the amount claimed."

The Court of Appeal held that, as a matter of principle, the clause was binding according to its terms and was not contrary to public policy.

5–104   The question arises whether there are any exceptions to the conclusive effect of the certificate. One is a clear case of fraud[1] and another is a mistake on the face of the certificate.[2] Indeed some clauses expressly create an exception for a "manifest error", which should be "plain and obvious" having regard to what the certificate was supposed to represent, (for example, if the amount stated as due was shown to be outside the

---

[96] *Sabemo Pty Ltd v De Groot* (1991) 8 B.C.L. 132.
[97] *ANZ Banking Group Ltd v Carnegie* (unreported, Vic Sup Ct, June 16, 1987) at 36; *Commonwealth Bank of Australia v Stow* (unreported, NSW Sup Ct, February 21, 1989); *ANZ Banking Group Ltd v Walsh* (unreported, Vic Sup Ct, May 8, 1991) at 3.
[98] *Commonwealth Bank of Australia v Stow* (unreported, NSW Sup Ct, February 21, 1989).
[99] [1973] 2 Lloyd's Rep. 437 at 440. See also *Dobbs v National Bank of A/Asia Ltd* (1935) 53 C.L.R. 643; *Papua & New Guinea Development Bank v Manton* [1982] V.R. 1000 (where the wording of the clause was also wide enough to be conclusive of the fact that a written demand for payment had been made upon the guarantor); *Balfour Beatty Civil Engineering v Technical & Guarantee Co Ltd* (1999) 68 Con. L.R. 180.
[1] *Bache & Co (London) Ltd v Banque Vernes et Commerciale de Paris* [1973] 2 Lloyd's Rep. 437 at 440; *Northern Crown Bank v Woodcrafts Ltd* (1917) 33 D.L.R. 367 at 371 (charges which were "improper" to the bank's knowledge).
[2] See *Bache & Co (London) Ltd v Banque Vernes et Commerciale de Paris* (*ibid.*) at 440. See also *Je Maintiendrai Pty Ltd v ANZ Banking Group Ltd* (1985) 38 S.A.S.R. 70 at 79, referring to an "obvious error".

scope of the certificate[3] or where two certificates were served, "gross inconsistencies" between the two documents).[4]

Conclusive evidence clauses will be interpreted strictly, with any ambiguity being resolved in favour of the guarantor.[5] Thus, the clause will not readily be construed as being conclusive of the legal *existence* of the indebtedness[6] or as precluding the guarantor relying on any equitable set off since this operates to reduce or extinguish the claim itself.[7]

The fact that conclusive evidence clauses are strictly construed also means that the guarantor may raise arguments as to whether the document served upon him can properly be described as a "certificate" or "statement"[8] and as to whether the person who has signed the certificate comes within the class of persons authorised to do so.[9] **5–105**

Sometimes other provisions are included in agreements which are designed to achieve the same effect as conclusive evidence clauses. Thus in *West of England Shipowners Mutual Insurance Association (Luxembourg) v Cristal Ltd (The "Glacier Bay")*[10] one of the parties was made "the sole judge in accordance with the terms [of the agreement] ... of the validity of any claim made hereunder". It was held that the clause effectively made that party the final arbiter on questions of fact, although subject to the duty to act fairly and subject to the jurisdiction of the courts to review issues of law. In the *"Glacier Bay"* the agreement itself was unusual since the relevant determining party had been specifically established to administer and adjudicate claims upon a fund set up by a consortium of oil companies to provide compensation[11] to members of the consortium in case of losses arising from oil pollution. So it was not unreasonable for that party to be the final arbiter on questions of fact. **5–106**

The extraordinary effect of this type of clause, and the more usual conclusive evidence clause, in the context of a guarantee, however, is that a guarantee which is not phrased in terms of a performance bond payable **5–107**

---

[3] *Try Build Ltd v Blue Star Garages Ltd* (1998) 66 Conv. R. 90 at 101–102. See in Australia *State Bank of New South Wales Ltd v Chia* [2001] 50 N.S.W.L.R. 587 at 608 where a "manifest error" was described as an "error which is easily demonstrable without extensive investigation, although some argument might be necessary" and it does not include errors which are "abstruse, obscure or inconsequential". See also *Promenade Investments Pty Ltd v New South Wales* (1992) 26 N.S.W.L.R. 203.

[4] See *Jenkins v National Australia Bank* [1999] A.N.Z. Conv. R. 544 at para.17, although not on the facts since the differences between the two certificates were minor.

[5] *British Linen Asset Finance Ltd v Ridgeway* (1999) G.W.D. 2–78.

[6] *ibid.* See also *Dobbs v National Bank of A/asia Ltd* (1935) 53 C.L.R. 643 at 651.

[7] See *State Bank of New South Wales v Chia* [2001] 50 N.S.W.L.R. 587 at 611, and the cases there cited. In Australia it has been suggested that it was a pre-condition for the operation of a conclusive evidence clause that it must be shown to have been prepared by a properly qualified official with due care and attention, with the burden of proof being on the bank to show this (*Shomat Pty Ltd v Rubinstein* (1995) 124 F.L.R. 284). But, even in Australia, this is thought to be incorrect. See also *Jenkins v National Australia Bank* [1999] A.N.Z. Conv. R. 544, which left the issue open.

[8] See the unsuccessful argument for the guarantors in *State Bank of New South Wales Ltd v Chia* [2001] 50 N.S.W.L.R. 587 at 608–609 that a "statement" should bear the technical meaning of "the periodic copy of the customer's account of the bank's ledger as it relates to the customer".

[9] See *Shomat Pty Ltd v Rubinstein* (1995) 124 F.L.R. 284.

[10] [1996] 1 Lloyd's Rep. 370.

[11] *ibid.*, at 379.

simply on demand without proof of default[12] becomes analogous to such a guarantee as a result of the inclusion of this clause. The difference is, however, that in the case of performance bond the guarantor is usually a bank, which has taken a counter-security from the principal and which may easily exercise its right of indemnity against the principal.[13] Where the guarantor is a private person, such as a company director or a consumer guarantor, there will usually be no such security. The guarantor, therefore, may be unable to recover sums paid to the creditor from an insolvent principal, and will have no redress if the amount which he has paid is in excess of the amount for which the principal is liable. The conclusive evidence clause is even more open to criticism where the clause is inserted in a guarantee by a creditor who is not a reputable banking institution, and there is one statement which has suggested that the practice of inserting such a clause is only acceptable because the bankers who insert them are known to be honest and reliable business persons.[14] Any rule of construction which rests on such a tenuous basis is questionable. Conclusive evidence, or similar clauses are likely to be subject to a successful challenge pursuant to the Unfair Terms in Consumer Contracts Regulations 1999 in circumstances in which those Regulations apply.[15]

3. SCOPE OF THE GUARANTOR'S LIABILITY WHERE THE PRINCIPAL CONTRACT IS DEFECTIVE

(i) The general principle

5–108   The general principle applicable to contracts of guarantee is that the guarantor's liability should be co-extensive with that of the principal.[16] It follows that, if no principal contract is concluded, the guarantor's liability never arises. As Lord Selborne said in *Lakeman v Mountstephen*,[17] "until there is a principal debtor there can be no suretyship. Nor can a man guarantee anyone else's debt unless there is a debt of some other person to be guaranteed".[18] The difficulty is that the parties to the principal contract may purport to conclude the principal contract, but for various reasons that contract is void, voidable or unenforceable.

---

[12] See, *e.g. Balfour Beatty Civil Engineering v Technical & Guarantee Co Ltd* (1999) 68 Con. L.R. 180 and the discussion on performance bonds, below, Ch.13.

[13] *Bache & Co (London) Ltd v Banque Vernes et Commerciale de Paris* [1973] 2 Lloyd's Rep. 437 at 441. The appropriate procedure for the guarantor is discussed in more detail below, Ch.12.

[14] *Bache & Co (London) Ltd v Banque Vernes et Commerciale de Paris* [1973] 2 Lloyd's Rep. 437 at 440 *per* Lord Denning M.R. In *Je Maintiendrai Pty Ltd v ANZ Banking Group Ltd* (1985) 38 S.A.S.R. 70 at 71 Jacobs J. hints that this is a possible basis for limiting the application of the decision in *Dobbs v National Bank of A/asia Ltd* (1935) 53 C.L.R. 643.

[15] See above, paras 4–160 to 4–176.

[16] See above, para.1–25.

[17] (1874) L.R. 7 H.L. 17.

[18] *ibid.*, at 24–25.

(ii) Void contracts

As Lord Selborne's statement indicates, a guarantee of a void obligation **5–109** is generally of no effect, and the guarantor does not come under any legal liability.[19] But the law is not entirely uniform in its approach, and a number of different situations whereby the contract is rendered void need to be considered.

(a) Illegal contracts

Where a statute expressly prohibits a contract so that it is void and of no **5–110** legal effect, it is clear that the creditor cannot enforce the guarantee.[20] Thus in *Heald v O'Connor*,[21] a guarantor of the principal moneys due under a debenture which was void by statute, so that no moneys became due under it, was not liable on the guarantee. The same principle will apply where the principal contract is void as against public policy and no action can be brought upon it, or where the sum which the creditor seeks to recover from the principal is held to be a penalty.[22]

Where the principal contract is entirely void, an alternative reason that **5–111** is sometimes given for the creditor's inability to claim upon the guarantee in this situation is that the guarantee itself never comes into operation because there is no consideration to support it. This is because the consideration is expressed in the guarantee to be the creditor entering into the principal contract, and if the contract is illegal and void, this consideration fails.

One commentator has suggested[23] that the illegality of the principal **5–112** transaction will inevitably nullify the creditor's rights against the guarantor, but there may be some circumstances in which this is not so. The term "void" in relation to illegal contracts may be misleading because a party to the contract who was unaware of the illegality and did not participate in the illegality may still be able to enforce the contract.[24] If this innocent party is the creditor, it is thought that the creditor should be able to recover from the guarantor when the principal has defaulted, despite the fact that the principal contract is to an extent tainted with illegality. The guarantor should not be allowed to plead the illegality of the principal transaction when the principal would not be able to do so. Similarly, if a particular term or part of the contract is illegal (for example, because it is a

---

[19] e.g. *Corser v Commonwealth General Assurance Co Ltd* [1963] N.S.W.R. 225 (principal contract void for uncertainty).
[20] *Swan v Bank of Scotland* (1836) 10 Bli. (NS) 627; 6 E.R. 231; *Lougher v Molyneux* [1916] 1 K.B. 718; *Heald v O'Connor* [1971] 1 W.L.R. 497; *Brown v Moore* (1902) 32 S.C.R. 93; *Dela Rosa v Prieto* (1874) 16 C.B. (NS) 578; 143 E.R. 1253; *Pearse v Morrice* (1834) 2 Ad. & El. 84; 111 E.R. 32.
[21] [1971] 1 W.L.R. 497.
[22] *Sterling Industrial Facilities Ltd (WA) v Lydiate Textiles Ltd* (1962) 106 SJ 669; *Citicorp Australia Ltd v Hendry* (1985) 4 N.S.W.L.R. 1 (sums therefore not "owing or payable" to the creditor); *Moreland Finance Corp (Vic) Pty Ltd v Brick & Masonry (Swann Hill) Pty Ltd* (1988) V. Conv. R. 54–315.
[23] J Steyn, "Guarantees: The Co-extensiveness Principle" (1974) 90 L.Q.R. 246 at 248.
[24] See generally J. Beatson, *Anson's Law of Contract* (28th ed., 2002), pp.397–400.

penalty or in restraint of trade) and can be severed from the rest of the agreement, which remains valid and enforceable, it is thought that the guarantor will be relieved from liability only in relation to that term or to that part of the contract.[25]

(b) Directors' guarantees of ultra vires transactions

5–113   Formerly, a contract entered into by a company when it had no power to do so was treated as void.[26] A number of decisions beginning in the 19th century have held that, despite the voidness of the principal obligation, a director's guarantee of such a transaction was still effective.[27] This is a clear exception to the general rule of co-extensiveness applicable to contracts of guarantee. It has been said that[28] some cases might be explained on the basis that the contracts were contracts of indemnity rather than contracts of guarantee, and others on the ground that on the facts the directors were estopped from relying on the ultra vires transaction because they had impliedly represented that the company had power to enter into the transaction. But these reasons are not stated in the relevant decisions. One justification offered for this exceptional rule is that "directors are more likely to be acquainted with the powers of the company than third parties".[29] But a similar justification is also applicable in other situations where the principal contract is void, yet the courts have nevertheless held the guarantee to be ineffective. In particular, a guarantee of a contract which is void due to the principal's infancy has been held to be unenforceable, even though the guarantor will often know that the principal is below the age of contractual capacity.[30]

5–114   It should be observed that the issue of guarantees of *ultra vires* transactions of companies is unlikely to occur in the future because of the operation of ss.108–110 of the Companies Act 1989. These provisions essentially abolish the doctrines of *ultra vires* to the extent that it operates to invalidate transactions with third parties, but at the same time retain the director's personal liability to the company for any loss arising out of *ultra vires* acts. But it is possible that the question of the validity of guarantees

---

[25] See *Silverton Ltd v Harvey* [1975] 1 N.S.W.L.R. 659 at 664, where Rath J. suggests that, if part of a debt is void, the guarantor's defence based on such invalidity would extend only to that part; *William E Thompson & Associates Inc v Carpenter* (1989) 69 O.R. (2d) 545.
[26] *Yorkshire Railway Wagon Co v Maclure* (1881) 19 Ch. D. 478.
[27] See, *e.g.*, *ibid.*; *Garrard v James* [1925] 1 Ch. 616. See also in Australia *Australian Joint Stock Bank v Croudace* (1899) 20 L.R. (NSW) 361. This case also represented an extension of the rule because a guarantee by a mayor and alderman of the principality's bank overdraft was held to be enforceable even though the principality had no power to borrow. *Cf.* in Canada *Macdonald-Crawford Ltd v Burns* [1924] 2 D.L.R. 977; *Communities Economic Development Fund v Maxwell* (1989) 64 D.L.R. (4th) 489.
[28] *Jowitt v Callaghan* (1938) 38 S.R. (NSW) 512 at 518. See also R. Else-Mitchell, "Is a Surety's Liability Co-extensive with that of the Principal Debtor?" (1947) 63 L.Q.R. 355 at 362–363.
[29] See J. Steyn, "Guarantees: The Co-extensiveness Principle" (1974) 90 L.Q.R. 246 at 251.
[30] At a time when such contracts were void pursuant to the Infants Relief Act 1874.

of *ultra vires* transactions may arise in other contexts (for example, where transactions entered into by a local authority are *ultra vires*).[31]

(iii) Minors' contracts

In the case of a principal contract entered into by a minor after June 9, 1987, the liability of a guarantor of that contract is prima facie preserved by s.2 of the Minors' Contracts Act 1987. This provides: **5–115**

"**2.** Where—

(a) a guarantee is given in respect of an obligation of a party to a contract made after the commencement of this Act, and

(b) the obligation is unenforceable against him (or he repudiates the contract) because he was a minor when the contract was made,

the guarantee shall not for that reason alone be unenforceable against the guarantor."

As regards principal contracts entered into by a minor prior to that date the guarantor's liability will be determined by the effect of the common law rules upon the validity of those contracts.[32] At common law contracts for necessaries and other beneficial contracts are binding upon the minor, so that the guarantor will remain liable. Other contracts are voidable, either requiring repudiation by the infant before or within a reasonable time after the infant attains majority (in the case of contracts of a class by which the infant acquires an interest of a permanent or continuing nature)[33] or requiring ratification by the infant in order to be binding (in the case of other contracts).[34]

In these cases the general principles applicable to voidable contracts which are guaranteed will apply, so that if, in relation to the former class of contracts, the infant repudiates or, in relation to the second class, the infant fails to ratify, this amounts to a rescission of the principal contract and both infant and guarantor will be released from liability.[35] As the principal contract has ended, the accessory obligation of the guarantor will also terminate.[36] If there is no repudiation by the infant of the principal contract where this is required or, alternatively, there is ratification, these actions will amount to an affirmation of the principal contract and the guarantor will probably be bound. It is not thought that the guarantor can rely upon the infancy of the principal when there has been such affirmation. Although, as will be seen,[37] the view has been advanced   **5–116**

---

[31] See, *e.g. Crédit Suisse v Borough Council of Allerdale* [1997] Q.B. 306.

[32] As the relevant statutory enactment (The Infants Relief Act 1874) was repealed by s.1 of the Minors' Contracts Act 1987. As to the common law rules see J. Beatson, *Anson's Law of Contract* (28th ed., 2002), pp.215–228.

[33] Referred to by Beatson (*op. cit.*) as "positive voidable contracts".

[34] Referred to by Beatson (*op. cit.*) as "negative voidable contracts".

[35] *Land & Homes (WA) Ltd v Roe* (1936) 29 W.A.L.R. 27.

[36] *ibid.*, at 29.

[37] See below, paras 5–118 to 5–122.

that a contract which is voidable as a result of the creditor's
misrepresentation or undue influence should render the guarantee
ineffective even if the principal debtor has affirmed the contract, it is
unlikely that such a view is tenable where the voidability arises simply
from the principal's infancy and not from a positive act by the creditor.[38]

5–117   The rules at common law governing infants' contracts mean, however,
that a number of more complicated situations can arise. The infant
principal, although ostensibly repudiating the contract, may fail to return
property acquired under it. In such case the guarantor should remain liable
because the principal has in fact retained the benefit of the contract and
the creditor has suffered loss. The principal may also repudiate the
contract and return the property, but by the date of the repudiation the
property may have diminished in value. Suppose that an infant purchases
land by instalments for £10,000, with the creditor taking a guarantee to
secure payment of the purchase price. After six months, the infant
repudiates the contract but the land in the vendor's hands is now worth
£8,000. As the creditor has suffered loss to the extent of £2,000, the
guarantor should be liable for this amount.[39]

(iv) Voidable contracts

5–118   Vitiating circumstances may exist making the principal contract voidable
by reason, for example, of the creditor's misrepresentation or undue
influence. If the principal elects to rescind the contract on this basis, or the
court sets aside the contract, no liability will attach to the guarantor.

5–119   A more difficult question is whether the guarantor can avoid liability
under the guarantee when the principal waives the right to rely on these
matters or elects to affirm the contract. There is no common law authority
on the issue, but a number of different views have been advanced. First, it
has been said that a guarantor should not be allowed to rely on possible
defences open to the principal when the principal chooses to affirm the
transaction because this would remove from the principal the right of
election to affirm or disaffirm.[40] In every case, the principal would need to
consult the guarantor before making the election. Secondly, a distinction
has been drawn between "fraud or other unconscionable conduct" on the
part of the creditor rendering the contract voidable and, for example, an
innocent misrepresentation by the creditor rendering the contract
voidable.[41] In the former situation, it is argued that the guarantor should
be able to take advantage of a defence which would have been open to the
principal if the contract had not been affirmed, but the conduct of the

---

[38] J. Steyn, "Guarantees: The Co-extensiveness Principle" (1974) 90 L.Q.R. 246 at 258–259.
[39] These conclusions are supported, albeit in a somewhat oblique manner, by Dwyer J. in
Land & Homes (WA) Ltd v Roe ((1936) 29 W.A.L.R. 27 at 29 who came to the conclusion
that the repudiation by the infant of the principal contact will usually discharge the guarantor
because "the creditor still retains the asset which he agreed to sell ... so that he has lost
nothing". The inference is that, if it can be shown that the creditor has suffered loss, the
guarantor will remain liable to the extent of the loss.
[40] S. Williston, *A Treatise on the Law of Contracts* (3rd ed., 1957), s.1218.
[41] J. Steyn, "Guarantees: The Co-extensiveness Principle" (1974) 90 L.Q.R. 246 at 257.

creditor in the latter situation does not justify a departure from the general rule that "it is in the interests of commerce that the effectiveness of guarantees be upheld".[42]

Finally, at the other extreme, it has been said, in the context of **5–120** guarantors of consumer transactions who might not be expected to seek legal advice, that the guarantor should not be subject to the caprice of the principal debtor in deciding whether or not to affirm a transaction.[43] This is because the guarantor may have no influence over the principal and as a practical matter may have little chance of recovering from the principal in an action for reimbursement.[44] Thus the guarantor should be able to rely on any defence, including rescission for innocent misrepresentation, which the principal could have relied upon in relation to the principal transaction. This right of the guarantor should in no way be limited by the principal's inability to rely on the defence.[45]

The lack of any definitive authority on the question of the guarantor's **5–121** right to rely on the voidability of the principal transaction makes it difficult to predict the likely outcome of the issue. A similar situation which might tend to support the wide view of the extent of the guarantor's ability to rely on the voidability of the principal transaction is where the principal is able to rely on the existence of an estoppel as against the creditor, there being some suggestion that the guarantor may also rely upon this defence.[46] But this is not a perfect analogy because the guarantor is relying upon a defence which is still open to the principal. The additional factor involved in the case of a voidable contract which has been affirmed is that the principal has waived the relevant defence (that is, the right to rescind).

On the other hand, it has been held[47] that the guarantor cannot rely on a **5–122** debtor's counterclaim for damages if the debtor is not a party to the proceedings, thus suggesting that the guarantor cannot rely on a defence of the principal based on the voidability of the principal transaction. However, one of the reasons for the denial of the right to rely on the principal's counterclaim is that the guarantor is not without a remedy because he can join the debtor as a third party, who in turn has a right to join the creditor as a fourth party claiming damages for breach of contract from the creditor.[48] This enables the rights of all persons to be determined together. This reasoning is not applicable where the principal debtor, having affirmed a voidable contract, cannot take action against the creditor at all. In this situation the courts are faced with the dilemma of either allowing the guarantor to rely on the defence which would have been open

---

[42] *ibid.*
[43] Law Reform Commission of British Columbia, *Report on Guarantees of Consumer Debts* (1979), pp.86–89 (see, especially, recommendations 34, 42).
[44] *ibid.*
[45] *ibid.* As to the guarantor's general right to rely on the defences of the principal, see below, paras 11–46 to 11–94.
[46] *International Leasing Corp (Vic) Ltd v Aiken* [1967] 2 N.S.W.R. 427 at 450.
[47] *Cellulose Products Pty Ltd v Truda* (1970) 92 W.N. (NSW) 561, discussed below, paras 11–46 to 11–94, especially 11–63.
[48] *ibid.*, at 588.

to the principal if the principal contract had not been affirmed or, on the other hand, refusing the guarantor this right.[49]

(v) Unenforceable contracts

5–123   As in the case of voidable contracts, the question of the guarantor's liability where the principal contract is unenforceable is also uncertain, although there is a little more authority. There are two lines of cases, those relating to the situation in which the principal contract is statute-barred, and those where the principal contract is unenforceable due to a failure to comply with the formalities of the Moneylenders Acts.

5–124   It may happen that the creditor's remedy against the principal is statute-barred whereas the creditor's claim against the guarantor is not. This result may occur, for example, because the creditor's claim against the principal arises on default, but the creditor's claim against the guarantor arises only after a demand is made upon the guarantor, with the period of limitation against the guarantor beginning to run only from the later time of the demand. It may also occur when the guarantee is under seal but the principal transaction is not, so that a longer limitation period applies to the guarantee. In these cases where the creditor's right to recover against the principal, but not the guarantor, is barred by the Statute of Limitations, it has been held that the guarantor is liable on the basis that the "mere omission to sue does not discharge the surety, because the surety can himself set the law in operation against the debtor",[50] that is, by paying off the debt and then claiming an indemnity from the debtor.

5–125   A different conclusion, however, has been reached where the main contract is unenforceable because of a failure to comply with statutory requirements relating to the principal obligation. Thus, where the principal contract was unenforceable because of a failure to comply with the requirements of the Moneylenders Act 1927, it was held that the guarantor was not liable on the broad ground that if the principal debtor is not liable, the guarantor will not be liable either.[51] But, significantly, a subsequent case concerning the same Act confined the reasons for reaching a conclusion that the guarantor was not liable to the basis that the Act itself specifically prohibited an action upon a promissory note in which the guarantee was embodied.[52] Thus explained, the authorities merely become examples, not of the effect of an unenforceable principal transaction on the

---

[49] Contracts which are voidable as a result of the lack of capacity of the principal are dealt with above, paras 5–115 to 5–117.

[50] *Carter v White* (1883) 25 Ch. D. 666 at 672, *per* Lindley L.J. See also *Re Powers; Lindsell v Phillips* (1885) 30 Ch. D. 291; *McPherson v McBain* [1932] 3 W.W.R. 617. The position may be different where the Statute of Limitations is worded so as to extinguish the principal obligation on the expiry of the relevant period: see Law Reform Commission of British Columbia, *Report on Guarantees of Consumer Debts* (1979), pp.69–70.

[51] *Eldridge and Morris v Taylor* [1931] 2 K.B. 416 at 418–420 per Scrutton L.J., 423 *per* Slesser L.J. *Cf.* Greer L.J. at 422, who treated the question as analogous to the creditor giving time to the principal.

[52] *Temperance Loan Fund Ltd v Rose* [1932] 2 K.B. 522: see an analysis of these cases in R. Else-Mitchell, "Is a Surety's Liability Co-extensive with that of the Principal Debtor?" (1947) 63 L.Q.R. 355 at 361–362.

liability of the guarantor, but of a statute specifically prohibiting an action on the guarantee itself.[53]

In sum, it can be said that the preservation of the liability of the **5–126** guarantor, despite the existence of a statute-barred principal transaction, is well established. In other cases, in which the principal contract is unenforceable because of a failure to comply with statutory requirements, the authorities are too limited to arrive at a definite conclusion, but tend to suggest that the guarantee cannot be enforced. In some of these cases there may be other bases for relieving the guarantor of liability. If the creditor fails to comply with statutory requirements in relation to a security which embodies the principal transaction and the value of the security is impaired, it is well established that the guarantor will be discharged to the extent of the loss.[54] Another possibility is that, by rendering the principal contract unenforceable, the creditor has committed "a positive act" to the prejudice of the guarantor, discharging the guarantor.[55]

(vi) Clauses in the guarantee preserving the guarantor's liability where the main contract is defective

Guarantees often contain express clauses specifically designed to **5–127** preserve the liability of the guarantor in the event of the principal contract being void, voidable or unenforceable. These may include:

1. The "principal debtor" clause by which the guarantor is stated to be liable "as a primary obligor and not merely as surety". In *Heald v O'Connor*,[56] Fisher J was of the opinion that such a clause did not render the guarantor liable where the principal contract was void for illegality, that is, it did not convert what was otherwise a contract of guarantee into a contract of indemnity.[57] The object of such a clause was merely to avoid the consequence of the creditor giving time or other indulgence to the principal, which acts would, without the inclusion of such a provision, discharge the guarantor.[58] It follows that the clause, standing alone, will probably not render the guarantor liable where the principal contract is void, voidable or unenforceable.[59]

2. A clause may specifically state that the guarantor is to be liable despite certain vitiating circumstances which render the principal contract void, voidable or unenforceable. Thus in *Alliance*

---

[53] See above, para.4–68.
[54] See below, para.8–49.
[55] But this principle is of doubtful validity. See below, paras 8–106 to 8–114.
[56] [1971] 1 W.L.R. 497.
[57] See also *Citicorp Australia Ltd v Hendry* (1985) 4 N.S.W.L.R. 1 at 20 *per* Clarke J., and above, para.1–101.
[58] But note that the "principal debtor" clause was held effective in *Fletcher Organisation Pty Ltd v Crocus Investments Pty Ltd* [1988] 2 Qd. R. 517 to preserve the guarantor's liability in the event of a release of a co-guarantor: see below, para.8–98, n.85.
[59] But it may well be different if no principal debtor is in existence at all: *Canadian Imperial Bank of Commerce v Patel* (1990) 66 D.L.R. (4th) 720.

Acceptance Co Ltd v Hinton[60] the defendant guarantor agreed that his liability would not be impaired "by reason of [the principal] being an infant or under other legal disability". It was held that the defendant was liable where the principal contract was void because of the principal's infancy either on the basis that this constituted a promise to indemnify the creditor or, alternatively, on the basis that the defendant was estopped by this clause from relying on the infancy of the principal as a defence to the creditor's claim.

5–128   A common form of drafting is to state that "the guarantor's liability shall not be affected or discharged by any partial or total invalidity, illegality or enforceablility of the principal obligation". One argument in this context[61] is that such a clause is ineffective because the drafting has been erroneously predicated on the basis that the guarantor has incurred an initial liability and the clause then simply refers to some subsequent illegality or unenforceability which affects that liability. On this view the guarantor never at any stage assumes a liability for the debt (for example, because the obligation giving rise to the debt is void *ab initio*).[62] This construction was, however, rejected by the Court of Appeal (in the context of interpreting a similar clause in a counter indemnity) in *Gulf Bank KSC v Mitsubishi Heavy Industries Ltd.*[63] Sir Thomas Bingham M.R. saw "no ground for distinguishing between illegality, invalidity or unenforceability from the beginning and illegality, invalidity or unenforceability occurring at some later stage".

5–129   It is also possible that a clause purporting to preserve the guarantor's liability in the event of a defective principal transaction will not be effective because the guarantee as a whole never becomes operative. Sometimes the creditor's consideration for the promise to guarantee is expressed to be the creditor entering into the principal transaction. If the principal transaction is void, this will not constitute good consideration and the guarantee, including the relevant clause, will be of no effect.

5–130   In respect of transactions regulated by the Consumer Credit Act 1974, clauses which purport to preserve the liability of the guarantor in the event of the unenforceability of the principal transaction will be ineffective. This arises because of the operation of s.113(1) of Consumer Credit Act 1974, which specifically applies the principle of co-extensiveness to guarantees and seeks to prevent the lender evading the regulatory provisions of the Act by seeking relief against a guarantor (or by enforcing a separate security). Section 113(1) states:

"**113.**–(1) Where a security is provided in relation to an actual or prospective regulated agreement, the security shall not be enforced so as to benefit the creditor or owner, directly or indirectly, to an extent

---

[60] (1964) 1 D.C.R. (NSW) 5.
[61] And successfully accepted in the Australian New South Wales Court of Appeal case of *Citicorp Australia Ltd v Hendry* (1985) 4 N.S.W.L.R. 1 (where the debt was void as being in the nature of a penalty).
[62] *ibid.*
[63] [1994] 2 Lloyd's Rep. 145 at 151.

greater (whether as respects the amount of any payment or the time or manner of its being made) than would be the case if the security were not provided and any obligations of the debtor or hirer, or his relative, under or in relation to the agreement were carried out to the extent (if any) to which they would be enforced under this Act."

(vii) Contracts of indemnity

If the contract is clearly one of indemnity, so that the indemnifier is 5–131 liable regardless of any default by the principal, or the existence of an effective principal obligation at all, the creditor may still recover the relevant losses in the event of the principal transaction being defective. Thus it has been held that the indemnifier will remain liable where the principal transaction is unenforceable due to a failure to comply with the Moneylenders Acts, without the necessity for any other special clauses rendering the indemnifier liable in the event of the unenforceability of the agreement to which the indemnity relates.[64] The same conclusion has been reached where the agreement to which the indemnity relates is void as a result of the infancy of one of the contracting parties.[65] The precise drafting of the indemnity will, however, be decisive, and it is often a difficult question of construction as to whether the agreement is in reality an indemnity against any loss regardless of the status of the principal transaction.[66]

Indeed, apart from any question of drafting, in the case of a sum held to 5–132 be in the nature of a penalty it has been suggested that it would be contrary to public policy to allow recovery from an indemnifier when the moneys were irrecoverable from the principal,[67] and that to allow recovery from the indemnifier on the basis of a formula which gives rise to an irrecoverable penalty would not reflect the creditor's true loss.[68] But it is not considered that this view is correct and the indemnifier's liability will be dependent on the interpretation of the particular instrument in question. Section 113(1) of the Consumer Credit Act 1974 (discussed above)[69] applies equally to indemnities, thus rendering an indemnity ineffective in respect of transactions regulated by the Act.

---

[64] *Argo Caribbean Group Ltd v Lewis* [1976] 2 Lloyd's Rep. 289 at 296–297. As to the distinction between a guarantee and an indemnity, see above, para.1–88.

[65] *Yeoman Credit Ltd v Latter* [1961] 1 W.L.R. 828. Discussed by M. P. Furmston, "Infants' Contracts-La Nouvelle Vague?" (1961) 24 M.L.R. 644.

[66] *e.g. Citicorp Australia Ltd v Hendry* (1985) 4 N.S.W.L.R. 1 (although the reasoning in that case now appears contrary to *Gulf Bank KSC v Mitsubishi Heavy Industries* [1994] 2 Lloyd's Rep. 145, discussed above, para.5–128).

[67] Clarke J. at first instance in *Citicorp Australia Ltd v Hendry* (1985) 4 N.S.W.L.R. 1 at 21. The matter was left open by Priestley J.A. on appeal: (1985) 4 N.S.W.L.R. 1 at 41.

[68] Clarke J. at first instance in *Citicorp Australia Ltd v Hendry* (1985) 4 N.S.W.L.R. 1 at 21.

[69] See above, para.5–130.

CHAPTER 6

DISCHARGE FROM LIABILITY BY THE DETERMINATION OF THE PRINCIPAL TRANSACTION

These methods of discharge from liability are considered together because they arise from the general principal of co-extensiveness applicable to contracts of guarantee, that is, the guarantee being a secondary obligation will cease to operate once the principal contract is determined.

1. DISCHARGE BY THE PRINCIPAL PERFORMING THE OBLIGATIONS UNDER THE PRINCIPAL CONTRACT

6–01   The guarantor will be discharged if the principal fully performs his obligations under the principal contract. Thus, if the guarantor undertakes that a vendor will deliver goods according to a particular contractual arrangement, the guarantor is discharged once the vendor has delivered in accordance with the contract. Similarly, a guarantor of a contractor's obligations under a building contract will be discharged when the contractor completes the construction work under the terms of the principal contract. In each case it is a question of fact whether there has been complete performance. In relation to a guarantee of a building contract, complete performance will generally occur when the architect issues a final certificate[1] except where the certificate is not binding, for example, because it has been procured by the fraud of the principal.[2] Sometimes, however, the contract of guarantee may be construed so that the obligations of the guarantor cease at the date of actual completion rather than at the date of the issue of the certificate.[3] Thus the guarantor will be discharged if actual completion can be shown, even if no certificate has been issued.

6–02   The most common example of the guarantor being discharged by the principal performing the obligations under the principal contract is where the principal debtor or the principal debtor's agent pays the creditor the full amount of a debt. It is necessary to consider discharge in this manner in detail.

---

[1] If the architect is required to specify certain stages of completion by means of the certificate, provision may be made for the reduction in the amount of the guarantee when a certain stage of completion is reached.
[2] *Kingston-Upon-Hull Corp v Harding* [1892] 2 Q.B. 494. Bowen L.J. was, however, of the view that if the issue of such a certificate had prejudiced the guarantors, altering their position to their detriment, the creditors would be estopped from denying the validity of the certificate (at 506–507).
[3] *Lewis v Hoare* (1881) 44 L.T. 66.

(i) Payment must be made in satisfaction of the principal obligation

One initial question that occasionally arises is whether the payment by **6–03** the principal was in fact made in satisfaction of the principal obligation. The reason for this difficulty lies in the fact that the debtor may have made payments in respect of the principal debt out of funds supplied to the debtor by one of the guarantors. Sometimes the funds have been supplied because of the close relationship between the guarantor and the principal, where, for example, the guarantor is a director of a family company, which is the principal. There are two possibilities in this situation. The first is that these payments are payments made by the principal debtor in discharge of the principal obligation—the guarantor merely supplying funds to improve the debtor's general financial position. The second is that the payments have been made by the guarantor in discharge of the guarantor's obligation under the guarantee—the principal merely acting as agent to remit the payments to the creditor. The issue is an important one if there are several guarantors because if the former view were adopted all the guarantors would be discharged, but if one guarantor were treated as satisfying his obligation under the guarantee by the payments then that guarantor would be able to claim contribution from any co-guarantor.

The most directly relevant decision is that of the High Court of Australia **6–04** in *Mahoney v McManus*,[4] where it was considered that the determination of this issue was a question of construction in each case. Although the normal inference might be that when the debtor makes a payment to the creditor, the debtor is acting on his own behalf with the intention of discharging the principal obligation,[5] on the facts of the case, the High Court (by a majority of three to two) held that the moneys had been paid by the debtor as the guarantor's agent to satisfy the guarantor's obligation under the guarantee. Gibbs C.J. (Murphy and Aickin J.J. concurring) reached this conclusion primarily because the moneys were paid to the principal debtor by the guarantor for the specific purpose of enabling the principal to pay the guaranteed creditors, not unsecured creditors generally. The payments had in fact been made after demands by the guaranteed creditors.[6] But this reasoning has rightly been criticised[7] on the basis that merely because the moneys were paid to the principal debtor in order to satisfy the guaranteed obligations does not inevitably lead to the inference that the principal debtor then paid the creditors on behalf of the guarantor in discharge of the contract of guarantee. Another plausible explanation was that the principal, having received funds from the guarantor, then paid the creditors on his own behalf to satisfy the principal obligation, which was guaranteed. This view was certainly open on the facts because certain documentary evidence and the principal debtor's

---

[4] (1981) 55 A.L.J.R. 673.
[5] *ibid.*, at 677.
[6] (1981) 55 A.L.J.R. 673 at 676 *per* Gibbs C.J.
[7] See the Note (1982) 56 A.L.J. 143 at 144–145.

internal records suggested that the amount paid by the guarantor to the principal debtor was merely a loan.[8]

6–05   Whatever criticism there may be of the decision on the facts, however, the case does illustrate clearly that the court may draw the inference that the obligations of the principal debtor have not been satisfied by payment even when the money has been actually paid by the debtor to the creditor and even when there has been no specific arrangement made with the creditor that the latter should accept the payment in discharge of the guarantor's liability rather than in discharge of the principal's obligation.

6–06   The High Court of Australia in *Mahoney v McManus* was concerned with the payment by the debtor from funds supplied by the guarantor. It is possible that the guarantor may pay money to the creditor on behalf of the debtor to satisfy the principal obligation,[9] rather than the obligation under the guarantee. Normally, however, the proper inference from the fact that the guarantor makes the payment will be that the guarantor intends to satisfy his obligations under the guarantee.

6–07   Even if there is no question of the principal debtor's payments being treated as a discharge of the guaranteed obligation, payment by the debtor to the creditor will discharge the guarantor only if it is a "good and satisfactory payment".[10] The following will not constitute such a payment.

(a) Balance owing from creditor to debtor

6–08   It may be the case that the guaranteed creditor owes a sum of money to the debtor by reason of other independent transactions. Even if that sum of money is of exactly the same amount as the guaranteed debt, the guarantor cannot claim that the principal debt has been discharged by treating the sum as payment of the guaranteed debt.[11] As will be seen,[12] however, a guarantor may be entitled to set off amounts owed by the creditor to the debtor, although usually the principal has to be joined as a party to the proceedings.[13]

(b) Assignment of security

6–09   If the debtor assigns to the creditor the means by which the debt may be paid (for example, by assigning a judgment debt),[14] this is not considered

---

[8] In *State Bank of New South Wales Ltd v Nepean Indoor Sport Centres Pty Ltd* (unreported, NSW Sup Ct, Rolfe J., April 28 1995), Rolfe J. thought that the minority view was "more compelling", but distinguished *Mahoney v McManus* (1981) 55 A.L.J.R. 673 on the basis that, on the facts before him, it was clear that no payment was made by the guarantor to the creditor in discharge of any liability under the guarantees. As to other criticisms of the decision see below, paras 12–167 to 12–171.
[9] This possibility is referred to in *Ulster Bank Ltd v Lambe* [1966] N.I. 161 at 169. As an example, see *Astilleros Espanoles SA & Banca Exterior De Espana SA v Bank of America National Trust and Savings Assoc* [1993] 2 Lloyd's Rep. 521.
[10] *Pritchard v Hitchcock* (1843) 6 M. & Gr. 151 at 166; 134 E.R. 844 at 851.
[11] *Harrison v Nettleship* (1833) 2 My. & K. 423; 39 E.R. 1005.
[12] See below, paras 11–46 to 11–94.
[13] *ibid.*
[14] *Halford v Byron* (1701) Prec. Ch. 178; 24 E.R. 86.

to be payment of the debt. But if, subsequently, the proceeds of the realisation of a collateral security given to the creditor are appropriated to the guaranteed debt, the guarantor will, of course, be discharged.

(c) Formal bookkeeping transactions

Only an actual payment will release the debtor and therefore discharge **6–10** the guarantor. It is not sufficient for the creditor merely to reorganise its accounts or bookkeeping procedures,[15] as where a bank merely transfers a customer's indebtedness from one account to another after first balancing the first account or treating it as in credit. The guarantor will not be discharged on the basis that the initial debt has been extinguished by the closure of the first account and a new debt incurred by the opening of the second account.[16]

(d) Part payment

If the guarantor is to be discharged, the creditor must be paid in full by **6–11** the principal debtor according to the terms of the principal agreement. Part payment will, however, operate to discharge the guarantor *pro tanto* in the case of a guarantee of a specific principal obligation.[17] Similarly where a guaranteed debt is compromised by the debtor and creditor, the guarantor is entitled to the benefit of the compromise in reduction of his liability.[18]

---

[15] *National Bank of New Zealand v Mee & Reid (Executors of Cramond)* (1878) 4 V.L.R. (L) 226; *Bank of A/asia v Crotchett* (1878) 4 V.L.R. (L) 226; *Lawrence v Finance Corp of Australia Ltd* (unreported, NSW Sup Ct, November 2, 1990), where the principal's accounting procedures were described as "extraordinary" and "eccentric"; *Boon v Australian Guarantee Corp (NZ) Ltd* (unreported, HC (NZ), December 14, 1991), where there was an amalgamation of two loans.

[16] *Bank of A/asia v Crotchett* (1878) 4 V.L.R. (L) 226, where an overdrawn "current account" was credited with a sum of £6,000 (which had been newly borrowed on the security of a mortgage), and a "secured" account opened with a debit of £6,000. *National Bank of New Zealand v Mee & Reid* (1885) N.Z.L.R. 3 CA 188. This general rule is subject to the qualification that if, on the wording of the guarantee, the guarantor has specifically guaranteed only the indebtedness of the first account rather than the general liability of the debtor to the bank the guarantor will be released by the closure of the first account. See the unsuccessful argument for the guarantor in *National Bank of New Zealand v Mee & Reid* (1885) N.Z.L.R. 3 C.A. 188.

[17] *Perry v National Provincial Bank of England* [1910] 1 Ch. 464; *Hancock v Williams* (1942) 42 C.B. (NSW) 252 at 257, *per* Jordan C.J. who equates part payment with partial release. But note the effect of payment if the guarantee is a continuing one: see above, para.5–22.

[18] *M'Clure v Fraser* (1840) 9 L.J.Q.B. 60. This assumes that the guarantor's liability is preserved, despite a release of the debtor (if the compromise has this result). See below, para.6–66.

(ii) Payment by the principal to the creditor which amounts to a preference

6–12   It was established pursuant to s.44(1) of the Bankruptcy Act 1914 that if the debtor's trustee in bankruptcy recovered the payment from the creditor on the basis that it was an undue preference over other creditors it was not a "good and satisfactory payment" resulting in discharge of the guarantor.[19] The guarantor remained fully liable. Under s.44(1), a payment was void as against the trustee in the bankruptcy and recoverable by the trustee if it was made with a view of giving "any creditor . . . or any surety or guarantor for the debt" a preference over other creditors.

6–13   Is the position the same pursuant to the provisions of the Insolvency Act 1986? Sections 239–241 (dealing with companies) and ss.340–342 (dealing with individuals) effected fundamental changes to the law relating to preferences. Pursuant to these provisions[20] a liquidator or a trustee in bankruptcy seeking to avoid payment or other transaction on the ground of preference has now to satisfy the court that at the material time the company or individual (as the case may be) was influenced by a desire to produce in relation to the person to whom a preference has been given the effect specified in s.239(4)(b) or s.340(3)(b). The effect specified in those provisions is that a preference is given if the company or individual does anything or suffers anything to be done which (in either case) has the effect of putting a creditor, or a surety or guarantor of the debtor's debts or other liabilities, into a position which, in the event of the company going into insolvent liquidation, or in the event of the individual's bankruptcy, will be better than the position that person would have been in if that thing had not been done.[21] This different test should not, it is thought, by itself create a different result than that arising pursuant to s.44(1) of the Bankruptcy Act 1914; a payment subsequently recovered as a preference is not on the face of it "a good and satisfactory payment". But a difficulty arises in that the legislation does not state that the payment is void.[22] Indeed, it gives the court power to make orders, one of which may specifically "provide for any surety or guarantor whose obligations to any person were released or discharged (in whole or in part) under the transaction, or by the giving of the preference, to be under such new or revived obligations to that person as the court thinks appropriate".[23] One possible implication is that, absent a court order imposing "revived obligations" upon the guarantor, he will

---

[19] *Petty v Cooke* (1871) L.R. 6 Q.B. 790; *Pritchard v Hitchcock* (1843) 6 M. & Gr. 151; 134 E.R. 844; *Re Conley* (1938) 107 L.J. Ch. 257 *Re Seymour* [1937] Ch. 668. If a payment is challenged as an undue preference, a guarantor of that payment should be joined as a party so as to give the guarantor, who would be affected by the court's decision, "the opportunity of adducing such evidence as he has and making such submissions as appear to him appropriate": *Re Idenden (a bankrupt)* [1970] 1 W.L.R. 1015 at 1015 *per* Stamp J.

[20] ss.239(5), 340(4)

[21] ss.239(4), 340(3)

[22] *Cf.* Insolvency Act 1986, s.127 which provides that "in a winding up by the court, any disposition of the company's property . . . made after the commencement of the winding up is, unless the court otherwise orders, void". It seems clear that in this case there is an exact parallel to s.44(1) of the Bankruptcy Act 1914.

[23] ss.241(1)(e), 342(1)(e).

be discharged by the initial payment, even if it is subsequently recovered as a preference.[24]

A liquidator in seeking to avoid a payment or other transaction on the ground of preference is assisted by a statutory presumption (in s.239(6)) that, in the case of persons connected to the company such as directors, the preference has been influenced by the desire to produce the specified effect. Yet it is still possible for a guarantor director to show that in making a payment to a particular creditor he had no desire to improve his own position.[25] There is a similar presumption in respect of associates of an individual bankrupt (in s.340(5)).   **6–14**

Another issue related to disposition upon insolvency is the extent to which the guarantor's liability may be affected by the debtor's bank continuing to honour cheques drawn on the company's overdrawn account in favour of third parties subsequent to a petition being presented for the winding up of the company and until the winding up order is made. The relevant provision is s.127 of the Insolvency Act 1986 which provides that: **6–15**

> "In a winding up by the court, any disposition of the company's property, and any transfer of shares, or alteration in the status of the company's members, made after the commencement of the winding up is, unless the court otherwise orders, void."

Section 127 was the subject of interpretation in *Coutts & Co v Stock*,[26] when at the date the winding up petition was presented the debtor's account with the bank was £500 in credit, but by the date the winding up order was made the overdraft had been increased as a result of the bank's honouring cheques to over £190,000. Lightman J. held that, although s.127 avoided, *as between the debtor company and the payee*, a disposition of the company's property made after presentation of the petition, it neither invalidated a loan made by someone else to the company to enable it to make that disposition, nor avoided a disposition as against the company's bank where the bank had merely fulfilled an agency or intermediary role between the company and the payee. As between the company and the bank, the money was validly borrowed and paid by the company to the payee.[27] The result was (on the facts of *Coutts & Co v Stock*)[28] that the guarantor remained liable for the full indebtedness of over £190,000, since the liquidators of the debtor company were unable to recover the payments from the payees. Lightman J. supported his view on these policy grounds:

---

[24] A similar argument may be made in respect of Pt.XV1 of the Insolvency Act 1986 which deals with provisions against debt avoidance (see ss.423–425, and especially the power of the court to make orders in respect of guarantors in s.425(1)(e)).

[25] See the unsuccessful argument for the guarantor in *Re Agriplant Services Ltd* [1997] 2 B.C.L.C. 598 at 609.

[26] [2000] 1 W.L.R. 906.

[27] Note Professor Goode's alternative reasoning that the acts of the bank in honouring cheques in this way constitute payments by the bank itself (by way of loan to the company) *of its own moneys* to the party in whose favour the cheques are drawn. The transaction is outside the scope of s.127 since the disposition is of the bank's property not the company's. (see R. Goode, *Principles of Corporate Insolvency Law* (2nd ed., 1997), p.432.

[28] [2000] 1 W.L.R. 906.

"This result accords with the underlying purpose of the section, namely to recover for the company moneys paid to a payee. The purpose does not extend to making the bank the guarantor of the payee's obligation to repay. It also means that there is no difference between a situation where the company withdraws the money from the bank and gives it to an agent to hand to the payee and a situation where the payment is made through a bank."[29]

These considerations appear compelling, although not all authority supports the reasoning and decision in *Coutts & Co v Stock*.[30]

(iii) Appropriation of payments and securities

6–16   One problem concerning the question of discharge by payment is whether the guarantor can in any way direct that the guaranteed debt be satisfied, or partially satisfied, by a payment from the debtor in preference to other obligations of the debtor. In general, it is clear that the guarantor cannot direct how the payment is to be appropriated.[31] The question is to be decided as if it arose solely between the creditor and the person making the payment; the fact that someone else is liable for the debt is irrelevant.[32] On this basis appropriation is in the first instance a matter for agreement between creditor and debtor.[33] In the absence of any agreement the debtor has the primary right of appropriating a payment to a particular debt, but if the debtor does not make the appropriation, the right to do so devolves upon the creditor.[34] If there is more than one debt owed by a debtor to a particular creditor, an appropriation can be made to any of these debts without regard to the fact that one or more of those debts is guaranteed.[35] It is irrelevant that the guarantor undertook the liability with no

---

[29] *ibid.*, at 910.

[30] [2000] 1 W.L.R. 906. *Cf. Hollicourt (Contracts) Ltd v Bank of Ireland* [2000] 1 W.L.R. 895 and Buckley L.J. (accepting concessions of counsel) in *Re Gray's Inn Construction Co Ltd* [1980] 1 W.L.R. 711 at 716. But in support of the position adopted by Lightman J. see *In re Mal Bower's Macquarie Electrical Centre Pty. Ltd* [1974] 1 N.S.W.L.R. 254; *In re Loteka Pty Ltd* [1990] 1 Qd. R. 322; *Tasmanian Primary Distributors Pty Ltd v RC and MB Steinhardt Pty Ltd.* (1994) A.C.S.R. 92. See also *Bank of Asia Ltd v Rogerio Sau Fungham* [1988] 1 H.K.L.R. 181.

[31] *Re Sherry* (1884) 25 Ch. D. 692; *Kirby v Duke of Marlborough* (1813) 2 M. & S. 18; 105 ER 289; *Williams v Rawlinson* (1825) 3 Bing. 71; 130 E.R. 440; *Lysaght v Walker* (1831) 5 Bli. (NS) 1; 5 E.R. 208.

[32] *Milverton Group Ltd v Warner World Ltd* [1995] 2 E.G.L.R. 28 at 31; *City Discount Co v McLean* (1874) L.R. 9 C.P. 692.

[33] *Milverton Group Ltd v Warner World Ltd* [1995] 2 E.G.L.R. 28 at 31; *Re Sherry* (1884) 25 Ch. D. 692; *Fahey v MSD Speirs Ltd* [1975] 1 N.Z.L.R. 240; *Fuller Brush Co Ltd v Hazell* (1975) 54 D.L.R. (3d) 22.

[34] If payments are received from a third party on behalf of the debtor, the debtor must be given the first right of appropriating those payments: *Waller v Lacy* (1840) 1 M. & Gr. 54; 133 E.R. 245.

[35] *Re Sherry* (1884) 25 Ch. D. 692; *Williams v Rawlinson* (1825) 3 Bing. 71; 130 E.R. 440; *Kirby v Duke of Marlborough* (1813) 2 M. & S. 18; 105 E.R. 289; *Hopkinson v Canadian Imperial Bank of Commerce* [1977] 6 W.W.R. 490; *Royal Bank of Canada v Bank of Montreal* [1976] 4 W.W.R. 721; *Palmer v Sutherland* [1869] 2 Q.S.C.R. 44; *Plomer v Long* (1816) 1 Stark. 153; 171 E.R. 430; *Fahey v MSD Speirs Ltd* [1975] 1 N.Z.L.R. 240.

knowledge of other debts already incurred by the debtor[36] or that the creditor made further unsecured loans to the debtor subsequent to the guaranteed loan.[37] An appropriation can be made to a debt which has not yet fallen due pursuant to the terms of the principal transaction (for example, a future instalment of rent under a lease)[38] and there is no implied term, arising out of the mere fact that the debt is guaranteed, that payments should be first appropriated to the debt secured by the guarantee.[39]

The debtor's intention to appropriate a payment to a particular debt need not be expressly stated but can be inferred from the circumstances. For example, if the debtor has paid the creditor an amount which is the exact sum owing in respect of a particular debt, this is evidence from which it may be inferred that the payment is intended to satisfy that particular debt rather than other debts owed to that creditor.[40] Similarly, when the creditor receives payment from the debtor following a joint demand from the guarantor and creditor and a voluntary promise by the debtor to pay, it may be inferred that the payment is intended to satisfy the guaranteed debt.[41] What usually happens, however, is that the debtor makes no express or implied appropriation, often having allowed the creditor complete freedom as to the appropriation of payments by a clause in the loan agreement or the guarantee. Such a clause might take this form:

6–17

"The lender has the right to appropriate either at the time of payment or at any time thereafter any moneys paid to it or otherwise coming into its possession or control on behalf of the debtor in or towards discharging or providing for whichever part or parts of any liability whatever of the debtor to the lender as the lender shall think fit."

Whether or not there then has been appropriation by the creditor is not governed by fixed rules, but will depend upon the creditor's intention, express, implied or presumed.[42]

These statements of general principle concerning appropriation of payments are subject to the following qualifications and limitations which may in some circumstances indicate that a particular payment should be applied in satisfaction of a guaranteed debt as opposed to another

6–18

---

[36] *Williams v Rawlinson* (1825) 3 Bing. 71; 130 ER 440; *Kirby v Duke of Marlborough* (1813) 2 M. & S. 18; 105 E.R. 289.
[37] *Bank of Nova Scotia v Neil* (1968) 69 D.L.R. (2d) 357.
[38] *Milverton Group Ltd v Warner World Ltd* [1995] 2 E.G.L.R. 28 at 31–32, but the guarantors are entitled to be credited with interest from the date when the payment was received until the date when the payment fell due. See also *Martin v Breknell* (1813) 2 M. & S. 39; 105 E.R. 297.
[39] *Fahey v MSD Speirs Ltd* [1975] 1 N.Z.L.R. 240 at 246.
[40] *Marryatts v White* (1817) 2 Stark. 101 at 102–103; 171 E.R. 586 at 587 where Lord Ellenborough described such payment as "irrefragable evidence". It should be noted that, on the facts of *Marryatts v White*, the case for implying an appropriation was stronger because the debtor also received a discount attributable only to the guaranteed account.
[41] *Shaw v Picton* (1825) 4 B. & C. 715; 107 E.R. 1226. As other examples, see *Young v English* (1843) 7 Beav. 10; 49 E.R. 965; *Field v Carr* (1828) 5 Bing. 13; 130 E.R. 964; *Newmarch v Clay* (1811) 14 East 239; 104 E.R. 592.
[42] *Milverton Group Ltd v Warner World Ltd* [1995] 2 E.G.L.R. 28 at 31.

unsecured debt, or, if only a part of a debt is secured by a guarantee, to that part as opposed to the unsecured part.

(a) An appropriation once made is conclusive

6–19   If the guarantor can show that the creditor has made a definite appropriation in favour of the guaranteed debt, the creditor is bound by that election.[43] If it is clear from the creditor's accounts that the payment has been applied to a particular debt, this will be binding, at least if this information has been communicated to the debtor or guarantor.[44] The creditor may choose to carry the payment to a "suspense account". If this is all that occurs, there is no appropriation to any particular debt,[45] but it is possible that even if the account is designated by the creditor as a "suspense account", additional facts may indicate that a specific appropriation has been made. For example, an appropriation may be inferred if the creditor pays a sum of money received as a result of the realisation of a security given to the creditor by the guarantor into a "suspense account",[46] but the creditor also charges interest on the principal debt, debited to another account, as if it had been reduced by the amount paid into the "suspense account".

6–20   One specific and important illustration of a situation where a creditor is bound by a particular appropriation is when a sum of money is simply carried into a current account without specific appropriation by creditor or debtor to a particular debt before it is placed in the account. In this situation, in accordance with the principle of *Devaynes v Noble (Clayton's Case)*,[47] the first sum paid in is deemed to be the first paid out, and the first debit in the account is extinguished by the first sum paid in. The operation of this rule[48] has been described in Chapter 5[49] and, in any event, it can be excluded,[50] for example, by a reference to the fact that the guarantee is "continuing".[51]

---

[43] *Deeley v Lloyds Bank Ltd* [1912] A.C. 756 at 783–784. *Simson v Ingham* (1823) 2 B. & C. 65; 107 E.R. 307; *McLean v Discount & Finance Ltd* (1939) 64 C.L.R. 312 at 353–354
[44] *Simson v Ingham* (1823) 2 B. & C. 65 at 71–74; 107 E.R. 307 at 310; *Ward v National Bank of New Zealand Ltd* (1889) 8 N.Z.L.R. (SC) 10 at 13, *per* Williams J.; *Cory Bros & Co Ltd v Owners of the Turkish Steamship "Mecca"* [1897] A.C. 286 at 292, *per* Lord Herschell; *Lyman v Miller* (1854) 12 U.C.Q.B. 215. These cases indicate that communication is necessary, but in *Deeley v Lloyds Bank Ltd* [1912] A.C. 756, no such limitation was expressed, and there was no indication on the facts that there was communication. See also *Hopkinson v Canadian Imperial Bank of Commerce* [1977] 6 W.W.R. 490 at 493–494, from which it appears that communication is not necessary in Canadian law.
[45] *Commercial Bank of Australia Ltd v Official Assignee of the Estate of John Wilson & Co* [1893] A.C. 181.
[46] See *Mclean v Discount & Finance Ltd* (1939) 64 CLR 312 *per* McTiernan J. at 358–359; *per* Rich J. at 339. *Cf.* Starke J. at 348; Evatt J. at 353 who were of the view that this was not sufficient evidence of appropriation.
[47] (1816) 1 Mer. 572; 35 E.R. 781.
[48] See above, para.5–22.
[49] *ibid.*
[50] *Henniker v Wigg* (1843) 4 Q.B. 792; 114 E.R. 1095. As this case illustrates, the continuing nature of the security may be inferred in a general way from the language and the conduct of the parties.
[51] See also the clause in *Westminster Bank Ltd v Cond* (1940) 46 Com. Cas. 60.

(b) Secret arrangements as to appropriation made between the principal and the creditor amounting to a fraud upon the guarantor

In certain cases, the contract of guarantee may be vitiated on the ground **6–21** of fraud because of a failure to disclose to the guarantor an arrangement regarding appropriation made between the creditor and the principal. Thus, in *Pidcock v Bishop*,[52] a guarantor for the purchase price of goods was discharged when the buyer and seller agreed that the buyer should pay in excess of the market price and apply that surplus to a pre-existing debt. Similarly, in *Vivian v Eynon*,[53] an indorser of a promissory note given to enable the principal to purchase a vehicle was held discharged from liability because of a secret arrangement to apply the first earnings of the truck towards liquidating an old debt that the principal owed to the creditor which was not secured by the guarantee. These cases are said to be based on the principle that the creditor has failed to disclose an unusual feature of the principal transaction to the guarantor which would have the effect that the position of the principal is different from that which the guarantor would naturally expect.

Two comments should be made in relation to these authorities. First, it is **6–22** clear that they only affect the creditor's freedom of appropriation where there is a specific arrangement between the creditor and the principal as to appropriation. There is no general duty to disclose to the guarantor that the creditor intends to appropriate payments in a particular way,[54] or even to disclose the existence of other loans not secured by the guarantee.[55] Secondly, it is arguable that both these cases conflict with established authority[56] which gives the creditor, in the absence of a specific appropriation by the debtor, complete freedom as to appropriation without the necessity for consultation with the guarantor at all. If such consultation is unnecessary, why is it that an arrangement between the creditor and the principal should discharge the guarantor?

(c) A security given by the principal or by a co-guarantor in relation to the guaranteed debt is to be appropriated to that debt

If a security is given by the principal in relation to a particular debt **6–23** which is guaranteed, the proceeds from the realisation of that security must be applied in reduction of that particular debt.[57] Thus, where a guarantee

---

[52] (1825) 3 B. & C. 604; 107 E.R. 857. See also *Re Mason Ex p. Sharp* (1844) 3 Mont. D. & De G. 490 (failure to disclose act of bankruptcy to guarantor).
[53] [1927] G.L.R. 447.
[54] *Bank of Nova Scotia v Neil* (1968) 69 D.L.R. (2d) 357.
[55] *Goodwin v National Bank of A/asia* (1968) 42 A.L.J.R. 110 (existing indebtedness need not be disclosed); *Bank of Nova Scotia v Neil* (1968) 69 D.L.R. (2d) 357 (future loans need not be disclosed). As to non-disclosure generally, see above, para.4–02 to 4–35.
[56] See the cases cited above, nn.33, 34.
[57] *Pearl v Deacon* (1857) 24 Beav. 186; 53 E.R. 328; *Royal Bank of Canada v Dickson* (1973) 33 D.L.R. (3d) 332 at 343–344; *Hancock v Williams* (1942) 42 S.R. (NSW) 252 at 256. A clause

of an independent debt due from a tenant to his landlord was further secured by a bill of sale over the tenant's furniture, it was held that the proceeds of sale of the furniture should be applied in reduction of the outstanding guaranteed debt, and not in reduction of arrears of rent due to the landlord.[58]

6–24   This rule of appropriation follows from the fact that the guarantor is entitled, after paying out the creditor, to the benefit of any securities held by the creditor to enforce the right of indemnity against the principal debtor or the right of contribution against a co-guarantor.[59] The creditor is not permitted to deprive the guarantor of the benefit of these securities by applying the proceeds to other debts of the principal debtor.[60] As securities held by a co-guarantor also enure for the benefit of all guarantors,[61] the same rationale should apply and the proceeds of those securities should also be appropriated to the guaranteed debt.[62]

6–25   This principle is not confined to where a security is given only in relation to the guaranteed debt. If the security is given in respect of two debts, one guaranteed and the other not, the guarantor is entitled to have a rateable proportion of the proceeds of the security deducted from the guaranteed debt.[63] For example, if there are two separate debts of £10,000, only one of which is guaranteed, and a security taken from the principal debtor to secure both debts realises £10,000, the guarantor is entitled to have the amount outstanding on the guaranteed debt reduced to £5,000.

6–26   As the rationale for this method of appropriation stems from the guarantor's right to the benefit of the securities held by the creditor, it will not be applicable in situations where no such right can be shown. Thus if the security is given to the same creditor for an entirely separate debt, which is not guaranteed, the guarantor, having no right to that security on satisfying the obligations under the guarantee, is not entitled to have the proceeds of the security applied in reduction of the guaranteed debt.[64] The same applies where the guarantee relates to a distinct part of one debt and a separate security is taken for the other part[65] (for example, the debt is £10,000, a guarantee is taken for a specific part, say £5,000, and a bill of sale is taken to secure the other £5,000). In effect, this arrangement converts one debt into two separate ones: one covered by the guarantee and the other by the separate security.

---

in the guarantee can reinforce this right: *Australian Bank Ltd v Daniberg* (unreported, Vic Sup Ct, April 9, 1987).

[58] *Pearl v Deacon* (1857) 24 Beav. 186; 53 E.R. 328. See also the comments of the High Court of Australia in *Hutchens v Deauville Investments Pty Ltd* (1986) 68 A.L.R. 367 at 374.

[59] *ibid.*

[60] For a detailed discussion of the rule that a creditor must not release or impair a security, which will result in the guarantor's discharge to the extent of the loss, see below, paras 8–46 to 8–105.

[61] See below, para.8–51.

[62] See *Re Butler's Wharf Ltd* [1995] 2 B.C.L.C. 43, where this result was assumed in respect of a guarantee assigned to the creditor.

[63] *Coates v Coates* (1864) 33 Beav. 249; 55 E.R. 363; *Perrie v Roberts* (1681) 1 Vern. 34; 23 E.R. 289. Such an appropriation should also occur where both debts are guaranteed so that each guarantor benefits rateably.

[64] *Wilkinson v London & County Banking Co* (1884) 1 T.L.R. 63.

[65] *Wade v Coope* (1827) 2 Sim. 155; 57 E.R. 747; *Re Butlers Wharf Ltd* [1995] 2 B.C.L.C. 43 at 50.

Another situation which sometimes occurs is where it is clear that the **6–27** additional security is given in relation to the whole debt but the guarantor's obligations extend only to a part of that debt. This may arise because the guarantor's liability is limited and the limitation is worded in such a way that the undertaking is construed as a guarantee of part of a debt rather than a guarantee of the whole debt with a specified limitation as to the guarantor's total liability. As a matter of general principle, a continuing guarantee limited in amount to secure a floating balance will prima facie be construed as applicable to a part only of the debt co-extensive with the amount of the guarantee.[66] An example would be a guarantee "of any debt which the principal may contract from time to time as a running balance of account to any amount not exceeding £400".[67]

If the guarantee is construed as a guarantee of part of a debt, the **6–28** guarantor would be entitled to the benefit of the securities upon payment of the guarantor's part of the debt in the same proportion as the debt satisfied by the guarantor bore towards the full amount of the debt.[68] This entitlement would arise because payment of the guarantor's part of the debt, as between the guarantor and the creditor, constitutes payment of the whole.[69] Thus, in appropriating the proceeds of the security, that proportion of the proceeds must be credited in diminution of the part of the debt for which the guarantor is liable. As an example, if the debt is £10,000, and the guarantor is liable for £5,000, being part of that debt, and the security given by the principal realises £4,000, the guarantor's liability is reduced by £2,000 to £3,000.

The position is probably different if the guarantee is of the whole debt **6–29** with a limitation upon the total liability. In this case, the guarantor's right to the benefit of the security cannot arise until the entire debt owing by the debtor has been paid, even though the guarantor has discharged the guarantee.[70] Thus, because the debt has not been paid and the guarantor has no right to the securities, there is no obligation on the creditor to appropriate the proceeds of any security in diminution of the guarantor's liability. The funds can simply be applied in reduction of the total indebtedness, so that if the debt is £10,000, with the guarantor's liability being limited to £5,000, and the security realises £4,000, the total debt is reduced to £6,000, but the guarantor remains fully liable to the upper limit of £5,000.[71]

---

[66] *Ellis v Emmanuel* (1876) 1 Exch. D. 157; *Re D (a lunatic patient) (No.2)* [1926] V.L.R. 467 at 486. In situations, however, where there is a guarantee of a fixed and ascertained sum (*e.g.* a mortgage debt), the guarantee will probably be construed as a guarantee of the whole indebtedness: *Ellis v Emmanuel* at 168–169.

[67] *Bardwell v Lydall* (1831) 7 Bing. 489; 131 E.R. 189. See also above, para.5–35.

[68] *Goodwin v Gray* (1874) 22 W.R. 312; *Re Butlers Wharf Ltd* [1995] 2 B.C.L.C. 43 at 50–51, where an argument that *Goodwin v Gray* (1874) 22 W.R. 312 was wrongly decided, was rejected. See also Jordan C.J. in *Tooth & Co Ltd v Lapin* (1936) 53 W.N. (NSW) 224 at 225.

[69] *Re Sass Ex p. National Provincial Bank of England Ltd* [1896] 2 Q.B. 12 at 15.

[70] This would appear to follow from *Re Sass Ex p. National Provincial Bank of England Ltd* [1896] 2 Q.B. 12, which specifically deals with the question in the context of the appropriation of dividends in bankruptcy.

[71] Although this view is thought to be correct, there is no definite authority to support it and, indeed, in *Tooth & Co Ltd v Lapin* (1936) 53 W.N. (NSW) 224 at 225 Jordan C.J. took the view that the guarantor is entitled to have a proportionate part of the net proceeds from the

6–30   Most modern guarantees assume that the authors' view is correct because they contain a provision which makes it clear that the *whole debt* is guaranteed with a limitation upon the total liability, thereby rebutting any suggestion that the instrument is a guarantee for part of a debt. An example is:

> "This guarantee is to be security *for the whole of the moneys hereby secured* but nevertheless the total sum payable hereunder by the guarantor shall not exceed the sum of £ ...."[72]

6–31   A special clause is also often included in a contract of guarantee stating that "until the whole of the principal's indebtedness to the creditor has been satisfied the guarantor shall not be entitled on any grounds whatsoever to claim the benefit of any security now or hereafter held by the creditor in respect of the debtor's liabilities".[73] Even if the guarantee, on its proper construction, is a guarantee of part of a debt, it is thought that this clause, by denying the guarantor's right to the securities at all until the whole debt is paid in full, would allow the creditor to appropriate the proceeds of the security in reduction of the general indebtedness rather than oblige the creditor to appropriate the proceeds in proportionate reduction of the guarantor's liability. But whether it be a guarantee of part of a debt on the one hand or a guarantee of the whole debt with a limit to the guarantor's liability on the other, such a clause would probably not allow a creditor to appropriate the proceeds of the security in respect of an entirely separate obligation not secured by the guarantee at all.[74] The clause does not negate the principle that the guarantor, having paid under the guarantee, is entitled to the security to enforce the right of indemnity against the debtor once the whole debt has been satisfied. An appropriation to an entirely different debt would thus prevent the security, or its proceeds, being restored to the guarantor at that point of time.

6–32   Sometimes, however, the guarantee states simply that "the guarantors will not in any way claim the benefit or seek the transfer of any security or part thereof". This clause has been interpreted as negating the guarantor's entitlement to the creditor's securities through subrogation and as relieving the creditor of the corresponding duty not to impair or release

---

realisation of a security credited in reduction of the guarantor's liability as surety even where there is a guarantee of "a general indebtedness with a limit as to the amount of his liability". See also Barwick C.J. in *Bank of Adelaide v Lorden* (1970) 45 A.L.J.R. 49 at 54, who does not draw the distinction made in the text in discussing the principles of appropriation when a security is provided by the guarantor: see below, paras 6–33 to 6–35 for a discussion of the relevant principles.

[72] (Emphasis added.) As another example, see *Ulster Bank Ltd v Lambe* [1966] N.I. 161 (guarantee to be available as an "ultimate security" for any balance).

[73] See a similar clause in *Buckeridge v Mercantile Credits Ltd* (1982) 56 A.L.J.R. 28.

[74] See *Re Butlers Wharf Ltd* [1995] 2 B.C.L.C. 43; *Re D (a lunatic patient) (No.2)* [1926] V.L.R. 467 at 486–487, where it is made plain that clear wording will be necessary before such an appropriation can be made. In *Re Butlers Wharf* (at 49), the relevant clause merely gave the bank the right to decide in which order the various liabilities (principal, interest, costs and other charges) would be discharged. It did not entitle the creditor to keep the proceeds of the security in a suspense account without appropriating them to the guaranteed debt.

those securities.[75] Thus the guarantor would have no right to the security at any stage. It is probable, therefore, that the effect of the clause is that the guarantor could not insist that the proceeds of such a security be appropriated to the guaranteed debt rather than to an entirely different debt.[76] Arguably, this result defeats the legitimate expectations of the guarantor who may well have been influenced in entering into the guarantee by the fact that the creditor is less likely to have recourse to the guarantee in the event of the principal's default since the principal obligation is secured.

(d) Security given by the guarantor for a particular debt to be appropriated in reduction of the guarantor's liability for that debt

If a guarantor gives a further security to the creditor to secure the guaranteed debt up to the limit of the guarantee and the creditor realises the security, that sum must be appropriated in diminution of the guarantor's liability for that debt.[77] Thus in *Bank of Adelaide v Lorden*,[78] there was a guarantee of the debts of the principal, the amount payable not to exceed a certain sum. One of the guarantors gave the creditor a charge over his interest in a deceased estate to secure the payment of the principal's account up to the same amount as that expressed in the instrument of guarantee. Barwick C.J. (Gibbs and Windeyer J.J. concurring) held that, because the guarantors would be entitled to the benefit of the security on payment of the amount properly demanded of them, the proceeds of the security must be applied in reduction of the guarantor's liability, and not merely in reduction of the principal debtor's account.[79] The result is that if the debt is £4,000, with a guarantee for that amount to a limit of £2,000, and the guarantor provides a security for the principal debt which realises £500, that sum must be applied to reduce the guarantor's liability to £1,500.

6–33

Barwick C.J. drew no distinction between a situation in which there is a guarantee of part of a debt and a situation in which there is a guarantee of the whole debt with a specified limitation to the guarantor's liability. The wording of the guarantee in *Bank of Adelaide v Lorden* would appear to justify the latter construction, and it is arguable that the guarantors, having guaranteed the whole debt, had no right to the benefit of the security until

6–34

---

[75] *Johnson v Australian Guarantee Corp Ltd* (1992) 59 S.A.S.R. 382 and below, para.8–97 for criticism of this interpretation.
[76] However, the fact that the principal has given the security for a specific debt could be regarded as a specific appropriation by the principal of the proceeds of that security to that particular debt.
[77] As to payments made by a guarantor in exchange for an absolute release, see *Milverton Group Ltd v Warner World Ltd* [1995] 32 E.G. 70, and below, para.9–07.
[78] (1970) 45 A.L.J.R. 49.
[79] *ibid.*, at 54. Note, however, that the creditor may still sue the principal or prove in the principal's bankruptcy or lquidation for the full amount of the debt (£4,000 in the example given) if the guarantee is for the whole of the principal's indebtedness: see below, para.10–35.

the whole debt was satisfied.[80] It has been seen[81] that the application of this reasoning in the context of a security provided by the principal led to the conclusion that the proceeds of the security can be appropriated by the creditor to reduce the general indebtedness. If this reasoning were applicable where the guarantor provided a security, it would mean that if there was a guarantee of the whole debt with a specified limitation to the guarantor's liability the guarantor's liability in the example given above would remain at £2,000. Only in the case of a guarantee of part of a debt would it be necessary to apply the sum to reduce the guarantor's liability to £1,500. But Barwick C.J.'s judgment, on the other hand, suggests that the guarantor's liability may be reduced whatever construction of the guarantee is adopted.

6–35   No doubt the guarantee can provide that the proceeds of a security furnished by the guarantor can be applied in reduction of the total indebtedness. An express term to this effect is not usually included, although most instruments of guarantee contain a clause stating that until the whole of the principal's indebtedness has been satisfied "the guarantor shall not be entitled on any grounds whatsoever to claim the benefit of any security now or hereafter held by the creditor in respect of the debtor's liabilities". If such a clause is construed or drafted to cover securities provided by the guarantor as well as the principal, it is arguable that such a clause inferentially allows the creditor to appropriate the proceeds of the security in reduction of the total indebtedness rather than compelling the creditor to apply them in diminution of the guarantor's liability. Again, the argument would be that, since the guarantor is not entitled to any benefit of the securities until the whole debt has been paid, the guarantor cannot insist on an appropriation of the proceeds of the security to reduce his liability.[82]

(e) Wording in the guarantee, or other documentation, may indicate that payments must be appropriated to the guaranteed debt or part of it

6–36   One situation in which the creditor is compelled to appropriate a payment by the debtor to the guaranteed debt is where the guarantee itself indicates that the guarantor will be discharged from liability if payments made by the debtor are not appropriated to that debt. In *Kinnaird v Webster*,[83] a creditor secured a bank loan with a number of promissory notes payable at intervals of a week. A guarantee of the loan was given "in the event of ... promissory notes ... not being paid at the due dates". This was interpreted to mean that the guarantor was to be discharged if the

---

[80] See this argument set out above, paras 6–23 to 6–32,, in the context of a situation where the principal provides a security.
[81] See above, paras 6–29 to 6–32.
[82] See *Johnson v Australian Guarantee Corp Ltd* (1992) 59 S.A.S.R. 382 and below, para.8–97, for criticism of this interpretation.
[83] (1878) 10 Ch. D. 139.

amount of the notes was not appropriated to the guaranteed debt.[84] *Kinnaird v Webster* might also be viewed, however, as an example of the principle that when additional security is given to the creditor to secure a particular debt the proceeds of the security, when realised, must be applied to a reduction of that debt. Other illustrations are difficult to find because guarantees are usually drafted by the creditor and therefore seldom contain clauses impairing the creditor's freedom of appropriation.

Sometimes other documentation may indicate that the creditor is under an obligation to appropriate payments in a particular way. In *Milverton Group Ltd v Warner World Ltd*[85] two guarantors made payments pursuant to a deed of release. The deed recited that a demand had been served upon them "in respect of outstanding rent and other obligations which [the debtor] had failed to perform under the lease". The demand itself had stated that the lessees had failed to pay a particular quarter's rent, and that there were substantial breaches of the repairing covenants. It was held[86] that the recital to the deed (with its reference to the prior demand) was impliedly an appropriation of part of the money paid to the stipulated quarter's rent, and the Court also expressed the view (without finally deciding)[87] that there was an argument that the remainder of the money should be appropriated to the unquantified claim for breach of the repairing covenants.

6–37

(f) Payments received under a compromise or scheme of arrangement should generally be distributed rateably over all the creditor's debts

Even if it is not expressly stated, a composition or scheme of arrangement will be generally construed as providing that the payments should be distributed rateably over all the debts.[88] A creditor, having some debts secured by guarantee and some not, cannot appropriate all of the payments in respect of the unsecured debts. The guaranteed debts must be treated as being reduced rateably to the extent of the payments received.[89] It has been suggested,[90] in reliance on American authority,[91] that the same rule applies when a creditor obtains a judgment in respect of several debts, some of which are covered by the guarantee and some of which are not. It is said that the proceeds of execution must be distributed rateably to all the

6–38

---

[84] *ibid.* at 144–145 *per* Bacon V.C. See also the explanation of the case in *Browning v Baldwin* (1879) 40 L.T. 248 at 249 *per* Bacon V.C. *Cf.* the interpretation of the guarantee in *Re Sherry* (1884) 25 Ch. D. 692 at 703.

[85] [1995] 2 E.G.L.R. 28.

[86] *ibid.*, at 31.

[87] On the facts it was unnecessary to decide this, since it would not have assisted the defendant's case.

[88] *Thompson v Hudson* (1871) L.R. 6 Ch. App. 320 at 330–331 although the wording of the arrangement may permit an appropriation in a particular manner. See the reference to the fact that "the payment must have been appropriated by the agreement" (at 332).

[89] *ibid.* See also the appropriation made in *Turner Manufacturing Co Pty Ltd v Senes* [1964] N.S.W.R. 692 at 697–698.

[90] *Rowlatt on The Law of Principal and Surety* (5th ed., 1999), para.4.88.

[91] *Blackstone Bank v Hill* (1830) 10 Pick. 129.

debts and cannot be appropriated by the creditor only to those debts which
are not guaranteed. There is, however, no English authority for this view,
although its adoption would be a sensible extension to the rule applying to
compromises, which would not unfairly affect the interests of the
creditor.[92]

(g) In the case of a guarantee of part of a debt or a debt payable by instalments dividends received on bankruptcy should be treated as appropriated rateably in favour of the guaranteed part of the debt

6–39   As has been seen,[93] if a guarantor's liability is limited the guarantee may
be drafted in such a way that it is either a guarantee for the whole debt,
with a specified limitation to the guarantor's liability, or a guarantee for a
part of the debt. If the latter formula is adopted, the guarantor has a right
to prove in the debtor's bankruptcy and to receive a dividend in respect of
the amount paid by the guarantor to the creditor.[94] It follows that, if the
creditor, at the time when the guarantor's liability has arisen, has proved
for the full amount of the debt and received a dividend, the part of the debt
guaranteed must receive a pro rata appropriation of the dividend.[95]

6–40   In the case of a guaranteed debt payable by instalments, the dividend
should be treated as appropriated rateably in part payment of each
instalment as it becomes due.[96] The guarantor cannot insist that the whole
amount of the dividend should be applied in discharge of the next
instalment due. This would result in the possibility of prejudice to the
creditor because the guarantor might become insolvent after the due date
for the payment of the instalment which had been reduced by the
appropriation, but before the liability for the full amount of the future
instalments arose. Indeed, for this reason in *Milverton Group Ltd v Warner
World Ltd*[97] it was held that the creditor could defer appropriation in such
circumstances, even to the final instalments, so long as the debt (in excess
of that amount) remained outstanding. Hoffmann J. said:

"The creditor is entitled to appropriate 'at any time' and I think it can
defer appropriation until it becomes necessary to do so. For example, it
can delay the appropriation of [the debtor's] £10,000 as long as there is
more than £10,000 owing. But when it has collected all but £10,000 from

---

[92] The South Australia Law Reform Commission approved of the rule in its *Report Relating
to the Reform of the Law of Suretyship*, Report No.39 (1979), para.4.
[93] See above, paras 5–35 to 5–40.
[94] *Re Sass Ex p. National Provincial Bank of England Ltd* [1896] 2 Q.B. 12 at 14–15.
[95] *ibid.*, *Raikes v Todd* (1838) 8 Ad. & El. 846; 112 E.R. 1058. See in detail, below, paras 10–28
to 10–43.
[96] *Martin v Brecknell* (1813) 2 M. & S. 39; 105 E.R. 297; *Milverton Group Ltd v Warner World
Ltd* [1995] 2 E.G.L.R. 28 at 31–32.
[97] [1995] 2 E.G.L.R. 28.

other debtors, that will amount to an appropriation of [the debtor's] £10,000 to the remaining debt."[98]

Most modern contracts of guarantee contain a clause making it clear   **6–41** that the guarantee is for the whole debt with a specified limit to the total liability and, in the case of a guarantee of part of a debt, negating the guarantor's right to have the dividends appropriated in reduction of the part of the debt guaranteed.[99]

(h) Creditor cannot appropriate to a principal contract that is void

It has been held[1] that the creditor cannot appropriate payments to a   **6–42** debt incurred during infancy because of the provisions of the Infants Relief Act 1874 (now repealed) which meant that there was effectively "no debt in respect of goods bought by an infant".[2] Presumably, this principle is also applicable to other situations in which it can be said there is "no debt" (for example, an illegal contract) although, somewhat inconsistently, the reasoning has not been applied when the contract is merely unenforceable (for example, where it is barred by the Statute of Limitations).[3] This prohibition on appropriating to a void contract may work to the advantage of a guarantor of another separate valid debt owed to the creditor by the same principal debtor because it means that any payments made must be appropriated by the creditor to the guaranteed debt.

(i) Limitations in certain circumstances exist on the right to appropriate payments to a new bank account

A bank generally acts on the instructions of the customer in regard to   **6–43** the opening of new bank accounts for the customer and, once the accounts are in operation, it will appropriate payments at the customer's direction.[4] This might affect the position of the guarantor in that payments which were formerly paid into a guaranteed overdrawn account might become directed, for example, to a new current account and be used for other purposes by the debtor. In *National Bank of Nigeria Ltd v Awolesi*,[5] the Privy Council indicated that in some circumstances there may be protection for the guarantor in this situation. First, the guarantee itself may on its true construction relate only to the existing account and

---

[98] *ibid.*, at 31. But note that in such a case the other debtors are entitled to be credited with interest from the date the payment was received until the date when the payment fell due. See *Milverton Group Ltd v Warner World Ltd* [1995] 2 E.G.L.R. 28 at 31.
[99] See also above, para.5–35.
[1] *Keeping v Broom* (1895) 11 T.L.R. 595.
[2] *ibid.*, at 596.
[3] *Mills v Fowkes* (1839) 5 Bing. (NC) 455; 132 E.R. 1174 (appropriation possible to a statute-barred debt).
[4] *National Bank of Nigeria Ltd v Awolesi* [1964] 1 W.L.R. 1311 at 1316.
[5] [1964] 1 W.L.R. 1311.

prohibit the establishment of new accounts. In *National Bank of Nigeria Ltd v Awolesi* the consideration for entering into the guarantee was expressed to be "the continuing of the existing account", and this was held to imply that "the parties had agreed that [the existing account] of the principal ... should be continued in an unbroken state and that they did not contemplate the opening of a second account".[6] The opening of a second account by the bank thus constituted a variation of the terms of the guarantee and the guarantor was discharged.

6–44   Moreover, even though the opening of a second account is contemplated by the guarantee and the guarantee is wide enough to cover the indebtedness in all the accounts, the Privy Council took the view that the guarantor will still be discharged if he is "substantially prejudiced"[7] by the operation of the new account. In *National Bank of Nigeria Ltd v Awolesi*, it was held that the guarantor was prejudiced. Although the guarantor, having guaranteed the total indebtedness of both the accounts, would receive the benefit of any capital sums in the new account in diminution of his liability,[8] he had been prejudiced because if the sums had been appropriated to the existing overdrawn account a proportion of the principal debt would have been paid off with a consequent reduction in the interest payable. The amount for which the guarantor was liable was therefore increased by this additional amount of interest payable.

6–45   The first ground given by the Privy Council is simply a question of the construction of the guarantee. The alternative basis of the Privy Council's decision has potentially serious consequences for banks, and is open to criticism in that it unduly restricts the right to open new accounts. It will mean that a bank holding a guaranteed account cannot act automatically on the instructions of its customer in opening a new account, and if a new account is opened it must be operated with a view to the interests of the guarantor; that is, by reducing the overdrawn account by the relevant amount of interest. It should also be emphasised that the Privy Council appeared to adopt the view that the guarantor was fully discharged once the prejudicial arrangement was carried into effect and not merely discharged to the extent of the loss resulting from the new arrangement.

6–46   A second criticism of the alternative basis of the Privy Council's decision is that its exact ambit is unclear. It is not thought that the decision would prohibit the opening of a subsequent loan account because this would effectively negate the well-established right of the creditor to make further unsecured loans to the principal debtor. However, the reasoning in *National Bank of Nigeria Ltd v Awolesi* might apply where the bank opens a "suspense account" during the currency of the guarantee for the receipt of payments not specifically appropriated by the debtor to a particular account. The appropriation of the payments to the "suspense account" could be said to operate to the prejudice of the guarantor because the amount of interest payable on the guaranteed debt would not be reduced.

---

[6] *ibid.*, at 1315.
[7] *ibid.*, at 1317.
[8] This is because two or more current accounts are in reality treated as one account and (if overdrawn) as one debt.

If the creditor wishes to guard against this possible consequence of the principle in *National Bank of Nigeria Ltd v Awolesi*,[9] the guarantee should contain a provision whereby the guarantor authorises the bank to open any new account, and stating that this arrangement shall not discharge the guarantor.

There is one situation in which the bank is clearly entitled to open a new account without the necessity for any specific authority in the contract of guarantee. When the guarantee has been validly determined as to future liabilities (for example, by notice or death) a new account can be opened by the creditor and payments can be appropriated by the creditor to the new account.[10] This conclusion has been reached despite the fact that the guarantor is in one sense prejudiced by this action, as the accounts for which he is liable are not credited with the new payments. Although it is not strictly necessary, a clause is often found in guarantees empowering the creditor to open fresh accounts for subsequent transactions of the customer on determination of the guarantee, and stating that payments appropriated to the new accounts shall not constitute a repayment of the guaranteed debt.[11]

6–47

(j) Combination of bank accounts

In some circumstances, the guarantor can compel the creditor to combine all the accounts of the principal debtor so that all those accounts must be taken into account in ascertaining the extent of the guarantor's liability.[12] This may be to the advantage of the guarantor because the guarantor will receive the benefit of any account in credit, the balance of which must be appropriated to reduce his liability.

6–48

(iv) Critique of rules relating to appropriation of payments and securities

Although, as has been seen, there are some qualifications on the general flexibility given to the debtor and, more importantly in practice, to the creditor to appropriate payments, they are often limited in effect. This is because of the limited circumstances where they arise—for example, the prohibition on appropriating to a void contract—or because of the impact of specific clauses in the guarantee. It might be argued that this flexibility given to the creditor operates to the prejudice of the guarantor. The creditor, after securing a guarantee for an initial loan, may make subsequent loans which are not secured by guarantee, and then appropriate all payments made, but unappropriated, by the debtor, in reduction of the subsequent borrowings.[13] The guarantor may be unaware

6–49

---

[9] [1964] 1 W.L.R. 1311. Note also doubts as to the validity of the alternative basis of the decision: see below, paras 8–06 to 8–14, especially 8–11 to 8–14.
[10] *Re Sherry* (1884) 25 Ch. D. 692.
[11] See S. Mather, "Guarantees and the Banker", *Gilbart Lectures on Banking* (1961), p.31.
[12] The question of the combination of accounts is discussed below, para.10–20.
[13] *Bank of Nova Scotia v Neil* (1968) 69 D.L.R. (2d) 357.

of the later loans and the increased likelihood that the loan for which he is liable will not be paid off.

6–50   Certainly the courts could have used existing principles to curtail the creditor's freedom of appropriation if they had so desired. For instance, since the courts have held that a bank cannot act prejudicially to the interests of the guarantor by opening new accounts on instructions of the customer, the courts could have used the same "prejudice" principle to prevent a bank appropriating payments to debts not secured by the guarantee.

6–51   But the law has not taken this course and, in response, some legislative reforms have been suggested. In Canada it has been proposed[14] that an obligation should be imposed on the creditor to apply payments to reduce or extinguish the guaranteed debt in preference to other debts owed by the debtor to the creditor and, if there are a number of guaranteed debts, the payments should be applied to extinguish the guaranteed debts in the order in which they were incurred. This solution appears to favour the guarantor unduly because it gives priority to the debts secured by tthe guarantee, even in respect of loans made before the guaranteed advance. The South Australian Law Reform Committee has recommended[15] a more balanced solution by concluding that payments should be distributed rateably amongst all the debts owing to the creditor by the debtor, unless the guarantor agrees otherwise at the time of appropriation.

6–52   Even this recommendation, however, is thought to be unworkable in respect of guarantees of commercial transactions in that it would impose an unfair burden on banks to ensure that the proper appropriation is made. If the principal operates its business over a large area, it is likely to have loans at different branches. In these circumstances, the banking system would need to become highly and efficiently centralised (with attendant costs) in order to ensure that payments were distributed rateably over all debts owing by that principal. The recommendation would also take away the discretion of the principal to appropriate payments and the principal may have good business reasons, which are quite independent of the fact that one of the loans is guaranteed, for paying off one loan rather than another.[16]

[14] Law Reform Commission of British Columbia, *Report on Guarantees of Consumer Debts* (1979), pp.57–58.
[15] *Report Relating to the Reform of the Law of Suretyship*, Report No.39 (1977), paras 4, 5. In the United States of America, different and inconsistent rules have been adopted in an effort to achieve an "equitable" result. Sometimes the payment has been applied to the oldest debt and sometimes to the debt for which there is a guarantor. Some States in the United States of America have adopted a rule whereby payments made by the debtor arising from the proceeds of a transaction covered by the obligation of the surety must be applied by the creditor who knows of this fact in discharge of that obligation. See generally A. A. Stearns and J. L. Elder, *The Law of Suretyship* (5th ed., 1972), para.7.23.
[16] As a result, the Tasmania Law Reform Commission in its Report *Suretyship and Guarantee*, Report No.50 (1987) recommended (at p.24) simply that advice should be given to the guarantor explaining that payments made by the principal debtor to the creditor need not necessarily be appropriated to the account guaranteed.

2. DISCHARGE BY THE RELEASE OF THE PRINCIPAL

(i) The general rule

If the creditor, without having received full payment or performance **6–53** from the debtor, nevertheless agrees to discharge the debtor from any further liability, the guarantor will be absolutely discharged.[17] There is no longer a debt to guarantee. The agreement to discharge the debtor must be a legally binding one, so that the guarantee (and other accompanying securities such as a mortgage) are discharged[18] being either under seal or supported by consideration,[19] but it can be in the form of a simple release or a composition and can be oral.[20] In circumstances where the creditor accepts part of the debt in satisfaction of the whole, it must be clear that the creditor is agreeing to discharge the whole debt, rather than merely relieving the debtor from paying a proportion of the debt.[21]

If the principal debt is secured by a mortgage, the release may be **6–54** effected by a discharge of the mortgage. Sometimes, however, the personal liability of the principal may remain despite the discharge as a result of agreement between principal and creditor, so that the guarantor will normally remain liable. But if the guarantee is drafted (for example, by a clause in the preamble) to relate to "moneys secured by the mortgage" it is arguable that the continuing personal liability will not come within the ambit of the guarantee[22] as the guarantee can be interpreted as limited in its terms only to those moneys which were formerly secured by the mortgage prior to its discharge.

The main judicial explanation of why a release of the principal debtor **6–55** discharges the guarantor in these circumstances emphasises the courts' desire to protect the position of the debtor. If the guarantor were not discharged it would amount to a "fraud on the principal debtor"[23] because the creditor could successfully proceed against the guarantor, and the

---

[17] *Cragoe v Jones* (1873) L.R. 8 Exch. 81; *Moss v Hall* (1850) 5 Ex. 46; 155 E.R. 20; *Re Lewis Ex p. Smith* (1789) 3 Bro. C.C. 1; 29 E.R. 370; *Jowitt v Callaghan* (1938) 38 S.R. (NSW) 512 at 518; *Hancock v Williams* (1942) 42 S.R. (NSW) 252 at 256; *South Australian Investment & Land Mortgage Co Ltd v Hart* (1895) 6 Q.L.J. 186; *Hill v Anderson Meat Industries Ltd* [1972] 2 N.S.W.L.R. 704 at 707–708. The rule also applies to situations in which there are a number of separate covenantors, each liable to perform the same obligation, *e.g.* two lessees, being the assignor and assignee of the lease: *Deanplan Ltd v Mahmoud* [1992] 3 All E.R. 945.
[18] *Cross v Sprigg* (1849) 6 Hare 552; 67 E.R. 1283. See also *Jerrad v Barclays Bank plc*, (unreported, CA, May 18, 1998).
[19] *Australian Joint Stock Bank v Armstrong* (1888) 5 W.N. (NSW) 9; *Bank of Montreal v Hawrish* (1967) 61 W.W.R. 16.
[20] As an illustration of a release under a composition, see *Bank of Adelaide v Lorden* (1970) 45 A.L.J.R. 49. As to difficulties of proving an oral release see *Scottish Electric plc v Piotr Ismestieff* (unreported, December 16, 1999).
[21] *Watters v Smith* (1831) 2 B. & Ad. 889; 109 E.R. 1373, and see the cases closely analysed in G.L. Williams, *Joint Obligations* (1949), para.53. A partial release of the principal will result in a partial release of the guarantor: see below, para.6–86.
[22] See, *e.g. Wadlow Pty Ltd v Lidums* (Unreported, SA Sup Ct, March 2, 1982).
[23] *Re Natal Investment Co (Nevill's Case)* (1870) 6 Ch. App. 43 at 47 *per* Mellish L.J.; *Mercantile Bank of Sydney v Taylor* (1891) 12 L.R. (NSW) 252 at 260 *per* Windeyer J.; *Mahant Singh v U Ba Yi* [1939] A.C. 601 at 607.

guarantor could then recover from the debtor as an indemnity any amount the guarantor has to pay the creditor.[24] One approach might have been to deny the guarantor the right to an indemnity in these circumstances but still permit the creditor to enforce the guarantee, but this would be to extinguish one of the guarantor's rights by an agreement of which he had no knowledge.[25]

(ii) Covenants not to sue

6–56   It is sometimes the case that the agreement between creditor and debtor is not phrased as an unconditional release, but as a covenant not to sue the debtor without any limitation as to time.

6–57   Most of the agreements in which the courts have been faced with an agreement not to sue have also contained a clause which have reserved the creditor's rights against the guarantor, and such a clause will be effective to preserve the liability of the guarantor, despite a release.[26] But what is the position if there is a simple covenant not to sue the debtor without any reservation?

6–58   In *Finley v Connell Associates*[27] Richards J. held that an agreement could not properly be characterised as a covenant not to sue at all unless it contained a reservation of rights against the guarantor, although such reservation could be implied[28] as well as express. Thus a simple promise not to sue the debtor without reservation would operate as an unqualified release of debtor and, consequently, the guarantor. With respect, this reasoning is erroneous. Although (as will be seen)[29] a reservation of rights clause might have the effect of converting an unqualified release of the debtor into a covenant not to sue,[30] such a provision has never been regarded as "an essential ingredient"[31] of a covenant not to sue. This can be achieved by other wording, it being a question of construction in each case in the light of the surrounding circumstances.[32]

6–59   Nevertheless, it is true that there is some authority (cited in *Finley v Connell Associates*)[33] that a bare covenant not to sue without a reservation of rights clause will discharge a guarantor. Thus in *Mahant Singh v U Ba Yi*[34] the Privy Council took the view that an undertaking by the creditor not to sue the debtor would not discharge the guarantor *provided that* there was a clause stating that the creditor's rights against the guarantor

---

[24] *ibid. Re Lewis Ex p. Smith* (1789) 3 Bro. C.C. 1; 29 E.R. 370; *Deanplan Ltd v Mahmoud* [1992] 3 All E.R. 945 at 960; *Bond & Bond Ltd v Rothery* [1935] G.L.R. 179.
[25] *Polak v Everett* (1876) 1 Q.B.D. 669 at 673–674.
[26] See below, para.6–67.
[27] [1999] Lloyd's Rep. P.N. 895.
[28] Following *Watts v Aldington, The Times*, December 16, 1993. See below, paras 6–64 and 6–72.
[29] See below, para.6–69.
[30] *ibid.*
[31] [1999] Lloyd's Rep P.N. 895 at 906.
[32] See *Deanplan Ltd v Mahmoud* [1993] Ch. 151 at 170 and generally G.L. Williams, *Joint Obligations* (1949), para.53.
[33] [1999] Lloyd's Rep P.N. 895.
[34] [1939] A.C. 601 at 609.

shall be preserved. The implication is that if the clause is absent then the guarantor would be discharged. There is a similar implication in *Kearsley v Cole*[35] where it was stated that a clause reserving rights against the guarantor "rebuts the implication that the surety was meant to be discharged".[36]

This view, it should be said, is not unanimous. In particular, in *Mallett v Thompson*,[37] (not cited in *Finlay v Connell Associates*),[38] which concerned a simple covenant by the creditor not to sue the debtor, Lord Ellenborough held that the guarantor was not discharged although the guarantor, upon paying the creditor, would have a right of indemnity against the debtor, thus rendering the creditor's covenant not to sue illusory from the debtor's point of view.   **6–60**

As a matter of principle, it is considered that the arguments favouring a release of the guarantor when the creditor covenants not to sue the debtor (without reserving rights against the guarantor) are compelling.   **6–61**

First, the distinction, at least in this context, between the effect of an agreement of absolute release and of a promise not to sue is artificial and unduly legalistic. The effect from the debtor's point of view of the two forms of agreement is exactly the same, and the effect on the guarantor's position should be the same, whether the expression "release" or "covenant not to sue" is used. As one court has commented: **6–62**

"We agree ... that distinction between a 'release' and a 'covenant not to sue' is entirely artificial. When one surrenders all means of enforcing his claim against another ... he effectively extinguishes the underlying right. Thereafter, if it is a right at all, it is a right without remedy ... When one wholly surrenders his recourse to the courts in such matters, he insulates his adversary against his claim as effectually as when he, in so many words, releases him ... Whether words of 'release' or of 'covenant' are used the effect should be the same."[39]

The second argument is simply one of consistency. There is clear authority for the proposition that if the creditor agrees to give time to the debtor, without the consent of the guarantor, then the guarantor is discharged.[40] It should, therefore, follow that if the creditor goes further   **6–63**

---

[35] (1846) 16 M. & W. 128 at 135; 153 E.R. 1128 at 1131. This is quoted with approval in *Cole v Lynn* [1942] 1 K.B. 142 at 146.
[36] *ibid.* See also *Re Lewis Ex p. Smith* (1789) 3 Bro. C.C. I; 29 E.R. 370; *Commercial Bank of Canada v Wilson* (1862) 11 U.C.C.P. 581 on the basis that a covenant not to sue the principal must be construed as a covenant not to sue the guarantor.
[37] (1804) 5 Esp. 178; 170 E.R. 778. See also *Hall v Thompson* (1860) 9 U.C.C.P. 257; *Deane v City Bank of Sydney* (1904) 2 C.L.R. 198 at 207, where Griffith J. appears to adopt a similar view during argument.
[38] [1999] Lloyd's Rep. P.N. 895. *Mallet v Thompson* was, however, approved by *Deanplan Ltd v Mahmoud* [1993] Ch. 151 in the context of a discussion of the assignment of a lease, when the assignee had been released by the lessor from liability.
[39] *McKenna v Austin* 134 F. 2d 659 (1943) at 661.
[40] See below, para.7–59. Although the fact that the guarantor is discharged by the creditor giving time to the principal has been criticised on the basis that the guarantor is not prejudiced by such action, where the creditor agrees never to sue the principal this criticism is not valid. There is clear prejudice because it is more likely that the creditor will have recourse to the guarantor.

and agrees *never* to sue the debtor the guarantor should also be discharged.[41] Finally, if the view of Lord Ellenborough in *Mallett v Thompson*[42] is correct and the guarantor can still recover an indemnity from the principal debtor despite the creditor's covenant not to sue that debtor, it would appear to be just as much a fraud on the principal as if this action were allowed to proceed after a release of a principal. In both cases the principal realistically expects that he will be immune from further action on receiving the creditor's promise, but then finds that an action for an indemnity by the guarantor may still be maintained.

6–64   As a result of these difficulties of distinguishing between the effect of a release on the one hand and a covenant not to sue on the other, Lord Neil, giving the leading judgment in the Court of Appeal decision of *Watts v Aldington*,[43] was of the view that "it will often be more satisfactory to consider whether the relevant document is an absolute release or a release with a reservation rather than to consider whether the document can be fitted into the strait jacket of a covenant or agreement not to sue". Although *Watts v Aldington*[44] was a case of a release of one joint debtors, the approach is now likely to be the same where the relationship is one of principal and surety. The question will then become whether, construing the contract as a whole in its factual matrix, there is an express or implied reservation of rights against the guarantor.

(iii) A release of the principal obtained by fraud

6–65   One commentator has unequivocally stated[45] that if the creditor has released the principal debtor as a result of the fraud of the principal the guarantor will not be discharged because, as a volunteer, the guarantor cannot take advantage of the fraud of another. The most relevant authority,[46] however, does not support this proposition, as it is based on the much narrower ground that the guarantor concurred in the fraudulent representations on the faith of which the release was given and was, therefore, estopped from relying on the release. The present law is therefore unclear, but one recommendation is that, when the guarantor is not a party to the fraud by the principal, the guarantor should be discharged.[47] In the United States of America the courts have adopted a similar position, but with the qualification that if the creditor, upon learning of the fraud, promptly rescinds the

---

[41] This point was stressed in *Re Lewis Ex p. Smith* (1789) 3 Bro. C.C. 1; 29 E.R. 370.
[42] (1804) 5 Esp. 178; 170 E.R. 778.
[43] *The Times*, December 16, 1993.
[44] *ibid.*
[45] *Halsbury's Laws of England* (4th ed., 1978), Vol. 20, para.286.
[46] *Scholefield v Templer* (1858) 28 L.J. Ch. 452; on appeal; (1859) 4 De G. & J. 429; 45 E.R. 166. G. Andrews and R. Millett, *Law of Guarantees* (3rd ed., 2000), pp.284–285 also cites *Kingston-Upon-Hull v Harding* [1892] 2 Q.B. 494, where a surety for a building contractor was not released when the architect's final certificate was procured by fraud. But the case is not directly relevant since the guarantee, on its proper construction, was a promise that the contractor should "well and truly" execute the work, and that had not been done.
[47] South Australia Law Reform Commission, *Report Relating to the Reform of the Law of Suretyship*, Report No.39 (1977), para.8.

release before the guarantor has been prejudiced by any change of position, the guarantor's liability will be revived along with that of the principal.[48] This qualification is desirable since it protects the interests of the creditor who acts promptly after discovery of the true facts.

(iv) The preservation of a right of action against the guarantor despite a release

Although it is now firmly established that an unconditional release of   **6–66** the debtor discharges the guarantor, it is also clear that in some circumstances the creditor's rights against the guarantor may be preserved despite the release. An attempt to preserve such creditor's rights may take three forms. First, in the agreement between creditor and debtor (whether it be an absolute release or a covenant not to sue), there may be an express or implied reservation of rights against the guarantor; secondly, such a clause may be inserted in the contract of guarantee; and, finally, when there is no reservation of rights clause in the guarantee itself, the creditor may obtain the consent of the guarantor to the continuation of the guarantor's liability at the time when the debtor is released by the creditor. Sometimes the creditor may rely on more than one of these methods in an attempt to preserve the liability of the guarantor despite the release.[49]

(a) A "reservation of rights" clause in the agreement of release between the creditor and the principal

Traditionally, a distinction has been drawn between an agreement which   **6–67** is phrased as an absolute release and one that is phrased as a covenant not to sue. If the agreement is properly construed as a covenant not to sue, then there is a clear authority that the "reservation of rights" clause is effective to preserve the liability of the guarantor, whether or not the guarantor consents to the release.[50] Thus in *Cole v Lynn*,[51] in a deed of arrangement executed by a debtor for the benefit of his creditors, the creditors covenanted not to sue the debtor or his estate with a further provision that the arrangement should not "in anywise prejudice or affect the rights or remedies of the creditors against any surety or sureties". It was held that this proviso preserved the creditor's rights against the guarantor and was also impliedly a consent by the debtor that the guarantor could still exercise a right of indemnity against him.[52]

---

[48] L.P. Simpson, *Handbook on the Law of Suretyship* (1950), p.307.
[49] As in *Bond & Bond Ltd v Rothery* [1935] G.L.R. 179 (where the first and second were relied on).
[50] *Greene King plc v Stanley* [2001] EWCA Civ 1966; *Cole v Lynn* [1942] 1 K.B. 142; *Kearsley v Cole* (1846) 16 M. & W. 128; 153 ER 1128 (where there was a covenant not to sue with a reservation of rights clause).
[51] [1942] 1 K.B. 142.
[52] *ibid.*, at 146. See also *Greene King plc v Stanley* [2001] EWCA Civ 1966.

6–68   In the case of an agreement which is phrased as an unconditional release, however, it has been held that a "reservation of rights" clause will not be effective to preserve the creditor's rights against the guarantor. The reasoning is that it is inconsistent with the absolute discharge of the debt, which the release accomplishes, to preserve rights against the guarantor. The "reservation of rights" clause is treated as void and full effect is given to the simple release, with the result that the guarantor is discharged.[53]

6–69   While this principle has never been specifically overruled, later decisions have sought to circumvent it, by construing the agreement between the creditor and debtor not as an unconditional release but as a covenant not to sue. This was done even though the agreement was worded as a "release", provided that the document also contained a clause reserving the creditor's rights against the guarantor.[54] The "reservation of rights" clause was thus treated as having a dual purpose. It converted what otherwise appeared to be an unconditional release into a covenant not to sue and, once that conclusion was reached, it was also held to preserve the creditor's rights against the guarantor. Given the rejection of the historical distinction between the effect of a release and covenant not to sue in *Watts v Aldington*,[55] the result is that any agreement between creditor and debtor, (whether worded as a covenant not to sue or as a release) which contains a clause preserving rights against the guarantor is effective for that purpose.[56]

6–70   The weight of early authority[57] was that extrinsic evidence could not be admitted to show that a document of release which is absolute in its terms is intended to reserve rights against the guarantor. Recently, however, in *Greene King plc v Stanley*[58] the Court of Appeal adopted a liberal approach to the admissibility of such evidence, in holding that the parol evidence rule did not preclude correspondence between the solicitors for the creditor and the debtor being admitted to show the existence of a reservation of rights against the guarantor. It was said that the construction of the voluntary scheme of arrangement entered between the debtor and his creditor should not be approached in "blinkers" so as to "exclude the

---

[53] *Webb v Hewitt* (1857) 3 K. & J. 438 at 442; 69 E.R. 1181 at 1183 *per* Sir William Page Wood V.C., relying on *Nicholson v Revill* (1836) 4 Ad. & El. 675; 111 E.R. 941; *Kearsley v Cole* (1846) 16 M. & W. 128; 153 ER 1128; *Mahant Singh v U Ba Yi* [1939] A.C. 601 at 607; *Industrial Acceptance Corp v Kennedy* (1966) 9 C.B.R. (NS) 113 at 126–127, 142.
[54] *Price v Barker* (1855) 4 El. & Bl. 760; 119 E.R. 281 (where the document executed by the creditor contained "general words of release"); *Bateson v Gosling* (1871) L.R. 7 C.P. 9; *Cragoe v Jones* (1873) L.R. 8 Exch. 81 at 84 *per* Kelly C.B.; *Green v Wynn* (1868) L.R. 7 Eq. 28. See also *Deanplan Ltd v Mahmoud* [1992] 3 All E.R. 945 at 957–960.
[55] *The Times*, December 16, 1993.
[56] See approval of this passage in *Greene King plc v Stanley* [2001] EWCA Civ. 1966.
[57] *Lewis v Jones* (1825) 4 B. & C. 506; 107 E.R. 1148; *Cocks v Nash* (1832) 9 Bing. 341; 131 E.R. 643. Cf. *Re Blakely Ex p. Harvey* (1854) 4 De G.M. & G. 881; 43 E.R. 752 at 759, where Turner L.J. was "not prepared to say that a reservation on the face of the deed is in all cases necessary". See also *Wyke v Rogers* (1852) 1 De G.M. & G. 408; 42 E.R. 609 at 612 where the Lord Chancellor said that "it is perfectly clear in law that an agreement that a transaction which would of itself operate to release the surety shall not have that effect, may be proved by parol evidence". But in this case the written document was not on its face an absolute release, but a promissory note which may not have been given for a release but for another purpose (for example, as additional security).
[58] [2001] EWCA Civ. 1966.

very evidence which establishes the existence of the reservation". The decision in *Green King plc v Stanley*[59] does not, however, unequivocally support the view that extrinsic evidence can be admitted, where the release is unambiguous (making no reference at all to a reservation of rights) since the voluntary arrangement in that case did refer to the relevant guarantee, which "effectively put the creditors on notice of ... the possibility that [the guaranteed] creditor intended to preserve its rights against the guarantors". Indeed the decision can be justified upon the narrower basis of the generally accepted principle that the parol evidence rule does not preclude the admissibility of extrinsic evidence to resolve an ambiguity in the terms of a written document.

The practice of inserting a reservation of rights clause in an agreement   **6–71**
of release is open to criticism because the debtor will not appreciate the effect of the reservation of rights clause contained in the release. There is a reasonable expectation on the part of the principal that the release operates to extinguish any further liability in respect of the debt, but in fact the principal has impliedly consented (by agreeing to the clause) to the guarantor exercising a right of indemnity.

(b) An implied reservation in the agreement of release between creditor and principal

Recent authority[60] concerning the release of one of a number of joint or   **6–72**
joint and several debtors have acknowledged the possibility of implying a reservation of rights against the other debtors. The term will be implied only if the test of strict necessity is satisfied, construing the contract as a whole in its factual matrix. Thus in *Watts v Aldington*[61] a judgment creditor (A) in respect of a judgment of £1.5 million (plus costs) against two persons as a result of a libel action against them agreed with one of those judgment debtors (W) to accept £10,000 "in full and final settlement of judgment and orders and any liability, however arising" and also in return for not opposing his bankruptcy order. W also made various undertakings not to repeat the libels against A and any breach of these undertakings would entitle A "to treat the contract as at an end and to proceed for the full entirety under those judgments as though the agreement had not been entered into". The Court of Appeal held that there was an implied reservation of rights against the other judgment debtor (T) because of, *inter alia*, the following considerations:

(i) The judgment was for £1.5 million plus costs and the sum to be provided by W (or his family) was £10,000. This sum represented only about 0.5 per cent of the total sum due to A including costs.

---

[59] *ibid.*
[60] *Watts v Aldington, The Times*, December 16, 1993; *Johnson v Davies* [1999] Ch. 117; *Finley v Connell Associates* [1999] Lloyd's Rep. P.N. 895. See also *Sun Life Assurance Society plc v Tantofex (Engineers) Ltd* [1999] 2 E.G.L.R. 135, where it was held that the release by the landlord of an assignee (and its surety) of a lease did not release the original tenant.
[61] *ibid.*

(ii) To the knowledge of W, A was seeking to recover an additional sum from T's trustee in bankruptcy. He told W that he hoped to recoup substantially more than £20,000.

(iii) There is no indication that at that stage either W or A gave any thought to the possibility that T might make a claim against W.

(iv) A entered into negotiations with W alone.

(v) W was under continuing obligations (*i.e.* not to repeat libels) pursuant to the agreement.

This, however, was a case of joint debtors, and (given the test of strict necessity) it is likely that an implied reservation of rights is less likely against a guarantor when a principal debtor is released. Indeed, conversely, the more usual implication is that the guarantor, as a party *secondarily liable*, is also to be released. Nevertheless, it is considered that circumstances may arise implying that the guarantor's liability is to be preserved despite an agreement of release. One situation is where the relevant agreement imposes obligations of a continuing nature upon the principal, for example, to make payments by instalments over a period of time. In these circumstances it is unlikely that the creditor would have intended to release the guarantor as at the date of the agreement so as to leave itself with rights only against the principal debtor if the latter defaulted upon its obligations. There were obligations of a continuing nature in *Watts v Aldington*[62] (that is, W's promise not to repeat certain libels), but, more significantly, it was a decisive factor in preserving the liability of the remaining debtors in *Johnson v Davies*.[63] There a debtor entered into a voluntary arrangement with his creditors pursuant to Pt.VIII of the Insolvency Act 1986 under which he was to pay to the supervisor 75 per cent of his net income for five years and any "windfall" assets he may receive within that period. Chadwick L.J. stated:[64]

"The proposals are for the debtor to make income payments—and to transfer windfall assets—to the supervisor over a period of five years. The words in paragraphs 4 and 19, 'When all moneys to be made available under these proposals have been realised and distributed to creditors', have to be read in that context. Failure by the debtor to make the income payments or to transfer windfall assets (if any) during the five-year term would give rise to the issue of a certificate of default, under paragraph 23, and, potentially, to an order for bankruptcy: ... In those circumstances it seems to me obvious that the creditors would wish to prove in the bankruptcy for the full amount of their debts; they would be appalled to find that those debts had been released and replaced by rights under the failed arrangement. It is for this reason, as it seems to me, that the further words in paragraphs 4 and 19, 'I will be released from any further liability to them relating to claims in respect of which

---

[62] *ibid.*
[63] [1999] Ch. 117.
[64] *ibid.*, at 128.

they were entitled to participate in this voluntary arrangement', look to the future. When all moneys 'to be made available ... have been ... distributed ... I will be released' means just that. The release is not to take effect (if at all) until the debtor's obligations under the proposals have been fulfilled."

It might be that this type of conditional agreement, however, is better viewed not as an implied reservation of rights against the surety, but simply as an agreement not amounting to an absolute release at all.

Yet even if the agreement is unconditional other circumstances may   **6–73**
indicate that the rights against the surety are to be preserved. Extrapolating from *Watts v Aldington*,[65] such circumstances might be if the amount paid by the principal upon his release is small in respect of the total indebtedness and there are circumstances known to the parties (guarantor, debtor and principal) indicating that the creditor would be seeking additional sums from the guarantor. Additionally, the fact that the guarantor has provided an additional security may also be a factor indicating the creditor does not intend to give up his (secured) rights against the guarantor upon a release of the principal.[66]

(c) A "reservation of rights" clause in the contract of guarantee

There is clear authority that a clause in the original contract of   **6–74**
guarantee can preserve a right of action against the guarantor.[67] In *Perry v National Provincial Bank of England*,[68] the guarantor mortgaged certain deeds to the bank to secure the indebtedness of a partnership customer, and the bank, without reference to the guarantor, released the customer from all further liability under an arrangement whereby it obtained instead debentures in a limited company incorporated to take over the assets of the original business. The guarantor claimed to be released from liability on the ground that, as the bank had released the principal debtor, his liability under the guarantee was discharged. The argument was rejected because the guarantee (embodied in the mortgage documents) contained a clause authorising the bank "to compound with and give time for payment of and accept compositions from and make any other arrangements with the debtors". In the words of Cozens-Hardy M.R.:

"it is perfectly possible for a surety to contract with a creditor in the suretyship instrument that notwithstanding any composition, release, or

---

[65] *The Times*, December 16, 1993.
[66] See this argument advanced in *Finley v Connell Associates* [1999] Lloyd's Rep. P.N. 895 at 907.
[67] *Perry v National Provincial Bank of England* [1910] 1 Ch. 464; *Cowper v Smith* (1838) 4 M. & W. 519; 150 E.R. 1534; *Union Bank of Manchester Ltd v Beech* (1865) 3 H. & C. 672; 159 E.R. 695; *Greene King plc v Stanley* [2001] EWCA Civ 1966 at para.77; *Bank of Adelaide v Lorden* (1970) 45 A.L.J.R. 49; *Fletcher Organisation Pty Ltd v Crocus Investments Pty Ltd* [1988] 2 Qd. R. 517 (concerning the release of a co-surety).
[68] [1910] 1 Ch. 464.

arrangement the surety shall remain liable although the principal does not."[69]

6–75   Although the law is clearly settled, it should be observed that the conclusion the courts have reached is arguably inconsistent with a number of earlier cases and, in particular, with the view of the Privy Council in *Commercial Bank of Tasmania v Jones*.[70] In that case, there was a novation—the creditor giving the debtor an absolute release and accepting a third party in his place. The Privy Council regarded the fact that there had been an absolute release of the debtor, rather than a mere covenant not to sue him, as important in coming to a conclusion that the guarantor was discharged in spite of a reservation of rights clause contained in the agreement of guarantee:

> "It may be taken as settled law that where there is an absolute release of the principal debtor, the remedy against the surety is gone because the debt is extinguished, and where such actual release is given no right can be reserved because the debt is satisfied, and no right of recourse remains when the debt is gone."[71]

6–76   It has been seen that when the reservation of rights clause is contained in the agreement of release between creditor and debtor it was at one time treated as void because the clause was treated as being incompatible with the absolute release. This passage appears to apply that reasoning to a situation where the reservation of rights clause is contained in the guarantee. The result would be that the reservation of rights clause in the guarantee would only be valid if the agreement between the creditor and the debtor is worded as a covenant not to sue rather than a release. The application of the reasoning of the Privy Council to the facts in *Perry v National Provincial Bank of England* would have rendered the reservation of rights clauses ineffective, because it is clear that absolute releases were given to the debtors in that case.[72] The releases could not be construed as covenants not to sue as the releases themselves did not contain reservation of rights clauses.

6–77   In *Perry v National Provincial Bank of England*, the court distinguished *Commercial Bank of Tasmania v Jones* on the ground that the acts done by the bank in the latter case did not fall within the meaning of the clause in the guarantee.[73] Yet this distinction is of doubtful validity because the relevant clause stated expressly that the guarantee was to continue notwithstanding that there was a "release" or "discharge",[74] and that is what occurred, even though a third party took on the liabilities. Whatever the merits of this argument, however, it is now

---

[69] *ibid.*, at 473.
[70] [1893] A.C. 313. See also *Re Mount Costigan Lead & Silver Mining Co Ltd* (1896) 17 L.R. (NSW) Eq. 80 at 91 *per* Manning J.
[71] [1893] A.C. 313 at 316.
[72] See *per* Cozens-Hardy M.R. in *Perry v National Provincial Bank of England* [1910] 1 Ch. 464 at 474.
[73] [1910] 1 Ch. 464 at 476 *per* Fletcher-Moulton L.J.
[74] See the clause set out in *Commercial Bank of Tasmania v Jones* [1893] A.C. 313 at 314. See also *Re Mount Costigan Lead & Silver Mining Co Ltd* (1896) 17 L.R. (NSW) Eq. 80.

overwhelmingly clear from the authorities that a reservation of rights clause embodied in the guarantee will be upheld whether the debtor is absolutely released by the creditor or whether the creditor covenants not to sue the debtor.[75]

A common type of clause which is inserted in the guarantee to preserve the liability of the guarantor in the event of a release of the principal debtor states "the creditor may at any time and from time to time compound with or release or discharge the principal debtor without impairing or releasing the guarantor".[76] The reference to a "composition" in such a clause has been defined as a "form of transaction ... by which an insolvent debtor ... contracts with his creditors as a body for his discharge extrajudicially, or for his reinstatement in his estate, in consideration of his payment to the creditors of an agreed proportion of their several debts".[77] It is probably sufficient in order to come within the term "composition" for the creditors to agree to take, in satisfaction of the debt, property of the debtor which, depending on the amount subsequently realised, might or *might not* be less than the full value of the debt.[78] But the word "composition" will probably not embrace an unqualified release of the debtor,[79] so in that event the guarantor will be discharged unless there is a reference to a "release" or "discharge". It should be noted that the clause not only contains a stipulation that the creditor is authorised to "release" or "compound with" the debtor, but also a statement by the guarantor that the guarantor's liability is to continue despite such action by the creditor. It may not be sufficient that the guarantee contains the former statement and not the latter, so that the courts are forced to draw the implication from the mere fact of the guarantor's authorisation of the release that the guarantor's liability should continue.

6–78

The above clause is often combined with a clause with permits the creditor "at all times ... to treat the guarantor as a principal debtor".[80] In New Zealand the view has been taken that this clause standing alone is effective to preserve the liability of the guarantor in the event of a release of the principal, even when there is no specific authority given to the creditor "to compound with or release or discharge the principal debtor" in the terms of the clause set out in the previous paragraph.[81] But there is

6–79

---

[75] See the authorities cited above, n.67.
[76] As similar examples, see *Cowper v Smith* (1838) 4 M. & W. 519; 150 E.R. 1534; *Perry v National Provincial Bank of England* [1910] 1 Ch. 464; *Bank of Adelaide v Lorden* (1970) 45 A.L.J.R. 49.
[77] *Aitken's Trustees v Bank of Scotland* [1944] S.C. 270 at 278.
[78] *Union Bank of Australia v Rogan* (1892) 13 L.R. (NSW) 285.
[79] See *Aitken's Trustees v Bank of Scotland* [1944] S.C. 270 at 278. Similarly, a clause by which the guarantor agrees that "any favour, grace or consideration" shown to the principal debtor will not discharge the debtor will probably not embrace an unqualified release: *Fletcher Organisation Pty Ltd v Crocus Investments Pty Ltd* [1988] 2 Qd. R. 517, although the decision concerned the release of a co-guarantor. Note also the dissenting judgment of Williams J.
[80] *Bond & Bond Ltd v Rothery* [1935] G.L.R. 179.
[81] *ibid.*, at 180; *General Produce Co v United Bank Ltd* [1979] 2 Lloyd's Rep. 255 at 259, where Lloyd J. appears inclined to this view. The clause in the latter case did, however, contain further specific wording referring to a continuation of the guarantor's liability despite a release, and the facts of the case were concerned with a release of the principal by operation of law. See also *Bank of New Zealand v Baker* [1926] N.Z.L.R. 462 at 487, which would also support the efficacy of such a clause standing alone to preserve the liability of the guarantor.

no decisive authority and the creditor would be unwise to rely on such a clause in isolation. This is especially so in view of other statements which have stressed that the effect of a "principal debtor" clause is not to enlarge the ambit of the guarantee[82] or to convert the contract of guarantee into an indemnity,[83] but merely to avoid the consequences of the guarantor being discharged where the creditor gives time or other indulgence to the principal.[84]

6–80   The effect of a clause in a contract of guarantee by which the guarantor promises to remain liable despite a release of, or compromise with, the principal will be different from when the agreement is contained in the agreement of release between creditor and debtor. One of the major reasons why a release of the principal debtor discharges the guarantor is that, if it were otherwise, the guarantor could claim an indemnity from the debtor on payment to the creditor, thus rendering the release illusory from the principal debtor's point of view. This would result in a fraud on the debtor.[85] This principle is not seen to be infringed where the reservation of rights clause is contained in the agreement of release because the debtor's assent to the clause constitutes an implied agreement to the continuation of the guarantor's right of indemnity against the debtor.[86] This implication cannot be drawn where the clause is contained in a separate agreement of guarantee because usually the debtor will not have assented to the clause.[87]

6–81   The issue therefore arises whether a reservation of rights contained in the guarantee should deprive the guarantor of his right of indemnity. On one view this may be the consequential result. In *Watts v Aldington*[88] Neil L.J. was of the view that, although it was "legitimate" to imply a term into the release of one joint debtor that there should be a reservation of rights against the other there was no "basis for making any implication as regards possible contribution rights"[89] by the latter.

6–82   Nonetheless, it is not clear why the guarantor should be deprived of his right of indemnity against the principal simply as an inference from

---

In Australia, see *Fletcher Organisation Pty Ltd v Crocus Investments Pty Ltd* [1988] 2 Qd. R. 517, where there is some support for the view that, the principal debtor clause is sufficient alone (see *per* Shepardson J. at 526–527, Ryan J. at 543), but the relevant clause also contained a promise by which the guarantor waived his rights in respect of the provisions of the instrument (see clause 6). The decision was also concerned with the release of a co-guarantor, not the principal debtor.

[82] *Parker v Bayly* [1927] G.L.R. 265 at 268.

[83] See above, para.1–101.

[84] *Heald v O'Connor* [1971] 1 W.L.R. 497 at 503. Note also that in *Payton v SG Brookes & Sons Pty Ltd* [1977] W.A.R. 91 it was specifically left open whether such a clause even had that effect.

[85] *Cole v Lynn* [1942] 1 K.B. 142 at 146; *Mercantile Bank of Sydney v Taylor* (1891) 12 L.R. (NSW) 252 at 260 per Windeyer J.; *Re Natal Investment Co (Nevill's Case)* (1870) 6 Ch. App. 43 at 47 *per* Mellish L.J.

[86] *Cole v Lynn* [1942] 1 K.B. 142 at 146.

[87] If the debtor does assent (as in *Atkins v Revell* (1860) 1 De G.F. & J. 360; 45 E.R. 398) then the right of indemnity should be preserved.

[88] *The Times*, December 16, 1993.

[89] The term "contribution" is probably being used here in a general sense to embrace the right of indemnity against a co-debtor.

a bare promise made *to the creditor* in the guarantee that he will remain liable despite a release, especially if he does not also consent to being treated as a "principal debtor". But if the guarantor is permitted to exercise his right of indemnity a "fraud on the debtor" will result since the debtor's legitimate expectation (arising from the release) is that his liability is extinguished. There is no easy answer to this question, but in the authors' view a reservation of rights clause in the guarantee should generally (and subject to the particular factual matrix of the contract) be interpreted as promise by the guarantor that his liability should continue but that his right of indemnity against the debtor should not.[90]

(d) Agreement by the guarantor to the continuation of liability

If there is no reservation of rights clause contained in the contract of guarantee, the creditor may seek to obtain the consent of the guarantor to the continuation of the guarantor's liability at the same time that the creditor releases the debtor. It has been held that such consent, when it is given before the release, will be effective to preserve the guarantor's liability, even if given verbally.[91] The relevant authority speaks of a binding agreement between guarantor and creditor.[92] If the guarantor requested the release, it can be argued this is so because the guarantor's promise to remain liable on the existing guarantee would be supported by the consideration of the creditor's release of the debtor.[93] This conclusion, however, is inconsistent with other authorities[94] which on similar facts have not adopted such an approach but have clearly held that when the release is in writing, parol evidence cannot be adduced to prove a contractual promise by the guarantor to remain liable. It has been suggested[95] that these cases are wrong, because the parol evidence is not being used to add to or vary the main contract, but to establish a separate collateral contract between the guarantor and the creditor. The parol evidence rule is not, therefore, infringed.

Another way in which the guarantor might be rendered liable in these circumstances is as a result of the application of the principles of estoppel, the guarantor being estopped from pleading the release because the guarantor had acknowledged that, notwithstanding the release, liability

6–83

6–84

---

[90] There is no definitive authority on this point, although in the Australian case *of Bank of Adelaide v Lorden* (1970) 45 A.L.J.R. 49 at 52 Barwick C.J. was of the view that the debtor when released was "effectively discharged ... from *any* further liability to pay *any* sum on account of that debt".

[91] *Davidson v M'Gregor* (1841) 8 M. & W. 755; 151 E.R. 1244. See also *Re Blakely Ex p. Harvey* (1854) 4 De G.M. & G. 881; 43 E.R. 752.

[92] *Davidson v M'Gregor* (1841) 8 M. & W. 755 at 767–768; 151 E.R. 1244 at 1249–1250.

[93] The pleadings in *Davidson v M'Gregor* (1841) 8 M. & W. 755; 151 E.R. 1244 did allege this request.

[94] *Brooks v Stuart* (1839) 9 Ad. & E. 854; 112 E.R. 1437; *Cocks v Nash* (1832) 9 Bing. 341; 131 E.R. 643 (a case of joint debtors but, in this context, the principles are the same). In both these cases the pleadings alleged that the release was at "the request" of the guarantor.

[95] G. L. Williams, *Joint Obligations* (1949), p.128, para.60.

under the guarantee should continue.[96] The creditor then relies on this assurance by releasing the principal debtor.

6–85 If the guarantor's consent to the continuation of liability is given after the creditor's release of the debtor, it has been said that the guarantor's liability will still revive if the guarantor makes a new promise to perform the obligation with knowledge of the release.[97] It is irrelevant that the promise is not supported by consideration.[98] This conclusion is based on authorities which have held that, where the creditor varies the principal contract by giving time to the principal[99] or impairs a security given by the principal,[1] the discharge of the guarantor, which would be the normal result of these actions, can be prevented by the subsequent consent of the guarantor. The basis of the continuation of the guarantor's liability in these situations is that the guarantor's subsequent promise "is valid, not as the constitution of a new, but the revival of an old debt".[2] But a giving of time or the impairment of a security given by the principal is unlike a release because those actions do not extinguish the debt. The guarantor is discharged because the guarantor's position has been prejudiced.[3] The reason for the continuation of the guarantor's liability based on a "revival of an old debt" is, therefore, less readily applied where the debt has been effectively extinguished by the release. Any argument that the subsequent consent is binding because it operates as an estoppel[4] may also fail because the release has already been given and the creditor could not therefore be said to be acting upon the guarantor's promise to remain liable.[5] But the position may be otherwise if there is some other evidence of reliance.

(v) Partial release

6–86 The creditor, instead of releasing the principal debtor absolutely, may release the principal debtor from only a portion of the debt, making it clear that liability remains for the balance. In this situation, it is considered that the guarantor will only be partially released by an amount corresponding

---

[96] A suggestion first made in G. L. Williams, *Joint Obligations* (1949), p.128, para.60.
[97] *Bogart v Robertson* (1905) 11 O.L.R. 295 at 306.
[98] *Mayhew v Crickett* (1818) 2 Swan 185; 36 E.R. 585. If there is consideration, this would constitute a new agreement, although if not in writing, it would be unenforceable: see above, Ch. 3.
[99] *Smith v Winter* (1838) 4 M. & W. 454; 150 E.R. 1507; *Phillips v Foxall* (1872) L.R. 7 Q.B. 666 at 676–677 *per* Quain J.
[1] *Mayhew v Crickett* (1818) 2 Swan. 185; 36 E.R. 585.
[2] *Mayhew v Crickett* (1818) 2 Swan. 185 at 191; 36 E.R. 585 at 587. It has been said that an analogous situation exists when a promise or acknowledgment may revive a debt already barred by the Statute of Limitations: *Wilson v Cristall* (1922) 63 D.L.R. 187 at 192 and see below, para.7–49, where consent to a variation is discussed.
[3] See the topic of discharge on these bases discussed below, paras 7–59 and 8–46.
[4] Estoppel has also been suggested as a basis for the continued liability of the guarantor where consent is given subsequent to a variation of the principal contract: see below, para.7–50.
[5] This is one of the requirements of an estoppel: see J. Beatson, *Anson's Law of Contract*, pp.112–126, esp. pp.115–117, heading "Alteration of position".

to the extent of the release of the principal.[6] Although the agreement of release constitutes a variation of the principal contract, such a variation does not lead to an absolute discharge of the guarantor because it is a variation which is obviously for the benefit of the guarantor, as it reduces the extent of the guarantor's liability.[7] The position would be different if the agreement of release with the principal in some way altered the nature of the guaranteed obligation, as, for example, where a mortgagor is released from an obligation to pay a portion of the mortgage debt *and* is also released from the covenant to insure.[8] The guarantor would then be fully discharged because the variation of the principal contract would not be one which was obviously beneficial to the guarantor.[9]

A clause in the guarantee will usually provide for the continuation of the guarantor's total liability despite a release of the principal. Ideally, such a clause should specifically refer to a "*partial* or absolute" release if the guarantor's liability is to be preserved in the event of a partial release.   **6–87**

(vi) The effect of the discharge of the principal in bankruptcy or in liquidation

Section 281(7) of the Insolvency Act 1986 expressly provides that discharge of the principal from his bankruptcy does not release any person from liability as surety for the principal or a person in the nature of such a surety. The reference to "in the nature of such a surety" probably encompasses the situation where there is no promise to be personally liable for the debt of another, but the "guarantor" simply provides a security.[10]   **6–88**

Similarly where a company is dissolved (pursuant to the Companies Act 1985, s.653) the guarantor remains liable for the obligations of the company he has guaranteed which are outstanding at the date of dissolution.[11] In the case of a company which was a lessee in *Hastings Corp v Letton*[12] it was held that the dissolution of the company was equivalent to a disclaimer, thereby discharging the guarantor of the lessee's obligation to pay the rent, but this decision cannot now stand with the House of Lord's decision *Hindcastle Ltd v Barbara Attenborough*   **6–89**

---

[6] See, in support, the Australian case of *Hancock v Williams* (1942) 42 S.R.(N.S.W.) 252. *Cf.* the view of the South Australia Law Reform Commission, *Report Relating to the Reform of the Law of Suretyship*, Report No.39 (1977), para.6. The Report quotes *Croydon Gas Co v Dickinson* (1876) 2 C.P.D. 46 at 51 as authority, but that case does not appear to support the Report's conclusion.

[7] *Croydon Gas Co v Dickinson* (1876) 2 C.P.D. 46 at 51 *per* Amphlett J.A. As to the effect of a variation of the principal contract, see below, Ch. 7.

[8] This example is given by Jordan C.J. in *Hancock v Williams* (1942) 42 S.R. (NSW) 252 at 257.

[9] See below, paras 7–01 to 7–03.

[10] See *Bank of New Zealand v Baker* [1926] N.Z.L.R. 462. Apart from the operation of the insolvency legislation it has been held that the creditor may take steps to bankrupt the principal without discharging the guarantor: *Browne v Carr* (1831) 7 Bing. 508; 131 E.R. 197; *Rainbow v Juggins* (1880) 5 Q.B.D. 422.

[11] *Re Fitzgeorge, Ex p. Robson* [1905] 1 K.B. 462.

[12] [1908] 1 K.B. 378.

Associates,[13] which held that a disclaimer of a lease does not operate to discharge a guarantor.

6–90   This general principle regarding discharge in bankruptcy or liquidation is subject to the effect of particular provisions either in the principal contract or the guarantee. For example, the principal contract may be conditional upon the principal remaining solvent so that upon the principal's bankruptcy or liquidation, the principal's liability will terminate and, therefore, the guarantor's liability will also determine.[14] Today this is unlikely in any practical sense, but, less obviously, particular drafting may effect the liability of the guarantor upon bankruptcy or liquidation. Thus in *Perar BV v General Surety & Guarantee Co Ltd*[15] the terms of a building contract provided that the employment of the contractor was to automatically determine in the event of the contractor having an administrative receiver appointed. This meant that, after such appointment, the guarantor of the contractor's obligations could not be liable for non-performance by the contractor, since the automatic determination meant it was not a breach of contract.

6–91   Some difficulty has also been occasioned by the words "due" and "owing". Thus a guarantor for the payment of interest whilst the principal sum remains either "due"[16] or "owing"[17] has been held to be released from liability for interest accruing after the principal debtor's discharge from bankruptcy, because after discharge the principal is no longer "due" or "owing", as the case may be. The same reasoning is probably applicable when a company is dissolved. Indeed, in *Re Moss Ex p. Hallett*,[18] in respect of the word "due", Bigham J. was of the view that a guarantee of the payment of interest will terminate at the earlier stage of adjudication of bankruptcy (or, presumably, winding up). Bigham J. stated:[19]

> "In my opinion, as soon as the principal debtor became bankrupt, which has happened, it would be untrue to say that the principal money remained due from him to [the creditor]. The only liability then existing was the liability on the trustee in bankruptcy in administering the bankrupt's estate to pay to [the creditor] a dividend in respect of that debt".

But these interpretations of the words "due" or "owing" will not relieve the guarantor from liability from all the principal sum, because it would be contrary to s.281(7) of the Insolvency Act 1986, (set out above)

---

[13] [1997] A.C. 70. Note that *Hastings Corp v Letton* was not followed in *Re Strathblaine* [1948] 1 Ch. 228. For further discussion see G. Andrews and R. Millett *Law of Guarantees* (3rd ed., 2000), p.286.
[14] *Smith v Watson* (1899) 1 G.L.R. 290.
[15] (1994) 66 B.L.R. 72. See also *Re Distributors & Warehousing Ltd* [1985] 1 B.C.C. 99, 570 at 99, 585.
[16] *Re Moss, Ex.p. Hallett* [1905] 2 K.B. 307; *Quainoo v NZ Breweries Ltd* [1991] 1 N.Z.L.R. 161.
[17] *Perrott v Newton King Ltd* [1933] N.Z.L.R. 1131, although there is no English decision on the effect of the word "owing".
[18] [1905] 2 K.B. 307.
[19] *ibid.*, at 310. See also *Re Gunson* [1966] N.Z.L.R. 187. *Cf.*, however, *Quainoo v NZ Breweries Ltd* [1991] 1 N.Z.L.R. 161 at 171–172.

expressly providing for the continuation of the principal's liability despite the discharge of the principal[20]

In any event, as regards guarantees in respect of the payment of interest, they can easily be drafted so as to avoid the difficulties occasioned by the use of the words "due" and "owing". Thus if the guarantor's obligation is expressed to be conditional upon *repayment* of the debt, a discharge in bankruptcy has no effect on the guarantor's liability because, even after that event, there has been no repayment.[21] Even where the words "due" or "owing" do appear, it is possible, depending on the exact terms of the guarantee, to adopt an interpretation that does not release the guarantor. Thus where the guarantee related to "the payment of all moneys which were *then* or should *thereafter become* due and owing", the guarantee was held to apply to debts immediately they became "due and owing". There was no stipulation that the debts had to continue to be "due and owing", so that the liquidation of the principal debtor had no effect on the liability of the guarantor since the debts had accrued at some previous point of time.[22]   **6–92**

Although a discharge in bankruptcy or a liquidation will generally not discharge the guarantor—that is, apart from the difficulties occasioned by the particular wording discussed in the previous paragraphs—it probably does not have the effect of making a guarantor liable for payment at a time earlier than that stipulated in the guarantee. If, for example, a company's liability for repayment of a debt only arises at a future date subsequent to the company's liquidation, the guarantor of that liability is not liable until that date arrives, even though it is probable that the company will not be able to repay the debt at that time.[23] This view has been advanced because it cannot be said with certainty that at the date for payment the debtor will make default, rendering the guarantor liable, since a change in circumstances may put the company in sufficient funds to enable it to pay the debt.   **6–93**

(vii) Voluntary schemes of arrangement

Voluntary arrangements in bankruptcy are governed by Pt XIII of the Insolvency Act 1986. In particular, the effect of such a scheme is prescribed by s.260(2) of the Act: **6–94**

"The approved arrangement—(a) takes effect as if made by the debtor at the meeting, and (b) binds every person who in accordance with the rules had notice of, and was entitled to vote at, the meeting (whether or not he was present or represented at it) as if he were a party to the arrangement."

---

[20] See also, in overseas jurisdictions, *Quainoo v NZ Breweries Ltd* [1991] 1 N.Z.L.R. 161 (New Zealand); *Bank of Montreal v McFatridge* (1959) 17 D.L.R. (2d) 557 (Canada); *Australian Credit Union v Pollard* (1991) A.S.C. 56, 093 (Australia).

[21] *Re Fitzgeorge, Ex p. Robson* [1905] 2 K.B. 307 at 310 (in argument); *Jowitt v Callaghan* (1938) 38 SR (NSW) 512 at 523.

[22] *Guthrie v Motor Credits Ltd* (1963) 37 A.L.J.R. 167 at 168. See also *Bank of Adelaide v Lorden* (1970) 45 A.L.J.R. 49 for a similar type of drafting.

[23] See the Australian case of *Re Sheezal, Ex p. Bercove* (1968) 11 F.L.R. 366 at 371.

There is no specific provision in this section governing the effect of a voluntary arrangement by the principal on the guarantor's liability. Indeed, there are competing policy considerations as to whether or not the guarantor should be discharged by such an arrangement. On the one hand, it might be argued that the liability of the guarantor should be preserved since otherwise a creditor might be dissuaded from voting in favour of a voluntary arrangement out of concern that he will lose his rights against his surety.[24] On the other hand, an argument favouring the release of the co-guarantor is that it is in the interests of the debtor that he should be able to propose a scheme under which he will obtain a complete release of his liabilities, including rights of contribution from any surety, or co-debtor, and that the scheme should not be frustrated by an action by a co-debtor or a surety enforcing rights of indemnity or contribution.[25]

6–95   In *Johnson v Davies*[26] the Court of Appeal, favouring the latter argument, held that an absolute release of a principal debtor pursuant to a voluntary arrangement in bankruptcy discharged the guarantor of the principal's obligation. In other words, it was equivalent to a consensual arrangement outside bankruptcy proceedings, which has the same effect of discharging the principal.[27] The result was derived from the wording of s.260(2), which did not purport, directly, to impose the arrangement on a dissenting creditor whether or not he has agreed to its terms; rather, he is bound by the arrangement as the result of a statutory hypothesis that requires him to be treated as if he had consented to the arrangement. Consequently, the legislature must be taken to have intended that the question whether the debtor and the co-debtors and sureties are discharged by the arrangement is to be answered by construing its terms as if they were the terms of a consensual agreement between the debtor and all those creditors who must be treated as being consenting parties.[28]

6–96   Another compelling factor was that s.260(2) itself did not refer to the preservation of the surety's liability, in sharp contrast to specific statutory provisions preserving his liability in the Bankruptcy Act 1914[29] and its predecessor, the Bankruptcy Act 1883.[30] This was especially so, since s.281 (7) of the Insolvency Act 1986 (set out above)[31] dealing with a statutory release from bankruptcy did include this earlier provision. Thus Chadwick L.J. concluded:[32]

---

[24] See *Johnson v Davies* [1999] Ch. 117 at 138.
[25] *ibid.* Now see s.263A of the Insolvency Act 1986 in respect of fast track voluntary arrangements as introduced by the Enterprise Act 2002.
[26] [1999] Ch. 117. and disapproving Jacobs J. in *RA Securities Ltd v Mercantile Credit Co Ltd* [1994] B.C.C. 598. See also, *March Estates plc v Gunmark Ltd* [1996] 2 B.C.L.C. 1.
[27] See above, para.6–53.
[28] Note that a creditor who is prejudiced by the decision of the majority to approve proposals which have the effect of releasing a co-debtor against whom he would otherwise have recourse can apply to the court, under s.262 of the Insolvency Act 1986, for the approval of the meeting to be revoked.
[29] s.28(4).
[30] s.30(4).
[31] See above, para.6–88.
[32] [1999] Ch. 117 at 131.

"It seems clear, therefore, that when the Act of 1986 was enacted the legislature was well aware of the problem: that is to say, that one consequence of releasing the debtor from debts owed to his creditors was that, under the general law, that release would or might have the effect of releasing co-debtors and sureties in respect of the same debts. In the context of a statutory release following bankruptcy that problem was dealt in the same way as it had been in legislation for the past 100 years. In the context of a release contained in a voluntary arrangement, which could be imposed on a dissenting creditor under Part VIII of the Act of 1986, the legislature did not adopt—or, at the least, did not adopt in express terms—the precedent which was offered by earlier legislature in relation to compositions or arrangements in bankruptcy proceedings. There is, to my mind, a strong inference that that was the result of a deliberate decision that, in this respect, voluntary arrangements should be treated as—and have the same consequences as—consensual deeds of arrangement, and not be regarded as a substitute for compositions or arrangements in bankruptcy proceedings".[33]

Thus as a matter of principle, a voluntary arrangement made pursuant to Pt.VIII of the Insolvency Act 1986 and discharging a debtor will also discharge his guarantor. But in each case it needs to be determined as a matter of construction whether or not there is an express or implied reservation of rights against the guarantor preserving his liability. Parol evidence is admissible to prove such a reservation, at least if the scheme of arrangement is ambiguous in its terms.[34] Indeed, as we have seen,[35] in *Johnson v Davies*[36] itself the arrangement was construed as preserving the guarantor's liability.

(viii) The effect of a release where the contract is one of indemnity

If the agreement is not one of guarantee, but can be categorised as a promise to indemnify the creditor against loss arising from the consequences of entering into a transaction, it is probable that the indemnifier will be discharged by the release of the debtor. One view is that "a liability to indemnify against a liability which has no existence, and

6–97

---

[33] Note also that certain cases decided under the Bankruptcy Act 1869 had held that arrangements made under the Bankruptcy Act 1869 did discharge the surety (See *Megrath v Gray, Gray v Megrath* (1874) L.R. 9 C.P. 216; *Ellis v Wilmot* (1874) L.R. 10 Ex. 10; *Ex p. Jacobs* (1875) 10 Ch. App. 211). The Court of Appeal in *Johnson v Davies* [1999] Ch. 117 at 132–137 thought that they had no bearing on voluntary arrangements under the Insolvency Act 1986 because under the Bankruptcy Act 1869 discharge of the debtor arose by operation of law and not as a result of the terms of the arrangement.

[34] *Greene King plc v Stanley* [2001] EWCA Civ. 1966, discussed above, para.6–70.

[35] See above, paras 6–72 to 6–73.

[36] [1999] Ch. 117. See also *Whitehead v Household Mortgage Corp.* [2002] 1 All E.R. 319, indicating that the courts should be slow to imply a term that the creditor would not rely on its security.

which can never arise, is a contradiction in terms",[37] so that, as in the case
of a guarantor, the indemnifier will be automatically discharged by the
release. Another suggestion is that the indemnifier will be discharged only
if the release prejudices the interests of the indemnifier.[38] Many
indemnities contain clauses effectively preserving the creditor's rights
where the debtor is released, or otherwise making it plain that the
indemnifier is liable for loss sustained by the creditor in cases where the
loss has arisen from the act of the creditor in discharging the debtor.

3. DISCHARGE BY NOVATION OF THE PRINCIPAL
TRANSACTION

(i) Novation of the principal contract by which one principal debtor is substituted for another

6–98   Novation of this kind takes place when the principal debtor, the creditor
and a third party all agree that the third party shall be substituted as the
new principal debtor. The consent of all parties must be obtained to the
novation,[39] which will be binding only if it is made with the appropriate
contractual intention and if it is supported by consideration, which is
usually the mutual release of existing obligations and the undertaking of
fresh obligations.[40] The effect of the novation is not to assign or transfer a
liability but to extinguish the original contract and replace it by another.
Thus the original debtor is released and it follows that, as in the case of a
simple release of the principal by the creditor, the guarantor is fully
discharged by such an agreement.[41]

6–99   Most of the situations involving a novation of this kind arise out of the
amalgamation of companies or changes in partnerships, the question being
whether, as a matter of fact, the creditor contracting with the company or
the firm accepts the new company or the new firm as its debtor in place of
the old company or firm.[42] The fact of novation may be implied from acts
or conduct.[43] However, the court will not draw this inference where,

[37] *Re Perkins* [1898] 2 Ch. 182 at 189 *per* Lindley M.R. See similarly *Taylor v Sanders* [1937]
V.L.R. 62 at 65 and, in the context of a statutory guarantee, *Housing Guarantee Fund Ltd v
Johnson* (unreported, Vic CA, March 17, 1995).
[38] This appears to be the approach taken by Asprey J.A. in *Total Oil Products (Aust) Pty Ltd
v Robinson* [1970] 1 N.S.W.R. 701 at 705, although on the facts the releases operated in the
indemnifier's favour. If the indemnifier is jointly or jointly and severally liable with
the debtor, the release of the debtor will, of course, discharge the indemnifier by virtue of the
general principle that the discharge of one joint contractor will discharge the other.
[39] As to novation generally, see J. Bailey, "Novation" (1999) 14 Journal of Contract Law 189
and *Chitty on Contracts* (28th ed., 1999), paras 20–084–20–087. See also *The "Tychy" (No.2)*
(unreported, July 24, 2001, CA).
[40] *R & I Bank of Western Australia Ltd v McNamee* (unreported, NSW Sup Ct, May 20,
1994).
[41] *Commercial Bank of Tasmania v Jones* [1893] A.C. 313; *Orchiston v Schlaepfer* [1924]
N.Z.L.R. 1170; *Re Mount Costigan Lead & Silver Mining Co Ltd* (1896) 17 LR (NSW) Eq 80.
[42] e.g. *Miller's Case* (1877) 3 Ch. D. 391.
[43] *Thomas v Welk* [1935] S.A.S.R. 165 at 168; *Re European Assurance Society Arbitration
Acts (Conquest's Case)* (1875) 1 Ch. D. 334; *Chatsworth Investments Ltd v Cussins
(Contractors) Ltd* [1969] 1 W.L.R. 1.

despite the existence of strong evidence to the contrary, the creditor indicates at the time of the events alleged to constitute the novation that there was to be no substitution of one debtor for another.[44] Such an indication shows a lack of agreement to a novation.

In *Commercial Bank of Tasmania v Jones*,[45] the Privy Council was of the opinion that a novation, as it involves an absolute release of the principal debtor, was incompatible with a clause contained in a guarantee preserving the creditor's rights against the guarantor. It has already been seen[46] that this reasoning was later studiously ignored in a situation where there was no novation, but merely an agreement by the creditor to release the debtor. **6–100**

Numerous authorities have held[47] that a reservation of rights clause upon a release of the principal is effective, despite this earlier view taken in *Commercial Bank of Tasmania v Jones* that the reservation of rights against the guarantor was inconsistent with an absolute release and, therefore, could not be relied upon. The legal position subsisting on a simple release should logically be equated with a novation, which also involves a release of the principal debtor. Thus, insofar as *Commercial Bank of Tasmania v Jones* suggests that a properly drafted reservation of rights clause contained in a guarantee cannot ever be effective to preserve the liability of the guarantor upon a novation, it should be regarded as a dubious authority.

Many contracts of guarantee do contain a clause whereby the guarantor is to remain reliable despite the release or discharge of the principal debtor, but such a clause might not be wide enough to embrace a release of the principal debtor arising from a novation as distinct from a simple release.[48] An effective clause would be one which referred to a "release or discharge by *novation*". This clause should render the guarantor liable for any outstanding obligations owed to the creditor before the novation, but the guarantor will not be liable for any new obligations incurred by the person who has been substituted as the debtor. This further liability will require a new guarantee, supported by consideration and evidenced in **6–101**

---

[44] See *Chitty on Contracts* (28th ed., 1999), para.23–031. As an example in the context of guarantees, see the Australian case of *Williams v Frayne* (1937) 58 C.L.R. 710 where a loan was made to a tenant of business premises, the loan being guaranteed. Successive sales of the business took place. The purchasers were entered in the accounts of the creditor so that it appeared that each new purchaser had replaced the previous one as his debtor. Despite this strong evidence indicating that the creditor had agreed to substitute each new purchaser as his debtor in respect of the balance of the advance, it was held that there was no novation because the original debtor and, indeed, the guarantor had been orally informed by the creditor when he gave approval for the first sale that the original principal debtor was to remain liable. The guarantor, therefore, also remained liable.

[45] [1893] A.C. 313.

[46] See above, paras 6–75 to 6–77.

[47] See above, para.6–74, n.67.

[48] In *Perry v National Provincial Bank of England* [1910] 1 Ch. 464 at 476, Fletcher Moulton L.J. was of the view that the clause in *Commercial Bank of Tasmania v Jones* [1893] A.C. 313 was insufficient to cover the novation in that case. Even though the clause referred to the "release" and "discharge" of the debtor, there was no reference to a "release by novation".

writing, unless the ambit of the original guarantee is such as to secure the obligations of those who might become liable by a novation.[49]

(ii) Transfer of the principal's liabilities under the principal contract

(a) Where the principal contract does not contemplate an assignment

6–102   The law does not recognise an assignment of contractual liability without the consent of the obligee.[50] Thus if the principal purports to assign the obligations arising from the principal contract without seeking the consent of the creditor, it will be ineffective. The guarantor, however, should still remain liable, although the guarantor will be discharged if a third party (the purported assignee) discharges the principal obligation by payment to the creditor.[51]

6–103   Furthermore, if the principal and the creditor agree to an assignment by the principal of the principal's contractual liability without notifying the guarantor (so as to make the assignment effective), the guarantor will probably be absolutely discharged because this will constitute a variation of the principal contract. Such a variation will discharge the guarantor, unless the variation is obviously immaterial or for the benefit of the guarantor. The introduction of another principal debtor could not be regarded as coming within these categories. If there is a condition of the guarantee that the guarantor shall be notified of any assignment and there is no such notification, the guarantor will be discharged on the alternative basis of the creditor's failure to comply with a condition of the guarantee.[52]

6–104   Conversely, if the guarantee contemplates that an assignment may take place, although the principal contract does not, the guarantor will not be absolutely discharged in the event of the creditor and the principal agreeing between themselves to an assignment as the guarantee has provided for the variation of the principal contract. But even in this case the guarantor will not be responsible for the debts of the new principal, unless they are specifically brought within the ambit of the guarantee.

---

[49] An example is the Australian decision of *Williams v Frayne* (1937) 58 C.L.R. 710 where Dixon J. (at 729) indicated that the guarantor would still have been liable even if there had been a novation because the borrower (the original principal debtor) was defined so as to include his transferees, which would have embraced future purchasers of the business.
[50] *Tolhurst v Associated Portland Cement Manufacturers Ltd* [1902] 2 K.B. 660 at 668.; *Linden Gardens Trust Ltd v Lenesta Sludge Disposals Ltd* [1994] 1 A.C. 85 at 103. See also J. Beatson, *Anson's Law of Contract* (28th ed., 2002), pp.484–485.
[51] A creditor cannot object to vicarious performance, unless prejudiced by the fact that the debtor does not perform personally: see G.H. Treitel, *The Law of Contract* (11th ed., 2003), p.756 and *British Wagon Co v Lea & Co* (1880) 5 Q.B.D. 149.
[52] Alternatively, the assignment may involve the creditor in breach of other conditions of the guarantee, for example, that possession of the goods shall remain with the original principal: e.g. *Ankar Pty Ltd v National Westminster Finance (Aust) Ltd* (1987) 162 C.L.R. 549. See below, paras 8–06 to 8–10.

(b) Where the principal contract contemplates an assignment

The principal contract may provide that the principal may assign his **6–105** interest in the contract. A common example is where the terms of a lease permit an assignment of the lessee's interest in the lease with the consent of the lessor. In this situation, the Court of Appeal in *Johnson Bros (Dyers) Ltd v Davison*[53] held, in a short judgment, that the guarantor remained liable when the lease was assigned and the assignee was unable to pay the rent. The court stressed two factors. The first was that the principal contract contemplated an assignment so that it could not be said that there was a variation of the principal contract discharging the guarantor. The second was that the guarantor knew of the terms of the lease. However, even in the absence of any actual knowledge by the guarantor of the clause in the principal contract permitting assignment, it is thought that a guarantor who undertakes to guarantee all the principal's obligations under a principal contract which permits an assignment should be deemed to be aware of the possibility of the assignment and should be regarded as having consented to it.[54]

In respect of leases of real property granted after January 1, 1996 s.5(2) **6–106** of the Landlord and Tenant (Covenants) Act 1995 operates to release a tenant from his obligations under the lease, so a guarantor of those obligations will be similarly relieved from liability.[55]

More generally, it is also possible that on its proper construction the **6–107** guarantee may still relate only to the obligations of the named principal whilst that principal is solely responsible for the obligations arising under the principal transaction. In this case the guarantor would not be liable for defaults subsequent to the assignment.

Another possibility is that, properly interpreted, the relevant documen- **6–108** tation does not constitute a mere assignment but creates significant changes to the obligations of the principal. This will constitute a variation of the principal contract thereby discharging the guarantee,[56] unless the guarantee contains clauses preserving the guarantor's liability in that event.[57]

The creditor, in order to guard against the possible assignment of the **6–109** principal's interest in the contract without reference to the guarantor, should specify in the guarantee itself that the principal may assign his interest under the principal transaction and that the guarantor shall be responsible not only for the obligations of the original principal but also the obligations of future assignees. Most guarantees of leases include a

---

[53] (1935) 79 S.J. 306.
[54] See also *Leishman v Mexted* (1991) A.N.Z. Conv. R. 394, where it was held that the guarantee applied to the duration of the lease, although there had been a deemed assignment of the lessee's interest according to the terms of the lease.
[55] See above, para.7–52 and note, especially the possibility of an authorised guarantee agreement (see below, para.6–154).
[56] *McNamee v R & I Bank Western Australia Ltd* (unreported, NSW CA, December 7, 1994). The majority (Meagher and Cole JJA) held, however, that the documentation amounted to an effective assignment of both the principal transaction and the guarantee. As to variation of the see below, Ch. 7.
[57] See below, para.7–81.

specific provision of this nature, but other wording may be interpreted as extending the guarantee to the entire lease term, including assignments during that term.[58]

(iii) Novation of the principal contract by which one creditor is substituted for another

6–110   Just as it is possible by novation to substitute one debtor for another, it is also possible by novation to substitute one creditor for another, the original contract being extinguished and replaced by another with a new creditor. In *Bradford Old Bank Ltd v Sutcliffe*,[59] the Court of Appeal was of the view that a novation by which an existing and ascertained debt is transferred to another creditor stands on a different footing from a novation by which the original debtor is released from the debt, and that a novation of the former type does not discharge the guarantor.[60] The reasoning given was that the position of the guarantor, whose liability is already ascertained, is not prejudiced by the novation, it being a "matter of no consequence to the surety to whom he has to pay [the debt]".[61] The Court of Appeal saw no difference in effect between an assignment by the creditor of his rights under the principal contract, where the dominant view is that the guarantor will not be released,[62] and a novation transferring the debt to another creditor. The two situations should, therefore, have the same consequence of preserving the liability of the guarantor.[63] Although this result is to be supported, it may be questioned whether it is theoretically correct. An assignment of the creditor's interest in the principal contract does not extinguish the original contract, but a novation does have this effect. Thus upon a novation, but not an assignment, the contract which the guarantee originally secured and upon which it depends no longer exists.

6–111   If the view expressed in *Bradford Old Bank Ltd v Sutcliffe* is correct and the guarantor remains liable, the new creditor will only be able to enforce the guarantee if it is assigned to the new creditor or if there is a novation of the contract of guarantee itself.

(iv) Assignment of the creditor's interest in the principal contract

6–112   The novation of the principal obligation whereby one creditor replaces another should be contrasted with the assignment of the

---

[58] See *Estates Gazette Ltd v Benjamin Restaurants Ltd* [1994] 1 W.L.R. 1528. *Cf. Johnsey Estates v Webb* [1990] E.G. 84 and see the discussion above, para.5–48.
[59] [1918] 2 K.B. 833.
[60] *ibid.*, at 841–842 *per* Pickford L.J., 846–847 *per* Bankes L.J. Scrutton L.J., at 852, expressly left the matter open.
[61] *ibid.*, at 842 *per* Pickford L.J.
[62] The question of assignment is discussed below, section (iv).
[63] [1918] 2 K.B. 833 at 842–843 *per* Pickford L.J.

principal obligation by the creditor.[64] Generally there is no restriction upon the creditor assigning the principal contract which is guaranteed. It cannot be argued that this prejudices the guarantor because it is immaterial, from the guarantor's point of view, to whom the guarantor owes the obligation.[65] It is possible that if the principal contract prohibits an assignment and the creditor and the principal alter its terms to permit an assignment the guarantor may be discharged on the basis that there has been a variation of the principal contract, but even here it is arguable that the variation is immaterial so that the guarantor will remain liable.

Generally, therefore, it is clear that if the principal obligation is **6–113** assigned and the benefit of the guarantee is also assigned, the assignee may enforce both the principal obligation and the guarantee.[66] The assignor will not, of course, then be able to enforce the guarantee.[67] An exception to this general rule is where the guarantee is construed as a guarantee of the performance of the obligations under the main contract only so long as those obligations are owed to the original creditor.[68] The guarantee will then be unenforceable by the assignee of the principal transaction, but it will be unusual for a contract of guarantee to be construed in this way.[69]

In order for the assignee to enforce the guarantee, no notice of the **6–114** assignment of the principal obligation need be given to the guarantor,[70] but if notice is not given, the guarantor may satisfy the obligation under the guarantee by paying the original creditor.[71] Notice to the guarantor of the assignment of the guarantee will usually be necessary to make the assignment effective,[72] but is otherwise unnecessary.[73]

---

[64] The major distinction between an assignment and a novation is that all the parties must consent to a novation and a new contract is established in place of the old contract. For an assignment, the consent of all the parties is unnecessary: see *Chitty on Contracts* (28th ed., 1999), paras 20-085–20-086.
[65] In *McNamee v R & I Bank Western Australia Ltd* (unreported, NSW CA, 7 December 1994), however, Mahoney JA (dissenting) considered that, exceptionally, a guarantee might be construed to inure for the personal benefit of the person named as creditor in the guarantee: "It is understandable that a guarantor may be content to bind himself to a creditor of known repute but not to one who is, *e.g.* regarded as 'a loan shark'."
[66] *Wheatley v Bastow* (1855) 7 De G.M. & G. 261; 44 E.R. 102; *Bradford Old Bank Ltd v Sutcliffe* [1918] 2 K.B. 833 at 841; *International Leasing Corp (Vic) Ltd v Aiken* [1967] 2 N.S.W.R. 427 at 439 *per* Jacobs J.A., 450–451 *per* Asprey J.A.
[67] *International Leasing Corp (Vic) Ltd v Aiken* [1967] 2 N.S.W.R. 427 at 438–439 *per* Jacobs J.A.
[68] *ibid.*, at 453 *per* Moffitt A.-J.A.
[69] *ibid.*, at 454 *per* Moffitt A.-J.A. As an example of a guarantee being construed as personal to the original creditor, see *Sheers v Thimbleby & Son* (1897) 76 L.T. 709.
[70] *Wheatley v Bastow* (1855) 7 De G.M. & G. 261 at 279–280; 44 E.R. 102 at 109; *Bradford Old Bank Ltd v Sutcliffe* [1918] 2 K.B. 833 at 841–842 *per* Pickford L.J. But in order for the principal contract to be effectively assigned, notice will usually have to be given to the principal.
[71] *Wheatley v Bastow* (1855) 7 De G.M. & G. 261 at 279–280; 44 E.R. 102 at 109.
[72] Law of Property Act 1925, s.136(1).
[73] See *Wheatley v Bastow* (1855) 7 De G.M. & G. 261 at 279–280; 44 E.R. 102 and its interpretation in *Sacher Investments Pty Ltd v Forma Stereo Consultants Pty Ltd* [1976] 1 N.S.W.L.R. 5 at 11.

6–115   Where the principal transaction is assigned without the benefit of the guarantee, it is likely that the assignor cannot enforce the guarantee.[74] The High Court of Australia in *Hutchens v Deauville Investments Pty Ltd*[75] referred with approval to comments by Jacobs J.A. in *International Leasing Corp (Vic) Ltd v Aiken*,[76] outlining the incongruous result which would occur if the position were otherwise:

> "If the debt is assigned but the guarantee is not assigned then the right in the original creditor to recover under the guarantee must at least be suspended so long as the debt is assigned. There cannot be two persons entitled to recover the amount of the same debt, one from the principal debtor, and so long as the principal debtor was in default, another from the surety. Let it be assumed otherwise and suppose that the original creditor, the assignor of the principal debt, could show that it was overdue and thereupon sued the surety. Let it be assumed that the surety paid. Then, the assignee sues the principal debtor. He must be entitled to succeed unless there are some special circumstances of estoppel in the particular case, a factor which I place to one side. The assignee under an absolute assignment could not be deprived of his right to recover from the debtor because the assignor had recovered from the surety."[77]

6–116   For similar reasons, in *Hutchens v Deauville Investments Pty Ltd* it was held that a guarantee (or the security for it) cannot be assigned without the benefit of the principal transaction.[78]

4. DISCHARGE BY THE PRINCIPAL VALIDLY TERMINATING THE PRINCIPAL CONTRACT AS A RESULT OF A STATUTORY OR CONTRACTUAL RIGHT OR UPON THE CREDITOR'S BREACH

(i) Termination arising from a statutory or contractual right

6–117   The principal debtor may validly terminate the principal contract on the basis of a provision in that contract permitting termination. Thus in *Western Credit Ltd v Alberry*[79] a hirer validly terminated a hire-purchase agreement pursuant to a clause giving him a right to do so, having fulfilled all the conditions of the agreement (including the payment of hire instalments) up to that date. It was held that the guarantor was relieved

---

[74] This may occur because there is no express assignment of the guarantee as discussed below, paras 10–173 to 10–199.
[75] (1986) 68 A.L.R. 367.
[76] [1967] 2 N.S.W.R. 427. See also *Clark v Dedvukaj* [1993] 2 Qd. R. 10 at 15.
[77] [1967] 2 N.S.W.R. 427 at 439. But the High Court did acknowledge that the legal consequences would be less clear if the assignee of the debt had rights of recourse against the original creditor in the event of default by the principal debtor.
[78] This was the factual situation in *Hutchens v Deauville Investments Pty Ltd* (1986) 68 A.L.R. 367.
[79] [1964] 1 W.L.R. 945. See also *William Hill (Southern) v Waller* [1991] E.G.L.R. 271 in the context of a lease.

from liability. Sometimes the principal may have a statutory right to terminate the principal contract and the guarantor will be similarly discharged.[80]

The effect of termination of the principal contract by the principal in the case of a guarantee will be to relieve the guarantor from any future obligations accruing subsequent to the date of termination, but this will not be the case if the contract is viewed as one of indemnity. Thus in *Goulston Discount Co Ltd v Clark*[81] the defendant "agreed to indemnify [the plaintiffs] against all losses and expenses which might be incurred by [the plaintiffs] in connection with [a] hire purchase agreement". It was held that the plaintiff was not limited to recovering simply unpaid instalments accruing prior to the termination of the hire-purchase agreement as this was an independent promise to indemnify the plaintiffs and was, therefore, unaffected by any valid termination of the hire-purchase agreement. **6–118**

(ii) Termination upon the creditor's breach

If the creditor repudiates the principal contract or is in breach of a condition of that contract, and the principal debtor accepts the repudiation or breach as terminating the contract, the guarantor will be discharged.[82] Again, the guarantor will be discharged in respect of obligations arising subsequent to the date of termination,[83] but will remain liable in respect of obligations accruing prior to that date.[84] Thus if the principal sum, with interest, is immediately payable upon the principal debtor's default without the necessity for any demand or notice, and default occurs, the guarantor's liability for the whole sum will be unaffected by the principal subsequently terminating the principal contract on the basis of the creditor's repudiation.[85] **6–119**

In this case, however, as the creditor is in breach of contract, the guarantor will be able to take advantage of the claim in damages that the **6–120**

---

[80] See *Insurance Office of Australia Ltd v Burke Pty Ltd* (1935) 35 S.R. (NSW) 438 (termination of a contract for the sale of land pursuant to a statutory right).

[81] [1967] 2 Q.B. 493. Note that there was a breach of the hire-purchase agreement in this case but the same principle is applicable in the case of a valid termination pursuant to a contractual term or a statutory right. *Cf. Unity Finance v Woodcock* [1963] 1 W.L.R. 455, which was doubted and distinguished in *Goulston Discount Co Ltd v Clark*. See also *Direct Acceptance Finance Ltd v Cumberland Furnishing Pty Ltd* [1965] N.S.W.R. 1504.

[82] *National Westminster Bank plc v Riley* [1986] F.L.R. 213, referring to repudiation, but the rule should logically apply to a breach of condition. G. Andrews and R. Millet, *Law of Guarantees* (3rd ed., 2000), p.287 cite *Watts v Shuttleworth* (1861) 7 H. 8 N. 353; 158 E.R. 510 as an example of this principle but on the facts there appeared only to be a simple breach of the principal contract. See below, para.8–110.

[83] *McDonald v Dennys Lascelles Ltd* (1933) 48 C.L.R. 457; *Elkhoury v Farrow Mortgage Services Pty Ltd (in liq)* (1993) 114 A.L.R. 541. Exceptionally, the guarantor will not be discharged because the principal's promise is independent of the creditor's obligations (*e.g.* a tenant's obligation to pay rent is independent of the landlord's covenant to repair): see *Chatfield v Elmstone Resthouse Ltd* [1975] 2 N.Z.L.R. 269 at 276.

[84] *Elkhoury v Farrow Mortgage Services Pty Ltd (in liq)* (1993) 114 A.L.R. 541.

[85] *ibid.*

principal has against the creditor provided that the principal is joined as a party to the proceedings.[86]

The dominant view is that a guarantor will not be discharged by a non-repudiatory breach of the principal contract by the creditor unless it can be shown that the relevant term of the principal contract has become a condition of the guarantee, and that there has been a departure from that condition.[87] But it has also been said that a non-repudiatory breach of the principal contract will discharge the guarantor if the breach is important in relation to the risk undertaken.[88]

5. DISCHARGE BY THE CREDITOR TERMINATING THE PRINCIPAL CONTRACT UPON THE PRINCIPAL'S BREACH

6-121   It is clear that if the creditor terminates the principal transaction according to its terms so as to discharge the principal from future liability, the guarantor of the transaction will be similarly relieved from liability. Thus if a lessor gives the lessee a notice to quit in accordance with the terms of the lease, the lessee and the guarantor of the lessee's obligations will be discharged from future liability for payment of the rent.[89] In respect of a lease, however, the mere service of a writ claiming forfeiture and possession will not in itself terminate the lease,[90] so that the guarantor of the tenant's obligations will remain liable for accrued instalments of rent between the date of service and the lease being determined in some other way (for example, by transfer to the landlord).[91]

6-122   It might reasonably be supposed, however, that if the creditor elects to terminate the principal contract for a breach of contract by the principal in circumstances in which the principal continues to remain liable to the creditor in damages, the guarantor will continue to remain liable for such liabilities. This follows from the fact that the reason for the creditor obtaining the guarantee in the first place is to secure protection against the

[86] *ibid.*, see below, para.11–46.
[87] *National Westminster Bank plc v Riley* [1986] F.L.R. 213 at 223: see below, paras 7–20 and 8–19.
[88] *The Mystery of Mercers of the City of London v New Hampshire Insurance Co* [1992] 2 Lloyd's Rep. 365 at 370, 371. And see below, para.7–20.
[89] *Giddens v Dodd* (1856) 3 Drew 485; 61 E.R. 988; *Tayleur v Wildin* (1868) L.R. 3 Exch. 303; *Associated Dairies v Pierce* (1981) 259 E.G. 562; *Apus Properties Ltd v Douglas Farrow & Co Ltd* [1989] 2 E.G.L.R. 265.
[90] *Ivory Gate Ltd v Spetale* (1998) 77 P. & C.R. 141. See also *Meadows v Clerical Medical & General Life Assurance Society* [1981] Ch. 70. Note that a guarantor has no right to claim relief against forfeiture pursuant to the Law of Property Act 1925, s.146(4) unless he has an "estate or interest in property" (*e.g.* as equitable mortgagee). See *Re Good's Lease* [1954] 1 W.L.R. 309.
[91] As in *Ivory Gate Ltd v Spetale* (1999) 77 P. & C.R. 141. But note that the lease has what has been described as a "trance like existence" (*Meadows v Clerical Medical & General Life Assurance Society* [1981] Ch. 70 at 75). Thus if the defence or any claim for relief from forfeiture fails, the forfeiture will take effect retrospectively from the date of service of the writ. It follows that the guarantor's liability for accrued instalments of rent will cease at that date, although the guarantor (depending on the terms of the guarantee) will be liable in damages to the landlord. See the following discussion, below, paras 6–127 to 6–136.

contingency of the principal's breach. However, it has been argued that, because the principal contract determines as a result of the creditor's acceptance of the debtor's breach in such circumstances, the consequence is that the obligation of the guarantor will also be extinguished.

Important to an understanding of such an argument is the distinction **6–123** between two forms of guarantee. The distinction was first drawn by Lord Reid in *Moschi v Lep Air Services Ltd*[92]:

> "With regard to making good to the creditor payments of instalments by the principal debtor there are at least two possible forms of agreement. A person might undertake no more than that if the principal debtor fails to pay any instalment he will pay it. That would be a conditional agreement. There would be no prestable obligation unless and until the debtor failed to pay. There would then on the debtor's failure arise an obligation to pay. If for any reason the debtor ceased to have any obligation to pay the instalment on the due date then he could not fail to pay it on that date. The condition attached to the undertaking would never be purified and the subsidiary obligation would never arise.
>
> On the other hand, the guarantor's obligation might be of a different kind. He might undertake that the principal debtor will carry out his contract. Then if at any time and for any reason the principal debtor acts or fails to act as required by his contract, he not only breaks his own contract but he also puts the guarantor in breach of his contract of guarantee."

An example of the first type of guarantee (hereafter called type (1)) **6–124** would be an undertaking that "in case the debtor is in default of payment I will forthwith make the payment on behalf of the debtor".[93] A guarantee of "the performance of all the terms and conditions of the contract" would be an illustration of the second type (type (2)). Sometimes the two forms of guarantee are combined. Thus in *NRG Vision Ltd v Churchfield Leasing Ltd*,[94] the guarantee was stated to be in respect of "the payment by the customer of all sums due under the agreement[95] ... *and* the due performance of all the customer's obligations thereunder".

---

[92] [1973] A.C. 331 at 344–345. See also *General Produce Co v United Bank Ltd* [1979] 2 Lloyd's Rep. 255 at 258; *Sunbird Plaza Ltd v Maloney* (1988) 166 C.L.R. 245 at 256; *Carlton Communications Plc v The Football League* [2002] EWHC 1650 (Comm.), paras 82–84.

[93] This is the second part of the guarantee in *Hyundai Heavy Industries Ltd v Papadopoulos* [1980] 1 W.L.R. 1129. See also the second part of the clause in *Sunbird Plaza Ltd v Maloney* (1988) 166 C.L.R. 245 (the payment of "all moneys payable by ... the purchaser") and the guarantee in *Keene v Devine* [1986] W.A.R. 217 (a guarantee "to make good any default on the part of [the principal] in the payment of the loan and all interest").

[94] (1988) 4 B.C.C. 56. See also *Sunbird Plaza Ltd v Maloney* (1988) 166 C.L.R. 245; *Bank of China v Hawkins* (1991) 7 A.C.S.R. 262 at 265–266; on appeal: (1992) 26 N.S.W.L.R. 562, where Gleeson C.J. (at 570) considered clauses 1 and 2 of the guarantee to be within the first category.

[95] But it is suggested below that in any event this first part of the clause should embrace a liability for damages.

6–125   If the guarantee is of type (1), the creditor's cause of action is in debt or for a money sum, the claim being for a liquidated amount.[96] In respect of a guarantee of type (2), the cause of action will generally be in damages for breach of contract, but, even in this case, an action for a liquidated sum will be appropriate if the amount claimed can be ascertained objectively by calculation.[97]

6–126   Bearing in mind the distinction between these types of guarantee, an examination is required of the effect of termination of the principal contract by the creditor on both accrued obligations and future obligations of the principal.

(i) Termination and the effect on subsequent obligations

6–127   The leading authority on this issue is *Moschi v Lep Air Services Ltd.*[98] A guarantee was given to secure a debt payable by instalments. The guarantor "personally guaranteed the performance by [the debtor] of its obligations to make the payments". When the debtor defaulted in making the payments, the creditor accepted this breach as putting an end to the contract and sought to recover the outstanding future payments from the guarantor. The guarantor argued that he was discharged from liability on the basis that, once the principal agreement had come to an end by the creditor's acceptance of the debtor's breach, the obligation of the debtor to make the future payments also ceased. Although the debtor would be liable in damages to the creditor, the guarantor argued that he had not guaranteed the obligation to pay damages but only the obligation to make the payments.[99]

6–128   The House of Lords rejected this argument on the basis that the guarantor by the terms of the guarantee had undertaken that the debtor would carry out his contract (that is, it was a guarantee of type (2), as described above). Thus the guarantor was liable in damages, the breach of the principal contract by the debtor putting the guarantor in breach of his contract of guarantee.[1] The measure of damages payable by the guarantor would be whatever sum the creditor could have recovered from the principal.[2]

6–129   The same reasoning can be applied to other types of transaction. Thus a guarantor of the "due performance ... and observance of all the ... conditions ... in [a] lease" was held liable in damages to the lessor

---

[96] As to the creditor's cause of action generally, see below, Ch. 10; *Sunbird Plaza Ltd v Maloney* (1988) 166 C.L.R. 245 at 255; *Bank of China v Hawkins* (1991) 7 A.C.S.R. 262 at 265–266; on appeal: (1992) 26 N.S.W.L.R. 562 at 569–570.

[97] *Spain v Union Steamship Co Ltd* (1923) 32 C.L.R. 138 at 142.

[98] [1973] A.C. 331.

[99] The guarantor also argued that the acceptance of the debtor's breach as putting an end to the contract was a material variation of the principal contract which extinguished the guarantor's liability. This argument was also rejected: see below, para.7–24.

[1] [1973] A.C. 331 at 345 *per* Lord Reid, 348 *per* Lord Diplock, 356–357 *per* Lord Simon of Glaisdale, 359 *per* Lord Kilbrandon.

[2] *ibid.*, at 339. But see below, para.10–208 as to the assessment of damages in an action against the guarantor.

despite the fact that the lease had been determined by the lessor's acceptance of the lessee's repudiation of the lease, which had brought the lease to an end and relieved the lessee from making future rental payments.[3] Similarly, the vendor of land recovered damages (being the deficiency on resale) from a guarantor of "the performance of the covenants and conditions by the purchaser" of the contract of sale. It was irrelevant that upon the vendor's acceptance of the purchaser's breach the contract came to an end and the vendor had no right to claim the contract price from the purchaser as a liquidated sum.[4]

As we have seen, however, Lord Reid, in *Moschi v Lep Air Services Ltd*[5]   **6–130** did indicate that if the guarantee only amounted to an undertaking by the guarantor that he would pay any instalment not paid by the debtor (a guarantee of type (1) as described above), the guarantor would be discharged in respect of subsequent instalments by a determination of the principal contract, even though the determination arises out of the creditor's acceptance of the principal's breach.

This result arises because the terms of the guarantee indicate that the   **6–131** guarantor has only promised to pay an instalment if the debtor fails to pay and that obligation to pay never arises because the contract has been determined. As a consequence, an action for a liquidated sum is not available because the payment has not yet accrued. A claim in damages is also not possible vis-à-vis the guarantor because the terms of the guarantee contemplate merely a guarantee of the instalment and not a liability in respect of damages.

No doubt this reasoning is in accordance with the general principles of   **6–132** strict construction applicable to guarantees. But given that the central object of the guarantee is to protect the creditor against the contingency of the principal's breach, the result is perhaps unfortunate. The guarantor escapes all liability in respect of future obligations subsequent to termination because of somewhat technical distinctions in drafting. It is to be hoped that the courts will strive for an interpretation of the guarantee that embraces a liability for damages as well as for the recovery of the instalment as a liquidated sum.[6] For example, a guarantee of "all sums due under the agreement", could be viewed as also imposing an obligation to *ensure* that the debtor pays those sums. Thus the agreement would be interpreted as a guarantee of both types (1) and (2) (as described above),[7] and render the guarantor liable for damages in the event of a determination of the principal contract relieving the principal (and

---

[3] *Nangus Pty Ltd v Charles Donovan Pty Ltd (in liq)* [1989] V.R. 184.
[4] *Womboin Pty Ltd v Savannah Island Trading Pty Ltd* (1990) 19 N.S.W.L.R. 364.
[5] [1973] A.C. 331 at 334–345. Note, however, that in *Moschi v Lep Air Services Ltd* itself, only Lord Reid specifically discusses this point of construction. The judgments of Lord Diplock and Lord Simon of Glaisdale, *e.g.* appear to contemplate the possibility of an action for damages against the guarantor, even though the guarantee is an undertaking to pay an instalment if the debtor fails to pay it.
[6] Note that in *Womboin Pty Ltd v Savannah Island Trading Co Pty Ltd* (1990) 19 N.S.W.L.R. 364 at 370, Rogers C.J. was of the view that "as a matter of general principle" a liability in damages should survive termination of the principal contract following the principal's breach, but his Honour's comments are limited to "a guarantor, who guaranteed *the performance* of the other party's obligation" (emphasis added). This was the case on the facts.
[7] See above, paras 6–123 to 6–125.

therefore the guarantor) from liability for the future instalments as liquidated sums.[8]

6–133   In any event, the message for the creditor is clear. The guarantee should contain a specific clause guaranteeing "the performance of the terms and conditions of the principal contract" so as to render the guarantor liable in damages in the event of a determination of the principal contract arising from the principal's breach before the date for payment of future instalments pursuant to the principal contract arises.

6–134   Even if no such clause is included and the agreement is simply a guarantee of all sums payable by the principal (type (1)), nevertheless the creditor will be able to enforce a liquidated damages clause in the principal contract (as is common in chattel leases). This will state that upon the principal's default the principal will become liable for future payments (subject to suitable rebates, for example, in the case of a lease, for the estimated rent obtainable from re-leasing for the balance of the term, and also a rebate for early repayment). In this case the guarantor's liability for the whole sum will arise on default by the principal and before the contract is determined by the creditor accepting the principal's repudiation.[9]

6–135   The benefit to the creditor of this mechanism is that the cause of action will be for a money sum (with its procedural advantages) and no duty to mitigate will arise, as would be the case in an action for damages.[10]

6–136   If the agreement is clearly one of indemnity whereby there is a promise to pay even in circumstances in which the principal never becomes liable for the future instalments, the creditor will not be affected by a determination of the principal transaction prior to the date for payment.[11]

(ii) Termination and the effect on accrued obligations

6–137   When the principal contract is terminated because of the principal's breach, payments which were due before the date of termination will be recoverable from the principal (and the guarantor) as a debt.

6–138   Some difficulty, however, arises when the accrued payments are recoverable by the principal debtor from the creditor despite the principal's breach.

6–139   In *Hyundai Heavy Industries Co Ltd v Papadopoulos*[12] a guarantee in these terms was given for the payment of sums due under a contract for the purchase and construction of a ship, the price payable by five instalments:

---

[8] In such a case, however, damages might be limited to the amount of the debt if consequential losses are not within the contemplation of the parties: see below, para.10–208.
[9] See *Direct Acceptance Finance Ltd v Cumberland Furnishing Pty Ltd* [1965] N.S.W.R. 1504 at 1509.
[10] But the danger is that the clause will be struck down as being in the nature of a penalty: see above, para.5–110.
[11] See *Direct Acceptance Finance Ltd v Cumberland Furnishing Pty Ltd* [1965] N.S.W.R. 1504.
[12] [1980] 1 W.L.R. 1129. See similarly *Hyundai Shipbuilding & Heavy Industries v Pournaras* [1978] 2 Lloyd's Rep. 502.

"we hereby jointly severally irrevocably guarantee the payment in accordance with the terms of the contract of all sums due or to become due by the buyer to you under the contract, and in case the buyer is in default of any such payment we will forthwith make the payment in default on behalf of the buyer."[13]

The buyer failed to pay the second instalment and the shipbuilding yard exercised its rights of cancellation and sued the guarantors for that instalment. The guarantors argued that they were not liable since the instalment was in any event recoverable by the buyer, just as in *Dies v British & International Mining & Finance Corp Ltd*[14] it had been held that if a contract for the sale of goods is discharged owing to the buyer's default, the seller must return any part of the price that has been pre-paid (less the amount payable in damages by the buyer). The House of Lords, however, distinguished *Dies v British & International Mining & Finance Corp Ltd*[15] since the contract for the construction and purchase of the ship (unlike a contract for the sale of goods) assumed that "the increasing proportions of the contract price represented by the five instalments bore some relation to the anticipated rate of expenditure".[16] On this basis, as the buyer remained liable for the instalment, the guarantors also remained liable.

Significantly, however, in the context of this debate the House of Lords **6–140** held that even on the assumption that the buyer was *not* liable for the instalment the guarantors nevertheless remained liable for those accrued payments.[17] There is little detailed legal analysis for this conclusion, except that any other result would offend "common sense".[18] Lord Fraser, for example, found it "difficult to believe that commercial men can have intended that the guarantors were to be released from liability for payments already due and in default just because the builder used his remedy of cancelling the shipbuilding contract for the future".[19]

It is not clear why the guarantor should have been liable for the **6–141** instalment when the buyer was not, since the principle of co-extensiveness applicable to guarantees should lead to the result that if the instalment is not payable by the purchaser it should not be recoverable from the guarantor as a liquidated sum. One explanation of the decision in *Hyundai Heavy Industries Co Ltd v Papadopoulos* is that the guarantor's obligation was construed by the court as being a liability to

---

[13] See [1980] 1 W.L.R. 1129 at 1133.
[14] [1939] 1 K.B. 724.
[15] *ibid.*
[16] [1980] 1 W.L.R. 1129, at 1148, *per* Lord Fraser. As one commentator has stated "another way of putting the same distinction, or a very similar one, would be to say that in *Dies* there was a total failure of consideration, since the buyer had received nothing, whereas in *Hyundai* there was no total failure of consideration, since the defendants had had the benefit of all the work which had been done before the date of termination": M. Furmston, *Cheshire & Fifoots Law of Contract* (13th ed., 1996), p.641.
[17] See a similar case in *Hyundai Heavy Industries v Pournaras* (1978) 2 Lloyd's Rep. 502 at 506, *per* Roskill L.J.
[18] [1980] 1 W.L.R. 1129 at 1151.
[19] *ibid.* See, similarly, Lord Edmund Davies at 1144, referring to Roskill L.J. in *Hyundai Shipbuilding & Heavy Industries v Pournaras* [1978] 2 Lloyd's Rep. 502 at 506, where he states that "the commercial purport and obvious intent and true construction of this document is such that the contrary ... is not really arguable".

pay regardless of the principal's position, that is, a primary liability in the nature of an indemnity was assumed. But the terms of the relevant instrument suggest that it was simply a guarantee.

6–142   A different and, in the authors' view, a correct approach was taken in the Australian case of *McDonald v Denys Lascelles Ltd*.[20] There the guarantee was given to secure the due payment of an instalment by a purchaser under a contract for the sale of land. Although the purchaser failed to pay the instalment when due, the purchaser still purported to rescind the contract for the vendor's breach, and this rescission was accepted by the vendor as discharging the contract. A valid rescission by the purchaser would certainly have discharged the guarantor because the purchaser would no longer have been under any liability either for payment of the instalment or in damages.

6–143   It was argued, however, that the purchaser had no valid ground for rescinding the contract, and that the contract was in fact discharged by the vendor's acceptance of the breach by the purchaser arising from his wrongful attempt to rescind. Dixon J. accepted this argument[21] and all the majority regarded the question of which party was in breach as irrelevant.[22] Their reasoning was that, as this was a contract for the sale of land and there had been a total failure of consideration (the purchaser obtaining no title to the land), the overdue instalment ceased to be payable by the purchaser when the contract was discharged and, indeed, was recoverable by him if he had paid it. It did not matter that the purchaser was in breach and subject to an action for damages by the vendor. It followed, according to the High Court, that the guarantors of the instalment must also be discharged as their liability was only accessory to the principal obligation.

6–144   Yet there is an outstanding question that was not discussed in that case. Why, on the facts of *McDonald v Dennys Lascelles Ltd*, was the guarantor not liable in damages? The answer at first glance is simple—the vendor did not bring an action for damages,[23] perhaps because the vendor could not show any loss because the value of the land had risen. More fundamentally, however, if Lord Reid's view in *Moschi v Lep Air Services Ltd*[24] (discussed above)[25] is correct, then an action for damages against the guarantor may not have been possible at all, even if the vendor had been able to show a loss of profit on the sale. The guarantee in *McDonald v Dennys Lascelles Ltd* was a guarantee to pay the instalment if the debtor did not[26] (type (1),

---

[20] (1933) 48 C.L.R. 457.

[21] *ibid.*, at 479. See also Evatt J., who dissented.

[22] *ibid.*, at 479 *per* Dixon J., 469 *per* Starke J., 467–468 *per* Rich J.

[23] Of course, the principal must be in breach of contract before an action can be maintained against the guarantor: *e.g. Hewison v Ricketts* (1884) 63 L.J.Q.B. 711 can probably be explained on the basis that the creditor by terminating a sale agreement and seizing the goods prevented the property passing so that the consideration for the sale agreement wholly failed. Thus the principal could not have been sued even in damages for the outstanding amounts owing so that the guarantor was also relieved from liability: see the explanation in *Brooks v Beirnstein* [1909] 1 K.B. 98. But in *McDonald v Dennys Lascelles* (1933) 48 C.L.R. 457, there was clearly a breach by the principal.

[24] [1973] A.C. 331.

[25] See above, paras 6–121 to 6–133.

[26] The guarantee was simply a guarantee of "the due payment" of the stipulated sum.

as described above)[27] and not a guarantee of the purchaser's obligations (type (2), as described above).[28] The result, according to Lord Reid's reasoning in *Moschi v Lep Air Services Ltd*, would be that the guarantee did not embrace a liability to pay damages but only to pay the instalment, which was no longer payable by the purchaser. The guarantor would, therefore, not be liable.

6. DISCHARGE BY DETERMINATION OF THE PRINCIPAL CONTRACT BY OPERATION OF LAW

(i) General principles

It has been seen[29] that, if the principal terminates the contract for the creditor's breach or by the exercise of a statutory right, the principal's future obligations under the contract will be discharged, and a guarantor of those obligations will also be discharged. The result is generally the same if the contract is discharged by operation of law.   **6–145**

Examples of a discharge of the guarantor's obligations by a discharge of the principal transaction by operation of law include situations where the principal contract is frustrated;[30] where a bailee is discharged from liability by theft of the goods in the bailee's care without any negligence on the part of the bailee;[31] where by statute the principal contract is determined;[32] where the parties to a lease purport to extend the term of a lease thus terminating the original lease;[33] and where the principal contract contains a provision for its automatic determination in the event of certain contingencies.[34]   **6–146**

Although in most cases the effect of a discharge of the guarantor in this way is to relieve the principal and, therefore, the guarantor of any liability for future (but not accrued) obligations,[35] it may be the case that the effect of determination of the principal transaction is to relieve the principal from all liability whether occurring before or after the determination. The guarantor will then also be relieved from all liability. This may happen as a result of the operation of statutory provisions. For example, where a finance company took possession of the goods from a hirer in breach of the   **6–147**

---

[27] See above, paras 6–123 to 6–125.
[28] *ibid.*
[29] See above, para.6–117.
[30] See the factual situation in *General Produce Co v United Bank Ltd* [1979] 2 Lloyd's Rep. 255.
[31] *Walker v British Guarantee Association* (1852) 21 L.J.Q.B. 257.
[32] *Unity Finance Ltd v Woodcock* [1963] 1 W.L.R. 455.
[33] But see *Goodaston Ltd v FH Burgess plc* [1999] L. & T.R. 46 which illustrates that the guarantee may be construed as extending to the new term.
[34] *Bruns v Colocotronis* [1979] 2 Lloyd's Rep. 412.
[35] Careful attention needs to be paid to the terms of the principal transaction to determine if the obligation has accrued or not. There may be some unexpected results. Thus in *Torminster Properties v Green* [1983] 1 W.L.R. 676 the guarantor of the obligation under a lease was held liable to pay rent which had not been quantified under a rent review clause at the date of termination. The obligation to pay such amounts was an "antecedent obligation" accruing before termination.

provisions of the Hire-Purchase Act, which stated that in the event of such a breach the principal shall be released from all liability, the guarantor was also absolutely discharged.[36]

6–148 Many contracts of guarantee provide that the liability of the guarantor is to continue despite the principal being released "by operation of law", or otherwise make it plain that the guarantor is to be liable for sums for which the principal never becomes liable to pay because of a determination of the principal contract by operation of the law.[37] Even a clause providing that the guarantor shall be treated as a principal debtor may be effective for this purpose.[38]

(ii) Disclaimer of leases

6–149 One specific aspect of a determination of the principal contract by operation of law arises as a result of a disclaimer of a lease by the liquidator of a company (pursuant to s.178 of the Insolvency Act 1986 or the principal's trustee in bankruptcy (pursuant to s.315 of the same Act). Additionally if a company is dissolved after being struck off the register:[39] the lease will vest in the Crown,[40] which then has the right to disclaim the lease.[41] The disclaimer is then deemed to take effect as if it were a disclaimer by the liquidator immediately prior to the dissolution of the company.[42] An administrator or receiver has no statutory authority to disclaim a lease.

6–150 The effect of a disclaimer is set out in s.178(4) of the Insolvency Act 1986, which provides that a disclaimer:

"(a) operates so as to determine, as from the date of the disclaimer, the rights, interests and liabilities of the company in or in respect of the property disclaimed; but

(b) does not, except so far as is necessary for the purpose of releasing the company from any liability, affect the rights or liabilities of any other person."[43]

---

[36] *Unity Finance Ltd v Woodcock* [1963] 1 W.L.R. 455.
[37] See *General Produce Co v United Bank Ltd* [1979] 2 Lloyd's Rep. 255 at 259. See also *Goulston Discount Co Ltd v Clark* [1967] 2 Q.B. 493; *Direct Acceptance Finance Ltd v Cumberland Furnishing Pty Ltd* [1965] N.S.W.R. 1504. The clauses in these cases were treated as promises to indemnify the creditor. *Cf. Unity Finance Ltd v Woodcock* [1963] 1 W.L.R. 455.
[38] See *General Produce Co v United Bank Ltd* [1979] 2 Lloyd's Rep. 255 at 259, where Lloyd J. is inclined to such a view, although there was also a specific provision in the contract providing for the continuation of the guarantor's liability despite a release of the principal "by operation of law".
[39] Pursuant to the Companies Act 1985, s.652.
[40] *ibid.*, s.654.
[41] *ibid.*, s.656. The execution of the notice of disclaimer means that the disclaimed lease is deemed not to have vested in the Crown (*ibid.*, s.657(1)).
[42] *ibid.*, s.657(2).
[43] [1997] A.C. 70. See also *Christopher Moran Holdings Ltd v Bairstow* [1999] 2 W.L.R. 396 (involving assessment of loss and damage upon a disclaimer pursuant to s.178(6) Insolvency Act 1986); *Basch v Stekel* [2000] L. & T.R. 1.

In *Hindcastle Ltd v Barbara Attenborough Associates Ltd*[44] the House of Lords held that, where only a landlord and an insolvent tenant is involved, the effect of a disclaimer pursuant to this provision is to determine the tenant's interest in property, namely the lease, as well as all the tenant's and landlord's rights and obligations arising from it.[45] But a guarantor of the tenant's obligations, or an original tenant, is not released by the disclaimer. Section 178(4)(b) operates as a "deeming provision" so far as other persons' rights and obligations are concerned. As Lord Nicholls (giving the leading judgment) stated:[46]

"The statute provides that a disclaimer operates to determine the interest of the tenant in the disclaimed property but not so as to affect the rights or liabilities of any other person. Thus when the lease is disclaimed it is determined and the reversion accelerated but the rights and liabilities of others, such as guarantors and original tenants, are to remain as though the lease had continued and not been determined. In this way the determination of the lease is not permitted to affect the rights or liabilities of other persons. Statute has so provided."

In so concluding the House of Lords overruled the Court of Appeal decision in *Stacey v Hill*.[47] This had held a hundred years earlier that the guarantor of a tenant's obligations was discharged upon a disclaimer of a lease, despite the earlier decision of *Hill v East & West India Dock Co*[48] which decided that a lessee who assigns the lease (as the law then stood)[49] remained liable for the rent.[50] The bases of the decision in *Stacey v Hill*[51] were, *inter alia*, that upon disclaimer the lease determines so that no rent can be due under it and, further, that the disclaimer operates as a release of the principal debtor (the tenant) which means, applying the usual rules of suretyship,[52] that the guarantor is also discharged. According to the House

---

[44] [1997] A.C. 70 at 87.
[45] Note, however, in respect of tenancies granted after January 1, 1996 if the original tenant assigns the lease, in whole or in part, he is released from his covenants pursuant to the lease, and ceases to have the benefit of the landlord's covenants as at the date of the tenancy. See Landlord and Tenant (Covenants) Act 1995, s.5. But as a condition of the assignment the tenant may be required to enter into an authorised guarantee agreement. See below, para.6–154.
[46] [1997] A.C. 70 at 88.
[47] [1901] 1 K.B. 660.
[48] (1884) 9 App. Cas. 448.
[49] But now see Landlord and Tenant (Covenants) Act 1995 s.5, below, paras 6–153 and 7–52, in respect of tenancies granted after January 1, 1996.
[50] It also followed that a guarantee of the original lessee's obligations remained effective: *Warnford Investments Ltd v Duckworth* [1979] 1 Ch. 127; *Harding v Preece* (1882) 9 Q.B.D. 281; *Re Distributors & Warehousing Ltd* [1985] 1 B.C.C. 99, 570 at 99, 576. As pointed out by Lord Nicholls *in Hindcastle Ltd v Barbara Attenborough Associates Ltd* this distinction has a consequence which makes "no sort of legal and commercial sense" [1977] A.C. 70 at 95. Applying *Stacey v Hill* ([1901] 1 K.B. 660) directors who guarantee their company's obligations as a tenant would not be liable if the company became insolvent and the lease was disclaimed, but applying *Hill v East & West India Dock Co* (1884) 9 App. Cas. 448 would be liable if an assignee from the company encountered financial difficulties and the lease was disclaimed.
[51] [1901] 1 K.B. 660.
[52] See above, paras 1–22 to 1–27.

of Lords, in *Hindcastle Ltd v Barbara Attenborough Associates Ltd*[53] this
analysis failed to take into account the "deeming" provision in s.178(4)(b).

6–151   Another reason given in *Stacey v Hill*[54] (and re-iterated by the Court of
Appeal in *Hindcastle Ltd v Barbara Attenborough Ltd*),[55] for concluding
that a disclaimer released the guarantor was that a guarantor's right to be
indemnified by the principal debtor (the tenant) "arose at the moment of
creation of the guarantee"[56] and "is to be regarded as inseparable from
it".[57] A release of the guarantor was necessary in order not to deprive the
guarantor of this right of indemnity, in the absence of clear statutory
wording (which was absent from s.178(4)(b)) depriving the guarantor of
this right. But as, Lord Nicholl pointed out in *Hindcastle Ltd v Barbara
Attenborough Associates Ltd*,[58] the statutory disclaimer provisions do not
remove the right of the guarantor to prove as a creditor in the insolvent
tenant's estate, and this continuing right has the effect of preserving the
right of indemnity:

> "The guarantor loses his right to an indemnity from the insolvent tenant,
> but in place the statute gives him a right to prove as a creditor of the
> insolvent tenant's estate. Thus there is no question of the guarantor's
> right to an indemnity being confiscated. After disclaimer the guarantor's
> position is no different from the position of any unsecured guarantor of a
> debtor who becomes insolvent. Had there been no disclaimer the
> guarantor's right of indemnity would have led only to a right to prove
> against the insolvent's estate. The disclaimer provisions do not change
> this. The Act leaves the loss consequent upon the tenant's bankruptcy
> where the parties to the guarantee intended."[59]

In *Hindcastle Ltd v Barbara Attenborough Associates Ltd*,[60] the House
of Lords also held that the interest of a sub-tenant continues and is
unaffected by the disclaimer of the lease of the head tenant, since
determination of the sub-tenant's interest in the property is not necessary
to free the tenant from liability (pursuant to the Insolvency Act 1986,
s.178(4)(a)).[61] As a result of the statutory deeming provision in s.178(4)(b)
the sub-tenant will hold the estate on the same terms, and subject to the
same rights and obligations, as would be applicable if the tenant's interest
had continued,[62] and the sub-tenant may apply to the court for an order
that the lease be vested in him.[63]

---

[53] [1997] A.C. 70 at 93.
[54] [1901] K.B. 660.
[55] [1995] Q.B. 95 at 105.
[56] [1977] A.C. 70 at 93.
[57] *ibid.* According to this reasoning this distinguished the position of the guarantor from the
position of the original tenant, who undertook liabilities without "any right of recourse against
anyone at that time": [1997] A.C. 77 at 93.
[58] [1977] A.C. 70.
[59] *ibid.*, at 94.
[60] [1977] A.C. 70.
[61] *ibid.*, at 89.
[62] *ibid.*
[63] *ibid.* And see *Re AE Realisations (1985) Ltd* [1987] 3 All E.R. 83. If the sub-tenant does not
perform the covenants in the original lease, he will be liable for forfeiture or the landlord can
distrain on the goods for rent (See *Hindcastle Ltd v Barbara Attenborough Associates Ltd*

Although *Hindcastle Ltd v Barbara Attenborough Associates Ltd*[64] **6–152** concerned disclaimer by liquidator, logically it should apply to disclaimer by the Crown after dissolution by the company.[65]

The result, therefore, of *Hindcastle Ltd v Barbara Attenborough* **6–153** *Associates Ltd*[66] is that a guarantor's liability will not be affected by a disclaimer of a lease, with the qualification that if the landlord takes possession the liability of the guarantor will then cease since the landlord is no longer "the involuntary receipient of a disclaimed lease".[67] As Lord Nicholls stated:[68]

"By his own act of taking possession he has demonstrated that he regards the lease as ended for all purposes. His conduct is inconsistent with there being a continuing liability on others to perform the tenant's covenants in the lease. he cannot have possession of the property and, at the same time, claim rent for the property from others."

The confirmation in *Hindcastle Ltd v Barbara Attenborough Associates Ltd*[69] (following *Hill v East & West India Dock* Co)[70] that the original tenant (and therefore the guarantor of that tenant) who assigns the lease remains liable[71] despite a disclaimer is now displaced in respect of tenancies granted after January 1, 1996 as a result of s.5(2) of the Landlord and Tenant (Covenants) Act 1995. This has the effect of releasing a tenant from his obligations under a lease as from an assignment of the tenancy and, conversely, at the same time the tenant ceases to be entitled to the benefit of the landlord's covenants. Section 5 also applies when only part of the premises is assigned (s.5(3)). In order to protect the landlord's position, however, s.16 of the Act does not preclude a tenant who has been released from a covenant of the tenancy form entering into an "authorised guarantee agreement" with respect to performance of the covenant by the assignee.

[1977] A.C. 70 at 89; *Re AE Realisations Ltd* [1987] 3 All E.R. 83). The sub-tenant can apply to the court for relief from forfeiture: *Barclays Bank plc v Prudential Assurance Co* [1998] 10 E.G. 15.

[64] [1997] A.C. 70.

[65] Thus *Re No.1 London Ltd* [1991] 1 B.C.L.C. 501 and *Re Yarmarine (IW) Ltd* [1992] B.C.C. 28, which followed *Stacey v Hill* [1901] 1 K.B. 660, in respect of disclaimer by the Crown should no longer be considered good law. See in more detail G. Andrews and R. Millett, *Law of Guarantees* (3rd ed., 2000), pp.545–546.

[66] [1997] A.C. 70.

[67] *ibid.*, at 89. This assumes there has been no vesting order pursuant to Insolvency Act 1986, s.181.

[68] *ibid.* See also *Basch v Stekel* [2001] L. & T.R. 1, in which it was also held that a notice by the landlord requiring the guarantor's executor to take a new lease (pursuant to a clause in the disclaimed lease) did not constitute an act of possession by the landlord.

[69] [1977] A.C. 70.

[70] (1884) 9 App. Cas. 448.

[71] Note that in *Allied London Investments Ltd v Hambro Life Assurance Ltd* (1984) 269 E.G. 41 (on appeal (1985) 50 P. & C.R. 207), it was held that, although the assignee is liable to indemnify the original lessee (if the latter pays the rent upon the assignee's default) the original lessee still remains under a primary liability. He is not therefore in a position of a co-surety with a guarantor who has guaranteed the assignee's obligation to pay rent. A release of the guarantor does not therefore release the original lessee on the basis of the general rule that a release of one co-guarantor discharges the others (see below, para.8–21).

(iii) Authorised guarantee agreements

6–154   The relevant provisions (ss.16–18) of the Landlord and Tenant (Covenants) Act 1995 governing such guarantee agreements have been discussed in detail elsewhere.[72] The general law relating to guarantees applies to them, and in particular those rules relating to the release of sureties.[73] The following key features of the "authorised guarantee agreements" should, however, be observed:

(a) An agreement will only be an "authorised guarantee agreement" if, under it, the tenant guarantees the performance of the relevant covenant to any extent by the assignee[74] and it is entered into in fulfilment of a condition "lawfully imposed" by the landlord on the giving of his consent to the assignment.[75] The words "lawfully imposed" import a requirement of reasonableness; a landlord can only require an "authorised guarantee agreement" as a condition on the granting his consent if in the circumstances that arise it is reasonable to do so.[76] It is not sufficient for a landlord, in an application for a new tenancy under Pt II of the Landlord and Tenant Act 1954, to insist on a term giving him a right to call for an "authorised guarantee agreement", simply on the basis that it is more convenient for a landlord with multiple leases in a given development to obtain uniformity in its lease agreements.[77] It is uncertain what circumstances would be regarded as reasonable in this context, but it should be sufficient if the landlord can show that the assignee is financially less sound than the former tenant.

(b) An agreement will not be an "authorised guarantee agreement" to the extent that it purports to impose upon the tenant any requirement to guarantee the performance of a relevant covenant by any other person than the assignee,[78] or to impose upon the tenant any liability in relation to any period after the assignee is released from liability in respect of that covenant by virtue of the Act.[79] Any agreement purporting to impose such liabilities is void as frustrating the operation of the Act.[80]

(c) An "authorised guarantee agreement" may, however, impose on the tenant "any liability as sole or principal debtor" in respect of any obligation owed by the assignee under the relevant

---

[72] See generally G. Andrews and R. Millet, *Law of Guarantees* (3rd ed., 2000), pp.536–539; Woodfalls *Law of Landlord & Tenant* Vol. 1, para.5.157A and Vol. 2, para.22.153: See also Law Commission Rep. No.174 *Landlord & Tenant Law: Privity of Contract & Estate*.
[73] s.16(8).
[74] s.16(2).
[75] s.16(3).
[76] *Wallis Fashion Group Ltd v CGU Life Assurance* [2000] L. & T.R. 520.
[77] *ibid.*
[78] s.16(4)(a).
[79] s.16(4)(b).
[80] s.25.

covenant.[81] Thus "a principal debtor" clause may be included in the agreement. The tenant may also be required to enter into a new tenancy in the event of the tenancy assigned by him being disclaimed, provided it corresponds in its covenants and duration with the assigned tenancy.[82]

(d) Section 17 sets out a procedural code for a notices to be served upon the guarantor pursuant to an "authorised guarantee agreement" informing him, *inter alia*, in respect of any fixed charge payable under the covenant, that the charge is now due and that the landlord intends to recover from the guarantor such amount as is specified in the notice.[83] The notice must be served[84] within six months of the charge becoming due.

[81] s.16(5)(a). See also the strangely worded s.16(5)(b) which re-enforces this by providing that an "authorised guarantee agreement" may "impose on the tenant liabilities as guarantor in respect of the assignee's performance of that covenant which are no more onerous than those to which he would be subject in the event of his being liable as sole or principal debtor in respect of any obligation owed by the assignee under that covenant".

[82] s.16(5)(c).

[83] s.17(3)(a)(b). Similar provisions in s.17 apply to a former tenant who remains bound by a covenant, (see s.17(2)) which will be the case in respect of tenancies granted prior to January 1, 1996. In such a case if there is also a guarantee of the former tenant's obligations the landlord is not required to serve notices on the tenant as a precondition of the guarantor's liability. This is despite the wording of s.17(2), which states that "the former tenant shall not be liable" under the agreement unless the required notice is served, thus suggesting (absent such a notice) that the primary liability is extinguished. See *Cheverell Estates Ltd v Harris* [1998] 1 E.G.L.R. 27, where it was held that s.17 was merely a procedural code.

[84] *ibid*. A notice under s.17 will be validly served if it is sent to his last residential address even if not received by him. (*Commercial Union L.ife Assurance Co Ltd v Moustafa* [1999] 24 E.G. 155). Note that s.17 probably has no application to actions for contribution or indemnity by the guarantor who has paid under his guarantee. See *Fresh (Retail) Ltd v Emsden* (unreported Ipswich county court January 18, 1999.)

CHAPTER 7

DISCHARGE FROM LIABILITY BY REASON OF THE CREDITOR'S CONDUCT TOWARDS THE PRINCIPAL

1. DISCHARGE BY THE CREDITOR AGREEING WITH THE PRINCIPAL TO VARY THE PRINCIPAL CONTRACT

(i) General scope of the rule

The general principle finds its rationale in the fact that the guarantor is **7–01**
responsible only for the obligations which are guaranteed. Thus, if the
principal and creditor without the guarantor's consent agree between
themselves to alter the nature of the principal obligation the guarantor is
discharged because the obligation in its altered form is not that which he
guaranteed.

The formulation of the principle as set out in *Holme v Brunskill*[1] has **7–02**
received wide judicial approval:[2]

---

[1] (1878) 3 Q.B.D. 495.
[2] *Crédit Suisse v Borough Council of Allerdale* [1995] 1 Lloyd's Rep. 315 at 361; *Melvin International SA v Poseidon Schiffahrt GMBH NV Kalma* [1999] 2 All E.R. (Comm) 761; *Metropolitan Properties Co. (Regis) Ltd v Bartholomew* [1995] 72 P.& C.R. 380 at 383; *Howard de Walden Estates Ltd v Pasta Place Ltd* [1995] 1 EGLR 79 at 80; *Ward v National Bank of New Zealand* (1883) 8 App. Cas. 755 at 763–764; *Hancock v Williams* (1942) 42 S.R. (NSW) 252; *Dunlop New Zealand Ltd v Dumbleton* [1968] N.Z.L.R. 1092 at 1096; *Ankar Pty Ltd v National Westminster Finance (Aust) Ltd* (1987) 162 C.L.R. 549 at 558–559; *Lloyds TSB Bank plc v Hayward* [2002] All E.R. (D) 351, para.5.

"The true rule in my opinion is that if there is any agreement between the principals with reference to the contract guaranteed, the surety ought to be consulted, and if he has not consented to the alteration, although in cases where it is without enquiry evidence that the alteration is unsubstantial, or that it cannot otherwise be beneficial to the surety, the surety may not be discharged; yet that if it is not self-evident that the alteration is unsubstantial, or one which cannot be prejudicial to the surety, the Court ... will hold that in such case the surety himself must be the sole judge whether or not he will consent to remain liable notwithstanding the alteration, and that if he has not so consented he will be discharged."[3]

Securities given by the guarantor to the creditor will also be released.[4] The principle is an equitable one[5] and is applied strictly. If the variation of the principal contract could prejudice the guarantor, he or she will be absolutely discharged whether or not the variation has in fact resulted in prejudice and whether or not it is likely to do so. The guarantor will remain liable only where the alteration to the principal contract is obviously "unsubstantial",[6] with no possible prejudice to the guarantor resulting, or where the alteration is *inevitably* for the benefit of the guarantor.[7]

7–03   It should be said that there were some earlier, more restricted interpretations of the rule. Writing in 1897, de Colyar was of the view that it must be clearly shown that there has been a material variation of the terms of the principal contract, unless it was clear that the guarantor undertook liability strictly on the faith of the principal contract after being given notice of its terms.[8] But even at that time the most significant authorities did not confine the rule in this way,[9] and most recent statements of the principle do not impose any such limitations, although there are exceptions. In *The Mystery of Mercers of the City of London v New Hampshire Insurance Co*[10] Scott L.J. (without finally deciding)

---

[3] (1878) 3 Q.B.D. 495 at 505.
[4] *Bolton v Salmon* [1891] 2 Ch 48; *Smith v Wood* [1929] 1 Ch 14; *Bolton v Darling Downs Building Society* [1935] Q.S.R. 237 at 246.
[5] *Polak v Everett* (1876) 1 Q.B.D. 669 at 673–674; *Holme v Brunskill* (1878) 3 Q.B.D. 495 at 505; *Ankar Pty Ltd v National Westminster Finance (Aust) Ltd* (1987) 162 C.L.R. 549 at 559; *Rees v Berrington* (1795) 2 Ves. Jun. 540; 30 E.R. 765. [1924] 4 D.L.R. 96). Note, however, it may be a term of the guarantee that the principal contract shall not be varied (*e.g. London Guarantee & Accident Co Ltd v Sweat-Comings* [1924] 4 D.L.R. 96).
[6] *Holme v Brunskill* (1878) 3 Q.B.D. 495 at 505 and the cases cited above n.2.
[7] See this expression in *Crédit Suisse v Borough Council of Allerdale* [1995] 1 Lloyd's Rep 315 at 366; *Holme v Brunskill* (1878) 3 Q.B.D. 495 at 505; See also the case cited n.2.
[8] H. A. de Colyar, *A Treatise on the Law of Guarantees and of Principal and Surety* (3rd ed., 1897), p.396.
[9] See, in particular, *Holme v Brunskill* (1878) 3 Q.B.D. 495 at 505–506. *Cf.*, however, *Sanderson v Aston* (1873) L.R. 8 Exch. 73 at 79, but this case was doubted in *Holme v Brunskill*.
[10] [1992] 2 Lloyd's Rep. 365. See also *Chatterton v Maclean* [1951] 1 All E.R. 761, in which Parker J. was of the opinion that the variation must "impinge on the rights of the guarantor", *e.g.* by affecting the guarantor's rights of subrogation. In Australia see *Sabemo Pty Ltd v De Groot* (1991) 8 B.C.L. 132 at 146, where Giles J. stated that "it may be necessary that the variation be material or operate to the prejudice of the guarantor".

considered that the strict rule in *Holme v Brunskill*[11] might not apply to a "professional compensated surety"[12] and, on a more general basis, that in order for a variation to discharge the guarantor it "must in some way alter the extent or nature of the risk undertaken by the guarantor".[13] As emphasised later in this chapter,[14] the authors regard the present law as unduly favourable to the guarantor, and would welcome a reformulation of the rule allowing discharge only in respect of alterations which are shown to be material.

(ii) Identification of the relevant contract and/or obligation

In applying the rule in *Holme v Brunskill*[15] care needs to be taken to identify the relevant principal transaction which is guaranteed, since only a variation of that transaction (not a related one) will discharge the guarantor. As an example, in *Metropolitan Properties Co (Regis) Ltd v Bartholomew*[16] company directors guaranteed the obligations of the company pursuant to a licence, which permitted the company to take possession as assignees of certain leased premises, when the lease itself had prohibited this. A subsequent variation of the terms of the lease (permitting multiple occupation) did not discharge the guarantors, since only the obligations pursuant to the licence had been guaranteed by the directors and these remained unaltered.

7–04

Where there is a guarantee of several distinct obligations within one contract, it will also be important to identify the precise obligation which has been varied. Decisions[17] concerning the discharge of the guarantor as a result of a variation whereby the creditor gives time to the principal indicate that a giving of time in respect of one obligation (for example, to make a periodical payment) will only discharge the guarantor from that obligation and not the remaining obligations (that is, in the example, to make the further periodic payments). The same principle has been said to apply to other types of variation of the principal contract.[18]

7–05

Even assuming that the rule applies to all types of variation, the guarantors will nevertheless be discharged from all liability if the

7–06

---

[11] (1877) 3 Q.B.D. 495.
[12] [1992] 2 Lloyd's Rep. 365 at 377.
[13] *ibid.*, at 375. (in discussing the concept of "embodiment" of the principal contract into the guarantee). Scott L.J. relies on *Stewart v M'Kean* (1855) 10 Exch. 675 and *Sanderson v Aston* (1873) L.R. 8 Ex. 73, but the latter was doubted in *Holme v Brunskill* (1877) 3 Q.B.D. 495. G. Andrews and R. Millet, *Law of Guarantees* (3rd ed., 2000), at p.297 appear to accept that this is the correct principle, relying upon *Bank of Baroda v Patel* [1996] 1 Lloyd's Rep 391, but this case does not depart from the accepted rule in *Holme v Brunskill* (at 396). The reference to the requirement of prejudice or the risk of default is only made generally in the context of an analysis of whether a variation of one of several distinct obligations discharges the guarantor from only that obligation or, alternatively, from the entire contract (see below, para.7–04).
[14] See below, para.7–56.
[15] (1878) 3 Q.B.D. 495.
[16] (1995) 72 P. & C.R. 380.
[17] See below, paras 7–77 to 7–80.
[18] See *Bank of Baroda v Patel* [1996] 1 Lloyd's Rep. 391 at 396.

contract is construed as a "global" indivisible obligation. Thus in *Bank of Baroda v Patel*[19] the guarantor was relased from all liability when the terms of a banking facility were varied to allow for some (but not all) foreign bill transactions to take place without ECGD cover. Potter J. said:[20]

> "It seems clear to me in this case, that the facility, while relating to several types of business, is essentially and properly to be regarded as a single agreement relating to liabilities arising from a spectrum of trading and financing activities by [the borrower] over a period of time which the bank was agreeing to finance, it being an integral and important part of the overall arrangement that ECGD cover should be provided in respect of foreign bill transactions. The obligation of the defendant as guarantor was a global obligation in respect of the sum of the net balance(s) arising from those activities, to be met if and when demand was made."

(iii) Distinction between a guarantee of the obligations of a specific contract and a future course of dealing

7–07   At first instance in *Mystery of the Mercers of the City of London v New Hampshire Insurance Co*,[21] Phillips J. was of the view that the rule regarding variation only applies where obligations arising under a specific contract are guaranteed and not in respect of obligations arising out of a future course of dealing:

> "Where on the other hand the guarantee is given in respect of obligations arising out of a contemplated course of dealing without reference, express or implied, to any specific contract it will be open to the creditor to vary the terms applying to the course of dealing so long as that course of dealing remains within the scope of the guarantee."[22]

7–08   The exclusion of guarantees of the obligations of a future course of dealing from the application of the rule is significant because modern contracts of guarantee often relate to a future series of transactions.[23] The result is that, if the guarantee is given, for example, to secure the performance of "all leasing arrangements" between the creditor and principal (without identifying a specific contract), it will be open to those parties to change the terms of any transaction yet to be executed between them, as long as the transaction can properly be described as a leasing

---

[19] [1996] 1 Lloyd's Rep. 391.
[20] *ibid.*, at 397.
[21] (Unreported, January 18, 1991, Q.B.) See, on appeal, (which was upheld) [1992] 2 Lloyd's Rep. 365, but not addressing this issue.
[22] See also *Pratapsing Moholalshai v Keshavlal Harilal Setalwad* (1934) 62 Indian Appeals 23 at 25; *Stewart v M'Kean* (1853) 10 Exch. 675; 156 E.R. 610; *Meney & Co v Birmingham* (1890) 34 N.B.R. 336 at 342.
[23] *e.g. Traders Finance Group Ltd v Brewster* (1967) 64 D.L.R. (2d) 554.

arrangement.[24] Although Phillips J. does not directly discuss the issue, it would even appear to follow from the general statement of principle in *Mystery of the Mercers of the City of London v New Hampshire Insurance Co* that once a specific agreement is concluded the creditor and principal should be able to vary its terms, because the guarantee does not relate only to the obligations of that specific contract. But it is arguable that at this stage the guaranteed obligation is crystallised and a subsequent variation means that the obligation in its altered form is not that which is guaranteed.[25]

(iv) Examples of variations discharging the guarantor

It is not instructive to catalogue all instances of variations of the principal contract which will result in the discharge of the guarantor, but in the case of an unlimited guarantee any increase in the potential liability of the principal (for example, by varying the agreement to permit additional funds to be advanced) will discharge the guarantor, since the potential liability of the guarantor is correspondingly increased.[26] It is not unduly difficult for the guarantor to establish a particular variation discharges him from liability since (as we have seen)[27] any variation will have this effect, unless there is no possibility of prejudice to the guarantor or the alteration is inevitably for the benefit of the guarantor. Thus in *Crédit Suisse v Borough Council of Allerdale*[28] a variation of a loan facility was agreed, which consolidated previous drawdowns to provide for a common interest period for all drawdowns. Depending upon the subsequent movement of interest rates this variation might have been beneficial to the borrower, but it might also have resulted in increased liability for interest. The variation had the consequence of discharging the guarantor since it would therefore not have been "inevitably" beneficial to the guarantor.[29]

In the context of a lease a variation increasing the rent payable when it is otherwise fixed by the terms of the lease will clearly discharge the

7–09

7–10

---

[24] See a similar example in *Stewart v M'Kean* (1855) 10 Exch. 675 at 687–688; 156 E.R. 610, in which a guarantee was given for a person's "intromissions, as your agent". Alderson B. simply posed the question whether on the facts the arrangements entered into could be properly viewed as "intromissions" (at 616).

[25] See the view taken in the first Australian edition of this work, J. O'Donovan & J. Phillips, *The Modern Contract of Guarantee* (1985), p.263. This result is also suggested by Pollock B in *Sanderson v Aston* (1873) L.R. 8 Exch. 73 at 79, who states that even when the "original contract was not part of the surety's contract", a material alteration of the principal contract will discharge the guarantor.

[26] See, *e.g. Guiness Mahon & Co Ltd v London Enterprise Investments Ltd* [1995] 4 Bank L.R. 184. In Australia in *Bond v Hong Kong Bank of Australia Ltd* (1991) 25 N.S.W.L.R. 286 at 309, Kirby P. (as he then was) considered that a very small increase in the guarantor's exposure (US$5,000 when the exposure was already US$194,000,000) could be regarded as "obviously unsubstantial". But in terms of the rule in *Holme v Brunskill* this is not thought to be correct.

[27] See above, paras 7–01 to 7–03.

[28] [1995] 1 Lloyd's Rep 315.

[29] *ibid.*, at 364–365.

guarantor. So, too, will any variation involving a change of use of,[30] or modification to,[31] the premises if there is any "argument"[32] that the potential burden on the tenant will be increased (for example, by potentially increasing the rent payable pursuant to a future rent review,[33] by increasing insurance payments,[34] or by imposing burdens upon tenants in respect of repairing obligations).[35] Other examples are an alteration in the area of the leased premises[36] or an agreement to allow a tenant to assign his interest in the lease contrary to its terms.[37]

7–11   In relation to a building contract, a change in the work or design from the original specifications,[38] a postponement of the date upon which the contractor was to take possession of the site in order to commence the building work,[39] or payments made to the building contractor before the due contractual date for payment stipulated in the principal contract,[40] will discharge the guarantor. Other examples are alterations in the terms of a mortgage or other security which embodies the principal contract[41] such as an increase in the interest rate payable[42] and, in the context of fidelity

[30] *Metropolitan Properties Co (Regis) Ltd v Bartholomew* (1995) 72 P. & C.R. 380 (variation allowing for multiple occupation), *Howard de Walden Estates Ltd v Pasta Place Ltd* [1995] 1 E.G.L.R. 79 (variation allowing wine to be served to diners and to use premises as an off-licence); *Apus Properties Ltd v Douglas Farrow Ltd* [1989] 2 E.G.L.R. 265 (variation permitting offices to be used by professional persons).
[31] *West Horndon Industrial Park Ltd v Phoenix Timber Group plc* [1995] 1 E.G.L.R. 77 (variation allowing lessor to re-enter premises to make external improvements).
[32] See this formulation in *Howard de Walden Estates Ltd v Pasta Place Ltd* [1995] 1 E.G.L.R. 79, at 81, referring and relying on *Selous Street Properties Ltd v Oronel Fabrics* [1984] E.G.D. 360.
[33] *West Horndon Industrial Park Ltd v Phoenix Timber Group plc* [1995] 1 E.G.L.R. 77 at 78. But if the rent is fixed for the duration of the lease and there is no other potential burden on the tenant caused by the variation, there may be no possibility of prejudice: *Metropolitan Properties Co (Regis) Ltd v Bartholomew* [1995] 72 P. & C.R. 380 at 386.
[34] *West Horndon Industrial Park Ltd v Phoenix Timber Group plc* [1995] 1 E.G.L.R. 77 at 78
[35] *ibid.*
[36] *Holme v Brunskill* (1878) 3 Q.B.D. 495.
[37] This would appear to follow from *Johnson Bros (Dyers) Ltd v Davison* (1935) 79 S.J. 306, although on the facts the assignment was made according to the terms of the lease: see below, para.6–105. For the position of the variation of leases after assignment see the Landlord and Tenant (Covenants) Act 1995, s.18 and below, para.7–52.
[38] As to variations in respect of building contracts, see, generally, *Hudsons Building and Engineering Contracts.* (11th ed., 1995) Ch. 7.
[39] *Mystery of the Mercers of the City of London v New Hampshire Insurance Co* (unreported, Q.B., January 18, 1991).
[40] *General Steam-Navigation Co v Rolt* (1858) 6 C.B (NS) 550; 141 E.R. 572; *Calvert v London Dock Co* (1838) 7 L.J. Ch. 90; *Thomas Fuller Construction Co (1958) Ltd v Continental Insurance Co* (1970) 36 D.L.R. (3d) 336; *Doe v Canadian Surety Co* [1937] S.C.R. 1. See similarly *Geelong Building Society v Encel* (unreported, Vic Sup Ct, August 31, 1993) (loan of money by creditor before it was contractually bound to do so).
[41] *Holland-Canada Mortgage Co v Hutchings* [1936] 2 D.L.R. 481; *Bolton v Darling Downs Building Society* [1935] Q.S.R. 237; *Bank of New Zealand v Baker* [1926] N.Z.L.R. 462; *Ford Motor Credit Co of Canada Ltd v Sorenson* (1973) 35 D.L.R. (3d) 253 (alteration of the terms of a conditional sales contract). In such cases, an alternative reason for the court's decision may be that the creditor has lost or impaired a security held for the enforcement of the principal obligation: see below, para.8–47 for a discussion of this overlap.
[42] *Crédit Suisse v Borough Council of Allerdale* [1995] 1 Lloyd's Rep. 315 at 364–365; *Invercargill Savings Bank v Genge* [1929] N.Z.L.R. 375; *Pioneer Trust Co v 220263 Ltd* (1989) 65 A.L.T.A. L.R. (2d) 220. See also *Sabemo Pty Ltd v De Groot* (1991) 8 B.C.L. 132 (increase of interest rate on overdue progress payments); *Tasman Finance Pty Ltd v Edwards* (unreported, NSW Sup Ct, December 8, 1992) (payment of interest three months earlier than it would otherwise have been due and payable pursuant to the original agreement).

guarantees, an alteration in the nature of the employee's duties.[43] In all these cases it should be emphasised that the variation was made in relation to the contract which was guaranteed. It is not sufficient if another contract, albeit a contract which is related to the guaranteed contract, is varied. Thus, where a surety guarantees to an owner who has entered into a building contract with a head contractor the performance of contracts between the head contractor and the subcontractors, the surety is not discharged by any change in a contract between the owner and the head contractor.[44]

(v) "Obviously unsubstantial" and "beneficial" variations

Whilst there are numerous instances of alterations to the principal contract discharging the guarantor, it is difficult to find in the cases many examples of alterations which are either "obviously unsubstantial" or clearly for the benefit of the guarantor. Changes made to the principal contract which do not affect the meaning of the agreement or which are made to clarify, or to correct minor errors in, the terms of the agreement[45] come within the former category.

7–12

Even though the non-prejudicial effect of the alteration must be apparent without a detailed inquiry as to its effects, some evaluative judgment as to whether a variation is "obviously unsubstantial" is necessarily required. There may be differing conclusions as illustrated by the New South Wales Supreme Court case of *Corumo Holdings Pty Ltd v C Itoh Ltd*.[46] Meagher J.A. held that a variation increasing the amount of the principal's potential liability could prejudice the guarantor, despite the fact that the principal's liability prior to the variation was already in excess of the guarantor's maximum limit of liability pursuant to the guarantee. The additional indebtedness meant that it was more likely that a demand would be made upon the guarantor and that the value of the guarantor's right of indemnity would be depreciated. Kirby P. (as he then was), however, was of the view, in the context of the commercial setting and the particular provisions of the guarantee, that the variation had prevented the

7–13

---

[43] *King v Herron and Montgomery* [1903] 2 I.R. 473.
[44] *Town of Truro v Toronto General Insurance Co* (1973) 38 D.L.R. (3d) 1 at 8.
[45] *Bond v Hong Kong Bank of Australia Ltd* (1991) 25 N.S.W.L.R. 286 at 297–298, 307–309; *Holland-Canada Mortgage Co v Hutchings* [1936] 2 D.L.R. 481; *Andrews v Lawrence* (1865) 19 C.B. (NS) 768; 144 E.R. 789; *Niagara & Ontario Construction Co v Wyse and United States Fidelity & Guaranty Co* (1913) 10 D.L.R. 116; *Hydro Electric Power Commission v Fidelity Insurance Co* [1937] 4 D.L.R. 626. In *Oakford v European American Steam Shipping Co Ltd* (1893) 1 H. & M. 182; 71 E.R. 80, Sir William Page Wood V.-C. even inclined to the view that when the principal contract is altered after a dispute as to a point of construction or interpretation, such alteration could not amount to a variation of the principal contract discharging the guarantor. It is difficult to see how this can be correct if the alteration does *in fact* substantially change the obligations of the creditor and the principal under the contract, even though the parties might have intended merely to clarify their obligations. The guarantor may well be prejudiced by this alteration, whatever the motives of the creditor and the principal.
[46] (1991) 5 A.C.S.R. 720 at 752.

guarantee being called upon at an earlier stage and might even be regarded as being for the benefit of the guarantor.[47]

7–14   Other examples of "obviously unsubstantial" variations include an alteration to the principal contract permitting the creditor to realise securities given by the principal and to hold the proceeds of such realisation in a nominated bank account[48] and, in the context of fidelity guarantees, minor alterations in the period of notice required to terminate the employment or a change in the salary payable.[49] Another possible illustration is an agreement between the creditor and the principal to allow the creditor to assign the interest in the principal transaction even though such an assignment is contrary to the original terms of the principal contract. Arguably, such a variation would be regarded as immaterial because it is a matter of no concern to the guarantor to whom the guaranteed obligation is owed.

7–15   Instances of alterations which are clearly for the benefit of the guarantor include an agreement between the principal and the creditor for a reduction in the amount of the principal's debt or in the interest rate.[50] This will be to the advantage of the guarantor because the guarantor's liability will be correspondingly reduced. Oddly it has been said[50a] in this situation that, despite the agreement to reduce the amount of the principal's liability, the surety will remain liable for the amount due under the contract as originally agreed. There is, however, no authority for this proposition and it is clear that the guarantor would only remain fully liable if a provision in the guarantee itself expressly stated this to be the case. Another example of an alteration which is clearly beneficial to the guarantor is a variation in the existing agreement by which the creditor takes an additional security from the principal. This is to the advantage of the guarantor because the guarantor is entitled to be subrogated to this additional security on satisfying the obligation under the guarantee.[51]

---

[47] *ibid.*, at 730–732. But note the effect of this reasoning in a variation giving time to the principal: see below, paras 7–63, 7–90 to 7–92.

[48] *Bank of South Australia v Benjamin* (1892) 14 A.L.T. 159.

[49] *Sanderson v Aston* (1873) L.R. 8 Exch. 73; *Frank v Edwards* (1852) 8 Exch. 214; 155 E.R. 1325; *Holland v Lea* (1854) 9 Exch. 430 at 439–441; 156 E.R. 184 at 188. It is different if the employee is made liable for additional losses (*Bonar v Macdonald* (1850) 3 H.L. Cas. 226), or there is an express or implied term of the contract of guarantee that the salary payable shall be at a certain level (*North Western Railway Co v Whinray* (1854) 10 Exch. 77; 156 E.R. 363).

[50] *Croydon Gas Co v Dickinson* (1876) 2 C.P.D. 46 at 51; *Ankar Pty Ltd v National Westminster Finance (Aust) Ltd* (1987) 162 C.L.R. 549 at 560.

[50a] See South Australia Law Reform Committee, *Report Relating to the Reform of the Law of Suretyship*, Report No. 39 (1977), para.6.

[51] *Traders Group Ltd v Brewster* (1968) 2 D.L.R. (3d) 390 at 395–396; *Matthews Thompson & Co Ltd v Everson* (1934) 34 S.R. (NSW) 114 at 123; *ANZ Banking Group Ltd v Taudien* (1981) 6 A.C.L.R. 289. But the guarantor may be discharged if there is an intention to discharge the earlier security: *Bell Basic Industries Ltd v Frisina* (unreported, WA Sup Ct, December 23, 1983) at 5. Note that in *Crédit Lyonnais (Aust) Ltd v Darling* (1991) 5 A.C.S.R. 703, however, a variation was held not to be "obviously unsubstantial" when the security was not registered, because this occasioned in practical terms the demand being made upon the guarantor. But the failure to register is more properly viewed not as a prejudicial variation, but as a breach of the creditor's equitable duty to perfect the security: see below, para.8–65. In any event, this decision did not concern a variation of the principal contract, but a variation of the guarantee itself.

(vi) Is a consensual, legally binding agreement essential?

One residual question is whether the variation needs to be legally   **7–16**
binding as between creditor and principal. In the case of a variation of the
principal contract by which the creditor gives the principal further time to
perform the obligations under the principal contract, it is firmly established
that the variation must be legally binding, being under seal or supported by
consideration.[52] Some of the authorities suggest that the same principle is
applicable to all types of variation.[53] Thus in *Egbert v National Crown
Bank*,[54] an alteration of the principal contract increasing the rate of
interest payable by the principal was statutorily invalid and of no effect. It
was held that the purported variation did not affect the liability of the
guarantor who, therefore, remained liable under his guarantee to repay the
original sum.

There are, however, a number of situations in which the guarantor has   **7–17**
been discharged by an alteration of the principal contract, even though
there appeared to be no consideration to support the variation. For
example, where a payment was made to a contractor under a building
contract before the due date for payment without the contractor providing
separate consideration, this was held to constitute a variation of the
principal contract discharging the guarantor of the contractor's obligations.[55]

More recently, Potter J. in *Bank of Baroda v Patel*[56] indicated that the   **7–18**
courts will not insist on the requirement of a variation in a strict
contractual sense. The lender made banking facilities available to the
borrowing company who acted as confirmer in respect of the importation
of goods into the Middle East. At the request of borrowing company, the
lender operated the facility without ECGD cover (as required by the
facility) in respect of a number of foreign bill transactions. The lender
argued that this constituted a waiver rather than a variation, but Potter J.
took a broader view:

"whether or not, in other contexts, it might properly be dubbed a waiver
rather than a variation, the operation of the facility by the bank at the

---

[52] *Clarke v Birley* (1889) 41 Ch. D. 422; *Rees v Berrington* (1795) 2 Ves. Jun. 540; 30 E.R. 765:
see below, para.7–65.
[53] *Price v Kirkham* (1864) 3 H. & C. 437 at 441; 159 E.R. 601 at 603, *per* Pollock C.B. and
Channel B., where the need for a valid contract is emphasised; *Egbert v National Crown Bank*
[1918] A.C. 903. In the leading case of *Holme v Brunskill* (1878) 3 Q.B.D. 495, there was also
clearly consideration to support the variation.
[54] [1918] A.C. 903. For similar cases in Canada, see *McHugh v Union Bank of Canada* [1913]
A.C. 299; *Royal Bank of Canada v McBride* [1927] 1 D.L.R. 909; *Merchants Bank of Canada v
Bush* (1918) 42 D.L.R. 236; *Northern Crown Bank v Woodcrafts Ltd* (1919) 46 D.L.R. 428.
[55] *General Steam—Navigation Co v Rolt* (1858) 6 C.B. (NS) 550; 141 E.R. 572. This and
similar cases may have another explanation (see below, para.8–106), but *Thomas Fuller
Construction Co* (1958) *Ltd v Continental Insurance Co* (1970) 36 D.L.R. (3d) 336 saw these
cases as examples of the rule regarding the variation of the principal contract. See also *Nelson
Fisheries Ltd v Boese* [1975] 2 N.Z.L.R. 233, as an example of where there was no real
evidence of consideration.
[56] [1996] 1 Lloyd's Rep. 391. See also *Bank of Scotland v Henry Butcher* [2001] 2 All E.R.
(Comm) 691 (but where the alleged variation to permit the customer's account to be used for
non-business purposes was not supported by the evidence, see paras 74–86).

request of [the borrower] without ECGD cover in respect of particular transactions, when both parties were well aware of the terms of the facility, amounts in broad terms to an agreement so to operate it and in effect as a variation of the terms of the facility."[57]

7–19   As the law now stands, provided that there is a consensual agreement to alter the principal contract, it is thought the guarantor should be discharged, whether or not the alteration is contractually binding. The guarantor is as prejudiced or potentially prejudiced by this informal agreement as if the alteration were contractually binding. Indeed, in many cases the creditor's voluntary promise may operate as an estoppel, thus preventing the creditor from insisting on the principal's compliance with the original contractual conditions.

7–20   If, however, there is no consensual agreement to vary the principal contract but simply a breach of that contract by the creditor, the dominant view is that the guarantor will not be discharged,[58] unless it is a repudiatory breach which is accepted by the principal debtor as terminating the principal contract[59] or unless the terms of the principal contract have become "embodied" in the guarantee.[60] But in *The Mystery of the Mercers of the City of London v New Hampshire Insurance Co*[61] Lord Scott was of the opinion that in the case of a breach of the principal contract by the creditor (whether the breach is repudiatory or otherwise) the guarantor's discharge should depend "on the importance of the breach in relation to the risk undertaken".[62] There is some merit in this latter approach since the guarantor's rights may be as prejudically affected by a breach of the principal contract by the creditor as by a consensual variation.

---

[57] *ibid.*, at 396. Potter J. also said that even if not a variation the operation of the facility in this manner could be regarded as "conduct by the creditor to the prejudice of its surety sufficient to discharge the defendant from liability" (at 396). But the validity of a general principle of this nature is very much in doubt (see below, paras 8–106 to 8–114, especially 8–114).

[58] *National Westminster Bank Plc v Riley* [1986] F.L.R. 213 apparently accepted by Parker L.J. and Nolan L.J. in *The Mystery of the Mercers of the City of London v New Hampshire Insurance Co* [1992] Lloyd's Law Rep. 365 at 370, 371. See above, paras 6–119 to 6–120 and below, para.8–19. See also *Bruns v Colocotronis* [1979] 2 Lloyd's Rep 412 at 420, where it was assumed that a failure to abide by a particular clause in arbitration proceedings did not amount to a variation.

[59] See above, paras 6–119 to 6–120.

[60] *National Westminster Bank Plc v Riley* [1986] F.L.R. 213: see below, paras 8–15 to 9–19. This is probably the explanation for *Watts v Shuttleworth* (1861) 7 H. & N. 353; 158 E.R. 510, where the guarantor of the performance of a contractor's work was discharged when there was no consensual variation but the owner of the building failed to insure as required by a term in the building contract. Another possibility where there is a breach of the terms of the principal transaction is that the guarantor is discharged because the creditor has acted in a prejudicial manner towards the guarantor. But the scope of this principle is limited: see below, paras 8–106 to 8–114.

[61] [1992] 2 Lloyd's Rep. 365.

[62] *ibid.*, at 376.

(vii) Where the terms of the principal contract provide for variation

Sometimes the principal contract itself contemplates and provides for a   **7–21**
variation of its terms. In such a case a variation in the way the principal
contract is performed will not discharge the guarantor because there is a
guarantee of a contract whereby the terms and obligations may change,
rather than of a fixed obligation. Common examples are a mortgage
permitting a variation in the interest rate payable by the mortgagor, and a
building contract permitting a variation of the construction work and
design.[63] Occasionally the variation may be permitted only if the parties to
the principal contract notify the guarantor and this condition must then be
satisfied.[64]

Even if the principal contract contemplates a variation, the guarantee   **7–22**
must make it clear that it relates to and encompasses whatever obligations
may from time to time exist under the principal transaction, rather than a
fixed obligation of the principal contract before the permitted variation
takes place.[65] For example, a general reference in the guarantee to the
principal transaction may be interpreted not as identifying a principal
transaction, which *may be varied from time to time*, but as referring only to
the particular obligations embodied in the principal transaction at the date
of execution of the guarantee. The guarantee will then relate to those
particular obligations and a departure from those terms will discharge the
guarantor.[66]

(viii) Variation distinguished from subsequent independent agreement

The rule that a variation of the principal contract discharges the   **7–23**
guarantor does not apply if the subsequent agreement between the
principal and the creditor amounts to the formation of a new contract
rather than a variation of the original agreement.[67] Thus the guarantor of a
loan will not be discharged if the creditor grants further loans to the debtor
under a separate and distinct contract, unless the subsequent[68] loan
agreement amounts to a rescission of the original loan agreement or a

---

[63] *e.g. Wren v Emmett Contractors Pty Ltd* (1969) 43 A.L.J.R. 213. As an example in another
context, see *Johnson Bros (Dyers) Ltd v Davison* (1935) 79 S.J. 306 (assignment of tenant's
interest in a lease permitted with consent of the landlord). See also *Gill Duffus SA v Rionda
Futures Ltd* [1994] 2 Lloyd's Rep. 67 at 82 (change to demurrage rate not a variation, but a
calculation reached upon a construction of the contractual terms).
[64] *Hayes v City of Regina* (1959) 20 D.L.R. (2d) 586.
[65] *Trade Credits Ltd v Burnes* [1979] 1 N.S.W.L.R. 630 at 634–635 *per* Mahoney J.A. The
decision was overruled on appeal, but not on this point: see *Burnes v Trade Credits Ltd* (1981)
34 A.L.R. 459. See also *Corumo Holdings Pty Ltd v C Itoh Ltd* (1991) 5 A.C.S.R. 720 at 728–
729.
[66] See *Corumo Holdings Pty Ltd v C Itoh Ltd* (1991) 5 A.C.S.R. 720 at 728–729. The
guarantor may also be discharged in this situation because of a breach of a condition of the
guarantee: see below, para.8–01.
[67] *Bank of Nova Scotia v Neil* (1968) 69 D.L.R. (2d) 357 at 365.
[68] *ibid.*

novation.[69] Where further loans are made to the principal, it is probable that the guarantee will be so drafted that such additional loans come within the ambit of the guarantee, for example, if it is a guarantee of "all present and future debts and liabilities of the debtor". The wording must, however, clearly indicate an intention to bring such loans within the scope of the guarantee. Thus a clause in a guarantee of a builder's obligations stating that any arrangement or alteration of the building contract shall not affect the guarantor's liability was not held to be sufficient to make the guarantor liable for independent borrowings made to enable the builder to perform the construction work.[70]

(ix) Exercise by the creditor of contractual rights

7–24   In *Moschi v Lep Air Services Ltd*,[71] it was argued that a guarantor is discharged when the creditor terminates the principal contract by an acceptance of a repudiatory breach of contract by the principal. One basis for this argument was that such an acceptance would constitute a variation of the principal contract. The House of Lords sensibly rejected the submission in forceful terms. Lord Simon of Glaisdale declared:

> "This seems to me to be, with all respect, an impossible argument. It is only in the jurisprudence of Humpty Dumpty that the rescission of a contract can be equated with its variation. The acceptance of the repudiation of an agreement does not alter its terms in any way—it merely transmutes the primary obligation of the promisor to perform the terms contractually into a secondary obligation, imposed by law, to pay damages for their breach."[72]

7–25   It should follow that any exercise of the contractual or statutory rights of the creditor against the principal will not constitute a variation of the principal contract discharging the guarantor.[73] This is generally so, although there have been a number of exceptional cases[74] where the guarantor was discharged simply because the creditor was exercising his contractual rights to enforce a security. The proper basis of such cases is explained elsewhere.[75]

---

[69] The guarantee will then be discharged because of the determination of the principal transaction (see above, Ch. 6). See the argument in *Adelaide Motors Ltd v Byrne* (1965) 60 D.L.R. (2d) 1.
[70] *Trade Indemnity Co Ltd v Workington Harbour & Dock Board* [1937] A.C. 1 at 21.
[71] [1973] A.C. 331.
[72] *ibid.*, at 355.
[73] See *Dunn v Thickett* [1925] 3 W.W.R. 736 (exercise of right of possession by the guarantor). *Cf. New Zealand Loan & Mercantile Agency Co Ltd v Smith* (1893) 15 A.L.T. 92 (consensual agreement by principal and creditor to convert debt into judgment debt discharged the guarantor).
[74] *Re Darwen and Pearce* [1927] 1 Ch. 176; *Matton v Lipscomb* (1895) 16 L.R. (NSW) Eq. 142.
[75] See below, para.8–83.

(x) Variation by statute

The rule that the guarantor is discharged by a variation of the principal   **7–26**
contract has been extended beyond the situation where there has been a
consensual variation by the creditor and the principal to where the
principal contract has been varied by statute. Thus in *Finch v Jukes*,[76] it
was held that a guarantor for the performance of obligations under a
construction contract was discharged when the obligations of the
contractor were altered by an Act of Parliament. It may need to be
shown in the case of variation by statute, however, that the variation is
material[77] and, in some cases, the legislation may, on its proper
interpretation, not discharge the guarantor but render the guarantor
liable, subject to the variation.[78] The insistence on the requirement of
materiality is probably explained by the fact that the variation has
occurred independently of the actions of the creditor.

(xi) Clauses in the guarantee excluding discharge on the ground of variation

A clause in the guarantee may purport to preserve the guarantor's   **7–27**
liability despite a future variation of the principal contract. The modern
form of guarantee invariably contains a clause, or a number of clauses,
designed to achieve this objective. There has been some judicial comment
on the effectiveness of some of the clauses and it will be useful here to
analyse some of the more common types of construction. Additionally the
validity of clauses of this nature may be subject to challenge pursuant to
the Unfair Terms in Consumer Contracts Regulations 1999, in circumstances where the regulations apply (as discussed in Chapter 4).[79]

(a) The "principal debtor" clause

The guarantee may state that the liabilities of the guarantor shall be   **7–28**
deemed to be those of the principal debtor or primary obligor.[80] It has
been held that such a clause prevents the guarantor being discharged in the
event of a variation of the principal contract whereby the principal is given
further time to perform the obligations under the contract.[81] There is

---

[76] [1877] W.N. 211. See also *Pybus v Gibb* (1856) 6 E. & B. 902; 119 E.R. 1100.
[77] This was the case in *Finch v Jukes* [1877] W.N. 211 and *Pybus v Gibb* (1856) 6 E. & B. 902;
119 E.R. 1100.
[78] *e.g. Public Trustee v T* [1933] N.Z.L.R. 889.
[79] See above, para.4–163. It is unlikely that the Unfair Contract Terms Act 1977 applies to
such clauses. See above, paras 4–160 to 4–162.
[80] *e.g. Heald v O'Connor* [1971] 1 W.L.R. 497.
[81] *Heald v O'Connor* [1971] 1 W.L.R. 497 at 503; *General Produce Co v United Bank Ltd*
[1979] 2 Lloyd's Rep. 255 at 259; *Brown Bros Motor Lease Canada Ltd v Ganapathi* (1982)
139 D.L.R. (3d) 227.

some, although not unanimous, authority[82] which suggests that the clause is effective to preserve the liability of the guarantor in the event of any type of variation of the principal contract, although in some of these cases there were further words in the clause, for example, a general waiver of the guarantor's rights or a specific statement to the effect that the guarantor's obligations were not to be affected by a variation.

7–29   Depending on the context, restrictive interpretations of the principal debtor clause are possible. The clause can be construed as operating only so long as the obligations remained as they were when the guarantee was executed[83] and sometimes the effect of the clause may be limited by other wording in the same clause precluding discharge as a result of specific events (for example, any defect in a security obtained from the principal or the incapacity of the principal). In *Crédit Suisse v Borough Council of Allerdale*[84] Colman J. construed such a clause narrowly to mean that the moneys could be recovered from the guarantor as a principal debtor *only* in respect of eventualities specified.

(b) Agreement that the guarantee is not to be affected by a variation

7–30   The guarantor may simply agree that the guarantee shall not be affected by any variation of the principal contract. A typical example is:

"we ... agree that the guarantee shall not be avoided, released or affected by the [creditor] making any variation or alteration in the terms of the [principal] agreement."[85]

7–31   Such a clause is effective to preserve the liability of the guarantor if a variation takes place,[86] although if there is any additional requirement to

---

[82] *Orme v De Boyette* [1981] 1 N.Z.L.R. 576; *Parker v Bayly* [1927] G.L.R. 265 at 267–268; *Fletcher Organisation Pty Ltd v Crocus Investments Pty Ltd* [1988] 2 Qd. R. 517 (although this was a case dealing with a release of a co-surety); *Greenwood v Francis* [1899] 1 Q.B. 312 at 323–324; *Perrott v Newton King Ltd* [1933] N.Z.L.R. 1131. Note, however, that in *Bank of New Zealand v Baker* [1926] N.Z.L.R. 462 at 487 it was held that the clause standing alone was sufficient to preserve the liability of the guarantor. See also *Orme v De Boyette* [1981] 1 N.Z.L.R. 576 at 580; *Dunlop New Zealand Ltd v Dumbleton* [1968] N.Z.L.R. 1092 at 1097; *Bridgestone Australia Ltd v GAH Engineering Ltd* [1977] Qd. R. 145; *Apus Properties Ltd v Douglas Farrow Ltd* [1989] 2 E.G.L.R. 265 where a clause (akin to a principal debtor clause) equating the position of the surety with the original tenant was not effective to preserve the guarantor's liability in the event of a variation of the lease agreed between the landlord and a subsequent tenant (at 271).
[83] As in *Bridgestone Australia Ltd v GAH Engineering Ltd* [1997] 2 Qd. R. 145. See also *Nelson Fisheries v Boese* [1975] 2 N.Z.L.R. 233 at 235–236 where the guarantor's position and liabilities were deemed to be "those of a principal debtor", but the phrase was qualified by the word "hereunder" (referring to the principal transaction).
[84] [1995] 1 Lloyd's Rep. 315 at 366.
[85] A similar clause appeared in *British Motor Trust Co Ltd v Hyams* (1934) 50 T.L.R. 230.
[86] *British Motor Trust Co Ltd v Hyams* (1934) 50 T.L.R. 230; *Hancock v Williams* (1942) 42 S.R. (NSW) 252 at 256; *Nelson Fisheries Ltd v Boese* [1975] 2 N.Z.L.R. 233 at 235–236; *Industrial Acceptance Corp v Lakeland Lumber Ltd* (1960) 26 D.L.R. (2d) 480 (BC); *Wood Hall Ltd v The Pipeline Authority* (1979) 53 A.L.J.R. 487 at 492; *Sabemo Pty Ltd v De Groot* (1991) 8 B.C.L. 132.

notify the guarantor of any variation, this must be observed.[87] If the word "variation" is not used, difficulties may arise. Thus, where it was provided that the liability of the guarantor shall not be affected by "any waiver or default" made by the creditor which might otherwise operate to discharge the guarantor, it was held that this expression did not include a contractual agreement for a variation between creditor and principal as opposed to a voluntary forbearance.[88] Similarly, a promise by a guarantor of a lease to perform the lessee's covenants "notwithstanding ... any other act or thing whereby but for this provision the guarantor would have been released" was held not to embrace a variation of the lease imposing additional burdens on the lessee through a right of re-entry.[89]

Even where, as is commonly the case, the clause specifically refers to a "variation", it is thought that this will not cover a release of the principal or a novation of the principal contract,[90] although it has already been seen that if appropriate wording is used the guarantor's liability can be maintained despite a simple release of the original principal debtor or a release by a novation.[91]   **7–32**

Although the word "variation" will not generally be interpreted only to include "minor" variations,[92] at the same time it will not encompass the situation where the alteration of the principal contract is so substantial as to raise an inference that the principal and the creditor have agreed to rescind the main contract and then substitute a new contract.[93] The guarantor will then be discharged on the basis that the principal contract which he guaranteed has been determined.[94] Thus a clause in a guarantee of a building contract preserving the guarantor's liability in the event of an "alteration" of the contract will not embrace fundamental changes involving the nature or location of the works.[95]   **7–33**

In this context, however, generally the courts have taken a broad view of what constitutes a variation; for example, where two hire-purchase   **7–34**

---

[87] *e.g. Midland Counties Motor Finance Co Ltd v Slade* [1951] 1 K.B. 346.

[88] *Nelson Fisheries Ltd v Boese* [1975] 2 N.Z.L.R. 233.

[89] *West Hordon Industrial Park Ltd v Phoenix Timber Group plc* [1995] 20 E.G. 137, where variation arose from a subsequent licence agreement. Cf the more robust approach to general wording in *Samuels Finance Group plc v Beechmanor Ltd* (1994) 67 P. & C.R. 282. As to variations of leases see now the Landlord and Tenant (Covenants) Act 1995, s.18, governing the position upon assignment see below, para.7–52.

[90] This conclusion is supported by *Dowling v Ditanda, The Times*, April 15, 1975, where it was held that there was an arguable case that a release of a security was not covered by a clause specifically referring to a variation. See also, by analogy, *Fletcher Organisation Pty Ltd v Crocus Investments Pty Ltd* [1988] 2 Qd. R. 517, where it was held that the words "favour, grace or consideration" did not cover an agreement for the release of a co-surety.

[91] See above, paras 6–74, 6–100 to 6–101.

[92] *Samuels Finance Group plc v Beechmanor Ltd* (1994) 67 P. & C.R. 282 at 285.

[93] For the distinction between a variation and a substituted contract, see *Chitty on Contracts* (28th ed., 1999), para.23–028.

[94] Although the guarantor's liability may be preserved if there is a clause preserving the guarantor's liability in case of a determination of the principal transaction by novation or otherwise.

[95] *Trade Indemnity Co Ltd v Workington Harbour and Dock Board* [1937] AC 1 at 21. See also *Dan v Barclays Australia Ltd* (1983) 57 A.L.J.R. 442 where a variation clause was assumed by the majority (Mason, Brennan and Deane JJ) not to embrace an extinction of the principal transaction governing the terms of credit and the substitution of another transaction governing such terms.

agreements for two separate vehicles were consolidated in one agreement, both vehicles being regarded as being hired together, this was treated as a variation rather than a substituted contract.[96] The terms of the revised agreement will also be important. Thus if the revised agreement, although making amendments in a particular respect (such as the instalments payable), states that the original agreement shall otherwise continue to be of "full effect" in other respects, this will be a factor indicating there has been a variation rather than a substituted contract.[97]

7–35 A substituted contract may also still be guaranteed if the guarantee is sufficiently widely drawn to embrace further contracts between the principal and the creditor. Thus if the guarantee relates to "all leasing contracts entered into between X and Y" during a specified period, any leasing contract will be guaranteed whether or not it is a substitution for an earlier one.

7–36 Even if the alterations are not so substantial as to result in the creation of a new contract in this way, it has been said that there may be "changes falling short of a novation which would yet be so fundamental that they could not properly be described as a variation at all".[98] In such a case the guarantor's liability will not therefore be preserved by a clause which simply embraces "variations" of the principal contract. In *Melvin International SA v Poseidon Schiffahrt Gmbh ("The Kalma")*[99] a guarantee was given in respect of a time charter "from Nemrut Bay, via the Black Sea to the Far East" (with a minimum duration of 57.5 days). When it was clear the agreement was to be completed in less time, addenda, *inter alia*, were entered into extending the agreement to a six/eight month time charter and giving the charterers an option to perform another voyage. This "new and separate adventure" did not come within a clause precluding the guarantor's discharge in the event of any "variation".[1]

(c) An authorisation to vary the principal contract

7–37 The guarantee may authorise the creditor to vary the principal contract and state that any such variation shall not affect the liability of the guarantor. An example of this type of clause, in the context of a mortgage transaction, is:

"The [creditor] shall be at liberty without discharging or in any way affecting the liability of the guarantors ... to vary or give up any

[96] *British Motor Trust Co Ltd v Hyams* (1934) 50 T.L.R. 230; *Co-op Trust Co of Canada v Kirby* [1986] 6 W.W.R. 90; *Esanda Ltd v Powell* (1986) 4 S.R. (WA) 22; *Crédit Lyonnais (Aust) Ltd v Darling* (1991) 5 A.C.S.R. 703 at 717–719.
[97] *Esanda Ltd v Powell* (1986) 4 S.R. (WA) 22. Note that an oral variation of a contract required to be in writing or evidenced in writing will be ineffective: see below, para.7–66.
[98] *Samuels Finance Group plc v Beechmanor* (1994) 67 P. & C.R. 282 at 285; *Melvin International SA v Poseidon Schiffahrt Gmbh ("The Kalma")* [1999] 2 All E.R. (Comm) 761.
[99] [1999] 2 All E.R. (Comm) 761. Cf. *Samuels Finance Group plc v Beechmanor* (1994) 67 P.&C.R. 282 (re-financing arrangement involving considerable injection of funds and removal of charges from some of the guarantors properties treated as a variation).
[1] Although, the changes here was so extensive that the case can reasonably be viewed as the substitution of a new contract.

mortgage ... covenant ... or other security or right of any kind whatsoever which the [creditor] may now or hereafter hold for payment of the said indebtedness."

In Australia it has been held that this clause effectively preserves the **7–38** liability of the guarantor in the event of a variation of the principal transaction even though the guarantor has not specifically consented to the variation or been consulted about it.[2] Sometimes the clause itself reinforces this conclusion by stating that the creditor shall be at liberty to vary the principal contract "without reference to the guarantor". As in a clause of type (b) (above), this wording will not encompass a novation of the principal contract or a rescission of the main contract between creditor and principal and the substitution of a new contract.

(d) A waiver of rights in the event of a variation

The guarantee may state that the guarantor waives any right to be **7–39** released in the event of a variation of the principal contract. The interpretation of such a provision arose for discussion in *Dunlop New Zealand Ltd v Dumbleton*,[3] where the guarantee declared:

"we hereby waive all and any of our rights as sureties (legal, equitable, statutory, or otherwise) which may at any time be inconsistent with any of the above provisions [of the guarantee]."

There seems to be no sound reason why such a declaration expressed in **7–40** terms of a waiver should have a different effect than if the guarantor simply agrees that the guarantee shall not be avoided or affected by the variation (see clause of type (b), above).[4] But in *Dunlop New Zealand Ltd v Dumbleton*, Wilson J. held[5] that the reason why a guarantor was discharged in the event of a variation of the principal contract was because of a term implied by law into the guarantee to that effect, and that this implied term could not be waived. With respect, it is submitted that this view is incorrect on two grounds. First, the rule regarding a variation of the principal contract is an equitable one and is not based upon an implied term of the guarantee. Secondly, even assuming that Wilson J. was correct on the first point, there is abundant authority that a contractual term that is for the benefit of one party can be waived by that party, and the implied

[2] *Duncombe v ANZ Bank Ltd* [1970] Qd. R. 202 at 207. See also *Dunlop New Zealand Ltd v Dumbleton* [1968] N.Z.L.R. 1092 at 1098, where Wilson J. supported the efficacy of an authorisation provision; *Bond v Hong Kong Bank of Australia Ltd* (1991) 25 N.S.W.L.R. 286 at 298, *per* Gleeson C.J.
[3] [1968] N.Z.L.R. 1092.
[4] Provided that the clause is drafted so as to operate as a waiver by the guarantor of the events which would otherwise discharge him. Cf. *Howard de Walden Estates Ltd v Pasta Place Ltd* [1995] 1 E.G.L.R. 79 at 81, where the clause was drafted so as to allow for waiver by the creditor/landlord in the event of breaches or apprehended breaches of the lease by the principal tenant.
[5] [1968] N.Z.L.R. 1092 at 1097–1098.

term that the guarantor shall be discharged in the event of a variation of the principal contract is certainly a term for the guarantor's benefit.

(e) A non-specific clause providing for all matters which might release the guarantor.

7–41   Sometimes a creditor relies on a general clause in the guarantee providing that the guarantor's liability shall continue notwithstanding "any act or thing whereby the guarantor would otherwise have been released". From the creditor's point of view the danger is that the clause can be interpreted restrictively so as not to include a variation. In *West Horndon Industrial Park Ltd v Phoenix Timber Group plc*,[6] for example, in the context of a guarantee of a lease, it was held that such a clause did not embrace a variation imposing additional burdens on a tenant arising from a subsequent licence agreement permitting the landlord to re-enter the premises to make improvements. It was to be more narrowly construed. As Mr Roger Kay Q.C. stated:

> "But I think Mr David Neuberger QC is right when he submits that what was contemplated was that this should cover such cases as the landlord refusing rent in a case where he wrongly believes there to be a breach of covenant or where, say as a condition of an assignment, he has received security for the rent which he subsequently releases. No doubt there are also other examples such as forebearance or where the landlord has agreed for a time with the tenant that the tenant might suspend payment of the rent for reasons best known to the tenant or the landlord. I do not attempt an exhaustive category of cases intended to be covered by those general words at the end of clause 10(1). Suffice it is to say that, in my judgement, they were not intended to cover and do not cover the additional burden imposed by clause 3 of the licence."[7]

Sometimes the guarantor only agrees by the relevant clause to remain liable despite a variation of the principal contract if he receives notice of it.[8] This will generally be construed as a condition precedent, requiring strict compliance.[9] The notice must accurately describe the variation[10] and should be given "in time for some sensible commercial action to be taken by the guarantors".[11] The fact that the guarantors may know of the variation does not excuse the creditor from its duty to comply with the notice provision.[12]

---

[6] [1995] 1 E.G.L.R. 77.
[7] *ibid.*, at 78.
[8] As in *Guiness Mahon & Co Ltd v London Enterprise Investments Ltd* [1995] 4 Bank L.R. 184 at 195.
[9] In *Guiness Mahon & Co Ltd v London Enterprise Investments Ltd* [1995] 4 Bank L.R. 184 it was said such a provision may be construed as an innominate term in appropriate cases, (at 194) but on normal contractual principles such clauses should operate as conditions precedent.
[10] *ibid.*, at 195.
[11] *ibid.*
[12] *Guiness Mahon & Co Ltd v London Enterprise Investments Ltd* [1995] 4 Bank L.R. 184 at 186.

(xii) Consent by the guarantor to the variation

(a) Where the consent is given before or at the time of the variation

If a clause in the guarantee does not preserve the liability of the   **7–42**
guarantor, he may still consent to the variation before or at the time that
the variation is agreed. The burden of proof is on the creditor to show that
there has been such consent,[13] but if the creditor can discharge this onus
the guarantor's liability will be effectively preserved despite the
variation.[14] The consent need not be in writing.[15] Nineteenth century
authority suggests that in order for the consent to be effective the
guarantor must be aware of the legal effect of such acquiescence[16] but in
the most recent decision of *Crédit Suisse v Borough Council of Allerdale*[17]
Colman J. held that it was irrelevant that the guarantors in consenting
might have failed to appreciate "at the time the need for specific consent
in order to make the guarantee effective".[18] This seems the better view.
Provided the guarantor is aware of the nature of the variation, he should
not escape liability simply because he is unaware of technical legal rules
relating to the discharge of guarantees.

Another suggested requirement for a valid consent (supported by   **7–43**
Canadian authority) is that the creditor must disclose all the material facts
surrounding the variation to the guarantor. In *Toronto Dominion Bank v
Calderbank*,[19] it was held that there was no valid consent where the
creditor did not disclose at the time of the variation that the main
operators of the principal company had established themselves in
competition. It is doubtful if English courts would require disclosure of
such extraneous facts, but they may well require a detailed explanation of
the type of variation envisaged.

It is clear, however, that mere knowledge of the variation is an   **7–44**
insufficient basis from which to infer consent. In *Wren v Emmett
Contractors Pty Ltd*,[20] Menzies J. drew a distinction between mere
knowledge of the variation and consent to the variation, stressing that
"mere knowledge of the variation ... does not of itself amount to

---

[13] *Provincial Bank of Ireland v Fisher* [1919] 2 I.R. 249; *General Steam-Navigation Co v Rolt*
(1858) 6 C.B. (NS) 550; 141 E.R. 572; *Williams v Frayne* (1937) 58 C.L.R. 710.
[14] *Clark v Devlin* (1803) 3 Bos. & Pul. 363; 127 E.R. 198; *Woodcock v Oxford & Worcester
Railway Co.* (1853) 1 Drew. 521; 61 E.R. 551; *Wren v Emmett Contractors Pty Ltd* (1969) 43
A.L.J.R. 213 at 220; *Harris v Rathbone* (1911) 13 G.L.R. 500; *Winstone Ltd v Bourne* [1978] 1
N.Z.L.R. 94.
[15] Except where the principal contract has itself to be in writing.
[16] *Strange v Fooks* (1863) 4 Giff. 408 at 412–413; 66 E.R. 765 at 768.
[17] [1995] 1 Lloyd's Rep. 315.
[18] *ibid.*, at 363.
[19] (1982) 142 D.L.R. (3d) 528. See also *Toronto Dominion Bank v Rooke* (1983) 3 D.L.R.
(4th) 715 and note that in *Mayhew v Crickett* (1818) 2 Swanst. 185 at 193; 36 ER 585 at 588,
Lord Eldon emphasised that the surety had "a knowledge of the circumstances". See above,
para.4–15, however, for criticism of the view that the duty to disclose unusual facts is a
continuing duty.
[20] (1969) 43 A.L.J.R. 213.

consent".[21] This distinction between knowledge and consent is exemplified by the fact that the guarantor is under no duty to warn the creditor against agreeing to a variation with the principal when the guarantor knows that the variation is going to occur.[22] In early cases, there was some suggestion that the guarantor could be liable merely because he had knowledge of the variation[23] and even that the guarantor might be under a duty to inquire whether dealings between the creditor and the principal constituted a variation,[24] but these views cannot now be considered correct.

7–45   Although mere knowledge of the variation is insufficient to establish consent, an implied consent may be inferred from the circumstances. The most obvious cases where an implication can be made are where the guarantor requests or instigates the variation,[25] arranges the variation[26] or is involved in the preparation of documents necessary for its execution.[27] The reason why the guarantor's liability will continue where the guarantor requests the variation is that there is a separate oral contract between guarantor and creditor, the creditor's assent to the variation being consideration for the guarantor's promise to remain liable.

7–46   Sometimes the guarantor or those acting for the guarantor may request or arrange the variation when acting in a capacity other than that of guarantor, but consent may nevertheless be inferred. In *Crédit Suisse v Borough Council of Allerdale*[28] a guarantee was given by the Council for debts of a company set up by the Council to assist with the Council's various capital projects. The giving of the guarantee was, as held, not within the statutory powers of the Council, but Colman J. also considered the effect upon the guarantee of variations to the loan agreement agreed between the company and the lending bank. The consent of the Council as guarantor to the amendments was inferred on the basis of these facts:[29]

(a) The Solicitor to the Council was the company secretary and the Chief Executive and Director of Finance of the Council was a company director.

---

[21] *ibid.*, at 220.
[22] *Matton v Lipscomb* (1895) 16 L.R. (NSW) Eq. 142 at 149; *Polak v Everett* (1876) 1 Q.B.D. 669 at 673 *per* Blackburn J.
[23] See *Tyson v Cox* (1823) Turn. & R. 395 at 399–400; 37 E.R. 1153 at 1155, where there is some suggestion that knowledge alone is sufficient. *Cf.*, however, in the context of a fidelity guarantee, *Enright v Falvey* (1879) 4 L.R. Ir. 397 at 402–403; *Warre v Calvert* (1837) 7 Ad. & E. 143 at 154–155; 112 E.R. 425 at 429–430 *per* Littledale J.
[24] *General Steam-Navigation Co v Rolt* (1858) 6 C.B. (NS) 550 at 595–599; 141 E.R. 572 at 589–590 *per* Cockburn C.J. and Crowder J. But they held that on the facts of the case there was no duty to inquire. *Cf.* Willes J. (1858) 6 C.B. (NS) 550 at 599–601; 141 E.R. 572 at 590–591, who denied the operation of constructive knowledge in this context.
[25] *Metropolitan Properties (Regis) Ltd v Bartholomew* (1996) 72 P. 8 C.R. 380; *Apus Properties Ltd v Douglas Farrow Ltd* [1989] 2 E.G.L.R. 265 at 271; *Harris v Rathbone* (1911) 13 G.L.R. 500; *Williams v Frayne* (1937) 58 CLR 710.
[26] *Apus Properties Ltd v Douglas Farrow Ltd* [1989] 2 E.G.L.R. 265 at 271; *Wren v Emmett Contractors* (1969) 43 A.L.J.R. 213 at 220; *Barns v Jacobsen* [1924] N.Z.L.R. 653. See also *Clyde Industries v Dittes* (unreported, NSW Sup Ct, June 5, 1992).
[27] *Woodcock v Oxford & Worcester Railway Co* (1853) 1 Drew 521; 61 E.R. 551; *Co-op Trust Co of Canada v Kirby* [1986] 6 W.W.R. 90. See also *Bond v Hong Kong Bank of Australia Ltd* (1991) 25 N.S.W.L.R. 286 at 309 *per* Kirby P. (as he then was).
[28] [1995] 1 Lloyd's Rep. 315.
[29] *ibid.*, at 362–363.

(b) These Council officers had a duty to submit to the Council on behalf of the company all relevant information, and they had a parallel duty to the company to receive such information on the Council's behalf.

(c) The Officers of the Council were empowered to make detailed financial arrangements (which included amendments to the loan agreement) provided that they did so in consultation with the Chair of the Council's Policy and Finance Committee. This requirement had been complied with.

(d) When the Council's solicitor (acting on instructions from the Council's Chief Executive) accepted the offer of variation from the bank the effect of this conduct was to inform the bank that the Council as well as the company were agreeing to the amendment, since the acceptance signed on behalf of the company was sent under the cover of a letter from the Council. Indeed there was an earlier letter on Council notepaper requesting the re-structuring.

Where, as here, the guarantor is an independent statutory authority such clear proof of consent will be required, but it is likely that consent will be more readily inferred in the more usual case where the guarantor is a director of the principal debtor company and negotiates with the creditor in that capacity. In this situation, the guarantor argued in *Winstone Ltd v Bourne*[30] that he had not assented to the variation in his capacity as a guarantor, but only in his capacity as a director of the principal company. Mahon J. rejected this argument:

"On the facts, *bearing in mind the clear knowledge of the defendants of their liabilities as guarantors*, I cannot hold that their informed and indorsed assent as directors of that company to the alteration in the debenture was not also an informed though unrecorded assent as guarantors of the [creditor's] debt."[31]

Aside from inferring consent, another basis for the continuing liability of the guarantor in this context is estoppel.[32] The creditor may have assumed as a result of the guarantor's conduct that the guarantee will remain effective[33] and relied upon that assumption by agreeing to the variation. Ignorance or mistake as to the guarantor's rights will not prevent the estoppel arising.[34] One potential advantage to the creditor of the principle of estoppel in this context is that it may arise when the facts do not clearly

7–47

---

[30] [1978] 1 N.Z.L.R. 94.
[31] *ibid.*, at 96 (emphasis added). See also *Wren v Emmett Contractors Pty Ltd* (1969) 43 A.L.J.R. 213 at 220 *per* Menzies J.; *Miles v Zuckerman* [1931] 1 D.L.R. 448 esp at 451.
[32] *Crédit Suisse v Borough Council of Allerdale* [1995] 1 Lloyd's Rep. 315.
[33] The application of estoppel in this way therefore leaves the original guarantee in place so that issues relating to the Statute of Frauds do not arise. See *Crédit Suisse v Borough Council of Allerdale* (*ibid.*) at 370–371.
[34] In *Crédit Suisse v Borough Council of Allerdale* [1995] 1 Lloyd's Rep. 315 at 370 it was said that ignorance of the variation itself would also not prevent the estoppel arising, but it is difficult to see why the guarantor's conduct should be treated as unconscionable and bind him if he is not aware of the altered circumstances.

indicate consent since it is based, not upon express agreement or the state of mind of the person who is estopped, but upon the unconscionability of permitting him to adopt inconsistent positions as to the relationship between himself and the other party. For example, in *Crédit Suisse v Borough Council of Allerdale*[35] fact (d) alone (as set out above)[36] would arguably have constituted an estoppel as against the Council.

7–48   As in the case of a clause in the guarantee permitting a variation,[37] a consent to a variation of the contract given by the guarantor at or before the date of the variation will render the guarantor liable only if what has taken place constitutes a variation as opposed to the formation of a new contract. Thus where a guarantor of an employment contract, in which the term of engagement was limited to one year, consented to remain liable when the term of employment was extended under a new contract, it was held that this required a new guarantee,[38] evidenced in writing. But if the guarantee had been worded so as to relate to future contracts, the guarantor would have remained liable without any need for a new guarantee.[39]

(b) Where the consent is given after the date of the variation

7–49   The creditor may negotiate the variation with the principal and only afterwards seek to obtain the consent of the guarantor to the variation. There is clear authority which suggests that an assertion of acceptance of liability by the guarantor at this time is binding on him, notwithstanding the absence of consideration and even though the guarantor simply assents to the variation (rather than specifically agreeing to be bound by the guarantee).[40]

7–50   It has been argued that the guarantor's continued liability is an analogous situation to that occurring when a promise or acknowledgment revives a debt already barred by the Statute of Limitations.[41] Another view[42] is that the continued liability is based on an estoppel or waiver.[43]

---

[35] *ibid.*

[36] See above, para.7–46.

[37] See above, paras 7–32 to 7–36.

[38] *Kitson v Julian* (1855) 4 E. & B. 854; 119 E.R. 317.

[39] *ibid.*, at 319.

[40] *Crédit Suisse v Borough Council of Allerdale* [1995] 1 Lloyd's Rep. 315 at 364; *Mayhew v Crickett* (1818) 2 Swanst. 185; 36 E.R. 585; *Smith v Winter* (1838) 4 M. & W. 454 at 467; 150 E.R. 1507 at 1513, *per* Parke B.; *Phillips v Foxall* (1872) L.R. 7 Q.B. 666 at 676–677 *per* Quain J.

[41] See this view discussed in *Wilson v Cristall* (1922) 63 D.L.R. 187 at 192. It is supported by *Mayhew v Crickett* (1818) 2 Swanst. 185 at 192; 36 E.R. 585 at 587, which refers to "a revival of an old debt".

[42] *Wilson v Cristall* (1922) 63 D.L.R. 187 at 192; *Crédit Suisse v Borough Council of Allerdale* [1995] 1 Lloyd's Rep. 315 at 364.

[43] For Australian criticism, see *Queensland Investment & Land Mortgage Co Ltd v Hart* (1894) 6 Q.L.J. 186 at 194. In that case *Mayhew v Crickett* (1818) 2 Swanst. 185; 36 E.R. 585 was confined to where a promise revives a debt barred by the Statute of Limitations and other exceptional situations. *Smith v Winter* (1838) 4 M. & W. 454; 150 E.R. 1507 was distinguished on the basis that, on the facts, the creditor did "a further act" in exchange for the guarantor's promise.

These seem to be doubtful bases for by-passing normal contractual principles.[44] Certainly the argument founded upon estoppel may well fail because it cannot be said that the creditor relies upon the guarantor's representation of consent, since the variation has already taken place before the guarantor's assurance is given.[45]

(xiii) Consent by the principal to the continuation of the guarantor's liability

There is authority which indicates in the context of a variation giving the principal further time to perform the principal obligation that the guarantor's liability will be preserved where the principal gives consent to the continuation of the guarantor's liability in the agreement of variation. The precise operation of this rule and the rationale for it are explained in the section dealing with a variation involving a giving of time.[46] There is no reported case where a similar conclusion has been reached in the context of a variation other than a giving of time and it is thought that the authorities may be confined to that situation.[47] Thus if the guarantor's liability is to continue in the event of a variation, there must be an appropriate clause in the guarantee which in some way authorises the variation, or the guarantor must otherwise consent to the variation.

7–51

(xiv) Variation and assignment of leases

Section 18 of the Landlord and Tenant (Covenants) Act 1995, contains provisions designed to protect the position of a leasehold tenant (and his guarantor) who remain liable under their leasehold covenants despite having assigned the lease. In the case of a new tenancy (that is, one entered into after January 1, 1996) such liability may arise because he has entered into an "authorised guarantee agreement" pursuant to s.16,[48] and in the case of an existing tenancy, because under the general law the original lessee remains bound by his covenants despite the assignment.[49]

7–52

---

[44] See J. Beatson, *Anson's Law of Contract* (28th ed., 2002), pp.112–126, 115 and the requirement of alteration of position. Note that it is possible, although unlikely, that the variation was made by the principal debtor or creditor acting as agent of the guarantor, and the subsequent consent operates as a ratification of the debtor or creditor's authority to negotiate the variation. See *Burnard v Lysnar* (1929) N.Z.P.C.C. 538, where the principal debtor was held to be agent of the guarantor. See also generally J. Beatson, *Anson's Law of Contract* (28th ed., 2002), pp.486–490.

[45] *ibid.*.

[46] See below, para.7–88, and the cases there cited.

[47] In *Holland-Canada Mortgage Co v Hutchings* [1936] 2 D.L.R. 481 at 489, Davis J. drew a distinction between these situations. See also *Reid v Royal Trust Corp of Canada* (1985) 20 D.L.R. (4th) 223 at 242.

[48] See above, para.6–154.

[49] See above, paras 6–149 to 6–153, especially 6–153. Now, however, see Landlord and Tenant (Covenants) Act 1995, s.5, which has the effect of releasing a former tenant from his covenants immediately upon assignment. His obligations devolve upon the assignee who is treated for all purposes as if he were the original tenant.

7–53   Section 18 provides that where there is such a liability and the terms of the lease have been varied since the assignment and after the commencement of the Act (January 1, 1996), the former tenant is not liable to pay any sum that is referable to the variation. The position of the guarantor of a former tenant is addressed in s.18(3). This states:

> "Where a person ('the guarantor') has agreed to guarantee the performance by the former tenant of a tenant covenant of the tenancy, the guarantor (where his liability to do so is not wholly discharged by any such variation of the tenant covenants of the tenancy) shall not be liable under the agreement to pay any amount in respect of the covenant to the extent that the amount is referable to any such variation."

The fact that the provision does not apply where the guarantor's liability is "not wholly discharged by any such variation" means that the normal rule as to variation prima facie applies. Thus if there are no clauses in the guarantee governing variation the guarantor will be wholly discharged by a variation that is not obviously insubstantial or for the benefit of the guarantor. But if the lease contains a clause preserving the liability of the guarantor in the event of a variation, s.18(3) limits the effectiveness of the clause since it means that the guarantor will not be liable for any increased liability referable to that variation. For example if the landlord agrees with the assignee to allow the premises to be used for commercial rather than residential purposes on payment of additional rent (contrary to the terms of the lease) neither the former tenant nor his guarantor will be liable for the resulting increased amount of rent.[50]

7–54   Section 18 only applies where "the landlord has, at the time of the variation, an absolute right to refuse to allow it".[51] Thus the section does not apply if the lease permits the tenant to vary the lease, albeit subject to certain conditions (for instance, in the example given, an option to use the premises for commercial purposes if an increased rent is paid).

(xv) Variation and contracts of indemnity

7–55   Where there is a contract of indemnity and the principal is given time to satisfy the obligation which is indemnified, the indemnifier will not be discharged.[52] It is thought, therefore, that the indemnifier will not be discharged in equity by other types of variation of the principal contract, although in particular cases it may be possible to identify an express or implied term in the indemnity to the effect that the contract which is indemnified should not be altered by the parties to it. For example, if the indemnifier promises to indemnify the lessor of a chattel against any loss

---

[50] Both s.18(2) and s.18(3) contemplate that the former tenant and guarantor, as the case may be, retain some liability. Thus it is unlikely that a guarantee containing a clause preserving the guarantor's liability in the event of a variation is void pursuant to s.25. See G. Andrews & R. Millett, *Law of Guarantees* (3rd ed., 2000) p.539.

[51] s.18(4)(a).

[52] *Way v Hearn* (1862) 11 C.B. (NS) 774; 142 E.R. 1000; *Wilson v Zealandia Soap & Candle Trading Co Ltd* [1927] G.L.R. 120 at 121.

arising from entering into the lease, it is arguable that the indemnity is given on the basis that the lessor and lessee do not radically alter the nature of the lease.

(xvi) Critique

Should there be any modification of the law relating to the rule that a variation of the principal contract discharges the guarantor? Clearly the adequacy of the existing law whereby the guarantor is discharged for almost every kind of minor variation needs reconsideration. It is thought that the present law, which only excludes "obviously unsubstantial" variations or variations which are clearly for the benefit of the guarantor from the application of the rule, unduly favours the guarantor. As an example, in *Mystery of the Mercers of the City of London v New Hampshire Insurance Co*,[53] (at first instance) Phillips J. released the guarantor of a building contractor's obligations from all liability only four months after receiving a fee of £45,600 because of an agreement between the owner and the contractor which extended by 24 days the latest date upon which the contractor was to take possession of the building site in order to commence work. The present rule of discharge also means that a variation which is intended to benefit all parties discharges the guarantor. For instance, it may be necessary to restructure the principal contract in order to avoid a temporary cash flow problem and thus avoid the principal's insolvency.

7–56

A preferable test is that the variation must be material in the sense that the guarantor will only be discharged when the potential liability under the guarantee is increased. Admittedly this imposes on the courts the function of deciding whether the variation is material, but this task is certainly no more difficult than ascertaining whether the variation is "obviously unsubstantial". The significant advantage of a test based upon materiality is that it protects a creditor who has sensibly agreed to a variation for the benefit of all parties.

7–57

Even in the case of a material variation the guarantor's liability should be preserved if there is an agreement in writing to remain liable at the time that the variation takes place. This would mean that a creditor could always protect the security by consulting the guarantor. This recommendation does involve the possibility of undue pressure being brought to bear on the guarantor to extract the guarantor's consent, but it is considered that this factor is outweighed by the need to allow the parties to the principal contract some freedom of action when circumstances change subsequent to the execution of the contract.

7–58

[53] (Unreported, Q.B., January 18, 1991). On appeal, it was held that the obliger's liability under the bond was not discharged by this variation because the bond was neither a guarantee nor an indemnity: *Mercers Co v New Hampshire Insurance Co* noted in [1992] 3 All E.R. 57. See also the comments of Kirby P. (as he then was) in *Corumo Holdings Pty Ltd v C Itoh Ltd* (1991) 5 A.C.S.R. 720 at 727 and in *Bond v Hong Kong Bank of Australia Ltd* (1991) 25 N.S.W.L.R. 286 at 307–308.

2. DISCHARGE BY THE CREDITOR AGREEING WITH THE PRINCIPAL TO GIVE TIME TO THE PRINCIPAL

(i) General scope of the rule

7–59   A binding agreement by the creditor to extend the time for the performance by the principal of the principal's obligations under the main contract releases the guarantor from liability.[54] The guarantor is released not only in respect of the guarantor's personal liability but also in respect of any additional security which has been given.[55] This is an aspect of the general rule that a variation of the principal contract discharges the guarantor, but it merits separate treatment because it is the most common example of a variation and it is distinctive since such an extension of time releases the guarantor whether or not the guarantor may be prejudiced by the extension.[56] Indeed, discharge occurs even if the giving of time is "manifestly for the benefit of the surety",[57] and even if the extension of time given is very short.[58]

7–60   As indicated later in this chapter,[59] it is considered that this formulation of the rule regarding the giving of time favours the guarantor to an extent that cannot be justified. Suffice to say, at present, there has been such judicial criticism of the rule that it cannot be considered beyond reversal.[60]

7–61   Indeed, one authority confines the rule to where the guarantee relates to the payment of a debt on a fixed date and that date is postponed. Thus in *Unigate Ltd v Bentley*,[61] it was held by the Court of Appeal not to apply where the date for completing certain tests pursuant to a joint venture agreement was extended, with the result that the guarantor of the agreement was not discharged. But this limitation has not gained general approval, and is not found in any of the older authorities.

7–62   One situation in which it is established that the guarantor will not be released is when he no longer remains in the capacity of a guarantor when

---

[54] *Moschi v Lep Air Services Ltd* [1973] A.C. 331; *Oakeley v Pasheller* (1836) 10 Bligh N.S. 548; 6 E.R. 202; *Rees v Berrington* (1795) 2 Ves. 540; 30 E.R. 765; *Polak v Everett* (1876) 1 Q.B.D. 669 at 673–674; *Samuell v Howarth* (1817) 3 Mer. 272 at 277–279; 36 E.R. 105 at 107–108; *Bank of Ireland v Beresford* (1818) 6 Dow. 233; 3 E.R. 1456; *Payton v SG Brookes & Sons Pty Ltd* [1977] W.A.R. 91 at 92–93; *Hancock v Williams* (1942) 42 S.R. (NSW) 252 at 255.
[55] *Bolton v Salmon* [1891] 2 Ch. 48; *Smith v Wood* [1929] 1 Ch. 14 at 23–24, 27–28.
[56] *Ward v National Bank of New Zealand* (1883) 8 App. Cas. 755 at 763; *Samuell v Howarth* (1817) 3 Mer. 272; 36 E.R. 105; *Polak v Everett* (1876) 1 Q.B.D. 669 at 673–674.
[57] *Samuell v Howarth* (1817) 3 Mer. 272 at 278; 36 E.R. 105 at 107. Note, however, that Amplett J.A. in *Croydon Gas Co v Dickinson* (1876) 2 C.P.D. 46 at 51 applied the general rule regarding variation. See also *Corumo Holdings Pty Ltd v C Itoh Ltd* (1991) 5 A.C.S.R. 720.
[58] *Polak v Everett* (1876) 1 Q.B.D. 669 at 674; *Brown v Aimers* [1934] N.Z.L.R. 414 at 423.
[59] See below, para.7–90.
[60] *Petty v Cooke* (1871) L.R. 6 Q.B. 790 at 795; *Polak v Everett* (1876) 1 Q.B.D. 669 at 674.
[61] Unreported, November 25, 1986, CA. See also *Bunting v MJN McNaughton Ltd* [1992] 2 N.Z.L.R. 513; *Matton v Lipscomb* (1895) 16 L.R. (NSW) Eq. 142 at 146; *Corumo Holdings Pty Ltd v C Itoh Ltd* (1991) 24 N.S.W.L.R. 370 where the New South Wales Court of Appeal did not specifically refer to the special rule regarding the giving of time where the principal contract obliged one joint venturer in a land development project to purchase the shares of the other joint venturers if a particular stage of development had not been approved by a certain date, and (*inter alia*) an extension of time was given for the purchase to take place.

time is given.[62] Hence a guarantor who has assumed a primary liability will not be discharged if the creditor gives time to the principal.[63] One specific illustration of this is where the creditor obtains judgment against both principal and guarantor, because after judgment both principal and guarantor are treated on an equal footing as principals.[64] Conversely, a guarantor will be released if, although originally a principal, the status of a guarantor has been acquired at the date when time is given and the creditor has notice of that fact.[65] The same applies if the creditor erroneously thinks the guarantor is a principal (because the guarantor has contracted vis-à-vis the creditor as such) but is later given notice of his true status.[66]

The rationale upon which the discharge of the guarantee is based is that the giving of time would prejudice the guarantor in circumstances where he chose to pay off the creditor and sue the principal for an indemnity. If the guarantor were prevented from suing until the relevant period of time had expired, the guarantor's position would be altered.[67] If, on the other hand, the law allowed the guarantor to proceed at once against the principal debtor, the agreement to give time would be effectively nullified from the principal's point of view, and a fraud on the principal would result.[68]

7–63

Before the guarantor is released there must exist a legally enforceable agreement which results in the principal being given time for the performance of the obligations under the principal contract.

7–64

(ii) Necessity for a binding agreement between creditor and principal

The agreement giving time must be legally binding, so as to put the creditor in a position where the principal cannot be sued in accordance with the terms of the original agreement between them.[69] This is not the case where an agreement to give time not under seal is unsupported by consideration,[70] or where the principal fails to comply with conditions that the creditor attaches to the undertaking to give time.[71] It also follows that

7–65

---

[62] *Payton v SG Brookes & Sons Pty Ltd* [1997] W.A.R. 91 at 93.
[63] e.g. *Reade v Lowndes* (1857) 23 Beav. 361; 53 E.R. 142.
[64] *Re a Debtor* [1913] 3 K.B. 11 at 13; *Jenkins v Robertson* (1854) 2 Drew. 351; 61 E.R. 755; *Duff v Barrett* (1869) 15 Gr. 632. *Cf.* the situation where the original principal debtor is released so that no debt remains: *Re a Debtor* [1913] 3 K.B. 11 at 14.
[65] *Rouse v Bradford Banking Co* [1894] A.C. 586 at 592–593; *Australian Joint Stock Bank v Hogan* (1902) 2 S.R. (NSW) 7 (defendant became a guarantor by retiring from a partnership).
[66] *Oakeley v Pasheller* (1836) 10 Bli. (NS) 548; 6 E.R. 202; *Overend, Gurney & Co Ltd (Liquidators) v Oriental Financial Corp Ltd (Liquidators)* (1874) L.R. 7 H.L. 348 at 360–361; *Burnard v Lysnar* [1927] N.Z.L.R. 757; on appeal: (1929) N.Z.P.C.C. 538.
[67] *Polak v Everett* (1876) 1 Q.B.D. 669 at 673–674.
[68] *Oriental Financial Corp v Overend, Gurney & Co* (1871) 7 Ch. App. 142 at 150.
[69] *Tucker v Laing* (1856) 2 K. & J. 745 at 751–752; 69 E.R. 982 at 985; *Rees v Berrington* (1795) 2 Ves. 540; 30 E.R. 765; *Jet Power Credit Union Ltd v Grant* (1974) 2 O.R. (2d) 657. Note an interesting example in *Clarke v Birley* (1889) 41 Ch. D. 422 at 434–435.
[70] *Thomas & Co Ltd v Welk* [1935] S.A.S.R. 165 at 168; *Mackenzie v West* (1890) 16 V.L.R. 588 at 590; *Williams v Frayne* (1937) 58 C.L.R. 710 at 717.
[71] *Vernon v Turley* (1836) 1 M. & W. 316; 150 E.R. 454.

mere failure of the creditor to sue the principal for any default does not release the guarantor.[72]

7–66   The agreement to give time need not be in writing,[73] except where the principal agreement itself is required to be in writing or is required to be evidenced in writing.[74]

7–67   Provided that a legally binding agreement exists, it need not be in express terms but can be implied.[75] Thus it has been held[76] that the acceptance of interest before it was due amounted to an implied promise by the creditor not to sue for the principal sum until the date on which the interest would have been payable. The principal could otherwise have been called up at any time. The court was prepared to infer this agreement even though the early payment of interest had not been requested by the creditor and even though there had been no express statement by the creditor forbearing to sue for the principal sum. Another example of an implied agreement to give time is where the creditor takes a promissory note or negotiable instrument from the debtor for the amount of an unsecured debt and the note or instrument is payable after the due date for payment of the debt.[77]

7–68   The question of whether there exists an implied agreement to give time arises in its most problematical form where the debt is secured and the creditor accepts a second security from the principal. In this context an agreement to give time may be inferred because of the application of the doctrine of merger by higher remedy.[78] This will apply if a creditor takes a security of "a higher nature" from the principal; for example, if a mortgage is subsequently taken from the principal to secure a debt which is only secured by a promissory note. The creditor's remedies on the "minor" security are merged in the "higher remedy" by operation of law and are extinguished, so that if the second security makes the debt payable at a subsequent date to that stipulated in the first security, this will amount to a giving of time.

7–69   Even where the doctrine of merger by higher remedy does not operate, for instance, where the subsequent security is of the same or lesser nature as the initial security, the mere acceptance of the new security by the creditor has often been interpreted as an implied and binding promise not

---

[72] *Trent Navigation Co v Harley* (1808) 10 East. 34; 103 E.R. 688; *Payton v SG Brookes & Sons Pty Ltd* [1977] W.A.R. 91 at 93; *Waung v Subbotovsky* [1968] 3 N.S.W.R. 499 at 508–509, where the creditor waited for a period of over twenty years after the principal defaulted before suing the guarantor (and unusually on the facts the plaintiff was not barred from taking proceedings by the Statute of Limitations).

[73] *Nisbet v Smith* (1789) 2 Bro. C.C. 579; 29 E.R. 317; *Deane v City Bank of Sydney* (1904) 2 C.L.R. 198 (agreement partly oral, partly in writing).

[74] *Goss v Lord Nugent* (1833) 5 B. & Ad. 58; 110 E.R. 713; *Dowling v Rae* (1927) 39 C.L.R. 363.

[75] *Blake v White* (1836) 1 Y. & C. Exch. 420; 160 E.R. 171; *Johnston and Ward v McCartney* [1934] 2 D.L.R. 800; *Mills v Schwass* [1929] G.L.R. 460.

[76] *Mills v Schwass* [1929] G.L.R. 460.

[77] *e.g. Harris v Rathbone* (1911) 13 G.L.R. 500 (although the guarantor also consented in this case). For an example of where the court refused to imply an agreement, see *York City & County Banking Co v Bainbridge* (1880) 43 L.T. 732. This is a somewhat harsh decision from the guarantor's point of view.

[78] For the requirements of the doctrine of merger, see G.L. Williams, *Joint Obligations* (1949), para.48. See also *Ward v National Bank of New Zealand* (1886) 4 N.Z.L.R. 35.

to sue for the debt on its due date.[79] Although the cases are not entirely consistent, it appears that the courts will readily imply such an agreement if, first, it is clear that the whole of the moneys secured by the first security are also secured by the second security;[80] and, secondly, the further security states that the money due under it shall be payable at a date subsequent to that specified in the first security[81] or can only be recovered after complying with time limits not imposed by the first security.[82] Thus in *Brown v Aimers*,[83] a guarantor of a mortgage was held to be discharged where the creditor took a bill of sale over the debtor's furniture for the repayment of money owing under a mortgage. The bill of sale made it plain that the moneys to be repaid were the moneys owing under the previous mortgage and imposed time limits (by the elapse of a reasonable period of time after demand) which were not contained in the previous mortgage.

A difficult question is whether the implied agreement to give time which is inferred from the taking of the second security can be negated if the second security contains a clause making it plain that the creditor's remedies under the first security remain. In *Twopenny v Young*[84] there was some suggestion that an appropriate clause could achieve this result because the conclusion that the taking of the second security did not amount to a giving of time was fortified by the fact that the second security was expressed to be "a further security". In *Bolton v Buckenham*,[85] however, the Court of Appeal was of the view that any provision preserving the remedies under the first security should be rejected as being inconsistent with the fact that a second security had been taken containing different terms. The relevant clause in the subsequent security stated specifically that the "full benefit" of the principal's covenants in the first security should be preserved. Esher M.R. said this:

7–70

> "But it is said that the benefit of the covenant by the principal debtor in the first deed is in terms reserved by the second. If that be so I do not think it makes any difference. I do not think that a person can in a deed reserve rights which, by other terms of the same deed, he has necessarily given up. The words of reservation are in such case idle words."[86]

[79] *Bolton v Buckenham* [1891] 1 Q.B. 278; *Brown v Aimers* [1934] N.Z.L.R. 414; *Munster and Leinster Bank v France* (1899) 24 L.R. Ir. 82; *Hatrick v Nicol* (1910) 30 N.Z.L.R. 257.
[80] *Bolton v Buckenham* [1891] 1 Q.B. 278 at 281, *per* Esher M.R., 281–282, *per* Kay L.J.; *Brown v Aimers* [1934] N.Z.L.R. 414 at 420, *per* Kennedy J. This was also the case in *Munster and Leinster Bank v France* (1899) 24 L.R. Ir. 82. *Cf. Twopenny v Young* (1824) 3 B. & C. 208; 107 E.R. 711, where it was not clear from the terms of the second security whether this requirement was satisfied.
[81] As in *Bolton v Buckenham* [1891] 1 Q.B. 278.
[82] As in *Brown v Aimers* [1934] N.Z.L.R. 414. If the two securities are given in pursuance of the original agreement, the inference is probably that they are independent securities, with the security enforceable at a later date not to be construed as affecting the enforcement of the other: *Boaler v Mayor* (1865) 19 C.B. (NS) 76; 144 E.R. 714, and its interpretation in *Munster and Leinster Bank v France* (1899) 24 L.R. Ir. 82 at 87, *per* Lord Ashbourne.
[83] [1934] N.Z.L.R. 414.
[84] (1824) 3 B. & C. 208; 107 E.R. 711 at 712.
[85] [1891] 1 Q.B. 278.
[86] *ibid.*, at 281. Similarly, *per* Kay L.J. at 282.

7–71   It is thought, however, that this conclusion is wrong because it is inconsistent with other authorities[87] which have held that even the doctrine of merger is subject to the intentions of the parties as expressed in the subsequent security. If an appropriate provision can negate the application of the principles of merger, it is also likely that it can negate an implied agreement to give time which would otherwise be inferred from the taking of the second security.

7–72   In the absence of evidence indicating that the whole of the moneys secured by the first security are also secured by the second security, which also provides that the money shall be due on a subsequent date, it is a question of fact in each case whether the court will be prepared to imply from other evidence a promise to forbear from suing for the debt at the earlier date.[88]

7–73   The agreement to give time must be made between the creditor and the principal. The guarantor is not released by an agreement between the creditor and an independent third party, by which the creditor gives time to the principal in consideration of the third party ensuring that the principal performs the contract.[89] This constitutes a new guarantee but it does not release the original guarantor of the principal contract. A similar situation exists where the agreement is between the creditor and a co-guarantor: the guarantor is not released by the creditor promising a co-guarantor that time will be given to the principal.[90] The reason for this is that the principal cannot enforce the creditor's promise to give time because it was not made to the principal, who was not a party to the agreement. In accordance with the rationale of the rule relating to the giving of time[91] it is permissible, therefore, for the guarantor to pay off the creditor and sue the principal at the original date for performance. The principal cannot argue that this operates as a fraud upon him by negating a binding agreement to give him time because he has never in fact been in a position to enforce such an agreement.

7–74   The agreement to give time must arise out of a voluntary agreement between creditor and principal and not as a result of a judicial order, even if the creditor consents to the order.[92]

---

[87] *Barclays Bank Ltd v Beck* [1952] 2 Q.B. 47; *Northern Crown Bank v Elford* (1917) 34 D.L.R. 280.

[88] Some Australian cases illustrate this point, although they are not entirely consistent. For example, in *Swan v National Bank* (1873) 4 A.L.J.R. 42 the creditor's action in taking a lien on the next clip of wool did not induce the court to imply a promise to forbear from enforcing a charge over the sheep (enforceable on demand) until the wool was sheared, but in *Queensland Investment & Land Mortgage Co Ltd v Hart* (1894) 6 Q.L.J. 186 a lien which was taken over future crops was held to constitute a promise not to enforce a mortgage over the farm property until the crops were harvested.

[89] *Frazer v Jordan* (1857) 8 E. & B. 303; 120 E.R. 113; *Lyon v Holt* (1839) 5 M. & W. 250; 151 E.R. 107.

[90] *Clarke v Birley* (1889) 41 Ch. D. 422.

[91] See above, para.7–63.

[92] *Provincial Bank v Cussen* (1886) 20 I.L.T. 73. *Cf.* however, dicta in *Jenkins v Robertson* (1854) 2 Drew. 351; 61 E.R. 755.

(iii) Necessity for an extension of time to be given

Where the principal agreement is an undertaking to repay a debt, the   **7–75**
giving of time has been defined as "extending the period, at which, by the
contract between them, the principal debtor was originally liable to pay the
creditor".[93] If the creditor accepts any performance which will take place
beyond the original date for performance, this constitutes a giving of time.
Thus where the creditor agrees in extinction of the debt to allow the debtor
to construct a ship, which would be completed after the original date for
payment of the debt, the guarantor is discharged.[94] The most common
examples of giving time are extensions of time to repay a loan under a
credit agreement such as a hire-purchase agreement[95] or a mortgage,[96] an
agreement to pay a lump sum by instalments[97] or, (as we have seen)[98] an
agreement to take further security, enforceable at a date subsequent to the
original date for performance.

In all cases it must be clear that there has been an extension of the date   **7–76**
on which the principal would otherwise be liable,[99] so that a simple
promise to increase the limit of a bank overdraft on the same terms as
before does not give time to the debtor but merely increases the amount of
the indebtedness.[1] This does not mean that a binding promise to increase
the limit of the overdraft can never constitute a giving of time.[2] It will do
so, for example, if an overdraft to be repaid within twelve months is made
repayable within eighteen months and, at the same time, the limit of the
overdraft is increased.[3]

(iv) Effect of the giving of time where the obligations of the principal contract are divisible

One problem in relation to the giving of time is whether the creditor's   **7–77**
promise to give an extension of time releases the guarantor from all the
obligations which are guaranteed. This question arises because there may
be a number of obligations involved, even within one principal contract. If
those obligations can be considered as being independent and distinct, the
giving of time in relation to one of those obligations will release the
guarantor only in relation to the guarantee of that obligation. Thus a
general guarantee of the performance of a hire-purchaser's obligations
under a hire-purchase agreement may include a guarantee of the

[93] *Howell v Jones* (1834) 1 Cr. M. & R. 97 at 107; 149 E.R. 1009 at 1014.
[94] *Davies v Stainbank* (1854) 6 De G.M. & G 679; 43 E.R. 1397.
[95] *e.g. Payton v SG Brookes & Sons Pty Ltd* [1977] W.A.R. 91.
[96] *e.g. Burnes v Trade Credits Ltd* (1981) 34 A.L.R. 459.
[97] *Clarke v Henty* (1838) 3 Y. & C. Exch. 187; 160 E.R. 667; *Bowsfield v Tower* (1812) 4 Taunt
456; 128 E.R. 405; *Wilson v Lloyd* (1873) L.R. 16 Eq. 60; *Burnard v Lysnar* [1927] N.Z.L.R.
757 and, on appeal to the Privy Council, [1929] N.Z.P.C.C. 538.
[98] See above, paras 7–68 to 7–72.
[99] *Rouse v Bradford Banking Co* [1894] A.C. 586 at 594–595.
[1] *ibid.*
[2] *Deane v City Bank of Sydney* (1904) 2 C.L.R. 198 at 213.
[3] *ibid.*

obligation to pay the instalments as well as a guarantee of the obligation to repair the property.[4] Where the creditor gives time to the principal to pay the instalments, the guarantor will not be released from the guarantee in relation to the latter obligation if the obligations are seen as independent and severable. There is no easy test for determining if this is so and the construction of the contract is decisive in each case. Many agreements, especially in the credit financing field, contain terms which expressly or impliedly indicate that all the provisions of the agreement are interlocking.[5]

7–78   The most difficult situation in deciding whether the obligations are distinct arises where the guarantor has promised to undertake that a sum of money will be repaid by the debtor and the debtor's obligation is not to repay a lump sum, but to make periodical repayments. If the periodical payments are viewed as a series of independent debts, the giving of time in relation to one instalment will not discharge the guarantor,[6] except in relation to the liability for that instalment. Again, the construction of the particular principal contract is vital, but it appears that if it is possible to quantify the money owing in terms of a total sum[7] and the contract requires its repayment by a number of periodic instalments of a fixed amount,[8] the contract will be construed as indivisible.[9] In this situation, a giving of time in relation to one instalment will release the guarantor from liability in relation to the whole of the amount owing. Most modern credit agreements and mortgages come within these guidelines.[10]

7–79   These situations should be contrasted with a guarantee of the payment of the price of goods supplied to the debtor where the amount of the payment is only to be calculated at the end of each month. In this case, each month's account can easily be construed as a separate debt, so that the giving of time in relation to one monthly account does not discharge the guarantor from liability for future monthly accounts.[11] There is some 19th-century authority to the effect that a guarantor of a general account for goods supplied, where there is no clear indication of separate accounts being given at regular intervals, is released from liability for only a proportion of the overdue account when time is given in relation to that proportion of the amount owing.[12] It is unclear how such a conclusion can be reached when it appears that the guarantee relates to one continuing

---

[4] *e.g. Midland Motor Showrooms Ltd v Newman* [1929] 2 K.B. 256.
[5] *e.g.*, in *Midland Motor Showrooms Ltd v Newman* [1929] 2 K.B. 256, at 261. For two early examples of obligations that were clearly divisible see *Skillett v Fletcher* (1866) L.R. 2 C.P. 469 and *Harrison v Seymour* (1866) L.R. 1 C.P. 518.
[6] *Croydon Gas Co v Dickinson* (1876) 2 C.P.D. 46; *WR Simmons Ltd v Meek* [1939] 2 All E.R. 645; *Burnard v Lysnar* [1927] N.Z.L.R. 757 at 775–776.
[7] See the wording of the agreement *Burnard v Lysnar* [1927] N.Z.L.R. 757 at 759. Such quantification was also possible in *Midland Motor Showrooms Ltd v Newman* [1929] 2 K.B. 256.
[8] See this fact stressed in *WR Simmons Ltd v Meek* [1939] 2 All E.R. 645 at 647.
[9] *Midland Motor Showrooms Ltd v Newman* [1929] 2 K.B. 256; *Burnard v Lysnar* [1927] N.Z.L.R. 757 at 775–776.
[10] See also *Eyre v Bartrop* (1818) 3 Madd. 221; 56 E.R. 491.
[11] *Croydon Gas Co v Dickinson* (1876) 2 C.P.D. 46; *WR Simmons Ltd v Meek* [1939] 2 All E.R. 645.
[12] *Dowden & Co v Levis* (1884) 14 L.R. Ir. 307; *Bingham v Corbitt* (1864) 34 L.J.Q.B. 37.

debt which cannot be severed into separate debts by evidence of the delivery of monthly or other periodic accounts.

The creditor may indicate that a debt which is originally indivisible has been converted into a number of separate debts. This may happen if the creditor takes promissory notes for separate amounts, which are in aggregate equivalent to the whole amount owing. It is arguable that separate debts are created because the creditor is then merely entitled to sue on the promissory notes.[13]

7–80

(v) Clauses in the guarantee excluding discharge on the ground of the giving of time

The guarantor may consent to the creditor granting an extension of time to the principal by a clause in the guarantee and the guarantor will then not be released. In this case the guarantor cannot exercise the right to pay off the creditor and then recover an indemnity from the principal until the new time limit has expired and, equally, the guarantor cannot be sued by the creditor until that date.[14]

7–81

Most modern documents of guarantee contain clauses which attempt to preserve the liability of the guarantor in these circumstances. The most common provision authorises the creditor "to give the principal time or any other indulgence or consideration" without impairing the liability of the guarantor.[15] The Privy Council examined such a clause in *Burnes v Trade Credits Ltd*,[16] where the term of the mortgage was extended for one year in return for an increase in the interest payable. The Privy Council, overruling the New South Wales Court of Appeal, held that this phrase did not contemplate a variation whereby the guarantor might be required to assume an additional liability. Thus, whereas a simple extension of the term of the loan might well come within this provision,[17] the superimposed requirement for the payment of additional interest meant that the new agreement went beyond the scope of the clause.[18] The Privy Council distinguished the earlier Australian decision of *Payton v SG Brookes & Sons Pty Ltd*,[19] where the Supreme Court of Western Australia held that a similar clause prevented the guarantor being discharged when time to pay the instalments was granted to a hirer under a hire-purchase agreement in consideration of an increase in the interest rate. The basis of the distinction was that in that case the hire-purchase agreement itself contemplated an

7–82

[13] A point left open in *Bell v Cahoon* (1964) 45 D.L.R. (2d) 249 at 263.
[14] The guarantor can agree to still remain liable on the original due date, but will then become a principal debtor.
[15] Sometimes the provision provides for any extension of time to be notified to the guarantor and this must then be complied with: *Midland Counties Motor Finance Co Ltd v Slade* [1951] 1 K.B. 346.
[16] (1981) 34 A.L.R. 459 (noted (1982) 56 A.L.J. 47).
[17] *Commercial & General Acceptance Ltd v Diab Pty Ltd* (unreported, NSW Sup Ct, March 11, 1977) supports this view. See also *Yates v Evans* (1892) 61 L.J.Q.B. 446 at 448, which indicates that a clause authorising the giving of time operates as an estoppel, preventing the guarantor relying on it as a defence; *Payton v SG Brookes & Sons Pty Ltd* [1977] W.A.R. 91.
[18] See also *Holland-Canada Mortgage Co v Hutchings* [1936] 2 D.L.R. 481 at 489.
[19] [1977] W.A.R. 91.

increase in the interest rate. Thus the variation in interest rate was made according to the terms of the principal contract itself with the guarantee relating to whatever obligations might from time to time be owed under the principal transaction.[20] The mortgage in *Burnes v Trade Credits Ltd*, on the other hand, did not authorise an increase in interest rates. Thus in *Payton v SG Brookes & Sons Pty Ltd*, unlike *Burnes v Trade Credits Ltd*, it was only necessary to rely on the clause in the guarantee allowing a granting of "time or any other indulgence" for the purpose of authorising a simple extension of the term of the loan. The result is that the usual "indulgence clause" in modern guarantees will not be effective to preserve the guarantor's liability if an agreement for an extension of time also imposes an additional liability, unless the additional burden is contemplated by the principal contract.

7–83   The courts have also considered whether several other common clauses in guarantees preserve the guarantor's liability when an extension of time is given to the principal debtor. In *Burnes v Trade Credits Ltd*, it was argued that the guarantor's promise to allow the creditor to make a "further advance" to the principal in effect authorised the creditor to give an extension of time to the principal. The argument was that the clause encompassed the situation in which the debtor, who had already obtained a loan, became entitled to retain it for a period beyond that which would otherwise have been the due date for its repayment. The Privy Council saw no merit in this argument, restricting the definition of "advance" to circumstances in which the creditor actually furnished the debtor with an additional principal sum.

7–84   Other relevant clauses have already been discussed in relation to the release of the guarantor by the variation of the principal contract.[21] Clearly, the fact that a guarantee is expressed to be a "continuing guarantee" will not authorise the giving of an extension of time.[22] It is likely, however, that a clause in the guarantee by which the creditor is "at liberty to act as if the guarantor were the principal debtor"[23] has this effect, although the point was specifically left open in *Payton v SG Brookes & Sons Pty Ltd*.

7–85   If the creditor wishes to prevent the guarantor being discharged by an extension of time, a clause should be inserted in the guarantee authorising the giving of time (in the same terms as that in *Burnes v Trade Credits Ltd*). But it should also be combined with a general clause authorising variation[24] which will prevent the guarantor being discharged even if the agreement giving time also involves the imposition of additional burdens upon the guarantor, such as an increase in the interest rate.

[20] *Burnes v Trade Credits Ltd* (1981) 34 A.L.R. 459 at 462.
[21] See above, para.7–27.
[22] *Trade Credits Ltd v Burnes* [1979] 1 N.S.W.L.R. 630.
[23] *Heald v O'Connor* [1971] 1 W.L.R. 497 at 503; *General Produce Co v United Bank Ltd* [1979] 2 Lloyd's Rep. 255; *Brown Bros Motor Lease Canada Ltd v Ganapathi* (1982) 139 D.L.R. (3d) 227; *Greenwood v Francis* [1899] 1 Q.B. 312 at 323.
[24] See above, para.7–27.

(vi) Where the principal contract provides for the giving of time

The principles discussed in relation to variation are equally applicable here.[25] One special application in relation to the giving of time is that the courts will imply into the principal contract a right to give credit according to the usage of trade in relation to that particular transaction, so that if a creditor grants credit in accordance with this usage the guarantor is not released.[26] Indeed, if the creditor brings an action against the guarantor before the period of credit has expired, the action against the guarantor will be premature because the principal will not be in default.[27] The most usual situation involving an implication that credit be given is in relation to a guarantee for the payment of goods supplied where no period of credit is stipulated.[28] There is some authority[29] that in this context the period of credit that the creditor can allow before the guarantor is discharged is not merely the normal trade credit but a further period of credit that the guarantor "could . . . reasonably expect might naturally be allowed".[30] The implication is that the guarantor may be obliged to inquire into the nature of the particular contractual relationship between the creditor and the principal.[31]

7–86

(vii) Consent by the guarantor to the giving of time

Even if there is no term in the guarantee by which the guarantor agrees to, or authorises, an extension of time, the guarantor will not be released if he consents to the giving of time to the principal before the extension is given. The same principle applies as in the case of variation generally.[32] As we have seen, if consent is given after the creditor has extended time, there is some doubt as to whether this is effective to prevent the guarantor's release.[33]

7–87

---

[25] See above, para.7–21.

[26] *Combe v Woolf* (1832) 8 Bing 156; 131 E.R. 360; *Samuell v Howarth* (1817) 3 Mer. 272 at 278; 36 E.R. 105 at 107, where, credit was given beyond the usual period. See also *Re Fox, Walker & Co, Ex p. Bishop* (1880) 15 Ch. D. 400; *Matthews Thompson & Co Ltd v Everson* (1934) 34 S.R. (NSW) 114.

[27] *Turner Manufacturing Co Pty Ltd v Senes* [1964] N.S.W.R. 692.

[28] As in *Allan v Kenning* (1833) 9 Bing. 618; 131 E.R. 746. But quaere whether such an arrangement attracts the application of the rule at all, because there is no fixed date stipulated for payment: see above, para.7–61.

[29] *Howell v Jones* (1834) 1 Cr. M. & R. 97 at 107–108; 149 E.R. 1009 at 1014; *A Tyree & Co v Symon* (1906) 9 G.L.R. 90 at 91–92, quoting with approval *Simpson v Manley* (1831) 2 Cr. & J. 12; 149 E.R. 5; *Matthews Thompson & Co Ltd v Everson* (1934) 34 S.R. (NSW) 114 at 122–123.

[30] *Matthews Thompson & Co Ltd v Everson* (1934) 34 S.R. (NSW) 114 at 122.

[31] *Howell v Jones* (1834) 1 Cr. M. & R. 97 at 107–108; 149 E.R. 1009 at 1014. Cf., however, *Bing, Harris & Co v Hislop* (1884) N.Z.L.R. 2 SC 311 at 313 where in a situation in which payment was not made according to that usual in the trade, it was said that the guarantor would only remain liable if he "was aware of and contemplated that the business was to be thus carried on".

[32] See above, para.7–42.

[33] See above, paras 7–49 to 7–50.

(viii) Consent by the principal to the continuation of the guarantor's liability

7–88   The guarantor's liability may be preserved if the principal agrees in the instrument giving time that the guarantor's liability will continue.[34] In this case, however, the promise is to be construed as preserving the right of the guarantor to recover from the principal as at the date of the original time for performance if the guarantor were successfully sued by the creditor or chose to exercise the right to pay the creditor off. The argument in this situation is that no fraud on the principal is involved because the principal has impliedly consented in the instrument giving time to the immediate exercise of this right by the guarantor, even though the creditor cannot sue the debtor until the extension of time has expired.

(ix) The giving of time and contracts of indemnity

7–89   If the contract is properly classified as one of indemnity, the giving of time by the creditor to the principal will not discharge the indemnifier,[35] unless it can be shown that it is an express or implied term of the contract of indemnity that time shall not be given.

(x) Critique

7–90   The rule that a guarantor is discharged by the creditor giving an extension of time to the principal even if the guarantor is not prejudiced by this concession favours the guarantor to an extent that cannot be justified. The rationale for the rule, namely, that the guarantor is deprived of the right to pay off the creditor and then recover from the principal, does not accord with commercial reality. As Justice Cardozo has commented:

> "The law has shaped its judgments upon the fictitious assumption that a surety, who has probably lain awake nights for fear that payment may some day be demanded, has in truth been smarting under a repressed desire to force an unwelcome payment on a reluctant or capricious creditor."[36]

7–91   Some common law jurisdictions have statutory provisions which permit an extension of time to discharge the guarantor only where the guarantor

---

[34] *Bailey v Edwards* (1864) 4 B. & S. 761 at 774–775; 122 E.R. 645 at 651; *Mahant Singh v U Ba Yi* [1939] A.C. 601 at 607; *Holme v Brunskill* (1878) 3 Q.B.D. 495 at 505; *Reid v Royal Trust Corp of Canada* (1985) 20 D.L.R. (4th) 223. The agreement by the principal must be specific: *Reid v Royal Trust Corp of Canada* at 239.

[35] *Way v Hearn* (1862) 11 C.B. (NS) 774; 142 E.R. 1000; *Wilson v Zealandia Soap & Candle Trading Co Ltd* [1927] G.L.R. 120.

[36] B. N. Cardozo, "The Nature of the Judicial Process" (*Storrs Lecture*, 1934) at 153–154. For judicial criticisms, see *Petty v Cooke* (1871) L.R. 6 Q.B. 790 at 795; *Polak v Everett* (1876) 1 Q.B.D. 669 at 674.

has been prejudiced.[37] Similarly, in the United States of America, a surety is discharged if it is shown that the extension of time results in material harm or prejudice.[38] This should be the law in this jurisdiction, which (as indicated above)[39] should also be the general test in respect of discharge arising from a variation of the principal contract. At the very least, the rule regarding the giving of time should be assimilated with the present law regarding other types of variation, that is, the guarantor will not be discharged if it can be shown that the variation is "obviously unsubstantial" or for the guarantor's benefit. There should be no separate rule whereby, if an extension of time is given, it inevitably results in the guarantor's discharge.

It is true that an extension of time granted to the principal may **7–92** sometimes prejudice the guarantor's interests, for example, if the principal transaction is embodied in a mortgage and the extension of time is given in a falling market so that the amount which could be obtained from an eventual sale of the mortgaged property is much reduced.[40] But often the result of the creditor's action is to improve the principal's financial position so that the guarantor's liability is lessened, or at least postponed.

3. DISCHARGE BY THE CREDITOR'S FAILURE TO TERMINATE THE PRINCIPAL CONTRACT BECAUSE OF THE PRINCIPAL'S BREACH

In the context of a guarantee of an employee's honesty and loyalty **7–93** towards his employer (a fidelity guarantee), it is clearly established that the guarantor will be discharged if the employer fails to dismiss the employee after discovering that the employee is in breach of the contract of employment.[41] The rule was originally confined to breaches involving fraud on the part of the employee, but was later extended to any breach of duty, whether involving dishonesty or not.[42] This conclusion appears to be based on the broad ground that the guarantor has a right in equity to require the creditor to use all remedies against the debtor, and the failure of the employer to terminate the principal contract deprives the guarantor of the benefit of one of those remedies.[43] The guarantor is, therefore, discharged. This reasoning is similar to that applied where the creditor loses or impairs a security to which the guarantor is entitled to be subrogated.[44]

---

[37] e.g. *The Mercantile Law Amendment Act* 1970, s.4 (Manitoba).
[38] *Guaranty Co v Pressed Brick Co* 191 U.S. 416 (1903).
[39] See above, para.7–57.
[40] *Reid v Royal Trust Corp of Canada* (1985) 20 D.L.R. (4th) 223 at 241.
[41] *Sanderson v Aston* (1873) L.R. 8 Exch. 73 at 76–77; *Phillips v Foxall* (1872) L.R. 7 Q.B. 666 at 680–681 *per* Blackburn J.; *Enright v Falvey* (1879) 4 L.R. Ir. 397.
[42] *Sanderson v Aston* (1873) L.R. 8 Exch. 73 at 76–77. But this extension was doubted in *Mayor of Durham v Fowler* (1889) 22 Q.B.D. 394 at 423 *per* Denman J.
[43] *Phillips v Foxall* (1872) LR 7 Q.B. 666 at 680, *per* Blackburn J.
[44] See this principle discussed below, para.8–46.

7–94   If this principle were extended to all types of guarantee, it would have a serious impact on creditors. The guarantor would be discharged whenever the principal breached a condition of the principal contract and the creditor failed to terminate the contract for that breach. Some (albeit oblique) support for a general principle to this effect is to be found in the comment of Bingham J. in *Bank of India v Transcontinental Commodity Merchants Ltd*[45] who was of the view that a surety is discharged if the creditor "causes or connives at the default by the principal debtor in respect of which the guarantee is given".[46]

7–95   Apart from these indications, however, there is no firm support for the view that this reasoning should be extended to guarantees generally.[47] Indeed, even in the context of a fidelity guarantee, there has been some attempt to confine the rule to the situation where the employer, upon discovery of the right of dismissal, enters into a *fresh arrangement* with the employee.[48] Thus confined, the cases simply become illustrations of the well-established principle that a variation of the principal contract discharges the guarantor. In any event, the reasoning upon which the rule is based, that is, that the creditor is under a duty to use all contractual remedies for the benefit of the guarantor, is defective and inconsistent with other authorities. If the reasoning were correct it would, in effect, extend the creditor's obligation not to impair any securities held for the debt to a duty not to impair any simple contractual remedy which can be exercised for the enforcement of the principal obligation. But, as will be seen, the definition of "a security" probably does not embrace a simple contractual remedy for the purpose of the rule.[49]

7–96   Thus there appears to be no general principle that if the creditor fails to terminate the principal contract upon a breach of condition by the principal the guarantor will be discharged, although there may be a term in the guarantee which makes the guarantor's liability conditional upon being notified by the creditor of a breach of a term of the principal contract by the principal.[50] This is the correct result as it is quite unreasonable for the guarantor to be discharged when the creditor has simply exercised a contractual right to affirm a contract, especially as the creditor may have often done so in order to enable the principal to achieve a sounder financial position.

---

[45] [1982] 1 Lloyd's Rep. 506. See also *Stone v Geraldton Brewery* (1898) 1 W.A.L.R. 23 at 27 where the guarantor of a tenant's obligations under a lease was discharged when the landlord failed to enter the premises for non-payment of rent.
[46] *ibid.*, at 515; approved on appeal: [1983] 2 Lloyd's Rep. 298 at 302–303. But the English Court of Appeal was of the view that there is no general principle that conduct prejudicial to the surety will discharge the surety: see below, para.8–106.
[47] Note, however, *Re Wolmershausen* (1890) 62 L.T. 541, where it was indicated that the creditor's failure to exercise a right of proof in bankruptcy was a breach of the creditor's duty not to impair a security.
[48] *Mayor of Durham v Fowler* (1889) 22 Q.B.D. 394 at 423 *per* Denman J.
[49] See below, paras 12–318 to 12–324, especially 12–322.
[50] e.g. *Clydebank & District Water Trustees v Fidelity & Deposit Co of Maryland* (1915) S.C. 362.

4. DISCHARGE BY THE CREDITOR AGREEING WITH THE PRINCIPAL TO GIVE TIME TO THE GUARANTOR

If the creditor agrees with the principal debtor to give the guarantor **7–97** time for the performance of the guarantor's obligations under the guarantee, there is some authority[51] to suggest that the guarantor is discharged. The rationale is that the creditor has entered into an arrangement which prevents the guarantor from satisfying the guarantor's obligations under the guarantee and pursuing the remedy of an indemnity against the principal.[52] This is because the guarantor, in exercising the right of paying off the creditor and taking action against the principal, would force the creditor to breach the contract with the principal. This would involve a fraud upon the principal. The guarantor is, therefore, not allowed to exercise this remedy but, being then deprived of such a right, is discharged from liability.

If one guarantor is discharged in this way, it follows that the remaining **7–98** guarantors also would be fully discharged, provided that it is a condition of the contract that all guarantors must remain parties to the agreement (for example, if they are described as "joint and several"[53] guarantors). The act of the creditor in releasing one guarantor breaches that condition and, therefore, all will be released. If there is no such condition, the other guarantors will be discharged to the extent that their rights of contribution are impaired.[54] This will invariably occur because there are fewer guarantors to share the loss.

It is considered that the guarantor should not be discharged where the **7–99** creditor agrees with the principal to give time to the guarantor. Once again, as in the case of the creditor agreeing to give the principal time, the premise upon which the rule is based is highly theoretical. It is most unlikely in any practical sense that the guarantor will wish to satisfy the principal debt so as to be able to exercise the right of indemnity against the principal.

Where there is an agreement between the creditor and *a guarantor* **7–100** giving the guarantor further time for the performance of the obligations under the guarantee, a different result is reached. This agreement is binding and that guarantor will remain liable subject to the agreement.[55] The liability of the principal or any co-guarantors is not affected.[56] It has been suggested[57] that the reason for this is that the agreement must be for the eventual benefit of all the guarantors since it postpones a claim for contribution by one guarantor against the others. But this is not the case

---

[51] *Clarke v Birley* (1889) 41 Ch. D. 422; *Oriental Financial Corp v Overend Gurney & Co* (1871) 7 Ch. App. 142 at 152.
[52] *ibid.*
[53] This wording generally has this effect: see below, para.8–21.
[54] This would appear to follow from the general principle in *Ward v National Bank of New Zealand* (1883) 8 App. Cas. 755, but there is no direct authority.
[55] *Clarke v Birley* (1889) 41 Ch. D. 422; *Dunn v Slee* (1817) 1 Moo. C.P. 2; 171 E.R. 284.
[56] *ibid.*
[57] R. Goff and G. Jones, *The Law of Restitution* (6th ed, 2002), para.14–015.

because if the creditor recovers from another guarantor, who is not a party to the agreement, that guarantor can immediately claim contribution from the guarantor to whom time has been given, despite the latter's arrangement with the creditor. Parke J. made this clear in *Dunn v Slee*[58] when he stated that "the surety who paid the whole would still have his action of contribution against a co-surety, notwithstanding any arrangement for time which might previously have taken place between the obligee [creditor] and such surety".[59] The result is that the agreement to give a guarantor time is rendered illusory from that guarantor's standpoint if the creditor recovers from other guarantors and those guarantors seek contribution from the guarantor to whom the creditor has given time.

7–101 In this case a real fraud does operate upon the guarantor to whom time has been given because it is very probable that the other guarantors, if sued by the creditor, will bring an action for contribution against the guarantor. There is therefore an arguable case that, if there is an agreement between the creditor and a guarantor giving the guarantor further time to pay, the creditor should be precluded from seeking recovery against the other guarantors until the relevant period of time has elapsed.

---

[58] (1816) Holt 399; 171 E.R. 284.
[59] *ibid.*, at 403; 285.

CHAPTER 8

DISCHARGE FROM LIABILITY BY REASON OF THE CREDITOR'S CONDUCT IN RELATION TO THE GUARANTOR

1. DISCHARGE BY THE CREDITOR'S FAILURE TO COMPLY WITH A CONDITION OF THE GUARANTEE

(i) General principles

8–01   The guarantor may be discharged because of a failure of a condition precedent to the operation of the guarantee or to the performance of the guarantor's obligations pursuant to the guarantee. Alternatively, the guarantor will be discharged if the creditor is in breach of essential promissory obligation or repudiates the guarantee.[1]

8–02   In the context of guarantees, however, the courts often do not draw a sharp distinction between a discharge on the basis of a failure of a condition precedent on the one hand, and a breach of a promissory obligation on the other, merely posing the question as to whether there has been "any departure ... from the terms as agreed upon in the guarantee".[2] As guarantees are usually unilateral instruments containing no substantive promises on the part of the creditor, probably the general tendency has been to view the creditor's promise as a condition precedent rather than as a promissory obligation.[3] Indeed, there is seldom any need to determine whether the creditor is in breach of a promissory term since the guarantor

---

[1] As to the general contractual principles applicable, see *Chitty on Contracts* (28th ed., 1999), Ch. 25. As examples of discharge by failing to comply with a condition of the guarantee, see *Philips v Astling* (1809) 2 Taunt. 206; 127 E.R. 1056; *Barber v Mackrell* (1892) 68 L.T. 29; *Archer v Hudson* (1844) 7 Beav. 551; 49 E.R. 1180; *Pickles v Thornton* (1875) 33 L.T. 658; *Bacon v Chesney* (1816) 1 Stark. 192; 171 E.R. 443; *Evans v Whyle* (1829) 5 Bing. 485; 130 E.R. 1148; *Greer v Kettle* [1938] A.C. 156; *Ankar Pty Ltd v National Westminster Finance (Aust) Ltd* (1987) 162 C.L.R. 549; *Lensworth Finance Ltd v Worner* [1979] Qd. R. 159. Examples in the context of fidelity guarantees are: *North-Western Railway Co v Whinray* (1854) 10 Exch. 77; 156 E.R. 363; *Holland v Lea* (1854) 9 Exch. 430; 156 E.R. 184. Specific examples of the principle are discussed elsewhere in the text.
[2] *Barber v Mackrell* (1892) 62 L.T. 108 at 109.
[3] *Ankar Pty Ltd v National Westminster Finance (Aust) Ltd* (1987) 162 C.L.R. 549 at 556.

is invariably seeking to show that he is discharged from liability rather than claiming damages.[4]

Different principles of construction, however, apply to promissory obligations as opposed to conditions precedent, and it is possible that the guarantor's continuing liability will be dependent upon which classification is adopted.

8–03

(ii) Breach of a promissory obligation

In this case, whether or not the guarantor is discharged will be dependent upon the classification of the term as a condition, warranty or intermediate term. If the creditor is in breach of a condition requiring strict performance or if there is substantial non-performance of an intermediate term, the guarantor will be relieved from liability, but not in situations in which the term is inessential or there is substantial compliance with an intermediate stipulation. Alternatively, the guarantor may be discharged if the creditor repudiates the guarantee, that is, evinces on intention no longer to be bound by its terms.[5]

8–04

Sometimes the relevant term is not construed as a condition and the evidence does not establish a repudiation. Thus in *Bowmaker (Commercial) Ltd v Smith*[6] a car dealer agreed to indemnify a finance company against losses if a customer defaulted in the performance of a hire-purchase agreement entered into with the finance company. It was a term of the indemnity that the finance company, upon payment of the amount due by the dealer, would transfer to him rights in the car. The finance company was unable to comply with this term since it had sold the vehicle, after a letter requesting the dealer to pay the outstanding amounts under the hire purchase agreement (when the customer defaulted) went astray, so that the dealer never responded. It was held that the dealer was not discharged absolutely (but merely had a contractual claim for damages against the finance company representing the value of the car) since "it was not a term of the contract non-performance of which in the ordinary way can properly be regarded as a repudiation of the contract".[7] Nor was there a repudiation of the agreement on the basis that the failure to transfer the rights in the car evinced an intention not to be bound by the agreement since this had resulted from the accidental loss of the letter[8] and not a deliberate act.[9]

8–05

---

[4] *ibid.*
[5] See *Chitty on Contracts* (28th ed., 1999), para.25–017. See *Skipton Building Society v Stott* [2001] Q.B. 261 at 269–270 where Evans L.J., in the case of guarantees, describes this as "probably" the position. The authors suggest it clearly is.
[6] [1965] 1 W.L.R. 855. See also *ANZ Banking Group Ltd v Beneficial Finance Corp Ltd* [1983] 1 N.S.W.L.R. 199 at 205.
[7] *ibid.*, at 858, *per* Diplock L.J.
[8] This is stressed at 858, *per* Diplock L.J. and at 859, *per* Sellers L.J.
[9] It may have been different if the finance company had deliberately retained the car when it was in a position to hand it over see [1965] 1 W.L.R. 855 at 859. G. Andrews and R. Millett,

8–06   The most useful illustration of a breach of condition of the guarantee by
the creditor discharging the guarantor, is the decision of the High Court of
Australia in *Ankar Pty Ltd v National Westminster Finance (Aust) Ltd*,[10]
where a guarantee (taking the form of a security deposit agreement) was
given by Ankar Pty Ltd (Ankar) in respect of the obligations of the
performance of a lessee's obligations under a chattel lease. The lessor,
Lombard Australia Ltd (Lombard), agreed that it would "use its best
endeavours" to ensure that the machinery referred to in the lease
remained in the lessee's possession and also agreed to notify Ankar if the
lessee proposed to sell or assign its interest in the machinery. Lombard
further promised to notify Ankar of any default by the lessee and, in the
event of default, to consult with Ankar with a "view to determine what
course of action" should be taken.

8–07   There was a breach of these terms in that Lombard did not notify Ankar
of a proposed assignment and the lessee's defaults and also failed to
consult as required.

8–08   The joint majority judgment of Mason A.C.J., Wilson, Brennan and
Dawson JJ. held that the relevant clauses were conditions of the contract
and Ankar as guarantor was discharged by reason of the relevant breaches.
Three reasons were referred to in reaching a conclusion that the terms
were conditions: the difficulty in assessing damages; the need to ensure
that Ankar was given an opportunity to protect its position, for example,
by persuading the lessee to remedy its default; and the danger that Ankar's
rights of subrogation might be set at naught by a transfer of possession of
the machinery in respect of which rent remained payable.[11]

8–09   Although the classification of a particular term as a condition, warranty,
or intermediate term is, of course, a question of construction in each case,
the strict approach to the construction of guarantees means that in cases of
ambiguity the term should be construed as a condition.[12]

8–10   *Halsbury's Laws of England* assert a more radical approach to discharge
for breach in respect of guarantees, taking the view that the guarantor is
discharged for any breach unless it is clearly insubstantial, without the
necessity for the guarantor to terminate the contract. But the relevant
passage from *Halsbury*[13] is not supported by authority. The cases which
are cited are (relevantly) examples of a variation of the principal contract

---

Law of Guarantees (3rd ed., 2000), p.289 have contrasted *Lloyds Bowmaker (Commercial)
Ltd v Smith* [1965] 1 W.L.R. 855 with *Watling Trust Ltd v Briffault Range Co Ltd* [1938] 1 All
E.R. 525, stating that "it is hard to draw any meaningful distinction between the two cases".
But in our view a distinction is clear because in the latter case (in the context of a similar
indemnity) the dealer agreed to "re-purchase" the car at a price fixed by the finance company.
Clearly in terms of this undertaking if the finance company is not in a position to give title and
delivery that is "the end of their action for the price." (See [1938] 1 All E.R. 525 at 528, *per*
Scott L.J.). No real question arose in this case therefore as to whether the relevant term was a
condition or whether the evidence constituted a repudiation.
[10] (1987) 162 C.L.R. 549.
[11] *ibid.*, at 557. As another example of a term being construed as a condition, see *Bank of
British Columbia v Turbo Resources Ltd* (1983) 148 D.L.R. (3d) 598 (term to make guarantor
party to renegotiations).
[12] This was the view of the Australian High Court in *Ankar Pty Ltd v National Westminster
Finance (Aust) Ltd* (1987) 162 C.L.R. 549 at 561.
[13] *Halsbury's Laws of England* (4th ed., re-issue), Vol. 20, para.332. The approach is
supported by Deane J. in *Ankar Pty Ltd v National Westminster Finance (Aust) Ltd* (1987) 162

or examples of the guarantee requiring strict compliance with the terms of the principal contract.[14]

(iii) A failure of a condition precedent

Although promissory obligations in guarantees will often be construed **8–11** as conditions, it is always open to the creditor to show that the relevant term is inessential or, alternatively, that it is an intermediate term, which the creditor has substantially performed. But if the term is construed not as a promissory obligation, but as a condition precedent to the operation of the contract or to the performance of the guarantor's obligations, no such categorisation is possible. The condition is either performed or it is not.[15] The consequence is that the guarantor is placed in a more favourable position if it is shown that the relevant term is a condition precedent and the condition is not fulfilled than if the creditor is in breach of a promissory stipulation. In the former situation, anything other than strict compliance means that the guarantor is automatically discharged, but in the latter case the guarantor may remain liable, depending on whether the stipulation is classified as a warranty, condition, or intermediate term. The determination of whether the term is a condition precedent or a promissory obligation however, is not always an easy question of construction. The term is likely to be a condition precedent if the guarantee is so drafted that it is dependent on particular *events* occurring[16] (for example, the service of written notices of default upon the principal debtor and notices upon the guarantor informing him of those defaults). But such provisions regarding notice may be so phrased as to impose obligations rather than provide for contingencies.[17]

The present law regarding the construction of conditions precedent is **8–12** unsatisfactory, allowing the guarantor to be discharged for the most trivial departure from the terms of the guarantee. On a proper construction of the instrument, it should be open for the courts to conclude that only substantial compliance with the condition precedent is required, and the courts should then be able to interpret the condition accordingly. Indeed, in *Oval (717) Ltd v Aegon Co (UK)*

C.L.R. 549 at 570–571 although it is not supported by the majority of the Court. The rule, however, is not given the status of a rule of law. Deane J. regards it as an expression of what can be presumed to be the intention of the parties (at 571). In *National Westminster Bank Plc v Riley* [1986] F.L.R. 213 at 223, the Court of Appeal also referred to this "special rule" applying to guarantees with apparent approval. There is reference to a proposition of counsel arising from the earlier Court of Appeal decision in *Vavasseur Trust Co Ltd v Ashmore* (unreported, April 2, 1976 CA). See, for more detailed comments, J.W. Carter & J.C. Phillips, "Construction of Contracts of Guarantee and the Hong Kong Fir Case" (1988) 1 J.C.L. 70 at 78–79.

[14] As discussed below, para.8–15.
[15] *Ritchie v Atkinson* (1808) 10 East. 295 at 306; 103 E.R. 787 at 791; *Tricontinental Corp Ltd v HDFI Ltd* (1990) 21 N.S.W.L.R. 689 at 704–705.
[16] *e.g. Tricontinental Corp Ltd v HDFI Ltd* (1990) 21 N.S.W.L.R. 689. See also *Oval (717) Ltd v Aegon Insurance Co (UK) Ltd* (1997) 85 B.L.R. 97.
[17] *e.g.*, in another context, *Bremer Handelsgesellschaft mbH v Vanden Avenne-Izegem PVBA* [1978] 2 Lloyd's Rep. 109; *Ankar Pty Ltd v National Westminster Finance (Aust) Ltd* (1987) 162 C.L.R. 549, in which the relevant clauses were defined in terms of obligations.

Ltd[18] it was suggested that (by analogy with the principles of suretyship applicable to *agreed* variations of the principal contract) breaches of a condition precedent that were obviously insubstantial or for the benefit of the guarantor would not discharge the guarantor. But this view is not in accordance with the usual approach to the construction of conditions precedent.

8–13   There are other possible advantages to the guarantor in attempting to establish that the relevant term is a condition precedent to the operation of the guarantee. Oral evidence can be adduced to prove the condition without such testimony being excluded by the parol evidence rule.[19] Furthermore, if the condition is a condition precedent to the operation of the guarantee, the creditor will not be able to rely on clauses in the main body of the guarantee which might otherwise have the effect of rebutting the condition, because the guarantee never becomes operative.[20] Another potential difference is that, applying usual contractual principles, in the case of an essential promissory obligation the guarantor will only be discharged if the guarantor elects to terminate the guarantee, whilst a failure of a condition precedent results in automatic discharge. But there is at least one overseas judicial view[21] that, in this context, the guarantor is not required to make a formal election to terminate for breach of an essential term. In any event, leaving aside questions of estoppel and laches, the guarantor's denial of liability under the guarantee may readily be construed as an election to terminate.

(iv) The effect of the statement of consideration or the recitals

8–14   The relevant condition (whether contingent or promissory) will often not be expressly stated in the operative part of the guarantee but may appear, expressly or impliedly, from a statement of the consideration for the guarantee or in the recitals to the guarantee. Thus in *National Bank of Nigeria Ltd v Awolesi*,[22] a guarantee was given in consideration of the bank "continuing the existing account with the principal". The Privy Council interpreted this as a promise by the bank to the guarantor that a second account would not be opened, and the bank departed from the terms of the guarantee when this was done. Other instances of a condition appearing in the expressed consideration for the guarantee or in the recital are where the guarantee is given on condition that the creditor obtains certain securities from the principal,[23] or abstains from taking proceedings against the principal to recover the debt, or in consideration of the creditor

---

[18] [1997] 85 B.L.R. 97. See also below, para.10–98.
[19] *Hawrish v Bank of Montreal* (1969) 2 D.L.R. (3d) 600 at 603; *Northern Rock Co Ltd v Newman and Calton* [1927] 1 R. 520 at 528; *Standard Bank of Canada v McCrossan* [1920] 60 S.C.R. 655; *Royal Bank of Canada v Girgulis* [1979] 3 W.W.R. 451.
[20] *Molsons Bank v Cranston* (1918) 45 D.L.R. 316.
[21] *Farrow Mortgage Services Pty Ltd (in liq.) v Slade* (1996) 38 N.S.W.L.R. 636 at 650–651.
[22] [1964] 1 W.L.R. 1311. As other examples, see *Pickles v Thornton* (1875) 33 L.T. 658; *Burton v Grey* (1873) 8 Ch. App. 932.
[23] See below, para.8–58.

providing the principal with a period of credit.[24] If the condition appears in the operative part of the guarantee and is repeated with different wording in the recitals, generally the courts will rely upon the wording of the clause as it appears in the main body of the guarantee.[25]

(v) When the terms of the principal contract are "embodied" in the guarantee

Halsbury's Laws of England[26] states that when there is a departure, **8–15** which is not clearly insubstantial, by the creditor from the express terms of the guarantee itself[27] or the "embodied terms of the principal contract"[28] the surety is discharged. It is not entirely clear what is meant by the reference to "the embodied terms of the principal contract". Some of the cases cited by *Halsbury*, however, constitute examples of the discharge of the guarantor by variation of the principal contract[29] (as discussed above)[30] or because the guarantor's obligation has been made conditional upon the terms of the principal contract being observed.[31]

It is the latter group of cases which properly identify the principle stated **8–16** by Halsbury. The guarantor is discharged because the creditor is in breach of a condition of the guarantee in failing to comply with the terms of the principal contract. Thus in *Blest v Brown*,[32] a guarantee was given for the due payment for flour to be supplied to a baker on credit, but the recital to the guarantee made the guarantee conditional on the flour being of such a quality that the baker could honour his contract to supply bread to a third party.

A general reference in the guarantee to the terms of the principal **8–17** contract will not, however, be sufficient to "embody" those terms within the guarantee. Thus in *Mystery of the Mercers of the City of London v New*

---

[24] *Bacon v Chesney* (1816) 1 Stark. 192; 171 E.R. 443; *Clarke & Walker Pty Ltd v Thew* (1967) 116 C.L.R. 465, where it was held that the condition not to sue was not breached by the service of a demand.
[25] *Evans v Earle* (1854) 10 Exch. 1; 156 E.R. 330. See generally as to construction of the guarantee, above, paras 5–01 to 5–09 and on this issue 5–08.
[26] (4th ed., re-issue), Vol. 20, para.332.
[27] See above, para.8–10, where the authors consider this proposition to be incorrect.
[28] *Halsbury's Laws of England* (4th ed., re-issue), Vol. 20, para.332.
[29] *Holme v Brunskill* (1878) 3 Q.B.D. 495.
[30] See above, Ch. 7.
[31] *Blest v Brown* (1862) 4 De G.F. & J. 367; 45 E.R. 1225. See also in relation to performance bonds *Paddington Churches Housing Association v Technical & Guarantees Co Ltd* [1999] B.L.R. 244, (see below, para.13–06). Note also that sometimes conditions of the principal contract need to be fulfilled before the guarantor is in default at all. See, *e.g. GMAC Commercial Credit Development Co v Sandhu* [2001] 2 All E.R. 782. See also, generally, below, Ch. 10.
[32] (1862) 4 De G.F. & J. 367; 45 E.R. 1225. See also *Horizon Aluminium Products v Parker* [1985] 1 N.Z.L.R. 506 (in respect of an indemnity); *Lensworth Finance Ltd v Worner* [1979] Qd. R. 159, where the guarantor was discharged because the guarantee contemplated that advances would be made to the principal only on the terms of the principal mortgage document referred to in the recital to the guarantee, but subsequently other conditions were attached to the loan.

Hampshire Insurance Co[33] it was held that the terms of principal transaction should not be "treated as embodied or incorporated in the contract of guarantee" simply where the guarantee referred to the principal building contract, and the guarantee was given as security against the failure of the builder to perform "in accordance with the terms and conditions" of the building contract. More specific wording of incorporation is required.

8–18   Matters relevant to determining whether the terms of the principal contract are embodied in the guarantee are the fact that the two documents (the guarantee and the principal transaction) are physically annexed[34] and that both the guarantor and the principal execute one instrument, which constitutes both the principal transaction and the guarantee.[35] But, again, these matters are probably insufficient in themselves without clear words of incorporation.

8–19   But in the absence of the terms of the principal contract being "embodied" in the guarantee, those terms will not constitute part of the contract between creditor and guarantor.[36] In such circumstances, breach of the principal contract by the creditor does not appear to have the effect of discharging the guarantor, unless it is a repudiatory breach which is accepted by the principal as terminating the principal contract[37] or possibly if the breach (even if non-repudiatory) is important "in relation to the risk undertaken".[38] Thus if the principal contract states that the creditor shall give notice to the guarantor of the principal's default[39] or (in the context of a guarantee of payment under a building contract) the principal contract states that the work is to commence at a certain date,[40] the guarantor will not be affected by a breach of these provisions.

(vi) Overlap with discharge on the ground of variation of the principal contract

8–20   A discharge of the guarantor on the ground of a failure to satisfy a condition upon which the guarantee is based often overlaps with another

---

[33] [1992] 2 Lloyd's Rep. 365, at 370, overruling the judge at first instance (unreported, January 18, 1991, Q.B.) But note that the Court of Appeal also held that the bond as a whole could not be described as a guarantee of performance.
[34] *Chambers v Rankine* [1910] S.A.L.R. 73 at 77.
[35] *British American Oil Co v Ferguson* [1951] 2 DLR 37. See, *e.g. Whitcher v Hall* (1826) 5 B. & C. 269; 108 E.R. 101, although the point is not expressly made.
[36] *Price v Kirkham* (1864) 3 H. & C. 437; 159 E.R. 601; *Brisbane City Council v Law Union & Rock Insurance Co Ltd* [1934] Q.S.R. 242; *Lunenburg Home for Special Care Corp v Duckworth* (1973) 33 D.L.R. (3d) 711.
[37] *National Westminster Bank Plc v Riley* [1986] F.L.R. 213 at 223: see above, para.7–20 (including criticism of this result). But it is possible that breach of the principal contract by the creditor will constitute an act which is prejudicial to the guarantor. For a discussion of this principle, see below, para.8–106.
[38] *The Mystery of the Mercers of the City of London v New Hampshire Insurance Co* [1992] 2 Lloyd's Rep. 365 at 370, 371. See also above, para.7–20.
[39] *Price v Kirkham* (1864) 3 H. & C. 437; 159 E.R. 601.
[40] *Brisbane City Council v Law Union & Rock Insurance Co* [1934] Q.S.R. 242.

basis for discharge, that is, a variation of the principal agreement.[41] For instance, it may be a condition of the guarantee that the guaranteed loan is to be made upon certain conditions, but the principal and the creditor vary the principal agreement to allow the loan to be given on other conditions. This involves both a failure of the condition upon which the guarantee is based and also a variation of the principal contract. Some authorities clearly state both these alternative grounds as reasons for the decision.[42] Sometimes, however, the courts have held that the guarantor was discharged, apparently on the basis of a variation of the principal contract, when in fact there was no evidence of a consensual variation[43] and the only legitimate basis for discharge was that there had been a failure or breach of the condition upon which the guarantee was given.[44]

2. DISCHARGE BY THE CREDITOR RELEASING A CO-GUARANTOR

(i) Where the continued existence of a co-guarantor is a condition of the guarantee

The guarantee may contain an express or implied term which makes the continued existence of a co-guarantor a condition of the contract of guarantee. A release of one guarantor in such a case releases the other guarantors from all liability,[45] including any additional security given by them for the enforcement of the principal obligation.[46] The term will be implied by the same wording that imposes an obligation on the creditor to obtain a co-guarantor. In particular, if the liability of the guarantors is

8–21

---

[41] See above, Ch. 7.

[42] *Holme v Brunskill* (1878) 3 Q.B.D. 495 at 506–507. Cotton L.J. decided the case primarily on the ground of there being a variation of the principal contract, but stated that the case could also be decided on the basis that there was a breach of a term of the contract of guarantee.

[43] A consensual variation is probably necessary before there can be discharge on this basis: see above, paras 7–16 to 7–20.

[44] *e.g. Blest v Brown* (1862) 4 De G.F. & J. 367; 45 E.R. 1225, where some of the language suggests that the guarantor was discharged on the basis of a variation of the principal contract. But there was no evidence of any variation, it simply being the case that the creditor was in breach of a term of the principal contract, in respect of which the guarantee required strict compliance.

[45] *Smith v Wood* [1929] 1 Ch. 14. In *Smith v Wood*, there was a release of the security given by the guarantor, but this was the equivalent of the guarantor himself being released because no personal liability was undertaken by the guarantor; the liability merely arising out of a charge created by the security. Sankey L.J. (at 25) and Hanworth M.R. (at 24) take the view that there was a breach of a term of the guarantee not to release the security. *Cf.* Russell L.J. (at 30–32), who appeared to base his decision favouring a release of the co-guarantors on the fact that their right of marshalling had been prejudicially affected. But it is unnecessary to show that the right of marshalling or contribution has been affected before the co-guarantor is discharged if there is an express or implied term not to release a guarantor. See also *Ward v National Bank of New Zealand* (1883) 8 App. Cas. 755 at 764–765; *Re Wolmershausen* (1890) 62 L.T. 541 at 545; *Robison Bros v Sloss* (1892) 14 A.L.T. 145.

[46] *Bolton v Salmon* [1891] 2 Ch. 48 at 53 (relying on *Hodgson v Hodgson* (1837) 2 Keen 704; 48 E.R. 800).

stated to be "joint" or "joint and several" this will be construed[47] as making the guarantee dependent on the execution of the guarantee by all those named as "joint and several" guarantors and also as making the guarantee dependent on those co-guarantors remaining parties to the agreement.[48] When this wording is used, therefore, the reason that is usually given by the courts for the fact that a release of one guarantor discharges the others from liability is that there has been a breach of the condition of the guarantee that all the guarantors shall remain parties to the agreement.[49]

8–22   The fact that the other guarantors are released in this situation can also be viewed, however, as an example of the general rule, which had a separate origin, that a release of one joint or joint and several promisor discharges the others, the joint promise being regarded as single so that if discharged for one it was discharged for all.[50] Historically the existence of this overlapping reason has led the courts to apply the normal rules relating to joint and several promisors, so that if the creditor covenants not to sue a co-guarantor or effects a compromise with a co-guarantor falling short of an absolute release, the other joint and several guarantors are not discharged.[51] The fact that the words "joint and several" make it a condition of the contract that all those named as guarantors shall remain as parties to the agreement does not appear to affect the position. While the courts, in the context of the construction of guarantees, have held that the words "joint" and "joint and several" imply that it is a condition of the guarantee that all guarantors remain parties to the agreement,[52] they have not implied from that expression a term that they must remain *effective* parties. On this traditional approach the creditor can avoid releasing the remaining guarantors if the agreement with a co-guarantor is worded as a covenant not to sue rather than a release.[53]

8–23   As we have seen[54] there has been recent judicial criticism of this traditional "straight jacket"[55] distinction between a release and a covenant not to sue in the context of an agreement releasing the principal debtor.

---

[47] See above, para.3–88.

[48] *Ward v National Bank of New Zealand* (1883) 8 App. Cas. 755 at 764; *Evans v Bremridge* (1855) 2 K. & J. 174; 69 E.R. 741; *Canadian Imperial Bank of Commerce v Vopni* (1978) 86 D.L.R. (3d) 383.

[49] *Ward v National Bank of New Zealand* (1883) 8 App. Cas. 755 at 764–765; *Walker v Bowry* (1924) 35 C.L.R. 48 at 57 *per* Starke J.; *Mahoney v McManus* (1981) 55 A.L.J.R. 673 at 677 *per* Gibbs C.J.

[50] *Re Wolmershausen* (1890) 62 L.T. 541 at 545 uses this explanation. Stirling J. refers to the release of joint and several sureties and approves the statement of Lord Denman in *Nicholson v Revill* (1836) 4 Ad. & El. 675 at 682–683; 111 E.R. 941 at 944: "We do not proceed on any doctrine as to the relation of principal and surety ... we give our judgment on the principle that the discharge of one joint and several debtor is a discharge of all". See also *Walker v Bowry* (1924) 35 C.L.R. 48 at 57–58 *per* Starke J.

[51] *Re Wolmershausen* (1890) 62 L.T. 541; *Mercantile Bank of Sydney v Taylor* (1891) 12 L.R. (NSW) 252 at 268–269 *per* Innes J.

[52] See also above, para.8–21.

[53] As to what constitutes a covenant not to sue or a compromise falling short of a release, see G.L. Williams, *Joint Obligations* (1949), paras 53, 55. See also *Re Vella; Ex p. Perpetual Finance Corp Ltd* (unreported, WA Fed Ct, September 18, 1992), which also approved this paragraph in the text.

[54] See above, para.6–64.

[55] *Watts v Aldington, The Times,* December 16, 1993.

Given this, it is likely in the future that the relevant inquiry in this context will also be rather whether or not the document, properly construed, constitutes a release which (expressly or impliedly) preserves the creditor's rights against co-guarantors as opposed to an absolute release.

The application of the normal rule as to joint and joint and several parties means that a release of one of two joint and several guarantors releases the other even if the release is given after judgment is obtained against the guarantor who is released.[56]

8-24

It is also necessary to be aware of the possibility of an implied release of a guarantor, which will then release the co-guarantors, but such a release will rarely be inferred. In particular, if a guarantee is given by two or more co-guarantors and a subsequent guarantee is given by only some of those guarantors, the guarantors who do not incur liability under the second security usually will not be impliedly released.[57]

8-25

(ii) Where the continued existence of a co-guarantor is not a condition of the guarantee

If there is no express or implied term that the co-guarantors shall remain parties to the agreement, the release of a co-guarantor will not discharge the other guarantors from all liability, but they will be released to the extent that their right of contribution has been taken away or prejudiced by the release.[58] The right of contribution will arise where there are guarantors of the same debt, whether the guarantors are bound by single or separate instruments.[59] The burden of proof is on the guarantor to show that the right of contribution has arisen and that it has been impaired by the release of the co-guarantor.[60] The precise circumstances in which a right to contribution arises are discussed elsewhere,[61] but it should be observed that the guarantor does not have to show that he has sustained loss by payment of more than his share of the principal debt. The surety's right to contribution prior to payment has not been clearly defined, but it has been said[62] that the guarantor may enforce a claim for contribution if the loss to be sustained by the guarantor is "imminent".[63] At the point in

8-26

---

[56] *Walker v Bowry* (1924) 35 C.L.R. 48 at 55–56, 57–58; *Re EWA (a debtor)* [1901] 2 K.B. 642 at 648; *Re Vella Ex p. Perpetual Finance Corp Ltd* (unreported, WA Fed Ct, September 18, 1992); *Mee v ANZ Banking Group Ltd* (unreported, NSW Sup Ct, July 16, 1982).

[57] *Mahoney v McManus* (1981) 55 A.L.J.R. 673 at 677 *per* Gibbs C.J. See in detail below, paras 9–12 to 9–17.

[58] *Re Wolmershausen* (1890) 62 L.T. 541 at 545; *Hancock v Williams* (1942) 42 S.R. (NSW) 252 at 256 *per* Jordan C.J.; *Ward v National Bank of New Zealand* (1883) 8 App. Cas. 755. It is also sufficient to show that the guarantor's right of marshalling has been affected: *Smith v Wood* [1929] 1 Ch. 14 at 28–32 *per* Russell L.J., and see above, para.8–21, n.45.

[59] But the fact that the guarantors are bound by separate instruments may indicate that they are not guarantors for the same principal debt, in which case no contribution will be available.

[60] *Ward v National Bank of New Zealand* (1883) 8 App. Cas. 755 at 766; *Hancock v Williams* (1942) 42 S.R. (NSW) 252 at 256; *Canadian Imperial Bank of Commerce v Vopni* (1978) 86 D.L.R. (3d) 383 at 390.

[61] See below, Ch. 12.

[62] *Wolmershausen v Gullick* [1893] 2 Ch. 514 at 527.

[63] See below, Ch. 12, for a detailed discussion of when the right of contribution arises and *quia timet* relief is available.

time when the guarantor acquires the right of contribution, the guarantor is entitled to a declaration that there is a right of contribution from a co-guarantor. This declaration can then be used in proceedings brought by the creditor against the guarantor.[64]

8–27   Provided that it can be shown that the right of contribution has arisen, it is then incumbent on the guarantor to show the extent to which the right of contribution has been affected. In the usual case, such proof will not be difficult. Unless the guarantors have made an agreement inter se varying their liability, each solvent guarantor must generally contribute equally to the common debt,[65] so that where there are two separate guarantors for one debt, prima facie the release of one will release the other from one half of his liability.[66]

8–28   But in some circumstances the guarantor may not be able to show that the right of contribution has been affected. First, if the agreement between the creditor and a guarantor amounts to a covenant not to sue rather than a simple release, one view[67] is that the other guarantors retain their right of contribution against that guarantor so that the other guarantors will not be discharged to any extent if sued by the creditor.[68] Secondly, if a guarantor has paid more than the guarantor's share of the common debt before the creditor's release of another guarantor, none of these amounts can be recovered from the creditor on the basis that he has been prejudiced by the release. This is because the right of contribution is not affected as the right has accrued at the time of payment and an action for contribution can still be maintained against the guarantor who has been released.[69]

---

[64] *Wolmershausen v Gullick* [1893] 2 Ch. 514: see below, paras 11–135 to 11–143 for a discussion of quia timet relief.

[65] *Dering v Earl of Winchelsea* (1787) 1 Cox 318; 29 E.R. 1184; *Ellesmere Brewery Co v Cooper* [1896] 1 Q.B. 75. Different considerations apply if the guarantors guarantee different amounts: see below, paras 12–217 to 12–244.

[66] *Hancock v Williams* (1942) 42 S.R. (NSW) 252 at 256. As to the issue of contribution see generally below, Ch. 12.

[67] The matter is not settled. G.L. Williams, *Joint Obligations* (1949), para.52, p.110, suggests that there is a right of contribution where the case concerns joint debtors *other than sureties*. But in the same paragraph it is made plain that Professor Williams really treats the situation where there is a release of the *principal debtor* by the creditor as a special case, and he would view co-guarantors as coming within the normal rule. His view, therefore, is that there is a right of contribution between co-guarantors when the agreement amounts to a covenant not to sue; *Re Wolmershausen* (1890) 62 L.T. 541 (where the court embarked on an analysis of whether the right of contribution had been taken away even though the relevant agreement was interpreted as a covenant not to sue). *Cf. South Australian Land Mortgage & Agency Co Ltd v McInnes* (1895) 6 Q.L.J. 289 (where it was held that, where there was a covenant not to sue one of two joint debtors, only half the debt could be recovered from the other).

[68] Note, however, recent criticism of the distinction between a covenant not to sue and a release (see above, para.6–64). But if the agreement of release of one guarantor contains a clause preserving rights against co-guarantors, such a clause will probably also constitute an implied consent to the exercise of the right of contribution against the guarantor released.

[69] *Reade v Lowndes* (1857) 23 Beav. 361; 53 E.R. 142. The case concerned the release of a principal debtor after the guarantor had paid more than his share, but the same principle is applicable in the context of a release of a co-guarantor.

(iii) Agreement of the guarantor to the release of a co-guarantor

The creditor may attempt to avoid the consequences resulting from a **8–29** release of a co-guarantor by inserting a clause in the guarantee itself which covers that contingency. A clause authorising the creditor "to grant releases and discharges as [it] thinks fit, without prejudice to or in any way limiting or lessening the liability of the guarantor" has been held sufficient to preserve the full liability of the guarantor who agrees to this clause in circumstances where the guarantor's liability might otherwise have been reduced to the extent that the right of contribution had been affected by the release of another guarantor.[70] By agreeing to the clause, the guarantor has consented to remain liable in full even though there is no right of contribution against the guarantor who has been released.

One possible limitation in the application of such a clause is that it does **8–30** not specifically refer to the release of a co-guarantor, so that it may be interpreted as referring to the release of other persons, such as the principal debtor. Some guarantees, however, contain a clause which is specifically directed to the contingency of the guarantor's release, for example, by authorising the creditor "to release *any guarantor* or enter into a composition with *any guarantor* without limiting or lessening the liability of the other guarantors". The word "release" should be specifically referred to in the clause. Depending on the context the words "favour, grace or consideration" may be insufficient to embrace an absolute release.[71]

This type of clause is probably also effective to preserve the liability of **8–31** the guarantors who are not released when there is other wording in the guarantee which implies that it is a condition of the guarantee that all must be parties to the agreement (for example, by the words "joint and several"). The effect of the clause is to rebut this normal implication.[72]

Sometimes the creditor's right to pursue a remedy against co-guarantors, **8–32** despite a release of another guarantor, may appear in the agreement of release.[73] This is effective to preserve the creditor's remedy against the guarantors who have not been released.[74] In this situation, however, the guarantors who remain liable still have a right of contribution against the guarantor released,[75] because the latter has impliedly consented to the exercise of that right by agreeing to the reservation of rights clause. The situation parallels that arising when the principal debtor consents to a reservation of rights clause in an agreement of release with the creditor

---

[70] *Canadian Imperial Bank of Commerce v Vopni* (1978) 86 D.L.R. (3d) 383 at 393–394.
[71] See *Fletcher Organisation Pty Ltd v Crocus Investments Pty Ltd* [1988] 2 Qd. R. 517, but upholding the effectiveness of a "principal debtor" clause: see below, para.8–98.
[72] Note, however, that in *Toronto Dominion Bank v Higgott* (1984) D.L.R. (4th) 5, it was held that a clause authorising releases only applied to a release of a co-guarantor given before the guarantors were called upon to pay by the making of a demand.
[73] See, *e.g.*, the clause in *Mee v ANZ Banking Group Ltd* (unreported, NSW Sup Ct, July 16, 1982).
[74] *Hallett v Taylor* (1921) 6 Lloyd's L.R. 416 at 418. Note, however, the special clause in this case, which negated this result on the facts.
[75] See G.L. Williams, *Joint Obligations* (1949), para.52.

and similar criticisms are applicable.[76] If a guarantor is released, it is unlikely that he will appreciate that the effect of the reservation of rights clause is that, indirectly, he will still be liable for a proportion of the debt as a result of the implied preservation of the co-guarantors' right of contribution.

8–33   If a clause in the agreement of release of one guarantor is to preserve the creditor's right of action against the co-guarantors, the reservation of rights clause must clearly indicate that it is to have this effect. The clause in the agreement of release must unequivocally stipulate that the rights against the co-guarantors are preserved, despite the release.[77] For example, a clause in an agreement of release which stated that "the release of the debtor [that is, the guarantor] hereinbefore contained shall not prevent any of the creditors from suing any other persons who may have become bound as sureties for the debtor or who are in any manner liable for the payment of any debts of the debtor" failed to achieve this objective.[78] This was because the remaining co-guarantor could not be regarded as a "surety" for the guarantor who had been released[79] and, equally, was not liable for the payment of the debts of the other co-guarantor but was merely liable to the creditor as a joint debtor with the other co-guarantor.[80] A clause which would effectively preserve the creditor's rights against a co-guarantor when another guarantor is released would state that "this release does not in any way prejudice or affect the creditor's rights against any other guarantor".

8–34   Even if there is no reservation of rights clause in the release or in the guarantee, the guarantor may still consent to the release of the co-guarantor. Where it is a condition of the contract that there must be co-guarantors, and one is released without the knowledge of some of the guarantors it has been said[81] that even those who gave their consent to the release are released from liability. The basis of this conclusion appears to be that those who assented could not have intended to take the whole burden of the guarantee upon themselves, having initially undertaken the liability not as a separate liability but as part of a contract with other guarantors.[82] But this reasoning is questionable where the guarantors clearly consent to a change in the contractual arrangements and agree to waive their right of contribution from the co-guarantors.[83] This would indicate clearly that the consenting guarantors are willing to remain liable despite the release of the co-surety. Provided that there is clear proof of consent, therefore, such guarantors should not be discharged.

---

[76] See above, para.6–71.
[77] *Liverpool Corn Trade Association Ltd v Hurst* [1936] 2 All E.R. 309.
[78] *ibid.*
[79] *ibid.*, at 314–315.
[80] *ibid.*
[81] *Ellesmere Brewery Co v Cooper* [1896] 1 Q.B. 75 at 82–83, *Australian Joint Stock Bank v Bailey (No 1).* (1897) 18 L.R. (NSW) 103. The latter decision was approved in *Deane v City Bank of Sydney* (1904) 2 C.L.R. 198 at 212.
[82] *Ellesmere Brewery Co v Cooper* [1986] 1 Q.B. 75 at 82–83 *per* Russell C.J.
[83] There was probably no such consent in *Ellesmere Brewery Co v Cooper* [1896] 1 Q.B. 75, but there may have been in *Australian Joint Stock Bank v Bailey (No.1)* (1897) 18 L.R. (NSW) 103.

(iv) Discharge of a co-guarantor pursuant to the insolvency legislation

Section 281(7) of the Insolvency Act 1986 expressly provides that a **8–35** "discharge does not release any person other than the bankrupt from any liability ... from which the bankrupt is released by the discharge." Thus a discharge of one co-guarantor will not release the other co-guarantors from liability. But as a matter of principle a voluntary arrangement of release made pursuant to Pt VIII of the Act will take effect in the same way as a consensual agreement of release, thereby discharging co-guarantors,[84] unless as a matter of construction the arrangement expressly or impliedly reserves rights against co-guarantors. The issue has already been considered in the context of a voluntary arrangement releasing the principal debtor.[85]

3. DISCHARGE BY THE CREDITOR MATERIALLY ALTERING THE TERMS OF THE GUARANTEE

If the creditor who holds the executed guarantee (whether under seal or **8–36** otherwise) in his possession deliberately makes a material alteration without the consent of the guarantor, the guarantor will be discharged even though the original words of the instrument remain legible.[86] This is an application of a general contractual principle, based on the rationale that "no man shall be permitted to take the chance of committing a fraud, without running any risk of losing by the event, when it is detected".[87] It follows that the guarantor will not be discharged if the creditor can show that the alteration is made by mistake[88] or by accident.[89]

Leaving aside negotiable instruments and banknotes (which fall into a **8–37** separate category governed by statute),[90] the test of materiality was recently formulated in ths way by the Court of Appeal in *Raiffeisen Zentralbank Osterreich AG v Crossseas Shipping Ltd*:[91]

---

[84] If it is a condition of the guarantee that the guarantors shall remain parties to the agreement, the co-guarantors will be released from all liability. Otherwise they will be released to the extent that their right of contribution has been effected. See above, paras 8–21 to 8–25.

[85] See above, paras 6–94 to 6–96.

[86] *Pigot's Case* (1614) 11 Co. Rep. 26b; 77 E.R. 1177; *Davidson v Cooper* (1844) 13 M. & W. 343; 153 E.R. 142; *Bank of Hindostan, China & Japan Ltd v Smith* (1867) 36 L.J.C.P. 241; *Master v Miller* (1791) 4 T.R. 320; 100 E.R. 1042; *Suffell v Bank of England* (1882) 9 Q.B.D. 555; *Koch v Dicks* [1933] 1 K.B. 307; *Birrell v Stafford* [1988] V.R. 281; *Vacuum Oil Co Pty Ltd v Longmuir* [1957] V.R. 456. The rule is of general application and should apply when the executed guarantee is in possession of the principal debtor or a co-guarantor: see *Citibank Savings Ltd v Vago* (unreported, NSW Sup Ct, 1 May 1992), where the allegedly material alteration was made either by the borrower's solicitor or a co-guarantor.

[87] *Master v Miller* (1791) 4 T.R. 320 at 329; 100 E.R. 1042 at 1047.

[88] *Wilkinson v Johnson* (1824) 3 B. & C. 428; 107 E.R. 792. But it must not be a mistake of law: *Bank of Hindostan, China & Japan Ltd v Smith* (1867) 36 L.J.C.P. 241.

[89] *Hong Kong & Shanghai Banking Corp v Lo Shee Shi* [1928] A.C. 181.

[90] See, Bills of Exchange Act 1882, s.64.

[91] [2000] 1 W.L.R. 1135.

"to take advantage of the rule, the would-be avoider should be able to demonstrate that the alteration is one which, assuming the parties act in accordance with the other terms of the contract, is one which is potentially prejudical to his legal rights or obligations under the instrument. I say 'potentially prejudicial' because I do not think it necessary to show that prejudice has in fact occurred. The rule remains a salutary one aimed at preventing fraud and founded upon inference of fraudulent or improper motive at the time of alteration. It seems to me that, absent any element of potential prejudice, no inference of fraud or improper motive is appropriate."[92]

There is no necessity for the guarantor to affirmatively prove fraud,[93] but (despite suggestions by some Commonwealth authority)[94] the rule is not confined to "fundamental" or "essential" obligations of the contract.[95] Nor, as presently formulated, does the application of the rule permit the adduction of evidence as to "the motives of the person effecting the alteration and the actual (as opposed to potential) effect of the alteration upon the liability of the avoiding party"[96]

8–38 On the facts of *Raiffeisen Zentral Bank Osterreich AG v Crossseas Shipping Ltd*[97] the creditor inserted the name and address of an agent to accept service for all legal processes issued in England in a blank space provided in the guarantee. It was held[98] that the alteration was not material. It had not altered or accelerated the guarantor's liability to make payment under the guarantee since the contract deemed the issue rather than the service of proceedings to be a demand under the guarantee and, in any event, it also required such demand to be sent to the guarantor's home address abroad. The only basis upon which the guarantor could claim potential prejudice was that he might seek to evade the service of proceedings upon him personally, which was not a satisfactory basis for the avoidance of the guarantee.

8–39 The application of the test in *Raiffeisen Zentralbank Osterreich AG v Crossseas Shipping Ltd*[99] means that the correction of misdescriptions will not constitute a material variation as, for example, in *Lombard Finance Ltd v Brookplain Trading Ltd*,[1] where the creditor altered the identity of principal borrower from "B Company Ltd" to "B Ltd".

8–40 Similarly, if the words "on demand" are added to the guarantee, but it is clear from the rest of the instrument that liability under the contract would

---

[92] *ibid.*, at 1148.
[93] *Warburton v National Westminster Finance Australia Ltd* [1988] 15 N.S.W.L.R. 238 at 244, which suggested the rule will not apply to non-fraudulent alterations.
[94] *Canadian Imperial Bank of Commerce v Skender* [1986] 1 W.W.R. 284.
[95] *Raiffeisen Zentralbank Osterreich AG v Crossseas Shipping Ltd* [2000] 1 W.L.R. 1135 at 1148–1149.
[96] *ibid.*, at 1149.
[97] [2000] 1 W.L.R. 1135.
[98] *ibid.*, at 1149–1150.
[99] [2000] 1 W.L.R. 1135.
[1] [1991] 2 All E.R. 762.

arise upon demand in any event, this will not be considered material.[2] Furthermore, an alteration which reduces the potential liability of the guarantor, for example, by inserting a limitation on liability to a stated amount[3] or to a particular account[4] or a reduction in the amount guaranteed[5] is probably not material.[6]

Decisions in Commonwealth countries[7] have held that the addition of a bank employee's name as a witness was not a material alteration. Although *Pigot's Case* has been less restrictively interpreted in those jurisdictions, it is likely that the same result will be reached applying the test in *Raiffeisen Zentralbank Osterreich AG v Crossseas Shipping Ltd*[8] provided that the guarantee was validly executed without the need for witnesses in any event, since the legal effect of the instrument remains unchanged.   **8–41**

Sometimes the creditor affixes a seal to the guarantee subsequent to the parties signing it. If the guarantee effectively operates as a contract under seal before the alteration by the creditor, the subsequent unauthorised affixing of a seal will not be material because the legal effect of the instrument remains the same.[9] Thus, when the guarantee contains the phrase "signed, sealed and delivered" and, on the line which the guarantor signs, the word "seal" is printed in parentheses, these facts constitute the document a deed from the outset, so that the subsequent addition of a gummed wafer seal by the creditor merely confirms the legal effect of the document and is not a material alteration.[10] If, however, the subsequent affixing of a seal changes the nature of the agreement from a simple contract to an instrument under seal, the alteration may be considered material because the change negatives the necessity for proof of consideration.[11] Additionally the limitation period applicable to the guarantee is extended.   **8–42**

The rule regarding material variations has been extended to an alteration by a stranger whilst the executed document is in the custody   **8–43**

---

[2] *Aldous v Cornwell* (1868) L.R. 3 Q.B. 573.
[3] *Walsh v Westpac Banking Corp* (1991) 104 A.C.T.R. 30.
[4] *Bank of Scotland v Henry Butcher* [2001] 2 All E.R. (Comm) 691 at paras 90–102 (alteration limiting guarantee to guarantee of the customer's business account, rather than guarantee of general indebtedness).
[5] *Farrow Mortgage Services Pty Ltd v Slade* (1996) 38 N.S.W.L.R. 636, where the principal sum (nominated in the mortgage and guarantee to be advanced) was altered. But it is arguable that an alteration reducing the principal sum may be material in some circumstances, *e.g.*, where the original amount of the loan is vital to the success of the venture and a lower advance may render the risk of default more likely.
[6] *Walsh v Westpac Banking Corp* (*ibid.*) was approved by Potter L.J. in *Raiffeisen Zentral Bank Osterreich AG v Crossseas Shipping Ltd* [2000] 1 W.L.R. 1135 at 1147–1148.
[7] *Birrell v Stafford* [1988] VR 281; *Canadian Imperial Bank of Commerce v Skender* [1986] 1 W.W.R. 284.
[8] [2000] 1 W.L.R. 1135.
[9] *Linton v Royal Bank of Canada* (1966) 60 D.L.R. (2d) 398; *Spear v Bank of Nova Scotia* (1973) 37 D.L.R. (3d) 130; *Royal Bank of Canada v Bermuda Holdings Ltd* (1975) 67 D.L.R. (3d) 316.
[10] *Royal Bank of Canada v Bermuda Holdings Ltd* (1975) 67 D.L.R. (3d) 316.
[11] *Linton v Royal Bank of Canada* (1966) 60 D.L.R. (2d) 398 at 400. On this basis, the court distinguished *Davidson v Cooper* (1844) 13 M. & W. 343; 153 ER 142. *Cf.*, however, *Royal Bank of Canada v Bermuda Holdings Ltd* (1975) 67 D.L.R. (3d) 316 at 323.

of the person to whom it was given.[12] Thus the odd result arises that a guarantor will be discharged by a stranger altering the guarantee in a material particular when it is in the possession of the creditor. It has been strongly and soundly argued[13] that the authorities extending the rule in this way are illogical and will probably not be followed. Exceptionally the guarantee may be altered by a stranger after signature by the guarantor, but prior to final execution by the creditor. In this case there is probably no proper agreement at all, unless an antecedent common intention can be identified to justify rectification of the document.[14]

8–44   Conversely, the rule in *Pigot's Case* has been confined to circumstances in which it is shown that the amendment to the document is an "operative and final alteration".[15] This is perhaps uncontentious, but in *Co-operative Bank plc v Tipper*[16] Judge Roger Cooke considered that "where a document consists otherwise of print, type and ink in writing the most natural inference to draw of an amendment to that in pencil is that it is not, and is not intended to be an operative and final alteration". This seems overstated. The operation of the rule should hardly be dependent upon the precise means or technique used to effect the alteration.

8–45   The guarantor will not be discharged by an alteration to the guarantee if it can be shown that the creditor has been expressly or impliedly authorised by the guarantor to effect the alteration. Sometimes a provision is included in the guarantee for this purpose. Indeed, even in the absence of a special clause to this effect, in *Armor Coatings (Marketing) Pty Ltd v General Credits (Finance) Pty Ltd*[17] the Full Court of the Supreme Court of South Australia held that when one of the parties executes the formal contract after agreement has been reached and hands it over to the other "he will readily be regarded as having conferred on that other implied authority to fill up blanks ... and to alter the document if necessary to make it conform to the common contractual intention where by mistake it does not do so".[18] It is thought, however, that this is incorrect. Such an inference should not so easily be drawn because it effectively confers power on the creditor to rectify the document unilaterally. Significantly, in *Raffeisen Zentralbank Osterreich AG v Crossseas Shipping Ltd*[19] no reference was made to this principle, even though the relevant alteration

---

[12] *Davidson v Cooper* (1844) 13 M. & W. 343; 153 E.R. 142; *Croockewit v Fletcher* (1857) 1 H. & N. 893; 156 E.R. 1463. This would include a co-guarantor or the principal debtor.
[13] *Chitty on Contracts* (28th ed., 1999), para.26–019. See also *Farrow Mortgage Services Pty Ltd v Slade* (1996) 38 N.S.W.L.R. 636 at 649.
[14] *Farrow Mortgage Services Pty Ltd v Williams* (unreported, NSW Sup Ct. April 5, 1993) at 17. But, on appeal in *Farrow Mortgage Sercies Pty Ltd v Slade* (1996) 38 N.S.W.L.R. 637 at 649 it was held that there was a common antecedent intention (by Clarke J.A.) and that the parties came into contractual relations (by Gleeson C.J.).
[15] *Co-operative Bank plc v Tipper* [1996] 4 All E.R. 366 at 372.
[16] *ibid.*
[17] (1978) 17 S.A.S.R. 259.
[18] (1978) 17 S.A.S.R. 259 at 277 (emphasis added). See also *Walsh v Westpac Banking Corp* (1991) 104 A.C.T.R. 30; *Warburton v National Westminster Finance Australia Ltd* [1988] 15 N.S.W.L.R. 238, where the Court of Appeal of New South Wales also held that if the party filling up the blanks makes an honest mistake and inserts incorrect material into the deed, the court is entitled to rectify the deed to make it conform to the common contractual intention of the parties.
[19] [2000] 1 W.L.R. 2000.

consisted of filling in a space left blank for the purpose of inserting the name and address of a service agent.

4. DISCHARGE BY THE CREDITOR RELEASING OR IMPAIRING SECURITIES HELD BY THE CREDITOR

(i) General scope of the rule

On satisfaction of the guaranteed obligation, the guarantor is entitled to be subrogated to any securities held by the creditor for the enforcement of the principal contract.[20] This equitable rule has been embodied in a statutory form.[21] As a result, if the creditor interferes with or impairs the value of such securities, the guarantor may be wholly or partially released from liability. A release on this basis can occur in three ways.

8–46

(a) A variation in the terms of the security forming part of the principal contract

It has already been seen that if the principal and the creditor consensually vary the terms of the principal agreement, the guarantor will be discharged from all liability unless the alteration is patently insubstantial or is obviously for the benefit of the guarantor.[22] A particular application of this principle is where the agreement between the principal and the creditor involves a variation in the terms of the security, which is itself part of the contract between principal and creditor.[23] It is irrelevant that the security for the most part is still effective (provided that the variation is not patently insubstantial)[24] or that the value of the security that is lost or impaired by the variation is far less than the amount of the debt guaranteed. The result is still that the guarantor is absolutely discharged.[25] Thus in *Polak v Everett*,[26] a guarantor was discharged from all liability on a debt of £6,000 when securities having a face value of £4,000 were improperly released to the principal by agreement between the creditor and the principal.[27]

8–47

---

[20] See below, Ch. 12.
[21] Mercantile Law Amendment Act 1856, s.5.
[22] *Holme v Brunskill* (1878) 3 Q.B.D. 495 at 505; *Dunlop New Zealand Ltd v Dumbleton* [1968] N.Z.L.R. 1092 at 1096. The question of variation of the principal contract is discussed above, Ch. 7.
[23] *Polak v Everett* (1876) 1 Q.B.D. 669; *Bolton v Darling Downs Building Society* [1935] Q.S.R. 237; *Bank of New Zealand v Baker* [1926] N.Z.L.R. 462 (although here the variation, which involved a release of the mortgage, was contemplated by a clause in the guarantee).
[24] See above, paras 7–01 to 7–03.
[25] *Polak v Everett* (1876) 1 Q.B.D. 669; *Taylor v Bank of New South Wales* (1886) 11 App. Cas. 596 at 603.
[26] (1876) 1 Q.B.D. 669.
[27] *ibid.*, at 677 *per* Quain J., 676–677 *per* Mellor J., 674–675 *per* Blackburn J., who (at 674) appears also to treat the case on the basis of a breach of the equitable duty (discussed below, para.8–49), but if that were so, the guarantor would be discharged only to the extent of the value of the security.

(b) A breach of a contractual obligation by the creditor in relation to the securities

8–48   Even if there is no variation of the terms of the main contract by agreement between creditor and principal, the guarantee may be given upon a condition that a specific security be obtained, perfected, protected, maintained or preserved by the creditor.[28] The term may be implied from the circumstances, and oral evidence is admissible to prove the condition if it amounts to a condition precedent to the operation of the guarantee.[29] If such a condition can be shown to exist, any failure in the performance of the condition will operate to release the guarantor from all liability because the creditor has not performed his part of the bargain. As in the case of a consensual variation (see (a), above), it is irrelevant that the security which is impaired or lost by the breach of condition has a substantially lower value than the amount guaranteed.[30]

(c) A breach of equitable duty

8–49   Even if the guarantor cannot show a consensual variation of the principal contract or a breach by the creditor of a condition of the guarantee relating to the securities, the creditor remains under an equitable duty to maintain such securities for the benefit of the guarantor. A breach of this duty will reduce the guarantor's liability to the extent that the value of the securities has been impaired as a result of the breach.[31] This was made clear recently by the Court of Appeal in *Skipton Building Society v Stott*[32] in approving the distinction drawn by Lord Watson in *Taylor v Bank of New South Wales*[33] between a consensual variation of the principal contract (as described in (a), above) and the unilateral act of the creditor in neglecting securities. Lord Watson had referred to cases where:

> "there had been an alteration of the original contract between the creditor and the principal debtor, without the consent of the surety, who

---

[28] *Northern Banking Co Ltd v Newman and Calton* [1927] I.R. 520 at 538; *Williams v Frayne* (1937) 58 C.L.R. 710 at 738 *per* Dixon J.; *Carter v White* (1883) 25 Ch. D. 666 at 670; *Hancock v Williams* (1942) 42 S.R. (NSW) 252 at 255.

[29] *Adelaide Life Assurance & Guarantee Co v Gandolphi* (1887) 21 S.A.L.R. 18; *Royal Bank of Canada v Girgulis* [1979] 3 W.W.R. 451; *Northern Banking Co Ltd v Newman and Calton* [1927] I.R. 520 at 538, where it is stated that the term may be "collateral" to the guarantee; *Hawrish v Bank of Montreal* [1969] 2 D.L.R. (3d) 600 at 603.

[30] *Carter v White* (1883) 25 Ch. D. 666 at 670; *Williams v Frayne* (1937) 58 C.L.R. 710 at 738 *per* Dixon J.; *Australian Joint Stock Bank v Hetherington* (1893) 14 L.R. (NSW) 503; *Northern Banking Co Ltd v Newman and Calton* [1927] I.R. 520 at 538.

[31] *Carter v White* (1883) 25 Ch. D. 666 at 670; *Williams v Frayne* (1937) 58 C.L.R. 710 at 738 *per* Dixon J.; *Australian Joint Stock Bank v Hetherington* (1893) 14 LR (NSW) 503; *Northern Banking Co Ltd v Newman and Calton* [1927] I.R. 520 at 539.

[32] [2001] Q.B. 261 at 269.

[33] (1886) 11 App. Cas. 596. See also *Williams v Frayne* (1937) 58 C.L.R. 710 at 738; *Taylor v Bank of New South Wales* (1886) 11 App. Cas. 596 at 602–603. See also *Northern Banking Co Ltd v Newman and Calton* [1927] I.R. 520 at 529; *Williams v Frayne* (1937) 58 C.L.R. 710 at 738; *Hancock v Williams* (1942) 42 S.R. (NSW) 252 at 256; *Buckeridge v Mercantile Credits Ltd* (1982) 56 A.L.J.R. 28 at 34.

was held to be wholly discharged, on the plain ground that he could not be made liable for default in the performance of a contract which he had not guaranteed. The present case would ... have been within the rule of *Pearl v Deacon*, 24 Beav 186; 1 De G & J 461, *where the creditor had, by his own act, rendered unavailable part of the security,* to *the benefit of which the surety was entitled, and the latter was held to be discharged, not absolutely, but only pro tanto."* [authors' italics].

This rule applies to securities taken by the creditor from the debtor or additional securities given by the guarantor,[34] provided that they were given to secure the guaranteed debt and not an entirely separate obligation.[35] It also applies to those securities which are taken by the creditor after the guarantee has been given.[36] The equitable rule is especially important in regard to such securities because, as they have been taken after the execution of the guarantee, there is unlikely to be a term in the guarantee imposing any obligation upon the creditor to preserve them.[37]   **8–50**

There is authority to suggest that the duty also extends to securities given by a co-guarantor in respect of the guaranteed obligation.[38] This is because the guarantor also has an interest in these securities since, if the guarantor satisfies the principal obligation, the guarantor is entitled to have the securities assigned to him to enforce contribution from a co-surety.[39] The exact nature of the creditor's duty in relation to securities given by a co-guarantor is not clear, it merely being stated that such securities shall not be "wasted".[40] The duty of the creditor in relation to securities given by the principal and the guarantor, which will be examined in the remainder of this section, should provide the appropriate guidelines for the determination of the duty in relation to securities given by a co-guarantor, but it has been suggested (without any elaboration and   **8–51**

[34] *Merchants Bank of London v Maud* (1870) 18 W.R. 312. As examples, see *Hunter v Zakus* (1968) 67 D.L.R. (2d) 355; *Re Darwen and Pearce* [1927] 1 Ch. 176. Where the security is given by the guarantor, a failure to maintain the security may also be a breach of the contract of guarantee by the creditor, so that there is no need to rely on the equitable doctrine. An exception is where the guarantor gives additional securities after having given the guarantee.
[35] *Wade v Coope* (1827) 2 Sim. 155; 57 E.R. 747; *Wilkinson v London & County Banking Co* (1884) 1 T.L.R. 63.
[36] *Pledge v Buss* (1860) John 663; 70 E.R. 585 (disapproving *Newton v Chorlton* (1853) 10 Hare 646; 68 E.R. 1087); *Forbes v Jackson* (1882) 19 Ch. D. 615; *Mayhew v Crickett* (1818) 2 Swan 185 at 191; 36 ER 585 at 587; *Polak v Everett* (1876) 1 Q.B.D. 669 at 676 *per* Blackburn J.
[37] Cf. *Crédit Lyonnais (Aust) Ltd v Darling* (1991) 5 A.C.S.R. 703, where the guarantor specifically arranged that the principal provide an additional security subsequent to the execution of the guarantee.
[38] *Margrett v Gregory* (1862) 10 W.R. 630. See also *Dobbs v National Bank of A/asia Ltd* (1935) 53 C.L.R. 643 (but here there was a contractual promise not to release the securities furnished by the guarantor's co-sureties and, in any event, the guarantee excluded liability on the part of the creditor).
[39] *Duncan, Fox & Co v North & South Wales Bank* (1880) 6 App. Cas. 1 at 19 *per* Lord Blackburn, citing *Dering v Earl of Winchelsea* (1787) 1 Cox 318; 29 E.R. 1184; *Craythorne v Swinburne* (1807) 14 Ves. Jun. 160; 33 E.R. 482; *Stirling v Forrester* (1821) 3 Bli. 575; 4 E.R. 712. *Cf.* Jessel M.R. at the first instance in *Duncan, Fox & Co v North & South Wales Bank* (1879) 11 Ch. D. 88 at 95–96.
[40] *Margrett v Gregory* (1862) 10 W.R. 630.

somewhat inconsistently) that the duty in the latter situation is a less onerous one.[41]

8-52   The creditor's obligations in equity do not extend to securities provided by a stranger without the authority of, or on behalf of, the principal debtor because the guarantor has no entitlement to these securities[42] since the guarantor cannot avail himself of them to seek an indemnity from the principal or to enforce contribution from a co-guarantor.[43] But it should be emphasised that this is a rare situation because a third party who gives the creditor a security will often thereby secure the principal obligation by the charge created by the security and assume a position analogous to a co-surety.[44] The equitable rule will apply to this security as it then becomes a security given by a co-guarantor.

8-53   The cases[45] do not always draw a clear distinction between a discharge of the guarantor by virtue of the breach of the equitable duty (situation (c), above), on the one hand, and by reason of a breach of condition to preserve or maintain a security (situation (b), above), on the other. Nevertheless, the distinction is important. It is clear from the above analysis that, if there is a breach of a condition of the guarantee, the guarantor is absolutely discharged even if the value of the security impaired is less than the amount guaranteed. But if the guarantor is discharged in equity, he will be released only to the extent that the security has been diminished in value.[46] In this situation there is, therefore, a necessity to show that the security has been destroyed or diminished in value due to the creditor's neglect, and the burden of proof is probably on the guarantor to show that there has been a breach of the relevant obligation.[47] Certainly, if the security is lost or destroyed and its value is equal to or in excess of the guaranteed debt, it is irrelevant on which basis the guarantor is discharged, but the basis is crucial if the value of the security impaired is less than the value of the guaranteed debt.

8-54   The distinction may also be significant because, whereas a condition of the contract may impose an obligation upon the creditor in relation to any

---

[41] *ibid.* But the *Times Law Report* of the case ((1862) 6 L.T. 543) does not make this distinction.
[42] *Chatterton v Maclean* [1951] 1 All E.R. 761 at 766–767; *Goodman v Keel* [1923] 4 D.L.R. 468 at 469–470.
[43] *ibid.*
[44] *Smith v Wood* [1929] 1 Ch. 14; *Bank of New Zealand v Baker* [1926] N.Z.L.R. 462; *Sherwin v McWilliams* (1921) 17 Tas. L.R. 94.
[45] This is especially so in some of the earlier cases, *e.g. Pearl v Deacon* 1857 24 Beav 186; 53 E.R. 328; *Strange v Fooks* (1863) 4 Giff. 408; 66 E.R. 765; *Pledge v Buss* (1860) John 663; 70 E.R. 585; *Mills v Schwass* [1929] G.L.R. 460. As explained in *Skipton Building Society v Stott* [2001] Q.B. 261 at 269, this is sometimes because the amount of pro tanto discharge is sufficient to extinguish the outstanding debt. But the distinction is well made in *Williams v Frayne* (1937) 58 C.L.R. 710 at 738 *per* Dixon J.; *Northern Banking Co Ltd v Newman and Calton* [1927] I.R. 520 at 538; *Carter v White* (1883) 25 Ch. D. 666 at 670; *Dale v Powell* (1911) 105 L.T. 291; *Hancock v Williams* (1942) 42 S.R. (NSW) 252.
[46] *Carter v White* (1883) 25 Ch. D. 666 at 670 *Williams v Frayne* (1937) 58 C.L.R. 710 at 738, *per* Dixon J.; *Northern Banking Co Ltd v Newman and Calton* [1927] I.R. 520 at 539.
[47] See *Skipton Building Society v Stott* [2001] Q.B. 261 at 271 para.27, *per* Evans L.J., but also holding that the creditor must show that he has obtained current market value, when the issue is whether the creditor has taken reasonable steps to market the property (see below, paras 8–85 to 8–87). *Cf.* Potter L.J. who left the matter open. See also *Buckeridge v Mercantile Credits Ltd* (1981) 147 C.L.R. 654 at 676 *per* Brennan J.

type of security, it is unclear whether the creditor's equitable duty extends to all kinds of securities. As the creditor's obligation to preserve and maintain securities stems from the guarantor's right to be subrogated to those securities upon payment of the debt, the equitable obligation should extend to all such securities.[48] But, as will be seen,[49] this criterion in itself does not provide an adequate test because it is not entirely clear to which securities the guarantor is entitled to be subrogated.[50]

(ii) Extent of the obligations of the creditor

It is not possible to make any statement in general terms as to the extent of the obligations of the creditor in regard to the securities which the creditor holds. Where there is a condition of the guarantee regarding the securities, the condition may impose any obligation on the creditor. But where the guarantor relies on a breach of the creditor's equitable duty, the exact nature of the duty has not been defined. Depending on the context, it is sometimes described as a duty to take reasonable care[51] and sometimes a duty to act bona fide.[52]
    8–55

Perhaps the most constructive approach to this complex area is to isolate the most common situations where the guarantor may be partially or wholly discharged by the creditor's actions in relation to securities held by the creditor and also to identify those instances where the guarantor will not be discharged.
    8–56

(a) Obtaining additional securities[53]

The creditor is under no equitable duty to the guarantor to seek additional securities from the principal.[54] Nor does the creditor have to renew a security, for example, by exercising an option to renew a lease.[55] If the guarantor is to argue successfully that other securities should be obtained by the creditor from the principal, the guarantor must establish an express or implied condition to that effect.
    8–57

Cases of express stipulations are rare and are unlikely to appear in modern contracts of guarantee. But although the courts are reluctant to
    8–58

---

[48] This will include securities coming within the *Mercantile Law Amendment Act* 1856, s.5. See below, Ch. 12. Thus, since the Act refers specifically to a "judgment", the creditor may be under a duty not to impair a judgment (*e.g.* by assigning it to a third party).

[49] See below, paras 12–312 to 12–324.

[50] *ibid.*

[51] *Northern Banking Co Ltd v Newman and Calton* [1927] I.R. 520 at 539; *Yorkshire Bank plc v Hall* [1999] 1 All E.R. 879 at 892 (in the context of exercising a power of sale).

[52] *Medforth v Blake* [1999] 3 W.L.R. 922 (receiver's duty in managing property to act bona fide, but also in some circumstances to act with due diligence).

[53] An aspect of this obligation is that the creditor may sometimes be obliged to obtain the execution of the guarantee by all those named as guarantors. This is discussed above, paras 3–88 to 3–99.

[54] *McDougal v Gariepy* (1922) 68 D.L.R. 560 at 561; *CBFC Ltd v Dryburgh* (unreported, NSW Sup Ct, March 18, 1995).

[55] *Williams v Frayne* (1937) 58 C.L.R. 710 at 723 *per* Latham C.J.

imply further terms "in a complex and carefully drawn document"[56] they are nevertheless sometimes prepared to infer a condition that additional securities be obtained and the basis for doing so often lies in the wording of the recital to the guarantee. In *Greer v Kettle*[57] the recital was in these terms:

> "Whereas the corporation have at the request of the guarantors advanced to [the borrowers] the sum of two hundred and fifty thousand pounds *on the security of a charge dated March 20 One Thousand nine hundred and twenty-nine on the shares particulars of which are set out in the schedule hereto.*"[58]

8–59   This wording, together with a provision in the body of the guarantee, led the court to conclude that there was a condition precedent to the guarantor's obligation that the debt must be secured by a charge on the shares specified in the schedule. It was not an undertaking to guarantee an unsecured debt and the guarantor was discharged from liability as the charge on the shares was never obtained. At a more general level the guarantee may state (perhaps in the recital or statement of consideration) that the guarantor will be answerable for advances which the creditor "agreed to make". In such a case it is possible that this will result in the guarantee being made conditional on a security being obtained if the principal transaction (or related documentation, such as an offer of loan) indicates that a security is required as a term of the advance.[59]

8–60   The precise wording of the recital will be decisive in each case. Thus in *ANZ Banking Group Ltd v Beneficial Finance Corp Ltd*[60] (which concerned the construction of an indemnity), the recital was interpreted as obliging the creditor only to obtain the security prior to the date when liability arose pursuant to the indemnity and not at the date of its execution. The creditor had complied with this condition precedent and was therefore able to enforce the agreement.

8–61   Where there is no specific wording in the guarantee from which it can be inferred that the guarantee is subject to a condition that a security shall be obtained, the task of the guarantor in establishing such a condition is likely to be much more difficult. The term may arise from the parties' negotiations and conduct, but it is not sufficient to show that the guarantor was aware that the principal debtor would provide an additional

---

[56] *Crédit Lyonnais Bank Nederland v Export Credit Guarantee Dept* [1996] 1 Lloyd's Rep. 200.
[57] [1938] AC 156. As other illustrations, see *Chambers v Rankine* [1910] S.A.L.R. 73; *Pratapsing Moholalshai v Keshavlal Harilal Setalwad* (1934) 62 Indian Appeals 23 *Malone v Wright, Heaton & Co* (1895) 6 Q.L.J. 270; *Ievins v Latvian (Toronto) Credit Union Ltd* (1977) 84 D.L.R. (3d) 248, although in one respect this case is wrongly decided, however, as the guarantor was only discharged pro tanto even though the obtaining of another security was a condition precedent to the operation of the guarantee; *BLM Holdings Ltd v Bank of New Zealand* (unreported, NSW Sup Ct, March 25, 1994), where the guarantor's liability was restricted to moneys advanced "in accordance with the terms of the facility", which required the creditor to obtain security prior to making funds available.
[58] Emphasis added. See this set out in [1938] A.C. 156 at 162.
[59] See as an illustration *Geelong Building Society (in liq) v Encel* (unreported, Vic Sup Ct, December 15, 1994).
[60] [1983] 1 N.S.W.L.R. 199.

security.[61] There must be a common understanding that the obtaining of the security is a condition of, or condition precedent to, the operation of the guarantee.[62] As the courts have pointed out, it is inherently unlikely that the creditor would agree to a condition of this nature, which would restrict the rights given to it pursuant to the formal documentation.[63] Indeed, in *Byblos Bank SAL v Al-Khudhairy*,[64] where it was argued that the evidence pointed to the existence of such a condition, Nicholls L.J. acknowledged that "little short of an express mention to the bank's officers that this guarantee was conditional would have been sufficient to give rise to the contractual term being contended for".[65] Nevertheless sometimes a condition is established on the basis of oral evidence. For example, in *NatWest Bank plc v Pickering*[66] the guarantor proved an oral understanding that it was a condition of the guarantee that another guarantee would be provided secured by a charge. Significantly, however, this oral evidence was supplemented by the postscript to a letter written by the guarantor to the creditor recording his recollection of the understanding, to which the creditor did not reply.

(b) Overlapping securities

The creditor may be in possession of a number of securities from the **8–62** principal debtor, and the question arises as to whether the creditor is under any liability if one of these securities is enforced rather than another. It is unlikely that there will be an express or implied condition of the guarantee that the creditor should enforce one of the securities in preference to the others. Hence any liability will rest on a breach of the equitable duty. In *Buckeridge v Mercantile Credits Ltd*,[67] the creditor was the mortgagee of the hotel premises of the debtor and was also given a debenture which created a specific charge over some of the debtor's assets and a floating charge over the balance.[68] The freehold land charged by the mortgage was also part of the land properly charged by the debenture. When the

---

[61] *JGL Investments Pty Ltd v Maracorp Financial Services Ltd* [1991] 2 V.R. 168. And there is no rule of law that the existence or continued availability of the security is a condition of the guarantee merely because the principal debt is secured: *Silverton Ltd v Harvey* [1975] 1 N.S.W.L.R. 659.

[62] *Byblos Bank SAL v Al-Khudhairy* (1986) 2 B.C.C. 99,549 at 99,557; *Socomex Ltd v Banques Bruxelles Lambert* [1966] 1 Lloyd's Rep. 156 at 177–178 (where it was argued that it was agreed that a period of notice be given before funding was to be withdrawn); *JGL Investments Pty Ltd v Maracorp Financial Services Ltd* [1991] 2 V.R. 168; *TCB Ltd v Gray* [1988] 1 All E.R. 108 at 113. See also *National Bank of New Zealand v Aherne* (unreported, HC (NZ), December 19, 1983). The pleading of the obligation as a condition precedent to the operation of the guarantee rather than as a simple condition will avoid the operation of the parol evidence rule.

[63] See *Socomex Ltd v Banque Bruxelles Lambert* [1966] 1 Lloyd's Rep. 156 at 178; *Den Norske Bank SA v Eustace-Stathis Porfyratos* (unreported, HC, January 17, 2001) at 8.

[64] (1986) 2 B.C.C. 99,549.

[65] *ibid.*, at 99,558; *JGL Investments Pty Ltd v Maracorp Financial Services Ltd* [1991] 2 V.R. 168. See also *Lloyds TSB Bank plc v Hayward* [2002] All E.R. (D) 351.

[66] Unreported, October 10, 2000.

[67] (1981) 147 C.L.R. 654. See a note on this case in (1982) 56 A.L.J. 421.

[68] *ibid.*

principal defaulted in the repayment of principal and interest, the creditor exercised a power under the debenture to appoint a receiver and manager of the hotel business. Further trading losses were incurred during the receivership and later the business was sold as a going concern. The guarantors argued, *inter alia*,[69] that they were not liable for any losses attributable to the exercise of the powers under the debenture because the creditor's action in exercising these powers, rather than the power of sale under the mortgage, had adversely affected the guarantors' entitlement to the benefit of the mortgage. The contract of guarantee in *Buckeridge v Mercantile Credits Ltd* contained special clauses excluding the creditor's duty in relation to securities which he held, but Aickin J. (Gibbs C.J. and Wilson J. concurring) passed some comments which can be regarded as of general application to the creditor's duty in the case of overlapping securities:

> "where ... there are two securities not capable of sensible concurrent exercise a bona fide choice of one rather than the other ... does not seem to me to be capable of being the basis of a complaint by the guarantors that the security to which they would have been entitled if they had paid in accordance with their obligations under the guarantee has been adversely affected."[70]

8–63   The duty is thus merely to make a bona fide choice. On the facts the court held that the creditor, far from acting mala fide, had followed the only sensible course of action because the best sale price could be expected to be obtained by operating and realising the hotel as a going concern.

8–64   The comments in *Buckeridge v Mercantile Credits Ltd* are probably limited to the facts of the case, that is, overlapping securities which cannot be sensibly exercised at the same time. If the securities are quite independent of each other (for example, a mortgage over real property and a bill of sale over chattels), the creditor should not be able to escape liability on the grounds that one security has been properly enforced if the creditor has improperly released the other.[71]

(c) Perfecting securities

8–65   It is clear that the creditor is under an equitable duty to perfect any securities obtained from the principal debtor to secure the guaranteed debt.[72] The majority of instances involve a neglect to register an instrument or to serve notice of an instrument when this is necessary to

---

[69] The guarantor's arguments are well summarised by Brennan J.: (1981) 147 C.L.R. 654 at 674.

[70] (1981) 147 C.L.R. 654 at 669–670.

[71] See below, para.8–71, as to the circumstances when a release will be improper.

[72] *Wulff v Jay* (1872) L.R. 7 Q.B. 756, and other cases cited below, nn. 73 to 77. The one exception to this general principle is *Wheatley v Bastow* (1855) 7 De G.M. & G. 261; 44 E.R. 102, where the creditor was held not to have discharged the guarantor when he failed to protect a fund in the hands of the court by applying for the necessary order. But that case may be treated as exceptional.

make it effective or to secure priority. Examples include a failure to register a bill of sale or chattel mortgage;[73] a failure to register an annuity bond under the relevant statutory provision;[74] a failure to make effective an equitable assignment by giving proper notice;[75] and a failure to register a registrable assignment or sale.[76] This principle has also been applied where the creditor fails to enter into possession to prevent chattels falling within the order and disposition of the bankrupt debtor, when this has not been achieved by registration of the security.[77] It should be emphasised that the obligation to enter into possession here is imposed merely for the purpose of establishing the creditor's rights as a secured creditor and not for the purpose of enforcement, which stands on a quite different footing.[78]

In some of the cases it is difficult to ascertain whether the guarantor is **8–66** released in equity or because of a breach of implied condition to perfect the security. This is sometimes because the value of the security lost is equal to or more than the amount guaranteed so that on either basis the guarantor would be fully discharged.[79] But most of the cases appear to be based on the creditor's breach of the equitable obligations.[80] It is clear that the mere fact that the principal debt is secured is not sufficient to make it an implied term of the guarantee that the security shall be perfected,[81] and it is thought that such a term will be implied only where a contractual obligation is also imposed to obtain a particular security.[82] In other cases, the likely approach is to discharge the guarantor in equity, leading to a partial release in the event of an impairment of a security which is less in value than that of the guaranteed debt.[83]

The equitable duty to perfect securities does not extend to securities **8–67** which are defective when received by the creditor as a result of a failure by the principal to make an effective transfer or to put the security documents

---

[73] *Wulff v Jay* (1872) L.R. 7 Q.B. 756; *Yorkshire Bank plc v Hall* [1999] 1 All E.R. 879 at 892; *Traders Finance Corp Ltd v Halverson* (1968) 2 D.L.R. (3d) 666; *Mills v Schwass* [1929] G.L.R. 460 at 462–463; *Re Kwan* (1987) 15 F.C.R. 264.
[74] *Straton v Rastall* (1788) 2 Term Rep. 366; 100 E.R. 197.
[75] *Northern Banking Co Ltd v Newman and Calton* [1927] IR 520; *Strange v Fooks* (1863) 4 Giff. 408; 66 E.R. 765.
[76] *Bank of Montreal v Bauer* (1978) 85 D.L.R. (3d) 752 (assignment of book debts, although on the facts a clause in the guarantee exonerated the creditors from liability); *Finning Tractor & Equipment Co Ltd v Mee* (1980) 110 D.L.R. (3d) 457 (registrable conditional sales contract); *Capel v Butler* (1825) 2 Sim. & St. 457; 57 E.R. 421 (registrable assignment of ships under applicable legislation).
[77] *Wulff v Jay* (1872) L.R. 7 Q.B. 756.
[78] See below, para.8–75.
[79] *Northern Banking Co Ltd v Newman and Calton* [1927] I.R. 520 at 539; *Strange v Fooks* (1863) 4 Giff. 408; 66 E.R. 765.
[80] *e.g. Wulff v Jay* (1872) L.R. 7 Q.B. 756; *Capel v Butler* (1825) 2 Sim. & St. 457; 57 E.R. 421.
[81] *Northern Banking Co Ltd v Newman and Calton* [1927] I.R. 520 at 538–539; *Silverton Ltd v Harvey* [1975] 1 N.S.W.L.R. 659.
[82] *Re Kwan* (1987) 15 F.C.R. 264 at 267, where Pincus J. implied a condition to perfect a bill of sale in circumstances in which the guarantee was given on the express stipulation that there should be a bill of sale; *Crédit Lyonnais (Aust) Ltd v Darling* (1991) 5 A.C.S.R. 703. See above, paras. 8–57 to 8–61 as to when a condition to obtain a security is imposed.
[83] *e.g.* if a delay in registering a mortgage meant that the creditor obtained a second rather than a first mortgage security, the loss will be the difference between the amount recovered on realising the second mortgage security and the amount which would have been recoverable if a first mortgage had been obtained: *Wambandry Pty Ltd v Amev-UDC Finance Ltd* (unreported, NSW Sup Ct, July 29, 1985).

in proper form. In Australia it has been held that when the creditor received an assignment of a lease from the principal, but the assignment is ineffective because the principal has not obtained the prior consent of the landlord, the creditor is not obliged to ensure that the assignment is perfected by obtaining such consent.[84] Another example of the application of this exception is where the creditor receives a registrable security from the principal in a patently unregistrable form.[85] In these cases, the guarantor may also be in breach of the guarantee if it contains an undertaking that the principal will perform the obligation to ensure the security is registered or in registrable form.[86]

8-68   The creditor's duty to perfect a security by registration does not appear to extend to circumstances in which re-registration becomes necessary because of some act of the principal. Thus in *Household Finance Corp v Foster*,[87] it was held that, where the principal removed the goods from the jurisdiction so that re-registration of a chattel mortgage became necessary under the relevant statute, the guarantor was not released from liability by the creditor's failure to register. On the facts, however, the creditor had no knowledge of the removal of the goods. It is possible that if the creditor does know of the matters necessitating re-registration, the creditor should take appropriate action to preserve the security.[88]

8-69   A final question is whether the creditor's duty to perfect securities extends beyond a duty to register and also embraces a duty to ensure that the security is adequate, for example, by ensuring that the goods which comprise the security are in existence. There is no authority supporting the imposition of any equitable duty in this respect, but in *Associated Japanese Bank (International) Ltd v Crédit du Nord SA*,[89] Steyn J. held that a guarantee of a chattel lease was ineffective when the goods which comprised the subject matter of the lease were not in existence on the date that the guarantee was executed. According to Steyn J. there was an express or implied condition precedent to the guarantee that the goods must be in existence and, in any event, the contract of guarantee was void for common mistake. The mistake was sufficiently fundamental since the guarantors (and, of course, the creditor) regarded the goods as their

---

[84] *Williams v Frayne* (1937) 58 C.L.R. 710 at 722 *per* Latham C.J., at 726 *per* Rich J., at 738–739 *per* Dixon J., at 741–742 *per* McTiernan J. In *Williams v Frayne* the landlord could not have perfected the security by subsequent action, and it is arguable that the creditor is obliged to perfect a security when the defect could be cured without difficulty. But even in this situation it is doubtful if any such obligation would be imposed because the creditor's general obligation to preserve securities stems from the corresponding duty of the guarantor to be subrogated to those securities in exactly the same condition as the creditor received them.
[85] *Traders Finance Corp Ltd v Halverson* (1968) 2 D.L.R. (3d) 666 at 674; *McDougal v Gariepy* (1922) 68 D.L.R. 560 at 561; *Continental Bank of Canada v Bradshaw* (1986) 74 N.S.R. (2d) 53. Indeed, the guarantor may have guaranteed the obligation of the principal to see that the security is registered or put in proper form: *Cerium Investments Ltd v Evans* [1991] 20 E.G. 189.
[86] *Cerium Investments v Evans* [1991] 20 E.G. 189, where a failure to register a licence was a breach of covenant by both the assignee and the sureties.
[87] [1949] O.R. 123.
[88] In *Household Finance Corp v Foster* [1949] O.R. 123 at 133–134, the question of the relevance of the creditor's knowledge is left open.
[89] [1989] 1 W.L.R. 255.

"prime security",[90] in respect of which the guarantors would acquire rights by subrogation on payment of the debt.

The decision has been rightly criticised[91] on the basis that the evidence supporting the existence of an express term was scant and that two requirements for the implication of a condition (obviousness and business efficacy) were not met. Furthermore, in respect of the finding of common mistake, it is probable, applying previous authority, that the mistake was not sufficiently fundamental.[92] Indeed, the decision is probably confined to where goods are not in existence at all. It is unlikely that the guarantor will be discharged on either basis where the goods are in existence but are much less valuable than both parties believe to be the case.

8–70

(d) Releasing securities

If a creditor holds a security for the enforcement of the principal obligation and the creditor destroys, releases or abandons the security, the guarantor will be released in equity to the extent that the value of the security has been impaired. Examples include a release of a mortgage,[93] delivery or reconveyance of the security to the debtor,[94] allowing the security to fall into the hands of a third party,[95] and a disposal of shares held as security.[96] The value of the security which is released is probably determined at the time of the surrender or release of the security.[97]

8–71

In order to be discharged in equity, the guarantor must show that he has suffered some injury as a result of the creditor's conduct,[98] and there are a number of instances where this cannot be shown. First, the creditor may release a valueless security (for example, a security which is a preference).[99] Secondly, the security may be released but later be recovered by the creditor. Examples are where the creditor assigns a promissory note to a third party and subsequently takes a reassignment of

8–72

---

[90] ibid., at 269.
[91] J. Carter, "An Uncommon Mistake" (1991) 3 J.C.L. 237.
[92] ibid., at 239–240. See Bell v Lever Bros Ltd [1932] A.C. 161.
[93] Pledge v Buss (1860) John 663; 70 E.R. 585; Bank of New Zealand v Baker [1926] N.Z.L.R. 462.
[94] Bank of Montreal v Robertson and Crothers [1976] 5 W.W.R. 680; Rose v Aftenburger (1969) 9 D.L.R. (3d) 42.
[95] Watts v Marac Finance Ltd (unreported, HC (NZ), July 14, 1988). But here the "security" involved was the goods which comprised the subject matter of the principal lease agreement and Doogue J (at 25) doubted whether such goods comprised a "security" within the general rule.
[96] Hunter v Zakus (1968) 67 D.L.R. (2d) 355; Bank of Victoria v Smith (1894) 20 V.L.R. 450.
[97] Bank of Victoria v Smith (1894) 20 V.L.R. 450 at 454. Cf. Rose v Aftenburger (1969) 9 D.L.R. (3d) 42 at 49, where the court raised the possibility of fixing the value at the date of judgment.
[98] Carter v White (1883) 25 Ch. D. 666 at 670 per Cotton L.J.; Williams v Frayne (1937) 58 C.L.R. 710 at 741 per McTiernan J.; Hancock v Williams (1942) 42 S.R. (NSW) 252 at 256 per Jordan C.J.; Trust & Agency Co of Australia v Greene (1870) 1 V.R. (L) 171 at 175.
[99] Hardwick v Wright (1865) 35 Beav. 133; 55 E.R. 845. As other examples, see Rainbow v Juggins (1880) 5 Q.B.D. 422 (an insurance policy which had lapsed and was of no value); Coates v Coates (1864) 33 Beav. 249; 55 E.R. 363 (an insurance policy which the bankrupt principal was unlikely to keep up).

it,[1] or where the creditor holding title deeds as security delivers them to the principal but subsequently recovers them.[2] A third situation where no injury may result is where the security is released and another security is substituted for it, at least if the guarantor is not prejudiced by the change of securities.[3]

8–73   As in the case of perfecting securities,[4] it is often difficult to ascertain from some of the judgments whether the guarantor is released in equity or because of a breach of an implied term in the contract of guarantee not to release the security.[5] Again, the reason often is that the value of the security surrendered is greater than the amount guaranteed so that the guarantor is fully discharged in any event.[6] If there is a contractual obligation to keep a particular security, a release of that security will discharge the guarantor even if the security was valueless or even if the guarantor was not injured by the release. In the case of co-guarantors who are jointly and severally liable, a breach of the obligation not to release a security given by one guarantor will release all from liability.[7]

8–74   Generally, the courts appear reluctant to imply a term that a particular security shall not be released. This undoubtedly leads to a balanced solution where the value of the security released is small in relation to the amount guaranteed. Probably the only situation where a term will be implied not to release a security is where an obligation is imposed in the first place to obtain that security,[8] because the court can then properly infer that the security should continue to be available.[9]

---

[1] *Armstrong v Widmer* (1975) 65 D.L.R. (3d) 345.

[2] *Bushell v Collett* (1862) 6 L.T. 20.

[3] *Caisse Populaire Notre-Dame Des Sept Douleurs Ltee v Picard* (1981) 129 D.L.R. (3d) 242. In *Bank of Victoria v Smith*, (1894) 20 V.L.R. 450 the debtor deposited share certificates with the creditor. Some of these share certificates were released to the debtor but, in part, were replaced by shares in another company. The court held that the guarantor was released pro tanto, but that the creditor was entitled to credit the value of the substituted shares against the amount lost by the surrender of the original share certificates to the debtor. It follows that if the value of the substituted shares had been equal to the value of the surrendered shares, the guarantor's liability would not have been diminished to any extent.

[4] See above, para.8–65.

[5] e.g. *Pledge v Buss* (1860) John 663; 70 E.R. 585.

[6] e.g. *Pledge v Buss* (1860) John 663; 70 E.R. 585. See its interpretation in *National Bank of New Zealand v Chapman* [1975] 1 N.Z.L.R. 480.

[7] *Smith v Wood* [1929] 1 Ch. 14. Note that here there was no personal liability. The guarantors merely charged their properties to secure the principal sum, so that the release of one of the securities operated as a total release of the guarantor who had provided it.

[8] See above, paras 8–57 to 8–61.

[9] *Smith v Wood* [1929] 1 Ch. 14 is an example of a breach of a term of the guarantee not to release a security. This was the basis of the judgments of Sankey L.J. (at 25) and Hanworth M.R. (at 24). Earlier in his judgment, Hanworth M.R. (at 22–23) appeared to view the case as an example of a variation of the principal transaction but this is not correct. Russell C.J. (at 30–32) based his decision on the fact that the guarantor's right of marshalling had been affected, but it is unnecessary to show such prejudice if there is a term of the guarantee that the security should not be relinquished.

(e) No general duty to enforce securities

Despite some early English dicta[10] and more recent Canadian authority to the contrary,[11] it is now established that the creditor has no duty in equity to enforce a security (for example, by exercising a power of sale) as distinct from perfecting it, even though it is shown that the security would have realised a greater amount if the power of sale has been exercised earlier. As the Privy Council explained in *China & South Seas Bank v Tan*:[12]

8–75

"The creditor is not obliged to do anything. If the creditor does nothing and the debtor declines into bankruptcy the mortgaged securities become valueless and the surety decamps abroad, the creditor loses his money. If disaster strikes the debtor and the mortgaged securities but the surety remains capable of repaying the debt then the creditor loses nothing. The surety contracts to pay if the debtor does not pay and the surety is bound by his contract."[13]

The rationale of this principle is that the guarantor has a remedy in this situation because the guarantor can pay off the debt and obtain by subrogation the benefits of the security.[14]

This general principle may be subject to certain qualifications, although most of these cannot be considered well established. First, it may be that the creditor will be liable if he acts mala fide.[15] It is thought that some affirmative duty should be imposed on the creditor. It is inconsistent to require a creditor to act positively to protect the creditor's security by registration,[16] yet allow the creditor to stand idly by and fail to realise the security at an appropriate time. It is true that in theory the guarantor can pay off the debt and exercise the remedy personally, but the guarantor might not know and might not be in a position to know of the declining value of the security.

8–76

---

[10] e.g. *Polak v Everett* (1876) 1 Q.B.D. 669 at 675–676, where Blackburn J. stated that if the creditor has by laches diminished the value of a pledge, the creditor is bound to give credit for the sum he or she ought to have made; *Williams v Price* (1824) 1 Sim. & St. 581 at 587; 57 E.R. 229 at 231, where Sir John Leach leaves open the question whether the creditor has to take steps actively to enforce a judgment.

[11] *Provincial Bank of Canada v Prince Edward Island Lending Authority* (1975) 59 D.L.R. (3d) 446 (guarantor discharged pro tanto when the creditor failed to enforce a chattel mortgage and permitted the goods subject to the charge to disappear).

[12] [1990] 1 A.C. 536. See also *O'Day v Commercial Bank of Australia Ltd* (1933) 50 C.L.R. 200 at 224

[13] *ibid.*, at 545.

[14] *China & South Seas Bank Ltd v Tan* [1990] 1 A.C. 536 at 545; *Carter v White* (1883) 25 Ch. D. 666 at 670.

[15] *O'Day v Commercial Bank of Australia Ltd* (1933) 50 C.L.R. 200 at 223–224 *per* McTiernan J., quoting with approval a passage from *Black v Ottoman Bank* (1862) 15 Moo. P.C.C. 472 at 483; 15 E.R. 573 at 577. See also statements that "the general duty" of a mortgagee is to use his powers for proper purposes and "to act in good faith": *Yorkshire Bank plc v Hall* [1999] 1 All E.R. 879 at 893; *Downsview Nominees Ltd v First City Corp Ltd* [1993] A.C. 295 at 315, referring to *Re B Johnson & Co (Builders Ltd)* [1955] Ch. 634 at 661–663, *per* Jenkins L.J.

[16] See above, para.8–65.

8–77   A second suggested qualification is that a duty to enforce may exist where the guarantor specifically requests that the security be enforced. In *Carter v White*,[17] where the guarantor argued that the creditor had failed to enforce a bill of exchange by presenting it for payment, Cotton L.J. thought that the guarantor might have been discharged if he had requested the security to be enforced and the creditor had refused. It is doubtful, however, that this is consistent with the right of the creditor to enforce the security at the time of his choosing as set out in *China & South Seas Bank v Tan*.[18]

8–78   More recently, in *Palk v Mortgage Services Funding plc*,[19] the Court of Appeal granted an application made by a borrower (who had granted a mortgage over a house owned by him and his wife as security) pursuant to the Law of Property Act 1925, s.91(2) seeking an order for sale of the mortgaged property. Section 91(2) states:

> "In any action, whether for foreclosure, or for redemption, or for sale, or for the raising and payment in any manner of mortgage money, the court, on the request of the mortgagee, or of any person interested either in the mortgage money or in the right of redemption, and, notwithstanding that—
>
> (a) any other person dissents; or
>
> (b) the mortgagee or any person so interested does not appear in the action;
>
> and without allowing any time for redemption or for payment of any mortgage money, may direct a sale of the mortgaged property, on such terms as it thinks fit, including the deposit in court of a reasonable sum fixed by the court to meet the expenses of sale and to secure performance of the terms."

The mortgagee wanted to delay selling the property in the hope that property prices would improve.

8–79   On the "extreme and exceptional"[20] facts the Court of Appeal held that a sale should be ordered. A delay would cause manifest unfairness to the third party mortgagors because the proposed letting of the property by the mortgagee would not have met the interest payments payable by the mortgagors, whose liability would therefore increase indefinitely and be open ended. If no sale was ordered the mortgage debt would increase at a rate of £43,000 a year, whereas a sale would reduce the capital debt to about £25,000, with liability for interest being reduced to about one twelfth.[21] Additionally, since the mortgagee had an expectation that property prices would increase it could purchase the property itself and

---

[17] (1883) 25 Ch. D. 666 at 670. See also *Bank of Toronto v Roeder* (1921) 63 D.L.R. 459 at 467, where the guarantor requested the creditor to seize goods subject to a chattel mortgage and the creditor promised to do so. The fact that the creditor made this promise is regarded as relevant.

[18] [1990] 1 A.C. 536.

[19] [1993] 2 All E.R. 481.

[20] *ibid.*, at 492.

[21] *ibid.*

"back [its] faith in the future value of the property".[22] Thus a sale would result in "fairness to both sides".[23]

Finally, a clear exception to the rule exempting the creditor from a duty **8–80** to enforce exists in the context of bills of exchange. An indorser of a bill of exchange, who is in a position of a surety, is discharged if the holder of the bill, the creditor, fails to take all the necessary steps to obtain payment by presenting it for payment and giving notice of dishonour.[24]

The prior discussion has centred on the creditor's duty in equity. It is **8–81** also possible that an express or implied term in the guarantee may oblige the creditor to enforce a particular security, but there are no illustrations of such a term being implied. Even if there were an obligation to obtain a particular security,[25] it would not be a necessary inference that the security should be properly enforced.

(f) Extent of duty if securities are enforced

Although there is no duty to enforce a security, what is the ambit of the **8–82** creditor's duty if the creditor chooses to do so? In general, when the creditor enforces a security, the creditor is entitled to exercise the rights given by the terms of the security or by the general law,[26] for example, by exercising a power of sale under a mortgage.[27]

While the general principles are clearly established, there are cases **8–83** where a guarantor has been released from liability despite the fact that the creditor has exercised a valid power of enforcement. Thus in *Re Darwen and Pearce*,[28] where the surety guaranteed payment of calls payable upon shares in a company, he was fully released when the company/creditor exercised its admitted power to forfeit the shares for non-payment of the calls. Similarly, in *Matton v Lipscomb*,[29] where the creditor validly foreclosed upon certain mortgages assigned to him by the principal as security for the debt, the court held that this constituted a material alteration in the security and the guarantor was completely discharged. The exact basis on which the guarantors were discharged in these cases is not clear from the judgments. Certainly in equity it would not be correct to discharge the guarantors absolutely (as in these cases) merely because the creditor has altered the security from its original form. The creditor would simply be under an obligation to hold the resulting proceeds of that security for the benefit of the guarantor and it would only be where the creditor could not do so or did not do so that

---

[22] *ibid.*
[23] *ibid.*
[24] *Goldfarb v Bartlett* [1920] 1 K.B. 639 at 648–649. The rule only applies to parties to bills of exchange, not to a guarantor under a separate instrument, and is thus not strictly a rule arising from the law of principal and surety: see *Carter v White* (1883) 25 Ch. D. 666 at 671 *per* Cotton L.J., 671–672 *per* Lindley L.J.
[25] See above, paras. 8–57 to 8–61.
[26] *Lep Air Services v Rolloswin Investments Ltd* [1971] 3 All E.R. 45 at 52–53 *per* Megaw L.J.
[27] *Taylor v Bank of New South Wales* (1886) 11 App. Cas. 596 at 601.
[28] [1927] 1 Ch. 176 at 187–188.
[29] (1895) 16 L.R. (NSW) Eq. 142.

the guarantor would be released to the extent of the loss. The proper explanation of these cases, it is suggested, lies in the fact that it was an implied term of the guarantee that the security should be kept in its original form, at least to the extent of not forfeiting the shares or foreclosing on the mortgages.[30] The creditor was in breach of this term and the guarantor was, therefore, fully discharged.

8–84   In exercising the powers of enforcement the creditor must comply with and exercise those powers as contemplated by the security document.[31] If the security is impaired as a result of a failure to do so, the guarantor will be discharged to the extent of the loss, unless there is an express or implied term of the contract of guarantee that a particular condition be observed.[32] No such term is usually implied, but, if it is, the guarantor will be absolutely discharged when the creditor is in breach of that term.

8–85   Sometimes the creditor may breach an express term of the principal contract regarding the enforcement of the security (for example, provisions regarding notice),[33] but the creditor also has a general duty to the guarantor when exercising a power of sale over securities held for the enforcement of the principal obligation.[34] The early cases did not precisely define that duty referring, for example, to the duty of creditors to make "the most of their security",[35] but it is now clear that it is a duty to take reasonable care to obtain a proper price[36] that is, the true market value of the mortgage property. Despite earlier authority to the contrary,[37] this obligation is not based upon the tort of negligence, (thus giving a right to claim damages), but is an aspect of the creditor's well established equitable

[30] This explanation seems to be supported by Megaw L.J. in *Lep Air Services Ltd v Rolloswin Investments Ltd* [1971] 3 All E.R. 45 at 52–53. See also Jordan C.J. in *Hancock v Williams* (1942) 42 S.R. (NSW) 252 at 255. Another explanation of the decision in *Matton v Lipscomb* (1895) 16 L.R. (NSW) Eq. 142 is that the foreclosure action and disposal of the property extinguishes the mortgagor's obligation and leaves no debt to guarantee: *Moose Jaw Credit Union Ltd v Kjarsgaard* (1982) 133 D.L.R. (3d) 543. But this explanation does not appear in the judgments.

[31] *Taylor v Bank of New South Wales* (1886) 11 App. Cas. 596 at 601; *Healy v Cornish* (1863) 3 S.C.R. (NSW) Eq. 28 at 31; *Bank of Nova Scotia v Ham* [1986] 5 W.W.R. 249 (exercise of rights pursuant to debenture, although no default had occurred).

[32] *Taylor v Bank of New South Wales* (1880) 11 App. Cas. 596 at 602–603.

[33] See the argument for the guarantors in *O'Day v Commercial Bank of Australia Ltd* (1933) 50 C.L.R. 200.

[34] *Mutual Loan Association Fund v Sudlow* (1858) 5 C.B. (N.S.) 449; 141 E.R. 183; *Skipton Building Society v Stott* [2001] Q.B. 261; *Re Wolmershousen* (1890) 62 L.T. 541 at 547.

[35] *Re Wolmershausen* (ibid.). See also *Mutual Loan Association Fund v Sudlow* (ibid.), where the judgments do not clarify whether the test is to take reasonable care or act bona fide.

[36] *Yorkshire Bank plc v Hall* [1999] 1 All ER 879 at 892; *Skipton Building Society v Stott* [2001] Q.B. 261, esp at 271 where Evans L.J. states that the creditor must show he has "taken reasonable steps to market the property"; *Meftah v Lloyds TSB Bank plc* [2001] 2 All E.R. (Comm) 741; *Cohen v TSB plc* [2002] 2 B.C.L.C. 32; *Cuckmere Brick Co Ltd v Mutual Finance Ltd* [1971] Ch. 949; *Downsview Nominees Ltd v First City Corp Ltd* [1993] A.C. 295. (The latter two cases assert the same principle in respect of the creditor/mortgagee's duty to the mortgagor).

[37] *Standard Chartered Bank Ltd v Walker* [1982] 3 All E.R. 938; (itself disapproving *Barclays Bank Ltd v Thienel* (1978) 122 S.J. 472 *Latchford v Beirne* [1981] 2 All E.R. 705); *American Express International Corp v Hurley* [1985] 3 All E.R. 564. Although in so far as these cases base the creditor's duty upon the tort of negligence they are no longer good law, it is considered that they do support the proposition that the equitable duty is to take reasonable care to obtain a proper price.

duty towards the guarantor.[38] A breach of the duty therefore means that the guarantor's liability is reduced to the extent that the value of the security has been impaired as a result of the breach.[39] The duty applies to the creditor exercising a power of sale as mortgagee[40] and logically should also apply to a receiver exercising a power of sale appointed by the creditor acting under the powers of a debenture. As to the latter, however, some difficulty has been occasioned by the fact that the basis of the receiver's duty in managing mortgaged property has been said to arise only in respect of "those with an interest in the equity of redemption."[41] In *Burgess v Auger*[42] Lightman J was of the view that a guarantor who has made no payment to the bank and has therefore presently acquired no right of subrogation to the security has insufficient standing to complain of the breach of duty. He "has yet to acquire an interest in the equity of redemption".[43] With respect, this is erroneous. The older authorities[44] clearly establish a general equitable duty towards the guarantor, and it should be sufficient that the guarantor has a contingent entitlement to subrogation on payment of the debt. Indeed Mr Justice Lightman's reasoning would mean that the guarantor could never assert a claim that for breach of duty until the whole debt had been paid off since it is only then that the right of subrogation arises. Significantly, in *Cohen v TSB plc*,[45] the Court of Appeal accepted that a duty to take reasonable care to obtain a proper price is owed to a guarantor by a receiver exercising a power of sale.

The burden of proof is probably upon the creditor to show that he has **8–86** taken reasonable care to obtain a proper price.[46] Reasonable steps must be taken to expose the property to the market[47] and where a business is carried on upon the property to be sold after re-possession account should be taken of the sale on the goodwill of the business.[48] These matters are considered in detail in other texts,[49] but generally a mortgagee exercising a power of sale can safely accept the highest bid for a correctly described and advertised property at a properly advertised auction.[50]

Sometimes the creditor will not exercise a power of sale, but will manage **8–87** the secured property, usually by the appointment of a receiver. The receiver has a duty towards the mortgagor and others "with an interest in the equity of redemption" to act bona fide and in some circumstances to

---

[38] *China & South Seas Bank Ltd v Tan* [1990] 1 A.C. 536; *Downsview Nominees Ltd v First City Corp Ltd* [1993] A.C. 295; *Yorkshire Bank plc v Hall* [1999] 1 All E.R. 879.
[39] *Skipton Building Society v Stott* [2001] Q.B. 261 at 269.
[40] e.g. *Skipton Building Society v Stott* (*ibid.*).
[41] *Medforth v Blake* [1999] 3 W.L.R. 922; *Burgess v Auger* [1998] 2 B.C.L.C. 478.
[42] [1998] 2 B.C.L.C. 478.
[43] *ibid.*, at 483.
[44] See above, cited in para.8–49.
[45] [2002] 2 B.C.L.C. 32.
[46] See *Skipton Building Society v Stott* [2001] Q.B. 261 at 271, *per* Evans L.J. (Alliot L.J. agreeing). Potter L.J. left the matter open.
[47] *Skipton Building Society v Stott* [2001] Q.B. 261 at 270.
[48] *AIB Finance Ltd v Debtors* [1997] 4 All E.R. 677.
[49] Fisher & Lightwood's *Law of Mortgage* (11th ed., 2002), paras 20.23–20.44; G. Lightman & G. Moss, *The Law of Receivers and Administrators of Companies* (2000) Ch. 7.
[50] Fisher & Lightwood (*ibid.*), para.20.17. As to the complex evidential questions that may arise, see *Cohen v TSB plc* [2002] 2 B.C.L.C. 32.

manage the property with due diligence.[51] Again, and despite Mr Justice Lightman's arguments in *Burgess v Auger*,[52] it is considered that, for the reasons previously advanced,[53] that a guarantor comes within the class of persons having an entitlement in the equity of redemption.

(g) Securities rendered ineffective by operation of law

8–88   The creditor will not be liable for breach of the equitable duty if a security held for the enforcement of the principal debt becomes ineffective or unenforceable simply by operation of law. The rule is directed to the creditor's own acts in relation to the security.[54] Thus if the secured property is recovered by the principal's trustee in bankruptcy or liquidator as a preference over other creditors, the guarantor will not be discharged in equity to the extent of the value of that security.[55] This is true even if the creditor voluntarily surrenders the security without the trustee in bankruptcy having to obtain a judgment against the creditor, provided that the facts justify the creditor's conclusion that the security amounts to a preference.[56]

8–89   It is possible in these circumstances that there may be an express or implied term of the contract that the continued availability of the security is a condition of the contract of guarantee so that the loss of the security even as a result of the operation of law would release the guarantor. This is unlikely in the usual case,[57] but may arise if the obtaining of the security itself (as in *Greer v Kettle*,[58] discussed above)[59] is a condition of the guarantee. Where such a provision exists, the courts may also imply the closely allied obligation that the security must continue to be effective and available during the continuance of the guarantee so that if the security is lost, even through no fault of the creditor, the guarantor will be discharged.

(h) Exercise of statutory rights by the creditor

8–90   Is a creditor liable for the loss or impairment of a security if that loss or impairment was caused simply by the creditor's acting under the provisions of a statute? In *Rainbow v Juggins*,[60] the creditor exercised an option given by s.16(4) of the Bankruptcy Act 1869 of surrendering a security to the principal's trustee in bankruptcy and proving for the whole debt. This was

---

[51] *Medforth v Blake* [1999] 3 W.L.R. 925.
[52] [1988] 2 B.C.L.C. 478, discussed above, para.8–85.
[53] See above, para.8–85.
[54] *NA Kratzmann Pty Ltd v Tucker* (1966) 123 C.L.R. 257 at 283.
[55] *NA Kratzmann Pty Ltd v Tucker* (1966) 123 C.L.R. 257; *Silverton Ltd v Harvey* [1975] 1 N.S.W.L.R. 659 at 664. As another example, see *Rainbow v Juggins* (1880) 5 Q.B.D. 422 (surrender of insurance policy which had become valueless through no fault of the creditor).
[56] *Canadian Imperial Bank of Commerce v Sitarenios* (1975) 63 D.L.R. (3d) 586.
[57] As an example of the court's refusal to imply a term see *Silverton Ltd v Harvey* [1975] 1 N.S.W.L.R. 659.
[58] [1938] A.C. 156.
[59] See above, para.8–58.
[60] (1880) 5 Q.B.D. 422.

held not to release the guarantor. But emphasis was placed on the fact that the possibility of the bankruptcy of the debtor is an event which the guarantor has in contemplation at the time of entering into the contract of guarantee so that the right to exercise the option becomes an implied term in the guarantee.[61] It would, therefore, be wrong to propound any firm principle that the creditor cannot be liable for impairing a security if the creditor acts under the provisions of a statute. Thus in *Metrocan Leasing Ltd v Virani*,[62] it was held that the creditor's action in giving up his right to seize the goods under s.22A of the British Columbia Bills of Sale Act 1961 released the guarantor even though the Act compelled the creditor to choose between seizing the goods and suing the debtor for the amount owing. The court thought that the policy of the legislation, which was designed to protect consumer debtors, favoured such an approach because otherwise a guarantor, who might be a close relative of the debtor, could still remain liable for the amount owing even though the creditor had seized the chattels. If the guarantor were closely associated with the debtor in this way, allowing the creditor to sue the guarantor would not be very different from allowing the creditor to sue the debtor as well as seizing the goods, which was the act prohibited by the statute.

This decision is questionable in that the creditor lost the benefit of the security even though the correct statutory procedures had been followed, simply because the policy of the statute appeared to the court to prohibit that course of action. The creditor should not have to anticipate such policy considerations, and the guarantor should not be discharged if the creditor acts under the clear provisions of the statute.

8–91

(iii) Clauses in the guarantee excluding liability for the creditor's action in releasing or impairing securities

Clauses in the guarantee may purport to absolve the creditor from liability for loss or impairment of any security. It will be helpful here to analyse the most common types of construction, bearing in mind that such exclusion clauses will be construed strictly against the creditor.[63] A number of different types will often appear together in one instrument of guarantee.[64]

8–92

1. The first type of clause authorises the creditor to deal in a variety of ways with the securities where such acts might otherwise discharge the guarantor. An example appeared in *Barclays Bank Ltd v Thienel*,[65] where the creditor was "at liberty ... to give up, modify, exchange or abstain

---

[61] *ibid.*, at 425.
[62] [1977] 1 W.W.R. 585. See also *Matton v Lipscomb* (1895) 16 L.R. (NSW) Eq. 142 (discussed above, para.8–83), where the creditor obtained a foreclosure of a mortgage under the provisions of the Real Property Act 1900 (NSW), but the guarantor was still released from liability. *Cf.* however, *Saanich Peninsula Savings Credit Union v Canada Instant Print Ltd* (1979) 94 D.L.R. (3d) 156.
[63] See above, para.5–01 for general rules of construction.
[64] *e.g. National Bank of New Zealand v Chapman* [1975] 1 N.Z.L.R. 480.
[65] (1978) 122 S.J. 472. See also a less comprehensive example in *Dobbs v National Bank of A/asia Ltd* (1935) 53 C.L.R. 643.

from perfecting or taking advantage of or enforcing securities in such manner as [it] might think expedient".

8–93   In order for this clause to be effective, it should contain an exhaustive list of the possible ways in which the creditor's dealings with the security may wholly or partially discharge the guarantor. For instance, if the creditor is to be absolved from liability to perfect a security, this event should be expressly stated. Thus in *Watson v Allcock*,[66] where the guarantee was not to be prejudiced by the execution of a warrant of attorney, this did not absolve the creditor from a failure to make the security effective.

8–94   As it stands, a clause of this type is probably comprehensive enough to preserve the liability of the guarantor in relation to most of the situations, discussed previously, where otherwise there would be a partial or total discharge of liability. As regards the question of the creditor's duty in enforcing a security, Thesiger J. held in *Barclays Bank Ltd v Thienel* that any implied duty to take reasonable care to obtain the best price for a security was excluded by this clause,[67] although it may not exclude a failure on the part of the creditor to act bona fide.[68]

8–95   Some possible limitations on the ambit of this clause, however, should be noted. It might be insufficient to cover a failure to obtain a security in the first place where this obligation is imposed on the creditor by other wording in the guarantee.[69] It may also be insufficient to embrace the contingency of a release by the creditor of a co-guarantor unless the definition of "securities" includes "guarantees".[70]

8–96   Finally, the wording of this clause does not make it absolutely clear that the "securities" referred to encompass all securities, whether obtained from the principal or the guarantor and whether obtained before or after the execution of the guarantee.[71] This can cause the creditor some difficulty, especially where the agreement guaranteed is itself a registrable security. Thus in *Traders Finance Corp Ltd v Halverson*,[72] a similar clause excluding the creditor from liability was construed as applying only to the registrable conditional sales contract which was guaranteed; it did not, therefore, absolve the creditor from a failure to register additional securities which he obtained. A reverse construction was adopted in *Finning Tractor & Equipment Co Ltd v Mee*,[73] where the clause exempted the creditor from a failure to perfect "collateral or other securities". The creditor was not thereby excused for a failure to register the agreement

---

[66] (1853) 4 De G.M. & G. 242; 43 E.R. 499.

[67] *Cf. Canadian Imperial Bank of Commerce v Haley* (1979) 100 D.L.R. (3d) 470 at 477–479, in which a clause exempting the creditor from "fault" was held not to cover negligence.

[68] See also *Bank of Nova Scotia v Ham* [1986] 5 W.W.R. 249, where a clause stating that the bank may "discharge, give up, realise or otherwise deal with such securities in such manner as [it] sees fit" was held not to embrace the bank's action in realising a security when there was no default.

[69] For an analysis of when this obligation is imposed, see above, paras 8–57 to 8–61.

[70] Often there is a separate clause stating that the guarantor's liability shall not be affected by a release of a co-guarantor: see above, paras 8–29 to 8–31.

[71] *Cf. Crédit Lyonnais (Aust) Ltd v Darling* (1991) 5 A.C.S.R. 703 at 708–709, where the clause referred to a security "held or taken *at any time*".

[72] (1968) 2 D.L.R. (3d) 666.

[73] (1980) 110 D.L.R. (3d) 457.

guaranteed, the clause being interpreted as being applicable only to a failure to perfect any additional securities that might be taken. Such problems can be avoided by a simple provision stating that the exclusion clause applies to all securities, whatever their source and whether obtained from the principal or the guarantor, at the date of the execution of the guarantee or otherwise.

2. A clause in the following form is common in a modern contract of guarantee:

"The liability of the guarantors shall not be affected or discharged ... by any act, neglect or default of the creditor whereby the liability of the guarantors or either of them would have been affected or discharged."

This, and similar clauses, probably preserve the liability of the guarantor in the case of the various events which would otherwise discharge the guarantor. Commonwealth authority[74] has interpreted such a clause as excusing any fault on the part of the creditor for mismanagement of the mortgaged premises when the creditor entered into possession under the terms of the mortgage and as relieving guarantor from liability arising from a failure to perfect a mortgage debenture by registration.[75] The same type of clause expressed as a waiver will also have an equivalent effect.[76]

3. Sometimes a clause in the guarantee clearly indicates that the guarantor has no right to the securities held by the creditor unless the guarantor has fully satisfied the obligations under the guarantee. An example is:

"until [the creditor] ... as mortgagee should have received all moneys owing to it by the mortgagor, the ... guarantors should not be entitled 'on any grounds whatsoever' to claim the benefit of any security now or hereafter held by [the creditor] as mortgagee."[77]

Such a clause should not negate the creditor's normal duties in relation to the securities. The guarantor is still entitled to the benefit of the securities on satisfying the obligation under the guarantee and the creditor, therefore, should do nothing to impair those securities.

4. A variant of the previous type of clause simply states that the "guarantors will not in any way or at any time claim the benefit or seek the transfer of any other security or any part thereof".[78] Unlike the previous

---

[74] *Hancock v Williams* (1942) 42 S.R. (NSW) 252 at 258.

[75] *Crédit Lyonnais (Aust) Ltd v Darling* (1991) 5 A.C.S.R. 703, although the clause was more specific, referring (*inter alia*) to "any omission by the creditor to complete any such collateral security". See also *Federal Business Development Bank v Mid-Can Dental Supply Co Ltd* (1982) 138 D.L.R. (3d) 723, where it was held a similar clause excluded the creditor's liability in respect of a failure to comply with a *statutory* requirement for the sale of goods repossessed under a chattel mortgage.

[76] *National Bank of New Zealand Ltd v Murland* [1991] 3 N.Z.L.R. 86 at 99; *National Mutual Life Assoc of Aust Ltd v Opie* (unreported, WA Sup Ct, December 12, 1994).

[77] See, *e.g. Buckeridge v Mercantile Credits* (1981) 147 C.L.R. 654.

[78] See a similar clause in *O'Day v Commercial Bank of Australia Ltd* (1933) 50 CLR 200.

clause (3, above), there is no part of the clause which clearly suggests that the guarantor is entitled to the security after paying the creditor. In *Johnson v Australian Guarantee Corp Ltd*,[79] the Supreme Court of South Australia held that, since such a clause negates the guarantor's entitlement to the creditor's securities through subrogation, it relieves the creditor of the corresponding duty not to impair or release those securities.

8–97 This result, although not without logic, is somewhat harsh from the guarantor's standpoint, especially if the clause covers mala fides on the part of the creditor. Such an interpretation means that the guarantor is being deprived of the equitable right to insist that the creditor does not impair a security, simply on the basis of a general clause which is directed only to the underlying rationale for the imposition of that duty.[80]

In any event, clear words will be required to exclude the right of subrogation, and as a consequence, the ancillary duty not to impair a security.[81] Thus a clause stating that the "security is in addition to and shall not affect or be merged in any bills, notes, guarantees, indemnities, undertakings, mortgages and charges" was held in *Re Butlers Wharf Ltd*[82] not to exclude the right of the surety to be subrogated to other securities of the creditor once he had paid the separate part of the debt for which he was liable.

8–98 5. A clause in the guarantee may state that the relationship between the creditor and the guarantor shall be deemed to be that of creditor and principal, for example:

"the relation constituted by virtue of this guarantee shall, as between the [defendant] and the bank be deemed for all purposes that of principal obligant and not that of a guarantor."[83]

There appears to be no direct authority in England on the effect of this clause, but in New Zealand[84] and Australia[85] it has been held to effectively preserve the guarantor's liability in the event of a loss of securities. This is on the basis that since the creditor is entitled to treat the guarantor as

---

[79] (1992) 59 S.A.S.R. 382. Even, according to King C.J., in the case of mala fides (at 385). But this would be a very wide construction of the clause.

[80] The dissenting judgment of Olsson J. has much to commend it: *ibid.* at 388.

[81] *Liberty Mutual Insurance Co (UK) Ltd v HSBC Bank Plc* [2001] Lloyd's Rep. 224 and, on appeal [2002] EWCA Civ 691, as discussed below, paras 12–270 to 12–271; *Re Butlers Wharf Ltd* [1995] 2 B.C.L.C. 43.

[82] [1995] 2 B.C.L.C. 43. See similarly the clause in *Liberty Mutual Insurance Co (UK) Ltd v HSBC Bank Plc* (*ibid.*): "This Agreement is separate from any other security or right of indemnity taken in respect of the guarantee from any person, including your above named customer".

[83] See a similar example in *Bank of New Zealand v Baker* [1926] NZLR 462. See also *Orme v De Boyette* [1981] 1 N.Z.L.R. 576; *Pogoni v R & WH Symington & Co (NZ) Ltd* [1991] 1 N.Z.L.R. 82.

[84] *Bank of New Zealand v Baker* [1926] N.Z.L.R. 462 at 487–488; *Pogoni v R & WH Symington & Co NZ Ltd* [1991] N.Z.L.R. 82 at 84–85.

[85] See *Fletcher Organisation Pty Ltd v Crocus Investment Pty Ltd* [1988] 2 Qd. R. 517. Although the principal debtor clause in that case was also combined with a clause by which the guarantor waived all his rights as surety, Shepherdson J. (at 527) and Williams J. (at 536) appeared to view the principal debtor clause standing alone as sufficient to preserve the guarantor's liability in the event of a loss of securities.

principal debtor,[86] the equitable rule discharging the guarantor in the event of a loss of securities has no application (even though a relationship of suretyship still exists between the guarantor and the person primarily liable).[87] Conversely, in Canada[88] it has been held that a "principal debtor" clause does not exclude the creditor's duty to preserve securities for the benefit of the guarantor.

The issue is an open one, but in an agreement which (principal debtor clause apart) is drafted as a guarantee it is perhaps a harsh construction to give an exclusionary effect to the clause, given the *contra proferentem* rule of interpretation applicable to guarantees and given that the creditor's action in impairing the securities may well deprive the guarantor (on payment of the debt) of an effective right of reimbursement from the party primarily liable.[89]

8–99

6. The guarantee may contain a clause which is directed specifically at the question of the failure of the creditor to realise the security to the best advantage, for example:

> "The security provided by the guarantee should not in any way affect or be affected by the creditor failing or neglecting to recover by the realisation of any collateral or other security."

Such a clause has been interpreted by the High Court of Australia in *Buckeridge v Mercantile Credits Ltd*,[90] as effectively preserving the liability of the guarantor if the actions of the creditor resulted in a deficiency in the amount received from the realisation of the security.[91] The clause would probably cover a negligent realisation,[92] but perhaps not a realisation where a lack of bona fides on the part of the creditor could be shown.

7. A clause in the guarantee may preserve the liability of the guarantor in the event of a variation of the principal contract.[93] Such a clause will be effective where the terms of a security, which is embodied in the principal contract, are changed.[94] But that is all. It will not be effective where the

---

[86] *Pogoni v R & WH Symington & Co (NZ) Ltd* [1991] 1 N.Z.L.R. 82 at 84–85.
[87] *ibid.* See this category of suretyship described above, para.1–29.
[88] *Brown Bros Motor Lease Canada Ltd v Ganapathi* (1983) 139 D.L.R. (3d) 227. In *Fletcher Organisation Pty Ltd v Crocus Investments Pty Ltd* [1988] Qd. R. 517 at 537, Williams J. thought the authority of little assistance, but it does represent a contrary view of the effect of the principal debtor clause.
[89] This is because on payment of the debt the guarantor would be entitled to be subrogated to those securities. But similar criticism in the first Australian edition of this work, J. O' Donovan and J. Phillips (1985) p.325 did not find favour in *Pogoni v R & WH Symington & Co (NZ) Ltd* [1991] 1 N.Z.L.R. 82 at 84–85.
[90] (1981) 147 C.L.R. 654.
[91] *ibid.*, at 675–676 *per* Brennan J. See also the clauses in *State Bank of Victoria v Parry* (1989) 7 A.C.L.C. 226; *Royal Bank of Canada v Savin* (1990) 71 O.R. (2d) 622, where a clause stating "the bank may ... otherwise deal with the customer and others as the bank may see fit" was viewed as excluding liability in respect of a negligent realisation of securities; *Continental Illinois National Bank & Trust Co of Chicago v Papanicolaou* [1986] 2 Lloyd's Rep. 441, where a clause stating that all amounts shall be paid "in full, free of set off or counterclaim" was also held to exclude such liability.
[92] See *Roynat Ltd v Denis* (1982) 139 D.L.R. (3d) 265, where a generally worded clause was held to exclude negligence.
[93] See above, paras 7–27 to 7–41, for examples of this type of clause.
[94] See above, para.8–47.

security is released[95] or where the creditor fails in other ways to preserve the security, for example, by failing to perfect the security or by failing to exercise reasonable care when enforcing it.

8–100   There are three final points to make about clauses excluding the creditor's liability for securities held by the creditor. First, the cases in this area have not drawn any distinction between the situation where the creditor's liability for the loss or impairment of a security is based on a breach by the creditor of a term of the guarantee and, alternatively, the situation where it is based on a breach of the creditor's equitable duty. Given the fact that exclusion clauses are to be construed contra proferentem, it is surprising that this approach has not been adopted, and it is no doubt arguable that if the clause is to cover both heads of liability, the clause should make this clear.[96] Secondly, if the obligation not to impair or release a security arises as a result of a condition precedent to the operation of the guarantee, the creditor will not be able to rely on an exclusion clause at all because the guarantee, and the exclusion clause which is part of it, never become legally binding.[97]

8–101   The validity of some of these clauses which purport to preserve the guarantor's liability in the event of the creditor improperly dealing with a security may be subject to challenge pursuant to the Unfair Terms in Consumer Contracts Regulations 1999, in circumstances where the Regulations apply.[98] In *Standard Chartered Bank Ltd v Walker*,[99] Denning M.R. considered that a clause excluding the liability of a mortgagee for negligence in realising a security was unreasonable within the meaning of the Unfair Contract Terms Act 1977. But *Standard Chartered Bank Ltd v Walker*[1] proceeded upon the now discredited basis that the creditor/mortgagee owed a duty of care in negligence to the guarantor. As the creditor's duty is now firmly based in equity,[2] it is unlikely (as explained in Chapter 4)[3] that the Unfair Contract Terms Act 1977 applies to clauses excluding such liability.

---

[95] *Dowling v Ditanda, The Times*, April 14, 1975.
[96] But a similar argument was rejected by Mahoney J.A. in *Crédit Lyonnais (Aust) Ltd v Darling* (1991) 5 A.C.S.R. 703 at 708.
[97] See *Molsons Bank v Cranston* (1918) 45 D.L.R. 316, where the condition precedent related to the obtaining of an additional guarantor.
[98] This in itself is a matter of some debate. See above, paras 4–163 to 4–176.
[99] [1982] 3 All E.R. 928 at 943.
[1] *ibid.*
[2] See above, para.8–85.
[3] See above, paras 4–160 to 4–162.

(iv) Guarantor's consent to the creditor's action in releasing or impairing securities

The guarantor will not be discharged by the loss or impairment of a **8–102** security if the guarantor requests,[4] or consents to,[5] the creditor's action in relation to the security. It is thought that the law applicable where the guarantor requests, or consents to, a variation of the principal contract is applicable also to a consent in this situation.[6] The guarantor must, therefore, expressly or impliedly consent to the creditor's dealing with the security. It is not sufficient that the guarantor merely has knowledge of such dealings.[7] But two points arising specifically from authorities relating to the loss or impairment of securities should be emphasised. First, there was an early suggestion that in order for there to be an effective consent, the guarantor had to know the legal effect of his acquiescence,[8] but this is no longer considered to be correct.[9] Secondly, there is authority indicating that, if the guarantor consents to remain liable after the security has been lost or impaired, the guarantor's liability will be preserved.[10] In *Mayhew v Crickett*,[11] the creditor took possession of the goods of the debtor, which were secured by a warrant of attorney, but then withdrew the execution. The guarantor was held not to be discharged because he had promised to remain liable subsequent to the withdrawal. But, as discussed in the context of variation,[12] the legal basis for the preservation of the guarantor's liability based upon subsequent consent is doubtful.

Finally, a difficulty may exist if there are several co-guarantors and only **8–103** some of them consent to the loss of the security. Where there is no condition of the contract of guarantee that the security shall be preserved, no doubt the guarantors who consent to the impairment will remain fully liable and those who do not will have their liability reduced to the extent that the value of the security has been impaired. But if there is such a condition, authorities[13] dealing with a release of a co-guarantor indicate that even the guarantors who consent to the release are discharged. It has already been suggested,[14] however, that the consenting guarantors in that situation should remain liable if the consent is clearly given, and the same

---

[4] *Sassoon & Sons Ltd v International Banking Corp* [1927] A.C. 711 at 730; *Stone v Geraldton Brewery Co* (1898) 1 W.A.L.R. 23 at 27 (guarantor requested the landlord (the creditor) to distrain for rent, resulting in the destruction of the right to enter into possession for unpaid rent).
[5] *Polak v Everett* (1876) 1 Q.B.D. 669 at 673 *per* Blackburn J.; *Routley v Gorman* (1920) 55 D.L.R. 58; *First City Capital Ltd v Hall* (1988) 67 O.R. (2d) 12; *Healy v Cornish* (1863) 3 S.C.R. (NSW) Eq. 28 at 32.
[6] See above, para.7–42.
[7] *Wren v Emmett Contractors Pty Ltd* (1969) 43 A.L.J.R. 213 at 220. See above, paras 7–44 to 7–45.
[8] *Strange v Fooks* (1863) 4 Giff. 408 at 413–414; 66 E.R. 765 at 768.
[9] See the discussion above, para.7–42, in the context of variation and especially *Crédit Suisse v Borough Council of Allerdale* [1995] 1 Lloyd's Rep. 315.
[10] *Mayhew v Crickett* (1818) 2 Swan 185; 36 E.R. 585.
[11] *ibid.*
[12] See above, paras 7–49 to 7–50.
[13] See above, para.8–34.
[14] See above, para.8–34.

principle should apply where the creditor is in breach of the contract of guarantee in releasing or impairing securities.

(v) Contracts of indemnity

8–104   If the contract is properly classified as one of indemnity rather than as a contract of guarantee, with the creditor being entitled to an indemnity in respect of losses arising out of a particular transaction, the indemnifier will still be entitled to be subrogated to the rights of the creditor on payment of the loss or damage.[15] Thus the indemnifier will be entitled to the benefit of any securities held by the creditor to seek reimbursement from the person primarily liable, and it should follow that the creditor must not impair or release those securities.[16] There is no specific authority on the extent of the creditor's equitable duty in the context of an indemnity, but, consistently, it should be the same as that imposed when the contract is one of guarantee,[17] and if impairment is shown the indemnifier should be discharged to the extent of the loss. This view is supported by Lord Selborne in *Duncan, Fox & Co v North & South Wales Bank*,[18] who states that the principles of equity will be applicable in "cases in which there is, strictly speaking, no contract of suretyship",[19] but a person secondarily liable has a right of reimbursement from a person primarily liable.

8–105   It is also possible for a term to be found in an indemnity whereby a particular security should not be released or impaired[20] in the same way as such a term can be found in a contract of guarantee. If there is a breach of such a condition, the indemnifier will be absolutely discharged.

5. DISCHARGE BY THE CREDITOR ACTING TO THE PREJUDICE OF THE GUARANTOR?

8–106   In *Black v Ottoman Bank*,[21] the Privy Council stated a general principle that a surety would be discharged if there has been "some positive act done by [the creditor] to the prejudice of the surety, or such degree of negligence, as in the language of Vice-Chancellor Wood in *Dawson v Lawes*,[22] 'to imply connivance and amount to fraud' ".[23] Fraud, in this

---

[15] *Morris v Ford Motor Co Ltd* [1973] Q.B. 792.
[16] Although there is no specific authority to support this conclusion. In relation to an insurance policy, see *Goulston Discount Co Ltd v Sims* (1967) 111 S.J. 682.
[17] For a detailed discussion of the extent of the duty, see above, paras 8–55 to 8–89.
[18] (1880) 6 App. Cas. 1.
[19] *ibid.*, at 13.
[20] *e.g. Guy-Pell v Foster* [1930] 2 Ch. 169.
[21] (1862) 15 Moo P.C.C. 472; 15 E.R. 573.
[22] (1854) 23 L.J. Ch. 434 at 441.
[23] (1862) 15 Moo P.C.C. 472 at 483; 15 E.R. 573 at 577. See also *Dawson v Lawes* (1854) 23 L.J. Ch. 434 at 441; *Mactaggart v Watson* (1835) 3 Cl. & Finn 525 at 543; *Mayor of Durham v Fowler* (1889) 22 Q.B.D. 394 at 420; *O'Day v Commercial Bank of Australia Ltd* (1933) 50 C.L.R. 200 at 223–224; *Australian Joint Stock Bank v Hogan* (1902) 2 S.R. (NSW) 7 at 11.

context, has been defined as conduct which is unfair to a surety.[24] Broadly construed, this general rule, especially the reference to "a positive act" by the creditor discharging the guarantor, is capable of radically extending the number of situations in which the creditor's actions may discharge the guarantor. It has been seen[25] that if the creditor impairs a security held for the enforcement of the principal obligation, the guarantor will be discharged, at least to the value of the security impaired. The guarantor will also be discharged if the creditor and principal agree to vary the principal obligation.[26] But although the application of these rules may be unclear in some situations, in general, the circumstances in which they apply are reasonably delineated. The rule enunciated in *Black v Ottoman Bank*, however, is potentially capable of applying to any action by the creditor which might prejudicially affect the guarantor, for example, a failure to insure,[27] a failure by the creditor to comply with relevant statutory requirements,[28] or the appointment of a receiver or liquidator in respect of the principal company when this is not the best course of action to preserve the assets and goodwill of the company.[29]

However, despite the apparent width of the principle it is difficult to find **8–107** any clear examples in either England or Australia of the discharge of a guarantor on this basis. There are three classes of cases. The first is where one of the bases for the decision is that the creditor must not act to the prejudice of the guarantor, but the fact that the guarantor has been discharged can be explained adequately on other well-established grounds. The second is where the principle in *Black v Ottoman Bank* has apparently been recognised, but its application has been negated on the facts. Finally, there are cases which have cast doubt on the principle either by expressly disapproving of it or by refusing to apply or even analyse the principle even though the facts of the case might have justified its application.

As an example of the first class, in *General Steam-Navigation Co v* **8–108** *Rolt*,[30] a guarantor for the due performance of a building contract was discharged when the contractor was paid sums before they became due under the principal contract. The basis of the decision was that the "prepayment must prejudice the surety in a case like this, inasmuch as it deprives him of the benefit of that which would be an inducement to the principal to perform the contract in due time".[31] Yet the agreement to

[24] *Mayor of Durham v Fowler* (1889) 22 Q.B.D. 394 at 419 *per* Denman J.
[25] See above, paras 8–46 to 8–89. See also *National Australia Bank Ltd v Drummond* (unreported, NSW Sup Ct, Giles J., July 7, 1995) (where a guarantor was not discharged simply because the bank granted another creditor priority over its mortgage).
[26] See above, Ch. 7.
[27] e.g. *Watts v Shuttleworth* (1861) 7 H. & N. 353; 158 E.R. 510 for a similar factual situation.
[28] e.g. *Unity Finance Ltd v Woodcock* [1963] 1 W.L.R. 455; *Traders Group Ltd v Garand* (1975) 65 D.L.R. (3d) 374.
[29] e.g. *Moase Produce Ltd v Royal Bank* (1987) 64 C.B.R. (NS) 191. See also the argument for the guarantors in *ANZ Banking Group Ltd v Carnegie* (unreported, Vic Sup Ct, June 16, 1987) at 45.
[30] (1858) 6 C.B. (NS) 550; 141 E.R. 572.
[31] *ibid.*, at 597; at 590 *per* Crowder J, 595–597; 589; *per* Cockburn C.J. See also *Calvert v London Dock Co* (1838) 7 L.J. Ch. 90, where Lord Langdale treated the question as analogous to where the creditor deprives the guarantor of the benefit of a security on paying the debt; *Warre v Calvert* (1837) 7 Ad. & El. 143; 112 E.R. 425; *Board of Trustees for the Macklin School District of Saskatchewan v Saskatchewan Guarantee & Fidelity Co* [1919] 2

allow the principal to be paid at an earlier date than that stipulated in the contract can also be viewed as a discharge of the guarantor as a result of a variation of the principal contract.[32] Again, in *Unity Finance Ltd v Woodcock*,[33] the guarantor of a hire-purchase contract was discharged when a finance company repossessed the goods from the hirer in breach of the provisions of the Hire Purchase Act 1938. One of the reasons for the decision was that "the conduct of the owners has much prejudiced the position of the [guarantor]".[34] But this decision can also be viewed as an example of the discharge of the guarantor arising as a result of the determination of the principal contract by operation of the law, because the provisions of the Hire Purchase Act stated that a hire-purchase transaction shall determine if the goods are repossessed in contravention of the Act.[35]

8–109   The application of the principle in *Black v Ottoman Bank* has invariably been denied in cases falling within the second category, because the act of the creditor was held not to be a positive act but merely an act of negligence[36] or passive inactivity[37] on the creditor's part. Thus the guarantor of the honest and faithful discharge of an employee's duties was not discharged in circumstances where the employer acquiesced in the principal's irregular mode of accounting,[38] or where the employer failed to demand[39] or check[40] accounts held by the principal. Similarly, it has been held that the creditor does not prejudice the position of and discharge the guarantor when the creditor fails to sue for the principal debt once it becomes due[41] or, in the context of a guarantee of a contractor's obligations under a building contract, when the owner fails to supervise the work properly.[42] The application of the rule has also been rejected where the creditor is bona fide exercising his rights under the principal contract. McTiernan J. made this clear in *O'Day v Commercial Bank of Australia Ltd*,[43] where it was alleged that the creditor wrongfully exercised its powers under a debenture given for the enforcement of the principal obligation. His Honour took the view that action by a creditor against a debtor which has no other colour or character than action taken bona fide

---

W.W.R. 396; *Thomas Fuller Construction Co* (1958) *Ltd v Continental Insurance Co* (1970) 36 D.L.R. (3d) 336.
[32] See this explanation in *Thomas Fuller Construction Co* (1958) *Ltd v Continental Insurance Co* (1970) 36 D.L.R. (3d) 336 at 355.
[33] [1963] 1 W.L.R. 455. As another example, see *National Bank of Nigeria Ltd v Awolesi* [1964] 1 W.L.R. 1311, discussed above, paras 6–43 to 6–46.
[34] [1963] 1 W.L.R. 455 at 461 *per* Lord Denning M.R.
[35] See above, paras 6–145 to 6–148.
[36] *Guardians of Mansfield Union v Wright* (1882) 9 Q.B.D. 683 at 688 *per* Jessel M.R.
[37] *Mayor of Durham v Fowler* (1889) 22 Q.B.D. 394 at 420 *per* Denman J.
[38] *Guardians of Mansfield Union v Wright* (1882) 9 Q.B.D. 683.
[39] *ibid.*
[40] *Black v Ottoman Bank* (1862) 15 Moo P.C.C. 472; 15 E.R. 573.
[41] *ibid., O'Day v Commercial Bank of Australia Ltd* (1933) 50 C.L.R. 200 at 224 *per* McTiernan J.
[42] *Kingston-Upon-Hull Corp v Harding* [1892] 2 Q.B. 494. *Cf.* however, *Stone v Geraldton Brewery Co* (1898) 1 W.A.L.R. 23 at 27, where it was held that a failure to re-enter the leased premises on the tenant's failure to pay the rent discharged the guarantor of the tenant's obligations under the lease. But there is no analysis of the principle underlying the decision.
[43] (1933) 50 C.L.R. 200.

by the creditor in pursuit of remedies will not discharge a surety, even though such action may be taken under a mistake of law as to the creditor's rights.[44]

As to the final class of cases, Goff L.J. in the Court of Appeal in *Bank of India v Trans Commodity Merchants Ltd and Patel*[45] clearly stated that "irregular" or prejudicial conduct in a general sense on the part of a creditor will not discharge a surety. Furthermore, there are also the factual situations in which the rule in *Black v Ottoman Bank* has been ignored. A striking example is *Watts v Shuttleworth*,[46] which indicates a clear tendency on the part of the courts to avoid a precise formulation and application of the rule. There, the guarantor of a contractors' obligation under a building contract was held to be discharged when the creditor failed to insure the building as required by the principal contract. Williams J. treated the case as analogous to a variation of the principal contract whereby the principal is given time to perform his obligations, although on the facts there was no consensual variation[47] but only a simple breach of the principal contract by reason of the creditor's failure to insure. Williams J. specifically rejected a submission that the rule on which the case should be decided was analogous to the principle that the guarantor is discharged by the creditor impairing a security held for the enforcement of the principal obligation. Yet *Watts v Shuttleworth* could have been viewed as an example of the principle enunciated in *Black v Ottoman Bank*. At the very least, even though the failure to insure might not be regarded as a positive act on the part of the creditor within the ambit of the rule, the principle should have merited some discussion.[48]

8–110

In conclusion, in the authors' view, the weight of authority is contrary to the existence of a general rule that the guarantor will be discharged if the creditor acts in a prejudicial manner towards the guarantor. The possibility of the guarantor being discharged outside the established categories such as variation of the principal contract or the impairment of a security cannot, however, be dismissed. Even Goff L.J., who disapproved of the rule in *Bank of India v Trans Commodity Merchants Ltd and Patel* did "not wish to be thought to be shutting the door upon further development of the law in this field by rigidly confining the circumstances in which a

8–111

---

[44] *ibid.*, at 224. *Cf.*, however, *Re Darwen and Pearce* [1927] 1 Ch. 176, where the creditor exercised his rights under the principal contract to forfeit shares. The guarantor was held to be discharged because the guarantor's rights had been interfered with. The proper explanation of this case, however, probably lies in the fact that the creditor was in breach of a term of the guarantee in forfeiting the shares: see above, para.8–83.

[45] [1983] 2 Lloyd's Rep. 298 at 302, approving Bingham J. at first instance: [1982] 1 Lloyd's Rep. 506 at 515. See also *Socomex Ltd v Banque Bruxelles Lambert SA* [1996] Lloyd's Law Rep. 156 at 198; *Westpac Securities Ltd v Dickie* [1991] 1 N.Z.L.R. 657 at 663–665 and note that in *National Westminster Bank Plc v Riley* [1986] F.L.R. 213 it was held that a non-repudiatory breach of the principal contract will not discharge the guarantor.

[46] (1861) 7 H. & N. 353; 158 E.R. 510.

[47] It has already been suggested that for a variation of the principal contract to discharge the guarantor there must be a consensual agreement to alter the terms between creditor and principal: see above, paras 7–16 to 7–20.

[48] A similar example is *Price v Kirkham* (1864) 3 H. & C. 437; 159 E.R. 601, where the guarantor was not discharged even though the creditor was in breach of a clause of the principal contract (although not of the guarantee) in failing to notify the guarantor of late payments by the principal.

surety may be discharged to specified instances".[49] Furthermore, Goff L.J. appeared to accept[50] the view of Bingham J. at first instance that the guarantor will be discharged if he "causes or connives at the default by the principal debtor".[51]

8–112   It should also be said that in Canada the principle that the guarantor is discharged appears to have been accepted where the prejudicial conduct materially increases the risk to the guarantor.[52] In *Bank of Montreal v Wilder*,[53] the guarantor was held to be discharged where the creditor was in breach of a term of the principal contract agreeing to increase the line of credit to the principal and honour the cheques of the principal, with the result that the principal could not carry on business as a viable commercial operation. The risk to the guarantor was, therefore, increased. The court held that the guarantor was absolutely discharged. This is a strange result because where the creditor releases or impairs a security held for the enforcement of the principal obligation the guarantor is discharged to the extent of the loss. Perhaps the reason is that the rule that the guarantor is discharged by the prejudicial conduct of the creditor was viewed in *Black v Ottoman Bank*[54] as a principle "*at law* and in equity",[55] rather than simply being a principle developed by the courts of equity. Whatever the rationale, it is thought that if the guarantor is to be discharged in this manner the guarantor should only be discharged pro tanto in respect of any additional liability sustained by reason of the creditor's prejudicial conduct towards the principal.[56]

8–113   There is no real support for the view that an indemnifier will be discharged on the basis that the person entitled to the indemnity has acted to his prejudice. However, Lord Denning M.R. has suggested[57] that recovery will not be permitted under a contract of indemnity if the person indemnified has acted illegally, for example, where the contract of indemnity relates to losses sustained by the owner as a result of entering into a hire-purchase contract, and the owner wrongfully repossesses the goods.[58] It is also the case that contracts of indemnity are construed strictly

---

[49] [1983] 2 Lloyd's Rep. 298 at 302. See also *Socomex Ltd v Banque Bruxelles Lambert SA* [1996] 1 Lloyd's Rep. 156 at 198.
[50] *ibid.* at 302. See also *Westpac Securities Ltd v Dickie* [1991] 1 N.Z.L.R. 657 at at 663–665.
[51] [1982] 1 Lloyd's Rep. 506 at 509.
[52] *Bank of Montreal v Wilder* (1983) 149 D.L.R. (3d) 193; approved on appeal by the Supreme Court of Canada: (1987) 1 W.W.R. 289. See also *Rumely v Leighton* (1916) 10 W.W.R. 817; *Traders Group Ltd v Garand* (1975) 65 DLR (3d) 374. *Cf. Royal Bank of Canada v Goff* (1988) 66 O.R. (2d) 701, in which *Bank of Montreal v Wilder* was distinguished on the basis that no breach of the principal agreement directly guaranteed occurred.
[53] (1983) 149 D.L.R. (3d) 193 at 227–232.
[54] (1862) 15 Moo P.C.C. 472; 15 E.R. 573.
[55] *ibid.*, at 483; 577 (emphasis added).
[56] Seaton J.A. in *Bank of Montreal v Wilder* (1983) 149 D.L.R. (3d) 193 at 203 took the view that the guarantors should be discharged only to the extent of any prejudice. In all the other cases, this possibility is not referred to.
[57] *Goulston Discount Co Ltd v Clark* [1967] 2 Q.B. 493 at 497–498, interpreting the earlier decision of *Unity Finance Ltd v Woodcock* [1963] 1 W.L.R. 455. Although it was held to be a guarantee in the latter case, Lord Denning clearly thought that it was an indemnity. See also *Hodgson v Hodgson* (1837) 2 Keen 704 at 710–712; 48 E.R. 800 at 803 (indemnifier prejudiced by release of a debtor against whom she would have had a right of contribution).
[58] *Goulston Discount Co Ltd v Clark* [1967] 2 Q.B. 493 at 497–498, interpreting *Unity Finance Ltd v Woodcock* [1963] 1 W.L.R. 455.

in favour of the indemnifier so that the holder of the indemnity will not be able to recover in respect of his own negligence or in respect of deliberate breaches of contract unless the contract of indemnity clearly encompasses such losses.[59]

It is considered that neither a guarantor nor an indemnifier should be **8–114** discharged on the basis of a prejudicial act by the creditor towards the principal. The rule is necessarily vague and uncertain, as the creditor would need to be extremely guarded in dealings with the principal, which may have unfortunate consequences. For example, the application of the principle would mean that the creditor would justifiably be wary of helping the principal overcome temporary financial difficulties by the supply of additional credit outside the limits of their original contract. If, despite this assistance, the principal's financial position still failed to improve, the creditor may be faced with the argument that this assistance had, in fact, caused a worsening of the principal's economic status, thus prejudicing the guarantor's interests and thereby discharging the guarantor.

6. NO GENERAL DUTY OF CARE

In the previous section, an analysis was made of the proposition that the **8–115** guarantor may be discharged in equity by conduct of the creditor which is prejudicial to the guarantor's interests. Decisions in New Zealand and Canada[60] have suggested that the guarantor is discharged if he acts negligently in respect of securities held for the enforcement of the principal obligation (outside the specific equitable grounds of discharge previously outlined) or even by general conduct of a negligent nature. As we have seen[61] in England the Court of Appeal in *Standard Chartered Bank Ltd v Walker*[62] did regard the creditor's duty in realising securities as based on negligence, but such a general duty of care was firmly rejected by the Privy Council in *China & South Seas Bank Ltd v Tan*.[63] Similarly in *Barclays Bank plc v Quinecare*[64] it was held that the creditor owes no duty to the guarantor to act reasonably to ensure that the loan is applied for the purpose for which it was given. It is now clear that if the guarantor is to be discharged, it must be by application of the equitable principles entitled in this Chapter.

---

[59] See above, paras 5–10 to 5–11. See also *Lord Newborough v Schroder* (1849) 7 C.B. 342; 137 E.R. 136 (losses not recoverable if they arise from the creditor's own voluntary act).
[60] *Clarke v UDC Finance Ltd* [1985] 2 N.Z.L.R. 636; *Communities Economic Development Fund v Cdn Pickles Corp* [1989] 3 W.W.R. 514 (without finally deciding). *Cf. Westpac Securities v Dickie* [1991] 1 N.Z.L.R. 657 at 664–665.
[61] See above, para.8–85.
[62] [1982] 3 All E.R. 938 at 944, 945. See also *American Express International Banking Corp v Hurley* [1985] 3 All E.R. 564.
[63] [1990] 1 A.C. 536 at 543–544.
[64] [1988] F.L.R. 166. See also *Shamji v Johnson Mathey Bankers Ltd* (1986) 2 B.C.C. 98, 910; *Burgess v Auger* [1998] 2 B.C.L.C. 478; *Yorkshire Bank plc v Hall* [1999] 1 All E.R. 879 at 893.

CHAPTER 9

DISCHARGE FROM LIABILITY BY THE DETERMINATION OF THE GUARANTEE

1. DISCHARGE BY PAYMENT BY THE GUARANTOR

9–01   Payment by the guarantor of the total amount of the guaranteed debt, or payment by the guarantor up to the limit of the specified liability under the guarantee, will discharge the guarantor from the guarantee.[1] Payment may be made by the creditor realising a collateral security provided by the guarantor since such a security must normally

---

[1] *e.g. Royal Bank v Sterns* [1924] 3 D.L.R. 1050.

be appropriated by the creditor in diminution of the guarantor's liability.[2] The removal of the guarantor's goods in execution[3] or the payment of sums to prevent execution is treated as being equivalent to payment,[4] and payment may even be effected by means of a loan from the creditor.[5] Payment will not be deemed to have been made, however, merely because the guarantor gives the creditor a promissory note or bond[6] for the amount due.[7]

The payment should be made to the person legally entitled to receive it,[8] **9–02** and at the place specified by the terms of the contract of guarantee.[9] If no place of payment is specified, the place of payment will be the place where the parties impliedly intend it should be made, having regard to all the circumstances including the course of conduct of the parties after the contract was signed.[10]

The most difficult problem[11] concerning payment by the guarantor **9–03** arises where the guarantor channels payments through the principal debtor so that it is unclear whether the payments have been made in satisfaction of the guarantor's obligations under the guarantee or whether the payments have in reality been made by the principal in discharge of the principal obligation, the guarantor merely supplying funds to strengthen the debtor's position. The issue is an important one if there are several guarantors because if the latter construction is adopted, all the guarantors will be fully discharged, the principal obligation having been satisfied, whereas if one guarantor is treated as satisfying his obligations under the guarantee by the payments, only that guarantor will be discharged and that guarantor will be able to claim contribution from any other co-guarantor.[12]

Similar problems arise if one guarantor is indebted to the creditor in **9–04** respect of another independent obligation so that it is unclear whether the guarantor intends the payment to satisfy the guarantor's obligations under the guarantee or under the separate undertaking.[13] The guarantor in all these cases should make it clear that an appropriation is being made in discharge of the guarantor's obligations under the guarantee if that is the intention. On payment of the principal debt, the guarantor may also ask

[2] See above, para.6–33.
[3] *Rodgers v Maw* (1846) 15 M. & W. 444; 153 E.R. 924.
[4] *Exall v Partridge* (1799) 8 Term Rep. 308; 101 E.R. 1405; *Edmunds v Wallingford* (1885) 14 Q.B.D. 811.
[5] *e.g. Brown, Shipley & Co Ltd v Amalgamated Investment (Europe) BV* [1979] 1 Lloyd's Rep. 488.
[6] *Taylor v Higgins* (1802) 3 East 169; 102 E.R. 562; *Maxwell v Jameson* (1818) 2 B. & Ald. 51; 106 E.R. 286; *Barclay v Gooch* (1797) 2 Esp. 571; 170 E.R. 459; *Re Parkinson Ex p. Sergeant* (1822) 1 Gl. & J. 183. *Cf. Re Roberts Ex p. Allen and Cazenove* (1858) 3 De G. & J. 447; 44 E.R. 1341; *Gore v Gore* [1901] 2 I.R. 269.
[7] A right of set-off will probably not be regarded as payment (*Bartlett v Pentland* (1830) 10 B. & C. 760; 109 E.R. 632), but the guarantor may be able to plead a set-off as a defence: see below, para.11–46.
[8] *BP Australia Ltd v Wales* [1982] Qd. R. 386.
[9] *ibid.*
[10] *ibid.*
[11] It is discussed in detail above, paras 6–03 to 6–07. See, especially, *Mahoney v McManus* (1981) 55 A.L.J.R. 673.
[12] See *Mahoney v McManus* (1981) 55 A.L.J.R. 673.
[13] *e.g. Waugh v Wren* (1862) 11 W.R. 244; *Commercial Bank of Australia v Wilson & Co's Estate* (Official Assignee) [1893] A.C. 181.

that the guarantee be delivered up to the guarantor, although there is probably no right to insist that this be done unless there is a real danger that it will be used for an improper purpose.[14]

9–05   When the guarantor pays the creditor under the guarantee a question arises as to the nature of the payment made. In particular, where the principal debt includes amounts representing both capital and interest, it may be necessary to determine whether the payments by the guarantor in satisfaction of the principal obligation still retain their character as separate payments of capital and interest. The guarantor may wish to establish that this is so for taxation purposes.[15] Although the cases are not entirely consistent,[16] and the result may be dependent on the precise wording of the guarantee,[17] the dominant view is that interest payable under the principal transaction does not, as between guarantor and creditor, lose its character as interest because it is paid in satisfaction of an obligation imposed by the guarantee.[18]

9–06   The consequences of the guarantor making full payment under the guarantee is that the guarantor will be entitled to a right of contribution from a co-guarantor and a right of indemnity from the principal. The guarantor will also be entitled to be subrogated to securities held by the creditor for the enforcement of the principal obligation.[19] As regards the position of the creditor, payments made by the guarantor to the full extent of the guarantor's liability, but which fall short of the total indebtedness of the principal,[20] will not usually prevent the creditor suing the principal or claiming in the principal's bankruptcy or winding-up for the full amount of the debt.[21]

9–07   Sometimes the guarantor makes a part payment in exchange for an absolute release. Such a payment will not be treated merely as consideration for the release, but also as part payment of the principal obligation.[22] Otherwise it would mean that the creditor could obtain payment for the release, without the overall indebtedness being reduced, thus prejudicing the principal debtor and any co-guarantors. As Hoffmann J. (as he then was) put it in *Milverton Group Ltd v Warner World Ltd*,[23] "a creditor could pick off his debtors one by one and recover in total more than the whole debt."[24] This appears to be a

---

[14] *Shewfelt v Kincardine* (1915) 35 O.L.R. 39. It is arguable, however, that the guarantee is itself a security to which the guarantor is entitled to be subrogated, especially if it is of assistance in proving the guarantor's right of contribution.
[15] e.g. *IRC v Holder* [1931] 2 K.B. 81; on appeal: [1932] A.C. 624; *Westminster Bank Executor & Trustee Co (Channel Islands) Ltd v National Bank of Greece SA* [1970] 1 Q.B. 256; on appeal: [1971] A.C. 945.
[16] See the authorities discussed in *Re Hawkins* (deceased) [1972] Ch. 714. See also F. G. Glover, "Interest Paid Under Guarantee" (1973) 123 N.L.J. 7.
[17] *Re Hawkins (deceased)* [1972] Ch. 714 at 728.
[18] *ibid. Re Amalgamated Investment & Property Co Ltd* [1984] 3 All E.R. 272.
[19] See these issues discussed below, Ch. 12.
[20] This conclusion presupposes that the guarantee is for the whole of the principal's indebtedness and not for part of the debt: see above, para.5–35.
[21] *Ulster Bank Ltd v Lambe* [1966] N.I. 161; *Westpac Banking Corp v Gollin & Co Ltd* [1988] V.R. 397: see below, paras 10–28 to 10–43.
[22] *Milverton Group Ltd v Warner World Ltd* [1995] 2 E.G.L.R. 28.
[23] *ibid.*
[24] *ibid.*, at 73.

principle of law, rather than one of construction, its basis stemming from the premise that both guarantor and principal debtor owe a common obligation to perform the principal transaction.[25] For the same reason (irrespective of any release) general payments by the guarantor to the creditor cannot be treated simply as payments in satisfaction of his liability as a third party rather than in satisfaction of the principal obligation.[26] Thus when a lessee defaults in paying rent, payments by the guarantor of the lessee's obligations will reduce the amount of outstanding rent owed to the landlord.[27]

2. DISCHARGE BY AGREEMENT

(i) Express agreement

The creditor and the guarantor may expressly agree to discharge the **9–08** guarantee. On normal contractual principles, this will operate as a rescission of the contract of gurantee provided that it is legally binding, being either under seal or supported by consideration[28] and provided that the creditor's agreement has not been procured by fraud.[29] The agreement may be oral, even though the original guarantee is required to be in writing.[30] Some difficulty may be occasioned by the requirement of consideration. The creditor's promise to release the guarantor may be supported by the guarantor agreeing to forfeit any rights the guarantor has under the guarantee (for example, the right to ensure that the creditor does not lose or impair a security). But such rights may be excluded by terms of the guarantee itself,[31] so that it is arguable that the guarantor is not relinquishing any rights at all in exchange for the creditor's promise to release the guarantor. The guarantor should, therefore, as a matter of caution ensure that separate consideration is provided for the creditor's promise or that the release is under seal. If there is no consideration,

---

[25] *ibid.* See also *P & A Swift Investments v Combined English Stores Group plc* [1989] A.C. 632 at 638 *per* Lord Templeman. *Cf.* suggestions to the contrary by Russell L.J. in *London & County (A & D) Ltd v Wilfred Sportsman Ltd* [1971] Ch. 764. In *Milverton Group Ltd v Warner World Ltd* [1995] 2 E.G.L.R. 28. Hoffmann J. considered that this decision could be explained on the basis of subrogation.

[26] *Milverton Group Ltd v Warner World Ltd* [1995] 2 E.G.L.R. 28 at 29–30 disapproving suggestions in *London County (A & D) Ltd v Wilfred Sportsman Ltd* [1971] Ch. 764 (see above n.25).

[27] *ibid.*

[28] G. H. Treitel, *The Law of Contract* (11th ed., 2003), pp.99–101. See also, in the context of a discharge of a guarantee, *Barclays Bank Ltd v Thomas* [1979] 2 Lloyd's Rep. 505 at 507.

[29] *Canadian Surety Co v The King* [1930] S.C.R. 434.

[30] *Morris v Baron & Co* [1918] A.C. 1 (a contract for the disposition of an interest in land could be rescinded orally); *Hamlet International plc v Billyphil Ltd* (unreported, November 5, 1999, CA), where it was accepted that an oral promise of discharge, together with the return of the guarantee, might constitute a valid defence. See, similarly, *Bank of Baroda v Shah* (unreported, July 30, 1999) where the bank gave an oral assurance that the guarantor would be released if he resigned as a director and shareholder of the principal company.

[31] See, *e.g.* the clauses set out above, para.8–92. As an example of an agreement not being supported by consideration, see *Rogers v ANZ Banking Group Ltd* [1985] W.A.R. 304.

however, the creditor's promise may still be effective as a waiver or as an estoppel.[32]

9–09   When the guarantee takes the form of a third party mortgage, it is a question of construction in each case whether or not the release of the mortgage releases the guarantor from the personal covenants created by the security.[33] But the most usual drafting will operate to discharge the guarantor from all personal obligations.[34]

9–10   A practice which occasionally takes place, is that a bank may physically "deliver up" the guarantee to the guarantor. This may be done either on payment of the amount due under the guarantee by the guarantor or on payment of the debt by the principal. This practice appears to prevent the creditor relying on the terms of the guarantee because the inference from this action is that the guarantee has been treated between the guarantor and the creditor as being at an end.[35]

9–11   This may be disadvantageous to the creditor in several situations. For example, the principal debtor may pay the whole debt, but the payment may be subsequently found to amount to a preference and be recovered by the principal's trustee in bankruptcy. If the guarantee contains a clause preserving the creditor's rights against the guarantor in the event of a preferential payment[36] (so as to rebut a possible inference that the guarantor is discharged by payment of the debt by the principal),[37] this clause will not operate in favour of the creditor as the delivery up of the guarantee will prevent the creditor relying on it. Similarly, when the guarantor is liable for part of a debt and pays that part to the guarantor, a creditor delivering up the guarantee will not be able to rely on a clause in it enabling the creditor to prove for the whole sum in the principal's bankruptcy without accounting to the guarantor for a proportionate part of the dividends received.[38]

(ii) Implied agreement

9–12   If there is no express agreement to discharge the guarantee, the facts may indicate that the guarantor and the creditor have intended to discharge the original guarantee by entering into a new guarantee which is

---

[32] As to waiver see G. H. Treitel, *The Law of Contract* (11th ed., 2003), p.102. As an example of an estoppel see *Marac Finance Ltd v Peters and Thompson* (unreported, HC (NZ), November 12, 1984). As to when one co-guarantor is released, see above, para.8–21.

[33] *Groongal Pastoral Co Ltd (in liq) v Falkiner* (1924) 35 C.L.R. 157; *Re Miller (a bankrupt) Ex p. Public Trustee* [1939] N.Z.L.R. 917 at 920; *Van Santen v Felix* [1994] A.N.Z. Con. R. 108. See generally note [1994] A.N.Z. Conv. R. 107.

[34] e.g. *Groongal Patoral Co Ltd (in liq) v Falkiner* (1924) 35 C.L.R. 157; *Van Santen v Felix* [1994] A.N.Z. Conv. R. 108.

[35] *MacKinnon's Trustee v Bank of Scotland* [1915] S.C. 411 at 418, although there is no discussion of the precise legal basis of the conclusion, which might be based on an implied release or an estoppel; *Simpson v Jack* (1948) S.L.T. (Notes 415). It would be otherwise if the delivery up was shown to be a mistake: *MacKinnon's Trustee v Bank of Scotland* [1915] S.C. 411 at 418.

[36] See this issue discussed above, para.6–12.

[37] See above, para.6–13.

[38] See this type of clause discussed below, para.10–38.

to be substituted for the original. The issue arose in the Australian High Court decision of *Mahoney v McManus*,[39] where a "joint and several" guarantee was given by A, B and C, who were shareholders and directors of the principal company, to secure a debt due to Chrysler Marine Australia Ltd from the principal company. At a later stage, another "joint and several" guarantee was given in respect of the same debt by A, B and D. Although C was not a party to the second guarantee, he claimed to be released from liability on the basis that A and B had been impliedly discharged from their obligation under the first guarantee by the execution of the second guarantee, and in consequence, C, as co-guarantor of the first joint and several guarantee, was also discharged. This argument was rejected by Gibbs C.J. (Aickin J. and Wilson J. concurring) because there was no evidence that the second guarantee was meant to be taken in substitution of the first guarantee so that it could be said that A and B were discharged from the first guarantee. As Gibbs C.J. stated:

"It is not inconsistent with the continued operation of a joint and several guarantee by A, B and C that a joint and several guarantee should be taken from A, B and D in respect of the same indebtedness. There is no reason why the two guarantees should not both be effective, so that the creditor can avail himself of either or both, and so that any surety can obtain contribution against all the others."[40]

In these cases where a further guarantee is taken, and there is an intention to release the guarantor who is excluded from the second guarantee, that guarantor should obtain a formal release from the creditor. **9–13**

Particular reliance was placed in *Mahoney v McManus*[41] on the fact that the parties to the second guarantee were not the same as the parties to the first guarantee. If this had been the case, Gibbs C.J. indicated that the conclusion might have been different: **9–14**

"If all the parties to both guarantees had been the same, it might have been easy to reach the conclusion that they intended, not that there should be two identical guarantees in respect of the same existing indebtedness, but that the latter guarantee was to be taken in substitution for, and to discharge, the former."

In this dictum Gibbs C.J. contemplates a situation in which the second guarantee is "identical" to the first guarantee. However, provided that the guarantees are between the same parties, major differences between the two guarantees should not preclude a finding that the original guarantee has been discharged and the second guarantee substituted for **9–15**

---

[39] (1981) 55 A.L.J.R. 673. As other examples, see *Lowes v Maughan and Fearon* (1884) 1 T.L.R. 6; *Lawrence v Finance Corp of Australia* (unreported, NSW Sup Ct, November 2, 1990).
[40] (1981) 55 A.L.J.R. 673 at 677.
[41] *ibid.*, at 676–677. Whether or not a subsequent agreement discharges an earlier guarantee can be a difficult question of evidence: see *e.g. Kateleigh Investments Pty Ltd v Grimbly Court* (unreported, Vic Sup Ct, October 30, 1985).

it.[42] Indeed traditionally, the fact that the difference between the two contracts relates to some essential matter has been relied upon by the courts as indicating that there has been a rescission of the original contract and a substitution of a new contract, as opposed to a mere variation of the original contract.[43]

9–16   In order to draw the necessary inference that the earlier guarantee is to be rescinded and replaced by a later guarantee, the second guarantee must have come into force. Thus in *Barclays Bank Ltd v Thomas*[44] no such inference was drawn when a guarantee was delivered in escrow, that is, it was not intended to have any legal effect until certain conditions were met.[45]

9–17   If the later guarantee has come into force but was made orally, it can be regarded as rescinding the earlier guarantee but it will itself be unenforceable because it is not evidenced in writing.[46] As indicated in the previous paragraphs, if the departure from the terms of the original guarantee relates to some essential matter, this might suggest that the original contract has been rescinded.[47] If the departure relates to an inessential matter, the new agreement will generally be interpreted not as a rescission of the original guarantee but merely as a variation of it. This variation will not be effective unless it is in writing,[48] and thus the first guarantee will remain in force according to its original terms. Unfortunately in the context of guarantees there is little guidance as to what matters will be regarded as essential, but it might be supposed that a change in the extent of the liability of the guarantor and the circumstances in which liability of the guarantor arises would be regarded as important differences.[49]

---

[42] See *National Australia Bank Ltd v Drummond* (unreported, NSW Sup Ct, 7 July 1995) (where Giles J. held that a later guarantee in respect of a greater amount was taken in substitution for, and to discharge, an earlier guarantee).

[43] *British & Beningtons Ltd v North Western Cachar Tea Co Ltd* [1923] A.C. 48 at 68. See also G. H. Treitel, *The Law of Contract* (11th ed., 2003), p.190.

[44] [1979] 2 Lloyd's Rep. 505.

[45] H. A. de Colyar in his *Treatise on the Law of Guarantees and of Principal and Surety* (3rd ed., 1897), p. 389 states another requirement that the substitution of the second contract must occur before any breach of the first contract (relying on *Taylor v Hilary* (1835) 1 Cr. M. & R. 741; 149 E.R. 1249). But this is not thought to be correct in circumstances where it is clear that a substitution has been effected.

[46] *Morris v Baron & Co* [1918] AC 1. And see generally G. H. Treitel, *The Law of Contract* (11th ed., 2003), p.189.

[47] *British & Beningtons Ltd v North Western Cachar Tea Co Ltd* [1923] A.C. 48 at 68.

[48] *Goss v Lord Nugent* (1833) 5 B & Ad 58; 110 E.R. 713. See also G. H. Treitel, *The Law of Contract* (11th ed., 2003), pp.189–190.

[49] In *Taylor v Hilary* (1835) 1 Cr. M. & R. 741; 149 E.R. 1249, it was held that a change in the time for payment was an essential difference, but in that case the second agreement was not another guarantee but an agreement by which the original guarantor assumed a primary liability. See also *Galloway v BNZ* (unreported, CA (NZ), February 25, 1991) (unlimited guarantee replaced by limited guarantee) and *National Australia Bank Ltd v Drummond* (unreported, NSW Sup Ct, July 7, 1995).

(iii) Merger by higher remedy

It is a general principle that, where a creditor takes a security of a higher   **9–18**
nature than that which is already held for the enforcement of the
obligation, the creditor's remedies on the minor security or cause of action
are normally merged in the higher remedy by operation of law and are
extinguished.[50] Thus if the creditor after the execution of the guarantee
subsequently takes a higher security, such as a mortgage from the
guarantor, the creditor's remedies against the guarantor will be confined to
those embodied in the mortgage. This may be of some significance as
various rights of the guarantor (for example, the right to be discharged in
certain circumstances) may be excluded by the guarantee but not by the
instrument of mortgage. This general principle of merger is subject to the
intentions of the parties,[51] so that the creditor's rights under the guarantee
may be preserved by a specific clause in the guarantee. An example is:

> "This guarantee shall be in addition to, and shall not be in any way
> prejudiced by, any collateral or other security now or hereafter held by
> the creditor, and the creditor's rights under this guarantee shall not be
> merged in any such other security."

In any event, apart from any special clauses, the doctrine of merger only   **9–19**
applies where the subsequent security is taken in respect of the same
obligation[52] and between the same parties,[53] and only where the security is
of a higher nature.[54] Thus if the original guarantee is embodied in a
mortgage of real property and the creditor subsequently takes a
promissory note or bill of sale from the guarantor there will be no merger.

Aside from the question of merger, it will not be an abuse of the court's   **9–20**
process[55] for the creditor to seek to enforce a subsequent security by way
of orders for the possession and sale of mortgaged property, simply
because it has previously brought proceedings pursuant to a personal
guarantee.[56] The creditor may have good reasons for not initially suing
upon the mortgage covenant, and cannot thereby be taken to waive its
rights to rely on the mortgage.[57] Questions of *res judicata* and issue
estoppel may, however, arise if in the subsequent proceedings an issue is

---

[50] *Owen v Homan* (1851) 3 Mac. & G. 378; 42 E.R. 307; *Bell v Banks* (1841) 3 Man. & G. 258;
133 E.R. 1140. See, generally, G. L. Williams, *Joint Obligations* (1949), para.49.
[51] *Barclays Bank Ltd v Beck* [1952] 2 Q.B. 47; *Stamps Commissioner v Hope* [1891] A.C. 476;
Twopenny v Young (1824) 3 B. & C. 208; 107 E.R. 711.
[52] *Barclays Bank Ltd v Beck* [1952] 2 Q.B. 47. Denning L.J., at 53, suggests in this case that
where there is a running account (as in the case of a continuing guarantee) the doctrine of
merger, even if applicable, would only apply to the indebtedness existing when the second
security was taken. This is because the doctrine of merger can only apply to existing debts.
[53] *White v Cuyler* (1795) 6 Term Rep. 176; 101 E.R. 497. This means that a subsequent
security given by a guarantor will not merge a simple contract debt of the principal debtor, or
vice versa.
[54] *Kidd v Boone, Evan's Claim* (1871) 40 L.J. Ch. 531; *Price v Moulton* (1851) 10 C.B. 561; 138
E.R. 222.
[55] Pursuant to CPR 3.4(2).
[56] *Securum Finance Ltd v Ashton* [2001] Ch. 291.
[57] *ibid*, at para.6. And see *National Westminster Bank plc v Kitch* [1996] 1 W.L.R. 1316.

raised which has been already adjudicated upon in the earlier proceedings.[58]

3. DISCHARGE BY EXPIRY OF THE PERIOD OF THE GUARANTEE

9–21   The guarantee may expressly provide that it is to expire at a specified date[59] or after a specified period.[60] The effect of such a provision is that the guarantor will not be liable for advances made to the principal or new transactions entered into with the principal after that date.

9–22   A difficulty exists, however, in respect of liabilities incurred or undertaken by the principal before the expiration of the period of the guarantee when those liabilities do not accrue until after the date on which the guarantee expires. For example, if a guarantee is given in respect of future advances to be made to the principal, and some of those advances, although made during the continuance of the guarantee, are repayable at a future date after the expiration of the guarantee, can the guarantor be made liable for those advances when the principal defaults? The guarantor may argue that as the principal is not in default during the period of the guarantee no liability is incurred in respect of such advances. The editors of *Halsbury* support such an argument, taking the view that "if ... the guarantee is for a specified period, it does not cover obligations undertaken, but not dischargeable, within that period unless it is so worded as to do so".[61]

9–23   In *National House-Building Council v Fraser*,[62] however, Sir Douglas Frank Q.C. in the English High Court expressly disapproved of this statement, thus suggesting that in all cases where the guarantee is for a specified period the guarantor will remain liable for advances which are repayable after the expiration of the period of the guarantee.[63] The case relied upon by the court in supporting its conclusion was *Westminster Bank Ltd v Sassoon*[64] where the contract stated that "This guarantee will expire on 30 June 1925" and no claim was made by the bank upon the guarantor until after that date. These words were interpreted as determining the

---

[58] See below, para.10–228. Such issues did not arise in *Securum Finance Ltd v Ashton* [2001] Ch. 291, because there was no adjudication, the earlier proceedings having been struck out.
[59] *Westminster Bank Ltd v Sassoon, The Times,* November 27, 1926.
[60] *e.g. National House-Building Council v Fraser* [1983] 1 All E.R. 1090, where the guarantee was expressed to expire "three years from the date hereof". Arguments by the guarantor that there is an implied term which limits the period of the guarantee, for example, during the period when the guarantors are directors of the principal debtor company, are unlikely to be successful: see *St George Commercial Credit Corp Ltd v Prior* (unreported, NSW Sup Ct, November 11, 1993).
[61] *Halsbury's Laws of England* (4th ed., 1978), Vol. 3, para.179. See also *McMartin v Graham* (1846) 2 U.C.Q.B. 363.
[62] [1983] 1 All E.R. 1090 at 1092–1093.
[63] Note that on the facts of *National House-Building Council v Fraser* [1983] 1 All E.R. 1090, the principal's default occurred within the period of the guarantee, it being treated as irrelevant that the loss was not quantifiable at that time. The case, therefore, does not directly address the present issue.
[64] *The Times,* November 27, 1926.

guarantor's liability in respect of any new advances after June 30, 1925, but not as determining the guarantee as at that date. Thus the guarantee was a continuing one and remained in existence when the claim was made and the principal's default arose.[65] Analysed in this way *Westminster Bank Ltd v Sassoon* is really only an example of a narrow interpretation being given to a phrase in the guarantee limiting its period of operation so that the conclusion could be reached that the guarantee remained in existence. Although this will usually be the preferred construction, the case does not provide an answer to the question of the guarantor's liability for obligations accruing after the relevant date, where the wording of the guarantee clearly indicates that the guarantee *itself* shall determine at that date.[66] In such a case, and despite the view expressed in *National House-Building Council v Fraser*, it is arguable that the guarantor will not be liable in respect of defaults by the principal accruing after the date of determination of the guarantee unless other wording in the guarantee itself specifically brings within its ambit liabilities of the principal which arise after that date.[67] This result may be achieved by stating that the guarantee shall apply to "liabilities which accrue subsequent to the determination of the guarantee in respect of transactions or advances incurred before its determination". A reference to the guarantor's liability for "contingent" obligations may also have this effect.[68]

Where the guarantee *itself* determines at a specified date and the guarantor's liability arises upon demand,[69] it will also be important that a demand be made by the creditor before the relevant date so as to avoid any argument that the cause of action did not arise against the guarantor during the period of the guarantee.   **9–24**

The procedure to be adopted upon expiry of the period of the guarantee is the same as that to be adopted when the contract of guarantee is revoked.[70]   **9–25**

---

[65] It is not clear from the very short report whether the principal's default arose before or after the stipulated date, but the conclusion that the guarantee was a continuing one meant that it was irrelevant whether or not the default arose after that date. As another example of default occurring within the period of the guarantee, see *Caisse Populaire de Ste Anne du Madawaska Ltee v Tardif* (1985) 61 N.B.R. (2d) 192.

[66] Note that in *Westminster Bank Ltd v Sassoon, The Times*, November 27, 1926, the court was influenced in deciding that the guarantee was a continuing one by the fact that there was a specific provision in the guarantee regarding revocation (by three months' notice on either side), which had not been complied with. In the absence of such a provision, the wording "This guarantee will expire on 30 June 1925" could be regarded as determining the guarantee itself.

[67] For a similar strict construction where a continuing guarantee is revocable, see *National Western Bank v Hardman* [1988] F.L.R. 302 discussed below, paras 9–32 to 9–35.

[68] See above, para.5–74, for a discussion of the meaning of liabilities which are "contingently owing".

[69] See below, para.10–110, for a discussion of the effect of a demand.

[70] See below, para.9–76.

4. DISCHARGE BY REVOCATION OF THE GUARANTEE

(i) Express revocation

9–26   This section analyses the circumstances in which the guarantor can revoke the guarantee. These circumstances can be classified in the following ways:

(a) Where there is no binding contract of guarantee

9–27   The consideration for the guarantee may be expressed to be the creditor entering into the principal transaction, or making further advances to the principal, or supplying goods to the principal. Even if the guarantor signs the guarantee, it does not become a binding legal agreement until the promise to guarantee is supported by consideration in the form stipulated.

9–28   Thus the guarantor can revoke the promise up to that point of time.[71] The creditor will not be able to avoid the possibility of such a revocation by a term in the guarantee itself which prevents revocation or restricts the power to revoke in some way (for example, by a clause which states that the guarantee shall not be determined by notice for a period of 12 months). Such a clause, being a part of the guarantee itself, is also unenforceable because the guarantee is not supported by consideration. The possibility of revocation by the guarantor in these circumstances can be avoided by taking a guarantee under seal, by the creditor furnishing a nominal consideration at the time when the guarantor signs the guarantee,[72] or by providing that the consideration is the creditor's *promise* to enter into the principal transaction.[73] Section 113(6) of the Consumer Credit Act 1974[74] now specifically provides for revocation of the guarantee before it becomes legally binding.

(b) Where the guarantee or principal transaction provides for revocation

9–29   The guarantor may revoke the guarantee when the contract of guarantee provides that it is revocable by notice.[75] Most commonly, the revocation is

---

[71] *Offord v Davies* (1862) 12 C.B. (NS) 748 at 752–753; 142 E.R. 1336 at 1338 (in argument); *North British Mercantile Insurance v Kean* (1888) 16 O.R. 117.
[72] *e.g.*, a nominal sum of money or credit: *Dutchman v Tooth* (1839) 5 Bing. N.C. 577; 132 E.R. 1222; *Johnston v Nicholls* (1845) 1 C.B. 251; 135 E.R. 535.
[73] This last method would, of course, require evidence of such a promise. Assuming this, the consideration would appear to be sufficient, applying normal contractual principles. But *cf.* the doubts expressed in G. Andrews and R. Millett, *Law of Guarantees* (3rd ed., 2000), p.24.
[74] See also s.106, which deems the security as never having effect.
[75] *Commercial Bank of Australia Ltd v Cavanaugh* (1980) 7 N.T.R. 12; *Je Maintiendrai Pty Ltd v ANZ Banking Group Ltd* (1985) 38 S.A.S.R. 70 (purported revocation ineffective because notice not delivered to creditor).

stipulated to take effect after the expiry of a period of time, often three months. The revocation must be clear and explicit,[76] not merely being the expression of a wish by the guarantor that the guarantee[77] be withdrawn, and must also comply strictly with the terms of the clause of revocation. Thus if the clause permitting revocation requires both notice in writing and the payment of any existing liability by the guarantor, these requirements must be complied with before the revocation is effective. In the case of co-guarantors it is a question of construction whether one co-guarantor may exercise his right of revocation without reference to the others. In *Egbert v National Crown Bank*[78] it was held that he could not do so when a joint and several guarantee provided that it should be a continuing guarantee "until the undersigned ... shall have given the bank notice in writing to make no further advances". The expression "the undersigned" was construed as "all the undersigned" rather than "all or any of the undersigned". Indeed this interpretation may be said to be in accordance with the general nature of a joint and several guarantee, which implies that all co-guarantors shall remain parties to it.[79]

Revocation clauses usually provide that notice must actually be **9–30** received by the creditor.[80] It has been argued[81] that such clauses may be invalid pursuant to the Unfair Terms in Consumer Contracts Regulations 1999[82] in the case of consumer transactions, if the same guarantee states that in the case of a demand by the creditor the demand shall be deemed to be received if, for example, it is sent to the guarantor's last known address. These different requirements for service create a "significant imbalance to the detriment of the consumer" within the meaning of Regulation 5(1). No doubt a similar argument can be put forward in determining the issue of reasonableness pursuant to the Unfair Contract Terms Act 1977, although it is doubtful if the Act applies to this type of clause.[83]

The usual effect of the guarantor revoking the guarantee in accordance **9–31** with a simple clause in the agreement permitting revocation is to prevent any future liability arising under the guarantee, but the revocation does not

---

[76] It is in the creditor's interests to draft the revocation clause in precise terms so as to avoid any challenge to the clause on the ground of uncertainty. See *Bank of Baroda v Patel* (unreported, CA, February 4, 1997), where the guarantor unsuccessfully argued that a clause providing that the guarantor may by notice revoke the guarantee and that, at a date "*not less than* three calendar months after receipt by [the creditor]" of such notice, the guarantee shall determine, was too uncertain. The Court of Appeal held, however, that the clause laid down the minimum period of notice, which should be the presumed period of notice if no period was specified by the guarantor.

[77] *Dickson v Royal Bank of Canada* (1975) 66 D.L.R. (3d) 242; *Benge v Hanna* (1979) 100 D.L.R. (3d) 218; *Preston v J Murray-More (NSW) Pty Ltd* (unreported, NSW Sup Ct, May 13, 1983.

[78] [1918] A.C. 903.

[79] See above, para.8–21, in the context of a release of one co-guarantor. *Cf.*, however, a construction more favourable to the guarantor in *Kalil v Standard Bank of South Africa Ltd* [1967] 4 S.A. 550. (AD).

[80] The creditor must be careful to specify the precise address where the notice must be sent. See *Royal Bank of Scotland plc v Slinn* (unreported, CA, March 10, 1989), where the failure to fill in the appropriate spaces in the guarantee left room for ambiguity.

[81] G. Andrews and R. Millett, *Law of Guarantees* (3rd ed., 2000), p.268.

[82] See above, para.4–160.

[83] See above, paras 4–160 to 4–162.

relieve the guarantor from liability already incurred.[84] This is the normal result of revocation[85] even though (as is often the case) the revocation clause does not expressly state that this is to be the effect.

9–32   Sometimes, however, in the case of revocable continuing guarantees which also provide that the obligation of the surety to pay arises only when a demand is made upon him by the creditor, the guarantee may be so drafted that the guarantor's liability is dependent upon the service of a demand upon the guarantor during the period of notice. If this is so, and the creditor fails to make a demand within the required time limit, the guarantor will be released from liability for the total indebtedness. An example is *National Westminster Bank plc v Hardman*,[86] where the relevant provision stated:

> "this guarantee shall be a continuing security and shall remain in force notwithstanding any disability or death of the guarantor until determined by three months' notice in writing from the Guarantor or the Personal Representatives of the Guarantor.
>
> But such determination shall not affect the liability of the Guarantor for the amount due hereunder at the date of expiration of the notice with interest as herein provided until payment in full."

Notice was given by the guarantor in accordance with this clause, but the bank only made a demand some eighteen months after the expiry of the three month notice period. The Court of Appeal held that this drafting clearly indicated that the guarantee itself "ceases to be in force" on the expiry of the three month notice period, and since no demand had been made by that time, nothing was "due hereunder" within the terms of the proviso.

9–33   The Court of Appeal sought to support its interpretation upon policy grounds. Any other construction would mean that the guarantor would remain liable indefinitely (since the limitation period would not commence unless and until there was a demand) and the bank would at any future time be entitled to apply any credit in the guarantor's accounts at the bank towards payment of the debt without making a demand at all. Others robustly assert[87] that "if the wording of the document is not clear, the banks only have themselves to blame if their security is not as extensive or valuable as they had hoped".

9–34   Nevertheless, from the creditor's point of view the result is unduly harsh. The guarantor escapes all liability as a result of a narrow, albeit not unreasonable, construction of the guarantee without any express obligation imposed upon the bank to make a demand during the notice period.

---

[84] See the general principle in *Silverburn Finance Ltd v Salt* [2001] 2 All E.R. (Comm) 438. See also *National House Building Council v Fraser* [1983] 1 All E.R. 1090; *Commercial Bank of Australia Ltd v Cavanaugh* (1980) 7 N.T.R. 12; *AG Canada v Bank of Montreal* (1984) 32 Man. R. (2d) 98.
[85] *Silverburn Finance (UK) Ltd v Salt* [2001] 2 All E.R. (Comm) 438, para.30.
[86] [1988] F.L.R. 302.
[87] G. Andrews and R. Millet, *Law of Guarantees* (3rd ed., 2000), p.267, referring to R. Goode [1988] J.B.L. 264.

This can hardly reflect the commercial intentions of the parties at the date of the agreement.[88]

In any event, the result in *National Westminster Bank plc v Hardman*[89] can be avoided if the relevant provisions indicate that at the end of the period of notice the character of the guarantee as a continuing security determines (rather than the guarantee contract itself), with the guarantor's liability being crystallised at that point of time. This was held to be the effect of the clause in the subsequent Court of Appeal case in *Bank of Credit and Commerce International v Simjee*,[90] which stated that:

9–35

"This guarantee is to be a continuing security to you notwithstanding any settlement of account or other matter or thing whatsoever but may and shall be determined (save as below provided) and the liability hereunder crytallised (except as regards unascertained or contingent liabilities and the interest charges costs and expenses hereinbefore referred to) at the expiration of three months after the receipt by you from the undersigned of notice in writing to determine it but notwithstanding determination as to one or more of the undersigned this Guarantee is to remain a continuing security as to the other or others."[91]

Less obviously, other wording may maintain the guarantor's liability. A proviso that states that the determination of the guarantee by notice "shall not affect the liability of the guarantor for the amount recoverable at the expiration of the notice" has been interpreted[92] as preserving the liability of the guarantor when a demand was not made before the expiry of the notice period. The amount is still "recoverable" in the sense of being "capable of being recovered" as at the date of the demand.

Some contracts of guarantee provide that even though a contract has been effectively revoked, the guarantee can be revived by the guarantor simply signing an acknowledgment to that effect. It is thought that such a clause is ineffective because the original guarantee has been effectively determined by the initial revocation, and any further liability would require another guarantee supported by consideration. The position might be otherwise, however, if it were expressly stated in the guarantee that the revocation suspended the obligations arising under the guarantee, rather than having the usual effect of terminating the guarantee.

9–36

In the case of guarantees of leases for a fixed term, it is sometimes provided by a term of the *principal transaction* (the lease) that the tenant may give notice that the guarantor be released, on condition that a substitute guarantor is provided (so-called substitution clauses). The term will usually require that the landlord must consent to the substitute guarantor, but probably such consent cannot be unreasonably withheld (by

9–37

---

[88] For criticism see D. Marks, "Guarantees—the Rights & Wrongs of Determination" [1994] J.B.L. 121.
[89] [1988] F.L.R. 302.
[90] [1977] C.L.C. 135.
[91] Other clauses of the agreement also supported this result (see especially clause 8, and the analysis at [1997] C.L.C. 135 at 139–140).
[92] *National Westminster Bank Ltd v French* (unreported, October 20, 1977).

analogy with the law regarding assignments).[93] From the landlord's point of view, care must be taken to ensure the drafting of the clause makes it clear that the release of the original guarantor does not come into effect until a substitute guarantor is provided.[94]

(c) A continuing guarantee where the consideration for the guarantee is divisible

9–38   If the guarantee is a continuing guarantee and the consideration for the guarantee is divisible, the guarantee is revocable in respect of liability to accrue in the future.[95] The most common example is a guarantee in respect of advances made or goods supplied from time to time by the creditor to the principal.[96]

9–39   Two explanations of the rule have been advanced. The first, which has attracted considerable judicial support, is that each advance which is made constitutes consideration for the promise to guarantee that advance so that in respect of a future advance the guarantee does not become a legally binding promise supported by consideration until that advance is made.[97] The promise to guarantee can be regarded as being in the nature of a standing offer which matures into a contract of guarantee when a new advance is made.[98] Thus explained, revocation in these circumstances is merely an example of revocation of the guarantee before it becomes legally binding (see (a) above).[99] This rationale explains why the guarantee cannot be revoked when the consideration for the guarantee is a single indivisible act which has been executed by the creditor[1] (for example, by the creditor entering into an indivisible principal transaction or the appointment of the principal by the creditor to a particular office).[2]

---

[93] See *Roux Restaurants Ltd v Jaison Property Development Co Ltd*, 74 P. & C.R. 357 (refusal of consent to assignment unreasonable if the landlord makes consent conditional on variations to the terms of the lease).

[94] See, *e.g. Greenwood (LE) Ltd v Lundy Properties Ltd*, 69 P. & C.R. 507, where the relevant clause was ambiguously drafted.

[95] *Coulthart v Clementson* (1879) 5 Q.B.D. 42 at 46; *Lloyd's v Harper* (1880) 16 Ch. D. 290 at 314, *per* James L.J., at 319–320, *per* Lush L.J.; *Re Crace; Balfour v Crace* [1902] 1 Ch. 733 at 737–738; *Beckett & Co v Addyman* (1882) 9 Q.B.D. 783 at 791; *Offord v Davies* (1862) 12 C.B. (NS) 748 at 757; 142 E.R. 1336; *Re Nicholson* (unreported, Fed Ct of Aust, May 23, 1989, No.854 of 1988); *Western Supplies Ltd v Montanini* (1989) 78 Sask. R. 119 (QB).

[96] *Coulthart v Clementson* (1879) 5 Q.B.D. 42 at 46–47 (advances); *Beckett & Co v Addyman* (1882) 9 Q.B.D. 783 at 791 (goods to be supplied). See also *Wingfield v De St Croix* (1919) 35 T.L.R. 432 (guarantor of rent payable under weekly tenancy may revoke guarantee on expiry of each week of the lease).

[97] *Coulthart v Clementson* (1879) 5 Q.B.D. 42 at 46–47; *Offord v Davies* (1862) 12 C.B. (NS) 748; 142 ER 1336 at 1340; *Lloyd's v Harper* (1880) 16 Ch. D. 290 at 319–320; *Re Crace; Balfour v Crace* [1902] 1 Ch. 733 at 737–738, approving *Offord v Davies*.

[98] *Coulthart v Clementson* (1879) 5 Q.B.D. 42 at 46–47; *Re Nicholson* (unreported, Fed Ct, May 23, 1989).

[99] See above, para.2–49.

[1] *Lloyd's v Harper* (1880) 16 Ch. D. 290 at 314 *per* James L.J., at 318, *per* Cotton L.J., at 319, *per* Lush L.J.; *Re Crace; Balfour v Crace* [1902] 1 Ch. 733 at 738; *Guinness v Box* (1879) 5 V.L.R. (L) 381; *Barclays NZ Ltd v Fogarty* (unreported, HC (NZ) December 1, 1989).

[2] *Lloyd's v Harper* (1880) 16 Ch. D. 290.

If the correct explanation for the rule regarding revocation is that there **9–40** is no consideration for the guarantee as to future advances until a particular advance is made, one result would be that a clause inserted in the guarantee limiting the power to revoke would be ineffective because, before each advance was made, the promise to guarantee would not be legally binding, being unsupported by consideration. Thus the clause, being part of that promise to guarantee, would also have no binding effect upon the guarantor.[3]

It seems unlikely that this explanation of the rule regarding revocation is **9–41** applicable to all guarantees of future advances or goods to be supplied. In particular, it does not explain why revocation is possible where the guarantee is at the outset a binding legal agreement.[4] This may occur because it is under seal or because it is clear from the proper construction of the guarantee that the first advance which is made by the creditor is consideration both for the promise to guarantee that advance *and* also future advances.[5] In such a case it cannot be argued that there is no binding guarantee as to a future advance until that advance is made.

The second explanation of the rule permitting revocation of a guarantee **9–42** where the consideration is divisible rests on general equitable grounds. James L.J. in *Lloyd's v Harper*[6] stated the principle in these terms:

"It may be considered equitable and right that where a man is not under any obligation to make further advances or to sell further goods, a person who has guaranteed repayment of such advances, or payment of the price of the goods, may say, 'Do not sell any further goods or make any further advances; I give you warning that you are not to rely upon my guarantee for any further advances which you make, or for any further goods you sell'. That might be in many cases a very equitable view. It perhaps might be hardly equitable for a banker or merchant to go on making advances after receiving a distinct notice from the guarantor that he would not be further liable."[7]

Some early formulations of such an equitable rule imposed a limitation **9–43** that before the guarantor could revoke in respect of future advances, the guarantor must have discovered that the principal was "unworthy of credit",[8] but such a limitation has now been discarded.[9] Yet the right to

---

[3] Lush L.J. in *Lloyd's v Harper* (1880) 16 Ch. D. 290 at 319, however, does contemplate that the guarantee may limit the power of revocation, even though he adopts the view that a guarantee of future advances is an arrangement in which "the consideration is supplied from time to time". See also *Offord v Davies* (1862) 12 C.B. (NS) 748 at 757; 142 E.R. 1336 at 1340 where Erle C.J. appears to assume that a clause which is properly drafted could prohibit revocation for a stipulated period.
[4] Joyce J. in *Re Crace; Balfour v Crace* [1902] 1 Ch. 733 at 737–738 stated that the rule applied to contracts under seal. See also *Beckett & Co v Addyman* (1882) 9 Q.B.D. 783 at 791 where this was assumed and *Lloyd's v Harper* (1880) 16 Ch. D. 290 at 314, 319, where the rule was stated sufficiently widely to encompass guarantees under seal.
[5] For a detailed discussion of consideration, see above, para.2–49.
[6] (1880) 16 Ch. D. 290.
[7] *ibid.*, at 314.
[8] *Burgess v Eve* (1872) L.R. 13 Eq. 450 at 459.
[9] As indicated by the formulation of the rule by James L.J. in *Lloyd's v Harper* (1880) 16 Ch. D. 290 at 314.

revoke will only be allowed where the consideration for the guarantee is divisible (for example, a guarantee of future advances or goods to be supplied from time to time).[10]

9–44   If the right of revocation is based on this general equitable rule, there is no difficulty in applying it to circumstances in which the guarantee is at the outset a binding agreement as to both present and future advances (for example, where it is under seal). The guarantee is then simply a binding agreement which contains an implied equitable right to revoke.

9–45   If the correct view is that the right to revoke is founded in equity, it is at least possible that the courts could have taken the view that the right could not be modified or excluded. But this has never been the case. There has merely been an insistence that the right to revoke should be explicit. Thus a general clause to the effect that the guarantors jointly and severally guarantee "for the space of 12 calendar months" future transactions will not exclude a right of revocation, because it may reasonably be interpreted as designating a period of time beyond which the guarantors' liability cannot extend, rather than making it clear that the guarantors cannot revoke within that period.[11]

(ii) Implied revocation

(a) Death of the guarantor

9–46   Where there is a continuing guarantee revocable during the lifetime of the guarantor because the consideration for the guarantee is divisible, the guarantee is determined upon the creditor receiving notice of the guarantor's death,[12] even though notice is received in an indirect way via a third party.[13] It is unnecessary for the guarantor's personal representatives to revoke the guarantee itself.[14] This conclusion was originally based on the belief that notice of death and the existence of a will represented notice to the creditor of the existence of trusts which might be incompatible with continuance of the guarantee.[15] Subsequently, however, the rule was extended to cases of intestacy.[16] The only possible, but unlikely, exception is where the guarantor's will contains an option to continue the guarantee so that the creditor may assume that, in spite of the guarantor's death, the guarantee is not to be determined.[17]

---

[10] *Re Crace; Balfour v Crace* [1902] 1 Ch. 733 at 738.
[11] See this clause and its interpretation in *Offord v Davies* (1862) 12 C.B. (NS) 748; 142 E.R. 1336 at 1340. As to the express wording of the guarantee overriding the equitable rule as to revocation, see also *W H Jones & Co (London) Ltd v Millar* (unreported, HC (NZ) November 26, 1991); on appeal: (June 5, 1991).
[12] *Coulthart v Clementson* (1879) 5 Q.B.D. 42; *Re Whelan* [1897] 1 I.R. 575. See above, para.9–38, for a discussion of the right of revocation where the consideration is divisible.
[13] *Re Whelan* [1897] 1 I.R. 575. But the creditor must have some knowledge of the death: *Bradbury v Morgan* (1862) 1 H. & C. 249; 158 E.R. 877; *Fennell v McGuire* (1870) 21 C.P. 134.
[14] *Coulthart v Clementson* (1879) 5 Q.B.D. 42 at 47.
[15] *ibid.*
[16] *Re Whelan* [1897] 1 I.R. 575.
[17] *Coulthart v Clementson* (1879) 5 Q.B.D. 42 at 47.

If the consideration for the guarantee consists of a single act which has **9–47** been undertaken by the creditor so that the guarantee is not revocable during the lifetime of the guarantor, the death of the guarantor has no effect (unless the terms of the guarantee prescribe otherwise).[18] On this basis in *Basch v Stekel*[19] the obligations of a guarantor of a fixed term lease were enforceable against his estate.

The fact that a continuing guarantee is determined by notice of death **9–48** has been criticised on the basis that it is inconsistent with earlier authority which reached a contrary conclusion by reference to the general rule that the contractual obligations of the deceased shall enure to the deceased's estate,[20] unless some personal element is involved in the transaction.[21] Indeed, there has been so much judicial disagreement[22] (albeit dicta) with the rule that it cannot be considered beyond reversal.

This issue is probably not of great importance because most contracts of **9–49** guarantee of a continuing nature negate the general rule by a term in the guarantee. A clause stating that "this guarantee shall not be determined by [the guarantor's] death" will be effective to preserve the guarantor's liability even after the creditor has notice of death.[23] The clause will not be interpreted as merely restating the general law that death will only have effect once the creditor receives notice of it.[24] A less specific clause will also achieve the same objective. Thus a provision that the guarantors "or their personal representatives" might determine their liability by a month's notice in writing to the creditor was interpreted to mean that the guarantee could only be determined upon the personal representative giving one month's notice in writing revoking the guarantee. Hence the guarantee was not determined simply by the creditor receiving notice that the guarantor was dead.[25] But if the clause states only that the guarantor may determine the guarantee on giving a period of notice, without any specific reference to the personal representatives of the guarantor, this is probably insufficient to negate the general rule that the mere receipt of notice of death by the creditor will determine the guarantee. The clause will be interpreted as merely imposing an obligation to give notice of revocation of the guarantee upon the guarantor during his lifetime, with no such obligation devolving upon the guarantor's personal representatives in the event of the guarantor's death.[26]

---

[18] As to those circumstances where the guarantee will not be revocable during the lifetime of the guarantor, see above, para.9–39.
[19] [2001] L. & T.R.I.
[20] See *Basch v Stekel* [2001] L. & T.R.I.
[21] This was clearly the reasoning in *Bradbury v Morgan* (1862) 1 H. & C. 249; 158 E.R. 877. As an example of a personal contract, see *Re Peacock* [1930] V.L.R. 9.
[22] *Re Crace; Balfour v Crace* [1902] 1 Ch. 733 at 739; *Re Silvester* [1895] 1 Ch. 573 at 577; *Beckett & Co v Addyman* (1882) 9 Q.B.D. 783 at 792. But note also that in *Harriss v Fawcett* (1873) 15 L.R. Eq. 311 at 313 Lord Romilly M.R. doubted the correctness of *Bradbury v Morgan* (1862) 1 H. & C. 249; 158 E.R. 877.
[23] *Carlton & United Breweries Ltd v Wilson* [1933] V.L.R. 113.
[24] *ibid.*
[25] *Re Silvester* [1895] 1 Ch. 573; *Toronto Dominion Bank v Brot* [1958] O.R. 152.
[26] *Harriss v Fawcett* (1873) 8 Ch. App. 866. But note that the guarantee stated specifically that the notice must be given in writing "under [the guarantor's] hand".

9–50   Where the liability of the guarantors is joint and several, the death of one guarantor will not discharge the others, even though the estate of the dead guarantor is itself released[27] since the death of one of the co-guarantors is a possible event which must have been in the contemplation of the parties at the time of the execution of the guarantee.[28] The position in respect of the death of a co-guarantor is thus different from the effect of the creditor releasing one of a number of co-guarantors who are jointly and severally bound. In these circumstances it has been held that the words "joint and several" impose an obligation upon the creditor not to release one of the guarantors and if the creditor does effect such a release, the others will be discharged.[29]

9–51   In the unlikely event that the liability of the co-guarantors is joint, the effect of the death of one of the co-guarantors is less clear. In *Ashby v Day*,[30] Lord Esher M.R. was of the view that the death of one joint surety terminates the obligations of the surviving sureties,[31] but this obiter dictum has been rightly criticised on the basis that it is contrary to the well-established principle that there is survivorship of joint obligations.[32]

(b) Certified mental illness of the guarantor

9–52   It has been held that the certified mental illness of the guarantor to the knowledge of the creditor will determine a continuing guarantee at the guarantor's option.[33] This view is in accordance with normal contractual principles,[34] although there is some suggestion that the plaintiff can sue on a contract even if there is knowledge of the disability, provided that the contract is fair.[35] This exception is, however, unlikely to apply to a guarantee. A provision is often included in the guarantee expressly preventing determination of the guarantee on the basis of the mental illness of the guarantor.

(c) A change in the constitution of the principal or the creditor

9–53   A change in the constitution of either the principal debtor or the creditor may occur in a variety of ways. For example, a sole trader may enter into a partnership, or the sole trader's business may be incorporated, or a business name may be changed; in the case of a partnership, there may be an increase or decrease in the number of partners; and in the case of a

---

[27] *Beckett & Co v Addyman* (1882) 9 Q.B.D. 783.
[28] *ibid.*
[29] See above, para.8–21.
[30] (1886) 54 L.T. 408.
[31] *ibid.*, at 410. Lindley L.J. at 410–411, and Lopes L.J. at 411 specifically left the point open.
[32] G. L. Williams, *Joint Obligations* (1949), para.71.
[33] *Bradford Old Bank v Sutcliffe* [1918] 2 K.B. 833, at first instance: see the findings of Lawrence J. at 835–836.
[34] See G.H. Treitel, *The Law of Contract* (11th ed, 2003), p.557. Under the general law, the contract is voidable at the patient's option.
[35] *ibid.*, *Dane v Kirkwall* (1838) 8 C. & P. 679; 173 E.R. 670.

company, it may be taken over by another company or there may be a change in its status.[36] In *First National Finance Corporation Ltd v Goodman*[37] the Court of Appeal (in the context of a company amalgamation) stated the general principle that a change in the identity of the creditor or debtor revokes the guarantee as to future transactions, unless there is an express or implied agreement in the guarantee to contrary effect.[38] But the case law and (in the case of partnership)[39] legislation requires analysis in those various situations which may arise.

(i) A principal who is a sole trader entering into a partnership

If the guarantee is drafted so as to secure the debts of a named individual, it will generally apply only to debts incurred by that individual whilst acting alone.[40] The guarantee will, therefore, be ineffective to secure further advances after the named individual enters into a partnership,[41] and any additional security given by the guarantor will be ineffective to secure such advances.[42] The guarantee, however, should be construed in the light of surrounding circumstances[43] and, having regard to these circumstances, the guarantee may be interpreted as extending to debts incurred by the partnership, even though it specifically refers to a named individual.[44] One factor that is relevant in this context is the guarantor's knowledge at the time of entering the guarantee that the principal intended to enter into a partnership.[45] Thus in *Leathley v Spyer*[46] the guarantor, after the cancellation of an initial guarantee, entered into a second guarantee with knowledge of a proposed partnership. It was held in the light of these facts that his guarantee extended to debts incurred after the formation of the partnership because otherwise the guarantee would have been meaningless.[47] Knowledge of the guarantor about a proposed partnership is, however, only one factor to be taken into account in determining the scope of the guarantee and, despite such knowledge, the wording of the guarantee itself or other surrounding circumstances may indicate that the guarantee should be limited to debts incurred by the named individual before entering the partnership.[48]

9–54

---

[36] *e.g.*, from a private to a public company.
[37] [1983] B.C.L.C. 203.
[38] *ibid.*, at 209.
[39] See below, para.9–57.
[40] *Bellairs v Ebsworth* (1811) 3 Camp. 53; 170 E.R. 1303; *Montefiore v Lloyd* (1863) 15 C.B. (NS) 203; 143 E.R. 761.
[41] *ibid.*
[42] *Bank of Scotland v Christie* (1840) 8 Cl. & Fin. 214; 8 E.R. 84 (security given by one partner to secure debts of the partnership).
[43] *Leathley v Spyer* (1870) L.R. 5 C.P. 595 at 602, *per* Willes. J; *Montefiore v Lloyd* (1863) 15 C.B. (NS) 203; 143 E.R. 761.
[44] In *Leathley v Spyer* (1870) L.R. 5 C.P. 595 the guarantee referred to a named individual. See also *Bank of British North America v Cuvillier* (1861) 4 L.T. 159.
[45] *Leathley v Spyer* (1870) L.R. 5 C.P. 595.
[46] (1870) L.R. 5 C.P. 595.
[47] *ibid.*, at 603, *per* Willes J., 605, *per* Keating J. In *Bank of British North America v Cuvillier* (1861) 4 L.T. 159, it was probably contemplated by the guarantee that the sole trader might take in partners.
[48] See *Montefiore v Lloyd* (1863) 15 C.B. (NS) 203; 143 E.R. 761, where the guarantor was held liable despite the fact that the guarantor had knowledge of the intending partnership. But

9–55   Some guarantees of debts incurred by sole traders avoid these problems of construction by specifically providing that the guarantee will apply to debts incurred by the sole trader after entry into a partnership.

(ii) A creditor who is a sole trader entering into a partnership

9–56   There is little authority on the effect of a creditor who is a sole trader entering into a partnership. It is likely that, if the guarantee is given to a named creditor, that creditor can recover only in respect of debts of other obligations which are owed to the creditor and future advances made by the partnership of which the creditor later becomes a member will not be caught by the guarantee.[49] The result is that the guarantee is revoked as to future liability. However, it may be possible to infer an agreement that the creditor referred to in the guarantee embraces the creditor while operating in partnership as well as while trading individually, so that the later advances made by the partnership will be within the scope of the guarantee.[50]

(iii) A change in constitution of the principal where it is a partnership

9–57   In the case of an already existing partnership, the law is governed by s.18 of the Partnership Act 1890 This provides:

> "A continuing guaranty or cautionary obligation given either to a firm or to a third person in respect of the transactions of a firm is, in the absence of agreement to the contrary, revoked as to future transactions by any change in the constitution of the firm to which, or of the firm in respect of the transactions of which, the guaranty or obligation was given."[51]

9–58   The section substantially re-enacted earlier statute law.[52] It has potential application not only to partnerships between individuals but also to corporate partnerships between companies in the same group.[53]

---

the decision was not reached without difficulty: see at 218–219; 767 *per* Byles J.; at 220; 768 *per* Keating J.

[49] See *Wright v Russel* (1774) 3 Wils. 530; 95 E.R. 1195 (fidelity guarantee). The conclusion in the text is supported by s.18 of the Partnership Act (which is discussed below) which provides that where there is a change in the constitution of a firm to which the guarantee is given the guarantee is revoked as to future transactions. The section does not strictly apply to the case of a sole trader entering into a partnership because the sole trader is not "a firm", *i.e.* "persons who have entered into partnership with one another", But the situation of a change of partnership is obviously analogous.

[50] *e.g. Barclay v Lucas* (1783) 1 Term Rep. 291; 99 E.R. 676, although this was a case of a change in the constitution of a partnership and not a situation where a sole trader enters into a partnership. The correctness of *Barclay v Lucas* was questioned in *Weston v Barton* (1812) 4 Taunt 673; 128 E.R. 495. Note also the possible application of the doctrine of estoppel by convention: see above, para.5–94.

[51] Partnership Act 1890, s.18.

[52] Mercantile Law Amendment Act 1856, s.4; Mercantile Law Amendment (Scotland) Act 1856, s.7. A similar rule previously existed at common law: see *Backhouse v Hall* (1865) 6 B. & S. 507 at 520; 122 E.R. 1283 at 1287–1288, *per* Blackburn J.

[53] *Re Rogers* (1989) 20 F.C.R. 561, where it was held that the existence of a common accounting system and the registration of a common business name did not establish that the group of companies was trading as a partnership.

The effect of the provision, insofar as it relates to changes in the **9–59** constitution of the principal debtor, is to revoke the guarantee in respect of future transactions where there is an increase in the number of partners, or a decrease in the number of partners due to death[54] or retirement.[55] The section will probably not operate where there are changes to the partnership deed of a less substantial nature, for example, by alterations to the share of partnership profits to be received by each partner. This is not a change in the constitution of the firm, but merely a change in its profit-sharing formula.

The section recognises that the general presumption of revocation may **9–60** be displaced if there is a contrary agreement. Presumably, as in the case where a sole trader enters into a partnership, the agreement may be inferred by construing the guarantee in the light of surrounding circumstances.[56] But such an agreement will not be inferred merely because the guarantee is expressed to operate for a definite period[57] or because the guarantee refers to the principal debtor in terms of a general business name without reference to the current partners.[58] In *Backhouse v Hall*,[59] the guarantee described the principal as "the firm of GW & WJ Hall, Shipbuilders", even though three different partners then carried on the business. It was held that the use of the general business name did not displace the general rule that the guarantee is discharged as to future dealings by a subsequent change in the firm's constitution. Nor will the general rule as to revocation be displaced by clauses in the partnership deed allowing for a transmission of the share of a deceased partner by providing that the executor shall be deemed to be a partner.[60]

There may be a clause in the guarantee specifically providing for a **9–61** guarantee of partnership debts to continue notwithstanding a change in the constitution of the firm. The clause, however, should be drafted so as to encompass all the situations which involve a change in the constitution. Thus an express clause stating that the liability of the guarantor was not to be affected by the *retirement* of any one of the partners did not prevent the guarantee being revoked as to future dealings by the *death* of one of the partners.[61] Conversely, if the clause contemplates the guarantee remaining in force despite the death of one of the partners, this will not cover the case of a partner's retirement.[62] A widely drafted clause along the following

---

[54] e.g. *Simson v Cooke* (1824) 1 Bing. 452; 130 E.R. 181.
[55] e.g. *National Mortgage & Agency Co of New Zealand Ltd v Tait* [1929] N.Z.L.R. 235 (dissolution of partnership); *University of Cambridge v Baldwin* (1839) 5 M. & W. 580; 151 E.R. 246.
[56] See *Leathley v Spyer* (1870) L.R. 5 C.P. 595. This is a case dealing with the entry by a sole trader into a partnership, where such an approach is permitted.
[57] *Hollond v Teed* (1848) 7 Hare 50; 68 E.R. 20. This is a case dealing with a change in the constitution of the creditor, but the same point of construction would apply here. Similarly if the guarantee is terminable only on written notice: *Colonial Bank of New Zealand v Smith* (1888) 6 N.Z.L.R. 659 at 661.
[58] *Backhouse v Hall* (1865) 6 B & S 507; 122 E.R. 1283.
[59] ibid.
[60] *Chapman v Beckinton* (1842) 3 Q.B. 703; 114 E.R. 676.
[61] *Huon v Dougharty* (1894) 20 V.L.R. 30.
[62] See *University of Cambridge v Baldwin* (1839) 5 M. & W. 580; 151 E.R. 246. See also *Pemberton v Oakes* (1827) 4 Russ 154; 38 E.R. 763.

lines would be effective to preserve the liability of the guarantor in all circumstances where the constitution of the principal debtor is changed:

> "Notwithstanding any change or changes in the name of the customer's firm or any change or changes in the membership of the customer's firm by death, retirement, introduction of a partner or partners, or any other change in the constitution of the firm the liability of the undersigned shall continue and the provisions hereof shall be applicable to any debts whether incurred before or after such changes."[63]

9–62   The agreement necessary to displace the general rule in S.18 of the Partnership Act as to revocation has generally been found in the terms of the guarantee itself, but it is possible that the necessary rebutting evidence may be in the form of a subsequent oral consent by the guarantor to remain liable for future advances at or before the date of the change in the constitution of the firm.[64]

(iv) A change in the constitution of the creditor where it is a partnership

9–63   Section 18 of the Partnership Act 1890, which is quoted above, also applies where there is a change in the constitution of the firm *to which* the guarantee is given. Thus where the creditor is a partnership, an increase in the number of partners,[65] or a decrease through retirement[66] or death,[67] will discharge the guarantor as regards future advances. The general rule may be displaced by agreement, but again an agreement to the contrary will not be inferred merely because the guarantee is expressed to operate for a definite period[68] or because the guarantee refers to the creditor in terms of a general business name without reference to the current partners.[69] One special example where an agreement has been inferred displacing the general rule is in the case of a promissory note payable to order given to a partnership to secure a debt where the maker does not appear on the face of the instrument to be merely a surety.[70]

9–64   If the creditor is a partnership, it is essential that the guarantee contains a specific provision preserving the liability of the guarantor for future advances despite a change in the constitution of the creditor. As in the case of a clause providing for the contingency of a change in the constitution of the principal debtor, the provision should be drafted so as to encompass all situations affecting the constitution of the firm.[71]

---

[63] See a similar clause in *Bank of Montreal v Berthelotte* [1953] O.W.N. 86.
[64] But quaere whether such consent amounts to an "agreement to the contrary" within the wording of the section.
[65] *Spiers v Houston* (1829) 4 Bli. (NS) 515; 5 E.R. 183.
[66] *Myers v Edge* (1797) 7 Term Rep. 254; 101 E.R. 960; *Dry v Davy* (1839) 10 Ad. & El. 30; 113 E.R. 12.
[67] *Strange v Lee* (1803) 3 East 484; 102 E.R. 682; *Barker v Parker* (1786) 1 Term Rep. 287; 99 E.R. 1098; *Weston v Barton* (1812) 4 Taunt 673; 128 E.R. 495.
[68] *Hollond v Teed* (1848) 7 Hare 50; 68 E.R. 20.
[69] *Backhouse v Hall* (1865) 6 B. & S. 507; 122 E.R. 1283. The general principles of construction which are discussed above in relation to the change in the constitution of the principal debtor would also be relevant in this context.
[70] *Pease v Hirst* (1829) 10 B. & C. 122; 109 E.R. 396.
[71] See this clause set out in the previous section.

(v) The incorporation of the principal

When the principal is incorporated after the execution of a guarantee, **9-65** the guarantor generally will be discharged as to future liability because the guarantee will relate only to the obligations of a principal which is unincorporated.[72] If, however, the incorporation of the company is contemplated at the date of the execution of the guarantee, it is possible (although unlikely) that the guarantee may be drafted so as to bring within its scope obligations owed by the new company.[73] Upon incorporation, there may be an assignment of the principal's interest in the contract to the new company with the creditor's consent, or, alternatively, there may be a novation whereby the company is substituted as the new principal debtor. The effect of such arrangements on the guarantor's liability is referred to elsewhere.[74]

(vi) The incorporation of the creditor

The incorporation of the creditor will discharge the guarantor as regards **9-66** the obligations of the principal incurred subsequent to the incorporation because the company constitutes a new legal entity and is not a party to the guarantee.[75] Thus in *Dance v Girdler*,[76] the guarantor's obligation to an unincorporated society was discharged when the society was incorporated, even though the guarantee was given to the governors of the society and "their successors".[77] It should be emphasised that in *Dance v Girdler* there was no suggestion that the fact of incorporation amounted to a variation of the principal contract,[78] which would discharge the guarantor absolutely. The usual procedure when the creditor is incorporated is for the benefit of the principal transaction and the benefit of the guarantee to be assigned to the company, which will then usually be able to enforce both contracts. Alternatively, there may be a novation whereby the company is substituted as the new creditor. The effect of such arrangements on the guarantor's liability is discussed in detail elsewhere.[79]

---

[72] For a similar situation, see *Massey-Ferguson Ltd v Crittenden* (1966) 56 W.W.R. 288, where a guarantor of partnership liabilities was held not to be responsible for liabilities incurred by a former partner when those liabilities had been incurred under a director's guarantee given by the former partner when the partnership was incorporated. See also above, para.5–63.

[73] Note also the possible application of the doctrine of estoppel by convention, above, para.5–94.

[74] See above, paras 6–98 to 6–109.

[75] *Dance v Girdler* (1804) 1 Bos & P.N.R. 34 at 43; 127 E.R. 370 at 374. Note, exceptional cases where the incorporating statute expressly provides for the transfer of rights and obligations: *Eastern Union Railway Co v Cochrane* (1853) 9 Exch. 197; 156 E.R. 84; *London Brighton & South Coast Railway Co v Goodwin* (1849) 3 Exch. 320; 154 E.R. 1042.

[76] (1804) 1 Bos & P.N.R. 34; 127 E.R. 370.

[77] In *Universal Co v Yip* (unreported, CA, June 18, 1986) a similar argument by the guarantor failed because no attempt was made to distinguish between liabilities incurred before and those incurred after incorporation. Note that the reference in *Dance v Girdler* (*ibid.*) to "successors" may mean that the new entity could enforce the guarantee pursuant to the Contracts (Rights of Third Parties) Act 1999 (see s.1) since it is arguable that the provision purports to confer a benefit on a third party expressly identified as a member of a class (see s.1(1)(b) and (3)).

[78] See above, Ch. 7.

[79] See above, paras 6–110 to 6–116 and below, paras 10–173 to 10–200.

(vii) Amalgamations and takeovers

9–67   As held in *First National Finance Corp Ltd v Goodman*,[80] if there is an amalgamation or takeover of the creditor so that a new legal identity is created, the guarantee will be revoked in respect of future transactions or advances entered into or made by that new identity.[81] The guarantor's liability in respect of future transactions will, however, often be preserved by a clause stating that the guarantee shall be binding and shall continue to operate notwithstanding any change of legal identity of the creditor,[82] or, alternatively, by a clause defining the creditor to include its "successors, assigns, and any company with which it may amalgamate"[83] (assuming in each case that the guarantee is assigned to the new identity).[84] Sometimes, however, despite such clauses, the substantive provisions of the guarantee may narrow the scope of the guarantee to embrace only obligations arising out of transactions between the principal and *original* creditor. In *Housing Guarantee Fund Ltd v Yusef*,[85] a guarantee was given in favour of the Master Builders' Housing Fund Ltd (MBHFL) to secure the obligations of a builder pursuant to the rules of that organisation. The guarantee was assigned to the Housing Guarantee Fund Ltd (HGFL), which was to replace MBHFL pursuant to a statutory scheme of arrangement. It was held that the guarantee could not be enforced in respect of the obligations of the builder to HGFL (and under the rules of HGFL) since the terms of the guarantee related only to liability arising from the rules of the pre-existing entity, MBHFL.

9–68   Similarly, if a new legal identity as principal is created by amalgamation or take-over, the guarantee will be revoked as to future transactions. This result is less easily avoided by drafting since the guarantee will have to embrace advances to a new principal debtor, which may not be in contemplation at the date of the execution of the guarantee. Otherwise the future advances will be outside the scope of the guarantee. As an example in *National Bank of New Zealand v West*,[86] a directors' guarantee was given "in consideration of advances or other banking accommodation ... made or given by The National Bank of New Zealand Ltd ... to Allied Wools (Otago) Ltd". It was planned to form a single new company by amalgamating three associated companies, including Allied Wools (Otago) Ltd, but in the interval before the new company was formed, it was agreed that loans by the bank should be

---

[80] [1983] B.C.L.C. 203.
[81] *ibid.*, at 209. A change of shareholding in a company will not constitute a new legal entity *Gill & Duffus SA v Rionda Futures Ltd* [1994] 2 Lloyd's Law Rep. 67 at 84.
[82] As referred to in *First National Finance Corp Ltd v Goodman* [1983] B.C.L.C. 203 at 212.
[83] See this clause in *First National Finance Corp Ltd v Goodman* [1983] B.C.L.C. 203 at 209. If the creditor holds the guarantee in an official capacity (*e.g.* public office holder or trustee) a change in the personal identity of the creditor will probably not discharge the guarantor. See *M'Gahey v Alston* (1836) 1 M. & W. 386; *Town of Truro v McCulloch* (1971) 22 D.L.R. (3d) 293.
[84] At least in respect of transactions to which the Contracts (Rights of Third Parties) Act 1999 does not apply. See below, paras 10–161 to 10–167.
[85] (1990) 8 A.C.L.C. 1197.
[86] [1978] 2 N.Z.L.R. 451. See also *Reid Murray Holdings Ltd (in liq) v David Murray Holdings Pty Ltd* (19720 5 S.A.S.R. 386, discussed above, para.5–63.

made to another of the associated companies, called International T & F (Wool) Co Ltd. It was held that advances made to International T & F (Wool) Co Ltd were not advances made to "Allied Wools (Otago) Ltd" within the meaning of the guarantee.

(viii) A change in business name

A change in business name (not involving a constitutional re-arrangement such as the formation of a partnership or incorporation) will probably not affect the guarantor's liability, provided that after the change the business is identifiable as the same creditor or principal, as the case may be.[87] For example, if a principal carries on business as a sole trader in the name of "XY painters" and later uses the name of "Y painters" whilst still carrying on business as a sole trader, the guarantor's liability will not be affected provided that it is clear from the evidence that the two concerns are the same.[88]

9–69

(ix) A change in place of business

In general, a change of the place of business will not affect the guarantor's liability unless it can be shown that there is a condition of the guarantee that either the creditor or the principal shall carry on business at a particular location. Thus in *Spencer, Turner and Boldero v Lotz*[89] the guarantee, which was stated to be "in consideration of your selling goods to Mr James Bennett, of 40–42 Hightown-road, Luton", was interpreted as being effective only whilst James Bennett, the principal debtor, carried on business at that address.

9–69A

(d) A change in the constitution of the guarantor

Whilst (as we have seen) a guarantee will be revoked by a change of identity of the creditor or principal, in *Gill & Duffus SA v Rionda Futures Ltd*[90] Clarke J. saw "no reason to extend" the principle to a change of identity of the guarantor. In the case of personal guarantees this will invariably be true, but it is possible to envisage changes to the identity of a guarantor which might revoke the guarantee as to future transactions (for example, in the case of a company guarantor when the company amalgamates and a new legal identity is created).[91]

9–70

---

[87] This is supported by *Wilson v Craven* (1841) 8 M. & W. 584 at 596; 151 E.R. 1171 at 1176 where the view was expressed that a change of name is immaterial so long as the creditor remains "the same body"; *Gill & Duffus SA, Rionda Futures Ltd* [1994] 2 Lloyd's Rep. 67 at 84.
[88] See also *Groux's Improved Soap Co Ltd v Cooper* (1860) 8 C.B. (NS) 800; 141 E.R. 1380.
[89] (1916) 32 T.L.R. 373.
[90] [1994] 2 Lloyd's Law Rep. 67 at 84.
[91] Although the statement in *Gill & Duffus SA v Rionda Futures Ltd* [1994] 2 Lloyd's Rep. 67 was given in the context of a company guarantee

(e) Termination of the principal transaction?

9–71   Sometimes it has been said that a continuing guarantee is impliedly revoked when the principal transaction is itself terminated. Thus in *Silverburn Finance Ltd v Salt*[92] guarantees securing money "in respect of any unpaid invoices" due to the creditor pursuant to a factoring agreement were revoked in respect of future liabilities by an agreed termination of the factoring agreement since "the legal relationship, in support of which the guarantees were supplied, was extinguished".[93] Yet this is really no more than an example of discharge of the future liabilities of the guarantor by determination of the principal transaction, which applies equally to guarantees of fixed obligations as well as continuing guarantees.[94]

(iii) Effect of revocation

9–72   The general effect of revocation is that the guarantor will be relieved of future liabilities but will remain liable in respect of accrued liabilities.[95] There are, however, two particular difficulties. The first is whether upon revocation the guarantor will remain liable in respect of liabilities which have been incurred or undertaken before the date of revocation but which only accrue after revocation. For example, if a guarantee is given in respect of future advances which are made to the principal before revocation but which are only repayable at a future date after the date of revocation, can the guarantor be made liable for those advances? The question has already been discussed elsewhere[96] in the context of the expiry of the period of the guarantee and the same considerations apply here. In the context of revocation, Sir Douglas Frank Q.C. was of the view in *National House-Building Council v Fraser*[97] that the guarantee cannot be revoked so as to exclude such outstanding liabilities. But this cannot be a matter of law and it will be a matter of construction in each case whether such liabilities are brought within the ambit of the guarantee.[98]

9–73   Some guarantees contain provisions designed to preserve the guarantor's liability in respect of liabilities of the principal which will accrue after revocation. For instance, the guarantee may state that it can only be

---

[92] [2001] 2 All E.R. (Comm) 438.
[93] *ibid.*, para.31.
[94] See above, Ch. 6.
[95] *Silverburn Finance (UK) Ltd v Salt* [2001] 2 All E.R. (Comm) 438; *Commercial Bank of Australia Ltd v Cavanaugh* (1980) 7 N.T.R. 12. See, however, the particular guarantee in *National Westminster Bank v Hardman* (unreported, CA, November 11, 1993), discussed above, paras 9–32 to 9–35.
[96] See above, paras 9–22 to 9–25.
[97] [1983] 1 All E.R. 1090. Sir Douglas Frank Q.C. appears to approve a passage in *Halsbury's Laws of England* (4th ed., 1978), Vol. 3, para.179 which states: "It appears that a continuing guarantee cannot be revoked so as to exclude outstanding liabilities properly undertaken by the banker on the faith of it, such as bills accepted by him current at the time of revocation".
[98] See *Hollond v Teed* (1848) 7 Hare 49 at 56; 68 E.R. 20 at 23, the decision usually cited in this context, where Sir James Wigram specifically states that "the language of the guarantee disposes of the question". See also *Parkes v Commonwealth Bank of Australia* (1990) A.S.C. 56–020 at 59–212.

revoked by the guarantor "making full provision up to the limit of the guarantee for any liabilities or obligations which are contingent at the time of revocation".[99] The reference to "contingent obligations" is probably sufficient to bring future liabilities of the principal within the ambit of the guarantee. In view of the ambiguity of the expression, however,[1] it would be wise for the creditor, if it is intended to include such liabilities, to refer specifically to "liabilities which accrue after revocation in respect of obligations or transactions incurred by the principal before revocation".

The second difficulty arises where there is a clause in the guarantee **9–74** providing for a specific period of notice to be given by the guarantor before the revocation becomes effective to determine the guarantee. Can the creditor grant further advances to the principal after receiving notice of revocation, but before the notice becomes effective? It has been suggested[2] that the creditor cannot increase the potential liability of the guarantor in this way once notice has been received, and that the creditor will be unable to recover these additional advances from the guarantor. This view is based on the general ground of "the duty of the guaranteed party to behave equitably towards the guarantor".[3]

There is, however, little concrete authority to support such a conclusion. **9–75** Reliance on the general principle that the creditor must not act to the prejudice of the guarantor would appear optimistic given the reluctance of the courts to accept this proposition.[4] More specifically, it is true that in *Lloyd's v Harper*,[5] the power of the guarantor to revoke a continuing guarantee was said to be based on considerations of equity,[6] but the comment was neither made in the context of the present issue, nor in the context of a guarantee which contained a contractual right to revoke upon a specified period of notice being given. However, given the doubts about the issue and the uncertain application of the creditor's duty not to prejudice the guarantor, the creditor should include a clause in the guarantee expressly stating that the guarantor will be liable for advances made to the principal during the continuance of the period of notice of revocation.

---

[99] See *National Bank of A/asia Ltd v Mason* (1976) 50 A.L.J.R. 362 for a similar clause. See also *Parkes v Commonwealth Bank of Australia* (1990) ASC 56–020 at 59–212, where a clause allowing for revocation in respect of "any further liability" and "further advances" was held not to "nullify" liability for contingent obligations existing up to the date of the giving of notice of revocation.

[1] See a discussion of the meaning of "contingently" above, para.5–74. The Law Reform Commission of Tasmania in its Report, *Suretyship and Guarantee*, Report No.50, (1987) p.25, specifically proposed that "guarantors should not be liable for continuing obligations of the principal debtor incurred after the creditor receives notice of revocation *except in the case where a commitment has been made by the creditor on behalf of the principal debtor, prior to receipt of the revocation, which has not been fulfilled at the time of the notice*". (Emphasis added).

[2] See *Paget's Law of Banking* (9th ed., 1982), p.510. The 11th edition (1994) does not appear to endorse this proposition.

[3] *ibid.*

[4] See the rule discussed above, para.8–106.

[5] (1880) 16 Ch. D. 290.

[6] *ibid.*, at 314 (quoted in the text above, para.9–42).

(iv) Procedure upon revocation

9–76   Once the guarantee has been determined, the creditor should open a new account for the debtor, appropriating all payments by the debtor to the new account and making any further advances to the debtor through that account. This is to avoid the operation of the principle in *Devaynes v Noble (Clayton's Case)*,[7] which provides that the first sum paid into a current account is deemed to be the first paid out and the first debit in the account is extinguished by the first deposit. The effect of this rule upon determination of the guarantee is that any payment made to a current account by the debtor after the guarantee has been determined will reduce the liability of the guarantor to the extent of that payment, while every new advance made to the debtor will constitute an additional liability for which the guarantor is not liable.[8] The creditor is, however, entitled to open a new account and appropriate payments made by the debtor to it,[9] unless the guarantee itself prohibits this.[10]

9–77   In order to guard against the failure of the creditor to open a new account, guarantees often contain a provision that the liability of the guarantor arising at the time of the determination of the guarantee shall remain notwithstanding any subsequent payments into or out of the account by or on behalf of the principal. Such a clause has been held to be effective to override the rule in *Clayton's Case* and to preserve the guarantor's liability for the amount quantified at the time of determination.[11] A reference in the guarantee to the fact that it is a "continuing" security, which prevents the operation of the rule in *Clayton's Case* during the continuance of the guarantee, will probably be insufficient to prevent its operation after the guarantee is determined because it could not at that time be described as a "continuing" security.

---

[7] (1816) 1 Mer. 572; 35 E.R. 767.
[8] As illustrations of this problem, see *National Mortgage & Agency Co of New Zealand Ltd v Mee* [1929] N.Z.L.R. 235; *Colonial Bank of New Zealand v Smith* (1888) 6 N.Z.L.R. 659.
[9] *Re Sherry* (1884) 25 Ch. D. 692.
[10] This is unlikely, but see the wording of the guarantee in *National Bank of Nigeria Ltd v Awolesi* [1964] 1 W.L.R. 1311.
[11] *Westminster Bank Ltd v Cond* (1940) 46 Com. Cas. 60.

Part III

THE RIGHTS OF THE PARTIES

CHAPTER 10

RIGHTS OF THE CREDITOR

1. Preliminary points

(i) The contractual rights of the creditor

Usually, the rights of the creditor are amply protected by the terms of **10–01** the guarantee which may provide that the creditor shall be at liberty to exercise its rights either by way of the guarantee or by way of the indemnity contained in the document at its discretion or concurrently. The guarantee may also state that if the creditor is unsuccessful in enforcing its rights under the guarantee contained in the document, it shall not thereby be prevented from proceeding to enforce its rights under the indemnity contained therein.[1] There will often be detailed provisions in the guarantee declaring that the creditor's rights shall not in any way be prejudiced or affected by a list of factors which might otherwise release or discharge the guarantor either absolutely or pro tanto to the extent that the guarantor is prejudiced thereby.[2] An express provision denying a waiver of the creditor's rights is not uncommon. Such a clause might provide:

> "No act or omission of the creditor shall operate as a waiver of its rights except to the extent indicated by it in writing whether with respect to a continuing, recurrent or subsequent breach of the guarantee by the guarantor or otherwise."

A waiver clause in these terms is often reinforced by the creditor's **10–02** dealings with the guarantor. For example, where the creditor requires comprehensive security documentation in connection with a guarantee and

---

[1] As to the effect of an indemnity clause, see above, paras 1–88 to 1–95.
[2] See generally above, Chapters 6–9 for a discussion of these clauses.

insists that the guarantee is a condition precedent of the loan to the
principal debtor, the court will be inclined to reject the guarantor's
allegation that the creditor stated that the guarantee was merely a
formality and would never be enforced.[3]

10–03   A well-drawn guarantee will also contain detailed clauses dealing with
the creditor's right of set-off and the creditor's right to prove in the
bankruptcy or liquidation of the principal debtor or the guarantor, the
creditor's rights to deal with securities held for the principal debt and
the creditor's rights to deal with the principal debtor or a co-surety without
discharging the guarantor.[4]

10–04   The guarantee may specifically allow the creditor to demand certain
financial information from the guarantor and may even contain a warranty
by the guarantor that any statement of assets and liabilities and/or trading
and profit and loss account and/or balance sheet and/or other financial
statement produced to the creditor by the guarantor in connection with the
guarantee is correct and complete.

(ii) Other remedies against the guarantor

10–05   A creditor's remedies against the guarantor may not be restricted to
enforcing the guarantee itself. The guarantor, by the guarantor's own
conduct, may have incurred other forms of liability, such as the tort of
deceit. In *CSR Ltd v Price*,[5] the plaintiff established a claim in deceit
against a wife who fraudulently signed her husband's signature on a
guarantee with the intention of inducing the plaintiff to supply goods on
credit to their company and with full knowledge that the document she had
forged was a guarantee.

(iii) The general rule

10–06   There is a general principle that, in equity, a creditor will not be bound
without its assent by any arrangement in derogation of its rights.[6] One
illustration of this general principle is that the court will rarely compel the
creditor to proceed against the principal debtor first before enforcing the
guarantee against the surety.[7]

---

[3] *Banque Cantonale Vandoist v Flizari Shipping Co Ltd* (unreported, Q.B.D. (Comm Ct) May
26, 1999) 1999 W.L. 1489523.
[4] See above paras 1–104 to 1–106; 6–74 to 6–82; 7–27 to 7–41; 7–81 to 7–85; 8–29 to 8–34; 8–92
to 8–101; 10–37; 11–48 to 11–51 and 11–88.
[5] (Unreported, NSW Sup Ct, Cole J, April 29, 1993).
[6] *Swire v Redman* (1876) 1 Q.B.D. 536.
[7] *Wright v Simpson* (1802) 6 Ves. Jun. 714 at 732; 31 E.R. 1272 at 1281: see below, paras 10–
108 to 10–109 and 1–11 to 11–25.

2. The creditor's rights to enforce the guarantee arise upon default of the principal debtor

As a guarantee is a contract to be answerable for the debt, default or   **10–07**
miscarriage of another, the creditor's right to enforce the guarantee does
not generally arise until the principal debtor defaults in the performance of
the principal obligation.[8] The guarantee itself may require the creditor to
observe certain formalities, for example, by serving a formal demand on
the guarantor,[9] or the principal debtor[10] or to take proceedings first against
the principal debtor.[11] Such conditions precedent to liability will be
construed strictly in favour of the guarantor in accordance with the normal
rule that the liability of the surety is strictissimi juris.[12] In the absence of
such provisions, however, the guarantor's liability arises immediately upon
default by the debtor.[13] Hence if the principal contract relates to the
supply of goods on certain terms of credit, say thirty days, the principal
debtor is not in default until the thirty days expires, and the creditor cannot
enforce the guarantee until the debtor defaults.[14]

Not every default justifies the creditor enforcing the guarantee. Where   **10–08**
the default is caused by the creditor's own conduct[15] or by the creditor's
failure to accept the debtor's proper performance of the principal
obligation, the guarantee cannot be enforced. Nor is the surety liable for
a default which occurs with the connivance of the creditor.[16] Indeed, even
though the principal debtor is in default, effective recovery of sums
payable by the guarantor may be affected by the specific terms of the
guarantee and the principal transaction as well as the course of litigation
pursued by the creditor in respect of the principal's breach.

An illustration of the effect of both these factors is *Sunbird Plaza Pty*   **10–09**
Ltd v Maloney.[17] The respondents in that case guaranteed "the
performance of all the terms and conditions of the contract including the
payment of all moneys *payable* by the purchaser *under the contract*". A
deposit was paid and the balance of the purchase price was to be paid

---

[8] *Keene v Devine* [1986] W.A.R. 217 at 223 (the guarantor was under no enforceable obligation unless and until the debtor failed to pay); *Rickaby v Lewis* (1905) 22 T.L.R. 130; *Pattison v Belford Union Guardians* (1856) 1 H. & N. 523; 156 E.R. 1309.
[9] See below, paras 10–108 to 10–124.
[10] See below, paras 10–101 and 10–145 to 10–151.
[11] See below, paras 10–107 to 10–124; and 11–11 to 11–25.
[12] *Tricontinental Corp Ltd v HDFI Ltd* (1990) 21 N.S.W.L.R. 689. See also above, paras 5–01 to 5–07 and below para.10–96.
[13] Hence guarantors are entitled to quia timet relief upon the principal debtor's default, even if no demand has been made on them. See below, paras 11–123 to 11–155. Note, however, the special case of performance bonds where no default needs to be shown: see below, Chapter 13. And a conclusive evidence clause in a standard form guarantee may obviate the need for proof of default: see above, paras 5–102 to 5–107.
[14] *Ex p. Gardom* (1808) 15 Ves. 286; 33 E.R. 762; *Antrobus v Davidson* (1817) 3 Mer. 569; 36 E.R. 219.
[15] *Halliwell v Counsell* (1878) 38 L.T. 176; *Blest v Brown* (1862) 4 De G. F. & J. 367; 45 E.R. 1225. Cf. *Re Barber & Co Ex p. Agra Bank* (1870) L.R. 9 Eq. 725.
[16] *Lodder v Slowey* [1904] A.C. 442, P.C.; *Sanderson v Aston* (1873) L.R. 8 Exch. 73; *M'Taggart v Watson* (1836) 3 Cl. & Fin. 525 at 543; 6 E.R. 227 at 230, *per* Lord Brougham; *Dawson v Lawes* (1854) Kay 280; 69 E.R. 119, VC.
[17] (1988) 166 C.L.R. 245.

pursuant to the contract of sale "upon settlement". On the day fixed for settlement, the purchaser wrongfully repudiated the contract but the vendor elected to affirm the contract and ultimately obtained an order for specific performance against the purchaser. The purchaser defied this order. The High Court of Australia held that the vendor could not recover the purchase price from the guarantors as a fixed sum because their liability was dependent "upon settlement" taking place and that had not occurred.

10–10   The purchase price would have been recoverable from the guarantor as a debt if the guarantor had undertaken to pay the purchase price on the *day fixed for settlement*, rather than upon settlement, and if the purchaser failed to pay the purchase price on or before that day. But Mason C.J., with whom Deane, Dawson and Toohey J.J. agreed, refused to accept that the guarantee in question could be given that interpretation:

> "No doubt a promise by a purchaser to pay the balance of the purchase price 'upon settlement' gives less protection to a vendor than a promise to pay on a date fixed for settlement. But this circumstance cannot justify reading the promise to pay 'upon settlement' ... otherwise than according to its terms."[18]

10–11   The terms of the guarantee in *Sunbird Plaza Pty Ltd v Maloney*, therefore, precluded a successful action in debt for a liquidated sum.

10–12   Furthermore, although the terms of the guarantee were wide enough to encompass an action in damages against the guarantor, the course of action taken by the vendor in affirming the contract of sale and obtaining an order for its specific performance prevented recovery of any loss of profit on the sale from the purchaser and, therefore, the guarantor. This was because, in accordance with general contractual principles, affirmed by the High Court of Australia, loss of bargain damages are only recoverable if the contract is brought to an end. Indeed, once an order for specific performance had been obtained, the contract could not be terminated without vacation of the order: a plaintiff cannot be permitted to act inconsistently by terminating a contract in the face of an order of the court requiring the plaintiff to complete.[19]

10–13   Another example of affirmation of the principal contract affecting the creditor's remedies against the guarantor is *Keene v Devine*.[20] In that case, the creditor affirmed a loan contract payable at a future date, despite a declaration (amounting to an anticipatory breach) by the principal debtor that it was unable to repay its debts. The contract, therefore, remained on foot unaffected by that breach. The guarantee obliged the guarantor "to

---

[18] *ibid.*, at 258. See also Gaudron J. at 268. If the guarantee had been appropriately drafted to allow recovery as a liquidated amount, presumably the guarantor would have been entitled on payment to be subrogated to the vendor's rights in the property to enforce his right of indemnity against the purchaser.

[19] *ibid.*, at 259–260. But the vendor could apply to the court to vacate the order of specific performance, terminate the contract, and claim damages in further proceedings: *ibid.*, at 264–265.

[20] [1986] W.A.R. 217.

make good any default on the part of the debtor in the payment of the said loan and of all interest ... thereon." Burt C.J. of the Supreme Court of Western Australian held that, since the date for "the payment of the said loan ... and interest ... thereon" arose only after the date of the issue of the writ, no cause of action had accrued.[21] The action was dismissed, leaving the plaintiff to commence proceedings again.

These are illustrations of the affirmation of the principal contract affecting the creditor's remedies. But, as has been seen,[22] the acceptance of the principal's breach by the creditor may also have an effect on the guarantor's liability.   **10–14**

A creditor can of course agree, for consideration, to defer enforcement of a guarantee. And such agreement will be binding upon the creditor according to its terms. In the absence of consideration, the creditor's agreement to suspend or defer its right to enforce a guarantee may constitute a promissory estoppel which will prevent the creditor from reverting to its original rights without giving the guarantors reasonable notice.[23] But the debenture-holder who entered into a realisation agreement in a written memorandum with the principal debtor and the guarantors expressed to be "without prejudice" to the rights of the parties and with an oral reservation of its right to demand repayment of the principal debt was not prevented from appointing a receiver and manager under its mortgage debenture.[24]   **10–15**

3. EXTRA-CURIAL METHODS OF ENFORCING THE GUARANTEE

(i) The creditor's right of set-off

On general principles, a creditor may be entitled to set off its claim against a guarantor after default by the principal debtor against a debt which the creditor owes to the guarantor.[25] As we have seen, the creditor's claim against the guarantor matures upon the debtor's default (or, at least when a demand is made upon the guarantor) and, provided the necessary mutuality is present, the creditor will be entitled to this set-off. Prior to the debtor's default, the creditor's claim against the surety is merely contingent and will not support a legal set-off.   **10–16**

Even after the principal debtor's default, a legal set-off will not be available where the guarantee takes the form of a promise that the debtor will perform the principal obligation. In enforcing this type of guarantee, the creditor is seeking unliquidated damages and this type of claim will not   **10–17**

---

[21] Although Burt C.J. did not finally decide whether this action did constitute a breach: see [1986] W.A.R. 217 at 223.
[22] See above, paras 6–121 to 6–144.
[23] See *Central London Property Ltd v High Trees House Ltd* [1947] K.B. 130.
[24] *Aitken v State Bank of New South Wales* (unreported, NSW CA, April 23, 1993).
[25] Indeed, the executor of a deceased creditor is entitled to retain the amount of the guarantor's liability from a legacy payable to the guarantor out of the creditor's estate, even though the principal debt is statute-barred: *Coates v Coates* (1864) 33 Beav. 249; 55 E.R. 363; *Re Melton; Milk v Towers* [1918] Ch. 37 at 49–50.

support a legal set-off: the claims must be mutual, liquidated and due and owing in order to justify a legal set-off.[26]

10–18   A different regime governs set-off where the creditor goes into liquidation. Where a bank loan to a company is guaranteed by the directors as principal debtors who enter into an agreement authorising the bank to withdraw money from their personal accounts to repay the company's debt, and the bank goes into liquidation, the liquidator is required by r.4.90 of the Insolvency Rules 1986 to set off the directors' credit balances against the company's debt to the bank. They are cross claims arising out of mutual dealings prior to the commencement of the winding up and the indebtedness of the company to the bank is thereby reduced by the amount of the credit balances in the directors' accounts.[27]

(ii) The creditor's right to set off a customer's liability under a guarantee against the credit balance of his account

10–19   It appears that where the creditor is a bank it may set off its customer's liability under a guarantee against the credit balance of the customer's account.[28] Indeed, in *Hill v Bank of Hochelaga*,[29] a bank was even allowed to set off a customer's liability under a guarantee against the credit balance in the guarantor's *joint account* with his wife. But if the other party to the joint account notifies the bank that he claims to be entitled to all the moneys in the joint account, the bank may not thereafter set off the liability of the other party under a guarantee against the credit balance in the joint account.[30]

(iii) The creditor's right to combine accounts

10–20   If the creditor is a bank, it may use its right to combine the debtor's accounts to obtain payment of the principal debt when it falls due, especially when it suspects that the principal's financial position is rapidly deteriorating.[31] In this way the creditor may secure payment of the principal debt. But this right of combination is not automatic: the bank must take action to exercise the right.[32]

---

[26] See *Crawford v Stirling* (1802) 4 Esp. 207; *Morley v Inglis* (1837) 4 Bing. N.C. 58; 132 E.R. 711; *National Bank of Australia v Swan* (1872) 3 V.R. 168.

[27] *MS Fashions Ltd v Bank of Credit and Commerce International SA* [1993] B.C.L.C. 280, affirmed [1993] Ch. 425, CA. *Cf. Re Bank of Credit and Commerce International SA (in liq) No. 8* [1998] 1 B.C.L.C. 68. See below, paras 11–115 to 11–118.

[28] See E.P. Ellinger, E. Lomnicka and R.J.A. Hooley *Modern Banking Law* (3rd ed., 2002), pp.199–220.

[29] [1921] 3 W.W.R. 430.

[30] *ibid.*

[31] But a bank which induces its customer to make a deposit simply to enable the bank to exercise its right to combine the accounts may be liable to disgorge the deposit as an unfair preference: see *Re Shaw* (1977) 31 F.L.R. 118 and ss.289 and 340 of the Insolvency Act 1986.

[32] P. Wood, *English and International Set-Off* (1989), paras 3.11, 3.12, 3.15 and 3.20; *Hamilton v Commonwealth Bank of Australia* (1992) 9 A.C.S.R. 90 at 106. If the bank takes no action to combine the accounts and the customer becomes bankrupt or goes into liquidation, the trustee

Subject to four exceptions, a bank can combine the separate current **10–21** accounts of its customer, even if they are held at different branches,[33] without the consent of the customer and, indeed, without reasonable notice.[34] The courts justify this principle on the ground that the customer must be taken to know the overall state of its accounts at the bank and should not be entitled to claim the credit balance in one account as a debt owing by the bank when there is a deficiency in its composite account with the bank.[35]

The first exception to the general principle is that a bank's right to **10–22** combine its customer's accounts, or more accurately its right to treat all its customer's accounts as the one composite account,[36] can be excluded by usage, a course of dealing or by a special agreement to keep the accounts separate.[37] In *Halesowen Presswork & Assemblies Ltd v National Westminster Bank Ltd*,[38] Roskill J. remarked that such an agreement "may be for a limited period or it may be indefinite in the duration or it may be only for such period as the banker-customer relationship subsists".[39] An obligation to maintain separate accounts may be implied simply from the designation of an account as something other than a current account,[40] the most usual example being a loan account.

Such an agreement to keep the customer's accounts separate may, **10–23** however, be determined by a change of circumstances, for example, where the customer becomes insolvent[41] or where a special resolution is passed

---

in bankruptcy or the liquidator will be required to exercise the statutory right to set off the accounts as mutual debts: see s.323 of the Insolvency Act 1986 and r.4.90 of the Insolvency Rules 1986 (SI 1986/1925). As to the cut-off date for the inclusion of claims in the taking of an account in relation to an insolvent company, see Insolvency Rules 1986 (SI 1986/1925), r.4.90(3). *Cf.* s.323(3) of the Insolvency Act 1986 in relation to bankruptcy. Any benefit which the bank receives as a result of this set-off is not a preference: see *Hamilton v Commonwealth Bank of Australia* (1992) 9 ACSR 90 at 106.

[33] *Garnett v M'Kewan* (1872) L.R. 8 Ex. 10; *National Bank of New Zealand v Heslop* (1882) 1 N.Z.L.R. 47.

[34] *Crosse v Smith* (1813) 1 M. & S. 545 at 556; 105 E.R. 204 at 208; *Garnett v M'Kewan* (1872) L.R. 8 Ex. 10; *Prince v Oriental Bank Corp* (1878) 3 App. Cas. 325 at 333, PC. *Cf. Greenhalgh v Union Bank of Manchester* [1924] 2 K.B. 153, which may be restricted to its particular facts.

[35] *Garnett v M'Kewan* (1872) L.R. 8 Ex. 10 at 13, *per* Kelly C.B. See also *Re European Bank, Agra Bank Claims* (1872) L.R. 8 Ch. App. 41; *James Kirkwood & Sons v Clydesdale Bank* 1908 S.C. 20 at 24.

[36] S.R. Derham, *Set-Off* (3rd ed., 2003), Ch. 15 and *Clark v Ulster Bank Ltd* [1950] N.I.L.R. 132 at 142. *Cf.* E.P. Ellinger, E. Lomnicka and R.J.A. Hooley, *Modern Banking Law* (3rd ed., 2002) who regard this right as a right of set-off.

[37] *Re Johnson & Co Ltd* [1902] 1 I.R. 439; *Garnett v M'Kewan* (1872) L.R. 8 Ex. 10 at 13, *per* Martin J.; *Greenwood Teale v William, Williams, Brown & Co* (1894) 11 T.L.R. 56.

[38] [1971] 1 Q.B. 1, affirmed by the House of Lords sub nom. *National Westminster Bank Ltd v Halesowen Presswork & Assemblies Ltd* [1972] A.C. 785.

[39] *ibid.*, at 21.

[40] See, *e.g. Re Gross, Ex p. Kingston* (1871) L.R. 6 Ch. App. 632, where the court held that an account opened by a customer as a "police account" could not be combined with the customer's personal account. See also *Re E. J. Morel (1934) Ltd* [1962] Ch. 21.

[41] See *British Guiana Bank v OR* (1911) 104 L.T. 754, PC Guiana. *Cf. Direct Acceptance Corp v Bank of New South Wales* (1968) 88 WN (NSW) (Pt.1) 498, where Macfarlan J. decided that the customer's insolvency did not determine the agreement to keep the accounts separate in the circumstances. In that case, another debenture-holder had appointed a receiver and a manager of the customer's business. But even when the customer becomes bankrupt or goes into liquidation, the bank should be able to fall back upon its statutory right of set-off under s.323 of the Insolvency Act 1986 and s.4.90 of the Insolvency Rules 1986. See *Hamilton v Commonwealth Bank of Australia* (1992) 9 A.C.S.R. 90 at 106–107.

for the winding-up of the customer,[42] but not where a debenture-holder (other than the bank) appoints a receiver and manager of the customer.[43] Hence, a current account and a loan account may be combined if the customer is insolvent since the express or implied agreement to keep the accounts separate is cancelled by the customer's insolvency.[44]

10-24   The second exception to the bank's right to treat its customer's accounts as one composite account arises where funds or property of the customer is remitted to the bank or appropriated for a particular purpose.[45] Hence, an account which is opened for the express purpose of carrying into effect a moratorium arrangement,[46] or an account containing money advanced to the customer by another party for the specific and exclusive purpose of paying a dividend to the customer's shareholders,[47] may not be combined with the customer's other accounts. It may also be the case that a bank may not combine a current deposit account with a fully-drawn loan account until the loan account is due and payable.[48]

10-25   The third exception to the general principle is that a bank may not combine a customer's private account with an account which is known to the bank to be a trust account[49] or to be used by the customer as trustee in the administration of a trust.[50] Similarly, a bank may not set off a credit balance in one account against a debit in another account held by the customer in a different capacity or in a different business.[51]

10-26   The final restriction upon a bank's right to combine accounts is that the customer's liability to the bank must have been incurred as part of the banker-customer relationship and not in connection with some other aspect of the bank's operations,[52] such as its travel or insurance business.

(iv) The creditor's right to vote on voluntary arrangements proposed by the debtor company

10-27   Where the creditors of a company are summoned to a meeting for the purpose of approving an arrangement put forward by the company, the voting rights of creditors holding guarantees from the company are

[42] See *National Westminster Bank Ltd v Halesowen Presswork & Assemblies Ltd* [1972] A.C. 785, where it was clear that the temporary arrangement to keep the accounts separate would determine if there was a material alteration in the circumstances.

[43] *Direct Acceptance Corp v Bank of New South Wales* (1968) 88 W.N. (NSW) (Pt.1) 498.

[44] However, *Re Johnson & Co Ltd* [1902] 1 I.R. 439 suggests that the insolvency of the customer is not sufficient to justify combining the customer's personal account with an account which is specifically designated as something other than a current account.

[45] *Rouxel v Royal Bank of Canada* [1918] 2 W.W.R. 791; *Greenwood Teale v William, Williams, Brown & Co* (1894) 11 T.L.R. 56.

[46] See *National Mutual Royal Bank Ltd v Ginges* (unreported, NSW Sup Ct, March 15, 1991) at p.18.

[47] *Barclays Bank Ltd v Quistclose Investments Ltd* [1970] A.C. 567.

[48] This appears to be a reasonable inference from *Hamilton v Commonwealth Bank of Australia* (1992) 9 A.C.S.R. 90 at 106 *per* Hodgson J.

[49] *Greenwood Teale v William, Williams, Brown & Co* (1894) 11 T.L.R. 56.

[50] *Union Bank of Australia v Murray-Aynsley* [1898] A.C. 693; *Bank of New South Wales v Goulburn Valley Butter Co Pty Ltd* [1902] A.C. 543.

[51] *Garnett v M'Kewan* (1872) L.R. 8 Ex. 10 at 14 *per* Pigott B.

[52] See *Halesowen Presswork v Westminster Bank* [1971] 1 Q.B. 1 at 20-21.

sometimes disputed on the basis that the liability under the guarantees has not yet arisen. Generally, however, such creditors are entitled to vote on the proposed arrangement and a rejection of their votes may constitute a material irregularity. Such an irregularity may persuade the court to revoke the other creditors' approval of the voluntary arrangement.[53] The chairman of the meeting is required to mark disputed claims as objected to and allow the disputed creditors to vote, subject to their votes being subsequently declared invalid if objection to their claims is sustained.[54]

(v) The creditor's right to prove in the bankruptcy or liquidation of the principal debtor

(a) The general principles

A creditor can prove for the amount of the principal debt in the **10–28** bankruptcy or liquidation of the principal debtor but is not obliged to do so.[55]

In general, all claims by creditors are provable as debts in both winding **10–29** up and bankruptcy whether they are present or future, certain or contingent, ascertained or sounding only in damages.[56] Where the principal debtor has not defaulted, it will be necessary for its liquidator or trustee in bankruptcy to estimate the value of the creditor's debt.[57] The amount provable in the winding up of the principal debtor company is the amount of the estimate.[58] The creditor's rights of set-off against the principal debtor in bankruptcy are similar to those available against a principal debtor company in liquidation.[59]

A central issue regarding the creditor's right of proof in the principal's **10–30** bankruptcy or liquidation is the difficulty of reconciling what has been described as "two potentially conflicting principles: that on the one hand a creditor should be entitled to obtain the full benefit of his guarantee; and that on the other a surety should be entitled to receive the full benefit of a

---

[53] *Re a Debtor (No.222 of 1990) Ex p. the Bank of Ireland* [1992] B.C.L.C. 137 (where the approval would not have been granted if the disputed creditors' votes had been taken into account).

[54] Rule 5.17(6) of the Insolvency Rules 1986.

[55] *National Bank of A/asia v Plummer* (1869) 6 WW & A'B (L) 165. As to the freedom of the creditor in exercising its remedies, see above, para.10–01. The principle stated in the text should apply equally to a creditor's right of proof in respect of a liability covered by a contract of indemnity.

[56] Insolvency Rules 1986, r.12.3 (SI 1986/1925). The court may fix the time limit within which creditors are to prove their debts or claims. Creditors who fail to prove their claims in time are excluded from current distributions: Insolvency Act 1986, s.153. As to the mode of proving a debt or claim, see I. F. Fletcher, *The Law of Insolvency* (3rd ed., 2002), paras 23–006 to 23–012.

[57] Insolvency Rules 1986, r.4.86. Compare s.322(3) and (4) of the Insolvency Act 1986 in relation to the bankruptcy of individual debtors.

[58] *ibid.*

[59] See s.323 of the Insolvency Act 1986 and r.4.90 of the Insolvency Rules 1986 (SI 1986/1925).

right of indemnity for his liability upon the guarantee".[60] How is this conflict to be resolved?

10-31   It is clear that, if the guarantor pays the whole of the principal debt, the guarantor will be subrogated to the creditor's proof.[61] If the creditor has in fact submitted a proof, it will be a trustee for the guarantor in respect of any dividends which it receives from the principal debtor's estate.[62]

10-32   In the absence of a payment of the whole of the principal debt, the amount for which the creditor can prove in the bankruptcy or liquidation of the principal debtor depends on whether the surety has guaranteed the whole or merely part of the principal debt.[63]

10-33   Where the creditor takes a guarantee for only part of the principal debt, the guarantor is entitled, on paying that part of the debt, to lodge a proof in respect of the amount so paid.[64] As cogently explained by Tadgell J. in *Westpac Banking Corp v Gollin & Co Ltd*:[65]

> "where part only of the debt is guaranteed, the part guaranteed [is] treated for the purposes of proof as a separate debt from the part not guaranteed .... Having paid the part guaranteed, and having thus discharged his whole obligation to the creditor, the surety becomes subrogated to the creditor's right to prove for that part. The surety being so entitled to prove and the creditor becoming to that extent disentitled, the rule against double proof is not infringed."[66]

10-34   Thus the rule against double proof[67] works against the creditor, who should reduce the proof by the amount paid by the guarantor in discharge of the guarantee. If the creditor has already lodged the proof, any dividends received by the creditor in respect of the part of the debt paid by the guarantor must be held in trust for the guarantor.[68] Thus if the total debt is £2,000 with a guarantee of part of that debt for £1,000 and the creditor receives a dividend of 20 pence in the pound (the dividend totalling £400) an amount equal to half the total dividends received (£200) must be debited from the guaranteed portion of the debt. Thus the

---

[60] *Westpac Banking Corp v Gollin & Co Ltd* [1988] V.R. 397 at 402.
[61] *ibid.*, at 403.
[62] *Ex p. Rushforth* (1805) 10 Ves. 409 at 414, 420; 32 E.R. 903 at 905, 907; *Re Sass Ex p. National Provincial Bank of England Ltd (hereafter Re Sass)* [1896] 2 Q.B. 12 at 15.
[63] As to this distinction, see above paras 5–35 to 5–40. Note especially that a guarantee of a fluctuating balance (as in the case of a guarantee of the debtor's current account with a bank) with a limit on the liability of the surety will prima facie be construed as a guarantee of part of the debt: *Barclays Bank Ltd v TOSG Trust Fund Ltd* [1984] 1 All E.R. 628 at 641–642.
[64] *Re Sass* [1896] 2 Q.B. 12 at 15 *per* Vaughan Williams. L.J.
[65] [1988] V.R. 397.
[66] *ibid.*, at 405. See also *Barclays Bank Ltd v TOSG Trust Fund Ltd* [1984] 1 All E.R. 628; *Gray v Seckham* (1872) L.R. 7 Ch. App. 680; *Ex p. Rushforth* (1805) 10 Ves. 409; 32 E.R. 903; *Re Butlers Wharf Ltd* [1995] 2 B.C.L.C. 43; *Seabird Corp Ltd (in liq) v Sherlock* (1990) 2 A.C.S.R. 111 at 116; *Re Sass* [1896] 2 Q.B. 12.
[67] The rule against double proof prevents two creditors of a bankrupt or a company in liquidation from proving in respect of what is, in substance, the same debt: *Re Oriental Commercial Bank* (1871) 7 Ch. App. 99. See also *Re Fenton Ex p. Fenton Textile Association Ltd* [1931] 1 Ch. 85 (CA) and below, paras 11–158 to 11–163 and 12–63 to 12–72.
[68] *Westpac Banking Corp v Gollin & Co Ltd* [1988] V.R. 397 at 403.

guarantor will be entitled to a refund of £200 and will, therefore, only be liable for £800.[69]

The position is different where the guarantee covers the whole of the **10–35** principal debt.[70] Where the surety has guaranteed the entire principal debt, even if the surety has paid to the extent of his liability, the surety may not prove in the debtor's bankruptcy or liquidation in competition with the creditor[71] because the surety has expressly or impliedly undertaken to be responsible for the full sum guaranteed. As Oliver L.J. observed in *Barclays Bank Ltd v TOSG Trust Fund Ltd*:[72]

"so long as any part of the whole debt remains outstanding, the surety, although he has paid up to the limit of his financial liability, is treated as not having discharged his liability to the creditor, presumably on the footing that there nevertheless remains an outstanding obligation on him to see that the whole debt is paid."[73]

The creditor, therefore, is entitled to prove for the whole debt[74] and a **10–36** payment by the guarantor of the amount of the guarantor's limited liability does not require the creditor to expunge part of the proof.[75]

All these principles are applicable whether the creditor first proves in **10–37** the estate of the bankrupt debtor before the creditor claims the balance of the principal debt from the guarantor, or whether the creditor claims against the guarantor first before proving in the estate of the bankrupt debtor for the balance.[76] But, of course, the creditor cannot retain more than 100 pence in the pound of the principal debt. If the creditor obtains more, it must hold the excess in trust for the paying guarantor.[77] Where a guarantor of a whole debt with a limitation on liability makes a payment to the creditor under his guarantee after the principal debtor has presented a bankruptcy petition or entered into a deed of arrangement, the guarantor

---

[69] See also above, paras 6–39 to 6–41.
[70] *Westpac Banking Corp. v Gollin & Co. Ltd* [1988] V.R. 397 at 403.
[71] *Re Sass* [1896] 2 Q.B. 12, applied in *Ulster Bank Ltd v Lambe* [1966] N.I. 161; *Seabird Corp Ltd (in liq) v Sherlock* (1990) 2 A.C.S.R. 111 at 115–116. It might be more accurate to state that the guarantor is not entitled to receive a dividend on his claim for an indemnity in competition with the creditor. See G. Andrews and R. Millett, *Law of Guarantee* (3rd ed., 2000), para.13.06. It appears that the same principle applies where the payment by the guarantor is made out of the proceeds of realisation of securities given to the guarantor by the principal debtor: *Midland Banking Co v Chambers* (1869) 4 Ch. App. 398. See also *Re Fernandes; Ex p. Hope* (1844) 3 Mont D. & De G. 720. Likewise, where the guarantee on its proper construction encompasses the amount remaining due to the creditor after payment of any dividends received from the principal's bankrupt estate, see *Westpac Banking Corp v Gollin & Co Ltd* [1988] V.R. 397 at 403.
[72] [1984] 1 All E.R. 628.
[73] *ibid.*, at 641. See also *Westpac Banking Corp v Gollin & Co Ltd* [1988] V.R. 397 at 401, 405; *Seabird Corp Ltd (in liq) v Sherlock* (1990) 2 A.C.S.R. 111 at 115. Cf. *Rowlatt on Principal & Surety* (4th ed., 1982), p.199, where the cases relied upon do not directly address this issue (*e.g. Ex p. Gilbey* (1878) 8 Ch. D. 248) or involve bills of exchange, which apply a different rule (see *Westpac Banking Corp v Gollin & Co Ltd* [1988] V.R. 397 at 399–401, 407–408). See also *Rowlatt on Principal and Surety* (5th ed., 1999), paras 11.05 and 11.07.
[74] *Re Sass* [1896] 2 Q.B. 12.
[75] *Re Rees, Ex p. National Provincial Bank* (1881) 17 Ch. D. 98 at 103.
[76] *Westpac Banking Corp v Gollin & Co Ltd* [1988] V.R. 397 at 403.
[77] *ibid.* See also *Midland Montagu Australia Ltd v Harkness* (1994) 124 A.L.R. 407.

will not be entitled to lodge a proof of debt for the amount of the payment unless the creditor accepted the payment in discharge of the whole debt.

Most guarantees now contain detailed provisions clearly indicating that the creditor is entitled to the benefit of all dividends from the principal debtor's estate in priority to the guarantor and that the guarantee covers the amount remaining due after the payment of such dividends. Even in the case of a guarantee of part of a debt, an express clause which clearly indicates that the guarantor has waived his rights in favour of the creditor will be effective to exclude the guarantor's right to prove in competition with the creditor.[78]

10–38   An example of a common clause is:

> "This guarantee shall not be considered as wholly or partially satisfied by the payment or liquidation at any time or times of any sum or sums of money for the time being due to the creditor, and all dividends, compositions and payments received by the creditor from the principal debtor or any other person or estate shall be applied as payments in gross without any right on the part of the guarantor to claim the benefit of any such dividends, compositions or payments or any securities held by the creditor until payment to the creditor of the amount hereby guaranteed, and this guarantee shall apply to and secure any ultimate balance due to the creditor."[79]

10–39   This type of clause is not the only term that can affect a creditor's right of proof. Where the guarantee contains a suspense account clause entitling the creditor to deposit all payments received from the sureties in a suspense account until it receives payment of the principal debt in full, the creditor is not required to reduce its proof in the insolvency of the principal debtor by the amount of the sureties' payments unless it appropriates them to the principal debt.[80]

(b) The effect of payments by the guarantor prior to the date of the debtor's bankruptcy or winding-up

10–40   On one view, the creditor's right of proof may be affected by payments by the guarantor before the date of the bankruptcy of the principal debtor or the date that the principal debtor company goes into liquidation, as the

---

[78] *Barclays Bank Ltd v TOSG Trust Fund Ltd* [1984] 1 All E.R. 628 at 641. For examples of different clauses see *Midland Banking Co v Chambers* (1869) L.R. 4 Ch. App. 398 (*Cf. Hobson v Bass* (1871) L.R. 6 Ch. App. 792).
[79] This provision is modelled on the clause accepted by the Ontario Supreme Court in *Kuproski v Royal Bank of Canada* [1926] 3 D.L.R. 801 at 806. See too *Ellis v Emmanuel* (1876) 1 Ex. D. 157 at 162. Such a clause, however, will not preclude the guarantor (or the guarantor's assignee) from exercising rights against a security obtained from the principal debtor: see *F. J. Hawkes & Co (Aust) Pty Ltd v International Hydrodynamics Pty Ltd* (unreported, NSW Sup Ct, October 17, 1979) at 10, and below, paras 10–82 to 10–87.
[80] *Commercial Bank of Australia Ltd v Wilson & Co's Estate* [1893] A.C. 181. *Cf. Re Butlers Wharf Ltd* [1995] 2 B.C.L.C. 43 at 49.

case may be. *MacKinnon's Trustee v Bank of Scotland*[81] suggests that a creditor is required to give credit for the sums received from the guarantor prior to the receiving order in the bankruptcy of the principal debtor because such sums reduce the principal's indebtedness to the creditor. This view would require the creditor to reduce its proof in the bankruptcy of the principal debtor by the amount of these sums. On similar reasoning, the creditor would be expected to give credit and reduce its proof in respect of the proceeds of securities given to the creditor by the guarantor as security for the principal debt and realised before the date of the receiving order.

Whilst *MacKinnon's Trustee v Bank of Scotland* is applicable where   **10–41** there is a guarantee of part of a debt because the amount of the *separate* debt for which the guarantor is liable is correspondingly reduced, it is thought to be incorrect where there is a guarantee of the total indebtedness.[82] Indeed, in *Ulster Bank Ltd v Lambe*,[83] which has been subsequently approved in Australia in *Westpac Banking Corp v Gollin & Co Ltd*,[84] Lowry J. held that, provided that the guarantee is construed as a guarantee of the whole debt rather than merely a guarantee of part of a debt, the creditor can sue the principal or prove in the principal's bankruptcy for the full amount of the debt.[85] Thus, if the guarantor's liability is limited to £1,000 and the total debt owed by the principal is £5,000 the creditor, even though he receives payment of £1,000 from the guarantor prior to the date of the principal's bankruptcy, may still prove in respect of the total debt of £5,000. If money is recovered in excess of the full amount of the debt, that surplus must be held in trust for the guarantor.[86]

Lowry J. specifically disapproved of *MacKinnon's Trustee v Bank of*   **10–42** *Scotland* and it is submitted that this view should be preferred. The decision in *Ulster Bank Ltd v Lambe*[87] appears to be correct because, in accordance with the principles outlined in the previous section,[88] if the guarantee is of the whole of the principal's indebtedness, the creditor is entitled at all times to treat the entire debt as owing and there remains "an outstanding obligation on [the guarantor] to see that the whole debt is paid".[89] It should be irrelevant whether the guarantor makes a payment before or after the principal's bankruptcy. Furthermore, as Lowry J. pointed out, the rights of other parties are not affected:

"the rights of other creditors of the principal debtor are not infringed, since the bank was at all times entitled to rank equally with other

---

[81] 1915 S.C. 411.
[82] See also R.M. Goode, *Legal Problems of Credit and Security* (3rd ed., 2003), para.8–18.
[83] [1966] N.I. 161.
[84] [1988] V.R. 397 at 406–407, 409.
[85] See above, paras 5–35 to 5–40, as to the distinction between a guarantee of the whole debt and a guarantee of part of a debt.
[86] Similar principles govern a creditor's right to prove under a scheme of arrangement in respect of the principal debtor after receiving a dividend in the liquidation of the guarantor: see *Midland Montagu Australia Ltd v Harkness* (1994) 124 A.L.R. 407 and *Bower v Marris* (1841) Cr. & Ph. 351; 41 E.R. 525.
[87] [1966] N.I. 161. See also *Westpac Banking Corp v Gollin & Co Ltd* [1988] V.R. 397 at 407.
[88] See above, paras 10–28 to 10–39.
[89] *Barclays Bank Ltd v TOSG Trust Fund Ltd* [1984] 1 All E.R. 628 at 641 *per* Oliver L.J.

unsecured creditors in the principal debtor's bankruptcy, and has independently of this right contracted to receive from the guarantor payment to supplement the dividend on the entire debt. If the entire debt is discharged, the creditor has no further interest, and the guarantor stands in his shoes. If the principal debtor remains solvent, the question of justice among his creditors does not arise."[90]

10–43   Many guarantees do in fact provide that the creditor shall not be required to give credit or reduce its proof in the principal's bankruptcy by reason of payments made by the guarantor. Additionally, clauses will permit the creditor complete freedom of appropriation as to payments received and, in particular, allow the creditor to appropriate payments to a suspense account[91] until such time that, in the creditor's discretion, it appropriates them to the guaranteed debt.[92] Although, on the authority of *Ulster Bank Ltd v Lambe* such clauses are strictly unnecessary where there is a guarantee of the whole debt, they will protect the position of the creditor in the case of a guarantee of part of a debt.

(c) The effect of payments by the guarantor after the date of the bankruptcy or winding-up

10–44   Sums received by the creditor after the date of the receiving order in the principal debtor's bankruptcy[93] and the proceeds of securities given to the creditor by the guarantor and realised after that date[94] do not reduce the indebtedness of the principal debtor[95] so the creditor need not reduce its proof in the bankruptcy of the principal debtor to take account of such amounts, whether the creditor receives them before or after it lodges the proof.[96] But the creditor is not entitled to receive more than 100 pence in the pound in respect of the guaranteed debt,[97] and after the creditor receives payment in full, it must hold any surplus in trust for any guarantors who are entitled to an indemnity from the principal debtor.[98]

---

[90] *Ulster Bank Ltd v Lambe* [1966] N.I. 161 at 169.
[91] *Commercial Bank of Australia v Official Assignee of the Estate of Wilson* [1893] A.C. 181.
[92] If payments are appropriated to a "suspense" account in accordance with this clause, the principal debt is, of course, not reduced, so that the amount of proof in the creditor's bankruptcy will not be affected: *Commercial Bank of Australia v Official Assignee of the Estate of Wilson* [1893] A.C. 181.
[93] *Westpac Banking Corp v Gollin & Co Ltd* [1988] V.R. 397 at 403, 405; *Re Rees* (1881) 17 Ch. D. 98; *Re Sass* [1896] 2 Q.B. 12. The corresponding date in the case of a company is generally the date that the company goes into liquidation. See Insolvency Rules 1986 (SI 1986/1925), r.13.12(a) and s.247(2) of Insolvency Act 1986.
[94] A creditor is a secured creditor only where it holds security over assets of the *bankrupt*. See Insolvency Act 1986, ss.67(a) and 248(a). Security taken from a guarantor does not fall into this category: see generally *Re Dutton, Massey & Co* [1924] 2 Ch. 199.
[95] *Ulster Bank Ltd v Lambe* [1966] N.I. 161 at 169.
[96] *Re Rees* (1881) 17 Ch. D. 98; *Re Sass* [1896] 2 Q.B. 12; *Westpac Banking Corp v Gollin & Co Ltd* [1988] V.R. 397 at 403.
[97] The guaranteed debt for this purpose must be taken to be the contractual debt and to include accruing interest, notwithstanding the bankruptcy or winding up of the principal debtor and the co-sureties or any of them: *Midland Montagu Australia Ltd v Harkness* (1994) 124 A.L.R. 407.
[98] *Westpac Banking Corp v Gollin & Co Ltd* [1988] V.R. 397 at 403.

Even the holder of a negotiable instrument is not required to reduce his **10–45** proof of debt in the insolvency of the acceptor to take into account part-payments received from the drawer or indorser as quasi-sureties of the acceptor's liability after the date of the acceptor's bankruptcy or liquidation.[99] The special rules that affect the holder's right of proof in other contexts[1] do not apply in this situation. It follows that the drawers or indorsers are not entitled to prove for the amount paid to the holder of the negotiable instrument in their capacity as quasi-sureties.[2]

In the rare case where a creditor takes a guarantee for only part of the **10–46** debt, any dividend received from the principal debtor's estate may not, in the absence of an agreement to the contrary, be appropriated to the part of the creditor's debt which is not covered by the guarantee. The dividend must be applied rateably to the whole debt so that the guarantor receives a proportionate benefit from the dividend.[3] Usually, however, the guarantee covers the whole debt and the guarantor is not entitled to any benefit from such a dividend.

(d) The effect of payments made or securities given by the principal debtor

Payments made to the creditor by or on behalf of the principal debtor **10–47** reduce the principal debtor's indebtedness, but securities given by the debtor to the creditor do not have this effect until they are realised and the proceeds are applied towards the principal debt.[4] Generally these securities will either be valued or realised by the creditor.

Indeed, a secured creditor has four options:

(a) to realise its security and prove for the outstanding balance of the debt;

(b) to assess and declare the value of its security so as to prove for the balance of its debt;

(c) to rely entirely on its security and refrain from proving; or

(d) to surrender the security and prove for its entire debt.[5]

---

[99] *Re London, Bombay & Mediterranean Bank Ex p. Cama* (1874) L.R. 9 Ch. App. 686 at 689; *Re Fothergill Ex p. Turquand* (1876) 3 Ch. D. 445; *Ex p. Leers* (1802) 6 Ves. 644; 31 E.R. 1228; *Re Stein Ex p. Royal Bank of Scotland* (1815) 19 Ves. 310; 34 E.R. 532. However, the holder is not entitled to more than 100 pence in the pound on the outstanding amount of the negotiable instrument: *Re Blakely Ex p. Harvey* (1854) 4 De G.M. & G. 881; 43 E.R. 752.

[1] See *Re Holder* [1929] 1 Ch. 205; *Re Blackburne* (1892) 9 Mor. 249; *Ex p. Taylor* [1893] A.C. 181.

[2] *Re London, Bombay & Mediterranean Bank Ex p. Cama* (1874) L.R. 9 Ch. 686; *Re Fothergill, Ex p. Turquand* (1876) 3 Ch. D. 445.

[3] *Re Sass* [1896] 2 Q.B. 12 at 15; *Raikes v Todd* (1838) 8 Ad. & E. 844; 8 L.J.Q.B. 35. See also above, paras 6–39 to 6–41.

[4] *Ulster Bank Ltd v Lambe* [1966] N.I. 161 at 169; *Re Hunter Ex p. Bank of New South Wales* [1982] Qd. R. 131 at 133; *Midland Banking Co v Chambers* (1869) 4 Ch. App. 398.

[5] See I.F. Fletcher, *The Law of Insolvency* (3rd ed., 2002), para.23–011; *Moor v Anglo-Italian Bank* (1879) 10 Ch. D. 681 at 689–690 where Sir George Jessel M.R. explained these options in detail. If the secured creditor assesses the value of its security and declares the value to the

10–48   The amount of the valuation[6] or the proceeds of realisation,[7] as the case may be, will then be deducted from the creditor's proof in the bankruptcy of the principal debtor. It is not essential, however, for the creditor to take this course of action. Although it is unlikely, the creditor may surrender the security to the trustee in bankruptcy or liquidator for the benefit of the creditors generally and may prove against the principal debtor's estate for the whole of its debt as an ordinary creditor, without thereby releasing the guarantor.[8]

10–49   The creditor need not value a lapsed security.[9] And if the creditor places a low value on the securities and receives a dividend in respect of the residue of the principal debt, this does not discharge the guarantors.[10] They are not relieved from liability to the extent of the valuation of the security in the principal debtor's bankruptcy or liquidation.[11] They remain liable to the creditor in respect of the whole of the guaranteed debt. Hence, if the security does not ultimately realise the amount of its valuation, the guarantors can be held liable for the deficiency.[12]

10–50   It is different where the creditor becomes a party to a composition or a deed whereby the principal debtor is discharged and the position of the surety is altered.[13] In *Canadian Bank of Commerce v Martin*[14] a creditor in the voluntary winding-up of a company under the Companies Act 1911 of British Columbia valued his securities at a certain sum and accepted in payment certain book debts of the company. The price was then deducted from the creditor's claim. This transaction was regarded as a purchase of the book debts and as being in substance a contract between the creditor and the company, discharging the company to the extent of the purchase price of the book debts. It is important to note that there was no provision in the Companies Act of British Columbia for valuing securities. The creditor's composition with the principal debtor was, therefore, unaffected by statute and it was held that the portion of the company's debt represented by the price of the book debts was satisfied and thus the sureties were partially released.

---

liquidator the liquidator has the right to redeem the security at the value put upon it in the creditor's proof: Insolvency Rules 1986 (SI 1986/1925), rr.4.97 and 4.99.
[6] Insolvency Rules 1986 (SI 1986/1925), r.6.115.
[7] Insolvency Rules 1986 (SI 1986/1925), rr.6.109 and 6.119.
[8] *Banque Canadienne Nationale v Dufour* (1979) 31 C.B.R. 300. *Cf. Ex p. Rushforth* (1805) 10 Ves. 409 at 414; 32 E.R. 903 at 905. If a secured creditor omits to disclose its security in its proof of debt, it must surrender the security for the general benefit of creditors unless the court grants relief on the ground of inadvertence or an honest mistake: Insolvency Rules 1986 (SI 1986/1925), r.6.116.
[9] *Rainbow v Juggins* (1880) 5 Q.B.D. 422.
[10] *Trust & Agency Co of Australia v Greene* (1870) 1 V.R. (L) 171. Where the creditor proves for a prospective liability on which it has placed too low a value it may be advisable for the surety to pay the creditor an amount equal to the value of the creditor's proof since this will discharge the surety's liability to the creditor and yet enable him to collect dividends in respect of the creditor's proof: see *Re Lennard* [1934] Ch. 235.
[11] *Kuproski v Royal Bank of Canada* [1926] 3 D.L.R. 801 at 804.
[12] *ibid.*
[13] As to the effect of a release of the principal, see above, paras 6–53 *et. seq.*
[14] (1918) 40 D.L.R. 155.

A similar decision might yet be possible in England even though the **10-51** Insolvency Rules 1986[15] allow a secured creditor to value its security when proving for its debt.

The secured creditor is not required to value its securities, so it could be **10-52** argued that the guarantors would be released to the extent of the valuation because the creditor's claim in the bankruptcy or liquidation of the principal debtor is restricted to the unsecured part of the debt by the voluntary act or agreement of the creditor. But the better view is that the sureties are not partially discharged by the valuation of the creditor's security since the valuation of the security is not a classical accord; so it does not extinguish that portion of the principal debt.[16] Indeed, if the creditor does not ultimately realise the value given to its security, it can apply to amend its proof, so it is clear that this portion of the principal debt is not liquidated simply by the valuation.[17]

(e) The effect of counter securities obtained by a guarantor from the principal debtor or a co-surety

The creditor need not reduce its proof in the bankruptcy of the principal **10-53** debtor so as to take into account counter securities obtained by a surety from the principal debtor or a co-surety. Since the creditor is not entitled to such securities[18] they do not affect its right of proof in the debtor's bankruptcy.

(vi) Special rules in relation to bills of exchange

(a) The holder's right to prove against the estate of the drawer or the indorsers in bankruptcy

Negotiable instruments constitute a curious exception to the general rule **10-54** relating to a creditor's right of proof against the principal debtor and a surety. Where the principal debtor and the surety are both liable on a negotiable instrument, for example, as acceptor and drawer or indorser respectively, the holder may not prove against the estate of the principal debtor without giving credit for sums received or dividends declared, even if not paid, from the surety's estate *before* the holder lodged its proof in the

---

[15] See *Re Jacobs* (1875) L.R. 10 Ch. 211 at 213–214 per Sir W. James L.J.; *Re London Chartered Bank of Australia* [1893] 3 Ch. 540 at 546 *per* Vaughan Williams J.; *Rainbow v Juggins* (1880) 5 Q.B.D. 422 at 423 *per* Bramwell L.J.

[16] This view is also consistent with *Midland Montagu Australia Ltd v Harkness* (1994) 124 A.L.R. 407 (receipt of dividends in the winding-up and under a scheme of arrangement approved by the court did not amount to pro tanto satisfaction of the debt to the extent of the amount of the admitted debt). See also *Moor v Anglo-Italian Bank* (1879) 10 Ch. D. 681 at 689–690.

[17] See Insolvency Rules 1986 (SI 1986/1925), r.6.15.

[18] *Re Walker; Sheffield Banking Co v Clayton* [1892] 1 Ch. 621; *Re Yewdall; Ex p. Barnfather* (1877) 46 L.J. Bcy. 87, affirmed in (1877) 46 L.J. Bcy. 109, CA: see below, paras 10–82 to 10–87.

estate of debtor. Similarly, in proving against the estate of the surety, the holder must give credit for sums received or dividends declared from the principal debtor's estate before the holder lodged its proof in the estate of surety.[19] In each case, however, the holder is not required to revise or reduce the proof for the full amount of the outstanding liability where a sum is received or a dividend is declared from the first estate *after* the holder lodged a proof against the second estate,[20] although the holder is not entitled to more than 100 pence in the pound upon the outstanding part of the bill.[21]

10–55 The holder of a joint and several promissory note made as security for a debt may be allowed to prove against the estate of the surety on the note even though the maker of the note, the principal debtor, assigns the property to the debtor's creditors in return for the debtor's own release and even though the deed of assignment contains no reservation of rights against the surety. The omission of such a reservation of rights will not discharge the surety where the surety himself requests the holder to execute the deed.[22]

(b) The effect of collateral securities upon the holder's right to prove.

10–56 The holder is not entitled to the benefit of collateral securities given by the acceptor to the drawer or the indorsers.[23] But the holder is allowed to take the benefit of collateral securities given to it by the acceptor. As a general rule, an indorsee can prove in the estate of the acceptor only to the extent of the actual debt owing to the indorsee. Thus, if the principal debtor puts his name on bills of exchange and then delivers them to the debtor's creditor as collateral security for the debt, the creditor can only prove in the bankruptcy of the debtor for the actual debt remaining due to the creditor and not for the amount of the bills.[24]

10–57 But where the creditor is given the collateral securities of *third persons* for a greater amount than the debt, the creditor can prove and receive dividends upon the full amount of the securities in the estates of those persons to the extent of 100 pence in the pound up to the amount of the actual debt owed by the principal debtor.[25] In *Ex p. Phillips*,[26] for example, A owed B £277 and, to secure this debt, deposited with him bills to the amount of £1,518 drawn by A and accepted by C. A and C both became

---

[19] *Re Holder* [1929] 1 Ch. 205; *Re Amalgamated Investment & Property Co. Ltd* [1985] 1 Ch. 349 at 380, *per* Vinelott J; *Re Blackburne* (1892) 9 Mor. 249; *Ex p. Taylor* [1893] A.C. 181; *Cooper v Pepys* (1741) 1 Atk. 107; 26 E.R. 70; *Re Stein, Ex p. Royal Bank of Scotland* (1815) 2 Rosa 197; *Re Houghton* (1857) 26 L.J. Bcy. 58.

[20] *Re Fothergill* (1876) 3 Ch. D. 445; *Re London, Bombay & Mediterranean Bank* (1874) 9 Ch. App. 686.

[21] *Ex p. Taylor* [1893] A.C. 181; *Ex p. Cama* (1874) 9 Ch. App. 686.

[22] *Re Blakely Ex p. Harvey* (1854) 4 De G.M. & G. 881; 23 L.J. Bcy. 26.

[23] *Re Walker; Sheffield Banking Co v Clayton* [1892] 1 Ch. 621. See also above, para.10–47.

[24] *Ex p. Bloxham* (1801) 6 Ves. 449 at 450; 31 E.R. 1215; *Re Willats, Ex p. Reader* (1819) Buck 381.

[25] *Ex p. Bloxham* (1802) 6 Ves. 600; 31 E.R. 1215.

[26] (1840) I Mont. D. & De G. 232.

bankrupt. It was held that B, the creditor and holder of the bills, could prove for the full amount of the bills against C's estate in bankruptcy, though he was not allowed to receive dividends beyond £277. Any other result would have meant that the creditor would be deprived of the full benefit of the bills given to the creditor by the principal debtor as collateral security.[27]

Notwithstanding Mellish L.J.'s remarks in *Re Gomersall*,[28] it appears   **10–58** that a similar principle applies to accommodation bills given to the creditor as collateral security for the principal debt. Mellish LJ suggested that a different rule should govern accommodation bills because on such bills the acceptor cannot be sued for any larger sum than the amount for which the drawer can be sued.[29] However, in *Ex p. Newton*,[30] the Court of Appeal held that, when a bill of exchange, accepted for the accommodation of the drawer, is deposited by the drawer as security for a debt less than the amount of the bill, the holder is entitled to prove in the bankruptcy of the acceptor for the full amount of the bill, although the holder cannot receive dividends in excess of the debt due to him by the drawer.

The result is different where the third party gives his bills of exchange   **10–59** *directly* to the creditor in payment for goods or services delivered or supplied to the principal debtor.[31] In such a case, the creditor can only prove in the estate of the third party for the actual sum due to the creditor, not the amount of the bills: the bills are, in effect, a pro tanto payment for the goods or services.[32] On a similar principle, in *Re Barned's Banking Co v Leech's Claim*,[33] the proceeds of sale of cotton specifically pledged to meet a bill of exchange were paid to the holder and it was held that these amounts had to be applied in reduction of his proof against the estate of the acceptor of the bill. But the acceptor's trustee in bankruptcy is not allowed to set off the proceeds against the holder's proof.[34]

Where the benefit of a guarantee for payment of a promissory note is   **10–60** transferred with the note, the transferee cannot prove in the bankruptcy of the guarantor but can claim that the amount of the guarantee be brought into account between the parties to it. Furthermore, the transferee can stand in the place of the transferor in respect of any balance found to be due to the transferee to the extent of the guarantee.[35] Generally, however, the acceptor's right to the benefit of a guarantee given to the acceptor is not transferred to the holder of the bill,[36] unless, of course, the guarantee is given for the express purpose of being exhibited to all the world.[37]

---

[27] *Ex p. Bloxham* (1802) 6 Ves. 600; 31 E.R. 1215.
[28] (1875) 1 Ch. D. 137. See this case on appeal: *Jones v Gordon* (1887) 2 App. Cas. 616.
[29] (1875) 1 Ch. D. 137 at 142.
[30] (1880) 16 Ch. D. 330. Perhaps this case can be explained on the basis that the holder had no notice that the bill was an accommodation bill.
[31] *Re Willats, Ex p. Reader* (1819) Buck 381 at 385.
[32] *ibid.*
[33] (1871) 6 Ch. App. 388.
[34] *ibid.*, at 392.
[35] *Re Barrington* (1804) 2 Sch. & Lef. 112.
[36] *Re Barned's Banking Co, Ex p. Stephens* (1868) 3 Ch. App. 753.
[37] *Re Agra and Masterman's Bank, Ex p. Asiatic Banking Co* (1867) 2 Ch. App. 391; *Re Barned's Banking Co, Ex p. Stephens* (1868) 3 Ch. App. 753 at 757.

(vii) The creditor's right to prove in the bankruptcy or liquidation of the guarantor

(a) The general principle

10–61   The creditor can prove in the bankruptcy or liquidation of the guarantor in respect of the guarantor's liability under the guarantee whether it is absolute, as on default by the principal debtor, or merely contingent,[38] for example, where the liability does not crystallise until a demand is made on the guarantor. The creditor can prove for the principal debt in the bankruptcy or liquidation of the guarantor even after the dissolution of the principal debtor since in that event the debtor is released by the operation of law not by the agreement of the parties.[39] But, depending upon the precise wording of the guarantee, the creditor may be unable to prove for interest on the debt subsequent to the date of the principal's bankruptcy or winding-up.[40] Furthermore, no interest which accrues subsequent to the guarantor's bankruptcy is recoverable as a provable debt.[41]

10–62   Although the creditor has the general right to prove in the bankruptcy or liquidation of the guarantor, the creditor cannot assume that the guarantor's liability will be admitted simply on the faith of a judgment or award against the principal debtor.[42] It will be necessary to prove the liability of the guarantor independently.[43]

(b) The effect of payment by or on behalf of the principal debtor before the date of the creditor's proof in the bankruptcy or liquidation of a guarantor

10–63   Payments by or on behalf of the principal before the date of the creditor's proof will reduce the amount of the guaranteed debt if appropriated by either the principal or creditor to that debt.[44] If as in the usual case the guarantor is liable for the whole debt but with a limit on his liability, such an appropriation means that the amount of the creditor's proof in the guarantor's bankruptcy or winding-up must

---

[38] See Insolvency Rules 1986 (SI 1986/1925), r.12.3. See also *Re Sudell Ex p. Simpson* (1834) 3 Deac. & Ch. 792; 3 L.J. Bcy. 113. Similar principles should apply to a creditor's right to prove in respect of a claim under a contract of indemnity.

[39] *Re Fitzgeorge* [1905] 1 K.B. 462: see above, para.6–88.

[40] See above, paras 5–51 to 5–53 and 6–88. Interest is limited to 8% per annum: Bankruptcy Act 1995, s.94(1) and Bankruptcy Rules, r.185.

[41] Bankruptcy Act 1995, s.94(1). See also I.F. Fletcher, *The Law of Insolvency* (3rd ed., 2002), para. 9–052. Compare *Re Ho Kok Cheong, Ex p. Banque Paribas* (unreported, High Court, Judith Prakash J., May 22, 2000) 2000–4 S.L.R. 742; 2000 S.L.R. Lexis 56.

[42] See above, paras 5–99 to 5–100.

[43] *Ex p. Young* (1881) 17 Ch. D. 668, discussed above, para.5–99.

[44] See generally above, paras 6–16 to 6–48. If a third party, such as a government department, reimburses the guarantor for the liability it has discharged under the guarantee, the guarantor is still entitled to enforce a right of indemnity against the principal debtor and a right to contribution against co-sureties, although the guarantor will, of course, be accountable to the government department for any sums recovered up to the amount of the reimbursement.

correspondingly be reduced.[45] For example, where there is a guarantee of a whole debt of £100,000 with a limit on the guarantor's liability to £20,000 and the debtor pays the creditor £50,000 in reduction of the principal debt, the creditor is only entitled to prove for a debt of £50,000 in the guarantor's bankruptcy or liquidation and can recover dividends up to £20,000. If the debtor had paid the creditor £90,000, the creditor would only be entitled to prove in the guarantor's bankruptcy or liquidation for a debt of £10,000 and recover dividends on that amount.

In the case where the guarantor is liable for part of the debt, as distinct **10–64** from a guarantee of the whole debt with a specified limitation on her or his liability,[46] whether such payments are attributed to the guaranteed portion of the debt or the other portion is a matter of appropriation between the creditor and the principal debtor.[47] In the absence of express provisions in the guarantee, the surety's trustee in bankruptcy cannot insist that the principal debtor's payments be applied solely to liquidate the guaranteed part of the debt.[48] Indeed, the principal contract may give the creditor an express right to appropriate the payments received from the debtor to the portion of the debt which has not been guaranteed or as the creditor sees fit.

(c) The effect of realising securities provided by the principal debtor before the creditor proves in the bankruptcy or liquidation of a guarantor

The proceeds of securities given by the principal to the creditor for the **10–65** enforcement of the principal obligation must normally be appropriated in reduction of the guaranteed debt[49] and, therefore, will have the same effect as actual payments by the principal which have been appropriated in respect of the guaranteed debt.[50] But in this situation there is a special rule (discussed elsewhere)[51] where the guarantee relates to only a part of a debt. Where a guarantor provides a security, the proceeds of the security must normally be appropriated in reduction of the guarantor's liability so that the creditor's right of proof in the guarantor's bankruptcy will be correspondingly reduced.[52]

---

[45] *Re Houlder* [1929] 1 Ch. 205 at 209; *Re Blakeley* (1892) 9 Mor. 173; *Re J Le Bar Seafoods Inc* (1981) 38 C.B.R. (NS) 64 at 68; *Re Amalgamated Investment & Property Co Ltd* (1984) 1 B.C.C. 99,104 at 99,120; *Re Agricultural Wholesale Society Ltd* [1929] 2 Ch. 261; *Re Parent Trust & Finance Co Ltd* [1936] 1 All E.R. 641.
[46] See above, paras 5–35 to 5–40.
[47] See above, paras 6–16 to 6–20.
[48] *Re Sherry* (1884) 25 Ch. D. 692. See also *Raikes v Todd* (1838) 8 Ad. & E. 844; 8 L.J. Q.B. 35.
[49] See above, paras 6–23 to 6–32.
[50] See previous paragraphs in this section and *Re Hunter Ex p. Bank of New South Wales* [1982] Qd. R. 131 at 133.
[51] See above, paras 6–23 to 6–32.
[52] See above, paras 6–33 to 6–35.

10–66   A creditor is not a secured creditor of the guarantor simply because it has securities from the principal debtor in respect of the principal debt;[53] these securities will not enure for the benefit of the separate estate of the guarantor.[54] Consequently, such a creditor is entitled to realise its securities to recover the principal debt, including contractual interest up to the date of disposal of the mortgaged properties.[55] It can then prove in the bankruptcy or liquidation of the guarantor for the outstanding balance of the principal debt whether it is principal or interest.[56] The creditor's proof is not restricted to pre-bankruptcy interest or post-liquidation interest at the prescribed rate, and the creditor can prove for pre-bankruptcy interest or post-liquidation interest up to the date of realisation of the securities even if there is no surplus in the guarantor's estate.

(d) The effect of payment by the principal debtor after the date of the creditor's proof in the bankruptcy or liquidation of a guarantor

10–67   It is not necessary for the creditor to reduce its proof to take into account payments received from the debtor or dividends declared in the debtor's bankruptcy or liquidation *after* the creditor lodges a proof in the bankruptcy or liquidation of a guarantor.[57] Otherwise, the creditor would be required to lodge an amended proof whenever it received or became entitled to a payment or dividend after the submission of its proof, but before the proof was admitted.[58] However, the creditor is not entitled to recover more than 100 pence in the pound of the principal debt and will be expected to account to the paying guarantors for any excess.[59] This is merely an illustration of the rule against double satisfaction.[60]

---

[53] *Re Ho Kok Cheong, Ex p. Banque Paribas* (unreported, High Court, Judith Prakash J., May 22, 2000) 2000–4 S.L.R. 742; 2000 S.L.R. LEXIS 56.

[54] *ibid.*; *Re Turner, Ex p. West Riding Union Banking Co* (1881–82) 19 Ch. D. 105.

[55] *Re Dutton, Massey & Co, Ex p. Manchester and Liverpool District Banking Co Ltd* [1924] 2 Ch. 199.

[56] *Re Ho Kok Cheong, Ex p. Banque Paribas* (unreported, High Court, Judith Prakash J., May 22, 2000) 2000–4 S.L.R. 742; 2000 S.L.R. LEXIS 56.

[57] *Re Amalgamated Investment & Property Co Ltd* [1985] Ch. 349; *Re Agricultural Wholesale Society Ltd* [1929] 2 Ch. 261; *Re Parent Trust & Finance Co Ltd* [1936] 1 All E.R. 641.

[58] See *Re Amalgamated Investment & Property Co Ltd* [1985] 1 Ch. 349 at 384.

[59] *Cf. Westpac Banking Corp v Gollin & Co Ltd* [1988] V.R. 397 at 409–410, where a similar conclusion was reached where the creditor proved in the bankruptcy of the *principal debtor*. See also *Re Houlder* [1929] 1 Ch. 205 at 213, where Astbury J. reached a similar conclusion in relation to a situation where the creditor received payments *otherwise than from the principal debtor* and proved in a surety's bankruptcy.

[60] *Windham v Wither* (1723) 1 Str. 515; 93 E.R. 671; *Midland Montagu Australia Ltd v Harkness* (1994) 35 N.S.W.L.R. 150. Compare *Farrow Finance Company Ltd (In Liq.) v ANZ Executors and Trustee Co Ltd* [1998] 1 V.R. 50, where the rule against double satisfaction did not apply.

(e) The effect of payment by a co-surety before the date of the creditor's proof in the bankruptcy or liquidation of a guarantor

In *Re Houlder*[61] Astbury J. declared: **10–68**

"a creditor who receives payments otherwise than from the principal debtor (before the date of the creditor's proof) can prove for his whole debt in the surety's bankruptcy so long as he does not get more than 20s in the pound."[62]

Any other result would give the unsecured creditors of the surety an unwarranted windfall because neither the creditor nor the paying surety would be entitled to prove for the amount of the payment.

In *Commercial Bank of Australia v Official Assignee of the Estate of* **10–69** *Wilson*,[63] after payment by three out of four co-sureties into a suspense account from which the creditor could at will appropriate in payment of their respective shares of the common liability, the creditor was allowed to prove for the full amount of the guaranteed debt in the bankruptcy of the fourth guarantor. The deposit in the suspense account was not even a partial discharge until the creditor appropriated the money in reduction of the guaranteed debt. There are statements in the Privy Council's judgment in this case, however, which suggest that, had an appropriation been made, the creditor would have been required to reduce his proof against the fourth surety.[64] With respect, this approach should not be adopted as it is inconsistent with authority and common sense.

A special rule applies to proofs of debt by holders of negotiable **10–70** instruments in the bankruptcy or liquidation of the drawer or indorsers who are liable as quasi-sureties in respect of the acceptor's debt. In *Re Amalgamated Investment & Property Co Ltd*[65] Vinelott J. expressed the principle in the following terms:

"In the case of a cheque a bill of exchange or a promissory note for valuable consideration the holder, while he may prove against the estate of all persons liable on it, must deduct in his proof all sums received from or dividends declared from the estates of all other parties liable and not only from the estate of the person principally liable."[66]

---

[61] [1929] 1 Ch. 205.
[62] *ibid.*, at 213.
[63] [1893] A.C. 181. See also above, paras 6–16 *et. seq.*
[64] See *Re Houlder* [1929] 1 Ch. 205 at 211.
[65] (1984) 1 B.C.C. 99,104.
[66] *ibid.*, at 99,117–8. It certainly is true that the holder must give credit for any payments received (or dividends declared) upon this proof against the acceptor when he lodges a proof of debt against the estate of the drawer: *Re Stein, Ex p. Royal Bank of Scotland* (1815) 19 Ves. 310; 34 E.R. 532; *Westpac Banking Corporation v Gollin & Co Ltd* [1988] V.R. 397 at 407–408. See P. Wood, *English and International Set-Off* (1989) para.10.120.

10-71   This statement summarises an old rule which has never been satisfactorily explained but which is confined to bills of exchange or kindred instruments.[67] In *Westpac Banking Corp v Gollin & Co Ltd*,[68] Tadgell J. placed the rule in its historical perspective:

> "Historically, the courts seem to have taken the view, in the light of the nature of a negotiable instrument, that the holder of a bill must be content, if one of the parties liable upon it becomes bankrupt, to prove in the bankruptcy for only so much of the value of the bill as he has not received before proof from the bankrupt and the other parties liable on the bill."[69]

10-72   In *Ex p. Leers*,[70] Lord Eldon applied the rule but expressed "considerable doubt whether a man having a bill, by virtue of which he has three debtors, is not entitled to prove the whole against each estate, until he has received 20s in the pound".[71] Perhaps the best explanation of the rule is that a payment of merely part of the face value of a bill of exchange is merely a part payment of what the *instrument itself* entitles the holder to receive.[72] Moreover, unlike a guarantee, the bill of exchange contains no stipulation that the persons occupying the position of sureties or quasi-sureties on the bill are guarantors of the whole debt.[73] It should follow, therefore, that a part payment by one of the parties liable on a bill of exchange should reduce the amount of the holder's proof on the bill as there is no other basis for maintaining that the parties remain liable for the full amount of the bill.

10-73   Whatever the correct explanation of the rule, it is generally accepted that it should be confined to bills of exchange[74] and it does not detract from the general principle espoused by Astbury J. in *Re Houlder*.

10-74   Nevertheless, the creditor's right to prove for the gross amount of its debt has not been universally recognised. In *Stotter & Downey as Liquidators of Equiticorp Industries Group Ltd (in liq) v Equiticorp Australia Limited (in liq)*[75] Fisher J. of the High Court of New Zealand held that a creditor could not lodge a proof of debt for the full amount of the principal debt in the liquidations of companies in a debtor group comprising borrowers and co-sureties, without giving credit for amounts

[67] See *Cooper v Pepys* (1741) 1 Atk. 107; 26 E.R. 70; *Ex p. Wildman* (1750) 1 Atk. 109; 26 E.R. 72; *Ex p. Leers* (1802) 6 Ves. Jun. 644; 31 E.R. 1237; *Ex p. Royal Bank of Scotland* (1815) 19 Ves. Jun. 310; 34 E.R. 532. An exception appears to be *Ex p. Gilbey* (1878) 8 Ch. D. 248, which involved a composition and can be explained on another basis: see *Westpac Banking Corp v Gollin & Co Ltd* [1988] V.R. 397 at 400.
[68] [1988] V.R. 397.
[69] *ibid.*
[70] (1802) 6 Ves. 644; 31 E.R. 1237.
[71] *ibid.*, at 645; 1238.
[72] *Ex p. Taylor* (1857) 1 De G. & J. 302 at 306; 44 E.R. 740 at 742, *per* Knight Bruce L.J.
[73] *Westpac Banking Corp v Gollin & Co Ltd* [1988] V.R. 397 at 408.
[74] *Re Blackburne* (1892) 9 Morr. 249 at 252; *Re Houlder* [1929] 1 Ch 205; R M Goode, *Legal Problems of Credit and Security* (3rd ed., 2003), para.8-32; *Muir Hunter on Personal Insolvency*, paras 2-710 to 2-715; E.F. McDonald, H.A. Henry & H.G. Meek, *Australian Bankruptcy Law and Practice*, (5th ed., 1977, Looseleaf) para.386.
[75] Unreported, High Court of New Zealand, Fisher J., November 15, 2001.

paid to the creditor prior to the liquidations. It was immaterial whether the pre-liquidation payment was made by the principal debtor or a surety. His Honour observed:

"As a matter of general principle, it would be surprising if, by a contract to which the general body of creditors were not a party, and which created no proprietary interest nor one of the recognised foundations for priority, a creditor could effectively gain priority over the general body of creditors. Were it contractually possible to make inflation of a debt conditional upon bankruptcy or liquidation one would expect such a term to be routinely included in every contract where credit is extended. ... [A]ttempts to contractually modify insolvency laws in that way would seem contrary to fundamental insolvency principles..."[76]

His Honour noted that such terms are ineffective where the member of **10–75** the debtor group that effected a reduction in the debt was the principal debtor. And he declined to follow Tadgell J. in *Westpac Banking Corp v Gollin & Co Ltd*[77] in applying a different rule to the situation where payment was effected by a surety, rather than the principal debtor. In that case Tadgell J. was prepared to allow the creditor to prove for the full amount of the principal debt in this situation without deducting the pre-liquidation payment received from the surety. Fisher J. in *Stotter & Downey as Liquidators of Equiticorp Industries Group Ltd (in liq) v Equiticorp Australia Limited (in liq)*[78] rejected this approach on the following ground:

"It is far from clear why, by a bilateral contract to which the general body of creditors were not a party, the creditor who happened to take a guarantee from a third party should receive a greater share than the others."[79]

With respect, the reason why the creditor stands to receive more than **10–76** the other unsecured creditors in the liquidation is because that is the basis on which the financial accommodation was provided to the principal debtor and the basis on which the guarantee was taken. In any event, the creditor does not receive a proportionately higher dividend on its debt; it is just that the principal debt is not reduced by the pre-liquidation payment so that the amount on which the creditor's dividend is calculated is the gross amount of the debt. This is a consequence of the creditor's right of appropriation. In any event, the creditor is not entitled to receive more than 100 pence in the pound and if it does so it will hold the surplus on trust for the paying surety.

---

[76] Paragraph 53 of the unreported judgment.
[77] [1988] V.R. 397.
[78] Unreported, High Court of New Zealand, Fisher J., November 15, 2001.
[79] Paragraph 58 of the unreported judgment.

While on the *Gollin*[80] view, a pre-liquidation payment by a surety should not be applied in reduction of the principal debt, unless it is appropriated to that debt,[81] it may be possible for the liquidator of an insolvent surety to challenge the pre-liquidation payment as a preference.[82]

10–77   The formal requirements relating to proofs of debts[83] do not displace the general rule that the creditor need not reduce its proof of debt in the bankruptcy or liquidation of a guarantor by the amount of any prior payments received from a co-surety.[84] A creditor who receives payments or dividends from a co-surety is still entitled to prove for the whole of its debt in the bankruptcy or liquidation of a guarantor because that guarantor is still indebted to the creditor for the whole debt.

10–78   In some respects, a set-off is a form of payment. If one of the co-guarantors in a joint and several covenant is sued by the creditor, can that co-guarantor set off a debt owing by the creditor to one of the co-sureties? *Bowyear v Pawson*[85] suggests that there is no such right of set-off, so it cannot be used to force the creditor to reduce the proof.

(f) The effect of payment by the co-surety after the date of the creditor's proof in the bankruptcy or liquidation of a guarantor

10–79   Even the strict rule which applies to bills of exchange[86] does not require the creditor to reduce its proof after it has been submitted in the bankruptcy or liquidation of a guarantor to take into account payments received from, or dividends declared by, a co-surety or co-surety's estate.[87] This saves the creditor from the expense and inconvenience of amending the proof whenever it receives or becomes entitled to a payment or dividend from a co-surety before the proof is admitted by the trustee in bankruptcy or the liquidator. By the same token, a creditor is not entitled to recover more than 100 pence in the pound of the principal debt, and will be expected to account to the guarantors for any excess.[88]

---

[80] [1988] V.R. 397.

[81] It may be noted that in *Stotter & Downey as Liquidators of Equiticorp Industries Group Ltd (in liq) v Equiticorp Australia Ltd (in liq)* the pre-liquidation payment was, in fact, appropriated to the principal debt.

[82] See Insolvency Act 1986, s.236.

[83] As to the formal requirements relating to proof of debt, see I.F. Fletcher, *The Law of Insolvency* (3rd ed., 2002), paras 23–006 to 23–007 and Insolvency Rules 1986, rr.4.73, 4.75, 4.182(2), Form 25 and *Practice Direction* [1987] 1 All E.R. 107.

[84] See above, paras 10–68 to 10–69.

[85] (1881) 6 Q.B.D. 540.

[86] See above, paras 10–70 to 10–73.

[87] *Re Amalgamated Investment & Property Co Ltd* [1985] Ch. 349 at 379–386; *Re Joint Stock Discount Co* (1869) L.R. 5 Ch. App. 86; *Re Blakeley. Ex p. Aachener Disconto Gesellschaft* (1892) 9 Morr. 173; *Midland Montagu Australia Ltd v Harkness* (1994) 124 A.L.R. 407 at 416.

[88] See *Westpac Banking Corp v Gollin & Co Ltd* [1988] V.R. 397 at 409–410; *Midland Montagu Australia Ltd v Harkness* (1994) 124 A.L.R. 407. Cf. *Re Houlder* [1929] 1 Ch. 205 at 213.

(viii) The creditor's right to prove where both the principal debtor and the guarantor are bankrupt or in liquidation

The general rule is that the creditor can lodge a proof against both **10–80** estates for the full amount of the principal debt and is not required to reduce its proof against one estate to take account of dividends declared or received from the other, provided of course that the creditor does not receive in total more than 100 pence in the pound.[89]

(ix) Proofs for interest

A creditor will not be entitled to prove for the full amount of the interest **10–81** payable on the principal debt. In the compulsory winding up of an insolvent company, a claim for interest on a debt carrying interest can only be admitted up to the date of presentation of the petition.[90]

(x) The creditor's entitlement to securities

The creditor may enforce any additional securities given to it by the **10–82** guarantor, although the proceeds of realisation must be appropriated in reduction of that guarantor's liability.[91] This will not, however, reduce the creditor's proof against the other guarantors of the whole debt. Similarly, securities taken from the principal may be realised, provided that the proceeds are appropriated in reduction of the principal debt.[92]

In general, however, the creditor has no equity or interest in any **10–83** securities which the guarantor has taken from a third party.[93] For example, if the guarantor's obligation is itself secured by an indemnity or a collateral security taken from a third party, then the creditor has no right to the benefit of this indemnity or collateral security.[94] Indeed, the creditor has no equity or interest in any counter-securities the guarantor may have taken from the principal in order to secure the guarantor's right of indemnity against the principal.[95] Thus in *Re Standard Insurance Co Ltd (in liq) and Companies Act 1936*[96] the guarantor company took from the principal debtor debentures as collateral security for its contingent liability under the guarantee. Both the principal debtor and the guarantor became

---

[89] *Re Sass* [1896] 2 Q.B. 12; *Re Rees* (1881) 17 Ch. D. 98; *Ex p. Rushforth* (1805) 10 Ves. 409 at 417; 32 E.R. 903 at 906; *Cooper v Pepys* (1741) 1 Atk. 107; 27 E.R. 710; *Re Fothergill Ex p. Turquand* (1876) 3 Ch. D. 445 at 450; *Re Blakeley* (1892) 9 Morr. 173; *Re Houlder* [1929] 1 Ch. 205.

[90] Insolvency Act 1986, ss.322(2) and 328(4); Insolvency Rules 1986, r.6.113; I.F. Fletcher, *The Law of Insolvency* (3rd ed., 2002), paras 9–052 to 9–053.

[91] See above, paras 6–33 to 6–35. Note, however, the contrary view in *Bank of Adelaide v Lorden* (1970) 45 A.L.J.R. 49.

[92] See above, paras 6–23 to 6–32.

[93] *Re Standard Insurance Co Ltd (in liq) and the Companies Act* 1936 [1970] 1 N.S.W.R. 392 at 396, and the cases cited therein.

[94] *Re Harrington Motor Co Ltd Ex p. Chaplin* [1928] 1 Ch. 105.

[95] *Re Standard Insurance Co Ltd (in liq) and the Companies Act 1936* [1970] 1 N.S.W.R. 599.

[96] [1970] 1 N.S.W.R. 599.

insolvent. It was held that the creditor had no right to enforce this security but was merely entitled to prove as an unsecured creditor in the winding-up of the guarantor. Street J. also took the view that the proceeds of the debenture in the guarantor's hands should be applied in meeting the amount of the creditor's dividend as an unsecured creditor in the winding-up of the guarantor company, and any surplus proceeds after covering the creditor's dividend should be returned to the principal for the benefit of its creditors generally.[97]

10–84   The rule that the creditor has no equity in collateral securities held by the guarantor means that the principal can create charges in favour of the guarantor after the execution of the guarantee even if they may prejudice the position of the creditor. Thus where the principal debtor granted an equitable charge to the guarantor, it was held[98] that the creditor was not entitled to the benefit of the security, even though the guarantor was the parent company of the principal debtor. The charge could, therefore, be enforced by a bank which had taken an assignment of the charge without notice of the guarantee. The conclusion was not affected by the fact that the guarantor had agreed by the terms of the guarantee not to claim the benefit of any dividend in the receivership of the debtor or diminish any payment which the creditor might receive. A specific clause prohibiting the guarantor from taking any securities from the principal would, however, mean that the guarantor would be in breach of the contract of guarantee in this situation.

10–85   There are two exceptions to the general rule prohibiting the creditor from claiming and enforcing collateral securities held either by the principal debtor or the guarantor. First, where a drawer of a bill of exchange lodges with an acceptor a security to meet the bill at maturity and both the drawer and acceptor become insolvent and fall under a forced administration, the holder of the bill is entitled to have the security appropriated towards payment of the bill. This is the so-called rule in *Ex p. Waring*.[99] Although the acceptor may be regarded as being in the position of a principal debtor and the drawer as being in the position of the surety, the rule has been specifically confined to the context of the concurrent insolvency of two parties liable on a bill of exchange.[1]

10–86   The second exception is that the creditor may be able to claim for its own benefit a counter-security given by the principal debtor to the guarantor if the guarantor is constituted a trustee of the security for the creditor.[2] A clause might specifically be included in the guarantee for this

---

[97] *ibid.*, at 399–400.
[98] *F. J. Hawkes & Co (Aust) Pty Ltd v International Hydrodynamics Pty Ltd* (unreported, NSW Sup Ct, October 17, 1979).
[99] (1815) 19 Ves. 345; 34 E.R. 546. See below, para.10–88.
[1] *Re Standard Insurance Co Ltd (in liq) and Companies Act 1936* [1970] 1 N.S.W.R. 599.
[2] *Ex p. Rushworth* (1805) 10 Ves. 409 at 421; 32 E.R. 903 at 907–908. Contrast *Wilding v Richards* (1845) 1 Coll. 655; 63 E.R. 584. This exception may explain the otherwise anomalous decision in *Re Richardson* [1911] 2 K.B. 705. See its interpretation, *e.g.* in *Hood's Trustees v Southern Union General Insurance Co of A/asia* [1928] 1 Ch. 793 at 805. Note also that in *F. J. Hawkes & Co (Aust) Pty Ltd v International Hydrodynamics Pty Ltd* (unreported, NSW Sup Ct, October 17, 1979), this possibility is recognised by Rath J. in his discussion of *Ford v Beech* (1846) 11 Q.B. 842; 116 E.R. 689.

purpose, although standard instruments of guarantee seldom contain such a provision.

Even if the creditor does not take any collateral securities from the **10–87** guarantor at the time the guarantee is given, the guarantee may provide that the creditor will be entitled to an equitable charge on the guarantor's property on default by the borrower. In *Murphy v Wright*,[3] the deed of guarantee contained a term that, on default by the borrower, the lender would be entitled to attach the debt to any real or personal property of the guarantor and to register a caveat against any of the guarantor's registered land. The New South Wales Court of Appeal held that the guarantee conferred an option to create an equitable charge over the registered land upon the borrower's default and that this was a caveatable interest; the option was exercisable by lodging a caveat.[4] However, the option to attach the debt to the guarantor's other property failed because the deed of guarantee did not specify how this option was to be exercised. This case offers lenders a better prospect of recovery than simply relying upon a personal action against the guarantors, but it is clear that the foundation of the equitable charge must be laid in the terms of the guarantee itself.

The rule in Ex p. Waring

In *Ex p. Dever; Re Suse (No.2)*,[5] the rule was expressed in the following **10–88** terms:

"Where, as between the drawer and the acceptor of a bill of exchange, a security has, by virtue of a contract between them, been specifically appropriated to meet that bill at maturity, and has been lodged for that purpose by the drawer with the acceptor; then, if both drawer and acceptor become insolvent, and their estates are brought under a forced administration, the bill-holder, though neither party nor privy to the contract, is entitled to have the specifically appropriated security applied in or towards payment of the bill."[6]

The specifically-appropriated securities are, therefore, available to the holder of the bill who can have them applied in or towards payment of the bill. Since such securities were deposited for the express purpose of covering the acceptor's liability on the bill, they are impressed with a trust for that purpose. Accordingly, they do not belong to the acceptor's general creditors, nor do they pass to his trustee in bankruptcy.

---

[3] (1992) 5 B.P.R. 11,734.
[4] The English equivalent of a caveat is a caution or restriction, See Land Registration Act 2002, Pt.4 and ss.15–19.
[5] (1885) 14 Q.B.D. 611.
[6] *ibid.*, at 620. In *Star v Silvia; Silvia v Genoa Resources & Investments Ltd (No.2)* (1994) 12 A.C.L.C. 608, the rule in *Ex p. Waring* (1815) 19 Ves. Jun. 345; 34 E.R. 546 did not apply because the relationship between the parties was not that of drawer and acceptor and because the security in question was inadequate.

10–89   Where the security lodged by the drawer with the acceptor takes the form of a deposit of money, the holder is entitled to have the funds paid to him in full upon the insolvency of both the drawer and the acceptor. [7] Moreover, the holder may prove in the drawer's insolvency for the balance of the guaranteed debt remaining after taking into account the deposit. But the holder must refund any dividends paid in excess of the amount of his reduced proof of debt.[8]

10–90   The rule in *Ex p. Waring*[9] is a positive rule dealing with the administration of estates and is not "the necessary result of equitable principles."[10] Nevertheless, it appears that the rule might not be applied where the value of the security is less than the liability owed to the holder of the bills.[11] To apply the rule in this situation would deprive the general creditors of the bankrupt acceptor of some part of the indemnity to which the acceptor is entitled under his contract with the drawer.[12] Where the value of the security exceeds the liability owed to the holder of the bills, this problem does not arise because the holder is not compelled to claim against the estates of both the drawer and the acceptor for a deficiency.

10–91   The rule will, in general, be restricted to the situation where two parties to a bill of exchange are concurrently insolvent,[13] although it is not necessary for both to have been formally adjudged bankrupt.[14] Moreover, the rule does not apply unless the holder is entitled to prove against both insolvent estates. Consequently, where the bill was dishonoured for non-acceptance, the rule in *Ex p. Waring* had no application.[15] But it is not essential that the securities be deposited by a party to the bill, as it is enough that the depositor is liable *in respect of the bill transaction*.[16]

---

[7] See *Re Suse, Ex p. Dever (No.2)* (1885) 14 Q.B.D. 611 at 623 *per* Brett M.R.
[8] *Re Barden's Banking Co* (1875) L.R. 10 Ch. App. 198.
[9] (1815) 19 Ves. Jun. 345; 34 E.R. 546.
[10] *Royal Bank of Scotland v Commercial Bank of Scotland* (1882) 7 App. Cas. 366 at 387.
[11] *ibid. Cf. Powles v Hargreaves* (1853) 3 De.G.M. & G. 430; 43 E.R. 169.
[12] *Royal Bank of Scotland v Commercial Bank of Scotland* (1882) 7 App. Cas. 366 at 387 *per* Lord Selborne L.C., 393 *per* Lord Blackburn. For a fairer method of calculating the respective dividends of the parties, see (1882) 7 App. Cas. 366 at 390–391 *per* Lord Blackburn. See also *Re Standard Insurance Co Ltd (in liq) and the Companies Act 1936* [1970] 1 N.S.W.R. 599 at 399–400 *per* Street J. (as he then was). See generally D Partlett, "The Right of Subrogation in Accommodation Bills of Exchange" (1979) 53 A.L.J. 694.
[13] *Re Standard Insurance Co Ltd (in liq) and the Companies Act 1936* [1970] 1 N.S.W.R. 599; *Commissioners of State Savings Bank of Victoria v Patrick Intermarine Acceptances Ltd (in liq)* [1981] 1 N.S.W.L.R. 175.
[14] *Powles v Hargreaves* (1853) 3 De. G.M. & G. 430; 43 E.R. 769; *Bank of Ireland v Perry* (1871) L.R. 7 Ex. 14; *City Bank v Luckie* (1870) 5 Ch. App. 773; *Re Barned's Bank, Ex p. Joint Stock Discount Co* (1875) L.R. 10 Ch. 198. *Cf. Royal Bank of Scotland v Commercial Bank of Scotland* (1882) 7 App. Cas. 366. The rule will not apply, however, unless the estate of the drawer who remits a bill of exchange to cover the bill on which he is liable as drawer is still within the jurisdiction of the court: *Ex p. General South American Co; Re Yglesias* (1875) 10 Ch. App. 639.
[15] *Vaughan v Halliday* (1874) 9 Ch. App. 561. Nor does the rule apply where the funds claimed for the benefit of the bill-holders are absolutely and entirely the property of, and in the possession of, only one of the parties, for example, where an agent consigns goods to the agent's principal, and both go bankrupt: *Ex p. Banner* (1876) 2 Ch. D. 278. See also *Ex p. Lambton* (1875) 10 Ch. App. 405.
[16] *Ex p. Smart* (1872) 8 Ch. App. 220.

(xi) The creditor's right to retain the title deeds of a third party mortgagor/guarantor

It is perhaps a reasonable expectation that a guarantor who has given a **10–92** mortgage to secure his secondary liability for the debts of a borrower should be entitled to the discharge of that mortgage and the return of the title deed when the lender is repaid in full. If the guarantor then decides to sell the property to a third party, it is reasonable to assume that the guarantor will be solely entitled to the proceeds of sale. In *Project Research Pty Ltd v Permanent Trustee of Australia Ltd*, [17] Hodgson J. exposed the flaws in these assumptions.

It seems a reasonable inference from *Project Research Pty Ltd v* **10–93** *Permanent Trustee of Australia Ltd* that a creditor will not be required to return a third party mortgagor's title deed upon payment of the principal debt where the mortgagor is threatening to institute proceedings for the taking of accounts between the mortgagor and the mortgagee, because in such proceedings the mortgagee may incur further costs and expenses. The mortgagee may wish to recover these costs and expenses under its security.

4. THE CREDITOR'S RIGHT TO ENFORCE THE GUARANTEE BY ACTION

(i) Conditions precedent to the guarantor's liability

In Chapter 8, we saw that the guarantor may be discharged by a breach **10–94** of a promissory condition of the guarantee or a failure of a condition precedent to the operation of the guarantee.[18] Common illustrations are a condition that a particular security be obtained by the creditor;[19] that a co-surety be made a party to the guarantee; [20] or that the principal loan be made upon certain terms.[21]

Such terms may be drafted as conditions precedent to liability but in the **10–95** context of the creditor's enforcement of the guarantee, the most relevant express conditions precedent are likely to be a requirement to serve notices of default or demand upon the principal or to submit disputes arising under the principal contract to arbitration.[22]

---

[17] Unreported, NSW Sup Ct, December 14, 1990.
[18] See above, paras 8–01 to 8–19.
[19] See above, paras 8–57 to 8–61. See, *e.g. W R Ruffler Pty Ltd v Idohold Pty Ltd* (unreported, NSW Sup Ct, November 19, 1990).
[20] See above, paras 3–87 to 3–98.
[21] See above, para.5–49 and paras 8–15 to 8–19.
[22] *Roux v Langtree* [1985] V.R. 799. *Cf. Thermistocles Navegacion SA v Langton (The "Queen Frederica")* [1978] 2 Lloyd's Rep. 164, where the Court of Appeal refused to imply a term that arbitration proceedings were a condition precedent to the defendant's liability because such a term was inconsistent with the express provisions of the guarantee. Where the loan facility agreement stipulated that the creditor could demand that the principal debtor pay within 48 hours all money owing, a demand requiring payment "forthwith" was defective: *Hong Kong Bank of Australia Ltd v McKenna* (unreported, Qld Sup Ct, December 13, 1993).

10–96   Although the matter has been discussed in detail elsewhere,[23] it should be emphasised that conditions precedent to liability require strict compliance.[24] Thus in *Tricontinental Ltd v HDFI Ltd*,[25] an Underpinning Agreement in the nature of a guarantee contained certain conditions precedent to the entitlement of the appellant to make a demand on the respondent for payment under the agreement. The relevant provision provided inter alia that, in the event of a default, which was capable of rectification by the principal debtor (Selkis), the appellant should serve a notice on Selkis requiring rectification of the default within seven days. Within 24 hours of issuing the notice to Selkis, the appellant was required to send a further notice to the respondent informing it of the event of default and of the notice served on Selkis. If Selkis failed to rectify the default within seven days, the appellant was required to notify the respondent of Selkis' failure to rectify the default.

10–97   The Court of Appeal of the Supreme Court of New South Wales held that these provisions were conditions precedent to the liability of the respondent. Hence strict, literal compliance with the conditions and the time limits was required. In the result, the respondent escaped liability to pay nearly £14 million because, inter alia, the appellant had failed to serve Selkis at its Perth address as stipulated in the guarantee and failed to give notice to the respondent of the failure of Selkis to remedy the default after the expiry of the seven-day period. It was not subsequently possible to serve other valid notices as the guarantee itself had expired.

10–98   In the United Kingdom it may be that strict compliance with a condition precedent to liability is not required. In *Oval (717) Ltd v Aegon Insurance Company (UK) Ltd*[26] it was a condition precedent to the plaintiff's right to recover under a performance bond that the plaintiff give defendant surety written notice of any "non-performance or non-observance on the part of the contractors of any of the stipulations or provisions contained in the" main contract within one month after the employer's supervisor learned of the default. Mr Recorder Colin Reese Q.C. held that a failure to comply with this condition precedent in respect of any *not-insubstantial breach* of the main contract prevented the plaintiff from enforcing the performance bond.

10–99   Oral evidence, although admissible to prove a condition precedent to the operation of the guarantee, is not admissible to prove a condition precedent to the liability of the guarantor.[27] It is permissible, however, in

---

[23] See above, paras 8–11 to 8–13 and note especially the criticisms of this approach.
[24] See also *BLM Holdings Pty Ltd v Bank of New Zealand* (unreported, NSW CA, March 25, 1994).
[25] (1990) 21 N.S.W.L.R. 689, Kirby P. dissenting. See also *Bond v Hong Kong Bank of Australia Ltd* (unreported, NSW CA, December 10, 1991); *Bechara v A & G Formworks Contractors Pty Ltd* (unreported, NSW CA, October 19, 1990); *Commonwealth Bank of Australia v Saunders* (unreported, SA FC Sup Ct, October 20, 1995).
[26] (1997) 85 B.L.R. 97; 54 Con. L.R. 74. But this is not in accordance with the usual approach to the construction of conditions precedent, see above, para.8–12.
[27] *Abrey v Crux* (1869) L.R. 5 C.P. 37; *Hitchings, Coulthurst Co v Northern Leather Co of America and Doushkess* [1914] 3 K.B. 907; *New London Credit Syndicate v Neale* [1898] 2 Q.B. 487, especially at 491 per Rigby and Vaughan Williams L.J.J; *Colonial Bank of New Zealand v Lewis and Moffett* [1887] N.Z.L.R. 5 S.C. 465 (but note the reference in that case to the possibility of establishing a collateral agreement). *Cf.* a condition precedent to the

accordance with normal principles, to have regard to the surrounding circumstances in the interpretation of the condition.

(a) Conditions precedent which will not be implied

It should be observed that the following are not implied conditions **10–100** precedent to the liability of the guarantor, although the recitals or the general terms of the guarantee may create express terms to similar effect.

(i) Notification of the principal's default.

The creditor is under no obligation to notify the principal debtor[28] or the **10–101** guarantor of the principal's default,[29] unless such notification is required by the terms of the guarantee.[30] The rationale for this rule is that the guarantor, when undertaking the obligation, must realise that there is a risk that the principal will not perform and the burden is, therefore, placed upon the guarantor to ascertain when the default has occurred.[31] Another justification proffered by the courts is that it is the guarantor's responsibility to ensure that the debtor performs the principal obligation, whether it is the payment of a debt or the performance of a duty or undertaking.[32]

The same rule regarding notification applies also to guarantors of bills of **10–102** exchange,[33] although if a party to a bill has assumed the position of surety (for example, by indorsing the bill), that party will not be liable before receiving notice of dishonour. This results from the provisions of the Bills of Exchange Act 1882[34] and, prior to its enactment, mercantile custom.[35]

---

operation of the guarantee, *e.g. Adelaide Life Assurance & Guarantee Co v Gandolphi* (1887) 21 S.A.L.R. 18.

[28] *Royal Bank v McMurchy* (1986) 46 Alta L.R. (2d) 388.

[29] *Moschi v Lep Air Services Ltd* [1973] A.C. 331 at 356 *per* Lord Simon of Glaisdale; *Commercial Bank of Australia Ltd v Colonial Finance, Mortgage, Investment & Guarantee Corp Ltd* (1906) 4 C.L.R. 57 at 70, *per* O'Connor J. Griffith C.J. left the point open, at 64–65. See also *Re Lockey* (1845) 1 Ph. 509; 41 E.R. 726; *Mulholland v Smith* (1894) 20 V.L.R. 403; *Thomas Fuller Construction Co (1958) Ltd v Continental Insurance* (1970) 36 D.L.R. (3d) 336; *Industrial Acceptance Corp v United Bus Co Ltd* (1954) 36 M.P.R. 1.

[30] See cases cited below, n.42.

[31] *Thomas Fuller Construction Co (1958) Ltd v Continental Insurance* (1970) 36 D.L.R. (3d) 336 at 353.

[32] *Re Lockey* (1845) 1 Ph. 509 at 511; 41 E.R. 726 at 727; *Wright v Simpson* (1802) 6 Ves. Jun. 714; 31 E.R. 1272, approved in *Moschi v Lep Air Services Ltd* [1973] A.C. 331 at 356, *per* Lord Simon of Glaisdale.

[33] *Carter v White* (1883) 25 Ch. D. 666 at 670–671; *Swinyard v Bowes* (1816) 5 M. & S. 62; 105 E.R. 974; *Warrington v Furbor* (1807) 8 East 242; 103 E.R. 334; *Hitchcock v Humphrey* (1843) 5 M. & G. 559; 6 R.R. 401. But it appears that the notorious insolvency of the acceptor before maturity excuses presentment and notice to the guarantors: *Holbrow v Wilkins* (1822) 1 B. & C. 10; 25 R.R. 285; *Warrington v Furbor* (1807) 8 East 242; 103 E.R. 334.

[34] ss.48–50 and 52(2)(a). See also *Byles on Bills of Exchange and Cheques* (27th ed., 2002), paras 15–29-15–41 and J.M. Holden, *The Law and Practice of Banking* (5th ed., 1991), p.189.

[35] *Carter v White* (1883) 25 Ch. D. 666 at 671; *Duncan, Fox & Co v North and South Wales Bank* (1880) 6 App. Cas. 1 at 13.

10–103   The fact that no notice of default needs to be given to the guarantor is open to criticism[36] on the basis that, if the guarantor were alerted to the true situation at an early stage, the guarantor could call on the debtor to pay[37] with some hope of obtaining payment from the debtor in whole or in part. Law reformers have questioned the wisdom and fairness of the general rule. In 1977, the Law Reform Commission of South Australia recommended that creditors be required by law to give guarantors notice of default in all cases.[38] The Commission observed:

> "The giving of notice to the surety immediately on the default of the debtor would alert him to the situation as between himself and the principal debtor. In many cases, he could call on the principal debtor to pay, with some hope at that stage of getting payment by the debtor in whole or in part and if he could not do that then he would be able to help himself."[39]

10–104   This proposal does not indicate the sanction for non-compliance and it places a substantial burden upon the creditor since it requires notice to be given to the guarantor immediately on default of the principal debtor. Would the guarantor be absolutely discharged where the creditor failed to provide the notice of default? Would a creditor who did not become aware of the principal debtor's default until a short period had elapsed forfeit the right to enforce the guarantee? And would every minor or technical default need to be disclosed?

10–105   A reasonable compromise appears in the report of the Law Reform Commission of British Columbia which recommended that a creditor should be obliged to provide notice of the default of the principal debtor to any guarantors of a consumer debt or obligation within 45 days of the default.[40] A failure to comply with this proposed requirement would reduce the liability of the guarantor by the extent that the guarantors could establish that they were prejudiced by the failure.[41] These recommendations appear to strike a fair balance between the interests of the parties to a consumer guarantee. They give the guarantors the opportunity of minimising their liability by urging the principal debtor to remedy the default or by attending to the default himself before the situation deteriorates. But if these proposals were applied to commercial guarantees, they would force creditors to police the principal transaction with greater diligence than is required under the current law.

10–106   Modern guarantees sometimes contain a provision requiring the creditor to give notice of the principal's default to the guarantor. The most common

---

[36] South Australia Law Reform Commission, *Report Relating to the Reform of the Law of Suretyship*, Report No.39 (1977), p.8.
[37] *ibid.*, p.8.
[38] *ibid.*, pp.7–8.
[39] *ibid.*, pp.7–8. See also Tasmania Law Reform Commission, *Suretyship and Guarantee* (Report No. 38, 1987), p.23, which emphasises the practical difficulties facing the guarantor in seeking to ascertain if the principal is in default.
[40] British Columbia Law Reform Commission, *Report on Guarantees of Consumer Debts* (1979), p.99, Recommendation 17.
[41] *ibid.* Recommendation 18.

recent examples occur in the context of guarantee of a contractor's obligations under a building contract whereby any departure from the terms of the building contract must be notified to the guarantor[42] or in respect of a guarantee given by a corporate body.[43] The guarantor must clearly establish that such a provision is a condition precedent to the guarantor's liability.[44] This burden will not be satisfied where the provision only appears as a term of the principal contract, which is not expressly or impliedly incorporated in the guarantee.[45] If notice of default is included as a condition precedent, but no time limit is specified within which the notice of default must be given, the court may imply a further term that notice of the particular default must be given within a reasonable time.[46] Even if no term appears in the guarantee requiring the creditor to notify the guarantor of any default, it has been suggested that the creditor is under a duty to notify if the guarantor requests information as to the principal's default,[47] but there is no definite authority to support this view.[48]

(ii) Prompt proceedings against the guarantor.

The creditor is under no duty to proceed against the guarantor promptly **10–107** after default by the principal.[49] This is so even if the principal debtor becomes insolvent during the delay and the guarantor is thereby prevented from effectively exercising his right of indemnity against the debtor.[50]

---

[42] e.g. Eshelby v Federated European Bank Ltd [1932] 1 K.B. 423; Clydebank and District Water Trustees v Fidelity & Deposit Co of Maryland 1915 S.C. 362. As other examples, see Stibbard v Dominion Banking & Investment Corp Ltd (1896) 17 A.L.T. 330 (mortgage guarantee); Batson v Spearman (1838) 9 Ad. & E. 298; 112 E.R. 1225 (loan guarantee); Bank of British Columbia v Turbo Resources Ltd (1983) 148 D.L.R. (3d) 598 (loan guarantee); Wright v Australian Alliance Assurance Co (1873) 7 S.A.L.R. 137 (fidelity guarantee); Fanning v London Guarantee & Accident Co Ltd (1884) 10 V.L.R. (L) 8 (fidelity guarantee); National Bank of A/asia v Brock (1864) 1 W.W. & A.B. (L) 208 (fidelity guarantee); Phillips v Fordyce (1771) 2 Chitty 676 (fidelity guarantee).
[43] Tricontinental Corp Ltd v HDFI Ltd (1990) 21 N.S.W.L.R. 689, discussed above, paras 8–11 to 8–13 and 10–96 to 10–97.
[44] Gordon v Rae (1858) 8 E. & B. 1065 at 1090; 120 E.R. 396 at 406; Directors of the London Guarantee Co v Fearnley (1880) 5 App. Cas. 911 especially at 917.
[45] Price v Kirkham (1864) 3 H. & C. 437; 159 E.R. 601.
[46] Corp of Chatham v McCrea (1862) 12 U.C. C.P. 352 and Wilson v R & I Bank of Western Australia Ltd (unreported, WA FC Sup Ct, December 11, 1992).
[47] Mulholland v Smith (1894) 20 V.L.R. 403 at 406–407 (the point was expressly left open).
[48] Indeed, it has been held that, although the surety is entitled to know the amount of his existing and contingent liabilities, the surety is not entitled to know the particulars of the principal debtor's account: Ross v Bank of New South Wales (1928) 28 S.R. (NSW) 539, and see above, para. 4–28.
[49] Waung v Subbotovsky [1968] 3 N.S.W.R. 499; Isbell Dean (Bean) Co v Avery [1923] 1 D.L.R. (NS) 708. Nor is the creditor required to enforce all the obligations of the guarantor if there is some doubt about the scope of the guarantee: Bank Negara Indonesia 1946 v Taylor [1995] C.L.C. 255. See G. Andrews and R. Millett, Law of Guarantees (3rd ed., 2000), para.7.27.
[50] Isbell Dean (Bean) Co v Avery [1923] 1 D.L.R. (NS) 708; Heinish v MCC Amusement Enterprises Ltd (1977) 42 N.S.R. (2d) 195.

(iii) Prior proceedings against principal debtor or a co-surety.

10–108   Lord Simon of Glaisdale in *Moschi v Lep Air Services Ltd*[51] made it clear that it is not an implied condition of a guarantor's liability that the creditor proceed first against the principal debtor before suing the guarantor or that the creditor exercises simultaneous recourse against other guarantors.[52] This arises from the fact that it is the duty of a guarantor to see that the principal pays the principal debt or performs the principal obligation, so that the guarantor is liable to the full extent of the guarantee's secondary obligation upon the principal's default.[53] It also follows that the creditor is under no duty to realise securities provided by the principal for the enforcement of the guaranteed obligation before proceeding against the guarantor.[54] All these statements of general principle are subject to the terms of the guarantee, which may require that certain remedies be taken against the principal or that certain collateral securities obtained by the creditor from the principal be realised before the guarantor is rendered liable.[55]

10–109   The Law Reform Commission of Tasmania has recommended that, where there is no agreement to the contrary, creditors be required to realise the principal debtor's securities before calling on the guarantor, except in circumstances where the creditor can establish that this would be ineffective.[56] This recommendation will probably have little effect because it is likely that creditors will exclude this proposed duty by the express provisions of the guarantee.

---

[51] [1973] A.C. 331 at 356–357. See also *Jackson v Digby* (1854) 2 W.R. 540; *Ewart v Latta* (1865) 4 Macq. H.C. 983; *TSB Bank plc v Dickson* [1998] EWCA Civ 1293 (unreported, Court of Appeal, Civil Division, July 24, 1998); *Bank of Nova Scotia v Vancouver Associated Contractors Ltd* [1954] 4 D.L.R. 72 (BC); *McLean v Discount & Finance Ltd* (1939) 64 C.L.R. 312 at 328; *Bank of Montreal v Stephen* (unreported, Can N.B.Q.B., August 31, 1989). This is so even if the principal has sufficient funds to pay the debt: *Coffey v DFC Financial Services Ltd* (unreported, NZ CA, October 2, 1991). But see below, para.10–209, as regards the duty to mitigate.

[52] See also *TSB Bank plc v Dickson* (unreported, Court of Appeal (Civil Division) July 24, 1998).

[53] [1973] A.C. 331 at 356–357, and see Lord Diplock in *Moschi v Lep Air Services Ltd* [1973] A.C. 331 at 347–348. See also this rule discussed in detail below, paras 11–11 to 11–28; *China & South Seas Bank v Tan* [1990] 1 A.C. 536 at 545; *TSB Bank plc v Dickson* [1998] EWCA Civ 1293 (unreported Court of Appeal, Civil Division, July 24, 1998).

[54] Lord Simon's statement does not specifically deal with the question of securities provided by the debtor, and no other authority specifically deals with this question. But if the creditor is under no duty to sue a solvent principal before taking action against the guarantor, it is difficult to see why the creditor should be under an obligation to realise a further security held for the enforcement of the principal obligation. Note that if the security is realised, it must be appropriated to the guaranteed debt: see above, paras 6–23 to 6–32. However, a creditor's attempt to extinguish the principal debt by other means does not prevent the creditor proceeding against the guarantor: *Barclays Bank plc v Williams* [1998] EWCA 700.

[55] See *Musket v Rogers* (1839) 8 Scott 51; 132 E.R. 1281; *Holl v Hadley* (1835) 2 Ad. & E. 758; 111 E.R. 292.

[56] Tasmania Law Reform Commission, *Suretyship and Guarantee*, Report No.38 (1987), p.23.

(iv) Is a demand necessary?

A. Demands on the principal debtor

A guarantor is liable upon the principal debtor's default.[57] To establish **10–110** the principal debtor's default, it is not necessary to show that the creditor requested the debtor to pay in the first instance.[58] Consequently such a request need not be pleaded in an action to enforce a guarantee.[59] It is sufficient to plead that the principal debtor neglected or refused to repay the creditor.[60] This is so even if the principal debt is repayable on demand because a person who agrees to pay upon demand what is to be considered his own debt is liable to be sued on that undertaking without any previous demand.[61] The demand is not necessary to complete the creditor's cause of action against the principal debtor. Consequently, the creditor is not required to make a prior demand on the principal debtor for repayment of the principal debt where there is no date fixed for repayment. The creditor can sue for the principal debt without any such demand.[62]

It is different, however, where a demand on the principal debtor is an **10–111** implied condition precedent to the creditor's cause of action against the debtor, for example, where the principal obligation is itself a collateral liability under a guarantee of another person's debts[63] or where the creditor intends to accelerate payment of a principal debt that would otherwise be payable by instalments.[64] In these cases, a prior demand on the principal debtor is necessary to establish the creditor's cause of action.[65]

B. Demands on the guarantor

Whether it is necessary for the creditor to make a demand on a **10–112** guarantor before enforcing the guarantee depends on the nature of the contract and the construction of its terms.[66] Where a guarantee stipulates that a demand is necessary before the creditor can sue the guarantor, the Statute of Limitations does not begin to run until a demand is made. The demand simply marks the time from which the surety's liability can be enforced.[67]

---

[57] See above, para.10–07 and below, para.10–143.
[58] *Lilley v Hewitt* (1822) 11 Price 494 at 505–506; 147 E.R. 543 at 546–547. See also *Sheppard & Cooper Ltd v TSB Bank plc (No.2)* [1996] 2 All E.R. 654, where the directors of the debtor company made it clear that funds were not available to meet the creditor's demand so there was no need to give the debtor company a reasonable opportunity to discharge the debt.
[59] *ibid.* See also *Cutler v Southern* (1667) 1 Saund. 116; 85 E.R. 125; *O'Connor v Sorahan* [1933] I.R. 591; *DFC Financial Services Ltd v Coffey* [1991] B.C.C. 218.
[60] *Lilley v Hewitt* (1820) 11 Price 494 at 505–506; 147 E.R. 543 at 546–547.
[61] *Rowe v Young* (1820) 2 Bli 391 at 465; 4 E.R. 372 at 406 *per* Bayley J. See also *Bradford Old Bank v Sutcliffe* [1918] 2 K.B. 833; *Jackson v Ogg* (1859) Johns 397; 70 E.R. 476.
[62] *ibid.*
[63] See *Bank of Scotland v Wright* [1991] B.C.L.C. 244.
[64] *Esso Petroleum Co Ltd v Alstonbridge Properties Ltd* [1975] 1 W.L.R. 1474.
[65] G. Andrews and R. Millett, *Law of Guarantees* (3rd ed., 2000), para.7.02A.
[66] *Moschi v Lep Air Services* [1973] A.C. 331; *Re Taylor, Ex p. Century 21 Real Estate Corporation* (1995) 130 F.L.R. 723.
[67] *Stimpson v Smith* [1999] 1 W.L.R. 1292 at 1304 *per* Tuckey L.J.

10–113   English courts have consistently assumed that the essential nature of a guarantee is a promise by the guarantor to see to it that the principal debtor performs his own obligations to the creditor.[68] Indeed, even where the principal obligation was to pay a sum of money, the original form of action against a guarantor was a claim in special assumpsit (a contract) rather than in indebitatus assumpsit (debt).[69] According to Lord Diplock in *Moschi v Lep Air Services*,[70] it follows that a guarantor is not entitled to notice from the creditor of the principal debtor's failure to perform the principal obligation.

10–114   It is submitted, however, that the essential nature of most guarantees is a secondary obligation to answer for the debt or default of another if that other person defaults.[71] In any event, even if a guarantor promises to see to it that the principal debtor performs his obligations to the creditor, the guarantee is still a collateral undertaking that creates a secondary liability which is contingent upon the principal debtor's default.[72] It does not necessarily follow, therefore, that a guarantor is not entitled to notice of the principal debtor's default or a demand before an action is commenced to enforce the guarantee.[73]

10–115   By mercantile custom, there is an implied contract in relation to bills of exchange requiring the holder to give notice of dishonour within a certain time to the drawer or indorser who stands in the position of surety for the acceptor.[74] This principle only applies to parties to the bill of exchange, not to persons who are interested in them as guarantors without being parties to the bill.[75] Hence, a surety for payment of a bill of exchange is not discharged by the holder's failure to give him notice of dishonour.[76] Indeed, a surety whose guarantee does not stipulate that he must be given notice of dishonour becomes immediately liable when due payment is not made on the bill of exchange to the holder.[77]

---

[68] *Wright v Simpson* (1802) 6 Ves. Jun. 714 at 734; 31 E.R. 1272 at 1282 *per* Lord Eldon; *Re Lockey* (1845) 1 Ph. 508 at 571; 441 E.R. 726 at 727; *M'Taggart v Watson* (1835) 3 Cl. & F. 525 at 540; 6 E.R. 227 at 230; *Moschi v Lep Air Services* [1973] A.C. 331 at 348 *per* Lord Diplock. See also at 357 *per* Lord Simon of Glaisdale. *Cf. Sunbird Plaza Pty Ltd v Maloney* (1988) 166 C.L.R. 245 at 256 *per* Mason C.J.

[69] *Moschi v Lep Air Services* [1973] A.C. 331 at 348–349 *per* Lord Diplock; *Mines v Sculthorpe* (1809) 2 Camp 215; 170 E.R. 1134; *Jordan's Castle* (1536) Y.B. 27 Hen. VIII Mich. fo. 24, pl. 3 *per* Fitz James C.J.; translation in Fifoot, *History and Sources of the Common Law Tort and Contract* (1949), pp.353, 355. For the correct date and citation, see Simpson, "The Place of Slade's Case in the History of Contract" 74 L.Q.R. 381 at 384 and Cheshire and Fifoot, *The Law of Contract* (7th ed., 1969), p.10, cited in *Moschi v Lep Air Services* [1973] A.C. 331 at 357 *per* Lord Simon of Glaisdale.

[70] [1973] A.C. 331 at 348–349.

[71] See *Sunbird Plaza Pty Ltd v Maloney* (1988) 166 C.L.R. 245 at 256 *per* Mason C.J.

[72] See *Re Athill, Athill v Athill* (1880) 16 Ch. D. 211 and *Re Taylor Ex p. Century 21 Real Estate Corporation* (1995) 130 A.L.R. 723 at 728.

[73] *Cf. Re Lockey* (1845) 1 Ph. 508; 41 E.R. 726.

[74] *Black v Ottoman Bank* 15 Moore's P.C. 472 at 484; 15 E.R. 573 at 577; *Hitchcock v Humfrey* (1843) 5 Man. & G. 559; 134 E.R. 683; *Walton v Mascall* (1844) 13 M. & W. 452; 153 E.R. 188; *Carter v White* (1883) 25 Ch. D. 666; *Barber v Mackrell* (1892) 68 L.T. (NS) 29. *Cf. Hartland v Jukes* (1863) 1 H. & C. 667; 158 E.R. 1052.

[75] *Carter v White* (1883) 25 Ch. D. 666.

[76] *Hitchcock v Humfrey* (1843) 5 M. & G. 559; 134 E.R. 683.

[77] *Barber v Mackrell* (1892) 68 L.T. (NS) 29 at 31; *Bank of Montreal v Hache* (1982) 38 N.B.R. (2d) 54 at 57–58.

Leaving aside guarantees of the obligations under a bill of exchange, the **10–116** general rule appears to be that a guarantor become liable as soon as payment is not made or as soon as default occurs under the principal contract, unless the guarantee itself provides that the guarantor is to be given a notice of default or demand for payment before the creditor can enforce the guarantee.[78]

This is consistent with the general doctrine relating to notice to the **10–117** effect that where a party undertakes to do a certain thing on a certain specific event which may become known to it, or with which it can make itself acquainted, the party is not entitled to any notice unless it stipulates for it.[79] In all cases, the question is whether, on a construction of the guarantee, the surety's collateral promise is to pay only "on demand".[80] If there is such a stipulation in the guarantee, the creditor must prove a real demand on the guarantor before it can enforce the guarantee.[81]

The presence of a "principal debtor" clause in a guarantee may dispense **10–118** with the need for a prior demand on the guarantor[82] because, on one

---

[78] *Bradford Old Bank Ltd v Sutcliffe* [1918] 2 K.B. 833; *Re Taylor, Ex p. Century 21 Real Estate Corporation* (1995) 130 A.L.R. 724; *Re J Brown's Estate, Brown v Brown* [1893] 2 Ch. 300 at 304–305; *Canadian Petrofina Ltd v Motormart Ltd* (1969) 7 D.L.R. (3d) 330 at 335–337. It is not necessary for the creditor to allow the guarantor a reasonable time to comply with the demand or even sufficient time to effect the mechanics of payment before instituting proceedings against the guarantor. The requirement to allow time for compliance with demands applies only to enforcement of securities: *Hong Kong Bank of Australia Ltd v Larobi Pty Ltd* (unreported, NSW Sup Ct, September 23, 1991).

[79] This general doctrine was stated in *Vyse v Wakefield* (1840) 6 M. & W. 442 at 452; 151 E.R. 485 at 489 *per* Lord Abinger C.B. (affirmed: *Vyse v Wakefield* (1840) 7 M. & W. 126; 151 E.R. 706). In *Commercial Bank of Australia Ltd v Colonial Finance, Mortgage, Investment and Guarantee Corp Ltd* (1906) 4 C.L.R. 57 at 65 and 70 the High Court of Australia left open the question whether this doctrine applied to guarantees.

[80] See, e.g. *Stibbard v Dominion Banking and Investment Corp Ltd* (1896) 17 A.L.T. 330 (where notice of default was held to be a condition precedent to the creditor's right to sue on the guarantee) and *Radley Court Pty Ltd v Hall* (unreported, NSW Sup Ct, O'Brien J., February 22, 1978) (a demand is required as a condition precedent of an action to enforce a guarantee). Contrast *Re Taylor, Ex p. Century 21 Real Estate Corporation* (1995) 130 A.L.R. 723, where clause 3(d) of the document stated that "these guarantees and indemnities shall be fully enforceable without Century 21 taking any step whatsoever against South Pacific or otherwise". The court held that a guarantor has no right to require a demand to be made on him, unless his contract so provides. See also *Partnership Pacific Ltd v Scott* (unreported, Qld Sup Ct, Skoien A.J., September 24, 1991). A conclusive evidence certificate may provide evidence that a demand was served on the guarantor: *Papua New Guinea Development Bank v Manton* [1982] V.R. 100. See also *Benson-Brown v Smith* (unreported, Vic Sup Ct, June 10, 1999) (certificate of indebtedness was only prima facie evidence of the quantum of the debt.)

[81] *Bradford Old Bank Ltd v Sutcliffe* [1918] 2 K.B. 833 at 848–849 *per* Scrutton L.J.; *Rowe v Young* (1820) 2 Bli 391 at 465 *per* Bayley J.; *Sicklemore v Thistleton* (1817) 6 M. & S. 9; 105 E.R. 1146. On the other hand, from the guarantor's point of view, the requirement of service of a written demand is an evidentiary or procedural requirement solely for his benefit so he can waive the requirement of a demand, pay the principal debt and seek contribution from his co-sureties: *Stimpson v Smith* [1999] 2 W.L.R. 1292. A person may waive a condition inserted for his sole benefit because of an implied term to that effect: *Gange v Sullivan* (1966) 116 C.L.R. 418. But quaere whether the requirement of a written demand is solely for the benefit of the surety as it determines the date from which the limitation period begins to run and that enables the creditor to determine its position under the contract of guarantee with certainty: *Toga Development No.10 Pty Ltd v Gibson* (1973) 2 B.P.R. 9260. Moreover, it is arguable that if one party waives a condition in his favour he should give the other party notice of the waiver: *Morten v Marshall* (1863) 2 H. & C. 365; 159 E.R. 127.

[82] *Esso Petroleum Co Ltd v Alstonbridge Properties Ltd* [1975] 1 W.L.R. 1471 at 1483 *per* Walton J (obiter dicta).

view,[83] the effect of this clause is to make the guarantor primarily liable for the principal debt as if it were his own debt. However, it could be argued that a principal debtor clause serves more modest purposes; it does not necessarily mean that the guarantor is to be treated as the principal debtor for all purposes from the inception of the guarantee but rather that the creditor is entitled to treat him as a principal debtor in certain events.[84] For instance, a principal debtor clause may prevent a guarantor from being discharged where the creditor gives time to the borrower.[85] In *DFC Financial Services Ltd v Coffey*[86] the Privy Council gave a principal obligation clause in a debenture provided as collateral security an even more limited operation: it enabled the debenture holder to proceed against the guarantors who provided the debenture as if they were primary obligors, *i.e.* by making a demand on them for payment.

10–119   Similarly, in *Commonwealth Bank of Australia v Stow*[87] a demand had been served on the principal debtor requiring payment within 14 days. Brownie J. held that the creditor was entitled to institute proceedings against the guarantor before this period expired because "principal debtor" clause rendered the guarantor liable to pay upon demand.

10–120   The principal debtor clause may not be the only provision suggesting that the guarantor may be liable without a prior demand. In *Stimpson v Smith*[88] the terms of a joint and several guarantee provided that the bank was entitled to set off a guarantor's liability against any credit balance in any account of either co-surety with the bank. The guarantee also provided that a demand had to be in writing and signed by the bank. After settling with the bank, one of the guarantors sought contribution from his co-surety. The co-surety argued that he was not liable because the bank had not made a written demand on the sureties.

10–121   The court held that the set off provisions in the guarantee could operate both before and after demand under the guarantee. Given the fact that the set off could be effected before a demand, the guarantee should not be construed as requiring a demand as a condition precedent to the liability of a guarantor.[89] The requirement of service of a written demand was a purely evidentiary or procedural requirement for the benefit of the guarantor. Consequently, the plaintiff was entitled to waive the requirement for a demand and seek contribution from his co-surety.

10–122   Where the contract takes the form of a hybrid guarantee and indemnity, the guarantee may stipulate that a prior demand is a condition precedent to liability as a surety but liability under the indemnity may arise without any prior demand. In *Re Taylor, Ex p. Century 21 Real Estate Corporation*[90] clause 1 of the document was a guarantee of payment of promissory notes by the guarantors but only "when demanded". Under

---

[83] *MS Fashions Ltd v Bank of Credit and Commerce International SA (in liq.) (No.2)* [1993] Ch. 425 at 447 *per* Dillon L.J.
[84] *General Produce Co v United Bank Ltd* [1979] 2 Lloyd's Rep. 255 at 259 *per* Lloyd J.
[85] See above, paras 1–01 and 5–127.
[86] [1991] B.C.C. 218, PC.
[87] Unreported, NSW Sup Ct, Brownie J., February 21, 1989).
[88] [1999] 2 W.L.R. 1292.
[89] See G. Andrews and R. Millett, *Law of Guarantees* (3rd ed., 2000), para.7.02A.
[90] (1995) 130 A.L.R. 723.

clause 2, which was expressed as a separate and severable covenant, the guarantors agreed that in the event of the maker of the promissory note failing to discharge its obligations they would "indemnify and keep indemnified" the holder of the note. Clause 3(d) purported to make clauses 1 and 2 principal obligations. It also provided that clause 1 and 2 "shall not be treated as ancillary or collateral to any other obligation — to the intent that those guarantees and indemnities shall be fully enforceable without [the holder] taking any step whatsoever against [the maker] or otherwise".

Burchett J. of the Federal Court of Australia held that the terms of **10–123** clause 3(d) were not strong enough to contradict the express provision in clause 1 requiring a demand to be made as a condition precedent to the liability under the guarantee. However, there was no such express provision in the indemnity contained in clause 2. Accordingly, the liability under that clause came into existence as soon as the maker failed to honour its obligations under the promissory notes, without the need for any prior demand on the guarantors.

This conclusion is consistent with the general rule in relation to **10–124** indemnities. As an indemnity creates a form of primary liability, it is not necessary to give an indemnifier any prior notice of loss or damage before enforcing the indemnity.[91]

C. Form of the demand

If a demand is necessary, the letter of demand must comply strictly in its **10–125** form and details with that which is required by the guarantee itself. Thus in *Re A & K Holdings Pty Ltd*,[92] the guarantee stated that the guarantors "jointly and severally guarantee on demand, which demand shall not be made before [a specified date], ... the payment in full of the amounts then owed by C company to each of its unsecured creditors". Sholl J. of the Supreme Court of Victoria held that, if a particular creditor made a demand under this clause, it was necessary for that creditor to make a demand for payment in full of *all debts owing* at the date of the demand by C company *to each of its unsecured creditors*. It was insufficient, for example, for the letter of demand merely to require payment of a debt owed to *the particular creditor* who made the demand.[93]

Generally, however, a demand addressed to a guarantor is valid if it **10–126** makes it clear to the guarantor that the creditor requires payment of a sum which is actually due.[94] Indeed, in the absence of a particular stipulation in

---

[91] *Cutler v Southern* (1667) 1 Wms Saund. 116; 85 E.R. 125.
[92] [1964] V.R. 257. See also *Bond v Hong Kong Bank of Australia Ltd* (unreported, NSW CA, December 10, 1991).
[93] *Cf.* the interpretation of the nature of the demand in *Commercial Banking Co of Sydney v Bennett* (1870) 9 S.C.R. (NSW) 238 (cases at law). See also *Household Finance Corp of Canada v Falconer* (1980) 80 A.P.R. 95 (Q.B.) and *Bank of Montreal v MacGregor* (1980) 21 B.C.L.R. 83 Sup Ct, as examples of the requirement of a particular demand.
[94] *NRG Vision Ltd v Churchfield Leasing Ltd* (1988) 4 B.C.C. 56 at 66. However, where the guarantee requires the payment of a certain sum as the amount agreed by the parties to represent the amounts payable under a contract for services rendered to the principal debtor, the guarantor cannot escape liability by showing that the creditor has made a "manifest error"

the guarantee, it is probably unnecessary in some cases for the demand to state the exact sum owing,[95] although in the case of an ordinary guarantee there is more justification for such a requirement than there is in the context of a mortgage where the mortgagor should be aware of the state of his account with the mortgagee.[96] As the High Court pointed out in *Bunbury Foods Pty Ltd v National Bank of A/asia Ltd*:[97]

"[T]o require the creditor in all cases to specify the amount of the debt may operate to impose an onerous burden upon him. Some accounts may be so complex and so constantly changing that it is difficult at any given time to ascertain or to assert the precise amount that is due and payable. Indeed, the ascertainment of the amount may in some instances require the resolution over time of complex issues of fact and law."[98]

While these comments related to demands on mortgagors, they are equally relevant in relation to demands on guarantors.

10–127   It appears, however, that the circumstances of the case may persuade the court to import a requirement that a demand upon the guarantors specify a precise sum. In *Donnelly v National Australia Bank*,[99] the Full Court of the Supreme Court of Western Australia granted the appellant guarantors unconditional leave to appeal against a summary judgment in favour of the respondent bank. It held it was arguable that the guarantee contained an implied term that the bank's demand should have specified the correct amount owing or otherwise provided the appellants with sufficient information to enable them to ascertain that amount. The guarantee defined the term "moneys hereby secured" broadly to include several items which appeared to be within the peculiar knowledge of the bank. Moreover, the guarantee provided that interest was to be "calculated in the manner and at the rate or rates determined by the bank for the time being, compounded and turned into principal accordingly". Consequently, it might have been difficult for the guarantors to ascertain their liability for interest on a particular date. The Full Court found that the guarantors had raised an arguable defence:

"Without the respondent providing the guarantors sufficient information when the letter of demand is sent so as to enable them to ascertain details of the amounts which, according to the respondent, are owing

---

in calculating the liabilities of the principal debtor: *Try Build Ltd v Blue Star Garages Ltd* [1999] 66 Con. L.R. 90.
[95] *Per* Starke J. in *O'Day v Commercial Bank of Australia Ltd* (1933) 50 C.L.R. 200 at 216. See also *Re A & K Holdings Pty Ltd* [1964] V.R. 257 at 262. Even in cases where a demand is made for an excessive amount, it may be effective for the amount actually owing: see *Bank of Montreal v Winter* (1981) 101 A.P.R. 385 (Can); *Bunbury Foods Pty Ltd v National Bank of A/asia* (1984) 58 ALJR 199 at 205; *Westpac Banking Corp v Evans* (1986) 1 N.Z.B.L.C. 102; [1986] B.C.L. 1129.
[96] *Bunbury Foods Pty Ltd v National Bank of A/asia* (1984) 58 A.L.J.R. 199 at 205.
[97] (1984) 58 A.L.J.R. 199 (a case involving a demand under a mortgage).
[98] *ibid.*, at 204–205.
[99] (Unreported, WA FC Sup Ct, May 19, 1992). [1992] ACL Rep 325 WA 79, followed in *ANZ Banking Group Ltd v Cooper* (1993) 9 W.A.R. 112. Cf. *Re A & K Holdings Pty Ltd* [1966] V.R. 257 at 262 per Sholl J.

under the guarantee and how those amounts are arrived at, it might well be impossible for the guarantors to ascertain those amounts. If that occurred, it would not be possible for the guarantors, on demand, to pay the correct amount owing."[1]

The Full Court of the Supreme Court of Western Australia noted that the guarantee was secured by a mortgage over the guarantors' family home and that they could lose this home if they did not pay the correct amount on demand.[2]

In *ANZ Banking Group Ltd v Cooper*[3] Master Bredmeyer refused an **10–128** application for summary judgment against guarantors and third party mortgagors because the demand on them did not enable them to ascertain how the creditor had calculated the amount demanded. This extra burden on the creditor was thought to be consistent with the reasoning in *Donnelly v National Australia Bank*.[4]

Even if one allows for the fact that *Donnelly v National Australia Bank* **10–129** was merely an application for leave to appeal against summary judgment and that the Full Court did not, therefore, determine the merits of the guarantors' defence, this case still represents a significant defeat for creditors. It adds to the growing list of technical defences which can be invoked by guarantors and tends to overlook the fact that a demand is merely a procedural step in the a creditor's action against guarantors.

In the particular circumstances of the case there was, with respect, little **10–130** justification for the court's conclusion. Both the guarantors were directors of the principal debtor company and should, therefore, have been aware of the current state of its indebtedness. Moreover, while the bank simply demanded on January 11, 1990 "the whole of the principal, charges, interest and other moneys owing under the guarantee and indemnity", it served a conclusive evidence certificate under its guarantee on September 28, 1990, specifying the amount of the moneys secured by the guarantee on that date. It appears that the writ in the action to enforce the guarantee was issued in either February or March 1990 and there was an amended statement of claim dated March 4, 1990 in the Appeal Book. The bank's application for summary judgment did not come before the Master until March 5, 1991. The guarantors had, therefore, been given ample opportunities to reach agreement with the bank about the precise amount owing under the guarantee before summary judgment was entered against them. Moreover, it would not have been possible for the bank to exercise its power of sale in respect of they guarantors' family home without complying with the statutory conditions as to notice. For these

---

[1] *ibid.*, at 11 *per* Rowland and Ipp J.J.
[2] Where the guarantors' residence is not at stake, it is unnecessary for the demand upon the guarantors to particularise how the amount of the claim was calculated: *Commonwealth Development Bank of Australia Ltd v Cochrane* (unreported, NSW Sup Ct, Giles J., October 28, 1998).
[3] (1993) 9 W.A.R. 112. See also *Citibank Savings Ltd v Justelle Nominees Pty Ltd and Thompson* (unreported, WA Sup Ct, Acting Master Hawkins, January 8, 1993).
[4] Unreported, WA FC Sup Ct, May 19, 1992.

reasons *Donnelly v National Australia Bank Ltd*[5] is unlikely to be embraced by the English courts.

10–131   Notification to the guarantor must be phrased in terms of immediate demand rather than in terms of a wish or vague request that payment should be made,[6] or a threat to take proceedings in the future or a general statement of the guarantor's indebtedness[7] or a mere notice of the principal debtor's default.[8]

10–132   The creditor should ensure that a demand is served on the guarantors in their capacity as guarantors rather than in their capacity as officers of the principal debtor company[9] and, in the case of joint creditors, all the creditors should, as a precaution, sign the notice of demand.[10] Furthermore, the demand must be served at the address for service as designated in the instrument of guarantee. In *Bond v Hong Kong Bank of Australia Ltd*,[11] the service of the notice was held to be invalid because it was sent to the guarantor's business address (as notified by the guarantor to the creditor) rather than the address designated in the guarantee, even though the latter premises were no longer occupied by the guarantor.

10–133   Sometimes the onus of establishing that a demand has been made is alleviated by a provision in the guarantee that the "demand shall be deemed to have been made when an envelope containing it is addressed to the guarantor at the last address of the guarantor known to the creditor is deposited in the Post Office". It appears that this clause precludes a defence by the guarantor that no demand was actually received.[12]

10–134   Another method of facilitating proof of the service of a demand is by invoking a conclusive evidence clause. It has been seen that the guarantee may contain a provision by which a statement by an officer of the creditor is to be conclusive evidence of the amount of the indebtedness. Such clauses may refer to matters other than the indebtedness and in *Papua*

---

[5] Unreported WA Fc Sup Ct, May 19, 1992.

[6] *Dow Banking Corp v Mahnakh Spinning & Weaving Corp* [1983] 2 Lloyd's Rep. 561; *Royal Bank of Canada v Ruben* (1978) 48 A.P.R. 707, QB.

[7] *Royal Bank of Canada v Oram* [1978] 1 W.W.R. 564.

[8] *Bank of Montreal v Agnew* (1986) 72 N.B.R. (2d) 276.

[9] *Canadian Petrofina Ltd v Motormart Ltd* (1969) 7 D.L.R. (3d) 330. See also *Edmunds v Westland Bank Ltd* (unreported, NZ CA, October 2, 1991).

[10] See *Manzo v 555/255 Pitt Street Pty Ltd* (1990) 21 N.S.W.L.R. 1 (a statutory demand in respect of a joint debt is invalid where equitable principles are applicable to the debt—as in the case of an implied right of indemnity available to co-guarantors against the principal debtor—if the notice is not signed by all the co-guarantors). Where the joint debt is not based on equitable principles, a payment to one of a number of joint creditors discharges the joint debt: see *Wallace v Kelsall* (1840) 7 M. & W. 264; 151 E.R. 765; *Steeds v Steeds* (1889) 22 Q.B.D. 537; *Powell v Brodhurst* [1901] 2 Ch. 160. It may be possible, therefore, for one of several joint creditors to make a valid demand for payment of the joint debt: *Manzo v 555/255 Pitt Street Pty Ltd* [1990] 21 N.S.W.L.R. 1 at 7. But if a guarantee is given to several persons jointly, they should all *sue* on it: *Pugh v Stringfield* (1857) 3 C.B. (NS) 2; 140 E.R. 637; (1858) 4 C.B. (NS) 364; 140 E.R. 1125 and below, para.10–160.

[11] (Unreported, NSW CA, December 10, 1991.) See also *Tricontinental Corp Ltd v HDFI Ltd* (1990) 21 N.S.W.L.R. 689.

[12] *Canadian Imperial Bank of Commerce v Haley* (1979) 100 D.L.R. (3d) 470; *State Bank of Victoria v Voss* (unreported, Vic Sup Ct, May 17, 1991). Even in the absence of such a clause, the courts generally assume that a document which is posted in a properly addressed envelope arrives at its intended destination. See, *e.g. Lloyd's TSB Bank plc (formerly Lloyd's Bank plc) v Mesologgides (a Bankrupt)* (unreported, Chancery Division, Stephen Tomlinson Q.C., December 17, 1999) 1999 W.L. 1425709.

New Guinea Development Bank v Manton,[13] where the clause provided that the statement was conclusive evidence of "all other matters stated herein", Beach J held that the clause was effective as being conclusive evidence that a written demand had been made on the guarantor within the terms of the guarantee.

Once a demand has been served, it appears that the guarantor must be **10–135** given a reasonable time to meet the obligation.[14] Generally, this will be interpreted as a period of time that is reasonably necessary for the guarantor to implement the mechanics of arranging the necessary bank transfer of funds, rather than a period of time that would enable the guarantor to arrange borrowing facilities to meet his obligations.[15]

D. Place of payment

In the absence of a specific contractual provision, the place of payment **10–136** shall be the place of the creditor's demand because that is where the guarantor's liability crystallises. Accordingly, in *Britten Norman Ltd (In Liq) v State Ownership Fund of Romania*[16] the respondent was not entitled to require payment under a bank guarantee to an account with a Romania bank. As there was no provision in the guarantee governing the place of payment, the court ordered the applicant bank to open an interest-bearing account in England in the name of the respondent and pay into the account the amount demanded under the guarantee.

(b) Waiver of conditions precedent

In accordance with normal contractual principles, any condition **10–137** precedent to the liability of the guarantor may be waived provided that notice is given and provided that the condition is solely for the benefit of

---

[13] [1982] V.R. 1000. See also *Bache & Co (London) Ltd v Banque Vernes et Commerciale de Paris SA* [1973] 2 Lloyd's Rep. 437 (where the Court of Appeal held that a conclusive evidence certificate requires the guarantor to pay the sum claimed but allows the guarantor to institute proceedings against the creditor to recover any excess). It is not necessary for a conclusive evidence certificate to itemise the principal and interest separately: *Je Maintiendrai Pty Ltd v Australia and New Zealand Banking Group Ltd* (1985) 38 S.A.S.R. 70. Note also the potential effect of the Unfair Terms in Consumer Contracts Regulations 1999.

[14] *Bond v Hong Kong Bank of Australia Ltd* (1991) 25 N.S.W.L.R. 286; *Thermo King Corp v Provincial Bank of Canada* (1981) 130 D.L.R. (3d) 256. In *Australia & New Zealand Banking Group Ltd v Cooper* (1993) 9 W.A.R. 112, Master Bredmeyer found that a guarantor of a debt repayable on demand is entitled to such time as is reasonably necessary to effect the mechanics of arranging for the necessary bank transfers of the funds. On the other hand, it may be argued that there was no justification for transposing the requirement that a mortgagor must be given a reasonable time to comply with a demand into the law of guarantees.

[15] *Bond v Hong Kong Bank of Australia Ltd* (1991) 25 N.S.W.L.R. 286. See also *Bank of Baroda v Panessar* [1987] 1 Ch. 335. Although a demand for payment "forthwith" is generally not reasonable, it appears that the creditor can nevertheless bring an action to enforce the guarantee following such a demand if the creditor has in fact allowed the guarantor a reasonable time to pay the debt: *Federal Business Development Bank v Dunn* [1984] 6 W.W.R. 46. See also *Good Motel Co Ltd (in liq) v Rodeway Pacific International Ltd* (1988) 94 F.L.R. 84.

[16] [2000] Lloyd's Rep. Bank 315.

the party waiving the condition.[17] This means that the guarantor may be able to waive the necessity for the creditor to make a demand or give notice of the principal's default since these provisions can be viewed as being for the guarantor's benefit.[18] The creditor, however, will not be able to waive compliance with such conditions.

(c) Joint proceedings against the principal debtor and the guarantors

10–138 As a general rule, it is not necessary for the creditor to institute joint proceedings against the principal debtor and the guarantors in the one action to recover the principal debt and enforce the guarantee.

10–139 It is not appropriate to join an application to wind up the principal debtor company with claims for other relief against the guarantors of the company's debts. Accordingly, it is not an abuse of process to commence proceedings to wind up the principal debtor company independently of separate court proceedings to recover the same principal debt from the company and to enforce the guarantee.[19]

(d) Conditions precedent and contracts of indemnity

10–140 It follows from the fact that no notice of default needs to be given to the guarantor and that the creditor does not have to take prior proceedings against the principal that an indemnifier is in the same position.[20] Similarly, in general, no demand needs to be made upon an indemnifier, although the position is unclear where the contract of indemnity expressly states that the indemnifier is only to be liable "upon demand". In the case of a guarantee, the reason why it is argued that a demand (in addition to the issuing of proceedings) is necessary where this wording is used is that the sum of money is payable under a collateral agreement.[21] Although a contract of indemnity is usually viewed as a primary obligation and does not come within the definition of a collateral agreement, liability under an express indemnity in this context will usually arise as a result of a breach of another transaction or events affecting that transaction, and in that sense the liability is collateral. This question is an open one but the creditor

---

[17] *Morten v Marshall* (1863) 2 H. & C. 305; 159 E.R. 127. Where the creditor has a right under a deed to insist upon a bank guarantee to secure performance, the creditor is entitled to waive the right without prejudicing its right to require performance of the remainder of the deed: *Tyms Enterprises Pty Ltd v Maranboy Pty Ltd* (unreported, NSW CA, March 17, 1994).
[18] *Stimpson v Smith* [1999] Ch. 340. Arguably, however, the term is not *solely* for the benefit of the guarantor because the creditor derives an advantage from it in that the creditor's cause of action will not accrue against the guarantor until the demand is made. This results in an advantage to the creditor because the Statute of Limitations will not begin to run until that point in time.
[19] *Permanent Custodians Ltd v Digital Enterprises Pty Ltd* (1992) 8 A.C.S.R. 542.
[20] *Cutler v Southern* (1667) 1 Saund. 116; 85 E.R. 125.
[21] *Bradford Old Bank Ltd v Sutcliffe* [1918] 2 K.B. 833 at 845–846; *Re Brown's Estate* [1893] 2 Ch. 300.

should as a precaution issue a demand even where the contract appears to be one of indemnity.

One special situation in which the creditor should give notice to the **10–141** indemnifier is where proceedings are brought against the creditor and the creditor wishes to compromise the action. This is because there is authority that the indemnifier is discharged if he is not given notice and can show that the agreement of compromise was improvident.[22]

(e) The effect of estoppel

A creditor may be estopped from enforcing its guarantee where it gives **10–142** the guarantor an unequivocal assurance that it will not enforce the guarantee if the guarantor complies with certain conditions. For example, in *Bank of Baroda v Shah*[23] the bank could not enforce its guarantee because it represented to the guarantor that he would be released if he resigned as a director of the principal debtor company and transferred his shares to the other guarantors.

(ii) The date on which the liability arises

The point of time at which the cause of action against the guarantor **10–143** arises is important for a number of reasons. First, the limitation period will begin to run against the creditor from the time when the debt could have been recovered by action against the guarantor. Secondly, where the guarantee is determined (for example, by revocation or by agreement) or is expressed to expire after a certain period of time has elapsed, the guarantor may only be liable in respect of liabilities which arise before the date of determination of the guarantee or before the date of its expiry, as the case may be.[24] Thirdly, if the cause of action against the guarantor has not arisen, the creditor cannot obtain a freezing order against the guarantor to prevent him dissipating assets or transferring them out of the jurisdiction. Such relief is intended to protect the fruits of the ultimate judgment in an action which has already been instituted.[25]

In order to ascertain when the cause of action against the guarantor **10–144** arises, it is necessary to have regard to the scope and conditions of both the principal contract and the contract of guarantee.

---

[22] *Smith v Compton* (1832) 3 B. & Ad. 407; 110 E.R. 146; *Newborough v Schroder* (1849) 7 C.B. 342; 137 E.R. 136. If the indemnifier is given notice and does not object, he will be estopped from impugning the compromise: *Duffield v Scott* (1789) 3 Term Rep. 374; 100 E.R. 628; *Jones v Williams* (1841) 7 M. & W. 493; 151 E.R. 860.

[23] Unreported, Court of Appeal, July 30, 1999.

[24] See this question discussed above, paras 9–21 to 9–25 and 9–26 to 9–45.

[25] *Riley McKay Pty Ltd v McKay* [1982] 1 N.S.W.L.R. 264. See also below, paras 12–30 to 12–33.

(a) The conditions of the principal contract

10–145   In the absence of particular wording in the guarantee, which may provide that certain conditions need to be fulfilled before the cause of action against the guarantor arises, the liability of the guarantor will arise upon the principal's default,[26] that is, at the same time that the creditor's cause of action against the principal debtor accrues.[27]

10–146   Whether default of the principal has occurred and at what point of time will be dependent on the nature and terms of the principal contract. Thus in *Eshelby v Federated European Bank Ltd*,[28] the guarantor of payments due under a building contract to a contractor was not liable on the guarantee because the work was performed defectively so that the principal debtor was not himself liable for the payments and, therefore, was not in default. Similarly, the guarantor of a bailee's obligations under a contract of bailment will not be liable where the goods are stolen from the bailee without any negligence on the bailee's part, because a bailee is not liable in the absence of negligence.[29] The guarantor for the payment of goods to be delivered is not liable when the goods are not delivered within the terms of the principal contract[30] or when the period of credit granted to the principal by the creditor has not expired,[31] because in both cases the principal's obligation to pay has not yet arisen. Conditions precedent to the liability of the principal debtor under the principal contract, such as the giving of notice, may also need to be satisfied before the principal's liability can properly be regarded as having arisen.[32]

10–147   A particular problem regarding the principal's default arises in the context of a guarantee of the repayment of advances made from time to time by the creditor to the principal through an overdrawn account. In

---

[26] It does not follow that a guarantor's right to bring an action in tort against a solicitor who allegedly negligently advised him to enter into the guarantee arises only on the principal debtor's default. The guarantor can sue his solicitor earlier and call upon the judge to assess the chance of the surety being called upon to pay under the guarantee: *Massoud Baradaran Tabarrok v EDC Lord & Co (a firm)* [1997] EWCA 481. In Australia, on the other hand, a claim for negligence arises when the plaintiff suffers loss or damage: *Wardley Australia Ltd v Western Australia* (1984) 3 B.P.R. 9500. However, a guarantee can be expressed in terms which make the guarantor liable upon the default of the principal debtor even if that debtor might not yet be liable for the amount of the principal debt because a proper demand has not been made upon him: *Hong Kong Bank of Australia Ltd v McKenna* (unreported, Qld FC Sup Ct, December 13, 1993) *per* Pincus A.J.

[27] See above, para.10–07 and *ANZ Banking Group Ltd v Elfakahani* (unreported, Vic Sup Ct, Harper J., July 31, 1992).

[28] [1932] 1 K.B. 423.

[29] *Walker v British Guarantee Association* (1852) 21 L.J.Q.B. 257. As an example of the absence of default by the principal in a fidelity guarantee, see *Jephson v Howkins* (1841) 2 Scott N.R. 605; 2 Man. & G. 366; 133 E.R. 787.

[30] *Schureck v McFarlane* (1923) 41 W.N. (NSW) 3.

[31] *Turner Manufacturing Co Pty Ltd v Senes* [1964] N.S.W.R. 642, CA. It would be premature to issue a writ in respect of payment for such goods. As another example, in the context of a loan, see *Keene v Devine* [1986] W.A.R. 217; discussed above, para.10–13.

[32] *Rickaby v Lewis* (1905) 22 T.L.R. 130; *Mayor of Wellington v Roberts and McNaught* (1883) N.Z.L.R. 2 C.A. 56. See also *Tricontinental Corp Ltd v HDFI Ltd* (1990) 21 N.S.W.L.R. 689, discussed above, paras 8–11, 8–13 and 10–96, where the guarantee itself provided that certain notices should be served on the principal. *Cf. DFC Financial Services Ltd v Coffey* [1991] B.C.C. 218.

Parr's Banking Co v Yates,[33] the Court of Appeal held that the liability of the guarantor was barred by the Statute of Limitations in respect of a particular advance after the expiration of six years from when that advance was made. This conclusion was based upon the assumption that the creditor's right of action accrues against the principal as soon as the first advance is made and the principal becomes indebted to the bank. Such a result is quite contrary to the true intentions of the principal and the creditor, being the provision of real working credit for the principal. As Lord Herschell stated in *Rouse v Bradford Banking Co*:[34]   **10–148**

> "[I]t is obvious that neither party would have it in contemplation that when the bank had granted an overdraft it would immediately, without notice, proceed to sue for the money; and the truth is that, whether there were any legal obligation to abstain from so doing or not, it is obvious that, having regard to the course of business, if a bank which has agreed to give an overdraft were to act in such a fashion, the results to its business would be of the most serious nature."[35]

Subsequently, in *Wright v New Zealand Farmers Co-op Association of* **10–149** *Canterbury Ltd*,[36] the Privy Council adopted a different conclusion in the context of a guarantee which stated (unlike the guarantee in *Parr's Banking Co v Yates*) that the guarantee "shall apply to the balance that is now or may at any time hereafter be owing". This was interpreted to mean that the repayment of every debit balance was guaranteed as it was constituted from time to time, the number of years which had expired since any individual advance was made being immaterial.[37] The decision in *Parr's Banking Co v Yates* was not overruled but it was distinguished on the basis that the guarantee did not contain the particular clause quoted above. From the creditor's point of view, it is important, therefore, that such a provision be included in a guarantee of future advances.[38] The result of *Wright v New Zealand Farmers Co-op Association of Canterbury Ltd* is that the creditor will not lose a right of action against the guarantor in respect of a particular advance after the expiration six years from the date of that advance being made.

In *Wright v New Zealand Farmers Co-op Association of Canterbury Ltd*, **10–150** the Privy Council did not specifically deal with the question of when the principal is in default. For example, if the principal borrows £2,000 through an overdrawn account by means of two separate advances of £1,000 each, the decision in *Wright v New Zealand Farmers Co-op Association of Canterbury Ltd* makes it plain that the Statute of Limitations in respect of the first £1,000 advanced will not run from the date of that first advance,

---

[33] [1898] 2 Q.B. 460.
[34] [1894] A.C. 586.
[35] *ibid.*, at 596.
[36] [1939] A.C. 439. See also *Hartland v Jukes* (1863) 1 H. & C. 667; 158 E.R. 1052.
[37] [1939] A.C. 439 at 449.
[38] Note, however, that the Privy Council did not express its approval of *Parr's Banking Co v Yates* [1898] 2 Q.B. 460: "Their Lordships express no opinion whether that particular decision was right or wrong": [1939] A.C. 439 at 450.

but it is not clear whether the principal can be regarded as being in default at all if the creditor simply sues the guarantor without any demand or notification to the principal. It is thought that in these circumstances the principal should be regarded as being in default only after a demand is made by the creditor upon the principal. This conclusion is reinforced by *Union Bank of Australia Ltd v Barry*.[39] The guarantor in that case was liable in case the principal "shall default in payment of such advances" (plus interest thereon) which had been made through an overdrawn account. Hood J. rejected the argument that, because the money was lent through an overdrawn account, the principal could be regarded as being in default from day to day and held that there was no default by the principal until a demand was made by the bank. His Honour observed:

> "At the time the guarantee was signed by the defendant, [the principal] owed a very large sum to the bank, and was in default in the sense that she owed it to the bank, which could at once enforce payment. If the defendant's contention is right, then if a fresh advance had been made a few minutes after the guarantee was signed, the bank could sue the surety. That I think was not the intention of the parties. The bank intended to carry on [the principal debtor] by overdrawn account. The defendant was expected to pay in case [the principal debtor], *having been asked to pay*, failed to do so."[40]

10–151   Section 6 of the Limitation Act 1980 deals with the limitation period where no time for performance has been specified in the principal contract. It provides that if a loan contract does not provide for repayment of the debt on or before a specific or determinable date, and does not make the obligation to repay conditional on a demand for payment by or on behalf of the creditor, time begins to run from the date on which the creditor makes a written demand for repayment of the debt.[41]

(b) Quantification of loss is unnecessary

10–152   Provided that it is shown that the principal debtor is in default, the creditor acquires a cause of action against the guarantor even if the creditor's loss is not yet quantified. This is apparent from *National House-Building Council v Fraser*.[42] The National House-Building Council was an organisation which compensated purchasers of houses which had been constructed defectively in breach of the Council's rules by any company placed on the national register of house-builders. The directors of one of the registered companies gave the National House-Building Council a guarantee that the company would perform the obligations imposed on it by the Council's rules and indemnify the Council against "all losses ...

---

[39] (1897) 23 V.L.R. 505.
[40] *ibid.*, at 507–508 (emphasis added). See also *ANZ Banking Group Ltd v Douglas Morris Investments Pty Ltd* [1992] 1 Qd. R. 478.
[41] See G. Andrews and R. Millett, *Law of Guarantees* (3rd ed., 2000), p.241.
[42] [1983] 1 All E.R. 1090.

incurred" by a failure to do so. The company built houses which were not in accordance with the rules regarding design and construction, and failed to honour an arbitrator's award made against the company in an action by the purchaser of one of the houses. The Council, in accordance with its rules, satisfied the award and claimed reimbursement from the company. The company failed to pay and the Council sought to enforce the guarantee. The guarantors argued that they were not liable because the guarantee, which was limited to a period of three years, had expired before the arbitrator's award quantifying the loss was made and, therefore, the Council had not incurred "a loss" within the scope of the guarantee. However, Sir Douglas Frank Q.C. held that the guarantors' liability arose upon the principal's default, in this case, upon the failure of the company to build the houses in accordance with the Council's rules regarding design and construction. This default had occurred within the three-year period of the guarantee and it was irrelevant that the loss was not quantified until a later date. Although this conclusion is correct as a matter of general principle, it is possible that, on the proper construction of the principal contract, or the guarantee, no default will occur until the loss is quantified.[43]

(c) The conditions of the guarantee

Even if the debtor is in default according to the terms of the principal **10–153** transaction, so that the creditor's action against the debtor accrues, no cause of action will arise against the guarantor if the terms of the guarantee make it clear that the creditor must comply with a condition precedent to the cause of action before suing the guarantor. The most familiar example is where the guarantor's obligation is to repay the moneys secured by the guarantee only after a demand is made upon the guarantor.[44] No cause of action arises until the demand is made and the limitation period will, therefore, only run from that point of time.[45] Consequently, once the guarantor's liability to pay an outstanding debt is crystallised by service of a demand, it is not possible to start the limitation period running again in respect of this debt by making a demand for a subsequent larger indebtedness.[46] As McPherson J. (as he then was) put it, "[Q]uite plainly, time cannot repeatedly be set running again by the simple expedient of making successive demands for precisely the same amount of balance; and I do not see that there is any difference if in a case like this the old balance

---

[43] A similar conclusion has been reached in relation to a contract of indemnity: see *Bosma v Larsen* [1966] 1 Lloyd's Rep. 22.
[44] *Bradford Old Bank Ltd v Sutcliffe* [1918] 2 K.B. 833; *Re Brown's Estate* [1893] 2 Ch. 300; *Dominion Bank v Elliott* [1938] O.W.N. 328; *National A/asia Bank Ltd v Bond Brewing Holdings Ltd* (1990) 1 A.C.S.R. 405 at 411; *Bond v Hong Kong Bank of Australia Ltd* (1991) 25 N.S.W.L.R. 286; *[CSJ ANZ Banking Group Ltd v Douglas Morris Investments Pty Ltd* [1992] 1 Qd. R. 478. See generally above, paras 10–125 to 10–135, as to the nature of a demand.
[45] *ibid.*
[46] *ANZ Banking Group Ltd v Douglas Morris Investments Pty Ltd* [1992] 1 Qd. R. 478; *Bank of Baroda v Patel* [1996] 1 Lloyd's Rep. 391.

forms part of the new."[47] Moreover, where the creditor proceeds on the basis that a demand was validly served on the guarantor and obtains a default judgment against the guarantor, the limitation period will run from the date of this valid formal demand even if the guarantor succeeds in an application to set aside judgment on the ground that he did not receive the demand. In these circumstances, the creditor cannot argue that the limitation period runs from the date of a later demand on the guarantor at his new address.[48]

10–154   Another example of a late start for the limitation period is where the right of action against the guarantor is made conditional upon the expiry of a period of time after the principal's default.[49] This may arise because the consideration for the guarantee is expressed to be the creditor allowing the principal that period of time to settle the debt.[50]

10–155   The creditor may serve a demand after the guarantors give notice terminating their liability. In *Bank of Credit and Commerce International SA v Simjee*[51] the terms of the guarantee provided that the expiry of the notice period crystallised the guarantor's obligations. Hobhouse L.J. held that the guarantee implied that the contract remained in force and that the creditor could make a demand even after the guarantor had revoked his guarantee.

10–156   A guarantee may also specify that the creditor has to comply with certain conditions in relation to the principal debtor before the guarantor can be sued. Thus in *Commercial Bank of Australia v Colonial Finance Mortgage Investment & Guarantee Corp*,[52] the guarantee stated that the guarantors undertook to pay the debts of the customer "in case the customer shall make default in payment thereof respectively or of any part thereof respectively on demand". The High Court of Australia held that a cause of action arose against the guarantor in respect of the principal debt once the customer was in default *and* a demand had been made on the customer. Thus the Statute of Limitations began to run against the creditor only when both these conditions were satisfied.

10–157   The terms of the guarantee may subordinate the claim of the guaranteed creditors to those of the guarantor's other creditors in the event of the guarantor's insolvency. In *Re Maxwell Communications Corporation plc (No.2)*,[53] Vinelott J. held that the waiver or subordination of a creditor's claim after the commencement of a bankruptcy or winding-up was not precluded by public policy considerations. Nor was the waiver or subordination of the guaranteed creditor's claim against the guarantor prohibited by the mutual dealings provision.[54]

---

[47] *ibid.*, at 489.
[48] *Bank of Baroda v Patel* [1996] 1 Lloyd's Rep. 391.
[49] *Holl v Hadley* (1835) 2 Ad. & E. 758; 111 E.R. 292; *Henton v Paddison* (1893) 68 L.T. 405.
[50] *Holl v Hadley* (1835) 2 Ad. & E. 758; 111 E.R. 292.
[51] [1997] C.L.C. 135. See also above, para.9–35.
[52] (1906) 4 C.L.R. 57.
[53] [1994] 1 All E.R. 737 at 746.
[54] *ibid.* See also *Deering v Hyndman* (1886) 18 L.R. Ir. 467; *Horne v Chester & Fein Property Developments Pty Ltd* [1987] V.R. 913. Cf. *National Westminster Bank Ltd v Halesowen Presswork & Assemblies Ltd* [1972] A.C. 785, as explained in *Re Maxwell Communications*

(d) The date on which the liability of an indemnifier arises

Under a contract of indemnity, the time at which the cause of action **10–158** against the indemnifier arises will be dependent on the terms of the indemnity.[55] As a general rule, an indemnifier will not be entitled to require a demand to be made upon him, unless the contract so provides.[56] A common form of indemnity is a promise to indemnify against "all consequences or liabilities" arising from the indemnified party entering into a particular transaction. In this case the cause of action against the indemnifer arises at the date when events occur which place the party indemnified under a liability, and it is unnecessary for the party indemnified to discharge that liability by payment or to have liability determined by judicial process.[57] Thus in *Bosma v Larsen*,[58] the charterer of a vessel agreed to indemnify the shipowner against liabilities arising from the master signing a bill of lading. The shipowner incurred such a liability when the goods were delivered in a damaged state at the port of destination. It was held that the cause of action arose from the date when these facts were established, and not at the later date when the liability was determined by judicial process. Similarly, in *Wardley Australia Ltd v Western Australia*,[59] the High Court of Australia held that the indemnity, in that case, on its true construction created a liability on the part of the respondent to pay the National Australia Bank Ltd a sum of money as soon as the bank's "net loss" was ascertained and quantified. This liability did not arise upon the execution of the indemnity but at the later date when the bank incurred actual loss or damage in settling proceedings instituted against the bank to recover an alleged preference.

It is possible that the contract of indemnity may be worded so that the **10–159** cause of action does not occur until a later date, for example, if it provides for an indemnity in respect of sums actually paid in pursuance of legal liability.[60] In *Telfair Shipping Corp v Inersea Carriers SA (The Caroline P)*,[61] for example, the owners of the vessel were entitled to be indemnified by the charterers under the terms of a charter party against the

---

Corp plc (No.2) [1994] 1 All E.R. 737 at 746. The mutual dealings provisions are s.323 of the Insolvency Act 1986 and r.4.90 of the Insolvency Rules 1986 SI 1986/1925.

[55] As to the effect of a condition precedent to the indemnifier's liability, see above, paras 10–140 to 10–141.

[56] See *Re Taylor, Ex p. Century 21 Real Estate Corp* (1995) 130 A.L.R. 723, where the liability of the debtors in their capacity as indemnifiers attached without the necessity for the making of a demand because the terms of the indemnity clause in the document did not require a demand. By the same token, the original tenant under a lease will be entitled to use the statutory demand procedure under the Insolvency Rules, r.6.5(4)(b) to obtain an indemnity from the guarantor of a later tenant to whom the lease has been assigned: *Cale v Assuidoman KPS (Harrow) Ltd* [1996] B.P.I.R. 245.

[57] See *Wardley Australia Ltd v Western Australia* (1992) 175 C.L.R. 514.

[58] [1966] 1 Lloyd's Rep. 22. See also *Chandris v Argo Insurance* [1963] 2 Lloyd's Rep. 65 and *ANZ Banking Group Ltd v Douglas Morris Investments Pty Ltd* [1992] 1 Qd. R. 478.

[59] (1992) 175 C.L.R. 514.

[60] See, *e.g.* *ANZ Banking Group Ltd v Douglas Morris Investments Pty Ltd* [1992] 1 Qd. R. 478.

[61] [1985] 1 All E.R. 243. See also *Paddington Churches Housing Association v Technical and General Guarantee Co Ltd* [1999] B.L.R. 244, where an action on an indemnity in respect of "the net established and ascertained damages" was dismissed as premature because the liability had not been calculated.

consequences of the master signing the bills of lading in terms more onerous than those of the charter party. This indemnity did not become enforceable until the shipowners' liability to the consignees had been determined by an award of damages against the shipowners. Hence, the limitation period for an action to enforce the indemnity began to run only when the award of damages was obtained. However, in *Bosma v Larsen*[62] McNair J. thought that the cause of action in these cases might be complete before the sums were paid and as soon as the person claiming to be indemnified obtained equitable relief in advance of payment or judicial determination of liability.[63]

(iii) Persons who may enforce the guarantee

(a) Joint creditors

10–160   If the guarantee is given to several persons jointly, they should all sue on it.[64] Where the joint creditors refuse to join in the action as claimants, they can be joined as defendants.[65] Occasionally, however, even though the guarantee names a number of parties as creditors, the interpretation of the agreement as a whole may indicate that the obligations of the guarantee are not owed jointly to all the parties named. In such a case, the proper claimant is the party (or parties) to whom the guarantee is in fact given.[66]

(b) Third parties

10–161   Additionally, the Contracts (Rights of Third Parties) Act 1999 created broad exceptions to the benefit side of the privity of contract doctrine. While Royal Assent to the Act was given on November 11, 1999, it does not apply to contracts entered into before May 11, 2000 unless expressly provided for in the contract.

10–162   Under the Act there can be an express or implied conferral of contractual rights on a third party.[67] Section 1(1)(a) provides that a third party may in his own right enforce a term of a contract if the contract expressly so provides. In addition, the Act impliedly confers rights on a third party where three conditions are satisfied: (i) the term purports to

[62] [1966] 1 Lloyd's Rep. 22.
[63] [1966] 1 Lloyd's Rep. 22 at 29. It is doubtful, however, whether quia timet relief is available in this situation as damages would provide an adequate remedy: see *McIntosh v Dalwood (No.4)* (1930) 30 S.R. (NSW) 415 at 418, and see below, paras 10–266 to 10–268.
[64] *Pugh v Stringfield* (1857) 3 C.B. (NS) 2; 140 ER 637; (1858) 4 C.B. (NS) 364; 140 E.R. 1125.
[65] See *Luke v South Kensington Hotel Co* (1879) 11 Ch. D. 121 (an action for foreclosure by one of the several mortgagees).
[66] *Boral Resources (Qld) Pty Ltd v Donnelly* [1988] 1 Qd. R. 506, discussed above, para.5–70.
[67] See A. Burrows, "The Contracts (Rights of Third Parties) Act 1999 and its Implications for Commercial Contracts" (2000) L.M.C.L.Q. 540 at 543. See also N. Andrews, "Strangers to Justice No Longer: The Reversal of the Privity Rule under the Contracts (Rights of Third Parties) Act 1999" (2001) C.L.J. 353; M. Bridge "The Contracts (Rights of Third Parties) Act 1999" (2001) 5 Edinburgh Law Review 85; and C. MacMillan, "A Birthday Present for Lord Denning: The Contracts (Rights of Third Parties) Act 1999" (2000) 63 M.L.R. 721.

confer a benefit on him (s.1(1)(b)); (ii) he is expressly identified in the contract by name, as a member of a class (for example, "unsecured creditor of ALC Plc")[68] or as answering a particular description (for example, the "creditor's assignee"); (iii) unless on a proper construction of the contract it appears that the parties did not intend the term to be enforceable by the third party. The third party does not need to be in existence when the contract is made.[69] Consequently, the contract may confer rights on a company that is not yet in existence or on an unborn child.

To enforce a term of the contract, the third parties will have available to **10–163** them any remedy that would have been available to them if they had been parties to the contract.[70] The rules relating to damages, injunctions, specific performance and other relief shall apply accordingly.[71]

The scheme of the Act is developed in subsequent sections. Section 2 of **10–164** the Act deals with the circumstances under which the contracting parties may vary or rescind the contract in a situation where the third party is entitled to enforce a term of the contract under s.1. Section 3 deals with the availability of any defences or set offs to the promisor (guarantor) in an action by a third party. Section 4 provides that s.1 does not affect any right of the promisee (the creditor) to enforce any term of the contract, while s.5 protects the promissor (the guarantor) against double liability to the promisee (the creditor) and the third party. There are specific exceptions in s.6 which prevent the third party from taking advantage of the Act.[72] Section 7 provides, *inter alia*, that s.1 does not affect any right or remedy of a third party that exists or is available apart from the Act. This preserves the existing common law and statutory exceptions to the doctrine of privity of contract.[73] Sections 8 and 9 deal with arbitration.

In the present context, the overall effect of the Act is that it will expand **10–165** the range of persons who may enforce guarantees. Where the enforceability tests in s.1 are satisfied, the creditor's successors or assigns[74] or even the creditor's nominees[75] or persons identified by reference to a particular class, for example, "all the unsecured creditors" of the principal debtor,[76]

---

[68] The purpose of these provisions is to enable the promisor (guarantor) to know with sufficient certainty who can claim the benefit of the guarantee: *Rattrays Wholesale Ltd v Meredyth-Young & A'Court Ltd* [1997] 2 N.Z.L.R. 363.

[69] Contracts (Rights of Third Parties) Act 1999, s.1(3).

[70] s.1(5).

[71] *ibid.*

[72] These exclusions are based on public policy and/or commercial grounds: G.H. Treitel in *Chitty on Contracts* (28th ed., 1999), pp.1012–1014.

[73] A. Phang, "On Justification and Method in Law Reform—The Contracts (Rights of Third Parties) Act 1999" (2002) 18 J.C.L. 32 at 36.

[74] In *Malyon v New Zealand Methodist Trust Association* [1993] 1 N.Z.L.R. 137 the New Zealand Court of Appeal held that a similar provision, s.4 of the Contracts (Privity) Act 1982 (NZ), did not allow a lessor to enforce a guarantee given in respect of an assignee's obligations as lessee on its construction in a deed of assignment of lease: the guarantee was intended to benefit the assignor of the lease but not the lessor.

[75] In *Rattrays Wholesale Ltd v Meredyth-Young & A'Court Ltd* [1997] 2 N.Z.L.R. 363 Tipping J. of the New Zealand High Court held that a person described as "the lessor's nominee" was a person designated by description for the purposes of s.4 of the Contracts (Privity) Act 1982 (NZ). *Cf. Field v Fitton* [1988] 1 N.Z.L.R. 482 (obiter dicta) and *Karangahape Read International Village Ltd v Holloway* [1989] 1 N.Z.L.R. 83.

[76] Compare, *e.g. Re A & K Holdings Pty Ltd* [1964] V.R. 257.

may be entitled to enforce a guarantee expressly or impliedly intended for their benefit.

10–166 It is possible to exclude the application of the Act by inserting a provision in the guarantee in the following terms:

"A person who is not a party to this agreement shall have no right under the Contracts (Rights of Third Parties) Act 1999 to enforce any of its terms except and to the extent that this agreement expressly provides for such Act to apply to any of its terms".[77]

Moreover, as we have seen, s.7(1) provides that s.1 does not affect any right or remedy of a third party that exists or is available apart from the Act. Accordingly, the common law doctrine of privity of contract and to exceptions will continue to be relevant.

10–167 It is still necessary, therefore, to examine the operation of guarantees expressed in the form of a deed not inter partes and the position of assignees, beneficiaries of a trust of the promise of guarantee and persons on whose behalf the creditor entered into the guarantee.

(c) Guarantees as deeds not inter partes

10–168 Where the guarantee is under seal, a distinction must be drawn between the case where the guarantee is embodied in a deed inter partes and the case where the guarantee takes the form of a deed not inter partes, the most common alternative form being a deed poll.[78] A deed inter partes is a document which records an agreement, covenant or some other arrangement entered into between two or more parties who, by the deed, evince an intention to be bound to each other. It is similar to a bilateral contract.[79] An example is a deed of guarantee between "The [named] guarantor of the first part and the [named] creditor of the second part" by which the guarantor promises to guarantee advances made to the principal debtor. A deed not inter partes, on the other hand, is not expressed in this bilateral form but is an expression of intention by one person or a group of persons which evidences a willingness by the maker (or makers) of the deed to be bound by its terms. Factors which will indicate that the deed is not inter partes are the absence of a clause at the beginning of the deed referring to the parties to the deed ("the parties clause") and the fact that the deed is expressed in the first person.[80] Thus, a guarantee in the following terms will be a deed poll rather than a deed inter partes:

---

[77] See A. Burrows, "The Contracts (Rights of Third Parties) Act 1999 and its Implications for Commercial Contracts" [2000] L.M.C.L.Q. 540 at 545 and s.1(2) of the Act.
[78] See generally R.J. Bullen, "The Rights of Strangers to Contracts under Seal" (1977–1978) 6 Adel. L.R. 119.
[79] *ibid.*, at 120.
[80] *Chelsea and Waltham Green Building Society v Armstrong* [1951] Ch. D. 853 at 857.

"We, the guarantors jointly and severally guarantee on demand ... the payment in full of the amounts then owed by C Company to each of its unsecured creditors."[81]

The distinction between the two forms of deed is not always an easy **10–169** question of construction, but it is significant in the context of determining those persons who may enforce the guarantee. If the deed is a deed inter partes, the covenantee can be regarded as being a party to the deed, and hence able to enforce it, *only* if the covenantee is named as one of the parties in the parties clause.[82] This established rule of privity has been held to apply even though it might appear from the remainder of the deed that it was intended that the covenantee should take the benefit of the deed.[83] For example, if the deed is expressed in the parties clause to be between the guarantor and a particular creditor, another person referred to in the body of the guarantee will not be able to enforce the guarantee even though it appears that the covenant was also made for that person's benefit. This may happen if, for instance, the other person has contracted jointly with the creditor referred to in the parties clause in respect of the principal transaction and so has an interest in being able to enforce the guarantee.

If, however, the deed is not inter partes, any person may sue to enforce **10–170** the covenant if it is clear from a construction of the deed of guarantee as a whole that the covenant is expressly or impliedly made for that person's benefit.[84]

Another possible difference between the two types of deed is that a deed **10–171** inter partes cannot be made with a person who is not in existence at the date of the deed or a person who is not ascertainable at that time[85] (for example, future creditors of the principal). Although the position is unclear in respect of a deed not inter partes,[86] it is arguable that such a deed can be validly made in respect of a class of persons not ascertainable at the date of the deed. If so, it would mean that a deed not inter partes could be made in respect of future creditors of the principal (for example, future assignees of the benefit of the principal transaction). In view of the uncertainty of this point, however, the creditor, if it wishes to contract for the benefit of future creditors, should expressly covenant as a trustee in respect of that class of persons.[87] Such a covenant must, of course, be made

---

[81] See, *e.g. Re A & K Holdings Pty Ltd* [1964] V.R. 257.

[82] R.J. Bullen, *op. cit.*, at 119–120. See also *Scudamore v Vandenstene* (1587) 2 Co. Inst. 673; *Windsmore v Hobart* (1584) Hob. 313; 80 E.R. 456; *Re A & K Holdings Pty Ltd* [1964] V.R. 257 at 261.

[83] *ibid.*

[84] *Re A & K Holdings Pty Ltd* [1964] V.R. 257 at 261. *Cf. Malyon v New Zealand Methodist Trust Association* [1993] 1 N.Z.L.R. 137, where a guarantee of the assignee's obligations as lessee in a deed of assignment of a lease was held to be covenant for the benefit of the assignor of the lease and not for the benefit of the lessor, even though the lessor was a party to the deed of assignment.

[85] *Re A & K Holdings Pty Ltd* [1964] V.R. 257 at 262.

[86] *ibid.*

[87] This suggestion is made in *Re A & K Holdings Pty Ltd* [1964] V.R. 257 at 262. See also *Metcalf v Bruin* (1810) 12 East 400; 104 E.R. 156.

where the contract is not under seal or if the guarantee is embodied in a deed inter partes.

10–172 Apart from those named as parties to the contract of guarantee or, in the case of a deed not inter partes, those for whose benefit the deed is expressed to be made, the following persons may also enforce a guarantee.

(d) Assignees

10–173 A contract of guarantee is assignable[88] as a legal chose in action.[89] Hence, the acquisition by a bank of the assets and choses in action of another bank carries with it the right to enforce a guarantee given to the other bank.[90] Usually, notice of the assignment of the benefit of the guarantee needs to be given to the guarantor to protect the assignee's priority,[91] but is otherwise unnecessary.[92]

10–174 The effect of an assignment, however, cannot be to enlarge the ambit of the guarantee and render the guarantor liable for obligations not encompassed within its terms.[93]

10–175 A guarantee or the security for it cannot be assigned without the benefit of the principal obligation[94] because otherwise "a creditor could effectively divorce the guarantor's liability from that of the principal debtor".[95] Similarly, an assignment of the guarantee is ineffective once the principal contract is determined, for example, by the creditor terminating the principal contract for the principal's breach.[96]

---

[88] See the Law of Property Act 1925, s.136. As to the enforcement of a legal chose in action assigned in equity, see *Raiffeisen Zentralbank Osterreich AG v Five Star General Trading LLC* [2001] EWCA Civ 68; [2001] 2 W.L.R. 1344. Where the assignment of the guarantee does not satisfy the statutory requirements because it is not in writing signed by the creditor and no written notice has been given to the guarantor, it may nevertheless take effect as an equitable assignment. This can arise where the guarantee is delivered to the assignee with the intention of passing the benefit of the guarantee and where there is consideration sufficient to support an equitable assignment: *Zaknic Pty Ltd v Svelte Corporation Pty Ltd* (unreported, Fed Ct, NSW District Registry, Lehane J., August 14, 1996) (B.C. 9603695 at 39). In such a case, the equitable assignee of the guarantee may enforce the guarantee in its own name: *Three Rivers District Council v Bank of England* [1996] Q.B. 292; *Long Leys Co Pty Ltd v Silkdale Pty Ltd* (1992) NSW Conv. R. 59, 476 and M. Leeming, "BCCI: the Real Party in Interest?" (1995) 111 L.Q.R. 549.

[89] *Loxton v Moir* (1914) 18 C.L.R. 360; *Housing Guarantee Fund Ltd v Yusef* (1990) 8 A.C.L.C. 1,197 at 1,212.

[90] *Bank of Montreal v Vineberg* (1925) 43 Que K.B. 363, Que CA.

[91] See the statutory provisions noted above, n.88.

[92] See *Wheatley v Bastow* (1855) 7 De G.M. & G. 261; 44 E.R. 102 and its interpretation in *Sacher Investments Pty Ltd v Forma Stereo Consultants Pty Ltd* [1976] 1 N.S.W.L.R. 5.

[93] *Housing Guarantee Fund Ltd v Yusef* (1990) 8 A.C.L.C. 1,197, discussed above, para.9–67. See also *Katsikalis v Deutsche Bank (Asia) AG* [1988] 2 Qd. R. 641, above, para.5–83.

[94] *Hutchens v Deauville Investments Pty Ltd* (1986) 68 A.L.R. 367.

[95] *ibid.*, at 373. See also *International Leasing Corporation Ltd v Aiken* [1967] 2 N.S.W.L.R. 427 at 439; *Sacher Investments Pty Ltd v Forma Stereo Consultants Pty Ltd* [1976] 1 N.S.W.L.R. 5 and *Gilmour v Pyramid Building Society (In Liq)* (unreported NSW CA, February 24, 1995). One possible result of this arrangement is the guarantor's rights of subrogation might be affected: see Note (1986) 68 A.L.R. 367 at 373.

[96] *Hughes v Fresh Pack Fruit & Vegetable Market Pty Ltd* [1965] W.A.R. 199 at 204, where it was held that such an assignment constituted a mere right to litigate in respect of accrued liabilities.

A guarantee can be enforced by an assignee of the creditor's rights **10–176** under the principal contract in two situations:

    (i) where the benefit of the guarantee is expressly or impliedly assigned along with the principal contract to which the guarantee relates;[97] and

    (ii) where the guarantee is properly classified as a covenant that touches and concerns land which is assigned by the creditor to the assignee.[98]

In the first situation, it is a question of construction whether the benefit **10–177** of the guarantee was intended to be assigned to the assignee. In the absence of an express assignment of the guarantee together with the principal contract,[99] the assignee must show that the express assignment of the principal contract has impliedly carried with it the benefit of the guarantee. A number of general points can be made about this question of construction.

First, where the creditor simply assigns the benefit of the principal **10–178** contract and the words of the assignment are limited to that transaction, the benefit of the guarantee securing it will not follow the assignment.[1] The assignee of the principal transaction is, therefore, unable to enforce the guarantee. An example of this situation is to be found in *International Leasing Corp (Vic) Ltd v Aiken*,[2] where the guarantee of a chattel lease was held not to be impliedly assigned by an assignment of the lease itself when the words of assignment were expressly limited to the lease, the goods which were the subject matter of the lease, and the moneys due thereunder.

Sometimes the guarantee may be incorporated in an instrument of **10–179** mortgage, and it was argued in *Consolidated Trust Co Ltd v Naylor*[3] that the benefit of a guarantee was effectively assigned with an express assignment of a mortgage (even where the words of assignment related only to the mortgage) because of the provisions of the Real Property Act 1900 (NSW). Section 51 of that Act provides that: "Upon the registration

---

[97] A guarantee of an assignee's obligations as lessee under a lease does not necessarily enure for the benefit of the lessor. In *Malyon v New Zealand Methodist Trust Association* [1993] 1 N.Z.L.R. 137, the New Zealand Court of Appeal held that the guarantee in that case was intended to benefit only the assignor of the lease, not the lessor.

[98] See below, paras 10–182 to 10–195.

[99] For a precedent for an express assignment, see "Note" [1989] A.N.Z. Conv R 358.

[1] *International Leasing Corp (Vic) Ltd v Aiken* [1967] 2 N.S.W.R. 427 at 439 *per* Jacobs J.A., 451 *per* Asprey J.A. See also *Sheers v Thimbleby & Son* (1897) 76 L.T. 709 especially at 713 (guarantee not running with assignment of a mortgage); *Blue Chip Investments Inc v Kavanagh* (1986) 60 Nfl'd & P.E.I.R. 85; *Blue Chip Investments Inc v Hicks* (1983) 50 Nfl'd & P.E.I.R. 60, affirmed on other grounds in (1985) 54 Nfl'd & P.E.I.R. 149. A contract of indemnity is also assignable: *Re Perkins* [1898] 2 Ch. 182; *British Union & National Insurance v Rawson* [1916] 2 Ch. 476. Note that in the event of the principal transaction being assigned without the benefit of the guarantee, the assignor cannot enforce the guarantee: *Hutchens v Deauville Investments Pty Ltd* (1986) 68 A.L.R. 367, and see above, paras 6–115 to 6–116.

[2] [1967] 2 N.S.W.R. 427.

[3] (1936) 55 C.L.R. 423, applied in *Farrow Mortgage Services Pty Ltd v Hogg* [1995] A.N.Z. Conv. R. 233.

of any transfer, the estate or interest of the transferor as set forth in such instrument, with all rights, powers and privileges thereto belonging or appertaining, shall pass to the transferee".[4] The High Court of Australia rejected the argument that, upon registration of the mortgage, s.51 effectively assigned not only the mortgage itself but the contract of guarantee contained in it.[5] The reasoning was that a guarantee is not an instrument within the meaning of the Real Property Act as it is not a document capable of registration under the Act.[6] It should be noted, however, that the decision in *Consolidated Trust Co Ltd v Naylor*[7] was at least partially based on the fact that a guarantee of a mortgage debt does not directly or indirectly affect the land. As we shall see, this conclusion may be open to debate in the light of recent case law.[8]

10–180   The second general point which should be made is that the courts may draw the inference that the benefit of the contract of guarantee has been assigned when the words of assignment, which are primarily intended to assign the principal transaction, are also wide enough to encompass an assignment of the benefit of the guarantee.[9] Thus in *Consolidated Trust Co Ltd v Naylor*, where the guarantee was contained in a mortgage, the assignor transferred "all moneys secured by the written contract of mortgage and all my rights, powers and remedies thereunder". This was held sufficient to transfer to the assignee the benefit of the guarantee as well as the mortgage.[10] In order for these or similar words of assignment to have this effect, it is probably essential that the guarantee be contained in the instrument of mortgage or other principal obligation so that it is abundantly clear that the guarantee is included in the "rights" or "powers" to be transferred.[11] It is also necessary for the principal transaction to be assigned expressly and not merely transferred by the operation of the relevant statutory provisions.[12] The court will decide that there is an

---

[4] Compare Land Registration Act 2002, ss.28 and 58.
[5] Compare *Gilmour v Pyramid Building Society (In Liq)* (unreported, NSWCA, February 24, 1995).
[6] See also *Farrow Mortgage Services Pty Ltd v Hogg* [1995] A.N.Z. Conv. R. 233 at 238–239.
[7] See especially the joint judgment of Dixon and Evatt J.J., (1936) 55 C.L.R. 423 at 434–435. The same argument was applied to a guarantee contained in a memorandum in *Sacher Investments Pty Ltd v Forma Stereo Consultants Pty Ltd* [1976] 1 N.S.W.L.R. 5 at 10. See also *Kumar v Dunning* [1987] 3 W.L.R. 1167 at 1179, CA.
[8] See below, paras 10–182 to 10–195.
[9] *Consolidated Trust Co Ltd v Naylor* (1936) 55 C.L.R. 423 and see its interpretation in *International Leasing Corp (Vic) Ltd v Aiken* [1967] 2 N.S.W.R. 427 at 439 *per* Jacobs J.A., at 451 *per* Asprey J.A.
[10] As other examples, see *Wheatley v Bastow* (1855) 7 De G.M. & G. 261; 44 E.R. 102 (assignment of mortgage debt and "the securities for the same", the securities being comprised of a mortgage containing a covenant for the payment of the debt given by one of the mortgagors in her capacity as surety); *Gilmour v Pyramid Building Society (in liq.)* (unreported, NSWCA, February 24, 1995) (B.C. 9504 209 at 4); *West v Lee Soon and Lee Shun* (1915) 24 D.L.R. 813.
[11] This fact is emphasised in the interpretation of *Consolidated Trust Co Ltd v Naylor* (1936) 55 C.L.R. 423 by Jacobs J.A. and Asprey J.A. in *International Leasing Corp (Vic) Ltd v Aiken* [1967] 2 N.S.W.R. 427 at 439, 451. See also *Pyramid Building Society (in liq) v Walker* (unreported, NSW Sup Ct, Rolfe J., December 1, 1993) and *Farrow Mortgage Services Pty Ltd v Hogg* [1995] A.N.Z. Conv. R. 233 (the consideration clause in the Memorandum of Transfer of Mortgage suggested that the continued provision of credit to the defendants was consideration for the guarantee).
[12] *Sacher Investments Pty Ltd v Forma Stereo Consultants Pty Ltd* [1976] 1 N.S.W.L.R. 5 at 12.

implied assignment of the benefit of the guarantee to the assignee of the mortgage debt if a reasonable person in the position of the contracting parties would have understood from the mortgage that, at the time of the loan and the execution of the mortgage, the benefit of the guarantee would run with the mortgage debt from time to time.[13] The conduct of the parties after the transfer of the mortgage may also persuade the court that there was an implied assignment of the guarantee.[14]

Finally, in *International Leasing Corp (Vic) Ltd v Aiken*,[15] Asprey **10–181** J.A. suggested that, where a guarantee, even one contained in a separate instrument, is drafted so as to refer to the "successors, transferees or assigns" of the original creditor, a simple assignment of the principal transaction, not containing terms sufficient to assign the guarantee itself, will still confer the benefit of the guarantee upon the assignee of the principal transaction. There are cases which can be explained on this ground,[16] but (subject to possible changes to the law of privity as outlined earlier)[17] this cannot be correct because in the absence of an assignment of the benefit of the guarantee, the assignee would not be a party to the guarantee. Indeed, in *Sacher Investments Pty Ltd v Forma Stereo Consultants Pty Ltd*,[18] Yeldham J. adopted this view and held that the assignees of a registered lease pursuant to the *Conveyancing Act* 1919 (NSW) could not enforce the guarantee even though the guarantor had covenanted with the original lessor and "its successors and assigns".[19]

The second situation in which an assignee of the principal contract may **10–182** be able to enforce a guarantee given to the creditor before the assignment is where the guarantee is a covenant that touches and concerns land assigned by the creditor to the assignee. This argument was not relevant in *International Leasing Corp (Vic) Ltd v Aiken* because there the guarantee related to a chattel lease. The argument was not even raised in *Consolidated Trust Co Ltd v Naylor* nor *Sacher Investments Pty Ltd v Forma Stereo Consultants Pty Ltd*. In the former, the guarantee was given in respect of a mortgage debt and it did not touch and concern the land in

---

[13] *Farrow Mortgage Services Pty Ltd v Hogg* [1995] A.N.Z. Conv. R. 233 at 238. In that case, there was nothing in the mortgage document or the guarantee contained in that document to suggest that the guarantee was intended to be solely for the benefit of the original mortgagee. Moreover, the mortgage document expressly provided for subsequent mortgagees. See also *Pyramid Building Society (in liq) v Walker* (unreported, NSW Sup Ct, Rolfe J., December 1, 1993).

[14] *Farrow Mortgage Services Pty Ltd v Hogg* [1995] ANZ Conv R 233 at 238.

[15] [1967] 2 N.S.W.R. 427 at 451.

[16] *e.g. Re Hallett & Co* [1894] 2 Q.B. 256 (guarantee given to original owners of a promissory note, and also "to holders of the promissory note for the time being", and it was held that the benefit of the guarantee passed to a subsequent holder of the note). See also *Re Agra and Masterman's Bank Ex p. Asiatic Banking Corp* (1867) L.R. 2 Ch. App. 391 (but the explanation here is probably that there was an offer to guarantee which could be accepted by subsequent parties to the principal transaction); See *Re Barned's Banking Co, Ex p. Stephens* (1868) 3 Ch. App. 753 at 756–757 and *Sassoon & Sons Ltd v International Banking Corp* [1927] A.C. 711 at 729–730.

[17] See above, paras 2–20 to 2–23.

[18] [1976] 1 N.S.W.L.R. 5. This case must now be read in the light of *P & A Swift Investments v Combined English Stores Group plc* [1988] 2 All E.R. 885; *Kumar v Dunning* [1987] 3 W.L.R. 1167 and *Lang v Asemo Pty Ltd* [1989] VR 773, as discussed below, paras 10–184 to 10–193.

[19] [1976] 1 N.S.W.L.R. 5 at 12.

the relevant sense. As Sir Nicholas Browne-Wilkinson V.-C. pointed out in *Kumar v Dunning*:[20]

> "A surety for a mortgage debt is a surety for the payment of the principal debt. The borrower's own covenant to pay the principal *has nothing to do with the land* and cannot touch and concern the land: there is, therefore, no reason why a covenant by way of surety for such a payment should touch and concern the land."[21]

10–183   But, with respect, a mortgagor's covenants may extend beyond mere payment of the mortgage debt to include covenants to repair, to insure and to pay rates and taxes which can affect the land as such. For this reason there is some doubt whether the recent cases on covenants touching and concerning land are consistent with the ultimate conclusion of the High Court of Australia in *Consolidated Trust Co Ltd v Naylor*.

10–184   While it might be possible to distinguish the guarantee in *Consolidated Trust Co Ltd v Naylor* as a guarantee of a mortgage debt and, therefore, as a covenant not touching and concerning land, no such distinction can be used to support the decision in *Sacher Investments Pty Ltd v Forma Stereo Consultants Pty Ltd*, which is clearly inconsistent with the recent cases insofar as it suggests that an assignee of the reversion of a lease is not entitled to enforce a guarantee of the lessee's obligations in the absence of a specific assignment of the guarantee.

In *Lang v Asemo Pty Ltd*,[22] the Full Court of the Supreme Court of Victoria drew heavily upon the earlier decisions of the Court of Appeal in *Kumar v Dunning*[23] and the House of Lords in *P & A Swift Investments v Combined English Stores Group plc*.[24] The defendants were the directors of a company which was the lessee of a strata title unit in a medical centre. They executed a deed of guarantee to secure the lessee's covenants when the lease was granted. On the same day that the lease and the guarantee were executed, the lessor sold the unit to Asemo Pty Ltd, which later sought to enforce the guarantee.

10–185   The defendants argued that the plaintiff could not enforce the guarantee because there was no privity of contract between them and the plaintiff, and the plaintiff was neither the lessor referred to in the guarantee nor the assignee of the benefit of the guarantee.

10–186   However, the Full Court held that the guarantee was enforceable by the plaintiff as a covenant touching and concerning the land. Gobbo J., with whom Murphy and Phillips J.J. concurred, applied the "satisfactory working test" propounded by Lord Oliver of Aylmerton in *P & A Swift Investments v Combined English Stores plc* for determining whether in any given case a covenant touched and concerned the land:

[20] [1987] 3 W.L.R. 1167.
[21] *ibid.*, at 1179 (emphasis added).
[22] [1989] V.R. 773.
[23] [1987] 3 W.L.R. 1167.
[24] [1988] 2 All E.R. 885.

"(1) The covenant benefits only the reversioner for the time being, and if separated from the reversion ceases to be of benefit to the covenantee. (2) The covenant affects the nature, quality, mode of user or value of the land of the reversioner. (3) The covenant is not expressed to be personal (that is to say neither being given only to a specific reversioner nor in respect of the obligations only of a specific tenant). (4) The fact that a covenant is to pay a sum of money will not prevent it from touching and concerning the land so long as the three foregoing conditions are satisfied and the covenant is connected with something to be done on, to or in relation to the land."[25]

Gobbo J. declared that there was "no reason in principle why the **10–187** decision of the House of Lords should not be followed by this court".[26] This appears to discount the analysis of a surety's covenant in the joint judgment of Dixon and Evatt J.J. in *Consolidated Trust Co Ltd v Naylor*:

"A surety's obligation stands in a different relation to the dealing. His liability is introduced by way of additional security. It is personal, and, except as a result of subrogation, does not directly or indirectly affect the land ... A guarantee is thus collateral to the mortgage transaction."[27]

Gobbo J. distinguished this case as one involving a guarantee of a **10–188** mortgage debt, as distinct from a guarantee of the performance of tenant's covenants: only the latter touched and concerned the land.[28] Moreover, his Honour did not refer to the Privy Council decision in *Hua Chiao Bank v Chiaphua Industries*,[29] where it was held that at the end of the term of a lease the assignee of the reversion was under no obligation to refund a security deposit given to support the tenant's covenants. In the Privy Council, Lord Oliver examined the relationship between the deposit and the land:

"It is bound up with the tenant's covenant only as it were, at one remove, as being an obligation correlative to a contractual obligation which is itself connected with the performance of covenants touching and concerning the land."[30]

---

[25] *ibid.*, at 891.
[26] *Lang v Asemo Pty Ltd* [1989] V.R. 773 at 776.
[27] (1936) 55 C.L.R. 423 at 434–435.
[28] [1989] V.R. 773 at 775, applying the distinction drawn by Sir Nicholas Browne-Wilkinson V.C. in *Kumar v Dunning* [1987] 3 W.L.R. 1167 at 1179. In *Farrow Mortgage Services Pty Ltd v Hogg* [1995] A.N.Z. Conv. R. 233, it was argued that a guarantee of a mortgage debt touched and concerned the land, but Nyland J. decided that the guarantee could be enforced by the assignee of the mortgage on the alternative basis of an implied assignment of the guarantee. In *Waydale v DHL Holdings* (1996) S.C.L.R. 391, a case decided under Scottish law, the court held that a guarantee of a tenant's obligation under a lease did not touch and concern the land; it merely provided protection to the landlord in the event of a default by the particular tenant.
[29] [1987] A.C. 99.
[30] *ibid.*, at 111.

10–189   By parity of reasoning, it could be argued that a guarantee to secure a tenant's obligations is not a covenant that touches and concerns the land.

10–190   Nevertheless, these arguments did not prevail. Applying Lord Oliver's "satisfactory working test" to the facts of the case, Gobbo J. found first that the surety's covenant benefited only the lessor for the time being; once separated from the reversion, it ceased to be of any benefit to the covenantee. But presumably the surety's covenant was also beneficial to the tenant in that it enabled it to obtain and retain the tenancy.[31] Secondly, the surety's covenant affected the land of the reversioner since the existence of the surety was an additional source of recovery and would, therefore, only add to the value. With respect, it is difficult to see how the existence of a guarantee enhances the value of the land *per se*. Indeed, in *Re Distributors & Warehousing Ltd*,[32] the guarantor's payment of the tenant's arrears of rent did not discharge the tenant's obligation to pay rent; the tenant continued in default and the landlord was entitled to forfeit the lease. Hence, the existence of a guarantee, and indeed payment by a guarantor, did not prevent the lease being forfeited, so how did the guarantee enhance the value of the land as such?

10–191   The third element of Lord Oliver's "satisfactory working test" involved an analysis of the terms of the guarantee. There was nothing in the instrument itself suggesting that it was intended to be limited to the specific lessor and the specific lessee. In fact, the identity of the parties and the essential steps in related transactions rebutted any such suggestion:

> "The lease was executed on the same day as the sale was completed in order to meet this requirement. The lessee was simply one of the two companies that were both lessors and vendors. It was not surprising that Asemo (the assignee) insisted on a guarantee being provided by the directors of the lessee company. Nothing in the content of progress of these related transactions suggests that the guarantee was not to benefit Asemo as assignee of the reversion which purchased the reversion *upon the basis of both the lease and the guarantee*."[33]

10–192   Nor was the guarantee limited to the period during which the lessee was in actual occupation of the premises, notwithstanding cl. 4 of the guarantee which provided: "This guarantee shall continue to be binding as long as the lessee remains in occupation of the demised premises." Gobbo J. expressed the view that this clause was intended to cover a holding over by the lessee at the conclusion of the term and suggested that the clause might be "equating occupation with entitlement to occupy and as merely providing confirmation of the fact that the guarantee ceased with the termination of the lease".[34] In any event, his Honour concluded that the

[31] R.R. Sethu, "Surety Covenants: Privity of Contract Estate?" (1989) 5 Aust. Bar. Rev. 153 at 166.
[32] [1985] 1 B.C.C. 99,570.
[33] [1989] V.R. 773 at 777–778 (emphasis added).
[34] *ibid.*, at 778.

trial judge was correct in rejecting the view that the guarantee was no longer binding once the lessee vacated the premises.

In the result, the Full Court of the Supreme Court of Victoria held that **10–193** the guarantee enabled Asemo Pty Ltd, the assignee of the reversion, to recover from the guarantors unpaid rent and unpaid rates for the balance of the lease but not unpaid charges levied by the body corporate because they did not fall within the tenant's covenants.

Despite several decisions at first instance to the contrary,[35] it appears **10–194** that guarantees of a tenant's obligations under a lease may be enforced by the assignee of the reversion whether the guarantee is given upon the granting of the lease[36] or on assignment.[37] It is immaterial whether the guarantor has undertaken to be answerable for all the tenant's obligations under the lease or merely the obligation to pay rent.

While this conclusion is defensible where the surety undertakes that he **10–195** will perform all the tenant's obligations under the lease if the tenant fails to do so, it is less compelling where the surety merely covenants to pay rent or other monetary amounts if the tenant defaults. Only in the former case is it true to say that: "A surety for a tenant is a quasi tenant who volunteers to be a substitute or twelfth man for the tenant's team and is subject to the same rules and regulations as the player he replaces."[38]

(e) Beneficiaries of a trust

A person who is not a party to a guarantee (whether under seal or not)[39] **10–196** will be able to enforce the guarantee if that person has a beneficial right under the guarantee which places him in a position of a cestui que trust under the contract.[40] The trustee is bound to enforce the security on behalf of the beneficiary.[41] The guarantee may be given expressly to a trustee on behalf of third persons, who can then be a fluctuating class[42] (for example, the members of an unincorporated association,[43] or the intending shareholders in a company[44]). The beneficiaries of the trust may be

[35] *Pinemain Ltd v Welbeck International* (1984) 272 E.G. 1166; *Re Distributors & Warehousing Ltd* [1985] 1 B.C.C. 99,570; *Coastplace v Hartley* [1987] 2 W.L.R. 1289. See also *Blue Chip Investments Inc v Kavanagh* (1986) 60 Nfl'd & P.E.I.R. 85 and *Blue Chip Investments Inc v Hicks* (1983) 50 Nfl'd & P.E.I.R. 60, affirmed on other grounds in (1985) 54 Nfl'd & P.E.I.R. 149.
[36] *P & A Swift Investments v Combined English Stores Group Plc* [1988] 2 All E.R. 885.
[37] *Kumar v Dunning* [1987] 3 W.L.R. 1167.
[38] *P & A Swift Investments v Combined English Stores Group Plc* [1988] 2 All E.R. 885 at 887 *per* Lord Templeman.
[39] *Lloyd's v Harper* (1880) 16 Ch. D. 290.
[40] *Metcalf v Bruin* (1810) 12 East 400; 104 E.R. 156; *Re A & K Holdings Pty Ltd* [1964] VR 257; *Don King Productions Inc v Warren* [2000] Ch. 291 at 321, affirmed at 335–336, CA. See generally H.A.J. Ford and W.A. Lee, *Principles of The Law of Trusts* (2nd ed., 1990), para.411; (3rd ed., 1995), para.4100; *Lewin on Trusts* (17th ed., 2000), paras 2–35 and 4–12.
[41] As to enforcement, see H.A.J. Ford and W.A. Lee, *Principles of the Law of Trusts* (2nd ed., 1990), para.411; (3rd ed., 1995), para.4100; *Lewin on Trusts* (17th ed., 2000), paras 12–47 and 12–48.
[42] *Re A & K Holdings Pty Ltd* [1964] V.R. 257 at 262; *Metcalf v Bruin* (1810) 12 East 400; 104 E.R. 156.
[43] *Metcalf v Bruin* (1810) 12 East 400; 104 E.R. 156.
[44] *Hallett v Taylor* (1921) 6 Lloyd's Rep. 416.

future assignees of the principal transaction[45] or, in the case of a performance bond guaranteeing the obligations of a contractor under a building contract, the owner may expressly contract as trustee on behalf of the suppliers of materials to the contractor.[46]

10–197　Where the guarantee does not expressly create a trust of the benefit of the guarantee in respect of a particular class of persons, there may be an implied trust as long as the intention to create a trust can be affirmatively proved.[47] According to an established line of authority, it must be shown that the promisor and promisee intended to contract on the basis that the promisee was to be trustee of the benefit of the promise;[48] it is not sufficient to establish a trust in favour of a third party merely from the fact that the terms of the contract indicate that a benefit was intended to be conferred upon the third party. Thus, it has been held that, if the guarantee indicates that the successors and assignees of the original creditor are to take the benefit of the guarantee, this will not be sufficient to create a trust for their benefit.[49] Similarly, if a performance bond entered into with a building owner merely states that the guarantor covenants to guarantee the payment by the contractor of the contractor's debts to the suppliers of materials, there will be no trust of the benefit of the guarantee in favour of those suppliers and, hence, they will not be able to enforce the guarantee.[50]

10–198　Commonwealth authority indicates that there is "considerable scope for the development of trusts".[51] Yet, despite some English cases indicating "less hostility"[52] towards their creation, it is unlikely a trust would be created simply by a reference in the guarantee to the fact that the benefit of the guarantee shall enure to the creditor's "successors and assignees".

(f) Where the person named in the guarantee is acting in the capacity of agent

10–199　The signatory to the guarantee may be acting in the capacity of agent for a principal, and in such a case the principal may enforce the guarantee even though not named within it.[53] Thus a partner may contract on behalf

---

[45] This possibility was recognised in *Sacher Investments Pty Ltd v Forma Stereo Consultants Pty Ltd* [1976] 1 N.S.W.L.R. 5 at 12.

[46] *Town of Truro v McCulloch* (1971) 22 D.L.R. (3d) 293; *Dominion Bridge Co Ltd v Marla Construction Co Ltd* [1970] 3 O.R. 125.

[47] *Vandepitte v Preferred Accident Insurance Co of New York* [1933] A.C. 70; *Re Schebsman* [1944] 1 Ch. 83; *Tobin Tractor (1957) Ltd v Western Surety Co* (1963) 40 D.L.R. (2d) 231. See generally H.A.J. Ford and W.A. Lee, *Principles of the Law of Trusts* (2nd ed., 1990), para.411; (3rd ed., 1995), para.4100; *Lewin on Trusts* (17th ed., 2000), para.4–12.

[48] H.A.J. Ford and W.A. Lee, *Principles of the Law of Trusts* (2nd ed., 1994), para.411 and (3rd ed., 1995), para.4100.

[49] See *Sacher Investments Pty Ltd v Forma Stereo Consultants Pty Ltd* [1976] 1 NSWLR 5 at 12.

[50] *Tobin Tractor (1957) Ltd v Western Surety Co* (1963) 40 D.L.R. (2d) 231.

[51] *Trident General Insurance Co. Ltd v McNiece Bros Ltd* (1988) 165 C.L.R. 107 at 166. There are some early English examples of this more liberal approach: *Kenney v Employers' Liability Insurance Corp* [1901] 1 I.R. 301; *Lloyd's v Harper* (1880) 16 Ch. D. 290.

[52] See J. Beatson, *Anson's Law of Contract* (28th ed., 2002), p.442. See also, *Darlington B.C. v Wiltshier (Northern) Ltd* [1995] 1 W.L.R. 68, esp. at 75, 81.

[53] *Garrett v Handley* (1825) 4 B. & C. 664; 107 E.R. 1208.

of the firm if that intention is clear from the circumstances.[54] Although there is no clear authority, the principles of agency may also enable persons who are not parties to the guarantee to sue upon the guarantee, even though they are unascertained at the date of the contract.[55] Thus a creditor may expressly execute a guarantee not only for its own benefit, but for the benefit of future assignees of the principal transaction. If an assignee later ratifies[56] the creditor's authority to contract on the assignee's behalf and provides consideration for the promise (for example, by assuming the obligations under the principal contract), it is arguable that such an assignee could enforce the guarantee.[57]

(g) The effect of an estoppel by convention

The doctrine of estoppel by convention[58] may be applied to allow **10–200** persons other than the named creditors to take the benefit of the guarantee, for example, when the guarantee is given expressly in favour of a specified company, but there is an agreed assumption that it would apply to all companies within the same group.[59] Reliance on estoppel in this way may be necessary when the guarantee is given to one party, but the financial accommodation is in fact provided to the principal debtor by another party.[60] An estoppel by convention may also be invoked by the assignee of a mortgage to establish that the assignee is entitled to enforce a guarantee of the mortgage debt, even though the guarantee was not expressly assigned to it.[61]

[54] ibid.
[55] This is by application of the test laid down by Lord Reid in Scruttons Ltd v Midland Silicones [1962] A.C. 446 at 474, and applied in New Zealand Shipping Co Ltd v Satterthwaite & Co Ltd [1975] A.C. 154. The contract of guarantee must be specifically drafted to satisfy those conditions.
[56] Lord Reid recognised the possibility of later ratification in Scruttons Ltd v Midland Silicones [1962] A.C. 446 at 474.
[57] This possibility is recognised in Sacher Investments Pty Ltd v Forma Stereo Consultants Pty Ltd [1976] 1 N.S.W.L.R. 5 at 12.
[58] See above, paras 5–94 to 5–96.
[59] Elsea Holdings Ltd v Butts (1986) 6 N.S.W.L.R. 175. See also Amalgamated Investment & Property Co Ltd v Texas Commerce International Bank Ltd [1982] Q.B. 84. See also above, paras 5–94 to 5–96. This form of estoppel may require some representation or conduct by the guarantors confirming that they are liable on the basis of the mutual assumption of the parties: Farrow Mortage Services Pty Ltd v Hogg (1995) 64 S.A.S.R. 450.
[60] See this difficulty arising in Amalgamated Investment & Property Co Ltd (in liq) v Texas Commerce International Bank Ltd [1982] Q.B. 84.
[61] See Farrow Mortgage Services Pty Ltd v Hogg (unreported, SA Sup Ct, Nyland J., November 17, 1994) (obiter dicta).

(iv) The nature and practice of proceedings to enforce the guarantee

(a) Nature of the action

10–201 If the principal transaction guaranteed is a debt or liquidated sum, the creditor's cause of action against the guarantor upon default of the principal will be an action on the guarantee for a money sum rather than a claim in damages.[62] This is because the guarantor has promised to pay an agreed sum upon default by the principal, that is, to pay (in terms of the usual form of guarantee) all sums "due", "owing" or "payable" to the creditor. Appropriate forms are to be found in the standard guides to practice and pleading.[63] The creditor may apply for summary judgment in respect of its claim under the guarantee.[64] In such proceedings, the court can decide disputed questions of law, including questions concerning the construction of documents.[65] Another significant advantage to the creditor, arising from the fact that an action on the guarantee is for a money sum, is that the creditor is under no duty to mitigate its damages.[66]

10–202 Some doubt as to correctness of this usual form of action against the guarantor arose from the decision in *Moschi v Lep Air Services Ltd*,[67] which suggested that the action against the guarantor should properly be framed only as a claim in damages. The reasoning was that the obligation of the guarantor should be regarded not as an obligation to pay a sum of money to the creditor but "to see to it" that the principal debtor performs the obligation.[68] However, in *Sunbird Plaza Pty Ltd v Maloney*,[69] Mason C.J. rejected this view:

> "It may be that as a matter of history the view that the guarantor has an obligation 'to see to it' that the debtor performs his obligation

---

[62] *Sunbird Plaza Pty Ltd v Maloney* (1988) 166 C.L.R. 245; *Scottish Midland Guarantee Trust v Woolley* (1964) 114 L.J. 272; *Re Standard Insurance Co Ltd (in liq) and Companies Act 1936* [1970] 1 N.S.W.R. 599; *Neptune Oil Co Pty Ltd v Fowler* (1963) 63 S.R. (NSW) 530. An action to enforce a guarantee may be struck out as an abuse of process in accordance with the Civil Procedure Rules 1998 (SI 1998/3132) but only in exceptional circumstances, such as where there has been an unconscionable delay: *Securum Finance Ltd v Ashton* [2001] Ch. 291. It is an abuse of process to pursue an action to enforce a guarantee solely for an ulterior motive unrelated to the subject matter of the litigation: *Whincup v Barclays Bank* 2000 W.L. 191238.
[63] *Atkin's Court Forms* (2nd ed., 1987 issue), Vol. 20, pp.154–161; *Bullen, Leake & Jacob's Precedents and Pleadings* (13th ed., 1990), pp.437–441; *Britt's Pleading Precedents* (5th ed., 1994), p.60. The particulars of claim must, of course, disclose a sufficient cause of action, but the particulars are not to be read in a strict and technical sense: *Jamieson v Mutual Acceptance Co Ltd* [1965] N.S.W.R. 1347. A guarantor alleging that he has been discharged should plead in any defence the facts from which a discharge could be implied: *Australian Joint Stock Bank v Hogan* (1902) 2 S.R. (NSW) 7.
[64] Civil Procedure Rules 1998, rr.24.2 and 24.3.
[65] *European Asian Bank v Punjab and Sind Bank* [1983] 1 W.L.R. 642 at 652.
[66] *Scottish Midland Guarantee Trust v Woolley* (1964) 114 L.J. 272; *Co-operation Mortgage Fund Ltd v Silver Bell Developments Ltd* (1985) 66 A.R. 316, Alta Q.B.
[67] [1973] A.C. 331.
[68] *ibid.*, at 348–349 *per* Lord Diplock, 352 *per* Lord Simon of Glaisdale. See also *Degman Pty Ltd v Wright* [1983] 2 N.S.W.L.R. 348 at 350–352.
[69] (1988) 166 C.L.R. 245.

explains why the guarantor is not entitled to notice of the debtor's default and why the creditor's cause of action arises on that default. But the view certainly does not accord with the nature of the guarantor's obligation as it is understood today. Rarely do guarantors have control of, or a capacity to influence, the principal debtor such that they would willingly assume an obligation to ensure that he performs his primary obligation. The fact that at common law the creditor sued the guarantor in special assumpsit gives some support to the view that the guarantor's cause of action is for damages for breach of contract. However, the modern view that the guarantor promises to answer for the debtor's debt or default has led to the practice of suing the guarantor for the money sum which the debtor has failed to pay, a practice which may well have been adopted on the introduction of the Judicature Acts."[70]

There will, however, be some circumstances in which the creditor's claim **10–203** is properly framed in damages. Most obviously, where there is a guarantee not of a debt or liquidated sum but of the general obligations under the principal contract (for example, a guarantee of a contractor's obligations to perform the work properly under a building contract,[71] or a guarantee of a tenant's obligations to maintain the property under a lease), the claim against the principal and, therefore, the claim against the guarantor will be in damages.

But even in the case of a guarantee of a debt or liquidated amount the **10–204** creditor may be relegated to a claim in damages if the debt or liquidated amount is not payable by the principal debtor in the events that occur, despite the fact that the principal debtor is in breach of contract.

This result may arise because, as in *Moschi v Lep Air Services Ltd*,[72] **10–205** there is a guarantee of a debt repayable by instalments and the creditor terminates the principal contract upon the principal's default. Neither the principal nor the guarantor are under an obligation to pay the agreed sums because the principal contract has been determined before the due date for the payment of the relevant instalments.[73] Any claim against the guarantor can only be properly framed in damages.[74]

In the case of a guarantee of a debt or a liquidated amount, another **10–206** situation in which an action for a money sum against the guarantor is not available is where the sum is irrecoverable from the principal because it amounts to a penalty[75] or because the specific event upon which it is payable never occurs. An illustration of the latter situation is *Sunbird Plaza Pty Ltd v Maloney*,[76] where a guarantee was given in respect of all

---

[70] *ibid.*, at 255–256. See also *Bank of China v Hawkins* (1992) 26 N.S.W.L.R. 562 and, for criticism, E. Peden, "A Classification of Contracts of Guarantee" (1991) 13 Syd. L. Rev. 221.
[71] e.g. *National Employers Mutual General Insurance Association Ltd v Herne Bay UDC* (1972) 70 L.G.R. 542. See also *Horsly v Ramsey* (1889) 10 L.R. (NSW) Eq. 41.
[72] [1973] A.C. 331. Discussed in detail above, paras 6–127 to 6–136 and 6–144.
[73] This assumes that the whole sum is not payable immediately as a result of an acceleration provision in the principal contract.
[74] See above, paras 6–127 to 6–136.
[75] See above, para.6–135.
[76] (1988) 166 C.L.R. 245, discussed in detail above, paras 10–09 to 10–12.

moneys payable by the purchaser under a contract of sale of land. Pursuant to the contract of sale, the moneys were payable "upon settlement", which did not occur, albeit as a result of the purchaser's breach. No action for a money sum was therefore available.

10–207   It should be emphasised that, in all these cases where an action for a money sum is not available, despite the guarantee being given in respect of a debt or liquidated amount, a claim in damages is only available where it is consistent with the terms of the guarantee.[77]

10–208   In any action for damages against the guarantor, the amount recoverable will generally[78] be whatever sum the creditor could have recovered from the principal: "the debtor's liability to the creditor is also the measure of the guarantor's."[79] Damages cannot generally be awarded for late payment of money,[80] although there is an exception in respect of interest charges incurred in obtaining finance from alternative sources (provided it is in the reasonable contemplation of the parties that such charges would arise).[81] In accordance with normal contractual principles, the creditor cannot maintain an action for loss of bargain damages without bringing the principal contract to an end.[82]

10–209   Where the creditor's claim is in damages, it will come under an obligation to mitigate its loss.[83] It is unclear, however, what steps the creditor should take as a reasonable course of mitigation. It is arguable that the creditor should have to proceed against a solvent principal or take action to prevent the principal running up large arrears of interest, but there is no clear indication in the cases that such an obligation will be imposed.[84] Indeed, it has been firmly stated that it is not a condition precedent to the guarantor's liability that the creditor should take prior

---

[77] See above, paras 6–123 to 6–126.
[78] But it is possible that some losses will be foreseeable by the principal but not the guarantor and therefore recoverable from the former but not the latter.
[79] *Moschi v Lep Air Services Ltd* [1973] A.C. 331 at 349 *per* Lord Diplock. This amount will often, of course, be less than the amount recoverable as a money sum, if that action had been available. Thus in *Sunbird Plaza Pty Ltd v Maloney* (1988) 166 C.L.R. 245 at 261, Mason C.J. points out that the vendor's claim for damages for breach by the purchaser of a contract for the sale of land would be the loss of profit on the sale, which would not have equalled the purchase price if an action had been available to recover the latter as a money sum.
[80] *London Chatham & Dover Ry. Co. v S.E. Ry. Co.* [1893] A.C. 429; *The President of India v La Pintada Co. Nav.* [1985] A.C. 104.
[81] *The Lips* [1988] A.C. 395; *Wadsworth v Lydal* [1981] 1 W.L.R. 598. See generally, G.H. Treitel, *The Law of Contract* (11th ed., 2003), p.997; J. Beatson, *Anson's Law of Contract* (28th ed., 2002), p.619. See also Late Payment of Commercial Debts (Interest) Act 1998.
[82] *Sunbird Plaza Ltd v Maloney* (1988) 166 CLR 245, where the creditor's claim for loss of bargain damages failed on this basis: see in detail above, paras 10–09 to 10–12.
[83] In *Sacher Investments Pty Ltd v Forma Stereo Consultants Pty Ltd* [1976] 1 N.S.W.L.R. 5 and *National Employers Mutual General Insurance Association Ltd v Herne Bay UDC* (1972) 70 L.G.R. 542, it appears to have been assumed that a duty to mitigate arises, although it was held in both cases that there was no breach of that duty on the facts. See also *Perrylease Ltd v Imecar AG* [1987] 2 All E.R. 373 at 381–382, where it was unsuccessfully argued that the creditor should have re-leased vehicles which had been repossessed from the principal debtor instead of selling them.
[84] Note, however, in *Dawson v Raynes* (1826) 2 Russ. 466; 38 E.R. 411, a surety for the performance of a receiver's obligations was not held liable for sums of interest because no steps were taken to have the receiver's accounts passed, when it was known that the receiver was bankrupt.

proceedings against the principal,[85] although this conclusion would not preclude a finding that the creditor in *mitigating its damages* should take action against the principal. Apart from any possible application of the rules regarding mitigation, it should be emphasised that there is a general equitable duty imposed upon the creditor not to impair securities held for the enforcement of the principal obligation.[86]

In some cases, the creditor may not wish to bring an action on the **10–210** guarantee for the money sum or for damages but simply to enforce a term of the guarantee itself. Relief analogous to specific performance is available to a party to an executed contract, such as a lessor who has supplied equipment to the principal debtor. That party may enforce a covenant by the guarantors to grant a legal or equitable mortgage and a fixed charge over their present and future property to secure the principal debtor's obligations under the lease.[87] In such a case, it is not necessary for the court to order that the entire contract be performed; it may simply order that individual obligations under the contract be carried into effect.[88]

In an action for possession of land secured by a legal charge, the chargee **10–211** may be granted leave to amend its pleadings to include a money claim under a guarantee included in the charge: the amendment raises no new factual issues, not already pleaded, and does not constitute a new cause of action.[89] A claim for a new remedy is not necessarily a new cause of action. But even if the money claim does involve raising a new cause of action, the court could exercise its discretion to allow the amendment of the pleadings[90]

Where the guarantee is secured by a mortgage over the guarantor's **10–212** dwelling house and the creditor brings an action for possession of the property, the court has a wide discretion under s.36 of the Administration of Justice Act 1970. The court can adjourn the proceedings, stay or suspend execution of the judgment or order, or postpone the date for delivery of possession. But these powers can only be exercised if it appears to the court that the guarantor is likely within a reasonable period to pay any sums due under the mortgage or to remedy a default consisting of a breach of any other obligation. Likelihood is a question of fact, to be determined by the judge on the evidence.[91]

A creditor who obtains a judgment for the total amount owing under a **10–213** mortgage and an order for possession in an action to enforce a mortgage securing a guarantee will not be able to institute fresh proceedings under the guarantee: the creditor's cause of action on the guarantee merges in the

---

[85] See above, paras 11–11 to 11–28.
[86] See above, paras 8–46 to 8–105.
[87] *Bridge Wholesale Acceptance Corp (Australia) Ltd v Burnard* (1992) 27 N.S.W.L.R. 415 at 423; *Burns Philp Trust Co Ltd v Kwikasair Freightlines Ltd* (1963) 63 S.R. (NSW) 492.
[88] Where the contract is an executory one the court may order specific performance of the entire contract: see *J C Williamson Ltd v Lukey* (1931) 45 C.L.R. 282 at 297.
[89] *Lloyds Bank Plc v Rogers* [1999] 3 E.G.L.R. 83; [1999] 3 E.G. 187.
[90] *ibid.* See also *Limitation* Act 1980, s.35(5)(a) and CPR Part 17, r.4 and Practice Direction 17.
[91] *Royal Trust Co of Canada v Markham* [1975] 3 All E.R. 433. The court will not exercise its discretion in favour of the guarantor if there is no evidence of likely payment or remedial action: *TSB Bank Plc v Dickson* (unreported, Court of Appeal, Civil Division, July 24, 1998).

judgment.[92] This is so even if the creditor makes further advances to the principal debtor after the date of the first proceedings in reliance on the guarantee, although a separate cause of action on the guarantee may be possible, *only in respect of these advances*, where the guarantee is a continuing guarantee supported by divisible consideration.[93]

10–214   Where the principal debtor company has been struck off the register, it may be necessary for the company's lessor to obtain an order under s.653 of the Companies Act 1985 restoring the company to the register before it can enforce a guarantee provided by a parent company in respect of its subsidiary's liabilities as a lessee. The restoration of the lessee company would rebut any argument that the liability of the guarantor company was determined because it ceased to exist before the rent fell into arrears.[94]

(b) Parties to the action

10–215   If the principal appears to be solvent, it is common for the creditor to sue both the principal and the guarantor in the one action. In these proceedings, the guarantor may claim an indemnity from the principal. If the creditor sues only the guarantor, the guarantor may claim an indemnity from the principal in third-party proceedings.[95] Where the guarantor claims the benefit of a set-off or cross-claim available to the principal, the principal should also be made a party to the action.[96] Similarly, if the creditor sues only one co-guarantor, that guarantor may claim contribution from other guarantors by means of third-party proceedings.[97] However, a creditor who takes proceedings against any one of the co-guarantors under a joint and several guarantee is not required to notify the other guarantors.[98]

10–216   Occasionally, the guarantor may undertake his obligations jointly with the principal or with another co-guarantor. In this case, it was essential at common law that all the parties jointly liable should be sued, because if a judgment was obtained against one joint contractor when sued alone, the other joint contractor was discharged.[99] This rule has now been reversed[1]

---

[92] *Lloyd's Bank Plc v Hawkins* [1998] EWCA Civ 1391 (unreported, Court of Appeal, August 12, 1998).
[93] *ibid.*
[94] *City of Westminster Assurance Co Ltd v Registrar of Companies* [1997] B.C.C. 960.
[95] Civil Procedure Rules 1998, Pt 20. As to practical guidance on the third party procedure, see *Bannister v Sgb Plc* [1997] P.I.Q.R. 165. See also *McIntosh v Williams* [1979] 2 N.S.W.L.R. 543.
[96] *Cellulose Products Pty Ltd v Truda* (1970) 92 W.N. (NSW) 561 at 588. But see the authors' views, below, para.11–63.
[97] Civil Procedure Rules 1998, Pt.20.
[98] *Stimpson v Smith* [1999] Ch. 340.
[99] See G. L. Williams, *Joint Obligations* (1949), para.43; *Chitty on Contracts* (28th ed., 1999), Vol. 1, para. 18–002; *Kendall v Hamilton* (1879) 4 App. Cas. 504; *Nicholson v Revill* (1836) 4 Ad. & E. 675; 111 E.R. 941; *Bank of A/asia v Miller* (1885) 6 A.L.T. 234. The rule does not apply to judgment on a cheque given by one for a joint debt (*Wegg-Prosser v Evans* [1895] 1 Q.B. 108) or where the judgment is set aside (*Greig Murray & Co Ltd v Hutchinson* (1890) 16 V.L.R. 334).
[1] See Civil Liability Contributions Act 1978, s.30; Civil Procedure Rules 1998, Pt 19, r.1 and *Chitty on Contracts* (28th ed., 1999), paras 18–009–18–010.

and, in any event, a guarantor will invariably be subjected to joint and several liability (rather than joint liability)[2] when bound together with other parties, whether co-guarantors or the principal.[3] Even where the guarantors are jointly and severally bound, however, the creditor must not release one guarantor after obtaining judgment against that guarantor because the normal rules relating to the release of a co-guarantor will apply.[4] The result is that, as the words "joint and several" impose an obligation that all the guarantors remain parties to the agreement, all the guarantors will be discharged by a release of one guarantor.[5] In the rare case where the guarantors are only severally liable, presumably each guarantor will be released to the extent that his right of contribution has been affected.[6]

Where the guarantee is given to a number of creditors jointly, all must **10–217** be made parties to an action upon it.[7]

(c) Summary judgment

A creditor may obtain a summary judgment against the guarantors **10–218** where there is no triable issue of law or fact.[8] Similarly, a mortgagee seeking possession of land pursuant to a third-party mortgage may obtain a summary judgment unless the mortgagor has an arguable ground of defence which cannot be disposed of summarily.[9] On applications for summary judgment the court may be satisfied by affidavit evidence that the defendant has not raised an arguable defence.[10] But the court's jurisdiction to grant summary judgment should be exercised with great care because it might deprive the guarantors of the chance to raise a genuine defence to the creditor's claim.[11]

If the mortgagor raises an arguable defence, the court may direct that **10–219** pleadings be filed and that the matter proceed to trial in the ordinary way.[12] As a condition of refusing summary judgment in an action for

[2] Note the effect of s.81 of the Law of Property Act 1925.
[3] A judgment against one joint and several contractor does not at common law release the other: see G.L. Williams, *Joint Obligations* (1949), para.48.
[4] See above, paras 8–21 to 8–34. However, a creditor can discontinue proceedings against two of four joint and several guarantors on the condition that it obtains judgment against the others: *National Bank Ltd v Moore* [2002] V.S.C. 221 (unreported, Vic Sup Ct, McDonald J., May 29, 2002).
[5] *Walker v Bowry* (1924) 35 C.L.R. 48; *Re EWA (a debtor)* [1901] 2 K.B. 642.
[6] This follows the general principles regarding the creditor's release of a co-guarantor: see above, paras 8–21 *et. seq.*
[7] *Pugh v Stringfield* (1857) 3 C.B. (NS) 2; 140 E.R. 637; (1858) 4 C.B. (NS) 364; 140 E.R. 1125. Where the joint creditors refuse to join in the action as plaintiffs, they can be joined as defendants: *Luke v South Kensington Hotel Co* (1879) 11 Ch. D. 121.
[8] See *Lawrence v Griffith* (1987) 47 S.A.S.R. 455; *Colonial Mutual Life Assurance Society Ltd v Glaser* (unreported, SA Sup Ct, Burley J, November 9, 1993). See also *Standard Chartered Bank Ltd v Walker* [1982] 3 All E.R. 938 and *Clarke v Union Bank of Australia Ltd* (1917) 23 C.L.R. 5 at 8.
[9] *Sabrino v Saunders* (unreported, SA Sup Ct, Burley J., November 19, 1993).
[10] *Ingram Coal Co v Nugent* 1991 S.L.T. 603.
[11] *Fancourt v Mercantile Credits Ltd* (1983) 154 C.L.R. 87 at 99.
[12] *ibid.*, and *Corporation of Moonta v Rodgers* (1980) 26 S.A.S.R. 143. Where a defendant seeks to set aside a judgment entered against him in default of appearance, he must show that

possession, the court may require the defendant mortgagor to pay into court a sum of money "so as to ensure adequate protection to the mortgagee and to otherwise do justice between the parties during the period pending the final hearing."[13] This principle, which was established in an application for an interlocutory injunction to restrain a mortgagee from enforcing a mortgage,[14] has been extended to summary applications for orders for possession.[15] However, the court will not direct the mortgagor to pay any sum into court where the validity of the mortgage itself is impugned.[16]

(d) Action for possession against a third party mortgagor

10–220   Some guarantees take the form of a third party mortgage under which the mortgagor offers his property as security for the payment of the principal debt or the performance of the principal obligation.[17] In these cases the mortgagee will not seek a judgment against the guarantor for a money sum but rather an order for possession of the secured property. Where the mortgaged property is a dwelling house the mortgagee will not necessarily be entitled to an order for possession even if the principal debtor is in default. Section 36(1) of the Administration of Justice Act 1970 provides that, where a mortgagee of a dwelling house brings an action in which it claims possession of mortgaged property, the court may exercise any of the powers conferred on it by s.36(2)[18] if it appears to the court that the mortgagor is likely to be able within a reasonable period to pay any sums due under the mortgage or to remedy a default consisting of a breach of any other obligation. In this context, the likelihood of the mortgagor being able to pay the sums due under the mortgage or remedy any other default is a question of fact to be determined by the judge on the evidence.[19] In the case of an instalment mortgage the court may exercise the power of suspension if the mortgagor establishes a likelihood of being able to pay instalments due to date.[20] The judge is entitled to take into account all the circumstances of the case including the fact that a large part of the debt was not challenged until a late stage, and that the defendant is trying,

---

the defence has a real prospect of success: *Re International Finance Corporation Claimant Utexafrica* 2001 W.L. 415566 (unreported, Q.B.D., Commercial Court, Mr Justice Moore-Bick, May 9, 2001).

[13] *Glandore Pty Ltd v Elders Finance & Investment Co Ltd* (1984) 4 F.C.R. 130 at 135 *per* Morling J. Summary judgment is not available in proceedings for possession of residential premises against a mortgagor: Civil Procedure Rules, r.24.3(2).

[14] *Inglis v Commonwealth Trading Bank* (1972) 126 C.L.R. 161; *Harvey v McWatters* (1948) 49 S.R. (NSW) 173.

[15] *Sabrino v Saunders* (unreported, SA Sup Ct, Burley J., November 19, 1993).

[16] See *Glandore Pty Ltd v Elders Finance & Investment Co Ltd* (1984) 4 F.C.R. 130.

[17] See above, para.1–23.

[18] Under s.36(2) the court can: adjourn the proceedings; stay or suspend execution of the judgment or order; or postpone the date for delivery of possession.

[19] *Royal Trust Co of Canada v Markham* [1975] 3 All E.R. 433 at 438.

[20] See Administration of Justice Act 1973, s.8 and *Royal Trust Co of Canada v Markham* [1975] 3 All E.R. 433 at 438, overcoming the effect of *Halifax Building Society v Clark* [1973] Ch. 307.

by whatever means, to avoid his responsibility to pay a debt for which he is clearly liable.[21] A defendant will not be entitled to a suspension order simply because the judge does not specify the amount outstanding under the mortgage, especially when it is clear that the defendant has incurred a substantial liability that he cannot discharge.[22]

Where a mortgagee obtains an order for possession against a principal **10–221** debtor company, it is also entitled to possession against the guarantors of the mortgage debt who voluntarily transferred the property to the mortgagor company in return for shares.[23]

(e) Interest to be awarded on judgment against the guarantor

The creditor will be entitled to receive interest in accordance with the **10–222** usual statutory provisions from the date when the cause of action arose against the guarantor until the date of judgment.[24] Usually, this rate of interest is at the court's discretion.

(f) No merger in judgment

Where a creditor obtains judgment against the principal debtor, the **10–223** creditor's cause of action against the guarantor does not merge in the judgment. As long as the principal debt is unsatisfied, the cause of action on the debt remains and the creditor retains the right to enforce collateral security. When a creditor obtains judgment in a debenture-holder's action against the principal debtor, there can be no further action on the debenture but the creditor is still entitled to enforce its remedies against the guarantor of the principal debt[25] in a separate and distinct action.[26]

In *Duchess Theatre Co v Lord*,[27] the terms of the mortgage documents **10–224** made it clear that no cause of action could arise under the collateral guarantees until a demand was made on the guarantors. As this demand was not made until after the judgment in the debenture-holder's action, there was no question of the claims against the guarantors merging in the judgment.

---

[21] *TSB Bank Plc v Dickson* [1998] EWCA 1293.
[22] *ibid.*
[23] *Stockholm Finance Ltd v Garden Holdings Inc* [1995] N.P.C. 162.
[24] Supreme Court Act 1981, s.35A and County Court Act 1984, s.89. A bank which is entitled to interest until judgment can, by custom and usage, charge compound interest on the principal debt. See *National Bank of Greece SA v Pinios Shipping Co (No.1)* [1990] A.C. 637; [1990] 1 Lloyd's Rep. 225. The effect of a judgment obtained against the guarantor and the principal debtor on the guarantor's liability for interest is discussed above, paras 5–50 to 5–53. Similarly, the effect of the principal debtor's or guarantor's winding-up or bankruptcy is discussed above, paras 5–56 to 5–58 and 6–88 to 6–96. Additional losses for late payment may be recoverable in excess of the relevant interest rate if they are forseeable: see above, para.10–208. See also Late Payment of Commercial Debts (Interest) Act 1998.
[25] *First City Capital Ltd v Ampex Can Inc* (1989) 75 C.B.R. (NS) 109 (Alta Q.B.). But see above, paras 5–50 to 5–53 as to the effect of a judgment against the principal on the guarantor's liability for interest.
[26] See *Economic Life Assurance v Usborne* [1902] A.C. 147.
[27] [1993] N.P.C. 163, CA.

10–225   Similarly in *Westpac Banking Corp v Comanos*,[28] the guarantor's judgment by consent in an action for possession by a mortgagee did not prevent the defendants from raising fresh defences in a subsequent action by the same plaintiff to enforce a guarantee given by the defendants. The cause of action which merged in the first judgment was the plaintiff's claim to possession of the defendants' property. This cause of action was quite distinct from the action to enforce the guarantee. Indeed, the plaintiff could not even raise an issue estoppel against the defendants in the subsequent action because their defences did not raise an issue of fact or law directly involved in the judicial determination in the action for possession. In *Westpac Banking Corp v Comanos* the default in the payment of the indebtedness of the defendants on their own account was sufficient to entitle the plaintiff to possession of the property. It was not necessary for the validity and enforceability of their guarantee to be determined in the action for possession. Consequently, no issue estoppel could be raised against them in the subsequent proceedings to enforce their guarantee. Moreover, it was not unreasonable for the defendants to concede the plaintiff's claim to possession while keeping alive their defences to the subsequent action to enforce their guarantee. On this basis, even the extended principle of res judicata founded on the rule in *Henderson v Henderson*,[29] as expounded in *Port of Melbourne Authority v Anshun Pty Ltd*,[30] was of no avail to the plaintiff in its application for summary judgment against the guarantors.

10–226   When the creditor obtains judgment against a guarantor, the debt owing by the guarantor merges in the judgment. But for the purposes of a petition in bankruptcy against the guarantor, the judgment is not taken to have extinguished the debt so that it ceases to exist.[31] It remains on foot so that it can support the bankruptcy petition even if the original bankruptcy order is annulled for any reason.[32]

10–227   In some cases a creditor has two separate sets of overlapping contractual rights: one a legal "all accounts" charge over the guarantor's property and the other a guarantee from the same party. If such a creditor obtains an order for possession and a money judgment in respect of the total amount outstanding under the charge, it will not be able to institute separate proceedings at a later date to enforce the guarantee because the guarantee merges in the judgment.[33] This is because the liability under the guarantee is automatically secured by the terms of the "all moneys" clause in the charge.

[28] Unreported, NSW Sup Ct, Giles J, May 9, 1991.
[29] (1843) 3 Hare 100; 67 E.R. 313.
[30] (1981) 147 C.L.R. 589. See also *Boles v Esanda Finance Corp Ltd* (1989) 18 N.S.W.L.R. 666.
[31] *Re King & Beesley, Ex p. King & Beesley* [1895] 1 Q.B. 189 at 191; *Wren v Mahoney* (1972) 126 C.L.R. 212 at 224.
[32] *Re Handby, Ex p. Flemington Central Spares Pty Ltd* (1967) 10 F.L.R. 378 at 381; *Re Baker, Ex p. Pioneer Industries Pty Ltd* (unreported, Fed Ct, Keifel J., August 11, 1995). See generally I.F. Fletcher, *The Law of Insolvency* (3rd ed., 2002), paras 11–028 to 11–034 as to annulment of bankruptcy. See s.282 of the Insolvency Act 1986, as amended by Sch.23, Pt 4 of the Enterprise Act 2002.
[33] *Lloyds Bank Plc v Hawkins* [1998] Lloyd's Rep. Bank 379, CA. See also *Chamberlain v Deputy Commissioner of Taxation* (1988) 164 C.L.R. 502.

(g) The effect of a judgment against the guarantor: res judicata

The doctrine of res judicata, meaning literally "the thing having been **10–228** determined", prevents a party from litigating again a matter which has already been determined by the court.[34] The purpose of the doctrine is twofold: first, to protect a litigant from having to answer a claim already resolved by the court; secondly, to ensure that justice is administered and dispensed fairly and efficiently and to avoid the possibility of inconsistent judgments on the same issues.[35] The doctrine of res judicata in its conventional form requires that, where judgment has been entered in an action, no other proceedings can then be maintained on the same cause of action because the cause of action has merged in the judgment and has lost its independent existence.[36]

Where the creditor obtains judgment against the guarantor and in **10–229** subsequent proceedings claims a further amount under the guarantee, the subsequent claim will be defeated by a plea of res judicata. Hence in *Sandtara Pty Ltd v Abigroup Ltd*,[37] a lessor who sought to claim additional rent in subsequent proceedings for the same period against a guarantor on the basis of a rent review provision in the lease was unsuccessful because the guarantor's liability to the lessor had been determined by the judgment in the original proceedings.

In *Securum Finance Ltd v Ashton*[38] a plea of res judicata did not **10–230** prevent a mortgagee from instituting proceedings against the mortgagors on the basis of their personal covenant in the mortgage even though earlier proceedings to enforce a separate guarantee given by the same parties were struck out for want of prosecution. It was no abuse of process that the mortgagee had confined itself in the first action to a claim on the guarantee (where there was a six year limitation period) and then decided to bring a second action based on the personal covenant in the mortgage (where the limitation period was 12 years). Clause 8.1 of the mortgage expressly provided that it was in addition to any other security held by mortgagee in respect of the obligations of the mortgagors.[39] And there was no abuse of process in allowing the mortgagee to enforce the personal covenant in the second action because the mortgagee was not raising arguments that it could have advanced in the earlier proceedings but failed to do so.

[34] As to the Scottish law on res judicata, see *Waydale Ltd v DHL Holdings (UK) Ltd (No.2)* 2000 S.C. 172; 2001 S.L.T. 224.
[35] See K. Wheelwright and R. Krever, "Recent Applications in Banking Law of Res Judicata and Issue Estoppel Doctrines" (1995) 23 A.B.L.R. 211.
[36] *Blair v Curran* (1939) 62 C.L.R. 464 at 532; *Jackson v Goldsmith* (1950) 81 C.L.R. 446 at 446; *Port of Melbourne Authority v Anshun Pty Ltd* (1981) 147 C.L.R. 589 at 597–598; *Chamberlain v Deputy Commissioner of Taxation* (1988) 164 C.L.R. 502 at 507–508; *Boles v Esanda Finance Corp Ltd* (1989) 18 N.S.W.L.R. 666 at 672–673.
[37] (1995) 13 A.C.L.C. 283. See generally G. Spencer Bower, A.K. Turner and K.R. Handley, *Res Judicata* (3rd ed., 1996).
[38] [1999] 2 All E.R. (Comm) 331.
[39] A different conclusion might be reached where the mortgage was provided simply to secure the covenant to pay another's debts to the mortgagee: *ibid.*

10–231 Issue estoppel, a kindred principle, prevents issues which have previously been judicially determined from being ventilated once again in subsequent proceedings between the same parties.[40]

10–232 In recent years, the courts have developed a different species of res judicata known as Anshun estoppel,[41] or estoppel by omission. This form of estoppel prevents a litigant from raising in a subsequent suit matters which *could have been* raised but were not raised in earlier litigation.

10–233 *Bryant v Commonwealth Bank of Australia*[42] is a recent illustration of the Anshun estoppel. In that case, Einfeld J. of the Federal Court of Australia held that most of the allegations in the applicant's statement of claim could have been raised in earlier proceedings between the parties so any judgment in the Federal Court might be inconsistent with the earlier judgment of the Supreme Court. Accordingly, these allegations offended the Anshun doctrine and the applicant was estopped from raising them in the Federal Court proceedings.

10–234 Einfeld J. acknowledged that the Anshun principle could apply to both defences and counterclaims, but was prepared to extend it to counterclaims only in exceptional cases. However, the present case fell in this category. All the applicant's cross-claims were connected with the subject matter of the Supreme Court proceedings and could have been raised and resolved in that forum. Accordingly, the Anshun estoppel prevented the applicant raising his counterclaims. The applicant was aware of all the relevant issues at the time of the original action and was, therefore, estopped from raising these matters by way of defence or counterclaim in the subsequent proceedings. This decision was affirmed by the Full Court of the Federal Court of Australia.[43]

10–235 Similarly, in *Triantafillidis v National Australia Bank Ltd*,[44] the plaintiff's claim floundered on an Anshun estoppel. Beach J. found that this principle prevented the plaintiff raising allegations of misrepresentation and unconscionable conduct more than two years after the bank had obtained judgment against the plaintiff in an action for possession of mortgaged property and exercised its power of sale. It would not have been reasonable to allow the plaintiff to raise these matters at this late stage and it might have produced results inconsistent with the judgment in the earlier proceedings.

10–236 In the third case in the trilogy, *Hong Kong Bank of Australia v McKenna*,[45] the plea of res judicata was successful. This time the plea was raised not by the bank, but by the guarantors. In its original action against the guarantors, the Hong Kong Bank of Australia (HKB) sought payment of a $1.8 million loan as a result of a default by Century, the borrower. The defendant guarantors alleged that the demand on the

---

[40] See generally G. Spencer Bower, A.K. Turner and K.R. Handley, *Res Judicata* (3rd ed., 1996).

[41] This doctrine is based on *Port of Melbourne Authority v Anshun Pty Ltd* (1981) 147 C.L.R. 589.

[42] (1994) 123 A.L.R. 642.

[43] (1995) 130 A.L.R. 129

[44] Unreported, Vic Sup Ct, Beach J., March 18, 1994.

[45] Unreported, Qld FC Sup Ct, December 13, 1993.

borrower was defective because it required payment "forthwith", whereas the loan facility agreement required payment within 48 hours after demand. The trial judge accepted this argument and rejected the bank's claim.

The bank instituted a separate action against the guarantors again **10–237** seeking the whole due amount to the bank. These proceedings were based on the borrower's default constituted by its failure to comply with a valid demand within the prescribed period of 48 hours. In this second action, the bank sought to recover only $852,470, not the $1.8 million claimed in the original proceedings. In the second action the bank was successful in its application for summary judgment; the presiding judge apparently was not aware that the loans in question were the same loans which were claimed in the earlier action. The defendant guarantors lodged an appeal against this summary judgment but later abandoned it.

HKB then appealed against the decision of the trial judge in the first **10–238** action, no doubt hoping to obtain a judgment for the larger amount of $1.8 million. It was met with a defence of res judicata and issue etoppel. The Queensland Full Court allowed the respondents to amend their notice of appeal to include these defences. Ultimately, the plea of res judicata was successful because the bank in both actions claimed the whole sum due under the loan facility and the judgment in the second action for $852,470 would be inconsistent with a judgment in the first proceedings for $1.8 million. This startling result could be attributed to the bank's flawed strategy of seeking summary judgment in the second action before its appeal in the first action was determined.[46]

To sum up, res judicata, issue estoppel and an Anshun estoppel can all **10–239** affect a creditor's right to enforce a guarantee and a guarantor's right to raise defences and counterclaims. These principles are designed to ensure that all matters which could be raised between the parties are in fact raised in the first proceedings relating to the matters in dispute.

(h) Proceedings to enforce the judgment

A judgment against the guarantors can be enforced through the **10–240** execution process or through bankruptcy proceedings. The creditor can give an undertaking not to seek to enforce the judgment for 28 days so as to give a third party mortgagor an opportunity to apply to the judge under the Administration of Justice Act 1970, s.36(2)(b) for a stay or suspension of execution on evidence that the mortgagor could pay the mortgage debt.[47] But a bankruptcy notice issued in respect of a judgment against the principal debtor and the guarantor as joint debtors is defective and may not be relied upon for a bankruptcy order. Such a notice is a nullity and must be set aside.[48] The principal debtor and the guarantor are not jointly

---

[46] Note, however, Thomas J.'s strong dissenting judgment.
[47] *National Westminster Bank Plc v Skelton* [1993] 1 W.L.R. 72. See Civil Procedure Rules 1998, Sch.1, Ord.48, r.1 and County Court Rules, Ord. 26, r.13.
[48] *Re Neate; Ex p. Pegasus Leasing Ltd* (unreported, Fed Ct, O'Loughlin J., 13 March 1995).

liable to the creditor. Their liability is normally several and a separate judgment against the guarantor is necessary to support a statutory demand.[49]

10–241   Where the guarantor is a company, the creditor may use the statutory demand procedure provided by s.123 of the Insolvency Act 1986 to establish the insolvency of the company for the purposes of a winding-up petition. This procedure requires the creditor to serve the company[50] with a written demand in a prescribed form[51] requiring payment of a present debt[52] in a sum exceeding 750 pounds[53] within three weeks.[54] If the company neglects to pay the sum or to secure or compound for it to the reasonable satisfaction of the creditor within this period, the company is presumed to be unable to pay its debts.[55]

10–242   A company does not neglect to pay the sum specified in the statutory demand if the debt itself is bona fide disputed upon substantial grounds.[56] But a mere dispute as to the amount, as distinct from the existence, of the company's debt will not prevent the creditor from relying on the statutory demand procedure to establish the company's insolvency.[57]

10–243   There is a general principle that the statutory demand procedure may not be used as a debt collecting agency.[58] Indeed, it is an abuse of process to invoke the procedure to enforce payment of a genuinely disputed debt.[59] While there is no express provision in the Insolvency Act 1986 or the Insolvency Rules 1986 for an application by the company to set aside a statutory demand based on a disputed debt, the company can apply for an injunction to prevent the creditor from presenting a winding up petition until the disputed indebtedness is resolved.[60]

---

[49] See generally, I.F. Fletcher, *The Law of Insolvency* (3rd ed., 2002), para.6–055 and Insolvency Act 1986, s.268.

[50] Service is normally effected at the registered office of the company but if there is no registered office the demand may be left at the company's actual place of business for the time being: *Re Fortune Copper Mining Co* (1870) L.R. 10 Eq. 390. If the demand is sent by registered post the court will require proof that the demand was left at the requisite location: *Re A Company (No.008790 of 1990)* [1992] B.C.C. 11. See I.F. Fletcher, *The Law of Insolvency* (3rd ed., 2002), para.20–014.

[51] As to the required form, see Insolvency Rules 1986, SI 1986/1925, rr.4.4–4.6 and Form 4.1.

[52] The debt must be presently due at the date when the creditor uses the statutory demand procedure: *Re Bryant Investment Co.* [1974] 1 W.L.R. 826.

[53] The prescribed amount is subject to alteration by order under s.416 of the Insolvency Act 1986.

[54] Insolvency Act 1986, s.123(1).

[55] See Insolvency Act 1986, ss.122(1)(f), 123(1).

[56] *Re London Wharfing and Warehousing Co Ltd* (1865) 35 Beav. 37; 55 E.R. 808; *Re London and Paris Banking Corp* (1875) 19 Eq. 444; *Mann v Goldstein* [1968] 1 W.L.R. 1091; *Re Lympne Investments Ltd* [1972] 1 W.L.R. 523; *Re LHF Wools Ltd* [1970] Ch. 27.

[57] *Re Tweeds Garages Ltd* [1962] Ch. 406; *Re Welsh Brick Industries Ltd* [1946] 2 All E.R. 197, CA. It is still necessary, however, for the undisputed amount of the debt to exceed the prescribed minimum amount.

[58] See generally *McPherson, The Law of Company Liquidation* (4th ed., 1999) (by A.R. Keay), pp.83–87.

[59] I.F. Fletcher, *The Law of Insolvency* (3rd ed., 2002), para.20–011; *McPherson, The Law of Company Liquidation* (4th ed., 1999) (by A.R. Keay), pp.103–104.

[60] *ibid.* Cf. *Cannon Screen Entertainment Ltd v Handmade Films (Distributors) Ltd* (1989) 5 B.C.C. 207; *Re A Company (No.0012209 of 1991)* [1992] 2 All E.R. 797. See also *Cadiz Waterworks v Barnett* (1874) L.R. 19 Eq. 182.

A failure to comply with a statutory demand is not the only way of **10–244** establishing the guarantor company's insolvency for the purpose of presenting a winding-up petition. The creditor can base its petition on the unsatisfied execution of a judgment obtained against the guarantor company[61] or positive proof of the company's insolvency.[62]

(v) The statutory liability of guarantors in respect of preferences granted by companies

In certain circumstances the liquidator of a company can recover **10–245** preferences from a guarantor who has caused the company's debts or liabilities to be liquidated or reduced to avoid liability under a guarantee. Section 239(4) of the Insolvency Act 1986 provides, in effect, that a surety or guarantor for any of the company's debts or other liabilities can obtain a preference if the company does anything or suffers anything to be done which has the effect of improving the surety or guarantor's position in the event of an insolvent liquidation of the company. Usually it is not difficult to satisfy the court that a payment discharging a debt or liability of the company has the effect of improving the position of the guarantor of that debt or liability. But an order will not be made against the surety or guarantor unless the company was influenced by a desire to produce a preferential effect in relation to the surety or guarantor.[63] However, there is a rebuttable presumption that a preference given by the company to persons connected with the company (otherwise than merely as its employees) was influenced by a desire to confer a preference on those persons.[64] In *Re Agriplant Services Ltd*,[65] for example, a guarantor who was a director and major shareholder of the company was held liable for a preferential payment that he caused the company to make in reduction of its liability under an equipment lease and his liability under an ancillary guarantee. The court had no difficulty in finding that the company was influenced by a desire to improve his position as a guarantor of the debts and liabilities of the company in liquidation.

It should be noted that there are material differences between s.239(4) **10–246** of the Insolvency Act 1986 and its predecessor, s.44 of the Bankruptcy Act 1914. In the first place, it is no longer necessary for a liquidator in a preference action to establish a dominant intention to prefer.[66] It is sufficient that the decision was *influenced* by a *desire* to prefer. This requirement is satisfied if the requisite desire was one of the factors that operated on the minds of the guarantors who decided to cause the company to confer the preference.[67]

---

[61] Insolvency Act 1986, s.123 (1)(b)(c) and (d).
[62] Insolvency Act 1986, s.123(1)(e). See I.F. Fletcher, *The Law of Insolvency* (3rd ed, 2002), paras 20–015 to 20–016 and *McPherson, The Law of Company Liquidation* (4th ed., 1999) by A.R. Keay, pp.56–58.
[63] Insolvency Act 1986, s.239(4) as amended by s.253 of the Enterprise Act 2002.
[64] Insolvency Act 1986, s.239(5) as amended by s.253 of the Enterprise Act 2002.
[65] [1997] B.C.C. 842.
[66] *Re MC Bacon Ltd* [1990] B.C.C. 78 at 87.
[67] *ibid.*

10–247 Secondly, it is no longer sufficient to establish an *intention* to prefer[68] under the current sub-section, there must be a subjective *desire* to produce the preferential effect. Moreover, it is not sufficient to prove a desire to make the payment or grant the security in question. There must have been a positive desire to improve the creditor's position in the event of an insolvent liquidation.[69] In its current form, the section extends the liability for preferential transactions to a surety or guarantor for any of the company's debts or other liabilities. It does not apply where an indemnifier causes a company to confer a preference in order to reduce the indemnifier's liability.[70] On the other hand, it is not restricted in its application to guarantors who are related entities of the principal debtor.[71]

(vi) The Statute of Limitations

10–248 The Limitation Act 1980 begins to run against the guarantor from the date when the cause of action against the guarantor is established, namely when the principal debtor defaults[72] or when the creditor satisfies any conditions precedent to the guarantor's liability. Where the principal debtor commits successive breaches of the principal contract, time begins to run afresh against the guarantors from the date of each breach. Hence, the creditor's claim may be barred in respect of earlier breaches but not later defaults.[73]

10–249 If the guarantors are only liable to pay on demand, time does not begin to run against the guarantors until the demand is made.[74] And the creditor cannot restart the limitation period by making a new demand for a larger sum that includes the amount of the original demand.[75]

---

[68] *ibid.*

[69] *ibid.*

[70] Compare s.588FH of the Australian Corporations Act 2001 (Cth) which applies where the liability discharged is a liability under a "guarantee of otherwise" and where the liability is "contingent or otherwise".

[71] Compare s.588FH of the Australian Corporations Act 2001 (Cth) which applies only where the liability of a related entity was discharged by the preferential payment.

[72] *Hampton v Minns* [2002] 1 W.L.R. 504; *Lep Air Services Ltd v Rolloswin Investments Ltd* [1973] A.C. 331 at 348–349, *per* Lord Diplock. However, the limitation period in an action to recover arrears of rent from a guarantor of a lessee's obligations runs not from the accrual of the arrears but from the demand for repayment under the guarantee: *Romain v Scuba TV Ltd* [1997] Q.B. 887. But in the special circumstances which arose in *Colvin v Buckle* (1841) 8 M. & W. 680; 151 E.R. 1212 time began to run when the creditors became aware of all the facts on which the guarantors' liability depended. See G. Andrews and R. Millett, *Law of Guarantees*, (3rd ed., 2000), para.707.

[73] G. Moss and D. Marks, *Rowlatt on Principal and Surety* (5th ed., 1999), para.1001 and G. Andrews and R. Millett, *Law of Guarantees* (3rd ed., 2000), para.707.

[74] *ibid.*

[75] *Hartland v Jukes* (1863) 1 H. & C. 667; 158 E.R. 1052; *Re Brown* [1893] 2 Ch. 300; *Romain v Scuba TV Ltd* [1996] 3 W.L.R. 117 at 123E. This is so even if the guarantor did not receive the demand, at least where he does not dispute service: *Bank of Baroda v Patel* [1996] 1 Lloyd's Rep. 391. Where the guarantee is given in consideration of forbearance to sue the principal debtor, time begins to run not later than the time when the forbearance expires: *Henton v Paddison* (1893) 68 L.T. 405.

(a) The limitation period

The period of limitation applicable to the creditor's claim against the **10–250** guarantor will vary with the circumstances. If the guarantee is not given under seal, the limitation period will be that applicable to simple contract debts (that is, six years), even though the creditor's claim against the principal may not be statute-barred,[76] which will occur where the principal transaction is under seal or is a mortgage debt. This is so even though the guarantee is physically attached to the memorandum of mortgage.[77] If the guarantee is given under seal, the period of limitation is 12 years[78] even though a different period of limitation applies to the principal transaction (for example, because it is not under seal[79] It follows that in some cases the limitation period against a guarantor might not have expired even though an action against he principal debtor is barred.)[80] However, an action against a guarantor of a lessee's obligations is subject to a six year limitation period under s.19 of the Limitation Act 1980 even if both the guarantee and the lease are under seal. Under s.19 "no action shall be brought to recover arrears of rent, or damages in respect of arrears of rent" after the expiration of a six year period. This provision applies not just to leases but also to guarantees of a lessee's obligation to pay rent.[81]

Where the action to enforce the guarantee is an action in debt, rather **10–251** than an action for damages, the special time limits under s.10 of the Limitation Act 1980 or s.1 of the Civil Liability (Contributions) Act 1978 do not apply.[82]

Sometimes the guarantor may covenant jointly and severally with the **10–252** principal debtor in a mortgage deed, rather than provide a separate deed. Even in this situation, it appears from *Re Frisby; Allison v Frisby*[83] that the period of limitation applicable to an action against the guarantor is the period applicable to specialties, and not the period applicable to actions to recover principal sums of money secured by mortgage. This point was of some importance under the Limitation Act then in force because the limitation period for actions upon a specialty was less than that for an action to recover principal sums secured by mortgage. The question is of only academic interest under the present Limitation Act as the two periods of limitation in these circumstances are in both cases the same, namely 12 years, but a difficulty may still arise if the creditor-mortgagee seeks to recover arrears of interest in respect of any sum of money secured by

---

[76] *Wallis v Crowe* [1942] S.A.S.R. 23; *Barnes v Glenton* [1899] 1 Q.B. 885. See Limitation Act 1980, s.5.
[77] *Wallis v Crowe* [1942] S.A.S.R. 23.
[78] Limitation Act 1980, s.8.
[79] *Re Powers; Lindsell v Phillips* (1885) 30 Ch. D. 291 (where in respect of the Limitation Act then in force, a different limitation period applied to the creditor's action against the principal, which was an action to recover money secured on land).
[80] *Carter v White* (1884) 25 Ch. D. 666.
[81] *Romain v Scuba TV Ltd* [1997] Q.B. 887, CA.
[82] *Hampton v Minns* (2001) 98 (20) L.S.G. 41.
[83] (1889) 43 Ch. D. 106. See especially Kay J. at first instance (at 112) and, on appeal, Bowen L.J. (at 117), Cotton L.J. (at 116). Fry L.J. left the question open (at 117). *Cf.*, *Colonial Investment & Loan Co v Martin* [1928] 3 D.L.R. 784.

mortgage. The Limitation Act provides that arrears of interest in respect of any sum of money secured by mortgage may not be recovered after the expiration of six years from the date on which the interest became due.[84] However, the period of limitation applicable to the action against the guarantor who has joined in the mortgage deed is, according to *Re Frisby; Allison v Frisby*, still that applicable to specialties, namely 12 years. The result is that a mortgagee would be able to recover 12 years of interest against the guarantor who has guaranteed the payment of interest, but would be able to recover only six years against the mortgagor himself. It is no defence for the guarantor to argue that such debts cannot be recovered from the principal because they are statute-barred.[85]

10–253 The limitation period for actions to recover moneys secured by a mortgage or change to recover the proceeds of sale of land is generally 12 years running from the date when the right to receive the money accrued.[86]

10–254 It was not an abuse of process for a creditor to bring an action on a guarantee, where the limitation period is six years, and then decide to bring a second action against the guarantors based on a covenant in their mortgage within the 12 year limitation period applicable to such actions.[87] The mortgage covenant was expressed to be in addition to all other securities held for the guarantors' obligations and there was no question of the creditor returning to court to raise arguments that could have been raised in the earlier proceedings.

10–255 The limitation period in an action to enforce an indemnity starts to run when the indemnified party incurs the loss or when the particular event covered by the indemnity occurs.[88] Until then, the liability under the indemnity is merely contingent.[89]

(b) The effect of part payment or acknowledgment of debt by the principal debtor

10–256 The question arises as to whether the period of limitation which is applicable to the creditor's claim against the guarantor is extended by a part payment or acknowledgment made by the principal to the creditor. Can a guarantor argue that the limitation period with respect to the guarantee has expired, even though such part payments or acknowledgments have extended the limitation period with respect to the creditor's

---

[84] See Limitation Act 1980, s.29(6).
[85] See above, paras 10–143 to 10–144 and below, para.10–259; *Carter v White* (1883) 25 Ch. D. 666.
[86] Limitation Act 1980, s.20.
[87] *Securum Finance Ltd v Ashton* [1999] 2 All E.R. (Comm) 331, appeal dismissed: [2001] Ch. 291.
[88] *Collinge v Heywood* (1839) 9 Ad. & El. 633; 112 E.R. 1352; *County District Properties Ltd v C. Jenner & Son Ltd* (1974) 230 E.G. 1589; *Adams v Dansey* (1830) 6 Bing. 506; 1030 E.R. 1376; *Carr v Roberts* (1833) 5 B. & Ald. 78, 10 E.R. 721.
[89] *Wardley Australia Ltd v Western Australia* (1992) 175 C.L.R. 514.

claim against the principal debtor? It has been held[90] that the guarantor cannot sustain this argument since the part payment or acknowledgement effectively interrupts the period of limitation with respect to the guarantee as well as the principal contract. In any event, the effect of ss.29–31 of the Limitation Act 1980 is that the limitation period starts again so far as the guarantor is concerned if the principal debtor makes a payment in reduction of the principal debt.[91] And part-payments of interest are treated as payments in respect of the principal debt.[92]

An acknowledgment of any debt or other liquidated amount binds the **10–257** party who acknowledges the debt and his successors but no other person.[93] Consequently, an acknowledgment of the debt by the principal debtor or a guarantor will not bind a co-surety so time will not begin to run afresh against him because of the acknowledgment.[94] Where the claim upon a guarantee is for an unliquidated amount, a part payment or acknowledgment by the principal does not extend the limitation period with respect to the creditor's claim against the guarantor.[95] This is so even if the guarantor is jointly and severally liable with the principal.[96]

(c) Part payment or acknowledgment by a co-guarantor

We saw in the previous section that the effect of part payment or **10–258** acknowledgment by the principal on the limitation period against the guarantor is dependent on the precise wording of the relevant section. The same applies to a payment or acknowledgment by a co-guarantor. If, however, *Re Frisby; Allison v Frisby*[97] is followed, then the payment or acknowledgment by one co-guarantor will interrupt the limitation period as against the other guarantors because all are persons liable to pay the debt.

---

[90] *Re Frisby; Allison v Frisby* (1889) 43 Ch. D. 106; *Re Powers; Lindsell v Phillips* (1885) 30 Ch. D. 291.
[91] See G. Andrews and R. Millett, *Law of Guarantees* (3rd ed., 2000), para.7.12; G. Moss and D. Marks, *Rowlatt on Principal and Surety* (5th ed., 1999), para.10.07.
[92] For this reason, a payment of interest by a principal debtor will make time to run afresh against the guarantor: *Re Powers* (1885) 30 Ch. D. 291 (payment of interest by mortgagor prevented the limitation period expiring against a surety who provided a bond for the payment of the mortgage debt); *Re Frisby* (1889) 43 Ch. D. 106 (the payment of interest by the mortgagor prevented the limitation period running in favour of a guarantor of the mortgage debt); *Lewin v Wilson* (1886) 11 App. Cas. 639. G. Andrews and R. Millett, *Law of Guarantees* (3rd ed., 2000), para.7.12, n.39 suggest that the converse is also true.
[93] Limitation Act 1980, s.31(6).
[94] G. Andrews and R. Millett, *Law of Guarantees* (3rd ed., 2000), para.7.12, n.41; G. Moss and D. Marks, *Rowlatt on Principal and Surety* (5th ed., 1999), para.10–07.
[95] *Re Wolmershausen* (1890) 62 L.T. 541 at 544–545; *Re Thomson* [1927] 2 D.L.R. 254.
[96] *Re Wolmershausen* (1890) 62 L.T. 541 at 544–545. *Rowlatt on Principal and Surety* (4th ed., 1982), p.194 suggests the opposite, but this conclusion is contrary to that stated in *Re Wolmershausen*.
[97] (1889) 43 Ch. D. 106.

(d) Recovery of interest

10–259   It may happen that the creditor may not be able to recover from the guarantor principal sums which have been guaranteed because the action in respect of those sums was brought after the expiry of the limitation period. The question which arises in such circumstances is whether the interest payable on those principal sums is recoverable. The recovery of at least a proportion of the interest may itself not be barred by the Limitation Act 1980 because the obligation to pay it has accrued by the terms of the principal transaction within six years before the action against the guarantor is brought.[98] If such interest is to be recoverable, the form of the guarantee must make it clear that the liability in respect of the interest is a separate liability rather than a liability which is merely accessory to the principal sum.[99] If the latter construction is adopted, the interest cannot be regarded as owing because the principal debt is not itself owing.[1] It is not an easy task to differentiate between these two possible constructions. Thus a guarantee of "all moneys and liabilities that may have been or may from time to time be owing ... with interest" has been held to guarantee separately both principal and interest and not just to guarantee the interest as accessory to the principal.[2] On the other hand, a guarantee of "all debts now owing or payable or hereafter to become owing or payable to the extent of £12,500 and *interest on the same respectively*" was taken to indicate that the interest was attached to and accessory to the principal sum.[3]

(e) The creditor's remedy against the guarantor when its action against the principal is statute-barred

10–260   A creditor's claim against the guarantor may not be statute-barred even though its claim against the principal is out of time. Such a situation may occur when the guarantee is under seal but the principal transaction is not, so that a longer period of limitation applies to the guarantee. It may also occur because the creditor's claim against the principal arises upon default, but its claim against the guarantor arises only after a demand is made upon him or her, so that the period of limitation against the guarantor begins to run only from the later time of the demand. In these circumstances it appears that the guarantor will still remain liable, despite the fact that the

---

[98] *e.g. Wallis v Crowe* [1942] S.A.S.R. 23; *Parr's Banking Co v Yates* [1898] 2 Q.B. 460; *Wright v New Zealand Farmers' Cooperative Association of Canterbury* [1939] A.C. 439. See also Limitation Act 1980, s.29(6).
[99] See *Commercial Bank of Australia Ltd v Colonial Finance, Mortgage, Investment & Guarantee Corp Ltd* (1906) 4 C.L.R. 57, especially at 69.
[1] *ibid.*
[2] *Parr's Banking Co v Yates* [1898] 2 Q.B. 460.
[3] *Commercial Bank of Australia Ltd v Colonial Finance, Mortgage, Investment & Guarantee Corp Ltd* (1906) 4 C.L.R. 57.

principal transaction is unenforceable.[4] This issue is discussed in more detail elsewhere.[5]

(vii) Rights of the holder or payee as creditor under a bill of exchange

General rights

A person who takes up a bill of exchange for the honour of anyone **10–261** whose name is on the bill becomes an indorsee of the bill and is entitled to all remedies against those whose names are on it.[6] A set-off for unliquidated damages cannot be successfully pleaded against an action on a bill of exchange.[7] Hence in *Rigg v Commonwealth Bank of Australia*,[8] in an action by the respondent bank against the appellants as drawers of a bill of exchange drawn on the bank in relation to advances made by the bank, the appellants were not entitled to raise any defences they might have had under separate guarantees executed in favour of the bank. This was because the court treated the execution of the bill of exchange as being analogous to a payment of cash or at least as involving an independent contract to be dealt with apart from the other aspects of the specific transaction giving rise to its existence.[9] Any other result would erode the commercial efficacy of bills of exchange.[10] But this general rule has no application where the general law or statutory provisions enable the bill of exchange itself to be struck down.[11]

An action on a promissory note given to a firm as a continuing security is **10–262** properly brought in the name of the original payees of the note if it has been delivered but not indorsed to a new firm constituted upon the retirement of some of the partners of the old firm.[12] Such an action is brought for the benefit of all interested parties.[13] But if the note is

---

[4] *Carter v White* (1883) 25 Ch. D. 666.
[5] See above, paras 10–143 to 10–144.
[6] *Mertens v Winnington* (1794) 1 Esp. 113, N.P.; 170 E.R. 297.
[7] On the other hand, in *John Shearer Ltd and Arrowcrest Group Ltd v Gehl Co* (1995) 17 A.C.S.R. 350, the Full Court of the Federal Court of Australia held that it did not follow that John Shearer Ltd did not have an "offsetting claim" under s.459H of the Australian Corporations Act 2001 merely because the debt referred to in the statutory demand under s.459E arose from a bill of exchange. Hence, such a claim might be sufficient to support an application to set aside the statutory demand even though it could not be relied upon as a defence by way of counterclaim in proceedings on the bill of exchange. See Insolvency Rules 1986, SI 1986/1925, r.6.4 (bankruptcy) and see I.F. Fletcher, *The Law of Insolvency* (3rd ed., 2002), paras 20–010 to 20–014 (company liquidations).
[8] (1989) 97 F.L.R. 261.
[9] *James Lamont & Co Ltd v Hyland Ltd* [1950] 1 K.B. 585.
[10] *Rigg v Commonwealth Bank of Australia* (1989) 97 F.L.R. 261. *Cf. Henriksens Rederi A/S v THZ Rolimpex (The Brede)* [1974] 1 Q.B. 233 and *Bank of Boston v European Grain & Shipping Ltd* [1989] 1 All E.R. 545.
[11] See *Ferro Corp (Aust) Pty Ltd v International Pools Aust Pty Ltd* (1993) 30 N.S.W.L.R. 539.
[12] *Pease v Hirst* (1829) 10 B. & C. 122; 109 E.R. 396.
[13] *ibid.*, at 127; 398.

indorsed to the newly constituted firm, the action must be brought in the names of the indorsees.[14]

10–263   In one special case, separate actions on a note may be necessary: a third person holding a note for the benefit of one joint indorser cannot maintain a joint action against the co-indorsers, as indorsers for the full amount of the note; the third person's proper course is to sue each of the co-indorsers separately in a special action to exact their shares of the liability.[15]

10–264   Recovery against one of the acceptor's sureties does not bar an action against a later indorser. Hence the indorsee of a bill, on default of the acceptor, can recover against the drawer and then bring a second action on the same bill against the first indorser, provided the indorsee does not take out execution against the drawer.[16] Without execution, the indorsee merely recovers damages from the drawer; he does not receive satisfaction. Judgment against the drawer without satisfaction is no bar to the action against the first indorser or indeed any subsequent indorser because it does not alter the indorser's undertaking.[17]

10–265   Usually an indorser will not be liable on a bill unless he is given notice of dishonour. But an absolute promise by the indorser to pay the bill is prima facie an admission that the bill has been presented to the acceptor for payment in due time and has been dishonoured, and further that due notice of dishonour has been given to the indorser.[18]

(viii) Quia timet relief in cases of indemnity

10–266   Where the contract between the promisor and the creditor is one of indemnity, as distinct from a contract of guarantee, it may be possible for the creditor to obtain quia timet relief even before it has suffered any loss. It is interesting to note that in this situation the court grants this form of relief in favour of "the creditor", who is the party indemnified, whereas in cases involving guarantees, quia timet relief is available to the guarantor who, in that context, is the person entitled to an indemnity from another, namely the principal debtor.

10–267   Whether quia timet relief is in fact available under a contract of indemnity depends upon the precise terms of the contract. Where an indemnifier undertakes to repay the party indemnified a sum of money after that party has paid it, or to reimburse that party for a loss sustained, quia timet relief will not be available to the party indemnified since damages will provide an adequate remedy.[19] But if the indemnifier undertakes to relieve the party indemnified by saving that party from the

---

[14] *ibid.*, at 127; 398.
[15] *Small v Riddel* (1880) 31 C.P. 373.
[16] *Claxton v Swift* (1685) 2 Show. K.B. 494; 89 E.R. 1062.
[17] *ibid.*
[18] *Lundie v Robertson* (1806) 7 East 231; 103 E.R. 89.
[19] *McIntosh v Dalwood* (No. 4) (1930) 30 S.R. (NSW) 415. See also *Lawrance v Dixon* (1991) 22 A.T.R. 256 at 267–268; *Newman v McNicol* (1938) 38 S.R. (NSW) 609. *Cf.* the tentative support which McNair J. gave the argument of counsel for the defendant in *Bosma v Larsen* [1966] 1 Lloyd's Rep. 22 at 29. In this type of indemnity, the suffering or incurring of loss, damage or expense is an essential element of the cause of action against the indemnifiers and

burden of having to pay a sum or incur a loss, equity will grant relief quia timet to the party indemnified.[20] In such a case, equity, "instead of compelling the party indemnified first to pay the debt, and perhaps to ruin himself in doing so, will specifically enforce the obligation by ordering the indemnifying party to pay the debt".[21]

Quia timet relief will not be available until the liability under the **10–268** contract of indemnity has crystallised into an actual and enforceable demand which the indemnifier has contracted to pay.[22] Moreover, it appears that this form of equitable relief will not be granted in respect of a claim for indemnity against a future contingent liability, as, for example, where there is a contract to indemnify the claimant against a future liability such as an electricity service charge which is contingent upon the determination of the owner of the property concerned to continue to use the electricity supply.[23] If quia timet relief is available, the claimant may seek the actual amount required to discharge his liability in addition to declaratory relief.[24]

---

must be pleaded: *Hawkesbury Valley Developments v Custom Credit Corp Ltd* (unreported, NSW Sup Ct, McLelland C.J. in Eq, May 12, 1995).

[20] *ibid.*

[21] *McIntosh v Dalwood (No. 4)* (1930) 30 S.R. (NSW) 415 at 418 *per* Street C.J.

[22] See *McIntosh v Dalwood (No. 3)* (1930) 47 W.N. (NSW) 85 at 86, *per* Harvey CJ; *Lawrance v Dixon* (1991) 22 A.T.R. 256 at 267. See also *Agnes & Jennie Mining Co v Zen* [1982] 4 W.W.R. 563. See also *Paddington Churches Housing Association v Technical and General Guarantee Co. Ltd* [1999] B.L.R. 244, where an action on an indemnity in respect of "the net established and ascertained damages" was dismissed as premature because the liability had not been calculated.

[23] *Newman v McNicol* (1938) 38 S.R. (NSW) 609 at 631 *per* Long Innes C.J.

[24] *Agnes & Jennie Mining Co v Zen* [1982] 4 W.W.R. 563.

CHAPTER 11

RIGHTS OF THE GUARANTOR BEFORE PAYMENT

1. Introduction

The onerous liabilities which fall upon persons who assume the **11–01** obligations of suretyship are offset to some extent by the rights which they enjoy at law, under statute and in equity. These rights are, of course, consistent with the fundamental principles of suretyship. One such principle is that the principal debtor is primarily liable for payment of the guaranteed debt, while the guarantors merely undertake a secondary obligation contingent upon the principal debtor's default.[1] This does not mean that the creditor is required to sue the principal debtor before enforcing the guarantee against the guarantors.[2] Nor is the creditor obliged

---

[1] See above, paras 1–18 to 1–27.
[2] See above, paras 10–107 to 10–109 and below, 11–11 to 11–28.

to realise collateral securities held in respect of the guaranteed debt before suing the guarantors.[3] The debtor's primary liability is, however, confirmed by the fact that a paying surety is entitled to an indemnity or reimbursement from the debtor.[4] It is also reflected in the right of a guarantor who pays the whole of the guaranteed debt to be subrogated to the rights and remedies which the creditor holds against the principal debtor, including the right to enforce any collateral securities for the guaranteed debt.[5] Prior to payment, a guarantor who is liable to pay the secured debt is merely entitled to a right of exoneration, a right to have the respective liabilities of the parties declared and to an order that the principal debtor pay the guaranteed debt so as to relieve the guarantor.[6] The guarantor's rights of reimbursement and subrogation are incidental to the guarantor's secondary liability. They enable the guarantor to throw the primary burden of the suretyship back onto the principal debtor or the principal debtor's property.[7]

11–02   Another seminal principle of the law of guarantees is that a surety who pays more than his proper share of the principal debt is entitled to contribution from the co-sureties.[8] Where the surety pays the guaranteed debt in full, the surety is entitled to be subrogated to the creditor's rights and remedies against the co-sureties for the debt.[9] In this way, guarantors are assisted to enforce their rights to contribution and the burden of suretyship is shared equitably.[10]

11–03   Since a guarantor assumes only a secondary liability and is not obliged to pay more than his proper share of the guaranteed debt, the guarantor may be discharged if the creditor does anything which is inconsistent with, or detrimental to, the guarantor's rights of exoneration, reimbursement, contribution or subrogation.[11]

11–04   This interplay of rights and liabilities demands that this chapter be read in conjunction with the other chapters in Pts II and III, as the rights of the parties should not be considered in isolation. Nor should they be discussed without reference to the context, in particular two crucial events: payment and default. For this reason, the rights of the guarantor will be examined both before and after payment of the whole or part of the guaranteed debt.

---

[3] See below, paras 11–15 to 11–17 and above, paras 10–107 to 10–109.
[4] See below, paras 12–01 to 12–115.
[5] See below, paras 12–254 to 12–360.
[6] See below, paras 11–123 to 11–156.
[7] See *Anson v Anson* [1953] 1 Q.B. 636.
[8] See below, paras 12–01 to 12–253.
[9] See below, paras 12–254 to 12–360.
[10] See *Wolmershausen v Gullick* [1893] 2 Ch. 514; *Duncan, Fox & Co v North and South Wales Bank* (1880) 6 App. Cas. 1 at 19–20 *per* Lord Blackburn.
[11] See above, Chapters 7 and 8.

2. RIGHTS OF THE GUARANTOR AGAINST THE CREDITOR BEFORE PAYMENT

(i) Right to information

As we saw in Chapter 4,[12] there is no universal obligation upon the   **11–05**
creditor to disclose all material facts to an intending guarantor. A
guarantor is, however, entitled to be informed of all features of the
principal transaction which, under the circumstances, the guarantor would
not expect to exist.[13] A failure to disclose that any such matters exist
amounts to an implied representation that they do not exist.[14]

Additionally, a guarantor has the right to inquire periodically from the   **11–06**
creditor the amount for which the guarantor is liable under the guarantee,
including both the guarantor's existing and contingent liabilities.[15] The
guarantor is also entitled to demand information as to the interest rate
charged on the principal debt and the amount, if any, realised by the
creditor under the collateral securities.[16] These rights are considered in
more detail in Chapter 4.[17]

A guarantor of a creditor's losses under a trade indemnity arrangement   **11–07**
is entitled to a discovery order in respect of documents relating to
discussions between the creditor and a company that was proposing to take
over the principal debtor. The creditor cannot resist the discovery order by
claiming privilege in respect of the documents because the creditor and the
guarantor have a common interest in the documents and the guarantor
would be subject to a duty of confidentiality if it received the documents.[18]

A guarantor is not an "accounting party" and is not generally entitled to   **11–08**
bring an action against the creditor for an account.[19] The court will not
order an account until the plaintiff's right to the account has been admitted
or established,[20] and there is no basis on which a guarantor *per se* can claim
to be entitled to an account or to access to the creditor's accounting
records in respect of the principal debtor in order to calculate the true
extent of his indebtedness.[21]

---

[12] See above, paras 4–01 to 4–35.
[13] See above, paras 4–06 to 4–35 and *Hamilton v Watson* (1845) 12 Cl. & Fin. 109; 8 E.R. 1339; *Goodwin v National Bank of A/asia* (1968) 117 C.L.R. 173; *London General Omnibus Co Ltd v Holloway* [1912] 2 K.B. 72.
[14] *National Mortgage & Agency Co of New Zealand Ltd v Stalker* [1933] N.Z.L.R. 1182.
[15] A. Holden, *The Law and Practice of Banking* (7th ed., 1986), Vol. 2, pp.198–199. See above, para.4–28.
[16] *Ross v Bank of New South Wales* (1928) 28 S.R. (NSW) 539.
[17] See above, paras 4–27 to 4–29.
[18] *Formica Ltd v Export Credits Guarantee Department* [1995] 1 Lloyd's Rep. 692.
[19] *A D & J A Wright Pty Ltd v Custom Credit Corp Ltd* (1992) 108 F.L.R. 45.
[20] *Batthyany v Walford* (1887) 36 Ch. D. 269 at 276–277.
[21] *A D & J A Wright Pty Ltd v Custom Credit Corp Ltd* (1992) 108 F.L.R 45.

(ii) Right to dispute the amount owing

11-09   When a guarantor is advised by the creditor of the amount of his liability under the guarantee, he is free to accept this statement. Indeed, he may have little choice if the guarantee expressly provides that such a statement by the creditor shall be conclusive evidence of the matters contained therein. But, in the absence of a contrary provision in the guarantee,[22] the guarantor is entitled to appear on a reference in an action by the creditor against the principal debtor in order to contest the amount of the principal debt outstanding.[23]

(iii) Right to notice of default or to a demand

11-10   Unless the guarantee specifically requires the creditor to give the guarantor notice of the principal debtor's default or provides for some other form of notice or condition precedent to liability, the guarantor may be sued immediately upon the default of the debtor.[24] In general, a guarantor is not entitled to a notice of default.[25] On the other hand, a demand upon the guarantor (in addition to the issue of proceedings) may be an essential prerequisite to the enforcement of the guarantee of a principal debt because no cause of action may arise under the collateral agreement until a demand is made.[26]

---

[22] See above, paras 5–99 to 5–107.

[23] *Essex v Wright; Essex v Duff* (1890) 13 Practice Reports 474 (Ont). See also above, paras 5–101 to 5–107.

[24] *Commercial Bank of Australia Ltd v Colonial Finance Mortgage Investment & Guarantee Corp Ltd* (1906) 4 C.L.R. 57; *George v Brayley* (1873) *Stevens Dig 398; Nares v Rowles* (1811) 14 East 510; 104 E.R. 697; *Stothert v Goodfellow* (1832) 1 Nev. & M. K.B. 202.

[25] See above, paras 10–101 to 10–106. One apparent exception to this rule is the right of the drawer or indorser of a bill of exchange to notice of dishonour. The drawer or indorser of a cheque has no such right; *Warrington v Furbor* (1807) 8 East 242 at 245; 103 E.R. 334 at 336; *Black v Ottoman Bank* (1862) 15 Moo P.C.C. 472 at 484; *Duncan, Fox & Co v North and South Wales Bank* (1880) 6 App. Cas. 1 at 18, *per* Lord Blackburn; *Carter v White* (1883) 25 Ch. D. 666 at 671. But this is not a true exception to the general rule. The liability of the drawer or indorser does not crystallise under the law merchant until he receives notice of dishonour. Moreover, it is different where the guarantor for payment of a bill of exchange or promissory note by the acceptor is not a party to the bill and has not contracted to be treated as such: the guarantor is not entitled to notice of dishonour: see *Warrington v Furbor*, above; *Swinyard v Bowes* (1816) 5 M. & S. 62; 105 E.R. 974; *Hitchcock v Humfrey* (1843) 5 Man. & G. 559; 134 E.R. 683; *Walton v Mascall* (1844) 13 M. & W. 452; 153 E.R. 188; *Carter v White* (1883) 25 Ch. D. 666.

[26] See above, paras 10–110 to 10–124.

(iv) Right to compel the creditor to proceed against the principal debtor or a co-surety or to realise collateral securities

(a) The general rule and its exceptions

Under Roman law, sureties could compel the creditor to sue the   **11–11**
principal debtor before having recourse to the sureties unless the sureties
had expressly waived this right or unless the creditor could show that such
a proceeding would be futile because the debtor was absent or insolvent.[27]
This principle has been adopted in many countries whose domestic law is
based on Roman civil law.[28]

Magna Carta contains a provision preventing the Crown from   **11–12**
distraining a surety "as long as the principal debtor is sufficient for the
payment of the debt".[29] However, the courts have consistently ruled that
this clause is restricted to the exceptional case where the surety's liability is
expressed to arise only after the creditor has proceeded against the
principal debtor first.[30]

The authors of the current edition of *Rowlatt on the Law of Principal*   **11–13**
and Surety[31] assert: "There is some authority for suggesting that a
surety ... has an equity against the creditor to prevent the creditor from
bringing down the whole weight of the debt upon the surety ... ".[32]
This is a departure from the view taken in earlier editions of that
learned book[33] and it is, therefore, necessary to assess the authorities
cited to support the new proposition. The current editors cite the obiter
dictum of Wright J in *Wolmershausen v Gullick*[34] that the Crown as a
creditor should in equity "be controlled and prevented from enforcing
its legal right inequitably against one alone of the sureties".[35] They also
rely upon Lord Eldon's comment in *Craythorne v Swinburne*[36] that
Dering v Earl of Winchelsea[37] decided that "the creditor, who can call

---

[27] *H.A. de Colyar on Guarantees* (3rd ed., 1897), p.148.

[28] See P.K. Jones, "Roman Law Basis of Suretyship in Some Modern Civil Codes" (1977) 52 Tul. L. Rev. 129 at 135, 139, 140 and W. D. Morgan, "The History and Economics of Suretyship" (1927) 12 Cornell L.Q. 153.

[29] (1215) 9 Henry III, c.8.

[30] *A-G v Resby* (1664) Hard. 377; 145 E.R. 506; *A-G v Atkinson* (1827) 1 Y. & J. 207; 148 E.R. 647; *R. v Fay* (1878) 4 L.R. Ir. 606. It is not entirely true, therefore, that this provision "has not been afforded a great deal of recognition": see *H.A. de Colyar on Guarantees* (3rd ed., 1897), p.147).

[31] D.G.M Marks and G.S. Moss, *Rowlatt on the Law of Principal and Surety* (5th ed., 1999) (hereinafter referred to as *Rowlatt on Principal and Surety*).

[32] *ibid.*, para.7–02.

[33] See, *e.g. Rowlatt on Principal and Surety* (3rd ed., 1936), pp.177–178.

[34] [1893] 2 Ch. 514.

[35] *ibid.*, at 522. There appears to be an error at para.7–02 of the current edition of *Rowlatt on Principal and Surety*. The learned editors state that Wright J. in *Wolmershausen v Gullick* considered by way of dictum that a surety could in equity "be controlled and prevented from enforcing its legal right inequitably against one alone of the sureties". It appears that if this alleged equity did exist, it would restrict the creditor in the enforcement of the guarantee.

[36] (1807) 14 Ves. Jun. 160; 33 E.R. 482.

[37] (1787) 1 Cox 318; 2 Bos. & P. 270; 29 E.R. 1184.

upon all, shall not be at liberty to fix one with payment of the whole debt."[38]

11–14   With respect, Wright J.'s remarks were directed at a guarantor's right to contribution from co-sureties and, in that context, it is true that equity can *in a sense* prevent the creditor from imposing the whole burden of the suretyship upon one guarantor. Equity adjusts this burden by allowing a guarantor who has paid more than his proper share to seek contribution from the co-sureties.[39] But this does not prevent a creditor from *initially* imposing the whole debt on one guarantor; it merely relieves that guarantor of part of this burden by applying the doctrine of contribution. Moreover, notwithstanding Lord Eldon's view of *Dering v Earl of Winchelsea*, a creditor remains at liberty to fix one guarantor with full payment of the principal debt provided that the guarantor is liable for the whole debt. The rights of the guarantors inter se may then be determined in an action for contribution. To quote Latham C.J. in *McLean v Discount & Finance Ltd*:[40]

> "A creditor to whom guarantees have been given may compel any surety to pay according to his contract. He is not bound to take any steps to distribute the burden among the sureties. Thus a surety who has guaranteed the whole of the debt may be compelled to pay the whole debt even though there are other sureties."[41]

11–15   The general rule is that a guarantor who has not paid the principal debt cannot require the creditor to proceed against the principal debtor[42] or a co-guarantor, or to enforce any securities held for the debt, before having recourse to the guarantor.[43] This is confirmed by the House of Lords decision in *Ewart v Latta*,[44] where Lord Westbury L.C. declared:

> "It is quite a misapprehension to suppose that there is any equity entitling the surety to compel the creditor to discuss the principal— unquestionably the surety has no such right unless he pays the whole debt."[45]

---

[38] (1807) 14 Ves. Jun. 160 at 163; 33 E.R. 482 at 483.
[39] See below, paras 12–254 to 12–360.
[40] (1939) 64 C.L.R. 312.
[41] *ibid.*, at 328.
[42] *Jackson v Digby* (1854) 2 W.R. 540; *Moschi v Lep Air Services Ltd* [1973] A.C. 331 at 356–357; *Ewart v Latta* (1865) S.C. 36; *Coffey v DFC Financial Services Ltd* (unreported, NZ CA, October 2, 1991); *Carter v White* (1883) 25 Ch. D. 666 at 670; *Morrison v Barking Chemicals Co Ltd* [1919] 2 Ch. 325. See also above, paras 10–107 to 10–109. In fairness to the current editors of *Rowlatt*, they acknowledge some of these authorities but they give no valid reasons why they should not apply: see *Rowlatt on Principal and Surety* (5th ed., 1999), para.7–02.
[43] *China & South Seas Bank Ltd v Tan* [1989] 3 All E.R. 839; *Jones v Bank of New South Wales* (unreported, Qld Sup Ct, April 19, 1979) and see above, paras 8–75 to 8–103.
[44] (1865) S.C. 36. This case concerned Scottish law but their Lordships took the view that the same principle applied in English law. See also *Fothergill, Re, ex p. Turquand* (1876) 3 Ch. D. 445.
[45] (1865) S.C. 36 at 41. See also *Moschi v Lep Air Services Ltd* [1973] A.C. 331 at 357 *per* Lord Simon of Glaisdale. Ironically, Lord Simon of Glaisdale refers to the third edition of *Rowlatt on the Law of Principal and Surety* (1936), p.144, which contains a correct statement of the rule.

The rationale of this principle is that it is the duty of the guarantor, not **11–16** the creditor, to ensure that the debtor performs the principal obligation[46] and that the creditor should have almost unbridled control over the remedies which the contract provides. The creditor should not be hampered in pursuing a specific course of legal action by a person who remains his debtor. By similar reasoning, a creditor cannot be compelled to sue co-sureties before proceeding against a guarantor who has not discharged his liability.[47]

This orthodox view is also consistent with the authorities which **11–17** indicate that a creditor will only be obliged to exhaust any particular remedy against the principal debtor before having recourse to the guarantor where there is an express provision to this effect in the guarantee.[48] The general principle is then subject to the terms of the guarantee which may require that certain remedies be taken against the principal debtor or that certain securities obtained by the creditor from the debtor be realised before the guarantor is rendered liable. Thus in *Holl v Hadley*,[49] it was a condition precedent to the liability of the guarantor that the "utmost efforts and legal proceedings" be taken against the principal debtor, and in *Musket v Rogers*,[50] the creditor undertook, before proceeding against the guarantor, to "avail himself to the uttermost of any actual or bona fide security" obtained from the debtor. In the absence of similar provisions in the guarantee or in some other contract between the creditor and the guarantor, the creditor is not obliged to take positive steps to obtain payment from the debtor or to realise any securities it has obtained from the debtor before proceeding against the guarantor.[51]

It has also been argued that the general rule admits exceptions. The **11–18** current editors of *Rowlatt* suggest that an exception should be made where there is a solvent principal debtor or solvent co-sureties who could be joined in the action to enforce the guarantee or where there is a security given by the principal debtor which could easily be realised to pay the whole debt.[52] However desirable this view may be, it is simply not the law. These matters are at present dealt with through the paying surety's right to indemnity and contribution and the right of subrogation to any securities or remedies held by the creditor for the principal debt.[53]

The current editors of *Rowlatt* argue that a further exception to the **11–19** general rule should be made "where the creditor has an opportunity to recover the debt from the principal debtor which will not be available to

[46] *Moschi v Lep Air Services Ltd* [1973] A.C. 331.
[47] *McLean v Discount & Finance Ltd* (1939) 64 C.L.R. 312 at 328 *per* Latham C.J.
[48] See *Abrey v Crux* (1869) L.R. 5 C.P. 37. See also *New London Credit Syndicate v Neale* [1898] 2 Q.B. 487; *Hitchings v Northern Leather Co* [1914] 3 K.B. 907. See *Rowlatt on Principal and Surety* (5th ed., 1999), p.114.
[49] (1828) 5 Bing 54; 130 E.R. 980. See also *Abrey v Crux* (1869) L.R. 5 C.P. 37, where such a condition precedent was not proved.
[50] (1839) 5 Bing N.C. 728; 132 E.R. 1281.
[51] *Musket v Rogers* (1839) 8 Scott 51; 132 E.R. 1281. Cf. *Holl v Hadley* (1835) 2 Ad. & E. 758; 111 E.R. 292; *Lawrence v Walmsley* (1862) 12 C.B. (NS) 799; 142 E.R. 1356. See also *Rowlatt on Principal and Surety* (4th ed., 1982), pp.113–114.
[52] See *Rowlatt on Principal and Surety* (5th ed., 1999), para.7–03.
[53] See below, Chapter 12.

the surety".[54] They rely on *Cottin v Blane*[55] as support for this proposition. *Cottin v Blane* was decided against the background of the French Revolution which precipitated war across Europe. In this conflict America remained neutral. A ship owned by an American, Mr Macauley, was chartered to Monsieur Changeur as agent for a French company. Cottin, the plaintiff, had guaranteed the obligations of the charterer and the charter-party. When the ship arrived at Bordeaux on August 30, 1793 to load its cargo it became subject to the embargo imposed on all neutral vessels. However, the Revolutionary Government promised to indemnify neutral ship owners for any losses caused by the embargo. When the charterer became bankrupt, Blane, an agent of the American ship owner, attempted to enforce Cottin's guarantee.

11–20   The issue was whether Cottin, the guarantor, could obtain an injunction to compel Blane, the ship owner's agent, to seek compensation from the French Government before enforcing the guarantee. The court granted the injunction on condition that the guarantor bring the amount of the guarantee into court.

11–21   *Cottin v Blane*[56] should not be regarded as authority for a general principle for three reasons: first, as the court itself observed, it was decided on its own "peculiar" facts;[57] secondly, it was merely an application for an interlocutory injunction; and finally, it has not been accepted as authority in subsequent cases.[58] It was not a case of a creditor being compelled to seek compensation from the *principal debtor* before suing the guarantor, but merely a case where the creditor-owner was compelled to claim first against a *fund provided by a third party*. It is submitted, therefore, that it should be treated as analogous to the creditor's obligation to perfect a security which is held for the enforcement of the guaranteed obligation.[59]

11–22   While *Cottin v Blane* does not support an exception in the general terms stated by the current editors of *Rowlatt*, it appears that the creditor can be restrained from first proceeding against the guarantor in two situations:

> (i) where the principal debtor's assets have been confiscated, subject to the claims of creditors of a particular nationality, allegiance or sympathy which includes the creditor but excludes the guarantor;[60] or

[54] See *Rowlatt on Principal and Surety* (5th ed., 1999), para.7–03.
[55] (1795) 2 Anstr. 544; 145 E.R. 962.
[56] (1795) 2 Anstr. 544; 145 E.R. 962.
[57] In *Laing Management Ltd (formerly Laing Management Contracting Ltd) v Aegon Insurance Co (UK) Ltd* (1997) 86 B.L.R. 70 at 116 Judge Humphrey Lloyd Q.C. observed that *Cotton v Blane* (1792) 2 Anstr. 544; 145 E.R. 962 is "merely pragmatic and decides nothing as a matter of principle."
[58] *Laing Management Ltd (formerly Laing Management Contracting Ltd) v Aegon Insurance Co (UK) Ltd* (1997) 86 B.L.R. 70 at 116. In that case *Cotton v Blane* did not apply in any event because the main contractor did not have any remedy that it could exercise against the owner before enforcing a performance bond given by a third party.
[59] See above, paras 8–65 to 8–70.
[60] *Wright v Simpson* (1802) 6 Ves. Jun. 714; 31 E.R. 1272. Lord Eldon at 732; 1281 thought that the creditor should be restrained from proceeding first against the guarantor rather than the confiscated assets only where the guarantor could not take advantage of the creditor's rights against the assets by assignment on payment of the principal debt.

(ii) where, on a similar basis, the guarantor is prevented from enforcing his right of indemnity against the principal debtor but the creditor alone is entitled to recover the principal debt by claiming against a *fund* specifically provided for the purpose of meeting such claims.[61]

An exception might possibly be made in certain circumstances where the guarantee provides that it can be determined by the creditor's closing the principal debtor's current account, ascertaining the amount due and demanding payment by the guarantor. If the creditor merely closed the debtor's account without taking the other steps to enforce the guarantee, the guarantor might be entitled to have his liability determined even though there would be no complete cause of action against the guarantor until demand.[62] In closing the debtor's account, the creditor might jeopardise the interests of the guarantor by preventing the debtor from trading on the debtor's current account, thereby making it more likely that the debtor would default in payment of the principal debt. In this situation, it might be inequitable to prevent the guarantor from seeking the assistance of equity to have his liability under the guarantee determined.[63] It might be otherwise where the guarantor has the right under the bargain with the creditor to determine his guarantee by giving notice to the creditor as, in this situation, the guarantor could terminate any further liability without the assistance of the court. **11–23**

There is some authority that a qualification to the general rule exists where the guarantor not only gives a personal guarantee but also assigns a further security to the creditor or provides a fund to satisfy the guaranteed obligation, if the principal debtor fails to pay. Thus in *Ex p. Goodman*,[64] it was said that "the sureties have an equity that [the creditor] should first prove his debt"[65] in the principal debtor's bankruptcy before proceeding against a security, namely, an assignment of copyhold premises, given by the sureties. There is little other authority to support this view[66] and it is thought to be incorrect. The guarantor is entitled to insist only that the fund which is provided through the proceeds of realisation of the security be appropriated to the guaranteed debt and not to other outstanding debts.[67] **11–24**

Some of the apparent exceptions to the general rule can be explained on other bases. On one view, *Law v East India Co*[68] supports an exception where payment is extracted from a guarantor by duress or oppression. **11–25**

---

[61] *Cottin v Blane* (1795) 2 Anstr. 544; 145 E.R. 962.
[62] *Morrison v Barking Chemicals Co Ltd* [1919] 2 Ch. 325 at 332 *per* Sargant J. (obiter dicta).
[63] The relief available would presumably be similar to that granted in *Ascherson v Tredegar Dry Dock & Wharf Co Ltd* [1909] 2 Ch. 401.
[64] (1818) 3 Madd. 373; 56 E.R. 542.
[65] *ibid.*, at 374; 542, *per* Sir John Leach V.C.
[66] *Rowlatt on Principal and Surety* (5th ed., 1999), para.7–04, n.21 cites *Re Westzinthus* (1833) 5 B. & Ad 817; 110 E.R. 992 in support of this proposition, but that case is really only an example of the guarantor's right to have the proceeds of the realisation of any collateral security applied to the guaranteed debt.
[67] See above, paras 6–23 to 6–35.
[68] (1799) 4 Ves. 824; 31 E.R. 427 at 430.

There, the defendant company forced its servant, who was guarantor for another servant, to pay a large sum as the amount due under the principal obligation. The defendant creditor had not proceeded against the principal, nor had an account been taken. The court ordered the defendant to refund the amount paid by the guarantor under duress, pending a determination of the rights of the parties. Although the Master of the Rolls commented that in these circumstances it would have been "but fairness"[69] for the creditor not to proceed directly against the guarantor, the court did not expressly compel the defendant to proceed against the principal debtor first. Moreover, the refund can be explained on the basis that a payment under duress is recoverable.

11–26   Another possible exception to the general rule that the creditor is not obliged to take proceedings against the principal debtor before enforcing the guarantee is where the creditor's action against the guarantor is an action for damages.[70] In such a case it is arguable that the creditor should take action against a solvent principal debtor in order to mitigate its damages. It is likely, however, that the terms and nature of the guarantee could easily displace this general duty of mitigation.

11–27   There is a statutory modification to the rule. In respect of transactions governed by the Consumer Credit Act 1974, no security (which includes a guarantee or indemnity) can be enforced until there has been service of notice of default upon the debtor or hirer. Pursuant to s.111(1) a copy of such notice must be served on any relevant third party surety. As no time limit is specified, however, the notice may be served at any time. If the creditor fails to serve a notice the security is enforceable against the surety (in respect of the breach or other matter to which the notice relates) on an order of the court only.[71]

11–28   A genuine exception arises as a result of the doctrine of marshalling. For example, where the principal debtor grants security over all its real and personal property in favour of the creditor in respect of the principal debt and a further security merely over its personal property in favour of the guarantors to secure their right of indemnity, the guarantor, even before he pays any amount off the principal debt,[72] can require the creditor to marshall its securities.[73]

This right of marshalling may be excluded by the express terms of the guarantee. Moreover, it will be of no practical benefit if the proceeds of realisation of the real property are insufficient to discharge the amount owing to the creditor. Ultimately, the creditor may resort to all its securities to recover any shortfall,[74] and the creditor's right to enforce its

---

[69] *ibid.*, at 430.
[70] See above, paras 10–201 to 10–209. It should be noted, however, that the creditor's usual action against the guarantor is an action for an agreed sum.
[71] s.111(2). See also ss.87(1)(e), 88. For a fuller discussion see R. Goode, *Consumer Credit Act 1974*, para.14.6; G. Andrews and R. Millett, *Law of Guarantees* (3rd ed., 2000), pp.523–524. Note that a land mortgage securing a regulated contract is enforceable (so far as is provided in relation to that agreement) on an order of the court only (s.126).
[72] See *Heyman v Dubois* (1871) L.R. 13 Eq. 158; *Praed v Gardiner* (1788) 2 Cox Eq. Cas. 86; 30 E.R. 40.
[73] See below, paras 11–40 to 11–45.
[74] See above, paras 10–82 to 10–87.

security over the debtor's personal property will depend simply upon its priority.

(b) Proposed reforms

Not all common law jurisdictions have adopted the general rule that the **11–29** creditor is not obliged to proceed first against the principal debtor. A significant minority of American States have embraced the doctrine of *Pain v Packard*[75] either by judicial decision[76] or legislation.[77] In that case, a New York court decided that, where the defendant is, to the creditor's knowledge, merely a surety and requests the creditor to proceed against a solvent principal when the debt is due, the creditor is bound to use due diligence against the principal to exonerate the surety. The surety will be discharged to the extent that the surety can show that he has been prejudiced by the creditor's failure to act on this request.

The legislative provisions which entrench the principle in *Pain v* **11–30** *Packard* either require the creditor to proceed against the principal debtor with due diligence within a reasonable time after being requested to do so by the guarantor[78] or they oblige the creditor to pursue the principal debtor *and* enforce any other security before proceeding against the guarantor.[79] This so-called "right of discussion" is not a peculiar creature of American law. It can be traced to Roman law[80] and is available to sureties in most civil law jurisdictions.[81]

The Law Reform Commission of South Australia recommended that a **11–31** creditor should be required to realise any collateral securities which would either extinguish or reduce the amount of the guarantor's liability before having recourse to the guarantor.[82] It further proposed that the creditor be subject to a duty to exercise due diligence in preserving and enforcing securities held in respect of the guaranteed debt.[83]

It is arguable that the person who enjoys the benefit of the guarantee, **11–32** namely the principal debtor, should bear primary responsibility for its burden. On this view, the guarantee is properly seen as an accessory obligation, a subsidiary security to be invoked after the creditor has

---

[75] 13 Johns (NY) 174 (1816).
[76] See *Cope v Smith* 8 Serge & R (Pa) 110; 11 Am. Dec. 582 (1822); *Martin v Skehan* 2 Colo 614 (1875). See also (1928) 37 Yale L.J. 971 and (1929) 1 Rocky Mt. L. Rev. 232.
[77] The following States have adopted the *Pain v Packard* doctrine by statute: Alabama, Arizona, Arkansas, Georgia, Illinois, Indiana, Iowa, Kentucky, Mississippi, Missouri, North Carolina, Ohio, Tennessee, Texas, Virginia, Washington, West Virginia, Wyoming. Five other States, California, Montana, North Dakota, South Dakota and Oklahoma have special statutes on the subject: see L. P. Simpson, *Handbook of the Law of Suretyship* (1950), p.179.
[78] See, *e.g.* s.12191 of the Ohio General Code.
[79] See, *e.g.* s.2850 of the California Civil Code.
[80] P.K. Jones, "Roman Law Basis of Suretyship in Some Modern Civil Codes" (1977) 52 Tul. L. Rev. 129 at 135, 139, 140; *H. A. de Colyar on Guarantees* (3rd ed., 1897), pp.147–148; W. D. Morgan, "The History and Economics of Suretyship" (1927) 12 Cornell L.Q. 153.
[81] *ibid.* See also the British Columbia Law Reform Commission, *Report on Guarantees of Consumer Debts* (1979), pp.44–45.
[82] South Australia Law Reform Commission, *Reform of the Law of Suretyship* (1977), p.7.
[83] *ibid.* See above, paras 8–82 to 8–87.

proceeded against the principal debtor or after the creditor has realised its collateral securities.

11–33   But there are both general and specific objections to such a right to discussion. In the first place, it diminishes the utility of the guarantee by imposing upon the creditor the delay and burden of pursuing the principal debtor first.[84] The creditor may have taken the guarantee for the very purpose of avoiding this expense and inconvenience. A right of discussion escalates the cost of enforcing a guarantee with few compensating benefits to the creditor.

11–34   It is not clear from the proposal of the Law Reform Commission of South Australia whether the creditor would be accountable to the guarantor for the amount which the creditor failed to realise because of a breach of its duty to exercise due diligence in preserving and enforcing securities held in respect of the guaranteed debt.[85] Nor is there any indication whether a guarantor would be entitled to invoke the proposed right of discussion at a time when the guarantor is not in a position to honour the guarantee.[86] And there is no suggestion that the guarantor should assist the creditor to proceed against the principal debtor first by providing an indemnity for the creditor's expenses or pointing to exigible assets of the principal debtor.

11–35   In 1977, the Civil Code Revision Office in Quebec recommended the repeal of the right of discussion in that province because it did not correspond with economic realities. It further proposed that a guarantee could expressly give the guarantor such a right, provided that the guarantor advanced to the creditor the necessary expenses and indicated what property could be seized.[87]

11–36   The Law Reform Commission of British Columbia took the opposite view: "[a] guarantor should be able, where the principal debtor has defaulted on ... [a] consumer transaction, to demand by notice in writing that the creditor commence an action against the principal debtor, or to enforce his security interest in any collateral given by the principal debtor to secure the principal obligation or both".[88] The Commission believed that such measures were desirable because consumer guarantors do not foresee the full extent of their contingent liabilities and cannot reasonably be expected to have sufficient available assets to honour their undertaking or to pursue their right of reimbursement against the principal debtor.[89] It could be argued, however, that the guarantors should have taken these factors into account when they assumed their obligation. Nevertheless, there is some merit in granting a consumer guarantor a right of discussion where the principal debtor is solvent or where there is a collateral security which could be realised to pay the guaranteed debt, provided that the

---

[84] This was one of the reasons why the doctrine in *Pain v Packard* was rejected by the American Law Institute: see American Law Institute, *Report on Security* (1941), pp.352, 355.
[85] See Commercial Law Note (1979) 53 A.L.J. 99 at 100.
[86] *ibid*. But on normal principles, the guarantor would be accountable: see above, paras 8–46 to 8–91.
[87] Civil Code Revision Office, *Report on the Quebec Civil Code* (1977), Vol II, Tome 2 (comment on recommended Art. 853 of Book 5).
[88] See *Report on Guarantees of Consumer Debts* (1979), p.47.
[89] *ibid*.

guarantor reimburses the creditor for any reasonable expenses incurred in suing the principal debtor or realising the securities. These considerations are reflected in the Credit Acts of the various Australian States which go even beyond the recommendations of the Law Reform Commission of British Columbia in requiring in certain circumstances prior proceedings against the principal debtor or against both the guarantor and the debtor jointly.

In commercial guarantees, it is thought that the guarantor is sufficiently protected by the guarantor's right of indemnity and subrogation and that the guarantor should not enjoy a right of discussion. A general right to insist that the creditor sue the principal debtor first would defeat the main purpose of the guarantee. But even in this context, a further exception to the general rule should be made where the security can be realised without prejudice to the creditor and a failure to realise it would cause unusual hardship to the guarantor.[90]   **11–37**

(v) No general right to the creditor's remedies and securities

Prior to actual payment of the guaranteed debt, a guarantor has, in general, no right to the remedies or securities held by the creditor for the debt.[91] A surety can, however, *acquire* such a right by paying the amount of the debt into court after the creditor refuses a tender of payment. Thus in *Goddard v Whyte*,[92] Sir John Stuart V.C. ordered the holder of a dishonoured promissory note to deliver up the principal's collateral security to a surety who had become liable on default of the principal and who had paid the amount into court on the creditor's refusal to accept payment.   **11–38**

Moreover, even before the guarantors pay their shares of the principal debt, guarantors of part of the principal debt may be entitled to a declaration of their rights to share proportionately in the proceeds of realisation of the creditor's securities once they pay their respective shares.[93] Such a declaration may assist the guarantors to raise the funds to pay their shares of the principal debt. A guarantor may even be entitled to apply for an injunction to restrain actions or appropriations which are inconsistent with the rights which the guarantors will acquire in respect of the creditor's remedies and securities upon payment of the amount of their respective parts of the principal debt.[94] It appears that these principles might not apply to a guarantor of the whole of the principal debt even if that guarantor's liability is limited to a certain amount.   **11–39**

[90] This suggestion is based on a provision in the Restatement, *Security* (1941) Q. 131.
[91] *Challenge Bank Ltd v Mailman* (unreported, NSW CA, May 14, 1993). See also below, paras 12–254 to 12–299. Even where the creditor has entered into possession of land mortgaged to secure the principal debt, this does not reduce the guarantor's liability until the land is sold and the proceeds are applied in reduction of the principal debt: *Re Debtor (No.90 of 1992)* (unreported, *The Times*, July 12, 1993) 1993 W.L. 965029.
[92] (1860) 2 Giff. 449; 66 E.R. 188.
[93] *Challenge Bank Ltd v Mailman* (unreported, NSW CA, May 14, 1993).
[94] *Graf v Auscan Timber Marketing Pty Ltd* (unreported, NSW Sup Ct, Young J., August 9, 1995).

(vi) Marshalling

11–40   The general rule is that, in the absence of independent and separate equities, the right of marshalling can only apply where the creditors have a common debtor and both funds are derived from that common debtor.[95] This general rule is qualified where there is an independent equity which requires one debtor to pay the debts of another.[96] In this situation, it does not matter that there is not one common debtor because the court will enforce the duty of the principal debtor to exonerate the secondary debtor by subjecting the principal debtor's funds to the discharge of the debt of the secondary debtor.[97] In other words, it is sufficient for the doctrine of marshalling that, as between the persons interested, the two debts *ought* to be paid by the same person even though that person may not be directly liable to the creditors for the two debts.[98]

11–41   In the context of a guarantee, this means that a creditor of the guarantor can require a creditor of the principal debtor to marshall its securities over the principal debtor and the guarantor's property, even though the securities were not granted by one common debtor. The guarantor is entitled to be exonerated by the principal debtor and this equity gives the creditor of the guarantor alone the right to require a creditor of both the principal debtor and the guarantor to marshall its securities to the benefit of the creditor of the guarantor.

11–42   Hence in *Ernst Bros Co v Canada Permanent Mortgage Corp*[99] a right of marshalling was allowed on the following facts. There were two brothers, Jeremiah (who owned Lot 14) and Frank (who wished to buy Lot 13). They joined in a mortgage on Lots 13 and 14 for £1,200. They agreed that £900 should go to Frank to pay for Lot 13, £200 to Jeremiah to buy machinery and the other £100 would go on expenses. Later, Frank conveyed Lot 13 to Jeremiah. This meant that Frank was entitled to be exonerated by Jeremiah for his liability under the mortgage. In a sense he was, as between the two brothers, only secondarily liable for the mortgage debt. The plaintiff had a lien on Lot 13 for the purchase money of a machine. The mortgagee of both Lots sold Lot 13, and the plaintiff sought to marshall against Lot 14. Marshalling was allowed even though the lien-holder and the mortgagee did not have one single common debtor. There were two separate debtors: Jeremiah and Frank. But Jeremiah had a duty to exonerate Frank in respect of his liability under the mortgage, so the lien-holder was entitled to call upon the mortgagee to marshall his security over Jeremiah's Lot 14.

---

[95] 53 American Jurisprudence 2d, para.9, cited with approval in *Sarge Pty Ltd v Cazihaven Homes Pty Ltd* (1994) 34 N.S.W.L.R. 658 at 661.
[96] *Savings & Loan Corp v Bear* 75 A.L.R. 980 (1930) at 995; *Ayres v Husted* 15 Conn. 504 (1843) at 516; *Newson v McLendon* 6 Ga. 392 (1849) at 400; *House v Thompson* 3 Head 512 (1859) at 516; *Story's Equity Jurisprudence* (13th US ed., 1886), para.642 at 650–651.
[97] Meagher, Gummow and Lehane's *Equity Doctrines and Remedies* (4th ed., 2002), by R. Meagher, D. Heydon and M. Leeming, para.11–045.
[98] R.H. McLaren and W.B. Rayner, *Falconbridge on Mortgages* (4th ed., 1977), p.315.
[99] (1920) 57 D.L.R. 500.

On the other hand, no right of marshalling was available in *Sarge Pty*   **11–43**
Ltd v Cazihaven Homes Pty Ltd[1] because there was no independent or
separate equity warranting a departure from the single common debtor
requirement. In that case, Mr and Mrs Masters lent £200,000 to Cazihaven
Homes Pty Ltd and took a first registered mortgage over its land; the
Thurms provided a third-party mortgage securing the indebtedness; the
ANZ Bank lent Cazihaven £130,000; the plaintiff guaranteed this loan and
took a second unregistered mortgage over the Thurms' land. When
Cazihaven defaulted, Mr and Mrs Masters exercised their power of sale
over the Thurms' land and then proposed to sell the Cazihaven land and
produce a surplus of £50,000.

On these facts, Young J. held that the plaintiff had no right to compel   **11–44**
Mr and Mrs Masters to enforce their security against the Cazihaven land
first. It was not as if the plaintiff had guaranteed Cazihaven's contingent
liability to the Thurms. Indeed, it was the other way around. Hence there
was no separate and independent equity to overcome the single common
debtor element necessary for marshalling.

Similarly, there was no right of marshalling available in *Morris v*   **11–45**
Rayners Enterprises Incorporated.[2] The House of Lords declared that
marshalling is a principle for doing equity between two or more creditors,
each of whom is owed debts by the same debtor but one of whom can
enforce its claim against more than one security or fund while the other
can resort to only one. This principle gives the latter an equity to require
that the first creditor satisfy itself so far as possible out of the security or
fund to which the other creditor has no claim. But it could not apply on
the facts of the case because there was only one debt owed by the
principal borrower to the bank, BCCI. Moreover, the bank had security
in the form of a charge over a deposit in the bank. There was no basis on
which the depositors could assert an equity to require the bank to
proceed against their deposits before claiming against the principal
debtors.

(vii) Right of the guarantor to rely on cross-claims and defences which the principal has against the creditor

In order that the guarantors be exonerated from liability, they may seek   **11–46**
to rely on any claims and defences which the principal has against the

---

[1] (1994) 34 N.S.W.L.R. 658.
[2] [1997] 3 W.L.R. 909.

creditor.[3] Sometimes the guarantors' rights in this regard have been widely expressed.[4] In *Bechervaise v Lewis*,[5] for example, Willes J stated:

> "[W]e have a creditor who is equally liable to the principal as the principal to him, and against whom the principal has a good defence in law and equity, and a surety who is entitled in equity to call upon the principal to exonerate him. In this state of things, we are bound to conclude that the surety has a defence in equity against the creditor."[6]

11–47   Indeed, to allow the guarantor to take advantage of such cross-claims or defences would prevent circuity of actions arising from the tripartite nature of the guarantee.[7] Moreover, it might be regarded as unjust that a guarantor cannot take advantage of a cross-claim when the principal debtor is not prepared or is unable to pursue the claim, especially where the guarantor is then forced to seek an indemnity from an insolvent debtor. Nevertheless, the law does not permit all cross-claims and defences available to the principal debtor to be pleaded by the guarantor,[8] at least without joining the principal as a party to the proceedings.[9]

11–48   Furthermore, the terms of the guarantee itself may preclude the guarantor from pleading cross-claims and defences available to the principal debtor. Clear and unequivocal words (or an obvious implication) are required to achieve this effect. If there is nothing in the guarantee to exclude the guarantor's right to counterclaim and set-off under the

---

[3] Directors who provided a guarantee of their company's *ultra vires* borrowings were not permitted to raise the defence that the principal transaction was *ultra vires* because they caused the company to enter into the transaction. See *Chambers v Manchester and Milford Rly Co* (1864) 5 B. & S. 588; 122 E.R. 951; *Yorkshire Railway Wagon Co v Maclure; Garrard v James* [1925] Ch. 616. These cases appear to be based on the view that the directors had agreed to be liable whether or not the principal debtor was liable. Sections 108, 109 and 111 of the Companies Act 1989 have abolished the doctrine of *ultra vires* so far as third parties are concerned but directors may be still liable to the company for any loss arising out of *ultra vires* acts: G. Andrews and R. Millett, *Law of Guarantees* (3rd ed., 2000), para.6.21.

[4] See *Hyundai Shipbuilding and Heavy Industries Co Ltd v Pournaras* [1978] 2 Lloyd's Rep. 502 at 508; *BOC Group PLC v Centeon LLC* [1999] 1 All E.R. (Comm) 53.

[5] (1872) L.R. 7 C.P. 372.

[6] *ibid.*, at 377; *Bowyear v Pawson* (1881) 6 Q.B.D. 540. See also *Oastler v Pound* (1863) 7 L.T. 852; *National Westminster Bank plc v Skelton* [1993] 1 All E.R. 242 at 250–251 (where the court assumed that the principal debtor was entitled to a claim for unliquidated damages by way of set-off against the plaintiff bank). The courts appear to take a different view in Australia: see below, para.11–63. Moreover, it is recognised even in England that the guarantor's claim to rely upon an equitable set-off available to the principal debtor is no obstacle to a legal mortgagee in an action for possession against a third-party mortgagor who has given a mortgage to secure repayment of the principal debt: *Ashley Guarantee plc v Zacaria* [1993] 1 All E.R. 254.

[7] *Ex p. Hanson* (1806) 12 Ves. Jun. 346; 34 E.R. 131.

[8] The guarantor must plea the set-off in his defence or counterclaim: *Commonwealth of Australia v Hallett* (unreported, SA Sup Ct, Burley J, January 16, 1995).

[9] It may be that English courts take a different view: see *Hyundai Shipbuilding & Heavy Industries Co Ltd v Pouranaras* [1978] 2 Lloyd's Rep. 502, where the Court of Appeal expressly accepted the correctness of the passage in Halsbury's Laws of England (4th ed), vol 20, para.190. See also *5K Construction Ltd (in receivership and liquidation) v Thakker* (unreported, Queen's Bench Division, Official Referees' Business, Judge Esyr Lewis Q.C., July 19, 1996).

common law and in equity, then these counterclaims and set-offs will be available to the guarantor.[10]

Thus, clauses providing that amounts are to be paid "without any **11–49** deduction" have been held to be insufficient to exclude an equitable set-off.[11] Similarly, more general provisions stating that the guarantor's obligations are to be unaffected "by any matter whatsoever" are unlikely to preclude the guarantor relying on the principal debtor's set-off.[12] A clause in a guarantee deeming the guarantor to be a "principal debtor in all respects" is also thought to be ineffective for this purpose. Indeed, a "principal debtor clause" would appear to reinforce the guarantor's claim to rely on the principal's set-off because it requires the guarantor to be treated *as if he were the principal debtor*.[13] Even if there is a specific provision in the guarantee purporting to exclude a right of set-off, a failure to distinguish between the different types of set-off (for example, legal as distinct from equitable) might lead to a restrictive interpretation that excludes some set-offs but not others.

From the creditor's point of view there is a more fundamental concern. **11–50** Even if the drafting is sufficiently wide to exclude the right of set-off, such clauses may in particular circumstances be held to be unreasonable pursuant to the Unfair Contract Terms Act 1977, where one party to a contract is dealing with the other on the basis of the other party's standard terms and conditions. Clauses excluding the right of set-off may fall within s.13(1)(b) of the Act as terms "excluding or restricting any right or remedy in respect of the liability".[14] If so, they will be ineffective unless they satisfy the requirement of reasonableness. This issue depends on a wide variety of factors set out in judicial decisions and Schedule 2 to the Act. It is significant, however, that in *Stewart Gill Ltd v Horatio Myer & Co Ltd*[15] Donaldson L.J. considered that "nothing could *prima facie* be more unreasonable" than the exclusion of a right of set-off when it arose from a credit or over-payment under another contract. All the decided cases under the Act have involved clauses excluding set-off in the principal transaction, but a similar analysis is applicable where the guarantee itself excludes the guarantor's right to rely on the principal debtor's set-off.

It appears, therefore, that a guarantor's right to invoke a set-off held by **11–51** the principal debtor as against the creditor may not be effectively excluded

---

[10] *Gilbert-Ash (Northern) Ltd v Modern Engineers (Bristol) Ltd* [1974] A.C. 689 at 709.
[11] *Connaught Restaurants Ltd v Indoor Leisure Ltd* [1994] 1 W.L.R. 501 (although the Court of Appeal did state that the context in which the words "without deduction" appeared could justify a contrary conclusion). Indeed, the Australian cases suggest that the issue of whether a guarantor may rely on a set-off which would have been open to the principal debtor depends, at least in part, on the terms of the guarantee. If the guarantor's obligation is not to pay the contract price without deduction but only to pay what the principal debtor could have been compelled to pay, the guarantor would be entitled to invoke an equitable set-off available to the principal debtor: *Beri Distributors Pty Ltd v Pulitano* (1994) 10 S.R. (WA) 274; *Langford Concrete Pty Ltd v Finlay* [1978] 1 N.S.W.L.R. 14.
[12] *BOC Group Plc v Centeon LLC* [1999] 1 All E.R. (Comm) 970.
[13] Contrast, however, Slade J. in *National Westminster Bank v Skelton* [1993] 1 W.L.R. 72 at 80 (although it was not a standard "principal debtor" clause in that case).
[14] The statutory guidelines are examined above, paras 4–160 to 4–176. See above, especially para.4–162 as to whether or not the Act applies to this type of clause.
[15] [1992] 1 Q.B. 600 at 606.

in some cases either because of imprecise drafting or because the clause as a matter of law is invalid.[16]

11–52   The guarantor's right to invoke any right of set off or counterclaim available to the principal debtor may, however, be excluded by the court's interpretation of the contract in its factual matrix. In determining whether the guarantor is liable to pay the creditor regardless of the rights of the creditor and the principal debtor *inter se*, the court can take a variety of factors into account: the inclusion in the guarantee of a conditional agreement to pay; the accruing of the guarantor's liability to pay before the principal debtor had any arguable right of set-off (where, for example, the default in question preceded the termination of the principal contract); the guarantor's obligation to pay "forthwith"; and the overall factual matrix of the contractual arrangements.[17]

11–53   A number of different situations need to be distinguished, although a common feature is that the principal debtor must be in a position to take advantage of the cross-claim or defence.

(a) Where the principal debt is directly reduced or extinguished

11–54   In *Cellulose Products Pty Ltd v Truda*[18] Isaacs J. expressed "the general rule" as follows:

> "the surety when sued can always show that the amount of the debt for which he is sued has been in fact reduced by the principal debtor, either by a direct payment or by receipt of moneys by the creditor on the debtor's account and for which the debtor is entitled to be credited."[19]

11–55   In a similar vein, in *Sun Alliance Pensions Life & Investments Services Ltd v RJL and Anthony Webster*[20] the court held that a guarantor can rely on a set-off available to the principal debtor as long as it arose out of the same transactions as the principal debt and was a claim for an amount which would reduce or extinguish the principal debt.

11–56   Thus payments to the creditor which must be appropriated or are appropriated to the principal debt will automatically reduce the guarantor's liability,[21] without the need to join the principal debtor as party to the proceedings.[22]

---

[16] Note, however, that a right of set-off arising within bankruptcy or winding up cannot be excluded: *National Westminster Bank Ltd v Halesowen Presswork & Assemblies Ltd* [1972] A.C. 785.

[17] See *BOC Group Plc v Centeon LLC* [1999] 1 All E.R. (Comm) 53. See also *National Westminster Bank Plc v Skelton* [1993] 1 W.L.R. 72, where the court held that in an action for possession a third party mortgagor was not entitled to invoke any right of cross-claim or set-off which the principal debtor company had against the mortgagee.

[18] (1970) 92 W.N. (NSW) 561.

[19] *ibid.*, at 586.

[20] [1991] 2 Lloyd's Rep. 410.

[21] As to the appropriation of payments, see above, paras 6–16 *et. seq.*

[22] See *Cellulose Products Pty Ltd v Truda* (1970) 92 W.N. (NSW) 561 at 588, where Isaacs J. indicated that, where the debt guaranteed is directly reduced, the principal debtor need not be

In determining whether a guarantor can rely on cross-claims and **11–57** defences which the principal debtor has against the creditor, it is convenient to deal separately with unliquidated and liquidated claims, not least because (in broad terms) different types of set-off apply to these claims.

(b) Where the principal debtor's claim against the creditor is for unliquidated damages

There is a threshold question here: does the principal's claim amount to **11–58** a defence in a strict sense, as distinct from a counter claim? If the principal debtor does not have a defence, the general principle of co-extensiveness will prevent the guarantor from resisting an application by the creditor for summary judgment. There are, however, two cross claims, in the nature of a defence, available to a guarantor: abatement and equitable set-off.

Under the doctrine of abatement a sum can be deducted from the **11–59** contract price in a contract for the sale of goods or a contract for work and labour in order to represent a diminution of the value of the goods or services arising directly from a breach of the contract.[23]

This principle has, of course, been enshrined in statute in relation to **11–60** contracts for the sale of goods.[24] Although it arises from an unliquidated claim for damages, abatement operates as a true defence[25] and it can, therefore, relieve a guarantor.

Illustrations of the abatement principle are where there is an agreement **11–61** between the principal and the creditor to reduce the contract price[26] or, in the context of a guarantee of the purchase price for the sale of goods, where the vendor fails to deliver a quantity of the goods as required by the contract.[27] The indebtedness of the principal towards the creditor is directly reduced in these circumstances because of the application of the formula laid down in the Sale of Goods Act[28] whereby the buyer, if he accepts the reduced quantity of goods, must pay for them at the contract price.[29]

Reliance by the guarantor on the fact that the principal debt has been **11–62** reduced or extinguished is an aspect of the total or partial discharge or the guarantor by payment, as described above, in Chapter 6.

---

joined. But, as is the case of equitable set-off, it is arguable that the principal should be joined where there is an issue as to the precise extent of the payments made.

[23] *Mondel v Steel* (1841) 8 M. & W. 858; 151 E.R. 1288; *Aries Tanker Corp v Total Transport Ltd* [1977] 1 W.L.R. 185 at 190; *Mellowes Archital Ltd v Bell Properties Ltd* (1977) 87 B.L.R. 26. See generally *Halsbury's Laws of England* 4th ed. re-issue (1999), Vol. 42, para. 411.

[24] Sale of Goods Act 1979, s.53(1).

[25] See generally *Halsbury's Laws of England* 4th ed. re-issue (1999), Vol. 42, para.411 and *Henrikens Rederi A/S v PHZ Rolimpex (The Brede)* [1974] Q.B. 233.

[26] *Cellulose Products Pty Ltd v Truda* (1970) 92 W.N. (NSW) 561 at 582.

[27] *ibid.*, at 565 and 582.

[28] Sale of Goods Act 1979, s.53(1).

[29] See also *Allen v Kemble* (1848) 6 Moore 314; 13 E.R. 704, where the guarantor was entitled to rely on the fact that, by the law of another jurisdiction which governed the contract, the principal debt was extinguished.

11–63   In *Cellulose Products Pty Ltd v Truda*,[30] however, Isaacs J. held that a *breach of warranty* affecting the value of the goods purchased does not have the effect of directly reducing or extinguishing the price. Rather the buyer has the option of suing the seller for the damages caused by the breach of warranty or waiting until he is sued for the contract price and then setting up the breach of warranty in diminution or extinction of the price. This is a personal option of the buyer and it cannot be exercised by his guarantors. Accordingly, the guarantors cannot argue that their liability has been reduced or extinguished by the damages arising from a breach of warranty by the vendor.

11–64   While abatement is limited in its operation to contracts for the sale of goods and contracts for work and labour, equitable set-off operates more broadly. The scope of equitable set-off is, however, rather imprecise, both in its judicial definition and its application to particular factual circumstances. In *Esso Petroleum Co Ltd v Milton*[31] Simon Brown L.J. stated two essential conditions for the existence of an equitable set-off:

> "First, that the counterclaim is at least closely connected with the same transaction as that giving rise to the claim; and second, that the relationship between the respective claims is such that it would be manifestly unjust to allow one to be enforced without regard to the other."[32]

This test does not entirely accord with the view of the House of Lords in *Bank of Boston Connecticut v European Grain & Shipping Ltd (The Dominique)*[33] where Lord Brandon of Oakbrook stated that an equitable set-off will arise if there is a cross claim "flowing out of and *inseparably connected* with the dealings and transactions which also give rise to the claim."[34] This is a more stringent formulation than the first limb of the test propounded by Simon Brown L.J., but, conversely, there is no reference to the second limb.

11–65   Judicial decisions about equitable set-off are difficult to reconcile. For example, in *Esso Petroleum Co Ltd v Milton*[35] itself the Court of Appeal refused to allow a petrol station operator to set off a claim for unliquidated damages for future losses arising from an alleged repudiatory breach of a petrol licence agreement by Esso against a claim by Esso for a specific delivery of petrol. Yet in *Dole Dried Fruit & Nut Co v Trustin Kerwood Ltd*[36] the defendant, who was the plaintiff's distribution agent in the United Kingdom, was held entitled to set off a claim for damages for a repudiatory breach of the agency agreement against a claim for the price of goods sold and delivered under a *separate* sale contract (albeit, one

---

[30] (1970) 90 W.N. (NSW) 561 at 570.
[31] [1997] 1 W.L.R. 938.
[32] *ibid.*, at 950.
[33] [1989] A.C. 1056.
[34] *ibid.*, at 1103 (emphasis added).
[35] 1997] 1 W.L.R. 938.
[36] [1990] 2 Lloyd's Rep. 309. See also *Federal Commerce Ltd v Molena Alpha Inc (The Nanfri)* [1978] Q.B. 927.

concluded in fulfillment of the agency agreement).[37] And, ironically, in *Dole Dried Fruit & Nut v Trustin Kerwood*[38] the Court of Appeal applied Lord Brandon's narrower formulation. There is a lack of coherence in the law relating to equitable set-off; or, perhaps, to put in the more charitable words of Slade L.J. in *National Westminster Bank v Skelton*,[39] "it appears that in deciding whether or not to allow a set-off the court will be much influenced by what it regards as the essential requirements of justice".[40]

The determination of the precise ambit of equitable set-off awaits **11–66** judicial resolution but, in the writers' view, the guarantor should be permitted to plead, not only an abatement, but also an equitable set-off possessed by the debtor as against the creditor. The very definition of equitable set-off means, even in its widest formulation, that it must be "closely connected" with the principal debt which is guaranteed. A creditor can have no reasonable objection to the guarantor relying on a set-off when this connection subsists, since it relates directly to the guaranteed debt and not to other debts owed by the debtor to that creditor. This is especially so since equitable set-off is now established as a true defence. Although the principal debt is not directly reduced, in equity, even prior to judgment, the existence of an equitable set-off means that the creditor cannot treat the debtor as being indebted to him to the extent of the set-off.[41]

The present authorities, however, give no firm guidance as to whether **11–67** the guarantor can plead the principal's abatement or equitable set-off when sued by the creditor in summary proceedings. There are two diverging views. In the first, Slade J., in *National Westminster Bank Plc v Skelton*[42] stated that the reasoning in the Australian case *Cellulose Products Pty Ltd v Truda*[43] was "impressive". In that decision Isaacs, J., held that, where a solvent principal debtor's claim against the creditor is for unliquidated damages in respect of the guaranteed transaction, the guarantor cannot plead the claim as a defence to an action on the guarantee, but must bring third party proceedings against the debtor claiming an indemnity. Thus, the guarantor of a purchaser's obligations under a contract for the sale of goods was not permitted to take advantage of a claim that the purchaser possessed against the creditor arising from a breach of the Sale of Goods Act 1923 (NSW), s.54(1).[44] In such

---

[37] In *Esso Petroleum v Milton* [1997] 1 WLR 938 at 951, Simon Brown L.J. stated that "[no] case as been cited to us in which payment of a debt presently due has been required to await the resolution of a cross claim for future losses". But in *Dole Dried Fruit and Nut v Trustin Kerwood Ltd* [1990] 2 Lloyd's Rep. 309, although it was not expressly stated, the claim for wrongful termination of the agency agreement must inevitably have involved a claim for future losses arising from that repudiation.
[38] [1990] 2 Lloyd's Rep. 309.
[39] [1993] 1 W.L.R. 72.
[40] *ibid.*, at 76. The guarantors of the mortgage debt will be entitled to an equitable set-off in respect of the value of the mortgagor's chattels and equipment which were lost while the mortgagee was in possession of the premises: *National Australia Bank Ltd v Jenkins* (unreported, Sup Ct, Vic., May 15, 1998).
[41] See S.R. Derham, *Set-off* (3rd ed., 2003), paras 4–29 to 4–30.
[42] [1993] 1 W.L.R. 72.
[43] (1970) 92 W.N. (NSW) 561. See also *Indrisie v General Credits Ltd* [1985] V.R. 251; *Covino v Bandag Manufacturing Pty Ltd* [1983] 1 N.S.W.L.R. 237 at 240–241.
[44] The equivalent of the Sale of Goods Act 1979, s.53(1).

circumstances the only procedure open to the guarantor, when sued by the creditor, is to join the debtor as a third party and claim an indemnity from the debtor. The debtor in turn has a right to join the plaintiff creditor as a fourth party, claiming damages for breach of warranty or otherwise, with all claims being heard and determined together.

11–68   The disadvantage of this procedure from the guarantor's point of view, however, is that it is cumbersome, especially in the context of resisting an application for summary judgment, and the guarantor is to some extent dependent on the eagerness of the principal debtor to prosecute the claim. It will also have adverse consequences in respect of costs.[45]

11–69   More recently, however, in *BOC Group Ltd v Centeon*[46] Rix J. gave an alternative view in the context of an application for summary judgment (and, indeed, without reference to *National Westminster Bank v Skelton*),[47] stating that, if the principal has an arguable set-off, then "it seems to me that the guarantor is entitled to rely on the alleged set-off as well".[48] For the reasons given earlier, the position adopted by Rix J. is to be preferred. Indeed, the authority of *Cellulose Products Ltd v Truda* is now somewhat diminished because at least one subsequent Australian authority appears to have taken a contrary view. In *Doherty v Murphy*[49] the Court of Appeal of the Supreme Court of Victoria permitted the guarantor to rely on an equitable set-off as a defence to the creditor's summary judgment application.

11–70   Moreover, the guarantor should be allowed to resist an application for summary judgment on the basis of this defence without joining the principal as a party to the proceedings at all.[50] It should be sufficient that the principal is joined before the ultimate determination of the validity of the claim, so that the principal is bound by the final orders. In the case of the guarantor showing an arguable defence to the application for summary judgment, leave to defend should only be granted on the condition that the guarantor join the principal as a party to the proceedings. The principal could be joined as a co-defendant on the ground that the relief sought requires the principal to be bound by the final orders.[51]

11–71   There may be an objection to the guarantor pleading the principal's claim as a defence in summary proceedings on the basis that the principal's

---

[45] See J. Phillips, "When Should the Guarantor be Permitted to Rely on the Principal's Set-Off?" [2001] L.M.C.L.Q. 382 at 387. See also Insolvency Act 1986, ss.130(2) and 285.
[46] [1999] 1 All E.R. (Comm) 53; aff'd *ibid.*, 970, CA. See also *Sun Alliance Pensions Life & Investment Service v RJL* [1991] 2 Lloyd's Rep. 410 at 417, where it appears to be contemplated (despite reliance on *Cellulose Products v Truda* (1970) 92 W.N. (NSW) 561) that an equitable set-off could be pleaded as a defence to a summary judgment application provided that the principal debtor has been joined as a party.
[47] [1993] 1 W.L.R. 72.
[48] [1999] 1 All E.R. (Comm) 53 at 67.
[49] [1996] 2 V.R. 535.
[50] *Tooth & Co Ltd v Rosier* (unreported, NSW Sup Ct, June 7, 1985) appears to support such an approach, although the principal debtor was insolvent in that case. *Cf. Sun Alliance Pensions Life & Investment Service v RJL* [1991] 2 Lloyd's Rep. 410.
[51] As suggested in S.R. Derham, *Set-off* (3rd ed., 2003), para.18–23, n.82, relying on *Amon v Raphael Tuck & Sons Ltd* [1956] 1 Q.B. 357 at 386.

right of election to claim unliquidated damages is negated.[52] But it is thought that this factor is outweighed by the prejudice to the guarantor that would otherwise occur.

This view draws support for the general principle that equitable set-off, **11–72** although not operating in reduction or extinction of the debt at law, does have a substantive effect.[53] As Derham has commented:

"But as far as equity is concerned, it is unconscionable for the creditor even before judgment to regard the debtor as a debtor to the extent of debtor's cross-demand, or to treat the debtor as having defaulted in payment to that extent, if circumstances exist which support an equitable set-off. In this sense, it operates in equity as a complete or a partial defeasance of the plaintiff's claim. A court of equity can protect the debtor's position by means of an injunction, and the debtor's right may be the subject of a declaration. This explains how equitable set-off can operate substantively without working an automatic discharge."[54]

Indeed, in this respect, the argument for allowing the guarantor to plead an equitable set-off as a defence is more compelling than a legal set-off which has only a procedural effect.[55]

Where the principal debtor is bankrupt or in liquidation, it has been **11–73** held[56] that the guarantor can plead a cross-claim for unliquidated damages without joining the principal debtor as a party to the proceedings at any stage, so that there may be a final determination of the claim without the principal debtor bring joined at all. The reasoning given is that the creditor is not prejudiced where the principal is insolvent because there is no risk of the subsequent action being taken against the creditor by the principal on the same claim, which is the primary reason for joinder.[57] But this reasoning is fallacious because there are circumstances[58] in which the trustee in bankruptcy or the liquidator of the principal debtor may pursue the claim against the creditor. The procedure suggested in the case of a solvent principal debtor should also be adopted in the context of insolvency; that is, the principal debtor should be joined before there is a final determination of the issues between the parties.

There is another and, from the guarantor's point of view, disturbing **11–74** circumstance when it has been clearly established that the guarantor

---

[52] This is one of the general objections used to deny the guarantor this right: see *Cellulose Products Pty Ltd v Truda* (1970) 92 W.N. (NSW) 561 at 575. See also *Indrisie v General Credits Ltd* [1985] V.R. 251 at 254; *Wilson v Mitchell* [1939] 2 K.B. 869 at 871.

[53] S.R. Derham, *Set-off* (3rd ed., 2003), para.4–29.

[54] *ibid.*, at para.4–30.

[55] *ibid.*, at paras 2–33 to 2–48.

[56] *Langford Concrete Pty Ltd v Finlay* [1978] 1 N.S.W.L.R. 14; *Western Motors (Distributors) Ltd v Palmer* [1979] 2 N.S.W.L.R. 93 at 97. *Cf.*, however, *Sun Alliance Pensions Life & Investments Services Ltd v R.J.L.* [1991] 2 Lloyd's Rep. 410 at 418 (where on the facts the principal was in voluntary liquidation).

[57] *ibid.*

[58] Where the principal debtor's cross-claim against the creditor is greater than the principal debt, the debtor's trustee in bankruptcy or liquidation may institute proceedings against the creditor, to recover the surplus, after taking into account the statutory right of set-off available.

cannot rely on a set-off. If the guarantor, as is commonly the case, has given additional security to the creditor in the form of a mortgage, it has been held that the guarantor/mortgagor cannot resist a claim for possession by relying on an equitable set-off.[59] This is so even if the extent of the cross-claim, upon which the equitable set-off is based, exceeds the amount of the mortgage debt.[60] In *National Westminster Bank v Skelton*[61] Slade L.J. justified the principle in this way:

> "The principle in my view has much to commend it, since it could lead to abuse if a mortgagee were to be kept out of his undoubted *prima facie* right to possession by allegations of some connected cross claims which might prove wholly without foundation."[62]

But this reasoning ignores the interests of the guarantor in the case of an arguable substantive claim. It is simply arbitrary to deny a right of set-off to a guarantor who gives additional security when the claim of the creditor is in substance for the recovery of the amount of the debt. Recovery of possession of the mortgaged property is in reality a procedural step in the creditor's ultimate objective of recovering what is owed to him by selling the property after taking possession. The present rule, justified on the basis of a separate cause of action for possession, is neither just nor in accordance with commercial reality.

(c) Where the principal debtor's claim against the creditor is for a liquidated amount

11–75   If a liquidated amount has been paid by the principal to the creditor and appropriated to the guaranteed debt, the amount of the guaranteed debt will be directly reduced. The guarantor's liability is then correspondingly reduced and no issue of set-off arises.[63] Indeed, there are some circumstances where the creditor must appropriate payments to the guaranteed debt, for example, in respect of the proceeds of a security given by the principal in respect of the guaranteed debt.[64]

11–76   But guarantors are not usually so fortunate. Far more commonly, of course, the principal merely has a claim for a liquidated amount against the creditor. Such a claim may give rise to a legal set-off originally conferred by the Statutes of Set-Off[65] in the early 18th Century, with the policy objective of preventing the imprisonment of a debtor when there was a

---

[59] *National Westminster Bank v Skelton* [1973] 1 W.L.R. 72; *Ashley Guarantee Co v Zacaria* [1993] 1 W.L.R. 62.
[60] *National Westminister Bank v Skelton* [1993] 1 W.L.R. 72, 78.
[61] [1993] 1 W.L.R. 72.
[62] *ibid.*, at 78.
[63] See, generally, J. O'Donovan and J. Phillips, *The Modern Contract of Guarantee* (3rd Aust. ed., 1996), pp.277–280.
[64] *Pearl v. Deacon* (1857) 24 Beav. 186; 53 E.R. 328. And see generally O'Donovan & Phillips *The Modern Contract of Guarantee* (3rd Aust. ed., 1996), pp.286–299.
[65] 2 Geo. 2 c.22 (Insolvent Debtors Relief) (1728) and 8 Geo. 2 c.24 (Set-off) (1734).

mutual debt owed by the creditor.[66] The Statutes of Set-Off are now repealed[67] but their effect has been legislatively preserved.[68]

Legal set-off applies to mutual debts so that there can be no legal set-off **11–77** against a claim for unliquidated damages; but, significantly in the context of this debate, the mutual debts may arise from transactions of a *different nature*.[69] Thus, the debtor may set off a claim for the price by the creditor in respect of a contract for the supply of materials with a credit claimed by him on an entirely different contract for the supply of materials.

The issue therefore arises as to whether or not the guarantor should be **11–78** permitted to rely on the principal's legal set-off as a defence to summary proceedings, where the legal set-off arises in this way, not from the guaranteed debt, but from an independent transaction. It is submitted that the argument for permitting such a defence is much weaker than in the context of equitable set-off. Leaving aside general criticisms of the nature of legal set-off to the effect that it operates to the detriment of other creditors of the debtor,[70] as a matter of policy it is unreasonable for the guarantor to be able to reduce his liability by reason of a debt, owed by the creditor to the debtor, which may be quite unrelated to the guaranteed transaction. As indicated, the original policy of the Statutes of Set-Off was to prevent imprisonment of the debtor; it was not to defeat the legitimate expectations of the creditor as against a separate debtor (the guarantor) who did not face this threat.

Moreover, in the case of the principal's legal set-off there are more **11–79** technical reasons which tend to suggest that the guarantor should not be allowed to rely on it. Unlike an equitable set-off, a legal set-off constitutes a procedural rather than a substantive defence.[71] This means that the creditor's claim to the principal debt is neither reduced not extinguished by the debtor's cross claim until judgment. Additionally, a legal set-off requires mutuality so that the cross-claim must arise between the same parties and in the same capacity. Here there is no mutuality in this sense, since the guarantor has no cross-claim in his own right, but is relying on the cross-claim of the principal.[72]

There may, of course, be cases in which the debtor's claim for a **11–80** liquidated amount is closely related to the debt guaranteed. In such a case there is no objection to the guarantor relying on the principal's set-off, provided that it is "closely connected with the same transaction as that giving rise to the [creditor's] claim"; that is, provided that it amounts to an equitable set-off (which can apply where both claims are liquidated).[73]

---

[66] *Halsbury*, para.420.
[67] Civil Procedure Acts Repeal Act 1879; Statute Law Revision and Civil Procedure Act 1883.
[68] Supreme Court Act 1981, ss.49(2), 84(2); and see Civil Procedure Rules rr.16.6 and 20.
[69] See, generally, *Halsbury's Laws of England* (4th ed., re-issued 1999), Vol. 42, para.421.
[70] Derham, "*Set-off*" (3rd ed., 2003), paras 5–139 to 5–153 and 6–11 to 6–12.
[71] *ibid.*, at paras 2–33 to 2–48.
[72] It may be argued, however, that this is not the issue. Rather, assuming mutuality between principal debtor and creditor, it is whether or not there is a special equitable principle that permits the guarantor to take advantage of this claim in his own right.
[73] Derham, "*Set-Off*" (3rd ed., 2003), para.4–08.

11–81   What then of judicial authority? There are cases of some antiquity, *Bechervaise v Lewis*[74] and *Murphy v Glass*,[75] which give some support to the proposition that the guarantor can plead a legal set-off which the principal has against the creditor even when the principal is not joined as a party to the proceedings. Yet both of these cases can be explained on the basis that they are simply illustrations of the principal debt being directly reduced or extinguished by the receipt of monies by the creditor for which the debtor is entitled to be credited. In *Bechervaise v Lewis*, the creditor, who was obliged to collect the debts guaranteed (pursuant to an arrangement between creditor and debtor), had in fact collected some of the debts, but failed to give the debtor credit for them. And in *Murphy v Glass* the debt, which was the purchase price of a farming property, could be regarded as being reduced by a final conclusive award of an arbitrator who had adjudicated on a dispute as to the acreage sold.

11–82   It is true that there is more modern authority, albeit dicta, reiterating the view that the guarantor may rely on the principal's legal set-off, with reliance being placed on statements from *Halsbury's Laws of England*. Thus, in *Hyundai Shipbuilding & Heavy Industries v Pournaras*[76] the Court of Appeal appeared to approve this passage from *Halsbury*'s fourth edition:[77]

> "On being sued by the creditor of the debt guaranteed, a surety may avail himself of any right to set-off or counterclaim which the principal debtor possesses against the creditor."

Yet *Halsbury* itself is far from conclusive with different editions citing the same authorities for somewhat different positions. The subsequent 1993 re-issue of the same edition adopts a different formulation:[78]

> "...a surety may avail himself of any set-off or counterclaim which the principal debtor could set up against the creditor in reduction of the guaranteed debt."

This is a much narrower view and, indeed, on one interpretation would even deny the right of the guarantor to rely on the principal's equitable set-off, since the effect of an equitable set-off is not to reduce the debt itself.

11–83   The most recent analysis by *Halsbury* does not avoid the confusion. In fact it reinforces uncertainty by providing two contrasting positions in different paragraphs. The relevant paragraphs state:

---

[74] (1872) L.R. 7 C.P. 372.
[75] (1869) L.R. 2 P.C. 408.
[76] [1978] 2 Lloyd's Rep. 502 at 508.
[77] 4th ed. (1978), para.190.
[78] Vol. 20, para.25. See also *Rowlatt on the Law of Principal & Surety*: (5th ed., 1999), para.4–91, where, it is stated: "Where the principal is entitled to a set-off against the creditor's demand arising out of the same transaction as the debt guaranteed, and in fact reducing that debt, the surety is entitled to plead it in an action by the creditor against the surety alone". This passage was quoted with approval in *National Westminster Bank v Skelton* [1973] 1 W.L.R. 72 at 79.

"422. It has been held that a guarantor can avail himself of any right of set-off held by the debtor against the creditor . . .

476. Claim against surety by third person. A surety for payment of a sum due under a contract is entitled to be exonerated by his principal, and in an action against himself as surety may therefore set off a debt due from the plaintiff to the principal arising out of the same transaction."

Paragraph 422 embraces both legal and equitable set-off, whilst para.476, in referring to a claim "arising out of the same transaction", appears to limit the guarantor's right to equitable set-offs.

11–84 Judicial pronouncements based on these inconsistent sources must be regarded as less than authoritative. Indeed, nowhere in the cases is there any real analysis of policy or, in particular, a careful consideration of whether or not a guarantor's claim to rely on a legal set-off available to the principal debtor should be treated differently from a guarantor's claim to rely on an equitable set-off available to the principal debtor.

11–85 Against this uncertain background, in the authors' view, the rights of a guarantor to be exonerated by relying on a cross claim or defence available to the principal debtor as against the creditor are as follows:

(a) The guarantor should be permitted to rely on the principal's claim as against the creditor when it amounts to an abatement or equitable set-off, since in such a case the claim will be 'closely connected' with the guaranteed debt. The claim may be for either a liquidated or unliquidated amount.

(b) The guarantor should not be able to rely on a legal set-off held by the principal as against the creditor, where the claim arises out of a transaction not closely connected to the guaranteed debt.

(c) In the case of a guarantee secured by a mortgage, the guarantor should not be denied the right to rely on the principal's set-off simply because the cause of action against the guarantor is for possession of the mortgaged property.

(d) A guarantor's liability may be reduced or extinguished by the application of the insolvency set-off provisions as a result of mutual dealings between the creditor and the principal debtor.

11–86 Rule 4.90 of the Insolvency Rules provides for the mutual credit and set-off of claims in both the bankruptcy of individuals and the liquidation, but not the administration, of companies. Under this rule, a set-off is deemed to have occurred at the date of the bankruptcy or liquidation (the relevant date) if the following conditions are satisfied:

1. Where, before the relevant date, there have been mutual credits, mutual debts or other mutual dealings between the debtor and any of its creditors proving or claiming to prove in the bankruptcy or liquidation.

2. An account shall be taken of what is due to the other in respect of mutual dealings and the sums due from one party shall be set off against the sums due from the other.

3. Only the balance of the account is provable in the bankruptcy or liquidation. Alternatively, any balance owing by the creditor shall be paid to the trustee in bankruptcy or liquidator as part of the debtor's assests.

11–87   Where the principal debtor is insolvent or in liquidation, the technical legal argument for permitting the guarantor to rely on the principal's set-off is much stronger because the principal debt is extinguished to the extent of the set-off.[79] The extinction takes place automatically on the date of bankruptcy or liquidation. Since the principal debt is then itself reduced, it follows that there should be a corresponding reduction in the guarantor's liability. Again, it is considered that this operates unfairly upon the creditor. The creditor has taken a security for a specific transaction, only to be deprived of it because of events quite unconnected to that transaction.

11–88   The terms of the guarantee may preclude the guarantor taking advantage of a cross-claim by the principal whether or not the principal is joined as a party to the guarantee.[80] This may be achieved by a specific clause, expressly stating that the guarantor shall not be entitled to invoke any cross-claim or set-off available to the principal, or by more general wording indicating that the guarantor has agreed to pay the principal debt without deduction.[81] In determining this question, regard may be had to the factual and commercial background of the transaction.[82] On this basis, parties who guaranteed "the payment of any monies advanced by way of credit" to a company were not entitled to rely upon an equitable set-off based on the company's claim that the goods supplied by the plaintiff were defective: the guarantors' liability was not limited to such amount as may become due and payable to the plaintiff for goods supplied.[83]

---

[79] *Stein v Blake* [1996] A.C. 243.

[80] *Beri Distributors Pty Ltd v Pulitano* (1994) 10 S.R. (WA) 274 at 276.

[81] *The "Fedora"* [1986] 2 Lloyd's Rep. 441; *Coca Cola Financial Corporation v Finsat International Ltd* [1998] Q.B. 43; *Covino v Bandag Manufacturing Pty Ltd* [1983] 1 N.S.W.L.R. 237; *Western Motors (Distributors) Pty Ltd v Palmer* [1979] 2 N.S.W.L.R. 93 at 99; *Beri Distributors Pty Ltd v Pulitano* (1994) 10 S.R. (WA) 274; *Langford Concrete Pty Ltd v Finlay* [1978] 1 N.S.W.L.R. 14 at 17; *Hyundai Shipbuilding & Heavy Industries v Pournaras* [1978] 2 Lloyd's Rep. 502; *ANZ Banking Group Ltd v Harvey* [1994] A.T.P.R. (Digest) 53,640; *Elkhoury v Farrow Mortgage Services Pty Ltd* (1993) 114 A.L.R. 541 at 549 (where the guarantor's claim to an equitable set-off was excluded by a general clause preserving the guarantor's liability notwithstanding any acts or omissions of the creditor); *P H Grace Pty Ltd v AEIBC* [1987] 1 M.L.J. 437. Cf. *Tooth & Co Ltd v Rosier* (unreported, NSW Sup Ct, June 7, 1985). See also above, paras 4–160 to 4–162 as to the potential application of the Unfair Contract Terms Act 1977 and the Unfair Terms in Consumer Contracts Regulations 1999 and G. Andrews and R. Millett, *Law of Guarantees* (3rd ed., 2000), para.7.28.

[82] *Hyundai Shipbuilding & Heavy Industries v Pournaras* [1978] 2 Lloyd's Rep. 502.

[83] *Beri Distributors Pty Ltd v Pulitano* (1994) 10 S.R. (NSW) 274. Cf. *Trafalgar House Construction (Region) Ltd v General Surety and Guarantee Co Ltd* [1995] 3 All E.R. 737.

(d) Where the principal has a legal set-off or a set-off in bankruptcy or liquidation against the creditor

Bechervaise v Lewis[84] and *Murphy v Glass*[85] give some support to the **11–89** proposition that the guarantor can plead a legal set-off which the principal has against the creditor pursuant to the *Statutes of Set-off*,[86] even when the principal is not joined as a party to the proceedings.

It would appear that where the basic requirements of the statutory right **11–90** of set-off are satisfied and none of the exceptions apply, the guarantor would have a valid defence to an action on the guarantee if the creditor failed to set off the creditor's mutual debts in its dealings with the debtor. In *National Mutual Royal Bank Ltd v Ginges*,[87] Brownie J. rejected a submission by the plaintiff that the guarantee on its proper construction did not require that the two accounts be set off. Relying on *Gye v McIntyre*[88] to support his conclusion, his Honour held that the mutual dealings provisions are self-executing, prevailing over any agreement of the parties to the contrary. Similarly, in *Tooth & Co Ltd v Rosier*[89] Wood J. held that a guarantor was entitled to resist an application by a creditor for summary judgment on the ground that the guarantor might be entitled to invoke the principal debtor's statutory right.[90] It has been argued[91] that this result is supported by the fact that the right of set-off is analogous to a security to which the surety is entitled on paying the principal debt.

It appears, therefore, that guarantors can rely upon the principal **11–91** debtor's right of statutory set off to reduce or extinguish their liability under their guarantees.[92] This is so even if the guarantors' liability crystallises before the principal debtor acquires its right of statutory set off against the creditor.[93] But the terms of the guarantee can prevent the guarantors from taking advantage of the principal debtor's statutory set off.[94]

On the other hand, as with legal set-offs, it is difficult to see how the **11–92** guarantor can argue that the principal debtor's cross-claim against the creditor is a mutual credit, a mutual debt or other mutual dealing between

---

[84] (1872) L.R. 7 C.P. 372, especially at 377, and see above, paras 11–46 and 11–81.
[85] (1869) L.R. 2 P.C. 408. See also *Alcoy & Gandia Railway & Harbour Co Ltd v Greenhill* (1897) 76 L.T. 542 at 553 (but in that case, the principal debtor was a party to the proceedings); *Board of Trade v Employers Liability Assurance Corp Ltd* [1910] 1 K.B. 401.
[86] (1729) 2 Geo II, c. XXII, s.13; 8 Geo II, c. XXIV, s.5.
[87] (Unreported, NSW Sup Ct, Brownie J., March 15, 1991).
[88] (1991) 98 A.L.R. 393.
[89] Unreported, NSW Sup Ct, June 7, 1985.
[90] See also *Emerson v Wreckair Pty Ltd* (1991) 103 A.L.R. 404, where the Full Court of the Supreme Court of Queensland allowed the appellant guarantors to claim a statutory set-off in respect of the proceeds of hire of equipment which, by agreement between the creditor and the principal debtor, should have been applied in reduction of the principal debt.
[91] See S.R. Derham, *Set-off* (3rd ed., 2003), paras 18–30 to 18–31.
[92] *5K Construction Ltd (in receivership and liquidation) v Thakker* (unreported, Queen's Bench Division (Official Referee's Business), Judge Esyr Lewis Q.C., July 19, 1996).
[93] *ibid.* Cf. G. Andrews and R. Millett, *Law of Guarantees* (3rd ed., 2000), para.12.12.
[94] *5K Construction Ltd (in receivership and liquidation) v Thakker* (unreported, Queen's Bench Division (Official Referee's Business), Judge Esyr Lewis Q.C., July 19, 1996).

the creditor *and the guarantor*.[95] Mutuality in this context involves an element of reciprocity.[96] Moreover, if the guarantor is allowed to take advantage of this wider right of statutory set-off, the guarantors may be able to reduce their liability (at the expense of other creditors) even though they could not have done so before the bankruptcy or liquidation.

11–93   Perhaps an equitable set-off might be available to the guarantors even where the principal debtor is bankrupt or in liquidation since it is unlikely that the statutory right of set-off constitutes a comprehensive code governing rights of set-off in this context. There may still be room for an equitable set-off to operate in favour of the guarantors, even though the mutuality requirement of the statutory right of set-off is not satisfied. On the other hand, both *Re ILG Travel*[97] and *Morris v Agrochemicals*[98] suggest that the contract between the parties cannot give better rights of set-off than those conferred by the Insolvency Rules, r.4.90, on grounds of public policy.

11–94   Conversely, while a guarantor's right to rely on a legal or equitable set-off available to the principal debtor can be excluded by the terms of the guarantee,[99] the parties cannot contract out of any statutory right of set-off.[1]

(e) Where the principal transaction is void, voidable or unenforceable

11–95   In Chapter 5, we saw that the guarantor may be able to rely on defences arising from the defective nature of the principal transaction,[2] including the fact that the moneys may be irrecoverable from the principal as being in the nature of a penalty.[3] Alternatively, the guarantor may be able to show that the creditor is estopped from recovering the debt from the principal.[4] In this case there is probably no need to join the principal

---

[95] *Ince Hall Rolling Mills Co Ltd v Douglas Forge Co* (1882) 8 Q.B.D. 179 at 183; *Shand v M J Atkinson Ltd (in liq)* [1966] N.Z.L.R. 551 at 571; *Peel v Fitzgerald* [1982] Qd. R. 544 at 547. The necessary mutuality might, however, be present where the guarantee contains a principal debtor clause which effectively renders the guarantor jointly and severally liable with the borrower for the principal debt.

[96] *Gye v McIntyre* (1991) 98 A.L.J.R. 393 at 402.

[97] Unreported, Jonathan Parker J., March 8, 1995.

[98] Unreported, Court of Appeal, December 20, 1995, reversed on appeal: but not on this point: [1997]3 W.L.R. 909, HL.

[99] See above, para.11–88.

[1] *National Westminster Bank Ltd v Halesowen Presswork & Assemblies Ltd* [1972] A.C. 785; *Re Cushla Ltd* [1979] 3 All E.R. 415; *Re Paddington Town Hall Centre Ltd (in liq)* (1979) 41 F.L.R. 239; *Re ILG Travel* (unreported, Jonathan Parker J., March 8, 1995); *Stein v Blake* [1995] 2 W.L.R. 710, HL; *Re Bank of Credit and Commerce International (No.8)* [1997] 3 W.L.R. 909. There are, however, compelling arguments in favour of the view that in a commercial transaction a solvent party should be able to waive its right to have its liability reduced by the amount it is owed by another party. See A. Berg, "Contracting Out of Set-Off in a Winding Up" (1996) 174 L.M.C.L.Q. 49.

[2] See above, paras 5–108 to 5–132.

[3] See above, para.5–112; *Citicorp Australia Ltd v Hendry* (1985) 4 N.S.W.L.R. 1. See also *Hewison v Ricketts* (1894) 63 L.J. Q.B. 711 as explained in *Brooks v Beirnstein* [1909] 1 K.B. 98 at 103.

[4] *International Leasing Corp (Vic) Ltd v Aiken* [1967] 2 N.S.W.R. 427 at 450 *per* Asprey J.A.

debtor as a party to the proceedings.[5] The reason is that such defences provide a legal reason why the creditor should not be allowed to recover against the principal debtor and the guarantor's liability arises only on default of the principal debtor.[6]

(f) The guarantor's general defences to an action on the guarantee

The guarantor's general defences to an action upon the guarantee can be **11–96** grouped into three broad categories: the first relates to the discharge of the guarantor by reason of the determination of the principal transaction; the second concerns the relationship between the creditor and the principal debtor; and the third focuses upon the guarantee itself and the creditor's relationship with the guarantor. These defences are analysed exhaustively above, in Chapters 6 to 8.[7]

(g) The guarantor's right to compel the creditor to combine accounts

Where the guarantor guarantees a particular account of a customer with **11–97** the customer's bank, can the guarantor require the bank to combine the customer's accounts so as to reduce or extinguish the indebtedness in the guaranteed account by reason of a credit balance in another account? It appears that a bank cannot be called upon to combine accounts maintained by the customer at different branches in order to meet a cheque that is not covered by the branch on which it is drawn.[8] It should follow that, prior to the bankruptcy or liquidation of the principal debtor, the debtor's bank cannot be compelled to combine the debtor's accounts before suing the guarantor. Naturally, if the guarantor pays the principal debt to the bank, the guarantor will be entitled to an indemnity from the debtor and can execute a judgment on the indemnity against the debtor's assets, including the chose in action constituted by the credit balance of the debtor's account at the bank.[9]

A different result occurs where the surety guarantees, not a particular **11–98** debt owing to the debtor's bank, but rather the general balance of the debtor's current account. Here, all the debtor's current accounts with the bank must be taken into account in determining the ultimate balance which is guaranteed.[10] It appears, therefore, that a guarantor's right to compel a bank to combine its customers' accounts depends upon the terms of the guarantee.

---

[6] *Stifel Estate Co v Cella* 291 S.W. 515 (1927).
[7] Again, there is probably no need to join the principal debtor as a party: see *Cellulose Products Pty Ltd v Truda* (1970) 92 W.N. (NSW) 561 at 565–566.
[8] See *Garnett v M'Kewan* (1872) L.R. 8 Ex. 10 at 14; *Halesowen Presswork & Assemblies Ltd v National Westminster Bank Ltd* [1971] 1 Q.B. 1 at 34. See also *Bank of New South Wales v Goulburn Valley Butter Co Pty Ltd* [1902] A.C. 543.
[9] See below, paras 12–01 to 12–115, especially paras 12–24 to 12–36.
[10] *Re Sherry* (1884) 25 Ch. D. 692 at 706; *Re Tonkin* (1923) 6 A.B.C. 197 at 210–211.

11–99   Where the principal debtor is bankrupt or in liquidation the bank also may be required to combine its customer's accounts in the interests of the general creditors of the customer.[11] In *Mutton v Peat*,[12] a firm of stockbrokers had both a current account and a loan account with its bankers. The stockbrokers were adjudged bankrupt and ceased to carry on business. At that time there was a credit balance of £1,362 10s in the current account and a balance of £7,500 was due to the bank on the loan account. The stockbrokers had deposited with their bank, as security, bonds and shares belonging to their clients, without the authority of the clients concerned. This deposit was made to secure the general indebtedness of the stockbrokers to the bank, not merely to secure their indebtedness on the loan account. The bank did not know that the deposited bonds and shares did not belong to the stockbrokers, and it ultimately realised the securities. The proceeds of sale, together with interest until sale, were more than sufficient to pay the outstanding balance of the loan account. The Court of Appeal held that the current account and the loan account should be combined and that the proceeds of sale of the deposited securities should be applied to liquidate the net indebtedness of the stockbrokers to the bank. Lindley M.R. concluded:

> "I do not care how the bankers may have manipulated their books or how many accounts they may have kept. When you come to ascertain which is the amount due from [the customer] to the bankers the question admits of only one solution—it is the balance due on the loan account after deducting the £1,362 10s."[13]

11–100   As the deposited securities had not been specifically appropriated to cover the debit balance in the loan account, they had to be used to satisfy the stockbrokers' net indebtedness to the bank. In *Mutton v Peat*[14] the issue arose between the bank and its customer; there was no guarantor involved. It is, however, a reasonable inference from the decision that the customer's accounts must be automatically combined to determine the true state of indebtedness for which a guarantor may be liable.

(viii) The guarantor's right to set off against the creditor a claim held by his co-surety

11–101   A surety's claim to set off a cross-claim held by a co-surety against the creditor's claim to enforce the guarantee against the surety is complicated by the rules governing co-obligors.[15] A joint debt cannot be set off against

---

[11] E.P. Ellinger, E. Lomnicka and R.J.A. Hooley, *Modern Banking Law* (3rd ed., 2002), p.219.
[12] [1900] 2 Ch. 79.
[13] *ibid.*, at 85.
[14] [1900] 2 Ch. 79.
[15] See G. Williams, *Joint Obligations* (1949), para.76.

a separate debt[16] any more than a separate debt can be set off against a joint debt.[17] But what is the position where the sureties sued are severally liable or where they are jointly and severally liable in respect of the guarantee and the creditor sues only one of them in respect of his several obligation? Can that surety set off the creditor's separate debt to the surety?

In *Bowyear v Pawson*,[18] it was argued that the defendant/surety was **11–102** entitled to set off the creditor's debt to his co-surety against his own liability under the guarantee. The defendant submitted that, upon payment of the guaranteed debt to the creditor, he would be entitled to seek contribution from his co-surety who enjoyed a right of set-off against the creditor. The court rejected this argument because the defendant guarantor could not show that he had any right to exonerate his own liability by appropriating the creditor's debt to his co-surety.[19] Upon payment of the principal debt, the defendant guarantor would be entitled to enforce the creditor's remedies against the co-sureties to support the guarantor's right of contribution, but the guarantor could not appropriate for his own purposes the creditor's debt to a co-surety.

The true basis for rejecting the defendant guarantor's right of set-off in **11–103** this case is unclear. Perhaps the court thought that the defendant guarantor's right to quia timet relief prior to payment should not extend to an appropriation of a co-surety's debt. But the expressed reason for its decision was that the defendant's argument was treating the defendant's liability with the co-surety as if it were joint, when in fact it was joint and several.[20]

The court's reluctance to allow the set-off in *Bowyear v Pawson* is not **11–104** shared by its American brethren. In the United States the general rule is that, where an action is brought against two or more defendants[21] to enforce a several debt or a joint and several debt, the defendants are entitled to set off a debt owed to one of them by the claimant.[22]

(ix) The guarantor's right to set off a claim the guarantor has against the creditor in his own right

Where the creditor's claim against the guarantor is in respect of **11–105** unliquidated damages, the guarantor will not be able to plead a defence of

---

[16] *Ex p. Riley* (1731) Kel. W. 24; 2 Digest (Re-issue) 430; *Kinnerley v Hossack* (1809) 2 Taunt 170; 40 Digest (Repl) 408; *Re Fisher Ex p. Ross* (1817) Buck 125; 40 Digest (Repl) 421; *Re Willis, Percival & Co Ex p. Morier* (1879) 12 Ch. D. 491, CA.
[17] *Jones v Fleeming* (1827) 7 B. & C. 217; 6 L.J.O.S. 113; *Watts v Christie* (1849) 11 Beav. 546; 18 L.J. Ch. 173.
[18] (1881) 6 Q.B.D. 540.
[19] *ibid.*, at 544.
[20] *ibid.*, at 544.
[21] *Commissioner of Banks v T C Lee & Co* 197 N.E. 88; 291 Mass 191 (1935); *Rossi Bros Inc v Commissioner of Banks* 186 N.E. 234; 283 Mass 114 (1933).
[22] See *Messick v Rardin* DC 111 6 F Supp. 200 (1934), appeal dismissed in *Rardin v Messick* 78 F 2d 643 (1933); *Merchants' National Bank of Los Angeles v Clark-Parker Co* 9 P 2d 826; 215 Cal 296 (1932); *Heiple v Lehman* 192 N.E. 858 (1934); *Commissioner of Banks v T C Lee & Co* 197 N.E. 88; 291 Mass. 191 (1935).

set-off pursuant to the Statutes of Set-off because those statutes are only applicable where there are mutual debts or liquidated sums.[23] Indeed it was at one time thought that the guarantor could not rely on a legal set-off because the nature of the creditor's claim against the guarantor as a matter of theory was always in respect of unliquidated damages,[24] but it is now clear that the creditor's claim can be (and commonly is) an action for a money sum.[25]

11–106   Where the creditor's action is for a money sum, the guarantor may claim a legal set-off arising out of the arrangement created by the guarantee. Indeed, the guarantor can set off against his liability on the guarantee a debt owing to him from the estate of the creditor as a result of dealings prior to the guarantee with a partnership comprising the creditor and the principal debtor. Thus in *Cheetham v Crook*[26] the plaintiff was able to set off the balance of a debt of £4,481 owed to him by the partnership of Pemberton and Milson against the liability he assumed as surety for Pemberton upon dissolution of the partnership in respect of a debt owed to Milson's estate.

11–107   But a guarantor seeking to assert a legal set-off must establish that there is mutuality between the guarantor's claim and the demand of the creditor; there can be no set-off unless the debts are mutual in the sense that they are both presently payable under mutual contracts or transactions, involving the same parties in the same capacities.[27] On this principle, the Supreme Court of Victoria in *National Bank of A/asia v Swan*[28] refused to allow the administrator of a deceased guarantor to set off debts due from a bank to the administrator in that capacity against a liability which had not yet accrued under the guarantee. In the absence of an express promise by the administrator to pay the guaranteed debt, the necessary mutuality was lacking as the administrator was not at the relevant time liable for the debt, and even when he became liable for it he would not be liable in his personal capacity, but as administrator of the deceased guarantor. Stawell C.J. declared:

"Unless the [administrator] makes an express promise to pay, the debt is the debt of the intestate, founded on a contract between the person suing and the intestate. It was not a debt, but a liability or duty imposed upon him, the administrator, to discharge the debt of another person, out of assets of that person which came to his, the administrator's hands—the debts consequently were not mutual."[29]

---

[23] *Crawford v Stirling* (1802) 4 Esp. 207; 170 E.R. 693; *Morley v Inglis* (1837) 4 Bing (NC) 58; 132 E.R. 711.

[24] *Moschi v Lep Air Services Ltd* [1973] A.C. 331. See also *Morley v Inglis* (1837) 4 Bing (NC) 58; 132 E.R. 711 and above, paras 10–201 to 10–214.

[25] *Sunbird Plaza Pty Ltd v Maloney* (1988) 166 C.L.R. 245; *National Bank of A/asia v Swan* (1872) 3 V.R. (L) 168: see above, para.10–202.

[26] (1825) M'Cle. & Yo. 307; 148 E.R. 429, approved in *Emerson v Wreckair Pty Ltd* (1991) 103 A.L.R. 404 at 412.

[27] *National Bank of A/asia v Swan* (1872) 3 V.R. (L) 168.

[28] *ibid.*

[29] *ibid.*, at 171.

The reason why demands due in different rights cannot be set off is essentially that "one man's money shall not be applied to pay another man's debt".[30]

In principle, the guarantor, even if the claim is in damages, may be able **11–108** to rely on equitable set-off where the guarantor's claim is so closely connected with that of the creditor that the title of the creditor to claim upon the guarantee can be regarded as being impeached.[31] But cases of equitable set-off are likely to be limited, probably to where the creditor is in breach of the terms of the guarantee.

A guarantee may provide that the guarantor must pay the creditor upon **11–109** the default of the principal debtor without raising any set-off or counterclaim. The parties are not prevented by s.49(2) of the Supreme Court Act 1981 or any ground of public policy from including such a provision in a guarantee.[32] In an action to enforce such a guarantee, the creditor may obtain summary judgment[33] even if the guarantor raises a set-off or counterclaim.[34] In *Continental Illinois Bank & Trust Co of Chicago v Papanicolaou*,[35] the Court of Appeal declared that the whole commercial purpose of a guarantee in these terms would be defeated if the set-off or counterclaim could be pleaded by the guarantor as a defence to an action to enforce the guarantee.[36] But such a guarantee does not prevent the guarantor pursuing his cross-claim in separate proceedings. Nor will a guarantee in these terms prevent a guarantor from raising a set-off in the bankruptcy or liquidation of the creditor because the statutory set-off provisions are mandatory and self-executing.[37]

In cases where the creditor is bankrupt or in liquidation and the **11–110** guarantor is subject to a claim by the trustee in bankruptcy or liquidator upon the guarantee, the guarantor may rely on the mutual credit provisions of the insolvency legislation to set off a debt owed by the creditor to the guarantor.[38] Rule 4.90 of the Insolvency Rules 1986

---

[30] *Jones v Mossop* (1844) 3 Hare 568 at 574; 67 E.R. 506 at 508, *per* Sir James Wigram V.C.
[31] See above, paras 11–58 to 11–74 and S.R. Derham, *Set-off* (3rd ed., 2003), paras 18–15 to 18–25.
[32] *Coca-Cola Financial Corporation v Finsat International Ltd* [1996] 3 W.L.R. 849 at 857, *per* Neill L.J. As to practical guidance in relation to counterclaims, see *Bannister v Sgb plc* [1997] P.I.Q.R. 165.
[33] As to applications for summary judgment, see CPR, Pt 24 and *Home and Overseas Insurance Co Ltd v Mentor Insurance Co (UK) Ltd* [1990] 1 W.L.R. 153 at 158 *per* Parker L.J.
[34] Where the contract between the parties contained a general provision prohibiting set off, subject to an exception permitting set off in respect of default by a non-performing party or its affiliates, the court held that the exception referred to a party to the actual contract and not to any of its affiliates. As a result, there could be no set off unless there had been a default by the contracting party. To set off a liability owed by an affiliate of a contracting party was not permissible unless that party itself was in default: *Sinochem International Oil (London) Co Ltd v Mobil Sales and Supply Corp (No.1)* [1999] 2 All E.R. (Comm) 522.
[35] [1986] 2 Lloyd's Rep. 441.
[36] Even a clause purporting to exclude a right of set-off in respect of a claim for misrepresentation or fraud by the creditor or a claim that the creditor had failed to exercise reasonable care in realising secured assets might be effective in a commercial guarantee because it might satisfy the requirements of reasonableness within the meaning of s.11(1) of the Unfair Contract Terms Act 1977.
[37] *Halesowen Presswork & Assemblies Ltd v National Westminster Bank Ltd* [1971] 1 Q.B. 1; *Gye v Mc Intyre* (1991) 98 A.L.R. 393.
[38] Insolvency Act 1986, s.323 (in relation to insolvent individuals) and Insolvency Rules 1986, r.4.90 (in relation to insolvent companies). See S.R. Derham, *Set-Off* (3rd ed., 2003), paras 6–

provides that an account must be taken where a company goes into liquidation in circumstances where there were mutual credits, mutual debts or other mutual dealings between the company and any creditor entitled to prove in the liquidation. Only the balance after the taking of the account is provable in the liquidation. There is a similar provision in relation to bankrupt debtors.[39]

11–111   The statutory right of set off available under the mutual credits provision in the insolvency legislation applies to both actual and contingent debts.[40] It is not difficult to apply this provision where the creditor's claim against the guarantor has accrued due as at the date of the commencement of the creditor's insolvency.[41] If the contingency has occurred and the creditor's claim against the guarantor has crystallised at the commencement of the creditor's insolvency, the amount of its claim is quantified and that amount is treated as having been due at the bankruptcy date.[42]

11–112   In this situation the guarantor may be entitled to require that his claim *against* the insolvent estate be set off against to creditor's claim under the guarantee. Only the balance remaining after taking this account of the mutual debts should be payable by the guarantor.

11–113   If there is a net balance owing to the creditor after the taking of this account, the liquidator or trustee in bankruptcy may assign the balance in realising the assets of the bankrupt or the company in liquidation.[43]

11–114   But the liquidator or trustee in bankruptcy may not assign the creditor's claim against the principal debtor or the guarantor as a chose in action without taking an account between the parties under the mutual credits provision.[44]

11–115   *MS Fashions Ltd v Bank of Credit & Commerce International SA*[45] provides a rare example of this type of set-off. Mr Sarwar guaranteed the debts of two companies to a bank and deposited approximately £300,000 with the bank to secure his obligation under the guarantee. The bank was wound up on the grounds of insolvency. Mr Sarwar and the two companies instituted what was in substance a redemption suit against the bank, arguing that the £300,000 deposited should be offset against the amount owing to the bank under the company's debentures. At first instance, Millett J. held that set-off operated by way of defence only and it could not be treated as a payment by the guarantor. It followed that the bank could

---

71 to 6–78 and J. O'Donovan, "The Banker's Lien and Right of Combination" (1994) 3(1) *International Insolvency Review* 1. Such a set-off will not be available unless the guarantor is clearly entitled to the sums owed by the creditor because otherwise the necessary mutuality or reciprocity is absent: *Bank of Credit and Commerce International SA (in liq) v Al-Saud* [1997] B.C.C. 63, CA. It is not sufficient that the beneficial interest in the money in the bank account could be established by the taking of an account between the parties claiming an interest in it. And where it is not clear that the credit balance in the creditor's accounts belongs to the guarantor, he is not entitled to invoke the statutory right of set-off against his liability as a guarantor: *ibid.*
[39] Insolvency Act 1986, s.323.
[40] *Stein v Blake* [1996] A.C. 243 at 252.
[41] See generally G. Andrews and R Millett, *Law of Guarantees* (3rd ed., 2000), para.13.18.
[42] *Stein v Blake* [1996] A.C. 243 at 252.
[43] *Stein v Blake* [1996] A.C. 243 at 258.
[44] *ibid.*
[45] [1993] B.C.L.C. 280 affirmed by *MS Fashions Ltd v BCCI (SA) Ltd (in liq) (No.2)* [1993] Ch. 425, CA.

proceed to enforce the company's debentures without taking into account any set-off which Mr Sarwar might have against the bank. However, the Court of Appeal granted the two companies leave to bring the redemption suit against the bank in liquidation under s.130 of the Insolvency Act 1986. Woolf and Scott L.JJ. found that it was arguable that the statutory right to set off the £300,000 deposit as a mutual debt or mutual credit under r.4.90 of the Insolvency Rules 1986 was the equivalent of payment of that sum to the bank by the guarantor, Mr Sarwar. Hence, it was arguable that the £300,000 deposit reduced the amount which the companies owed to the bank under its debentures, and leave should be granted to the companies to raise this issue in the redemption suit against the bank. If this argument ultimately prevailed, the bank would not be entitled to enforce their debentures for the full £600,000 secured debt and pay Mr Sarwar only a dividend in the liquidation in respect of his deposit of £300,000. The bank would be required by the mutual debts provision to offset the amount of the deposit against the amount owing under the debentures.

The guarantor was allowed to invoke the statutory set-off against the **11–116** creditor in *MS Fashions v Bank of Credit and Commerce International SA*[46] because under the terms of the guarantee the guarantor's liability was expressed to be that of a principal debtor. In other words, the guarantors were under a personal, principal obligation to pay the creditor. Accordingly, the guarantor could require the creditor to set off its claim under the guarantee against the guarantor's claim to recover the funds deposited with the creditor as security for the principal obligation.

The terms of the guarantee may not be the only source of a guarantor's **11–117** personal covenant to repay the guaranteed debt as a principal debtor. Where the security provided by the guarantor is registered land, s.28 of the Land Registration Act 1925 implies a personal covenant for repayment unless this covenant is negatived by "suitable words" in the instrument. The terms of any clause purporting to exclude this implied covenant will be construed in favour of the mortgagor/guarantor, particularly where he has received no funds from the mortgagee.[47] However, if the mortgagor's personal covenant is not excluded, it could allow the mortgagor to claim a statutory set-off against an insolvent mortgagee.

While a guarantor may rely on the mutual credit provisions of the **11–118** insolvency legislation to set off a debt owed by the creditor to the guarantor, the principal debtor cannot take advantage of sums deposited with the creditor by the guarantor by way of security for the principal debt unless the guarantor undertook a personal liability as principal debtor to a pecuniary demand by the creditor. In *Re Bank of Credit and Commerce International SA (No.8)*[48] the guarantors deposited certain sums with the bank on terms that they were not entitled to repayment until the bank's loans to the principal debtor companies were repaid in full. The guarantors

---

[46] [1993] B.C.L.C. 280, affirmed on appeal: [1993] Ch. 425, CA.
[47] See *Fairmile Portfolio Management v Davies Arnold Cooper (a firm)* (1998) E.G.C. 5417, *The Times*, November 17, 1998 and G. Andrews and R. Millett, *Law of Guarantees* (3rd ed., 2000), para.13.22.
[48] [1997] 3 W.L.R. 909, H.L. See generally S. Elwes, "Claims in Insolvency and the Right of Set-Off" (1998) 14 *Insolvency Law and Practice* 321.

purported to secure the loans by charges over their deposits. The bank had the right to appropriate the security deposits under its control and the right to discharge the principal debt out of the deposits but it did not have the right to make a pecuniary demand on the guarantors because they were not personally liable for the principal debt. In these circumstances, there were no mutual claims between the guarantors and the bank and there was no basis for a statutory set-off under r.4.90 of the Insolvency Rules 1986.[49] Consequently, in recovering the loans from the principal debtor companies, the liquidators of the bank were not required to set off the amounts deposited by the guarantors by way of security.

11–119   The insolvency of the bank involved no breach of its duty as chargee of the security deposits so there was no basis on which the bank could be liable to the guarantors for loss arising from the insolvency of the bank. Nor was there any basis for any claim to an indemnity by the principal debtor companies against the bank or any right to set off this claim against those companies' liability for the full amount of the principal debt.

11–120   *MS Fashions Ltd v Bank of Credit and Commerce International SA*[50] was distinguished on the ground that the security document in that case expressly referred to the liability of the depositor as that of a principal debtor. The principal debtor was discharged by the automatic set-off between the depositor and the bank in that case because the depositor and the principal debtor were jointly, severally and unconditionally liable for the same debt. In *Re Bank of Credit and Commerce International SA (No.8)*,[51] on the other hand, the depositors were not personally liable for the principal debt and there was, therefore, no mutuality between the claim of the bank against the principal debtor companies and the claim of the guarantors against the bank so to justify a set-off under r.4.90.[52]

11–121   There is no similar procedure for quantifying contingent or unascertained claims by the insolvent estate *against* the guarantor.[53] The creditor's claim against the guarantee may be merely contingent at the date the creditor became insolvent (because, for example, the principal debtor was not in default at the time). The statutory set off is not available to the insolvent creditor in this situation because the contingency cannot be valued.[54] There is no way of telling whether the principal debtor will default and, if so, the amount of the guarantor's liability. Indeed if a set off were allowed in this situation, the principal debt would be effectively paid even thought the guarantor was not yet liable to pay and even though there was only a slight risk of default by the principal debtor.[55]

11–122   On the other hand, if the contingency that causes the guarantor's liability to crystallise occurs after the creditor's insolvency but before an account is taken between the parties, then a statutory set-off should be

[49] SI 1986/1925.
[50] [1993] B.C.L.C. 280.
[51] [1997] 3 W.L.R. 909, HL.
[52] See also *Tam Wing Chuen v Bank of Credit and Commerce Hong Kong Ltd* [1996] B.C.C. 388, PC.
[53] *Stein v Blake* [1996] A.C. 243 at 253.
[54] See *Stein v Blake* [1996] A.C. 243 at 253 and *Tam Wing Chuen v Bank of Credit and Commerce Hong Kong Ltd* [1996] B.C.C. 388 at 389, PC.
[55] G. Andrews and R. Millett, *Law of Guarantees* (3rd ed., 2000), para.13.18.

effected, provided that the obligations giving rise to the guarantor's liability existed at the date of the commencement of the creditor's insolvency.[56] In this situation the creditor's claim has accrued due and the set-off can be effected in the taking of the account between the insolvent creditor's estate and the guarantor. If there is still an outstanding debt owing to the creditor after the statutory set-off is effected, the guarantor will not be entitled to an injunction to restrain the creditor from enforcing its securities for the balance of the principal debt.[57]

3. THE RIGHTS OF THE GUARANTOR AGAINST THE PRINCIPAL DEBTOR BEFORE PAYMENT

(i) The right of exoneration

(a) When it arises at law

In general, a guarantor's right to an indemnity from the principal debtor **11–123** does not crystallise at law prior to payment.[58] But where, independently of the guarantee, the debtor covenants with the guarantor to pay the debt on a given day, the guarantor can bring an action for breach of contract against the debtor for the whole sum when that date has passed, even if the guarantor himself has not paid the debt.[59]

An express contract of indemnity between the principal debtor and the **11–124** guarantor may confer upon the guarantor a right of exoneration, as distinct from a right of reimbursement of losses sustained by reason of the guarantor's liability as guarantor. It appears that the guarantor might be able to maintain an action against the principal debtor for exoneration even before the guarantor is sued by the creditor where the debtor covenants not merely to indemnify the guarantor but also to "save, protect,

---

[56] *Re Daintrey* [1900] 1 Q.B. 546 at 556–557; *Re Charge Card Services Ltd* [1986] 3 All E.R. 289 at 311; *Day & Dent Construction Ltd v North Australian Pty Ltd* (1982) 56 A.L.J.R. 347; *Hiley v People's Prudential Assurance Co Ltd (in liq)* (1938) 60 C.L.R. 468 at 496. Cf. *Carreras Rothmans Ltd v Freeman Mathews Treasure Ltd (in liq)* [1985] Ch. 207 at 230.
[57] *MS Fashions Ltd v Bank of Credit & Commerce International SA* [1992] B.C.C. 571, CA.
[58] *Collinge v Heywood* (1839) 9 Ad. & E. 633; 112 E.R. 1352; Re Bruce David Realty Pty Ltd (in liq) [1969] V.R. 240.
[59] *Wooldridge v Norris* (1868) L.R. 6 Eq. 410. See *Loosemore v Radford* (1842) 9 M. & W. 657 at 658–659; 152 E.R. 277 at 278, where Alderson B. stated: "The question is, to what extent has the plaintiff been injured by the defendant's default? Certainly to the amount of the money that the defendant ought to have paid according to his covenant." See also *Carr v Roberts* (1833) 5 B. & Ad. 78; 110 E.R. 721; *Re Allen* [1896] 2 Ch. 345; *Carpenter v Park* 19 Cal. App. 2d 567; 66 P 2d 224 (1937); *Gustavson v Koehler* 177 Minn. 115; 224 N.W. 699 (1929); *Toussaint v Martinnant* (1787) 2 T.R. 100; 100 E.R. 55; *Spark v Heslop* (1859) 1 E. & E. 563; 120 E.R. 1020; *Martin v Court* (1788) 2 Term Rep. 640; 100 E.R. 344. Equally, where the guarantor is bankrupt or in liquidation, the trustee in bankruptcy or the liquidator is entitled to recover the same amount as damages for the breach of contract as the guarantor himself could have recovered: *Ashdown v Ingamells* (1880) 5 Ex. D. 280. See also *Re Perkins* [1898] 2 Ch. 182; *Carr v Roberts* (1833) 5 B. & Ad. 78; 110 E.R. 721. If the principal debtor pays the creditor after the appointed date but before the surety obtains judgment against the principal debtor for breach of the covenant to pay, only nominal damages may be awarded to the guarantor: *Loosemore v Radford* (1842) 9 M. & W. 657 at 658; 152 E.R. 277 at 278, *per* Baron Parke. Cf. *Re Richardson* [1911] 2 K.B. 705, discussed below, para.11–126.

defend and keep him harmless" from all debts and liabilities and all actions in respect of such debts and liabilities.[60] But the general rule at common law is that a person who is entitled to an indemnity cannot enforce it until that person has made a payment to the third party or sustained loss or damage.[61]

11–125   On one view, the guarantor may be required to apply the amount recovered from the principal debtor in reduction of the guaranteed debt. To quote Parke B. in *Loosemore v Radford*:[62] "The defendant (debtor) may perhaps have an equity that the money he may pay to the plaintiff (surety) shall be applied in discharge of his debt."[63] On the other hand, in *Re Law Guarantee Trust & Accident Society Ltd*,[64] Buckley L.J. suggested that, once a person entitled to an indemnity receives payment from the person giving the indemnity, that person is entitled to deal with the money as he thinks proper. This is the dominant view.[65] In *Carr v Roberts*,[66] both Littledale and Patteson J.J. confirmed that it is the duty of the party giving the indemnity to pay the full amount whether or not it is applied in discharge of the principal debt. Moreover, in *Re Walker*,[67] Stirling J. observed: "Upon principle, I cannot see why a surety who takes from the principal debtor a bond or indemnity at once becomes a trustee of that for the principal creditor."[68]

11–126   It may be different where the principal debtor is himself concerned in some way independently of the guarantee with the application of the money which the principal debtor pays to the guarantor by way of exoneration. This suggestion is based upon *Re Richardson*,[69] where a woman, who was bound as a beneficiary of a trust to indemnify her husband as trustee of a lease, had a vested interest in ensuring that the money which she paid to her husband's trustee in bankruptcy was passed on to the lessor so as to relieve the leased property from the conseqences of non-payment of rent and damages for breach of covenant. The trustee in bankruptcy sought to exercise the husband's right of exoneration against the wife for the benefit of the general creditors of the bankrupt estate. In other words, he wanted to obtain an indemnity from the wife but not pay the amount received to the lessor, leaving the lessor merely with a right of proof in the husband's estate. The Court of Appeal held, however, that the trustee in bankruptcy could invoke the husband's right of exoneration against the wife *only for the purpose of passing the amount recovered on to*

---

[60] See *Carr v Roberts* (1833) 5 B. & Ad. 78 at 82; 110 E.R. 721 at 722–723 *per* Parke J. (in arguendo). See also Patteson J. at 85; 723. In that case, however, the defendant had covenanted not merely to indemnify and protect the plaintiff but also to pay the plaintiff's debts.

[61] *M'Gillivray v Hope* [1935] A.C. 1 at 10 *per* Lord Tomlin; *Collinge v Heywood* (1839) 9 Ad. & E. 633 at 640; 112 E.R. 1352 at 1354.

[62] (1842) 9 M. & W. 657; 152 E.R. 277. See also *Re Richardson* [1911] 2 K.B. 705.

[63] *ibid.*, at 658; 278.

[64] [1914] 2 Ch. 617 at 633. See also at 640 *per* Kennedy L.J.; *Re Fenton Ex p. Fenton Textile Association* [1931] 1 Ch. 85 at 105, *per* Lord Hayworth M.R., 114 *per* Lawrence LJ.

[65] *Cf.* G. Andrews and R. Millett, *Law of Guarantees* (3rd ed., 2000), para.10.31.

[66] (1833) 5 B. & Ad. 78; 110 E.R. 721.

[67] [1892] 1 Ch. 621.

[68] *ibid.*, at 629.

[69] [1911] 2 K.B. 705. See also *Cruse v Paine* (1868) L.R. 6 Eq. 641; *Re Perkins* [1898] 2 Ch. 182.

the lessor. There is nothing in the unanimous judgments of the Court of Appeal to indicate that this principle is restricted to the context of trustees and beneficiaries. Indeed, Cozens-Hardy M.R. specifically referred to the analogous situation of a surety claiming an indemnity from the principal debtor.[70]

Subsequent cases,[71] however, have been at pains to distinguish *Re* **11–127** *Richardson* and it will probably be restricted to its special facts. In reference to *Re Richardson*, Kennedy L.J. said in *Re Law Guarantee Trust & Accident Society Ltd*:[72] "The circumstances were peculiar".[73] Like the cases of *Cruse v Paine*[74] and *Re Perkins*,[75] *Re Richardson* involved a situation where the party providing the indemnity had an interest in the ultimate discharge of the liability in full in order to avoid forfeiture of property. These cases do not cast doubt on the general rule that any money recovered by the guarantor from the principal debtor by way of exoneration belongs to the guarantor in his own right. Indeed, this is the very reason why the court will not order quia timet relief in equity in the form of a direction to the principal debtor to pay *the guarantor.* Such a payment does not discharge the principal debtor from liability to the creditor and the money paid over to the guarantor can be distributed among the general creditors of the guarantor, without relieving the principal debtor of liability to pay the principal debt to the creditor.[76]

Any payments by the principal debtor to the creditor after the date fixed **11–128** for payment under the debtor's covenant with the guarantor relieve the guarantor pro tanto from responsibility.[77] Accordingly, if the debtor pays the creditor in full after the due date, the guarantor will merely be entitled to nominal damages for breach of the covenant.[78]

Since actual payment to the creditor is generally required before a **11–129** guarantor can enforce the right of indemnity against the principal debtor at law, it is not sufficient that the guarantor has simply given a promissory note in extinguishment of the principal debt.[79] Payment or something akin

---

[70] [1911] 2 K.B. 705 at 709.
[71] *Re Richardson* [1911] 2 K.B. 705 is difficult to reconcile with *Re Harrington Motor Co* [1928] 1 Ch. 105, which attempted to explain and distinguish that case. Moreover, *Re Richardson* was expressly doubted in *Hood's Trustee v Southern Union General Insurance Co of A/asia* [1928] 1 Ch. 793 at 805. See also *Re Law Guarantee Trust & Accident Society Ltd* [1914] 2 Ch. 617 at 633, 640; *Loosemore v Radford* (1842) 9 M. & W. 657; 152 E.R. 277; *Carr v Roberts* (1833) 5 B. & Ad. 78; 110 E.R. 721; *Re Fenton Ex p. Fenton Textile Association* [1931] 1 Ch. 85 at 104–105.
[72] [1914] 2 Ch. 617.
[73] *ibid.*, at 641.
[74] (1868) L.R. 6 Eq. 641. There, stock jobbers were interested in seeing that the money which they provided was applied in discharging the calls on the shares; otherwise the shares could be forfeited.
[75] [1898] 2 Ch. 182. There, executors of an assignee of a lease were interested in the application of the amount they paid in discharging the obligations under the lease; otherwise the lease could be forfeited.
[76] *Re Fenton, Ex p. Fenton Textile Association* [1931] 1 Ch. 85 at 114.
[77] *Loosemore v Radford* (1842) 9 M. & W. 657 at 658; 152 E.R. 277 at 278 *per* Parke B.
[78] *ibid.*, at 659; 278 *per* Alderson B.
[79] *Maxwell v Jameson* (1818) 2 B. & Ald. 51; 106 E.R. 286; *Taylor v Higgins* (1802) 3 East 169; 102 E.R. 562; *Whelan v Crotty* (1868) 2 Ir. L.T. 285. *Cf. Barclay v Gooch* (1797) 2 Esp. 571, 170 E.R. 459; which was followed by the Court of Exchequer in Ireland in *McKenna v Harnett* (1849) 13 Ir. L.R. 206. See also Pollock C.B. in *Rodgers v Maw* (1846) 15 M. & W. 444 at 449;

to payment is necessary.[80] In Ireland, it is established that the handing over of property can be equivalent to payment in this context.[81] This principle has not yet gained a wider acceptance, although it appears that the guarantor can recover the value of such property by bringing an action against the principal debtor for breach of the debtor's implied promise to indemnify the guarantor.[82]

(b) The quia timet action in equity

11–130   The hardship which common law imposed upon a guarantor by requiring the guarantor to pay the principal debt before pursuing the right of indemnity against the principal debtor is partially mitigated by the quia timet action in equity.[83] The rationale for equity's intervention is that guarantors should be able to remove the cloud hanging over their heads before it starts to rain.[84] Quia timet relief is intended to protect guarantors from first having to pay the debt. Such relief is not restricted to the context of guarantees. It is available in equity whenever a person has a reasonable apprehension of imminent inconvenience or detriment because of the neglect, inadvertence or culpability of another.[85] It requires the principal debtor to take appropriate steps to ensure that the debt will be discharged or the guarantor relieved of the liability the guarantor might incur in consequence of the debtor's default.[86] It is consistent with the secondary liability of the guarantor because it casts the primary burden upon the debtor.

---

153 E.R. 924 at 926. It is submitted that the proposition in the text is valid because, as nothing was paid on the surety's note before action, he had not sustained any damage and could not, therefore, claim an indemnity: see *Fahey v Frawley* (1890) 26 L.R. Ir. 78 at 90 *per* Holmes J.
[80]   *Maxwell v Jameson* (1818) 2 B. & Ald. 51; 106 E.R. 286; *Power v Butcher* (1829) 10 B. & C. 329; 109 ER 472. As to what constitutes discharge by payment, see above, paras 9–01 to 9–07.
[81]   *Fahey v Frawley* (1890) 26 L.R. Ir. 78; *Gore v Gore* [1901] 2 I.R. 269.
[82]   *ibid.* See also *British Dominions Insurance Co v Duder* [1915] 2 K.B. 394; *Hope v M'Gillivray* [1935] A.C. 1. See also *Rowlatt on Principal and Surety* (5th ed., 1999), p.192.
[83]   Quia timet means literally "because one fears" so it is an appropriate term to describe this type of proceedings.
[84]   This metaphor was first used by Lord Keeper in *Ranelaugh v Hayes* (1683) 1 Vern. 189; 23 E.R. 405. See also *Nisbet v Smith* (1789) 2 Bro. C.C. 579 at 582; 29 E.R. 317 at 318; and *Thomas v Nottingham Inc Football Club Ltd* [1972] Ch. 596. As to the form of the writ and the statement of claim in an action for quia timet relief, see *Atkin's Court Forms* (2nd ed., 1982), Vol. 20, pp.140 and 143.
[85]   See *Papamichael v National Westminster Bank Plc* [2002] 1 Lloyd's Rep. 332; *Higgins v Potter* (1949) 50 S.R. (NSW) 77 at 88; *Metropolitan Bank Ltd v Christensen* (1895) 21 V.L.R. 288 (trespass); *Woollahra Municipal Council v James S Samson Pty Ltd* (1959) 4 L.G.R.A. 321; *Maxwell v Ditchburn* (1845) 5 L.T.O.S. 405; *Guardian Assurance Co Ltd v Matthew* [1919] 1 W.W.R. 67; *Patterson v T J Moss Tie Co* 330 S.W. 2d 344; 46 Tenn. App. 405 (1959) Where two debtors are expressed to be jointly liable for a debt but, as between themselves, one debtor is a surety for the other, the surety is entitled to quia timet relief against the other debtor: *Watt v Mortlock* [1964] Ch. 84. See also *Tate v Crewdson* [1938] Ch. 869.
[86]   *National Commercial Bank v Wimborne* (1978) 5 B.P.R. 11,958. But quia timet relief is also available to sureties who have charged their property with payment of the principal debt: *Watt v Mortlock* [1964] Ch. 84. But quia timet relief is unlikely to be granted in an ex parte application or by way of interlocutory order: see *Felton v Callis* [1969] 1 Q.B. 200 at 218–218; G. Andrews and R. Millett, *Law of Guarantees* (3rd ed., 2000), para.10.28.

Quia timet relief is based on the principal debtor's duty to indemnify **11–131** and "save harmless" the guarantor. As a result, one would not expect it to be available to recourse guarantors since the principal debtor is usually unaware of their existence and might not, therefore, owe them such a duty. Nevertheless, at least in the context of negotiable instruments, recourse guarantors such as the indorsers of a bill of exchange have been allowed quia timet relief.[87] But where a motor car dealer, at the request of a finance company, guarantees the due performance of a hire-purchase agreement entered into between the finance company and a hirer, quia timet relief might not be available to the dealer. In the absence of an express or implied promise by the hirer to indemnify the dealer, it would be difficult to establish that the hirer was under a duty to indemnify and "save harmless" the dealer. An indemnity might be available to the dealer on restitutionary grounds but this claim to an indemnity might not qualify the dealer for quia timet relief. A hire-purchase agreement, unlike a bill of exchange, is not a negotiable instrument, so it is difficult to argue in this context that the hirer should be liable on an implied promise of reimbursement based on constructive knowledge that another party would become secondarily liable on the hire-purchase agreement.

It is doubtful whether quia timet relief is available to a person who **11–132** provided a guarantee without an express or implied request of the principal debtor. In this case the claim to an indemnity is based not on an express or implied contract but rather on restitutionary grounds and there is no right to restitution before payment of the principal debt. The court should not, therefore, require the principal debtor to exonerate the guarantor in this situation.[88]

Although most choses in action can be reached by the process of **11–133** sequestration, this is not true of a guarantor's right to call upon the debtor to discharge the principal debt. It appears that this equitable right of exoneration is not a chose in action in the nature of property.[89] Thus a mortgagee cannot through a sequestration avail itself of the mortgagor's right to require the assignee of the equity of redemption to pay the secured debt even though, as between the mortgagor and the assignee, the latter is primarily liable.[90]

Where directors guarantee the overdraft of a company whose assets vest **11–134** in the Crown as *bona vacantia* and are disclaimed by the Crown, the

---

[87] Where an indorser pays the holder of the bill because the indorser is forced to do so, he is entitled to an indemnity from the acceptor. Indeed, it appears that the indorser may even be entitled to quia timet relief against the acceptor prior to actual payment. This can be justified on the basis of an implied promise of reimbursement since the acceptor should have known that the bill could be negotiated: see *Double Diamond Bowling Supply Ltd v Eglinton Bowling Ltd* (1963) 39 D.L.R. (2d) 19. See also *D J Morris v Ellis* (1974) 7 N.B.R. 516 (NBSC); *Pownal v Ferrand* (1827) 6 B. & C. 439; 108 ER 513. *Cf. Chitty on Contracts* (26th ed., 1989), Vol. II, para.1802. Compare (28th ed., 1999), Vol. II, para.44–104. See also *Moschi v Lep Air Services Ltd* [1973] A.C. 331 at 348.

[88] G. Andrews and R. Millett, *Law of Guarantee* (3rd ed., 2000), para.10.26.

[89] *Cf. Octavo Investments Pty Ltd v Knight* (1979) 144 C.L.R. 360; *Kemtron Industries Pty Ltd v Commissioner of Stamp Duties* [1984] 1 Qd. R. 576. These cases suggest that a trustee's right of indemnity is in the nature of a proprietary right. See also *Custom Credit Corp Ltd v Ravi Nominees Pty Ltd* (1992) 8 W.A.R. 42.

[90] *Irving v Boyd* (1868) 15 Gr. 157.

directors may not obtain a vesting order under s.181 of the Insolvency Act 1986 on the ground that they are under a liability in respect of the disclaimed property. The liability of the directors arose because of their guarantees, and it was not a liability in respect of the disclaimed assets. Consequently, the directors will not be able to obtain the disclaimed assets by way of exoneration.[91]

(c) When is quia timet relief available?

11-135   A guarantor is entitled to this form of equitable relief as soon as the principal debt becomes due and the guarantor owes the creditor a definite sum, even if the guarantor has not paid that amount.[92] Relief is available when the account between the creditor and the principal debtor is closed and the guarantor incurs an actual accrued or absolute liability giving the creditor a right to immediate payment.[93] Quia timet relief will not be granted where the surety's liability is not yet established.[94] It is not sufficient, therefore, that a demand has been made on the guarantor and that, upon the taking of accounts, a debt *might* become due to the creditor.[95] But a guarantor may apply for relief even if the precise *amount* of the guarantor's liability will be determined only in subsequent proceedings. In *Re Anderson-Berry*,[96] Lord Hanworth M.R. observed:

"It is not contested by Mr Preston that there is a right on the part of the surety to exoneration by his principal, and that as soon as any definite sum of money has become payable to the creditor, the surety has a right to have it paid by the principal and his own liability in respect of it brought to an end. *But it is said that that right only arises as and when a definite sum of money has become payable. I think this is too narrow a*

---

[91] *Re Spirit Motorsport Ltd (in liq)* [1996] 1 B.C.L.C. 684.
[92] *Ranelaugh v Hayes* (1683) 1 Vern. 189; 23 E.R. 405; *Nisbet v Smith* (1789) 2 Bro. C.C. 579 at 582; 29 E.R. 317 at 319; *Wolmershausen v Gullick* [1893] 2 Ch. 514; *Re Ledgard* (1922) 66 S.J. 405; *Morrison v Barking Chemicals Co Ltd* [1919] 2 Ch. 325; *Ascherson v Tredegar Dry Dock & Wharf Co Ltd* [1909] 2 Ch. 401; *Double Diamond Bowling Supply Ltd v Eglinton Bowling Ltd* (1963) 39 D.L.R. (2d) 19; *Milne v Yorkshire Guarantee & Securities Corp* (1906) 37 S.C.R. 331 at 342; *Thomas v Nottingham Inc Football Club* [1972] 1 Ch. 596; *Moulton v Roberts* [1977] Qd. R. 135; *Holden v Black* (1905) 2 C.L.R. 768 at 784; *National Commercial Bank v Wimborne* (1978) 5 B.P.R. 11,958; *Woolmington v Bronze Lamp Restaurant Pty Ltd* [1984] 2 N.S.W.L.R. 242; *Rogers v ANZ Banking Group Ltd* [1985] W.A.R. 304. Quia timet relief is available to a surety even if he is a principal debtor vis-à-vis the creditor: *Tate v Crewdson* [1938] 1 Ch. 869. This occurs where borrowers agree to be jointly liable to the lender but occupy the positions of principal and surety inter se: see above, paras 1–29 to 1–30.
[93] *Thomas v Nottingham Inc Football Club Ltd* [1972] 1 Ch 596, approved in *Moulton v Roberts* [1977] Qd. R. 135 per Williams J; *Stimpson v Smith* [1999] Ch. 340; *Wolmershausen v Gullick* [1893] 2 Ch. 514 at 527.
[94] *Hughes-Hallett v Indian Mammoth Gold Mines Co* (1882) 22 Ch. D. 561 at 564 *per* Fry J.; *Re Ledgard; Attenborough v Ledgard* (1922) 66 Sol. Jo. 404. Where a person has provided a guarantee or indemnity in respect of all sums which may be assessed against the party for income tax, that person's right of indemnity from the party arises upon the making of the income tax assessments because they establish conclusively the income tax liability even if the assessments are contested: *Re Dixon* [1994] 1 Qd. R. 7.
[95] *Morrison v Barking Chemicals Co Ltd* [1919] 2 Ch. 325; *Antrobus v Davidson* (1817) 3 Mer. 569; 36 E.R. 219. *Cf. Holden v Black* (1905) 2 C.L.R. 768 at 783–784.
[96] [1928] 1 Ch. 290.

view. I think that from the cases that have been cited there is a right of the surety to ask that he should be protected from a cloud that hangs over him if and when it is quite clear that there is a cloud hanging over him, and if there is a liability, even though the amount of that liability will be ascertained in subsequent proceedings, I think the surety has a right to ask for protection. There is the liability, quantified though it may be by subsequent proceedings and at a subsequent date, but once the liability has appeared then I think the right of the surety has accrued."[97]

There were special circumstances in *Re Anderson-Berry*,[98] which may **11–136** have influenced the granting of the relief. There the court granted quia timet relief to sureties under an administration bond to prevent the administrator from carrying out his persistent threats to distribute the estate even though he was well aware that there were still outstanding and indeterminate liabilities. The administration bond, which the administrator was required to furnish to the Registrar of the Probate, Divorce and Admiralty Division, contained a condition that the administrator would well and truly administer the estate according to law. If the court had allowed the administrator to defy this condition it would have been stultifying its own jurisdiction. In this special situation then, the Court of Appeal had no hesitation in taking control of the estate before the wrong actually occurred and before the sureties incurred a liability under their bond. But Lawrence L.J. warned against a wider application of this reasoning:

"If the action had been brought merely to get a principal debtor to discharge a debt of his own, it may very well be that the circumstances would have to be very special before such a *quia timet* action would be held to be justified."[99]

Nevertheless in *Papamichael v National Westminster Bank plc*[1] Judge Chambers Q.C. sitting as a judge of the High Court appeared to accept that the right to quia timet relief arises even when no accrued right to "a definite sum of money has become payable." On this basis, quia timet may be available even where the claim against the guarantor is for unliquidated damages.[2]

Whatever the position regarding accrued rights, before the court can **11–137** exercise its discretion to grant quia timet relief the guarantor must show a sufficiently clear right to an indemnity together with a clear indication that the indemnifier (*i.e.* the principal debtor) is going to ignore his obligations.[3] The first requirement will usually not be difficult to satisfy

---

[97] *ibid.*, at 304. See also *Holden v Black* (1905) 2 C.L.R. 768 at 783–784.
[98] [1928] 1 Ch. 290.
[99] *ibid.*, at 309. *Cf. Rowlatt on Principal and Surety* (5th ed., 1999).
[1] [2002] 1 Lloyd's Rep. 332 at 338 para.59.
[2] As to circumstances when this arises see below, para.11–138.
[3] *Rowland v Gulfpac Ltd* [1999] 1 Lloyd's Rep. Bank. 86. But a "clear indication" probably does not mean that there has to be a "clear threat". See *Papamichael v National Westminster Bank plc* [2002] 1 Lloyd's Rep. 332 at 338, para.61.

since in most cases the right to indemnity will automatically arise if the guarantor satisfies the principal debt. The second reinforces the notion (as expressed by Lord Hanworth in *Re Anderson-Berry*),[4] that the guarantor must show that he should be protected from "a cloud that hangs over him".[5] But it has been said that "the cloud" does not have to be "especially ominous".[6] Thus in *Ascherson v Tredegar Dry Dock & Wharf Co Ltd*[7] the estate of a deceased guarantor was able to obtain quia timet relief, even though there was no immediate threat of the bank attempting to recover that debt. Certainly, however, the guarantor must show that the cloud that hangs over him is no less than one which shows a good arguable case.[8]

11–138   On this basis a guarantor may seek quia timet relief even if the guarantor is not yet in jeopardy[9] and even if there is no immediate probability that the creditor will press him for payment in the near future.[10] The guarantor need not wait until the creditor institutes proceedings against the principal debtor or the guarantor, or both the debtor and the guarantor.[11] Equally, the guarantor may seek quia timet relief even if the creditor has not sued the guarantor or the principal debtor and even if the creditor has not refused to sue the principal debtor.[12] Quia timet relief is certainly available where the principal debtor denies the obligation to indemnify the sureties and asserts a right to leave the principal debt unpaid indefinitely, even though the sureties are under no immediate threat from the creditor.[13] Conversely, it is not necessary to establish that the creditor has refused to exercise its right to sue the principal debtor.[14] A guarantor who pays all or part of the principal debt

[4] [1928] 1 Ch. 209.
[5] *ibid.*, at 304.
[6] *Papamichael v National Westminster Bank plc* [2002] 1 Lloyd's Rep. 322 at 338, para.61.
[7] [1909] 2 Ch. 401.
[8] *Papamichael v National Westminster Bank* [2002] 1 Lloyd's Rep. 332 at 339, para.66. But in that case Judge Chambers considered that a good arguable case was itself sufficient (at 341 para.86).
[9] But quia timet relief will be granted with alacrity where the guarantor is at risk because funds are being controlled by the directors of a company in a manner adverse to the guarantor's interest: *Salcedo v Mawarie Mining Co Pty Ltd* (1991) 6 A.C.S.R. 197 at 203. See also *Graf v Auscan Timber Marketing Pty Ltd* (unreported, Sup Ct, NSW, Young J., August 9, 1995). Relief will not be available, however, to a surety of a bankrupt or a company in liquidation to restrain the trustee in bankruptcy or liquidator from acting to the prejudice of the surety by selling a security for the principal debt at undervalue: *Pratt's Trustee in Bankruptcy v Pratt* [1936] 3 All E.R. 901; *Hibernian Fire & General Insurance Co v Dargon* [1941] I.R. 514.
[10] *Ranelaugh v Hayes* (1683) 1 Vern. 189; 23 E.R. 405; *Bechervaise v Lewis* (1872) L.R. 7 C.P. 372 at 377; *Ferguson v Gibson* (1872) L.R. 14 Eq. 379; *Re Giles* [1896] 1 Ch. 956; *Double Diamond Bowling Supply Ltd v Eglinton Bowling Ltd* (1963) 39 D.L.R. (2d) 19; *Ex p. Snowdon* (1881) 17 Ch. D. 44 at 47; *Ascherson v Tredegar Dry Dock & Wharf Co* [1909] 2 Ch. 401.
[11] *ibid.*, *National Commercial Bank v Wimborne* (1978) 5 B.P.R. 11,958.
[12] *National Commercial Bank v Wimborne* (1978) 5 B.P.R. 11, 958 at 11, 978. See also *Mathews v Saurin* (1893) 31 L.R. Ir. 181; *Ascherson v Tredegar Dry Dock & Wharf Co Ltd* [1909] 2 Ch. 401 at 408–409. By the same token, it appears that the guarantor will not be entitled to quia timet relief unless the guarantor admits his liability under the guarantee: *Mathews v Saurin* (1893) 31 L.R. Ir. 181.
[13] *Rogers v ANZ Banking Group Ltd* [1985] W.A.R. 304 at 313–314, *per* Burt C.J.
[14] *Mathews v Saurin* (1893) 31 L.R. Ir. 181; *Ascherson v Tredegar Dry Dock & Wharf Co Ltd* [1909] 2 Ch. 401 at 408–409.

before it is due does not thereby forfeit the right to seek quia timet relief, but the court will not require the principal to pay the creditor before the due date.[15]

Once the requirements for the exercise of the court's discretion to grant **11–139** quia timet relief have been met, "the discretionary exercise"[16] involves balancing "the severity of the relief sought against the degree of the perceived threat".[17] Of particular relevance here (as in the case of a freezing order) is the potential dissipation of assets by the defendant.[18]

The requirement that the guarantor be liable for an ascertained sum due **11–140** and owing before quia timet relief can be granted[19] presents a problem where the contract of guarantee is revocable at the option of the guarantor after the expiration of a specified period of notice. In *Morrison v Barking Chemicals Co Ltd*,[20] a guarantor whose notice of revocation had not yet expired was denied quia timet relief because he incurred no accrued or definite liability prior to the determination of the guarantee at the end of the period of notice. In the result, a provision which was intended to allow a guarantor to revoke his guarantee on notice prevented him from qualifying for quia timet until his notice of revocation expired.

Where the guarantee makes a demand a condition precedent of the **11–141** guarantor's liability, one would expect that the guarantor would not qualify for quia timet relief until a formal demand was made; but this is not the case.[21] A guarantor is entitled to this type of relief whether or not the guarantee itself requires that a prior demand be made on the guarantor or the principal debtor and whether or not such a demand has, in fact, been made.[22]

Another exception to the rule that quia timet relief is available only **11–142** where the guarantor has incurred an accrued and fixed liability is where the principal debtor agrees with the guarantor to make specific provision for the guarantor's contingent liability to the creditor.[23] In such a special case, the guarantor can demand that the principal debtor make provision for the guarantor's liability or bring sufficient funds into court for this purpose.[24]

---

[15] *Drager v Allison* (1959) 19 D.L.R. (2d) 431. Quia timet relief may be granted even though the payment ordered to be made to the creditor might afterwards be recovered as a preference: *Salcedo v Mawarie Mining Co Pty Ltd* (1991) 6 A.C.S.R. 197.
[16] *Papamichael v National Westminster Bank plc* [2002] 1 Lloyd's Rep. 332 at 338–339, para.64.
[17] *ibid.*
[18] *ibid.*, para.66.
[19] This requirement does not prevent an action for quia timet relief being brought where the amount payable by the principal debtor to the creditor can only be ascertained by taking an account or making inquiries: see above, n.97.
[20] [1919] 2 Ch. 325 at 331 *per* Sargant J.
[21] See *Thomas v Nottingham Inc Football Club Ltd* [1972] 1 Ch. 596, where Goff J. applied *Ascherson v Tredegar Dry Dock & Wharf Co Ltd* [1909] 2 Ch. 401 and declined to follow *Bradford v Gammon* [1925] Ch. 132.
[22] *ibid.* See also *Tate v Crewdson* [1938] 1 Ch. 869 at 882.
[23] *Toussaint v Martinnant* (1787) 2 T.R. 100.
[24] *Dale v Lolley* (1808) Exch. Trin. T., referred to in a note to *Nisbet v Smith* (1789) 2 Bro C.C. 579 at 582; 29 ER 317 at 319. See also *Bellingham v Freer* (1837) 1 Moo. P.C. 333; 12 E.R. 841 and *Coppin v Gray* (1842) 1 Y. & C. Eq. 205; 62 E.R. 856.

Quia timet relief in the form of a declaration may not in itself protect the estate of the principal debtor. A freezing order would confer this protection, but an applicant for such an injunction is required to show that he has a complete and maintainable cause of action at the date of the hearing of the application.[25] The courts will not grant a freezing order in respect of a contingent cause of action, however close to fruition that cause of action may be and however just or convenient it may otherwise be to grant such an order.[26]

11–143   It is not necessary for a guarantor to assume a personal liability in order to claim a right of exoneration.[27] Where jointly owned property is mortgaged to secure the debt of one of the co-owners, the other is entitled to a right of exoneration in the form of a charge over the borrower's interest in the property.[28] However, there will be no such charge where both parties derived a benefit from the mortgage of the jointly-owned property.[29]

(d) Exclusion of the right to quia timet relief

11–144   The guarantor's right to be exonerated by the principal debtor as soon as the principal debt is payable can be excluded by express agreement.[30] This right can also be excluded by the nature of the principal liability.[31] Thus in

---

[25] See Mr Justice Andrew Rogers, "The Scope of the Mareva Injunction", in M. Hetherington (ed.), *Mareva Injunctions* (1983), p.27 and R. Meagher, D. Heydon and M. Leeming, *Equity Doctrine and Remedies* (4th ed., 2002) paras 21-430–21-455. See also *Siskina v Distos Compania Naviera SA* [1979] A.C. 210 at 256 *per* Lord Diplock; *The Tatiangela* [1980] 2 Lloyd's Rep. 193 at 197 *per* Parker J.

[26] *The Niedersachsen* [1983] 2 Lloyd's Rep. 600; *Steamship Mutual Underwriting Association v Thakur Shipping* [1986] 2 Lloyd's Rep. 439; *Siporex Trade SA v Comdel Commodities* [1986] 2 Lloyd's Rep. 428; *The Veracruz* [1992] 1 Lloyd's Rep. 353; *Zucker v Tyndall Holdings Plc* [1992] 1 W.L.R. 1127. Quaere, whether a repudiatory breach of contract would be sufficient to justify a Mareva injunction. See *Zucker v Tyndall Holdings Plc* [1992] 1 W.L.R. 1127 at 1135 where Neill L.J. left open this question.

[27] See, *e.g. Re Conley* [1938] 2 All E.R. 127 at 131; *Barclays Bank Plc v O'Brien* [1994] 1 A.C. 180; *Re A Debtor (No.24 of 1971); Ex p. Marley v Trustee of the Property of the Debtor* [1976] 1 W.L.R. 952.

[28] *Re Pittoriou, Ex p. Trustee of Property of Bankrupt* [1985] 1 W.L.R. 58 at 61–62; *Morgan v Seymour* (1638) 1 Rep. Ch. 120; 21 E.R. 525; *Ex p. Crisp* (1744) 1 Atk. 133; 26 E.R. 87; *Greerside v Benson* (1745) 3 Atk. 248; *Mayhew v Crickett* (1818) 2 Swanst. 185 at 191; 36 E.R. 585 at 587; *Goddard v Whyte* (1860) 2 Giff. 449 at 452; 66 E.R. 188 at 189.

[29] See *Rowlatt on Principal and Surety* (5th ed., 1999), p.156.

[30] *Wooldridge v Norris* (1868) L.R. 6 Eq. 410 at 414 *per* Sir G.M. Giffard V.C. It is doubtful whether a provision in a guarantee purporting to exclude the guarantor's right to apply for quia timet relief would be effective unless the principal debtor is a party to the guarantee and is, therefore, bound by its provisions: see G. Andrews and R. Millett, *Law of Guarantees* (3rd ed., 2000), para.10.29 where it is suggested that a provision in a guarantee excluding the guarantor's right to quia timet relief might be contrary to public policy or invalid as a clog on the equity of redemption. However, the real problem is that the principal debtor is rarely a party to the contract of guarantee. There may, however, be an estoppel preventing the guarantor from applying for quia timet relief. See also *Bradford v Gammon* [1925] Ch. 132 where no quia timet relief was available because of the terms of an indemnity agreement between partners.

[31] *Morrison v Barking Chemicals Co Ltd* [1919] 2 Ch. 325 at 331.

Hungerford v Hungerford,[32] a guarantor of a mortgage debt was precluded from demanding that the mortgagor pay the debt on the day specified in a covenant by the guarantor and the mortgagor because the transaction was founded upon the use of the land as a long-term security. This was a special case where both a tenant for life and the remainderman joined in a mortgage, both covenanting and giving a bond to pay the mortgage debt. In this situation, the land was "at Stake to enable the Principal to owe it (the mortgage debt), as well as the Security to pay it, or borrow thereon". Hence the remainderman, who was in the position of a guarantor, could not compel the tenant for life or his executors to redeem the mortgage on the specified date. In this rather abstruse case, it appears that the guarantor was not in imminent danger of being called upon to pay the principal debt because of "the sense of the principal transaction",[33] so he was not entitled to quia timet relief. Nor will the guarantor qualify for quia timet relief where the nature of the principal obligation is such that it will not be extinguished for a definite period.[34]

(e) Parties to the quia timet action

While it is established that a guarantor's right to apply for quia timet **11–145** relief is independent of the wishes of the creditor,[35] the guarantor should join the creditor in the proceedings.[36] This enables the guarantor to seek an order that the principal debtor pay the guaranteed debt direct to the creditor.[37] If the creditor is not a party, the court cannot order the debtor to pay the debt to the *surety instead* as this would not discharge the debtor's liability to the creditor.[38]

Clearly the principal debtor must be joined as a defendant in **11–146** proceedings for quia timet relief[39] even if the principal debtor is insolvent and unable to pay any money to the creditor, because this fact alone should not prevent the guarantor obtaining a declaration of the debtor's primary liability.

---

[32] (1708) Gilb. Eq. Rep. 67 at 69; 25 E.R. 47 at 48. See *Chitty's Equity Index* (4th ed., 1886), Vol.4, p.3632 and *Viner's Abridgement of Law and Equity* (2nd ed., 1791–1795), Vol. 20, p.105.
[33] *Rowlatt on Principal and Surety* (5th ed., 1999), para.7–15.
[34] *Bellingham v Freer* (1837) 1 Moo P.C. 333; 12 E.R. 841.
[35] *Tate v Crewdson* [1938] 1 Ch. 869; *Thomas v Nottingham Inc Football Club Ltd* [1972] 1 Ch. 596; *Ascherson v Tredegar Dry Dock & Wharf Co Ltd* [1909] 2 Ch. 401.
[36] *Wolmershausen v Gullick* [1893] 2 Ch. 514; *Woolmington v Bronze Lamp Restaurant Pty Ltd* [1984] 2 N.S.W.L.R. 242. While it is desirable to make the creditor a party to the action, it is not *necessary* to join the creditor or the co-sureties: *Ascherson v Tredegar Dry Dock & Wharf Co Ltd* [1909] 2 Ch. 401 at 405. The creditor was not joined in the quia timet proceedings in *Tate v Crewdson* [1938] Ch. 869; *Watt v Mortlock* [1964] 1 Ch. 84 and *Thomas v Nottingham Incorporated Football Club Ltd* [1972] Ch. 596.
[37] *ibid.*, at 405.
[38] *ibid.*, at 405.
[39] Quia timet relief will not be granted on an *ex parte* application: *Felton v Callis* [1969] 1 Q.B. 200.

(f) The form of quia timet relief

11–147   Quia timet relief is intended to protect the guarantor from first having to pay the principal debt. It requires the debtor to take appropriate steps to ensure that the debt will be discharged or the guarantor relieved of the liability he might incur in consequence of the debtor's default.[40] The minimum relief available in a quia timet action is a declaration that the guarantor is entitled to be exonerated from liability to the creditor and discharged on payment by the principal debtor.[41] The order may further require the debtor to pay the creditor the full amount owing forthwith so as to obtain the cancellation and return of the guarantee and to take any other steps necessary for the discharge and exoneration of the guarantor.[42]

11–148   In *Salcedo v Mawarie Mining Co Pty Ltd*,[43] McLelland J granted quia timet relief in the form of a declaration of the guarantor's right to be discharged and exonerated from all liability under the guarantee and a further order that funds realised through a sale of the principal debtor's assets by a receiver appointed by the court in earlier proceedings be paid direct to the guaranteed creditor. His Honour was mindful of the fact that this payment might later be challenged as a preference in the ultimate winding-up of the principal debtor company, but saw no alternative because there was a substantial risk that the funds would be dissipated by the directors if they were paid to the debtor company.

11–149   While the debtor will not be ordered to pay the outstanding debt to the plaintiff surety, the court can order that the amount of the debt be paid into court or that the defendant debtor give security[44] or set aside a fund to indemnify the claimant.[45] Where there already exists a definite

---

[40] *National Commercial Bank v Wimborne* (1978) 5 B.P.R. 11,958. In an appropriate case, quia timet relief may also be ordered against a party who has given the surety a bond by way of counter-indemnity: see *Wooldridge v Norris* (1868) L.R. 6 Eq. 410.

[41] *Wooldridge v Norris* (1868) L.R. 6 Eq. 410 at 413 *per* Giffard V.-C.; *Ascherson v Tredegar Dry Dock & Wharf Co Ltd* [1909] 2 Ch. 401; *National Commercial Bank v Wimborne* (1978) 5 B.P.R. 11, 958. See also *Woolmington v Bronze Lamp Restaurant Pty Ltd* [1984] 2 N.S.W.L.R. 242; *Rogers v ANZ Banking Group Ltd* [1985] W.A.R. 304 at 312 and *Watt v Mortlock* [1964] 1 Ch. 84. The costs will follow the event: *Ascherson v Tredegar Dry Dock & Wharf Co Ltd* [1909] 2 Ch. 401 at 409. If the creditor is not itself in default, costs should not be awarded against the creditor: *Holden v Black* (1905) 2 C.L.R. 768 at 785.

[42] *Thomas v Nottingham Incorporated Football Club* [1972] Ch. 596; *Re Dixon* [1994] 1 Qd. R. 7; *McIntosh v Dalwood (No.4)* (1930) 30 S.R. (NSW) 415 at 418. In *Leeds Industrial Co-op Society v Slack* [1924] A.C. 851 at 857, Lord Finlay suggested that damages may be awarded although no injury has been sustained; but see Lords Sumner and Carson, dissenting. It appears that quia timet relief may include an order that provision for payment be made: *Agnes & Jennie Mining Co v Zen* [1984] 1 W.W.R. 90 (BCSC); *McLean v Discount Finance Ltd* (1940) 64 C.L.R. 312.

[43] (1991) 6 A.C.S.R. 197.

[44] *Flight v Cook* (1755) 2 Ves. Sen. 619; 28 E.R. 394.

[45] *Re Richardson* [1911] 2 K.B. 705 at 709, 713; *Rankin v Palmer* (1912) 16 C.L.R. 285 at 290–291 *per* Griffith C.J. See also *Graf v Auscan Timber Marketing Pty Ltd* (unreported, NSW Sup Ct, Young J., August 15, 1995), where a guarantor was granted an order restraining the principal debtor from dissipating funds it was about to receive because it was likely that the principal debtor would act adversely to the guarantor.

fund for this purpose, the court may order that payment be made from that fund.[46]

Quia timet relief may be available against a third party who has given **11–150** the guarantor a counter-indemnity or security. Thus in *Wooldridge v Norris*[47] quia timet relief was claimed against the estate of the principal debtor's father who had given the guarantor a bond by way of counter-indemnity. The correct approach in such a case is for the third party to be required to perform his obligation to indemnify the guarantor.

Quia timet relief will be tailored to the particular circumstances of each **11–151** case so as to protect the guarantor as far as possible from being required to pay.[48] As Judge Chambers Q.C. pointed out in *Papamichael v National Westminster Bank Plc*,[49] "The nature of the relief is not fixed".[50] The severity of the relief sought against the principal debtor must be balanced against the degree of the perceived threat to the guarantor. But unless there is plain evidence before the court that the principal debtor clearly has the means to pay the debt, the court may merely make a general declaration exonerating the guarantor and grant him liberty to apply for further relief if the debtor fails to discharge the principal debt.[51] In other words, the court will not make a specific order enforcing the plaintiff's claim to quia timet relief, but it will make a declaration and grant liberty to apply.[52] On an application for further relief at a later date, the court can consider all the circumstances of the case (particularly the defendant's position) before making a specific order.[53] In an appropriate case, the

---

[46] *Re Anderson-Berry* [1928] Ch. 290 at 305–308; *Wooldridge v Norris* (1868) L.R. 6 Eq. 410. Indeed, in *Re Richardson* [1911] 2 K.B. 705 at 709, Cozens-Hardy M.R. recalled: "Another way in which the indemnity was often worked out in the Court of Chancery was by ordering a fund to be set apart to meet the liability as and when it arose" (emphasis added). See also Fletcher Moulton L.J. at 713 and *Salcedo v Mawarie Mining Co Pty Ltd* (1991) 6 A.S.C.R. 197, where the court ordered the debtor company to pay the proceeds of sale of its plant and equipment to the creditor. A quia timet action can, of course, be brought even if there is no particular fund which can be protected by the court's order: *Watt v Mortlock* [1964] 1 Ch. 84. It is not, therefore, necessary for the plaintiff to establish that the defendant is in possession of funds sufficient to discharge the principal debt.

[47] (1868) L.R. 6 Eq. 410.

[48] *National Commercial Bank v Wimborne* (1978) 5 B.P.R. 11,958.

[49] [2002] 1 Lloyd's Law Rep. 332.

[50] *ibid.*, at 338.

[51] *Rogers v ANZ Banking Group Ltd* [1985] W.A.R. 304 at 312–313. The form of the usual order appears in *Thomas v Nottingham Inc Football Club Ltd* [1972] 1 Ch. 596 at 607; *Watt v Mortlock* [1964] 1 Ch. 84. See also *Ascherson v Tredegar Dry Dock & Wharf Co Ltd* [1909] 2 Ch. 401 at 409; *Woolmington v Bronze Lamp Restaurant Pty Ltd* [1984] 2 N.S.W.L.R. 242.

[52] *Watt v Mortlock* [1964] 1 Ch. 84 at 88; *Woolmington v Bronze Lamp Restaurant Pty Ltd* [1984] 2 N.S.W.L.R. 242 at 244. In *Graf v Auscan Timber Marketing Pty Ltd* (unreported, Sup Ct NSW, August 9, 1995) Young J. declared that the principal debtor company was obliged to collect certain debts owed to it and set aside these funds as soon as practicable for the purpose of discharging the debt owed to certain guarantors who had discharged the principal debt. His declaration was intended to exonerate other guarantors whose residence was subject to a mortgage which had been transferred to the paying guarantors on discharge of the guaranteed debt.

[53] As Andrews and Millett point out, the Debtors Acts 1869 and 1878 would probably preclude any order for committal or sequestration in the normal case: see RSC Ord.45, r.1, especially the commentary at *The Supreme Court Practice 1997* (1996), Pt 1, 45/1/24 and 45/1/32–36; Administration of Justice Act 1970 s.11 and *Felton v Callis* [1969] 1 Q.B. 200 (where the court refused to issue a writ of *ne exeat regno* against a defendant who was proposing to leave the jurisdiction): G. Andrew and R. Millett, *Law of Guarantees* (3rd ed., 2000),

court might decide in these subsequent proceedings to make a sequestra-tion order or appoint a receiver,[54] but there are no instances of this form of relief in the authorities.

11–152   The court is not able to declare that the guarantor is entitled to set off his contingent liability under the guarantee against a separate debt which the guarantor owes to the principal debtor. The guarantor's contingent right of indemnity before payment, this right of exoneration, affords no defence to an action by the principal debtor to recover a distinct debt.[55]

(g) The utility of quia timet relief

11–153   The Law Reform Commission of British Columbia reported that the quia timet action was "exceedingly inefficient" and "fraught with technicalities".[56] One of the main problems with the equitable remedy is that the creditor is not a necessary party to the proceedings.[57] When the creditor is not joined, it remains free to enforce its contractual rights under the guarantee notwithstanding the guarantor's inchoate right of indemnity from the principal debtor prior to payment. Even if the creditor is joined, it is only in exceptional circumstances (which the courts are reluctant to specify)[58] that this inchoate right will persuade the court to restrain the creditor from enforcing the guarantee against the surety.[59] Exceptional circumstances may include proof of fraud and collusion on the part of the creditor, for example, where the creditor has assisted the principal debtor in dissipating the principal debtor's assets so that the primary burden of the debt can be cast upon the guarantor. The creditor might also be restrained from enforcing the guarantee where there is clear evidence that a

---

para.10.28. See also S. Sime, *A Practical Approach to Civil Procedure* (5th ed., 2002), pp.390–391 and 489–490.

[54] See *Graf v Auscan Timber Marketing Pty Ltd* (unreported, Sup Ct NSW, Young J., August 9, 1995).

[55] Under the Statutes of Set-Off, only mutual debts which were both presently existing and payable at the date of the action could constitute a defence. A debt which is merely contingent cannot support a legal set-off: *R. v Ray Ex p. Chapman* [1936] S.A.S.R. 241 at 247; *Fromont v Coupland* (1824) 2 Bing 170; 130 E.R. 271; *Leman v Gordon* (1838) 8 Car. & P. 392; 173 ER 546; *Re Smith Fleming & Co* (1866) L.R. 1 Ch. App. 538.

[56] British Columbia Law Reform Commission, *Report on Guarantees of Consumer Debts* (1977), p.43.

[57] *ibid. Cf. Wolmershausen v Gullick* [1893] 2 Ch. 514. There are numerous examples of cases where quia timet relief has been granted without the creditor being joined in the proceedings: see *Ascherson v Tredegar Dry Dock & Wharf Co Ltd* [1909] 2 Ch. 401; *Tate v Crewdson* [1938] Ch. 869; *Watt v Mortlock* [1964] 1 Ch. 84; *Thomas v Nottingham Inc Football Club Ltd* [1972] Ch. 596.

[58] See, *e.g. Re Anderson-Berry* [1928] 1 Ch. 290 at 309, *per* Lawrence L.J.; *Mahoney v McManus* (1981) 55 A.L.J.R. 673 at 675 *per* Gibbs C.J.

[59] *Cf. Elian and Rabbath v Matsas and Matsas* [1966] 2 Lloyd's Rep. 495, where a bank guarantee was given on the understanding that a shipowners' lien on cargo would be lifted and no further lien imposed. When the shipowners, in breach of that understanding, imposed a further lien through the ship's master, they were enjoined from enforcing their guarantee. The Court of Appeal granted an injunction to prevent what might have been an irretrievable injustice being done to the shippers who would ultimately have to reimburse the bank guarantor. Strictly speaking, this was not a case involving quia timet relief, but it suggests that in an appropriate case the court might enjoin the creditor from enforcing the guarantee.

condition precedent to the operation of the guarantee or to the liability of the guarantor has not been satisfied.

Should a guarantor qualify for quia timet relief and should such relief be **11–154** granted, there remains the problem of enforcement. Declarations granted by the court in a quia timet action are binding on the parties, but it appears that if they are disobeyed they can only be enforced by committal proceedings for contempt of court.[60] There are grave doubts whether an order that the principal debtor pay the creditor the amount outstanding can be enforced in a more specific manner.[61]

Despite these practical problems, the advantage of quia timet relief to **11–155** the guarantor is that a court order can be obtained requiring the principal debtor under threat of contempt to discharge the principal debt, thereby relieving the guarantor of his secondary obligation. This is particularly useful where there is some doubt about the precise amount of the principal debt or the guarantor's share of the liability or where there is a distinct possibility that the principal debtor might dissipate the assets which are presently available for the payment of the principal debt, although it is not necessary for the guarantor to show any fraudulent disposition of property on the part of the principal debtor or any special reason for fearing a loss.[62] All the plaintiff has to do is to make out a reasonable and probable cause of prejudice from the threatened act.[63] A further advantage of quia timet is that the principal debt may be reduced or extinguished without any need for the guarantor to pay the creditor out of his own money and then seek an indemnity from the principal. Finally, the very threat by one guarantor to seek quia timet relief may prompt the principal debtor to provide the creditor with further security or additional guarantees, thereby enabling the guarantor to restrict or escape liability.

(h) Proposed reforms

To achieve some balance in the competing interests of the parties, the **11–156** Law Reform Commission of British Columbia recommended that the guarantor be required to join the creditor in any proceedings for quia timet relief.[64] Where the creditor is joined, it will be bound by the declarations of the court and may be prevented from pursuing its normal remedies against

[60] See *National Commercial Bank v Wimborne* (1978) 5 B.P.R. 11,958 and *Practice Direction—Enforcement of Judgments and Orders*. 70 Practice Direction 1, cl.1.2.
[61] See British Columbia Law Reform Commission, *Report on Guarantees of Consumer Debts* (1977), p.43. The reluctance of the courts to specify the mode of enforcing a declaration of quia timet relief can be seen in *Watt v Mortlock* [1964] 1 Ch. 84 at 88; *Ascherson v Tredegar Dry Dock & Wharf Co Ltd* [1909] 2 Ch 401 at 409; *Woolmington v Bronze Lamp Restaurant Pty Ltd* [1984] 2 N.S.W.L.R. 242. This uncertainty limits the utility of quia timet relief.
[62] *Doster v Continental Casualty Co* 268 Ala 123; 105 So 2d. 83 (1958).
[63] *Briseis Tin Mining Co v New Brothers Home No.1 Tin Mining Co* (1891) 12 A.L.T. 223. But a quia timet action will not lie where the plaintiff's fear or apprehension of injury or damage arises, not from anything done or threatened by the defendant, but from the plaintiff's own view of his rights and disabilities: *Higgins v Potter* (1949) 50 S.R. (NSW) 77 (an injunction case).
[64] British Columbia Law Reform Commission, *Report on Guarantees of Consumer Debts* (1977), p.44.

the guarantor. This is a substantial fetter to place upon the creditor's contractual rights and it may defeat the whole purpose of the guarantee. It can only be justified if quia timet relief ensures that the creditor will be paid in full. Given the current uncertainty about specific methods of enforcing an order that the principal debtor pay the creditor, it does not seem fair to restrict the creditor's right of redress against the guarantor. Legislation may be required to confer upon the creditor a specific right to enforce an order to pay made in a quia timet action by some means such as execution, attachment or a charging order.[65]

(i) The guarantor's limited right to prospective indemnity from a stranger

11–157   While a guarantor's right to a prospective indemnity from the principal debtor arises as soon as the debt becomes payable, the guarantor's right to quia timet relief against a stranger who provides an indemnity does not crystallise until he is about to sustain a loss or incur a liability under the guarantee.[66] This difference is attributable to the fact that the stranger is not ultimately responsible for the principal debt, whereas the debtor is so liable.[67] Quia timet relief will, however, be available against the stranger before the guarantor sustains any actual damage.[68] It appears, however, that a surety who obtains payment from a stranger pursuant to quia timet relief is not obliged to apply the sum in paying off the creditor.[69]

(j) The guarantor's right of proof in the principal debtor's bankruptcy or liquidation

11–158   Prior to payment, a guarantor is merely a contingent or prospective creditor of the principal debtor in relation to his indemnity. Nevertheless, as such a creditor, the guarantor is entitled by statute to apply for a winding-up order in respect of the principal debtor.[70] But a surety's right to quia timet relief does not constitute an existing debt.[71] Thus a guarantor

---

[65] As to the enforcement of judgments, see Civil Procedure Rules 1998, Sch.1, RSC Orders 71–73, Pts 70 to 73, Sch.1, RSC Ords 45, 46, 47, 51 and 52 and Sch.2 and CCR Ords 25–27, and 35; *Practice Direction—Enforcement of Judgments and Orders*, 70 Practice Direction 1, and S. Sime, *A Practical Approach to Civil Procedure* (5th ed., 2002), pp.490–491.
[66] *Antrobus v Davidson* (1817) 3 Mer. 569; 36 E.R. 219.
[67] *Rowlatt on Principal and Surety* (5th ed., 1999), p.152.
[68] *Wooldridge v Norris* (1868) L.R. 6 Eq. 410. See also *Re Anderson-Berry* [1928] 1 Ch. 290; *Re Law Guarantee, Trust & Accident Society Ltd* [1914] 2 Ch. 617.
[69] See *Re Law Guarantee Trust & Accident Society Ltd, Liverpool, Mortgage Insurance Company's Case* [1914] 2 Ch. 617, CA.
[70] Insolvency Act 1986, s.124(1). This reverses the effect of *Re Vron Colliery Co* (1882) 20 Ch. D. 442 at 447. This right to present a winding-up petition may be useful where the guarantor is a director of the principal debtor company and wishes to prevent the company incurring further debts when he knows it is insolvent: see generally Insolvency Act 1986, ss.213 and 214, as amended by s.253 of the Enterprise Act 2002. On the other hand, a guarantor's right of exoneration cannot, it appears, found a petition in bankruptcy against the principal debtor. *Cf.*

who has not paid cannot prove in the principal debtor's bankruptcy for his right of indemnity as an *accrued liability*.[72]

In *Ex p. Whittaker*,[73] Cave J. did not finally determine whether a **11–159** guarantor for a liquidated debt presently owing could prove before payment, but his Lordship suggested that any such proof could only be in respect of a *contingent liability*. Section 328(3) of the Insolvency Act 1986 provides that, for the purposes of any references to a debt or liability within those parts of the Act which are concerned with personal insolvency, it is immaterial whether the debt or liability is present or future, certain or contingent, fixed or unliquidated, or capable of being ascertained by fixed rules or as a matter of opinion.[74] This suggests that even before payment a surety can in theory prove in the principal debtor's bankruptcy in respect of his contingent liability.[75] But even this proposition is subject to the provisions of the bankruptcy legislation regarding mutual credits, the rule against double proof and the terms of the guarantee itself.

While the surety may prove for a liability which is contingent at the date **11–160** of the bankruptcy or liquidation of the debtor, the surety will only be entitled to a dividend if he subsequently pays the whole of the principal debt. But as long as the surety actually pays all of the principal debt before an account is taken of the mutual dealings between the principal debtor and the surety, a statutory set-off should be available to the surety.[76] To quote Mason J. (as he then was) in *Day & Dent Constructions Pty Ltd v North Australian Properties Pty Ltd*:[77]

"As the surety's claim is a provable debt ... it is natural that it should also be capable of being set off under [the mutual dealings provision], provided of course that it has become an actual liability by the time the account is taken."[78]

Wolmershausen v Gullick [1893] 2 Ch. 514. See also *Re Lennard* [1934] Ch. 235 and *cf. Re Snowdon, Ex p. Snowdon* (1881) 17 Ch. D. 44; *McIntosh v Shashoua* (1931) 46 C.L.R. 494.
[71] *Re Mitchell* [1913] 1 Ch. 201.
[72] *Re A.R. Maddren* (1895) 1 A.L.R. 100; *Re Hyams, Ex p. Balfour* (1883) 5 A.L.T. 112; *Re Fenton* [1931] 1 Ch. 85; *Re Paine* [1897] 1 Q.B. 122; *Re Blackpool Motor Car Co* [1901] 1 Ch. 77; *Re Oriental Commercial Bank* (1871) 7 Ch. App. 99.
[73] [1891] 39 W.R. 400.
[74] There is a similar provision in relation to provable debts in company liquidations. See Insolvency Rules 1986 SI 1986/1925, r.13.12(3).
[75] See *Re Paine* [1897] 1 Q.B. 122; *Re Herepath and Delmar* (1890) 7 Mor. 129; *Re Blackpool Motor Co* [1901] 1 Ch. 77. As to the guarantor's rights of set-off in the debtor's bankruptcy, see below, paras 12–87 to 12–92.
[76] See s.323 of the Insolvency Act 1986 and r.4.90 of the Insolvency Rules 1986 SI 1986/1925.
[77] (1982) 150 C.L.R. 85.
[78] *ibid.*, at 108. The High Court of Australia disapproved of obiter dicta to the contrary in *Re Bruce David Realty Pty Ltd (in liq)* [1969] V.R. 240 at 243 (a case where no payment was ever made by the surety). See *Day & Dent Constructions Pty Ltd v North Australian Properties Pty Ltd* (1982) 150 C.L.R. 85 at 95. See also *Re Fenton* [1931] 1 Ch. 85, CA, applied in *Colquhoun v Simpson* (1990) 19 N.S.W.L.R. 306.

11–161   A guarantor cannot prove in the principal debtor's bankruptcy if the creditor has already proved or may prove in respect of the principal debt.[79] In substance, the guarantor and the creditor would be proving in respect of the same debt, a debt for which the creditor has priority.[80]

11–162   In *Re Bruce David Realty Pty Ltd (in liq)*,[81] a principal debtor, who was later declared bankrupt, advanced part of his bank overdraft to a company which in turn provided a guarantee of the overdraft. The company went into liquidation and the debtor's trustee in bankruptcy lodged a proof of debt in respect of the advance. The company's liquidator rejected the proof, claiming a set-off against the debtor in respect of the company's right to an indemnity as a guarantor.

11–163   One of the reasons which Adam J. of the Supreme Court of Victoria gave for denying the company's right of set-off was that it would have contravened the rule against double proof. As the principal creditor had lodged a proof of debt in the debtor's estate in respect of the guaranteed debt,

> "[i]t would clearly be contrary to principle to permit the assets of the bankrupt estate, available to the principal creditor for payment of a dividend in the bankruptcy on account of its unsatisfied debt, to be depleted for the benefit of the guarantor of the very same debt."[82]

In effect, the set-off would have allowed the guarantor to prove in the principal debtor's bankruptcy in competition with the creditor in respect of what was in substance the same debt.

11–164   The entrenched rule against double proof is not the only restriction on the guarantor's right to prove in the bankruptcy of the principal debtor. The guarantor's theoretical right to prove in respect of the guarantor's contingent liability (subject to the rule against double proof) will usually be extinguished by an express term in the guarantee restraining the guarantor from proving in the debtor's bankruptcy until the creditor has received payment in full.

11–165   Where the rule against double proof and the terms of the guarantee present no obstacle because, for example, the creditor has renounced its right to prove,[83] the guarantor can prove in respect of the guarantor's own liability. The guarantor is not prevented from proving by the fact that the creditor has already received a dividend in the bankruptcy of the principal debtor.[84] Nor is the guarantor bound by the creditor's valuation of its securities.[85] But the guarantor's proof in respect of his contingent liability

---

[79] *Re A.R. Maddren* (1895) 1 A.L.R. 100; *Re Hyams Ex p. Balfour* (1883) 5 A.L.T. 112; *Re Fenton* [1931] 1 Ch. 85 at 110, 114–115; *Re Paine* [1897] 1 Q.B. 122; *Re Blackpool Motor Car Co* [1901] 1 Ch. 77; *Re Oriental Commercial Bank* (1871) 7 Ch. App. 99; *Western Australia v Bond Corp Holdings Ltd* (1992) 8 A.C.S.R. 352 at 354.
[80] *ibid.* But it is different if the guarantee is of part of the debt: see above, paras 10–33 to 10–34.
[81] [1969] V.R. 240.
[82] *ibid.*, at 243. See also *Re Fenton* [1931] 1 Ch. 85.
[83] See *Re Fenton* [1931] 1 Ch. 85 at 119 *per* Romer L.J.
[84] *Trust & Agency Co of Australia v Greene* (1870) 1 V.R. (L) 171.
[85] *ibid.*

will not necessarily be accepted as the full amount of the guarantee. The debtor's trustee in bankruptcy will be required to make an estimate of the value of the guarantor's contingent claim[86] as at the date of the bankruptcy on the basis of the facts known at that date.[87] Any person aggrieved by this estimate may appeal to the court.[88]

Although a non-paying surety has a theoretical right to prove as a **11–166** contingent creditor, such a surety is not entitled to vote at a meeting of the creditors in respect of the full amount of his contingent debt.[89] The chairperson of the creditors' meeting would be justified in attaching only a nominal value of £1 to a prospective claim to an indemnity by the guarantor who has not paid any amount of the principal debt.

(k) Quia timet relief in the principal debtor's bankruptcy or liquidation

Rowlatt argues that, by analogy with *Re Anderson-Berry*,[90] quia timet **11–167** relief should be given to a guarantor of a bankrupt or a company in the course of winding-up if the trustee in bankruptcy or the liquidator is threatening to prejudice the guarantor's position.[91] An example would be where the trustee in bankruptcy or the liquidator threatens to realise a security which is available for the debt at a gross undervalue. It appears, however, that for the reasons outlined earlier in this chapter, this exceptional case will be confined to its special facts and that it does not support the proposition advanced by Rowlatt.[92]

Pratt's Trustee in Bankruptcy v Pratt[93] confirms this assessment. There, a **11–168** husband and wife were co-sureties of a company's overdraft at a bank. Each deposited property as collateral security and they agreed as between themselves that the husband was primarily liable. When the husband later went bankrupt, his trustee in bankruptcy, with the consent of the bank, sold the property he had given as collateral security. Farwell J. rejected the wife's claim that the property had been sold at an undervalue. Even though it was alleged that the wife had already suffered a detriment through the sale, quia timet relief was not granted to reinforce her claim to an indemnity from her husband. It appears then that *Re Anderson-Berry*, which was neither cited in argument nor mentioned in Farwell J.'s judgment, will be confined to its distinctive facts.

In one special situation, namely, where the guarantor obtains a charge **11–169** over the principal debtor's property, the guarantor's right of exoneration prior to payment will prevail against the estate of the principal debtor in

---

[86] See Insolvency Act 1986, s.322(3) and Insolvency Rules 1986 SI 1986/1925, r.4.86 and I.F. Fletcher, *The Law of Insolvency* (3rd ed., 2002), paras 9–025 to 9–027 and 23–004.
[87] *Ellis & Co's Trustee v Dixon-Johnson* [1924] 1 Ch. 342 at 357.
[88] Insolvency Act 1986, s.168(3), (5) and s.303(1).
[89] Insolvency Rules 1986 SI 1986/1925, rr.4.67(5) and 6.93(3).
[90] [1928] 1 Ch. 290.
[91] *Rowlatt on Principal and Surety* (5th ed., 1999), para.7–11.
[92] See above, paras 11–135 to 11–136.
[93] [1936] 3 All E.R. 981. See also *Hibernian Fire & General Insurance Co v Dorgan* [1941] I.R. 514.

bankruptcy. *Re Marley*[94] provides an illustration. To assist his son in obtaining a bank loan for business ventures, James Marley conveyed his freehold house into their joint names, and the house was then charged to the bank. It was accepted that he thereby assumed the position of surety for his son's business debts. When the business failed and the son was adjudged bankrupt, the son's interest in the freehold property vested in his trustee in bankruptcy. Since James Marley as guarantor had not paid the principal debt, his claim to an indemnity was inchoate. Nevertheless, Foster and Fox J.J. held that he acquired a charge over his son's interest when the freehold property was originally charged for the payment of the principal debt. This charge was enforceable as against the son's trustee in bankruptcy and the court declared that the bank's debt was payable primarily out of the son's share of the property.[95] In effect, the son's interest in the property vested in his trustee in bankruptcy subject to the father's inchoate right of indemnity as a surety. There was no need for a sale of the property in the circumstances as the bank was not seeking to enforce its security, but the court's order effectively reduced the equity of the son's trustee in bankruptcy in the property to reflect his primary liability for the principal debt. This result is similar to that which would have been produced by the doctrine of marshalling in the event of a sale of the charged property.

(l) The guarantor's right to set-off a claim to an indemnity from the principal debtor

11–170   A guarantor who has not paid any sum in reduction of the principal debt may not set off his contingent or prospective claim to an indemnity against a claim by the trustee in bankruptcy or liquidator of the principal debtor under s.323 of the Insolvency Act 1986 or r.4.90 of the Insolvency Rules 1986.[96] Any such set-off is precluded by the rule against double proof which prevents a surety from competing with the creditor in the bankruptcy or liquidation of the principal debtor if any part of the principal debt is outstanding.

Moreover, a corporate guarantor will not be able to resist a statutory demand served by the principal debtor under the Insolvency Act 1986 by raising its contingent or prospective claim to an indemnity from the principal debtor.[97]

---

[94] [1976] 1 W.L.R. 952. See also *Gee v Liddell* [1913] 2 Ch. 62 at 72–73.
[95] *Re Marley* [1976] 1 W.L.R. 952 is in accordance with the general rule that the creditor cannot restrain the guarantor from exercising his rights in respect of any securities the guarantor has obtained from the principal debtor: see above, paras 10–82 to 10–87.
[96] *Re Fenton Ex p. Fenton Textile Association Ltd* [1931] 1 Ch. 85. As to the rule against double proof, see above, paras 11–158 to 11–163 and 12–63 to 12–72.
[97] See *Mideb Nominees Pty Ltd v Begonia Pty Ltd* (1994) 15 A.C.S.R. 70 (a case involving a claim against a co-surety for an indemnity pursuant to a deed of indemnity.

(m) No right of discussion

In general, a guarantor has no right to compel the creditor to proceed **11–171** first against the principal debtor or to enforce collateral securities in respect of the principal debt.[98] However, a guarantor may be able to persuade the court not to grant an administration order under the Insolvency Act 1986 in respect of a principal debtor company where the applicant has ample security that it could enforce without court intervention and where the making of an administration order could have a disastrous effect on the guarantor and his property.[99]

(n) The guarantor's right to petition for the winding-up of the principal debtor

As a contingent creditor of the principal debtor company, a guarantor **11–172** who has not paid the principal debt is entitled to present a petition to wind up the principal debtor.[1] However, this course of action may rebound on the guarantor because it will usually precipitate a default by the principal debtor and crystallise the guarantor's liability. Moreover, a contingent creditor will be unable to obtain a dividend in the liquidation of the principal debtor[2] to relieve that creditor of his contingent liability. It would be better for the guarantor to revoke his liability under a continuing guarantee. At least this would crystallise the guarantor's accrued liabilities[3] and give the company, as a going concern, the chance to obtain a new guarantor.

(o) Marshalling

A surety may be entitled to invoke the equitable doctrine of marshalling **11–173** by way of exoneration before he has paid the principal debt.[4]

(p) An indemnifier's right to quia timet relief

Even indemnifiers are entitled to quia timet relief. In *Rowland v* **11–174** *Gulfpac Ltd*,[5] for example, Rix J. granted a freezing order to support an indemnity claim even though the cause of action to enforce the indemnity

---

[98] See above, paras 11–11 to 11–37.
[99] *Re Imperial Motors (UK) Ltd* [1990] B.C.L.C. 29. In considering whether to make an administration order, the court does not attach as much weight to the interests of secured creditors because they do not stand to lose as much as unsecured creditors: *Re Consumer and Industrial Press Ltd* [1998] B.C.L.C. 177.
[1] Insolvency Act 1986, s.124(1).
[2] *Re Fenton Ex p. Fenton Textile Association Ltd* [1931] 1 Ch. 85, CA.
[3] See above, paras 9–26 to 9–45.
[4] See *Heyman v Dubois* (1871) L.R. 13 Eq. 158. See above, paras 11–40 to 11–45.
[5] [1999] Lloyd's Rep. Bank. 86 at 98. See G. Andrews and R. Millett, *Law of Guarantees* (3rd ed., 2000), para.12.18.

was not yet complete at law. It was enough that the right to the indemnity was clear and that there was clear evidence that the indemnifier intended to ignore his obligations.

4. THE GUARANTORS' RIGHTS AGAINST CO-SURETIES BEFORE PAYMENT

(i) The right to contribution at law and in equity

11–175   Upon payment of more than their just shares of the guaranteed debt, guarantors have a right to contribution from their co-sureties.[6] Yet even before guarantors make a payment or incur a loss under the guarantee, they will be entitled to a declaration of the right to contribution if the creditor has obtained judgment or its equivalent against them.[7] Thus, in the leading case of *Wolmershausen v Gullick*,[8] the executor of a deceased surety brought a quia timet action against the co-sureties where the creditor had merely lodged a claim against the deceased's estate for the whole amount of the principal debt. If the creditor's claim had been allowed in the administration action, this would have been equivalent to judgment against the estate for the total debt guaranteed. Hence, quia timet relief was granted. Wright J. held that contribution could be effected either by an order that the defendant co-surety pay his proportionate share to the creditor if he is joined in the proceedings or, if the creditor is not a party, by a prospective order that the co-surety indemnify the plaintiff from further liability when he pays his fair share of the common liability.

11–176   An issue arises as to whether, as a precondition to the granting of quia timet relief, the guarantor must become liable to pay more than his fair share of the whole of the principal debt. For example, if there are three guarantors of a mortgage debt comprising principal of £90,000, interest, insurance premiums and taxes, and the creditor demands payment of £18,000 from one surety for arrears of interest and unpaid premiums and taxes, can that surety seek quia timet relief against the co-sureties to obtain a declaration that each of the sureties is liable for £6,000? For reasons which will be explained later,[9] it is submitted that the better view is that quia timet relief should be available only when a surety incurs an accrued and definite liability to pay more than his fair share of the whole of the common debt; it is not sufficient that the surety has become liable for more than the fair share of the amount demanded by the creditor. On this basis, quia timet relief should not be granted to the guarantor in the above example because that guarantor has not been called upon to pay more than

---

[6] See below, paras 12–158 to 12–171.
[7] *Wolmershausen v Gullick* [1893] 2 Ch. 514; *Craythorne v Swinborne* (1807) 14 Ves. 160 at 164; 33 E.R. 482 at 483–484. If a judgment is obtained, it is probably unnecessary for the guarantor to show that he is ready and willing to pay it: *Bond v Larobi Pty Ltd* (1992) 6 W.A.R. 489 at 503 *per* Owen J.
[8] [1893] 2 Ch. 514.
[9] See below, paras 12–158 to 12–171.

his one third share of the total mortgage debt, which is well in excess of £90,000.[10]

Even where the creditor has not obtained a judgment or its equivalent, **11–177** on one view[11] quia timet relief may be granted when the guarantor's loss or liability is threatened or imminent,[12] at least if the guarantor can show he was willing, able and prepared to pay the debt or his share of it.[13] Thus it appears that it will be available where the accounts between the creditor and the principal debtor are closed[14] and there is an accrued and definite liability immediately due and payable.[15] It is immaterial that the creditor has not yet formally demanded payment or that the creditor is unlikely to do so in the near future.[16] This is so even where a demand for payment is a condition precedent to the guarantor's liability under the terms of the guarantee, because a guarantor is entitled to dispel the ominous cloud hanging over his head by obtaining a declaration of the right to contribution.[17] In this sense, a guarantor's right to quia timet relief against the co-sureties depends less on the creditor's intentions than on the amenability of the guarantor to suit. It is enough that the creditor *could* enforce the guarantee against the surety forthwith[18] or after making a demand.[19] It is no defence that the co-surety had no knowledge of the payment made by the guarantor.[20] Nor does there appear to be any justification for limiting quia timet relief to cases where the creditor cannot recover against the principal debtor.[21]

A guarantor seeking quia timet relief should bring an action in equity **11–178** joining the co-sureties and the creditor as defendants. Where all these

[10] See *Woolmington v Bronze Lamp Restaurant Pty Ltd* [1984] 2 N.S.W.L.R. 242 at 245, where Needham J. stated that "the plaintiff [surety] would be entitled to the declaration only if he had paid *the full amount or had paid his share of the amount*, or satisfied the court that he was willing, able and prepared to pay that amount" (emphasis added).
[11] But the specific circumstances in which quia timet relief can be granted have not been precisely defined: *Mahoney v McManus* (1981) 55 A.L.J.R. 673 at 675 *per* Gibbs C.J.
[12] R. Goff and G. Jones, *The Law of Restitution* (6th ed., 2002), para.14–011. See also *McLean v Discount & Finance Ltd* (1939) 64 C.L.R. 312 at 343 *per* Starke J.
[13] See this limitation in *Woolmington v Bronze Lamp Restaurant Pty Ltd* [1984] 2 N.S.W.L.R. 242 at 245 ("willing, able and prepared to pay") and *Moulton v Roberts* [1977] Qd. R. 135 at 138 ("being prepared to pay it off to the advantage of his co-sureties"). Contrast *Bond v Larobi Pty Ltd* (1992) 6 W.A.R. 489, where Owen J. held that it was not an essential prerequisite to the "accrual of the cause of action for contribution" (meaning the guarantor's right to quia timet relief) that the guarantor demonstrated an ability and willingness to pay his just proportion of the principal debt. It is simply a factor to be taken into account in determining what, if any, quia timet is available to the guarantor.
[14] *Thomas v Nottingham Inc Football Club Ltd* [1972] Ch. 596, as applied to a surety's right to contribution in *Moulton v Roberts* [1977] Qd. R. 135 at 138 *per* Williams J.
[15] ibid. See also *Patterson v Arcade Buildings Ltd* [1930] G.L.R. 312 at 316.
[16] *Stimpson v Smith* [1999] Ch. 340, CA; *Thomas v Nottingham Inc Football Club Ltd* [1972] Ch. 596, as applied to a surety's right to contribution in *Moulton v Roberts* [1977] Qd. R. 135 at 138 *per* Williams J. See also *Woolmington v Bronze Lamp Restaurant Pty Ltd* [1984] 2 N.S.W.L.R. 242 and *Davis v First National Bank*, 86 Or. 474; 161 P. 93 (1916). However, in Canada it has been held that it is at least necessary that the guarantor has been called upon to pay more than his fair share: *Tucker v Bennett* [1927] 2 D.L.R. 42 at 47–48 *per* Orde J.A.
[17] ibid.
[18] *Tate v Crewdson* [1938] 1 Ch. 869; *Morrison v Barking Chemicals Co* [1919] 2 Ch. 325.
[19] *Thomas v Nottinghamshire Inc Football Club Ltd* [1972] 1 Ch. 596, as applied to a surety's right to contribution in *Moulton v Roberts* [1977] Qd. R. 135 at 138 *per* Williams J.
[20] *Stimpson v Smith* [1999] Ch. 340, CA.
[21] Cf. *Wolmershausen v Gullick* [1893] 2 Ch. 514.

parties are joined, the claimant can obtain an order requiring the co-sureties to pay their shares of the principal debt directly to the creditor.[22] This distributes the burden of the suretyship fairly and may prevent the creditor from enforcing a judgment solely against the claimant.[23] Such an order may be vacated when payment is made pursuant to its terms.[24]

11–179 Where the creditor is not joined in the proceedings the relief available is more circumscribed. The court cannot order payment to the creditor or enjoin the creditor from enforcing a judgment against the guarantor who is seeking quia timet relief.[25] Nor can the court order the co-sureties to pay their respective shares to the claimant surety, because the claimant surety cannot give them a valid discharge as against the creditor.[26] But the court can *declare* the claimant's right to contribution and even make a prospective order directing the co-sureties to indemnify the claimant against any liability he might incur after paying more than his share of the guaranteed debt.[27] The court's declaration of the claimant's right to contribution will specify an amount which is in proportion to the limits of the respective liabilities of the guarantors.[28]

11–180 The court's declaration will be futile if the co-sureties are free to dispose of their assets and property so as to defeat the surety's claim to contribution. In the United States, it has been suggested that a guarantor, even before payment of the principal debt, may restrain a fraudulent conveyance by a co-surety.[29] The current English provisions are intended to protect the victims of transactions entered into at an undervalue[30] but a guarantor who has not yet paid more than his share of the principal debt might still be classified as a victim for this purpose.[31]

---

[22] *Morgan v Seymour* (1638) 1 Ch. Rep. 120; *Dering v Earl of Winchelsea* (1787) 1 Cox 318; 29 E.R. 1184; *Wolmershausen v Gullick* [1893] 2 Ch. 514 at 528–529. The form of the writ and the statement of claim can be adapted from the forms in *Atkin's Court Forms* (2nd ed., 1982), pp.140, 143 which deal with the surety's action for quia timet relief against the principal debtor. For the form of the order, see *Kent v Abrahams* [1928] W.N. 266.
[23] *ibid.*
[24] *Patterson v Arcade Buildings Ltd* [1930] G.L.R. 312 at 317 (an indemnity case).
[25] *Wolmershausen v Gullick* [1893] 2 Ch. 514 at 528–529.
[26] *ibid.*, at 528–529.
[27] *ibid.*, at 528–529. But a surety will not be able to enforce an order for contribution until he has paid more than his fair share of the principal debt: *Wolmerhausen v Gullick* [1893] 2 Ch. 514 at 529. See also below, paras 12–158 to 12–171.
[28] *Ellesmere Brewery Co v Cooper* [1896] 1 Q.B. 75, approved in *McLean v Discount & Finance Ltd* (1939) 64 C.L.R. 312 at 341 *per* Starke J.
[29] *Bowen v Hoskins* 45 Miss. 183 (1871); *Pashby v Mandingo* 42 Mich. 172; 3 N.W. 927 (1897). See also *Clinton v Sellars* (1908) 6 W.L.R. 788 (Can) (court has power to grant an interim injunction quia timet in an action by an execution creditor to recover a fraudulent conveyance).
[30] See Insolvency Act 1986, ss.423–425, replacing s.172 of the Law of Property Act 1925. See generally I.F. Fletcher, *The Law of Insolvency* (3rd ed., 2002), paras 8–083 to 8–086. Section 423 of the Insolvency Act 1986 was amended by s.253 of the Enterprise Act 2002.
[31] It appears that a surety with a right of proof in respect of his contingent liability was regarded as a creditor for the purposes of the rule as to fraudulent preferences: *Re Blackpool Motor Car Co Ltd; Hamilton v The Company* [1901] 1 Ch. 77. See also *Re J F Aylmer (Manildra) Pty Ltd* (1968) 12 F.L.R. 337; *Re Jaques McAskell Advertising Freeth Division Pty Ltd* [1984] 1 N.S.W.L.R. 249. Moreover, in the context of fraudulent preferences it may be sufficient for the surrounding circumstances to show that the disposition of property was made with a view to hindering or delaying *future creditors* from recovering their debts: *Ex p. Russell; Re Butterworth* (1882) 19 Ch. D. 588; *Lloyd v Blumenthal* (1884) 5 L.R. (NSW) Eq. 99, and *Cf. Payne v McDonald* (1908) 6 C.L.R. 208 at 211, 213; *Perpetual Executors, etc Ltd v Wright*

Moreover, there is a burgeoning jurisdiction in both Australia and **11–181** England which can be invoked, prior to judgment, to prevent the dissipation or removal abroad of assets and property of the defendant which ultimately might be needed to satisfy the judgment.[32] But even if this form of relief were extended to a claimant in a quia timet action, it would only be available in cases where there was a distinct risk that the assets of the defendant would be removed overseas[33] or dissipated.

In *Cohen v Tranquille*[34] a guarantor who had been served with a demand **11–182** by the creditor was refused injunctive relief to prevent another guarantor from transferring his half interest in his residence to his wife who alleged that she was not liable as a co-surety. The plaintiff had no present contractual entitlement to contribution or subrogation and it was not appropriate to grant an injunction that might inhibit the creditor's enforcement of its securities when the creditor was not a party to the proceedings.

(ii) Practical problems with quia timet relief

Against this background there are grave doubts about the utility of quia **11–183** timet relief as a means of enforcing contribution by co-sureties. All the deficiencies of the quia timet action to enforce the guarantor's right of indemnity against the principal debtor apply mutatis mutandis in this context.[35] The method of enforcing the court's declaration of quia timet relief is uncertain and, in many cases, ineffectual.[36] Even in the exceptional case[37] where the creditor is joined as a party in the proceedings and the court declares that the creditor is not entitled to enforce the guarantee, it appears that the creditor may still elect to pursue its remedies or to realise securities given to the creditor by the guarantor in respect of the principal debt. The creditor's only risk is that contempt proceedings may be instituted against it. It is difficult to see why the courts are reluctant to grant quia timet relief in the form of an injunction actually restraining the creditor from enforcing the guarantee. This form of relief is similar to a feeezing order. In that context, as has been seen, the courts require the applicant to show that he has a complete and maintainable cause of action

---

(1917) 23 C.L.R. 185 at 193, 198. A surety who has not yet paid more than his just share of the principal debt might be regarded as a future creditor within this principle.

[32] *Mareva Compania Naviera SA v International Bulkcarriers SA* [1975] 2 Lloyd's Rep. 509, CA; *Third Chandris Shipping Corp Unimarine SA* [1979] Q.B. 645, CA; *Chartered Bank v Daklouche* [1980] 1 W.L.R. 107, CA; *Barclay Johnson v Yuill* [1980] 1 W.L.R. 1259; *Allen v Jambo Holdings Ltd* [1980] 1 W.L.R. 1252, CA; *Riley McKay Pty Ltd v McKay* [1982] 1 N.S.W.L.R. 264; I.C.F. Spry, "Mareva Injunctions" (1990) 20 U.W.A. Law Rev. 169; A. Rogers, "The Extra-territorial Reach of the Mareva Injunction" (1991) L.M. & C.L.Q. 231; B. J. Davenport, *Mareva Injunctions and Anton Piller Relief* (1990); P. Matthews, *Mareva Injunctions* (1990); R. Meagher, D. Heydon and M. Leeming, *Equity Doctrine and Remedies* (4th ed., 2002), paras 21-430–21-455.

[33] *ibid.*

[34] [2001] F.S.C. (unreported, Vic Sup Ct, Beach J., December 7, 2001).

[35] See above, paras 11–153 to 11–155.

[36] *ibid.*

[37] For some suggestions as to what cases may be regarded as exceptional, see above, paras 11–135 to 11–143.

at the date of the hearing of the application.[38] Whatever the correct explanation, clearly some reform of the quia timet action is warranted and the solution may lie in the recommendations of the Law Reform Commission of British Columbia, which were considered earlier in this chapter.[39]

(iii) The guarantor's right to set off a prospective claim to contribution against a debt owed to a co-surety

11–184   A guarantor's prospective right to contribution from the co-sureties in respect of payments of more than his fair share of the principal debt provides no justification for an application to the court for an order setting aside a statutory demand served by a co-surety on the guarantor.[40]

(iv) The guarantor's right to enforce contribution before payment through securities held for the principal debt

11–185   Sometimes it will not be necessary to proceed against the co-sureties themselves to enforce a claim to contribution. For example, where the principal debtor gives the guarantors a mortgage over the principal debtor's property as a counter-security, any one of the co-guarantors can probably institute proceedings to have the property made available for the purpose of contribution.[41] Such an action can be brought at any time after the principal debtor's default, and it is evidently available whether or not the plaintiff has paid the principal debt.[42]

11–186   Similar relief is available where the principal debtor gives only one of the guarantors a counter-security: the other co-sureties are entitled to share the benefit of this security on equitable principles.[43] This rule applies whether or not the claimant has paid off the principal debt, and it requires

---

[38] See above, paras 11–135 to 11–143.
[39] See above, para.11–156.
[40] See Insolvency Rules 1986, rr.6.1–6.5 (individual bankruptcy). There are no similar provisions in relation to company liquidations, although a company can apply for an injunction to restrain a creditor from presenting a winding up petition where the indebtedness is genuinely disputed; I.F. Fletcher, *The Law of Insolvency* (3rd ed., 2002), para.20–011. See also *Mideb Nominees Pty Ltd v Begonia Pty Ltd* (1994) 15 A.C.S.R. 70, where the guarantor's prospective right to contribution from the respondent company was reinforced by a deed of indemnity.
[41] *Moorhouse v Kidd* (1898) 25 O.A.R. 221, affirming (1896) 28 O.R. 35 *per* MacLennan J.A.
[42] The relevant action is probably an action for a declaration and for an order for sale of the secured property, with the proceeds to be applied in reduction of the principal debt or in settling the guarantors' right to contribution *inter se*. Naturally, the principal debtor should be joined in any such proceedings. It is true that the plaintiff in *Moorhouse v Kidd* (1898) 25 O.A.R. 221 had paid the principal debt, but the main point of the case was that it was not necessary for him to enforce the counter-security before paying the debt and seeking contribution from his co-surety; the co-surety himself could have brought an action to make the mortgaged land available for his indemnity at any time after the debtor's default. Accordingly, it was no defence for the co-surety to claim that the counter-security had depreciated in value.
[43] *Steel v Dixon* (1881) 17 Ch. D. 825; *Menzies v Kennedy* (1876) 23 Gr. 360. See also below, paras 12–248 to 12–250.

the counter-security to be shared by the co-sureties in proportion to their respective liabilities. A guarantor cannot exclude the co-sureties from enjoying any benefits or securities which the guarantor receives from the principal debtor.[44] The guarantor cannot deny the claims of the co-sureties even if he only agreed to become a guarantor in return for the counter-security and even though the other guarantors were unaware of the existence of the counter-security at the time that they entered into the contract of suretyship.[45]

This relief, however, is not available in respect of securities provided to **11–187** one guarantor by a stranger, because the ability of the principal debtor to discharge the principal debt has not been diminished and the co-sureties are not disadvantaged by the grant of such security. Thus in *Goodman v Keel*,[46] the court soundly rejected the argument that a guarantor should bring into hotchpot the wages which the principal debtor's son had assigned to him, because it was at least morally certain that the debtor would have received the benefit of her son's wages if they had not been assigned to protect the guarantor. The son's assignment of his wages to the guarantor in no way impaired or withdrew anything which the co-sureties could have hoped to reach through legal process.

Where the guarantors themselves provide the creditor with securities for **11–188** the payment of the principal debt, they may be entitled to have the securities marshalled so as to distribute the burden of the principal debt equitably.[47] It appears that this right to invoke the doctrine of marshalling is not dependent upon prior payment of the whole or part of the debt, but it may be excluded by an express provision in the guarantee.

(v) The guarantor's right to contribution in the bankruptcy or liquidation of a co-surety

For the reasons outlined earlier in relation to a guarantor's prospective **11–189** right to an indemnity from his principal debtor, a guarantor's contingent right to contribution from a co-surety prior to payment of the principal debt is, in theory, provable in the bankruptcy or liquidation of the co-surety.[48] This theoretical right of proof is, however, usually extinguished, or at least curtailed, by the rule against double proof and the terms of the guarantee. The rule against double proof precludes a guarantor from proving in a co-surety's bankruptcy or liquidation in competition with the

---

[44] *Jones v Hill* (1893) 14 L.R. (NSW) Eq. 303 at 309; *Ellesmere Brewery Co v Cooper* [1896] 1 Q.B. 75 at 80–81.
[45] *Steel v Dixon* (1881) 17 Ch. D. 825; *Trerice v Burkett* (1882) 1 O.R. 80, CA.
[46] [1923] 4 D.L.R. 468. See also *American Surety Co v Boyle* 65 Ohio L.R. 486; 63 N.E. Rep. 73 (1902). *Cf. Sherwin v McWilliams* (1921) 17 Tas. L.R. 94.
[47] *Smith v Wood* [1929] 1 Ch. 14. See also *Re Hodgetts Ex p. Official Receiver* (1949) 16 A.B.C. 201 at 211–212, where Paine J. indorsed a similar view of *Smith v Wood*.
[48] See above, paras 11–158 to 11–166. Once again, however, this right to prove in the bankruptcy or liquidation of a co-surety is subject to the rule against double proof and the terms of the guarantee: see above, para.11–163. But the fact that the amount of contribution is unascertained at the date of the bankruptcy is no bar to a surety's right to prove in the estate of a co-surety for contribution: *Wolmershausen v Gullick* [1893] 2 Ch. 514 and *Re Lynch Ex p. Hungerford; Lynch (Respondent)* (1937) 9 A.B.C. 210.

creditor for what is in substance the same debt.[49] Moreover, the guarantee itself may expressly prohibit the guarantor from proving at all until the creditor is paid in full or it may allow the guarantor to prove but require the guarantor to hold any dividends received in trust for the creditor. Curiously, a guarantor's contingent liability before payment of more than his just share of the principal debt will not support a petition in bankruptcy against a co-surety,[50] but it appears that it could sustain an application to wind up a company which is liable to contribute as a co-surety.[51] To support a creditor's petition for a winding up order, the debt must be in a liquidated form as at the date of the presentation of the petition,[52] even if the debt may be payable at a future date or subject to a contingency.[53]

---

[49] See above, para.11–163.
[50] *Wolmershausen v Gullick* [1893] 2 Ch. 514. See also *Re Lennard* [1934] Ch. 235 and Insolvency Act 1986, s.267(1) and (2)(b) and I.F. Fletcher, *The Law of Insolvency* (3rd ed., 2002), paras 6–026 to 6–027.
[51] See Insolvency Act 1986, ss.124.
[52] This is the crucial date, not the date of the hearing: I.F. Fletcher, *The Law of Insolvency* (3rd ed., 2002), paras 21–005 to 21–006. *Cf. Re Karnos Property Co Ltd* (1989) 5 B.C.C. 14.
[53] *Re Midford Docks Co* (1883) 23 Ch. D. 292.

CHAPTER 12

RIGHTS OF THE GUARANTOR AFTER PAYMENT

1. The guarantor's right of reimbursement or indemnity from the principal debtor

(i) The basis of the right of indemnity

(a) Where the principal debtor requested the guarantee

12-01   The guarantee itself seldom confers an express right of indemnity upon the guarantor,[1] but if it does, the guarantor's right to an indemnity will be governed by that provision. The legal foundation of the guarantor's right of indemnity usually depends upon the circumstances in which the guarantor assumed the burdens of suretyship. Where the guarantor gave the guarantee at the valid request[2] of the principal debtor, there is, in the absence of an express right of indemnity,[3] an implied contract of indemnity[4] or an implied term in the contract of guarantee to a similar

---

[1] See, *e.g. Cooper v Jenkins* (1863) 32 Beav. 337; 55 E.R. 132; *Re Moss, Ex p. Hallett* [1905] 2 K.B. 307. Where there is an express agreement between the principal debtor and the sureties as to their right of indemnity, the sureties may find that their right to prove in the principal's bankruptcy or liquidation is constrained by the rule against double proof: See, *e.g. Re Moss, Ex p. Hallett* [1905] 2 K.B. 307 and compare *Re Simons, Ex p. Allard* (1881) 16 Ch. D. 505 (where the counter-indemnity provided to the surety was unenforceable because it was not consistent with the terms of a composition accepted by the principal debtor's creditors) with *Re Robinson, Ex p. Burrell* (1876) 1 Ch. D. 537 (where under the terms of the composition the debtor was left free to deal with his assets and was therefore able to grant a valid security over the assets in favour of a surety who guaranteed payments to the creditors under the composition).

[2] If the principal debtor's request was void or unenforceable, it is as if no request had been made and the guarantor's claim to an indemnity can only lie in quasi-contract. But the request may be inferred from the circumstances, *e.g.* where the guarantor is the parent company of the borrower: *Seabird Corp Ltd v Sherlock* (1990) 2 A.C.S.R. 111 at 115. A surety who acts on an *ultra vires* request from a principal debtor company may be protected by ss.108–111 of the Companies Act 1989. But this would probably not assist a director who discharged debts of his company at the *ultra vires* request of the company secretary because the director remains personally liable to the company for any loss arising out of *ultra vires* acts. See *Re Cleadon Trust Ltd* [1939] 1 Ch. 286 at 299–300 and G. Andrews and R. Millett, *Law of Guarantees* (3rd ed., 2000), para.10.11.

[3] *Bradford v Gammon* [1925] Ch. 132; *Cooper v Jenkins* (1863) 32 Beav. 337; 55 E.R. 132; *Shiel v Stables* [1933] N.Z.L.R. s.45; *Israel v Foreshore Properties Pty Ltd (in liq)* (1980) 54 A.L.J.R. 421; *Re Moss, Ex p. Hallet* [1905] 2 K.B. 307. If there is an express agreement between the principal debtor and the guarantor providing for a right of indemnity, the court will not imply such a right: *Toussaint v Martinnant* (1787) 2 Term Rep. 100. See also *Re Richmond Gate Property Co* [1965] 1 W.L.R. 335 at 337; *Upton v Ferguson* (1833) 3 Moo & S. 88. A guarantor's right of indemnity can be expressly limited below the extent of the guarantor's liability under the guarantee: see *Weatherly v Mann* (unreported, NSW CA, August 16, 1973). As to the right of a guarantor to an indemnity where the express contract of indemnity with the principal debtor is unenforceable or void, see *Craven-Ellis v Canons* [1936] 2 K.B. 403; *Britain v Rossiter* (1879) 11 Q.B.D. 123. It appears that a restitutionary claim for an indemnity may be available even if the express contract of indemnity is void: see G. Andrews and P. Millett, *Law of Guarantees* (3rd ed., 2000), para.10.05. It may be different where the express contract of indemnity is merely unenforceable. See *Brittain v Rossiter* (1879) 11 Q.B.D. 123, although the implied agreement in that case appears to have circumvented s.4 of the Statute of Frauds 1677.

[4] *Johnson v Royal Mail Steam Packet Co* (1867) L.R. 3 C.P. 38 at 43; *Harris v Carnegie* [1933] 4 D.L.R. 760 (a case analogous to suretyship); *Re a Debtor* [1937] Ch. 156. See also *Anson v Anson* [1953] 1 Q.B. 636; *Re Salisbury-Jones* [1938] 3 All E.R. 459; *Manzo v 555/255 Pitt St Pty Ltd* (1990) 21 N.S.W.L.R. 1 at 5; *Batard v Hawes* (1853) 2 E. & B. 287 at 296; 118 E.R. 775 at 778.

effect.[5] In such cases the guarantor will be entitled to an indemnity whether or not his payment conferred a benefit on the principal debtor.[6] Indeed, a guarantor is entitled to an indemnity from the principal debtor even if the guarantee was given to secure money borrowed by the debtor for the use of a third person.[7] But there can be no express or implied contract of indemnity when the guarantee is furnished without the request or knowledge of the principal debtor who is sued on the alleged indemnity.[8] It is sufficient, however, that the majority of the directors of the debtor company knew that the surety intended to guarantee the company's debts and acquiesced in the provision of the guarantee for the benefit of the company. In such a case, the debtor company will be taken to have requested the guarantee, and the guarantor will have an implied right of indemnity.[9] Moreover, an indemnity will be available from the principal debtor where the principal debtor ratifies the guarantee after learning of its existence.[10]

(b) Where the principal debtor did not request the guarantee

If the debtor did not request the guarantee, the guarantor's right of reimbursement can only be based on a restitutionary claim.[11] On this basis, a guarantor[12] can recoup the amount he pays in reduction of the principal debt upon satisfying the following conditions:[13]   **12–02**

---

[5] See *Israel v Foreshore Properties Pty Ltd (in liq)* (1980) 54 A.L.J.R. 421 at 424.
[6] *Brittain v Lloyd* (1845) 14 M. & W. 762; 153 E.R. 683. See also *Warlow v Harrison* (1859) 1 E. & E. 309 at 317; 120 E.R. 920 at 928. Hence in *Argo Caribbean Group Ltd v Lewis* [1976] 2 Lloyd's Rep. 289, the guarantor was entitled to an indemnity even though the principal contract was unenforceable because of a breach of the Money Lenders Acts. See also *Re Chetwynd's Estate* [1938] Ch. 13 and *Alexander v Vane* (1836) 1 M. & W. 511; 150 E.R. 537 (indemnity available even though principal contract unenforceable) because there was no written note or memorandum as required by s.4 of the Statute of Frauds 1677. On the other hand, a surety who paid a statute-barred debt was not entitled to an indemnity on restitutionary grounds: *Re Morris; Coneys v Morris*; [1922] 1 I.R. 81, affirmed on appeal [1922] 1 I.R. 136.
[7] *Bolton v Cooke* (1825) 3 L.J.O.S. Ch. 87.
[8] *Conaghan v Cahill* (1932) Q.J.P. 54. See also *Weatherly v Mann* (unreported, NSW CA, August 16, 1973).
[9] *Rogers v ANZ Banking Group Ltd* [1985] W.A.R. 304 at 313 *per* Burt C.J.
[10] *ibid.* Burt C.J. suggested that it might be necessary for the company to enjoy the benefit of the guarantee it ratifies, but ratification should in itself be sufficient to justify an indemnity.
[11] See generally R. Goff and G. Jones, *The Law of Restitution* (6th ed., 2002), Chs 14 and 15; *Exall v Partridge* (1799) 8 Term Rep. 308; 101 E.R. 1405; *Moule v Garrett* (1872) L.R. 5 Ex. 132; 7 Ex. 101. See also *Morrice v Redwyn* (1731) 2 Barn. K.B. 26; 94 E.R. 333 (an *indebitatus assumpsit* claim); *Woffington v Sparks* (1744) 2 Ves. Sen. 569; 28 E.R. 363; *Taylor v Mills* (1777) 2 Cowp. 525; 98 E.R. 1221; *Toussaint Martinnant* (1787) 2 Term Rep. 100 at 105; 100 E.R. 55 at 57. *Ware v Horwood* (1807) 14 Ves. 28; 33 E.R. 432; *Alexander v Vane* (1836) 1 M. & W. 511; 150 E.R. 537; *Kearsley v Cole* (1846) 16 M. & W. 128; 153 E.R. 1128.
[12] It appears that recourse guarantors have a right of reimbursement even though the principal debtor may be unaware of their existence: *D.J. Morris v Ellis* (1974) 7 N.B.R. 516 (NB SC). See also *Pownal v Ferrand* (1827) 6 B. & C. 439; 108 E.R. 513; *Double Diamond Bowling Supply Ltd v Eglinton Bowling Ltd* (1963) 39 D.L.R. (2d) 19.
[13] *Cf.* R. Goff and G. Jones, *The Law of Restitution* (6th ed., 2002), Ch. 15.

    (i) that the payment was made under the compulsion of law, not under a mere moral compulsion;[14]

    (ii) that the payment was reasonably necessary in the interests of the principal debtor or the guarantor or both of them;[15] and

    (iii) that the payment discharged the liability of a debtor who, as between himself and the guarantor, was primarily and ultimately responsible for the debt and consequently obtained the benefit of the payment by an absolute or pro tanto discharge.[16]

12–03   Such a claim will succeed only where the guarantor was compelled by some necessity to incur the obligation and where it was just and reasonable in all the circumstances for the guarantor to be reimbursed.[17] This was the reason why the plaintiff's claim to a reimbursement failed in *Owen v Tate*.[18] There, the plaintiff acted initially behind the backs of the defendants who had obtained a loan from a bank on the security of a mortgage of land owned by a third party. To assist this third party, the plaintiff, without consulting the defendants, deposited a sum equivalent to the loan with the bank and signed a guarantee to pay money due from the defendants to the bank up to the amount of his deposit. In this way he obtained the release of the third party's deeds. When the defendants learned of the plaintiff's action they protested but later, when pressed for payment of their debt, they requested the bank to have recourse to the amount deposited by the plaintiff. In this sense, they ultimately accepted the benefit of the plaintiff's actions, but initially they neither requested not wanted this benefit. In these circumstances the Court of Appeal held it was neither just nor equitable to require them to reimburse the plaintiff.

---

[14] *Moule v Garrett* (1872) L.R. 7 Ex. 101 at 104; *Brook's Wharf & Bull Wharf Ltd v Goodman Bros* [1937] 1 K.B. 534, CA; *Exall v Partridge* (1799) 8 T.R. 308 at 310; 101 E.R. 1405 at 1406 *per* Lord Kenyon C.J.; *Johnson v Royal Mail Steam Packet Co* (1867) L.R. 3 C.P. 38 at 43; *Re Cleadon Trust* [1939] 1 Ch. 286, CA. Cf. *Alexander v Vane* (1836) 1 M. & W. 511; 150 E.R. 537 and Restatement of Restitution, para.78.

[15] *Owen v Tate* [1976] 1 Q.B. 402 at 409–410 *per* Scarman L.J. Note that Goff and Jones describe this second element in terms that the guarantor must not have officiously exposed himself to make the payment: see R. Goff and G. Jones, *The Law of Restitution* (6th ed., 2002), para.15–009. Cf. *The Zuhal K The Selin* [1987] 1 Lloyd's Rep 151. Further, a volunteer who performs the obligations of the principal debtor and confers an unsolicited benefit upon the principal debtor has no restitutionary claim to a reimbursement: see *Hodgson v Shaw* (1834) 3 Myl. & K. 183 at 190; 40 E.R. 70 at 73; *Leigh v Dickeson* (1884) 15 Q.B.D. 60 at 64; *Falcke v Scottish Imperial Insurance Co* (1886) 34 Ch. D. 234.

[16] *Moule v Garrett* (1872) L.R. 7 Ex. 101 at 104; *The Ripon City* [1898] P. 78 at 85–86, *per* Sir F.H. Jeune P.; *Brook's Wharf & Bull Wharf Ltd v Goodman Bros* [1937] 1 K. B. 534 at 544 *per* Lord Wright M.R.; *Johnson v Royal Mail Steam Packet Co* (1867) L.R. 3 C.P. 38 at 43; *Re Law Courts Chambers Co Ltd* (1889) 61 L.T. 669; *Garrard v James* [1925] Ch. 616 (director/guarantors were held liable on their guarantees even though the principal contract was *ultra vires*); *Roberts v Crowe* (1872) L.R. 7 C.P. 629 at 637; *Duncan, Fox & Co v North and South Wales Bank* (1880) 6 App. Cas. 1 at 19.

[17] *Owen v Tate* [1976] 1 Q.B. 402. See also *Re a Debtor* [1937] Ch. 156 at 166 *per* Stephenson L.J. Cf. *Anson v Anson* [1953] 1 Q.B. 636 at 642–643.

[18] [1976] 1 Q.B. 402. This case has been cogently criticised by the leading commentators on the law of restitution: see P. Birks and J. Beatson, "Unrequested Payment of Another's Debt" (1976) 92 L.Q.R. 188 and R. Goff and G. Jones, *The Law of Restitution* (6th ed., 2002), para.15–011. Indeed, if *Owen v Tate* is followed, there will be little scope for a restitutionary claim to an indemnity.

Consequently, the mere fact that the guarantor's payment confers a benefit upon the debtor does not always ensure the success of the guarantor's restitutionary claim for a reimbursement where the benefit was unwanted or unnecessary. Certainly, where the debtor derives no advantage from the payment, the guarantor will not be entitled to a reimbursement.[19]

The position is different if the payment made also relieves the payer **12–04** from his own liability.[20] For example, where two persons are liable for the same debt, and, as between them, one is primarily liable and the other is secondarily liable, the former is obliged to indemnify the latter if the latter discharges the liability.[21] This restitutionary right to an indemnity is not founded on a request for payment and there is no question of the secondary obligor officiously exposing himself to the liability to pay the principal debt: the secondary obligor is, after all, liable in his own right. The right to an indemnity arises simply because the secondary obligor discharges the liability of the primary obligor. This principle allows a lessee, who had assigned the lease, to obtain an indemnity after payment to the lessor, not only against the assignee,[22] but also against a surety for the assignee.[23] The indemnity arises despite the absence of privity of contract between the lessee and the surety for the assignee.

Because of the potential difficulties associated with the restitutionary **12–05** claim to an indemnity, a guarantor usually seeks an indemnity founded on an express or implied contract and, therefore, a prospective guarantor would be unwise to accept the burdens of suretyship in the absence of a specific request by the principal debtor.[24]

(c) A surety's or quasi-surety's right of indemnity in a bill transaction

In *Duncan, Fox & Co v North and South Wales Bank*,[25] Lord Selborne **12–06** L.C. explained the right of an indorser to an indemnity from the acceptor for any sum the indorser pays off the bill in the following terms:

---

[19] See R. Goff and G. Jones, *The Law of Restitution* (6th ed., 2002), para.15–015; *Re Morris; Coneys v Morris* [1922] 1 I.R. 81, affirmed on appeal [1922] 1 I.R. 136.
[20] *Becton Dickinson Ltd v Zwebner* [1988] 3 W.L.R. 1376.
[21] *Moule v Garrett* (1872) L.R. 7 Ex. 101; *Duncan, Fox & Co v North and South Wales Bank* (1880) 6 App. Cas. 1 at 11–12; *Becton Dickinson UK Ltd v Zwebner* [1989] 1 Q.B. 208; *Selous Street Properties Ltd v Oronel Fabrics Ltd* (1984) 270 E.G. 643.
[22] *Moule v Garrett* (1872) L.R. 5 Ex. 132; 7 Ex. 101; *Walker v Bartlett* (1856) 18 C.B. 845; *Re Cleadon Trust Ltd* [1939] 1 Ch. 286; *Becton Dickinson Ltd v Zwebner* [1989] Q.B. 208; *Selous Street Properties Ltd v Oronel Fabrics Ltd* (1984) 270 E.G. 643. A similar principle applies to a transferee of shares if the transferer is made a contributory: *Nevill's Case* (1870) L.R. 6 Ch. App. 43; *Roberts v Crowe* (1872) L.R. 7 C.P. 629; *Kellock v Enthoven* (1882) L.R. 8 Q.B. 458.
[23] *Becton Dickinson Ltd v Zwebner* [1989] 1 Q.B. 208; *Selous Street Properties Ltd v Oronel Fabrics Ltd* (1984) 270 E.G. 643; *Cale v Assuidoman KPS (Harrow) Ltd* [1996] B.P.I.R. 245. It is not necessary for the original lessee to serve notices on the assignees of the lease or their guarantors under s.17 of the Landlord and Tenant (Covenants) Act 1995 to enforce this restitutionary claim to an indemnity or contribution: *Fresh (Retail) Ltd v Emsden* (unreported, Judge Brandt C.C. (Ipswich), January 18, 1999).
[24] Since the request must be made by the principal debtor, a request in the guarantee itself will generally not suffice as the debtor is seldom a party to the guarantee.
[25] (1880) 6 App. Cas. 1.

"The acceptor, though he may know nothing of any particular indorser, knows that by his acceptance he does an act which will make him liable to indemnify any person who may indorse, and may afterwards pay the bills; and he knowingly and intentionally undertakes that liability, as much as if the indorsement were the result of direct communication between himself and that person."[26]

Although the drawer of a bill of exchange is not strictly a surety for the acceptor, such a drawer enjoys a similar right of indemnity against the acceptor.[27]

12–07   In *Ex p. Bishop*,[28] the drawer's right of indemnity was based upon an implied authority given to him by the acceptor. In that case, it was established that it was the common practice of London bill brokers not to indorse each bill of exchange which may have been discounted for a customer when they rediscounted the bill with their bankers. Instead, the brokers gave the bankers a general guarantee covering all the bills to be rediscounted with the bankers. The Court of Appeal held that, when an accommodation bill was drawn and accepted to raise money for the drawer and acceptor, the drawer by discounting the bill with the London bill brokers had an implied authority from the acceptor to deal with them in the ordinary course of their business. Since the brokers had an implied authority from the acceptor to make themselves liable on the bill under their guarantee to their bankers, they were entitled to an indemnity from the acceptor for what they had paid to the bankers in respect of the bill under their guarantee.

12–08   Successive indorsers are also prima facie liable to indemnify one another in respect of their liabilities on the bill or note, so that a prior indorser must indemnify a subsequent one.[29] But where the successive indorsers are all accommodation indorsers for another party, or where they have reached an independent collateral agreement to share the liability, they may merely be liable to contribute inter se.[30]

12–09   The acceptor of an accommodation bill is merely a surety as between himself and the drawer. As such, the acceptor is entitled to recover from the drawer whatever he is required to pay in discharge of the suretyship.[31] The rights of other accommodation parties to a bill to an indemnity from

---

[26] *ibid.*, at 14. See also *Pownal v Ferrand* (1827) 6 B. & C. 439; 108 E.R. 513.
[27] *Ex p. Yonge* (1814) 3 V. & B. 31; 35 E.R. 391; *Pownal v Ferrand* (1827) 6 B. & C. 439; 108 E.R. 513.
[28] (1880) 15 Ch. D. 400.
[29] *Macdonald v Whitfield* (1883) 8 App. Cas. 733.
[30] See *Macdonald v Whitfield* (1883) 8 App. Cas. 733; *Vallée v Talbot* (1892) 1 Que. S.C. 223, CA.
[31] *Jones v Broadhurst* (1850) 9 C.B. 173; 137 E.R. 858. It is doubtful whether an accommodation acceptor would be entitled as a matter of law to recover by way of indemnity the costs of an action brought against him: *Pierce v Williams* (1854) 23 L.J. Ex. 322; *Beech v Jones* (1848) 5 C.B. 696; 136 E.R. 1052, doubting *Jones v Brooke* (1812) 4 Taunt 464; 128 E.R. 409; *Stratton v Mathews* (1848) 3 Exch. 48; 154 E.R. 750.

the party accommodated are implied from his request to them to put their names on the bill.[32] In the absence of such a request, an accommodation indorser cannot claim an indemnity from one of the joint makers of a promissory note even if there is proof that that maker was not a principal but merely a surety for the other maker without the knowledge of the indorser.[33] In such a case, however, the accommodation indorser may be able to claim contribution from the maker as a co-surety.[34]

By contrast, a person who pays on maturity a joint and several **12–10** promissory note signed by that person as surety and another person as principal can recover the amount from the principal even if the payment was made without any request or compulsion by the holder.[35]

(ii) When is the indemnity enforceable?

The principal debtor and the guarantor can, of course, expressly agree **12–11** that the guarantor's right of indemnity is enforceable even before the guarantor has paid any part of the principal debt.[36] In the absence of such an agreement, a guarantor is not entitled to claim an indemnity until he pays the principal debt or some part of it.[37] The guarantor need not wait to be called upon by the creditor to pay the debt even if the undertaking is couched in terms that the guarantor will pay a certain sum "when called

---

[32] *Godsell v Lloyd* (1911) 27 T.L.R. 383. It is not necessary for the contract of indemnity which arises out of an accommodation transaction to be in writing: *Batson v King* (1859) 4 H. & N. 739; 157 E.R. 1032.

[33] *ibid.*

[34] *ibid.*

[35] *Davies v Humphreys* (1840) 6 M. & W. 153; 151 E.R. 361.

[36] See, *e.g. Spark v Heslop* (1859) 1 El. & El. 563; 120 E.R. 1020, where a guarantor was held to be entitled to recover from the principal debtor a sum equal to the costs of an action under the terms of an express covenant of indemnity even though he had not yet paid the costs. See also *Re Allen* [1896] 2 Ch. 345 (covenant between the principal debtor and surety that debtor would pay the principal debt on a certain day; surety had immediate right to recover damages for breach of covenant on that day). See also *Bosma v Larsen* [1966] 1 Lloyd's Rep. 22 (shipowners' claim to any indemnity was statute-barred because it arose when facts came into existence which created their liability to cargo-owners and insurers); *National House-Building Council v Fraser* [1983] 1 All E.R. 1090. Guarantors will be entitled to enforce their right of indemnity in equity even before they have paid any part of the principal debt: *Meates v Westpac Building Corp Ltd* [1991] 3 N.Z.L.R. 385. See above, paras 11–130 to 11–152.

[37] *Stirling v Forrester* (1821) 3 Bli. 575; 4 E.R. 712; *Re Fenton, Ex p. Fenton Textile Association Ltd* (hereinafter *Re Fenton*) [1931] 1 Ch. 85 at 113–114; *Re Mitchell* [1913] 1 Ch. 201; *Davies v Humphreys* (1840) 6 M & W 153; 151 ER 361; *Israel v Foreshore Properties Pty Ltd (in liq)* (1980) 54 A.L.J.R. 421. But note that a contractual right of indemnity may arise (as a result of the principal's request for the guarantee) at the date of the execution of the guarantee, although there is no enforceable debt until payment by the guarantor: *Re a Debtor* [1937] Ch. 156. But where the guarantors' obligation to pay the principal debt ceases upon termination of the principal transaction according to its terms, so too does the principal debtor's obligation to indemnify the guarantors against their liability as guarantors: *Pace v Ireland* (unreported, NSW CA, September 10, 1993), reversing *Pace v Ireland* (unreported, NSW Sup Ct, February 13, 1991) (a case where the guarantors agreed to indemnify the "borrower" against any liability they might incur under bank loans which the guarantors agreed to repay). See also quia timet relief, above, paras 11–130 to 11–152. Unless the right of indemnity exists at the time of payment by the guarantor or immediately thereafter, it will never arise: *Scholefield Goodman & Sons Ltd v Zyngier* [1984] V.R. 445. This decision was affirmed by the Privy Council on other grounds in *Scholefield Goodman & Sons Ltd v Zyngier* (1985) 59 A.L.J.R. 770.

upon".[38] Where guarantors have no reasonable defence to the creditor's claim on the guarantee, they may pay the debt as soon as it becomes due.[39] But a guarantor cannot accelerate his remedy against the principal debtor by a premature payment.[40] If the guarantor discharges the principal debt before the due date, the right to an indemnity from the debtor does not crystallise until the debtor could be sued for the debt.[41]

12–12   By the same token, guarantors who pay off the principal debt after the principal debtor's default but before receiving any demand from the creditor are entitled to an indemnity from the debtor. It is not necessary for the guarantors to wait until a demand is served on them if their liability is clear. Even if a demand is a condition precedent to their liability they can waive this condition because it is in their favour. A guarantor who pays off the principal debt before receiving any demand from the creditor does not have the immediate right to an indemnity from the principal debtor which a guarantor enjoys upon discharging the principal debt after default by the debtor and demand by the creditor.[42] A sub-surety, who is in effect a surety for a surety, can also invoke this right of indemnity once he has settled the creditor's claim in his capacity of subsurety.[43]

12–13   Where the guarantor obtains the discharge of the principal debt by giving the creditor a promissory note or bond payable on a certain date,

[38] *Green v Parr* (1870) 4 S.A.S.R. 126.

[39] *Pitt v Purssord* (1841) 8 M. & W. 538; 151 E.R. 1152. See also *Green v Parr* (1870) 4 S.A.S.R. 126 at 127. In equity it was clearly established that a surety could pay the principal debt when it fell due: *Swire v Redman* (1876) 1 Q.B.D. 536 at 541. See also *Lord Newborough v Schroder* (1849) 7 C.B. 342 at 399; 137 E.R. 136 at 159; *Pettman v Keble* (1850) 9 C.B. 701; 137 E.R. 1067. It is immaterial that the payment under the guarantee was made for an ulterior motive or that the guarantor derives a collateral benefit from the payment: *Baker v Microdos Computers Australia Pty Ltd (in liq)* (1996) 20 A.C.S.R. 148 (where the guarantor was able to set off the amount of the payment against any liability that he might incur in the principal debtor company's action against him in relation to the transfer of the company's stock). As to whether the principal debtor is liable to reimburse the guarantor for expenses incurred by the guarantor in unnecessarily contesting for some time the payment of a valid debt covered by the guarantee, see *Re Garway Ex p. Marshall* (1751) 1 Atk. 262; 26 E.R. 167.

[40] See *Drager v Allison* (1959) 19 D.L.R. (2d) 431; [1959] S.C.R. 661 (Can). See also *Coppin v Gray* (1842) 1 Y. & C. Eq. 205; 62 ER 856; *Re Moss; Ex p. Hallet* [1905] 2 K. B. 307; *Good Motel Co Ltd (in liq) v Rodeway Pacific International Ltd* (1988) 94 F.L.R. 84. Where a company guaranteed the performance of the obligation of its subsidiary to make progress payments to a builder under a building contract, the company did not confer an unfair preference on the builder by making payments before it was required to do so under its guarantee. The company was not actually or contingently liable to the builder under the performance guarantee at the time of the payments. *Walsh v Salzer Constructions Pty Ltd* [2001] 3 V.L.R. 305.

[41] *ibid.*

[42] See *Green v Parr* (1870) 4 S.A.L.R. 126 (Aus); *Read v McLean* [1925] 3 D.L.R. 716; and *Stimpson v Smith* [1999] Ch. 340 (a contribution claim, but a similar principle should apply to a claim to an indemnity from the principal debtor). *Cf. Good Motel Co Ltd (in liq) v Rodeway Pacific International Ltd* (1988) 94 F.L.R. 84 at 93 (where Miles C.J. was not persuaded that the payments by the guarantor were made pursuant to the guarantee). Where the guarantors' right of indemnity is based on an express or implied contract, they might be able to sue the principal debtor even before payment for an anticipatory breach of this contract if the debtor asserts that he intends to ignore his obligation to indemnify the guarantors: G. Andrews and R. Millett, *Law of Guarantees* (3rd ed., 2000), para.10.16. Compare *Rowland v Gulfpac Ltd* [1999] Lloyd's Rep. Bank. 86 at 98. It is unlikely that guarantors would be entitled to sue the principal debtor in this situation if their claim to an indemnity was based on restitutionary grounds.

[43] *Standard Brands Ltd v Fox* 29 (1972) D.L.R. (3d) 167 affirmed in (1974) 44 D.L.R. (3d) 69. See also *Fox v Royal Bank of Canada* (1975) 59 D.L.R. (3d) 258.

the better view appears to be that the guarantor cannot claim an indemnity from the principal debtor before the bond or note matures, for only then does the guarantor sustain a loss.[44] Similarly, there is a presumption that a bill of exchange or cheque operates only as a conditional payment and the surety does not effect payment until the condition is satisfied. However, if this presumption can be rebutted by express or implied agreement,[45] the guarantor should be entitled to seek an indemnity from the principal debtor for the amount of the bill of exchange or cheque paid to the creditor. But, there is no right of indemnity where the bond given by the surety to the creditor is replaced by another bond which discharges the original debt.[46]

(iii) Exclusion, waiver or forfeiture of the right of indemnity

A guarantor's right of reimbursement or indemnity can be limited or **12–14** excluded expressly by agreement[47] or impliedly by the type of liability secured by the guarantee.[48] Where the nature of the principal liability is such that it cannot be discharged before a certain period elapses, the guarantor will not be entitled to an indemnity in respect of a premature payment.[49] Nor can the guarantor compel the principal debtor to pay off the creditor before that period expires. So too, where a mortgagor and the mortgagor's guarantor jointly covenant to pay the mortgage debt on a specified day on the understanding that the land is to be used as a continuing security to assist the mortgagor to pay the secured debt, the guarantor cannot require the mortgagor to redeem the mortgage on that date.[50] On the other hand, the guarantor's right of indemnity cannot be

---

[44] *Maxwell v Jameson* (1818) 2 B. & Ald. 51 at 54; 106 E.R. 286 at 287; *Taylor v Higgins* (1802) 3 East 169; 102 E.R. 562. See also *Re Parkinson; Ex p. Sergeant* (1822) 2 Gl. & J. 23. *Cf. Barclay v Gooch* (1797) 2 Esp. 571; 170 E.R. 459; *Gore v Gore* [1901] 2 I.R. 269; *Fahey v Frawley* (1890) 26 L.R. Ir. 78, which may be explained as applications for quia timet relief: see T. D. Putnam, *Suretyship* (1981), p.72.

[45] *Allen v Royal Bank of Canada* (1926) 95 W.P.C. 17; *Re Romer & Halsam* [1893] 2 Q.B. 286 (the handing of a negotiable security and the giving of a receipt does not amount to payment if the security is later dishonoured); *Bolt & Nut Co (Tipton) Ltd v Rowlands Nicholls & Co Ltd* [1964] 2 Q.B. 10 (a cheque is a conditional payment). See G. Andrews and R. Millett, *Law of Guarantees* (3rd ed., 2000), para.10.22.

[46] *Re Parkinson, Ex p. Sergeant* (1822) 1 Gl. & J. 183, affirmed in (1825) 2 Gl. & J. 23.

[47] *Bradford v Gammon* [1925] Ch. 132; *Shiel v Stables* [1933] N.Z.L.R. s.45; *Israel v Foreshore Properties Pty Ltd (in liq)* (1980) 54 A.L.J.R. 421. If the guarantee itself excludes the guarantor's indemnity, the principal debtor cannot enforce this provision unless the guarantor was a party to the guarantee or unless the guarantor falls within the Contracts (Rights of Third Parties) Act 1999. As we have seen, a guarantor's right of indemnity can be expressly limited below the extent of the guarantor's liability under the guarantee: see *Weatherly v Mann* (unreported, NSW CA, August 16, 1973).

[48] See *Hungerford v Hungerford* (1708) Gilb. Eq. Rep. 67 at 69; 25 E.R. 47; *Bellingham v Freer* (1837) 1 Moo. P.C. 333; 12 E.R. 841. *Cf. AGC (Advances) Ltd v West* (1984) 5 N.S.W.L.R. 590 (implied contract will rarely displace right of indemnity); *Close v Close* (1853) 4 De G.M. & G. 176; 43 E.R. 474.

[49] See *Bellingham v Freer* (1837) 1 Moo P.C. 333; 12 E.R. 841; *Drager v Allison* (1959) 19 D.L.R. (2d) 431; [1959] S.C.R. 661 (Can). See also above, paras 11–35 *et seq.*

[50] *Hungerford v Hungerford* (1708) Gilb Eq. Ca. at 69; 25 E.R. 47 at 48: see *Chitty's Equity Index* (4th ed., 1886), Vol.4, p.3632; *Viner's Abridgment of Law and Equity* (2nd ed., 1791–1795), Vol 20, p.105. See also above, para.11–144.

excluded by a provision in the principal transaction which is intended to govern the obligation of the principal debtors inter se.[51] Nor can a guarantor's right of indemnity be excluded by an undertaking by the creditor that it will not sue the principal debtor or that it will not prove in the principal's bankruptcy or liquidation.[52] Even a compromise between the creditor and the principal debtor will not prevent the guarantors from invoking their right of indemnity if they are called upon to pay and are liable to pay the principal debt.[53] But a surety's right of indemnity from the principal debtor can be excluded by a compromise agreement between the creditor and the surety even where the agreement preserves "any subrogated claims" by the surety in respect of sums paid to the creditor. The preservation of the "subrogated claims" does not extend to the surety's rights to an indemnity relating to sums which were payable and paid by the surety to the creditor but which were not payable by the principal debtor to the creditor.[54]

12–15   The sureties can waive their right of indemnity by representations which amount to a binding promise that the right of indemnity will not be enforced or which constitute an estoppel preventing its enforcement.[55] But clear language is required to waive or exclude the guarantor's right of indemnity. In *Re Mitchell, Freelove v Mitchell*,[56] for example, the surety clearly intended that his estate should not enforce the right of indemnity against the principal debtor in respect of a debt arising after his death but the surety's will only released the principal debtor in respect of debts existing at the date of the surety's death. Accordingly, the estate's right to an indemnity in respect of the subsequent debt was not effectively excluded.

12–16   When a trustee, carrying on the business of an insolvent builder under a deed of assignment for the benefit of his creditors, reported to the creditors that he intended to treat his guarantor's claim to an indemnity as a preferential one out of the available funds in accordance with an express term of the deed, the guarantor did not thereby forfeit his right of personal indemnity from the trustee: the trustee's statement purporting to affect his rights was not specifically drawn to the guarantor's attention and there could be no waiver without knowledge.[57] Only the guarantor himself could waive his rights as a surety.

---

[51] *Israel v Foreshore Properties Pty Ltd (in liq)* (1980) 54 A.L.J.R. 421.
[52] See *Brown v Coughlin* (1914) 50 S.C.R. 100 at 109.
[53] G. Andrews and R. Millett, *Law of Guarantees* (3rd ed., 2000), para.10.03.
[54] *Re Empire Paper Ltd (in liq)* [1999] B.C.C. 406.
[55] See *Chadwick v Manning* [1896] A.C. 231, PC; *Jorden v Money* (1854) 5 H.L. Cas. 185; 10 E.R. 868.
[56] [1913] 1 Ch. 201. See G. Andrews and R. Millett, *Law of Guarantees* (3rd ed., 2000), para.10.23.
[57] *Shiel v Stables* [1933] N.Z.L.R. s.45.

(iv) Who can invoke the right of indemnity?

In general, a guarantor who has paid *any* amount off the principal debt **12–17** can claim an indemnity from the principal debtor.[58] This is an independent right of the guarantor; it is not acquired by way of subrogation to the rights of the creditor.[59] Where a guarantor makes payments to the creditor to serve the guarantor's own business purposes and not in response to any demand from the creditor, the court may conclude that the payments were not made pursuant to the guarantee and deny the guarantor an indemnity in respect of the payments.[60] As we have seen, this right of indemnity can also be invoked by a sub-surety of a surety once the sub-surety has settled the creditor's claim in his capacity of sub-surety.[61] Moreover, it is available to a person who pays on guarantees given in respect of the carrying on of a business by an executor or trustee as part of an estate, or given by a trustee carrying on a business assigned to the trustee for the benefit of creditors of the former owner.[62]

The presumption of advancement which operates between a husband **12–18** and his wife will not, in general, preclude the husband's claim to an indemnity in respect of a liability he has incurred under a guarantee of his wife's debts. Neither his entry into the guarantee nor any payments which he is compelled to make thereunder will be presumed to be a gift to his wife. Thus, the husband is entitled to reimbursement from the wife or her estate for any payments he has made in reduction of the guaranteed debt.[63]

The right of indemnity is also available in cases analogous to suretyship **12–19** where one party pays at the request and for the benefit of another.[64] Equally, whenever a person who is merely secondarily liable makes a payment under compulsion of law in discharge of another's primary liability, that person is entitled to claim an indemnity from the other party.[65] On this basis the assignor of a lease and the transferor of shares can recover from the assignee and transferee respectively if they are compelled to discharge any obligations or make any payments in discharge of the primary liability of the assignee or the transferee, as the case may

---

[58] It appears that it is even available to recourse guarantors: see above, para.12–01. It should also be available to the government in respect of a bare statutory guarantee. The fact that the guarantee is contained in a statute should not preclude the government's right of indemnity.

[59] K.P. McGuiness, *The Law of Guarantee* (1986), pp.212–213; *Morris v Ford Motor Co* [1973] 2 All E.R. 1084 at 1089, CA.

[60] *Good Motel Co Ltd (in liq) v Rodeway Pacific International Ltd* (1988) 94 F.L.R. 84, where the guarantor made payments of rent under a sublease to preserve the business of a motel which was in the hands of one of its subsidiaries.

[61] *Standard Brands Ltd v Fox* (1972) 29 D.L.R. (3d) 167, affirmed in (1973) 44 D.L.R. (3d) 69. See also (1975) 59 DLR (3d) 258.

[62] *Shiel v Stables* [1933] N.Z.L.R. s.45.

[63] *Re Salisbury-Jones* [1938] 3 All ER 459; *Anson v Anson* [1953] 1 Q.B. 636. It is different, however, where there is concrete evidence that the husband's payment of the principal debt was intended to be a gift to his wife. It may also be noted that the High Court of Australia has recently held that the presumption of advancement applies to gifts by fathers and mothers to their children: *Nelson v Nelson* (1995) 132 A.L.R. 133.

[64] *Israel v Foreshore Properties Pty Ltd (in liq)* (1980) 54 A.L.J.R. 421.

[65] *Roberts v Crowe* (1872) L.R. 7 C.P. 629 at 637 *per* Willes J. See also *Duncan, Fox & Co v North and South Wales Bank* (1880) 6 App. Cas. 1 at 19 and *Rowlatt on Principal and Surety* (5th ed, 1999), para.7–06.

be.[66] A similar situation arises where a creditor lawfully seizes one person's property in payment of another's debt.[67] The owner's right to indemnity exists although there may be no agreement to indemnify the owner and even though, in that sense, there may be no privity between the owner and the debtor.[68]

12–20 By analogy with the rights of a guarantor, these parties who are secondarily liable are entitled to the creditor's remedies against the primary obligor upon payment or discharge of the primary obligation.[69] They should, therefore, be entitled to an indemnity even if the primary obligor was unaware of the existence of their secondary obligation.[70] The right of an indorser, who is secondarily liable on a bill of exchange, to an indemnity from the acceptor[71] of the bill is even clearer because the acceptor should expect that there will be indorsers, even if they are not known to the acceptor.[72]

(v) Can a right of indemnity be invoked by an indemnifier?

12–21 Where a contract of indemnity rather than a contract of guarantee is entered into at the request of a debtor, there appears to be no sound reason why the indemnifier should not be entitled to recoup from the debtor any amounts the indemnifier pays pursuant to the contract.[73] Through payment, the indemnifier, in effect, incurs a liability at the request and for the benefit of another person who should, therefore, be obliged to indemnify the indemnifier.[74] It may be difficult to establish the necessary request where the debtor is an infant[75] and there may be some problems in calculating the amount of this indemnity where the indemnifier's liability is more extensive than that of the debtor,[76] but

---

[66] See *Moule v Garrett* (1872) L.R. 5 Ex. 132; 7 Ex. 101; *Walker v Bartlett* (1856) 18 C.B. 854; 139 E.R. 1604; *Nevill's Case* (1870) 6 Ch. App. 43; *Roberts v Crowe* (1872) L.R. 7 C.P. 629; *Kellock v Enthoven* (1882) L.R. 8 Q.B. 458; 9 Q.B. 241.
[67] *Exall v Partridge* (1799) 8 Term Rep. 308; 101 E.R. 1405; *Johnson v Royal Mail Steam Packet Co* (1867) L.R. 3 C.P. 38; *Edmunds v Wallingford* (1885) 14 Q.B.D. 811.
[68] *Edmunds v Wallingford* (1885) 14 Q.B.D. 811.
[69] *Rowlatt on Principal and Surety* (5th ed., 1999), para.7–07.
[70] See *Powers v Nash* 37 Maine 322 (1853).
[71] See *Sleigh v Sleigh* (1850) 5 Exch. 451; 155 E.R. 224; *Ex p. Bishop* (1880) 15 Ch. D. 400 at 410.
[72] See *Ex p. Bishop* (1880) 15 Ch. D. 400 at 416; *Duncan, Fox & Co v North and South Wales Bank* (1880) 6 App. Cas. 1 at 13, 14 *per* Lord Selborne.
[73] *Cf. Sheffield Corp v Barclay* [1905] A.C. 392. See *Chitty on Contracts* (28th ed., 1994), Vol. 2, para.42–103.
[74] *Israel v Foreshore Properties Pty Ltd (in liq)* (1980) 54 A.L.J.R. 421; *Duncan, Fox & Co v North and South Wales Bank* (1880) 6 App. Cas. 1 at 13–14. See also *Moule v Garrett* (1872) L.R. 7 Ex. 101, the *"Zuhall K"* and *"The Selin"* [1987] 1 Lloyd's Rep. 151, 1 F.T.L.R. 76 and Goff and Jones, *The Law of Restitution* (6th ed., 2002), paras 15–009 to 15–019.
[75] The defendant in *Yeoman Credit Ltd v Latter* [1961] 1 W.L.R. 828 would not have been entitled to an indemnity from the infant hirer under the hire-purchase contract. Even though a guarantee of a minor's contract may be enforceable, it does not follow that the guarantor is entitled to an indemnity from the minor See Minors' Contracts Act 1987, s.2.
[76] Although this in itself should not bar relief.

generally the indemnifier should be entitled to an indemnity from the debtor.

In *Versteeg v Court*,[77] White J. of the Supreme Court of Western **12–22** Australia confirmed that the applicants, who had provided a guarantee and indemnity at the request of the principal debtor company, were entitled to an indemnity from the company in respect of amounts paid to a bank pursuant to the indemnity clause in the guarantee and indemnity. This indemnity applied to any liability which the applicants lawfully incurred at the specific request and for the benefit of the company. The right of indemnity extended beyond amounts which the principal debtor company could be required to pay and even beyond amounts which could be demanded under the guarantee. The applicants were held to be entitled to an indemnity from the principal debtor company in respect of certain loan charges and the legal costs incurred by, and awarded against, the creditor in its unsuccessful defence of a preference claim arising out of a payment by the principal debtor company. If the creditor's defence had been successful, the liability of the applicants would have been reduced. Hence, the legal costs fell within the scope of the term "moneys hereby secured" in the guarantee and indemnity. Accordingly, when the applicants paid these amounts to the creditor they acquired a right of indemnity against the principal debtor company. But the creditor was not entitled to recover interest either from the principal debtor company or from the applicants on their guarantee and indemnity. Consequently, the applicants were not entitled to an indemnity from the company for the amount paid to the creditor as interest.

If the debtor did not request the indemnifier to provide the indemnity, it **12–23** appears that the latter would be restricted to a restitutionary claim for reimbursement of any amounts paid for the benefit of the debtor,[78] and the debtor's liability on the indemnity would probably be limited by the terms of the principal transaction.[79]

(vi) How is the right of indemnity enforced?

In one special case, the guarantor's right of indemnity may be enforced **12–24** by a form of self-help. Thus, an executor, who is guarantor for the debt of the testator, can retain from the estate amounts equal to the sum the executor has paid to the creditor in reduction of the principal debt.[80]

---

[77] (Unreported, WA Sup Ct, July 17, 1992).
[78] R. Goff and G. Jones, *The Law of Restitution* (6th ed., 2002), para.15–015.
[79] See *Chitty on Contracts* (28th ed., 1999), Vol. 2, para.44–103. In other words, the principal debtor's liability to the indemnifier would be limited to the liability imposed on the debtor under the principal transaction. See also Goff and Jones, *The Law of Restitution* (6th ed, 2002), para.15–020. As to the principal debtor's rights of set-off against the guarantor's claim to an indemnity, see below, para.12–52.
[80] *Re Beavan; Davies Banks & Co v Beavan* [1913] 2 Ch. 595. Cf. *Re Giles* [1896] 1 Ch. 956, which was not followed in *Re Beavan* and which may have been merely an application for quia timet relief.

12–25   Generally, however, it will be necessary for guarantors who wish to enforce their rights of indemnity to bring actions in their own names[81] against the principal debtor for indemnification.[82] The statement of claim should describe the way in which the guarantors' suretyship arose. Where the debtor has expressly agreed to indemnify the guarantors, they should sue on that agreement.[83]

12–26   Apart from statute, if an indemnity is given *to* more than one guarantor, it is a question of construction as to whether it is joint or several.[84] Conversely, s.81 of the Law of Property Act 1925 provides, in effect, that a covenant made by two or more persons jointly to pay money or do any other act shall be construed as being made with each of them. Hence, an express promise of indemnity by two or more principal debtors can, in the absence of evidence to the contrary, be construed under this provision as a promise made jointly and severally by each principal debtor and be enforced accordingly.

12–27   Where there is no express agreement by the principal debtor to indemnify the guarantor, the guarantor can enforce the right of reimbursement by bringing an action in the guarantor's own name[85] against the debtor for money paid to the defendant's use and at the defendant's request.[86] It is not necessary that there should be an actual request[87] as the request is often implied. Where a guarantor pays the principal debt after the debtor dies intestate, the guarantor can apply for an administration order as a creditor of the intestate estate.[88]

12–28   The right of the guarantor to sue the principal debtor on the indemnity is not extinguished by a judgment obtained by the creditor against the guarantor, and the limitation period for the guarantor's action against the debtor begins to run from the time of the guarantor's payment of any

---

[81] As a result of s.5 of the Mercantile Law Amendment Act 1856 it is no longer necessary for the guarantor to sue the principal debtor in the creditor's name, joining the creditor as a party and providing an indemnity for the creditor's costs. Compare *Wright v Simpson* (1802) 6 Ves. 714; 31 E.R. 1272, LC. See G. Andrews and R. Millett, *Law of Guarantees* (3rd ed., 2000), para.11.03. The guarantor's right of indemnity does not arise by subrogation to the rights of the creditor; it is an independent right of the guarantor: *Morris v Ford Motor Co* [1973] 2 All E.R. 1084 at 1089 per Lord Denning M.R.

[82] As to the form of the writ and the statement of claim in an action by a guarantor to enforce the guarantor's right of indemnity against the principal debtor, see *Atkin's Court Forms* (2nd ed., 1982), Vol. 20, pp.140 and 142.

[83] See *Ahern v O'Donovan* (1881) 15 I.L.T. 7.

[84] *Toussaint v Martinnant* (1787) 2 Term Rep. 100 at 104. See also *Palmer v Sparshott* (1842) 4 Man. & G. 137 at 140–141; 134 E.R. 57 at 58, where Tindal C.J. declared: "where a man covenants with two or more jointly, yet if the interest and cause of action of the covenantees be several and not joint, the covenant shall be taken to be several, and each of the covenantees may bring an action for his particular damages, notwithstanding the words of the covenant are joint."

[85] See *Morris v Ford Motor Co* [1973] 2 All E.R. 1084. Where the party who discharges the liability is not a surety but an indemnifier, that party cannot bring an action in the party's own name against the party on whose behalf he made the payment: *Morris v Ford Motor Co*, above. In equity, the surety was entitled to pay the debt at maturity and sue the principal debtor in the name of the creditor: *Swire v Redman* (1876) 1 Q.B.D. 536 at 541.

[86] *Israel v Foreshore Properties Pty Ltd (in liq)* (1980) 54 A.L.J.R. 421 at 424; *Pitt v Purssord* (1841) 8 M. & W. 538; 151 E.R. 1152; *Stirling v Forrester* (1821) 3 Bli. 575; 4 E.R. 712; *Re a Debtor* [1937] 1 Ch. 156; *Anson v Anson* [1953] 1 Q.B. 636.

[87] *Re Morris; Coneys v Morris* [1922] 1 Ir. R. 81 at 83.

[88] *Williams v Jukes* (1864) 34 L.J.P.M. & A. 60.

amount in reduction of the guaranteed debt.[89] When the guarantor pays only part of the debt, the limitation period begins to run only in respect of that part.[90]

If the creditor sues the guarantor and does not join the principal debtor **12–29** as a defendant, the guarantor may institute third-party proceedings against the debtor to enforce the right of indemnity.[91] In deciding whether leave should be granted to issue a third-party notice, the court will simply consider whether the applicant's claim is in good faith and whether it will result in indemnity or contribution.[92] Usually, however, both the principal debtor and the guarantor are joined as defendants in an action to enforce the guarantee, and the guarantor's right of reimbursement or indemnity is determined in accordance with Pt.20 of the Civil Procedure Rules 1998.

A guarantor claiming a reimbursement or indemnity from the principal **12–30** debtor may obtain a freezing order to prevent the debtor removing from, or even perhaps dissipating within, the jurisdiction, assets which may be necessary to satisfy the ultimate judgment.[93] The purpose of this remedy is to prevent the defendant from abusing his dispositive powers to defeat the plaintiff's claim. It operates in personam[94] and it does not give the plaintiff any security or any priority over the debtor's other creditors.[95] As Ackner L.J. pointed out in *A J Bekhor Co Ltd v Bilton*,[96] "[t]he purpose of the Mareva [freezing order] was not to improve the position of claimants in an insolvency but simply to prevent the injustice of a defendant removing his assets from the jurisdiction which might otherwise have been available to satisfy a judgment".[97]

Lingering doubts about the jurisdiction to grant a freezing order[98] were **12–31** dispelled by s.37(3) of the Supreme Court Act 1981 and it is now clear that

---

[89] *Re Mitchell* [1913] 1 Ch 201; *Collinge v Heywood* (1839) 9 Ad. & El. 633; 112 E.R. 1352. See also *Angrove v Tippett* (1865) 11 L.T. 708; *Considine v Considine* (1846) 9 I.L.R. 400 (Ir). The limitation period is six years.

[90] *Davies v Humphreys* (1840) 6 M. & W. 153; 151 E.R. 361.

[91] See the CPR 1998, Pt.20, r.20.6, and S. Sime, *A Practical Approach to Civil Procedure* (5th ed., 2002), pp. 185–186, and *McIntosh v Williams* [1979] 2 N.S.W.L.R. 543; *Gurtner v Circuit* [1968] 2 Q.B. 587 at 595. Where the guarantor invokes this procedure to enforce an express contract by the principal debtor to indemnify the guarantor, he can enter judgment against the debtor before anything has been paid under the guarantee: *English & Scottish Trust Co v Flatau* (1887) 36 W.R. 238. Usually, however, the principal debtor does not have a similar right to call in the guarantor: *Re Kitchin Ex p. Young* (1881) 17 Ch. D. 668 at 670 *per* James L.J.

[92] *Carshore v North Eastern Railway Co* (1885) 29 Ch. D. 344, CA.

[93] See M.S. Hoyle, *The Mareva Injunction and Related Orders* (3rd ed., 1997); S. Sime, *A Practical Approach to Civil Procedure* (5th ed., 2002), pp.377–391; M. Hetherington (ed.) *Mareva Injunctions* (1983) and R. Meagher, D. Heydon and M. Leeming, *Equity Doctrine & Remedies* (4th ed., 2002), paras 21–430–21–455.

[94] *J Bekhor & Co Ltd v Bilton* [1981] Q.B. 923 and R. Meagher, D. Heydon and M. Leeming, *Equity Doctrine & Remedies* (4th ed., 2002), para.21–450. *Cf. Z Ltd v A-Z* [1982] Q.B. 558 at 573

[95] *PCW (Underwriting Agencies) Ltd v Dixon* [1983] 2 All E.R. 158; *Babanaft International Co SA v Bassatne* [1990] Ch. 13 at 25.

[96] [1981] Q.B. 923.

[97] *ibid.*, at 941–942.

[98] It was once thought that the jurisdiction to grant Mareva injunctions was based on s.45 of the Judicature Act 1925, which re-enacted s.18 of the Supreme Court of Judicature Act 1873 empowering the court to grant interlocutory injunctions whenever it was "just or convenient." There is even a strong argument that there was no sound jurisdictional basis for granting

a freezing order may be made not only in interlocutory proceedings but also after the final hearing "in aid of execution".[99] But there is no jurisdiction to grant a freezing order unless the claimant has a pre-existing cause of action which can be enforced immediately against the defendant arising out of an actual or theoretical infringement of the claimant's legal or equitable rights.[1]

12-32 Freezing orders are not confined to cases initiated in the Commercial Court[2] or to cases of debt.[3] Nor are they restricted to foreigners or foreign residents. It is now accepted that freezing orders can be granted against local residents who are threatening to remove their assets from the jurisdiction.[4] In some cases they have even been granted to prevent local defendants from dissipating their assets *within* the jurisdiction.[5] Indeed, many of the original fetters upon freezing orders have been removed as they have evolved in response to the changing demands of modern commercial life.[6] Nevertheless, the courts require the plaintiff to make out a strong prima facie case before they will grant a freezing order.[7]

12-33 On this basis, a guarantor who has paid some or all the principal debt and who can show that there is a real danger that the principal debtor intends to remove assets from the jurisdiction or dissipate them within the jurisdiction to frustrate the guarantor's claim to an indemnity may be entitled to a freezing order against the debtor.[8]

12-34 If the principal debtor is a company, the guarantor has an alternative method of enforcing the right of indemnity: the guarantor can serve a statutory demand on the debtor company pursuant to s.123 of the Insolvency Act 1986. If the company fails to pay the guarantor the amount of the demand within three weeks after it is served, the guarantor can petition for a winding-up order under s.124. Where the proceeds of sale of property jointly owned by two guarantors are applied in payment of the guaranteed debt, both guarantors must sign the statutory demand: the

---

Mareva injunctions prior to s.37(3) of the Supreme Court Act 1981. See R. Meagher, D. Heydon and M. Leeming, Equity Doctrines & Remedies (4th ed., 2002), para.21–435.
[99] *Faith Panton Property Plan Ltd v Hodgetts* [1981] 2 All E.R. 877.
[1] *Zucker v Tyndall Holdings Plc* [1993] 1 All E.R. 124. See also *Mareva Compagnia Naviera v International Bulk Carriers* [1980] 1 All E.R. 213; *Rasu Maritima SA v Perusahaan Pertambangan Minyak Dan Gas Bumi Negara (Pertamina)* [1978] Q.B. 644.
[2] *Siskina (Cargo Owners) v Distos Compania Naviere SA* [1979] A.C. 210 at 261–262 *per* Lord Hailsham. See also *Barclay-Johnson v Yuill* [1980] 3 All E.R. 190.
[3] *Barclay-Johnson v Yuill* [1980] 3 All E.R. 190 at 197 See also *Seven Seas Properties Ltd v Al-Essa* [1989] 1 All E.R. 164 (a case involving specific performance).
[4] *Barclay-Johnson v Yuill* [1980] 3 All E.R. 190; *Rahman (Prince Abdul) bin Turki al Sudairy v Abu-Taha* [1980] 3 All E.R. 409.
[5] *Rahman (Prince Abdul) bin Turki al Sudiary v Abu Taha* [1980] 3 All E.R. 409 at 412; *Kirby v Banks* [1980] C.A.T. 624; *Z Ltd v A-Z* [1982] Q.B. 558.
[6] See A. Rogers, "The Scope of the Mareva Injunction" Ch. 2 in M. Hetherington (ed.) *Mareva Injunctions* (1983), pp.33–34 and R. Meagher, D. Heydon and M. Leeming, *Equity Doctrine and Remedies* (4th ed., 2002), para.21–430.
[7] *MBPXL Corp v Intercontinental Banking Corp Ltd* (unreported, Court of Appeal, August 28, 1975); *Z Ltd v A-Z* [1982] Q.B. 558. Cf. *Rasu Maritima SA v Perusahaan Pertambangan Minyak Dan Gas Bumi Negara (The Pertamina)* [1978] Q.B. 644 (only a "good arguable case" was required). See R. Meagher, D. Heydon and M. Leeming, *Equity Doctrines and Remedies* (4th ed., 2002), para.21–445.
[8] The court considers the balance of convenience and evaluates general discretionary factors. See *Riley McKay Pty Ltd v McKay* [1982] 1 N.S.W.L.R. 264 at 276.

common law rule that a payment to one of a number of joint creditors discharges a joint debt[9] has no application because of equitable principles of contribution between the guarantors.[10] However, while one such guarantor may not sign a statutory demand under the section on behalf of both guarantors, that guarantor may nevertheless apply for a winding-up order on the general ground of insolvency in his own right as a prospective or contingent creditor pursuant to s.124(1).[11]

Where the principal debtor company is in liquidation, it may not have   **12–35** sufficient assets to satisfy the guarantors' claim to an indemnity. If the liquidator is unwilling to conduct litigation in the name of the company to recover its assets the court may authorise the guarantors, as persons in whose interests the winding-up is being carried out and who are entitled to benefit from the assets of the company, to conduct litigation in the name of the company to recover its debts or assets.[12]

The guarantor's right of indemnity can also be enforced by exercising   **12–36** the right of subrogation or marshalling, which are discussed below.[13]

(vii) Counter-indemnities provided by the principal debtor

The principal debtor may provide one or more of the co-guarantors with   **12–37** securities by way of counter-indemnity. These securities will not necessarily be valid and enforceable by the guarantors.[14] Where a surety guarantees a composition between the principal debtor and its creditors, a provision in the deed of composition purporting to transfer any surplus remaining in the debtor's estate after paying off his creditors will not necessarily be invalid. But if the guarantor is a creditor of the debtor's insolvent estate and if the guarantor has reached a secret arrangement with the principal debtor for payment in full, the entire arrangement may be set aside in the debtor's bankruptcy or liquidation.[15] Similarly, where an existing guarantor obtains a counter security from an insolvent principal debtor as a result of pressure, the security may constitute a voidable preference.[16]

---

[9] *Wallace v Kelsall* (1840) 7 M. & W. 264; 151 E.R. 765; *Steeds v Steeds* (1889) 22 Q.B.D. 537; *Powell v Broadhurst* [1901] 2 Ch. 160.
[10] See *Manzo v 555/255 Pitt Street Pty Ltd* (1990) 21 N.S.W.L.R. 1.
[11] *ibid.*, at 9.
[12] *Russell v Westpac Banking Corp* (1994) 61 S.A.S.R. 583.
[13] See above, paras 11–40 to 11–45 and below, paras 12–254 to 12–355.
[14] A failure to comply with the bills of sale legislation may render these securities invalid: see *Hughes v Little* (1886) 18 Q.B.D. 32.
[15] See generally *Wood v Barker* (1865) L.R. 1 Eq. 139. See also *McKewan v Sanderson* (1875) L.R. 20 Eq. 65.
[16] See Insolvency Act 1986, ss.239 and 340 as amended by ss.253 and 262 of the Enterprise Act 2002; *Re MC Bacon Ltd* [1991] Ch. 127 and *Jackman v Mitchell* (1807) 13 Ves. 581; 33 E.R. 412.

(viii) Defences

12–38   The defences open to a principal debtor who is sued by the debtor's surety for reimbursement of an amount the surety has paid off the guaranteed debt depends upon how the guarantee was obtained. As already noted, if it was provided at the request of the debtor, the claim is founded upon a contract of indemnity.[17] In the absence of such a request, the surety may have only a restitutionary claim for reimbursement.[18]

(a) Where there is a contract of indemnity

12–39   If the guarantor pays the amount demanded by the creditor without availing himself of defences which were available either to the principal debtor or himself as guarantor, the guarantor might still be entitled to indemnity from the debtor based on an express or implied contract.[19] The court will examine the precise terms of the debtor's request for the guarantee. If the guarantor was asked to pay on default by the debtor such amounts as the debtor himself was legally compellable to pay, then the guarantor will not be entitled to an indemnity where the guarantor pays amounts which the debtor was not obliged to pay.[20] But the usual implication is simply that the guarantor is requested to pay if the principal debtor does not, regardless of whether the principal debtor could have been legally compelled to pay. In these circumstances, the principal debtor cannot deny the guarantor the right of indemnity merely because the guarantor did not avail himself of the relevant defences.[21] In the result, the principal debtor may be held liable to indemnify the guarantor for payments which could not have been extracted from the debtor himself.[22]

12–40   This reasoning explains the indemnity granted in *Re Chetwynd's Estate*,[23] where the guarantor paid the creditor despite the fact that the principal transaction was unenforceable because it offended the Money Lenders Act 1929. A similar principle apparently also determines the

---

[17] See above, para.12–01.

[18] See above, para.12–02.

[19] *Brittain v Lloyd* (1845) 14 M. & W. 762; 153 E.R. 683. See also *Warlow v Harrison* (1859) 1 E. & E. 309; 120 ER 920.

[20] *Chambers v Manchester & Milford Rly Co* (1864) 5 B. & S. 588 at 612; 122 E.R. 951 at 960; *Bryant v Christie* (1816) 1 Stark. 329, N.P.; 171 E.R. 488. See *Argo Caribbean Group Ltd v Lewis* [1976] 2 *Lloyd's Rep.* 289 at 295. As an example, see *Sleigh v Sleigh* (1850) 19 L.J. (NS) Ex. 345; 155 E.R. 224.

[21] *ibid.* See also *Re Chetwynd's Estate* [1938] Ch. 13.

[22] See *Whitlam v Bullock* [1939] 2 K.B. 81 at 88; *Argo Caribbean Group Ltd v Lewis* [1976] 2 Lloyd's Rep. 289; *Alexander v Vane* (1836) 1 M. & W. 511; 150 E.R. 537; *Re Chetwynd's Estate* [1938] Ch. 13 (guarantor entitled to prove as a creditor to recover on his indemnity for the money he paid to the moneylenders even though the promissory note they held did not comply with s.6 of the Moneylenders Act 1929). *Cf. Re Morris; Coneys v Morris* [1922] 1 I.R. 81, affirmed on appeal [1922] 1 I.R. 136. See also *Penley v Watts* (1841) 7 M. & W. 601; 151 E.R. 907. If the principal debtor is not liable, the surety's proper course is to deny liability on the guarantee: *Re Nott & Cardiff Corp* [1918] 2 K.B. 146, reversed on a different point in the House of Lords in [1919] A.C. 337. *Cf. Jefferys v Gurr* (1831) 2 B. & Ald. 833; 109 E.R. 833.

[23] [1938] Ch. 13. See also *Argo Caribbean Group Ltd v Lewis* [1976] 2 Lloyd's Rep. 289.

principal debtor's liability to indemnify the guarantor where the guarantee itself is unenforceable, as in *Alexander v Vane*,[24] where a guarantor was allowed to enforce his indemnity against a principal debtor even though his guarantee was unenforceable because of a failure to satisfy the Statute of Frauds. In both cases, the guarantor was allowed an indemnity because he was originally requested by the principal debtor to pay on default, whether or not the debtor or the guarantor himself could be compelled to pay.[25] It should be emphasised that in these cases the guarantor was not obliged to pay because of the *unenforceability* of the guarantee or the principal transaction. Further, it is unlikely that the principal's promise to indemnify the guarantor will be interpreted as extending to the situation where there is no default by the principal debtor at all.[26]

A different result was reached in *Re Morris; Coneys v Morris*.[27] There, **12–41** Powell J. of the Irish Court of Appeal held that a guarantor who paid a debt which was not recoverable because it was statute-barred against both the principal *and* himself had no right of indemnity from the principal. This case appears to be inconsistent with *Re Chetwynd's Estate* but it may be reconcilable if the guarantor in *Re Morris; Coneys v Morris* was merely requested to pay on default what the debtor could have been compelled to pay.[28] In any event, *Re Morris; Coneys v Morris* may be distinguishable from *Re Chetwynd's Estate* on the ground that *neither* the principal debtor *nor* the guarantor in the Irish case could have been compelled to pay the principal debt. But this should not in itself make any difference to an absolute promise of indemnity; nor would it distinguish *Alexander v Vane*. A more rational distinction may be that the claim to an indemnity in the former case may have been regarded by the court as a restitutionary claim, where a different rule applies.

Where a guarantor concedes the amount of the principal debt and **12–42** judgment is entered against the guarantor, the principal debtor will not generally have standing to appeal against the judgment unless the court considers it just and convenient, where for example, the principal debtor is prejudiced in some way by the judgment.[29] The general rule is that a judgment is not binding on a person who was not a party to the proceedings in which it was granted.[30] Hence, it will be difficult for the principal debtor to establish that he may be prejudiced by the judgment against the guarantor because no part of that judgment can be used against

---

[24] (1836) 1 M. & W. 511 at 515–516; 150 E.R. 537 at 538. See also *McColl's Wholesale Pty Ltd v State Bank (NSW)* [1984] 3 N.S.W.L.R. 365.
[25] See *Argo Caribbean Group Ltd v Lewis* [1976] 2 Lloyd's Rep. 289 at 295 *per* Orr L.J., explaining *Re Chetwynd's Estate* [1938] Ch. 13.
[26] See below, paras 12–50 to 12–51.
[27] [1922] 1 Ir. R. 81, applied in *Fuller v Perano* [1941] N.Z.L.R. 44. See also *Good Motel Co Ltd (in liq) v Rodeway Pacific International Ltd* (1988) 94 F.L.R. 84.
[28] See also [1922] 1 Ir. R. 136.
[29] See *Gracechurch Holdings Pty Ltd v Breeze* (1992) 7 W.A.R. 518 (a case involving a contract of indemnity between two guarantors). See also *Asphalt & Public Works Ltd v Indemnity Guarantee Trust Ltd* [1969] 1 Q.B. 465; *Helicopter Sales (Australia) Pty Ltd v Rotor-Work Pty Ltd* (1974) 132 C.L.R. 1.
[30] See *King v Norman* (1847) 4 C.B. 884.

the principal debtor.[31] It is unlikely, therefore, that the principal debtor will be granted leave to appeal against a judgment entered against a guarantor. The guarantor's right to an indemnity from the principal debtor may be disputed in separate proceedings, but the guarantor will gain no assistance from the creditor's judgment against him in these proceedings.[32] It is only where the principal debtor is estopped from denying the validity of the judgment or where the principal debtor elects to be bound by it that the judgment against the guarantor can be used in proceedings against the principal debtor for an indemnity.[33]

12–43   Nor is it likely that the terms of a contractual indemnity granted by the principal debtor in favour of the guarantor will be broad enough to capture liabilities arising out of a judgment. The creditor's judgment against the guarantor is a separate and independent source of liability and it does not constitute a liability arising under the guarantee.[34] Hence, the terms of the indemnity will not generally provide any justification for the creditor's judgment against the guarantor being admitted in the guarantor's action against the principal debtor for an indemnity.[35]

(b) The restitutionary claim to an indemnity

12–44   When the guarantor's claim to an indemnity from the principal debtor sounds in contract, it is not necessary for the guarantor to establish that his payment conferred a benefit on the debtor by discharging the whole or part of the principal debt.[36] It is quite different where the guarantee was not requested by the principal debtor or where the debtor's request proves to be void or unenforceable, for then the guarantor can only rely on a restitutionary claim to a reimbursement. Such a claim requires the guarantor to show that his payment conferred a direct, tangible benefit upon the principal debtor by discharging the debtor's liability in whole or in part.[37] Consequently, a guarantor may not on this basis seek a reimbursement of amounts paid in respect of debts which could not be enforced against the principal debtor. The court may also deny equitable relief on the ground that it would be contrary to public policy or that the surety did not "come to equity with clean hands".[38]

12–45   To sum up, whether the guarantor claims an indemnity on an express or implied contract or a reimbursement in restitution, the guarantor can in certain circumstances forfeit the right of redress against the principal debtor if he does not or cannot[39] take full advantage of his legal rights to

---

[31] See *Gracechurch Holdings Pty Ltd v Breeze* (1992) 7 W.A.R. 518 at 523 (a case involving a contract of indemnity between two guarantors).
[32] *ibid.* See also *King v Norman* (1847) 4 C.B. 884.
[33] *Gracechurch Holdings Pty Ltd v Breeze* (1992) 7 W.A.R. 518 at 523–524.
[34] See *Isaac & Sons v Salbstein* [1916] 2 K.B. 139 at 141.
[35] See *Gracechurch Holdings Pty Ltd v Breeze* (1992) 7 W.A.R. 518 at 525.
[36] R. Goff and G. Jones, *The Law of Restitution* (6th ed, 2002), para.15–015.
[37] *ibid.*
[38] See above, paras 12–39 to 12–44.
[39] G. Andrews and R. Millett, *Law of Guarantees* (3rd ed., 2000), para.10.24. *Meyers v Casey* (1913) 17 C.L.R. 90 at 124 *per* Isaacs J.; *Dering v Winchelsea* (1787) 1 Cox 318 at 320; 29 E.R.

dispute the principal debt. Conversely, in the case of a contractual right of indemnity, the principal debtor may be liable to indemnify the guarantor against a liability which neither the principal debtor nor the guarantor could be compelled to discharge.

(c) Practical considerations

The safest course of action for a prospective guarantor is to take from **12–46** the principal debtor an express, comprehensive indemnity under which the guarantor is entitled to be indemnified for whatever he actually pays off the principal debt. On the other hand, it is in the interests of the principal debtor to restrict such an indemnity to amounts which the debtor himself could be compelled to pay,[40] or at least to give the guarantor advance warning not to discharge the disputed liability.[41] One of the debtor's problems is that he might lack the bargaining power to secure the guarantor's consent to limitations upon the right of indemnity under an express or implied contract. Another is that the debtor may often be unaware that the guarantor is about to make a payment to the creditor and cannot, therefore, always warn the guarantor in advance that the creditor's claim is disputed. In any event, once the guarantor assumes the obligations of a surety at the request of the principal debtor, it is difficult to see how the guarantor can be relieved of this burden simply by the debtor countermanding his request. The guarantor's liability will continue despite the countermand and so will the guarantor's right to an indemnity from the principal debtor.[42]

(d) Proposed reforms

The Law Reform Commission of British Columbia recommended a **12–47** statutory solution to this problem. It proposed that in an action by a consumer guarantor[43] against the principal debtor for reimbursement the debtor should not be able to rely on any matter of fact, law, or mixed fact and law, upon which the debtor could have relied to reduce or extinguish his obligations to the creditor.[44] To compensate the debtor for this burden, the Commission proposed that the debtor should be allowed to recover from the creditor an amount of money equal to the amount by which the debtor's liability to the consumer guarantor would have been reduced had

---

1184 at 1185; *Yango Pastoral Co Pty Ltd v First Chicago Australia Ltd* (1978) 139 C.L.R. 410 at 432 *per* Jacobs J.
[40] See *Argo Caribbean Group Ltd v Lewis* [1976] 2 Lloyd's Rep. 289 at 295 *per* Orr L.J. (obiter dicta); *Sleigh v Sleigh* (1850) 19 L.J. (NS) Ex. 345; 155 E.R. 224; *Re Chetwynd's Estate* [1938] Ch. 13 at 19–20.
[41] *Argo Caribbean Group Ltd v Lewis* [1976] 2 Lloyd's Rep. 289 at 295 *per* Orr L.J.
[42] See *Exall v Partridge* (1799) 8 Term Rep. 308; 101 E.R. 1405 *per* Lord Kenyon C.J. *Cf. Argo Caribbean Group Ltd v Lewis* [1976] 2 Lloyd's Rep. 289 at 295–296 *per* Orr L.J.
[43] Recourse guarantors were excluded from this proposal: British Columbia Law Reform Commission, *Report on Guarantees of Consumer Debts* (1979), p.55.
[44] British Columbia Law Reform Commission, *Report on Guarantees of Consumer Debts* (1979), p.56, Recommendation 25.

he been able to rely on the matter in resisting the guarantor's claim of indemnity.[45]

12–48   In some cases, the current law imposes a greater burden upon the principal debtor when sued by the guarantor than the principal debtor would carry if the debtor were sued by the creditor and invoked his own defences. But it could be argued that it is equally unfair to deny a guarantor the right of indemnity or reimbursement because the guarantor does not avail himself of the defences open to the principal debtor. The proposal of the Law Reform Commission of British Columbia attempts to balance and reconcile the competing interests of the parties. Nevertheless, the prospect of a multiplicity of suits between principal debtors and creditors for unwarranted payments made by guarantors detracts from these recommendations. Why should a guarantor be free to pay in response to the creditor's demand without first checking to ensure that the guaranteed debt is valid and enforceable or without, at least, joining the principal debtor in the proceedings so that the debtor himself can raise a defence or counterclaim?

(e) Defences in relation to indemnity claims under bills of exchange

12–49   A drawer or indorser of a bill of exchange who chooses to pay even though he could not be compelled to do so because no notice of dishonour has been received is, on one view, not entitled to an indemnity from a prior party.[46] But the fact that the bill is unenforceable is not necessarily a bar to his claim to an indemnity from the acceptor or the party accommodated in respect of the amount paid.[47] Once the surety has paid the holder on behalf of the principal debtor, he becomes a creditor of the principal and can be barred by a composition deed entered into by the principal with the principal's creditors even if he did not assent to it.[48] The principal can, therefore, plead such a deed as a defence to the surety's claim to an indemnity.

(ix) Compromises

12–50   Similar problems arise when a guarantor effects a reasonable compromise of a dubious claim and then seeks to recover on the indemnity, at least where the claim is on a restitutionary basis. The guarantor need not give the principal debtor notice of the compromise, but runs the risk that the debtor may later argue that the guarantor has acted precipitately or unreasonably or that the guarantor could have obtained more favourable

[45] British Columbia Law Reform Commission, *Report on Guarantees of Consumer Debts* (1979), p.56, Recommendation 26.
[46] N. Elliott, J. Odgers and J.M. Phillips, *Byles on Bills of Exchange* (27th ed., 2002), p.472, n.69. *Cf. Horne v Rouquette* (1878) 3 Q.B.D. 514 at 519. *Cf.* above, paras 12–39 to 12–44.
[47] *Re Chetwynd's Estate* [1938] Ch. 13.
[48] *Hooper v Marshall* (1869) L.R. 5 C.P. 4; 39 L.J.C.P. 14.

terms.[49] By giving the principal debtor notice of a proposed compromise, the guarantor avoids such disputes and robs the debtor of this defence in an action for an indemnity or reimbursement. If the debtor ignores the notice, the guarantor may take any reasonable steps towards settlement of the creditor's claim; the debtor is then estopped from contesting the fairness of the result when the guarantor later sues for a reimbursement or an indemnity.[50]

In a case where the right of indemnity is contractual (the debtor **12–51** promising to pay the guarantor regardless of whether or not the debtor is obliged to pay), these difficulties will probably not arise. As the debtor is obliged to reimburse the guarantor even if the guarantor is not liable, it is unlikely that the debtor can complain of an unfavourable settlement.

(x) Set-offs

A guarantor's right to an indemnity is subject to any right of set-off **12–52** which the principal debtor may raise against the guarantor.[51] A legal set-off will be available to the guarantor only where the guarantor has already paid the creditor, because the Statutes of Set-Off allowed a set-off only where the mutual debts were both presently existing and payable at the date of the action.[52]

Conversely, where a surety is liable as a contributory in the liquidation **12–53** of the debtor, the surety can set off the debtor's liability under a promissory note taken by the creditor and acquired by the surety through subrogation as a result of a payment of the principal debt after the commencement of the debtor's liquidation. It is no objection to this right of set-off that the surety's claim to an indemnity was merely contingent and prospective at the date of the debtor's liquidation.[53]

(xi) Releases

A simple release of the principal debtor by the creditor discharges the **12–54** guarantor and prevents the guarantor from claiming reimbursement or an indemnity.[54] But where the creditor "releases" the debtor but, in the

---

[49] *Smith v Compton* (1832) 3 B. & Ad. 407; 110 E.R. 146; *Ince v Sampson* (unreported, NSW Sup Ct Eq. Div, Young J., September 27, 1991). *Cf. Webster v Petre* (1879) 4 Ex. D. 127. The guarantor may make the best compromise possible in the circumstances and then recover from the principal debtor the loss sustained in paying the compromised debt: *Lord Newborough v Schroder* (1849) 7 C.B. 342 at 399; 137 E.R. 136 at 159. See also *Pettman v Keble* (1850) 9 C.B. 701; 137 E.R. 1067.
[50] *Hornby v Cardwell* (1881) 8 Q.B.D. 329. See also *Duffield v Scott* (1789) 3 Term Rep. 374 at 377; 100 E.R. 628 at 630.
[51] *Rogers v Maw* (1846) 15 M. & W. 444; *Thornton v Maynard* (1875) L.R. 10 C.P. 695.
[52] See S.R. Derham, *Set-Off* (3rd ed., 2003), para.2–08.
[53] *Re Moseley Green Coal & Coke Co Ltd; Barrett's Case (No.2)* (1864) De G.J. & S. 756; 46 E.R. 1116. *Cf. Re Glen Express Ltd* (unreported, Neuberger J., October 19, 1999, *New Law Digest*), where the rule against double proof prevented the guarantor from succeeding in his claim to an insolvency set-off because the guarantor had not paid anything to the creditor.
[54] See *Bateson v Gosling* (1871) L.R. 7 C.P. 9; *Nicholson v Revill* (1836) 4 Ad. & E. 675; 111 E.R. 941.

agreement of release, reserves its rights and remedies against the guarantor, the latter retains his rights against the debtor.[55] In such a case, the "release" takes effect merely as a covenant by the creditor not to sue the principal debtor, and the guarantor's rights against the debtor are unimpaired.[56] The principal debtor is held, by agreeing to the creditor's right of action against the guarantor, to have impliedly consented to the guarantor subsequently exercising a right of indemnity against him.[57]

12–55   Releases granted by the creditor are not the only releases which can affect the guarantor's right of indemnity. The guarantor himself may by will release all debts due to the guarantor by the principal debtor. But such a release will not include the debtor's liability to indemnify *the guarantor's estate* where payment is made after the guarantor's death out of his estate to satisfy the principal debt. The right of indemnity does not give rise to a debt until the estate pays the debt, and hence the payment creates a debt due to the estate, not to the testator personally.[58]

(xii) Limitation periods

12–56   Subject to any agreement to the contrary, the limitation period in an action to enforce the right of indemnity starts when the guarantor pays the creditor.[59] If the guarantor pays the creditor only part of the principal debt, the limitation period in the action to recover that part runs from the date of payment; the limitation period for the balance begins when it is paid to the creditor.[60]

(xiii) The amount of the indemnity

12–57   A guarantor is entitled to an indemnity in respect of any amount paid by him in reduction of the guaranteed debt.[61] It is not necessary for the

---

[55] *Baterson v Gosling* (1871) L.R. 7 C.P. 9; *Kearsley v Cole* (1846) 16 M. & W. 128; 153 E.R. 1128.

[56] *Kearsley v Cole* (1846) 16 M & W 128; 153 E.R. 1128. As to the distinction between an accord and satisfaction operating as a release, as distinct from a covenant not to sue, see *Deanplan Ltd v Mahmoud* [1992] 3 All E.R. 945. See also above, paras 6–56 to 6–64.

[57] *Cole v Lynn* [1942] 1 K.B. 142. See also above, para.6–56.

[58] See *Re Mitchell; Freelove v Mitchell* [1913] 1 Ch. 201 at 206 *per* Parker J.

[59] See Limitation Act 1980, s.5; *Collinge v Heywood* (1839) 9 Ad. & E. 633; 112 E.R. 1352; *Re Mitchell* [1913] 1 Ch. 201; Consequently, a provision in a guarantor's will releasing all debts of the principal debtor to the guarantor did not apply to amounts paid by the guarantor's estate to the creditor after the surety's death because the guarantor's right to an indemnity from the principal debtor did not arise until he or his estate paid the creditor: *Re Mitchell; Freelove v Mitchell* [1913] 1 Ch. 201. See also *Re Orme; Evans v Maxwell* (1883) 50 L.T. 51 and *Re Harrison* [1886] L.R. 32 Ch. D. 295 (an executor, who is surety for an unpaid debt of his testator cannot exercise his right of retainer in respect of his liability as a surety unless he pays the debt). *Cf. Re Giles* [1896] 1 Ch. 596, not followed in *Re Beavan, Davies, Banks & Co* [1913] 2 Ch. 595.

[60] *Davies v Humphreys* (1840) 6 M. & W. 153; 151 E.R. 361. See *Rowlatt on Principal and Surety* (5th ed., 1999), para.10–11.

[61] *ibid.*, at 167; 367. *Rowe v Willcocks* [1923] G.L.R. 149. A guarantor is not entitled to an indemnity from the principal debtor unless the amount paid by the guarantor was due to the principal debtor's default as distinct from a claim by the guarantor against the principal debtor

guarantor to pay the full amount of his liability before seeking the indemnity.[62] If the guarantor obtains a discharge of the debt by paying less than its full amount, then his indemnity is restricted to the amount actually paid to the creditor.[63] While it may be difficult in some cases to extract even this lesser amount from the principal debtor, the fact that the debtor is incapable of satisfying the guarantor's claim to an indemnity does not deny its existence.[64]

The principal debtor will not be obliged to indemnify a guarantor in respect of a payment made to protect a collateral security. Thus a guarantor was not allowed to recover a sum paid to protect a prior mortgage securing the promissory note which he had guaranteed.[65] It is different, however, where the guarantor is not merely personally liable but has incurred a *distinct* liability as equitable mortgagee. Amounts paid to protect the debtor's property in these circumstances are chargeable to the debtor as a just allowance for the protection of the mortgage security, even though the amount was not paid under the guarantee.[66] In this situation, however, the guarantor enjoys a right of indemnity in his capacity as a mortgagee, not as a surety.   **12–58**

The indemnity extends to any liability which the surety incurs as a result of satisfying the obligations under the guarantee. But a payment in excess of the amount for which the principal was liable or a payment in the absence of any evidence that the principal was in default might not be recoverable from the principal.[67] In *US Fidelity & Guaranty Co v Webber*,[68] for instance, the plaintiffs' claim to an indemnity was rejected because there was no evidence that they were liable to pay the amounts which they paid to an employer under a fidelity bond: the employer's shortages in grain and coal were attributable to shrinkage and waste and not to the negligence or improper conduct of the employee.   **12–59**

A guarantor is also entitled to recover interest on the sum paid to the creditor from the date of payment[69] even if the principal debt itself did   **12–60**

---

in its own right: *Re Empire Paper Ltd (in liq)* [1999] B.C.C. 406. It appears that the mere production of a judgment signed against the guarantor by the creditor is not, in itself, sufficient evidence of the loss sustained by the guarantor who seeks to recover from the principal debtor under an indemnity bond: *King v Norman* (1847) 4 C.B. 884; 136 E.R. 757. See also *Price v Burva* (1857) 6 W.R. 40.

[62] *Davies v Humphreys* (1840) 6 M. & W. 153 at 167; 151 E.R. 361 at 367.

[63] *Jamieson v Trustees of the Property of Hotel Renfrew* (1941) 4 D.L.R. 470; *Soulten v Soulten* (1822) 5 B. & Ald. 852.

[64] *Re Franco-Can Mortgage Co; Re Bank of Montreal* [1927] 1 W.W.R. 403 (Alta).

[65] *Fitzgerald v Jenkins* (1975) 15 N.S.R. (2d) 707, affirmed in (1976) 17 N.S.R. (2d) 265 (CA).

[66] *O'Brien v Mackintosh* (1904) 34 S.C.R. 169.

[67] British Columbia Law Reform Commission, *Report on Guarantees of Consumer Debts* (1979), p.54. Even in a contractual claim for indemnity, it is unlikely that such payments will be recoverable: see above, paras 12–39 to 12–43.

[68] (1915) 24 D.L.R. 113 at 117.

[69] Interest runs from the date of the guarantor's payment to the creditor: *Re Fox, Walker & Co, Ex p. Bishop* (1880) 15 Ch. D. 400; *Hitchman v Stewart* (1855) 3 Drew. 271; 61 E.R. 907; *Re Watson* [1896] Ch. 925 at 937.

not carry interest.[70] On one view only simple interest is recoverable[71] at the appropriate rate.[72] Where a higher rate of interest is charged on the principal debt, the guarantor should discharge the outstanding debt as soon as possible; otherwise the guarantor's own claim to interest on the amount he pays may be reduced[73] because such interest could have been saved by a prompt payment. In exercising its discretion to award interest at the judicial rate,[74] the court would probably award compound interest.[75]

12–61   The guarantor's indemnity is not restricted to the amount the guarantor pays off the principal debt, plus interest. The guarantor can recover any additional damages which the guarantor has been compelled to pay by reason of non-payment of the principal debt.[76] The guarantor can also recover costs from the principal debtor, including additional costs reasonably incurred in resisting the creditor's claim.[77] The latter are awarded on a common fund basis.[78] Generally, it is immaterial that the

[70] *Re Swan's Estate* (1869) 4 I.R. Eq. 209. *Cf. Rigby v Macnamara* (1795) 2 Cox Eq. Case 415 30 E.R. 192; *Re Maria Anna & Steinbank Coal & Coke Co; McKewan's Case* (1877) 6 Ch. D. 447; *A E Goodwin Ltd (in liq) v A G Healing Ltd (in liq)* (1979) 7 A.C.L.R. 481; *Shiel v Stables* [1933] N.Z.L.R. s.45; *Re Fox, Walker & Co, Ex p. Bishop* (1880) 15 Ch. D. 400, CA; *Re Swan's Estate* (1869) 4 Ir. Eq. 209; *Re Watson* [1896] 1 Ch. 935 at 937. A failure to pay promptly does not deprive a surety of the right to receive interest by way of damages: see *McColl's Wholesale Pty Ltd v State Bank (NSW)* [1984] 3 N.S.W.L.R. 365.
[71] *Rigby v Macnamara* (1795) 2 Cox 415. *Cf. Re Maria Anna & Steinbank Coal & Coke Co; McKewan's Case* (1877) 6 Ch. D. 447 at 455 (obiter dicta) (which suggests that the guarantor will be entitled to a full indemnity, including compound interest). This is the better view because the guarantors should be entitled to a comprehensive indemnity for the full amount of their loss.
[72] In a business context the rate of interest generally reflects the current commercial rate. *Cf. The Mecca* [1968] P. 665 at 672 and *Chitty on Contracts* (28th ed., 1999), Vol. 1. para.27–146. In other contexts the court has a discretion as to the rate awarded: Supreme Court Act 1981, s.35A and County Court Act 1984, s.69. See also the Late Payment of Commercial Debts (Interest) Act 1998 which confers on a creditor a right of "statutory interest" under an implied term on "qualifying debts" where both parties are acting in the course of a business. The initial rate has been fixed at 8 per cent over the official dealing rate of the Bank of England. This Act will probably only be relevant to compensated sureties such as guarantor corporations.
[73] *Hawkins v Maltby* (1868) L.R. 6 Eq. 505 at 509. *Cf. Rowlatt on Principal and Surety* (5th ed., 1999), p.149, where it is suggested that the principal debtor should not be entitled to claim a reduction in the amount of the indemnity because the surety was tardy in discharging the principal debt because the debtor was primarily liable for that debt.
[74] Under s.35A of the Supreme Court Act 1981, added by the Administration of Justice Act 1982, s.15(1), Sch.1, Pt.I. See also *Practice Direction (interest: pleading)* [1983] 1 All E.R. 934 and *IM Properties Plc v Cape & Dalgleish (a firm)* [1998] 3 All E.R. 203, CA; *Walkers v Rome* [1999] 2 All E.R. (Comm) 961; [2000] 1 Lloyd's Rep. 116.
[75] See Supreme Court Act 1981, s.35A and G. Andrews and R. Millett, *Law of Guarantees* (3rd ed., 2000), para.10.18.
[76] See *Badeley v Consolidated Bank* (1886) 34 Ch. D. 536 at 556, reversed on other grounds in (1888) 38 Ch. D. 238, CA.
[77] *Garrard v Cottrell* (1847) 10 Q.B. 679; 116 E.R. 258; *Smith v Howell* (1851) 6 Exch. 730 at 731; 155 E.R. 739 at 740; *Hornby v Cardwell* (1881) 8 Q.B.D., 329, CA; *Re Garway, Ex p. Marshall* (1751) 1 Atk. 262; 26 E.R. 167; *Jones v Brooke* (1812) 4 Taunt 464; 128 E.R. 409; *Stratton v Mathews* (1848) 3 Exch. 48; 154 E.R. 750. Such costs are allowed as damages for breach of an implied contract to indemnify the surety: *McColl's Wholesale Pty Ltd v State Bank (NSW)* [1984] 3 N.S.W.L.R. 365. The surety is entitled to be reimbursed the costs he reasonably incurs in investigating the validity and quantum of the creditor's claim against the principal debtor: *Re Empire Paper Ltd (in liq)* [1999] B.C.C. 406 at 412.
[78] *Howard v Lovegrove* (1870) L.R. 6 Ex. 43. It may well be that a guarantor is now entitled to an order that the costs recoverable from the principal debtor be taxed on the indemnity basis. See now *Gomba Holdings (UK) Ltd v Minorities Finance Ltd (No. 2)* [1993] Ch. 171. See G. Andrews and R. Millett, *Law of Guarantees* (3rd ed., 2000), para.10.20.

principal debtor did not authorise the guarantor's expenditure[79] as long as the costs were incurred in reasonably defending the proceedings in the interests of the debtor[80] or as long as they were a necessary expense.[81] It appears that even a guarantor who claims an indemnity on a restitutionary basis will be entitled to such costs[82] because they were reasonably necessary in the interests of the principal debtor or the guarantors or both of them.[83] But a guarantor may be denied the costs of contesting the creditor's claim where there was clearly no defence[84] or where the guarantor defends the creditor's action solely for his own benefit.[85] Similarly, the guarantor will not be allowed to recover the costs of execution by the creditor because he is expected to pay the guaranteed debt when the creditor obtains judgment.[86]

Finally, a guarantor can seek an indemnity not just in respect of amounts **12–62** paid in reduction of the principal debt but also in respect of property transferred to the creditor for this purpose.[87]

[79] *Smith v Compton* (1832) B. & Ad. 407; 110 E.R. 146; *Hornby v Cardwell* (1881) 8 Q.B.D. 329.

[80] *South v Bloxam* (1865) 2 Hem. & M. 457; 71 E.R. 541; *Baxendale v London, Chatham & Dover Railway Co* (1874) L.R. 10 Exch. 35 at 44 *per* Quain J. See also *Gillett v Rippon* (1829) Mood & M. 406; 173 E.R. 1204, where a guarantor was denied recovery of costs of £60 incurred in contesting a creditor's claim for £6. Guarantors will not, however, be entitled to the costs of litigation conducted entirely for their own benefit, for example, to show that they had been discharged: *Re International Contract Co, Hughes' Claim* (1872) L.T. 13 Eq. 623 at 624, 625 *per* Wickens V.C. See also *South v Bloxam* (1865) 2 Hem. & M. 457; 71 E.R. 541.

[81] Thus in *Pierce v Williams* (1854) 23 L.J. Ex. 322, the costs of the writ in a suit against the guarantor were allowed since the writ was the first notification to him of the amount due and unpaid by the principal debtor and a demand was a condition precedent to liability. The costs of subsequent proceedings were, however, disallowed as the guarantor could have paid the creditor after the writ had been served on him. See also *Gillett v Rippon* (1829) Mood & M. 406; 173 E.R. 1204.

[82] *Shepheard v Bray* [1906] 2 Ch. 235 at 254. But, *cf.* R. Goff & G. Jones, *The Law of Restitution* (6th ed., 2002), para. 14–013, n.74. Clearly, costs incurred with the authority of the principal debtor are recoverable: *Garrard v Cottrell* (1847) 10 Q.B. 679 and *Crampton v Walker* (1860) 3 E. & E. 321; 121 E.R. 463.

[83] *Owen v Tate* [1976] Q.B. 402 at 409–410. *Cf. Shepheard v Bray* [1906] 2 Ch. 235 at 254. *Shepheard v Bray* was reversed on appeal: [1907] 2 Ch. 571 (the Court of Appeal was not prepared to assent to all that Warrington J. had decided at first instance); and R. Goff and G. Jones, *The Law of Restitution* (6th ed., 2002), para.15–021, n.25.

[84] *Roach v Thompson* (1830) M. & M. 487; 173 E.R. 1233; *Beech v Jones* (1848) 5 C.B. 696; 136 E.R. 1052; *Gillett v Rippon* (1829) Mood & M. 406; 173 E.R. 1204. See also *South v Bloxam* (1865) 2 H. & M. 457; 71 E.R. 541. A guarantor who has no defence may pay the creditor in full before he is sued and then claim an indemnity from the principal debtor: *Lord Newborough v Schroder* (1849) 7 C.B. 342 at 399; *Pitt v Purssord* (1841) 8 M. & W. 538; 151 E.R. 1152 (a case involving a promissory note).

[85] *Re International Contract Co; Hughes' Claim* (1872) L.R. 13 Eq. 623 at 624, 625 *per* Wickens V.C.; *Baxendale v London, Chatham & Dover Rly Co* (1874) L.R. 10 Exch. 35. On this basis, it is even doubtful whether a guarantor is entitled to recover the costs of investigating the enforceability of the guarantee itself: *Re Empire Paper Ltd (in liq)* [1999] B.C.C. 406 at 412.

[86] *Pierce v Williams* (1854) 23 L.J. Ex 322.

[87] *Fahey v Frawley* (1890) 26 L.R. Ir. 78 at 90 *per* Holmes J.; *Rodgers v Maw* (1846) 15 M. & W. 444; 16 L.J. Ex. 137 (execution levied against guarantor's property and money paid over to judgment creditor by the sheriff). With the consent of the creditor the guarantor can satisfy the principal obligation by assigning securities granted to him by the principal debtor by way of counter-indemnity: *Paton Wilkes* (1860) 8 Gr. 252 (Can).

(xiv) The right of indemnity in the bankruptcy or liquidation of the principal debtor

(a) The rule against double proof and the terms of the guarantee

12–63   For the purposes of determining whether a debt or liability is provable it is immaterial whether the debt or liability is present or future, certain or contingent, fixed or unliquidated, and ascertainable by fixed rules or as a matter of opinion.[88]

12–64   A surety or quasi-surety who pays a bill or note is entitled to be indemnified in respect of the amount paid plus interest.[89] On a more general plane, s.57 of the Bills of Exchange Act 1882 governs the measure of damages which a quasi-surety, such as a drawer or indorser, who has been compelled to pay the amount of a bill or note to the holder, can recover from the principal debtor who may be the acceptor, the maker or a prior indorser.[90] But the indemnity does not extend to an amount paid to protect a prior mortgage which was security for the promissory note because that amount was not a debt due from the principal debtor to the creditor.[91]

12–65   A guarantor's prospective right of exoneration by the principal debtor in respect of the guarantor's contingent liability under the guarantee is provable in the debtor's bankruptcy or liquidation. Since this prospective liability does not bear a definite value, the debtor's trustee in bankruptcy or liquidation will be required to make an estimate of its value.[92]

12–66   The statutory schemes that apply in bankruptcy and liquidation appear to make a payment by a guarantor in reduction or discharge of the guarantor's liability under the guarantee provable as a liquidated sum in the bankruptcy of the principal debtor.[93] The payment could take the form of a remittance to the creditor or dividends paid to the creditor in the guarantor's own bankruptcy or liquidation. But even after a guarantor makes such a payment in reduction or discharge of the guaranteed debt, the guarantor's right to seek reimbursement by proving in the principal debtor's bankruptcy or liquidation is subject to the rule against double proof and the terms of the guarantee itself. However, where the principal debtor has incurred a debt to a creditor and another creditor advances

---

[88] See the Insolvency Act 1986, s.382(3) in respect of individual debtors and the Insolvency Rules 1986, r.30.12, in respect of companies.

[89] *Petre v Duncombe* (1851) 20 L.J.Q.B. 242, *Ex p. Davies* (1897) 66 L.J.Q.B. 499; *Fitzgerald v Jenkins* (1975) 15 N.S.R. (2d) 707, affirmed in (1976) 17 N.S.R. (2d) 265, CA.

[90] N. Elliott, J. Odgers & J.M. Phillips, *Byles on Bills of Exchange and Cheques* (27th ed., 2002), paras 25–49, 25–52 and 28–01.

[91] *Fitzgerald v Jenkins* (1975) 15 N.S.R. (2d) 707, affirmed in (1976) 17 N.S.R. (2d) 265, CA.

[92] Insolvency Act 1986, s.322(3); Insolvency Rules 1986 SI 1986/1925, r.4.86. Where the creditor permanently covenants not to sue the principal debtor but reserves its rights against the guarantor, the guarantor should be entitled to have his contingent liability to the creditor valued by the debtor's trustee in bankruptcy: *Ex p. Whittaker* (1891) 39 W.R. 400.

[93] See Insolvency Act 1986, ss.322 and 382(1) and I.F. Fletcher, *The Law of Insolvency* (3rd ed., 2002), paras 23–001 to 23–004. See also *Hardy v Fothergill* (1888) 8 App. Cas. 351; *Wolmenshausen v Gullick* [1893] 2 Ch. 514 at 518. See also *Re Maddren* (1895) 1 A.L.R. 100; *Re Lynch, Ex p. Hungerford* (1937) 9 A.B.C. 210.

funds to the debtor to repay that existing debt, the rule against double proof will not prevent the other creditor from proving in the bankruptcy or liquidation of the principal debtor.[94] This is because the other creditor is not a guarantor who assumes liability for the principal debt. Rather, the other creditor has merely provided the debtor with funds to meet the principal debt.

Mellish L.J .captured the substance of the rule against double proof in *Re Oriental Commercial Bank*:[95] "The true principle is, that there is only to be one dividend in respect of what is in substance the same debt, although there may be two separate contracts."[96] This rule effectively prevents a surety from lodging a proof in the bankruptcy or liquidation of the principal debtor unless the surety has paid the creditor in full before a certain date. On one view this date is the date on which the creditor lodges his proof of debt.[97] This view is supported by the argument that if the rule against double proof did not operate until the creditor was paid, a surety could invoke his statutory right of insolvency set-off against the principal debtor even before he paid the creditor[98] and, in effect, receive a payment from the debtor through the set-off. This would offend the rule against double proof because the creditor would still entitled to lodge a proof of debt in the insolvency of the principal debtor and receive a dividend in respect of the amount set off by the surety.[99]

It could be argued, however, that the rule against double proof should **12–67** come into operation on the date only when the creditor's dividend is paid, not the earlier date on which the creditor lodges its proof of debt.[1] The rationale of the rule against double proof is to prevent two dividends being paid in respect of what is essentially the same debt. This rationale is not served by applying the rule at the date the creditor lodges its proof because this is merely a procedural step and the rights of the surety should not be determined by something as arbitrary as the date on which the creditor lodges its proof.[2] On this approach it is not the lodging of two proofs in respect of the same debt that is offensive but rather the payment of two dividends in respect of the same debt.

---

[94] *Re Parkfield Group Plc (in liq)* [1998] 1 B.C.L.C. 451; [1997] B.C.C. 778.
[95] (1871) 7 Ch. App. 99. See also *Re Fenton* [1931] 1 Ch 85; *Re Moss Ex p. Hallett* [1905] 2 K.B. 307; *Barclay's Bank v TOSG Fund Ltd* [1984] A.C. 626.
[96] (1871) 7 Ch. App. 99 at 101. This principle applies equally to company liquidations. See I.F. Fletcher, *The Law of Insolvency* (3rd ed., 2002), paras 23–002 to 23–004.
[97] *Re Fenton* [1931] 1 Ch. 85 at 119. See also P. Wood, *English and International Set-Off* (1989), para.10.97; *Muir Hunter on Personal Insolvency*, para.3–2103.
[98] See P. Wood, *English and International Set Off* (1989), para.10.98. This argument was rejected in *Re Glen Express Ltd* [2000] B.P.I.R. 456, where the rule against double proof prevented a director from setting off his contingent liability as a guarantor of a company's debts against his liability to repay his loan account to the company.
[99] See G. Andrews and R. Millett, *Law of Guarantees* (3rd ed., 2000), para.13.03.
[1] G. Andrews and R. Millett, *Law of Guarantees* (3rd ed., 2000), para.13.03 favours this view, citing *Barclays Bank Ltd v TOSG Fund Ltd* [1984] A.C. 626 in support. However, this case contains no explicit support for the proposition advanced by the learned authors. In any event, the case did not concern a right of proof by a guarantor.
[2] G. Andrews and R. Millett, *Law of Guarantees* (3rd ed., 2000), para.13.03. The fact that insolvency set-off is now recognised as automatic and self-executing is not inconsistent with this view. See *Stein v Blake* [1996] A.C. 243 at 254.

12–68   Most modern guarantees are drafted so that the guarantee is of the whole principal debt, even where the guarantor's liability is expressly limited. For example, a clause may state that "the guarantee is to be security for the whole of the moneys hereby secured, but nevertheless the total sum payable by the guarantor shall not exceed £10,000". The result is that there is only one debt and the guarantor is precluded from proving in the principal debtor's bankruptcy until the creditor has been paid in full, even though the guarantor has satisfied his maximum liability under the guarantee.[3] It is only in the comparatively rare circumstances where the guarantee is for part of the debt that the guarantor will be able to prove in the principal debtor's bankruptcy when he has paid that part;[4] in this case there are, in effect, two separate debts, and the rule against double proof in respect of the same debt does not apply. The question of construction as to whether the guarantee is a guarantee for the whole debt or merely part of the debt is discussed elsewhere.[5]

12–69   Where a holding company sets up a subsidiary company to raise funds through bond issues guaranteed by the holding company and the funds are then advanced to the holding company, the rule against double proof does not prevent the subsidiary company proving in the holding company's scheme of arrangement in respect of these funds even though the holders of the bonds have also lodged a proof of debt. The court will not ignore the separate corporate personality of the companies and treat the claims as, in legal substance, claims in respect of the same debt.[6]

12–70   Modern guarantees usually contain a further provision restricting the guarantor's right of proof. It is common to provide that the guarantor is not to be entitled as against the creditor, or the creditor's successors and assigns, to any right of proof in the bankruptcy or insolvency of the principal unless and until the whole of the principal's indebtedness to the creditor has been satisfied.[7] Such a clause will probably be effective to preclude the guarantor proving in the principal's bankruptcy even where the guarantee is for part of the debt and the guarantor has paid that part.[8]

12–71   Some guarantees go even further, prohibiting the guarantor from proving in the principal debtor's bankruptcy not only in respect of the guaranteed debt, but in respect of any debt or liability whatsoever which

---

[3] *Re Sass* [1896] 2 Q.B. 12; *Ellis v Emmanuel* (1876) 1 Ex. D. 157; *Re Rees* [1896] 2 Q.B. 14; *Re Fitness Centre (South East) Ltd* [1986] B.C.L.C. 518 at 521 *per* Hoffman J; *Re Fothergill; Ex p. Turquand* (1876) 3 Ch. D. 445. See also above, paras 10–33 to 10–39.
[4] *Re Sass* [1896] 2 Q.B. 12. See also above, para.5–36.
[5] See above, paras 5–35 to 5–40.
[6] *Re Polly Peck International Plc (in administration)* [1996] 2 All E.R. 433.
[7] See, *e.g. Midland Banking Co v Chambers* (1869) 4 Ch. App. 398; *Re Sass* [1896] 2 Q.B. 12. The terms of the guarantee are of paramount importance: *Re Lynch Ex p. Hungerford; Lynch (Respondent)* (1937) 9 A.B.C. 210.
[8] However, a clause merely stating that the guarantee was a continuing security and additional to and without prejudice to any other security held by the creditor from the principal debtor may not be sufficient to exclude the right of proof of a guarantor of part of the principal debt: *Re Butter's Wharf Ltd* [1995] 2 B.C.L.C. 43 at 55. *Cf. Barclays Bank Ltd v TOSG Fund Ltd* [1984] 1 All E.R. 628 at 644 *per* Oliver L.J. (where the guarantee was construed as a guarantee of a part of the principal debt even though it appeared to be a guarantee of the whole debt with a limitation on the amount of the guarantor's liability).

the principal may owe to the guarantor.[9] From the creditor's point of view, it may be preferable to insert a provision in the guarantee requiring the guarantor to prove in respect of the distinct and independent debt and to hold any dividends received on this proof in trust for the creditor.[10] Arguably, such a provision could be enforced as a contract to create a trust.[11] In this way the creditor could enjoy the benefit of his own proof in respect of the principal debt *and* the guarantor's proof in respect of the distinct and independent debt.

A guarantor's right to prove in the bankruptcy of the principal debtor **12–72** must always be considered against this background of the rule against double proof and in the light of the terms of the guarantee. Most of the following discussion proceeds on the assumption that the guarantee is of the whole debt and that, therefore, a proof by the guarantor would, in general, offend the rule against double proof. Different results flow where the guarantee is merely for part of the debt; these will be noted in passing.

(b) The guarantor's rights where the creditor has proved or can prove in the principal's bankruptcy

If the creditor proves in the bankruptcy of the principal debtor and is **12–73** paid in full, the guarantor who has paid off the principal debt can claim the benefit of the creditor's proof as it stands, with the same degree of priority.[12] The guarantor would be entitled to credit for all dividends already paid to the creditor[13] and to share in all future dividends from the estate of the principal debtor so as to recoup himself for the sums paid to the creditor.[14] In a sense the guarantor acquires this remedy of the creditor by subrogation.[15] But if the guarantee is for the whole debt, the guarantor has no right to receive anything in the principal debtor's bankruptcy until the creditor has been paid in full,[16] even though the guarantor has paid an amount equivalent to his maximum liability under the guarantee.[17] Thus a guarantor is not entitled to prove in his own right for the balance remaining due after the creditor has proved in the principal debtor's estate

---

[9] *Cf. Re D (a lunatic patient)* (No.2) [1926] V.L.R. 467.
[10] See R.M. Goode, *Legal Problems of Credit and Security* (3rd ed., 2003), para.8–24.
[11] See *Tailby v Official Receiver* (1888) 13 App Cas 523.
[12] *Re Whitehouse* (1887) 37 Ch. D. 683 at 695; *Stammers v Elliott* (1868) L.R. 3 Ch. 195.
[13] *Ford v London Chartered Bank of Australia* (1879) 5 V.L.R. (E) 328 at 331, 338. See also *Re Whitehouse* (1887) 37 Ch. D. 683.
[14] *Re Sass* [1896] 2 Q.B. 12.
[15] See *American Surety Co of New York v Bethlehem National Bank of Bethlehem* 314 US 314 (1941). See below, paras 12–254 *et seq.*
[16] *Re Fothergill; Ex p. Turquand* (1876) 3 Ch. D. 445.
[17] *Re Sass* [1896] 2 Q.B. 12; *Re Rees, Ex p. National Provincial Bank of England* (1881) 17 Ch. D. 98; *Re Fernandes, Ex p. Hope* (1843) 3 Mont. D. & D. 720; 8 Jur. 1128; *Earle v Oliver* (1848) 2 Ex. Ch. 71; 154 E.R. 410; *Midland Banking Co v Chambers* (1869) 4 Ch. App. 398; *Seabird Corpn Ltd (in liq) v Sherlock* (1990) 2 A.C.S.R. 111 at 115-116; *Westpac Banking Corporation v Gollin & Co Ltd* [1988] V.R. 397 at 409. *Cf. MS Fashions Ltd v Bank of Credit and Commerce International SA (in liq)* [1993] Ch. 425 at 448.

and received a dividend in respect of the debt.[18] Nor is the guarantor entitled to prove in the principal debtor's estate in respect of a payment in partial reduction of the principal debt.[19] But where the creditor accepts a part payment by the guarantor in discharge of the whole debt, the guarantor can prove in the bankruptcy or liquidation of the principal debtor for the amount of the payment.[20] Similarly, a guarantor may be able to prove in the principal's insolvency for the amount he paid the creditor if the creditor receives the balance of the principal debt from the debtor or a co-surety. This right of proof is not precluded by the rule against double proof because the creditor is not entitled to prove in its own right in the insolvency of the debtor once it has received payment in full.[21]

12–74   As has been seen, these principles stem from the rule against double proof and they do not apply where the guarantee is for merely part of the debt.

12–75   In this situation, a guarantor who pays the creditor the part of the debt for which he is liable before the creditor receives a dividend from the principal debtor's estate is entitled by subrogation to lodge a proof of debt in the name of the creditor for the amount of his payment.[22] Where the guarantor pays the creditor after the creditor receives the dividend, the creditor will hold that part of the dividend attributable to the guarantor's part of the debt on trust for the guarantor.[23]

12–76   Where the guarantee is of the whole debt, the rule against double proof also affects the guarantor's right to enforce the indemnity where both the principal debtor and the guarantor are bankrupt. Once the creditor proves in the debtor's estate, no proof can be lodged on behalf of the guarantor's estate in the bankruptcy of the debtor in respect of dividends paid to the creditor in the guarantor's bankruptcy.[24] Yet if the creditor receives payment in full from the dividends from the guarantor's estate combined with the dividends from the debtor's estate, the guarantor's estate is

---

[18] *Re Pyke; Davis v Jeffreys* (1955) S.J. 109. The guarantor is, however, entitled to prove for interest on such balance.
[19] *Re Fenton* [1931] 1 Ch. 85, CA.
[20] *Re An Arranging Debtor No.A1076* [1971] N.I. 96 (a case involving an arrangement with creditors under s.343 of the Irish Bankrupt and Insolvent Act 1857).
[21] See G. Andrews and R. Millett, *Law of Guarantees* (3rd ed., 2000), para.13.06.
[22] *Re Sass* [1896] 2 Q.B. 12 at 15; *Ex p. Rushforth* (1805) 10 Ves. Jun. 409; 32 E.R. 903; *Paley v Field* (1806) 12 Ves. 435; 33 E.R. 164; *Bardwell v Lydall* (1831) 7 Bing. 489; 131 E.R. 189; *Hobson v Bass* (1871) 6 Ch. App. 792; *Gray v Seckham* (1872) L.R. 7 Ch. App. 680; *Barclays Bank Ltd v TOSG Fund Ltd* [1984] 1 All E.R. 628; *Re Butler's Wharf* [1995] 2 B.C.L.C. 43; *Westpac Banking Co v Gollin & Co Ltd* [1988] V.R. 397 at 405.
[23] *Re Sass* [1896] 2 Q.B. 12 at 15; *Westpac Banking Co v Gollin & Co Ltd* [1988] V.R. 397 at 406.
[24] *Re Oriental Commercial Bank Ex p. European Bank* (1871) 7 Ch. App. 99 at 103 *per* Sir G. Mellish L.J. See also *Re Fenton; Ex p. Fenton Textile Association (No.2)* [1932] 1 Ch. 178. See also *Re Fenton* [1931] 1 Ch. 85 at 115 *per* Lawrence L.J. This view is difficult to reconcile with Australian cases suggesting that a surety who pays part of the principal debt will be entitled to a *pro tanto* right of subrogation if the balance of the principal debt is paid by the debtor or co-sureties or by the realisation of securities. See *A E Goodwin Ltd (in liq) v A G Healing Ltd* (1979) 7 A.C.L.R. 481; *McColl's Wholesale Pty Ltd v State Bank (NSW) Ltd* [1984] 3 N.S.W.L.R. 365; *Raffle v AGC Advances Ltd* [1989] A.S.C. 58,528; *Bayley v Gibsons Ltd* (1993) 1 Tas. R. 385; and *Equity Trustees Executors & Agency Co Ltd v New Zealand Loan & Mercantile Agency Co Ltd* [1940] V.L.R. 201 at 207–208. *Cf. Ex p. Brett; Re Howe* (1871) 6 Ch. App. 838 and *Re Fothergill; Ex p. Turquand* (1876) 3 Ch. D. 445.

entitled to the benefit of the creditor's proof in the debtor's bankruptcy
and can claim any future dividends payable on that proof.[25]

The rule against double proof is so pervasive that it enjoins a guarantor   **12–77**
of the whole debt from proving in competition with an unpaid creditor who
has not proved but who might prove at some later date prior to the
declaration of the final dividend from the principal debtor's estate.[26] Thus
the mere likelihood of a double proof prevents the guarantor from proving
in the principal debtor's bankruptcy. But where the creditor renounces its
right of proof against the principal debtor's insolvent estate or releases the
debtor while reserving its rights against the guarantors, the rule against
double proof does not apply because the creditor cannot prove in the
debtor's estate.[27] However, if the creditor reserves its rights against the
guarantors, *they* are entitled to prove against the principal debtor's estate
to enforce their right of indemnity.[28]

(c) *The effect of counter-securities held by the guarantor*

Sometimes the guarantor holds a counter-security from the debtor.[29]   **12–78**
What is the entitlement of the parties to the proceeds of the security if both
the principal debtor and the guarantor are bankrupt? The rule appears to
be that the creditor, having no entitlement to the security,[30] may simply
prove in the guarantor's bankruptcy. The guarantor may then recoup from
the security the amount of the dividend paid to the creditor. Any surplus
funds should then be applied for the benefit of the principal.[31] But if the
proceeds of the security are insufficient to reimburse the guarantor for the
amount of the dividend paid to the creditor in his bankruptcy, they must be
applied as far as they will go to relieve the principal debtor's estate of its
liability to reimburse the guarantor. The guarantor must then seek the
balance of the amount of the indemnity as an unsecured creditor in the

---

[25] *Re Whitehouse* (1887) 37 Ch. D. 683 at 695. If the creditor has released the principal debtor,
this course of action will not be attractive because the release will bar the guarantor's recovery
also. In such a case, the guarantor would probably prefer to sue the principal debtor's estate
on the basis of the right to an indemnity.
[26] *Re Fenton* [1931] 1 Ch. 85 at 114.
[27] G. Andrews and R. Millett, *Law of Guarantees* (3rd ed., 2000), para.13.12.
[28] *Perry v National Provincial Bank of England* [1910] 1 Ch. 464; *Cowper v Smith* (1838) 4 M.
& W. 519; 150 E.R. 1534; See above, paras 12–11 to 12–13.
[29] A bill of sale granted to a guarantor by way of counter-indemnity is void because it cannot
comply with the form prescribed by the Bills of Sale Act 1878 and the Bills of Sale
Amendment Act 1882, ss.8 and 9: *Hughes v Little* (1886) 18 Q.B.D. 32. See also *Brown Shipley
& Co Ltd v Amalgamated Investment (Europe) BV* [1979] 1 Lloyd's Rep. 488 (where a right of
subrogation was lost when a guarantor received reimbursement under a counter-guarantee
even though the money paid by way of counter-guarantee was provided by a loan from the
guarantor). See below, para.12–333.
[30] *Re Walker* [1892] 1 Ch. 621 at 629; *Re Standard Insurance Co Ltd (in liq) and the
Companies Act* (1969) 91 W.N. (NSW) 654. Cf. *Re Richardson* [1911] 2 K.B. 705.
[31] See *Royal Bank of Scotland v Commercial Bank of Scotland* (1882) 7 App. Cas. 366 at 390–
391, per Lord Blackburn, approved in *Re Standard Insurance Co Ltd (in liq) and the
Companies Act* (1969) 91 W.N. (NSW) 654 at 663 per Street J. See also *Commissioners of State
Savings Bank of Victoria v Patrick Intermarine Acceptances Ltd (in liq)* [1981] 1 N.S.W.L.R.
175. Cf. *Ex p. Waring* (1815) 19 Ves. Jun. 345; 34 E.R. 546. See above, para.10–85 and below,
para.12–325.

principal debtor's bankruptcy.[32] For example, if the guarantor's bankrupt estate pays a dividend of £10,000 to the creditor and the guarantor recovers £8,000 on realisation of a counter-security provided by the principal debtor, the guarantor can then prove in the principal debtor's bankruptcy as an unsecured creditor and recover a dividend on the balance of £2,000. The rule against double proof will be no obstacle where the creditor has been paid the principal debt in full from other sources.

12–79   This rule is not usually affected by provisions in the guarantee. The usual clause stipulating that the guarantor cannot prove in the principal debtor's bankruptcy would probably not alter the guarantor's right to *apply the security* in this way. However, it may be possible for a clause in the guarantee to confer upon the creditor a right to the benefit of the counter-security by constituting the guarantor a trustee for the creditor in respect of the security. The creditor could then insist that the security be realised for the creditor's benefit and the proceeds be applied in reduction of the principal debt.

12–80   Where the guarantor holding the counter-security from the principal debtor is not himself bankrupt, the guarantor's right of indemnity upon payment is limited to the amount by which the guaranteed debt exceeds the value of the counter-security.[33] Thus, if the guarantor holds a security valued at £50,000 and pays the full amount of a principal debt of £80,000, he can stand in the place of the creditor in respect of dividends on £30,000.

12–81   Usually a proof by the creditor does not affect a counter-security held by a guarantor. Most modern guarantees provide that the creditor can take all dividends from the principal debtor's estate and yet hold the guarantor liable to the full amount of the guarantee until the creditor receives 100 pence in the pound.[34] In such a case, a proof by the creditor will not affect any counter-security given by the principal debtor to the guarantor.[35]

12–82   Where the guarantee is merely of a part of the debt, however, a proof by the creditor can affect a counter-security held by the guarantor. Assume again that the principal debt stands at £80,000, while the counter-security is worth £50,000. If the creditor proves in the principal debtor's bankruptcy for the full amount of the debt and receives a total dividend of £800, and then the guarantor realises the counter-security and pays the creditor the full amount of the part of the debt he has guaranteed, the guarantor, in taking the account as regards his security, must bring in the difference between the dividend actually received by the creditor, namely £800, and the dividend the creditor would have received had the security been valued and a dividend paid on the balance of £30,000. In short, the guarantor must bring in £500, being the difference between the dividend paid to the creditor, namely £800 and the dividend of £300 which the creditor would have received had the counter-security been valued and a dividend paid on the balance of the principal debt. The guarantor must bring this amount into account because he could have saved the principal debtor's estate this

---

[32] *ibid.*
[33] *Baines v Wright* (1885) 15 Q.B.D. 102; (1885) 16 Q.B.D. 330, CA.
[34] See, *e.g.*, *Midland Banking Co v Chambers* (1869) L.R. 7 Eq. 179; 4 Ch. App. 398.
[35] *Midland Banking Co v Chambers* (1869) L.R. 7 Eq. 179; 4 Ch. App. 398; *Re Melton* [1918] 1 Ch. 37; *Re Lennard* [1934] Ch. 235.

expense by valuing the counter-security in accordance with the ordinary rules of bankruptcy.[36] This problem does not arise in relation to a guarantee of the whole debt because generally the guarantor has no right to prove or to value his counter-securities in the bankruptcy of the principal debtor.

(d) For what can the guarantor prove?

Even where a guarantor is entitled to exercise a right of proof in the principal's liquidation, he may not prove for interest paid on the principal debt after a winding-up order has been made in respect of the principal debtor, where the debt was payable at the date of the winding-up order.[37] As between the company's creditors, the order nullifies all contracts for interest.[38] A similar principle applies where the principal debtor is in bankruptcy.[39]   **12–83**

(e) The guarantor's right to prove where the creditor has lost or renounced his right of proof

Payment of the principal debt is not the only way in which a guarantor of the whole debt can acquire a right to prove in the principal's bankruptcy without offending the rule against double proof. A guarantor is free to exercise his right of proof where the creditor renounces in some binding way the creditor's own right to prove in the principal's bankruptcy.[40] The creditor might forgo its right to prove, for instance, where it receives some consideration from the guarantor. However, the creditor will not be taken to have renounced this right to prove simply by failure to exercise the right promptly. As long as the creditor proves prior to the declaration of the final dividend,[41] it will abort any attempt by a guarantor of the whole debt to prove in the principal's bankruptcy in respect of amounts which the guarantor has paid in reduction of the principal debt.   **12–84**

---

[36] *Baines v Wright* (1885) 15 Q.B.D. 102; (1885) 16 Q.B.D. 330, CA. As to the provisions for valuation of securities, see above, para.10–48.
[37] *Re International Contract Co* (1872) L.R. 13 Eq. 623; *Re Standard Insurance Co Ltd (in liq)* [1970] 1 N.S.W.L.R. 392. See also above, paras 12–63 to 12–72.
[38] *ibid.* Only in special circumstances can a surety prove for interest in the winding-up: *McColl's Wholesale Pty Ltd v State Bank (NSW)* [1984] 3 N.S.W.L.R. 365. See generally I.F. Fletcher, *The Law of Insolvency* (3rd ed., 2002), para.24–017 and s.189 of the Insolvency Act 1986.
[39] As a general rule there can be no proof for interest accruing after the date of the bankruptcy: *Re Savin* (1872) 7 Ch. App. 760 at 764; *Re London, Windsor & Greenwich Hotels Co* [1892] 1 Ch. 639 at 648. But this rule applies only as between the proving creditor and the trustee in bankruptcy; it does not apply as between the creditor and subsequent mortgagees after the annulment of the bankruptcy: *Re Pearce* [1909] 2 Ch. 492 at 504. See also above, paras 5–50 to 5–58. See also ss.322(2) and 328(4) of the Insolvency Act 1986 and I.F. Fletcher, *The Law of Insolvency* (3rd ed., 2002), paras 9–052 to 9–053.
[40] *Re Fenton* [1931] 1 Ch. 85 at 114.
[41] See generally, Insolvency Act 1986, s.153; *Butler v Broomhead* [1975] Ch. 97 and Insolvency Rules 1986, rr.4.182 and 6.104.

12–85   Another situation in which a surety as a contingent creditor may acquire a right to prove against the estate of the principal debtor is where the creditor releases the debtor but reserves its rights against the surety.[42] Here the rule against double proof does not apply because only the surety can lodge a proof of debt.

12–86   The rule against double proof presents no obstacle to a guarantor of merely part of a debt from proving in the principal's bankruptcy after payment of that part.[43] In this situation it is immaterial to consider whether or not the creditor has renounced its right of proof because it does not override the guarantor's right of proof.

(f) The guarantor's right of set-off in the bankruptcy or liquidation of the principal debtor

12–87   In *Jones v Mossop*,[44] Sir James Wigram V.-C. held that, where an obligor in a bond becomes surety for advances to the obligee and is compelled to pay the principal debt on the insolvency of the obligee, that obligor is entitled to set off the amount of that payment against the sum due on the bond. This suggests that, if a guarantor pays the creditor on demand (whether before or after the sequestration order) under a guarantee entered into before the bankruptcy of the principal, the guarantor will be able to set off such payment against debts owed to the principal.

12–88   In relation to individual insolvency the mutual credits provision is s.323 of the Insolvency Act 1986; the mutual credits provision in relation to companies is r.4.90 of the Insolvency Rules 1986, which is couched in similar terms. Section 323 applies where before the commencement of the bankruptcy there have been mutual credits, mutual debts or other mutual deals between the bankrupt and any creditor of the bankrupt proving or claiming to prove for a bankruptcy debt.[45] Section 323(2) provides that in this situation an account shall be taken of what is due from each party to the other in respect of the mutual dealings, and the sums due from one party shall be set off against the sums due from the other. Only the balance (if any) is provable in the bankruptcy or, as the case may be, payable to the trustee in bankruptcy.[46]

12–89   There is some doubt whether debts which were not due and payable at the commencement of the bankruptcy can be set off under s.323 of the Insolvency Act 1986. Some authorities suggest that "due" means "payable" or "recoverable by action".[47] This would exclude the liabilities of guarantors who have not paid the creditor as at the date of

---

[42] See *Re Fenton* [1931] 1 Ch. 85 at 119 *per* Romer L.J.
[43] See above, paras 12–63 to 12–72.
[44] (1844) 3 Hare 568 at 571; 67 E.R. 506 at 508.
[45] Insolvency Act 1986, s.323(1). For the definition of "bankrupt" and "bankruptcy debt" see s.382(1).
[46] Insolvency Act 1986, s.323(4).
[47] *Re European Life Assurance Society* (1869) L.R. 9 Eq. 122; *Re Stockton Iron Co* (1875) 2 Ch. D. 101; *Potel v IRC* [1971] 2 All E.R. 504.

commencement of the debtor's bankruptcy.[48] On one view, unless the guarantors pay the creditor on or before this date, there is no debt due from the bankrupt to the guarantors capable of forming the subject matter of a set-off under s.323.[49] On the other hand, in *Re A Debtor Ex p. the Debtor v Trustee of Property of Waite*[50] Hodson L.J. suggested that an amount could be due at the date of the bankruptcy order even if it had to be calculated at a later date. In *Stein v Blake*[51] Lord Hoffman took a similar view of the meaning of the word "due" in s.323(2). His Lordship declared:

> "It is clear ... that when section 323(2) speaks of taking an account of what is 'due' from each party, it does not mean that the sums in question must have been due and payable, whether at the bankruptcy date or even the date when the calculation falls to be made. The claims may have been contingent at the bankruptcy date and the creditor's claim against the bankrupt may remain contingent at the time of calculation, but they are nevertheless included in the account."[52]

Consequently, the contingent nature of the guarantors' obligation does not prevent them from qualifying for a set-off under the mutual credits provision. It is enough that at the bankruptcy date mutual dealings exist between the guarantor and the debtor which involve absolute or contingent rights or obligations that later mature or develop in the course of events into pecuniary demands capable of set-off before an account is taken between the parties.[53] Prior to payment, however, the guarantors are not entitled to a set-off but merely a limited right to be protected against any claims that the creditor might make upon them as guarantors.[54]

Even if the guarantors pay under their guarantees before the date of the bankruptcy or liquidation they might yet be denied the benefit of the mutual credits provision. Guarantors will not be entitled to set off their payments under their guarantees against debts owed to them by a bankrupt debtor if they had notice at the time their liabilities became due

12–90

---

[48] See *Re A Debtor (No.66 of 1955), Ex p. The Debtor v The Trustee of the Property of Waite* [1956] 1 W.L.R. 1226; *Re Fenton* [1931] 1 Ch. 85.
[49] *ibid.*
[50] [1956] 1 W.L.R. 1226 at 1238.
[51] [1996] A.C. 243.
[52] *ibid.*, at 252.
[53] *Day & Dent Constructions Pty Ltd (in liq) v North Australian Properties Pty Ltd* (1982) 56 A.L.J.R. 347. *Cf. Hiley v People's Prudential Assurance Co Ltd* (1938) 60 C.L.R. 468 at 483, 496–497. Indeed, in *Re Last, Ex p. Butterell* (unreported, Fed Ct of Aust, NSW District Registry, Davies J., August 12, 1994) a guarantor was entitled to set off the amount of his indemnity from a bankrupt principal debtor against a debt which the guarantor owed the bankrupt debtor even though the bankrupt had purported to assign the latter debt to his children in a voidable settlement.
[54] *Re Fenton* [1931] 1 Ch. 85 at 104. For this reason a guarantor who has not paid any amount of the principal debt is not able to invoke an insolvency set-off against the claim of the liquidator of the principal debtor company to recover a debt owing to the company by the guarantor: the guarantor's contingent claim against the debtor company is not a provable debt because of the rule against double proof and it cannot, therefore, be set-off: *Re Glen Express Limited* (unreported, Neuberger J., October 19, 1999, *New Law Digest*).

that a bankruptcy petition relating to the bankrupt debtor was pending.[55] A similar restriction applies in relation to company liquidation.[56] The effect of r.4.90(3) is that sums due from the debtor company to guarantors must not be included in the account if the guarantors had notice at the time the sums became due that a meeting of creditors had been summoned under s.98 of the Insolvency Act 1986 or (as the case may be) a petition for the winding up of the debtor company was pending. If the guarantors had such notice they are required to pay the company's liquidator the full amount of their debts to the company but they are only entitled to receive a dividend on the amount they have paid under their guarantees of the company's debts.[57]

12–91   In certain circumstances, the rule against double proof does not prevent the personal representatives of a deceased guarantor from invoking a right similar to a set-off in the bankruptcy of the principal debtor to recoup amounts paid by them in discharge of the guaranteed debt. Where the guarantor leaves property by will to the principal debtor, who later becomes bankrupt, the right of the guarantor's executors to set off, against the debtor's share of the estate, amounts paid by them in reduction of the principal debt depends upon whether the testator died before or after the debtor's bankruptcy. In *Re Watson*,[58] it was held that the executors of a testator who had guaranteed the debt of a mortgagor were entitled in the *subsequent* bankruptcy of the mortgagor to deduct from the mortgagor's share of the testator's estate all payments made by them under the guarantee, together with interest. The mortgagor had never obtained a discharge from his bankruptcy, and neither the executors nor the mortgagee proved in the bankruptcy. This was not a case of set-off as there were no mutual debts. There was no suggestion, therefore, that the rule against double proof was being indirectly infringed by a set-off. Thus, there was no bar to the executors extracting the testator's indemnity from the mortgagor's share of the estate.

12–92   Similarly, the rule against double proof did not affect the right of the executors of a testator who had guaranteed the debt of a principal debtor from deducting from the debtor's reversionary interest in the testator's estate the amount paid by them under the guarantee.[59] This right will be forfeited, however, where the executors prove in the bankruptcy of the principal debtor for the full amount of the debt without making any allowance for, or assigning any value to, the bankrupt's interest under the

---

[55] Insolvency Act 1986, s.323(3).
[56] Insolvency Rules 1986, r.4.90.
[57] See generally S. Rajani, *Tolley's Corporate Insolvency* (1994), para.C14.26.
[58] [1896] 1 Ch. 925. See also *Re Whitehouse, Whitehouse v Edwards* (1887) 37 Ch.D. 683.
[59] The assignee of the bankrupt's share of the estate was in no better position vis-à-vis the executors than the bankrupt would have been: *Re Melton* [1918] 1 Ch. 37. The application of these principles is not affected by the rule against double proof and they apply even where the creditor has proved in the bankruptcy of the principal debtor: *Re Melton*, above. But where a creditor entitled to an annuity proved in the bankruptcy of the legatee who was principal debtor, and the liability in respect of the annuity was therefore quantified, the surety's personal representatives were entitled to obtain an indemnity out of the legatee's interest in the deceased surety's estate to the extent of the creditor's proof, less the dividends paid to the creditor: *Re Lennard* [1934] Ch. 235.

will.[60] If the legatee's bankruptcy precedes the testator's death, the executors can retain only an amount proportionate to the declared dividends distributable in the bankruptcy.[61]

(g) The right of indemnity in bankruptcy as between joint and separate estates

The general rule is that a separate estate, such as the estate of a partner, **12–93** cannot prove against a joint estate, such as the estate of a partnership, and a joint estate cannot prove against a separate estate until all the creditors of the respective estates sought to be proved against are satisfied. The joint estate's proof against the separate estate is deferred in this way, however much the insolvency of the joint estate may be attributed to the conduct of the partner whose separate estate is being administered in bankruptcy.[62]

The rule as to proof between two separate estates of two partners may **12–94** be relaxed in certain cases. In *Lacey v Hill*,[63] however, no such concession was made because the relation of principal and surety never in reality existed between two partners. In fact, the joint estate of the partners was primarily liable for the principal debt even though one partner was ostensibly guarantor for the other. In these circumstances the court denied the separate estate of the solvent partner who was "guarantor" the right to prove for the amount of his indemnity in the estate of his bankrupt partner. Any dividend paid would in effect, through the solvency of the guarantor's estate, simply augment the joint estate of the partnership which was primarily liable and which caused the default. Moreover, the court found that such a proof should not be allowed because it would prejudice the insolvent partner's separate creditors.

(h) The priority of the guarantor's proof

A guarantor's right to prove against the estate of the bankrupt principal **12–95** debtor does not enjoy any special priority.[64] Indeed, as we have seen, it may be relegated by the rule against double proof and the terms of the guarantee.[65] But once the guarantor's right of proof is enforceable, it may acquire the priority granted to the creditor whose debt was paid by the guarantor. Thus, a guarantor who pays a Crown debt is entitled to the Crown's rights of priority in the bankruptcy of the principal debtor.[66]

---

[60] *Stammers v Elliott* (1868) L.R. 3 Ch. 195.
[61] There is no right to withhold the bankrupt's share as beneficiary, except to the extent of any dividend declared or composition payable in the bankruptcy: *Cherry v Boultbee* (1839) 4 My. & Cr. 442; 41 E.R. 171; *Re Rees* (1889) 60 L.T. 260; *Re Pink* [1912] 1 Ch. 498, affirmed in [1912] 2 Ch. 528, CA.
[62] *Lacey v Hill* (1872) 8 Ch. App. 441 at 444.
[63] *ibid.*
[64] *Re Whitehouse* (1887) 37 Ch. D. 683 at 695; *Stammers v Elliott* (1868) LR 3 Ch 195.
[65] See above, paras 10–28 to 10–39 and below, paras 12–63 to 12–72.
[66] *Re Lord Churchill* (1888) 39 Ch. D. 174; *R. v Fay* (1878) 4 L.R. Ir. 606. See below, paras 12–337 to 12–343.

Similarly, a surety who pays a debt which is afforded a statutory priority enjoys the same priority as the preferential creditor.[67]

(i) Proof by persons in situations analogous to suretyship

12–96   Guarantors are not the only persons who enjoy a right to prove in the estate of a primary obligor because of their secondary liability. The courts have granted similar rights to persons in analogous positions.[68] But the suretyship analogy has not been extended to an under-tenant whose goods were distrained for arrears of rent due from his immediate lessor,[69] nor to a lessee who incurred expenses through an assignee's failure to observe the covenants of the lease.[70]

(j) The effect of bankruptcy on the surety's or quasi-surety's right of indemnity under a bill transaction

12–97   Where a surety or quasi-surety pays the amount of a note or bill after the maker or acceptor becomes bankrupt, that surety or quasi-surety can only prove against the estate of the bankrupt if the holder of the note or bill does not prove against the estate.[71] The surety or quasi-surety is enjoined from lodging a separate proof in the bankrupt's estate by the rule against double proof.[72] If the holder has already proved in the bankrupt's estate, the surety or quasi-surety is, upon payment of the note or bill, entitled to the benefit of this proof,[73] but even this benefit is limited to the sum by which the guaranteed part of the debt exceeds the value of securities given to him by the maker or acceptor.[74] Thus in *Baines v Wright*,[75] the acceptor deposited certain wool with the drawer to secure payment of a bill. The

---

[67] *Re Lamplugh Iron Ore Co* [1927] 1 Ch. 308. *Cf. Re Walters Deed of Guarantee* [1933] Ch. 321. See also Insolvency Act 1986, ss.175, 328, 386 and Sch. 6.

[68] See, *e.g. Stedman v Martinnant* (1811) 3 East 427 (accommodation acceptor). *Cf. Filbey v Lawford* (1841) 3 Man. & G. 468; 133 E.R. 1227, *Ex p. Lobbon* (1810) 17 Ves. Jun. 334; 2 Ves. Jun. Supp 480; 34 E.R. 129, 1188 (drawer); *Haigh v Jackson* (1838) 13 M. & W. 598; 150 E.R. 1283 (indorser of a bill of exchange); *Wood v Dodgson* (1813) 2 M. & S. 195; 105 E.R. 355 (retired partner); *Ex p. Yonge* (1814) 3 V. & B. 31 at 40; 35 E.R. 391 at 394; *Aflalo v Foudrinier* (1829) 6 Bing 306; 130 E.R. 1298 (solvent partner paying whole of partnership debt); *Lincoln v Wright* (1841) 4 Beav. 427; 49 E.R. 404 (executor liable for default of co-executor).

[69] *Hoare v White* (1857) 3 Jur. (NS) 445.

[70] *Hardy v Fothergill* (1888) 3 App. Cas. 351.

[71] *Re Lynn, Ex p. Read* (1822) 1 Gl. & J. 224 at 226. It appears, however, that the drawer of a foreign bill of exchange upon an acceptor in England may be entitled, on dishonour and protest of the bill, to prove in the bankruptcy of the acceptor for damages in the nature of re-exchange, which the drawee is liable to pay to the holder, but which he has not yet paid to the holder: *Re Gillespie* (1886) 18 Q.B.D. 286. In this case the common law was applied under s.97(2) of the Bills of Exchange Act 1882 because s.57(1) was not intended to deal with this situation: N. Elliott, J. Odgers and J.M. Phillips, *Byles on Bills of Exchange and Cheques* (27th ed., 2002), para.28–21.

[72] *ibid.*

[73] *ibid.*

[74] *Baines v Wright* (1885) 16 Q.B.D. 330, CA. See also above, paras 9–47 to 9–49.

[75] (1885) 16 Q.B.D. 330, CA.

drawer indorsed the bill and the acceptor later became bankrupt. By an arrangement with the drawer and indorser, the indorsee proved for the full amount of the bill and the drawer argued that he was entitled to retain the wool as security for the difference between the dividend paid to the indorsee by the acceptor's estate and the amount of the bill. This argument was rejected on the ground that it would enable the drawer to circumvent the bankruptcy rules as to valuation of securities.[76]

Where the holder of accommodation bills proves in the liquidation of **12–98** the drawer or indorser as the principal debtor and in the liquidation of the acceptor as surety, the rule against double proof prevents the acceptor from proving against the estate of the drawer or indorser for the amount of the dividend paid to the holder in the acceptor's liquidation.[77] No such indemnity can be enforced in the bankruptcy or liquidation of the drawer or indorser.

In *Gray v Seckham*,[78] a bank proved in the winding-up of a company for **12–99** £3,659 and was declared entitled to a dividend of £1,051 on that sum. Later, the bank brought an action against one of the makers of a promissory note given as security for the company's debt and indorsed to the bank. The defendant paid the bank £2,067 for the principal debt and interest due on the note and then claimed a proportionate share in the dividend received by the bank in the company's winding-up. The court held that he was entitled to a share in the dividend paid to the bank in the same proportion as the amount he paid bore to the amount of the bank's proof.

In a modern contract of guarantee there are generally provisions **12–100** excluding a surety's right to share dividends paid to the creditor in the principal debtor's bankruptcy, but in the less formal context of a bill of exchange these provisions are absent and, therefore, the usual contractual restrictions on the rights of the sureties or quasi-sureties do not exist.

It is not necessary for the parties claiming an indemnity from the estate **12–101** of the person primarily liable to be sureties. Consequently, solvent partners, who strictly speaking are not sureties, can prove in the bankruptcy of an insolvent partner where they have paid the joint debts since the bankruptcy, on account of a fraudulent misapplication by the insolvent partner to that partner's own use, without authority or the privity of his co-partners. The co-partners can claim a right of indemnity by proving against the estate of their insolvent partner simply because they have paid the joint debts.[79]

(k) Mutual accommodation and the right of indemnity

(i) **Where there is no specific exchange of acceptances.** If two parties **12–102** enter into an arrangement for the mutual accommodation of each other but there is no specific exchange of acceptances, one in consideration for

---

[76] *Insolvency Rules* 1986 SI 1986/1925, rr.6.115 and 4.95.
[77] *Re Oriental Commercial Bank Ex p. European Bank* (1871) 7 Ch. App. 99.
[78] (1872) 7 Ch. App. 680.
[79] *Ex p. Yonge* (1814) 3 V. & B. 31; 35 E.R. 391.

the other, one party is not entitled to prove against the bankrupt estate of the other until he pays the other party's bills as acceptor.[80] Only then does that party become entitled as surety on such accommodation bills to an indemnity from the party accommodated. The mere reciprocal acceptances do not, of themselves, constitute a debt provable by either party in the bankruptcy of the other.[81] To quote Grose J. in *Cowley v Dunlop*:[82] "[W]hen a man accepts without consideration, he is never a creditor of the person for whom he accepts until he pays."[83] Thus the accommodating party's right to an indemnity as surety of the party accommodated is dependent upon the accommodating party honouring his acceptance of that party's bills. There is, therefore, no material difference between this transaction and an ordinary guarantee.

12–103   **(ii) Where there is a specific exchange of acceptances.** Where two parties enter into an arrangement for the mutual accommodation of each other with a specific exchange of acceptances, the position is quite different. In this situation, the acceptance of one party constitutes an absolute debt payable to the other party from the beginning, whether or not that other party honours his own acceptance.[84] Each party is answerable only on the bills which were exchanged, and one party cannot maintain an action against the other on an implied promise of indemnity simply because that party has paid his own acceptance. The party's remedy is against the other party on the other bills, and not as surety on the bills accepted by the first party.[85]

12–104   Lord Ellenborough C.J. explained this complex principle in *Buckler v Buttivant*:[86]

> "There was no promise of indemnity on either side, in case their respective acceptances were not provided for: but each party was to look to the liquidation of his claim on the other to the bills which he took in lieu of his own, and his remedy thereon, and to those only: then the law will not raise any implied promise ultrà those bills."[87]

And further:

> "The holder of the bills has his remedy first against the acceptor, and if he fails to pay, then against the drawer. So if the acceptor refuses payment, the drawer has his remedy on the bill against him. But the plaintiff as acceptor has no remedy against the drawers for the payment

---

[80] *Re Lynn, Ex p. Read* (1822) 1 Gl. & J. 244. See also *Cowley v Dunlop* (1798) 7 Term Rep. 565 at 572; 101 E.R. 1135 at 1138.
[81] *Re Dyer, Ex p. Solarte* (1834) 3 Deac. & Ch. 419 at 422.
[82] (1798) 7 Term Rep. 565; 101 E.R. 1135.
[83] *ibid.*, at 576; 1140.
[84] *Rolfe v Caslon* (1795) 2 H. Bl. 571; 126 E.R. 708; *Cowley v Dunlop* (1798) 7 Term Rep. 565; 101 E.R. 1135; *Buckler v Buttivant* (1802) 3 East 72; 102 E.R. 523. But it appears that the debt created by the specific exchange of acceptances will not support a bankruptcy petition: *Sarratt v Austin* (1811) 4 Taunt 200; 128 E.R. 305. See also *Re Knowles, Ex p. Solarte* (1832) 2 Deac. & Ch. 261 at 268.
[85] *ibid.*
[86] (1802) 3 East 72; 102 E.R. 523.
[87] *ibid.*, at 80; 527.

of his own acceptances, because he did not accept in consideration of a promise of indemnity, but in consideration of an agreement, or rather of an *actual and executed delivery of other acceptances to the same amount*."[88]

This principle applies even if the amounts and due dates of the mutual **12–105** acceptances do not correspond exactly, as long as the parties intended that the exchange of their bills would be treated as a specific exchange.[89] Moreover, it does not appear to matter whether the acceptances so exchanged by one party are that party's own or procured by him from friends.[90]

It was originally thought that since a specific exchange of acceptances **12–106** created an absolute debt payable on either side from the beginning, the drawer holding a bill accepted by the other party might prove in the bankruptcy of the acceptor, even though that drawer's own counter-acceptance was outstanding.[91] But such a proof placed a demand upon the fund for paying the holder of the outstanding bill, and the party seeking to prove, namely the drawer, was also liable on this outstanding bill. It was eventually established, therefore, that the drawer could not prove in the bankruptcy of the acceptor unless the drawer took up the counter-acceptance.[92] This removed the objection that the drawer was proving in competition with his own creditor.

(iii) Mutual accommodation and double bankruptcies. Where accep- **12–107** tances for mutual accommodation have been exchanged between two persons, both of whom are bankrupt, neither trustee in bankruptcy can prove against the other estate in respect of any such bills which may have remained in the hands of the bankrupt whose estate the trustee represents, until the holders of all the bills have been paid in full.[93] This is so even though an unequal negotiation of bills by the two parties in accommodation transactions has caused greater damage to the bankrupt's estate of which he is trustee than to the other estate.[94] No proof can be made in respect of the bills dishonoured or even the excess of damage ultimately sustained on that account until the holders of all the bills have been fully paid.[95]

---

[88] *ibid.*, at 81; 527 (emphasis added).
[89] Thus in *Buckler v Buttivant* (1802) 3 East 72 at 81; 102 E.R. 523 at 527, Lord Ellenborough C.J. remarked that the only difference between that case and *Rolfe v Caslon* (1795) 2 H. Bl. 571; 126 E.R. 708 was "the trifling circumstance of some of the bills becoming due two days before the counter-acceptances of the plaintiff, a circumstance not regarded by the parties at the time".
[90] *Buckler v Buttivant* (1802) 3 East 72 at 85; 102 E.R. 523 at 529 *per* Le Blanc J.
[91] *Ex p. Beaufoy* (1787), cited in W. Cooke, *Bankruptcy Laws* (8th ed., 1823), vol.1, p.180; *Ex p. Clanricarde* (1787), W. Cooke, *Bankruptcy Laws* (8th ed., 1823), vol.1, p.183. See also *Ex p. Rawson* (1821) Jac. 274 at 278; 37 E.R. 854 at 856 *per* Lord Eldon.
[92] See *Re Bainess and Padmore* (1789), cited in W. Cooke, *Bankruptcy Laws* (8th ed., 1823), vol.1, p.183; *Ex p. Rawson* (1821) Jac. 274 at 278; 37 E.R. 854 at 856 *per* Lord Eldon.
[93] *Ex p. Walker* (1798) 4 Ves. 373; 31 E.R. 190, followed in *Ex p. Earle* (1801) 5 Ves. 833; 31 E.R. 883.
[94] *ibid.*
[95] *ibid.*

12–108   This recondite principle is known as the rule in *Ex p. Walker*.[96] Those confused by the rule can draw comfort from the fact that they are in good company. In *Ex p. Rawson*,[97] Lord Eldon, who argued *Ex p. Walker* before Lord Loughborough, confessed: "I have no difficulty in saying that I never understood it. I am satisfied that though, no doubt, the court understood that judgment, yet none of the counsel did."[98] The rule is now firmly established,[99] though its rationale is elusive.

12–109   When two parties, A and B, exchange acceptances for their mutual accommodation they are both liable in different capacities in respect of all the outstanding bills. A is liable as acceptor of the bills he has accepted for B's accommodation and liable as drawer or indorser of the bills accepted by B for his accommodation. The same is true of B mutatis mutandis. If both A and B are solvent, the only way of determining whether there is any debt owing between them in respect of the mutual accommodation transactions is to ascertain the balance which would result if all the bills had been duly met and the accounts adjusted. This exercise disentangles the parties and fixes their shares of the liability. But this method of calculating the balance of accommodation mutually given and received between the parties is inappropriate where both of them are bankrupt. In this situation, their respective shares of the total liability would depend upon the dividends paid by each of their estates, and this is largely a matter of chance.[1] Again, if one estate were allowed to prove in the bankruptcy of the other, it would be proving in competition with its own creditors, namely the holders of the bills. The courts will not countenance such a double proof. Moreover, if one estate were allowed to prove for the amount by which it was damnified more than the other estate, the court would be allowing a proof in respect of a debt created by the bankruptcy.

12–110   How then, do the two insolvent estates share the liabilities arising out of the mutual accommodation transactions? For what amount can one estate prove against the other? The rights and liabilities of the bankrupt estates are adjusted by excluding the dishonoured paper on both sides; in other words by laying the bills on both sides out of the account, and allowing proof only in respect of any cash balance outstanding between the parties, or bills actually paid.[2] Even a proof in respect of a cash balance will be rejected where that balance is covered by outstanding bills.[3]

12–111   **(iv) The scope of the rule in *Ex p. Walker*.** The rule in *Ex p. Walker*[4] is not restricted to the situation where the acceptances exchanged in a mutual accommodation arrangement between the two parties who later become insolvent are drawn on those parties. It can be applied to reject a proof made on behalf of the estate of a bankrupt who has given accommodation acceptances, which have been discounted and which are

---

[96] (1798) 4 Ves. 373; 31 E.R. 190.
[97] (1821) Jac. 274; 37 E.R. 854.
[98] *ibid.*, at 278; 856.
[99] See *Ex p. Earle* (1801) 5 Ves. 833; 1 E.R. 883; *Ex p. Solarte* (1834) 3 Deac. & Ch. 419; *Ex p. Laforest* (1833) 2 Deac. & Ch. 199.
[1] See *Ex p. Walker* (1798) 4 Ves. 373; 31 E.R. 190 *per* Lord Loughborough.
[2] See *Re Lynn, Ex p. Read* (1822) 1 Gl. & J. 224; *Ex p. Macredie* (1873) 8 Ch. App. 535.
[3] *Re Lynn, Ex p. Read* (1822) 1 Gl. & J. 224.
[4] (1798) 4 Ves. 373; 31 E.R. 190.

outstanding, against the estate of the drawer of other accommodation bills which were *drawn on a third party* and given by the drawer to the acceptor of the outstanding bills in exchange for the acceptor's acceptances. Thus in *Re Knowles Ex p. Solarte*,[5] Knowles & Co sent Alzedo five bills drawn by it on Dyer and Swayne. In return, Knowles & Co received from Alzedo acceptances for the precise amount of the five bills. Knowles & Co discounted Alzedo's acceptances with its bankers. Alzedo became bankrupt before his acceptances became due and he paid none of the bills which he accepted. The holders of these bills did, however, prove in the winding-up of Knowles & Co and they thereby recovered dividends of roughly five shillings in the pound on Alzedo's acceptances. Since Alzedo had not negotiated the five bills he received in exchange for his acceptances, his trustee in bankruptcy then sought to prove the bills in Knowles & Co's winding-up on the ground that Knowles & Co was liable as drawer. The court held that to admit the trustee's claim would be to allow a double proof. The only way in which Alzedo's trustee in bankruptcy could prove in respect of these five bills would be for Alzedo to deliver up the bills to Knowles & Co or otherwise to relieve it of all liability in respect of those bills.

The principle in *Ex p. Walker* will not apply unless all the necessary **12–112** elements of the rule are present. It is predicated upon a mutual accommodation arrangement. It does not, therefore, apply where only one party has given accommodation paper.[6] Thus in *Ex p. Metcalfe*,[7] where Williamson and Palmer were both bankrupt, a proof in respect of a cash balance due from Williamson to Palmer was allowed in Williamson's bankruptcy but his trustee was allowed to apply the dividends in respect of that proof for the exoneration of his estate in respect of another proof lodged against the estate in respect of dishonoured bills which had been advanced from Williamson to Palmer.

It has been suggested that the rule in *Ex p. Walker* might not apply **12–113** where one bill was, in some aspects, the consideration for another bill.[8] Moreover, the rule has no application where the cross-accommodation bills are in the hands of third parties.[9] In *Ex p. Cama*,[10] Sir G. Mellish L.J. remarked:

"I cannot see how the doctrine of *Ex parte Walker* 4 Ves 373 can possibly apply to a case where there are, in fact, three firms, and where the firm which seeks to prove is not the same as that which made the arrangement about the exchange of acceptances."[11]

---

[5] (1832) 2 Deac. & Ch. 261, explained in *Re Dyer, Ex p. Solarte* (1834) 3 Deac. & Ch. 419; 1 Mont. & A. 270.
[6] *Ex p. Metcalfe* (1805) 11 Ves. 404; 32 E.R. 1143.
[7] *ibid.*
[8] *Ex p. Cama* (1874) 9 Ch. App. 686 at 689 *per* Sir G. Mellish L.J. *Cf. Ex p. Macredie* (1873) 8 Ch. App. 535 at 539.
[9] *ibid.*
[10] (1874) 9 Ch. App. 686.
[11] *ibid.*, at 689.

Consequently, where A gave his own accommodation acceptances to B, and B indorsed them to C in exchange for acceptances of C, and all three became bankrupt, it was held that no proof could be made on behalf of the estate of C against the estate of B as indorser of A's acceptances in the hands of C at the date of his bankruptcy.[12] But this did not prevent such a proof on behalf of the estate of C being made against the estate of A, the acceptor, even though there had been cross-acceptances given by B to A, some of which were outstanding.[13] Pending the final adjustment of the equities between the three estates, A's trustee in bankruptcy was entitled to retain the dividends payable in respect of such proof.[14]

12–114   The rule in *Ex p. Walker* admits a further exception where one of the bankrupt estates realises a surplus because it suffers less than the other estate as a result of the accommodation given. Where after all the holders of the bills are satisfied there remains a surplus in one estate, the other estate may prove for any debt owing to it from the accommodation transactions.[15]

12–115   In general, however, the rule in *Ex p. Walker*[16] will prevent a proof by the person who entered into the arrangement for the exchange of acceptances[17] and will prevent outstanding acceptances being taken into account between bankrupt estates. However, where the giving of the acceptance constitutes a debt provable in bankruptcy, this is good consideration for a bill. It may allow the estate of the bankrupt indorser who gave such an acceptance to a previous holder in return for the bill to claim future dividends from the bankrupt estate of the acceptor by subrogation to the proof of the current holder who has been paid in full.[18] In this situation, the rule in *Ex p. Walker* would not bar the estate of the bankrupt indorser from recovering future dividends up to the amount of the dividends already paid to the holder by the indorser's estate.

The other major right of a guarantor after payment of the principal debt is to seek contribution from his co-sureties.

2. The guarantor's right to contribution from co-sureties

(i) Historical background

12–116   It is doubtful whether there was a common law action for contribution between co-sureties until the latter part of the 18th century:[19] the common law courts believed that to admit such a claim would be "a

---

[12] *Re Knowles, Ex p. Solarte* (1832) 2 Deac. & Ch. 261, explained in *Re Dyer, Ex p. Solarte* (1834) 3 Deac. & Ch. 419; 1 Mont. & A. 270.
[13] *Re Dyer, Ex p. Solarte* (1834) 3 Deac. & Ch. 419; 1 Mont. & A. 270.
[14] *ibid. Cf. Ex p. Metcalfe* (1805) 11 Ves. 404; 32 E.R. 1143.
[15] *Ex p. Rawson* (1821) Jac. 274 at 279; 37 E.R. 854 at 856 *per* Lord Eldon.
[16] (1798) 4 Ves. 373; 31 E.R. 190.
[17] *Ex p. Cama* (1874) 9 Ch. App. 686 at 689. *Cf. Ex p. Macredie* (1873) 8 Ch. App. 535 at 539.
[18] *Ex p. Greenwood* (1834) Buck 237.
[19] See *Toussaint v Martinnant* (1737) 2 T.R. 100 at 105; 100 E.R. 57–58 and R. Goff and G. Jones, *The Law of Restitution* (5th ed., 1998), p.399. In 1584 in *Offley v Johnson* (1584) 2 Leo. 166; 74 E.R. 448 it was held that there was no action for contribution between co-sureties. As

great cause of suits".[20] In London, however, it was enforceable by custom.[21]

Eventually, the common law courts recognised a guarantor's claim for **12–117** contribution through an action for money paid to the use of a co-surety: the amount of the principal debt was thus divided equally among the guarantors. At common law, the insolvency of one guarantor did not proportionately increase the liability of the solvent sureties to contribute.[22] By contrast, equity required solvent guarantors to make good the contributions of their insolvent co-sureties,[23] and this rule now prevailed as a result of s.25(ii) the Judicature Act of 1873 and its modern counterpart, s.49 of the Supreme Court Act 1981.[24]

The courts of equity were particularly equipped to deal with contribution suits between sureties because of their procedures and facility with accounts.[25]

(ii) The basis of the right to contribution

The doctrine of contribution recognises that guarantors for the same **12–118** principal debtor and for the same debt or obligation have a common interest and a common burden.[26] The right to contribution depends on whether the liabilities were "of the same nature and to the same extent".[27] This is an independent right of a guarantor which is not acquired through subrogation to the rights of the creditor.[28] Accordingly, if one guarantor who is directly liable to the creditor pays the principal debt, that guarantor can claim contribution from the co-sureties because he has discharged their obligations to the creditor.[29] The common burden of the suretyship should

---

to the history of contribution in the context of insurance, see *Albion Insurance Co Ltd v Government Insurance Office* (NSW) (1969) 121 C.L.R. 342 at 349–352 *per* Kitto J.

[20] *Wormleighton and Hunter's Case* (1614) Godb. 243 at 243; 78 E.R. 141 at 142.

[21] *Offley v Johnson* (1584) 2 Leon 166; 74 E.R. 448.

[22] *Batard v Hawes* (1853) 2 El. & Bl. 287; 118 E.R. 775; *Browne v Lee* (1827) 6 B. & C. 689; 108 E.R. 604. On Scots law, see *Buchanan v Main* (1900) 3 F. 215.

[23] *Dallas v Walls* (1873) 29 L.T. 599; *Hole v Harrison* (1673) 1 Chan. Cas. 246; 22 E.R. 783; *Lawson v Wright* (1786) 1 Cox. Eq. Cas. 275; *Peter v Rich* (1830) 1 Ch. R. 19; 21 E.R. 499; *Ellesmere Brewery Co v Cooper* [1896] 1 Q.B. 75 at 80.

[24] *Lowe v Dixon* (1885) 16 Q.B.D. 455; *Mahoney v McManus* (1981) 55 A.L.J.R. 673. See also below, paras 12–173 to 12–177.

[25] See *Tucker v Bennett* (1927) 60 O.L.R. 118 at 124.

[26] *Ellesmere Brewery Co v Cooper* [1896] 1 Q.B. 75 at 79 *per* Lord Russell C.J.; *Dering v Winchelsea* (1787) 1 Cox Eq. Cas. 318; 29 E.R. 1184; *Albion Insurance Co Ltd v Government Insurance Office of New South Wales* (1969) 121 C.L.R. 342 (an insurance case) at 350–351 *per* Kitto J.; *Eagle Star Ltd v Provincial Insurance plc* [1993] 3 W.L.R. 257 at 263. But contribution will not be available simply because the respective liabilities of the parties arise out of similar relationships on related transactions: *Smith v Cock* [1911] A.C. 317.

[27] *BP Petroleum Development Ltd v Esso Petroleum Co Ltd* [1987] S.L.R. 345 at 348 *per* Lord Ross.

[28] *Gardner v Brooke* [1897] 2 I.R. 6 at 19, QB. Hence a surety's right to recover a contribution from a co-surety is not affected by the fact that the co-surety has a right of set-off against the creditor: *Wilson v Mitchell* [1939] 2 K.B. 869.

[29] *Ellesmere Brewery Co v Cooper* [1896] 1 Q.B. 75 at 79 *per* Lord Russell CJ; *Dering v Winchelsea* (1787) 1 Cox Eq. Cas. 318; 29 E.R. 1184; *Stirling v Forrester* (1821) 3 Bli. 575; 4 E.R. 712; *Ramskill v Edwards* (1885) 31 Ch. D. 100; *Shepheard v Bray* [1906] 2 Ch. 235; *Eagle Star Ltd v Provincial Insurance Plc* [1993] 3 W.L.R. 257; *American Surety Co of New York v*

be borne equitably so that no guarantor can be required, as between the guarantor and the co-sureties, to pay more than his due share.[30] In this light, the right to contribution is firmly founded upon natural justice[31] and equitable principles.[32] On a more general plane, Goff and Jones assert that it is an illustration of the broader principle of unjust enrichment,[33] while some cases[34] previously saw its basis as an implied contract.

12–119   In *Craythorne v Swinburne*,[35] Lord Eldon L.C. attempted to explain the true basis of a contribution claim on the ground that the universal acceptance of the equitable principle of contribution allowed a guarantor to assume the burdens of suretyship on the faith of an implied promise of contribution from his co-sureties. While it is true that the principle of contribution has gained wide acceptance in the courts, this is not in itself sufficient to justify the implication of a promise to contribute without reference to the expressed intentions and conduct of the parties. For this reason, the orthodox view that the doctrine of contribution is founded on equitable principles should generally prevail. As contribution is based on equitable principles, it is not necessary for a guarantor to plead any agreement with his co-sureties in a contribution suit.[36]

(iii) Rights of contribution of a surety or quasi-surety against his co-sureties in a bill transaction

12–120   The drawer and the indorsers of a bill are not co-sureties as between themselves.[37] In general, they are not, therefore, entitled to contribution from one another. But the circumstances surrounding the making, issue and negotiation of a bill or note may be considered for the purpose of ascertaining the true relationship existing between the parties who put

---

Wrightson (1910) 103 L.T. 663 at 667. See also R. Meagher, D. Heydon and M. Leeming, *Equity Doctrine and Remedies* (4th edn., 2002), para.10–020.

[30] *Mahoney v McManus* (1981) 55 A.L.J.R. 673 at 675 *per* Gibbs C.J.; *McLean v Discount & Finance Ltd* (1939) 64 C.L.R. 312 at 328 *per* Latham C.J.; *Albion Insurance Co Ltd v Government Insurance Office (NSW)* (1969) 121 C.L.R. 342 at 350–352. See also *Duncan, Fox & Co v North and South Wales Bank* (1880) 6 App. Cas. 1 at 19; *Craythorne v Swinburne* (1807) 14 Ves. Jun. 160 at 165; 33 E.R. 482 at 484 *per* Lord Eldon L.C.; *Dering v Earl of Winchelsea* (1787) 1 Cox 318; 29 E.R. 1184; *Menzies v Kennedy* (1876) 23 Gr. 360.

[31] See *Mahoney v McManus* (1981) 55 A.L.J.R. 673.

[32] *Stirling v Forrester* (1821) 3 Bli. 575 at 590; 4 E.R. 712 at 717; *Dering v Earl of Winchelsea* (1787) 1 Cox 318; 29 E.R. 1184; *Craythorne v Swinburne* (1807) 14 Ves. Jun. 160; 33 E.R. 482; *Re Ennis* [1893] 3 Ch. 238; *Moulton v Roberts* [1977] Qd. R. 135 at 139; *Tucker v Bennett* [1927] 2 D.L.R. 42; *Ostrander v Jarvis* (1909) 18 O.L.R. 17, Ont Div Ct; *Stirling v Burdett* [1911] 2 Ch. 418; *Ward v National Bank of New Zealand* (1883) 8 App. Cas. 755 at 765, PC; *Albion Insurance Co Ltd v Government Insurance Office of NSW* (1969) 121 C.L.R. 342.

[33] *Bonner v Tottenham & Edmonton Permanent Investment Building Society* [1899] 1 Q.B. 161 at 174 *per* Vaughan Williams L.J.; *Armstrong v Commissioner of Stamp Duties* (1967) 69 S.R. (NSW) 38 at 47 *per* Walsh J.A.; *Mahoney v McManus* (1981) 180 C.L.R. 370 at 388 *per* Brennan J. (as he then was); R. Goff and G. Jones, *The Law of Restitution* (6th ed., 2002), paras 14–006 to 14–007. See also K.P. McGuinness, *The Law of Guarantee* (1986), p.225.

[34] See, *e.g. Shire of Windsor v Enoggera Divisional Board* [1902] Q.S.R. 23 at 30 *per* Griffith C.J.; *Patterson v Arcade Buildings Ltd* [1930] G.L.R. 312.

[35] (1807) 14 Ves. Jun. 160; 33 E.R. 482.

[36] *Henderson v Skinner* 1990 S.L.T. 24, Sh Ct.

[37] See above, paras 1–44 to 1–52.

their signatures upon a bill or note either as makers or indorsers.[38] The court can draw reasonable inferences from these facts and circumstances even if such inferences qualify, alter or invert the relative liabilities which the law merchant would assign to the parties to the bill or the bill transaction.[39] In *Macdonald v Whitfield*,[40] the directors of a company mutually agreed with each other to become sureties to a bank for the same debts of the company and pursuant to that agreement successively indorsed three promissory notes of the company. In these circumstances, the Privy Council held that the directors were entitled, and, indeed, liable to equal contribution *inter se*, and that they were not liable to indemnify each other successively according to the order of their indorsements. Hence, contribution was ordered among the directors on proof of the common purpose with which they successively indorsed the promissory notes of the company.

Contribution may also be available in certain cases even in the absence **12–121** of such a common purpose.[41] In *Godsell v Lloyd*,[42] a husband and wife were parties to a promissory note as makers, and the husband's brother was the payee who indorsed the note with the intention of accommodating both the husband and the wife. In fact, the wife herself signed the note for the accommodation of her husband. Scrutton J. held that the wife and the payee were co-sureties, and that as between them the wife was only liable for half the amount of the dishonoured note, even though the payee was not aware that the wife was merely an accommodation maker when he indorsed the note.

Successive indorsers of a bill or note can displace their normal liability **12–122** under the law merchant and assume the liability of co-sureties by an independent collateral agreement to contribute equally or on some other basis upon the principal debtor's default.[43] Such an agreement will be unenforceable unless it satisfies the Statute of Frauds.[44]

Successive indorsers of a bill or note are not necessarily co-sureties **12–123** merely on proof that the bill or note was made for the accommodation of another.[45] In the absence of agreement to the contrary, the indorsers of an accommodation bill or note may be considered to have entered into a contract of suretyship only in the terms in which the bill or note and their indorsements are known to create, and no contribution may be available to them *inter se*.[46] But where two parties sign a promissory note as accommodation parties and one pays the note when it is due, that party

---

[38] *Macdonald v Whitfield* (1883) 8 App. Cas. 733 at 745.
[39] *ibid.*
[40] (1883) 8 App. Cas. 733.
[41] See *Reynolds v Wheeler* (1861) 10 C.B. (NS) 561; 142 E.R. 572; *Godsell v Lloyd* (1911) 27 T.L.R. 383.
[42] (1911) 27 T.L.R. 383.
[43] See *Macdonald v Whitfield* (1883) 8 App Cas 733 at 745; *Lacombe v Labonte* (1920) 59 Que. S.C. 17, CA.
[44] See *Macdonald v Whitfield* (1883) 8 App. Cas. 733 at 745.
[45] *Ianson v Paxton* (1874) 23 U.C.C.P. 439 (Can). *Cf. Fox v Toronto General Trusts Corp* [1934] 4 D.L.R. 579.
[46] *ibid.*

can claim contribution from the other.[47] In such a case, the position and order of the indorser's signatures are immaterial. Contribution is available even if one accommodation indorser signs a promissory note after and under the signature of another such indorser: both are liable to contribute equally if the maker of the note had so agreed with each of them respectively.[48] *Cockburn v Johnston*[49] suggests that contribution will be restricted to the situation where the second indorser knows when the second indorser indorses the note that the first indorser is, like himself, merely an accommodation indorser. The flaw in this argument is that a surety's right to contribution does not depend upon the surety's knowledge of the existence of co-sureties.[50]

12–124   Contribution is also available to an accommodation drawer who has paid the whole of a bill against another accommodation indorser.[51] This is consistent with *Steele v M'Kinlay*,[52] which merely decided that a drawer could not sue an indorser *on the bill itself*. A claim for contribution is based on equitable principles which impose a liability quite distinct from that created by the bill.[53]

12–125   Where the evidence establishes that one of the three joint and several makers of a promissory note is, in fact, the principal debtor, and that the other makers are the debtor's sureties, they can claim contribution from one another as co-sureties.[54] If one of these co-sureties pays the note when it is due, that co-surety can sue for contribution, and it is no defence for another co-surety to assert that there had been no demand made or action brought against him by the holder.[55] It is not even necessary for the claimant to establish that he paid the bill or note at the request or under the compulsion of the holder.[56]

12–126   Contribution is available to a person who assumes the position of co-surety with other sureties. Thus, in certain circumstances, it can be claimed by a person who purchases a business and whose name is inserted on a promissory note as surety in substitution for that of the vendor.[57] Again in *Harper v Knowlson*,[58] two retired partners were liable as co-sureties for the continuing partners and were each liable to contribute in respect of outstanding promissory notes drawn by one of their former partners and indorsed by themselves and their two other partners before their retirement.

---

[47] *Fox v Toronto General Trusts Corp* [1934] 4 D.L.R. 759; *Clipperton v Spettigue* (1868) 15 Gr. 269. See also *Rutherford v Taylor* (1915) 8 W.W.R. 790; 24 D.L.R. 882.
[48] *Steacy v Stayner* (1904) 7 O.L.R. 684, CA.
[49] (1869) 15 Gr. 577.
[50] See *Dering v Lord Winchelsea* (1787) 2 Bos. & Pul. 270; 29 E.R. 1184. See also *Godsell v Lloyd* (1911) 27 T.L.R. 383.
[51] *Reynolds v Wheeler* (1861) 10 C.B. (NS) 561; 142 E.R. 572.
[52] (1880) 5 App. Cas. 754.
[53] *Reynolds v Wheeler* (1861) 10 C.B. (NS) 561; 142 E.R. 572.
[54] *Davies v Humphreys* (1840) 6 M. & W. 153; 151 E.R. 361; *Pitt v Purssord* (1841) 8 M. & W. 538; 151 E.R. 1152.
[55] *Pitt v Purssord* (1841) 8 M. & W. 538; 151 E.R. 1152.
[56] *ibid.*
[57] *Robinson v Ford (No.2)* (1913) 25 W.L.R. 674 (Sask).
[58] (1863) 2 E. & A. 253 (Can).

It appears that contribution will not be available to the drawer of a bill **12–127** of exchange in the drawer's capacity as quasi-surety against a person who assumes the position of a surety under a mortgage covering the ultimate balance of the principal debtor's indebtedness on a general account. Contribution cannot be ordered in such a case because the parties are not co-sureties for the same debt and are not, therefore, liable to a common demand.[59]

(iv) Modification or exclusion of the right to contribution

Whatever the basis of the doctrine of contribution, it is clear that a **12–128** guarantor can, by an express agreement with the co-sureties, modify or exclude the right to contribution.[60] If the guarantors agree that they shall each be answerable only for a specified and separate portion or amount of the principal debt, there is no right of contribution.[61] The equitable doctrine is also excluded where the guarantors agree that one surety will be solely liable to pay the first £50,000 of the principal debt[62] and where their agreement incorporates a statutory formula which does not distribute the liability equally among them.[63] A right to contribution can also be waived by some clear and unequivocal representation.[64]

A guarantor can also postpone the right of contribution by agreeing with **12–129** the creditor in *the guarantee* not to "make a claim or enforce" that right so long as any part of the principal debt remains unpaid. Such a clause, at least if it is drafted in such form that it can be characterised as a modification of the equitable rights rather than an abrogation of the entitlement to go to court, will not constitute an ouster of the court's

---

[59] *Scholefield Goodman & Sons v Zyngier* [1984] V.R. 445, affirmed on appeal in (1985) 59 A.L.J.R. 770; *Molsons Bank v Kovinsky* [1924] 4 D.L.R. 330. *Cf. Maxal Nominees Pty Ltd v Dalgety Ltd* [1985] 1 Qd. R. 51; *D & J Fowler (Aust) Ltd v Bank of New South Wales* [1982] 2 N.S.W.L.R. 879.

[60] *Craythorne v Swinburne* (1807) 14 Ves. Jun. 160; 33 E.R. 482; *Dering v Earl of Winchelsea* (1787) 1 Cox 318 at 321; 29 E.R. 1184 at 1185; *Pendlebury v Walker* (1841) 4 Y. & C. Ex. 424 at 441–442; 160 E.R. 1072 at 1079 *per* Alderson B.; *Re Ennis* [1893] 3 Ch. 238; *Arcedeckne v Lord Howard* (1875) 45 L.J. Ch. 622; *Steel v Dixon* (1881) 17 Ch. D. 825; *Stimpson v Smith* [1999] Ch. 340; *A/asian Conference Association Ltd v Mainline Constructions Pty Ltd (in liq)* (1978) 141 C.L.R. 335; 53 A.L.J.R. 66; *Morgan Equipment Co v Rodgers (No.2)* (1993) 32 N.S.W.L.R. 467. Such an agreement does not, of course, affect the rights of the creditor: *Bater v Kare* [1964] S.C.R. 206 (Can). Conversely, sureties for distinct debts of a principal debtor in different combinations may agree to share the burden equally in certain events. Such an agreement would exclude any right of contribution which might arise in respect of any particular debt: see *Arcedeckne v Lord Howard* (1872) 27 L.T. 194. See also *Official Trustee in Bankruptcy v Citibank Savings Ltd* (1995) 38 N.S.W.L.R. 116, where contribution was not allowed between the co-sureties because one group was obliged to indemnify the other on equitable principles.

[61] *Pendlebury v Walker* (1841) 4 Y. & C. Ex. 424; 160 E.R. 1072. Just as co-sureties can control or limit their right to contribution from one another by agreement, successive indorsers of a bill or note for the accommodation of another can, by contract among themselves, exclude or restrict their claims to contribution: *Mitchell v English* (1870) 17 Gr. 303; *Ianson v Paxton* (1874) 23 C.P. 439 (Can).

[62] *Bater v Kare* [1964] S.C.R. 206 (Can); *Molson's Bank v Kovinsky* [1924] 4 D.L.R. 330.

[63] *Shire of Windsor v Enoggera Divisional Board* [1902] Q.S.R. 23.

[64] See, *e.g. Woodhouse AC Israel Coco Ltd SA v Nigerian Produce Marketing Co Ltd* [1972] A.C. 741 at 761.

jurisdiction.[65] Moreover, contribution can be excluded by an express clause in the guarantee itself stating that the creditor's several guarantors under that guarantee are not co-sureties but that some are primarily liable and others secondarily liable as between themselves.[66] Even a provision in a surety's guarantee that he cannot be sued unless the other guarantors default exempts that surety from an obligation to contribute, because that surety and the other guarantors are not liable to a common demand.[67]

12–130   The courts will, however, not readily draw an inference that a guarantor has excluded a right of contribution, even if it is clear that his other rights, such as the right of subrogation, are excluded. In *Cornfoot v Holdenson*,[68] a bank which held a guarantee from the defendant took a further guarantee in respect of its customer's account from the plaintiff. In effect, the plaintiff and the defendant were answerable for the whole of the floating balance of the customer's account up to the limits of their respective liabilities. The second guarantee, which was expressed to be independent of the first guarantee, stated that the plaintiff would not claim the benefit of any former guarantee or security. It was argued that these provisions excluded the plaintiff's right of contribution. However, Mann J. found that, while they excluded the plaintiff's right to be subrogated to the position of the creditor and his right to have the customer's other contracts delivered to him, they did not impair his right to contribution from the defendant. By the same token, it is not true that the prima facie rule of equal sharing of the common burden of the principal debt can only be displaced by the express agreement of the co-sureties.[69] Unequal sharing may be ordered where the court can discern a clear implication that this is what the parties must have intended or where unequal sharing is necessary to do justice in the circumstances of the case.[70]

12–131   Although a guarantor may modify or exclude his own right of contribution by a provision in the guarantee, the co-guarantors' rights to claim contribution or share in the benefit of a security will not be excluded by an agreement to which they are not a party, unless the claim is barred by estoppel.[71]

---

[65] *Hong Kong Bank of Australia Ltd v Larobi Pty Ltd* (1991) 23 N.S.W.L.R. 593; *Bond v Larobi Pty Ltd* (1992) 6 W.A.R. 489. It appears, however, that this principle will be limited in its application to the situation where all the sureties agree to restrict their right to contribution and there is equality of treatment and proportionality between all the co-sureties: *Bond v Larobi Pty Ltd* (1992) 6 W.A.R. 489 at 496. Quaere, however, whether co-sureties who are liable under *separate instruments* can take advantage of the guarantor's promise as they are not parties to the agreement. Possible defences, however, may be based on common law or statutory exceptions to privity (see above, paras 2–20 to 2–23) or estoppel. If the co-sureties have given a similar undertaking, another possibility is an implied contract between the sureties: see, in another context, *Clarke v Dunraven* [1897] A.C. 59.
[66] *Molson's Bank v Kovinsky* [1924] 4 D.L.R. 330 at 332. See also *Turner v Davies* (1796) 2 Esp. 478; 170 E.R. 425.
[67] *Re Denton's Estate* [1904] 2 Ch. 178. See also *Craythorne v Swinburne* (1807) 14 Ves. Jun. 160; 33 E.R. 482 and below, para.12–145.
[68] [1932] V.L.R. 4. See also *Gardner v Brooke* [1897] 2 I.R. 6 at 19 (Q.B.) per Gibson J.; *Bater v Kare* [1964] S.C.R. 206.
[69] *Trotter v Franklin* [1991] 2 N.Z.L.R. 92 at 98.
[70] *ibid.*
[71] *Steel v Dixon* (1881) 17 Ch. D. 825 at 832 (agreement between one guarantor and the principal debtor); *Bond v Larobi Pty Ltd* (1992) 6 W.A.R. 489.

An agreement to modify or exclude a surety's right to contribution can **12–132** be vitiated on grounds of fraud,[72] fraudulent concealment[73] or a failure to satisfy a condition precedent.[74] It might also be set aside for innocent misrepresentation or undue influence.[75]

A right to contribution can be impliedly excluded[76] but the courts should **12–133** be reluctant to draw such an inference.[77] Clearly there can be no implied exclusion of the right to contribution where the guarantors have reached a specific agreement on this matter.[78] Sometimes, however, the right to contribution can be displaced by the parties' conduct or the course of events. It has been suggested that contribution is excluded where one guarantor enjoys the whole benefit of the guarantee in another capacity to the exclusion of the co-surety:[79] in this special situation, it might be inequitable to require the co-surety to contribute.

Equally, where it is clear from the substance of the transaction and the **12–134** relationship of the co-sureties that the liability of one would rank ahead of the others, it may not be appropriate to grant contribution against the other co-sureties. For example, in *Official Trustee in Bankruptcy v Citibank Savings Ltd*[80] the trustee in bankruptcy of one co-surety was not

---

[72] *Pendlebury v Walker* (1841) 4 Y. & C. Ex. 424; 160 E.R. 1072.

[73] *Macreth v Walmesley* (1884) 51 L.T. 19 at 20 *per* Kay J. But there is no general duty of disclosure between co-sureties, so a surety is not obliged to inform the co-sureties that the principal debtor owes the surety a debt: *Macreth v Walmesley* (1884) 51 L.T. 19 (Ch).

[74] *Arcedeckne v Lord Howard* (1875) 45 L.J. Ch. 622, HL.

[75] See R. Goff and G. Jones, *The Law of Restitution* (6th ed., 2002), para.14–008. See also above, Chapter 4. See also *Rae v Rae* (1857) 61 Ch. R. 490 (right to contribution excluded where the surety was induced to provide a guarantee on the understanding that the paying surety would indemnify the co-surety against any liability he might incur as a result of his giving the guarantee).

[76] *Israel v Foreshore Properties Pty Ltd (in liq)* (1980) 30 A.L.R. 631 at 635; *Re Wygoda and Poconowski* (unreported, NSW Fed Ct, November 28, 1991); *Official Trustee in Bankruptcy v Citibank Savings Ltd* (1995) 35 N.S.W.L.R. 116. See also *Trotter v Franklin* [1991] 2 N.Z.L.R. 92, below, para.12–218. Contrary to Lord Kenyon's suggestion in *Turner v Davies* (1796) 2 Esp. 478; 170 E.R. 425 (NP), it is doubtful whether the right of contribution is impliedly excluded simply because the guarantor requested the co-surety to join the guarantor in providing the guarantee. In so far as *Trotter v Franklin* suggests that the right of contribution may be modified if the justice of the case demands it, it is not clear that this represents a correct statement of English law in the absence, for example, of something in the nature of an estoppel.

[77] *Bater v Kare* [1964] S.C.R. 206; *Pacanowski v Wygoda* (unreported, Full Court of the Federal Court, Neaves, Wilcox and Spender J.J., December 18, 1992). The courts appear reluctant to conclude that a surety has surrendered his equitable claim to contribution: *AGC (Advances) Ltd v West* (1984) 5 N.S.W.L.R. 590. *Cf. Swain v Wall* (1641) 1 Ch. R. 149; 21 E.R. 534.

[78] *Patterson v Arcade Buildings Ltd* [1930] G.L.R. 312.

[79] As, for example, where one of the guarantors has withdrawn from the company on whose behalf the guarantee was given and the other guarantors continue as directors or controlling shareholders of the company: *Bater v Kare* [1964] S.C.R. 206 (Can). The court might even be prepared to imply a term that the remaining directors will use their best endeavours to release the retiring director from his personal guarantee by providing alternative security, if necessary. The proper measure of damages for breach of this implied term is the loss resulting from the creditor enforcing the personal guarantee and collateral security against the retiring director: *Marsden v Elston* [2001] 2 C.L. 269 (Norwich County Court). See also *Woolmington v Bronze Lamp Restaurant Pty Ltd* [1984] 2 N.S.W.L.R. 242 at 246 (where such a claim was rejected on the evidence); *AGC (Advances) Ltd v West* (1984) 5 N.S.W.L.R. 590 (on appeal, the Court of Appeal did not address this issue, and it held that Mrs West was nevertheless liable *to the creditor* for the principal debt). See also below, para.12–218.

[80] [1999] B.P.I.R. 754 (Sup Ct, NSW, Bryson J., October 12, 1995).

entitled to contribution from other co-sureties who entered into the transaction for no consideration and on the basis that the security offered by that co-surety would be more than sufficient to meet the principal debt. But in the absence of an estoppel, it is doubtful whether English law requires a guarantor's prima facie right of contribution to be modified simply on the grounds of justice between the parties.[81] Certainly a mere imbalance of power and responsibility between the guarantors in their capacities as shareholders and directors in a private company is not sufficient to justify an implied term that they will share the burden of the principal debt unevenly.[82] Nor is it likely that one guarantor's share of the common liability will be increased because he has acted improperly in his capacity as a director of the principal debtor, thereby increasing the potential liability of his co-sureties.[83]

12–135 A guarantor's right to contribution may be waived by subsequent transactions[84] or forfeited by the guarantor's failure to perform his duties towards the co-sureties.[85] Accordingly, if a guarantor refuses to join with a co-surety, who has paid more than his share, in suing the principal debtor for an indemnity, the guarantor might not be able to complain if that co-surety later refuses to share the amount recovered from the debtor.[86]

12–136 In the absence of an express or implied agreement between the co-sureties, the general rule that they must contribute equally to the common debt can be modified or excluded by the common intention of the sureties.[87] In *Morgan Equipment Co v Rodgers (No.2)*,[88] Giles J. found that the common intention of the co-sureties was that their respective liabilities to contribute were to be measured by shareholdings in the principal debtor company which was the vehicle for their joint venture.[89]

12–137 A right to contribution can be deferred, rather than excluded. A clause in a guarantee which merely defers the guarantor's right to pursue a right of contribution against the co-sureties until the creditor is paid in full is not offensive to public policy and is enforceable according to its terms. The clause is not an abrogation of the right of contribution but rather a deferral of the right to enforce the claim to contribution.[90]

---

[81] *Hampton v Minns* [2002] 1 W.L.R. 504. *Cf. Trotter v Franklin* [1991] 2 N.Z.L.R. 92.
[82] *Hampton v Minns* [2002] 1 W.L.R. 504.
[83] *ibid.*
[84] *Coope v Twynam* (1823) Turn. & R. 426; 37 E.R. 1164.
[85] *Steel v Dixon* (1881) 17 Ch. D. 825 at 832 (*e.g.* a failure to bring benefits into hotchpot). But there was no breach in *Hampton v Minns* [2002] 1 W.L.R. 504. As possible examples, see below, paras 12–200 to 12–213.
[86] *ibid.*, at 828–829 and 832.
[87] See *Coulls v Bagot's Executor & Trustee Co Ltd* (1967) 119 C.L.R. 460 at 488; *Muschinski v Dodds* (1985) 160 C.L.R. 583 at 597, 617; *Robinson v Campbell (No.2)* (1992) 30 N.S.W.L.R. 503.
[88] (1993) 32 N.S.W.L.R. 467. See also *Leigh-Mardon Rly Ltd v Wawn* (1995) 17 A.C.S.R. 741.
[89] Compare *Bater v Kare* [1964] S.C.R. 206 and *AGC (Advances) Ltd v West* (1984) 5 N.S.W.L.R. 590.
[90] *Bond v Larobi Pty Ltd* (1992) 6 W.A.R. 489.

(v) To whom is contribution available?

The right to contribution is restricted to co-sureties who are liable in **12–138** respect of the same principal debt owed by the same principal debtor.[91] The co-sureties must share a common obligation[92] and be liable to a common demand.[93] For this reason, the guarantors of a company's debts are not entitled to seek contribution from the company's directors who are liable under ss.213 and 214 of the Insolvency Act 1986 for wrongful or fraudulent trading: the liabilities are not of the same order because the guarantors' liability is secondary in the sense that it is dependent upon the default of the principal debtor company, whereas the liability of the directors is a primary statutory liability.[94]

A payment by a surety under his guarantee may justify a contribution **12–139** claim even if it was made for the ulterior motive of deflecting another liability of the guarantor. In *Baker v Microdos Computers Australia Pty Ltd (in liq)*,[95] for example, it was immaterial that a guarantor who made a payment under his guarantee thereby acquired a right of indemnity which he could set off against any liability which he might incur in the principal debtor's action against him in relation to the transfer of the debtor's plant and stock.

It does not matter whether the co-sureties are bound as to different **12–140** amounts and in different terms,[96] save that no guarantor can be required to pay more than the limit of his guarantee.[97] If A, B and C are liable in terms of their guarantees for the whole of the principal debt, they can claim contribution from one another even if their liability is expressed to be limited in varying amounts, say, £1,000, £2,000 and £3,000 respectively, provided that none of them can be held liable beyond the stated limit of his guarantee.[98]

---

[91] *Ellesmere Brewery Co v Cooper* [1896] 1 Q.B. 75 at 79; *Moulton v Roberts* [1977] Qd. R. 135 at 139; *Cornfoot v Holdenson* [1932] V.L.R. 4; *Mahoney v McManus* (1981) 55 A.L.J.R. 673. Thus, where the principal debtor assigns the burden of a guaranteed principal debt with the consent of the creditor, and then a second guarantee is taken securing the obligations of the assignee, the guarantors will not be liable to contribute.

[92] *Smith v Cook* [1911] A.C. 317; *Ellesmere Brewery Co v Cooper* [1896] 1 Q.B. 75; *Scholefield Goodman & Sons Ltd v Zyngier* (1985) 59 A.L.J.R. 770. See also *Johnson v Wild* (1890) 44 Ch. D. 146. For this reason, there is no right of contribution where one surety pays off the creditor and demands reimbursement from the principal debtor who then finds another surety. Cf. *Cornfoot v Holdenson* [1932] V.L.R. 4 at 14.

[93] *Hunter v Hunt* (1845) 1 C.B. 300; 135 E.R. 555; *Johnson v Wild* (1890) 44 Ch. D. 146 (an indemnity case); *American Surety Co of New York v Wrightson* (1910) 103 L.T. 663 at 665. See also *Burke v LFOT Pty Ltd* (2002) 187 A.L.R. 612. Consequently, if the principal debt is assigned by the creditor and the assignee takes a new guarantee to secure the debt, the new surety cannot seek contribution from the original guarantor: *Ellesmere Brewery Co v Cooper* [1896] 1 Q.B. 75 at 79.

[94] *Street v Retravision* (1995) 16 A.C.S.R. 780. See s. 215 of the Companies Act 1985.

[95] (1996) 20 A.C.S.R. 148.

[96] *Molson's Bank v Kovinsky* [1924] 4 D.L.R. 330 at 332; *Dering v Earl of Winchelsea* (1787) 1 Cox 318; 29 E.R. 1184.

[97] *Dering v Earl of Winchelsea* (1787) 1 Cox 318; 29 E.R. 1184.

[98] See *Pendlebury v Walker* (1841) 4 Y. & C. Ex. 424; 160 E.R. 1072.

12–141   It is enough for the guarantors to share a common liability for *part* of the principal debt.[99] Thus if one guarantor is liable for the first £10,000 of the principal debt and another surety is liable for the whole of the principal debt without limitation, they can claim contributions from each other since they share a common liability for the first £10,000 of the debt.

12–142   Contribution is not available, however, where the guarantors are liable for different debts or obligations of the same principal debtor[1] or different parts of the same principal debt.[2] For example, where A guarantees repayment of the principal debtor's overdraft and B guarantees repayment of a separate advance by the bank to the debtor, no action for contribution will lie between A and B. Nor is contribution open to sureties who are answerable for distinct and specific portions of the same debt.[3] Accordingly, an action for contribution will not lie between one guarantor who is liable for a discrete portion of the principal debt, say the first £50,000, and another who is liable for the ultimate balance owing by the debtor beyond the first £50,000.[4]

12–143   The same lack of mutuality prevents a guarantor claiming contribution from a sub-surety of one of the guarantor's co-sureties: the claimant and the sub-surety are not subject to a common demand and a common liability.[5] Thus, if A, B and C are co-sureties, and D is surety for A, then B and C cannot claim contribution from D.

12–144   The right to contribution can be invoked by guarantors who are liable for the same debt or obligation whether they are bound jointly, jointly and severally, or merely severally;[6] whether they are bound by the same or different instruments[7] and, indeed, whether or not they knew of each other's existence.[8] Nor does it matter whether the obligations of the co-

---

[99] *Molson's Bank v Kovinsky* [1924] 4 D.L.R. 330 at 332. This may occur where one surety is liable for a part of the total debt and the other sureties are liable for the whole indebtedness, although modern documentation makes this result unlikely.

[1] *Coope v Twynam* (1823) 1 Turn & R. 426 at 429; 37 E.R. 1164 at 1166; *Pendlebury v Walker* (1841) 4 Y. & C. Ex. 424; 160 E.R. 1072. Cf. *Dering v Earl of Winchelsea* (1787) 1 Cox 318; 29 E.R. 1184. See also *Ellis v Emmanuel* (1876) 1 Ex. D. 157 at 162 *per* Blackburn J.

[2] See *Pendlebury v Walker* (1841) 4 Y. & C. Ex. 424; 160 E.R. 1072; *Coope v Twynam* (1823) T. & R. 426; 37 E.R. 1164; *Collins v Prosser* (1823) 1 B. & C. 682; 107 E.R. 250; *Ellis v Emmanuel* (1876) 1 Ex. D. 157, CA.

[3] *Pendlebury v Walker* (1841) 4 Y. & C. Ex. 424; 160 E.R. 1072; *Coope v Twynam* (1823) 1 Turn & R. 426; 37 E.R. 1164. Cf. *Collins v Prosser* (1823) 1 B. & C. 682; 107 E.R. 250; *Ellis v Emmanuel* (1876) 1 Ex. D. 157. See above, paras 5–35 to 5–40.

[4] See *Molson's Bank v Kovinsky* [1924] 4 D.L.R. 330.

[5] *Craythorne v Swinburne* (1807) 14 Ves. Jun. 160; 33 E.R. 482; *Re Denton* [1904] 2 Ch. 178; *Standard Brands Ltd v Fox* (1974) 44 D.L.R. (3d) 69; *Fox v Royal Bank of Canada* (1975) 59 D.L.R. (3d) 258; *Ward v National Bank of New Zealand* (1883) 8 App. Cas. 755.

[6] *Stirling v Forrester* (1821) 3 Bli. 575 at 590; 4 E.R. 712 at 717, *per* Lord Redesdale; *Dering v Winchelsea* (1787) 1 Cox Eq. Cas. 318; 29 E.R. 1184; *Mahoney v McManus* (1981) 55 A.L.J.R. 673 at 675 *per* Gibbs C.J.; *McLean v Discount & Finance Ltd* (1939) 64 C.L.R. 312. Cf. *Underhill v Horwood* (1804) 10 Ves. Jun. 209; 32 E.R. 824, which suggests contribution is not available where the sureties are bound severally.

[7] *McLean v Discount & Finance Ltd* (1939) 64 C.L.R. 312 at 328; *Pendlebury v Walker* (1841) 4 Y. & C. Ex. 424; 160 E.R. 1072; *Dering v Earl of Winchelsea* (1787) 1 Cox 318; 29 E.R. 1184; *Re Ennis* [1893] 3 Ch. 238; *Ellesmere Brewery v Cooper* [1896] 1 Q.B. 75; *Mayhew v Crickett* (1818) 2 Swanst. 185; 36 E.R. 585; *Ostrander v Jarvis* (1909) 18 O.L.R. 17, CA; *Molson's Bank v Kovinsky* [1924] 4 D.L.R. 330 at 335–336; *Mahoney v McManus* (1981) 55 A.L.J.R. 673.

[8] *Smith v Wood* [1929] 1 Ch. 14 at 21; *Dering v Earl of Winchelsea* (1787) 1 Cox 318; 29 E.R. 1184; *Craythorne v Swinburne* (1807) 14 Ves, Jun. 160 at 165; 33 E.R. 482 at 484; *Molson's Bank v Kovinsky* [1924] 4 D.L.R. 330; *Mahoney v McManus* (1981) 55 A.L.J.R. 673 at 675. On

sureties arose at the same or at different times.[9] Thus, where a creditor takes one guarantee jointly binding A and B as sureties of the whole indebtedness up to a limit of £10,000, and another guarantee from B, C and D binding them jointly and severally for the total amount of the same principal debt, and yet another guarantee from E in respect of the first £5,000 of the principal debt, E can claim contribution from A, B, C and D in respect of any amounts E pays up to the limit of his liability whether or not E was aware of the other guarantees when E became a surety. It is not even necessary to establish that the different instruments binding the guarantors are expressly connected with each other.[10] Nor does it matter that the co-sureties are liable under different causes of action as long as the respective liabilities are of the same nature[11] and the parties are liable to perform substantially the same obligation.[12] The court will look at the substance of the transactions to determine whether the parties are sureties for the same debt or obligation.[13] It is not sufficient that the respective obligations arose out of related transactions[14] or that the claimant's payment has benefited or relieved the defendant financially.[15]

(vi) Who is obliged to contribute?

Contribution is available only against co-sureties[16] on the basis that **12–145** persons who bear co-ordinate liabilities to make good one loss or to

the other hand, if the surety provides his guarantee on condition that other parties become co-sureties, then he will be discharged if this condition is not satisfied: *Leaf v Gibbs* (1830) 4 C. & P. 466; *Evans v Bremridge* (1855) 2 K. & J. 174; 69 E.R. 741, on appeal (1856) 8 De G.M. & G. 100; *National Provincial Bank of England v Brackenbury* (1906) 22 T.L.R. 797. See also *James Graham & Co (Timber) Ltd v Southgate Sands* [1986] Q.B. 80, where the signature of one of the co-sureties was forged and this nullified the agreement of the others to provide their guarantees. See above, paras 3–87 to 3–98, 3–134, and 4–222.
[9] *Whiting v Burke* (1871) 6 Ch. App. 342; *Scholefield Goodman & Sons Ltd v Zyngier* [1986] A.C. 562.
[10] *Molson's Bank v Kovinsky* [1924] 4 D.L.R. 330 at 335.
[11] *BP Petroleum Development Ltd v Esso Petroleum* 1987 S.L.T. 345 at 348; *Street & Halls v Retravision (NSW) Pty Ltd* (1995) 56 F.C.R. 588 at 597; *Burke v LFOT Pty Ltd* (2000) 187 A.L.R. 161 at 183 and 187.
[12] *Cockburn v GIO Finance Ltd (No.2)* [2001] N.S.W.C.A. 177 (unreported judgment of the New South Wales Court of Appeal, June 14, 2001) (where it was held that contribution was not available between a lender who discharged a mortgage pursuant to a court order on grounds of undue influence, and a solicitor who was held liable for negligence in relation to advice about the mortgage; the mortgagee suffered no loss as a result of the mortgage being set aside; the mortgagee's loss was incurred as a result of the advance in reliance on the mortgage and this was not a liability or obligation owed concurrently with the solicitor to the plaintiff. In short, contribution was not available between the mortgagee and the solicitor because they were not under co-ordinate liabilities for the same loss.
[13] *Reynolds v Wheeler* (1861) 10 C.B. (NS) 561; 142 E.R. 572; *AGC (Advances) Ltd v West* (1984) 5 N.S.W.L.R. 590; *Sherwin v McWilliams* (1921) 17 Tas. L.R. 94. See also *Davies v Humphreys* (1840) 6 M. & W. 153; 151 E.R. 361.
[14] *Re La Rosa, Ex p. Norgard* (1991) 31 F.C.R. 83; *Cummings v Lewis* (1993) 41 F.C.R. 559.
[15] *Ruabon Steamship Co v London Assurance* [1900] A.C. 6; *Mahoney v McManus* (1981) 180 C.L.R. 370.
[16] *Craythorne v Swinburne* (1807) 14 Ves. Jun. 160; 33 E.R. 482; *Re Denton's Estate* [1904] 2 Ch. 178. It is also available as between co-indemnifiers: *Johnson v Wild* (1890) 44 Ch. D. 146. It is even available against a co-guarantor who is not personally liable for the principal debt but who has pledged or charged his property with payment of the debt: see *Mahoney v*

meet a common demand can be held liable to contribute.[17] The parties can be under co-ordinate liabilities in the relevant sense even if they can choose different methods of discharging their obligations, for example by a contribution of equity capital to the principal debtor rather than an advance of loan capital or a payment to the creditor on behalf of the principal debtor.[18] By the same token, a guarantor will not be entitled to contribution from the co-sureties unless the guarantor directly or indirectly pays more than his just share of the principal debt.

12–146   Where one guarantor enjoys the whole benefit of the guarantee through his shareholding in a company from which his co-surety has withdrawn, the co-surety is not liable to contribute.[19] Since the first guarantor enjoys all the benefits of the guarantee he alone must bear its burden, and his co-surety has a sound defence to an action for contribution.[20] There is, however, no direct English or Australian authority for this proposition. On the other hand, it is consistent with the equitable genesis of the right of contribution.[21] It is at least clear that a co-surety can resist a claim for contribution by relying on an indemnity granted by the claimant in a contribution suit. This indemnity can take the form of a verbal promise since the Statute of Frauds does not apply to such an undertaking.[22]

12–147   Co-sureties in a prior degree may not claim contribution from a sub-surety of one of their co-sureties.[23] As we have seen, where A, B and C are co-sureties and D is surety for A, it appears that B and C may not demand contribution from D because D is not subject to a common demand.[24] Similarly, A may not claim contribution from his sub-surety,[25] but D can claim an indemnity from A, as his principal.[26]

12–148   It is not enough for the parties to be liable for the same principal debt if their liability to pay arises at different times. Thus in *Re Denton's Estate*,[27]

McManus (1981) 44 A.L.J.R. 673; *Re Hodgetts; Ex p. Official Receiver* (1949) 16 A.B.C. 201; *McLean v Discount & Finance Ltd* (1939) 64 C.L.R. 312 at 325. But a guarantor is not entitled to an indemnity from a person who has himself agreed to indemnify the debtor in respect of the debt because this is an independent obligation for which the guarantor is not secondarily liable: *Re Law Courts Chambers Co* (1889) 61 L.T. 669.

[17] See *Albion Insurance Co Ltd v Government Insurance Office (NSW)* (1969) 121 C.L.R. 352 at 350; *Coope v Twynam* (1823) Turn. & R. 426 at 429; 37 E.R. 1164 at 1166 *per* Lord Eldon L.C.

[18] *Capita Financial Group Ltd v Rothwells Ltd* (1992) 30 N.S.W.L.R. 619.

[19] *Bater v Kare* [1964] S.C.R. 206.

[20] *ibid.*

[21] This passage was cited with apparent approval in *Official Trustee in Bankruptcy v Citibank Savings Ltd* (1995) 38 N.S.W.L.R. 116 at 125.

[22] See above, paras 3–07 to 3–18.

[23] *Standard Brands Ltd v Fox* (1974) 44 D.L.R. (3d) 69; *Fox v Royal Bank of Canada* (1975) 59 D.L.R. (3d) 258; *Craythorne v Swinburne* (1807) 14 Ves. Jun. 160; 33 E.R. 482. However, a sub-surety who pays the principal debt will be entitled to an indemnity from the surety: *Re Denton's Estate* [1904] 2 Ch. 178.

[24] *ibid.*

[25] *Craythorne v Swinburne* (1807) 14 Ves. Jun. 160; 33 E.R. 482 at 484; *Re Denton's Estate* [1904] 2 Ch. 178 at 192–193 *per* Stirling L.J.

[26] *Standard Brands Ltd v Fox* (1974) 44 D.L.R. (3d) 69; *Fox v Royal Bank of Canada* (1975) 59 D.L.R. (3d) 258.

[27] [1904] 2 Ch. 178. The right of contribution must exist at, or immediately after, the moment of payment by the paying surety; otherwise it will never arise: *Scholefield Goodman & Sons Ltd v Zyngier* [1984] V.R. 445, affirmed on other grounds in (1985) 59 A.L.J.R. 770 PC. *Cf. Davies v Humphreys* (1840) 6 M. & W. 153; 151 E.R. 361.

the defendant, Denton, was not allowed contribution from the plaintiff because his liability as surety to pay the principal debt arose immediately on demand, whereas the plaintiff's liability as guarantor crystallised only after the expiration of six months from the creditor's becoming entitled to exercise its power of sale under its mortgage deed and giving notice thereof to the plaintiff. In short, the plaintiff was not a co-surety with Denton but in fact a guarantor to the creditor against the default of both Denton and the principal debtor.

12–149 The estate of a deceased joint tenant is not obliged to contribute to mortgage repayments made by the surviving joint tenant. Through the principle of survivorship, the death of one joint tenant vests the property in the survivor who is not, therefore, entitled to claim contribution from the deceased joint tenant's estate in respect of mortgage repayments after the date of the death.[28]

12–150 No contribution can be extracted from a guarantor who is surety for the principal debtor *and* the party claiming contribution.[29] For example, if A guaranteed repayment of the whole of the principal debt by B, the principal debtor, and also repayment to a limited extent by C, a surety, A will not be liable to contribute to C because B and C are both principal debtors so far as A is concerned. A and C are not subject to a common demand and are not, therefore, co-sureties even though they are liable for the same principal debt.[30]

12–151 Contribution is not available against persons who gave a guarantee without consideration at the request and for the benefit of other co-sureties by way of the provision of credit to a company which the co-sureties owned and controlled.[31] These persons are entitled to an indemnity from the other co-sureties and are not, therefore, liable to a contribution suit by the other co-sureties,[32] although under a joint and several guarantee they would be liable to the creditor for the full amount of the principal debt. Contribution is based on equitable principles and not the actual or imputed agreement of the co-sureties.[33]

12–152 A guarantor can claim contribution from another guarantor only where they are co-sureties *as between themselves*.[34] Where a bill of exchange is given as security for a debt, the drawer and the acceptor are sureties vis-à-vis the principal debtor, but as between themselves the drawer is only surety for the acceptor. In the absence of an agreement to the contrary, the drawer and the acceptor are not co-sureties and the primary burden must be borne by the acceptor with no right of contribution against the drawer.[35] However, contribution will be available between parties whose names appear as successively liable on a bill of exchange where they intended as

---

[28] *Lumley v Robinson* [2002] EWCA Civ 94 (unreported decision of the Court of Appeal, January 25, 2002).
[29] *Re Denton's Estate* [1904] 2 Ch. 178.
[30] *ibid.*
[31] *Official Trustee in Bankruptcy v Citibank Savings Ltd* (1995) 38 N.S.W.L.R. 116.
[32] *ibid.*
[33] *ibid.*, at 123.
[34] *Ex p. Hunter* (1825) 2 Gl. & J. 7; *Molson's Bank v Kovinsky* [1924] 4 D.L.R. 330.
[35] *Ex p. Hunter* (1825) 2 Gl. & J. 7. See also *Duncan, Fox & Co v North and South Wales Bank* (1880) 6 App. Cas. 1 at 20 *per* Lord Blackburn.

between themselves to assume the positions of co-sureties in equal degree.[36]

12–153   Even outside the context of bills of exchange, a person can be held liable to contribute if he assumes the position of a co-surety with the plaintiff and it is immaterial whether that person is a co-surety so far as the creditor is concerned.[37] It is true that in *Turner v Davies*[38] Lord Kenyon suggested that a party who became a joint surety at the request of another guarantor, without the knowledge of the creditor, is not required to pay that guarantor a contribution of a moiety. With respect, there appears to be no justification for such a general principle. It should be a question of fact in each case whether the party induced to enter into the guarantee at the request of the other guarantor has agreed to share the secondary liability and be liable to a common demand from the creditor.[39] It may be more difficult to draw such an inference where the guarantor who requested the other party to provide a guarantee has taken a security for himself from the principal debtor only because this might suggest that the guarantors are not as between themselves co-sureties.[40]

12–154   As the right to contribution is founded upon equitable principles and not an express or implied contract between the guarantors, it is available against co-sureties whether or not they were aware of each other's existence when they provided their guarantees.[41]

12–155   It is often said that only solvent co-sureties are required to contribute.[42] But a guarantor who pays the whole of the principal debt and claims contribution from the solvent co-sureties may be required to share with them any dividends later received on proving in the estate of an insolvent co-surety for that guarantor's share of the principal debt.[43] Thus where A, B, C and D are equal co-sureties and A pays the whole of the principal debt, amounting to £60,000, A can claim contribution from

---

[36] *Reynolds v Wheeler* (1861) 10 C.B. (NS) 561; 142 E.R. 572; *Batson v King* (1859) 4 H. & N. 739; 157 E.R. 1032; *Macdonald v Whitfield* (1883) 8 App. Cas. 733.

[37] *Sherwin v McWilliams* (1921) 17 Tas. L.R. 94: see above, para.12–145.

[38] (1796) 2 Esp. 478; 170 E.R. 425.

[39] *Done v Walley* (1848) 2 Exch. 198; 154 E.R. 463. Where the circumstances suggest that the surety who requested a guarantee from another party provided that party with a security to induce him to provide the guarantee, it may well be that the other party is, in fact, a sub-surety who is not entitled to contribution. See G. Andrews and R. Millett, *Law of Guarantees* (3rd ed., 2000), para.12.10.

[40] *Turner v Davies* (1796) 2 Esp. 478; 170 E.R. 425. See *Rowlatt on Principal and Surety* (5th ed., 1999), para.7–53, which suggests that this proposition is probably limited to the situation where the proper inference is that the additional surety was asked to join on that basis. Strictly speaking, the fact that one surety holds a counter-security from the principal debtor does not prevent that surety from being a co-surety with another guarantor of the principal debt. But where a surety takes a security from another guarantor, this suggests that they are not liable to a common demand and are not, therefore, co-sureties.

[41] *Mahoney v McManus* (1981) 55 A.L.J.R. 673 at 675 *per* Gibbs C.J.; *McLean v Discount & Finance Ltd* (1939) 64 C.L.R. 312 at 328, 336–337; *Albion Insurance Co Ltd v Government Insurance Office* (NSW) (1969) 121 C.L.R. 342 at 350–352; *Dering v Earl of Winchelsea* (1787) 1 Cox 318; 29 E.R. 1184; *Craythorne v Swinburne* (1807) 14 Ves. Jun. 160 at 165; 33 E.R. 482; *Smith v Wood* [1929] 1 Ch. 14 at 21.

[42] *Mahoney v McManus* (1981) 55 A.L.J.R. 673 at 675; *Re Price* (1978) 85 D.L.R. (3d) 554; *Ellesmere Brewery Co v Cooper* [1896] 1 Q.B. 75 at 80; *Trusts & Guarantee Co v Dodds* (1922) 23 O.W.N. 69. At common law the burden of the principal debt was simply divided among both solvent and insolvent co-sureties: *Batard v Hawes* (1853) 2 El. & Bl. 287; 118 E.R. 775.

[43] *Re Hendry, Ex p. Murphy* [1905] S.A.L.R. 116.

the solvent co-sureties. If D is insolvent, B and C will each be liable to contribute £20,000, that is, one third of the principal debt. In other words, where one of the co-sureties is insolvent, the contribution of the other co-sureties is increased proportionately to meet the common debt.[44] Any dividends which A receives in D's insolvent estate on a proof for D's one quarter share of the principal debt must be shared equally with B and C. Should A be paid a dividend of £6,000 on his proof for £15,000 in D's estate (that is, D's share of the principal debt), A can be called upon to pay B and C £2,000 each.[45] The end result would be that A, B and C would each pay £18,000 of the principal debt and D's estate would pay £6,000 in the form of a dividend. It is not strictly true, therefore, that insolvent sureties are entirely exempt from the obligation to contribute; it is just that the *initial* burden of the suretyship is borne by the solvent co-sureties.

12–156 Guarantors can claim loss relief from corporation tax under s.136(4) of the Capital Gains Tax Act 1979 for payments made under a joint and several guarantee only to the extent that they could not recover from their co-sureties at the time they made the payments. No such relief will be available in respect of amounts they could have recovered but chose not to pursue.[46]

12–157 There is no right of contribution available to co-guarantors against parties who may be personally liable for a restoration order made under s.214 of the Insolvency Act 1986 because of wrongful trading.[47] The liability of the company's directors under s.214 is a primary liability and it is not in the same degree as the obligation of those who have given a guarantee or indemnity in respect of the company's indebtedness.[48] As there is no common burden and no co-ordinate liability, the guarantors cannot obtain contribution from the delinquent directors.[49]

(vii) When can contribution be enforced?

12–158 As soon as a guarantor has paid more than that guarantor's fair share of the principal debt as between himself and the co-sureties, the guarantor is entitled to demand contribution from them in proportion to their

---

[44] *Lowe v Dixon* (1885) 16 Q.B.D. 455 at 458; *Dallas v Walls* (1873) 29 L.T. 599.
[45] *Re Hendry, Ex p. Murphy* [1905] S.A.L.R. 116. Of course, the rule against double proof will preclude a guarantor from proving in competition with the creditor in the bankruptcy or liquidation of the principal debtor or a co-surety. It is only where the principal debt is paid in full that a guarantor is entitled to prove in the bankruptcy or liquidation of a co-surety for the amount paid in excess of his fair share of the common debt.
[46] *Leisureking Ltd v Cushing (Inspector of Taxes)* [1993] S.T.C. 46.
[47] *Street v Retravision* (1995) 16 A.C.S.R. 780. See also *Re Terry's Sound Lounge Pty Ltd* (unreported, Fed Ct, Gummow J., April 11, 1995). Section 214 of the Insolvency Act 1986 was amended by s.253 of the Enterprise Act 2002.
[48] *ibid.*
[49] *Dering v Earl of Winchelsea* (1787) 1 Cox. Eq. Cas. 318; 29 E.R. 1184; *Street v Retravision* (1995) 16 A.C.S.R. 780.

respective liabilities.[50] Even a guarantor who pays more than his fair share with the aid of a stranger will be entitled to contribution, the guarantor and the stranger being treated as one claimant.[51] The right to contribution, in the sense of the cause of action for contribution, does not arise as soon as there is a judgment against the surety,[52] although the judgment will clearly provide the guarantor with ample grounds for seeking quia timet relief.[53] Clearly, contribution is also available to a guarantor who pays the whole debt or a part in satisfaction of the whole debt,[54] even if the amount paid is less than the limit of the guarantor's liability.[55] A guarantor who pays an amount in return for a release of both co-sureties from a joint and several guarantee is entitled to seek contribution from his co-guarantor even if there was no written demand by the creditor for payment. It is enough that the amount of the liability was ascertained or ascertainable, that a demand could realistically be anticipated in the absence of a negotiated settlement and that the arrangement reached with the creditor was not disadvantageous to the co-surety.[56] A sub-surety who pays the principal debt is entitled to a similar remedy by way of indemnity against the co-sureties in a prior degree.[57]

12–159 A guarantor who pays less than his share of the principal debt, however, will not be allowed contribution unless the payment *becomes more* than the guarantor's due proportion of the principal debt as the result of a subsequent payment by the debtor or another guarantor.[58] For example, if

---

[50] *McLean v Discount & Finance Ltd* (1939) 64 C.L.R. 312 at 328; *Mahoney v McManus* (1981) 55 A.L.J.R. 673; *Lang v Le Boursicot* [1993] 5 B.P.R. 97,406 (contribution is only available to guarantors who have made payments in excess of their proportionate shares of the common liability under the guarantee); *Stirling v Burdett* [1911] 2 Ch. 418 at 425; *Ex p. Gifford* (1802) 6 Ves. Jun. 805 at 808; 31 E.R. 1318 at 1319; *Holmes v Williamson* (1817) 6 M. & S. 158; 105 E.R. 1202; *Davies v Humphreys* (1840) 6 M. & W. 153 at 168–169; 151 E.R. 361 at 367; *Ex p. Snowdon* (1881) 17 Ch. D. 44 at 48 (the word "not" appearing in the judgment is clearly a mistake and should be ignored); *Tucker v Bennett* [1927] 2 D.L.R. 42; *Blancher v Russell* (1980) 11 B.L.R. 1 (Ont Co Ct); *Godfrey v Hennelly* (1893) 19 V.L.R. 70 (where a joint indorser of a promissory note received a notice of dishonour and paid when called upon to do so). Where a guarantor waives a condition precedent to liability, such as a requirement of a prior written demand, the guarantor can pay the principal debt and seek contribution from a co-surety: *Stimpson v Smith* [1999] Ch. 340. A surety who would not otherwise be liable to contribute may be estopped from denying contribution "if for a great length of time acts had been done": *Underhill v Horwood* (1804) 10 Ves. Jun. 209 at 223–224; 32 E.R. 824 at 830. Presumably, the party claiming contribution in such a case would have to establish the other elements of estoppel.
[51] See *Arcedeckne v Lord Howard* (1872) 27 L.T. 194, affirmed (1875) 45 L.J. Ch. 622.
[52] Contrast *Bond v Larobi Pty Ltd* (1992) 6 W.A.R. 489 at 503, where Owen J. appeared to confuse a guarantor's claim for contribution with his right to apply for quia timet relief.
[53] See above, paras 11–135 to 11–143 and 11–153 to 11–155.
[54] *Stimpson v Smith* [1999] Ch. 340, applying *Thomas v Nottingham Inc Football Club* [1972] Ch. 596.
[55] *Dominion of Can Invt Etc Co v Gelhorn* (1917) 36 D.L.R. 154, CA; *Walker v Bowry* (1924) 35 C.L.R. 48. See also *Lawson v Wright* (1786) 1 Cox Eq. Cas. 275; 29 E.R. 1164; *Re Snowdon, Ex p. Snowdon* (1881) 17 Ch. D. 44 at 47 *per* James L.J.. Note, however, the cause of action for contribution for the purpose of obtaining quia timet relief arises prior to payment: see above, paras 11–175 to 11–182. But only when the guarantor has paid more than his fair share of the principal debt is there a debt to support a petition in bankruptcy against a co-surety: *Ex p. Snowdon* (1881) 17 Ch. D. 44.
[56] *Stimpson v Smith* [1999] Ch. 340 at 353.
[57] *Standard Brands Ltd v Fox* (1974) 44 D.L.R. (3d) 69; *Fox v Royal Bank of Canada* (1975) 59 D.L.R. (3d) 258.
[58] *Davies v Humphreys* (1840) 6 M. & W. 153; 151 E.R. 361.

there are three guarantors, A, B and C equally liable for a principal debt of £60,000, each with a limit on liability of £20,000, and A pays £6,000 in reduction of the principal debt, then A will be entitled to a contribution of £2,000 from both B and C if the balance of the principal debt is liquidated upon realisation of a security provided by the principal debtor. It is immaterial that A has not paid more than the expressed limit of his liability.

The early editions of *Rowlatt on Principal and Surety*[59] suggested that a **12–160** guarantor who paid more than his share of the principal debt *then due* could insist on contribution from the co-sureties even though a larger sum might later be demanded by the creditor. However, Rowlatt later appeared to resile from this position by stating, "A surety paying more than his share of what is due cannot insist on contribution if a larger sum may later become due," citing *Stirling v Burdett*[60] in support.[61] On the other hand, *De Colyar on Guarantees*[62] states that a surety's right to contribution does not arise until that surety has paid more than his just proportion or share of the totality of the common debt. It is submitted that this is the better view. The right of contribution among co-sureties is based on equitable principles.[63] In a contribution suit, a court of equity was able to take a complete account of the amounts paid by each surety and the amounts still to be contributed by those sureties who had paid less than their fair share of the common debt. It could deal with the rights of contribution in one decree and even make provision for the actual or possible bankruptcy of any contributing surety. Having regard to the nature of contribution proceedings in equity and the public policy against a multiplicity of suits, equity should not entertain contribution suits unless the plaintiff has paid more than his fair share of the total principal debt.[64] As Parke B. put it in *Davies v Humphreys*:[65]

"until the one has paid more than his proportion either of the whole debt, or of that part of the debt which remains unpaid by the principal, it is not clear that he ever will be entitled to demand anything from the other, and before that, he has no equity to receive a contribution and consequently no right of action."[66]

---

[59] *Rowlatt on Principal and Surety* (3rd ed., 1936), p.245. The current editors of Rowlatt have apparently resiled from this position, or at least they have expressed no firm approval: see *Rowlatt on Principal and Surety* (5th ed., 1999), para.7–56. *Cf. Thomas v Nottingham Inc Football Club Ltd* [1972] Ch. 596.
[60] [1911] 2 Ch. 418.
[61] *Rowlatt on Principal and Surety* (5th ed., 1999), p.171.
[62] *H.A. De Colyar on Guarantees* (3rd ed., 1897), pp.343–344.
[63] See above, paras 12–116 to 12–119.
[64] *Tucker v Bennett* [1927] 2 D.L.R. 42 at 48.
[65] (1840) 6 M. & W. 153.
[66] *ibid.*, at 168–169. See also *Stirling v Burdett* [1911] 2 Ch. 418, where Warrington J. reached a similar conclusion in relation to a contribution suit involving sureties whose liabilities were limited in varying amounts. See also *Walker v Bowry* (1924) 35 C.L.R. 48; *McFarlane v Calhoun* (1879) 2 P.E.I.R. 283; *Blancher v Russell* (1980) 11 B.L.R. 1 Ont Co Ct; *Gardner v Brooke* [1897] 2 I.R. 6, QB; *Pagratide v Davis* [1922] 2 W.W.R. 1114; *Re Snowdon, Ex p. Snowdon* (1881) 17 Ch. 44, CA; *Moorooka Shopping Town (Nominees) Pty Ltd v Kilmartin* [1999] Q.S.C. 195 (unreported decision of Qld Sup Ct, Chief Justice de Jersey, August 20, 1999); *Tucker v Bennett* [1927] 2 D.L.R. 42 at 47–48.

This approach enables the rights of the sureties inter se to be determined in the one action. Any perceived hardship to a paying surety is mitigated to some extent by that surety's right of indemnity against the principal debtor.

12–161   Where the guaranteed debt is payable by instalments, a guarantor does not acquire a right to contribution simply by paying more than the guarantor's share *of each instalment* unless such instalments amount to separate debts or unless each instalment creates a discrete liability.[67] Nor does a payment by a guarantor to a suspense account justify a claim for contribution from the co-sureties, because the amount so paid has not been appropriated to the principal debt.[68]

12–162   While it might be more convenient to require that the whole amount of the principal debt should be settled before allowing one guarantor to call upon a co-surety for contribution,[69] this is not the law: a guarantor is entitled to contribution in respect of each payment made in excess of the guarantor's due proportion of the debt.[70] Nor is a claimant required to wait until the rights as between the principal debtor and the co-sureties have been settled.[71] Hence the claimant need not seek an indemnity or reimbursement from the principal debtor before proceeding against the co-sureties for contribution.

12–163   A guarantor can pay more than his share of the principal debt when it becomes due and then seek contribution.[72] The guarantor need not wait until the creditor makes a demand,[73] issues a writ,[74] or even obtains judgment against him.[75] Indeed, it is not even necessary for the creditor to resort to the guarantee at all prior to payment, provided that there is a distinct possibility that the creditor may do so.[76] Where the principal debt exceeds the limit of the guarantors' liability and the creditor is pressing for a reduction, a guarantor is entitled to pay the creditor and seek a contribution from his co-sureties even if the creditor has not closed the principal debtor's account.[77] These principles apply a fortiori where the guarantor's payment is made with the knowledge, approval and encouragement of the co-sureties.[78]

---

[67] *Stirling v Burdett* [1911] 2 Ch. 418 at 429. *Cf. Re Macdonald* [1888] W.N. 130. Equally, a surety who has paid all the interest but less than half the principal of the common debt cannot claim contribution by treating the principal and the interest as separate debts: *Lever v Pearce* [1888] W.N. 105.
[68] *Commercial Bank of Australia Ltd v Wilson & Co's Estate* [1893] A.C. 181, PC.
[69] See *Davies v Humphreys* (1840) 6 M. & W. 153; 151 E.R. 361. *Cf.* the cases cited at n.50 above.
[70] See *Davies v Humphreys* (1840) 6 M. & W. 153; 151 E.R. 361.
[71] *A E Goodwin Ltd (in liq) v A G Healing Ltd (in liq)* (1979) 7 A.C.L.R. 481.
[72] *Pitt v Purssord* (1841) 8 M. & W. 538; 151 E.R. 1152.
[73] *Moulton v Roberts* [1977] Qd. R. 135. Even if the guarantor is only liable to pay "on demand", a written demand for payment is not a condition precedent of the right to claim contribution from co-sureties: the requirement of a demand may be waived by the guarantors because it is for their benefit: *MS Fashions Ltd v Bank of Credit and Commerce International SA* [1993] Ch. 425; *Stimpson v Smith* [1999] Ch. 340.
[74] *Pitt v Purssord* (1841) 8 M. & W. 538; 151 E.R. 1152.
[75] *ibid.*
[76] *Moulton v Roberts* [1977] Qd. R. 135; *Stimpson v Smith* [1999] Ch. 340.
[77] *Stimpson v Smith* [1999] Ch. 340.
[78] *ibid.*

Contribution will not be available, however, where the guarantor's **12–164** payment is premature or unjustified in the sense that it was made before he was under a liability to pay.[79] The payment made by the guarantor seeking contribution must have been in respect of an accrued liability, such as instalments of rent then due and payable by a lessee and interest thereon.[80] A payment by a guarantor of the whole of the balance of the rent for the unexpired term of the lease will not be in respect of an accrued liability because the lessor might not have accelerated the lessee's liability to pay this rent by giving a notice to determine the lease.[81]

The payment must be one which the guarantor was legally bound to **12–165** pay[82] and which the co-surety could have been compelled to pay.[83] Payment of the guaranteed debt without the prior consent of the co-guarantors or a court order imposing liability on the co-guarantors to pay a contribution does not preclude the co-guarantors from arguing that the payment was officious or voluntary and that no right of contribution arose.[84] If the guarantor has a valid procedural or substantive defence to the creditor's claim but nevertheless pays the principal debt, the guarantor will not be entitled to contribution from the co-sureties.[85] This is equally true where the payment was effected by the realisation of a security given by the guarantor in support of the principal debt.[86] A premature realisation of the security and payment of the proceeds to the creditor cannot accelerate the guarantor's right to contribution; the co-sureties will be liable to contribute only on the due date.[87] To avoid these difficulties, a guarantor should give the co-sureties notice of intention to dispute the

---

[79] *McLean v Discount & Finance Co Ltd* (1939) 64 C.L.R. 312 at 335 *per* Latham C.J., who dissented, but not on this point; *Barry v Moroney* (1837) I.R. 8 C.L. 554; *Cumberlege v Lawson* (1850) 1 C.B. (NS) 709; 140 E.R. 292; *Pawle v Gunn* (1838) 4 Bing. (NC) 445; 132 E.R. 859.

[80] *Lang v Le Boursicot* [1993] 5 B.P.R. 97, 406.

[81] *ibid.*, at 11,786. For the same reason, a guarantor may not seek contribution in respect of a payment of an "appraisal value" because the lessor does not have an unconditional right to require this payment from the lessee: *ibid.*, at 11,787.

[82] *McFarlane v Calhoun* (1879) 2 P.E.I.R. 283; *Tucker v Bennett* (1927) 60 O.L.R. 118, HC; *Carney v Phalen* (1883) 16 N.S.R. 126, CA; *Barry v Moroney* (1837) I.R. 8 C.L. 554.

[83] *Russell v Arnold* (1922) 70 D.L.R. 849 at 851, CA. The payment must also be made by the guarantor qua guarantor and not for a different purpose: *Trotter v Franklin* [1991] 2 N.Z.L.R. 92 at 102.

[84] *Stimpson v Smith* [1999] Ch. 340 at 350 *per* Peter Gibson L.J.

[85] *Patterson v Campbell* (1910) 44 N.S.R. 214, CA; *Smith v Compton* (1832) 3 B. & Ad. 407; 110 E.R. 146; *Pettman v Keble* (1850) 9 C.B. 701; 137 E.R. 1067. However, the guarantor may have a statutory right to contribution under s.1(1) of the Civil Liability (Contribution) Act 1978 where his liability under the guarantee can be classified as a liability for damages, as distinct from debt. Note that s.6(1) of that Act provides that the entitlement to compensation operates "whatever the legal basis of [the] liability, whether tort, breach of contract, breach of trust *or otherwise*" (emphasis added). See *Friends Provident Life Office v Hillier Parker May & Rowden (a firm)* [1995] 4 All E.R. 260 and *Moschi v Lep Air Services* [1973] A.C. 351. Cf. Goff & Jones *The Law of Restitution* (6th ed., 2002), paras 14–001 to 14–004. The better view is that generally a claim to enforce a guarantee is a claim for a money sum but the position might be different in relation to guarantees of a builder's obligations under a construction contract or a tenant's obligations under a lease.

[86] *McLean v Discount & Finance Ltd* (1939) 64 C.L.R. 312 at 335 *per* Latham C.J. who dissented, but not on this point. See also *Fahey v Frawley* (1890) 26 L.R. I.R. 78 (where payment was effected by the transfer of mortgage security held by the guarantor) and *Paton v Wilkes* (1860) 8 Gr. 252 (Can.)

[87] *ibid.*

creditor's claim, agree terms with the creditor or pay his due proportion of the principal debt. It may also be necessary for the guarantor to join the principal debtor as a party to the action instituted by the creditor so that the guarantor can invoke any valid defences available to the debtor.[88] Unless this procedure is adopted the co-sureties may later resist an action for contribution on the ground that the creditor's claim was unfounded or excessive.[89] A notice in these terms, in effect, prevents the co-sureties from claiming that the creditor was paid improperly or prematurely.[90]

12–166   Prior to payment of more than the guarantor's share of the principal debt, there is no right to claim contribution. As has been seen, payment can be effected by the surety personally or by the realisation and application of the proceeds of a security which the surety has provided in support of the principal debt.[91] It may even be sufficient if it is made by a third party on the guarantor's behalf where the guarantor is liable to reimburse the third party.[92]

12–167   The payment need not even be made directly to the creditor but can be made indirectly through the principal debtor. In *Mahoney v McManus*,[93] the High Court of Australia by a majority of three to two held that a guarantor who paid the principal debtor an amount in excess of his share of the principal debt was entitled to contribution from co-guarantors provided that it could be shown that the guarantor made the payment not for the debtor's general purposes, but through the agency of the debtor in diminution or discharge of his liability under the guarantee. If the payment were made to the principal debtor generally, it would be the principal who paid off the principal debt, thereby discharging all the guarantors. In this latter case, therefore, a payment by the debtor in reduction of the principal debt from an advance by a person who happens to be a guarantor will not entitle that guarantor to claim contribution from the co-sureties.[94] However, the majority judgments stressed that the court should not be too technical in determining what amounts to payment.[95] By the same token, the guarantor's right to contribution only arises if the guarantor has discharged his obligations under the guarantee. This should be established as a matter of fact before any notions of natural justice are

---

[88] *Wilson v Mitchell* [1939] 2 K.B. 869; *McLean v Discount & Finance Ltd* (1939) 64 C.L.R. 312.

[89] *Duffield v Scott* (1789) 3 Term Rep. 374; 100 E.R. 628, approved in *Jones v Williams* (1841) 7 M. & W. 493 at 501; 151 E.R. 860 at 864; *Pettman v Keble* (1850) 9 C.B. 701; 137 E.R. 1067.

[90] See *Smith v Compton* (1832) 3 B. & Ad. 407; 110 E.R. 146. See also *Stewart v Braun* [1925] 2 D.L.R. 423; *Pettman v Keble* (1850) 9 C.B. 701; 137 E.R. 1067.

[91] *Mahoney v McManus* (1981) 55 A.L.J.R. 673; *Re Hodgetts Ex p. Official Receiver* (1949) 16 A.B.C. 201; *McLean v Discount & Finance Ltd* (1939) 64 C.L.R. 312 at 335 *per* Latham C.J. dissenting, but not on this point.

[92] *Trotter v Franklin* [1991] 2 N.Z.L.R. 92 at 101.

[93] (1981) 55 A.L.J.R. 673. See also above, paras 6–03 to 6–06.

[94] *ibid.*, at 675. Although the principal debtor is a third party who may pay off the debt on behalf of the guarantor (see above, n.92), in this situation the principal debtor is paying off the debt *on the principal debtor's own account* to discharge the principal debt.

[95] (1981) 55 A.L.J.R. 673 at 676. The minority, Wilson and Brennan J.J., concluded that the debtor had merely sought to discharge its own indebtedness. Indeed, Brennan J. at 680 found on the evidence that there was no arrangement between the debtor company and the creditors concerned that the payment should be accepted in discharge of the guarantor's liability, as distinct from the principal debt.

invoked to determine how the co-sureties should contribute to the common debt.[96]

A right of contribution was allowed in *Mahoney v McManus*[97] since it **12–168** was held that the payment was made by the guarantor through the agency of the principal debtor in reduction of his liability under the guarantee. This was so even though the amount which the guarantor paid to the principal debtor was different from the amount of the principal debt and despite the fact that the debtor's internal records suggested that the amount was merely a loan, not a payment in reduction of the guarantor's liability for the principal debt. With respect, the ease with which the majority in *Mahoney v McManus* inferred that the guarantor had made payments in reduction of his own liability under his guarantee is disturbing. It might be possible for a guarantor who advanced money to the principal debtor as a loan to claim later that the advance was a payment in reduction of the guarantor's own liability as guarantor. In this way, the guarantor might be able to acquire by subrogation any priority which the creditor enjoys under collateral securities or any remedies which the creditor has to enforce payment of the principal debt. In effect, the guarantor might be able to convert his unsecured debt into a secured debt by subrogation to the creditor's securities. This appears to be inconsistent with the statutory provisions governing the distribution of the assets of insolvent persons since it allows one creditor, namely, the guarantor, to acquire an improper advantage over unsecured creditors.[98]

The reasoning of the majority of the High Court of Australia in **12–169** *Mahoney v McManus* also appears to be inconsistent with the principle in *Barclay's Bank Ltd v Quistclose Investments Ltd*.[99] On this principle, money paid to a company which subsequently goes into liquidation will not be available for distribution among its general creditors where it was lent to the company specifically and exclusively for a particular purpose and this purpose has not been carried out.[1] In such a case, the money is to be held on trust for the person who advanced the money for the particular purpose. In finding that the amount paid by the guarantor to the principal debtor did not become part of the general assets of the debtor as a loan, the High Court of Australia in *Mahoney v McManus* produced a similar result, but it is important to note that the payment by the guarantor was not specifically earmarked for reduction of the principal debt. With respect, there was little evidence to support the finding of Gibbs C.J. that "the moneys were not paid to the company to be used for its general purposes, but only for the purpose of enabling it to pay the creditors which held guarantees and which, as all those present at the meetings knew,

---

[96] Contrast (1981) 55 A.L.J.R. 673 at 676 *per* Gibbs C.J., with whom Aickin and Murphy J.J. concurred.
[97] See also *Bernhardt v Brassington* (unreported, NSW Sup Ct, Grove J., February 10, 1993).
[98] See *Mahoney v McManus* (1981) 55 A.L.J.R. 673 at 678 *per* Wilson J.
[99] [1970] A.C. 567, HL.
[1] See P.J. Millett Q.C., "The Quistclose Trust : Who Can Enforce It?" (1985) 101 L.Q.R. 269 and The Hon Mr Justice L.J. Priestley, "The Romalpa Clause and the Quistclose Trust" in P.D. Finn ed., *Equity and Commercial Relationships* (Law Book Co Ltd, 1987), p.217. See also *Twinsectra Ltd v Yardley* [1999] Lloyd's Rep. Bank. 438.

would resort to the guarantees if the company's debts were not paid".[2] The essential element of the principle in *Barclay's Bank Ltd v Quistclose Investments Ltd*, which insists on the payment of money for a specific and exclusive purpose, was therefore missing. By relaxing this requirement, the majority of the High Court of Australia in *Mahoney v McManus* has exposed serious weaknesses in the statutory provisions which are intended to protect the interests of unsecured creditors in the bankruptcy or winding-up of the principal debtor.[3]

12–170   The problems created by the majority view in *Mahoney v McManus* are not confined to the situation where the principal debtor is insolvent. A fundamental condition of the right to contribution is payment to the creditor by the guarantor, which should be affirmatively proved. As Wilson J pointed out in his dissenting judgment, "[a]ny relaxation of that principle can only be destructive of that certainty which it is the purpose of the law to provide".[4]

12–171   Where payment is made to the creditor by a guarantor with the assistance of funds from a third party, to whom the creditor then assigns securities held for the principal debt, the court will treat the third party and the surety as the one person for the purposes of contribution. In enforcing his right of contribution, the surety must give credit for any amounts be receives from the net proceeds of realisation of these securities.[5]

(viii) The limitation period in a contribution suit

12–172   Where the sureties agree to pay to the creditor whatever the principal debtor owes to the creditor, the sureties are liable in debt and the normal limitation period applies to the sureties' claim to contribution. On the other hand, where the sureties guarantee the principal debtor's performance of his obligations under, say, a building contract or a lease, the sureties are liable to the creditor in damages if the principal debtor does not perform the principal obligation. However, it is unlikely that these contribution claims by the sureties *inter se* will be governed by a two-year limitation period under s.10 of the Civil Liability (Contribution) Act 1978, because this result would not be consistent with the purpose of the Act.[6]

(ix) The effect of bankruptcy of a co-surety upon a right to contribution

12–173   Once a guarantor pays a larger sum than the guarantor's share of the principal debt, any co-sureties who have not paid their share owe that

---

[2] (1981) 55 A.L.J.R. 567 at 676.
[3] See Insolvency Act 1986, ss.239(4), 328(3) and 340 and Insolvency Rules 1986 SI 1986/1925, r.4.181.
[4] (1981) 55 A.L.J.R. 673 at 679. Brennan J. also dissented on similar grounds.
[5] *Re Arcedeckne; Atkins v Arcedeckne* (1883) 24 Ch. D. 709.
[6] *Hampton v Minns* [2002] 1 W.I.R. 1 (obiter dicta). See below, para.12–186.

guarantor a debt which can support a petition in bankruptcy against them.[7] A guarantor can also prove in the estate of a bankrupt co-surety when the guarantor has paid the whole of the principal debt.[8] If the creditor *has already lodged* a proof in the estate of the bankrupt co-surety, a guarantor who pays the creditor in full will be entitled to take over the creditor's proof for the principal debt and to recover dividends upon the whole of that sum.[9] Where the creditor has *not lodged* a proof in the estate of the bankrupt co-surety before the creditor is paid in full by the guarantor, that guarantor can still prove in the name of the creditor for the whole amount of the principal debt and recover dividends on that amount.[10] Any dividends recovered by the guarantor in excess of the guarantor's proportionate share of the principal debt can later be claimed in contribution proceedings by the co-sureties.[11]

A guarantor who has paid the whole of the principal debt *before the* **12–174** *creditor has proved* against the estate of a bankrupt co-surety can lodge a proof in his own name, but such a proof is limited to the bankrupt surety's share of the principal debt.[12] For this reason, a guarantor who has paid the principal debt in full will usually take over the proof already lodged by the creditor or, if no such proof has been made, may lodge a proof in the name of the creditor.

A guarantor of the whole debt who has paid more than that guarantor's **12–175** share of the debt but less than the full debt cannot prove in the bankruptcy of a co-surety because the proof would be in competition with the right of the creditor to prove against the estate and would, therefore, offend the rule against double proof.[13] It is only where the unpaid creditor has renounced in some binding way the right to prove in the bankruptcy of the co-surety[14] that the guarantor will be entitled to prove against that estate, since in this situation there is no possibility of a double proof.

Often, of course, the rule against double proof is not the only obstacle **12–176** preventing a guarantor who has paid less than the full amount of the principal debt from proving in the bankruptcy of a co-surety. The terms of the guarantee may expressly prohibit a proof by the guarantor unless the creditor has been paid in full. Indeed, the guarantee may even preclude the guarantor from proving in the co-surety's estate in competition with a proof by the creditor in respect of a distinct debt other than the one guaranteed.

---

[7] *Ex p. Snowdon* (1881) 17 Ch. D. 44; *McIntosh v Shashoua* (1931) 46 C.L.R. 494 and see Insolvency Act 1986, s.267. See also above, paras 12–159 to 12–160.
[8] See *Re Parker; Morgan v Hill* [1894] 3 Ch. 400; *Re Hendry, Ex p. Murphy* [1905] S.A.L.R. 116; below, paras 12–312 to 12–317.
[9] See below, paras 12–312 to 12–313; *Re Parker; Morgan v Hill* [1894] 3 Ch. 400.
[10] *Re Parker; Morgan v Hill* [1894] 3 Ch. 400. The Mercantile Law Amendment Act 1856, s.5 confirms this principle: see below, paras 12–312 to 12–317.
[11] See *Re Parker; Morgan v Hill* [1894] 3 Ch. 400. See also *Re Hendry, Ex p. Murphy* [1905] S.A.L.R. 116 at 119.
[12] *ibid.*
[13] See above, paras 10–28 to 10–39 and paras 12–67 to 12–68; *Re Hendry, Ex p. Murphy* [1905] S.A.L.R. 116. See also *Ex p. Stokes* (1848) De G. 618. *Cf. Commercial Bank of Australia v Wilson & Co* [1893] A.C. 181.
[14] See *Re Fenton* [1931] 1 Ch. 85 at 119 *per* Romer LJ.

12–177   Where a bankrupt surety obtains a discharge from his bankruptcy, that surety is usually but not necessarily relieved of liability to contribute towards payment of the principal debt. If the surety's liability to contribute was incurred by means of a breach of trust, for example, where as a director of a company the surety guaranteed repayment of money advanced to the company on unauthorised security or in an *ultra vires* transaction, this liability will be excluded from the discharge in bankruptcy.[15]

(x) The effect of the death of a co-surety upon the right to contribution

12–178   While the bankruptcy or winding-up of a guarantor can proportionately increase the amounts for which the co-sureties will be liable to the creditor, it is not clear whether the death of a surety has a similar effect. Much depends upon the nature of the liability assumed by the surety and the terms of the arrangement with the co-sureties.

12–179   Modern guarantees often provide that a guarantor's liability shall not be terminated by his death or even by notice of his death, and that the guarantor's liability shall continue until his legal personal representative gives notice that the guarantor's liability is terminated. In the absence of such a provision, a creditor cannot enforce the guarantee against the estate of a deceased surety once the creditor has notice of the surety's death.[16] But the joint and several co-sureties remain liable and it does not necessarily follow that the co-sureties forfeit their right to contribution from the estate of the deceased surety. An action for contribution against the executors of a deceased surety can be maintained provided that it is consistent with the terms of the guarantor's implied original engagement.[17] On this approach, the court looks not at the guarantor's liability to the creditor at the time of payment of the principal debt but rather at the implied terms of the guarantors' original arrangement among themselves.[18] This is a departure from the general principle that contribution is solely based

---

[15] *Ramskill v Edwards* (1885) 31 Ch. D. 100; Insolvency Act 1986, s.281(3).

[16] *Other v Iveson* (1855) 3 Drewry 177; 61 ER 870. See also *Re Denton's Estate* [1904] 2 Ch. 178, CA.

[17] It appears that joint and several sureties remain liable notwithstanding the death of one of the sureties, and the deceased's estate should be liable for his share. Possibly the estate of a joint surety cannot be compelled to contribute his share: *Ashby v Ashby* (1827) 7 B. & C. 444 at 451; 108 E.R. 789 at 791 *per* Littledale J.; *Batard v Hawes* (1853) 2 El. & Bl. 287 at 298–299; 118 E.R. 775 at 779; *Prior v Hembrow* (1841) 8 M. & W. 873 at 889–890; 151 E.R. 1294 at 1301 per Alderson B. See also *Dering v Earl of Winchelsea* (1787) 1 Cox 318; 29 E.R. 1184. See also *Rowlatt on Principal and Surety* (5th ed., 1999), para.7.55 and Meagher, Gummow and Lehane's, *Equity Doctrine and Remedies* (4th ed., by R. Meagher, D. Heydon and M. Leeming (Butterworths Lexis Nexis Australia 2002), para.10–015.

[18] *ibid.* But the estate of the deceased guarantor might not be liable to contribute where the surviving surety enjoys all the benefit of the joint guarantee: *Cunningham-Reid v Public Trustee* [1944] 1 K.B. 602. See also *Bater v Kare* [1964] S.C.R. 206 (Can); *Woolmington v Bronze Lamp Restaurant Pty Ltd* [1984] 2 N.S.W.L.R. 242; *AGC (Advances) Ltd v West* (1984) 5 N.S.W.L.R. 590. See also below, para.12–215.

upon equitable principles but, in theory, there is no reason for barring such a claim in equity.[19]

Where the guarantors are bound severally or jointly and severally and **12–180** their estates do remain liable to the creditor (because the creditor has not received notice of the death of a surety), the estate of a deceased surety cannot escape the liability to contribute to the co-sureties.[20] In this context, contribution is based upon equitable principles and it is unnecessary to consider further the terms of the guarantor's original engagement.

Where the guarantors are merely bound jointly, it appears to be **12–181** necessary to establish something beyond the mere fact of co-suretyship before the estate of a deceased surety can be compelled to contribute to the payment of the principal debt.[21] Although the liability of the joint surety *to the creditor* probably terminates on the joint surety's death,[22] his estate might yet be required to contribute in exceptional circumstances where the court infers from the dealings of the parties that the deceased surety intended his estate to pay the surety's original share of the principal debt. The cases in which a court might be prepared to infer such an arrangement are described in *Prior v Hembrow*[23] as those which "stand on the same footing as that of several persons jointly contracting for a chattel to be made or procured for the common benefit of all—the building of a ship, for instance, or the furnishing of a house—and as to which the executors of any party dying before the work is completed are by agreement to stand in the place of the party dying".[24] In *Ashby v Ashby*,[25] Bayley J. gave a clear illustration of this principle:

"To put a plain case, suppose two persons are jointly bound as sureties, one dies, the survivor is sued and is obliged to pay the whole debt. If the deceased had been living, the survivor might have sued him for contribution in an action for money paid, and I think he is entitled to sue the executor of the deceased for money paid to his use as executor ... and when money is paid to his use as executor, justice requires that the person who has made that payment should have the liberty of looking to the fund which the executor has in that character."[26]

---

[19] As to the basis of the right of contribution between co-sureties in equity, see R. Goff and G. Jones, *The Law of Restitution* (6th ed, 2002), paras 14–006 to 14–007. See *Dering v Earl of Winchelsea* (1787) 1 Cox 318; 29 E.R. 1184.
[20] *Rowlatt on Principal and Surety* (5th ed., 1999), para.7–55. See also above, paras 9–46 to 9–51.
[21] *ibid.*
[22] See above, paras 9–50 to 9–51.
[23] (1841) 8 M. & W. 873; 151 E.R. 1294.
[24] *ibid.*, at 889–890 *per* Alderson B.
[25] (1827) 7 B. & C. 444; 108 E.R. 789.
[26] *ibid.*, at 451; 791. A similar situation might arise where a loan by the creditor to the estate would be called in unless the estate of the deceased surety contributed to the payment of the principal debt: *Rowlatt on Principal and Surety* (5th ed., 1999), p.166, para.7–55 n.97. However, as Andrews and Millett point out, it is not easy to see why his Lordship thought that the estate would benefit from the payment in that case. G. Andrews and R. Millett, *Law of Guarantees* (3rd ed., 2000), para.12.25.

But the payment by the survivor can only be regarded as a payment to the use of the deceased's executor where the executor is thereby released of something which would otherwise be a burden on the estate. While the courts are prepared to infer such an arrangement from the dealings of the parties, the inference will not be drawn lightly.[27]

(xi) How is the right to contribution enforced?

12–182   At common law, a guarantor who has paid more than his just proportion of the principal debt could maintain an action for contribution or an action for money paid to the use of the co-sureties.[28] To succeed in the latter action, the plaintiff had to prove a payment of more than his share of the debt at the express or implied request of the co-sureties.[29] One direct result of the Judicature Act of 1873 was to avoid this technicality by making such actions largely redundant.[30] After the Judicature Act fused the administration of common law and equity, it was established that the rule of equity prevailed.[31] An action for contribution in the Chancery Division of the High Court then became the usual method of enforcing a guarantor's rights against the co-sureties.[32] Where a contribution claim arises between co-guarantors under the same instrument, it may properly be brought as a claim at law for a simple contract debt in quasi-contract.[33] If there is any dispute as to the liability of the defendants, the claimant should seek a general declaration of the extent of their liability.[34] But unless all interested parties are joined in the proceedings, the court will not *enforce* a guarantor's claim to contribution.[35]

12–183   The common practice is to join the principal debtor and all solvent co-sureties in the action for contribution; the rights of all the parties can then be determined in the one inquiry.[36] The principal debtor should be joined unless clearly insolvent or unless there is some other sound reason for excluding him.[37] This principle is a reminder that the debtor is primarily

---

[27] *Rowlatt on Principal and Surety* (5th ed., 1999), p.166, para.7–55. See also G. Andrews and R. Millett, *Law of Guarantees* (3rd ed., 2000), para.12.25.
[28] See *McLean v Discount & Finance Ltd* (1939) 64 C.L.R. 312 at 341.
[29] See *Batard v Hawes* (1853) 2 El. & Bl. 287 at 296; 118 E.R. 775 at 778.
[30] R. Goff and G. Jones, *The Law of Restitution* (6th ed., 2002), paras 14–006 to 14–007.
[31] Supreme Court Act 1981, s.49.
[32] See *Atkin's Court Forms* (1982 Issue), Vol. 20, pp.165–167, Forms 61–63, for the forms of writs and Forms 64–66, for statements of claim. The plaintiff must claim a specific sum, as distinct from an account: *Blackie v Osmaston* (1884) 28 Ch. D. 119. If the plaintiff is unable to claim a specific sum, he should seek a general declaration of the extent of the parties' respective liabilities. See above, paras 11–175 to 11–183.
[33] See, *e.g. Davies v Humphreys* (1840) 6 M. & W. 153; 151 E.R. 361; *Lang v Le Boursicot* [1993] 5 B.P.R. 97,406 at 11,785.
[34] See *A E Goodwin Ltd (in liq) v A G Healing Ltd (in liq)* (1979) 7 A.C.L.R. 481.
[35] *Ibid.*
[36] *Hampton v Minns* [2002] 1 W.L.R. 1; *Hay v Carter* [1935] Ch. 397; *Lawson v Wright* (1786) 1 Cox 275; *Hitchman v Stewart* (1855) 3 Drew 271; 61 E.R. 907; *Craythorne v Swinburne* (1807) 14 Ves. 160 at 164; 33 E.R. 482 at 483 *per* Lord Eldon L.C. The form of the appropriate order appears in *Kent v Abrahams* [1928] W.N. 266.
[37] *Hay v Carter* [1935] Ch. 397 ; *Lawson v Wright* (1786) 1 Cox Eq. Cas. 275; 29 E.R. 1164; *Cowell v Edwards* (1800) 2 Bos. & P. 268; 126 E.R. 1275. Indeed, where one of the co-sureties is insolvent, his trustee or personal representative should be joined: *Hole v Harrison* (1673)

liable for the principal debt. The guarantors are entitled to an indemnity from the debtor, but where the debtor is patently insolvent it is unnecessary to join him because the indemnity is worthless.[38] All solvent co-sureties should be joined in the action for contribution to avoid a multiplicity of suits against the different co-sureties for their respective proportions of the principal debt.[39] Even the creditor should be made a party so that the court can order payments by the co-sureties direct to the creditor, thereby discharging the principal debt. In the absence of the creditor, the court will merely make a prospective order under which a guarantor can recover sums paid in excess of the guarantor's share.[40]

Where the creditor brings an action against a guarantor on the **12–184** guarantee, the defendant can claim contribution against the co-sureties who are not already parties through third-party proceedings.[41] Similar proceedings can be taken for contribution against co-sureties who are already parties to the action.[42] The purpose of these procedures is to avoid a multiplicity of proceedings[43] and the possibility of the same questions being litigated twice or more with possibly different results.[44] However, a guarantor who is sued by the creditor on a guarantee cannot set off debts owing by the creditor to one of the co-sureties in respect of separate transactions apart from the guarantee, because this is not a genuine claim for contribution from a co-surety.[45]

The claim of a guarantor against the co-sureties for contribution is **12–185** generally not a specialty but that of a simple creditor.[46] The limitation

---

1 Chan. Cas. 246; 22 E.R. 783. This will facilitate any proof of debt that might later be lodged in that surety's bankruptcy by establishing his share of the common liability. Equally, where a co-surety has died, his personal representative should be joined in the contribution proceedings because he may be liable to the extent of the deceased estate: *Primrose v Bromley* (1739) 1 Atk. 89; 26 E.R. 58; *Batard v Hawes* (1853) 2 El. & Bl. 287; 118 E.R. 775. Although it was declared in *Hay v Carter* that a joinder of the principal debtor was a necessity, it is probably unnecessary to join the principal debtor as a defendant, given the modern rules permitting third party claims: *Griffith v Wade* (1966) 60 D.L.R. (2d) 62, Alta CA. See CPR, Pt.20.

[38] However, it is perhaps going too far to suggest that it is an essential condition precedent of a contribution claim that the surety "demonstrate at least by inference that a claim against the principal would be futile because he is insolvent or otherwise not worth pursuing": G. Andrews and R. Millett, *Law of Guarantees* (3rd ed., 2000), para.12.07. This principle relates to joinder of parties.

[39] See *Craythorne v Swinburne* (1807) 14 Ves. Jun. 160 at 164; 33 E.R. 482 at 484 *per* Lord Eldon.

[40] *Wolmershausen v Gullick* [1893] 2 Ch. 514.

[41] See Civil Procedure Rules SI 1998/3132, Pt.20. Before a Pt.20 claim can be made, it is necessary to obtain the court's permission under Pt.20.7, unless the claim is issued before or at the same time as the defence is filed. A co-surety who is joined as a third party may be liable for his own costs if he mounts a separate defence even if the creditor fails in his action against the surety: *Williams v Buchanan* (1891) 7 T.L.R. 226, CA. See also below, para.12–245.

[42] See Civil Procedure Rules SI 1998/3132 Part 20: G. Andrews and R. Millett, *Law of Guarantees* (3rd ed., 2000), para.12.17.

[43] See *Standard Securities Ltd v Hubbard* [1967] Ch. 1056 at 1059; *Baxter v France* [1895] 1 Q.B. 455 at 493 *per* Lord Esher M.R.; *Barclays Bank Ltd v Tom* [1923] 1 K.B. 221 at 223, 225.

[44] See *Beneckne v Frost* (1876) 1 Q.B.D. 419 at 422 *per* Blackburn J.; *Ex p. Young* (1881) 17 Ch. D. 668; *Re Salmon* (1889) 42 Ch. D. 351 at 360.

[45] See *Bowyear v Pawson* (1881) 6 Q.B.D. 540. See also *Wilson v Mitchell* [1939] 2 K.B. 869.

[46] *Walker v Bowry* (1924) 35 C.L.R. 48. See also *Jones v Hill* (1893) 14 L.R. (NSW) Eq. 303 at 305; *Copis v Middleton* (1823) Turn. & R. 224; 37 E.R. 1083. But a guarantor who pays the whole of the principal debt guaranteed by a deed can obtain the deed by subrogation and then sue the co-sureties for contribution as a specialty creditor: see below, paras 12–303 to 12–317.

period[47] in an action for contribution does not begin to run against the plaintiff until the plaintiff pays more than his share of the principal debt[48] even if the plaintiff's liability to the creditor was established at some earlier date.[49] Similarly, the limitation periods for contribution claims in respect of successive payments to the creditor in excess of the guarantor's share run from the date of each payment.[50]

12–186   Even where the guarantee takes the form of a promise by the guarantors that the principal debtor will perform its obligations it is unlikely that a two-year limitation period will apply to a co-surety's claim for contribution on the ground that it is a claim for contribution in respect of damages by virtue of s.1 of the Civil Liability (Contribution) Act 1978.[51] If the guarantor's claim for contribution fell within s.1 of the Civil Liability (Contribution) Act 1978 it would be statute-barred two years after the principal debtor's default even though the creditor had not attempted to enforce the guarantee within that two year period and even though creditor would have a further four years within which to enforce the guarantee. This absurd result suggests that s.1 of the Civil Liability (Contribution) Act 1978 was intended to apply to contribution between joint tortfeasors, not co-sureties. The better view is that a six-year limitation period should apply to all actions for contribution between co-sureties.

12–187   It is immaterial that the guarantor was entitled to apply for quia timet relief more than six years before he instituted contribution proceedings. Quia timet relief is available as soon as the guarantor's liability is ascertained and immediate, whereas contribution is only available where the guarantor has paid more than his fair share of the principal debt.[52]

12–188   In *Brown v Cork*,[53] the Court of Appeal suggested that where a surety institutes a contribution suit against a co-surety, the defendant can set-off unsecured liabilities of the claimant against the defendant's liability to

---

[47] A surety's claim for contribution is not a speciality debt so a six-year limitation period applies: Limitation Act 1980, ss.5 and 8. The six-year limitation period applies even though the claim for contribution is based on equitable principles: *Lang v Le Boursicot* [1993] 5 B.R.P. 97,406; *Rowlatt on Principal and Surety* (5th ed., 1999), para.10–12.
[48] *Walker v Bowry* (1924) 35 C.L.R. 48; *Davies v Humphreys* (1840) 6 M. & W. 153 at 168; 151 E.R. 361 at 367; *Ex p. Gifford* (1802) 6 Ves. 805; 31 E.R. 1318; *Re Snowdon, Ex p. Snowdon* (1881) 17 Ch. D. 44. If a guarantor pays less than his fair share of the principal debt and then the principal debtor discharges the debt at a later date, the guarantor's right to contribution arises at the date of the discharge of the principal debt if he has paid more than his rateable share of that debt: *Davies v Humphreys* (1840) 6 M. & W. 153; 151 E.R. 361.
[49] See *Wolmershausen v Gullick* [1893] 2 Ch. 514.
[50] *Pitt v Purssord* (1841) 8 M. & W. 538; 151 E.R. 1152; *Davies v Humphreys* (1840) 6 M. & W. 153; 151 E.R. 361.
[51] See *Hampton v Minns* [2002] 1 W.L.R. 1 and G. Andrews and R. Millett, *Law of Guarantees* (3rd ed., 2000), para.12.18.
[52] See *Rowland v Gulfpac Ltd* [1999] Lloyd's Rep. Bank. 86 at 98 where Rix J. granted quia timet relief in relation to an indemnity even though the cause of action to enforce the indemnity was not complete at law. It was enough that the right to the indemnity was sufficiently clear and that there was clear evidence that the indemnities intended to ignore his obligation. See G. Andrews and R. Millett, *Law of Guarantees* (3rd ed., 2000), para.12.18.
[53] [1986] P.C.C. 78 (obiter dicta). Contrast *A E Goodwin Ltd (in liq) v A G Healing Ltd (in liq)* (1979) 7 A.C.L.R. 481, which suggests that the doctrine of subrogation cannot be used to justify a right of set-off because it is a class right enjoyed by all the co-sureties who have not contributed to the common debt.

contribute to the common debt. Such a right of set-off would also be available under the mutual dealings provisions in the bankruptcy or winding up of either surety.[54]

In relation to bills of exchange the cause of action in a contribution suit **12–189** accrues when the claimant takes up the bill or note and pays it, not when it is dishonoured.[55] The action must be brought within the limitation period which commences as soon as the claimant pays more than his due proportion of the total principal debt owed by the maker or acceptor or the party accommodated.[56] Moreover, the claimant has a fresh cause of action each time and for every sum he pays more than his share of the total principal debt.[57] Whereas a contribution suit against a surety or quasi-surety originally took the form of an action for money paid to the surety's use,[58] it now appears that the usual procedure is to bring an action in equity for contribution.[59]

When a lender advances money to companies operating in a group it **12–190** usually takes cross-guarantees and charges to secure all the indebtedness of all the companies in the group. Upon default, the lender may appoint receivers and managers of all the companies in the group under the cross charges.

When the receivers and managers have collected and realised all the **12–191** secured assets and applied the proceeds in payment of each company's liabilities as a borrower, there may be a surplus. How should this surplus be applied? Naturally, the receivers are expected to adjust the rights of the respective parties and respect the rights of the paying guarantors to claim a proportionate share of the surplus by subrogation. But should the receivers allow set-offs claimed by some members of the group against others in respect of dealings apart from the guaranteed transactions?

In *Brown v Cook*[60] the Court of Appeal examined these issues and **12–192** concluded that the surplus should be distributed by the receivers and managers among the companies in the group that had paid more than their just share of the common debt. In other words, they were expected to apply the surplus in accordance with the companies' respective rights of contribution *inter se*. No allowance should be made for set-offs which the companies had against each other in respect of other transactions such as inter company loan accounts. Even the proviso to s.5 of the Mercantile Law Amendment Act 1856 required no more of the receivers and managers: it merely ensured that a surety was only entitled to claim from its co-sureties the "just proportion" of the common debt for which

---

[54] *Brown v Cork* [1986] P.C.C. 78 at 85. See Insolvency Act 1986, s.323 and Insolvency Rules 1986 SI 1986/1925, r.4.90
[55] *Constantine v Drew* (1869) 1 N.W. 100 (Ind).
[56] *Davies v Humphreys* (1840) 6 M. & W. 153; 151 E.R. 361; *Browne v Lee* (1827) 6 B & C 689; 108 E.R. 604.
[57] See N. Elliott, J. Odgers and J.M. Phillips, *Byles on Bills of Exchange* (27th ed., 2002), p.473. See also *Davies v Humphreys* (1840) 6 M. & W. 153; 151 E.R. 361; *Re Snowdon; Ex p. Snowdon* (1881) 17 Ch. D. 44; *Walker v Bowry* (1924) 35 C.L.R. 48.
[58] See, *e.g.*, *Reynolds v Wheeler* (1861) 10 C.B. (NS) 561; 142 E.R. 572.
[59] See above, paras 12–182 to 12–183.
[60] [1985] B.C.L.C. 363.

it was "justly liable". The words "just proportion" referred to the common debt or loss sustained by the co-sureties. They did not require a consideration of the whole state of accounts between the parties in order to determine what was "justly" due from one to the other.

12–193   This approach draws support from *A E Goodwin Ltd v AG Healing Ltd*,[61] where Powell J. held that the right of paying sureties to enforce the creditor's securities by subrogation was in the nature of a class right. It was enjoyed by the paying sureties as a group according to the amounts by which their payments in reduction of the principal debt exceeded their fair share or just proportion of that debt. As the right of subrogation was not an individual right, the paying sureties could enforce their right of subrogation without having to take into account any other debts which they owed one another as a result of dealings outside the relationship of co-sureties. Consequently, in the context of corporate group guarantees, the paying sureties were entitled to share any surplus realised by the receivers and managers appointed over the assets of all the companies in the group without any deductions in respect of inter-company debts which they owed one another in respect of other dealings.

12–194   In the rare case where a creditor has a claim against one guarantor who is entitled to contribution from a co-guarantor who, in turn, is entitled to an indemnity from the creditor, the court may simply dismiss the claims for contribution and indemnity and enter judgment for each guarantor against the creditor to avoid a multiplicity of suits.[62]

(xii) Defences to an action for contribution

(a) Defences arising out of the nature of the guarantee

12–195   A guarantor's liability to contribute to the co-sureties depends not only upon the terms of the guarantee but also upon the terms of the instruments by which the other sureties are bound.[63] From these instruments it might be clear that the defendant in an action for contribution is not the claimant's co-surety but rather a surety of *both* the principal debtor and the claimant and therefore liable only on the default of both parties.[64] Again, the terms of the respective guarantees may indicate that the defendant is answerable only for a distinct and separate portion of the principal debt and that the defendant is not, therefore, liable to the claimant.[65] In some cases, the guarantee itself may

---

[61] (1979) 7 A.C.L.R. 481 at 489.

[62] *Cf. Schenker & Co. (Aust) Pty Ltd v Maplas Equipment & Services Pty Ltd* [1990] V.R. 834, a decision based in part on s.29 of the Supreme Court Act 1986 (Vic).

[63] *Molson's Bank v Kovinsky* [1924] 4 D.L.R. 330 at 336. A surety's right to contribution also depends, to a large extent, upon a principle of equity: *Craythorne v Swinburne* (1807) 14 Ves. Jun. 160; 33 E.R. 482.

[64] See above, paras 12–147 and 12–150. For a precedent for this form of defence, see *Atkin's Court Forms* (1982 issue), Vol. 20, Form 69, pp.168–169.

[65] See above, para.12–145. For a precedent for this form of defence, see *Atkin's Court Forms* (1982 issue), Vol. 20, Form 70, p.169.

specifically exclude a right of contribution.[66] These matters should be expressly pleaded as defences. Indeed, a surety may expressly plead as a defence any matter which indicates that there is no right of contribution, for example, the fact that the parties are not co-sureties because they are not liable to a common demand.[67]

(b) Defences relating to payment

A guarantor's defence to an action for contribution may simply deny the **12–196** claimant's claim by alleging that the claimant has not paid any money under the guarantee or that the claimant has not paid an amount in excess of his share.[68] Where payment is admitted, the defence may allege that payment was premature in the sense that the claimant paid before he was under a liability to pay,[69] or unjustified, in the sense that the claimant was under no legal obligation to pay.[70] For these reasons, the guarantor should give notice to his co-sureties to defend the creditor's claim, reach a compromise or pay their contributions. However, it is no defence to a contribution suit that one guarantor paid the creditor without any formal demand for payment being made on any of the co-sureties, as required by the terms of their joint and several guarantee. Service of a written demand is merely a procedural or evidentiary requirement for the benefit of the guarantors. Accordingly it can be waived by any of the guarantors under a joint and several guarantee.[71]

(c) Defences arising out of actions of the creditor

The creditor's conduct may discharge a guarantor either wholly or pro **12–197** tanto (for example, by giving time to the principal debtor[72] or by releasing

---

[66] See above, paras 12–128 to 12–137.

[67] See above, paras 12–138 to 12–144. The fact that the several guarantees given for the principal debt are expressed to be "independent" or "additional" does not, in itself, relieve the guarantors of their common liability: *Cornfoot v Holdenson* (1931) A.L.R. 376; 5 A.L.J. 305. Nor does a provision in a guarantee requiring a new bond to be obtained on the death of one of the sureties afford a defence to the estate of the deceased guarantor since a new bond would not release the estate of its liability under the original guarantee: *Re Ennis; Coles v Peyton* [1893] 3 Ch. 238.

[68] For precedents for the forms of defence, see *Atkin's Court Forms* (1982 issue), Vol. 20, Forms 67 and 68, p.168.

[69] *McLean v Discount & Finance Co Ltd* (1939) 64 C.L.R. 312 at 335 *per* Latham C.J. who dissented, but not on this point. It is not, however, necessary for the guarantor to wait until the creditor institutes proceedings before making payment: *Pitt v Purssord* (1841) 8 M. & W. 538; 151 E.R. 1152.

[70] *Russell v Arnold* (1922) 70 D.L.R. 849, CA; *McFarlane v Calhoun* (1879) 2 P.E.I.R. 283; *Carney v Phalen* (1883) 16 N.S.R. 126, CA; *Patterson v Campbell* (1910) 44 N.S.R. 214, CA. No right to contribution arises where the payment was voluntary or officious: *Stimpson v Smith* [1999] 2 All E.R. 833. See also *Duffield v Scott* (1789) 3 Term Rep. 374; 100 E.R. 628; *Pettman v Keble* (1850) 9 C.B. 701; 137 E.R. 1067; *Smith v Compton* (1833) 3 B. & Ad. 407; 110 E.R. 146; *Cumberlege v Lawson* (1857) 1 C.B. (NS) 709.

[71] *Stimpson v Smith* [1999] 3 All E.R. 833.

[72] *Worthington v Peck* (1894) 24 O.R. 535, Ch (where three out of four co-sureties on a promissory note obtained from the holder an extension of time by renewal of the note without the consent of the fourth co-surety: held there was no right of contribution against this co-

or impairing securities held for the principal debt[73] or by releasing the principal debtor or a co-guarantor)[74] and this conduct may be pleaded as a defence to an action for contribution.[75] In *Griffith v Wade*[76] Johnson J.A. delivered the judgment of the Alberta Supreme Court, Appellate Division. His Lordship stated: "I cannot see how a co-surety who has been called upon to contribute only his share can complain if other co-sureties are released or have to pay a lesser sum".[77] It would be different if the creditor (or a surety who has paid in full)[78] releases the principal debtor (without reserving its rights or a covenant not to sue) because this would prejudice a co-surety's right of indemnity.[79] But the co-sureties will not be released or discharged where the creditor grants a concession or gives time to the surety claiming contribution because this type of indulgence benefits all

---

surety); *Sword v Victoria Super Service Ltd* (1958) 15 D.L.R. (2d) 217; *Griffith v Wade* (1966) 60 D.L.R. (2d) 62. *Sword v Victoria Super Service Ltd* (1958) 15 D.L.R. (2d) 217 was a case where the surety (not the creditor) gave time to the principal debtor: it was held that he thereby released his co-sureties from an obligation to contribute. But Lord J. of the Supreme Court of British Columbia approved of the reasoning in *Worthington v Peck* 24 O.R. 535 (where the holder of a promissory note granted three co-sureties an extension of time by renewing the note without the consent of the fourth co-surety). As to the liability of a surety who consents to the creditor giving time to the principal debtor, see *Deane v City Bank of Sydney* (1904) 2 C.L.R. 198. On the other hand, a surety's right to contribution is not affected by the fact that the creditor has given time to the co-surety: *Dunn v Slee* (1817) Holt N.P. 399; 171 E.R. 284. See also above, Ch. 8.

[73] See above, paras 8–46 to 8–103.

[74] See above, paras 8–21 to 8–35. This presupposes that the other guarantors remain liable. Note that sometimes the liability of the remaining guarantors will either be extinguished (if there is joint and several liability) or reduced to the extent to which their right of contribution has been affected: see above, paras 8–21 to 8–28. See *Mercantile Bank of Sydney v Taylor* [1893] A.C. 317; *Cheetham v Ward* (1797) 1 Bos. & P. 630; 126 E.R. 1102; *Bonser v Cox* (1841) 4 Beav. 379; 49 E.R. 767; *Nicholson v Revill* (1836) 4 Ad. & El. 675; 111 E.R. 941; *Re EWA* [1901] 2 K.B. 642; *Watts v Baron Aldington, The Times* December 16, 1993; *Johnson v Davies* [1999] Ch. 117 at 138–139 and Insolvency Act 1986, s.260(2) (a voluntary arrangement that the creditor opposed can be revoked on an application to the court). But see s.3 of the Civil (Liability) Contribution Act 1978, which provides that judgment for a debt or damages against a person jointly liable does not preclude an action against any other person jointly liable. The release of a surety who is severally liable will not discharge the co-sureties absolutely but they will be discharged to the extent that their right of contribution has been prejudiced: *Ward v National Bank of New Zealand* (1883) 8 App. Cas. 755 at 766 *per* Sir Robert Collier. See also *Re Wolmershausen; Wolmershausen v Wolmershausen* (1890) 62 L.T. 541; 38 W.R. 537. *Brandt on Suretyship and Guarantees* (2nd ed.), s.277 states "The release of one surety, without the consent of his co-surety, from liability to the creditor, will not discharge him from liability to contribute to the co-surety, who is *subsequently* compelled to pay the debt." (emphasis added): *Griffith v Wade* (1966) 60 D.L.R. 62 at 70 and *Walker v Bowry* (1924) 35 C.L.R. 48 at 50 and 58; *Ward v National Bank of New Zealand* (1883) 8 App. Cas. 755; *Molson's v Kovinsky* [1924] 4 D.L.R. 330 at 335–357. Where the principal loan agreement is varied in a way which is not obviously "unsubstantial" without the consent of one guarantor, that guarantor will be discharged and cannot be liable to contribute: *Cantred Pty Ltd v Contingency Investments Pty Ltd* (unreported, Vic Sup Ct, Gobbo J., August 26, 1991). The reason why the non-paying surety is released from his obligation to contribute appears in *Hobart v Stone* (1830) 10 Pick 215 at 218–219. (Massachusetts Supreme Judicial Court, Shaw C.J., Putnam, Wilde & Morton J.J.), *i.e.*, the liability of the co-surety is contingent on the principal debtor's liability to indemnify).

[75] See also *Begbie v State Bank of New South Wales Ltd* [1994] A.T.P.R. 41,881 (where the court held that a guarantor released by the creditor's unconscionable conduct was not obliged to contribute).

[76] (1966) 60 D.L.R. 62.

[77] *ibid.*, at 70.

[78] See *Hobart v Stone* (1830) 10 Pick 215 at 218–219.

[79] *Griffith v Wade* (1966) 60 D.L.R. 62.

the guarantors.[80] A release of one joint guarantor will not necessarily discharge the other. In *Ebert v Wolff*,[81] the joint guarantee provided that the creditor could release or discharge one guarantor without thereby releasing or discharging the other guarantor or otherwise prejudicing or affecting the creditor's rights and remedies against the other guarantor. In that case a friend of one of the joint guarantors purchased his release and obtained a transfer of the creditor's rights against the other guarantor. Neuberger J. held that the friend was entitled to claim the whole of a judgment debt due from the other guarantor to the creditor because it was assigned to him. Moreover, it appears that the remaining co-surety was not entitled to contribution from the guarantor who was released. It would be advisable, therefore, for guarantors to ensure that the terms of their guarantees do not destroy or prejudice their rights of contribution if the creditor releases one of their co-sureties.

Presumably if one guarantor has been induced to enter the guarantee as **12–198** a result of undue influence, duress, unconscionability, or any other vitiating factor,[82] it is also a defence to an action for contribution.[83] But a co-surety may not defend a contribution suit by raising a counterclaim that he has against the creditor.[84]

(d) Defences attributable to the conduct of the principal debtor

Actions taken by the maker or acceptor of a promissory note or bill of **12–199** exchange as principal debtor in his dealings with the claimant in a contribution suit may constitute a defence. For instance, if the principal debtor gave the claimant another promissory note for the principal debt, this might relieve the defendant from liability to contribute to the common debt.[85] But it is no defence to an action by the first indorser for contribution that the maker of the promissory note had misrepresented to the defendant that the first indorser would be in funds to take up the note at maturity.[86]

[80] See *Kearsley v Cole* (1846) 16 M. & W. 128; 153 E.R. 1128 (where rights against the sureties were reserved); and *Dunn v Slee* (1817) 1 Moore C.P. 2; Holt N.P. 399, NP.
[81] Unreported, Chancery Division, Neuberger J, April 30, 1998.
[82] See above, Chapter 4.
[83] This assumes that the other guarantors continue to be liable (but see above, paras 8–21 to 8–28).
[84] *Wilson v Mitchell* [1939] 2 K.B. 869; *Gillespie v Torrance* 25 N.Y. 306 82 Am. Dec. 355; *Newton v Lee* 139 N.Y. 332 (1893); 34 N.E. 905 (guarantors could not set off the damages suffered by the principal debtor in the absence of an assignment of the claim or an allegation of insolvency or on some other ground of equitable jurisdiction).
[85] See *Done v Walley* (1848) 2 Exch. 198; 154 E.R. 463. On the other hand, it might be argued that the second promissory note should merely be brought into "hotchpot" for the benefit of all parties liable to contribute: see above, paras 12–248 to 12–250.
[86] *McKelvey v Davis* (1870) 17 Gr. 355.

(e) Defences attributable to conduct of the claimant or another co-surety

12–200 Some of these defences relate to inducements offered to the guarantors to provide their guarantees. Thus, where the defendant gave the guarantee in reliance on a misrepresentation by the claimant or another co-surety as to the extent of the defendant's liability, he will have a valid defence to an action for contribution beyond the amount which his liability was represented to be.[87] But it is no defence to allege that the claimant was paid to act as guarantor for this does not necessarily deprive him of the right of contribution.[88] And it is no defence to allege that the claimant failed to inform his co-sureties that he was owed a debt by the principal debtor because there is no obligation between co-sureties to disclose dealings with the principal debtor.[89]

12–201 Where the principal debt is compromised by an agreement between the creditor and the claimant, the latter will be unable to claim contribution in respect of a payment under the limit of the guarantee[90] unless the payment is accepted by the creditor in full satisfaction of the debt.[91] Co-guarantors should be informed of a proposed compromise to give them the opportunity to show that it would be an improvident bargain. If they are not so advised, they might be able to defend a subsequent action for contribution on the grounds that the creditor's claim could have been resisted or that settlement could have been reached on better terms.[92] There is no such defence, however, where the co-sureties decline an opportunity to participate in the arrangement.[93]

12–202 It is no defence to a contribution suit in relation to a bill of exchange or promissory note that the claimant paid the holder of a bill or note without receiving notice of dishonour,[94] or without a demand being made or an

---

[87] *Council of the Shire of Windsor v Enoggera Divisional Board* [1902] Q.S.R. 23. See also *AGC (Advances) Ltd v West* (1984) 5 N.S.W.L.R. 590 (a surety who is guilty of a breach of fiduciary obligation in relation to a co-surety may have his share of the common liability increased by the amount of the benefit derived from the breach). It is a defence to a contribution suit that the plaintiff orally agreed to indemnify the defendant: *Rae v Rae* (1857) 61 Ch. R. 490. It will not be necessary for such an agreement to satisfy the Statute of Frauds 1677. See also *Robinson v Campbell (No.2)* (1993) 30 N.S.W.L.R. 503 at 508; *Staples v Baker* [1999] 1 Qd. R. 317 at 327–328; *Brooks v Marshall* (unreported, NSW CA, February 11, 1996).
[88] *Rawlings and Ball v Galibert* (1920) 59 S.C.R. 611 at 619 *per* Idington J. (Can).
[89] *MacKreth v Walmesley* (1884) 51 L.T. 19; 32. W.R. 819.
[90] *Walker v Bowry* (1924) 35 C.L.R. 48 at 53 *per* Isaacs A.C.J.
[91] *ibid.*
[92] *Smith v Compton* (1832) 3 B. & Ad. 407; 1 L.J. K.B. 146; 110 E.R. 146. Section 1(4) of the Civil Liability (Contribution) Act 1978 entitles a person who has entered into a bona fide settlement or compromise of a claim in respect of any damage to recover contribution. This is so whether or not he was ever in fact liable provided that the factual basis of the claim against him could be established. However, it is unlikely that this provision applies to a contribution claim between co-sureties because a claim against a guarantor is generally a claim for a money sum, as distinct from damages. G. Andrews and R. Millett, *Law of Guarantees* (3rd ed., 2000), para.12.19.
[93] *Stewart v Braun* [1925] 2 D.L.R. 423 (Man).
[94] *Fox v Toronto General Trusts Corp* [1934] 4 D.L.R. 759 (where a note signed by two persons as accommodation parties, apparently as makers, was on maturity paid in full by one party without notice of dishonour). It is not necessary for both indorsers of a promissory note as co-sureties to receive notice of dishonour: *Godfrey v Hennelly* (1893) 19 V.L.R. 70.

action being brought against the claimant by the holder.[95] It is enough that the claimant paid the bill or note (or at least more than his due proportion thereof) when it matured.[96]

Nor is mere delay in bringing the action for contribution a defence. **12–203** Thus, a first indorser of a promissory note was still entitled to contribution from the other indorsers even though he did not bring his action for five years after he had paid more than his due share and even though one of the other indorsers had become insolvent in the meantime: each defendant could have had his liability determined and paid his share before he was sued by the claimant for contribution; hence they were not prejudiced by the delay.[97]

As the right to contribution is based on equitable principles, a person **12–204** who is guilty of fraud, illegality, wilful misconduct or gross negligence may not be entitled to contribution from co-sureties.[98]

(i) Guarantor releasing the principal debtor. It is important to consider **12–205** whether there is a defence to an action for contribution where the claimant has released the principal debtor or given the principal debtor time or granted some other indulgence without the consent of the co-sureties.[99] One guarantor may be in a position to release the principal because he has satisfied the guaranteed obligation and acquired the creditor's rights.[1] In *Greenwood v Francis*,[2] Smith L.J. took the view that a guarantor who is sued by a co-guarantor for contribution cannot rely on defences (such as a release of the principal debtor) which would normally be open to the guarantor when sued by the creditor.[3] But this view was specifically rejected in *Griffith v Wade*[4] in the context of a release of a principal by the guarantor, who had paid off the principal debt. There the Appellate Division of the Alberta Supreme Court held that a co-guarantor could raise a defence that the principal debtor had been released, and the co-guarantor would be discharged if the co-guarantor were deprived of the right of reimbursement from the debtor.[5] This will invariably be the case when a co-guarantor is sued for contribution by another guarantor who has paid off the principal debt and then released the principal, because the absolute release, which bars all claims against the principal, will prevent[6]

---

[95] *Pitt v Purssord* (1841) 8 M. & W. 538; 151 E.R. 1152.
[96] *Fox v Toronto General Trusts Corp* [1934] 4 D.L.R. 759.
[97] *McKelvey v Davis* (1870) 17 Gr. 355.
[98] See *Burke v LFOT Pty Ltd* (2002) 209 C.L.R. 282 at 287.
[99] See *Sword v Victoria Super Service Ltd* (1958) 15 D.L.R. (2d) 217; *Way v Hearn* (1862) 11 C.B. (NS) 774 at 781, 782; 142 E.R. 1000 at 1003; *Griffith v Wade* (1966) 60 D.L.R. (2d) 62. Cf. *Greenwood v Francis* [1899] 1 QB 312, where the giving of time was authorised by the guarantee. Cf. also R. Goff and G. Jones, *The Law of Restitution* (6th ed., 2002), para.14–016.
[1] Once the guarantor has paid off the principal debt, it is the guarantor, and not the creditor, who has authority to release the principal: *Griffith v Wade* (1966) 60 D.L.R. (2d) 62 at 68.
[2] [1899] 1 Q.B. 312 (obiter dicta).
[3] *ibid.*, at 320.
[4] (1966) 60 D.L.R. (2d) 62.
[5] *ibid.*, at 68–69. See also *Sword v Victoria Super Service Ltd* (1958) 15 D.L.R. (2d) 217. But not if it is a covenant not to sue: see above, paras 6–56 to 6–64. A surety who releases the principal debtor and then claims contribution from a co-surety carries the onus of showing that the release of the principal debtor has not prejudiced the co-surety's right of indemnity: *Griffith v Wade* (1966) 60 D.L.R. (2d) 62 at 69–70.
[6] *Griffith v Wade* (1966) 60 D.L.R. (2d) 62.

the co-guarantor seeking reimbursement from the principal of the amount the co-guarantor has to pay in contribution.[7] Thus if there are co-guarantors, A and B, for a debt of £10,000, and A pays off the principal debt, releases the principal, and seeks a contribution of £5,000 from B, B will be released from all liability because the effect of the release is to deprive B of the right to recover his share of the principal debt, namely £5,000, from the principal. It is thought that the decision in *Griffith v Wade* is correct. As Johnson J.A. states:

> "If ... a surety is discharged by an act of the creditor which affects his right of contribution,[8] it should follow that the co-surety should also be released from contribution by any act which deprives him of his right of reimbursement from the principal debtor. The test would therefore be whether prejudice had been suffered by the surety's act in dealing with the principal debtor."[9]

12–206   There is unlikely to be any provision in a modern contract of guarantee which specifically governs this situation. A clause will usually authorise *the creditor* to grant releases without discharging the guarantor, but it is doubtful if *a guarantor*, even where the guarantor steps into the shoes of the creditor after payment of the principal debt, can take advantage of the clause.[10] But a clause which deems the co-guarantors to be principal debtors as between themselves and the creditor may effectively prevent one guarantor from relying on the release of the principal debtor by another guarantor who has paid off the principal debt as a ground for discharging that other guarantor from liability.[11]

12–207   **(ii) Giving time or varying the principal contract**. The guarantor who has paid off the principal debt may agree with the principal to give the principal time to perform his obligations under the principal contract, or otherwise agree to vary that contract, without obtaining the consent of the other guarantors. Can such a guarantor seek contribution from the co-sureties? No doubt the co-sureties would argue that they should be discharged because of the variation of the principal contract, just as if the creditor had agreed to vary the contract. The question was specifically left open in *Greenwood v Francis*[12] because a clause in the guarantee constituted the co-guarantors principal debtors between themselves and the creditor, thus preventing them from relying on such defences normally available to guarantors. This clause was held, therefore, to exclude liability for the act of the creditor in giving time to the principal and, as a result, also to exclude liability for the act of the guarantor who had placed himself

---

[7] If a surety pays the principal debt to the creditors and then releases the principal debtor, he will have no right to compel contribution from his co-sureties because he has extinguished their right of indemnity against the principal debtor: *Griffith v Wade* (1966) 60 D.L.R. (2d) 62.

[8] *e.g.*, see above, paras 6–53 to 6–55 and 8–26 to 8–28; *Ward v National Bank of New Zealand* (1883) 8 App. Cas. 755.

[9] (1966) 60 D.L.R. (2d) 62 at 67.

[10] See *Sword v Victoria Super Service Ltd* (1958) 15 D.L.R. (2d) 217 at 224.

[11] As to the effect of this clause on a release of the principal, see above, paras 6–74 to 6–82 and 8–26 to 8–28.

[12] [1899] 1 Q.B. 312.

in the position of the creditor by satisfying the guaranteed obligation.[13] Smith L.J., however, expressed the view[14] that the defences available to a guarantor when sued by the creditor (such as a giving of time by the creditor to the principal) are not available to a guarantor when sued by a co-guarantor for contribution. In Canada, however, a guarantor who gave time to a principal debtor in these circumstances was held to have discharged the co-guarantors.[15]

In view of the judicial criticism[16] relating to the discharge of a guarantor **12–208** when the creditor gives an extension of time to the principal, the courts might be reluctant to extend the rule to a situation where the guarantor (who in fact steps into the creditor's shoes) gives time to the principal. On the other hand, there is a compelling argument that the co-sureties should be released or discharged to the extent that the surety's actions have prejudiced their right of indemnity against the principal debtor.[17] Moreover, the argument favouring a discharge of co-guarantors is more likely to succeed if the guarantor substantially varies the principal obligation to the prejudice of the co-guarantors. The co-guarantors would be fully discharged in this situation by analogy with the rule which applies when the creditor agrees with the principal to vary the principal obligation.[18]

In *Capita Financial Group Ltd v Rothwells Ltd*,[19] one guarantor paid off **12–209** the full amount of the principal debt and then entered into an agreement with the principal debtor not to charge interest on the debt, or alternatively agreed to forbear to bring proceedings against the principal debtor for such interest. In a contribution suit, a co-guarantor argued that these actions discharged the co-guarantor from its co-ordinate liability for the principal debt and absolved it of its obligation to contribute. The New South Wales Court of Appeal rejected this argument on the ground that the guarantor's actions occurred after the right of contribution had arisen and could not, therefore, impair it.[20] With the greatest respect, the agreement between the guarantor and the principal debtor did effectively release the principal debtor from its obligation to pay interest on the principal debt and this

---

[13] *ibid.*, at 321 *per* Smith L.J. 323 *per* Collins L.J. *Cf.* the clause in *Sword v Victoria Super Service Ltd* (1958) 15 D.L.R. (2d) 217.

[14] [1899] 1 Q.B. 312 at 320. See also *Way v Hearn* (1862) 11 C.B. (NS) 774; 142 E.R. 1000.

[15] *Sword v Victoria Super Service Ltd* (1958) 15 D.L.R. (2d) 217. See also *Griffith v Wade* (1966) 60 D.L.R. (2d) 62; (1966) 58 W.W.R. 344 (Can). But in s.280 Brandt on *Suretyship and Guarantees* (2nd ed.) states: "If one of two co-sureties consents to the giving of time to the principal (debtor), and the other does not, and the one who so consents afterwards has the debt to pay, he cannot recover contribution from the surety who did not consent to the extension: *Sword v Victoria Super Service Ltd* (1958) 15 D.L.R. (2d) 217 at 224. The latter was discharged from his obligation to the creditor, and likewise from contribution by the extension." In *Worthington v Peck* (1894) 24 O.R. 535 (Ch) at 540. Ferguson J. accepted these statements as propositions of law.

[16] See, *e.g. Swire v Redman* (1876) 1 Q.B.D. 536 at 541–542 *per* Blackburn J. See generally below, paras 7–59 to 7–64 and 7–89 to 7–92.

[17] *Ward v National Bank of New Zealand* (1883) L.R. 8 App. Cas. 755. See also *Way v Hearn* (1860) 11 C.B. (NS) 774 at 781 and 782; 142 E.R. 1000 at 1003. See also *Greenwood v Francis* [1889] 1 Q.B. 312, CA, where the giving of time was authorised by the guarantee.

[18] See above, paras 7–01 to 7–58 for a discussion of this rule. *Cf.* R. Goff and G. Jones, *The Law of Restitution* (6th ed., 2002), para.14–016.

[19] (1992) 30 N.S.W.L.R. 619.

[20] *ibid.*, at 631.

could compromise the other guarantor's prospective right of indemnity from the principal debtor. It should be immaterial that this right of indemnity had not arisen before the guarantor's right to contribution. It should be preserved for the benefit of both guarantors in respect of any amount they pay in respect of the principal debt whether the payment is made directly to the creditor or to a co-guarantor by way of contribution. Guarantors seeking contribution should do nothing to prejudice their co-guarantors' right of indemnity from the principal debtor. In this respect, a guarantor who pays off the principal debt stands in no better position than the creditor.

12–210   **(iii) Loss or impairment of securities**. If a guarantor satisfies the guaranteed obligation and acquires securities from the creditor, all co-sureties are entitled to share in the benefit of these securities.[21] The guarantor who actually acquires the securities will, therefore, be under a duty to preserve them in the same plight and condition as they were when they were handed over to him.[22] In an action for contribution by the paying surety, the liability of the other guarantors will be reduced to the extent that they have been prejudiced by the loss or impairment of the securities.[23] This loss or impairment will generally operate to their detriment because the securities would have been available to them as a means of enforcing their claim to indemnity or reimbursement from the principal debtor or their claim to contribution from another co-surety.

12–211   The exact nature of a guarantor's duty of care in this situation has not been clearly delineated but, in the context of realising a security, it has been described as a duty to take reasonable care.[24] Elsewhere it has been said that there must not be a "substantial alteration" in the securities.[25] No doubt, the nature of the guarantor's duties in relation to these securities will be similar to the nature of the creditor's duty in relation to securities the creditor holds for the principal debt.[26] At least one thing is clear. While the plaintiff in a contribution suit has a duty to preserve the collateral securities, the claimant is under no obligation to enforce them even if they are depreciating in value.[27]

12–212   **(iv) Counter-securities obtained by the surety**. Where the surety claiming contribution obtains from the principal debtor a bond for his own security as guarantor, this is not necessarily a defence to that surety's action for contribution.[28] The co-sureties are still liable to contribute even if the claimant furnished the guarantee on the express condition that he

---

[21] *Greenwood v Francis* [1899] 1 Q.B. 312 at 324 *per* Collins L.J.
[22] *Monk v Smith* (1893) 14 L.R. (NSW) Eq. 311; *Trader's Finance Corp Ltd v Marks* [1932] N.Z.L.R. 1176.
[23] *Greenwood v Francis* [1899] 1 Q.B. 312 at 322, *per* Smith L.J., 324 *per* Collins L.J. See also *Ramsey v Lewis* 30 Barb. (NY) 403 (1859). For precedents for this form of defence, see *Atkin's Court Forms* (1982 issue), Vol. 20, Form 71, p.169.
[24] *Greenwood v Francis* [1899] 1 Q.B. 312 at 324 per Collins L.J.
[25] *Monk v Smith* (1893) 14 L.R. (NSW) Eq. 311 at 318 *per* Owen C.J.
[26] The scope of the creditor's duty in relation to securities which the creditor holds for the principal debt is discussed below, paras 12–335 to 12–336. See also above, paras 8–46 to 8–105.
[27] *Moorhouse v Kidd* (1898) 28 O.R. 35, affirming (1896) 25 O.A.R. 221.
[28] *Knight v Hughes* (1828) 3 C. & P. 467; 172 E.R. 504; *Cf. Swain v Wall* (1641) 1 Ch. R. 149; 21 E.R. 534.

alone would be entitled to enjoy the benefit of the counter-security.[29] Yet, despite the existence of such an agreement between the principal debtor and the claimant, the security given to the claimant will enure for the benefit of all the co-sureties[30] and he is under a duty to preserve it for their benefit.[31] In such a case, loss or impairment of the security is a good defence in an action for contribution and it will discharge the co-sureties pro tanto.[32] Conversely, where a surety releases his co-surety from an obligation to contribute, he also releases pro tanto a third party who has provided an indemnity in respect of his liability as a guarantor.[33]

(v) Release of a co-guarantor. There is little authority on the effect of a **12–213** guarantor's release of a co-guarantor on the remaining guarantors. The guarantor may be in a position to give such a release because the guarantor has satisfied the principal debt. Presumably a release of one guarantor by another who has paid the principal debt in full will discharge the other co-sureties absolutely if they are jointly and severally bound.[34] A similar result occurs where the creditor releases a co-surety.[35] But where the co-sureties are not jointly and severally bound, a release of one co-surety by the paying guarantor will not discharge the other co-sureties, although they will not be liable to make good the released surety's share of the principal debt.[36]

(vi) Onus of proof. It has been suggested that, before contribution can **12–214** be obtained, the onus is on the surety seeking to recover contribution to show that nothing has been done by that surety or at his direction that would prejudice the rights of the co-sureties.[37] However, it is difficult to see why the claimant in a contribution suit should be expected to establish not just his claim to contribution but also any defences open to a co-surety. There would appear to be no reason for departing from the normal principle that a defendant is required to establish his own defences.

---

[29] *Steel v Dixon* (1881) 17 Ch. D. 825; *Re Arcedeckne; Atkins v Arcedeckne* (1883) 24 Ch. D. 709. The co-sureties may, however, have a defence to the action for contribution where the counter-security given to the plaintiff was intended to discharge the plaintiff as surety.

[30] This is merely an application of the hotchpot principle discussed below, paras 12–248 to 12–250.

[31] *Steel v Dixon* (1881) 17 Ch. D. 825; *Berridge v Berridge* (1890) 44 Ch. D. 168. It will be different if the co-sureties agree to renounce this equity in their favour or are otherwise estopped: *Steel v Dixon* at 832.

[32] *Ramsey v Lewis* 30 Barb. (NY) 403 (1859), cited in *Rowlatt on Principal and Surety* (5th ed., 1999), p.172.

[33] *Hodgson v Hodgson* (1837) 2 Keen 704; 48 E.R. 800.

[34] Except where there is a special clause in the guarantee preserving their liability: see above, paras 8–29 to 8–34. But R. Goff and G. Jones, *The Law of Restitution* (6th ed., 2002), para.14–014 doubt whether a surety's release of co-surety discharges any remaining co-sureties from contributing such a proportion of the principal debt as they would have recovered from the released surety and *Cf.* McGuinness, *The Law of Guarantee* (2nd ed., 1996) para.9.25, where it is suggested that the release of a co-surety by a surety does not discharge the other co-sureties from their obligations to contribute.

[35] See also above, paras 8–21 to 8–28.

[36] See *Griffith v Wade* (1966) 60 D.L.R. (2d) 62 at 70. See also *Fletcher v Grover* (1840) 11 N.H. 368; *Hodgson v Hodgson* (1837) 2 Keen 704; 48 E.R. 800.

[37] K.P. McGuinness, *The Law of Guarantee* (1986), p.233.

(f) Where one guarantor enjoys the whole benefit of the guarantee

12–215   It has been held that, where one guarantor enjoys the whole benefit of the guarantee through his shareholding in a company from which the co-surety has withdrawn, the co-surety is not liable to contribute. Since the guarantor enjoys all the benefits of the guarantee, he alone must bear its burden and the co-surety had a sound defence to an action for contribution.[38] There is, however, no English authority for this proposition which would allow one guarantor to escape liability to contribute on the basis that he received no benefit from the guarantee even though the guarantor is jointly and severally liable according to its terms. On the other hand, the proposition is consistent with the equitable genesis of the right of contribution. If this proposition gains acceptance, the courts will no doubt require the defendants in the contribution suit to provide affirmative proof that the claimant derived some quantifiable financial benefit which was not contemplated by the parties at the time the guarantee was given.[39] In *Lang v Le Boursicot*,[40] the principal debtor entered into two commercial leases for equipment and furniture for use in the office and factory space of its premises. There were several guarantors of the obligations under the commercial leases. One of these guarantors, Ravenscar Pty Ltd, was the owner of the business premises. When the principal debtor went into liquidation, its liquidator surrendered possession of its premises to Ravenscar and abandoned the principal debtor's interest in the leases. Ravenscar made payments to the lessor under the leases and ultimately purported to assume full ownership of the leased equipment and furniture. In a suit by Ravenscar for contribution, the other co-guarantors claimed that Ravenscar was not entitled to contribution because of the benefits it had derived from its continued possession of the leased equipment and furniture. McLelland J. rejected this argument, holding that Ravenscar did not derive any benefits which were not contemplated by the parties at the time the guarantees were given. Any benefits which Ravenscar had derived in the circumstances were attributable to the fact that the principal debtor carried on business on Ravenscar's premises and that the liquidator of the principal debtor had abandoned that company's claim to the leased equipment and furniture. However, McLelland J. did acknowledge that a guarantor's claim to

---

[38] See *Bater v Kare* [1964] S.C.R. 206; *Woolmington v Bronze Lamp Restaurant Pty Ltd* [1984] 2 N.S.W.L.R. 242. See also *AGC (Advances) Ltd v West* (1984) 5 N.S.W.L.R. 590, where Hodgson J declined to depart from the usual principle requiring equal contribution from co-sureties who prima facie were equally liable for the common debt. But his Honour's judgment suggests that the burden might have been shared unequally where one surety enjoyed a disproportionate benefit from the guarantee. *Cf. Bahin v Hughes* (1886) 31 Ch. D. 390 (defaulting trustee's right to contribution).

[39] *Lang v Le Boursicot* (1993) 5 B.P.R. 97,406 (where there was no evidence that the plaintiff guarantor derived any identifiable benefit from the fact that the liquidator of the principal debtor had abandoned certain leased equipment and furniture on premises owned by the guarantor).

[40] (1993) 5 B.P.R. 97,406.

contribution could be affected by benefits not contemplated by the other co-guarantors at the time the guarantees were given:

"If it could be affirmatively demonstrated that Ravenscar derived some quantifiable realised financial gain from the leased items remaining in its possession ... it might be proper to debit the amount of that gain against amounts paid by Ravenscar in respect of which it might otherwise be entitled to claim contribution."[41]

Another basis on which contribution may be resisted is where the other guarantors are deprived of any benefits of the guarantee through the wrongful acts of the claimant.[42]

(g) *Where the claimant has indemnified the defendant*

Where the claimant has granted the defendant guarantor an indemnity **12–216** in respect of his liability as a guarantor, the defendant guarantor can resist a contribution suit instituted by the claimant.[43] This indemnity can be constituted by a verbal promise since the Statute of Frauds does not apply to such an undertaking.

(xiii) The amount of contribution

Once it is clear that the defendant has no defence to the action for **12–217** contribution, it becomes necessary to consider how the court calculates the amount of contribution which can be awarded to the claimant. While the common law judges ordered equal contributions from all the co-sureties whether they were solvent or insolvent,[44] the equitable rule which now prevails[45] requires all solvent sureties to divide the burden rateably and to contribute in proportion to the amounts for which they are respectively liable under the terms of their guarantees.[46] This proportionate division of the principal debt among the solvent co-sureties can be varied or excluded by express agreement among the sureties.[47]

[41] *ibid.*, at 11,788.
[42] See, *e.g. Connelly v Joose* (unreported, NSW Sup Ct, May 28, 1990).
[43] *Port of Melbourne Authority v Anshun Pty Ltd* (No. 2) (1982) 55 A.L.J.R. 621.
[44] *Russell v Arnold* (1922) 70 D.L.R. 849; *Brown v Lee* (1827) 6 B. & C. 689; *Batard v Hawes* (1853) 2 E. & B. 287; 118 E.R. 775.
[45] See *Lowe v Dixon* (1885) 16 Q.B.D. 455; *Dallas v Walls* (1873) 29 L.T. 599; *Re Price* (1978) 85 D.L.R. (3d) 554; Supreme Court Act 1981, s.49.
[46] *Hitchman v Stewart* (1855) 3 Drew. 271; 61 E.R. 907; *Lowe v Dixon* (1885) 16 Q.B.D. 455; *Mahoney v McManus* (1981) 55 A.L.J.R. 673 at 675; *De Sousa v Cooper* (1992) 106 F.L.R. 79 at 81; *Ellesmere Brewery Co v Cooper* [1896] 1 Q.B. 75 at 80–81; *Pendlebury v Walker* (1841) 2 Y. & C. Ex. 424; 160 E.R. 1072; *Re Denton's Estate* [1903] 2 Ch. 670; *Re Price* (1978) 85 D.L.R. (3d) 554; *Hole v Harrison* (1673) 1 Ch. Ca 246; 22 E.R. 783; *Lawson v Wright* (1786) 1 Cox. Eq. Cas. 275; 29 E.R. 1164; *Dallas v Walls* (1873) 29 L.T. 599; *Peter v Rich* (1630) 1 Ch. R. 34; 21 E.R. 499 at 500.
[47] *Dering v Earl of Winchelsea* (1787) 1 Cox 318; 29 ER 1184; *Steel v Dixon* (1881) 17 Ch. D. 825.

12–218   It may also be possible to infer an implied agreement to vary the general rule providing for equal contribution. Thus in *Trotter v Franklin*,[48] a solicitor's partnership and a stockbroker each held a 50 per cent shareholding in the principal company, and made equal financial contributions. In the circumstances, it was held that the three solicitors in the partnership, who were individual guarantors for the company's liabilities, should each pay one sixth of the outstanding debt, and the stockbroker, who was also a co-guarantor, should pay the remaining half of the debt. Similarly, in *Morgan Equipment Co v Rodgers (No.2)*,[49] the contribution was measured by the guarantors' respective shareholdings in a joint venture at the time the guarantee was enforced.

12–219   If contribution is ordered in respect of a bill of exchange or a promissory note, it will be in the terms in which the bill or note and its indorsements are known to create.[50] In other words, it will be in the proportions for which each party has assumed liability. Beyond this, the normal rules of contribution will determine the amount of contribution from each party.[51]

12–220   In the absence of such an express or implied arrangement between the sureties the general equitable rule will govern the amount of contribution payable and it is no answer to claim that ordinary business people who enter into a modern guarantee might expect, and indeed assume, that the secondary liability would be shared equally by all the co-sureties, whether solvent or not.[52] The equitable mode of distributing the burden of suretyship is for the solvent co-sureties to contribute equally if each is a guarantor to an equal amount, and if not equally, then proportionately to the amount for which each is liable.[53] There are several variations on this theme.

(a) Where all the co-sureties have undertaken unlimited liability and all are solvent

12–221   If all the guarantors have assumed unlimited liability for the principal debt and all are solvent, they must bear the total liability equally.[54] Thus if the creditor claims a principal debt of £60,000 against three solvent guarantors, A, B and C, whose liability is unlimited, the guarantors will share the debt as follows:

---

[48] [1991] 2 N.Z.L.R. 92.
[49] (1993) 32 N.S.W.L.R. 467.
[50] *Ianson v Paxton* (1874) 23 U.C.C.P. 439 (Can).
[51] See below, paras 12–221 to 12–244.
[52] *Re Price* (1978) 85 D.L.R. (3d) 554 at 557.
[53] *Pendlebury v Walker* (1841) 4 Y. & C. Ex. 424 at 441; 160 E.R. 1072 at 1079, approved in *Ellesmere Brewery Co v Cooper* [1896] 1 Q.B. 75 at 85; *Re MacDonaghs* (1876) 10 Ir. Eq. 269; *Commercial Union Assurance Co Ltd v Hayden* [1977] Q.B. 804 at 815; *Newby v Reed* 1 Wm. Bl. 416; 96 E.R. 237; *Dering v Earl of Winchelsea* (1787) 1 Cox Eq. 318; 29 E.R. 1184.
[54] *ibid.* As contribution is based on equitable principles, there may be circumstances in which the burden is not shared equally because one of the guarantors has derived a benefit from the guarantee to the exclusion of the others: see above, paras 12–128 to 12–137.

A's share	£20,000
B's share	£20,000
C's share	£20,000
Principal debt	£60,000

If the creditor's claim against the principal debtor is compromised on terms that the guarantors remain liable and one of two equal co-sureties pays the amount of the compromise, that co-surety can claim contribution from the other co-surety in respect of half the amount paid.[55]

(b) Where all the guarantors have undertaken unlimited liability and one or more of the guarantors is insolvent

Where one of the guarantors is insolvent, the other guarantors' share of **12–222** the burden of the principal debt is proportionately increased.[56] In the above example if A were insolvent, B and C would each be answerable for £30,000 of the principal debt, subject of course to any reimbursement they may receive as dividends in A's bankruptcy.

(c) Where each guarantor's liability for the principal debt is limited

The dominant view[57] is that in this situation the guarantor's liability is **12–223** assessed on what is known as the "maximum liability basis", that is, the burden of the principal debt is borne in the proportion which each guarantor's limited liability bears to the total of the guarantors' limited liabilities. For example, suppose A, B and C are co-sureties for the whole of a principal debt of £60,000, and their liabilities are limited to £20,000,

---

[55] *Murray v Gibson* (1880) 28 Gr. 12. Similarly, if a creditor releases a guarantor who has been adjudged bankrupt on receipt of an amount in satisfaction of a judgment debt against the guarantor, the other guarantors will be liable to contribute in respect of that amount, not the whole of the principal debt: *Walker v Bowry* (1924) 35 C.L.R. 48.

[56] *Re Price* (1978) 85 D.L.R. (3d) 554. See also *Trusts & Guarantee Co v Dodds* (1922) 23 O.W.N. 69 (Can); *Mahoney v McManus* (1981) 55 A.L.J.R. 673 at 675; *Peter v Rich* (1629) 1 Ch. R. 34; *Hole v Harrison* (1673) 1 Chan. Cas. 246; 23 E.R. 783; *Lawson v Wright* (1786) 1 Cox Eq. Cas. 275; 29 E.R. 1164; *Hitchman v Stewart* (1855) 3 Drew 271; 61 E.R. 907; *Dallas v Walls* (1873) 29 L.T. 599; *Lowe v Dixon* (1885) 16 Q.B.D. 455.

[57] *Ellesmere Brewery Co v Cooper* [1896] 1 Q.B. 75 at 81–82 (although on the facts it was held there was no right of contribution); *Steel v Dixon* (1881) 17 Ch. D. 825 at 830; *Pendlebury v Walker* (1841) 4 Y. & C. Ex. 429 at 441; 160 E.R. 1072 at 1079, in which Alderson B was of the view that if the sureties were not liable for an equal amount then they should contribute "proportionably to the amount for which each is surety"; *Ostrander v Jarvis* (1909) 18 O.L.R. 17 at 19, Div Ct; *Commercial Union Assurance Co Ltd v Hayden* [1977] Q.B. 804 at 814; *Re MacDonaghs* (1876) 10 Ir. Rep. Eq. 269. See also *Cornfoot v Holdenson* [1931] A.L.R. 376, where the parties agreed to contribute on this basis and *Ellis v Emmanuel* (1876) 1 Ex. D. 157 at 162, where Blackburn J. expressed the view that "the limits put on the amounts which could be recovered from the sureties respectively would affect the amount which each was to contribute" The "maximum liability" basis appears to be the dominant test in the United States. See *Malone v Stewart* 235 Pa. 99; 83 A. 607 (1912), *contra Burnett v Millsaps* 59 Miss. 333 at 337 (1881).

£30,000 and £50,000 respectively. If C pays an amount of £30,000 claimed by the creditor in full satisfaction of the principal debt, the liability will be shared as follows:

$A(\frac{1}{5})$	£6,000
$B(\frac{3}{10})$	£9,000
$C(\frac{1}{2})$	£15,000
Amount paid to creditor	£30,000

12–224 A few comments about this approach are warranted. First, in *Ellesmere Brewery Co v Cooper*,[58] Lord Russell stated that "*where the claim of the creditor is to the full amount*, each must pay up to the fixed limit of his liability".[59] This would mean that, if the creditor claimed the full £60,000 of the principal debt, each of the three sureties would be liable for £20,000, but it is clear from Lord Russell's judgment[60] that if the creditor had claimed only £20,000 the sureties would be required to share this burden on the maximum liability basis described above.

12–225 Indeed, in *Ellesmere Brewery Co v Cooper* it was assumed that the four co-sureties (two with liability limited to £50 each; two with liability limited to £25 each) would share a common debt of £48 as follows: £16; £16; £8; £8.[61]

12–226 There is no sound reason for drawing a distinction based upon whether or not the creditor claims the full amount of the principal debt, and it is thought to be incorrect.[62] The only justification for Lord Russell's suggestion is that, since all the sureties have agreed to be liable up to a certain amount, they may be taken to have assumed equal liability up to that amount. This reasoning should not, however, override the general principle that the co-sureties should bear the burden equally if liable in equal shares or *proportionately* if they are liable in different shares or in different amounts.[63]

12–227 The second comment which may be made is that, although the "maximum liability" basis is the preferred approach, Cairns L.J. in *Commercial Union Assurance Co Ltd v Hayden*[64] specifically stated that there was no decision binding the Court of Appeal to adopt it. It is, therefore, still open for the courts to adopt an alternative method of determining each guarantor's share of the principal debt. The "independent liability" basis discussed below[65] is one such alternative. Indeed, its application is likely to avoid a disproportionate burden being placed on

[58] [1896] 1 Q.B. 75.
[59] *ibid.*, at 81 (emphasis added).
[60] *ibid.*, at 81–82.
[61] *ibid.*, at 81–82.
[62] No such distinction is made elsewhere: see esp *Re MacDonaghs* (1876) 10 Ir. Rep. Eq. 269.
[63] See *Pendlebury v Walker* (1841) 4 Y. & C. Ex. 424 at 441; 160 E.R. 1072 at 1079.
[64] [1977] Q.B. 804 (a decision regarding contribution between co-insurers).
[65] See below, paras 12–231 to 12–233.

one guarantor, whose upper limit of liability is high in comparison with the other guarantors.[66]

(d) Where each guarantor's liability is limited and one or more of the guarantors is insolvent

As has been seen, where one guarantor is insolvent, the burden borne by **12–228** each of the co-sureties is proportionately increased.[67] Hence, if the creditor claims a principal debt of £50,000 against three co-sureties, A, B and C whose liabilities are limited to £20,000, £30,000 and £50,000 respectively and C is insolvent, A and B will share the burden of the principal debt according to the "maximum liability method" as follows:

A($\frac{2}{5}$)	£20,000
B($\frac{3}{5}$)	£30,000
Principal debt	£50,000

These figures result from an application of the "maximum liability" method to the stated problem.

(e) Where the guarantors share liability for part of the principal debt

Assume that there are three guarantors, A, B and C and that A is liable **12–229** for the first £9,000 of the principal debt of £49,000 and that B and C are liable for the whole debt. Since the guarantors share a common liability only in respect of the first £9,000 of the principal debt, contribution between A, on the one hand, and B and C, on the other, is restricted to that portion.[68] As B and C are guarantors of the whole debt they will share the balance of the debt equally. The guarantors must, therefore, share the burden of the principal debt in the following amounts:

A	£3,000
B	£23,000
C	£23,000
Principal debt	£49,000

[66] For instance, in the example given at the beginning of the section, if C's limit of liability were £150,000 (not £50,000) the "maximum liability" formula would distribute the debt of £30,000 in the ratio 2:3:15. Thus C would bear $\frac{3}{4}$ of the debt. The "independent liability" basis (discussed below, paras 12–231 to 12–233) would distribute the debt in the ratio 2:3:3. Thus C would be liable for $\frac{3}{8}$ of the debt. As to the application of the independent liability basis to *Ellesmere Brewery Co v Cooper* [1896] 1 Q.B. 75, see *Commercial Union Assurance Co Ltd v Hayden* [1977] Q.B. 804 at 814.
[67] See above, para.12–155.
[68] *Molson's Bank v Kovinsky* [1924] 4 D.L.R. 330 at 332.

12–230   Where the sureties are guarantors of *different* parts of the principal debt, they are not co-sureties and contribution is not available.[69]

(f) Where the liability of some of the guarantors is limited and the liability of others is unlimited

12–231   In this situation, the "maximum liability" method is an inappropriate basis for distributing the burden of the principal debt. The difficulties which this method would produce in this context would make it, at best, unfair and, at worst, unworkable.[70] It is thought that the "independent liability" principle, which determines the right of contribution between co-insurers in indemnity insurance, is a more appropriate basis for sharing the burden of suretyship among the guarantors in this situation.[71] On this method, the guarantors who are liable to contribute to the common burden bear the debt equally up to the amount of their limited liability.[72] Thus if A's liability is limited to £20,000 and B's liability is unlimited, they will share the burden of a principal debt of £10,000 equally.[73]

12–232   Where the amount claimed by the creditor exceeds the limit of A's liability, the independent liability principle would require the court to determine what would have been the liability of each guarantor had each been the only surety. The amount claimed is then divided among the guarantors in proportion to these independent liabilities. In this way the common debt is borne in the proportions which each guarantor's limited liability bears to the total of the guarantors' limited liabilities.[74] For example, if the liability of A under A's guarantee is limited to £20,000 and B's liability under B's guarantee is unlimited, the parties will share the burden of a principal debt of £60,000 as follows:

> A's independent liability as a sole guarantor would be £20,000; B's independent liability as a sole guarantor would be £60,000; therefore A and B would share the principal debt in the proportion 2:6; thus A would be liable to pay $\frac{1}{4}$ or £15,000 and B would be liable to pay $\frac{3}{4}$ or £45,000.

12–233   This is a much fairer method of apportionment since it divides the *actual amount* of the principal debt and does not impose an unduly onerous burden on one guarantor simply because a larger principal debt would still

---

[69] See above, paras 12–138 to 12–157.
[70] See *Commercial Union Assurance Co Ltd v Hayden* [1977] Q.B. 804, where the Court of Appeal considered the apportionment of liability between co-insurers. Cf. *Government Insurance Office (NSW) v Crowley* [1975] 2 N.S.W.L.R. 78.
[71] But in *Commercial Union Assurance Co Ltd v Hayden* [1977] Q.B. 804 at 814, Cairns L.J. was "prepared to assume" that "the maximum liability" basis determined apportionment between co-sureties.
[72] *Naumann v Northcote* (unreported, CA, February 7, 1978) cited in *Rowlatt on Principal and Surety* (5th ed., 1999), para.7–52. See also *Commercial Union Assurance Co Ltd v Hayden* [1977] Q.B. 804; *American Surety Co of New York v Wrightson* (1910) 103 L.T. 663.
[73] See *Commercial Union Assurance Co Ltd v Hayden* [1977] Q.B. 804.
[74] *Rowlatt on Principal and Surety* (5th ed., 1999), p.168.

be within that guarantor's guarantee.[75] In short, the independent liability method shares the burden of the principal debt as it is, not as it might have been.

(g) Cumulative guarantees

Special problems arise in calculating the amount of contribution **12–234** between guarantors who are bound in respect of different amounts of a common debt or obligation by separate guarantees. Contribution will be ordered even if the guarantees are expressed to be "independent" and "additional" as long as the parties are co-sureties for the same debt or share a common liability for part of the debt.[76] In certain contexts, the words "independent" and "additional" might delineate the portions of a debt to which each guarantee primarily applies by indicating that the earlier guarantees are intended to cover the initial advances and the subsequent guarantees are to cover subsequent advances to the principal debtor.[77] But generally, the mere existence of a second and subsequent guarantee by some of the original guarantors in respect of the same indebtedness will not prevent the creditor from enjoying the benefit of both guarantees[78] and will not, therefore, bar contribution.

There are at least two possible bases on which contribution between co- **12–235** sureties under cumulative guarantees might be determined: the "maximum liability" method and the "independent liability" method. Both these methods have been described above.[79] It remains to consider their application to cumulative guarantees.

The "maximum liability" method is applied where the liabilities of the **12–236** guarantors are limited to different amounts. In calculating the liability of each guarantor, the court simply ascertains what is the limit of the liability of each guarantor under that guarantor's guarantee and then distributes the burden in accordance with the proportions which these liabilities bear to the aggregate of each guarantor's maximum liability. Thus if the principal debt is £40,000 and A has limited her or his liability under his guarantee to £20,000 while B's liability under a separate guarantee is limited to £30,000, they will share the common liability as follows:

---

[75] *Commercial Union Assurance Co Ltd v Hayden* [1977] Q.B. 804.
[76] See *Cornfoot v Holdenson* [1931] A.L.R. 376; *Ellis v Emmanuel* (1876) 1 Ex. D. 157 at 162; *Ellesmere Brewery Co v Cooper* [1896] 1 Q.B. 75 at 80–81.
[77] See F.A.A. Russell, "Co-Sureties: Rights of Contribution" (1935) 9 A.L.J. 42 at 44.
[78] See *Mahoney v McManus* (1981) 55 A.L.J.R. 673 at 677.
[79] See above, paras 12–223 to 12–227 and 12–231 to 12–233. For a discussion of alternative methods of calculating the amount of contribution, see F.A.A. Russell, "Co-Sureties: Rights of Contribution" (1935) 9 A.L.J. 42, and R.P. Meagher, D. Heydon and M. Leeming, *Equity—Doctrines and Remedies* (4th ed., 2002), paras 10–090–10–095.

$$A\text{'s share} = \frac{A\text{'s maximum liability}}{\text{Total of maximum liability of A and B}}$$

$$= \frac{£20,000}{£50,000} = \frac{2}{5} = £16,000$$

$$B\text{'s share} = \frac{B\text{'s maximum liability}}{\text{Total of maximum liability of A and B}}$$

$$= \frac{£30,000}{£50,000} = \frac{3}{5} = £24,000$$

12–237   Contribution can also be assessed on a maximum liability basis where several parties are liable on separate guarantees limited to varying amounts of the same indebtedness. In this situation, perhaps the most equitable method of distributing the burden of the principal debt is to divide the amount payable first among the different guarantees on a maximum liability basis and then further divide each guarantee's share of the liability among the solvent sureties in each group.[80]

12–238   For example, where a principal debt of £30,000 is to be shared among the following guarantors:

(i)   A, B and C, whose maximum liabilities on the First Guarantee are £6,000, £3,000 and £1,000 respectively;

(ii)   B, C and D, whose maximum liabilities on a Second Guarantee are £12,000, £8,000 and £4,000 respectively; and

(iii)   D, E and A, whose maximum liabilities on a Third Guarantee are £15,000, £6,000 and £5,000 respectively,

the parties will share the principal debt as follows:

12–239   The First Guarantee would bear one-sixth $(\frac{1}{6})$ of the principal debt. This share is calculated by dividing the aggregate of A, B and C's maximum liabilities under the First Guarantee, that is, £10,000 (£6,000 + £3,000 + £1,000) by the aggregate of the maximum liabilities of all the guarantors under all three guarantees, that is £60,000. Thus the First Guarantee would be answerable for one-sixth $(\frac{1}{6})$ of the principal debt of £30,000, namely £5,000.

12–240   A's share of this liability of that £5,000 would be:

£6,000/£10,000 (the maximum limit of A's liability)/(the total maximum limits of all parties to the First Guarantee) $= \frac{3}{5} = £3,000$

12–241   B's share of this liability of £5,000 would be:

£3,000/£10,000 $= 3/10 = £1,500$

---

[80] This is the approach adopted in the United States of America: *United States Fidelity & Guarantee Co v Naylor* 237 F 314 (1916).

12-242

C's share of this liability of £5,000 would be:

$$£1,000/£10,000 = 1/10 = £500$$

Similar calculations could be made for the Second and Third Guarantees.

As has been seen, the "maximum liability" method presents difficulties **12-243** when some of the guarantors have undertaken an unlimited liability. Similar problems occur where some of the cumulative guarantees impose limits on the guarantors' liabilities and others do not. The "independent liability" method avoids these difficulties by allowing the court to determine what would have been the liability of each surety had that surety been the only surety. For example, if A's liability under his guarantee is limited to £10,000 and B's liability under a separate guarantee for the same debt is unlimited, the parties will be liable for a principal debt of £40,000 in the following proportions and amounts:

A's independent liability as sole guarantor would be £10,000.

B's independent liability as sole guarantor would be £40,000.

Therefore, A and B should share the principal debt in the proportion 1:4.

Thus, A would be liable to pay $\frac{1}{5}$ or £8,000 and B would be liable to pay $\frac{4}{5}$ or £32,000.

In the case of cumulative guarantees with several parties (some with **12-244** limited and some with unlimited liability), the independent liability basis should also be used to determine not just the burden to be carried by each guarantee, but also each guarantor's liability under each separate guarantee.

(xiv) Costs

In a claim for contribution at law it was doubtful whether a guarantor **12-245** could recover from the co-surety the costs of defending proceedings brought against the guarantor by the creditor.[81] By contrast, a claim for contribution is now recognised as a substantially equitable claim which is founded on principles of natural justice.[82] While co-sureties are not, strictly speaking, under co-ordinate liabilities to pay the costs incurred by one of the co-sureties in defending the creditor's action to enforce the guarantee,[83] they should all contribute to the costs of a successful defence

---

[81] See *Knight v Hughes* (1828) 3 C. & P.467; 172 E.R. 504 (an action for assumpsit).
[82] See *Albion Insurance Co Ltd v Government Insurance Office* (NSW) (1969) 121 C.L.R. 342 at 350–352; *AGC (Advances) Ltd v West* (1984) 5 N.S.W.L.R. 590 at 604.
[83] *Morgan Equipment Co v Rodgers* (No. 2) (1993) 32 N.S.W.L.R. 467 at 482.

by one co-surety which enures for their benefit.[84] Hence, any co-surety who benefits from the successful defence, in whole or in part, of the creditor's claim is liable to contribute to the reasonable and proper costs of that defence.[85] But, apart from a special contract between the co-sureties in relation to such costs, a guarantor will only be liable to contribute in respect of payments or expenses which have benefited the co-sureties.[86] This claim to indemnity is based on restitutionary principles. Only where the costs were incurred in raising a reasonable defence against the creditor's claim on grounds which would also have relieved the co-sureties will the guarantor be able to obtain contribution for a proportionate share of the costs.[87] No contribution will be ordered in respect of the costs of raising a defence which is personal to the guarantor because this defence would not benefit the co-sureties.[88]

(xv) Interest

12–246   In an action for contribution, a guarantor is entitled to recover from the co-sureties interest on amounts paid to the creditor in excess of the guarantor's proportionate share of the common liability, even if the principal debt itself did not carry interest.[89] In the early cases, the courts applied the "trustee rate" of 8 per cent.[90] While this rate is appropriate in actions for breaches of trust, there is no cogent reason for applying it in an action for contribution. It is now recognised that an action for contribution is founded upon equitable principles, but this, in itself, is no justification for applying the "trustee rate" of interest. Guarantees are common features of most modern commercial transactions and the burden which a

---

[84] *Wolmershausen v Gullick* [1893] 2 Ch. 514 at 529–530 *per* Wright J.; *Kemp v Finden* (1844) 12 M. & W. 421; 152 E.R. 1262; *Tindall v Bell* (1843) 11 M. & W. 228; 152 E.R. 786; *Broom v Hall* (1859) 7 C.B. (NS) 503; 141 E.R. 911; *Morgan Equipment Co v Rodgers* (1993) 32 N.S.W.L.R. 467 at 482; *James Hardie & Co Pty Ltd v Wyong Shire Council* (2000) 48 N.S.W.L.R. 679.
[85] *Morgan Equipment Co v Rodgers (No. 2)* (1993) 32 N.S.W.L.R. 467.
[86] See particularly *Wolmershausen v Gullick* [1893] 2 Ch. 514 at 529–530 *per* Wright J. See also *Kemp v Finden* (1844) 12 M. & W. 421; 152 E.R. 1262; *Tindall v Bell* (1843) 11 M. & W. 228; 152 E.R. 786; *Broom v Hall* (1859) 7 C.B. (NS) 503; 141 E.R. 911; *Morgan Equipment Co v Rodgers* (1993) 32 NSWLR 467 (successful defence of creditor's claim resulted in settlement for two-thirds of claim; hence co-guarantor was liable to contribute to the costs of the defence on the same basis as his co-ordinate liability).
[87] *Williams v Buchanan; Anderson (Third Party)* (1891) 7 T.L.R. 226 at 227 *per* Lord Esher; *Wolmershausen v Gullick* [1893] 2 Ch. 514 at 529–530; *Broom v Hall* (1859) 7 C.B. (NS) 503; 141 E.R. 911.
[88] *Re International Contract Co; Hughes Claim* (1872) L.R. 13 Eq. 623 at 624; *South v Bloxham* (1865) 2 Hem. & M. 457; 71 E.R. 541, VC.
[89] *Lawson v Wright* (1786) 1 Cox Eq. Cas. 275; 29 E.R. 1164; *Hitchman v Stewart* (1855) 3 Drew 271; 61 E.R. 907; *Re Fox Walker & Co; Ex p. Bishop* (1880) 15 Ch. D. 400; *Re Swan's Estate* (1869) 4 Ir. Eq. 209.
[90] *Re Swan* (1865) 4 Ir. R. Eq. 209; *CS Lawson v Wright* (1786). 1 Cox 275; 29 E.R. 1164; *Hitchman v Stewart* (1855) 3 Drew 271; 61 E.R. 907; *Ex p. Bishop* (1880) 15 Ch. D. 400; *A E Goodwin Ltd (in liq) v A G Healing Ltd (in liq)* (1979) 7 A.C.L.R. 481; *McColl's Wholesale Pty Ltd v State Bank of New South Wales* [1984] 3 N.S.W.L.R. 365 at 377.

paying guarantor incurs is essentially a commercial loss.[91] Certainly, the "opportunity cost" of a paying guarantor is far greater than the opportunity cost which is caused by a defaulting trustee whose rate of return on authorised trustee investments is more modest than a guarantor could obtain in commercial transactions.[92] In deciding what contribution should be available to a paying guarantor, the court should ensure that the guarantor receives proper compensation for assuming more than his fair share of the common debt.[93] This can only be achieved by awarding a commercial rate of interest in contribution suits.[94]

Interest is calculated from the date or dates on which the guarantor's **12–247** payments exceeded the guarantor's proportionate share of the common liability, and this is not necessarily the same as the dates of the payments.[95]

(xvi) The "hotchpot principle"

The equitable rule of contribution demands not merely that the **12–248** common burden be shared proportionately but that co-sureties share in the securities or other benefits given to a guarantor by the principal debtor or assigned by the creditor to the guarantor on payment of the principal debt.[96] No guarantor, not even an insolvent one,[97] can retain for his own advantage, securities or benefits given to that guarantor by the principal debtor, even if the co-sureties were unaware of such securities and even if they were a condition of the guarantor entering into the guarantee.[98] The guarantor must bring them into hotchpot so that they can be shared pro tanto with the co-sureties.[99] These securities or benefits will enure to the benefit of all the guarantors until they are recouped in full or until the securities or

---

[91] *Morgan Equipment Co v Rodgers* (1993) 32 N.S.W.L.R. 467. *Cf. A E Goodwin Ltd (in liq) v A G Healing Ltd (in liq)* (1979) 7 A.C.L.R. 481; *McColl's Wholesale Pty Ltd v State Bank of New South Wales* [1984] 3 N.S.W.L.R. 365 at 377.

[92] *Morgan Equipment Co v Rodgers* (1993) 32 N.S.W.L.R. 467 at 487.

[93] See *Nixon v Furphy* (1926) 26 S.R. (NSW) 409 at 413; *Re Dawson; Union Fidelity Trustee Co Ltd v Perpetual Trustee Co Ltd* (1966) 84 W.N. (NSW) (Pt.1) 399.

[94] *Morgan Equipment Co v Rodgers (No.2)* (1993) 32 N.S.W.L.R. 467. The court could exercise its discretion to award an interest rate reflecting the current commercial rate. *Cf. The Mecca* [1968] P.665 at 672 and *Chitty on Contracts* (28th ed., 1998), Vol. 1, para.27–146. See above, para.12–60, n.72.

[95] *Davies v Humphreys* (1840) 6 M. & W. 153; 151 E.R. 361; *Lawson v Wright* (1786) 1 Cox Eq. Cas. 275; 29 E.R. 1164; *Hitchman v Stewart* (1855) 3 Drew 271; 61 E.R. 907; *Re Swan's Estate* (1869) 4 Ir. Eq. 209; *Re Fox Walker & Co; Ex p. Bishop* (1880) 15 Ch. D. 400.

[96] *Ellesmere Brewery Co v Cooper* [1896] 1 Q.B. 75 at 80–81; *Ex p. Crisp* (1744) 1 Atk. 133 at 135; 26 E.R. 87 at 88; *Berridge v Berridge* (1890) 44 Ch. D. 168; *Duncan, Fox & Co v North and South Wales Bank* (1880) 6 App. Cas 1 at 19; *Jones v Hill* (1893) 14 L.R. (NSW) Eq. 303 at 309; *Sherwin v McWilliams* (1921) 17 Tas. L.R. 94; *Re Arcedeckne; Atkins v Arcedeckne* (1883) 24 Ch. D. 709 ; *Knight v Hughes* (1828) 3 C. & P.467; Mood & M. 247, NP; *Cf. Steel v Dixon* (1881) 17 Ch. D. 825.

[97] *Duncan, Fox & Co v North and South Wales Bank* (1880) 6 App. Cas. 1 at 19.

[98] *Steel v Dixon* (1881) 17 Ch. D. 825; *Re Arcedeckne; Atkins v Arcedeckne* (1883) 24 Ch. D. 709

[99] *Sherwin v McWilliams* (1921) 17 Tas. L.R. 94; *Re Arcedeckne; Atkins v Arcedeckne* (1883) 24 Ch. D. 709. Bringing into hotchpot involves giving credit for the securities and allowing set-off in relation to the securities: *Re Albert Life Assurance Co Ltd* (1870) L.R. 11 Eq. 164 at 172 *per* Bacon V.C.; *Re Arcedeckne, Atkins v Arcedeckne* (1883) 24 Ch. D. 709.

benefits are exhausted.[1] Moreover, in the absence of any agreement among the co-sureties, a guarantor cannot exclude the co-sureties from sharing any benefit the guarantor obtains from the principal debtor.[2]

12–249   The same principle applies to payments made by the principal debtor to one guarantor[3] or in relief of the co-sureties.[4] The benefit of such payments must be shared among the co-sureties in proportionate reduction of their respective liabilities.[5] Accordingly, a guarantor who claims contribution must give credit for the amount of any payments received from the principal debtor.[6]

This principle does not, however, extend to securities or benefits given to a guarantor by a stranger, as distinct from the principal debtor. These need not be brought into hotchpot because they were never part of the principal debtor's estate and therefore were never available to assist the sureties to enforce their right of reimbursement or indemnity against the debtor.[7] Since the co-sureties suffer no injury or harm in being deprived of these securities or benefits, they have no claim to them as part of their right of contribution. Similarly, a benefit secured by a guarantor on the guarantor's own initiative and maintained at his own expense need not be shared with the co-sureties. For this reason, an insurance policy on the principal debtor's life taken out and serviced by one guarantor at the guarantor's own expense and for his own benefit is not subject to the "hotchpot principle".[8]

12–250   The "hotchpot principle" is not restricted to securities and benefits given to a guarantor by the principal debtor. It applies equally to benefits assigned to a guarantor by the creditor on payment of the principal debt. The paying surety is taken to have purchased these benefits on behalf of the co-sureties and must take their value into account when seeking contribution.[9]

(xvii) The right of contribution in cases of indemnity

12–251   Where there are several parties liable under contracts of indemnity, as distinct from contracts of guarantee, contribution should be ordered on

[1] *Berridge v Berridge* (1890) 44 Ch. D. 168.
[2] *Jones v Hill* (1893) 14 LR (NSW) Eq. 303 at 309 *per* Owen C.J. in Eq; *Steel v Dixon* (1881) 17 Ch. D. 825: see above, paras 12–130 to 12–131.
[3] *Knight v Hughes* (1828) 3 C. & P.467; 172 E.R. 504; *Steel v Dixon* (1881) 17 Ch. D. 825.
[4] *Stirling v Forrester* (1821) 3 Bli. 575 at 590; 4 E.R. 712 at 717.
[5] *ibid.*
[6] *Knight v Hughes* (1828) 3 C. & P.467; 172 E.R. 504.
[7] *Goodman v Keel* [1923] 4 D.L.R. 468.
[8] *Re Albert Life Assurance Co* (1870) L.R. 11 Eq. 164 at 172 *per* Bacon V.C. See also *Re Arcedeckne; Atkins v Arcedeckne* (1883) 24 Ch. D. 709 at 715–717.
[9] See above, paras 12–182 to 12–194.

similar principles to those governing contribution between insurers.[10] On this basis, contribution will only be available to indemnifiers where they are under co-ordinate liabilities to make good the one loss.[11] It has been suggested that if one party is liable under a contract of indemnity and another under a guarantee, contribution will not be ordered because the indemnifier may be under a more extensive liability than the guarantor.[12] But this should not preclude contribution where the two parties in fact share a common liability.[13] Any other result would distribute the burden inequitably. The exact share to be borne by each party could be determined by applying the independent liability test used to calculate contribution between co-sureties.[14]

A failure by one co-indemnifier to inform the other of a proposed **12–252** compromise or settlement of the claim against them does not excuse the other co-indemnifier of a liability to contribute to the settlement sum, particularly where an agreement between the indemnifiers expressly preserved their rights to challenge any settlement on grounds of unreasonableness.[15]

Having considered the guarantor's right of indemnity against the **12–253** principal debtor and right to contribution from the co-sureties, it will be convenient to examine the guarantor's right of subrogation.

3. THE GUARANTOR'S RIGHT OF SUBROGATION

(i) Meaning and purpose of subrogation

Once the principal debt or obligation has been wholly satisfied, a **12–254** guarantor has the right to be subrogated to the rights of the creditor: the

---

[10] See *Albion Insurance Co Ltd v Government Insurance Office (NSW)* (1969) 121 C.L.R. 342 at 349–352 *per* Kitto J.; *Government Insurance Office (NSW) v Crowley* [1975] 2 N.S.W.L.R. 78. An insurer is not entitled to claim contribution for a voluntary payment over and above its share of the liability: *Legal and General Assurance Society Ltd v Drake Insurance Co Ltd* [1992] Q.B. 887. As to contribution between co-insurers, see *Legal and General Assurance Society Ltd v Drake Insurance Co Ltd* [1992] Q.B. 887 (the right to contribution was limited by "rateable proportion" clauses in the policies).

[11] *Albion Insurance Co Ltd v Government Insurance Office of NSW* (1969) 121 C.L.R. 342 at 350; *CIBC Australia Ltd v Parkston Ltd* (1995) 18 A.C.S.R. 429 at 435.

[12] *Chitty on Contracts* (28th ed., 1998), Vol 2, para.44–107. See also *Re Law Courts Chambers Co* (1889) 61 L.T. 669, which held that a guarantor is not entitled to an *indemnity* from a person who has agreed to indemnify the debtor in respect of the debt, because this is an independent obligation for which the guarantor is not secondarily liable. On this basis, contribution between the guarantor and the indemnifier would be denied because they do not share a common liability. See also *Crafts v Tritton* (1818) 8 Taunt. 365; 129 E.R. 423.

[13] In *Parr's Bank v Albert Mines Syndicate* (1900) 5 Com. Cas. 116, where a loan was both guaranteed and insured, it was held that the insurer was subrogated to the rights of the creditor against the surety. As Bingham points out, only a slight change of facts would be necessary to allow contribution between the insurer and the surety, as distinct from subrogation: see P. Bingham, "The Surety's Rights to Contribution" (1984) 12 A.B.L.R. 394 at 404–405.

[14] See *Government Insurance Office (NSW) v Crowley* [1975] 2 N.S.W.L.R. 78; *Commercial Union Assurance Co Ltd v Hayden* [1977] Q.B. 804.

[15] *Newcastle Protection and Indemnity Association Ltd v Assurance Foreningen Gard Gjensidig* [1998] 2 Lloyd's Rep. 387 at 400 *per* Colman J.

guarantor has the right to take under, or to stand in the shoes of, the creditor in enforcing the principal obligation of the debtor as well as any securities, priorities and remedies which the creditor enjoyed prior to the performance of the principal obligation.[16] In the suretyship context, subrogation is a method of adjusting the rights of the parties in the interests of justice.[17] Here the doctrine of subrogation has dual application: first, it can be invoked by a guarantor against the principal debtor as a way of enforcing the guarantor's right of reimbursement or indemnity;[18] secondly, it can be used by a guarantor who wishes to enforce a contribution claim against co-sureties.[19]

12–255   Subrogation is not, however, a cause of action but rather an equitable remedy against a party who would otherwise be unjustly enriched.[20] As Millett L.J. pointed out in *Boscawen v Bajwa*,[21] it is a means by which the court regulates the legal relationship between a claimant and a defendant in order to prevent unjust enrichment.[22] Strictly speaking, it does not necessarily keep the security alive[23] because upon payment of the full amount of the secured debt, the security would be discharged under the general law and cease to exist.[24] Nor does it require that the claimant must for all purposes be treated as an actual assignee of the benefit of the security.[25] But it does mean that the security is treated as if it were still available to assist the claimant to recover the amount he has paid in reduction or discharge of the principal debt.[26]

---

[16] *Duncan, Fox & Co v North and South Wales Bank* (1880) 6 App. Cas. 1; *Traders' Finance Corp Ltd v Marks* [1932] N.Z.L.R. 1176; *Craythorne v Swinburne* (1807) 14 Ves. Jun. 160 at 162; 33 E.R. 482 at 483; *Morgan v Seymour* (1638) 1 Rep. Ch. 120; 21 E.R. 525; *Ex p. Crisp* (1744) 1 Atk. 133; 26 E.R. 87; *Mayhew v Crickett* (1818) 2 Swanst. 185 at 191; 36 E.R. 585 at 587; *Goddard v Whyte* (1860) 2 Giff. 449 at 452; 66 E.R. 188 at 189.

[17] *Aldrich v Cooper* (1803) 8 Ves. Jun. 382 at 389; 32 E.R. 402 at 405, approved by the High Court of Australia in *A/asian Conference Association Ltd v Mainline Constructions Pty Ltd* (in liq) (1978) 141 C.L.R. 335; 53 A.L.J.R. 66 at 71; *Duncan, Fox & Co v North and South Wales Bank* (1879) 6 App. Cas. 1 at 12 and 19; *Parsons and Cole v Briddock* (1708) 2 Vern. 608; 23 E.R. 997; *Wright v Morley* (1805) 18 Ves. 12 at 22 and 23; 32 E.R. 992 at 995–996. As to the practical and conceptual problems that might arise from this approach to subrogation where there are other unsecured and priority creditors, see M. Bridge, "Failed Contracts, Subrogation and Unjust Enrichment: *Banque Financière de la Cité v Parc (Battersea) Ltd*" (1998) J.B.L. 323.

[18] *R. v Doughty* (1702) Wight. 3; 145 E.R. 1152; *Regina Brokerage & Investment Co v Waddell* (1916) 27 D.L.R. 533, CA; *Gedye v Matson* (1858) 25 Beav. 310; 53 E.R. 655; *Re Empire Paper Ltd (in liq)* [1999] B.C.C. 406 at 408 *per* Stanley Burnton Q.C.; *Liberty Mutual Insurance Co (UK) Ltd v HSBC Bank plc* [2001] Lloyd's Rep. 224.

[19] *Stirling v Forrester* (1821) 3 Bli. 575 at 590; 4 E.R. 712 at 717; *Re Parker* [1894] 3 Ch 400 CA; *McNeill v Short* [1926] 4 D.L.R. 951, Alta CA. See also *Sherwin v McWilliams* (1921) 17 Tas. L.R. 94.

[20] *Banque Financière de la Cité v Parc (Battersea) Ltd* [1998] 1 All E.R. 739 at 749 *per* Lord Hoffmann. See also P. Birks, *An Introduction to the Law of Restitution* (1985), p.93 and C. Mitchell, *The Law of Subrogation* (1994), p.4.

[21] [1995] 4 All E.R. 769.

[22] *ibid.*, at 777.

[23] This is more a metaphor or an analogy than a legal principle. See P. Birks, *An Introduction to the Law of Restitution* (1985), pp.93–97.

[24] *Banque Financière de la Cité v Parc (Battersea) Ltd* [1998] 1 All E.R. 739 at 749 *per* Lord Hoffmann.

[25] *ibid.*

[26] *ibid.* The remedy of subrogation can be invoked to enforce rights in personam as well as rights in rem. See *Banque Financière de la Cité v Parc (Battersea) Ltd* [1998] 1 All E.R. 739 at

(ii) Historical basis of subrogation

Roman law recognised a right of subrogation[27] but the history of its **12–256** reception into English law is largely uncharted. While it is clear that it was originally a creature of equity[28] and that it developed primarily out of the principal-surety relationship, little else is known of its early history in the English legal system. Prior to the enactment of the Mercantile Law Amendment Act 1856, there was a difference between the English and the Scottish law of suretyship: in England, a guarantor paying a debt was not entitled at law to the benefit of securities[29] which the creditor held, whereas in Scotland the guarantor was so entitled.[30] In England, only the courts of equity allowed the guarantor a remedy, and relief was granted on principles borrowed from the civil law and administered with regard to the respective rights and immunities of all parties subject to contribution.[31]

Subrogation is in the nature of a class right and for this reason a claim of **12–257** set-off based on it will fail since the necessary mutuality does not exist. Hence in *A E Goodwin Ltd (in liq) v A G Healing Ltd (in liq)*,[32] all the guarantors who contributed towards the payment of the principal debt were entitled to be subrogated to the creditor's rights against the debtor, even though some of the guarantors owed the debtor more through inter-company loans than they contributed to the principal debt.

Under s.5 of the Mercantile Law Amendment Act 1856 a guarantor on **12–258** satisfying the principal debt is entitled to an assignment of every judgment, specialty or other security held by the creditor in respect of the principal debt or obligation. This right can be enforced by an action for specific performance or for damages for breach of the statute.[33] The Act was intended to give sureties and co-debtors the same rights in a court of law which they enjoyed previously in a court of equity.[34] The guarantor's rights under the section arise at the time the guarantee is given.[35] It follows that the guarantor has the right to require the creditor to marshal its

---

742, *per* Lord Steyn. In that case subrogation gave a bank a personal remedy against a subsequent mortgagee.

[27] See *John Edwards & Co v Motor Union Insurance Co* [1922] 2 K.B. 249 at 252 *per* McCardie J.; *Aetna Life Insurance Co v Middleport* 124 US 534 (1887) at 548.

[28] See *Commissioners of State Savings Bank of Victoria v Patrick Intermarine Acceptances Ltd (in liq)* [1981] 1 N.S.W.L.R. 175 at 178. Subrogation was also, however, recognised by the common law: *Ex p. Crisp* (1744) 1 Atk. 133; 26 E.R. 87.

[29] *Cf. Ex p. Crisp* (1744) 1 Atk. 133; 26 E.R. 87.

[30] *Embling v McEwan* (1872) 3 V.R. (L) 52 at 53.

[31] *ibid.*

[32] (1979) 7 A.C.L.R. 481 at 489. See above, para. 12–193. Compare *Brown v Cork* [1985] B.C.L.C. 363 which dealt with enforcement of the right of subrogation against co-sureties. See below, paras 12–272 to 12–283. See above, paras 12–182 to 12–194.

[33] *Dale v Powell* (1911) 105 L.T. 291. In *Batchellor v Lawrence* (1861) 9 C.B. (NS) 543 at 556; 142 E.R. 214 at 218, Byles J. stated that s.5 affords a guarantor "at least the same remedy at law as he would have had in equity". See also *Atkin's Court Forms* (1982 Issue), Vol. 20, pp.141, 144–145 for the form of the writ and the statement of claim in an action to compel transfer of securities.

[34] *Hardy v Johnson* (1880) 6 V.L.R. (L) 190; *Dering v Earl of Winchelsea* (1787) 1 Cox Eq. Cas. 318; 29 E.R. 1184. It appears that a person who satisfies the principal debtor's liabilities under a mistake of fact or law will not be entitled to the rights of subrogation conferred on a paying surety: *Rowlatt on Principal and Surety* (5th ed., 199), p.157.

[35] *Dixon v Steel* [1901] 2 Ch. 602.

securities,[36] and the creditor is under a duty not to lose or impair the securities held for the principal debt.[37] The Act also furnished a summary mode of implementing the principles of equity in a contribution suit, which differed from an action at law both in its general principle and its operation.[38] In some respects, the Act extended the rights of the paying guarantor,[39] but at the same time it adopted the equitable principles on which that guarantor's right of subrogation was based.[40] Indeed, the equitable basis of the doctrine of subrogation is both explicitly and implicitly recognised in the statute itself.[41]

12-259   A guarantor's right of subrogation, then, is founded on the general rules of equity which are now enshrined in statute; it does not depend on a special stipulation in the contract of guarantee.[42] Specifically, it rests on the guarantor's equity not to have the entire burden of the debt cast upon him simply by the creditor's choice not to resort to its other remedies or securities.[43] It is only fair and equitable that a guarantor should be placed in the same position as a fully-paid creditor who declines to enforce such remedies or securities or who deals with them to the prejudice of the guarantor. Story explains the equitable basis of subrogation in the following terms:

"[N]o one ought to profit by another man's loss where he himself has incurred a like responsibility. Any other rule would put it in the power of the creditor to select his own victim; and, upon motives of mere caprice or favouritism, to make a common burden a most gross personal oppression. It would be against equity for the creditor to exact or receive payment from one, and to permit, or by his conduct to cause, the other debtors to be exempt from payment."[44]

---

[36] See below, paras 12–344 to 12–355.
[37] See below, paras 12–335 to 12–336.
[38] *Hardy v Johnson* (1880) 6 V.L.R. (L) 190; *Dering v Earl of Winchelsea* (1787) 1 Cox Eq. Cas. 318; 29 E.R. 1184.
[39] See below, paras 12–303 to 12–311.
[40] *Batchellor v Lawrence* (1861) 9 C.B. (NS) 543 at 550–551; 142 E.R. 214 at 216. See also *Duncan, Fox & Co v North and South Wales Bank* (1880) 6 App. Cas. 1 at 19.
[41] *Batchellor v Lawrence* (1861) 9 C.B. (NS) 543 at 555; 142 E.R. 214 at 218, where Byles J. noted that the preamble of the Act recited that it was intended to give to sureties and co-debtors the same rights in a court of law which they previously had in a court of equity. Moreover, the proviso to the section limits recovery to the "just proportion" for which the co-surety or co-debtor is "justly liable".
[42] *National Bank of New Zealand v Ward* [1882] N.Z.L.R. 1 at 51, CA. For this reason, the right of subrogation should be available in respect of a bare statutory guarantee given by government under legislation.
[43] *Craythorne v Swinburne* (1807) 14 Ves. Jun. 160 at 162; 33 E.R. 482 at 483; *Aldrich v Cooper* (1803) 8 Ves. Jun. 382 at 389; 32 ER 402 at 405; *Duncan, Fox & Co v North and South Wales Bank* (1880) 6 App. Cas. 1 at 12, 19; *Parsons v Briddock* (1708) 2 Vern. 608; 23 E.R. 997; *Wright v Morley* (1805) 11 Ves. Jun. 12 at 22–23; 32 E.R. 992 at 995–996.
[44] *Story's Equity Jurisprudence* (1st English ed., 1884), art.493, p.315, quoted with approval in *Commissioners of State Savings Bank of Victoria v Patrick Intermarine Acceptances Ltd (in liq)* [1981] 1 N.S.W.L.R. 175 at 179 *per* Meares J. It appears likely that subrogation in the context of guarantees will be justified in terms of unjust enrichment. See *Banque Financière de la Cité v Park (Battersea) Ltd* [1998] 2 W.L.R. 475, HL, where Lord Hoffmann explained that a lender who advances money to a borrower to pay off a secured debt is entitled to be subrogated to the original creditor's securities on grounds of unjust enrichment. See also *Registrar-General v Gill* (unreported, NSW CA, August 16, 1994) and *Boscawen v Bajwa*

(iii) **Exclusion or waiver of subrogation**

While the right of subrogation exists independently of contract, it can, of **12–260** course, be excluded or curtailed by an express provision or an implied term in the contract of guarantee.[45] The guarantor therefore, can bargain the right of subrogation away, but it cannot be excluded by an agreement between the principal debtor and the creditor that the guarantor will not be entitled to the securities held for the principal debt.[46] To exclude the right of subrogation, the guarantee must be explicit.[47] In *Equity Trustees Agency etc v New Zealand Loan & Mercantile Agency Co Ltd*[48] the following provision in the guarantee was not enough to waive the guarantor's right of subrogation:

"[Y]ou shall be at liberty to act as though I were the principal debtor and I hereby waive in your favour all and any of my rights as surety (legal, equitable, statutory or otherwise) which may at any time be inconsistent with any of the above provisions."[49]

Nor will a provision stating that the guarantee is in addition to other securities exclude a guarantor's right of subrogation.[50]

On the other hand, the High Court of Australia in *O'Day v Commercial Bank of Australia Ltd*[51] held that the following clause effectively disentitled the guarantor to any interest in, and to any rights in respect of, the securities held for the principal debt by way of subrogation or otherwise:

"this guarantee shall be considered to be in addition to any other guarantee or security either from the guarantors or any other person or company which the bank now has or may hereafter take for the debts of the company and that *the guarantors will not in any way claim the benefit or seek the transfer of any other security or any part thereof*' (emphasis added).

[1995] 4 All E.R. 769 at 777. With respect, it is preferable to base subrogation on equitable principles rather than the ambiguous concept of unjust enrichment. *Cf. Banque Financière de la Cité v Parc (Battersea) Ltd* [1999] 1 A.C. 221.

[45] *Liberty Mutual Insurance Co Ltd v HSBC Bank plc* [2001] Lloyd's Rep. 224 (on appeal, see [2002] EWCA Civ. 691). See *Morris v Ford Motor Co Ltd* [1973] 2 All E.R. 1084 (an indemnity case where similar principles were applied); *O'Day v Commercial Bank of Australia Ltd* (1933) 50 C.L.R. 200 at 213 *per* Rich J., 220 *per* Dixon J, 223 *per* McTiernan J. See also *Equity Trustees Executors & Agency Co Ltd v New Zealand Loan & Mercantile Agency Co Ltd* [1940] V.L.R. 201 at 207; *Midland Banking Corp v Chambers* (1869) 4 Ch. App. 398; *Ex p. National Provincial Bank* (1881) 17 Ch. D. 98. Contrast *Re Manawatu Transport Ltd* (1984) 2 N.Z.C.L.C. 99,084, which suggests that guarantors cannot validly waive rights of subrogation that would benefit the unsecured creditors or shareholders of a company.

[46] *Cf. Steel v Dixon* (1881) 17 Ch. D. 825.

[47] *Liberty Mutual Insurance Co Ltd v HSBC Bank plc* [2001] Lloyd's Rep. 224 (on appeal [2002] EWCA Civ. 691, discussed below, para.12–270). See also *Re Butler's Wharf Ltd* [1995] 2 B.C.L.C. 43.

[48] [1940] V.L.R. 201.

[49] See also *Re Kirkwood's Estate* (1878) 1 L.R. Ir. 108.

[50] *Re Butler's Wharf Ltd* [1995] 2 B.C.L.C. 43.

[51] (1933) 50 C.L.R. 200.

12–261   It appears that such a provision can also exclude the guarantor's statutory right of subrogation.[52] A person may by express contract or stipulation exclude a right conferred upon that person for his own benefit,[53] but may not waive a right in which the public has an interest.[54] As the public has no interest in a guarantor's statutory right of subrogation, it may be renounced or relinquished by an express provision in the guarantee.[55]

12–262   Clauses in a guarantee or third party mortgage intended to exclude the right of subrogation until the creditor receives payment in full will not necessarily achieve this result where the creditor acts in a way that materially prejudices the guarantor's position. In *Lloyds TSB Bank plc v Shorney*[56] Mr Shorney gave the bank a guarantee to secure the running account of a company up to £150,000. As security for Mr Shorney's liabilities as a guarantor, he and his wife gave the bank a mortgage over their residence.

12–263   Clause 21 of the mortgage relevantly provided:

> "Until all money and liabilities and other sums due owing or incurred by the [Company] to the bank shall have been paid or discharged in full notwithstanding payout in whole or in part of any sum recoverable from the Mortgagor hereunder or any purported release or cancellation hereof the Mortgagor shall not by virtue of such payment or by any other means or any other ground (save as hereunder provided): . . .
>
> (d) be entitled to claim or have the benefit of any security or guarantee now or hereafter held by the bank for any money or liabilities or other sums due or incurred by the customer to the bank or to have any share therein."

12–264   Mr Shorney later executed further guarantees of the company's liabilities, thereby increasing his liabilities to the bank to the sum of £290,000. Mrs Shorney was not informed of these further guarantees. When the company defaulted, the bank obtained a judgment against Mr Shorney for approximately £252,900. The bank then instituted proceedings

---

[52] *Johnson v Australian Guarantee Corp Ltd* (1992) 59 S.A.S.R. 382; *Drummond v National Australia Bank Ltd* (1997) 7 B.P.R. 14, 985; *Austin v Royal* (1999) 47 N.S.W.L.R. 27. In *O'Day v Commercial Bank of Australia Ltd* (1933) 50 C.L.R. 200, the High Court of Australia held that the surety's right of subrogation was excluded by the terms of his guarantee and the court did not consider whether such an exclusion was prevented by the predecessor of the Supreme Court Act 1958 (Vic), s.72.

[53] *Rumsey v North Eastern Railway Co* (1863) 14 C.B. (NS) 641 at 649; 143 E.R. 596 at 600; *Rowbotham v Wilson* (1857) 8 E. & B. 123 at 151; 120 E.R. 45 at 56; *Morten v Marshall* (1863) 2 H. & C. 305 at 309; 159 E.R. 127 at 128. These cases are merely illustrations of the Latin maxim: quilibet potest renunciare juri pro se introducto (anyone may, at his pleasure, renounce the benefit of a stipulation or other right introduced entirely in his favour).

[54] *Equitable Life Assurance of the United States v Bogie* (1905) 3 C.L.R. 878 at 897; *Graham v Ingleby* (1848) 1 Exch. 651 at 656; 154 E.R. 277 at 279. See also *Caltex Oil (Aust) Pty Ltd v Best* (1990) 170 C.L.R. 516; *Felton v Mulligan* (1971) 124 C.L.R. 367 at 377, 390.

[55] In *Johnson v Australian Guarantee Corp Ltd* (1992) 59 S.A.S.R. 382, a case on s.17 of the Mercantile Law Act 1936 (SA), the South Australian Supreme Court reluctantly agreed with these propositions.

[56] [2001] EWCA 1161.

against Mr and Mrs Shorney to enforce the mortgage. A suspended possession order was made by consent. Some months later the bank sought to enforce its judgment against Mr Shorney by obtaining a charging order absolute in respect of his interest in the matrimonial home.

When the Shorneys settled some other litigation against their financial **12–265** advisers in relation to a failed business venture, £210,000 was paid to the bank on terms that £150,000 be applied to discharge Mr Shorney's indebtedness secured by the mortgage and £60,000 in reduction of Mr Shorney's liabilities to the bank as a guarantor of the company's debts. It was common ground that the £210,000 were almost exclusively funds of Mrs Shorney.

In essence, the issue for the court was whether an order should be made **12–266** for the sale of the property. This depended on whether the bank's charging order prevailed over the charge that Mrs Shorney obtained by subrogation when her funds were used to discharge Mr Shorney's indebtedness to the bank.

The court found the replacement of Mr Shorney's original guarantee for **12–267** £150,000 with further guarantees for £290,000 meant that the principal transaction was materially different from that which the joint mortgage was intended to secure. An increase in Mr Shorney's liabilities was not within Mrs Shorney's contemplation as a third party mortgagor and there was nothing in the mortgage that allowed the bank to prejudice Mrs Shorney's position by taking further guarantees from her husband. In the absence of Mrs Shorney's consent, this additional liability was not included in the scope of the bank's charging order. Accordingly, Mrs Shorney's charge took priority over the bank and the bank was not entitled to an order for the sale of the property. This case will prompt drafters to review clauses in guarantees that attempt to preserve the liability of the guarantor where the creditor's dealings with the principal debtor adversely affect the guarantor.

Where the assets of a group of companies which have provided **12–268** debentures and cross-guarantees are realised by their respective receivers, it is not open to the receivers to waive the rights of subrogation which some of these companies enjoy as sureties, as this may prejudice the unsecured creditors and shareholders of those companies.[57] It is different, of course, where the doctrine of marshalling applies, but this requires a common debtor or a group of common debtors.

A guarantor may be guilty of conduct which makes it unjust or **12–269** inequitable for that guarantor to assert the right of subrogation.[58] This highlights the equitable basis of the doctrine. But a guarantor will not be taken to have waived or forfeited the right of subrogation simply because a stranger makes payments in reduction of the principal debt.[59] Moreover,

---

[57] *Re Manawatu Transport Ltd* (1984) 2 N.Z.C.L.C. 99,084.
[58] *Equity Trustees Executors & Agency Co Ltd v New Zealand Loan & Mercantile Agency Co Ltd* [1940] V.L.R. 201 at 207. See also *Morris v Ford Motor Co* [1973] 2 All E.R. 1084. A surety may also impliedly waive his right of subrogation by his own conduct: *Brandon v Brandon* (1869) L.R. 4 Ch. App. 398.
[59] See *Heyman v Dubois* (1871) L.R. 13 Eq. 158; *Re Arcedeckne*; *Atkins v Arcedeckne* (1883) 24 Ch. D. 709.

where the guarantor takes a mortgage or charge from the principal debtor by way of counter-indemnity, this is unlikely to constitute a waiver of the guarantor's right of subrogation in respect of the creditor's securities.[60]

12–270   Clear words are also required to postpone the right of subrogation. The issue of whether or not the right of subrogation is postponed is of particular importance in the case of what have been called "partially overlapping securities". An illustration is *Liberty Mutual Insurance Co (UK) Ltd v HSBC Bank Plc*[61] A bank provided admiralty bonds at the request of its customer (the Ocean Marine Mutual Insurance Association Ltd, called "Omnia") to claimants who had arrested, or threatened to arrest, its members' vessels in various parts of the world in respect of maritime claims arising out of the carriage of goods or collisions (the bonds providing security in place of the arrested vessel). The bank held a fixed charge from "Omnia" covering both the bank's claims to be indemnified by "Omnia" against the bank's losses arising out of its engagements in respect of the admiralty bonds *and* the bank's other general claims against "Omnia". Additionally the bank was the beneficiary of a bond from a third party (Liberty Mutual Insurance Co (UK) Ltd, called "Liberty") which indemnified the bank but only against liabilities and losses it might sustain by reason of it having executed the admiralty bonds. Hence there existed "partially overlapping" securities. The third paragraph of the bond stated that:

> "This Agreement is separate from any other securities or right of indemnity taken in respect of the Guarantee from any person, including your above-mentioned customer."

12–271   "Liberty" argued that, to the extent that it had discharged by payment any of its bonds given to the bank, it was entitled to be subrogated to the bank's security under its fixed charge *pari passu* with the bank's claims against Omnia. The bank's case, on the other hand, was that the third paragraph of the bond (set out above) operated to postpone Liberty's right of subrogation until it had utilised the fixed security to obtain a complete indemnity in respect of losses for which it had no indemnity from Liberty (*i.e.* those losses not arising from the bank having executed the admiralty bonds).[62] The Court of Appeal[63] held that the third paragraph of the bond was not sufficiently clear to postpone the right of subrogation, for a number of reasons,[64] *inter alia*:

---

[60] *Cf. Cooper v Jenkins* (1863) 32 Beav. 337; 55 E.R. 132 and *Rowlatt on Principal and Surety* (5th ed., 1999), para.7.43. This is true, *a fortiori*, where the sureties were not aware of the existence of the creditor's securities at the time they took their security: *Lake v Brutton* (1856) 8 De G.M. & G. 440 at 451–452; 44 E.R. 460 at 464–465.

[61] [2002] EWCA Civ 691.

[62] The bank accepted that in the case of "totally overlapping securities" (*i.e.* securities covering the same claims) the clause would not affect the surety's right of subrogation. (see cl.25).

[63] The leading judgment is given by Rix L.J.

[64] See especially paras 59–70.

(a) The clause neither expressly mentioned subrogation nor the concept of postponement. Indeed, the concept of postponement of a security was not necessarily synonymous with separation of the security, since the concept of postponement does not insist upon a complete separation; it allowed the surety to share in the security, but only after the creditor had satisfied himself completely in respect of the *other* debts.[65]

(b) The clause focused upon the separateness of surety bond ("This agreement is separate from any other securities or right of indemnity" taken "in respect of the guarantee"), thus emphasising the separateness of the bond itself, not the separateness of any other security or indemnity.

(c) The clause was wide enough to embrace a personal right of indemnity as well as secured rights, and this would lead to "odd results"[66] if it was interpreted as postponing the right of subrogation. For example, in an insolvency situation, even in the absence of a fixed charge, Liberty's right to share rateably in the bank's dividend in the liquidation would be postponed until the bank had a complete indemnity.

(d) Other clauses could have been utilised, which would have been more appropriate to postpone the right of subrogation (*e.g.* the surety will have no right of subrogation "unless and until the whole of such principal moneys and interest shall have first been completely discharged and satisfied").

(e) The clause could realistically be interpreted as emphasising other rights of the bank, for example, that the rights afforded by the bond could be exercised separately from any other security or right in respect of the guaranteed debt; or, where a bond is taken as part of a package of securities, to make it clear that each security is independent; or to protect the bank against arguments that the surety is not discharged by the release of the debtor or by the debtor being given time to pay.[67]

(iv) When is subrogation available?

The equitable right of subrogation only arises when the creditor is paid **12–272** in full,[68] although it is not necessary for the guarantor claiming the right to

---

[65] See para.62.
[66] See para.61.
[67] Although it may be doubted whether the clause would be sufficiently specific for this purpose.
[68] *Duncan, Fox & Co v North and South Wales Bank* (1880) 6 App. Cas. 1; *Globe & Rutgers Fire Insurance Co v Truedel* [1927] 2 D.L.R. 659; *Ex p. Brett*; *Re Howe* (1871) 6 Ch App 838 at 841, CA; *Dixon v Steel* [1901] 2 Ch. 602 at 607 per Cozens-Hardy J. This is equally true of the statutory remedy provided by s.5 of the Mercantile Law Amendment Act 1856: see below, paras 12–274 to 12–275. There will be no right of subrogation unless the surety's right of

THE RIGHTS OF THE PARTIES

have discharged the whole of the principal debt himself: subrogation is available even if part of the debt was paid by the principal debtor or another guarantor.[69] A guarantor who claims a right of subrogation must, however, have paid an amount in reduction or liquidation of the principal debt.[70]

12–273   Once the creditor has been fully paid, a guarantor is entitled to share in the securities to the extent of that guarantor's payment of the debt.[71] In the absence of a contrary provision in the guarantee, a surety who guarantees merely part of the principal debt is, upon payment of that amount, entitled to a proportionate part of the securities held for the debt.[72] Such a surety is entitled to participate pro tanto in the benefit of the securities held by the creditor. But where, as is usually the case, there is a guarantee of the whole debt with a limitation on the amount of the guarantor's liability, the guarantor is not entitled to any securities upon payment of that limited amount.[73] Nor is the guarantor entitled to a transfer of a proportionate interest in the creditor's securities equivalent to the share of the principal

---

contribution or indemnity existed at the time of payment of the principal debt or immediately thereafter: *Scholefield Goodman & Sons Ltd v Zyngier* [1984] V.R. 445, affirmed on other grounds in (1985) 59 A.L.J.R. 770, PC. Subrogation is not, of course, confined to guarantors. Where a debtor borrows money to pay off a secured debt, the lender may in certain circumstances be subrogated to the security of the creditor whose debt was discharged: *State Bank of South Australia v Rothschild Australian Ltd* (1990) 8 A.C.L.C. 925. In this area subrogation is not based on contract, as in insurance cases, but on unjust enrichment: *Banque Financière de la Cité v Park (Battersea) Ltd* [1998] 2 W.L.R. 475, HL. See T. Villiers, "A Path Through the Subrogation Jungle: Whose Right Is It Anyway?" (1999) L.M.C.L.Q. 223. A right of subrogation can also be acquired where the guarantor pays out a prior secured creditor: See *State Bank of South Australia v Rothschild Australia Ltd* (1990) 8 A.C.L.C. 925.
[69] *A E Goodwin Ltd (in liq) v A G Healing Ltd (in liq)* (1979) 7 A.C.L.R. 481; *Gedye v Matson* (1858) 25 Beav. 310; 53 E.R. 655; *Equity Trustees Executors & Agency Co Ltd v New Zealand Loan & Mercantile Agency Co Ltd* [1940] V.L.R. 201 at 207, *per* Lowe J.; *McColl's Wholesale Pty Ltd v State Bank (NSW)* [1984] 3 N.S.W.L.R. 365; *Raffle v AGC (Advances) Ltd* [1989] A.S.C. 58,528. A surety's statutory right of subrogation is not available unless the whole principal debt is paid: see *Bayley v Gibsons Ltd* (1993) 1 Tas. R. 385, although it is not necessary for the surety to pay the whole debt himself. A surety's right to subrogation is not affected by payments made by strangers: *Heyman v Dubois* (1871) L.R. 13 Eq. 158; *Re Arcedeckne, Atkins v Arcedeckne* (1883) 24 Ch. D. 709 and *A E Goodwin Ltd v AG Healing Ltd* (1982) 7 A.C.L.R. 481 at 487.
[70] See *Equity Trustees Executors & Agency Co Ltd v New Zealand Loan & Mercantile Agency Co Ltd* [1940] V.L.R. 201 at 207. The mere admission of a proof in the bankruptcy or liquidation of the guarantor is not the equivalent of payment. See *Ewart v Latta* (1865) 4 Macq. 983; *Re Fothergill; Ex p. Turquand* (1876) 3 Ch. D. 445. *Cf. Re Howe; Ex p. Brett* (1871) 6 Ch. App. 838. But the payment of a dividend on the creditor's proof would entitle the trustee in bankruptcy or the liquidator of the surety to a claim on the creditor's securities to enforce the surety's right of indemnity once the creditor had been paid in full: *Ewart v Latta* (1865) 4 Macq. 983.
[71] *Gedye v Matson* (1858) 25 Beav. 310 at 312; 53 E.R. 655 at 656 *per* Romilly M.R. *Duncan, Fox & Co v North & South Wales Bank* (1880) 6 App. Cas. 1 at 12. Where the creditor agrees to compromise the principal debt, in return for the payment of a lesser amount by the guarantor, the guarantor's right of recoupment through subrogation will be limited to the amount actually paid: See *Reed v Norris* (1837) 2 My. & Cr. 361; 40 E.R. 678; *Ex p. Rushworth* (1805) 10 Ves. 409; 32 E.R. 903; *Butcher v Churchill* (1808) 14 Ves. Jun. 567; 33 E.R. 638; and the proviso to s.5 of the Mercantile Law Amendment Act 1856.
[72] *Ward v National Bank of New Zealand Ltd* (1889) 8 N.Z.L.R. 10; *Re Butler's Wharf Ltd* [1995] 2 B.C.L.C. 43; *Goodwin v Gray* (1874) 22 W.R. 312; *Hobson v Bass* (1871) L.R. 6 Ch. App. 792 at 794: see above, paras 5–35 to 5–40. See also *Wade v Coope* (1827) 2 Sim. 155; 57 E.R. 747.
[73] *Re Sass* [1896] 2 Q.B. 12; *Re Howe* (1871) L.R. 6 Ch. App. 838 at 841; *Austin v Royal* (1999) 47 N.S.W.L.R. 27. *cf. Re Fothergill; Ex p. Turquand* (1876) 3 Ch. D. 445. A guarantor may,

762

debt paid by the guarantor. Hence, a guarantor of 25 per cent of the principal debt will not, upon payment of that share, be entitled to a transfer of 25 per cent of the creditor's securities as a tenant in common.[74] But that guarantor may be entitled to a declaration that, upon payment of his share in the principal debt, he will be entitled to a proportionate interest in the *proceeds* of realisation of the creditor's securities.[75] The guarantee itself often reinforces this conclusion by providing that there shall be no subrogation until the principal debt is paid in full.

The statutory right of subrogation conferred by the Mercantile Law Amendment Act 1856 is available to a surety who has paid the entire amount which that surety can be called upon to pay under the guarantee, provided that the whole of the principal debt has been paid.[76] The words "the debt" in the statutory provision do not require the surety to pay the whole of the principal debt himself.[77] In *Bayley v Gibsons Ltd*,[78] Zeeman J. declared that the statutory right of subrogation was available to guarantors who paid the full amount of their limited liability before the balance of the principal debt was repaid through the realisation of the creditor's securities. Accordingly, the creditor's registered mortgage debenture was preserved for the benefit of the guarantors by force of the statute even though the creditor had been paid the secured moneys in full. Where the creditor's security takes the form of a registered mortgage which is released when the creditor exercises a power of sale personally or through a receiver and manager, the doctrine of subrogation does not artificially preserve that security, but the guarantors can hold the creditor accountable for the proceeds of sale.[79]

In *Bayley v Gibsons Ltd*[80] Zeeman J. left open the question as to **12–274** whether a surety who pays only part of what he is obliged to pay under the guarantee is entitled to the statutory right of subrogation. It is submitted that the statutory right of subrogation should also be available in this situation as long as the creditor is paid in full by the guarantor and another source. Subrogation should be available to recover, by way of indemnity from the principal debtor, *any amount* paid in reduction of the principal debt and any amount which ultimately proves to be more than the guarantor's common liability shared by the co-sureties. It should not be available, however, until the principal debt is paid in full from a source or

---

however, have a claim against a creditor or a co-surety if securities held by them for the principal debt are lost or impaired: see below, paras 12–335 to 12–336.
[74] *Challenge Bank Ltd v Mailman* (unreported, NSW CA, May 14, 1993).
[75] *ibid.*
[76] There is authority to the effect that a guarantor will not be entitled to any right of subrogation unless he has satisfied the liability of the principal debtor, even if the guarantor has paid up to the limit of his liability under the guarantee: *Re Howe, Ex p. Brett* (1871) 6 Ch. App. 838 at 841 *per* Mellish L.J. Contrast *A E Goodwin Ltd v A G Healing Ltd* (1979) 7 A.C.L.R 481 at 487 and *Bayley v Gibsons Ltd* [1993] 1 Tas. R. 385 at 400–401 *per* Zeeman J.
[77] See *A E Goodwin Ltd (In Liq) v A G Healing Ltd (In Liq)* (1979) 7 A.C.L.R. 481 at 487; *McColl's Wholesale Pty Ltd v State Bank of New South Wales* (1984) 3 N.S.W.L.R. 365 at 378–379; *Russet Pty Ltd (in liq) v Bach* (unreported, NSW Sup Ct, Young J., June 23, 1988); *The Equity Trustees Executors and Agency Co Ltd v NZ Loan and Mercantile Agency Co Ltd* [1940] V.L.R. 201 at 207.
[78] (1993) 1 Tas. R. 385.
[79] *Re Sass* [1896] 2 Q.B. 12.
[80] (1993) Tas. R. 385.

sources that include the guarantor. As Cohen J. observed in *State Bank of New South Wales v Geeport Developments Pty Ltd*,[81] "[i]t may well be that the right to exercise that subrogation may not come into existence until the whole of the debt has been paid, whether by the principal debtor or another person so that the right until then remains dormant. This however seems more a matter of enforcement rather than a question of rights which exist".[82]

12–275 The discharge of a creditor's security at law is certainly not a bar to subrogation in equity; indeed it is a precondition of the remedy of subrogation.[83] Hence, the Mercantile Law Amendment Act 1856 was merely intended to confirm this principle and provide legal redress to paying guarantors who were having difficulties exercising their right of subrogation.

12–276 A sub-surety is, upon payment, entitled to be subrogated to the rights of the creditor against the co-sureties in prior degree.[84] In other words, a surety for a surety is entitled to contributive subrogation only against a co-surety of the principal surety.[85] Conversely, where a surety pays out the principal debt, that surety has no right of subrogation in respect of securities which the creditor has taken from a sub-surety since subrogation is intended to assist a surety to obtain contribution from the *co-sureties*, not the sub-sureties.[86]

12–277 Subrogation is also available to a person who charges his property for the debt of another. Accordingly, the chargor is entitled to the benefit of any securities held by the creditor over the property of the debtor and can require that the debt be discharged out of the debtor's property covered by such securities.[87] The principle of subrogation even enables an indorser who is only secondarily liable but who pays on a bill of exchange to be subrogated to the benefit of a security taken by another indorser who was secondarily liable and who took that security against the contingent liability of having to pay out on the bill.[88]

12–278 Where a wife mortgages her interest in the matrimonial home to secure a limited amount of her husband's liabilities under specific guarantees, she will be subrogated to the creditor's securities to that extent when the property is sold and the proceeds applied in reduction of the secured

---

[81] (1991) 5 B.P.R. 11,947.

[82] *ibid.*, at 11,953–1,954. See also *Patten v Bond* (1889) 60 L.T. 583; *Chetwynd v Allen* [1899] 1 Ch. 353; *Burston Finance Ltd v Speirway Ltd (in liq)* [1974] 1 W.L.R. 1648 at 1652 and C. Mitchell, "Subrogation and Part Payment of Another's Debt" (1998) L.M.C.L.Q. 14.

[83] *Boscawen v Bajwa* [1996] 1 W.L.R. 328. See also *D & J Fowler (Australia) Ltd v Bank of New South Wales* [1982] 2 N.S.W.L.R. 879 at 887.

[84] *Standard Brands Ltd v Fox* (1974) 44 D.L.R. (3d) 69; *Fox v Royal Bank of Canada* (1975) 59 D.L.R. (3d) 258.

[85] *Crow v Murphy* 12 B. Mon. 444 (Ky 1851), cited in S.I. Langmaid, "Some Recent Subrogation Problems in the Law of Suretyship and Insurance" (1934) 47 Harv. L.R. 976 at 995.

[86] *Raffle v AGC (Advances) Ltd* [1989] A.S.C. 58,528.

[87] See *Dixon v Steel* [1901] 2 Ch. 602; *Re Marley* [1976] 1 W.L.R. 952, DC. As to the rights of marshalling in this situation, see *Smith v Wood* [1929] 1 Ch. 14.

[88] *Commissioners of State Savings Bank of Victoria v Patrick Intermarine Acceptances Ltd (in liq)* [1981] 1 N.S.W.L.R. 175. See also *Maxal Nominees Pty Ltd v Dalgety Ltd* [1985] 1 Qd. R. 51.

debt.[89] She is entitled to have these securities kept alive for her benefit even if the husband's liabilities to the creditor have been increased by his execution of further guarantees and even if there is a clause in the wife's mortgage stating that she may not claim the benefit of any security held by the creditor until it is paid in full. Equity will not allow the creditor to rely on this type of clause to justify increasing the husband's liabilities beyond those contemplated by his wife without her consent because this would prejudice her rights on indemnity against her husband.[90]

Co-debtors can change their relationship inter se by agreement.[91] If one co-debtor constitutes himself guarantor for the others by express agreement or otherwise, that co-debtor will, upon giving notice to the creditor of this change, be entitled on payment to a right of subrogation in respect of any securities held by the creditor for the principal debt.[92] While it is necessary to inform the creditor of such an agreement between the debtors, it is sufficient for the creditor to be notified after the principal transaction has been effected.[93] Conversely, where one guarantor assumes the primary liability as between himself and a co-surety, that co-surety will be entitled by subrogation to the securities and remedies of the creditor upon payment of the principal debt.[94]

The remedy of subrogation applies equally in situations which are **12–279** analogous to suretyship. Consequently, where a party to a mortgage is bound as between himself and the mortgagee to pay on the default of the mortgagor arrears of taxes to prevent a sale of the land, that party is entitled to a form of subrogation: the party can require the mortgagee to allow him to use the mortgagee's name in a suit against the mortgagor to enforce payment of the amount of the arrears.[95]

But guarantors who have given a performance bond to support a **12–280** construction contract have no legal right on the default of the contractor to take possession of the construction site and to complete the work. There is, therefore, no general principle that, upon the default of the principal, a guarantor is entitled immediately to discharge the principal obligation and to this end to put himself in the place of the person primarily liable under the principal obligation. The guarantor's proper course is to discharge his

---

[89] *Lloyds TSB Bank plc v Shorney* [2001] EWCA Civ 1161.

[90] *ibid.*

[91] The change in the status and relationship of the parties can arise by inference from the circumstances or by express agreement: *Re Marley* [1976] 1 W.L.R. 952, DC ; *Re Pittoriou (a bankrupt) Ex p. Trustee of the Property of the Bankrupt* [1985] 1 W.L.R. 58. See also above, paras 1–29 to 1–30.

[92] *Duncan, Fox & Co v North and South Wales Bank* (1880) 6 App. Cas. 1 at 12. See also *Re Marley* [1976] 1 W.L.R. 952, DC.

[93] *Rouse v Bradford Banking Co* [1894] A.C. 586.

[94] *Parsons v Briddock* (1708) 2 Vern. 608; 23 E.R. 997, approved in *Wright v Morley* (1805) 18 Ves. 12 at 22–23; 32 E.R. 992 at 995–996. *Cf. Hodgson v Shaw* (1834) 3 My. & K. 189; 40 E.R. 70; and *Armitage v Baldwin* (1842) 5 Beav. 278 which cast doubt upon *Parsons v Briddock* (1708) 2 Vern. 608; 23 E.R. 997, although the objections to the case appear to be based on the proposition that there was no right to the securities–an argument that is no longer tenable in the light of s.5 of the Mercantile Law Amendment Act 1856. See *Rowlatt on Principal and Surety* (5th ed., 1999), p.158.

[95] *Harris v Carnegie* [1933] 4 D.L.R. 760.

secondary liability and then sue the principal for an indemnity[96] or the co-sureties for contribution. As Edwards J. pointed out in *Slowey v Lodder*:[97]

> "The surety for payment of a debt, it is true, may insist upon paying the debt, but he has this right *not as a right to substitute himself for and to claim the rights of the person primarily liable upon the obligation*, as against the creditor, but as a right necessarily incident to his right to put himself in the place of and to acquire the rights of the creditor against the principal debtor."[98]

12–281   Payment of the whole principal debt or discharge of the principal obligation is a condition precedent to the remedy of subrogation. The ordinary principles which regulate payment between debtor and creditor will determine whether the principal debt has been paid in full.[99] These principles are dealt with in Chapter 6 in the section dealing with appropriation.[1]

12–282   Apart from statute, subrogation might not be available where the guarantor officiously assumes the burdens of suretyship without any request by the principal debtor to do so and then pays the principal debt. The guarantor has no contractual right of indemnity in this situation[2] and may be denied an equitable right of subrogation unless his payment to the creditor discharges the principal debt.[3] A debt can only be discharged in this situation with the consent or subsequent ratification of the debtor.[4] Generally, the debtor will accept the guarantor's payment as discharging his debt, and therefore, it may be argued that the guarantor should be entitled to a right of subrogation in this situation. But is it consistent for equity to deny the guarantor a right of indemnity where the guarantor has officiously undertaken the obligations of suretyship and yet allow that guarantor a right of subrogation upon payment of the principal debt?[5] After all, the right of indemnity and the right of subrogation are, in theory, based on the same equity.[6] Even if there may be some difficulty in

---

[96] *Slowey v Lodder* (1901) 20 N.Z.L.R. 321 at 337. See also *Purcell v Raphael* (1867) 7 S.C.R. (NSW) 138. *Cf. Crown Lumber Co Ltd v Smythe* [1923] 3 D.L.R. 933, approved in *Royal Bank of Canada v Wilson* (1963) 41 W.W.R. 465, where the Appellate Division of the Supreme Court of Alberta held that sureties who complete a building contract abandoned by the contractor are entitled to reimburse themselves out of the moneys owing by the owner. See also *Employers Liability Assurance Corp Ltd v The Queen* [1968] 2 Ex. C.R. 246.

[97] (1900) 20 N.Z.L.R. 321.

[98] *ibid.*, at 337. Emphasis added.

[99] *Equity Trustees Executors & Agency Co Ltd v New Zealand Loan & Mercantile Agency Co Ltd* [1940] V.L.R. 201 at 205.

[1] See above, paras 6–16 to 6–52.

[2] See *Owen v Tate* [1976] 1 Q.B. 402, CA.

[3] See R. Goff and G. Jones, *The Law of Restitution* (6th ed., 2002), para.3–027 and P. Birks J. Beatson, "Unrequested Payment of Another's Debt" (1976) 92 L.Q.R. 188.

[4] R. Goff and G. Jones, *The Law of Restitution* (6th ed., 2002), para.1–018, n.17.

[5] See T.D. Putnam, *Suretyship* (1981), p.85. See also above, paras 12–01 to 12–05.

[6] See *Yonge v Reynell* (1852) 9 Hare 809 at 818; 68 E.R. 744 at 748; *Nicholas v Ridley* [1904] 1 Ch. 192. It might be different if the doctrine of subrogation were founded on a concept of unjust enrichment. There is some merit in this view since the creditor should not be entitled to retain the surety's payment and still recover from the principal debtor without acknowledging the surety's right to be subrogated to the creditor's rights and remedies to prevent unjust enrichment: see generally R. Goff and G. Jones, *The Law of Restitution* (6th ed. 2002), para.3–

invoking a right of subrogation in equity in this situation, there should be no problem where the guarantor relies upon the statutory right of subrogation. Under the statute, it is enough that the guarantor, being liable with another for a debt or duty, pays the debt or performs the duty. It is immaterial that the guarantor was officious in making the payment or that the principal debtor did not accept the payment. So in this situation it is advisable for the guarantors to invoke the statutory right of subrogation.

Where the creditor's remedies against co-guarantors arose under a deed, **12–283** a guarantor's claim to enforce those remedies by *subrogation* is, or is analogous to, a "cause of action founded on a deed" and, hence, a limitation period of 12 years applies.[7] This is so even if the paying guarantor's claim to contribution against the co-guarantors was statute-barred after six years.[8] The right of subrogation, in this instance, is similar to a specialty debt which carries a longer limitation period.

(v) Subrogation and negotiable instruments

Rights of subrogation can arise in the context of negotiable instruments. **12–284** A guarantee can be incorporated in the instrument itself or it may be embodied in a separate document.[9] Moreover, negotiable instruments create a chain of liability under which one party is primarily liable as acceptor or maker and other parties, such as drawers and indorsers, are treated as quasi-sureties for the primary obligors. Among themselves, however, those quasi-sureties are not co-sureties.[10] A series of Australian cases has examined the rights of subrogation in this context. For present purposes, the central question in all these cases is whether the claimants were entitled to enforce their right of contribution through subrogation.

In the first case, *D & J Fowler (Aust) Ltd v Bank of New South Wales*,[11] **12–285** the plaintiffs, as drawers of bills of exchange, paid the bank as holder of the bills when they were dishonoured upon presentment to the acceptor, Tramore Pty Ltd (Tramore). The issue was whether the plaintiffs were entitled by subrogation to the bank's rights under certain mortgages and guarantees held from Tramore and certain other parties who had covenanted to pay the bank upon demand. It was not necessary for Helsham C.J. to decide whether the plaintiffs were sureties within s.8A of the Usury Bills of Lading and Written Memoranda Act 1902 (NSW); it was sufficient that they were persons "being liable with another" for the debt to the bank within the meaning of the section. His Honour held that the plaintiffs were entitled to the securities provided to the bank by the principal debtor, Tramore, as well as the other parties as co-sureties. It was

---

008 ("subrogation should be permitted only so far as it is necessary to enable a claimant to recover the loss he has suffered"); Low Kee Yang, *The Law of Guarantees in Singapore and Malaysia* (1992), pp.231–232.

[7] See, *e.g.* Limitation Act 1980, s.8; *Lang v Le Boursicot* (1993) 5 B.P.R. 97,406 at 11,786.

[8] *Lang v Le Boursicot* (1993) 5 BPR 97,406.

[9] See above, paras 1–53 and 1–54.

[10] See above, paras 1–43 to 1–52.

[11] [1982] 2 N.S.W.L.R. 879.

immaterial that no demands had been made under the mortgages and guarantees. While such demands were necessary to crystallise causes of action against the mortgagors and guarantors, the failure to make demands did not extinguish the third parties' liability for the debt to the bank. Hence, the plaintiffs as drawers were entitled to the benefit of the mortgages and guarantees. It is implicit in this conclusion that the third parties were liable for the bank's debt as co-debtors or as co-sureties.

12–286 In *Scholefield Goodman & Sons Ltd v Zyngier*,[12] the Victorian Full Court reached the opposite conclusion on similar facts. In that case, the plaintiff company drew bills upon Zinaldi & Co Pty Ltd (Zinaldi) which were accepted by Zinaldi and negotiated to a bank to finance the import of goods by Zinaldi. The bills of exchange accepted by Zinaldi were delivered to and discounted by the bank, the discounted value being paid to Zinaldi. To secure Zinaldi's future indebtedness to the bank, Zyngier had given a mortgage over certain land. In this mortgage, Zyngier agreed to pay the bank the balance for the time being owing on her own current account and on Zinaldi's current account, and all other sums owing by her or by Zinaldi, including any sums owing in respect of bills of exchange discounted by the bank.

12–287 Zinaldi dishonoured all the bills presented by the bank on their maturity dates, but the bills were paid when the bank presented them to the plaintiff company as drawer.

12–288 The bank called upon Zyngier under her mortgage to discharge Zinaldi's overdraft of around $20,000. Zyngier paid off the overdraft and sought a discharge of her mortgage. The bank replied that it was unable to discharge the mortgage because the plaintiff company was claiming equal contribution from Zyngier as a co-surety in respect of the amount paid by the plaintiff company on the dishonoured bills.

12–289 The Victorian Full Court held that the plaintiff company and Zyngier were not co-sureties so that the plaintiff company was not entitled to be subrogated to the bank's mortgage over her property. It found that the parties were liable for different debts: the plaintiff company was liable merely for the amount of the dishonoured bills, whereas Zyngier was liable for Zinaldi's *total* indebtedness. Moreover, there were provisions in the mortgage which allowed the bank recourse against Zyngier if the plaintiff company failed to pay in response to a demand. This suggested that the parties were not co-sureties but rather that Zyngier was a "surety for a surety" or a "sub-surety". Hence, the plaintiff company had no right of contribution against Zyngier, nor any right to be subrogated to her mortgage either under the equitable doctrine of subrogation or under the equivalent of s.5 of the Mercantile Law Amendment Act 1856.

12–290 Faced with these two apparently conflicting decisions and a similar factual matrix, the Full Court of the Supreme Court of Queensland in *Maxal Nominees Pty Ltd v Dalgety Ltd*[13] distinguished *Scholefield Goodman & Sons Ltd v Zyngier*. In the Queensland case, the respondent drew bills of exchange on Brisbane Cap Co Pty Ltd to cover the price of

[12] [1984] V.R. 445.
[13] [1985] 1 Qd. R. 51.

goods imported by that company. The bills were accepted by the company and then negotiated by the respondent, which indorsed and delivered them to a bank. After the bills were presented to the company by the bank and dishonoured, the respondent, as drawer and indorser, paid the bank £66,831 on account of its liability on the bills. It then claimed contribution from the appellant as a co-surety, and claimed to be entitled by subrogation to the bank's mortgage over the appellant's property. The appellant had given the bank a guarantee in respect of the total indebtedness of the acceptor company, including all moneys paid or advanced in respect of any bill of exchange.

It was argued that the respondent and the appellant were not co-sureties **12–291** because they were not liable to a common demand: their liabilities as drawer and indorser, on the one hand, and guarantor, on the other, were not co-ordinate or of the same degree. This argument was based on the view that the surety was unlikely to assume a co-extensive liability on the same level with the drawers and indorsers upon bills to which it was not a party.

The Full Court of the Supreme Court of Queensland held, however, that **12–292** the respondent's liability was also only a secondary liability in the same degree: "By drawing the bills [the respondent] engaged not that it would meet those bills but simply that on due presentment they would be paid according to their tenor" and if dishonoured that "he [would] compensate the holder or any indorser who [was] compelled to pay the bills".[14]

In the result, the respondent and the appellant were held to be co- **12–293** sureties and the respondent was entitled to the bank's mortgage by subrogation.

With respect, the respondent's liability was secondary only so far as the **12–294** acceptor's primary liability was concerned. The fact that the acceptor was primarily liable and that the respondents and the appellant were secondarily liable did not necessarily establish that the appellant and the respondents were liable to a common demand for a liability of the same degree. On a bill of exchange, the acceptor is primarily liable and the drawer and the indorsers are secondarily liable but, as between themselves, the drawer is liable before the first indorser, and the first indorser is liable before the second indorser and so on. This confirms that parties can share a common principal debtor and yet not be co-sureties.

The Full Court of the Supreme Court of Queensland distinguished **12–295** *Scholefield Goodman & Sons Ltd v Zyngier* on two grounds. First, in that case the guarantee was confined to the ultimate balance due to the bank, which suggested that the guarantor was liable for the residual indebtedness after the bank had exhausted its remedies against the parties liable on the bills.[15] There was no such restriction in the present case.

It is relatively common, however, for guarantees to provide that the **12–296** guarantor shall be liable for the ultimate balance due to the creditor. This provision is intended to have the effect that the guarantee is a guarantee of the whole debt so that the creditor's right of proof in the bankruptcy or

---

[14] [1985] 1 Qd. R. 51 at 55; see s.60(1)(a) of the Bills of Exchange Act 1909 (Cth).
[15] By analogy with *Molson's Bank v Kovinsky* [1924] 4 D.L.R. 330.

liquidation of the principal debtor or a co-surety will not be compromised or restricted by the rule against double proof.[16] If it were intended to render the guarantor liable only for the ultimate amount owing to the creditor after the creditor has pursued all other parties liable for the debt, how would it apply where there were several guarantees in this form? Furthermore, the reference to the ultimate balance surely cannot mean that the guarantor is immune from suit until the creditor recovers against all other parties liable for the principal debt, as this would be inconsistent with the general principle that a creditor is not obliged to have prior recourse to the principal debtor or co-sureties before enforcing a guarantee.[17]

12–297   According to the Full Court of Queensland, the second distinguishing feature between *Scholefield Goodman & Sons Ltd v Zyngier* and *Maxal Nominees Pty Ltd v Dalgety Ltd* was that in the Victorian case the guarantor was not capable of being made liable in the capacity of guarantor in respect of the dishonoured bills of exchange as a separate item of indebtedness. Hence, the element of mutuality necessary to make her a co-surety with the drawer of the bills was absent. This conclusion involves a strained reading of the terms of Zyngier's guarantee which obliged her:

> "to pay the bank on demand the balance *for the time being* owing by Zinaldi on its account and all other sums which the bank may advance to Zinaldi or which *now or hereafter* become owing from or payable by Zinaldi for or in respect of any moneys which may be payable by Zinaldi *or* for or in respect of any bills of exchange to which Zinaldi *is or may hereafter* be a party or *is or may hereafter* be liable."[18]

This wording would appear to indicate that if, at a certain date, the only amounts owing to the bank by Zinaldi were amounts for which Zinaldi was liable under bills of exchange, then this separate item of indebtedness could be claimed under Zyngier's guarantee. Moreover, the fact that the guarantee covered indebtedness apart from the liability on the bills does not deny that *both* the guarantor and the drawers could be held liable for the dishonoured bills. In retrospect, the grounds on which the Full Court of Queensland sought to distinguish the Victorian case appear to be unsatisfactory.

12–298   The decision of the Victorian Full Court in *Scholefield Goodman & Sons Ltd v Zyngier* was affirmed by the Privy Council on appeal.[19] The Privy Council held that the drawer of a dishonoured bill of exchange who paid the discounting bank the amount of the bill on its presentation had no claim to contribution against a third party who had guaranteed the bill of exchange by providing security to the bank. The fundamental question was

---

[16] See above, paras 5–35 to 5–40 and 10–33 to 10–37, where further effects of such a clause are noted.
[17] See above, paras 10–107 to 10–109 and 11–11 to 11–28.
[18] This is a paraphrase of Zyngier's guarantee used in the Privy Council decision in *Scholefield Goodman & Sons Ltd v Zyngier* (1985) 59 A.L.J.R. 770.
[19] (1985) 59 A.L.J.R. 770.

whether upon the true construction of the contract between the bank and Zyngier she had placed herself in the position of a co-surety on the same footing as the drawer or indorser of the bill of exchange accepted by Zinaldi, or whether her liability to the bank arose only upon default by all the parties liable upon the bill of exchange. Lord Brightman, delivering the advice of their Lordships, stated that the "normal understanding"[20] when a third party such as Zyngier guaranteed a bill of exchange for the benefit of a discounting bank was that the surety guaranteed that payment would be made by one or other of the parties liable upon the bill as acceptor, drawer or indorser. His Lordship continued:

> "It will not be the normal understanding that the surety intends to place himself on a level with the drawer, so as to be answerable equally with the drawer if the acceptor defaults. There is no reason why he should. There is no reason to suppose that, in a contract between the bank and the surety, the surety desires to confer a benefit on the drawer and to share with him the responsibility for a dishonoured acceptance. Nor is there any reason why the bank should wish to call upon the surety for payment until the parties to the bill have defaulted."[21]

Hence, Zyngier and the parties to the bill were not co-sureties and the drawer was not entitled to contribution from her.

In *Scholefield Goodman & Sons Ltd v Zyngier*, the Privy Council **12–299** suggested that the decision in *D & J Fowler (Aust) Ltd v Bank of New South Wales*[22] was not correct. Their Lordships doubted whether on a true construction of the documents in that case the individual defendants had constituted themselves as co-sureties with the plaintiffs or had indemnified them against their liability as drawers. It was more likely that the defendants had merely undertaken a liability secondary to that of the plaintiffs as drawers of the bills. Similarly, their Lordships doubted the correctness of the decision of the Queensland Full Court in *Maxal Nominees Pty Ltd v Dalgety Ltd* on the true construction of the bill of mortgage and guarantee in that case. It appeared more likely that the appellant had undertaken that the bank as holders of a bill would be duly paid by the parties liable on the bill.[23] In other words, the appellant was not a co-surety with the parties liable on the bill but rather a guarantor who became liable upon their default. It is submitted that this will be the normal construction placed upon the undertaking of a guarantor of a bill of exchange. Accordingly such a guarantor and the parties liable on the bill will not be entitled to contribution from one another as co-sureties, nor to any right of subrogation.

---

[20] *ibid.*, at 774.
[21] *ibid.*, at 774.
[22] [1982] 2 N.S.W.L.R. 879.
[23] *Scholefield Goodman & Sons Ltd v Zyngier* (1985) 59 A.L.J.R. 770 at 775.

(vi) The amount recoverable by subrogation

12–300   The equitable principle that a guarantor who invokes the remedy of subrogation cannot recover more than the guarantor has paid[24] is recognised in the proviso to s.5 of the Mercantile Law Amendment Act 1856. While it is true that a guarantor who pays the whole debt is entitled under the section to sue the co-sureties for the whole debt, that guarantor may not "bring into his pocket by means of the judgment more than a just proportion", namely, the amount by which the guarantor's payment exceeded his share of the principal debt.[25] Where there are several co-sureties, each is only entitled to a proportionate share of the net proceeds of realisation of the securities held by the creditor[26] and the creditor is not entitled to charge interest on the costs of realising the securities.[27]

12–301   The terms "just proportion" and "justly liable" in the proviso to s.5 do not refer to the full state of accounts between the co-sureties but only to their indebtedness to one another as co-sureties. Hence, in *Brown v Cork*,[28] the other indebtedness between the co-sureties was not taken into account in dividing up the surplus of £195,000 realised by a receiver upon the sale of assets covered by securities, which were provided by a group of seven companies in a joint and several mutual guarantee. The receiver appointed by the creditor under these securities was merely obliged to pay the surplus to the co-sureties. The surplus could then be marshalled among the sureties on the assumption that each surety had borne an equal share of the total liability for the principal debt. Once this was achieved, the other indebtedness between the co-sureties could be taken into account.

12–302   The doctrine of subrogation does not give a guarantor any greater rights than the creditor had. This is equally true of the statutory remedy provided in s.5. Thus in *A/asian Conference Association Ltd v Mainline Constructions Pty Ltd (in liq)*[29] the guarantor of a building contract was not entitled to the surplus which remained after the retention fund required by the contract was used to complete the work on the default of the contractor: since the owner was not entitled to this surplus under the building contract, the guarantor could not acquire a right to it by subrogation.

(vii) The scope of the remedy of subrogation

12–303   The equitable principle of subrogation, which is entrenched in s.5 of the Mercantile Law Amendment Act 1856 entitles a surety, upon payment of the whole of the principal debt or upon performance of the principal obligation, to an assignment of all the securities held by the creditor in

---

[24] *Reed v Norris* (1837) 2 My. & Cr. 361; 40 E.R. 678; *Ex p. Rushforth* (1805) 10 Ves. 409; 32 E.R. 903; *Butcher v Churchill* (1808) 14 Ves. Jun. 567; 33 E.R. 638.
[25] *Re Parker; Morgan v Hill* [1894] 3 Ch. 400 at 404–405, CA.
[26] *Ward v National Bank of New Zealand* (1889) 8 N.Z.L.R. 10; *Brown v Cork* [1986] P.C.C. 78, CA.
[27] *ibid.*
[28] [1986] P.C.C. 78, CA. Compare *Baldwin v Torvale Group Ltd* [1998] C.L.Y. 3314.
[29] (1978) 141 C.L.R. 335; 53 A.L.J.R. 66.

respect of the principal debt or obligation.[30] The fact that the creditor is the Crown does not excuse it from complying with the statute.[31] Nor is it material whether the securities were given to the creditor by the principal debtor,[32] a co-debtor,[33] a co-surety[34] or the debtor's partner,[35] as long as they relate to the transaction guaranteed.[36] The right of subrogation extends to such securities whether or not the guarantor was aware of their existence[37] and whether or not the guarantor relied upon them when he furnished the guarantee.[38] It is not even necessary for the securities to be in existence at that time.[39]

The guarantor will be entitled to the securities at the time he pays[40] in **12–304** whatever form and to whatever extent they are held by the creditor.[41] The guarantor will also be entitled to the benefit of any securities taken by the creditor in substitution for the original securities.[42] But if the creditor has

---

[30] *Duncan, Fox & Co v North and South Wales Bank* (1880) 6 App. Cas. 1 at 19; *A E Goodwin Ltd (in liq) v A G Healing Ltd (in liq)* (1979) 7 A.C.L.R. 481; *Traders' Finance Corp Ltd v Marks* [1932] N.Z.L.R. 1176. The surety does not, however, necessarily obtain through subrogation the benefit of all the covenants contained in the securities: *McColl's Wholesale Pty Ltd v State Bank (NSW)* [1984] 3 N.S.W.L.R. 365 (interest not necessarily allowed at rate in security document). Where the creditor refuses to hand over the securities, the surety can bring an action against the creditor: see *Goddard v Whyte* (1860) 2 Giff. 449 at 452; 66 E.R. 188 at 189. See also *Atkin's Court Forms* (1982 Issue), Vol. 20, pp.141, 144–145 for the form of the writ and the statement of claim in an action to compel transfer of securities.

[31] *R v Doughty* (1702) Wight. 2; 145 E.R. 1152.

[32] *Traders' Finance Corp Ltd v Marks* [1932] N.Z.L.R. 1176; *Morgan v Seymour* (1638) 1 Ch. Rep. 120; *Greerside v Benson* (1745) 3 Atk. 248; 26 E.R. 944; *Mayhew v Crickett* (1818) 2 Swanst. 185 at 191; 36 E.R. 585 at 587; *Goddard v Whyte* (1860) 2 Giff. 449 at 452; 66 E.R. 188 at 189.

[33] *D & J Fowler (Aust) Ltd v Bank of New South Wales* [1982] 2 N.S.W.L.R. 879 at 885.

[34] *Smith v Wood* [1929] 1 Ch. 14; *Ex p. Crisp* (1744) 1 Atk. 133 at 135; 26 E.R. 87 at 88; *Greerside v Benson* (1745) 3 Atk. 248; 26 E.R. 944; *Stirling v Forrester* (1821) 3 Bligh 575 at 590; 4 E.R. 712 at 717; *Dering v Earl of Winchelsea* (1787) 1 Cox 318; 29 E.R. 1184; *Duncan, Fox & Co v North and South Wales Bank* (1880) 6 App. Cas. 1 at 19; *D & J Fowler (Aust) Ltd v Bank of New South Wales* [1982] 2 N.S.W.L.R. 879 at 885; *Brown v Cork* [1985] B.C.L.C. 363, CA. See also s.5 of the Mercantile Law Amendment Act 1856.

[35] In *Goddard v Whyte* (1860) 2 Giff. 449; 66 E.R. 188, the principle of subrogation was extended to securities given to the creditor by the debtor's partner. But subrogation does not cover securities which the creditor has received from a stranger in its own right without reference to the principal transaction: *Chatterton v Maclean* [1951] 1 All E.R. 761 at 766–767.

[36] *Duncan, Fox & Co v North and South Wales Bank* (1880) 6 App. Cas. 1 at 19; *Re Hodgetts; Ex p. Official Receiver* (1949) 16 A.B.C. 201.

[37] *Mayhew v Crickett* (1818) 2 Swanst. 185 at 191; 36 E.R. 585 at 587; *Newton v Chorlton* (1853) 10 Hare 646 at 651; 68 E.R. 1087 at 1089; *Pearl v Deacon* (1857) 24 Beav. 186; 53 E.R. 328; *Coates v Coates* (1864) 33 Beav. 249; 55 E.R. 363; *Goddard v Whyte* (1860) 2 Giff. 449; 66 E.R. 188; *Duncan, Fox & Co v North and South Wales Bank* (1879) 6 App. Cas. 1; *Leicestershire Banking Co Ltd v Hawkins* (1900) T.L.R. 317; *Re Jeffrey's Policy* (1872) 20 W.R. 857.

[38] *Forbes v Jackson* (1882) 19 Ch. D. 615; *Mayhew v Crickett* (1818) 2 Swanst. 185 at 191; 36 E.R. 585 at 587; *Newton v Chorlton* (1853) 10 Hare 646 at 651; 68 E.R. 1087 at 1089; *Pearl v Deacon* (1857) 24 Beav. 186; 53 E.R. 328; *Coates v Coates* (1864) 33 Beav. 249; 55 E.R. 363; *Goddard v Whyte* (1860) 2 Giff. 449; 66 E.R. 188; *Duncan, Fox & Co v North and South Wales Bank* (1880) 6 App. Cas. 1 at 19; *Leicestershire Banking Co Ltd v Hawkins* (1900) 16 T.L.R. 317; *Re Jeffery's Policy* (1872) 20 W.R. 857.

[39] *Scott v Knox* (1838) 2 Jo. Ex. Ir. 778. The right of subrogation extends to all securities taken by the creditor in respect of the principal debt, whether taken before or after the contract of suretyship was concluded: *Forbes v Jackson* (1882) 19 Ch. D. 615 at 621 *per* Hall V.C.

[40] *Pearl v Deacon* (1857) 24 Beav. 186; 53 E.R. 328. See also *Bank of Victoria v Smith* (1894) 20 V.L.R. 450.

[41] *Jones v Hill* (1893) 14 L.R. (NSW) Eq. 303.

[42] *Ward v National Bank of New Zealand Ltd* (1889) 8 N.Z.L.R. 10.

abandoned any of these securities or accepted substitutes for them without the consent of the guarantor, this may reduce the guarantor's liability. The value of the abandoned securities should be deducted from the amount of the principal debt when the securities were abandoned. So the guarantor is entitled to be credited with an equivalent amount in reduction of the guarantor's liability.[43] Similarly, where the guarantor derives no benefit from the substitution of the securities, he is entitled to a proportionate part of the securities originally held and later given up by the creditor without his consent.[44] This too will, in effect, reduce the guarantor's liability.

12–305   A guarantor, however, has no right to dictate the form of any subsequent security taken by the creditor from the principal debtor,[45] although he will be entitled to this security if it is given in respect of the principal debt or obligation.[46] For this reason, a guarantor will not be entitled to an additional security taken by the creditor for a further advance not covered by the guarantee.[47]

12–306   Section 5 of the Mercantile Law Amendment Act 1856 introduced several material changes to the guarantor's equitable right of subrogation. The term "security" in equity included every security which the creditor could invoke against the principal debtor.[48] It did not apply to a security which had been paid and satisfied and which could not, therefore, be used by the creditor against the principal debtor.[49] Under the statute, the courts give a broader meaning to the term "security" in s.5.[50] Under the section, it is now possible for a guarantor who pays the principal debt to obtain an assignment from the creditor of the securities which the debtor has paid and satisfied and which are, therefore, worthless in the hands of the creditor.[51] Thus, the surety's right of subrogation is extended to securities that originally secured a principal debt which has been discharged.[52] To quote Helsham C.J. in *D & J Fowler (Aust) Ltd v Bank of New South Wales*:[53] "the section artificially keeps alive, if necessary, the security and lets the person who has paid the debt in effect get his hands on it".[54]

12–307   The section does not restrict the method of assignment of the securities to any particular form.[55] The guarantor is entitled to have the securities

[43] *Pearl v Deacon* (1857) 24 Beav. 186; 53 E.R. 328; *Bank of Victoria v Smith* (1894) 20 V.L.R. 450: see above, paras 8–71 to 8–75.
[44] *Ward v National Bank of New Zealand Ltd* (1889) 8 N.Z.L.R. 10.
[45] *Jones v Hill* (1893) 14 L.R. (NSW) Eq. 172.
[46] *Forbes v Jackson* (1882) 19 Ch. D. 615. *Re Hodgetts Ex p. Official Receiver* (1949) 16 A.B.C. 201.
[47] *Jones v Hill* (1893) 14 L.R. (NSW) Eq. 172; *Swan v National Bank* (1873) 4 A.J.R. 42.
[48] *Brandon v Brandon* (1859) 28 L.J. Ch. 147.
[49] *Everingham v Waddell* (1881) 7 V.L.R. (L) 180.
[50] Indeed, the courts have interpreted the whole section liberally: *Everingham v Waddell* (1881) 7 V.L.R. (L) 180 at 184–185 *per* Stawell C.J.
[51] *Everingham v Waddell* (1881) 7 V.L.R. (L) 180. See also *Hardy v Johnson* (1880) 6 V.L.R. 190.
[52] See *Everingham v Waddell* (1881) 7 V.L.R. (L) 180; *Hardy v Johnson* (1880) 6 V.L.R. 190. The section removes the technical difficulty which previously existed, namely that the remedy of subrogation was taken away by payment of the principal debt: *Batchellor v Lawrence* (1861) 9 C.B. (NS) 543 at 556; 142 E.R. 214 at 218 *per* Byles J. See also *Copis v Middleton* (1823) Turn. & R. 224 at 229; 37 E.R. 1083 at 1085.
[53] [1982] 2 N.S.W.L.R. 879.
[54] *ibid.* at 885.
[55] *Everingham v Waddell* (1881) 7 V.L.R. (L) 180 at 186.

assigned to him by any effectual means he considers fit.[56] If the guarantor tenders an assignment by deed prepared at his own expense and allows the creditor a reasonable time to examine it, there can be no objection.[57] Moreover, the assignment can be to the guarantor or to a trustee for the guarantor.[58] If the creditor fails to assign the securities, the guarantor can bring an action for specific performance to enforce the statutory right to an assignment[59] or sue the creditor for damages.[60]

12–308 Where one guarantor pays off a judgment obtained against that guarantor and his insolvent co-surety, it is not necessary for the guarantor to take an assignment of the judgment in order to support a claim for contribution from the co-surety's insolvent estate. In *Re M'Myn*,[61] the testator and her mother and others signed a guarantee to certain bankers to secure an advance made to a relative. Eventually, the testator's mother paid off the judgment obtained by the bankers against the co-guarantors. The question was whether the legal personal representatives of the mother were entitled to claim contribution from the estate of the testator in priority to the other creditors of that estate. Chitty J. declared that the personal representatives of the mother were entitled to obtain what she had paid in excess of her fair contribution in priority to the unsecured creditors of the testator. In the circumstances, it was immaterial that the mother had neither brought an action nor obtained an assignment of the judgment awarded to the bankers. Given the fact that the co-surety was apparently insolvent, her trustee or administrator in bankruptcy could accept a proof of debt for the guarantor's claim to contribution without requiring the guarantor to prove as a judgment creditor.[62] The guarantor's statutory right to an assignment of the creditor's judgment was sufficient to support the proof of debt; a formal assignment of the creditor's judgment was unnecessary. Otherwise the paying surety's claim for contribution against the insolvent estate would have been increased by the costs and expenses incurred in obtaining an assignment of the creditor's judgment. No useful purpose would have been served by adding this extra burden to the insolvent estate. This analysis should also apply where the paying surety purports to exercise, through subrogation, one of the options open to the creditor under the creditor's securities in the bankruptcy or winding-up of an insolvent co-surety.[63]

12–309 But outside the context of bankruptcy or winding-up, the paying surety will need to obtain an assignment of the creditor's securities before he can exercise any of the remedies conferred by the securities. Hence, the paying

---

[56] *ibid.*, at 186.
[57] *ibid.*, at 186.
[58] *ibid.*, at 186.
[59] *Dale v Powell* (1911) 105 L.T. 291 at 292; *Oddy v Hallett* (1855) Cab. & El. 532.
[60] *Dale v Powell* (1911) 105 L.T. 291; *Batchellor v Lawrence* (1861) 9 C.B. (NS) 543 at 546; 142 E.R. 214 at 215; *Goddard v Whyte* (1860) 2 Giff. 449: 66 E.R. 188; *Oddy v Hallett* (1885) Cab. & El. 532.
[61] (1886) 33 Ch. D. 575. See also *Re Lord Churchill; Manisty v Churchill* (1888) 39 Ch. D. 174 at 176; *Re Lamplugh Iron Ore Co Ltd* [1927] 1 Ch. 308.
[62] *Re M'Myn* (1886) 33 Ch. D. 575. See also *Re Jason Construction Ltd* (1975) 25 D.L.R. (3d) 340 (Can).
[63] See *Moor v Anglo-Italian Bank* (1879) 10 Ch. D. 681 and I.F. Fletcher, *The Law of Insolvency* (6th ed., 2002), para.23–011. See above, para.10–47.

surety cannot appoint a receiver and manager or exercise a power of sale without first obtaining an assignment of the creditor's security.

12–310   The principle in *Re M'Myn* should be restricted to the situation where the paying surety invokes the statutory right of subrogation to enforce his claim to contribution from an *insolvent co-surety*. Any extension of the principle beyond these boundaries would be inconsistent with the cases where a paying surety was forced to bring an action for damages for breach of statutory duty against a creditor who refused to assign the judgment or securities to which the surety was entitled.[64]

12–311   Naturally, a guarantor's statutory right of subrogation is not restricted to an assignment of the securities held by the creditor for the payment of the principal debt. The guarantor is also entitled to exercise both the curial and the extra-curial remedies attached to those securities.[65]

(a) Securities, rights and remedies covered by subrogation

12–312   A wide variety of securities is covered by the equitable principle of subrogation now enshrined in the Mercantile Law Amendment Act 1856. Examples include: the benefit of a contract assigned by the principal debtor to the creditor,[66] a deposit of title deeds,[67] an equitable mortgage which is not void as against the liquidator of the mortgagor,[68] a lien on shares[69] or a vendor's lien on goods,[70] a right of stoppage in transitu,[71] leases,[72] promissory notes,[73] bills of exchange,[74] guarantees and

---

[64] See, *e.g. Dale v Powell* (1911) 105 L.T. 291; *Batchellor v Lawrence* (1861) 9 CB (NS) 543 at 556; *Goddard v Whyte* (1860) 2 Giff. 449 at 452. Subrogation may also be enforced by a suit for specific performance: R. Meagher, D. Heydon and M. Leeming, *Equity Doctrines and Remedies* (5th ed., 2002), para.9–225 and *Dale v Powell* (1911) 105 L.T. 291. See also *Atkin's Court Forms* (1982 Issue), Vol. 20, pp.141 and 144–145.

[65] *D & J Fowler (Aust) Ltd v Bank of New South Wales* [1982] 2 N.S.W.L.R. 879.

[66] *Edwards v Lennon* (1866) 6 S.C.R. (NSW) Eq. 18.

[67] *A M Spicer & Son Pty Ltd (in liq) v Spicer and Howie* (1931) 47 C.L.R. 151.

[68] *Mount Burnett Ltd (in liq) v Chambers* [1929] N.Z.L.R. 609. See also *D & J Fowler (Aust) Ltd v Bank of New South Wales* [1982] 2 N.S.W.L.R. 879 (subrogation extends to collateral mortgages under which no demand for payment has been made).

[69] Thus in *Brandon v Brandon* (1859) 3 De G. & J. 524; 44 E.R. 1371 sureties for a receiver of a testator's estate were allowed, upon the receiver's default and their payment of the principal debt, to recoup their indemnity from his shares. See also *Glossop v Harrison* (1814) 3 V. & B. 134; 35 E.R. 478.

[70] Thus in *Imperial Bank v London & St Katherine's Dock Co* (1877) 5 Ch. D. 195, a surety who paid the price of goods to the vendor was held to be entitled to the unpaid vendor's lien. A broker who acts for an unnamed buyer and who is by a trade custom personally liable for the principal's default is entitled to a similar lien: *Imperial Bank v London & St Katherine's Dock Co.* See also *Re Westzinthus* (1833) 5 B. & Ad. 817; 110 E.R. 992.

[71] A surety for the price of goods might be able to stop them in the name of the vendor, who might then be bound to authorise or ratify the stoppage: see *Imperial Bank v London & St Katherine's Dock Co* (1877) 5 Ch. D. 195. It appears, however, that the surety cannot stop the goods in transitu against the principal in his own name: *Siffken v Wray* (1805) 6 East 371; 102 E.R. 1328.

[72] Thus a surety for the performance of covenants under a lease will be entitled to an indemnity out of the land in respect of any rental payments made by him: *Lord Harberton v Bennett* (1829) Beat. 386.

[73] *Everingham v Waddell* (1881) 7 V.L.R. (L) 180.

[74] *ibid.* Moreover, the surety is not obliged to accept an assignment of the bill of exchange or promissory note indorsed by the creditor "without recourse".

indemnities,[75] certain insurance policies[76] and funds standing to the credit of the principal but appropriated to a particular purpose under a contract.[77] Upon payment, a guarantor of a purchaser's obligations under a contract for the sale of goods may be subrogated to the rights of the vendor under a reservation of title clause (a Romalpa clause) contained in the contract.[78] Accordingly, the guarantor may be entitled to the goods supplied or, where they have been sold, to the proceeds of sale if they are traceable. This will strengthen the guarantor's position if the purchaser becomes bankrupt and is unable to satisfy the guarantor's right of indemnity.[79]

12–313 A guarantor's remedy of subrogation is not confined to the securities held for the principal debt. Through subrogation, a guarantor who pays the debt is entitled to any moneys appropriated to the principal transaction between the creditor and the debtor.[80] This right extends to dividends which the creditor receives in the debtor's bankruptcy since these amounts are paid in reduction of the principal debt.[81]

12–314 The equitable principle of subrogation embodied in the Mercantile Law Amendment Act 1856 also gives the guarantor a right to use the remedies available to the creditor in any action or other proceeding in order to obtain indemnification from the principal debtor or contribution from a co-surety.[82] In any such action or other proceeding, the payment of the debt may not be pleaded in bar.[83] A surety under a hire-purchase agreement is, upon payment, entitled to the securities held by the owner in order to obtain an indemnity from the hirer, but is not entitled to exercise the owner's remedy of repossessing the property.[84] A guarantor who has satisfied a judgment obtained against the principal debtor and the

---

[75] *D & J Fowler (Aust) Ltd v Bank of New South Wales* [1982] 2 N.S.W.L.R. 879. Subrogation extends to other guarantees under which no cause of action has arisen because no demand was made upon the guarantors before payment of the principal debt by the person invoking the right of subrogation: *D & J Fowler (Aust) Ltd v Bank of New South Wales* at 886.

[76] Thus in *Aylwin v Witty* (1861) 30 L.J. Ch. 860, a person who guaranteed the payment of insurance premiums was able to claim a reimbursement out of the policy moneys. But a surety will not be entitled to an insurance policy taken out by a co-surety on the co-surety's own initiative to protect himself against his own liability: *Re Albert Life Assurance Co, Ex p. Western Life Assurance Society* (1870) L.R. 11 Eq. 164, at 172–173.

[77] *Re Sherry* (1884) 25 Ch. D. 692 at 702.

[78] See *Aluminium Industrie Vaassen BV v Romalpa Aluminium Ltd* [1976] 1 W.L.R. 676, CA.

[79] T.D. Putnam, *Suretyship* (1981), p.86.

[80] *Employers' Liability Assurance Corp v The Queen* [1968] 2 Ex. C.R. 246.

[81] *Ford v London Chartered Bank of Australia* (1879) 5 V.L.R. (E) 328 at 331, where it was suggested that the surety was entitled to recover a proportionate part of such dividends either by an action at law for money had and received or a suit in equity. In *Re Parker* [1894] 3 Ch. 400, it was held that a surety who has paid the debt can prove in the bankruptcy of a co-surety for the whole debt, but cannot actually recover more than his due share.

[82] The person who has paid the principal debt is not, of course, limited to bringing curial proceedings on any judgment, specialty or other security: *D & J Fowler (Aust) Ltd v Bank of New South Wales* [1982] 2 N.S.W.L.R. 879 at 886. In an appropriate case, a paying guarantor will be entitled to be subrogated to the rights of the creditor's representative, such as a trustee for debenture holders: *A E Goodwin Ltd (in liq) v A G Healing Ltd (in liq)* (1979) 7 A.C.L.R. 481.

[83] *D & J Fowler (Aust) Ltd v Bank of New South Wales* [1982] 2 N.S.W.L.R. 879.

[84] See *Chatterton v MacLean* [1951] 1 All E.R. 761 at 765–766 *per* Parker J.; P. Bingham, "The Surety's Right to Contribution" (1984) 12 A.B.L.R. 394 at 396.

guarantor may even enforce the judgment for his own benefit.[85] Thus, it is not necessary for the guarantor to sue the principal debtor to recover on the indemnity, and the guarantor will not forfeit the right to enforce the judgment because of a lapse of time unless the delay would bar the judgment itself.[86]

12–315   Similarly, the statutory right of subrogation includes judgments obtained against several co-sureties.[87] If one of the sureties technically satisfies the judgment by payment of the debt and damages and costs, that surety is entitled to have the creditor's judgment assigned to him.[88] If the creditor refuses, the surety can sue the creditor for damages, being the full amount paid by the surety to satisfy the judgment debt.[89] Moreover, after the surety obtains an assignment of the judgment, he is entitled to stand in the place of the creditor and continue in the creditor's name proceedings already instituted to enforce the judgment against the co-sureties until he receives from them payments representing their respective shares of the common liability.[90] But where a guarantor sued as sole defendant satisfies the judgment obtained by the creditor, that guarantor cannot insist upon an assignment of the judgment because it will not help him to enforce contribution from the co-sureties.[91] The guarantor can, however, require the creditor to assign to him the guarantee signed by the guarantor and the co-sureties as this may assist the guarantor to enforce the right of contribution.[92] It should at least assist the paying guarantor to establish who were the co-sureties and what were their respective shares of the principal debt.

12–316   Through subrogation, a guarantor who pays the debt may in certain circumstances acquire the creditor's remedies against third parties.[93] In City of Prince Albert v Underwood McLellan & Associates Ltd,[94] for example, the creditor's right to sue a supervising engineer for damages arising from the collapse of the city's reservoir was assigned to a guarantor on discharge of the principal obligation. The assignment of this right to sue the engineer was, however, reinforced by an agreement between the

[85] Smith v Burn (1880) 30 U.C.C.P. 630. See also Done v Walley (1848) 2 Exch. 198; 154 E.R. 463.
[86] ibid. See also Cockburn v Gillespie (1858) 11 Gr. 465 (Can).
[87] Done v Walley (1848) 2 Exch. 198; 154 E.R. 463. In this context, the term "judgment" means a judgment which could be treated as unsatisfied for the purpose of obtaining contribution from co-sureties: Silk v Eyre (1875) 9 Ir. Rep. Eq. 393.
[88] Batchellor v Lawrence (1861) 30 L.J.C.P. 39; Hardy v Johnson (1880) 6 V.L.R. (L) 190; Embling v McEwan (1872) 3 V.R. (L) 52; Stirling v Forrester (1821) 3 Bli. 575; 4 E.R. 712, HL.
[89] Embling v McEwan (1872) 3 V.R. (L) 52. The onus of proving that any of the co-debtors was insolvent rests with the defendant and the plaintiff need not plead any special damage: Embling v McEwan at 55.
[90] Fast v Osachoff [1926] 4 D.L.R. 355 at 360, CA. See also s.5 of the Mercantile Law Amendment Act 1856.
[91] Hardy v Johnson (1880) 6 V.L.R. (L) 190. It is different where the judgment is obtained against all the co-sureties. See Batchelor v Lawrence (1861) 9 C.B. (NS) 543; Embling v McEwan (1872) 3 V.R. (L) 52.
[92] ibid., at 192 per Stawell C.J.
[93] In Re Miller, Gibb & Co Ltd [1957] 1 W.L.R. 703, the Board of Trade, which had guaranteed an exporter's losses due to foreign exchange control, was held to be subrogated to the exporter's right to a certain fund as soon as it ultimately came to hand when payment was eventually permitted by the foreign exchange authority.
[94] (1968) 3 D.L.R. (3d) 385.

guarantor and the city when the surety liquidated the principal debt. Again, in *Sanders v Sanders*,[95] a guarantor was, upon payment of the principal debt, subrogated to a creditor's right to set aside a fraudulent preference conferred upon another creditor.

It has even been held, in the context of a fidelity guarantee, that the **12–317** doctrine of subrogation extends to the creditor's remedies for breach of contract, so that if the creditor fails to exercise his right to terminate the principal contract for breach, this impairs one of the "securities" to which the guarantor is entitled on payment and, consequently, it discharges the guarantor pro tanto.[96] This extremely liberal view[97] is difficult to accept since a simple contractual right under the main contract cannot reasonably be regarded as a security to enforce it. A more restrictive approach was seen in *Re Russell; Russell v Shoolbred*,[98] where it was held that a right of distress for rent was not a security within the meaning of the statute since the section deals with securities which are in their nature assignable and does not include a simple contractual remedy arising from non-payment of rent.[99]

(b) Securities, rights and remedies not covered by subrogation

In general, the creditor is not entitled to securities provided to the **12–318** guarantor by the principal debtor by way of counter-indemnity.[1] However, the creditor will be able to claim the benefit of securities provided by the principal debtor to the guarantor on trust to apply the proceeds in reduction of the principal debt.[2]

(i) Floating charges. There is some doubt as to whether the doctrine of **12–319** subrogation applies to floating charges. A floating charge is an hypothecation which creates merely an inchoate equitable assignment by

---

[95] 49 Idaho 733; 291 P. 1069 (1930). See *Re Walters' Deed of Guarantee* [1933] Ch. 321; *Re Dutcher* 213 F. 908 (1914), DC.
[96] *Phillips v Foxall* (1872) L.R. 7 Q.B. 666 at 680–682 *per* Blackburn J. As other examples, see *Re Wolmershausen* (1890) 62 L.T. 541 (a right of proof in bankruptcy proceedings treated as coming within the rule); *Stone v Geraldton Brewery* (1898) 1 W.A.L.R. 23 at 26 (right to re-enter or reject tenant for non-payment of rent treated as coming within the rule). *Cf.*, however, *Re Russell; Russell v Shoolbred* (1885) 29 Ch. D. 254 (right of distress for rent not a security within s.5 of the Mercantile Law Amendment Act 1856). See also *Forsyth v MacLeod* [1864] Mac. 293 (NZ).
[97] *Phillips v Foxall* (1872) 7 Q.B. 666: see above, paras 7–93 to 7–96.
[98] (1885) 29 Ch. D. 254.
[99] *ibid.*, at 265. But since a "specialty" is mentioned in the section, it is arguable that a remedy for a breach of a contract under seal comes within its ambit.
[1] *Ex p. Waring* (1815) 19 Ves. 345 at 349; 34 E.R. 546 at 547, unless the rule in *Ex p. Waring* itself is applicable. Where the principal debtor provides security by way of counter-indemnity to the guarantor and then becomes insolvent, it may be difficult for the guarantor to use the statutory demand procedure against the debtor. See Insolvency Rules 1986, r.6.5(4)(d) and *Re a Debtor (No.1 of 1987)* [1989] 1 W.L.R. 271 at 276. The court has a discretion to set aside a statutory demand where it would be unjust for the debtor to be subjected to a bankruptcy petition founded on his failure to comply with a defective demand. See also *Smith v Braintree District Council* [1989] 3 All E.R. 897 at 901–902 and G. Andrews and R. Millett, *Law of Guarantees* (3rd ed., 2000), para.11.03.
[2] *Ex p. Waring* (1815) 19 Ves. 345; 34 E.R. 546; *Ex p. Rushforth* (1805) 10 Ves. 409; 32 E.R. 903. *Cf. Wilding v Richards* (1845) 1 Coll. 655; 63 E.R. 584.

way of charge, giving the chargee neither possession nor title to the charged assets. In *O'Day v Commercial Bank of Australia Ltd*,[3] a guarantor argued that the creditor's failure to comply with the requirements for the enforcement of a debenture creating a floating charge over the debtor's assets had not been satisfied and hence the security was destroyed. The essence of this argument was that the unlawful action of the creditor had rendered it impossible for it to restore the security to the principal debtor upon payment by the debtor of the money secured by the debenture and that the principal debt was thereby extinguished. It should be noted that the guarantor was unable to argue that his remedy of subrogation was prejudiced by the loss or impairment of the security because the guarantee itself expressly excluded the right of subrogation. Strictly speaking, therefore, the High Court in *O'Day v Commercial Bank of Australia Ltd* did not exclude floating charges from the doctrine of subrogation. It merely decided that the equitable principle that a chargee is bound on payment of the secured debt to restore the secured property to the chargor did not apply to floating charges: as the floating charge did not vest anything in the chargee, the chargee could not be expected to hand anything back to the chargor on payment of the principal debt. As Dixon J. observed:

"A floating charge operates to secure moneys over an undertaking without giving to the creditor any legal or equitable interest in any specific piece of property comprised in the undertaking until the event occurs upon which it becomes a fixed security. The creditor obtains neither the possession nor property in any part of the assets. He has nothing to retransfer or to redeliver to the debtor upon payment of the debt. The debtor retains control of the assets and the power to dispose of them in the course of business. The rule of equity invoked is that 'if a creditor holding security sues for his debt, he is under an obligation on payment of the debt to hand over the security; and if, having improperly made away with the security, he is unable to return it to his debtor, he cannot have judgment for the debt' (*per* Viscount Cave L.C., *Ellis & Co's Trustee v Dixon-Johnson* [1925] A.C. 489 at 491). This doctrine is entirely inapplicable to a charge which remains floating where nothing is vested in or handed over to the creditor."[4]

12–320   Nevertheless, it is submitted that the doctrine of subrogation should extend to floating charges[5] even though they are merely hypothecations. They still contain a range of remedies and rights which will assist a paying

---

[3] (1933) 50 C.L.R. 200.

[4] *ibid.*, at 220. Rich J. concurred in Dixon J.'s judgment. See also at 217 *per* Starke J., 224 *per* McTiernan J.

[5] In *Roynat Ltd v Denis* (1982) 139 D.L.R. (3d) 265 at 278, it appears to have been assumed that a debenture creating a floating charge came within the doctrine of subrogation. See also *ANZ Banking Group Ltd v Carnegie* (unreported, Vic Sup Ct, June 16, 1987) where Crockett J held that a right of subrogation was available in respect of a floating charge); *Re Selvas Pty Ltd (in liq): Westell v Craddock* (1989) 52 S.A.S.R. 449 (to similar effect); *Bayley v Gibsons Ltd* [1993] 1 Tas. R. 385; *National Bank of New Zealand Ltd v Chapman* [1975] 1 N.Z.L.R. 480 at 484.

guarantor to enforce the right of indemnity or contribution. They should, therefore, be available to guarantors who liquidate the principal debt.

(ii) Private insurance policies. The doctrine of subrogation does not **12–321** extend to a policy on the life of the principal debtor taken out and maintained by the creditor at its own expense; the creditor may retain the policy and recoup it even if the debt is paid.[6] Nor will a guarantor be entitled by subrogation to an insurance policy effected and maintained by a co-surety at the co-surety's own expense and on his own initiative to protect himself against any liability under the guarantee.[7] But it appears that, on payment of the principal debt, a guarantor will be entitled to an insurance policy deposited with the creditor by the principal debtor.[8]

(iii) Personal rights. The guarantor's claim to subrogation may be **12–322** resisted where the security claimed is a personal right of the creditor which does not pass to the guarantor under the Mercantile Law Amendment Act 1856. In *Chatterton v Maclean*,[9] it was held that the right of a finance company to seize goods let on hire-purchase did not pass to a guarantor on payment because it was a personal right. It is submitted, however, that this right to take possession should have passed to the finance company under s.5 of the Mercantile Law Amendment Act since it was not a right personal to the finance company. This case was cited without disapproval in *Moschi v Lep Air Services Ltd*,[10] but there it was used to support another proposition, that is, that a guarantor may remain liable in damages even after the vendor has accepted the buyer's repudiation of an instalment contract.[11]

Subrogation will not necessarily entitle the guarantor to the benefit of all **12–323** the covenants under the principal contract. For example, the court may decline to award the guarantor interest at the higher rate specified in the principal contract.[12]

A guarantor will not be entitled to be subrogated unless the amount it paid to the creditor was due to the principal debtor's default. If the guarantor's claim was merely part of its own claim against the principal debtor, subrogation will not be available.[13]

---

[6] *Dalby v India & London Life Assurance Co* (1854) 15 C.B. 365; [1843–60] All E.R. Rep. 1040. See also P. Bingham, "The Surety's Rights to Contribution" (1984) 12 A.B.L.R. 394 at 397 as to comprehensive insurance policies.
[7] *Re Albert Life Assurance Co, Ex p. Western Life Assurance Society* (1870) L.R. 11 Eq. 164 at 172–173.
[8] *Rainbow v Juggins* (1880) 5 Q.B.D. 422 appears to assume this, although on the facts the insurance policy was valueless. See also *Rowlatt on Principal and Surety* (5th ed., 1999), p.162.
[9] [1951] 1 All E.R. 761. See also *Re Russell; Russell v Shoolbred* (1885) 29 Ch. 254, CA (as to distraint for rent).
[10] [1973] A.C. 331.
[11] In Canada, it has been held that if a creditor retakes possession under a conditional sales contract, the creditor must not impair the property repossessed: *Crain v Hoffman* (1917) 37 D.L.R. 435; *Traders' Finance Corp Ltd v Ross* [1943] 1 D.L.R. 49. Note that if the right of repossession can be regarded as a security, s.5 of the Mercantile Law Amendment Act 1856 will preserve the guarantor's rights, even though the hire purchase agreement is discharged as a result of the guarantor's payment.
[12] *McColl's Wholesale Pty Ltd v State Bank of New South Wales* [1984] 3 N.S.W.L.R. 365 at 379 and R. Meagher, D. Heydon and M. Leeming, *Equity Doctrines and Remedies* (4th ed., 2002), para.9–225.
[13] *Re Empire Paper Ltd (in liq)* [1999] B.C.C. 406.

12–324 **(iv) Preferences and wrongful pledges**. Subrogation will not be available in respect of a mortgage granted by the principal debtor to the creditor and later avoided a preference.[14] Nor will a surety be entitled to the benefit of a wrongful pledge by the debtor to the creditor of the property of a third party.[15] Indeed, the third party will be allowed to use the guarantee to secure the release of the property.[16] The third party is entitled to have the property relieved of the encumbrance by realising any property of the principal debtor pledged for the same debt at the expense of any guarantors for the debt.[17]

(viii) Effect of bankruptcy upon the guarantor's right of subrogation

12–325 In the special situation to which the rule in *Ex p. Waring*[18] applies, bankruptcy can affect a guarantor's right of subrogation. This rule states:

"Where, as between the drawer and the acceptor of a bill of exchange, a security has, by virtue of the contract between them, been specifically appropriated to meet the bill at maturity, and has been lodged for that purpose by the drawer with the acceptor; then, if both drawer and acceptor become insolvent, and their estates are brought under a forced administration, the billholder, though neither party nor privy to the contract, is entitled to have the specifically appropriated security applied in or towards payment of the bill."[19]

12–326 The rationale of the rule in *Ex p. Waring* is that the security cannot be applied in paying the general creditors of the acceptor because in the hands of the acceptor it is impressed with a trust. Nor should it be applied for the benefit of the general creditors of the drawer because the drawer is not entitled to have the security returned without meeting the acceptances. Accordingly, in an attempt to achieve justice between the insolvent estates of the drawer and the acceptor, the court applies the security towards paying the acceptances it was intended to cover.[20]

12–327 This special rule applies where the value of the security was more[21] than the amount due under the bills of exchange but only where there is a

---

[14] *Duncan, Fox & Co v North and South Wales Bank* (1880) 6 App. Cas. 1 at 19; *Re Hodgetts; Ex p. Official Receiver* (1949) 16 A.B.C. 201. See also *Wade v Coope* (1827) 2 Sim. 155; 57 E.R. 747; *Wilkinson v London & County Banking Co* (1884) 1 T.L.R. 63.
[15] *Chatterton v Maclean* [1951] 1 All E.R. 761 at 766–767.
[16] *Re Stratton, Ex p. Salting* (1883) 25 Ch. D. 148; *N A Kratzmann Pty Ltd v Tucker* (1966) 123 C.L.R. 257; 40 A.L.J.R. 373. See also *McColl's Wholesale Pty Ltd v State Bank (NSW)* [1984] 3 N.S.W.L.R. 365. *Cf. Mount Burnett Ltd (in liq) v Chambers* [1929] N.Z.L.R. 609.
[17] *Ex p. Altson* (1868) 4 Ch. App. 168; *Ex p. Salting* (1883) 25 Ch. D. 148.
[18] (1815) 19 Ves. Jun. 345; 34 E.R. 546.
[19] *Ex p. Dever; Re Suse (No.2)* (1885) 14 Q.B.D. 611 at 620.
[20] *Ex p. Dever; In re Suse (No.2)* (1885) 14 Q.B.D. 611 at 623 *per* Cotton L.J.
[21] This was the case in *Ex p. Waring* (1815) 19 Ves. Jun. 346; 34 E.R. 546 itself, although this point does not appear clearly in this report of the case. See E.P. Ellinger, "Securitbank's Collapse and the Commercial Bills Market of New Zealand" (1978) 20 *Malaya Law Review* 84.

concurrent insolvency of two parties liable on a bill of exchange and there is no obviously correct and simple way of dealing with the competing claims.[22] Given the criticism that the rule has attracted, it is unlikely to be extended beyond its narrow boundaries.[23] However, within this compass it does interfere with a guarantor's normal right to securities held for the principal debt.[24] It is not consistent with general equitable principles but it is too entrenched to reverse.[25]

Under the rule in *Ex p. Waring* the specifically-appropriated securities **12–328** are, therefore, available to the holder of the bill who can have them applied in or towards payment of the bill. Since such securities were deposited for the express purpose of covering the acceptor's liability on the bill, they are impressed with a trust for that purpose. Accordingly, they do not belong to the acceptor's general creditors, nor do they pass to her or his trustee in bankruptcy.

The rule in *Ex p. Waring*[26] is a positive rule dealing with the **12–329** administration of estates and is not "the necessary result of equitable principles."[27] Nevertheless, it appears that the rule might not be applied where the value of the security is less than the liability owed to the holder of the bills.[28] To apply the rule in this situation would deprive the general creditors of the bankrupt acceptor of some part of the indemnity to which the acceptor is entitled under his contract with the drawer.[29] Where the value of the security exceeds the liability owed to the holder of the bills, this problem does not arise because the holder is not compelled to claim against the estates of both the drawer and the acceptor for a deficiency.

The rule will, in general, be restricted to the situation where two parties **12–330** to a bill of exchange are concurrently insolvent,[30] although it is not necessary for both to have been formally adjudged bankrupt.[31] Moreover,

[22] In *Royal Bank of Scotland v Commercial Bank of Scotland* (1882) 7 App. Cas. 366 the House of Lords accepted that the rule was too entrenched in English law to discard but their Lordships did not incorporate it into Scottish law.
[23] *Re Standard Insurance Co Ltd (in liq) and the Companies Act* (1969) 91 W.N. (NSW) 654 at 661, approved in *Commissioners of State Savings Bank of Victoria v Patrick Intermarine Acceptances Ltd (in liq)* [1981] 1 N.S.W.L.R. 175.
[24] See above, paras 12–303 to 12–317.
[25] See *Royal Bank of Scotland v Commercial Bank of Scotland* (1882) 7 App. Cas. 366 at 386–387 *per* Lord Selborne L.C.
[26] (1815) 19 Ves. Jun. 345; 34 E.R. 546.
[27] *Royal Bank of Scotland v Commercial Bank of Scotland* (1882) 7 App. Cas. 366 at 387.
[28] *ibid.* Cf. *Powles v Hargreaves* (1853) 3 De G.M. & G. 430; 43 E.R. 169, a case which was doubted in *Star v Silvia; Genoa Resources & Investments Ltd* (unreported, NSW Sup Ct, Eq Div, Brownie J., August 1, 1994).
[29] *Royal Bank of Scotland v Commercial Bank of Scotland* (1882) 7 App. Cas. 366 at 387 *per* Lord Selborne L.C., 393 *per* Lord Blackburn. For a fairer method of calculating the respective dividends of the parties, see (1882) 7 App. Cas. 366 at 390–391 *per* Lord Blackburn. See also *Re Standard Insurance Co Ltd (in liq) and the Companies Act 1936* [1970] 1 N.S.W.R. 599. See generally D Partlett, "The Right of Subrogation in Accommodation Bills of Exchange" (1979) 53 A.L.J. 694.
[30] *Re Standard Insurance Co Ltd (in liq) and the Companies Act 1936* [1970] 1 N.S.W.R. 599; *Commissioners of State Savings Bank of Victoria v Patrick Intermarine Acceptances Ltd (in liq)* [1981] 1 N.S.W.L.R. 175.
[31] *Powles v Hargreaves* (1853) 3 De G.M. & G. 430; 43 E.R. 769; *Bank of Ireland v Perry* (1871) L.R. 7 Ex. 14; *City Bank v Luckie* (1870) 5 Ch. App. 773; *Re Barned's Bank Ex p. Joint Stock Discount Co* (1875) L.R. 10 Ch. 198. Cf. *Royal Bank of Scotland v Commercial Bank of Scotland* (1882) 7 App. Cas. 366. The rule will not apply, however, unless the estate of the

the rule does not apply unless the holder is entitled to prove against both insolvent estates. Consequently, where the bill was dishonoured for non-acceptance, the rule in *Ex p. Waring* had no application.[32] But it is not essential that the securities be deposited by a party to the bill, as it is enough that the depositor is liable *in respect of the bill transaction.*[33]

12–331   In other contexts, the bankruptcy or liquidation of the principal debtor or a co-surety will have no effect on the right of the surety who pays off the creditor and obtains its securities to enforce them in respect of any excess which remains after set-offs are allowed.[34]

(ix) Loss of the right of subrogation

12–332   If the creditor realises the securities held for the principal debt and applies the proceeds in reduction of the debt, the securities are exhausted and the guarantor loses the right of subrogation.[35] This is fair and equitable, provided that the full value of the securities is credited. On the other hand, if the creditor fails to preserve or realise the securities in a proper manner, the guarantor will be discharged either absolutely or to the extent that he is prejudiced.[36] There will be an absolute discharge where obtaining or preserving securities was a condition of the guarantee;[37] otherwise there will be a pro tanto discharge.[38] Again, this is a fair and equitable result.

12–333   Payment under a counter-guarantee can deprive the original sureties of their right of subrogation. In *Brown Shipley & Co Ltd v Amalgamated Investment (Europe) BV,*[39] the claimants guaranteed a loan by a bank to the defendant. As a precaution, they took a counter-guarantee from the defendant's parent company. When the claimants were compelled to pay on their guarantee, they made a demand on the parent company under its counter-guarantee. The parent company answered its liability under the counter-guarantee with the aid of a loan from the claimants who then sued the defendant as principal debtor, claiming that they were subrogated to the rights and remedies of the bank as creditor. Donaldson J. reluctantly

---

[32] drawer who remits a bill of exchange to cover the bill on which he is liable as drawer is still within the jurisdiction of the court: *Ex p. General South American Co; Re Yglesias* (1875) 10 Ch. App. 639.

[32] *Vaughan v Halliday* (1874) 9 Ch. App. 561. Nor does the rule apply where the funds claimed for the benefit of the bill-holders are absolutely and entirely the property of, and in the possession of, only one of the parties, for example, where an agent consigns goods to the agent's principal, and both go bankrupt: *Ex p. Banner* (1876) 2 Ch. D. 278. See also *Ex p. Lambton* (1875) 10 Ch. App. 405.

[33] *Ex p. Smart* (1872) 8 Ch. App. 220.

[34] *McColl's Wholesale Pty Ltd v State Bank (NSW)* [1984] 3 N.S.W.L.R. 365.

[35] *Regina Brokerage & Investment Co v Waddell* (1916) 27 D.L.R. 533, CA.

[36] See above, paras 8–46 to 8–105.

[37] There is rarely an express or implied condition in guarantees requiring creditors to realise collateral securities in a proper manner. Contrast *Skipton Building Society v Stott* [2000] 1 All E.R. (Comm) 257, where the implied term was justified on the basis the building society's statutory duty under para.1(1)(a) of Sch.4 to the Building Societies Act 1986. Compare *China and South Seas Bank Ltd v Tan Soon Gin* [1990] 1 A.C. 536.

[38] See above, paras 8–49 to 8–51.

[39] [1979] 1 Lloyd's Rep. 488.

held that these rights of subrogation had been transferred by operation of law to the parent company when it discharged its liability under its counter-guarantee. Since the claimants had surrendered their rights under the counter-guarantee, they also lost their rights of subrogation against the defendant. This unfortunate result could have been avoided if the claimants had themselves discharged the guarantee given to the bank instead of providing the parent company with the loan which it used to discharge its counter-guarantee. The case is a stern reminder that rights of subrogation can be lost through inadvertence and by the operation of law.

(x) Effect of the death of the guarantor upon the right of subrogation

Far from destroying the right of subrogation, the death of a guarantor **12–334** may sometimes enhance the enforcement of it. Where the principal debtor happens to be a legatee under the guarantor's will, the executors may retain the amount of the guarantor's claim to an indemnity plus reasonable interest out of the legacy due to the debtor.[40] This is so even if the debtor is declared bankrupt after the guarantor's death and even if the surety's action would be statute-barred.[41] Equally, where the principal debtor has executed a deed of assignment for the benefit of his creditors for payment according to the laws of bankruptcy and the guaranteed creditor has assented to the deed, the guarantor's executors can retain the amount of the guarantor's indemnity out of the legacy payable to the principal debtor instead of proving in the creditor's place.[42]

(xi) Duties attending subrogation

A guarantor who pays the principal debt and is, therefore, entitled to the **12–335** creditor's securities by subrogation is subject to a correlative duty to hold these securities upon trust and to bring into account, as between himself and the co-sureties, any moneys that might be received from them.[43] The guarantor's right to immediate contribution from the co-sureties is subject to this duty.[44] If the co-sureties are not prepared to allow the guarantor to hold the securities on these terms, the court may order that the securities be transferred to a trustee to administer and to pay the moneys arising therefrom in such a manner as to secure to each co-surety his respective rights in relation to the securities.[45]

Because the guarantor is, upon payment of the principal debt, entitled to **12–336** be subrogated to all securities and remedies held by the creditor for the

[40] *Re Watson* [1896] 1 Ch. 925.
[41] *ibid.*
[42] *Re Whitehouse* (1887) 37 Ch. D. 683.
[43] *Margrett v Gregory* (1862) 6 L.T. 543; *Re Arcedeckne; Atkins v Arcedeckne* (1883) 24 Ch. D. 709; *Traders' Finance Corp Ltd v Marks* [1932] N.Z.L.R. 1176.
[44] *Monk v Smith* (1893) 14 L.R. (NSW) Eq. 311: see above, paras 12–210 to 12–211.
[45] *Traders' Finance Corp Ltd v Marks* [1932] N.Z.L.R. 1176 at 1182.

debt, the creditor is subject to an equitable duty to preserve these securities and remedies for the guarantor.[46] The scope of this equitable duty is not always clearly delineated,[47] but it probably extends to all securities, remedies and rights to which a guarantor would be entitled by subrogation. Any loss or impairment of these benefits will discharge the guarantor pro tanto.[48] Where there is an express or implied condition in the contract of guarantee that the creditor will perform a particular obligation in relation to a security, a failure to perform this obligation will discharge the guarantor absolutely even if the security concerned did not fall within the scope of the equitable doctrine of subrogation or the guarantor's statutory right of subrogation.[49]

(xii) Effect of subrogation upon priorities

12–337   The doctrine of subrogation entitles a guarantor to stand in the place of the creditor upon payment of the principal debt. Hence if the creditor was the Crown, a guarantor who pays the principal debt acquires the same priority, if any, as the Crown enjoyed;[50] if the creditor was a specialty creditor[51] or a preferential creditor,[52] the guarantor acquires that status upon payment of the principal debt. Moreover, if a guarantor receives the benefit of a security through subrogation, that guarantor should also enjoy the priority accorded to that security. The guarantor should, therefore, take priority over encumbrancers whose securities were subsequent and inferior to the security held by the creditor.[53] The same principle should apply where the guarantor acquires a right to a security held by a co-surety upon payment of the principal debt. The guarantor's payment of the

[46] Carter v White (1883) 25 Ch. D. 666 at 670; Dale v Powell (1911) 105 L.T. 291.
[47] The equitable duty is discussed elsewhere: see above, paras 8–46 to 8–91.
[48] Carter v White (1884) 25 Ch. D. 666; Taylor v Bank of New South Wales (1886) 11 App Cas 596: see above, paras 8–49 to 8–54.
[49] The obligation may relate, e.g., to the preservation of a floating charge, an insurance policy, or even the exercise of a contractual remedy under the main contract: see Coyte v Elphick (1874) 22 W.R. 541 (insurance policy). But see above, para.12–317. See also Watson v Allcock (1853) 4 De G.M. & G. 242; 43 E.R. 499 (express term of the guarantee that a warrant of execution be enforced).
[50] Re Lord Churchill; Manisty v Churchill (1888) 39 Ch. D. 174.
[51] Re Lord Churchill; Manisty v Churchill (1888) 39 Ch. D. 174.
[52] Re Lamplugh Iron Ore Co Ltd [1927] 1 Ch. 308. Similarly, where rent paid by a guarantor is a cost and expense of the winding-up of the principal debtor company, the guarantor acquires the preferential status of the landlord to whom the guarantor paid the rent: Re Downer Enterprises Ltd [1974] 1 W.L.R. 1460. See also Insolvency Act 1980, s.115; Insolvency Rules 1986 SI 1986/1925, r.4.218 and I.F. Fletcher, The Law of Insolvency (3rd ed., 2002), paras 24–011 to 24–013.
[53] Cf. Forbes v Jackson (1882) 19 Ch. D. 615. See also Drew v Lockett (1863) 32 Beav. 499; 55 E.R. 196; Silk v Eyre (1875) 9 I.R. 393; Aylwin v Witty (1861) 30 L.J. Ch. 860; Dawson v Bank of Whitehaven (1877) 4 Ch. D. 639. Similarly, a lender who pays out a secured creditor is entitled to that creditor's security with its inherent defects and limitations: Castle Phillips Finance v Piddington (1995) 70 P. & C.R. 592, CA. By the same token, it may be entitled to priority over a subsequent mortgagee on restitutionary grounds even if that was not the mutual intention of the parties because otherwise the subsequent mortgagee would be unjustly enriched by the discharge of the prior mortgage: Banque Financière de la Cité v Parc (Battersea) Ltd [1998] 1 All E.R. 739.

principal debt has not prejudiced the subsequent encumbrancers. Thus, it should not matter whether or not they had notice of the suretyship.[54]

Subrogation will not give a guarantor priority over prior encumbrancers **12–338** or assignees.[55] Thus in *Re Jason Construction Ltd*,[56] a bank which took a general assignment of the book debts of a building contractor (including any amounts owing or payable by building owners) by way of a floating charge as security for continuing advances was not postponed to a guarantor who completed the work under the contract after the contractor's default and who was, through a subsequent agreement, subrogated to the contractor's claim against the building owner for amounts outstanding. Since both the bank's assignment and the guarantor's right of subrogation were equitable claims, the priority was given to the party who first perfected his interest by notifying the building owner, who was liable as debtor to the building contractor.[57]

Further advances by the creditor on the same securities cannot affect a **12–339** guarantor's right of subrogation in respect of such securities.[58] Nor can they postpone the guarantor's priority since he is entitled to all securities taken by the creditor from the principal debtor either at the time of the guarantee or at a later date.[59] Thus, the creditor's right to resort to the securities in respect of the subsequent advances will be postponed to the guarantor's right to be subrogated to the securities upon payment of the initial advance.[60] It is, however, usual to override this priority by an express provision in the guarantee stating that further advances are covered by the guarantee and that the guarantee is of the whole indebtedness. In this situation, the entire principal debt must be paid to the creditor before the guarantor acquires a right of subrogation.[61]

In *Lloyds TSB Bank plc v Shorney*[62] it was argued that surety was **12–340** entitled to priority over a mortgagee in respect of an increase in the liabilities of a joint mortgagor beyond the limit of the surety's liability. The surety entered into a joint mortgage with her husband over their home to secure his liability as a guarantor of the debts of a company. The husband's liability as guarantor was initially limited to £150,000 but it was later

---

[54] See *Drew v Lockett* (1863) 32 Beav. 499 at 506; 55 E.R. 196 at 199. In G. Andrews and R. Millett, *Law of Guarantees* (3rd ed., 2000), para.11.15 this case is discussed as an illustration of the doctrine of marshalling but it is more correctly classified as a case on the surety's right of subrogation.

[55] *ibid.*

[56] (1972) 25 D.L.R. (3d) 340.

[57] This is the rule in *Dearle v Hall* (1828) 3 Russ. 1; 38 E.R. 475.

[58] *Jones v Hill* (1893) 14 L.R. (NSW) Eq. 303 at 309–310; *Forbes v Jackson* (1882) 19 Ch. D. 615; *Dawson v Bank of Whitehaven* (1877) 4 Ch. D. 639, reversed on another point in (1877) 6 Ch. D. 218. Cf. *Williams v Owen* (1843) 13 Sim. 597; 60 E.R. 232, which was followed in *Farebrother v Wodehouse* (1856) 23 Beav. 18; 26 L.J. Ch. 81; 53 E.R. 7.

[59] *Forbes v Jackson* (1882) 19 Ch. D. 615.

[60] It might be different where the creditor is obliged to make further advances when called upon by the principal debtor. But even in this situation the guarantor should be entitled to priority over the creditor in respect of further advances made after the initial advance was repaid by the guarantor. *Cf. Rowlatt on Principal and Surety* (5th ed., 1999), p.161.

[61] See *Jones v Hill* (1893) 14 L.R. (NSW) 303. *Cf. Re Pelechet; McLeod & Co Ltd v Lysnar* [1928] G.L.R. 208 (where advances were made beyond the sum to which the guarantee was limited).

[62] *Lloyds TSB Bank Plc v Shorney* [2002] 1 F.L.R. 81; [2002] Fam. Law 18.

increased to around £290,000 as a result of the execution of further guarantees.

12–341 After a judgment was awarded against the husband under his guarantees, the bank obtained a charging order absolute against the husband's interest in the matrimonial home. It was common ground that a payment of £210,000 to the bank came almost exclusively Mrs Shorney's funds. £150,000 of this sum was paid to discharge the mortgage. It was argued, therefore, that she was entitled to keep the mortgage alive under s.5 of the Mercantile Law Amendment Act 1856 to enforce her restitutionary claim against her husband for the money paid out to discharge his indebtedness.

12–342 The issue for the court was whether Mrs Shorney's charge by subrogation took priority over the charging order obtained by the bank. The issue was complicated by the fact that clause 21 of the bank's mortgage over the matrimonial home provided that the mortgagor was not to make any claim in competition with the bank or assert any right to a security until the bank was paid in full.

12–343 The Court of Appeal held that clause 21 allowed the bank to prevent Mrs Shorney exercising her equitable rights but, in the absence of her consent, the clause did not allow the bank to put her in a position that she would not reasonably have contemplated. As Mrs Shorney reasonably contemplated a liability of £150,000 under her charge securing her husband's guarantee limited to that amount, her liability under her mortgage could not be increased to £210,000. Accordingly, she took priority over the bank in respect of the liabilities assumed by her husband in excess of £150,000. This case is an example of tailored equitable relief and its effect on the respective priorities of a mortgagee and a paying surety.

(xiii) Marshalling

12–344 The doctrine of marshalling[63] applies where there are two secured creditors of the same principal debtor.[64] If one of the secured creditors, A (the double claimant), has the right to resort to two funds or items of property,[65] whereas the other secured creditor, B (the single claimant), is

---

[63] As to the difference between contribution and marshalling, see *Tombs v Roch* (1846) 2 Coll. 490 at 499–500; 63 E.R. 828; *Ramsay v Lowther* (1912) 16 C.L.R. 1 at 24.
[64] If there is more than one debtor, marshalling will not operate where only one of the funds has been charged by a debtor jointly with another person: *Ex p. Kendall* (1811) 17 Ves. Jun. 514; 34 E.R. 199. A surety is not entitled to marshal securities held in respect of different debts or in respect of a different part of the same debt. *Wilkinson v London & County Banking Co* (1884) 1 T.L.R. 63 (where a guarantor of the balance of a borrower's account was not entitled to marshal the securities handed back to the borrower after repayment of each specific advance to the creditor); *Wade v Coope* (1827) 2 Sim. 155. Compare *Heyman v Dubois* (1871) L.R. 13 Eq. 158 which is thought to be incorrect.
[65] The right of marshalling does not operate unless the double claimant has a free and unbridled choice as to which fund to use first and the same type of rights against each fund: B. MacDonald, "Marshalling", in *Laws of Australia*, Vol. 15, para.29; *Miles v Official Receiver in Bankruptcy* (1963) 109 C.L.R. 501 (mortgagee obliged by terms of mortgage to resort to mortgagor's life assurance policy first: no marshalling); *Webb v Smith* (1885) 30 Ch. D. 192

entitled to resort to only one of the funds or items of property, then B can require A to marshall the fund or property over which A alone has security.[66] If, A, the double claimant, has already enforced its security over the funds or assets available to both A and B under their securities, B will be entitled to stand in the shoes of A in respect of A's exclusive securities.[67] In this way, the secured funds and assets of the principal debtor are marshalled so that both secured creditors will be paid as much as possible of their secured debts.[68]

These marshalling principles can be readily applied in the suretyship **12–345** context. As a general rule, marshalling applies only between two secured creditors of the same debtor. If the principal debtor grants security over all the principal assets in favour of the creditor and a limited security over merely some of his assets, say Blackacre, in favour of the guarantor to protect the guarantor's right of indemnity, the court can compel the creditor, the double claimant, to marshall the proceeds of realisation of all the secured property other than Blackacre in order to recover the principal debt.[69] If the double fund is sufficient to satisfy the double claimant, the single claimant can apply for a marshalling order which will entitle him to take over the double claimant's call on the single fund. But if the double claimant's remedies against the double fund are exhausted without satisfying the double claimant's debt, then it may enforce the security over Blackacre without any constraints from the doctrine of marshalling. In this sense, marshalling generally operates against the principal debtor or mortgagor, not against the double claimant, namely the creditor. It is only where the double claimant is in possession of a surplus of the alternative fund or its proceeds that the marshalling order will be directed to the creditor as double claimant.[70]

Where the guaranteed debt is secured by the mortgage of two funds, one **12–346** of which is subject to a second mortgage, the doctrine of marshalling can be applied *against a guarantor* who pays the principal debt: the guarantor will be compelled to marshal the securities in favour of the second mortgagee. Consequently, if the proceeds of the fund on which there are

---

(defendants were not obliged by doctrine of marshalling to exercise their inferior right of set-off against a fund arising on the sale of furniture rather than their superior lien upon a fund produced by the sale of a brewery over which the plaintiff also had a charge).
[66] But equity will not restrain the double claimant from exercising its security over the fund to which he alone is entitled because this would enable an unsecured creditor to interfere with his priority. See R. Meagher, D. Heydon and M. Leeming, *Equity Doctrines and Remedies* (4th ed., 2002), para.11.010.
[67] *Aldrich v Cooper* (1803) 8 Ves. Jun. 382; 32 E.R. 402; *Webb v Smith* (1885) 30 Ch. D. 192 at 200. See also *Trimmer v Bayne (No.2)* (1803) 9 Ves. 209; 32 E.R. 582; *Re Cohen (decd) sub nom National Provincial Bank v Katz* [1960] 1 Ch. 179 at 190; *Re a Debtor (No.24 of 1971) Ex p. Marley* [1976] 1 W.L.R. 952 at 955 *per* Foster J.
[68] In this sense, marshalling is similar to subrogation. There can be no claim for marshalling where only one debt is owed: R. Meagher, D. Heydon & M. Leeming, *Equity Doctrines and Remedies* (4th ed., 2002), para.11–040; *Re Bank of Credit and Commerce International SA (No.8)* [1998] A.C. 214 at 231.
[69] *Aldrich v Cooper* (1803) 8 Ves. Jun. 382; 32 E.R. 402; *Re Kendall* (1811) 17 Ves. Jun 514; 34 E.R. 199; *Webb v Smith* (1885) 30 Ch. D. 192; *Re Westzinthus* (1833) 5 B. & Ad. 817; 110 E.R. 992; *Re Stratton, Ex p. Salting* (1883) 25 Ch. D. 148.
[70] *Commonwealth Trading Bank v Colonial Mutual Life Assurance Society Ltd* [1970] Tas. S.R. 120 at 131. See also *Praed v Gardiner* (1788) 2 Cox Eq. Cas. 86; 30 E.R. 40.

two mortgages are applied in discharging the guaranteed debt, the second mortgagee will be entitled to the balance of the other fund remaining after satisfying the first mortgage.[71] Equally, where several persons charge their properties by way of counter-indemnity to a surety who has guaranteed a company's overdraft, the mortgagors are entitled as against the surety to have the charges marshalled so as to distribute the burden of the counter-indemnity equitably.[72]

12–347 The doctrine of marshalling is often raised in relation to corporate groups. It is common for members of the group to borrow money from, and grant securities to, different lenders. Cross-guarantees whereby each member of the group guarantees the repayment of the debts of the other members of the group are also common. When a default occurs under the securities, receivers are appointed in respect of all the companies in the group and all the secured assets are realised. It is then necessary to decide how the proceeds of realisation will be applied. Is it necessary for the receivers to marshall the proceeds?

12–348 In *Re Manawatu Transport Ltd*,[73] three associated companies, Manawatu Transport Ltd (Manawatu), Wanganui Freighters Ltd (Wanganui) and Reliance Transport (Wellington) Ltd (Reliance), each granted a mortgage debenture to the Bank of New Zealand (BNZ). Later, Manawatu gave further debentures to BP Oil New Zealand Ltd (BP) and to UDC Finance Ltd (UDC). All the companies in the group gave cross-guarantees in respect of each other's indebtedness. The applicants were appointed as receivers of the companies by the debenture holders. After realising the secured assets, they sought directions as to how the funds were to be applied.

12–349 Eichelbaum J. had no hesitation in deciding that the doctrine of marshalling did not apply in this situation. In essence, one of the fundamental elements of the doctrine was missing because the lenders did not have a common debtor. More specifically, the secured creditor who was seeking a marshalling order had not advanced funds to *all* the parties who were debtors of the secured creditor against whom marshalling was sought. In the circumstances of the case, one secured creditor, BNZ, who had a claim against all three associated companies and their assets, could not be required by another secured creditor, UDC, who had a claim against only Manawatu and its assets, to proceed against the assets of Wanganui and Reliance to the exclusion of the common debtor, Manawatu.

12–350 The only way in which marshalling would be available in this situation would be if the principal and surety exception to the common debtor rule applied. Under this exception, marshalling is available where the parties who are not common debtors have assumed the position of surety in relation to the common debtor. In *Re Manawatu Transport Ltd*, there was no evidence that Wanganui and Reliance were primarily liable and Manawatu only secondarily liable as surety for Manawatu's debts to BNZ.

---

[71] *South v Bloxham* (1865) 2 Hem. & M. 457; 71 E.R. 541. *Cf. Dixon v Steel* [1901] 2 Ch. 602.
[72] *Smith v Wood* [1929] 1 Ch. 14.
[73] (1984) 2 N.Z.C.L.C. 99,084.

On the contrary, the effect of the cross-guarantees was that Wanganui and Reliance were merely secondarily liable as guarantors for Manawatu's debts to BNZ. Consequently, the principal and surety exception could not make up for the fact that there were no common debtors. In the result, the proceeds of realisation of the assets of the respective companies were applied in reduction of their liabilities. There was no justification for a ratable division of the net proceeds across the three companies in proportion to their respective indebtedness. When the assets were applied in the order required by the court, Wanganui and Reliance finished up with a surplus of £238,247 and £115,349 respectively and Manawatu had a deficiency of £88,943.

The terms of the guarantee itself may prevent the guarantor from **12–351** invoking the equitable doctrine of marshalling.[74] But even if the doctrine does apply, it will not give the guarantor any greater rights than the doctrine of subrogation where the creditor ignores its obligation to marshall and enforces its securities without regard to the guarantor's limited recourse to some of the principal debtor's property. In this situation, the guarantor may be entitled to stand in the shoes of the creditor *in respect of the proceeds* of realisation of the assets to which the creditor had exclusive recourse.[75] But if these proceeds have been handed over to the principal debtor and dissipated in trading or in paying the unsecured creditors, the guarantor will have no redress against either the creditor or the principal debtor and no right to trace the proceeds into the hands of third parties,[76] even if they took the proceeds with notice of the single claimant's right to marshall. Certainly, the double claimant does not become a trustee for the single claimant in respect of the alternative security or its proceeds; nor does the double claimant incur any liability to the single claimant for failing to make the fund available to the single claimant before it was paid over to the principal debtor or otherwise dissipated.[77]

---

[74] See *Buckeridge v Mercantile Credits Ltd* (1981) 147 C.L.R. 654, where the High Court of Australia held that the doctrine of subrogation could be excluded by the terms of the guarantee. See above, paras 11–40 to 11–45.

[75] *Aldrich v Cooper* (1803) 8 Ves. Jun. 382; 32 E.R. 402; *Re Kendall* (1811) 17 Ves. Jun. 514; 34 E.R. 199; *Webb v Smith* (1885) 30 Ch. D. 192. See also *Farebrother v Wodehouse* (1856) 23 Beav. 18; 26 L.J. Ch. 81; on appeal: (1857) 26 L.J. Ch. 240. Moreover, a surety may be discharged to the extent that he has been prejudiced by improper "marshalling": see *Smith v Wood* [1929] 1 Ch. 14. This case actually involved a discharge of co-sureties as a result of the creditor's release of one of the securities which he held for the principal debt.

[76] The right of marshalling confers no more than a mere equity; it does not give the guarantor an equitable proprietary interest which can form the basis of a right of tracing: *Flint v Howard* [1893] 2 Ch. 54 at 73 *per* Kay L.J.; *Commonwealth Trading Bank v Colonial Mutual Life Assurance Society Ltd* [1970] Tas S.R. 120 at 125, 128 per Veasey J. See also R. Meagher, D. Heydon and M. Leeming, *Equity Doctrines and Remedies* (4th ed., 2002), para.11–055. Hence, purchasers for value or even volunteers can defeat the single claimant's right to marshall: see *Dolphin v Aylward* (1870) L.R. 4 H.L. 486 at 502.

[77] See B. MacDonald, "Marshalling", in *Laws of Australia*, Vol. 15, para.25; *Commonwealth Trading Bank v Colonial Mutual Life Assurance Society Ltd* [1970] Tas. S.R. 120 at 122, 132. But see *South v Bloxam* (1865) 2 Hem. & M. 457; 71 E.R. 541. Note the explanation of *South v Bloxam* in *Dixon v Steel* [1901] 2 Ch. 602 at 607 and see R. Meagher, D. Heydon and M. Leeming, *Equity Doctrines and Remedies* (4th ed., 2002), para.11–020.

12–352　　Notwithstanding the views expressed in some authorities,[78] the doctrine of marshalling is not available to a guarantor who is merely an unsecured contingent creditor of the principal debtor. A creditor with securities over different assets of the principal debtor cannot be compelled to marshall those securities so as to preserve the value of any security granted by the principal debtor in respect of the guaranteed debt, as distinct from his other debts.[79] But where a creditor has taken security for two debts, only one of which is guaranteed, the guarantor is entitled as against the creditor to the benefit of a proportion of the security.[80] However, this is more an application of the principle of appropriation of securities than the doctrine of marshalling.[81]

12–353　　Nor is a guarantor entitled to have a security granted to the creditor by the principal debtor enforced before a security which the guarantor himself granted to the creditor in respect of the principal debt.[82] An essential element of marshalling is lacking. This is not a situation where the principal debtor has provided two securities; one security was granted by the principal debtor, the other by the guarantor.

12–354　　A second mortgagee may not be entitled to marshall securities against a surety. In *NZ Loan & Mercantile Agency Co Ltd v Loach*,[83] Joseph Loach granted a first mortgage over A to Hope. Mrs Loach, as surety, gave a mortgage to Hope over B in respect of Joseph Loach's principal debt. Loach then gave a second mortgage over A to the plaintiff. Denniston J. held that the plaintiff was not entitled to insist that Hope realise Mrs Loach's property and apply the proceeds in reduction of the principal debt. Nor was he entitled to require Mrs Loach's property to stand charged with the moneys owing to him if Loach's property was realised first.

12–355　　These limitations upon the application of the doctrine of marshalling in the suretyship context are consistent with the general principle that a guarantor cannot require the creditor to realise any securities obtained from the principal debtor before proceeding against the guarantor.[84]

---

[78] See *Praed v Gardiner* (1788) 2 Cox Eq. Cas. 86; 30 E.R. 40; *Heyman v Dubois* (1871) L.R. 13 Eq. 158. See also T. D. Putnam, *Suretyship* (1981), p.89.

[79] See *Halsbury's Laws of England* (4th ed.), Vol. 20, para.191; *Re Kendall* (1811) 17 Ves. Jun. 514; 34 E.R. 199; Low Kee Yang, *The Law of Guarantees in Singapore and Malaysia* (1992), p.224. Contrast *Coates v Coates* (1864) 3 Beav. 249; 55 E.R. 363, which suggests that the guarantor is entitled to have the creditor's securities marshalled *pro rata* in order to reduce his liability. Even if this right were available it would normally be overridden by the creditor appropriating a security to a particular debt: *Perrie v Roberts* (1681) 1 Vern. 34; 22 E.R. 857. However, a security given to the creditor in respect of the principal debt must be appropriated to that debt, see above, paras 6–16 to 6–18.

[80] *Perrie v Roberts* (1681) 1 Vern. 34; 22 E.R. 857; *Coates v Coates* (1864) 33 Beav. 249; 55 E.R. 363; *Huggard v Representative Church Body* [1916] 10 I.R. 1 at 19.

[81] See above, paras 6–16 *et seq.*

[82] Contrast *NZ Loan & Mercantile Agency v Loach* (1912) 31 N.Z.L.R. 292; *Ex p. Marley* [1976] 1 W.L.R. 952. See also *Ex p. Goodman* (1818) 3 Madd. 373.

[83] (1912) 31 N.Z.L.R. 292.

[84] See above, paras 11–11 to 11–28.

(xiv) Consolidation

Under the doctrine of consolidation a creditor, who holds two **12–356** mortgages, can stipulate that the mortgagor cannot redeem one mortgage without redeeming the other.[85] Contrary to the suggestion in *Farebrother v Woodhouse*,[86] a creditor should not be entitled to invoke a right of consolidation against a surety because this would place an unfair burden on the surety and would be contrary to the equitable principle of subrogation.[87]

(xv) The right of subrogation in cases of contracts of indemnity

Where a creditor takes a contract of indemnity, as distinct from a **12–357** guarantee, or where a creditor takes a guarantee which contains an indemnity as a separate, independent undertaking, the party liable thereunder will, upon payment to the creditor of the amount of the loss or damages covered by the indemnity, be entitled to the benefit of any right of action held by the creditor, whether in contract or in tort, provided the enforcement of the right will diminish the loss.[88] This right of indemnity arises from the nature of the contract of indemnity and is founded on equitable principles.[89] While it is not based on an implied term in the contract between the parties, it can be limited or excluded by that contract.[90]

Presumably, an indemnifier invoking this right of subrogation will be entitled to the same range of securities as is available to a guarantor through subrogation. It should be noted, however, that an indemnifier may not enjoy the statutory right of subrogation under the equivalent of s.5 of the Mercantile Law Amendment Act 1856 because an indemnifier is probably not "liable *with* another for any debt or duty", nor is he a "co-contractor" or a "co-debtor".

Unlike the right of indemnity available to a guarantor against a principal **12–358** debtor, this right of indemnity cannot be enforced by an action in the indemnifier's own name. The right of action is not assigned to the indemnifier; nor does the indemnifier have a statutory right to have the right of action assigned to him. In this context, subrogation involves the enforcement of the indemnified party's right of action. As Derham points out, "[t]he doctrine of subrogation does not confer a new and

---

[85] There will be no right of consolidation unless the mortgages expressly provide for consolidation: See Law of Property Act 1925, s.93.

[86] (1856) 23 Beav. 18; 53 E.R. 7 (1857) 26 L.J. Ch. 240. This case was doubted in *Re Butler's Wharf Ltd* [1995] 2 B.C.L.C. 43 and the appeal from the trial judge's decision was compromised: See (1857) 26 L.J. Ch. 240.

[87] It might be different where the creditor takes a security containing a right of consolidation *after* the guarantee was executed. See *Rowlatt on Principal and Surety* (5th ed., 1999), p.161.

[88] *Morris v Ford Motor Co Ltd* [1973] Q.B. 792, CA; *Re Miller Gibb & Co* [1957] 1 W.L.R. 703.

[89] *ibid.*, at 800–801 *per* Lord Denning M.R. 805 *per* Stamp L.J.

[90] *Morris v Ford Motor Co Ltd* [1973] Q.B. 792 at 814–815 *per* James L.J.

independent right of action on the [indemnifier], but merely gives [him] the benefit of any personal right that the [indemnified party] himself has against the third party".[91] Hence, the indemnifier must sue in the name of the party indemnified.[92] Equity will compel that party to allow his name to be used in these proceedings on such terms as are just and equitable.[93] But equity will not assist an indemnifier to enforce the right of subrogation in this way if it would not be just and equitable to do so.[94]

12–359   An indemnifier can invoke the right of subrogation to assist him to enforce the right of reimbursement or indemnity against the principal[95] and, presumably, the right to contribution from co-indemnifiers.

12–360   Where an indemnifier exercises its right of subrogation against a third party and recovers a sum in excess of the amount which it was entitled to recoup, it will hold the surplus on trust for the indemnified party.[96] This principle did not apply in *Lonrho Exports Ltd v Export Credits Guarantee Department*[97] because the indemnifier in that case, ECGD, recovered moneys from the Zambian government pursuant to a bilateral agreement between the UK Government and the Zambian Government in their sovereign capacities. Accordingly, the sum received by the ECGD was not received as a trustee or agent for the indemnified party pursuant to the export credit guarantee. Accordingly, the indemnified party was not entitled to any share in the sums received by the ECGD either under the express or implied terms of its export credit guarantee or on the basis of a fiduciary duty. The fact that the ECGD had, in fact, paid the indemnified party a share of the moneys received from the Zambian Government was simply a matter of bounty. The indemnified party had no right to these payments and could not, therefore, claim interest on its share of the amounts received for the period between the date of the receipt and the date of the ex gratia payments to the indemnified party some seven years later.

---

[91] S. R. Derham, *Subrogation in Insurance Law* (1985), p.69. See also *Simpson v Thomson* (1877) 3 App. Cas. 279; *Hobbs v Marlowe* [1978] A.C. 16 at 37.
[92] *Morris v Ford Motor Co Ltd* [1973] Q.B. 792 at 800–801 *per* Lord Denning M.R.; *Mason v Sainsbury* [1782] 3 Dougl. 61; 99 E.R. 538; *Simpson v Thomson* (1877) 3 App. Cas. 279; *King v Victoria Insurance Co Ltd* [1896] A.C. 250 at 256, PC.
[93] *e.g.* the indemnifier may be required to give security for costs: see *John Edwards & Co v Motor Union Insurance Co* [1922] 2 K.B. 249 at 254.
[94] *Morris v Ford Motor Co Ltd* [1973] Q.B. 792.
[95] *ibid.*
[96] *Lonrho Exports Ltd v Export Credits Guarantee Department* [1996] 4 All E.R. 673 at 691. Compare *Lord Napier and Ettrick v Hunter; Lord Napier and Ettrick v R F Kershaw Ltd* [1993] A.C. 713 where the House of Lords stated that the indemnifier has an equitable lien on any amounts recovered by the indemnified party to secure the amount due to the indemnifier from the recoveries).
[97] [1996] 4 All E.R. 673.

Part IV

GUARANTEES IN PARTICULAR CONTEXTS

CHAPTER 13

PERFORMANCE BONDS

1. The nature of performance bonds

13–01 Performance bonds are a common mechanism in commercial transactions to protect against a failure of a contracting party to perform.[1] In the context of a contract for the sale of goods a performance bond may secure the seller's obligation to deliver, or the buyer's obligation to pay the price. Similarly in construction contracts performance bonds are a means of guaranteeing the performance of the head contractor to the proprietor or, alternatively, the performance of a sub-contractor to the head-contractor.

---

[1] As to the commercial role and advantages of performance bonds see G. Andrews and R. Millett *Law of Guarantees* (3rd ed., 2000), pp.481–480.

Performance bonds are seen as a preferable alternative to insurance since the charges are generally less than the relevant insurance premium,[2] and the bank issuing the bond will normally not be able to resist a claim for payment, especially in the case of unconditional bonds.[3] This chapter is written with special reference to construction contracts, since performance bonds are an especially common security in such contracts.

13–02   Performance bonds are of two types. The first type is a conditional performance bond whereby the guarantor only becomes liable upon proof of a breach of the terms of the principal contract by the builder, and the proprietor sustaining loss as a result of such breach. The guarantor's liability, therefore, will only arise in the usual way as a result of the principal's default. The second type of performance bond is an unconditional or "on-demand" performance bond, which is so drafted that the guarantor will become liable merely when demand is made upon the guarantor by the proprietor with no necessity for the proprietor to prove any default by the principal in performance of the building contract.

2. Conditional bonds

13–03   A common form of a conditional bond is illustrated in *Paddington Churches Housing Association v Technical & General Guarantee Co Ltd*[4] is:

> "Now the Condition of the above written Bond is such that if the Contractor shall duly perform and observe all the terms provisions conditions and stipulations of the said Contract on the Contractor's part to be performed and observed according to the true purport intent and meaning thereof or if *on default* by the Contractor or for the avoidance of doubt a valid determination of the Contractor's employment under clause 27 of the said Contract the Surety shall satisfy and discharge the *net established and ascertained damages* sustained by the Employer thereby up to the amount of the above written Bond then this obligation shall be null and void but otherwise shall be and remain in full force and otherwise shall be and remain in full force and effect up to the date of issue of the Statement of Practical Completion ..." [authors' emphasis]

---

[2] As to the role of the Export Credits Guarantee Department in insurance, see G. Andrews and R. Millett, *Law of Guarantees* (3rd ed., 2000), Ch. 15. Insurance may be given for an unjustified call on a performance bond.

[3] See below, paras 13–12 to 13–53. Note that unconditional performance bonds may also be used to secure the performance of obligations where there is otherwise an absence of a binding principal obligation, as in the case of tender bonds (taken to ensure that a successful bidder for the tender does not subsequently refuse to sign a contract upon the terms of his tender) or a bond taken to secure a counter trade obligation (that is, an agreement by the supplier of goods to purchase another commodity from the buyer at a future date which might be void for uncertainty or as being an agreement to agree).

[4] [1999] B.L.R. 244. See similarly *Trafalgar House Construction (Regions) Ltd v General Surety & Guarantee Co Ltd* [1996] A.C. 199.

Such an agreement will be construed as a guarantee since it is predicated **13-04** upon breach and the occasioning of loss and damage (as indicated by the italicised words).[5] Sometimes a provision is also included stating that no alteration in the terms of the agreement between employer and employee, and that no forbearance or indulgence granted by the employer, shall release the bond issuer from liability. Such a clause also points to the existence of guarantee since its inclusion is only consistent with the agreement being a guarantee since those events will discharge a guarantor, but not a primary obligor.[6]

The normal incidents of suretyship will apply to such bonds. Thus the **13-05** bond will prima facie be interpreted as being co-extensive with liability under the underlying contract so that a bond securing the contractor's obligations under a building contract will remain in force until there has been practical completion according to the terms of the building contract (for example, by the issue of an architect's certificate). The bond issuer is in the same position as the contractor.[7] Furthermore, in accordance with usual principles of suretyship the bond issuer will be discharged by a release of the party whose obligations are secured,[8] a variation of the underlying construction contract,[9] and a release of any securities held by the beneficiary of the bond.[10] The bond issuer may also rely on a set off or counterclaim possessed by the party whose obligations are secured and is entitled to rights of indemnity and subrogation. All these rights may be excluded by the terms of the guarantee, but clear wording is required to do so.[11]

Strict compliance with any conditions precedent is required before the **13-06** bond issuer will incur any liability. Such conditions precedent may arise because the bond itself incorporates the terms of the construction contract as terms of the bond. Thus in *Paddington Churches Housing Association v Technical & General Guarantee Co Ltd*[12] the recital to the guarantee specifically referred to the construction contract and additionally (as set out above)[13] the substantive part of the guarantee referred to clause 27 of that contract. As a result it was held that the bond issuer incurred no

---

[5] See *Trafalgar House Construction (Regions) Ltd v General Safety & Guarantee Co Ltd* [1996] A.C. 199.
[6] *ibid.* But not if the "language of suretyship" is absent from the clause, which can then be explained on the basis that the rule applicable to true guarantees was intended to apply to the agreement: *Gold Coast Ltd v Caja de Ahorros del Meditarraneo* [2002] 1 Lloyd's Rep. 617, para.25.
[7] *City of Glasgow District Council v Excess Insurance Co Ltd* [1986] S.L.T. 585, where it was held that on a proper construction of the building contract there might be liability on the contractor after practical completion and that what was envisaged by the expression "practical completion" was practical completion by the contractors named in the bond. See also *De Vere Hotels Ltd v Aegon Insurance Co (UK) Ltd* (unreported, October 15, 1977).
[8] See above, para.6-53.
[9] See above, Ch.7.
[10] See above, para.8-71.
[11] See in respect of the exclusion of the right of set-off *Trafalgar House Construction (Regions) Ltd v General Surety & Guarantee Co Ltd* [1996] A.C. 1999 and in respect of the exclusion of the right of subrogation, *Liberty Mutual Insurance Co (UK) Ltd v HSBC Bank Ltd* [2001] Lloyd's Rep. Bank. 224 and, on appeal, [2002] EWCA Civ. 691, discussed above, para.12-270.
[12] [1999] B.L.R. 244.
[13] See above, para.13-03.

liability in the event of a determination of the construction contract pursuant to clause 27 until it had received a statement of the "net established and ascertained damages" in accordance with the method of calculation set out in that clause.[14]

13-07   A condition precedent may also provide that the bond issuer will incur no liability unless a demand for payment is made prior to the date of termination of the bond. Thus in *Lorne Stewart plc v Hermes Kreditversicherungs*[15] such a condition precedent meant that the bond issuer was held to incur no liability when a demand for payment was posted to the bond issuer only on the termination date itself. The bond may also impose by way of a condition precedent that a breach by the contractor of the terms of the construction contract must be notified to the bond issuer. In *Oval (717) Ltd v Aegon Insurance Co (UK) Ltd*[16] a clause required the bond issuer to be informed in writing of any "non-performance or non-observance on the part of the contractors of any of the stipulations or provisions contained [in the underlying contract] and on their part to be performed and observed within one month after such non-performance or non-observance shall have come to the notice of the employer". The employer was unable to call on the bond when he failed to notify the bond issuer of the contractor's failure to complete the works on time within the stipulated one month time period (there being an extended completion date).[17] Whilst the contractor's breach in *Oval (717) Ltd v Aegon Insurance Co (UK) Ltd*[18] was relatively serious, the clause was interpreted literally as embracing every (*i.e.* "any") breach. This construction means that the burden placed upon the employer to notify the bond issuer of events of non performance is high since pursuant to the terms of most construction contracts the contractor may non-perform in a variety of ways (for example, by failing to supply the employer with the relevant number of working drawings or with copies of vouchers to prove that the materials used are in compliance with specified requirements).[19]

---

[14] See also *Alstrom Combined Cycles Ltd v Henry Boot plc* (unreported May 1, 2001) where there was specific reference in the bond to the bond issuer's liability determining, *inter alia*, upon "the date specified therein" of a Defects Correction Certificate issued by the engineer. Clause 61 of the building contract defined that date as "the date on which the Contractor shall have completed his obligations to construct and complete the works to the engineer's satisfaction".

[15] Unreported October 22, 2001.

[16] (1997) 85 B.L.R. 97.

[17] See, however, *Odebrecht Oil & Gas Services Ltd v North Sea Production Co Ltd* (unreported May 10, 1999) where the notification clause stated that "if the employer reasonably believes that there has been a breach by the contractor, he shall give written notice to the Contractor and the Guarantor, specifying the nature of such breach and his estimate of the amount of Damages arising therefrom". It was held that the notice did not need to state with precision the acts or omissions alleged to constitute each breach or the date of the alleged breach.

[18] (1997) 5 B.L.R. 97.

[19] By analogy with the general principles of suretyship applicable to agreed variations of the principal contract (see above Ch.7) the Recorder held that breaches that were obviously unsubstantial (without evident inquiry) or for the benefit of the guarantor, did not come within the ambit of the clause. But it is doubtful if this view is in accordance with the usual approach to the construction of conditions precedent (see above para.8–12, and below, para.10–98).

A final issue in respect of conditional bonds is that if the employer is to **13–08**
recover under the bond in respect of damages incurred by a defaulting
contractor for failure to complete the work, the employer must ensure that
the right to recover damages against the contractor is preserved. The
general contractual principle is that damages for loss of bargain (in this
situation damages for the additional cost of completing the work) are only
recoverable in the event of a repudiation (or breach of condition) of the
building contract by the contractor, which is then accepted by the
employer. Terminating the construction contract in reliance on a provision
permitting termination (or providing for automatic termination) upon
stipulated events occurring will not necessarily have this effect. A salutary
warning is *Perar BV v General Surety and Guarantee Co Ltd*.[20] That case
concerned a claim made on a bond which arose out of the termination of a
building contract which incorporated the conditions of the JCT Standard
Form of Building Contract with Contractor's Design (1981 Edn), cl.27.2 of
which stated:

> "In the event of the Contractor ... having an administrative receiver, as
> defined in the Insolvency Act 1986, appointed ... the employment of the
> Contractor under this Contract shall be forthwith automatically
> determined but the said employment may be reinstated and continued
> if the Employer and the Contractor ... [and] receiver ... shall so agree."

The contractor went into administrative receivership. No further work **13–09**
was done on site and the employer subsequently considered that the
contractor had abandoned the contract. Four days later the employer
notified the administrative receiver that it was not intended to reinstate or
continue the contractor's employment. The Court of Appeal held that the
employer was not entitled to treat the cessation of the work following the
automatic termination as an abandonment and repudiation of the contract
since, once the employment had been thus automatically terminated, the
contractor ceased to be under his primary obligation to carry out the
works.[21] The contract by setting out an exclusive code as to what was to
happen in the event of insolvency, and the appointment of an administrative receiver, precluded the appointment of the receiver being treated as
an anticipatory breach of contract or repudiation.

The latter point is important since a list of events stipulated in the **13–10**
contract, for which the employer is entitled to terminate the contract, may
be construed an exclusive code of termination, thus precluding termination
for repudiatory conduct. Any provision of this type should be qualified by
wording in these terms: "without prejudice to any other legal or equitable
right or remedy which the owner or employer would otherwise possess
hereunder or as a matter of law". It was this provision that, in part, enabled
enforcement of the bond in *Laing Management Ltd v Aegon Insurance Co*

[20] (1994) 66 B.L.R. 72.
[21] *ibid.*, at 82–83.

(UK) Ltd.[22] Here, although it was held that the termination of the principal contract when the contractor was put in receivership did not constitute acceptance of any repudiation by the contractor, effective termination of the contract for other (admitted) acts of repudiation took place by the issue of the statement of claim. This generated a claim in damages against the contractor, and thus against the issuer of the bond.

13–11   Even if this general saving provision is included, however, there are dangers for the employer, especially if the employer terminates the contract on the basis that the contractor has been placed in receivership. By itself the appointment of receiver is unlikely to constitute a repudiation of the contract since the main purpose of an administrative receiver is to enable the company to continue to trade. Worse, for the employer's point of view, the letter of appointment may be construed as an affirmation of the contract, preventing terminating for repudiation at a later stage since an election to affirm has then been made. There is also the additional argument that if the employer terminates the contract upon the basis of a clause permitting termination for specified events, then it is the employer's act of termination rather than the conduct of the contractor which prevents the contractor completing the work.[23]

3. UNCONDITIONAL BONDS

13–12   An unconditional bond is usually drafted so that it is clear that the bond issuer is liable to pay upon demand. *Wood Hall Ltd v Pipeline Authority*[24] provides an example:

> "1. The bank unconditionally undertakes and covenants to pay on demand any sum or sums which may from time to time be demanded in writing by the owner up to a maximum aggregate sum of ONE MILLION FIVE HUNDRED THOUSAND DOLLARS ($1,500,000.00) to be held by the owner."[25]

13–13   Drafted in this way, unconditional performance bonds are analogous to letters of credit[26] or even promissory notes payable on demand.[27] They are to be treated as the equivalent of cash. Generally no term will be implied that a breach of the underlying contract is required before the bond can be

---

[22] (1997) 55 Con. L.R. 1. Note that in this case the bond was given to a contractor in respect of the obligations of a sub-contractor.
[23] This argument was rejected in *Laing Management Ltd v Aegon Insurance Co Ltd* (1997) 55 Con. L.R. because it was clear that the contractor was not going to complete the work in any event.
[24] (1979) 141 C.L.R. 443.
[25] *ibid.*, at 447.
[26] *R D Harbottle (Mercantile) Ltd v National Westminster Bank Ltd* [1978] Q.B. 146; *Howe Richardson Scale Co Ltd v Polimex-Cekop and National Westminster Bank Ltd* [1978] 1 Lloyd's Rep. 161; *Edward Owen Engineering Ltd v Barclays Bank International Ltd* [1978] Q.B. 159; *Intraco Ltd v Notis Shipping Corp* [1981] 2 Lloyd's Rep. 256; *Solo Industries UK Ltd v Canara Bank* [2001] 1 W.L.R. 1800 at 1804.
[27] *Edward Owen Engineering Ltd v Barclays Bank International Ltd* [1978] 1 Q.B. 159 at 170–171.

called in.[28] It is now clear, despite earlier doubts, that the relationship between the bank and proprietor pursuant to an unconditional performance bond is not one of suretyship,[29] which reinforces the view (subject to the following discussion) that a performance bond operates independently of the underlying transaction. As Lord Denning stated in *Edward Owen Engineering Ltd v Barclays Bank International Ltd*:[30]

"A bank which gives a performance guarantee must honour that guarantee according to its terms. It is not concerned in the least with the relations between the supplier and the customer; nor with the question whether the supplier has performed his contracted obligation or not; nor with the question whether the supplier is in default or not. The bank must pay according to its guarantee, on demand, if so stipulated, without proof or conditions."[31]

The fact that the performance bond does not result in a contract of **13–14** suretyship will also mean that the obligor under the bond will not be discharged by such matters as a variation of the underlying contract or by the proprietor giving time to the principal contractor for the performance of the contractor's obligations under the principal contract.[32] The bank's liability may also not be affected by the loss or impairment of securities held by the proprietor for the enforcement of the principal's obligation if the obligor (not being in the position of a surety) is not entitled to be subrogated to those securities on making payment under the performance bond.[33] For similar reasons, since no element of suretyship is involved, it follows that the bank will be obliged to pay when a demand is made upon it, even if the underlying transaction has been determined, for example by the proprietor terminating the contract for the contractor's breach[34] or by frustration.[35]

Where the underlying transaction is illegal or unenforceable, the **13–15** position is less clear. In *Standard Bank (London) Ltd v Canara Bank*[36] it was held (obiter) that a valid demand could be made upon a

---

[28] *State Trading Corp of India Ltd v E D & F Man (Sugar) Ltd* [1981] Com.L.R. 235; *Costain International Ltd v Davy McKee (London) Ltd* (unreported, CA, November 26, 1990). As to the reluctance of the courts to imply terms into an unconditional bond, providing for a limitation upon the proprietor's right to call on the bond see *Britten Norman Ltd (in liq) v State Ownership Fund of Romania* [2000] Lloyd's Rep. Bank. 315 at 320.
[29] *Wood Hall Ltd v Pipeline Authority* (1979) 141 CLR 443 at 445.
[30] [1978] 1 Q.B. 159.
[31] *ibid.*, at 171. See also *Gulf Bank KSC v Mitsubishi Heavy Industries Ltd* [1994] 2 Lloyd's Rep. 145.
[32] See above, Ch. 7.
[33] See above, para.8–46.
[34] *Geraldton Building Co Ltd v Christmas Island Resort Pty Ltd* (unreported, WA Sup Ct, May 30, 1994), where it was held that it was the parties' common intention that the right to call on the bond should survive termination, and also that there was no basis for limiting resort to the bond only to where the claim under the agreement was liquidated.
[35] See *Emerson Electric Industries Controls v Bank of America* (unreported, Eng CA, July 10, 1979) (frustration of the principal contract was held to have no effect on the guarantor's liability). As to the general rules governing the guarantor's liability in these circumstances, see above, paras 6–117 to 6–148.
[36] Unreported, HC, May 22, 2002.

performance bond in such circumstances, but in that case not only did the parties to the bond have in contemplation the absence of an enforceable underlying contract, but the bond contained a clause specifically stating the guarantor's liability should not be extinguished or reduced by the "invalidity, illegality or unenforceability" of the principal obligation.[37] Nevertheless, the autonomous nature of the bond should mean that the beneficiary of the bond is not affected by the invalidity or illegality of the underlying contract even in the absence of such a clause.

13–16   The making of a demand pursuant to an unconditional performance bond will have serious consequences for the contractor. Invariably the obligor under the bond will be a bank which, upon payment to the proprietor, will immediately debit the contractor's account or exercise its rights in respect of a counter-indemnity obtained from the contractor. As a result, the creditor may suffer liquidity problems and may also be concerned that the moneys received by the proprietor may be dissipated.

The contractor may therefore seek to restrain the proprietor from making a demand upon the guarantee and/or seek to obtain an injunction against the bank restraining it from paying under the guarantee. The circumstances in which relief may be obtained are discussed below.

(i) Limitations on the proprietor's right to demand payment pursuant to the bond

13–17   Although the law is not entirely clear, it is possible to identify a number of situations in which the contractor may obtain relief, although in some of them only against the proprietor and not the bank.

(a) *Where the bond is not unconditional*

13–18   In every case the terms of the guarantee need to be carefully scrutinised to ascertain whether the obligation of the bank pursuant to the bond is unconditional in the sense that the obligation arises merely upon demand being made by the proprietor. Another possible construction is that the moneys are only payable by the bank if there is evidence of a breach by the contractor. In determining this question, the overall commercial purpose of the contractual relationship is important, as well as the form and language of the guarantee.[38] Nomenclature is not decisive. Thus in *Trafalgar House Construction (Regions) Ltd v General Surety & Guarantee Co Ltd*,[39] a deed described as a "bond" was held to be a guarantee rather

---

[37] See a similar clause in *Gulf Bank KSC v Mitsubishi Heavy Industries Ltd (No.2)* [1996] 1 Lloyd's Rep. 499.

[38] *Attaleia Marine Co Ltd v Bimeh Iran (Iran Insurance Co)* [1993] 2 Lloyd's Rep. 497 at 502; *Gold Coast Ltd v Caja de Ahorros del Mediterraneo* [2002] 1 Lloyd's Rep. 617.

[39] [1996] A.C. 199.

than an unconditional performance bond, as the obligor's liability was
predicated upon breach.[40]

The tendency of the courts, however, has been to treat the bond as **13–19**
unconditional if there is a clear statement that the amount is payable by
the bank simply upon a written demand being made, even though there are
some indications to the contrary elsewhere in the document. Thus in *Esal
(Commodities) Ltd v Oriental Credit Ltd*,[41] where the bank "undertook to
pay the said amount on your written demand *in the event that the supplier
fails to execute the written performance*", it was held that the latter words
did not alter the fact that the moneys were payable upon a written demand
being made as stated in the earlier part of the clause.[42] The beneficiary of
the bond did not have to show a failure to perform by the supplier in order
to claim upon the bond. Similarly, in *Standard Bank (London) Ltd v
Canara Bank*[43] a guarantee which stated that Canara Bank "hereby
irrevocably and unconditionally agree to pay ... upon your first written
demand" was treated as an unconditional performance bond, even though
the bond contained a clause stating that it was given for "the due and
punctual payment by [the supplier] of its obligations under the said
purchase contract" and, additionally, the usual provisions preserving the
liability of the guarantor in respect of events which would normally
discharge a guarantor pursuant to a conditional bond (for example, a
variation of the principal contract).[44] Indeed, in *IE Contractors Ltd v
Lloyd's Bank plc*,[45] Staughton L.J. was of the view that in cases of
ambiguity there was "a bias or presumption" that performance bonds were
not payable upon proof of facts, but merely upon the presentation of the
appropriate document(s) (that is, in the case of unconditional bonds, upon
the making of a written demand).

Even if a bond might otherwise be regarded as being conditional, the **13–20**
inclusive of a "conclusive evidence clause"[46] may also have the effect of
creating an unconditional obligation. In *Balfour Beatty Civil Engineering v
Technical & General Guarantee Co Ltd*[47] the instrument required
payment upon the "first written demand" and provided that "such

---

[40] As another example, see *Guyana & Trinidad Mutual Fire Insurance Co Ltd v R K Plummer
& Associates Ltd* (1992) 8 Const. L.J. 171.
[41] [1985] 2 Lloyd's Rep. 546.
[42] See also *Gold Coast Ltd v Caja de Ahorros del Mediterraneo* [2002] 1 Lloyd's Rep. 617. As
this case illustrates the document may be interpreted as an "on demand" guarantee even
though the demand has to be accompanied by the provision of a certificate. *Cf. Re Butler's
Wharf Ltd* [1995] 2 B.C.L.C. 43, where the wording clearly indicated there was a
"conventional guarantee", but the guarantee was subsequently stated to be payable "upon
first demand following demand for repayment under the terms of the ... facility". It was held
that this simply made the guarantee conditional upon the service of a demand upon the
principal debtor and the guarantor, but did not convert the obligation into a performance
bond payable without proof of default.
[43] Unreported, CA, May 22, 2002.
[44] See also *Gold Coast Ltd v Caja de Ahorros del Mediterraneo* [2002] 1 Lloyd's Rep. 617. *Cf.*
the importance given to the existence of such clauses in *Trafalgar House Construction
(Regions) Ltd v General Surety & Guarantee Co Ltd* [1996] A.C. 199. See above, para.13–04.
[45] [1990] 51 B.L.R. 1. See also *Siporex Trade SA v Banque Indosuez* [1986] 2 Lloyd's Rep. 146
at 159, where Hirst J. indicated that precise wording might not be essential.
[46] See above, para.5–02.
[47] (1999) 68 Con. L.R. 180 at 183.

demand should be accepted by the surety as conclusive evidence that the sum of demand is due hereunder". Waller L.J. in the Court of Appeal concluded in this way:

> "This bond contains language which seems to me to make it absolutely clear that this is a bond intended to be met without the surety having either the right or the duty to make any detailed inquiry provided the demand letter conforms with the conditions of the bond. It requires payment on 'first demand'; it provides that the statements required to be made should be conclusive evidence of the facts stated therein. That is the clearest possible indication that as between the surety, and the promisee, there will be no investigation into the underlying facts."

(b) Where the written demand required by the terms of the bond itself is deficient

13–21   Even if the bond is unconditional in the sense described above, the contractor may restrain the bank from paying the proprietor pursuant to the bond if the written demand fails to assert facts which the bond requires it should assert, that is, if the demand has not been made in proper form. Thus in *Franz Maas (UK) Ltd v Habib Bank AG. Zurich*[48] a bond was given to secure the payment of certain liquidated sums falling due pursuant to the underlying agreement. The bond provided that the claims made by the beneficiary should be in writing, and should state that the other party to the underlying contract "had failed to pay ... under [its] contractual obligations". On the facts the statement of demand did not allege "a failure to pay" but a "failure to meet contractual obligations". It was held that a demand which stated that a person had failed "to meet contractual obligations" was not equivalent to a statement that a person "had failed to pay" since "the former concept is wide enough to include any claim for damages for unliquidated or unascertained sums arising from any breach of [the underlying agreement] which would ... widen the scope of the guarantee far beyond that which the parties intended",[49] namely, the failure to pay the liquidated and unascertained sums falling due under the underlying agreement. Similarly, it will constitute a wrongful demand if it is made by someone who is not, within the terms of the bond, a named beneficiary.[50]

13–22   The precise wording of the demand as stated in the bond does not, however, always have to be repeated. In *IE Contractors Ltd v Lloyd's Bank plc*,[51] each bond provided:

---

[48] [2001] Lloyd's Rep. Bank. 14.
[49] *ibid.*, at 25.
[50] *e.g. GKN Contractors v Lloyds Bank plc* (1985) 30 B.L.R. 48, where the demand was made not by the named beneficiary, but by the apparent successor in title to the beneficiary under Iraqi legislation, and it was held arguable that it was not a valid demand.
[51] [1990] 51 B.L.R. 1; on appeal from Leggatt J.: [1989] 2 Lloyd's Rep. 205. See also *Esso Petroleum Malaysia Inc v Kago Petroleum* [1995] 1 M.L.J. 149 at 157.

"We undertake to pay you unconditionally the said amount on demand, *being your claim for damages brought about by the above named principal.*"[52]

The Court of Appeal held that the second part of the clause *did not* **13–23** make the amounts payable only on proof of default (that is, the bond remained unconditional). But the wording *did* have the effect that the written demand must state "in substance", although not in express terms, that the claim was in respect of damages for breach of contract. On the facts, however, the demand was valid because, although it did not refer specifically to a claim for damages, it did assert that the claim was for breach of contract. This was sufficient "in substance" to be treated as an assertion of a claim for damages.

It should be emphasised that the obtaining of an injunction on the basis **13–24** of a deficient demand in practical terms is only a delaying tactic until a proper demand is made, although of some help to the contractor when its liquidity problems are critical.

(c) Where the construction contract itself qualifies the proprietor's right to make a demand?

There is some authority[53] in other common law jurisdiction (notably **13–25** Australia) that the contractor may obtain relief where the construction contract itself contains some qualification upon the proprietor's right to make a demand. The relief envisaged here is not to obtain an injunction against the bank which must pay according to the unconditional terms of the bond, but against the proprietor who is to be restrained from making a demand upon the bank and thus converting the bond into cash.

This principle was applied in *Selvas Pty Ltd v Hansen Yuncken (SA) Pty* **13–26** *Ltd*[54] where the relevant clause in the construction contract stated:

"Any security provided by the sub-contractor in terms of this contract shall be available to the contractor *upon default of the sub-contractor* or whenever the contractor may be otherwise entitled to the payment of moneys by the sub-contractor under or in consequence of this contract or whenever the contractor may be entitled to reimbursement of any moneys paid to the other under this contract, in all such cases as if the security were a sum of money due or to become due to the sub-contractor by the contractor."

It was held that the contractor was entitled to an injunction restraining the proprietor from making a demand to call on the moneys secured by the bond. This was because the clause in the construction contract stipulated

---

[52] *ibid.*, (emphasis added).
[53] *Wood Hall Ltd v Pipeline Authority* (1979) 141 C.L.R. 443 at 459; *Selvas Pty v Hansen Yuncken (SA) Pty Ltd* (1987) 6 A.C.L.R. 36; *Pearson Bridge (NSW) Pty Ltd v State Rail Authority of New South Wales* (1982) 1 A.C.L.R. 81.
[54] (1987) 6 Australian Construction Law Rep. 36.

preconditions to the proprietor's right to call up the security, for example, by reference to the "default of the sub-contractor", and the contractor could show that there was a "real dispute" between the parties as to whether the precondition had been satisfied. The balance of convenience was also in the contractor's favour.

13–27   The possibility of the contractor obtaining an injunction in this way is disturbing from the point of view of the proprietor, who might well have imagined that it could convert the performance bond into cash at any time according to the unconditional terms of the bond. Indeed, the result is contrary to the general nature of an unconditional performance bond that it is to be independent of the underlying contract. It is considered that wording in the principal building contract should only be relevant in determining the obligation of the proprietor to account once the proprietor has made a demand and has received the moneys from the bank.[55]

(d) Fraudulent demands

13–28   **(i) Restraining the bank from making payment**. It is established that the bank may be restrained from making a payment pursuant to the bond if it is shown that the beneficiary is guilty of fraud to the knowledge of the bank. There is some difficulty, however, in defining fraud for this purpose. In respect of letters of credit, where a similar principle applies, fraud can be shown if the documents that are required to be presented contain material misrepresentations of fact, which are untrue to the beneficiary's knowledge.[56] But unconditional performance bonds usually require no documentation apart from the serving of a notice of demand, so in this context fraud has been defined as the beneficiary making a claim for payment to which the beneficiary knows that he was not entitled.[57] If the view that performance bonds are independent of the underlying transaction is taken to the extreme, however, so that the beneficiary is always honestly entitled to assume a call can be made simply by the making of a demand (because that is what the bond states), the fraud exception will be rendered meaningless. This appeared to be the view of Moore-Bick J. in *Standard Bank (London) Ltd v Canara Bank*[58] when he stated (albeit obiter) that "even in a case where the beneficiary knew that [the underlying contract] was void or unenforceable it would still be open to him to make a valid demand under the guarantee because that is what it contemplates".[59] Yet there is other authority stating that fraud can be established by showing that when the beneficiary made the demand he knew that the sum was not due from the other party to the underlying

---

[55] See below, para.13–54.
[56] *United City Merchants (Investments) Ltd v Royal Bank of Canada* [1982] 2 All E.R. 720 at 725; *Themehelp v West* [1995] 4 All E.R. 215 at 219. See also *Contronic Distributors Pty Ltd v Bank of New South Wales* [1984] 3 N.S.W.L.R. 110.
[57] *GKN Contractors v Lloyd's Bank plc* [1985] 30 B.L.R. 48 at 63; *Deutsche Ruckversicherung AG v Walbrook Insurance Co Ltd* [1994] 4 All E.R. 181 at 187.
[58] Unreported, CA, May 22, 2002.
[59] *ibid.*, at para.71.

contract, and the beneficiary dishonestly made the demand despite such knowledge,[60] (for example, where other party is not in breach of contract and/or has fully performed its obligations, to the knowledge of the beneficiary.)[61] This was the manner in which the issue was addressed by the Court of Appeal in *Balfour Beatty Civil Engineering v Technical & General Guarantee Co Ltd,*[62] where the bond was given in favour of a contractor to secure the obligations of a sub-contractor (called Leadrail):

"In the assessment one is entitled to remind oneself that the question is not whether Leadrail or its liquidator might be able to show that the sum claimed under the bond was not in fact due.[63] Nor is the question whether the beneficiary in the light of the evidence might not have some-anxiety as to whether the sum was due and have some anxiety about whether Leadrail might not have a good claim to the return of the money if it is paid by the surety. The question is whether when the demand was made the persons acting on behalf of the plaintiffs knew that the sum claimed was not due from Leadrail, and dishonestly made a demand despite that knowledge."

In determining whether or not the beneficiary is guilty of fraud much **13–29** may turn on the precise terms of the bond. In *Standard Bank (London) Ltd v Canara Bank*[64] it was perhaps not insignificant that the bond contained a clause providing that the guarantor's liability should not be reduced or extinguished in the event of the underlying transaction being unenforceable or illegal, and no doubt a clause in the bond can also provide that a demand shall be valid even though the beneficiary knows that the relevant sum is not due because there is no breach of the underlying contract. But in the usual case it is considered that the approach adopted in *Balfour Beatty Civil Engineering v Technical & General Guarantee Co Ltd*[65] is correct.

Whatever the precise nature of fraud in this context, it is clear that **13–30** where an injunction is sought against a bank restraining the bank from making payment under the bond, the burden of proof is high, although there have been slightly different formulations of the appropriate test. In *R D Harbottle (Mercantile) Ltd v National Westminster Bank Ltd*[66] it was said that there must be a "clear" case of fraud, (of which the bank has notice), even upon the making of a interlocutory application. In *United Trading*

---

[60] Assuming the bank's knowledge of such fraud. See below, paras 13–33 to 13–34.
[61] See *CDN Research & Development Bank Ltd v Bank of Nova Scotia* (1980) 18 C.P.C. 62 (buyer of goods making a claim upon a bond guaranteeing delivery of goods when those goods have been delivered).
[62] (1999) 68 Con. L.R. 180 at 190–191. See also *Consolidated Oil Ltd & American Express Bank Ltd* (unreported, CA, January 21, 2000).
[63] Cf. *Potton Homes Ltd v Coleman Contractors Ltd* (1984) 28 B.L.R. 19 at 30 where Eveleigh J. at one point in his judgment appears to treat a demand following the mere fact of a breach as equivalent to fraud: "It cannot be said that the plaintiffs have proved that there are no breaches of the original contract and that *a demand would therefore be fraudulent*".
[64] Unreported, HC, May 22, 2002.
[65] (1999) 68 Con. L.R. 180. Note that another instance of fraud might be where the beneficiary knows that the performance bank has been discharged.
[66] [1978] Q.B. 146 at 155–156. See also *Edward Owen Engineering Ltd v Barclays Bank International Ltd* [1978] 1 Q.B. 159 at 175.

Corp SA v Allied Arab Bank Ltd,[67] however, the test was expressed at an interlocutory stage as being (under the old civil procedure rules) whether "it is seriously arguable that, on the material available, the only realistic inference is that [the beneficiary] could not honestly have believed in the validity of its demands on the performance bonds".[68] Pursuant to the new Civil Procedure Rules the words "it is seriously arguable" would now need to be replaced by "there is a real prospect".[69] It has been suggested that this re-formulation lowers the standard of proof since it is a "comparatively low hurdle"[70] to establish that there is a "real prospect" of success, the expression being identified with "some chance of success".[71] But in *Solo Industries UK Ltd v Canara Bank*[72] Mance L.J. doubted that there was any substantive change to the burden of proof:

"The courts in the *Harbottle* and *Edward Owen* cases were concerned with the interlocutory stage. The test that they stated was undiluted by any reference to 'arguable case'. The defence that they and later authorities identify, of established fraud known to the bank, is, by its nature, one which, if it is good at all, must be capable of being established with clarity at the interlocutory stage. On any view, as Rix J. observed [in *Czarnikow-Rionda Sugar Trading Inc v Standard Bank London Ltd*[73]] the court should be careful not to allow too extensive a dilution of the presumption in favour of the fulfilment of independent banking commitments. The introduction of the balancing concept of 'the only realistic inference' and the actual conclusion on the facts in the *United Trading* case suggest that the court there also had this consideration in mind."

In any event, there will clearly be no fraud if there is a mere assertion of fraud,[74] or if the beneficiary is acting bona fide,[75] but is simply uncertain as to the right to payment pursuant to the underlying transaction.[76] The difficulty of establishing fraud is accentuated when performance bonds are

---

[67] [1985] 2 Lloyd's Rep. 554.
[68] *ibid.*, at 561. See also *Sunderland Association Football Club Ltd v Uruguay Montevideo FC* [2001] 2 All E.R. (Comm.) 828 at 834.
[69] *Solo Industries UK Ltd v Canara Bank* [2001] 1 W.L.R. 1800 at 1812 para.32.
[70] *ibid.*, at 1812 para.31.
[71] *ibid.*
[72] [2001] 1 W.L.R. 1800 at 1813, para.32.
[73] [1999] 2 Lloyd's Rep. 187.
[74] *United Trading Corp SA v Allied Arab Bank Ltd* [1985] 2 Lloyd's Rep. 554 at 561.
[75] In *GKN Contractors v Lloyd's Bank plc* (1985) 30 B.L.R. 48, Parker L.J. indicated that it might constitute fraud if the beneficiary bona fide made a demand, believing that there was a breach of the underlying contract, but the bank knew there was not. But this is an unlikely factual situation.
[76] *Deutsche Ruckversicherung AG v Walbrook Insurance Co Ltd* [1994] 4 All E.R. 181. Note that, if there is clear evidence of fraud and the bank does make payment when a demand is made, the bank has a potential liability in negligence. In *United Trading Corp SA v Allied Arab Bank Ltd* [1985] 2 Lloyd's Rep. 554 at 560, Ackner L.J. thought that "it is arguable that a bank owes a duty of care to the party ultimately liable at the end of the chain not to pay out on the performance bond if ... there is clear evidence that the beneficiary's demand is fraudulent because it is the party at the end of the chain who may have to bear the ultimate loss". See also *GKN Contractors v Lloyd's Bank plc* (1985) 30 B.L.R. 48; *Consolidated Oil Ltd v American Express Bank Ltd* (unreported, CA, January 21, 2000).

given in respect of an overseas beneficiary. The courts are reluctant to infer fraud from a failure of the beneficiary in the overseas country to respond to the allegations because there is another explanation of the beneficiary's silence,[77] namely, an "understandable" reluctance to submit to legal jurisdiction outside the beneficiary's own country, when it is clear from the documentation that the proper law in relation to the settlement of disputes arising from the underlying transaction is that of the beneficiary's country.[78] The only remaining evidence, therefore, may be the uncorroborated statement of the contractor, upon which the court will be reluctant to rely.[79]

An example of the reluctance of the courts to grant an injunction **13–31** restraining the bank from making payment on the basis of fraud is *Edward Owen Engineering Ltd v Barclays Bank International Ltd*,[80] where the beneficiary of the goods was a buyer in Libya who had failed to establish any mechanism for payment through a confirmed letter of credit. Lane L.J. analysed the evidence in this way:

"The way [counsel] seeks to establish fraud is this. He points to the undoubted fact that the buyers in Libya have failed to reply to any of the requests for a proper confirmed letter of credit according, [counsel] submits, to the terms of the contract and, moreover, have failed to produce any suggestion of any default or breach of contract on the part of the sellers in England which would possibly justify a demand that the performance guarantee be implemented.

I disagree that that amounts to any proof or evidence of fraud. It may be suspicious, it may indicate the possibility of sharp practice, but there is nothing in those facts remotely approaching true evidence of fraud."[81]

A more recent example is *Turkiye IS Bankasi AS v Bank of China*[82] **13–32** where the performance bond was given to the main contractor in respect of the obligations of a sub-contractor. On the facts Waller J. found that it "would be likely to be found"[83] that the main contractor (rather than the sub-contractor) was in breach of contract, having failed to make advance payments and supply machinery and labour to the sub-contractor as agreed. Despite the resulting conclusion that "it would thus seem likely

---

[77] In other cases the unexplained failure of the beneficiary to respond may point to the "only realistic inference" being that of fraud. See *United Trading Corp SA v Allied Arab Bank Ltd* [1985] 2 Lloyd's Rep. 554 at 561; *Sunderland AFC v Uruguay Montevideo FC* [2001] 2 All E.R. (Comm.) 828 at 834.

[78] This explanation of the beneficiary's silence led the court in *United Trading Corp SA v Allied Arab Bank Ltd*, above, to conclude that no arguable case had been made out "on the available evidence", even though it was reasonably clear that the beneficiary had enforced certain performance bonds not related to the contract in respect of which the parties were in dispute.

[79] *Bolivinter Oil SA v Chase Manhattan Bank NA* [1984] 1 W.L.R. 392.

[80] [1978] Q.B. 159. See also *Intraco Ltd v Notis Shipping Corp* [1981] 2 Lloyd's Rep 256; *R D Harbottle (Mercantile) Ltd v National Westminster Bank Ltd* [1978] 1 Q.B. 146.

[81] *ibid.*, at 175.

[82] [1996] 2 Lloyd's Rep. 611, approved on appeal [1998] 1 Lloyd's Rep. 250.

[83] [1996] 2 Lloyd's Rep. 611 at 617.

that [the contractor] had no right to claim under the performance bonds"[84] this was insufficient to establish fraud. Waller J. stated:

> "But, even now, if I, having examined the material which is before me, had to ask myself whether the demand was 'fraudulent', I am left in a state of doubt. I do not have the material before me to enable me to be clear that the arrangements did not leave [the contractor] with some argument that the sub-contractor had broken its contract."

13–33   Even if fraud can be established, it has also often been difficult to prove the additional element of the bank's clear knowledge of the fraudulent claim. The bank is under no obligation to inquire into the dealings in relation to the principal contract[85] and knowledge of any fraud will not be imputed to the bank[86] merely because the claimant upon the guarantee fails to produce any evidence of default or breach of contract by the principal contractor.[87] Even if the bank is aware of matters whereby the beneficiary of the bond may not be justified in making a claim (for example, because that beneficiary has broken a condition of the contract), the bank will still be obliged to pay.[88] Such questions are regarded as contractual disputes to be settled between the parties to the principal contract.[89] The same is probably the case even if the claim is made upon the performance bond with the object of inducing the contractor to settle its claims with the owner on terms which are favourable to the owner.[90]

13–34   The bank's knowledge of fraud must exist prior to payment, but it is sufficient if that knowledge is established by the date of the court hearing, even if the bank has no notice of the fraud at the time of the demand.[91] If the only relevant date for determining the existence of knowledge was the date of demand it would result in the "absurdity"[92] that the court would be bound not to grant an injunction, despite it concluding that knowledge of fraud was sufficiently established at the time of the court hearing. As Mance L.J. remarked in *Solo Industries UK Ltd v Canara Bank*[93] "it would

---

[84] *ibid.*
[85] *Discount Records Ltd v Barclays Bank Ltd* [1975] 1 W.L.R. 315 at 318–319 (a case dealing with irrevocable confirmed letters of credit, where the same principle applies); *Edward Owen Engineering Ltd v Barclays Bank International Ltd* [1978] 1 Q.B. 159 at 174; *Consolidated Oil Ltd, American Express Bank Ltd* (unreported, CA, January 21, 2000); *Howe Richardson Scale Co Ltd v Polimex Cekop & Nat West Bank* [1978] Lloyd's Rep. 161.
[86] *ibid.*
[87] *Edward Owen Engineering Ltd v Barclays Bank International Ltd* [1978] 1 Q.B. 159 at 175. See also *CDN Research and Development v Bank of Nova Scotia* [1982] 39 O.R. (2d) 13.
[88] See *R D Harbottle (Mercantile) Ltd v National Westminster Bank Ltd* [1978] 1 Q.B. 146, where in relation to one of the performance bonds in that case, the bank was probably aware that the beneficiary of the bond had failed to establish a condition precedent to the operation of the guarantee by establishing a confirmed letter of credit: see especially at 153, 155.
[89] *R D Harbottle (Mercantile) Ltd v National Westminster Bank Ltd* [1978] 1 Q.B. 146 at 155.
[90] This was apparently the case in *Wood Hall Ltd v Pipeline Authority* (1979) 141 C.L.R. 443 and the court did not grant the contractor relief.
[91] *Solo Industries UK Ltd v Canara* [2001] 1 W.L.R. 1800 at 1809 para.21. See also *Deutsche Ruckversicherung AG v Walbrook Insurance Co Ltd* [1994] 4 All E.R. 181; *Rajaram v Ganesh t/a Golden Harvest Trading Corp* [1995] 1 S.L.R. 159.
[92] *Solo Industries UK Ltd v Canara Bank* [2001] 1 W.L.R. 1800 at 1809, para.21.
[93] *ibid.* See also the more technical analysis by Waller L.J. in *Balfour Beatty Civil Engineering v Technical & General Guarantee Co Ltd* (1999) 68 Con. L.R. 180 at 188–190.

affront good sense, and probably general principles relating to illegality, if courts were obliged to give judgment in favour of a beneficiary now shown to be acting fraudulently".[94]

(ii) Restraining the beneficiary from making a demand. The foregoing discussion has centred upon the relevant law in respect of an application for an injunction restraining the bank from making payment under the guarantee. Recently, in *Themehelp Ltd v West*,[95] the English Court of Appeal indicated that the requirements of proof might not be so stringent where the application was to restrain the beneficiary from making a demand upon the guarantee since, in such a case, there was no risk to the "integrity of the performance bond".[96] Waite L.J. stated:

13–35

> "In a case where fraud is raised as between the parties to the main transaction at an early stage ... before any question of the enforcement of the guarantee (as between the beneficiary and the guarantor) has yet arisen at all ... it does not seem to me that the slightest threat is involved to the autonomy of the performance guarantee if the beneficiary is injuncted from enforcing it in proceedings to which the guarantor is not a party."[97]

On the facts, the performance bond secured payments pursuant to a contract of sale and an interlocutory injunction was granted on the basis that the sale had been induced by fraudulent misrepresentations by the seller. The court concluded that the granting of the injunction was required to protect the interests of the buyer—otherwise the seller, who was out of the jurisdiction, may not have had sufficient assets remaining within the jurisdiction to satisfy a judgment for damages for fraudulent misrepresentation if fraud was proved at the trial. A Mareva injunction, freezing the proceeds of payment under the guarantee in the hands of the seller until trial of the action, would not be sufficient to protect the position of the buyer because, if the seller were allowed to claim under the guarantee, the guarantor would be immediately entitled to claim against the buyer pursuant to the counter-guarantee. On the other hand, if an injunction were granted, the seller would not be prejudiced if the buyer failed to establish fraud at the trial since the seller could then proceed to enforce the performance bond in the normal way.

13–36

If, as *Themehelp Ltd v West* suggests, separate principles are to apply to an application for an injunction where the beneficiary has not yet claimed under the guarantee, with respect, the decision itself does little to elucidate them. Waite L.J. left open in this context both the question of whether or not the burden of proof should be less onerous than "the sole realistic inference from the facts" test adopted when an injunction is sought against

13–37

---

[94] *Cf. Banco Santander SA v Bayfern Ltd* [2000] Lloyd's Rep. Bank. 165 where it was held that where knowledge of the beneficiary's fraud had come to the notice of the confirming bank after it had made a discounted payment, the issuing bank was not obliged to reimburse it.
[95] [1996] Q.B. 84.
[96] *ibid.*, at 98–99.
[97] *ibid.*

the bank, and the issue of whether or not non-fraudulent breaches of the underlying contract would support the granting of an injunction.[98] Indeed, it is somewhat odd that the court should consider applying different principles simply because an injunction is sought at an earlier point of time prior to the demand being made upon the bank. This means that the beneficiary's rights will be dependent upon fine issues of timing as to when the proceedings are commenced. It is not easy to perceive why the "integrity of the performance bond" and general commercial understandings in the banking industry are not at risk simply because an injunction is sought against the beneficiary of the bond prior to the demand being made upon the bank.[99]

13–38   Indeed the decision in *Themehelp Ltd v West*[1] is arguably contrary to the earlier Court of Appeal decision in *Dong Jin Metal Co Ltd v Raymet Ltd*[2] which, in the context of a letter of credit, rejected the view that there should be a different test depending on whether the relief is sought against the beneficiary or the bank. Subsequently, there has also been judicial criticism of the view expressed in *Themehelp v West*,[3] most notably by the Court of Appeal in *Group Josi v Walbrook Insurance Co Ltd*[4] where Staughton L.J. said:

> "However, it is argued ... that the case is altogether different, and the rule which I have been discussing does not apply, when an injunction is sought not against the bank but against the beneficiary of a letter of credit. In my opinion that cannot be right. The effect on the life blood of commerce will be precisely the same whether the bank is restrained from paying or the beneficiary is restrained from asking for payment."

13–39   It is likely, therefore, that *Themehelp v West*[5] (although not yet specifically overruled) will not be followed and the burden of proving fraud will not be different where the injunction is sought against the beneficiary. Arguably, however, where an injunction is sought against the beneficiary, proof that the bank has knowledge of that fraud should not be a prerequisite for relief. If the bank is not yet a party to the proceedings, it is difficult to see why the bank's knowledge of fraud should be relevant.

13–40   **(iii) Balance of convenience and freezing injunctions**. Even in the case of a fraudulent demand an interlocutory application to restrain the bank from making payment pursuant to the bond (or to restrain the beneficiary from making a demand) will not necessarily be successful, since the balance of convenience may not favour the applicant. It is true that payment by the

---

[98] [1996] Q.B. 84.
[99] See the dissenting judgment of Evans LJ ([1996] Q.B. 84 at 101–105), which has much to commend it.
[1] [1996] Q.B. 84.
[2] Unreported, CA, July 13, 1993.
[3] [1996] Q.B. 84.
[4] [1996] 1 Lloyd's Rep. 345 at 361. See also *Bolvinter Oil S.A v Chase Manhattan Bank NA* [1984] 1 Lloyd's Rep. 251 at 256; *Britten Norman (in liq) v State Ownership Fund of Romania* [2000] Lloyd's Rep. Bank. 315 at 321; *Intraco Ltd v Notis Shipping Corp* [1981] 2 Lloyd's Rep. 256; *Deutsche Ruckversicherung AG v Walbrook Insurance Co Ltd* [1994] 4 All E.R. 181.
[5] [1996] Q.B. 84.

bank may have serious consequences for an applicant contractor in terms of its immediate liquidity position (since the contractor will be required to reimburse the bank). Payment may also affect its business reputation, affecting its ability to obtain future contracts, especially overseas (where proprietors will invariably inquire if the contractor is reliable by asking whether or not the contractor has been the subject of a previous demand).[6] Yet, even in the case of fraud, the interests of the financial community in preserving the autonomy of the bond have been held to be dominant, in particular, if the applicant is able to obtain a freezing order (sometimes called a Mareva injunction). Witness, as an example, the approach of Rix J. in *Czarnikow-Rionda Sugar Trading v Standard Bank London Ltd*:[7]

"the balance of convenience would seem to me to come down firmly in favour of the bank. Ex hypothesi, the bank would be entitled, in the absence of an injunction, to pay the beneficiary and would not be in breach of contract to the claimant in doing so. Why, therefore, should the interests of the claimant overtop the public and general interests in the maintenance of banking commitments and in the autonomy of such commitments? The preference of concern about the private loss of the defrauded claimant to the general weal might arguably in a particular case fall in favour of the former, if the claimant could be in no other way protected. But it seems to me that the presence of the *Mareva* injunction or freezing order, which the Courts can grant in a case of fraud even on a worldwide basis and even as merely ancillary relief to litigation abroad, militates very strongly against that argument."

Thus, as an alternative to granting an injunction preventing payment **13–41** upon the bond, the courts may grant a freezing order (which then precludes the beneficiary dealing with the proceeds of the bond), providing that the conditions for its granting are met. Thus there must be an existing cause of action over which the English court has jurisdiction[8] and a real risk that the relevant assets (in this case the moneys received by the beneficiary) will be dissipated so that the judgment or award will be unsatisfied.[9] It is not relevant to the inquiry that the beneficiary may become insolvent so as to give the applicant a priority over other creditors.[10] A freezing order will, however, be of much less value to the contractor if (as is often the case) the bond is payable in a foreign jurisdiction.[11] Although, exceptionally, a freezing

---

[6] See generally *Pearson Bridge (NSW) Pty Ltd v State Rail Authority of New South Wales* (1982) 1 A.C.L.R. 81; *United Trading Corp SA v Allied Arab Bank Ltd* [1985] 2 Lloyd's Rep. 554 at 560 (inability to raise further credit).
[7] [1999] 2 Lloyd's Rep. Bank. 187 at 203. See also *United Trading Corp SA v Allied Arab Bank Ltd* [1985] 2 Lloyd's Rep. 554 at 566.
[8] *The Siskina* [1979] A.C. 210. See also S. Gee, *Mareva Injunctions & Anton Piller Relief* (4th ed., 1998), pp.178–183.
[9] See generally S. Gee, *Mareva Injunctions & Anton Piller Relief* (4th ed., 1998), Ch. 10 as to the requirements for the granting of a Mareva injunction.
[10] *Themehelp Ltd v West* [1996] Q.B. 84 at 103, *per* Evans L.J.
[11] Note also that a freezing order, even if granted, will be of little value if a third party has a prior right to the assets, for example, by assignment. See G. Andrews and R. Millet *Law of Guarantees* (3rd ed., 2000), p.510.

order may be granted in respect of assets of the defendant in a foreign jurisdiction,[12] there is a reluctance of the courts to do so[13] and, additionally, an obvious difficulty of enforcement of the order in some States.

13–42   It should also be emphasised that a freezing order may be obtained even in the absence of fraud if the applicant can show another existing cause of action, for example, a breach of the underlying contract by the beneficiary, provided that the other conditions for the granting of the injunction exist.[14]

(e) A demand where the underlying contract is avoided or there is a total failure of consideration?

13–43   There has been one suggestion that an injunction may be obtained, even as against the bank, to prevent payment under the bond even in the absence of fraud. In *Potton Homes Ltd v Coleman Contractors Ltd*[15] Eveleigh L.J. considered that:[16]

> "–in principle I do not think it possible to say that in no circumstances whatsoever, apart from fraud, will the court restrain the buyer. The facts of each case must be considered. If the contract is avoided or if there is a failure of consideration between buyer and seller for which the seller undertook to procure the issue of the performance bond, I do not see why, as between seller and buyer, the seller should not be unable to prevent a call upon the bond by the mere assertion that the bond is to be treated as cash in hand."

13–44   There is, however, no other English authority[17] supporting such a claim. Cases where there is a total failure of consideration (for example, in the case of a bond securing the buyer's obligation to pay pursuant to a contract of sale, a failure to supply goods)[18] may on the same facts also involve fraudulent misrepresentations which induce the execution of the performance bond itself and where (as will be seen)[19] a separate principle

---

[12] See *Derby v Weldon (No.1)* [1990] Ch. 48; *Derby v Weldon (Nos 3&4)* [1990] Ch. 65; *Maclaine Watson v International Tin Council (No.2)* [1989] Ch. 286; *Republic of Haiti v Duvalier* [1990] 1 Q.B. 202.

[13] See *Intraco Ltd v Notis Shipping Corp* [1981] 2 Lloyd's Rep. 256. Similarly where the bond is payable outside the jurisdiction the court would probably not order payment into court, which was a suggestion made by Evans L.J. in *Themehelp v West* [1996] Q.B. 84 at 103. See *Britten Norman Ltd v State Ownership of Romania* [2000] Lloyd's Rep. Bank. 315.

[14] See S. Gee, *Mareva Injunctions and Anton Piller Relief* (4th ed., 1998), Ch. 10.

[15] (1984) 28 B.L.R. 19.

[16] *ibid.*, at 28.

[17] Note that in *Kvaerner Singapore Pty v UDL Shipping (Singapore) Pty Ltd* [1993] 3 S.L.R. 350 the Singapore High Court quoted this passage with approval but that case is probably explained on the basis that it was a conditional bond (given to secure the obligations of a seller) so that the failure of the seller to fulfil his obligations under the contract was "a condition precedent to the buyer making a demand" (at 354).

[18] See, as an example, the American case *Szkejin v Henry Schroder Banking Corp* (1941) 31 N.Y.S. 2d 631 (seller shipped rubbish instead of the contract goods).

[19] See below, paras 13–46 to 13–50, and especially *Solo Industries UK Ltd v Canara Bank* [2001] 1 W.L.R. 1800.

applies, giving ground for relief. Nor, as Eveleigh L.J. envisages, should the fact that the other party to the underlying contract avoids that contract constitute in itself a basis for restraining payment, at least unless the bank knows that the beneficiary has acted dishonestly in making a demand in full knowledge that it is in default and has no valid counterclaim.[20]

One decision where an injunction was granted in the absence of fraud **13–45** was *Elian & Rabbath v Matsas & Matsas*[21] where the charterers of a vessel procured the issuing of a bond in order to secure a release of their cargo, which was subject to a lien by the owners of the vessel in respect of demurrage charges. Yet, immediately upon release, the owners purported to exercise a fresh lien on the cargo–this time in respect of delay. An injunction was granted restraining the owner from making a demand upon the bond. It has been said[22] that this decision can be explained on the basis that, in accordance with the dictum of Eveleigh L.J. in *Potton Homes Ltd v Coleman Contractors Ltd*,[23] there had been a total failure of consideration. Yet a more likely explanation of this "special case"[24] is that the bond was subject to a term that no further lien would be imposed so that the bond was not truly unconditional. Lord Denning M.R. stated[25] specifically that:

"It can well be argued that the guarantee was given on the understanding that the lien was raised and no further lien imposed: and that when the shipowners, in breach of that understanding, imposed a further lien, they were disabled from acting on the guarantee."

(f) Where the performance bond itself is invalid

As has been seen[26] the bank's obligation to pay pursuant to an **13–46** unconditional performance bond means that the bank is to be insulated from the underlying commercial disputes. In *Solo Industries UK Ltd v Canara Bank*[27] it was held, however, that it does not follow from this general proposition that banks accept the risk that the instrument itself has been induced by a conspiracy between its customer and the beneficiary or a misrepresentation by the beneficiary. On the facts the beneficiaries had fraudulently induced the issue of bond by falsely creating the impression of the existence of valid and subsisting supply contracts, which were in reality largely fictitious. The claimant argued that once the bond had been issued

---

[20] Note also that in *Gulf Bank KSC v Mitsubishi Heavy Industries Ltd* [1994] 2 Lloyd's Rep. 145 it was held that the performance bond was enforceable even on the assumption that the underlying contract had never come into effect, although in that case there was a clause preserving the guarantor's obligation in the event of its invalidity, illegality, or unenforceability.

[21] [1966] 2 Lloyds Rep. 495.

[22] See G. Andrews and R. Millet, *Law of Guarantees* (3rd ed., 2000), p.507.

[23] (1984) 28 B.L.R. 19 at 28.

[24] See [1996] 2 Lloyd's Rep. 495 at 497, *per* Denning M.R.

[25] [1999] 2 Lloyd's Rep. 495 at 495. See also Danckwerts L.J. at 498, who referred to the existence of "a breach of faith in regard to the arrangement between the parties".

[26] See above, paras 13–12 to 13–16.

[27] [2001] 1 W.L.R. 1800.

the bank was obliged to pay under it upon receiving a demand (despite the fact that, applying normal contractual principles, the bond was voidable for misrepresentation) unless it could show that the bank knew the demand was fraudulent. Mance L.J. rejected[28] this view:

"I cannot see any principled basis for this conclusion. It has nothing to do with autonomy. It cannot flow from the terms of the instrument, or the fact that banks are concerned with documentary compliance. It seeks to impose on banks the risk of being misled into entering into the instrument, when the only risks that the bank may fairly be taken to have accepted are the risks undertaken under the instrument, *assuming* it to be valid. It does not reflect the limits of a defence or right of set off (like the fraud exception). It deprives the bank of a defence that it has under ordinary contractual principles, and of its right to trial of that defence, which if tried and proved would mean that the bank should not have been held liable in the first instance."

The result is that the bank may refuse to pay under the bond if it is shown that there is a "reasonable or real prospect that the relevant bond was procured by, and has been validly avoided . . . on account of fraudulent conspiracy and fraudulent misrepresentation".[29]

13–47 On the same basis it may be that the customer may restrain the bank from making payment, although this does not necessarily follow, since it is arguable that the decision whether or not to avoid the bond should be that of the bank's alone. Despite the reference to "ordinary contractual principles" (in the passage quoted above) it is unlikely that the bank could be restrained from making payment in the case of innocent, as opposed to fraudulent misrepresentations, which would also render the bond voidable.

13–48 The approach taken in *Solo Industries UK Ltd v Canara Bank*[30] had been previously supported by a dictum of Donaldson M.R. in *Bolvinter Oil S.A v Chase Manhattan Bank*[31] and by suggestions of a similar approach in respect of cheques[32] and letters of credit.[33] At the same time it is difficult to reconcile *Solo Industries UK Ltd v Canara Bank*[34] with the earlier Court of Appeal decision in *Gulf Bank KSC v Mitsubishi Heavy Industries Ltd*,[35] in which it was held that the bank was obliged to pay under the bond (in this case a counter-indemnity) even on the assumption (agreed for the purposes of argument) that not only the underlying transaction, but the bond itself "never had any legal effect". It is true that the bond in that case contained a clause specifically stating that the obligation should not be "discharged or diminished" in the event that the bond was invalid, illegal or unenforceable. But if the bond is void, or if it is voidable and avoided

---

[28] *ibid.*, at 1814, para.36.
[29] *Solo Industries UK Ltd v Canara Bank* [2001] 1 W.L.R. 1800 at 1814, para.41.
[30] [2001] 1 W.L.R. 1800.
[31] [1984] 1 Lloyd's Rep. 251.
[32] *Clovertogs v Jean Scenes Ltd* (unreported, March 5, 1982) discussed in *Solo Industries UK Ltd v Canara Bank* [2001] 1 W.L.R. 1800 at 1810–1811.
[33] *Safa Ltd v Banque du Caire* [2000] 2 Lloyd's Rep. 600 at 608.
[34] [2001] 1 W.L.R. 1800.
[35] [1994] 2 Lloyd's Rep. 145.

ab initio, it is difficult to see why the clause should have the effect of preserving the bond issuer's liability since, as part of an invalid agreement, it was never, or is no longer, operative.

The fact that the bank may refusepayment under the bond if it is **13–49** procured by fraudulent misrepresentation leaves unclear the position of assignees of the bond who, on normal principles, will take subject to equities.[36] This result will be subject to the terms of the assignment construed in the light of the surrounding circumstances, which may make it clear that the assignee shall take the benefit of the guarantee free from any defences which might be raised against the assignor.[37]

Another difficulty is where there is a chain of banks and the **13–50** misrepresentation is directed to the first bank in the chain and not the issuing bank, Mance L.J. in *Solo Industries UK Ltd v Canara Bank*[38] was prepared to adopt[39] a broad approach as to the effect of the misrepresentation:

> "Where, as here, a fraudulent conspiracy or misrepresentation is alleged, involving the pretence of a genuine commercial transaction, it would not seem difficult to treat the pretence as directed to all bankers who become involved. Each, no doubt, acts on that basis. Further the law constructs a contract between the issuing bank and the beneficiary. The law may in appropriate circumstances be capable of recognising or constructing an implicit representation as to the genuineness of the underlying commercial transaction as far as the beneficiary is aware."

(g) Where the bond issuer itself is involved in the underlying transaction

In respect of claims upon letters of credit it has been held that a bank **13–51** issuing the letter [or its assignees] may rely on a set off or counter-claim in the rare case where the bank is involved in the underlying transaction, and has a set off or counterclaim arising from that transaction. By analogy, the same principle may be applicable to performance bonds. The relevant authority concerning letters of credit is *Safa Ltd v Banque du Caire*.[40] Safa were assignees of two letters of credit opened in the sums of £5.55m and £3.7m by the bank in favour of Paul Group International Insurance Brokers/T L Dallas Ltd (The Paul Group), a Lloyd's broker. The context

---

[36] See *Solo Industries UK Ltd v Canara Bank* [2001] 1 W.L.R. 1800 at 1815 para.38. *Cf.* the position in respect of bills of exchange which creates an exception in respect of holders in due course. (See s.38 Bills of Exchange Act 1882.)

[37] See *Standard Bank (London) Ltd v Canara Bank* (unreported, CA, May 22, 2002) where the relevant clause stated "We agree with the Assignee that all sums payable by us to the assignee pursuant to the assigned property shall be paid in full without any set-off or counterclaim and fully clear of all deductions or withholding on account of taxes".

[38] [2001] 1 W.L..R 1800.

[39] *ibid.*, at 1815 para.39.

[40] [2000] 2 Lloyd's Rep. 600. The following facts are taken from *Solo Industries UK Ltd v Canara Bank* [2001] 1 W.L.R. 1800 at 1809, para.22.

was proposed loans of £30m and £40m by the bank to Aboul Fatouh Establishment (AFE). The credits were available for drawdown against the presentation of a financial insurance guarantee to be issued in favour of the bank by Merrion Reinsurance Co Ltd, covering repayment of the loans. Payments under the credits were intended to cover the premium on the financial insurance guarantee. The Paul Group was on the face of it acting as broker for the bank in arranging such insurance. But the bank never in fact agreed to make the loans and concluded that Merrion Reinsurance Co Ltd was not financially sound. A demand was made by the Paul Group, which the bank refused to pay.

13–52   In refusing the application for summary judgment by the Paul Group, it was held that the bank had a reasonable argument that it could rely on a set off and counterclaim as against the Paul Group because of the "unusual circumstances"[41] that the bank was involved in the underlying transaction. This arose because the Paul Group, whilst the beneficiary under the letter of credit, was also procuring the financial insurance guarantees for the bank's benefit, in return for which the bank was to pay the premiums direct to the Paul Group. The Paul Group knew that the bank was to be beneficiary of the proposed letter of credit and the bank's precise requirements by way of insurance. In the Court of Appeal Waller L.J. stated[42] the principle in these terms:

"When a bank is involved in the related transaction it may be unjust for that bank to be forced to pay on a summary judgment where it has a real prospect of succeeding by reference to a claim on the underlying transaction, and particularly if that claim is a liquidated claim, the Court should not give summary judgment either because a set-off has a reasonable prospect of success or because there is a compelling reason to have a trial of the letter of credit issue."

13–53   The decision in *Safa Ltd v Banque du Caire*[43] may be explained on the narrower basis that the bond itself was voidable, being induced on the basis of fraudulent misrepresentations by the Paul Group as the creditworthiness of Merrion Reinsurance Co Ltd, but the Court of Appeal does identify as a separate exception to the autonomy of the bond circumstances in which the bank is involved in the underlying transaction.

(ii) The application of moneys which are received by the beneficiary of an unconditional performance bond

13–54   Unless the special circumstances outlined in the previous sections apply, the beneficiary of an unconditional bond is entitled to receive the amount stipulated in the guarantee from the bank guarantor on the making of a

[41] See a close examination of the facts by Walker J. at first instance (unreported, October 21, 1999).
[42] [2000] 2 Lloyd's Rep. 600 at 608.
[43] [2000] 2 Lloyd's Rep. 600.

demand. A further, and separate, question is the application of those moneys once they have been received by the proprietor. In *Cargill International SA v BSFIC*[44] (in respect of a bond relating to a seller's obligation under a contract of sale) the Court of Appeal, approving Morison J. at first instance, stated that:

"It is implicit in the nature of a performance bond that in the absence of clear contractual words to a different effect there will be an accounting between the parties at some stage after the bond has been called, in the sense that their rights and obligations will be determined at some future date. If the amount of the bond is not sufficient to satisfy the beneficiary's claim for damages he can bring proceedings for his loss, giving credit for the amount received under the bond. *Conversely, if the amount received under the bond exceeds the true loss sustained, the party who provided the bond is entitled to recover the overpayments.*"[45] [authors' emphasis].

Australian authorities[46] support this proposition in the context of a performance bond securing the contractor's obligation under a building contract.

The passage (quoted above) in *Cargill International SA v BSFIC*[47] **13–55** contemplates the possibility of "clear contractual words" in the underlying contract or the performance bond itself negating these "implicit" features of the bond. In the case itself, a reference in the contract of sale to the fact that "The performance bond is liable to be forfeited by the buyer if the seller fails to fulfil any of the terms and conditions of [the contract of sale]" was correctly interpreted as simply as a reference to the position between the buyer and the bank, rather than negating any obligation on the part of the beneficiary buyer to account. The reference to "forfeiture" was simply being used as a "shorthand" expression for the buyer's right to call for payment under the bond. Indeed, if it had been intended to exclude the duty to account a reference to forfeiture by the seller would have been more appropriate.[48]

But what if the wording does clearly negative such duty? At first **13–56** instance in *Cargill International SA v BSFIC*[49] Morison J. considered that:

"Had I been persuaded that there was a term of the contract between the parties which enabled the buyer to call on the bond when he had suffered no damage, and to retain the moneys, I would have held the provision to have been penal."[50]

[44] [1998] 2 All E.R. 406.
[45] *ibid.*, at 410. See also *Comdel Commodities Ltd v Siporex Trade SA* [1997] 1 Lloyd's Rep. 424 at 431.
[46] *Australasian Conference Association Ltd v Mainline Construction Pty Ltd* (1978) 141 C.L.R. 335; *Woodhall Ltd v Pipeline Authority* (1979) 141 C.L.R. 443 at 454.
[47] [1998] 2 All E.R. 406.
[48] *ibid.*, at 414.
[49] [1996] 4 All E.R. 563.
[50] *ibid.*, at 573.

The Court of Appeal did not specifically comment on this proposition, although the approach to the issue appears to be simply one of construction. In any event, it is not entirely clear why on the facts of *Cargill International SA v BSFIC*[51] a provision stating that the beneficiary could forfeit the moneys would inevitably by penal, as the bond was limited to 10 per cent of the purchase price. This amount might be regarded a genuine pre-estimate of damage since it would not be extravagant in relation to the greatest possible loss that could flow from the breach. Indeed, at a more fundamental level, the application of the law regarding penalties would be novel in this context because the doctrine is invariably applied to moneys payable by one party to another under the same contract. It is difficult to see how striking down a clause in the underlying transaction as a penalty provision could have a bearing on the application of moneys received under what is regarded as an independent agreement.

13–57   Clearly the decision in *Cargill International SA v BSFIC*[52] provides some protection for the contractor if the proprietor has received substantial sums from the bank, but the proprietor's true loss is small. But such protection might be illusory if the principal transaction is governed by foreign law where different rules may apply. There is also no suggestion in *Cargill International SA v BSFIC*[53] that the proprietor holds the moneys received subject to any trust, with the result that the contractor will not have any proprietary claim in the case of the employer's insolvency.[54]

13–58   If the beneficiary is subsequently found liable to account for a specific amount of the moneys which he has received pursuant to the bond, it is unclear if the beneficiary is only liable to pay interest from the date that the duty to account for a specific surplus is established, or from the date when he first received the total amount paid by the bank.[55] The former is perhaps the preferable view since the beneficiary should not be penalised for the exercise of his proper legal rights to call upon the bond, especially if the precise determination of the state of accounts between the parties to the underlying contract is unclear and can only be ascertained by arbitration or litigation.

4. DRAFTING A PERFORMANCE BOND

13–59   The principal will be concerned to ensure that any performance bond which is taken to secure the principal's obligation under the principal contract is not unconditional in nature, because any payment by the

---

[51] [1998] 2 All E.R. 406.
[52] *ibid.*
[53] *ibid.*
[54] Although a constructive trust is a possibility (see *Barclays Bank Ltd v Quistclose Investments Ltd* [1970] A.C. 567) it is more likely that the proprietor is simply a stakeholder in respect of the money received from the bank: see *Hastingwood Property Ltd v Saunders Bearman Anselm* [1990] 3 W.L.R. 623.
[55] See the issue discussed more fully in G. Andrews and R. Millett, *Law of Guarantees* (3rd ed., 2000) pp.515–516.

guarantor will immediately expose the principal to the exercise of the guarantor's indemnity against it. The guarantor will usually be a bank which has taken a security from the principal, or insisted that the principal has set aside funds to meet any obligations of the bank under the performance bond, so that the right of indemnity may be easily exercised.[56]

Thus, if its bargaining position permits, the principal in these **13–60** circumstances should take steps to ensure that the performance bond cannot be called up simply by the beneficiary of the bond making a demand. The demand should be required to be evidenced by documentation, preferably by an independent arbitrator, showing that the principal contract has not been performed.[57] A less desirable alternative is to impose an obligation upon the beneficiary of the bond to provide a sworn statement indicating in what respect the principal has not complied with the contract. Such a clause might at least provide some deterrent to the making of an arbitrary demand. The performance bond should also contain a provision to ensure that a demand cannot be made where performance of the principal contract becomes impossible (for example, through frustration), or where the beneficiary is in breach of the principal contract. The bond should also contain a definite expiry date so that a demand cannot be made after the principal obligations have been performed. Finally, the principal should attempt to include a clause stipulating for a pro rata reduction in the amount that may be demanded under the bond as performance under the principal contract progresses; that is, in the case of a building contract, by completion of the construction work to a certain stage, or, in a contract for the supply of goods, by the supply of a certain quantity of the goods.

5. PERFORMANCE BONDS IN INTERNATIONAL TRADE

The use of unconditional performance bonds in international construc- **13–61** tion contracts and contracts for the sale of goods is common. As the beneficiary under the bond, which will often be a foreign government or government agency, can call upon the guarantor to pay without proving any default by the principal, the principal is placed at an immediate disadvantage. The principal has virtually no power to prevent payment by the bank/guarantor to the beneficiary and will eventually become liable for this amount by virtue of the counter-indemnity required by the bank guarantor. The pitfalls of such unconditional performance bonds have been well catalogued,[58] and they may be compounded by national

---

[56] The principal can, of course, take action against the beneficiary of the bond where the demand has been made in circumstances where the principal is not in breach of the principal contract, but the principal bears the burden of proving this breach.

[57] If this provision is included, the performance bond would not in fact be unconditional.

[58] See A. Pierce, *Demand Guarantees in International Trade* (1993); P.S. Parsons, "Commercial Law Note" (1979) 53 A.L.J. 224; G. Andrews and R. Millett, *Law of Guarantees* (1992), Ch. 15; R. Edwards, "The Role of Bank Guarantees in International Trade" (1982) 56 A.L.J. 281; K. P. Williams, "On Demand and Conditional Performance Bonds" (1981) *Journal of Business Law* 8; R. Gould, "Construction Financing—Effects on

legislation of the beneficiary, affecting provisions in the performance bond which would otherwise operate in favour of the principal (for example, the legislation may render invalid an expiry date for the guarantee).[59] The risk to the exporter can be minimised by obtaining insurance cover against an arbitrary demand by the beneficiary[60] or, where a construction contract is involved, by the principal taking an indemnity in relation to such loss from the subcontractors employed in the project.[61] Additionally, the principal may seek to make payment by the bank dependent upon a certificate by an independent party certifying a breach of the underlying contract, or to include a provision stating that the performance bond is to determine upon production of evidence that the underlying transaction has been fully performed.[62] There is, however often little prospect of the beneficiary agreeing to these stipulations.

13–62   The International Chamber of Commerce has at various times formulated uniform rules for contract guarantees.[63] These rules have as one of their objectives the protection of the principal from unjustified claims under the guarantee by imposing an obligation upon the beneficiary to provide evidence of default by the principal. But the rules only apply if the parties agree to incorporate them into the guarantee, and many foreign governments still insist that the principal enter into an unconditional performance bond whereby the demand can be made without proof of default and without the necessity of any documentation.

13–63   In the context of international trade, a not infrequent issue[64] which arises is the proper law applicable both to the performance bond and also to the counter indemnity, which is invariably given to the bank by the principal. The usual conflict of laws rules apply so that, in the absence of an express choice of law by the parties, the court will infer the intention of the parties as to choice of law from the terms and nature (as well as the surrounding circumstances) of the contract. When it is not possible to infer such intention, the contract will be governed by the system of law with which the transaction has the closest and most real connection.[65]

Other Contractual Provisions" (1985) (March) *International Business Lawyer* 117; M. Rubino-Sammartano, "Performance Bonds—Primary or Secondary Obligations" (1985) (March) *International Business Lawyer* 125; G. Penn, "On Demand Bonds—Primary or Secondary Obligations?" (1986) 4 J.I.B.L. 224; G. Jones, "Letters of Credit in the United States Construction Industry" (1986) (February) *International Business Lawyer* 17; F. Schwank, "New Trends in International Guarantees" (1987) (August) *International Banking Law* 35; F. Cahill, "Security for Performance Clauses" (1988) 4 BCL 18; A.J. Barclay, "Court Orders against Payment under First Demand Guarantees Used in International Trade" [1989] 3 J.I.B.L. 110.
[59] *ibid.*
[60] R. Edwards, "The Role of Bank Guarantees in International Trade" (1982) 56 A.L.J. 281 at 285.
[61] *ibid.*
[62] Alternatively, the performance bond could be given for a limited period.
[63] See P. S. Parsons, "Commercial Law Note" (1979) 53 A.L.J. 224; R. Edwards, "The Role of Bank Guarantees in International Trade" (1982) 56 A.L.J. 281 at 286–287.
[64] See S.K. Chatterjee, "The Method of Determining the Governing Law of Performance Bonds and Counter—Guarantees: A Commercial Approach" [1994] 1 J.I.B.L. 20.
[65] See below, Ch.14. See also, in this context, *Wahda Bank v Arab Bank plc* [1994] 2 Lloyd's Rep. 411 at 412–413.

In respect of the performance bond itself, the law applicable to the **13–64** underlying transaction will not necessarily be applied as the proper law of the performance bond. The bond is properly treated as an autonomous contract and is thus distinguishable from a guarantee, when the courts will often infer that the parties intended that the guarantee should be governed by the same law as the principal obligation.[66] As an example, in *Attock Cement Co Ltd v Romanian Bank for Foreign Trade*,[67] the contract for the construction of a cement plant in Pakistan, which was expressed to be governed by English law, contained a requirement that the Romanian contractor should provide a performance bond. It was held that there was no good arguable case that the performance bond was governed by English law as payment was to be made in Romania. The performance bond therefore had its closest and most real connection with Romanian law.[68]

The proper law of the performance bond may however be important in **13–65** determining the proper law of the counter-indemnity given by the principal. There is a close connection between these transactions since the performance bond is usually only issued in consideration of a counter-indemnity being provided. In *Wahda Bank v Arab Bank Plc*,[69] for instance, it was held that the proper law of the counter-indemnity was Libyan law. A decisive factor was that Libyan law governed the performance bond, and it was "the natural expectation of both parties" that "the two contracts would be governed by the same law so that there was no risk of the plaintiffs being liable on the performance bond but not liable on the counter guarantee".[70]

---

[66] *Attock Cement Co Ltd v Romanian Bank for Foreign Trade* [1989] 1 W.L.R. 1147 at 1159.
[67] [1989] 1 W.L.R. 1147.
[68] But there is no absolute rule of law that the place of payment should determine the proper law. A range of factors will be considered: see below, Ch.14. See also, in the context of letters of credit, *Bank of Credit & Commerce Hong Kong Ltd v Sonali Bank* [1995] 1 Lloyd's Rep. 227.
[69] [1994] 2 Lloyd's Rep. 411.
[70] *ibid.*, at 419. See also *Turkiye IS Bankasi AS v Bank of China* [1993] 1 Lloyd's Rep. 132. As to the terms of a counter-indemnity see *Mitsubishi Heavy Industries Ltd v Gulf Bank KSC* [1996] 1 Lloyd's Rep. 499.

CHAPTER 14

SURETYSHIP IN PRIVATE INTERNATIONAL LAW

1. Introduction

14-01   The tripartite nature of guarantees and the rights and obligations they create pose some intriguing questions in the field of private international law. The principal transaction may be entered into in one jurisdiction and the guarantee in another. If so, which law governs the operation, validity and effect of the guarantee? And which law determines whether the principal obligation has been performed or discharged? Is it possible for the principal debtor to be in default according to the law of the country where the principal transaction is to be performed and yet for the guarantors to be discharged according to the law governing the guarantee itself? By what law are the rights of the guarantors vis-à-vis the creditor and the principal debtor to be determined? Does a different regime govern the rights and obligations of the guarantors *inter se*? Given the United Kingdom's membership of the European Community and its central position in international trade, these questions cannot be overlooked. Naturally, definitive answers must be sought in the standard textbooks on private international law and international trade law but the purpose of this chapter is to provide a roadmap to assist in navigating this vast domain.

14-02   In this chapter, we shall examine the private international law rules relating to the enforcement of guarantees with particular reference to three issues:

    (i) jurisdiction;

    (ii) choice of law; and

    (iii) recognition and enforcement of judgments[1]

2. Jurisdiction

14-03   The threshold issue is to identify the appropriate forum to resolve the dispute. There are several restrictions on the jurisdiction of English courts in the cases. First, an English court might not have jurisdiction because English law does not recognise the capacity of the particular claimant or defendant to sue or be sued in England or because the defendant is entitled to immunity from suit. Secondly, the jurisdiction of the English court may be circumscribed by the rules of private international law.

---

[1] For a detailed analysis of these issues, see J. Hill *The Law Relating to International Commercial Disputes* (1998), Ch.12 and Dicey & Morris, *The Conflict of* Laws (13th ed., 2000), Vol. 1, Ch.14.

(i) Foreign corporations

A foreign corporation that is duly created under the law of the place **14-04** where it is constituted can sue or be sued in England.[2] A business incorporated in a territory that is not recognised by the UK government as a State is nevertheless treated as a foreign corporation from a recognised state by force of s.1 of the Foreign Corporations Act 1991.

(ii) Foreign states

A foreign state which is recognised by the United Kingdom Foreign **14-05** Office[3] has the capacity to sue in England.[4] Subject to the doctrine of state immunity as refined by statute, a recognised foreign state can also be sued in England.[5] On the other hand, an unrecognised state cannot sue or be sued in England.

A recognised foreign state which provides a commercial guarantee can **14-06** be sued in England because s.3 of the State Immunity Act 1978 provides that a "State is not immune as respects proceedings relating to—

(a) a commercial transaction entered into by the State; or

(b) an obligation of the State which by virtue of a contract (whether a commercial transaction or not) falls to be performed wholly or partly in the United Kingdom."[6]

Section 3(3) defines the term "commercial transaction" to include:

---

[2] *Lazard Brothers & Co v Midland Bank* [1933] A.C. 289. See Dicey & Morris, *The Conflict of Laws* (13th ed., 2000), Rule 155. The fact that a foreign corporation which establishes a place of business in England is required to lodge certain documents with the Registrar of Companies does not mean that this branch of the foreign corporation will be recognised as a separate legal entity. See Companies Act 1985, ss.690A and 691. As to the jurisdiction over international organisations, see the International Organisations Act 1968 and *Arab Monetary Fund v Hashim (No.3)* [1990] 3 W.L.R. 139. See also Hill, *International Commercial Disputes* (1998) pp.17–23. The International Tin Council has been held to lack a legal personality in private international law so it cannot not sue or be sued: See *J H Rayner (Mincing Lane) Ltd v Department of Trade and Industry* [1989] Ch. 72. Compare *Arab Monetary Fund v Hashim (No.3)* [1991] 2 A.C. 114. See also F.A. Mann, "International Organisations as National Corporations" (1991) 107 L.Q.R. 357.

[3] *Cf. GUR Corporation v Trust Bank of Africa Ltd* [1987] Q.B. 559, which suggests that a foreign state's locus standi in England is determined by its recognition in the international community, not by the Foreign Office.

[4] Hill, *International Commercial Disputes*, p.23. See also G. Marston, "The Personality of the Foreign State in English Law" [1997] 56 C.L.J. 374 and G. Badr, *State Immunity: An Analytic and Prognostic View* (1984).

[5] *ibid.* Under English law, a successful plea of sovereign immunity does not confer immunity from legal liability, but only exemption from the local jurisdiction of the English court: *Cardinal Financial Investments Corporation v Central Bank of Yemen* [2001] Lloyd's Rep. Bank. 1 at 3.

[6] The State Immunity Act 1978, s.3(1). However, s.3(2) provides that this section does not apply if the parties to the dispute are states or have otherwise agreed in writing. A central bank of a foreign government will not be entitled to state immunity under the State Immunity Act 1978 in respect of a commercial transaction even if it was intended to serve the interests of the state: *Banca Carige Spa v Banco National de Cuba* [2001] Lloyd's Rep. Bank. 203 at 212.

"(a) any contact for the supply of goods or services; and

(b) any loan or other transaction for the provision of finance or *any guarantee or indemnity* in respect of any such transaction or of any other financial obligation . . ."[7]

Recognised states can also be sued in respect of mortgages granted over immovable property in the United Kingdom.[8] This is relevant to third party mortgages or collateral securities granted by a recognised state.

14–07   The fact that a recognised foreign state is subject to the adjudicative jurisdiction of an English Court does necessarily mean that the recognised state is subject to the enforcement jurisdiction.[9] However, an English court has jurisdiction to enforce a judgment against a recognised foreign state in two situations: first, where the defendant has waived state immunity;[10] and secondly, where the judgment relates to property used or intended to be used for "commercial purposes".[11] The term "commercial purposes" is defined[12] by reference to "commercial transaction" in s.3(3), which includes "any contract for the supply of goods or services". Only where a bank account of a foreign embassy is used solely for commercial purposes will it be subject to the process of attachment.[13]

(iii) Actions *in personam* against other parties

(a) Sources of jurisdiction

14–08   An action to enforce a guarantee involves an *in personam* action against the guarantors. English courts derive their jurisdiction in an *in personam* action from three sources: first, international regulations, principally the Council Regulation 44/2001 ("the Judgments Regulation") and, to a lesser extent, the Brussels and Lugano Conventions (the "International Conventions"); secondly, the Modified Rules, which in certain circumstances confers jurisdiction on the courts of one or more of the countries comprised in the United Kingdom; and thirdly, the traditional rules of

---

[7] But a claim for an indemnity against member states who were parties to the International Tin Council Agreement was not justiciable under English law because of sovereign state immunity: *JH Rayner (Mincing Lane) Ltd v Department of Trade and Industry* [1990] 2 A.C. 418. Sovereign state immunity will not be available to private parties to a promissory note even if the maker of the note was an agent for a state in the transaction underlying the promissory note: *Cardinal Financial Investments Corporation v Central Bank of Yemen* [2001] Lloyd's Rep. Bank. 1 at 3.
[8] See State Immunity Act 1978, s.6(1).
[9] Hill, *International Commercial Disputes*, para.2.3.43.
[10] State Immunity Act 1978, s.13(3). See *A Co Ltd v Republic of X* [1990] 2 Lloyd's Rep. 520 and F.A. Mann, "Waiver of Immunity" (1991) 107 L.Q.R. 362.
[11] State Immunity Act 1978, s.13(4).
[12] In s.17(1) of the State Immunity Act 1978.
[13] *Alcom Ltd v Republic of Columbia* [1984] A.C. 580; H. Fox, "Enforcement Jurisdiction, Foreign State Property and Diplomatic Immunity" (1985) 34 I.C.L.Q. 115.

private international law which are based on the principles which were contained in RSC Orders 10 to 12.[14]

(b) Jurisdiction under the Judgments Regulation and the International Conventions

By force of s.21(1) of the European Communities Act 1972, the **14–09** Judgments Regulation came into force in the United Kingdom on March 1, 2002, without the need for any implementing legislation. The Judgments Regulation leaves certain matters, in particular the determination of domicile, to be governed by the national law. The relevant national law in relation to the Judgments Regulation is the Civil Jurisdiction and Judgments Orders 2001 (SI 2001/3929) which plays a similar role to that performed by the Civil Jurisdiction and Judgments Act 1982 in relation to the Brussels and Lugano Conventions.[15]

The International Conventions have diminished in importance since the Judgments Regulation came into force. The Brussels Convention continues to apply but only to Denmark, which did not participate in the Judgments Regulation. The Lugano Convention continues to apply only as regards Iceland, Norway, Switzerland and Poland.

This mosaic of international regulation is not as diverse as it appears. The jurisdictional rules under the Judgments Regulation and the International Conventions are broadly similar and it is expected that cases decided under the International Conventions will be relevant to the Judgments Regulation. For these reasons a composite account of the Judgments Regulation and the International Conventions will be provided and any material differences between these regimes will be noted.

The general jurisdictional rule under these regimes is that a person **14–10** domiciled in a contracting state must be sued in the courts of that state.[16] However, there are exceptions. First, a person domiciled in a contracting state may be sued in another contracting state in matters relating to a contract, in the courts of the place of performance of the main obligation[17] in question.[18]

---

[14] See generally Hill, *International Commercial Disputes*, para.1.2.7. See now Supreme Court Act 1981, ss.15 and 19.
[15] The Brussels and the Lugano Conventions have the force of law in the United Kingdom by virtue of ss.2 and 3A respectively of the Civil Jurisdiction and Judgments Act 1982. As to the Judgments Regulation, see Beaumont in *Reform and Development of Private International Law* (Fawcett ed., 2002), p.9, and P. North, "Rethinking Jurisdiction of Judgments" (2002) 55 *Current Legal Problems* 395.
[16] Judgments Regulation, Art.2; International Conventions, Art.2. As to the domicile of corporations, see Art.60 of the Judgments Regulation and Art.53 of the International Conventions.
[17] *W H Martin Ltd v Spezialfahrzeugwerke GmbH*, Trans.Ref: QBENI 97/112 CMS1, April 8, 1998, Peter Gibson L.J., CA; *Raiffeisen Zentralbank Osterreich AG v National Bank of Greece SA* [1999] 1 Lloyd's Rep. 408, Tuckey J., QBD (Comm Ct). Even an implied term can be the principal obligation in a contract: *ibid.*
[18] See Judgments Regulation, Art.5(1); International Conventions, Art.5 and *Gamelstaden plc v Casa de Suecia SA and Thulin* [1994] 1 Lloyd's Rep. 433; *The Governor and Company of the Bank of Scotland v SA Banque Nationale de Paris* [1996] I.L.Pr. 668; *The Governor and Company of the Bank of Scotland v Seitz* [1991] I.L.Pr. 426; 1990 S.L.T. 584; *Bio Medical*

14–11   In *Seitz's case*[19] a German national domiciled in Germany granted two
guarantees in favour of the Bank of Scotland in relation to the accounts of
two companies held at a Glasgow branch of the bank. The Court of Session
held that the bank could enforce the guarantees in Scotland because the
place of performance of the contractual obligation was the bank's Glasgow
branch, in the absence of an express provision as to the place of
performance. This conclusion was consistent with the Brussels Convention
which carried no implication that the pre-eminent jurisdiction was
conferred on the courts of the guarantor's domicile.

14–12   Secondly, a person domiciled in a contracting state may also be sued:

> (i)   where he is one of several defendants, in the courts of the place
>   where any one of them is domiciled;[20]
>
> (ii) as a third party in an action on a guarantee or in any other third
>   party proceedings, in the court seised of the original proceedings,
>   unless these proceedings were instituted solely for the purpose of
>   removing him from the jurisdiction of the court which would be
>   competent in his case;[21]
>
> (iii) on a counter-claim arising from the same contract or facts on
>   which the original claim was based, in the court in which the
>   original claim is pending;[22]
>
> (iv) in matters relating to a contract, if the action may be combined
>   with an action against the same defendant in matters relating to
>   rights *in rem* in immovable property, in the court of the
>   contracting state in which the property is situated.[23]

Where the proceedings assert rights *in rem* in immovable property,
exclusive jurisdiction, regardless of domicile, is conferred on the courts of

---

Research Ltd (Trading As Slenderstone) v Delatex SA [2000] I.L.Pr. 23. The place of
performance of the main contractual obligation is determined by the conflict of laws principles
of the court seised: *GIE Groupe Concorde v Master of the Vessel Suhadiwarno Panjan* [1999] 2
All E.R. (Comm) 700 (G.C. Rodriguez Iglesias President, ECJ); *Industrie Tessli Italiana
Como v Dunlop AG* [1976] E.C.R. 1473; [1977] C.L.Y. 1281; *Custom Made Commercial Ltd v
Stawa Metallbau GmbH* [1994] E.C.R. I–2913; [1994] C.L.Y. 4800. In the case of a letter of
credit the place or performance of the main obligation is the place of payment: *Crédit Agricole
Indosuez v Chailease Finance Corp* [2000] 1 All E.R. (Comm) 399. Under the Judgments
Regulation, Art.5(1) there are now specific provisions dealing with the place of performance
in relation to contracts for the sale of goods and the provision of services. Unless otherwise
agreed, the place of performance, in the case of the sale of goods or the provision of services,
is the place in a Member State where, under the contract, the goods or services are delivered
or provided or should be delivered or provided, as the case may be. In other cases, the general
rule that a person domiciled in a Regulation State, may in another Regulation State, be sued,
in matters relating to contract in the courts of the place of performance of the obligation in
question: Art.5(1)(a). There are also special provisions relating to contracts of employment
(Arts 18–21), consumer contracts (Arts 15–17) and insurance contracts (Arts 8–14).
[19] *The Governor and Company of the Bank of Scotland v Seitz* 1991 1 L. Pr. 426; 1990 S.L.T.
584.
[20] Judgments Regulation, Art.6(1); International Conventions, Art.6(1), as amended. This
convention is Sch.1 to the Civil Jurisdiction and Judgments Act 1982 (c.27).
[21] Judgments Regulation, Art.6(2); International Conventions, Art.6(2).
[22] Judgments Regulation, Art.6(3); International Conventions, Art.6(3).
[23] Judgments Regulation, Art.6(4); International Conventions, Art.6(4).

the contracting state in which the property is situated.[24] This rule is relevant in relation to proceedings to enforce collateral securities or third party mortgages over immovable property.

The parties can agree to confer exclusive jurisdiction on the courts of a **14–13** particular contracting state.[25] If the parties, one or more of whom is domiciled in a contracting state, have agreed that the courts of a contracting state are to have jurisdiction, then those courts shall have exclusive jurisdiction.[26] Where there is a non-exclusive jurisdiction clause in a guarantee, the effect of Art.17 of the International Conventions is to give exclusive jurisdiction to a particular contracting state once the parties exercise their choice to institute proceedings in that country.[27]

If the defendant is not domiciled in a contracting state the jurisdiction of **14–14** the courts of each contracting state shall, subject to Art.16, be determined by the law of that state. This rule does not override the exclusive jurisdiction of the courts of a contracting state in which immovable property is situated to entertain proceedings which assert rights *in rem* in relation to that property.[28]

Nothing in the Conventions prevents a court of a contracting state from **14–15** acquiring jurisdiction where the defendant, regardless of domicile,[29] appears and submits to the jurisdiction.[30] But the entry of an appearance will not be taken as a submission to the jurisdiction of the contracting state where it was entered solely to contest the jurisdiction or where the courts of another contracting state have exclusive jurisdiction because the proceedings assert rights *in rem* in relation to immovable property situated in that other contracting state.[31]

Even where proceedings are commenced in a court of another **14–16** contracting state, an English Court has jurisdiction to grant interim relief, including freezing orders, in aid of the foreign proceedings.[32]

---

[24] Judgments Regulation, Art.22(1); International Conventions, Art.16(1)(a). See Hill, *International Commercial Disputes*, p.93.
[25] Judgments Regulation, Art.23; International Conventions, Art.17.
[26] *ibid.* See Hill, *International Commercial Disputes*, para.5.3.1. and *The Governor and Company of the Bank of Scotland v SA Banque Nationale de Paris* [1996] 1 L. Pr. 668. An agreement as to jurisdiction may be deemed to have been reached where one party specifies the court which is to have jurisdiction over disputes arising from a contract and the other party does not object and if the conduct of the parties was consistent with accepted practice in that particular branch of trade or commerce: *Mainschiffahrts Genossenschaft eG (MSG) v Les Gravieres Rhenanes Sarl* [1997] 3 W.L.R. 179 (J.L. Murray, President ECJ). Proceedings commenced in a foreign country in breach of an exclusive jurisdiction clause can be restrained by an injunction: *Bouygues Offshore SA v Ultisol Transport Contractors Ltd* [1996] 2 Lloyd's Rep. 153 (Note).
[27] *Gamelstaden plc v Case de Suecia SA and Thulin* [1994] 1 Lloyd's Rep. 433 (a case involving a loan agreement).
[28] Judgments Regulation, Arts 4(1) and 22(1); International Conventions, Art.16(1).
[29] *Brenner & Noller v Dean Witter Reynolds Inc* Case C–318/93 [1994] E.C.R. I–4275, 4280 (para.15).
[30] Judgments Regulation, Art.24; International Conventions, Art.18. See Hill, *International Commercial Disputes*, para.5.2.1.
[31] *ibid.*
[32] *Alltrans Inc v Interdom Holdings Ltd* [1993] I.L.Pr. 109, CA.

(c) Service in actions under the Judgments Regulation and the International Conventions

14–17   If the foreign defendant is physically present in England at the time of service, the claimant may serve the defendant within the jurisdiction.[33] Where the defendant is not physically present in England at the time of service, it might be thought that the claimant would require leave of the court to serve the defendant out of the jurisdiction. But this is not the case. It is established that the claimant does not require leave to serve the defendant abroad in cases falling within the scope of the International Conventions.[34] Leave to serve the writ out of the jurisdiction will, however, be required where the writ includes several claims some of which fall within the scope of the conventions and some of which do not.[35] It is likely that the same rules as to service will apply under the Judgments Regulation.

(d) Jurisdiction under the Modified Rules within the United Kingdom

14–18   Within the United Kingdom, there are three distinct legal systems: England and Wales; Scotland; and Northern Ireland. The Modified Rules for the allocation of jurisdiction within the United Kingdom apply by force of Schedule 4 to the Civil Jurisdiction and Judgments Act 1982.[36] Consequently, an English court cannot assume jurisdiction in relation to disputes falling within the scope of Art.1 of the Modified Rules, including an action to enforce a guarantee, if the defendant is domiciled in Scotland or Northern Ireland. But where the dispute falls outside the scope of the Modified Rules, jurisdiction is governed by the traditional rules of private international law.[37]

14–19   **(i) Scope of the Modified Rules**. In practice, the Modified Rules determines the jurisdictional rules in two cases: first, where the Judgments Regulation or the International Conventions simply confer jurisdiction in relation to a particular matter on the courts of the United Kingdom without specifying whether the courts of England, Scotland or Ireland are to have jurisdiction; and secondly, where the questions of jurisdiction are internal to the United Kingdom and do not involve a foreign legal system outside the United Kingdom.[38]

14–20   **(ii) General rule: defendant must be sued in his domicile**. The general jurisdictional principle under the Modified Rules is that a person

---

[33] *Union Bank of Finland Ltd v Lelakis* [1997] 1 W.L.R. 590. See Hill, *International Commercial Disputes*, para.4.3.2.
[34] Hill, *International Commercial Disputes*, para.4.3.2.
[35] Hill, *International Commercial Disputes*, para.4.3.3. As to the form of the claim in such a case, see Civil Procedure Rules 1998, rr.6.17–6.23. See also *Gascoince v Pyrah, The Times,* November 26, 1991 and Hill, *International Commercial Disputes*, para.4.3.4 and S. Sime, *A Practical Approach to Civil Procedure* (5th ed., 2002), pp.108–134.
[36] As substituted by SI 2001/3929, Sch.2, para.4.
[37] *ibid.* See below, paras 14–29 to 14–32.
[38] Hill, *International Commercial Disputes*, paras 6.1.1. and 6.1.2.

domiciled in a part of the United Kingdom must be sued in the courts of that part.[39] This general rule is subject to a number of exceptions which are similar to the exceptions to the general jurisdictional rule in the Judgments Regulation and the International Conventions.

(iii) Exceptions: place of performance. The first exception is that a 14–21 person domiciled in a part of the United Kingdom may be sued in another part of the United Kingdom, in matters relating to a contract, in the courts of the place of performance of the obligation in question.[40]

(a) Multiple defendants, multiple claims. The second series of exceptions 14–22 relates to actions against multiple defendants, third party proceedings, counter claims and proceedings in which a contractual claim is combined with a claim asserting rights *in rem* in immoveable property. Rule 5 of the Modified Rules provides:

"A person domiciled in a part of the United Kingdom may, in another part of the United Kingdom, also be sued:
1. where he is one of a number of defendants, in the courts of the place where any of them is domiciled,[41]
2. as a third party in an action on a warranty or guarantee or in any third party proceedings, in the court seised of the original proceedings, unless these were instituted solely with the object of removing him from the jurisdiction of the court which would be competent in his case;[42]
3. on a counterclaim arising from the same contract or facts on which the original claim was based, in the court in which the original claim is pending;[43]
4. in matters relating to a contract, if the action may be combined with an action against the same defendant in matters relating to rights *in rem* in immovable property, in the court of the part of the United Kingdom in which the property is situated."[44]

(b) Debts secured over property. A person domiciled in one part of the 14–23 United Kingdom may be sued in proceedings concerning a debt secured on immovable property in another part of the United Kingdom where the property is situated.[45] Indeed, the same rule applies to proceedings which are brought to assert, declare or determine proprietary or possessory rights, or rights of security in or over movable property, or to obtain authority to dispose of movable property.[46]

(c) Consumer contracts. There are special provisions dealing with 14–24 jurisdiction in relation to consumer contracts.[47] Generally, proceedings

---

[39] Rule 1.
[40] Rule 3(a).
[41] Rule 5(a).
[42] Rule 5(b).
[43] Rule 5(c).
[44] Rule 5(d).
[45] Rule 3(h)(i).
[46] Rule 3(h)(ii). See Hill, *International Commercial Disputes*, para.6.2.9.
[47] Rules 7–9. See Hill, *International Commercial Disputes*, para.6.2.12.

may be instituted against a consumer only in the part of the United Kingdom in which he is domiciled.

14–25   **(d) Immovable property**. Where the proceedings against the defendant have as their object rights *in rem* in immovable property or tenancies of immovable property, they must be instituted in the courts of the part of the United Kingdom in which the property is situated.[48] This principle is particularly relevant to the enforcement of third party mortgages or collateral securities provided by guarantors.

14–26   **(iv) Choice of jurisdiction**. The parties are allowed to confer jurisdiction on courts of a part of the United Kingdom to settle any disputes which have arisen or may arise in connection with a particular legal relationship.[49] This prorogation of jurisdiction can be made in the guarantee itself or when a dispute arises between the parties.

14–27   **(v) Submission to jurisdiction**. Like the traditional rules of private international law, Rule 11 of the Modified Rules confers jurisdiction on a court of a part of the United Kingdom before which a defendant enters an appearance in the proceedings. But this rule does not apply where the appearance was entered solely to contest the jurisdiction or where a court in another part of the United Kingdom has exclusive jurisdiction because the proceedings assert rights *in rem* in immovable property[50] situated in that other part of the United Kingdom.

14–28   **(vi) Service under the Modified Rules**. It appears that where an English Court has jurisdiction under the Modified Rules the defendant may be served out of the jurisdiction in another part of the United Kingdom without the leave of the court.[51] Leave to serve outside the jurisdiction may, however, be necessary where some claims against the defendant fall within the Civil Jurisdiction and Judgments Act 1982 and some do not.[52] But if the defendant is physically present in the jurisdiction at the time of service, naturally he can be served within the jurisdiction. Presumably, the court will not exercise jurisdiction over such a defendant in an *in personam* action if it considers that another forum is more appropriate.

(e) The traditional rules of private international law: jurisdiction and service

14–29   In cases falling outside the scope of the Judgments Regulation, the International Conventions and the Modified Rules, the traditional rules of private international law determine the jurisdiction of the court. In this sense the traditional rules have a residual operation.

---

[48] Rule 11.
[49] Rule 12. See Hill, *International Commercial Disputes*, para.6.2.6.
[50] Rules 11(a) and 13(2).
[51] Hill, *International Commercial Disputes*, para.4.3.2.
[52] Hill. *International Commercial Disputes*, para.4.3.3. See also SI 2001/3929, Sch.2, para.4. As to the form of the claim in such cases, see Civil Procedure Rules 1998, rr.6.17–6.23 and Hill, *International Commercial Disputes*, para.4.3.4. See also Art.20 which provides some procedural safeguards for defendants.

Under the traditional rules of private international law, an English court **14–30** has jurisdiction in relation to *in personam* actions in three situations.[53] First, a defendant may submit to the jurisdiction of the court. But the mere entry of an appearance in the proceedings for the sole purpose of contesting the court's jurisdiction does not constitute a submission to jurisdiction.[54] Secondly, an English court has jurisdiction over a defendant who is duly served within the jurisdiction provided that the principle of *forum non conveniens* does not apply.[55] Under this principle, "a court which has jurisdiction over a defendant may decline to exercise it on the grounds that it is not the appropriate venue for the action and that considerations of justice require that the plaintiff litigate in another jurisdiction".[56] The House of Lords accepted the principle of *forum non conveniens* as part of English law in *Spiliada Maritime Corp v Cansulex Ltd*.[57]

The third basis on which an English Court may assume jurisdiction over **14–31** an absent defendant is where the claimant obtains leave under r.6.20 of the Civil Procedure Rules 1998 to serve a writ on the defendant out of the jurisdiction.[58] To persuade the court to exercise its discretion to grant leave to serve the defendant outside the jurisdiction, the claimant must satisfy the court, *inter alia*, that it is the most appropriate forum.[59] In other words, the principle of *forum non conveniens* is a factor in the exercise of the court's discretion. The English court would appear to be the most appropriate forum for dealing with disputes arising under contracts that have a close connection with England.[60] In deciding whether to exercise its discretion, the court will also consider the merits of the claimant's claim and decide whether there is a serious question to be tried.[61] Finally, the claimant must establish a good arguable case that the claim falls within one of the paragraphs r.6.20 of the Civil Procedure Rules 1998.[62] An action to be enforce a guarantee could fall within these paragraphs as: (a) a claim to enforce a contract made within the jurisdiction;[63] (b) a claim in respect of a breach committed within the jurisdiction of a contract made within or out

---

[53] See Hill, *International Commercial Disputes*, para.1.2.7. See also *National Commercial Bank v Wimborne* (1979) 11 N.S.W.L.R. 156.

[54] See *Carmel Exporters (Sales) Ltd v Sea-Land Services Inc* [1981] 1 All E.R. 984: Compare *Harris v Taylor* [1915] 2 K.B. 580. See also CPR, Pt.II and S. Sime, *A Practical Approach to Civil Procedure* (5th ed., 2002), p.110.

[55] *Australian Assets Co Ltd v Higginson* (1897) 18 N.S.W. Eq 189; 14 W.N. (NSW) 97.

[56] M.C. Pryles, "The Struggle for Internationalism in Transnational Litigation" (1987) 61 A.L.J. 434 at 434. See also L. Marasinghe, "International Litigation: Choice of Forum" (1993) 23 U.W.A.L.R. 264; F.K. Juenger, "What's Wrong With Forum Shopping?" (1994) 16 Syd. L.R. 1; B.R. Opeskin, "The Price of Forum Shopping" (1994) 16 Syd. L.R. 14; F.K. Juenger, "Forum Shopping: A Rejoinder" (1994) 16 Syd. L.R. 28; B.J. Davenport, "Forum Shopping in the Market" (1995) 111 L.Q.R. 366; A.G. Slater, "Forum Non Conveniens: A View from the Shop floor" (1988) 104 L.Q.R. 554 and Hill, *International Commercial Disputes*, paras 9.2.1–9.2.58.

[57] [1987] A.C. 460. See also Hill, *International Commercial Disputes*, paras 9.2.33–9.2.34.

[58] Hill, *International Commercial Disputes*, paras 7.3.1–7.3.3.

[59] Hill, *International Commercial Disputes*, para.1.2.7.

[60] See *Spiliada Maritime Corporation v Consulex Ltd* [1987] A.C. 460.

[61] *Seaconsar Far East Ltd v Bank Markazi Jomhouri Islami Iran* [1994] A.C. 438.

[62] *ibid.*

[63] Civil Procedure Rules 1998, r.6.20(5).

of the jurisdiction;[64] (c) a claim to enforce a contract expressly or impliedly governed by English law;[65] or (d) a claim to enforce a contract which provides that the High Court of Justice has jurisdiction to determine any action in respect of the contract.[66]

14–32   Having identified the court which has jurisdiction to determine the dispute, it is necessary to consider what law should be applied by the court in relation to different aspects of the contract. At the outset, it may be noted that there are two separate regimes governing the choice of law issue.

3. CHOICE OF LAW RULES

14–33   Two consequences flow from the fact that a contract of guarantee is accessory to, and to some extent dependent upon, the principal debt or obligation.[67] The first consequence of the accessory nature of a guarantee is that a guarantor cannot be liable for more that the outstanding principal debt or the damages caused by the principal's failure to perform the primary obligation;[68] indeed, the guarantor may be liable for considerably less if the guarantor has limited his liability by the terms of the guarantee.[69] Secondly, the law regulating the principal transaction determines when and to what extent the principal debtor is in default in payment of the principal debt or performance of the principal obligation.[70] Since a guarantor is not usually liable unless the principal debtor is in default, the law regulating the principal transaction will determine when the guarantor's liability arises.[71]

(i) The proper law for principal contracts entered into on or before April 1, 1991

14–34   In respect of contracts entered into on or before April 1, 1991, the law governing the principal transaction is referred to as the "proper law" of the contract.[72]

---

[64] *ibid.*, r.6.20(6).
[65] *ibid.*, r.6.20(5)(c).
[66] *ibid.*, r.6.20(5)(d). See also r.6.20(1).
[67] See above, paras 1–22 to 1–26.
[68] *ibid.*
[69] See above, paras 1–22 to 1–26.
[70] *Rouquette v Overmann* (1875) L.R. 10 Q.B. 525 at 537; *Kirsten v Chrystmos* (1939) 14 N.Y.S. (2d) 442.
[71] *ibid.*
[72] The uniform rules of the Rome Convention, implemented in the United Kingdom by the Contracts (Applicable Law) Act 1990, govern contracts entered into from April 1, 1991. See below, paras 14–45 to 14–55.

(a) Rules for identifying the proper law

To determine the proper law of the principal contract, one must consider **14–35** three situations.[73] The first is where the parties have made an express choice of law.[74] This express choice of law will govern the contract[75] provided that the intention expressed is bona fide and legal and there is no reason for avoiding the choice on the grounds of public policy.[76] As a general rule, therefore, the parties' express choice of law should prevail unless there are strong reasons to the contrary.[77] However, the court will not accept the parties' choice of foreign law if it was made simply to avoid local statutory restrictions on exclusion of liability.[78]

In the absence of an express stipulation, the court will examine all the **14–36** facts surrounding the contract to determine whether it can infer a choice of the proper law by the parties.[79] The terms of the contract, principally the choice of jurisdiction or arbitration clauses, give rise to a strong inference that the same law is the proper law of the contract.[80]

---

[73] See *James Miller & Partners Ltd v Whitworth Street Estates (Manchester) Ltd* [1969] 1 W.L.R. 377 at 383, reversed in [1970] A.C. 583. See also Law Reform Commission, *Choice of Law*, Report No.58 (1992).

[74] In theory, the parties could choose two or more proper laws to govern different aspects of the contract but this rarely occurs: *Hamlyn & Co v Talisker Distillery* [1894] A.C. 202 at 207; *Kahler v Midland Bank* [1950] A.C. 24 at 42; *Re Helbert Wagg & Co Ltd* [1956] Ch. 323 at 340; *Forsakringsiktieselskapet Vesta v Butcher* [1986] 2 All E.R. 488 at 504–505, aff'd on other grounds: [1988] 2 All E.R. 43; [1989] 1 All E.R. 402; *Libyan Arab Foreign Bank v Bankers' Trust* [1989] 3 All E.R. 252 at 267.

[75] *Vita Food Products Inc v Unus Shipping Co* [1939] A.C. 277; *Dalmia Dairy Industries Ltd v National Bank of Pakistan* [1978] 2 Lloyd's Rep. 223; *Indian & General Investment Trust Ltd v Borax Consolidated Ltd* [1920] 1 K.B. 539; *O'Donovan v Dussault* (1973) 35 D.L.R. (3d) 280, Alta, CA; *Scandanavian American National Bank v Kneeland* (1914) 16 D.L.R. 565; *Sharn Importing v Babchuk* (1971) 21 D.L.R. (3d) 349. An express choice of law usually takes the following form: "The parties agree and declare that this contract shall be construed according to the laws of the United Kingdom", or simply "The laws of the United Kingdom shall apply to this contract". Since the choice of law is intended to cover not just the construction of the contract but also its validity, operation and effect and the rights and liabilities of the parties, the second formula is preferable.

[76] *Vita Food Products Inc v Unus Shipping Co Ltd* [1939] A.C. 277 at 290; *Dalmia Dairy Industries Ltd v National Bank of Pakistan* (1978) 2 Lloyd's Rep. 223; *Kay's Leasing Corp Pty Ltd v Fletcher* [1964–1965] N.S.W.R. 25; *Golden Acres Ltd v Queensland Estates Pty Ltd* [1969] Qd. R. 378; *Queensland Estates Pty Ltd v Collas* [1971] Qd. R. 75.

[77] *Kutchera v Buckingham International Holdings* [1988] I.R. 61.

[78] For example, under the Unfair Contract Terms Act 1977, s.27(1) or s.27(2), the Carriage of Goods by Sea Act 1971, s.1(2) (applying the revised Hague-Visby Rules relating to limits on a sea carrier's liability) or Sale of Goods Act 1979, s.56.

[79] See *James Miller & Partners Ltd v Whitworth Street Estates (Manchester) Ltd* [1970] A.C. 583; *Dennys Lascelles Ltd v Borchard* [1933] 3 N.S.W.R. 261, *sub nom Waung v Subbotovsky* [1968] 3 N.S.W.R. 499 (an appeal to the High Court of Australia was restricted to the Statute of Limitations issue): *Waung v Subbotovsky* (1969) 43 A.L.J.R. 372; *Papua New Guinea Development Bank v Manton* [1982] V.R. 1000, *Sharn Importing Ltd v Babchuk* (1971) 21 D.L.R. (3d) 349; *O'Donovan v Dussault* (1973) 35 D.L.R. (3d) 280; *Scandanavian American National Bank v Kneeland* (1914) 16 D.L.R. 565.

[80] *Amin Rasheed Shipping Corpn v Kuwait Insurance Co* [1984] A.C. 50 at 64–67; *Compagnie Tunisienne de Navigation SA & Compagnie d'Armement Maritime SA* [1971] A.C. 572. A choice of jurisdiction can be expressed in the following manner in the contract:

> "Any proceedings in respect of any claim, dispute or cause of action arising hereunder shall at the option of the creditor be instituted, heard and determined in a court of competent jurisdiction in London and such court shall possess territorial jurisdiction to hear and determine such proceedings."

But the form and language of the contract[81] and the place where a bank account is kept[82] are important factors in some cases.

14–37 Where the clause states that a foreign court has exclusive jurisdiction, the clause will be strictly enforced no matter how inconvenient it is to the local party.[83] If there is a foreign jurisdiction clause in the contract, the local court will normally grant a stay of proceedings unless a strong case is shown for the local court to assume jurisdiction.[84] If the court infers that the parties intended the contract to be governed by a foreign law, that law is the proper law even if the contract is to be performed in the United Kingdom.[85]

14–38 If the court cannot find an express or inferred choice, it should objectively determine and apply "the system of law with which the transaction has the closest and most real connection".[86] All the facts and circumstances of the contract are scrutinised.[87] Perhaps the most useful guideline is the place where the contract was made and is to be performed[88] but any one or more of the following factors may be equally

---

[81] *The Adriatic* [1931] P. 241, CA; *Whitworth Street Estates (Manchester) Ltd v James Miller v Partners Ltd* [1970] A.C. 583. But, given the widespread use of the English language in business contracts, not much significance is attached to the fact that the contract is expressed in English: *Amin Rasheed Shipping Corpn v Kuwait Insurance Co* [1984] A.C. 50 at 65 and 70–71.

[82] *X A/G v A Bank* [1983] 2 All E.R. 464. Indeed, it is sometimes said that there is a rebuttable presumption that the law governing a contract between a bank and its customer is the law of the country where the account is kept: *Libyan Arab Foreign Bank v Manufacturers Hanover Trust Co* [1988] 2 Lloyd's Rep. 494.

[83] *Akai Pty Ltd v People's Insurance Co Ltd* (1995) 8 A.N.Z. Insur. Cases 75,837, applying *Eleftheria (Owners of Cargo) v Eleftheria (Owners)* [1970] P.94.

[84] *Leigh-Mardon Pty Ltd v PRC Inc.* (1993) 44 F.C.R. 88; *KH Enterprise v Pioneer Container* [1994] 2 All E.R. 250, PC (the fact that the claim was statute-barred in the foreign jurisdiction was not sufficient reason for granting a stay in the local jurisdiction). See also *Dalmia Dairy Industries Ltd v National Bank of Pakistan* [1978] 2 Lloyd's Rep. 223; *Hamlyn & Co v Talisker Distillery* [1894] A.C. 202; *N V Kwik Hoo Jong Handel Maatschappij v James Finlay & Co* [1927] A.C. 604 at 608 (choice of jurisdiction clauses); *Vita Food Products Inc v Unus Shipping Co Ltd* [1939] A.C. 277 at 290 (arbitration clause).

[85] *St Pierre & South American Stores (Gath & Chaves) Ltd* [1936] 1 K.B. 382.

[86] *Bonython v Commonwealth* [1951] A.C. 201 at 219; *Tomkinson v First Pennsylvania Banking & Trust Co* [1961] A.C. 1007 at 1068, 1081–1082; *James Miller & Partners Ltd v Whitworth Street Estates (Manchester) Ltd* [1970] A.C. 583; *Amin Rasheed Corp v Kuwait Insurance Co* [1982] C.L.Y. 326; *JMJ Contractors v Marples Ridgway* (1985) 31 Build. L.R. 100; *Dubai Electricity Co v Islamic Republic of Iran Shipping Lines* [1984] 2 Lloyd's Rep. 380 at 383; *Rossano v Manufacturers Life Insurance Co* [1962] 2 All E.R. 214 at 218. See also B. Davenport, "Proper Law Now Not So Proper" (1991) 6 I.B.F.L. 157. The better view is that it is the system of law, rather than the country, with which the transaction must have the connection. Compare *Re United Railways of Havana* [1961] A.C. 1007 at 1068.

[87] *The Assunzione* [1954] P. 150; *Coast Lines v Hudig & Veder Chartering NV* [1972] 2 Q.B. 34; *Lindsay v Miller* [1949] V.L.R. 13; *Subbotovsky v Waung* [1968] 3 N.S.W.R. 261, affirmed *sub nom. Waung v Subbotovsky* [1968] 3 N.S.W.R. 499.

[88] *P & O Steam Navigation Co v Shand* (1865) 3 Moo. P.C. (NS) 272 (place of making the contract). A contract is presumed to be made where the last assent or act necessary for its execution as a contract takes place: See *Albeko Schuhmaschinen v Kamborian Shoe Machine Co Ltd* (1961) 111 L.J. 519; *CIT Corp v Sanderson* 43 F. (2d) 985 (1930); *Brinkibon Ltd v Stahag Stahl and Stahlwarenhandelsgesellschaft mbH* [1982] 2 W.L.R. 264. See also *R. v International Trustee for the Protection of Bondholders AG* [1937] A.C. 500; (place of payment); *Subbotovsky v Waung* [1968] 3 N.S.W.R. 261, affirmed *sub nom. Waung v Subbotovsky* [1968] 3 N.S.W.R. 499; *O'Donovan v Dussault* (1973) 35 D.L.R. (3d) 280, Alta, CA; *Scandanavian American National Bank v Kneeland* (1914) 16 D.L.R. 565; *Sharn Importing Ltd v Babchuk* (1971) 21 D.L.R. (3d) 349; *Rothwells Ltd (in liq) v Connell* (1993) 93 A.T.C. 5106 (place of payment).

significant in an appropriate case: the places of residence[89] or business[90] of the parties; the nature of the legal personality of the parties;[91] the nature and location of the subject matter of the contract;[92] the currency expressed in the contract;[93] the location of the funds that are available for the security or discharge of the principal obligation;[94] the place of performance or delivery;[95] or the place where a bank must perform its obligation under a letter of credit.[96] The place where the contract was executed may have been entirely fortuitous, so this factor is seldom important.[97] Moreover, the fact that security for the performance of the principal obligation has been given over land in another jurisdiction does not necessarily mean that the contract will be governed by the law of that jurisdiction.[98]

Whatever legal system is selected by the parties or determined by the court to be the proper law of the principal contract, the contract is governed by that proper law as it stood at the time the contract was made.[99] In the absence of a contrary provision in the contract itself, subsequent changes to the proper law are generally disregarded.

14–39

(b) The functions of the proper law in relation to the principal contract

The importance of the proper law of the principal contract can be seen in the range of issues it governs. It determines the formation, validity, operation, construction and effect of the contract.[1] It probably determines

14–40

---

[89] *Jacobs v Crédit Lyonnais* (1884) 12 Q.B.D. 589 at 600 and 602.

[90] *Re Anglo-Austrian Bank* [1920] 1 Ch. 69 at 75. See also *Sharn Importing Ltd v Babchuk* (1971) 21 D.L.R. (3d) 349, BC.

[91] *R. v International Trustee for the Protection of Bondholders AG* [1937] A.C. 531 at 557 and 574; *The Assunzione* [1954] P. 150; *National Bank of A/Asia Ltd v Scottish Union & National Insurance Co* [1952] A.C. 493.

[92] *British South Africa Co v De Beers Consolidated Mines Ltd* [1910] 1 Ch. 354 at 383. See also *Dennys Lascelles Ltd v Borchard* [1933] V.L.R. 46.

[93] *Papua and New Guinea Development Bank v Manton* [1982] V.R. 1000.

[94] *Dennys Lascelles Ltd v Borchard* [1933] V.L.R. 46. See also *Spurrier v La Cloche* [1902] A.C. 446 at 450; *Bonython v Commonwealth* [1951] A.C. 201 at 221. See too Dicey & Morris, *The Conflict of Laws* (13th ed., 2000), Vol. 2, para.33–299, p.1424.

[95] *Jacobs v Crédit Lyonnais* (1884) 12 Q.B.D. 589.

[96] *Power Curber International Ltd v National Bank of Kuwait SAK* [1981] 1 W.L.R. 1233; *Offshore International SA v Banco Central SA* [1977] 1 W.L.R. 399.

[97] *Sharn Importing Ltd v Babchuk* (1971) 21 D.L.R. (3d) 349.

[98] See *British South Africa Co v De Beers Consolidated Mines Ltd* [1910] 2 Ch. 502 and *Dennys Lascelles Ltd v Borchard* [1933] V.L.R. 46.

[99] *Subbotovsky v Waung* [1968] 3 N.S.W.R. 261, affirmed *sub nom. Waung v Subbotovsky* [1968] 3 N.S.W.R. 499; *Everts v Matteson* 132 P. (2d) 476 (1942); *Ingalls v Bell* 110 P. 2 1068 (1941). But the proper law may change during the currency of the contract: see *Black Clawson International Ltd v Papierwerke Waldorf-Aschaffenburg AG* [1981] 2 Lloyd's Rep. 446 at 456. Cf. *The "Blue Wave"* [1982] 1 Lloyd's Rep. 151 at 153; *Armar Shipping Co Ltd v Caisse Algérienne d' Assurance et de Reassurance* [1981] 1 W.L.R. 207. Perhaps the parties should be allowed to change the proper law during the life of the contract only if the agreement to change the proper law is allowed by the original proper law. See P. Kaye, "The New Private International Law of Contract of the European Community" (1993), p.10.

[1] *St Pierre v South American Stores (Gath & Chaves) Ltd* [1936] 1 K.B. 382; *Permanent Trustee Co (Canberra) Ltd v Permanent Trustee Co (NSW)* (1969) 14 F.L.R. 246 at 254; *Horne v Rouquette* (1878) 3 Q.B.D. 514; *Wilson v Metcalfe Construction Co* [1947] 3 D.L.R. 491, on

whether the parties have the capacity to enter into the contract[2] and whether consideration[3] and privity of contract[4] are necessary to render the contract enforceable. The effect of duress and mistake are governed by the proper law.[5] The proper law of the contract also determines whether or not the principal obligation has been discharged by performance,[6] the outbreak of war,[7] bankruptcy or liquidation,[8] accord and satisfaction,[9] a moratorium[10] or legislation.[11] The proper law of the principal contract governs the rights and obligations of the parties.[12] Consequently, it is the proper law that determines the substance of performance of the principal contract,[13] although the mode of performing contractual obligations is governed by the *lex loci solutionis*.[14]

(c) Matters not governed by the proper law

14–41   Logically, the proper law of the contract cannot be used to determine whether a contract has been concluded for the purposes of jurisdiction or to assist in determining an objective choice of law.[15] One approach to these threshold questions is to say that the objective putative proper law should

---

appeal [1947] 4 D.L.R. 472; *Scandinavian American National Bank v Kneeland* (1914) 16 D.L.R. 565; *Gibbs v Fremont* (1853) 9 Exch. 25; 156 E.R. 11; *Vita Food Products Inc v Unus Shipping Co Ltd* [1939] A.C. 277, PC; *White Cliffs Opal Mines Ltd v Miller* (1904) 4 S.R. (NSW) 150; *The Parouth* [1982] 2 Lloyd's Rep. 351, CA. *Cf. Oceanic Sun Line Special Shipping Co Inc v Fay* (1988) 62 A.L.J.R. 389 at 401 *per* Brennan J. and at 419 *per* Gaudron J.
[2] *Bondholders Securities Corp v Manville* [1934] 4 D.L.R. 679; *M'Feetridge v Stewarts and Lloyd's* (1913) S.C. 773; *Kent v Salmon* [1910] T.P.D. 637 (S.Afr); *Charron v Montreal Trust Co* (1958) 15 D.L.R. (2d) 240; *Male v Roberts* (1790) 3 Esp. 163; 170 E.R. 574, NP; *Bodley Head Ltd v Flegon* [1972] 1 W.L.R. 680.
[3] *Re Bonacina* [1912] 2 Ch. 394 at 400 and 404.
[4] *Scott v Pilkington* (1862) 2 B. & S. 11; 121 E.R. 978. *Cf. Hartmann v Konig* (1933) 50 T.L.R. 114.
[5] *The Parouth* [1982] 2 Lloyd's Rep. 351; *Albeko Schuhmaschinen v The Kamborian Shoe Machine Co Ltd* [1961] 111 L.J. 519.
[6] *Bellingham v Freer* (1837) 1 Moo P.C.C. 333; 12 E.R. 841; *Adams v National Bank of Greece SA* [1961] A.C. 255. However, the currency in which the debt is to be paid will be governed by the *lex loci solutionis*: *Jacobs v Crédit Lyonnais* (1884) 12 Q.B.D. 589 at 604.
[7] *Dalmia Dairy Industries Ltd v National Bank of Pakistan* [1978] 2 Lloyd's Rep. 223; *Re Anglo-Austrian Bank* [1920] 1 Ch. 69.
[8] *Potter v Brown* (1804) 5 East 124; 46 E.R. 628; *Gardiner v Houghton* (1862) 2 B. & S. 743; 121 E.R. 1247.
[9] *Ralli v Dennistoun* (1851) 6 Exch. 483; 155 E.R. 633.
[10] *Re Helbert Wagg & Co Ltd* [1956] Ch. 323, *National Bank of Greece and Athens SA v Metliss* [1958] A.C. 509; *Adams v National Bank of Greece SA* [1961] A.C. 255; *Dennys Lascelles Ltd v Borchard* [1933] V.L.R. 46.
[11] *Mount Albert Borough Council v A/Asian Temperance & General Mutual Life Assurance Society* [1938] A.C. 224; *Perry v Equitable Life Assurance Co* (1929) 45 T.L.R. 468; *R v International Trustee* [1937] A.C. 500.
[12] *St Pierre v South American Stores (Gath & Chaves) Ltd* [1937] 3 All E.R. 349 at 352; *Horne v Rouquette* (1878) 3 Q.B.D. 514.
[13] *Mount Albert Borough Council v A/Asian Temperance & General Mutual Life Assurance Society* [1938] A.C. 224.
[14] Unless some other law is chosen: *Jacobs v Crédit Lyonnais* (1994) 12 Q.B.D. 589. The method of performing the contract will include such matters as the hours for payment and delivery and the currency of payment
[15] See generally, P. Kaye, *The New Private International Law of Contract of the European Community*, p.11.

determine these matters.[16] In other words, these questions should be decided on the basis of the law that would be the proper law if the contract were validly concluded. Another approach is for an English court to apply English law as the *lex fori* on the basis that these are essentially procedural matters.[17] While there is no clear support in the authorities or the commentaries on private international law for either of these approaches or any other approach, it is thought that there is much to be said for the application of the *lex fori*.

Other matters that are not governed by the proper law of the contract **14–42** are the mode of performance and the value and identification of the contractual money of account. The former is governed by the *lex loci solutionis*, unless the parties choose some other law.[18] The latter are governed by the *lex pecuniae*, the law of the money of account specified in the contract.[19] However, the money of payment is governed by the *lex loci solutionis* as this is an aspect of the mode of performance.[20] Procedural matters, such as the assessment of damages, the currency of the judgment[21] and possibly the rate of interest on damages for breach of contract are governed by the *lex fori*.[22]

Under the traditional rules of private international law, the appro- **14–43** priate limitation period for an action to enforce the principal contract was regarded as a procedural matter to be determined by the *lex fori*.[23] However, the The Foreign Limitation Periods Act 1984, which came into force on October 1, 1985, provides that limitation matters are generally to be governed by the applicable law.[24] Section 1(1) of the Act provides:

"Subject to the following provisions of this Act, where in any action or proceedings in a court in England and Wales the law of any other country falls (in accordance with rules of private international law applicable by any such court) to be taken into account in the determination of any matter–

(a) the law of that other country relating to limitation shall apply in respect of that matter for the purposes of the action or proceedings . . ."

---

[16] Kaye, *The New Private International Law of Contract of the European Community*, p.15. See also *The Parouth* [1982] 2 Lloyd's Rep. 351 at 353 and Cheshire and North, *Private International Law* (11th ed., 1987), p.475.
[17] Kaye, *The New Private International Law of Contract of the European Community*, pp.16–17.
[18] *Jacobs v Crédit Lyonnais* (1884) 12 Q.B.D. 589.
[19] *Re Chesterman's Trusts* [1923] 2 Ch. 466. However, revalorisation, which affects the value of the debt rather than currency, is governed by the proper law: *Anderson v Equitable Assurance Society of the United States* (1926) 134 L.T. 557.
[20] *Miliangos v George Frank (Textiles) Ltd* [1975] A.C. 443.
[21] *D'Almeida Araujo LDA v Sir Frederick Becker & Co Ltd* [1953] 2 Q.B. 329; *Kohnke v Karger* [1951] 2 K.B. 670; *The Despina R* [1979] A.C. 685.
[22] *Miliangos v George Frank (Textiles) Ltd (No.2)* [1977] Q.B. 489. The liability to pay interest on damages for breach of contract is governed by the proper law of the contract: *ibid.*
[23] *Arab Monetary Fund v Hashim* [1996] 1 Lloyd's Rep. 589 at 600; *Subbotovsky v Waung* [1968] 3 N.S.W.R. 261, affirmed *sub nom. Waung v Subbotovsky* [1968] 3 N.S.W.R. 499.
[24] See Hill, *International Commercial Disputes*, para.19.1.2.

While the applicable law governs most questions of limitation, it does not determine whether and when proceedings have been commenced in respect of any matter. This is determined by the law of England and Wales.[25]

14-44   There are further exceptions to the general rule in s.1(1) based on public policy. The English court may decide not to apply the general rule where its application would to any extent conflict with public policy,[26] in particular where the application of the general rule would cause undue hardship to a party or a potential party to the action or proceedings.[27] Where the English court decides not to apply the foreign limitation period pursuant to s.2 of the Foreign Limitation Periods Act 1984, the English limitation period will apply to the action or proceedings.[28]

(ii) The "applicable law" for principal contracts entered into after April 1, 1991: The Rome Convention

14-45   The Contracts (Applicable Law) Act 1990 implements the 1980 Rome Convention on the Law Applicable to Contractual Obligations and the 1984 Luxembourg Convention on Greek Accession to the Rome Convention in the United Kingdom as from April 1, 1991.[29] Subject to certain exceptions, the Rome Convention replaces the English private international rules relating to the applicable law in international contracts. The Convention replaces the term "proper law of the contract" with the term "applicable law". It prescribes how the "applicable law" in relation to contractual obligations is determined "in any situation involving a choice between the law of different countries".[30]

(a) Territorial scope of the Convention

14-46   In the United Kingdom, where there are three legal systems, (English and Welsh, Scottish and Northern Irish) within a single political entity, the Rome Convention will be applied in the United Kingdom court even where conflicts arise between the laws of different nations within the

---

[25] Foreign Limitation Periods Act 1984, s.1(3).
[26] s.2.
[27] s.2(2). See also *Liberian Shipping Corporation "Pegasus" v A King & Sons* Ltd [1967] 2 Q.B. 86 at 98.
[28] *Arab Monetary Fund v Hashim* [1996] 1 Lloyd's Rep. 589 at 600. Compare *The Komninos* [1991] 1 Lloyd's Rep. 370 at 377.
[29] The Rome Convention was ratified in the 1980's by Belgium, Denmark, France, Germany, Italy and Luxembourg. It was implemented into domestic law by Germany and Denmark before the Convention came into force on January 1, 1991, when the United Kingdom ratified the Convention. However, the Rome Convention was implemented in the United Kingdom by the Contracts (Applicable Law) Act 1990, which came into force on April 1, 1991. See generally R. Plender, *The European Contracts Convention: The Rome Convention on the Choice of Law for Contracts* (1991).
[30] Art.1 of the Rome Convention, which is attached, as Sch.1, to the Contracts (Applicable Law) Act 1990.

United Kingdom.[31] Moreover, where the Rome Convention applies it can be used to determine the applicable law where conflicts arise not just between the laws of different parts of the United Kingdom or between the laws of the United Kingdom and those of other contracting states; it even applies to conflicts between the contract law of the United Kingdom or parts of the United Kingdom and non-contracting states.[32]

(b) Retrospectivity

The Rome Convention only applies to contracts made after the date on which the Convention came into force in the contracting states. For the United Kingdom, Belgium, Denmark, France, Germany, Greece, Italy and Luxembourg it applies to contracts made after April 1, 1991. For the Netherlands and Ireland it applies to contracts concluded after September 1, 1991 and January 1, 1992 respectively.[33]   **14–47**

(c) Termination

Under Art.30, the Rome Convention has a finite duration of ten years from April 1, 1991 but it is automatically renewable for five-year terms thereafter, except in contracting states where it has been denounced not less than six months before the expiration of the period of ten or five years, whereupon it ceases to have any further effect at the end of the relevant period.[34]   **14–48**

(d) Agreements relating to applicable law

As in the pre-existing private international law rules, the Rome Convention gives effect to express or implied choice of law agreements. The parties' express choice of applicable law must be expressed or "demonstrated with reasonable certainty by the terms of the contract or the circumstances of the case".[35] For example, a loan agreement conferring jurisdiction on the courts of a particular country where the lender does business may demonstrate that the applicable law governing the loan contract is to be the law of that country.[36] Moreover, the past conduct of the parties in dealing with one another subject to an express choice of law may suggest that that choice of law should apply in relation to the current loan contract even if there is no express choice of law in that contract.[37] Finally,   **14–49**

---

[31] The Contracts (Applicable Law) Act 1990, s.2(3).
[32] Art.2. See Hill, *International Commercial Disputes*, para.14.4.19 and Kaye, *The New Private International Law of Contract of the European Community*, pp.32–34.
[33] Kaye, *The New Private International Law of Contract of the European Community*, pp.34–35.
[34] Kaye, *The New Private International Law of Contract of the European Community*, p.35.
[35] Art.3(1). See Dicey & Morris, *The Conflict of Laws* (13th ed., 2000), Vol. 2, paras 32R–059 *et seq.*
[36] Dicey & Morris, *The Conflict of Laws* (13th ed., 2000), Vol. 2, para.33–294.
[37] Dicey & Morris, *the Conflict of Laws* (13th ed., 2000), Vol. 2, para.33–294, p.1421.

the fact that the principal contract is supported by a guarantee that contains an express choice of law may indicate that that choice of law should govern the principal contract to which it is accessory.[38]

14–50   The parties are permitted to stipulate that one part of a contract is to be governed by the law of one country and the remainder of the contract by the law of another country.[39] Moreover, the parties can vary the applicable law after the conclusion of their contract.[40]

(e) Restrictions on the parties' choice of the applicable law

14–51   The parties' freedom to choose the law of a particular country as the applicable law is constrained by Art.3(3) of the Convention. It provides that where the parties choose a particular country's law, even though the contractual context at the time of that choice is otherwise wholly connected with the law of one other country, the parties' choice is not to prejudice the application of the mandatory rules of the law of the other country. Mandatory rules are defined as rules that "cannot be derogated from by contract".[41] Examples include ss.12–15 of the Sale of Goods Act 1979 and s.6 of the Unfair Contract Terms Act 1977.

(f) The applicable law in the absence of choice

14–52   Under Art.4(1) of the Rome Convention, in the absence of choice by the parties, the applicable law shall be the law of the country with which the contract is most closely connected.[42] This Article also provides several rebuttable presumptions that can be used to determine the applicable law in the absence of a choice by the parties. For present purposes, it is sufficient to note the general presumption that the contract is most closely connected with the country where the party who is to effect the

---

[38] Dicey & Morris, *The Conflict of Laws* (13th ed., 2000), Vol. 2, para.33–294, p.1421, *Cf. Turkiye IS Bankasi AS v Bank of China* [1993] 1 Lloyd's Rep. 132; *Wahda Bank v Arab Bank plc* [1996] 1 Lloyd's Rep. 470, CA.
[39] Art.3(1). This appears to correspond with the pre-existing private international law rules: *Forsakringsiktieselskapet v Butcher* [1986] 1 All E.R. 488. Compare *Kahler v Midland Bank* [1950] A.C. 24 at 42 and *Libyan Arab Foreign Bank v Bankers Trust Co* [1989] 3 All E.R. 252 at 267.
[40] Art.3(2). Under the pre-existing rules of private international law there was a dichotomy of opinion on what law should govern the parties' ability to vary the original proper law of the contract. See *James Miller and Partners Ltd v Whitworth Street Estates (Manchester) Ltd* [1970] A.C. 583 at 603 and Dicey & Morris, *Conflict of Laws* (11th ed., 1987), Vol. 2, p.1168. See now Dicey & Morris, *Conflict of Laws* (13th ed., 2000), Vol. 2, p.1222.
[41] See also Art.7(2). See generally Kaye, *The New Private International Law of Contract of the European Community* (1993), pp.159–167 and Dicey & Morris, *The Conflict of Laws* (13th ed., 2000), Vol. 2, para.33–312, p.1429. If the contract is a consumer contract within Art.5, then the mandatory rules of the consumer's habitual residence may be relevant: Art.3(3).
[42] See generally, Kaye, *The New Private International Law of Contract of the European Community*, pp.179–180.

performance which is characteristic of the contract[43] has at the time of the conclusion of the contract:

(i) his habitual residence, or, in the case of a body corporate or unincorporated, its central administration;[44]

(ii) his principal place of business;[45] or

(iii) where, under the contract, performance is to be effected through a place of business other than the principal place of business, the former place of business.[46]

There are special rebuttable presumptions to assist in identifying the applicable law relating to contracts involving a rights in or to use immovable property;[47] contracts for the carriage of goods;[48] consumer contracts;[49] and individual employment contracts.[50]

(g) *The functions of the applicable law in relation to principal contracts entered into after April 1, 1991*

It is expressly provided that the following substantive aspects of contractual obligations are governed by the applicable law: **14–53**

(a) the existence and material validity of the contract and its terms;[51]

(b) the interpretation of the contract;[52]

(c) the substance[53] but not the manner[54] of performance;

---

[43] The performance which is characteristic of the contract is a concept foreign to English law. As to the meaning of this term, see Kaye, *The New Private International Law of Conflict of the European Community*, pp.179–180.
[44] See generally Kaye, *The New Private International Law of Contract of the European Community*, pp.183–185.
[45] *ibid.*
[46] *ibid.*
[47] Art.4(3), which provides that the country of the situs of the immovable property is generally presumed to be the country most closely connected with the contract. See Kaye, *The New International Law of Contract of the European Community*, p.191. This presumption can be rebutted. See Art.4(5).
[48] Art.4(4). See generally Kaye, *The New Private International Law of Contract of the European Community*, pp.197–202.
[49] Art.5. See generally, Kaye, *The New Private International Law of Contract of the European Community*, pp.203–220.
[50] Art.6. See generally Kaye, *The New Private International Law of Contract of the European Community*, pp.221–238.
[51] Art.8(1). Under Art.10(1)(e) the consequences of nullity are expressly included in the law of contract. See *Grupo Torras SA v Sheikh Fahad Mohammed Al Sabah* [1996] 1 Lloyd's Rep. 7 (a swaps contract). See generally Kaye, *The New Private International Law of Contract of the European Community*, pp.269–279.
[52] Art.10(1). See generally Kaye, *The New Private International Law of Contract of the European Community*, pp.298–299.
[53] Art.10(1). See generally Kaye, *The New Private International Law of Contract of the European Community*, pp.299–301.
[54] Art.10(2). See generally Kaye, *The New Private International Law of Contract of the European Community*, pp.301–304.

(d) the consequences of a breach of the contract,[55] including the assessment of damages;

(e) the extinction of obligations through frustration and supervening illegality;[56]

and

(f) the limitation of actions.[57]

A different regime applies to the formal validity of contracts entered into after April 1, 1991. Article 9(1) provides that a contract concluded between persons in the *same country* is formally valid if it satisfies the formal requirements of the applicable law or of the law of the country where it is concluded. Where the contract is between persons in *different countries* it is formally valid if it satisfies the formal requirements of the applicable law or of the law of one of those countries.[58]

14–54　　There is a special rule dealing with incapacity. In a contract concluded between persons in the same country, a natural person who would have capacity under the law of that country may invoke his incapacity resulting from another law only if the other party was aware of this incapacity at the time of the conclusion of the contract or was not aware of the incapacity as a result of negligence.[59]

14–55　　While the substance of performance is governed by the applicable law,[60] the manner of performance and the steps to be taken in the event of a defective performance are determined by the law of the country in which performance takes place.[61]

(iii) The law governing the guarantee

(a) Identifying the proper law and the applicable law of the contract of guarantee

14–56　　The principles used to identify the proper law of the principal contract[62] are equally relevant to the proper law of the guarantee.

14–57　　It is possible, but unlikely, that a guarantee could expressly stipulate a proper law or an applicable law different from that expressly chosen in the

---

[55] Art.10(1)(c). See generally Kaye, *The New Private International Law of Contract of the European Community*, pp.304–305.
[56] Art.10(1)(d). See generally Kaye, *The New Private International law of Contract of the European Community*, p.308.
[57] Art.10(1)(d). See generally Kaye, *The New Private International Law of Contract of the European Community*, p.308.
[58] Art.9(2). See generally Kaye, *The New Private International Law of Contract of the European Community*, p.285.
[59] Art.11. See generally Kaye, *The New Private International Law of Contract of the European Community*, pp.311–319.
[60] See above, para.14–53.
[61] Art.10(2). See generally Kaye, *The New Private International Law of Contract of the European Community*, pp.301–304.
[62] See above, paras 14–49 to 14–52.

principal contract. It would, of course, be preferable for the guarantor's secondary obligation to be governed by the same law that governs the debtor's principal obligation.[63] By the same token, if the parties to a guarantee do expressly choose the law of a different country as the proper law of the guarantee, then that law will generally prevail.[64]

In the absence of an express choice of law, the courts are likely to infer **14–58** that the proper law or the applicable law of the guarantee is the proper law or the applicable law of the principal contract on the ground that the same law should govern the principal and the secondary obligations.[65] The same approach should be applied in determining the proper law or applicable law of a counter-guarantee: the parties may be presumed to have intended the proper law or the applicable law of the guarantee to govern the counter-guarantee.[66]

This principle does not necessarily apply to a bank guarantee, a letter of **14–59** credit or a performance bond because these undertakings are not so closely linked to the principal transaction. They are autonomous undertakings that warrant a different rule. Under both the common law rules of private international law and the Rome Convention, it is necessary to identify the different contracts involved in these undertakings. The relevant contract is between the issuing bank and the beneficiary of the bank guarantee, letter of credit or performance bond. This contract has its closest and most real connection with the law of the country where payment is to be made on presentation of confirming documents.[67] This then should be the proper law of the undertaking according to the common law rules of private international law. The Rome Convention, on the other hand, suggests that the applicable law is the law of the country where the principal place of

---

[63] *Broken Hill Pty Co Ltd v Xenakis* [1982] 2 Lloyd's Rep. 304. See also Dicey & Morris, *The Conflict of Laws* (13th ed., 2000), Vol. 2, para.33–294, p.1421.

[64] See *Vita Food Products Inc v Unus Shipping Co Ltd* [1939] A.C. 277.

[65] Dicey & Morris, *The Conflict of Laws* (13th ed., 2000) Vol. 2, para.33–313 n.67 and *Broken Hill Co Pty Ltd v Xenakis* [1982] 2 Lloyd's Rep. 304. In *Governor and Company of the Bank of Scotland of the Mound v Butcher* (unreported, Court of Appeal, Civil Division, July 28, 1998) the following factors indicated that the contract of guarantee was most closely connected with Scotland:
   (i) the guarantee related to an overdraft of a bank account in Scotland of a Scottish company that traded in the Middle East;
   (ii) the contract of guarantee was between a Scottish Bank and two guarantors who were directors of the Scottish company, even though one of the guarantors was resident in England; and
   (iii) the contract of guarantee contained terms that were apt for a guarantee governed by Scottish law. See also *Anton Durbeck GmbH v Den Norske Bank ASA* [2003] Q.B. 1160, CA.

[66] *Wahda Bank v Arab Bank plc* [1996] 1 Lloyd's Rep. 470; *Turkiye IS Bankasi AS v Bank of China* [1993] 1 Lloyd's Rep. 132, (where there was an implicit agreement that the counter-guarantee was to be governed by Turkish law which was the proper law of the principal obligation, namely a performance bond). On the hand, under the Rome Convention the characteristic performance under a counter-guarantee may be the performance of the bank that issues the counter guarantee. *Cf. Bank of Baroda v Vysya Bank Ltd* [1994] 2 Lloyd's Rep. 87. It may well be therefore that the applicable law under Art.4(2) of the Convention will be the law of the country where the branch of the bank that issued the counter-guarantee is situated. See Dicey & Morris, The *Conflict of Laws* (13th ed., 2000), Vol. 2, para.33–309, p.1428.

[67] *Attock Cement Co v Romanian Bank for Foreign Trade* [1989] 1 Lloyd's Rep. 572 at 580. See also *Bank of Baroda v Vysya Bank Ltd* [1994] 1 Lloyd's Rep. 87 and Dicey & Morris, *The Conflict of Laws* (13th ed., 2000), Vol. 2, paras 33–301–33–303, p.1425.

business or, as the case may be, where the place of business of the issuing bank is situated.[68] However, this result could prove to be inconvenient in the context of international trade and it may be possible to avoid this problem by invoking Art.4(5) of the Convention so that the applicable law can be declared to be the law of the country where payment is to be made in response to confirming documents.[69]

(b) Negotiable instruments

14–60   The uniform rules of the Rome Convention do not apply to "obligations arising under bills of exchange, cheques and promissory notes and other negotiable instruments to the extent that the obligations arising under such negotiable instruments arise out of their negotiable character".[70] The conflict of law rules in relation to bills of exchange or promissory notes must be determined in accordance with the provisions of the Bills of Exchange Act 1882.[71] But this Act does not contain a comprehensive code of private international law rules relating to negotiable instruments and it is necessary to have to resort to a supplementary rule, probably the *lex loci contractus* or law of the place where the contract was made, to govern the formation of the contract and the capacity of the parties.[72]

(c) The functions of proper law and the applicable law of the contract of guarantee

14–61   The functions of the proper law and the "applicable law" in relation to the guarantee are similar to the function of the proper law of the principal contract in relation the principal contract. These functions were outlined earlier.[73] It remains to note that the proper law and the applicable law of the contract of guarantee generally govern the rights and liabilities of the guarantors vis-à-vis the creditor.[74] For example, the proper law of the

---

[68] Dicey & Morris, *The Conflict of Laws* (13th ed., 2000), Vol. 2, para.33–302, p.1425. See also *Bank of Baroda v Vysya Bank Ltd* [1994] 2 Lloyd's Rep. 87 at 92 and *Sierra Leone Telecommunications Co Ltd v Barclays Bank plc* [1998] 2 All E.R. 820.
[69] Dicey & Morris, *The Conflict of Laws* (13th ed., 2000) Vol. 2, para.33–302, p.1425.
[70] Art.1(2)(c) of the Rome Convention. See Kaye, *The New Private International Law of Contract of the European Community*, pp.116–118.
[71] See generally Dicey & Morris, *The Conflict of Laws*, (13th ed., 2000), Vol. 2, paras 33R–314–33–324, pp.1431–1433 and Hill, *International Commercial Disputes*, paras 16.7.1–16.7.24.
[72] Dicey & Morris, *The Conflict of Laws* (13th ed., 2000), Vol. 2, paras 33R–326 *et seq.*, pp.1434–1454.
[73] See above, para.14–40. Where the proper law of a contract of guarantee is determined to be Scottish law in accordance with Art.4 of the Rome Convention, the guarantee will not be enforceable unless the guarantor's signature is witnessed by two witnesses: *Governor and Company of the Bank of Scotland of the Mound v Butcher* (unreported, Court of Appeal, Civil Division, July 28, 1998).
[74] *St Pierre v South American Stores (Gath & Chaves) Ltd* [1937] 3 All E.R. 349 at 352; *Horne v Rouquette* (1878) 3 Q.B.D. 514. See also Art.10(1)(c) of the Rome Convention and Kaye, *The New Private International Law of Contract of the European Community*, pp.304–305. There is, however, a separate rule on subrogation under Art.13 of the Rome Convention. See below, para.14–63.

guarantee determines whether the creditor is entitled to hold one of several joint sureties liable notwithstanding the discharge of one or more of the co-sureties.[75] The decision in *Allen v Kemble*[76] can be viewed in this light. There the court allowed a surety under a foreign guarantee governed by a foreign law to claim a set-off which was available to the principal debtor against the creditor in England because under the foreign law this set off extinguished the principal debt. The surety was entitled to rely on this set-off as a defence even though under English law it would not have extinguished the principal debt.

(d) Rights of the sureties inter se

As a general rule, the rights and liabilities of the sureties *inter se* are **14–62** determined by the *lex fori* as they generally depend not on contract but on equitable principles. A surety's right to contribution should, therefore, be governed by the *lex fori*.[77] In general, a surety's right of indemnity from the principal debtor depends upon an express or implied contract with the debtor and it should be determined by the proper law or applicable law of *that* contract.

(e) Subrogation

Under the traditional rules of private international law, the surety's right **14–63** of subrogation is based on equitable principles so it should be governed by the *lex fori*.[78] This principle should apply to sureties who entered into their guarantees on or before April 1, 1991.

The Rome Convention applies to guarantees executed after that date by **14–64** force of the Contracts (Applicable Law) Act 1990. Article 13 of that Convention provides, in effect, that the law governing the guarantors' obligation to pay the principal debt shall determine whether the guarantors are to be subrogated to the creditor's rights against the principal debtor under the law governing the creditor's relationship with the debtor. Consequently, under the Rome Convention, the applicable law governing the guarantee determines whether and to what extent the guarantor is entitled to subrogation.

But where a government department, such as the Export Credits **14–65** Guarantee Department, agreed to pay an exporter 95 per cent of any loss it might suffer by reason of political events or economic difficulties in relation to its customer, a foreign country, and the government recovered a settlement sum as a Sovereign State from the foreign country as a result of a multilateral agreement to reschedule its debts, the exporter was not

---

[75] *Scandanavian American National Bank v Kneeland* (1914) 16 D.L.R. 565.
[76] (1848) 6 Moore 314; 13 E.R. 704, PC.
[77] *American Surety Co of New York v Wrightson* (1910) 103 L.T. 663 at 665.
[78] By analogy with the equitable right of contribution. See *American Surety Co of New York v Wrightson* (1910) 103 L.T. 663 at 665.

entitled to claim the amount of the settlement. The moneys recovered were not held in trust for the exporter.[79]

(f) Rules of evidence and procedure

14-66   In an action to enforce a guarantee in an English court the local rules of evidence and procedure apply as part of the *lex fori*, whatever the proper law or the applicable law of the guarantee.[80] English law, therefore, governs whether the claimant is entitled to a freezing order or an injunction to prevent a litigant from proceeding abroad.[81] Moreover, English rules will determine whether the judgment is given in a foreign currency.[82] Under the Foreign Limitation Periods Act 1984, however, questions of limitation are governed by the applicable law, not the *lex fori*.[83]

(g) Formal requirements and remedies

14-67   Under the traditional rules of private international law applicable to guarantees entered into on or before April 1, 1991, formal requirements[84] and remedies available to the parties[85] are treated as matters of procedure and are governed by the *lex fori*. Hence, a foreign contract of guarantee which does not satisfy the Statute of Frauds could not be enforced by an English court.[86] But where the proper law of the contract requires the guarantee to be accompanied by a notarial certificate, this is not merely a procedural matter governed by the *lex fori*. Rather it is a substantive issue determined by the proper law of the guarantee. Thus, such a guarantee may be unenforceable in England even though English domestic law does not require a notarial certificate.[87]

14-68   On the other hand, the so-called "right of discussion", under which a guarantor can in some jurisdictions require the creditor to proceed against a defaulting principal debtor first has been classified as merely a foreign formal requirement. It can, therefore, be ignored by an English court in an action to enforce the guarantee.[88] Similarly, an English court cannot be

---

[79] *Lonrho Exports Ltd v Export Credits Guarantee Department* [1999] Ch. 158.
[80] Hill, *International Commercial Disputes*, p.9. See also Art.14 of the Rome Convention, discussed in Hill, *International Commercial Disputes*, at p.773.
[81] Hill, *International Commercial Disputes*, p.9 and Chapters 10 and 11.
[82] Hill, *International Commercial Disputes*, p.9 and para.18.3.
[83] The *lex fori* governed this issue under the common law rules of private international law. See *Arab Monetary Fund v Hashim* [1996] 1 Lloyd's Rep. 589 at 600; *Subbotovsky v Waung* [1968] 3 N.S.W.R. 261, affirmed *sub nom. Waung v Subbotovsky* [1968] 3 N.S.W.R. 499.
[84] *Leroux v Brown* (1852) 12 C.B. 801; 138 E.R. 1110. See also *English v Donnelly* (1958) S.C. 494. *Cf. Halloran v Jacob Schmidt Brewing Co* 162 N.W. 1082 (1917) at 1084.
[85] See *De La Vega v Vianna* (1830) 1 B. & Ad. 284; 109 E.R. 792; *Baschet v London Illustrated Standard* [1900] 1 Ch. 73; *Chaplin v Boys* [1971] A.C. 356 at 378, 381–382 and 394. *Cf. Scandanavian American National Bank v Kneeland* (1914) 16 D.L.R. 565.
[86] See above, n.84.
[87] *O'Donovan v Dussault* (1973) 35 D.L.R. (3d) 280, Alta, CA.
[88] *Subbotovsky v Waung* [1968] 3 N.S.W.R. 261, affirmed *sub nom. Waung v Subbotovsky* [1968] 3 N.S.W.R. 499.

expected to provide a remedy in an action to enforce a guarantee if it is unknown according to the *lex fori*. By the same token, the claimant's remedies will be determined by the *lex fori* as a procedural matter, even if the claimant is thereby awarded relief unknown to the *lex causae*.[89]

A different regime applies to contracts of guarantee entered after **14–69** April 1, 1991. The Rome Convention, which is applied as a law of the United Kingdom by force of the Contracts (Applicable Law) Act 1990, contains specific provisions dealing with the formal validity of contracts. Under Art.9 of the Rome Convention, a contract concluded between persons who are in the same country is formally valid if it satisfies the formal requirements of the applicable law of the law of the country where it is concluded. A contract concluded between persons who are in *different countries* is formally valid if it satisfies the formal requirements of the applicable law or of the law of *one* of those countries.[90] However, where the subject matter of the contract is a right to immovable property, the contract will be subject to the mandatory formal requirements of the law of the country where the property is situated if by that law those requirements are imposed irrespective of the country where the contract is concluded and irrespective of the applicable law.[91]

(h) Guaranteed debts expressed in foreign currency

The general rule is that a debtor who owes a creditor a debt expressed in **14–70** foreign currency can elect to pay the debt in England either in that foreign currency or in pounds sterling.[92] If the debtor chooses to pay in pounds sterling, the rate of exchange at the date of payment will determine the precise amount to be paid.[93] This rate of exchange may be different from that which applied at the time when the debt was contracted or when it fell due. If so, the creditor bears the loss or reaps the benefit, as the case may be.[94] Similar rules should apply to the payment of the principal debt by a guarantor.

---

[89] *Phrantzes v Argenti* [1960] 2 Q.B. at 35–36. But if the *lex fori* does not provide a form of action appropriate for the enforcement of the foreign right, the action may not be maintained.
[90] Art.9(5). A different rule applies to consumer contracts under Art.5 of the Rome Convention.
[91] Art.9(6) of the Rome Convention.
[92] See *Pyrmont Ltd v Scholt* [1939] A.C. 145 at 158; *Adelaide Electric Supply Co v Prudential Assurance Co Ltd* [1934] A.C. 122 at 151. As to payment in a foreign currency, see *Marrache v Ashton* [1943] A.C. 311 at 317; *Barclays Bank International Ltd v Levin Bros (Bradford) Ltd* [1977] Q.B. 270 at 277–278. As to payment in pounds sterling according to the law of the place of performance, see *Adelaide Electric Supply Co v Prudential Assurance Co Ltd* [1934] A.C. 122 at 148 and 151; *Auckland Corp v Alliance Assurance Co Ltd* [1937] A.C. 587; *Mount Albert Borough Council v A/Asian Temperance & General Mutual Life Assurance Society Ltd* [1938] A.C. 244 at 240–241. The debt can be discharged by a payment into court: *Miliangos v George Frank (Textiles) Ltd* [1976] A.C. 443 at 469.
[93] *Barclay's Bank International Ltd v Levin Bros (Bradford) Ltd* [1977] Q.B. 270; *George Veflings Rederi A/S v President of India* [1979] 1 W.L.R. 59.
[94] See *British Bank for Foreign Trade Ltd v Russian Commercial and Industrial Bank* (1921) 38 T.L.R. 65; *Re Chesterman's Trust* [1923] 2 Ch. 466; *Anderson v Equitable Assurance Society of the United States* (1926) 134 L.T. 557; *Broken Hill Pty Ltd v Latham* [1933] 1 Ch. 373 at 408.

14–71   Drafters have attempted to protect creditors against any losses they might incur through an application of these principles. The usual formula is to provide:

> "All payments to be made by the guarantors under this guarantee shall be made in [the foreign currency] or in such currency or currencies as the creditor shall direct."

But there is some doubt whether such a provision can exclude the general rule that payment in England of a foreign currency debt may be made in pounds sterling, since the law of the place of payment, not the proper law of the guarantee or the applicable law, should determine *how* payment can be made.[95]

(i) Judgments relating to foreign currency obligations

14–72   The law relating to currency obligations draws a distinction between the money of account and the money of payment.[96] As Lord Denning M.R. observed in *Woodhouse AC Israel Cocoa Ltd v Nigerian Produce Marketing Co Ltd*,[97] "The *money of account* is the currency in which an obligation is to be measured. It tells the debtor *how much* he has to pay. The *money of payment* is the currency in which the obligation is to be discharged. It tells the debtor *by what means* he is to pay."[98]

14–73   Under the traditional rules of private international law, the money of account is determined by the proper law of the contract, in the absence of an express indication by the parties of some other law.[99] Hence is *Boython v Commonwealth of Australia*[1] the money of account was taken to be the currency of the country with which the contract had its closest and most real connection. In deciding upon this currency, the English courts have applied a presumption that the parties intend the money of account to be the currency of the place of payment, although this presumption is not a rigid rule.[2]

14–74   Similarly, under the Rome Convention, which applies to contracts entered into after April 1, 1991, the applicable law governs the "interpretation" of the contract[3] and "the consequences of breach including the assessment of damages in so far as it is governed by rules of law".[4] The applicable law should also govern the liability to pay interest

[95] See Dicey & Morris, *Conflict of Laws* (13th ed., 2000), Vol. 2, pp.1600–1604. *Cf. Anderson v Equitable Assurance Society of the United States* (1926) 134 L.T. 557 at 562; *Heisler v Anglo-Dal Ltd* [1954] 1 W.L.R. 1273 at 1278.
[96] See generally Hill, *International Commercial Disputes*, para.18.2.1.
[97] [1971] 2 Q.B. 23.
[98] *ibid.*, at 54 (emphasis in original quotation).
[99] Hill, *International Commercial Disputes*, p.567.
[1] [1951] A.C. 201.
[2] See Hill, *International Commercial Disputes*, p.568.
[3] Art.10(1)(a).
[4] Art.10(1)(c).

on damages for breach of contract.[5] Consequently, where the contract of guarantee is governed by English law it will generally, but not invariably, be appropriate to award damages in pounds sterling. But where the contract is not governed by English law, damages will be assessed in accordance with the foreign applicable law.

Where English law is the applicable law damages are not necessarily   **14–75** assessed in pounds sterling. The parties can stipulate or imply that another currency is to be the currency of the contract. If so, an English court will generally award damages in that currency.[6] In the absence of such an agreement between the parties in a contract for which English law is the applicable law, the general principle is that the "plaintiff should be compensated for the expense or loss in the currency which most truly expresses his loss".[7] This may, for example, be the currency in which the claimant carries on its business as this is the currency it will have to spend to meet its loss.[8]

The defendant will not be required to indemnify the claimant against   **14–76** any fall in the value of the currency in which the claimant operates his business after the date on which the cause of action accrues.[9] But the court will award interest in the appropriate currency to compensate for the delay between the breach of contract and the award of damages.[10]

While the substance of the obligation to pay (the money of account) is   **14–77** determined by the applicable law of the contract,[11] in the manner of performance "regard shall be had to the law of the country in which performance takes place".[12] For example, where the applicable law is foreign law but the contract provides for payment in England, the court must have regard to English law as governing the money of payment but

---

[5] *Miliangos v George Frank (Textiles) Ltd* [1976] A.C. 443 at 463 and 467. The liability to pay contractual interest and the rate applicable to such interest payable in respect of a debt are, in general, determined by the law applicable to the loan contract: Art.10(1)(b). Similarly, the liability to pay interest *as damages for non-payment of a debt* is governed by the law applicable to the contract under which the debt was incurred: Art.10(1)(c). But the rate of such interest is apparently determined by English law as the *lex fori: Miliangos v George Frank (Textiles) Ltd (No.2)* [1977] Q.B. 489 at 497. But see *Helmsing Schiffahrts GmbH v Malta Drydocks Corporation* [1977] 2 Lloyd's Rep. 444 at 449–450. The rate of interest awarded under this rule is a matter for the discretion of the court under s.35A of the Supreme Court Act 1981, and in exercising this discretion the court will generally award the rate applicable to the currency in which the debt is expressed: *Miliangos v George Frank (Textiles) Ltd (No.2)* [1977] Q.B. 489 at 497. See Dicey & Morris, *The Conflict of Laws* (13th ed., 2000) Vol. 2, para.33R–371, p.1454 and Art.1(2)(h) which states that the Rome Convention does not apply to questions of procedure. The Late Payment of Commercial Debts (Interest) Act 1998 would appear to apply only where English law is the applicable law. See Dicey & Morris, *The Conflict of Laws* (13th ed., 2000) Vol. 2, paras 33–377–33–378.
[6] *Services Europe Atlantique Sud (SEAS) v Stockholms Rederiaktiebolag Svea* [1979] A.C. 685 at 700 *per* Lord Wilberforce.
[7] *Services Europe Atlantique Sud (SEAS) v Stockholms Rederiaktiebolag Svea* [1979] A.C. 685 at 701 *per* Lord Wilberforce.
[8] See *The Texaco Melbourne* [1994] 1 Lloyd's Rep. 473 at 478 and *The Despina R* [1979] A.C. 685 at 697 and Hill, *International Commercial Disputes*, pp.570–572.
[9] Hill, *International Commercial Disputes*, p.572.
[10] *The Texaco Melbourne* [1994] 1 Lloyd's Rep. 473 at 476–477 *per* Lord Goff.
[11] Art.10(1) of the Rome Convention.
[12] Art.10(2) of the Rome Convention. See generally Hill, *International Commercial Disputes*, pp.572–574.

English law will not be allowed to distort the substance of the obligation in accordance with the foreign law.[13] Under English law where a defendant is obliged to pay the claimant in England a sum of money expressed in a foreign currency, the defendant can elect to pay the appropriate amount in the foreign currency or pay the equivalent in pounds sterling at the rate of exchange prevailing at the due date.[14]

14–78   It would appear that when an English court orders payment of a debt or damages it may give judgment for an amount expressed in a foreign currency or its equivalent in pounds sterling at the date when the court authorises enforcement of the judgment.[15] This rule governs contractual actions whether the proper law is English[16] or foreign law.[17] It covers judgments given in actions to enforce a guarantee whether they take the form of a claim for unliquidated damages for failure to perform the principal obligation or for a liquidated sum being the amount of the outstanding principal debt.[18]

14–79   Currency conversion clauses are sometimes inserted in guarantees to safeguard creditors against any losses they might incur as a result of a court converting the currency expressed in the guarantee to another currency for the purpose of giving judgment. Such clauses may provide:

"If, for the purpose of obtaining judgment in any court in any country it becomes necessary to convert into any other currency (hereinafter called "the judgment currency") an amount due (in the currency expressed in the guarantee) under this guarantee, then the conversion shall be made, in the discretion of the creditor, at the rate of exchange prevailing either on the date of default or on the day before the day on which the judgment is given (the "conversion date").

If there is a change in the rate of exchange prevailing between the conversion date and the date of payment of the amount due, the guarantors will pay such additional amounts (if any, but in any event not

---

[13] Hill, *International Commercial Disputes*, p.573.
[14] *Barclays Bank International Ltd v Levin Brothers (Bradford) Ltd* [1977] Q.B. 270 at 277 *per* Mocatta J. See also *Re Lines Brothers Ltd* [1983] Ch 1. As to problems arising out of foreign exchange control legislation, see Hill, *International Commercial Disputes*, paras 18.4.1–18.4.9.
[15] See *Miliangos v George Frank (Textiles) Ltd* [1976] A.C. 443 and S. Stern, "The Courts and Foreign Currency Obligations" (1995) 4 L.M.C.L.Q. 494 at 504–518.
[16] See, *e.g. Federal Commerce & Navigation Co Ltd v Tradax Export SA* [1977] Q.B. 324, reversed on another ground in [1978] A.C. 1; *Barclay's Bank International Ltd v Levin Bros (Bradford) Ltd* [1977] Q.B. 270 (a bill of exchange expressed in a foreign currency). See also *The Despina R* [1979] A.C. 685. But this proposition is only true where the currency of the contract is the foreign currency: see *ANZ Banking Group Ltd v Cawood* [1987] 1 Qd. R. 131.
[17] See, *e.g. Miliangos v George Frank (Textiles) Ltd* [1976] A.C. 443; *Kraut AG v Albany Fabrics Ltd* [1977] Q.B. 122.
[18] *Miliangos v George Frank (Textiles) Ltd* [1976] A.C. 443; *Barclay's Bank International Ltd v Levin Bros (Bradford) Ltd* [1977] Q.B. 270; *The Despina R* [1979] A.C. 685; *Services Europe Atlantique Sud (SEAS) v Stockholms Rederiaktiebolag Svea (The Folias)* [1979] A.C. 685; *Federal Commerce & Navigation Co Ltd v Tradax Export SA* [1977] Q.B. 324 at 341–342; 349 and 354, reversed on another point in [1978] A.C. 1. There is an apparent exception to the rule that courts may give judgments in foreign currency relating to the conversion of foreign currency debts in company liquidations. See *Re Dynamics Corp* [1976] 1 W.L.R. 757; *Re Lines Bros Ltd* [1983] Ch. 1; S. Stern, "The Courts and Foreign Currency Obligations" (1995) 4 L.M.C.L.Q. 494 at 515.

a lesser amount) as may be necessary to ensure that the amount paid in the judgment currency when converted at the rate of exchange prevailing at the date of payment will produce the amount then due in [the currency expressed the guarantee]"

There may be further provisions declaring that any additional amount so payable shall be due as a separate debt unaffected by any judgment being obtained for any other sums due or in respect of the guarantee and that the rights of the creditor to recover any such amount shall not merge in the judgment. Finally, the drafter will usually define the term "rate of exchange" for the purposes of the currency conversion clauses.

It is doubtful, however, whether these clauses can achieve their **14-80** objectives. Even if the proper law of the guarantee or the applicable law is foreign and the amount payable under the guarantee is expressed in that foreign currency, *the law of the place of payment* should determine in what currency a judgment in an action on the guarantee can be expressed, and, indeed, the date on which any conversion from the currency expressed in the guarantee can be made.[19] Where the law of place of payment is inconsistent with these specific provisions of the guarantee, the former should prevail.

But where the discharge of a foreign currency obligations involves **14-81** payment in England or abroad in a currency other than the money of account, the exchange rate to be applied should be determined by the law applicable to the obligation, not the law of the place of payment.[20] This is the position under both the common law and the Rome Convention.[21]

4. RECOGNITION AND ENFORCEMENT OF FOREIGN JUDGMENTS

(i) Rationale

Slade L.J. explained the rationale for the system of recognising and **14-82** enforcing foreign judgments in *Adams v Cape Industries plc*[22] as "an acknowledgement that the society of nations will work better if some foreign judgments are taken to create rights which supersede the underlying cause of action, and which may be directly enforced in countries where the defendant or his assets are to be found".[23]

---

[19] See Dicey & Morris, *Conflict of Laws* (13th ed., 2000), Vol. 2, pp.1600–1604. *Cf. Anderson v Equitable Assurance Society of the United States* (1926) 134 L.T. 557 at 562; *Heisler v Anglo-Dal Ltd* [1954] 1 W.L.R. 1273 at 1278. See also *Miliangos v George Frank (Textiles) Ltd* [1976] A.C. 443 at 465; *Despina R* [1979] A.C. 685 at 704.
[20] Hill, *International Commercial Disputes*, p.573 and *Report on Foreign Money Liabilities* Law Com No 124 (1983), p.4, n.15. See also Dicey & Morris, *The Conflict of Laws* (13th ed., 2000), p.1600 (Rule 210) and *George Veflings Rederi A/S v President of India* [1979] 1 W.L.R. 59.
[21] Hill, *International Commercial Disputes*, p.573.
[22] [1990] Ch. 433.
[23] *ibid.*, at 552. See generally M.J. Whincop, "The Recognition Scene: Game Theoretic Issues in the Recognition of Foreign Judgments" (1999) 23 Melbourne University Law Review 416 and P. Kaye, *Civil Jurisdiction and Enforcement of Foreign Judgments* (1987).

14-83   Obtaining a judgment against a defendant, particularly a foreign defendant, may be a phyrric victory if the defendant has no assets in the jurisdiction. In this situation, the claimant will be interested in having the judgment recognised and enforced in a jurisdiction where the defendant's assets are situated. Conversely, where a defendant has been successful in proceedings abroad he may wish to have the judgment in his favour recognised by an English court if the claimant institutes an action in England based on the same subject matter. In this section, we shall examine the rules for recognition and enforcement of foreign judgments.

14-84   There are, in fact, several regimes under which foreign judgments may be recognised and enforced. In some of these regimes the court's jurisdiction to recognise and enforce a foreign judgment is based on the doctrine of obligation; in others, on the principle of reciprocity. The doctrine of obligation holds that, if there is a sufficient nexus between the defendant and the court which awarded the foreign judgment, then the local court should recognise the judgment and, perhaps assist in its enforcement. This is the dominant theory underlying the recognition and enforcement of foreign judgments under the traditional English rules of private international law.[24] By contrast, the system of recognition and enforcement of foreign judgments under the Judgments Regulation and the International Conventions (the Brussels and Lugano Conventions) is based on the doctrine of reciprocity.[25] On this approach, the courts of the United Kingdom are generally required to recognise and enforce the judgment of a court of another contracting state because the court of the other contracting state is required to recognise and enforce judgments of courts of the United Kingdom. The general thrust of these regimes is that the courts of each contracting state are to be treated as equal. This underlying rationale overrides any juridical advantage that one court might have over another in relation to the ability to obtain summary judgment.[26]

14-85   Before we examine the different systems that govern the recognition and enforcement of foreign judgments it is necessary to draw a distinction between the central concepts of recognition and enforcement. Recognition is a relatively passive process which does not involve the court in the enforcement of the judgment. For example, an English court could recognise a foreign judgment in favour of the defendant by allowing the defendant to rely on the foreign judgment as a defence in proceedings instituted against him in England. Enforcement, on the other hand, involves the court in rendering assistance to the claimant in taking steps to recover the amount of the judgment.

---

[24] Hill, *International Commercial Disputes*, p.338.
[25] Hill, *International Commercial Disputes*, p.376.
[26] *Virgin Aviation Services Ltd v CAD Aviation Services* [1991] I.L.Pr. 79.

(ii) The different regimes

There are, in fact, several regimes under which judgments can be **14–86** recognised and enforced:[27]

(i) the traditional common law rules of private international law;

(ii) the regime governing the enforcement of judgments of Superior Courts of Commonwealth Countries;

(iii) the regime governing the recognition and enforcement of judgments given by foreign courts outside the Commonwealth under certain bilateral treaties or international treaties;

(iv) the regimes governing the recognition and enforcement of foreign judgments pursuant to the Judgments Regulation or the Brussels and Lugano Conventions (the "International Conventions").

(v) the regime governing the recognition and enforcement of judgments granted by courts of another part of the United Kingdom.

(iii) The traditional common law rules of private international law

These rules are largely procedural in character and they have a residual **14–87** operation when no other regime governs the recognition and enforcement of foreign judgments in the United Kingdom.[28] Essentially, an English court will enforce a final and conclusive judgment[29] for a fixed sum of money[30] granted by a foreign court of competent jurisdiction.[31]

(a) Final and conclusive judgment

The foreign judgment must be final and conclusive in the sense that it is **14–88** neither interim nor provisional.[32] It must constitute a definitive determination of the litigation between the parties.[33] The fact that the judgment is or may be subject to an appeal abroad does not prevent it from being final and conclusive in the relevant sense,[34] although an English court will

---

[27] For a comprehensive analysis of these different regimes, see Hill, *International Commercial Disputes*, Ch.12.

[28] See generally, Hill, *International Commercial Disputes*, Ch.12.

[29] See Hill, *International Commercial Disputes*, paras 12.2.25–12.2.27.

[30] See Hill, *International Commercial Disputes*, paras 12.2.28–12.2.30.

[31] See Hill, *International Commercial Disputes*, paras 12.2.2–12.2.24.

[32] See *Desert Sun Loan Corporation v Hill* [1996] 2 All E.R. 847 at 863; *Nouvion v Freeman* (1889) 15 App. Cas. 1; *Carl Zeiss Stiftung v Rayner & Keeler Ltd (No.2)* [1967] 1 A.C. 853; *Kirin-Amgen Inc v Boehringer Mannheim GmbH* [1997] F.S.R. 289.

[33] Hill, *International Commercial Disputes*, p.347.

[34] *Nouvion v Freeman* (1889) 15 App. Cas. 1.

normally stay enforcement of the judgment pending the determination of the appeal.[35]

(b) Judgment for a fixed sum of money

14–89   The foreign judgment must be for a fixed sum of money,[36] but not a tax or a penalty.[37] Moreover, it will not be enforced if it involves specific performance of a contract, rather than damages for its breach.[38]

(c) Judgment of a court of competent jurisdiction

14–90   Only a judgment of a court of competent jurisdiction will be enforced. The foreign court will be a court of competent jurisdiction if the defendant voluntarily submitted to the jurisdiction[39] or agreed to confer jurisdiction on the foreign court.[40] Where the defendant entered an appearance in the foreign proceedings to protest the jurisdiction of the court, this will not be taken as a submission to the foreign court's jurisdiction.[41] But if the defendant voluntarily enters an appearance and defends the action on its merits, he cannot deny that he has submitted to the jurisdiction.[42]

14–91   Where the defendant was served out of the jurisdiction of the foreign court, it will not be assumed that the foreign court was a court of competent jurisdiction. The claimant will be required to prove that there was an appropriate territorial connection between the defendant and the foreign jurisdiction. For individuals, a voluntary physical presence within the jurisdiction at the time of service of the originating proceedings will suffice.[43] So too would residence within the jurisdiction even if the defendant was not physically present at the time the proceedings were commenced.[44] But the fact that the defendant is a national of the foreign

---

[35] *Colt Industries Inc v Sarlie (No.2)* [1966] 1 W.L.R. 1287. The court has a discretion to vary proceedings to enforce a foreign judgment which is subject to an appeal. See *Dr Wolfgang Petereit (As Receiver of Ibh-Holdings AG) v Babcock International Holdings Ltd* [1992] I.L.Pr. 331.

[36] *Sadler v Robins* (1808) 1 Camp. 253; *Beatty v Beatty* [1924] 1 K.B. 807.

[37] *Huntington v Attrill* [1893] A.C. 150; *Government of India v Taylor* [1955] A.C. 491.

[38] Hill, *International Commercial Disputes*, p.347.

[39] Civil Jurisdiction and Judgments Act 1982, s.33. See Hill, *International Commercial Disputes*, p.339. An agreement to submit to the jurisdiction can be implied: *Blohn v Desser* [1962] 2 Q.B. 116; P.R.H. Webb, "Enforcement of Foreign Judgments: Implied Submission" (1962) 25 M.L.R. 96.

[40] Hill, *International Commercial Disputes*, p.341.

[41] Civil Jurisdiction and Judgments Act 1982, s.33(1)(a) and (b).

[42] See *Boissière & Co v Brockner & Co* (1889) 6 T.L.R. 85 and Hill, *International Commercial Disputes*, p.340.

[43] *Adams v Cape Industries plc* [1990] Ch. 433. See also *Carrick v Hancock* (1895) 12 T.L.R. 59 at 60.

[44] This question was expressly left open in *Adams v Cape Industries plc* [1990] Ch. 433 but Hill argues cogently that residence itself should be sufficient. See Hill, *International Commercial Disputes*, p.343.

country[45] or domiciled[46] there is not sufficient to justify enforcement of the foreign judgment. Nor is the fact that the foreign court appeared to be the most appropriate forum to resolve the dispute between the parties[47] or even that the defendant had assets within the foreign jurisdiction.[48]

English courts are likely to treat an overseas corporation as present **14–92** within the jurisdiction of the courts of a foreign country if the corporation has established and maintained at its own expense a fixed place of business there or has carried on business there for a reasonable period through a branch office or a representative.[49] However, it appears that an overseas corporation will not be taken to be present within the foreign country if its representative there has no authority to bind the corporation and carries on business principally on his own account.[50]

(d) Recognition of foreign judgments

The traditional rules governing mere recognition of a foreign judgment **14–93** are simpler. An English court will recognise a foreign judgment on the merits[51] between the same parties as a defence to proceedings in England if the judgment creates either a cause of action estoppel or an issue estoppel.[52]

(e) Defences

There are numerous defences to the recognition and enforcement of **14–94** foreign judgments by English courts. If the foreign judgment offends English standards of procedural[53] or substantive justice[54] or public policy[55]

---

[45] Hill, *International Commercial Disputes*, p.346. There are, however, dicta to the contrary. See, *e.g. Emanuel v Symon* [1908] 1 K.B. 302.
[46] Hill, *International Commercial Disputes*, p.346.
[47] See *Schibsby v Westenholz* (1870) L.R. 6 Q.B. 155.
[48] *Emanuel v Symon* [1908] 1 K.B. 302. It is not even sufficient that the cause of action arose within the jurisdiction of the foreign court: *Sirdar Gurdyal Singh v Rajah of Faridkofe* [1894] A.C. 670.
[49] *Adams v Cape Industries plc* [1990] Ch. 433 at 530–531 and Hill, *International Commercial Disputes*, p.344.
[50] *Adams v Cape Industries Plc* [1990] Ch. 433.
[51] See generally, Hill, *International Commercial Disputes*, p.351. As a result of the Foreign Limitation Periods Act 1984 a foreign judgment based on limitation is to be regarded as a decision on the merits.
[52] Hill, *International Commercial Disputes*, pp.348–351.
[53] A foreign judgment obtained in breach of the principles of natural justice will not be recognised and enforced. See *Jet Holdings Inc v Patel* [1990] 1 Q.B. 335 and *Muhl v Ardra Insurance Co Ltd* [1997] 6 Re. L. R. 206, Richard Ground, Sup Ct (Ber).
[54] *Owens Bank Ltd v Etoile Commerciale SA* [1995] 1 W.L.R. 44 (fraud); *Owens Bank Ltd v Bracco* [1992] 2 A.C. 443. See generally Hill, *International Commercial Disputes*, pp.360–363.
[55] The public policy defence relates to the substance of the foreign judgment, not to the underlying cause of action: Hill, *International Commercial Disputes*, p.363. It is therefore difficult to justify the Court of Appeal's reasoning in *Israel Discount Bank of New York v Hadjipateras* [1984] 1 W.L.R. 137, which suggests that a foreign judgment based on a guarantee that was tainted with undue influence may be unenforceable on grounds of public policy. *Cf. Maronier v Larmer* [2002] Q.B. 621 at 624–627 and 637–638 where the court refused to enforce a foreign judgment obtained without notice.

it will not be recognised or enforced. Moreover, the principle of *res judicata* will prevent the English court from recognising a foreign judgment that conflicts with an earlier English judgment creating an estoppel between the parties.[56] Finally, the judgment of a foreign court will not be recognised or enforced if the institution of the proceedings in the foreign court was contrary to an agreed dispute resolution procedure under an agreement between the parties.[57]

(iv) Judgments of superior courts of Commonwealth countries

14–95   Part II of the Administration of Justice Act 1920 provides for the enforcement of judgments awarded by the superior courts of Commonwealth countries.[58] Section 9(1) provides that where a judgment has been obtained in a superior court of a territory to which the Act applies, the judgment creditor may apply to the High Court "at any time within twelve months after the date of the judgment, or such longer period as may be allowed by the court, to have the judgment registered in the court". On any such application the court may, if in all the circumstances of the case it thinks it is just and convenient that the judgment should be enforced in the United Kingdom, order the judgment to be registered.[59] The High Court, therefore, has a discretion whether or not to order registration of the foreign judgment.

14–96   Section 9(2) of the Act lists the circumstances in which the court must refuse registration, and these grounds correspond roughly with the defences to enforcement of foreign judgments at common law.[60] The list in s.9(2) is not comprehensive. Other grounds for refusing registration include *res judicata* and the fact that the institution of proceeding in the foreign court was contrary to the parties' agreement as to the dispute resolution procedure.[61] If a judgment is registered under s.9 of the Administration of Justice Act 1920 it will, as from the date of registration, have the same force and effect as if it had been obtained or entered up on the date of registration in the registering court.[62] This will enable the claimant to enforce the judgment in the United Kingdom. Indeed, the Act is concerned only with the registration and enforcement of foreign

[56] Hill, *International Commercial Disputes*, p.364.
[57] Civil Jurisdiction and Judgments Act 1982, s.32. See generally Hill, *International Commercial Disputes*, p.364.
[58] The Administration of Justice Act 1920 still remains generally in force but its application to territories to which it had not already been applied was excluded by an Order in Council made under the Foreign Judgments (Reciprocal Enforcement) Act 1933, s.7(1). See Reciprocal Enforcement of Judgments (General Application to H.M. Dominions, etc.) Order S.R. & O. 1933 No.1073: Dicey & Morris, *Conflict of Laws* (13th ed., 2000), Vol. 1, p.472. Consequently, many Commonwealth countries are covered by the Foreign Judgments (Reciprocal Enforcement) Act 1933, namely Australia, Bangladesh, Canada, Guernsey, India, Isle of Man, Jersey, Pakistan, and Tonga.
[59] See generally Dicey & Morris, *Conflict of Laws* (13th ed, 2000) Vol.1, pp.471–472.
[60] Hill, *International Commercial Disputes*, p.369. It is true, however, that s.9(2)(f) is more limited than the common law.
[61] Civil Jurisdiction and Judgments Act 1982, s.32.
[62] Administration of Justice Act 1920, s.9(3)(a).

judgments; it does not deal with recognition of a foreign judgment by way of defence in proceedings instituted in the United Kingdom.[63]

(v) Recognition and enforcement of judgments given by the courts of non-Commonwealth countries pursuant to bilateral treaties or certain international conventions

(a) Conditions for recognition and enforcement

The Foreign Judgments (Reciprocal Enforcement) Act 1933 provides **14–97** for the recognition and enforcement of: (a) judgments awarded by the courts of foreign countries outside the Commonwealth to which the United Kingdom has assumed obligations under bilateral treaties and (b) foreign judgments granted in proceedings under certain international conventions.[64] The original intention was that this Act would supersede the Administration of Justice Act 1920 in respect of foreign judgments. However, the 1933 Act applies to relatively few Commonwealth countries[65] and the two regimes continue to exist as mutually exclusive domains.[66] Registration under the 1933 Act is mandatory and the provisions of the Act supersede the common law rules.

Basically there are three conditions which must be satisfied before a **14–98** foreign judgment can be enforced under the 1933 Act: first, the judgment must be final and conclusive between the parties; secondly, the judgment must be for a sum of money, but not including a tax for a penalty; thirdly, the Act must have been extended to the foreign country in question by delegated legislation.[67]

If these conditions are satisfied, the judgment creditor may apply to have **14–99** the judgment registered in the High Court at any time within six years after the date of the foreign judgment.[68] There are certain procedural requirements relating to applying for registration, taking out the order for registration and serving the debtor with notice of the registration.[69] A foreign judgment registered under the 1933 Act has the same force and

---

[63] Hill, *International Commercial Disputes*, p.368.
[64] Hill, *International Commercial Disputes*, p.368. The Act applies to judgments given by the superior courts of the following non-Commonwealth countries: Austria, Belgium, the Federal Republic of Germany, France, Israel, Italy, The Netherlands, Norway and Surinam. But judgments given by the courts of a contracting state (as defined in s.1 of the Civil Jurisdiction and Judgments Act 1982) fall within the scope of the Brussels and Lugano Conventions if the judgment concerns civil or commercial matters. Most judgments relating to guarantees fall in this category. Certain Commonwealth countries are also covered by the regime in the Foreign Judgments (Reciprocal Enforcement) Act 1933, namely Australia, Bangladesh, Canada, Guernsey, India, Isle of Man, Jersey, Pakistan and Tonga.
[65] Hill, *International Commercial Disputes*, p.368.
[66] *ibid.*
[67] See Foreign Judgments (Reciprocal Enforcement) Act 1933, s.1(2) and (3) and Hill, *International Commercial Disputes*, p.370.
[68] Foreign Judgments (Reciprocal Enforcement) Act 1933, s.2(1).
[69] Civil Procedure Rules 1998, Pt 74 and *Practice Direction–Enforcement of Judgments in Different Jurisdictions* 74 PD.1. See Hill, *International Commercial Disputes*, pp.370–371.

effect as a judgment of the High Court, and the judgment can be executed in the same manner as a local judgment.[70]

(b) Bars to registration

14–100   Registration will be refused if the foreign judgment has been wholly satisfied[71] or if it cannot be enforced by execution in its country of origin.[72]

(c) Setting aside registration

14–101   The judgment debtor can apply to have the registration of the foreign judgment set aside on grounds of improper registration,[73] lack of jurisdiction of the foreign court,[74] procedural or substantive injustice[75] or public policy.[76] Moreover, the registration may be set aside if there was an inconsistent judgment of a court of competent jurisdiction in existence at the time that the foreign court gave its judgment. The fact that the foreign judgment is or may be subject to an appeal does not prevent the enforcement of the foreign judgment under the 1933 Act.[77] But the court may, on the application of the judgment debtor, set aside registration or adjourn the application to set the registration aside in order to enable the foreign appeal to be determined.[78]

(d) Recognition without enforcement

14–102   It is not necessary to register a foreign judgment on the merits[79] under the 1933 Act in order for the court to recognise the judgment as a defence

[70] Foreign Judgments (Reciprocal Enforcement) Act 1933, s.2(2).
[71] Foreign Judgments (Reciprocal Enforcement) Act 1933, s.2(4).
[72] Foreign Judgments (Reciprocal Enforcement) Act 1933, s.2(1), proviso (b).
[73] Foreign Judgments (Reciprocal Enforcement) Act 1933, ss.4(1)(a)(i) and 4(1)(a)(vi).
[74] Foreign Judgments (Reciprocal Enforcement) Act 1933, s.4(1)(a)(ii). See generally Hill, *International Commercial Disputes*, pp.372–373.
[75] Lack of notice of the proceedings and fraud are grounds for setting aside registration of the foreign judgment. See Foreign Judgments (Reciprocal Enforcement) Act 1933, s.4(1)(a)(iii) and s.4(1)(a)(iv). But a judgment of a foreign court against a guarantor will not be set aside if he chose not to defend himself in the foreign proceedings: *Habib Bank Ltd v Mian Aftab Ahmed* 2000 W.L. 1544656 (unreported, Queens Bench Div, Carnwath J., October 12, 2000). Where the defendant's right of appeal from the judgment of the foreign court was compromised by political upheavals in the foreign country, the English court may hear expert evidence from the Foreign Office on this issue but only if the defendant raises the issue promptly: *ibid.*
[76] Foreign Judgments (Reciprocal Enforcement) Act 1933, s.4(1)(a)(v). See Hill, *International Commercial Disputes*, paras 12.4.14–12.4.16.
[77] Foreign Judgments (Reciprocal Enforcement) Act 1933, s.4(1)(b).
[78] Foreign Judgments (Reciprocal Enforcement) Act 1933, s.5(1). The judgment creditor can re-apply to have the judgments registered when the foreign appeal has been determined: s.5(2).
[79] A foreign judgment will not be entitled to recognition unless it is a judgment on the merits: *Black-Clawson International Ltd v Papierwerke Waldhof-Aschaffenburg AG* [1975] A.C. 591. The meaning of the phrase "on the merits" is discussed in Hill, *International Commercial Disputes*, paras 12.3.7–12.3.20.

in proceedings[80] in the United Kingdom. The defences to enforcement are also defences to recognition of the foreign judgment.[81]

(vi) The recognition and enforcement of judgments under the Judgments Regulation and the International Conventions

(a) Recognition of foreign judgments under the Judgments Regulation and the International Conventions

Part I of the Civil Jurisdiction and Judgments Act 1982 implements the **14–103** Brussels and Lugano Conventions (the "International Conventions") on the recognition and enforcement of judgments in civil and commercial matters[82] by contracting states.[83] This regime is diminishing in importance but it will be examined alongside the regime for the recognition and enforcement of foreign judgments under the Judgments Regulation because the two regimes are broadly similar. These mandatory regimes are based largely on the principle of reciprocity, rather than a doctrine of obligation.[84]

Several basic conditions must be satisfied before a judgment of a court **14–104** of another contracting state will be recognised in the United Kingdom. First, the judgment must fall within the scope of the Judgments Regulation or the International Conventions in the sense that it must be a judgment given in a contracting state other than the state in which recognition and enforcement is sought. Moreover, the judgment must be in a civil and commercial matter, whatever the nature of the foreign court or tribunal. The term "judgment" in this context means any judgment given by a court or tribunal of a contracting state, whatever the judgment may be called, including a decree, order, decision or writ of execution and even the determination of costs or expenses by an officer of the court.[85] Finally, the judgment must have been granted after the Judgments Regulation or the International Conventions, as the case may be, come into force.[86]

If these conditions are satisfied the judgment must be recognised in **14–105** another contracting state even if the judgment debtor was not domiciled in the state where the judgment was granted and even if the court assumed jurisdiction over the debtor on an exorbitant basis.[87] This problem is more acute for outsiders because they are not entitled to the protection of the

---

[80] Foreign Judgments (Reciprocal Enforcement) Act 1933, s.8(1).
[81] Hill, *International Commercial Disputes*, p.374, para.12.6.22.
[82] The term "civil and commercial matters" is not defined but it would include a judgment relating to the enforcement of a guarantee. See Hill, *International Commercial Disputes* paras 3.3.5–3.3.8.
[83] The contracting states are Belgium, Denmark, the Federal Republic of Germany, Greece, Spain, France, Ireland, Italy, Luxembourg, the Netherlands, Portugal and the United Kingdom.
[84] Hill, *International Commercial Disputes*, para.13.0.3.
[85] Judgments Regulation, Art.32; International Conventions, Art.25. See generally Hill, *International Commercial Disputes*, paras 13.1.2–13.1.8.
[86] See Hill, *International Commercial Disputes*, para.13.0.1.
[87] Judgments Regulation, Arts 33 and 36; International Conventions, Art.26. See Hill, *International Commercial Disputes*, paras 13.2.1–13.2.3.

jurisdictional and procedural safeguards contained in the Judgments Regulation and the International Conventions.[88]

14–106   While these regimes provide that a judgment given in a contracting state a regulation state shall be recognised in the other contracting states without any special procedure being required, it is still necessary to comply with certain formalities. The party seeking recognition of the foreign judgment should produce a copy of the judgment and, in the case of a default judgment, proof that the other party was served with the document instituting the proceedings.[89]

(b) Defences

14–107   There are numerous defences to recognition of foreign judgments under the Judgments Regulation and the International Conventions. A judgment of a court of a contracting state shall not be recognised if recognition is contrary to public policy in the state in which recognition is sought.[90] A judgment obtained by fraud may in certain cases offend the public policy of the state in which recognition of the judgment is sought.[91] Moreover, the Judgments Regulation and the International Conventions contain provisions that are intended to protect the defendant's right to proper service of proceedings and a fair hearing.[92]

14–108   Recognition will be refused if the foreign judgment is irreconcilable with a judgment given in a dispute between the same parties in the state in which recognition is sought.[93] It will also be refused where the foreign judgment cannot be reconciled with an earlier judgment *given in a non-contracting state* or a non-regulation state involving the same cause of action between the same parties, provided that this latter judgment satisfies the conditions necessary for recognition in the state where recognition is sought.[94]

14–109   On the other hand, an appeal in the state of origin does not bar recognition of the foreign judgment, although it may cause a court in the contracting state in which recognition is sought to stay the proceedings on

---

[88] Judgments Regulation, Arts 26, 31 and 35; International Conventions, Art.46. Hill, *International Commercial Disputes*, para.13.1.11 and Von Mehren, "Recognition and Enforcement of Sister-State Judgments: Reflections on General theory and Current Practice in the European Economic Community and the United States" (1981) 81 Col. L.R. 1044.
[89] See Judgments Regulation, Art.33; International Conventions, Art.46.
[90] Judgments Regulation, Art.34(1); International Conventions, Art.27(1). See Hill, *International Commercial Disputes*, paras 13.3.11–13.3.17.
[91] See Hill, *International Commercial Disputes*, para.13.3.15 and *Société d'Informatique Service Réalisation Organisation (SISRO) v Ampersand Software BV* [1994] 1 L. Pr. 55.
[92] Judgments Regulation, Arts 34 and 35; International Conventions, Art.20(2) and 27(2). See Hill, *International Commercial Disputes*, paras 13.3.18–13.3.88; *Adams v Cape Industries plc* [1990] Ch. 433 and *Alivon v Furnival* (1834) 1 Cr. M. & R. 277; 149 E.R. 1084.
[93] Judgments Regulation, Art.34(4); International Conventions, Art.27(3). See Hill, *International Commercial Disputes*, paras 13.3.39–13.3.41. Art.22 provides that where related actions are brought in different contracting states, any court other than the court first seised of the dispute may stay its proceedings.
[94] Judgments Regulation, Art.34(4); International Conventions, Art.27(5). See Hill, *International Commercial Disputes*, para.13.3.42.

the application of either party or of its own motion.[95] Moreover, under no circumstances may a foreign judgment be reviewed as to its substance, so the court in the state in which recognition is sought may not review the merits of the foreign judgment. Indeed, the court in which recognition is sought is not generally entitled to examine the basis on which the foreign court assumed jurisdiction over the defendant.[96]

(c) Enforcement of judgments under the Judgments Regulation and the International Conventions

(i) **Principles and procedure**. The general principle is that a judgment **14–110** granted in one contracting state or one regulation state should have the *same effect* in the jurisdiction in which enforcement is sought as it does in its state or origin,[97] although it may be enforced in a different manner than it would have been enforced in the state of origin.[98]

The procedure for making an application for enforcement of a foreign **14–111** judgment is governed by the law of the state in which enforcement is sought. An application for enforcement of a foreign judgment of a court of a contracting state in England must be submitted to the High Court.[99] The applicant must attach to his application a copy of the judgment which satisfies the conditions necessary to establish its authenticity[1] and documents which establish that, according to the law of the state of origin, the judgment is enforceable and has been duly served.[2] The applicant must also provide an address for service of process within the jurisdiction of the court in which enforcement is sought.[3] This enables the applicant to be informed promptly of the court's decision and allows the defendant to institute an appeal.[4]

Once the foreign judgment is registered for enforcement in England, it **14–112** shall have the same force and effect as if the judgment had originally been given by the High Court.

(ii) **Security for costs**. A party making an application under s.4 of the **14–113** Civil Jurisdiction and Judgments Act 1982 for enforcement of a foreign judgment under the International Conventions shall not be required solely on the ground that he is not domiciled or resident within the jurisdiction to

---

[95] Judgments Regulation, Art.37(1); International Conventions, Art.30. See Hill, *International Commercial Disputes*, paras 13.3.44–13.3.46; *Dr Wolfgang Petereit (As Receiver of Ibh-Holdings AG) v Babcock International Holdings Ltd* [1992] I.L.Pr. 331 and *Industrial Diamond Supplies v Riva* [1977] E.C.R. 2175.
[96] Judgments Regulation, Art.36; International Conventions, Arts 28 and 29. See Hill, *International Commercial Disputes*, paras 13.3.2–13.3.10.
[97] Case 145/86 *Hoffmann v Krieg* [1988] E.C.R. 645 at 666.
[98] Hill, *International Commercial Disputes*, paras 13.4.1–13.4.3. There is a separate regime for the enforcement of court settlements: Judgments Regulation, Arts 57 and 58; International Conventions, Art.51. See Hill, *International Commercial Disputes*, paras 13.5.4–13.5.5.
[99] Judgments Regulation, Art.53; International Conventions, Art.32(1) and s.4 of the Civil Jurisdiction and Judgments Act 1982.
[1] Judgments Regulation, Art. 53(1); International Conventions, Art.46(1).
[2] Judgments Regulation, Arts 53–55; International Conventions, Art.47(1).
[3] Judgments Regulation, Art.40(2); International Conventions, Art.33.
[4] Jenard Report [1979] O.J. C59/50 cited in Hill, *International Commercial Disputes*, para.13.4.6.

give security for costs of the application.[5] The courts could, however, require the applicant to provide security for costs on other grounds.[6]

14–114		**(iii) Ex parte applications.** An application for the enforcement of a foreign judgment under these regimes shall be heard ex parte and the defendant is not entitled to make any submissions at this stage of the proceedings.[7] This is intended to minimise the defendant's opportunities to dissipate his assets or remove them from the jurisdiction.

14–115		**(iv) Appeals against registration.** The judgment debtor may appeal against the High Court's decision to register the judgment of a court in a contracting state or a regulation state within one month of the date of the service of the notice of registration.[8] If the debtor is domiciled in a contracting state other than that in which the decision authorising enforcement was given, the time for lodging an appeal is extended to two months from the date of service of the notice of registration of the judgment.[9]

14–116		Certain limitations are placed on enforcement of the judgment pending the resolution of an appeal against registration. No measures of enforcement other than protective measures against the defendant's property may be taken during this period.[10] The protective measures that may be taken against the defendant's property are intended to prevent the defendant from removing his assets from the jurisdiction in order to abort the execution process.[11]

14–117		When the High Court has resolved the judgment debtor's appeal against registration there is only one further right of appeal, generally heard by the Court of Appeal. This final appeal is restricted to an appeal against the judgment given on an appeal brought under Art.37(1) of the International Conventions or Art.44 of the Judgments Regulation. This is confined to the decision relating to the merits of an appeal lodged against a decision authorising the enforcement of a foreign judgment.[12] Consequently, there is no appeal against a decision refusing to stay enforcement proceedings pending the resolution of an appeal in the state of origin.[13]

---

[5] See Art.45 and Civil Procedure Rules 1998, r.25.13. See also Judgments Regulation, Art.51.
[6] See *Chequepoint SARL v McClelland* [1996] 3 W.L.R. 341 (a decision under RSC Ord.23, r.1). Compare the position in relation to security for costs under the common law rules of private international law, see *Barton v Minister for Foreign Affairs* (1984) 2 F.C.R. 463 and *Farmitalia Carbo Erba Srl v Delta West Pty Ltd* (1994) A.I.P.C. 91–085 at 38,495.
[7] Judgments Regulation, Art.41; International Conventions, Art.34(1). See generally Hill, *International Commercial Disputes*, para.13.4.13.
[8] Judgments Regulation, Art.43; International Conventions, Arts 36(1) and 37(1); Civil Procedure Rules 1998, Pt.74.
[9] Judgments Regulation, Art.43(5); International Conventions, Art.36(2); Civil Procedure Rules 1998, Pt.74. See also Civil Procedure (Amendment) Rules 2002 SI 2002/2058, r.29(a) and Sch.8.
[10] Judgments Regulation, Art.47(1); International Conventions, Art.39. Hill, *International Commercial Disputes*, paras 13.4.21–13.4.27.
[11] See Judgments Regulation, Art.47(3); International Conventions, Art.39(2).
[12] Hill, *International Commercial Disputes*, paras 13.4.28–13.4.29.
[13] See *Delloye v Lamberts* [1996] I.L.Pr. 504.

(vii) Recognition and enforcement of judgments given in other parts of the United Kingdom

There is a separate regime for the reciprocal recognition and **14–118** enforcement of judgments given within the United Kingdom in ss.18 and 19 of the Civil Jurisdiction and Judgments Act 1982.

(a) Recognition

Section 19 of the Act provides: **14–119**

"A judgment to which this section applies given in one part of the United Kingdom shall not be refused recognition in another part of the United Kingdom solely on the ground that, in relation to that judgment, the court which gave it was not a court of competent jurisdiction according to the rules of private international law in force in that other part."

While it is clear that a judgment given in another part of the United Kingdom may not be refused recognition simply on the ground that the court giving the judgment lacked jurisdiction in private international law, the precise impact of s.19 is far from clear.

A judgment procured by fraud or in breach of natural justice in another **14–120** part of the United Kingdom might yet be entitled to recognition[14] but it is unlikely that an English court would be required to recognise a judgment which offended English public policy.[15] Moreover, recognition may be refused if the judgment given in one part of the United Kingdom conflicts with an earlier judgment in another part where recognition is sought.[16]

(b) Enforcement

There is a mandatory registration regime under s.18 for the enforcement **14–121** of monetary provisions contained in any judgment given by a court in another part of the United Kingdom. The party seeking enforcement must obtain a certificate from the court of the country of origin and register it in the country where enforcement is sought.[17] Once registered in the High Court, the judgment is of the same force and effect as if it had been given by the High Court.[18]

---

[14] Hill, *International Commercial Disputes*, para.13.6.5.
[15] *ibid.*
[16] Civil Jurisdiction and Judgments Act 1982, Sch.6, para.10(b) and Sch.7, para.9(b). See Hill, *International Commercial Disputes*, para.13.6.3.
[17] Civil Jurisdiction and Judgments Act 1982, Sch.6, para.2. See generally, Hill, *International Commercial Disputes*, paras 13.6.8–13.6.11.
[18] Civil Jurisdiction and Judgments Act 1982, Sch.6, para.6.

(c) Setting aside registration and staying enforcement

14–122　　The court may set aside registration if it is contrary to the provisions of Sch.6 to the Act and if the court is satisfied that there is a prior irreconcilable judgment of another court having jurisdiction in the matter.[19] Moreover, the court may stay proceedings for the enforcement of any judgment if it is satisfied that the judgment debtor is entitled and intends to apply to have the judgment quashed or set aside in the country of origin.[20]

---

[19] Civil Jurisdiction and Judgments Act 1982, Sch.6, para.10.
[20] Civil Jurisdictions and Judgments Act 1982, Sch.6, para.9.

INDEX